Pro SQL Server Internals, Second Edition

Dmitri Korotkevitch
Tampa
Florida, USA

ISBN-13 (pbk): 978-1-4842-1963-8 ISBN-13 (electronic): 978-1-4842-1964-5
DOI 10.1007/978-1-4842-1964-5

Library of Congress Control Number: 2016959812

Distributed to the book trade worldwide by Springer Science+Business Media New York, 233 Spring Street, 6th Floor, New York, NY 10013. Phone 1-800-SPRINGER, fax (201) 348-4505, e-mail `orders-ny@springer-sbm.com`, or visit `www.springer.com`. Apress Media, LLC is a California LLC and the sole member (owner) is Springer Science + Business Media Finance Inc (SSBM Finance Inc). SSBM Finance Inc is a Delaware corporation.

For information on translations, please e-mail `rights@apress.com`, or visit `www.apress.com`.

Apress and friends of ED books may be purchased in bulk for academic, corporate, or promotional use. eBook versions and licenses are also available for most titles. For more information, reference our Special Bulk Sales–eBook Licensing web page at `www.apress.com/bulk-sales`.

Any source code or other supplementary materials referenced by the author in this text are available to readers at `www.apress.com`. For detailed information about how to locate your book's source code, go to `www.apress.com/source-code/`. Readers can also access source code at SpringerLink in the Supplementary Material section for each chapter.

Printed on acid-free paper

To my family. Thank you for letting me disappear behind the keyboard and ignore all my chores and duties!

Contents at a Glance

Contents

About the Author

Dmitri Korotkevitch is a Microsoft Data Platform MVP and Microsoft Certified Master (SQL Server 2008) with more than 20 years of IT experience, including years of experience working with Microsoft SQL Server as an application and database developer, database administrator, and database architect.

Dmitri specializes in the design, development, and performance tuning of complex OLTP systems that handle thousands of transactions per second around the clock.

Dmitri regularly speaks at various Microsoft and SQL PASS events, and he provides SQL Server training to clients around the world. He regularly blogs at `http://aboutsqlserver.com`, rarely tweets as `@aboutsqlserver`, and can be reached at `dk@aboutsqlserver.com`.

About the Author

About the Technical Reviewers

Victor Isakov is a database architect and Microsoft certified trainer. He provides consulting and training services globally to various organizations in the public, private, and NGO sectors, and has been involved in different capacities at various international events and conferences.

He has authored a number of books on SQL Server and worked closely with Microsoft to develop the new generation of SQL Server 2005 certification and the Microsoft Official Curriculum for both ILT and e-learning.

Specialties include Microsoft SQL Server; Microsoft analysis services; designing database solutions; re-factoring database solutions; performance tuning database solutions; and SQL Server training.

Mike McQuillan is a software and database specialist who lives with his wife and daughter in the United Kingdom. Mike is a polyglot programmer who began messing around with computers in the 1980s, first with an Atari 800XL and then a Sinclair Spectrum. He took up databases in the 1990s and quickly fell in love with SQL. He's been working with SQL Server since version 7 and is an SQL Server MCSA.

When he's not tinkering with computers, Mike and his family enjoy lengthy walks around Cheshire with the family pups, Dolly and Bertie (who keep his feet warm when he's writing).

Acknowledgments

First and foremost, I am enormously grateful to my technical reviewers, Victor Isakov and Mike McQuillan. Their suggestions and comments were extremely helpful and dramatically improved the quality of the book. It would have been impossible for me to complete the project without their help.

The same applies to the entire Apress team and especially to Jill Balzano, Douglas Pundick, and April Rondeau. Special thanks go to Jonathan Gennick, who is keeping the series alive.

I would also like to thank Tom LaRock, who reviewed the first edition of the book. Even though he was unable to participate in this project, you can see his influence all over the place.

Next, I would like to thank Thomas Grohser, who helped me to write Chapter 5 and provided great feedback on a few other topics. He is a Microsoft Data Platform MVP with more than 20 years of experience working with SQL Server. He specializes in designing and building SQL Server solutions that focus on high availability, disaster recovery, scalability, security, and manageability.

I would like to thank Niko Neugebauer, who is the one of the world's best experts in columnstore indexes and data warehousing. Niko reviewed Chapters 33 and 34 and gave me great feedback on them. Niko is a Microsoft Data Platform MVP and has, perhaps, the best columnstore indexes–related blog on the Internet, which can be found at `http://www.nikoport.com/columnstore`. He also published the Columnstore Indexes Scripts Library at GitHub, which you can access at `https://github.com/NikoNeugebauer/CISL`.

The same thanks apply to Dmitry Pilugin for his help with Chapters 3 and 29. Dmitry is one of very few people outside of Microsoft who knows how Query Optimizer *actually* works, and he generously reviewed those chapters for me. You can read Dmitry's blog about Query Processor at `http://www.queryprocessor.com`.

Obviously, a book about SQL Server would be meaningless without the product itself. I would like to thank the entire Microsoft team for all their hard work and the wonderful platform they created. Special thanks go to Jos de Bruijn, Sunil Agarwal, Ajay Jagannathan, Gjorgji Gjeorgjievski, Alexey Eksarevskiy, Borko Novakovic, Arvind Shyamsundar, and many others who patiently answered my questions.

I would like to thank Ian Stirk and Nazanin Mashayekh for the great feedback on the first-edition content. It helped me to improve the quality of this edition.

Finally, I would like to thank all my friends from the SQL Server community for their support and encouragement. It is impossible to list everyone here, but there is one group of people I want to thank in particular. Those are my Nepali friends: Dibya Shakya, Shree Khanal, Ravi Chandra Koirala, and Raghu Bhandari. It was very motivating to meet such a wonderful community!

Thank you very much! It was a pleasure and honor to work with all of you!

Introduction

Four years ago, when I had just started to work on the first edition of *Pro SQL Server Internals*, many people asked me, "Why have you decided to write yet another book on the subject? There are plenty of other Internals books already published." It was–and, as a matter of fact, still is–a very valid question, which I feel obligated to answer.

I set myself two goals when I started to work on the series. First, I wanted to explain how SQL Server works in the most practical way, demonstrating dependencies between particular aspects of SQL Server Internals and the behavior of your systems. Perhaps it deserves some explanation.

There is a joke in the SQL Server community: "How do you distinguish between junior- and senior-level database professionals? Just ask them any question about SQL Server. The junior-level person gives you the straight answer. The senior-level person, on the other hand, always answers, 'It depends.'"

As strange as it sounds, that is correct. SQL Server is a very complex product with a large number of components that depend on each other. You can rarely give a straight *yes* or *no* answer to any question. Every decision comes with its own set of strengths and weaknesses and leads to consequences that affect other parts of the system.

Pro SQL Server Internals covers on what, exactly, "it depends." I wanted to give you enough information about how SQL Server works and to show you various examples of how specific database designs and code patterns affect SQL Server's behavior. I tried to avoid generic suggestions based on best practices. Even though those suggestions are great and work in a large number of cases, there are always exceptions. I hope that, after you read this series, you will be able to recognize those exceptions and make decisions that benefit your particular systems.

My second goal was based on the strong belief that the line between database administration and development is very thin. It is impossible to be a successful database developer without knowledge of SQL Server Internals. Similarly, it is impossible to be a successful database administrator without the ability to design efficient database schema and write good T-SQL code. That knowledge helps both developers and administrators to better understand and collaborate with each other, which is especially important nowadays in the age of agile development and multi-terabyte databases.

This belief came from my personal experience. I started my career in IT as an application developer, slowly moving to backend and database development over the years. At some point, I found that it was impossible to write good T-SQL code unless I understood how SQL Server executed it. That discovery forced me to learn SQL Server Internals, and it led to a new life in which I design, develop, and tune various database solutions. I do not write client applications anymore; however, I perfectly understand the challenges that application developers face when they deal with SQL Server. I have "been there and done that."

My biggest challenge during the transition to the *Internals* world was to find good learning materials. There were plenty of good books; however, all of them had a clear separation in their content. They expected the reader to be either developer or database administrator–never both. I tried to avoid that separation in this book. Obviously, some of the chapters are more DBA-oriented, while others lean more toward developers. Nevertheless, I hope that anyone who is working with SQL Server will find the content useful.

You should not, however, consider *Pro SQL Server Internals* to be a SQL Server tutorial. Nor is it a beginner-level book. I expect you to have previous experience working with relational databases, preferably with SQL Server. You need to know RDBMS concepts, be familiar with different types of database objects, and be able to understand SQL code if you want to get the most out of this series.

As you may have already noticed, this book covers multiple SQL Server versions, from SQL Server 2005 up to recently released SQL Server 2016. With a few exceptions, I did not specifically cover Microsoft Azure SQL Databases; however, they are based on the most recent SQL Server codebase, and the majority of the book's content can be applied to them.

I also need to mention that I completed the manuscript shortly after SQL Server 2016 RTM was released. The recent development process changes have made Microsoft significantly more agile, and we should expect enhancements and improvements to be delivered in service packs and even CU releases. Some of them would even appear in the previous versions of the product, as we have already seen with SQL Server 2012 SP3 and SQL Server 2014 SP2.

With the agile nature of development and the *cloud-first* model adopted by Microsoft, I would expect that some of the limitations that the new SQL Server 2016 features have in the RTM release will be lifted in the future. Check the latest documentation and do not rely strictly on this book as your source of information. While it is challenging to work with and write about a product that evolves all the time, it is a good challenge to have.

I was extremely nervous two and half years ago when the first edition of *Pro SQL Server Internals* was about to be published. I did not know if I would succeed in my goals. I was very happy to find that many of you liked the book and found it useful. I hope you will enjoy the second edition, which I *subjectively* think is even better than the first one.

Finally, I want to thank you again for all your feedback, encouragement, and support–and, most important, for your trust in me. I would have been unable to write it without all your help!

How This Book Is Structured

The book is logically separated into eight different parts. Even though all of these parts are relatively independent of each other, I would encourage you to start with Part I, "Tables and Indexes," anyway. This part explains how SQL Server stores and works with data, which is the key point in understanding SQL Server Internals. The other parts of the book rely on this understanding.

The parts of the book are as follows:

> **Part I: Tables and Indexes** covers how SQL Server works with data. It explains the internal structure of database tables; discusses how and when SQL Server uses indexes; and provides you with basic guidelines about how to design and maintain them. The second edition of the book brings a new chapter about new SQL Server 2016 features, along with some additional SQL Server 2016–related changes in the other chapters.

> **Part II: Other Things That Matter** provides an overview of different T-SQL objects and outlines their strengths and weaknesses; it also supplies use cases showing when these objects should or should not be used. It also includes a long, architecture-focused discussion on data partitioning. The second edition adds content on JSON support and geospatial types enhancements, and it has several other minor improvements in other areas.

> **Part III: Locking, Blocking, and Concurrency** talks about the SQL Server concurrency model. It explains the root causes of various blocking issues in SQL Server, and it shows you how to troubleshoot and address them in your systems. Finally, this part provides you with a set of guidelines on how to design transaction strategies in a way that improves concurrency in systems. This area has not been changed in SQL Server 2016; however, I rewrote a couple of chapters to make them better.

Part IV: Query Life Cycle discusses the optimization and execution of queries in SQL Server. Moreover, it explains how SQL Server caches execution plans, and it demonstrates several issues related to plan caching commonly encountered in systems. As with the SQL Server concurrency model, there are not many changes in SQL Server 2016; however, I tried to improve content here and there.

Part V: Practical Troubleshooting provides an overview of the SQL Server execution model and explains how you can quickly diagnose systems and pinpoint the root cause of a problem. The second edition introduces a new chapter on the new and exciting SQL Server 2016 feature called *Query Store*. Moreover, the "System Troubleshooting" chapter has also been extended and improved.

Part VI: Inside the Transaction Log explains how SQL Server works with the transaction log, and it gives you a set of guidelines on how to design backup and High Availability strategies in systems. The second edition adds content on SQL Server 2016 and Microsoft Azure improvements in those areas.

Part VII: Columnstore Indexes provides an overview of columnstore indexes, which can dramatically improve the performance of data warehouse solutions. SQL Server 2016 adds many improvements in that area, including the use of columnstore indexes in operational analytics scenarios, which are now covered the second edition.

Part VIII: In-Memory OLTP Engine discusses In-Memory OLTP implementation in both SQL Server 2014 and 2016. There are many technology improvements in SQL Server 2016 that are described in this book.

It is also worth noting that most of the figures and examples in this book were created in the Enterprise Edition of SQL Server 2012-2016, with parallelism disabled on the server level in order to simplify the resulting execution plans. In some cases, you may get slightly different results when you run scripts in your environment using different versions of SQL Server.

Downloading the Code

You can download the code used in this book from the Source Code section of the Apress website (`www.apress.com`) or from the *Publications* section of my blog (`http://aboutsqlserver.com`). The source code consists of SQL Server Management Studio solutions, which include a set of the projects (one per chapter). Moreover, it includes several .Net C# projects, which provide the client application code used in the examples in Chapters 13, 14, and 15.

Contacting the Author

You can visit my blog at `http://aboutsqlserver.com` and email me at `dk@aboutsqlserver.com`. I am always happy to answer any of your questions, and I would be enormously grateful for any feedback you provide–both privately and publicly on Amazon and in other web sites. Trust me, it makes a difference and helps improve the quality of future books in the series.

PART I

Tables and Indexes

CHAPTER 1

Data Storage Internals

A SQL Server database is a collection of objects that allow you to store and manipulate data. In theory, SQL Server supports 32,767 databases per instance, although the typical installation usually has only several databases. Obviously, the number of databases SQL Server can handle depends on the load and hardware. It is not unusual to see servers hosting dozens or even hundreds of small databases.

In this chapter, we will discuss the internal structure of databases and how SQL Server stores data.

Database Files and Filegroups

Every database consists of one or more transaction log files and one or more data files. A *transaction log* stores information about database transactions and all of the data modifications made in each session. Every time the data is modified, SQL Server stores enough information in the transaction log to undo (roll back) or redo (replay) this action, which allows SQL Server to recover the database to a transactionally consistent state in the event of an unexpected failure or crash.

Every database has one primary data file, which by default has an `.mdf` extension. In addition, every database can also have secondary database files. Those files, by default, have `.ndf` extensions.

All database files are grouped into filegroups. A *filegroup* is a logical unit that simplifies database administration. It permits the logical separation of database objects and physical database files. When you create database objects–tables, for example–you specify what filegroup they should be placed into without worrying about the underlying data files' configuration.

Listing 1-1 shows the script that creates a database with the name `OrderEntryDb`. This database consists of three filegroups. The `primary` filegroup has one data file stored on the `M:` drive. The second filegroup, `Entities`, has one data file stored on the `N:` drive. The last filegroup, `Orders`, has two data files stored on the `O:` and `P:` drives. Finally, there is a transaction log file stored on the `L:` drive.

Listing 1-1. Creating a database

```
create database [OrderEntryDb] on
primary
(name = N'OrderEntryDb', filename = N'm:\OEDb.mdf'),
filegroup [Entities]
(name = N'OrderEntry_Entities_F1', filename = N'n:\OEEntities_F1.ndf'),
filegroup [Orders]
(name = N'OrderEntry_Orders_F1', filename = N'o:\OEOrders_F1.ndf'),
(name = N'OrderEntry_Orders_F2', filename = N'p:\OEOrders_F2.ndf')
log on
(name = N'OrderEntryDb_log', filename = N'l:\OrderEntryDb_log.ldf')
```

Electronic supplementary material The online version of this chapter (doi:10.1007/978-1-4842-1964-5_1) contains supplementary material, which is available to authorized users.

D. Korotkevitch, *Pro SQL Server Internals*, DOI 10.1007/978-1-4842-1964-5_1

You can see the physical layout of the database and data files in Figure 1-1. There are five disks with four data files and one transaction log file. The dashed rectangles represent the filegroups.

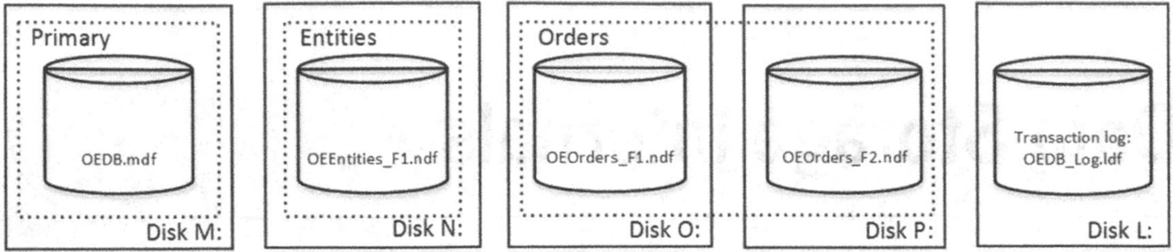

Figure 1-1. *Physical layout of the database and data files*

The ability to put multiple data files inside a filegroup lets us spread the load across different storage drives, which could help to improve the I/O performance of the system. You should consider, however, the redundancy of the storage subsystem when you do that. A database would become fully or partially unavailable if one of the storage drives failed.

Transaction log throughput, on the other hand, does not benefit from multiple files. SQL Server works with transactional logs sequentially, and only one log file would be accessed at any given time.

■ **Note** We will talk about the transaction log's internal structure and best practices associated with it in Chapter 30, "Transaction Log Internals."

Let's create a few tables, as shown in Listing 1-2. The `Customers` and `Articles` tables are placed into the `Entities` filegroup. The `Orders` table resides in the `Orders` filegroup.

Listing 1-2. Creating tables

```
create table dbo.Customers
(
    /* Table Columns */
) on [Entities];

create table dbo.Articles
(
    /* Table Columns */
) on [Entities];

create table dbo.Orders
(
    /* Table Columns */
) on [Orders];
```

Figure 1-2 shows the physical layout of the tables in the database and on the disks.

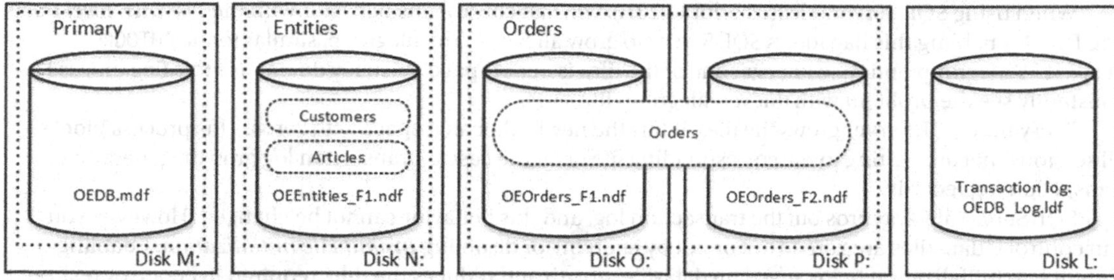

Figure 1-2. *Physical layout of the tables*

The separation between logical objects in the filegroups and the physical database files allows us to fine-tune the database file layout to get the most out of the storage subsystem without worrying that it breaks the system. For example, independent software vendors (ISV) who are deploying their products to different customers can adjust the number of database files during the deployment stage based on the underlying I/O configuration and the expected amount of data. These changes will be transparent to developers who are placing the database objects into the filegroups rather than into database files.

■ **Best Practice** Do not use the `PRIMARY` filegroup for anything but system objects. Creating a separate filegroup or set of filegroups for the user objects simplifies database administration and disaster recovery, especially in the case of large databases. We will discuss this in greater depth in Chapter 31, "Backup and Restore."

You can specify initial file sizes and auto-growth parameters at the time that you create the database or add new files to an existing database. SQL Server uses a *proportional fill* algorithm when choosing to which data file it should write data. It writes an amount of data proportional to the free space available in the file–the more free space a file has, the more writes it handles.

■ **Tip** OLTP systems and filegroups with volatile data usually benefit from multiple data files regardless of the underlying storage configuration. The optimal number of files depends on workload and the underlying hardware. As a rule of thumb, create four data files if the server has up to 16 logical CPUs, keeping a 1/8th ratio between files and CPUs afterward.

Set the same initial size and auto-growth parameters, with grow size being defined in megabytes rather than by percentage for all files in a same filegroup. This helps the proportional fill algorithm balance write activities evenly across data files.

Setting the same initial size and auto-growth parameters for all files in the filegroup is usually enough to keep the proportional fill algorithm working efficiently. However, in some rare cases SQL Server can grow filegroup files unevenly, even with this setup.

SQL Server 2016 introduces two options–`AUTOGROW_SINGLE_FILE` and `AUTOGROW_ALL_FILES`–which control auto-growth events on a per-filegroup level. With `AUTOGROW_SINGLE_FILE`, which is the default option, SQL Server 2016 grows the single file in the filegroup when needed. With `AUTOGROW_ALL_FILES`, SQL Server grows all files in the filegroup whenever one of the files is out of space.

When using SQL Server releases prior to 2016, you can control this behavior with the *instance-level* trace flag `T1117`. Enabling this flag forces SQL Server to grow all files in the filegroup, similar to the `AUTOGROW_ALL_FILES` filegroup option, whenever one of the files is out of space. I usually do not use this flag unless I constantly see the problem with uneven filegroup file sizes.

Every time SQL Server grows the files, it fills the newly allocated space with zeros. This process blocks all sessions that are writing to the corresponding file or, in the case of transaction log growth, generating transaction log records.

SQL Server always zeros out the transaction log, and this behavior cannot be changed. However, you can control if data files are zeroed out or not by enabling or disabling *Instant File Initialization*. Enabling Instant File Initialization helps speed up data-file growth and reduces the time required to create or restore the database.

■ **Note** There is a small security risk associated with Instant File Initialization. When this option is enabled, an unallocated part of the data file can contain information from previously deleted OS files. Database administrators are able to examine such data.

You can enable Instant File Initialization by adding an `SA_MANAGE_VOLUME_NAME` permission, also known as a *Perform Volume Maintenance Task*, to the SQL Server startup account. This can be done under the Local Security Policy management application (`secpol.msc`), as shown in Figure 1-3. You need to open the properties for the Perform Volume Maintenance Task permission and add a SQL Server startup account to the list of accounts there.

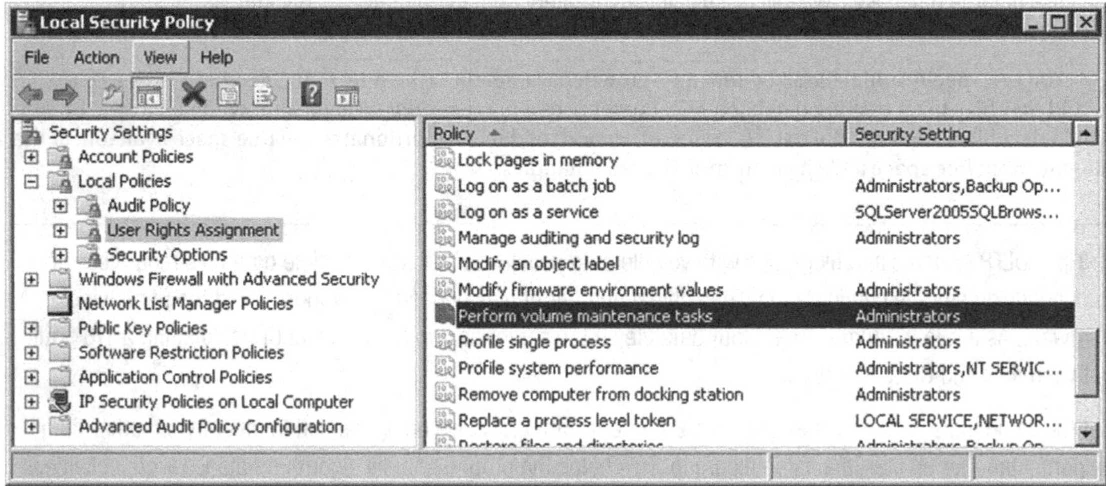

Figure 1-3. *Enabling Instant File Initialization in secpol.msc*

■ **Tip** SQL Server checks to see if Instant File Initialization is enabled on startup. You need to restart the SQL Server service after you give the corresponding permission to the SQL Server startup account.

SQL Server 2016 allows you to enable Instant File Initialization by granting Perform Volume Maintenance Task permission to the SQL Server startup account during setup. Figure 1-4 illustrates that.

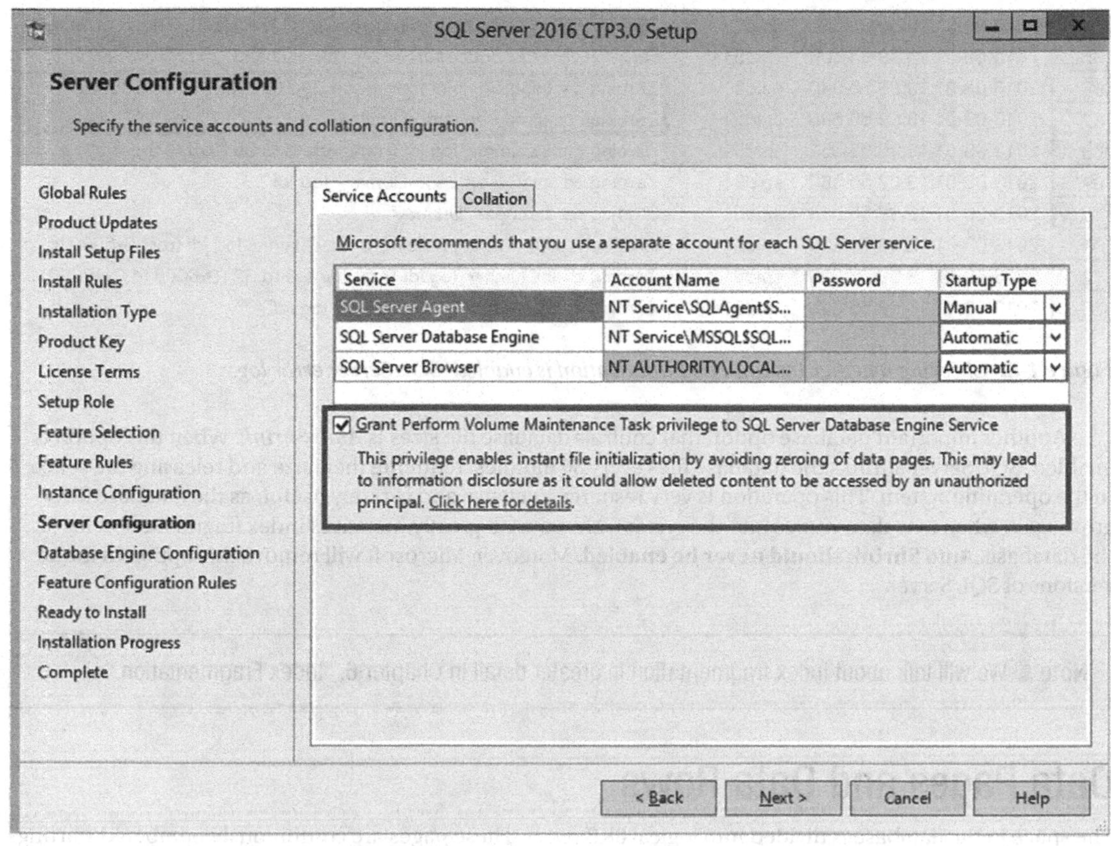

Figure 1-4. *Enabling Instant File Initialization in SQL Server 2016 setup*

In order to check if Instant File Initialization is enabled, you can use the code shown in Listing 1-3. This code sets two trace flags that force SQL Server to put additional information into the error log, create a small database, and read the content of the error log file.

Listing 1-3. Checking to see if Instant File Initialization is enabled

```
dbcc traceon(3004,3605,-1)
go
create database Dummy
go
exec sp_readerrorlog
go
drop database Dummy
go
dbcc traceoff(3004,3605,-1)
go
```

If Instant File Initialization is not enabled, the SQL Server error log indicates that SQL Server is zeroing out the .mdf data file in addition to zeroing out the log .ldf file, as shown in Figure 1-5. When Instant File Initialization is enabled, it would only show the zeroing out of the log .ldf file.

64	2013-09-01 13:39:55.500	spid51	DBCC TRACEON 3004, server process ID (SPID) 51. This is an infor...
65	2013-09-01 13:39:55.500	spid51	DBCC TRACEON 3605, server process ID (SPID) 51. This is an infor...
66	2013-09-01 13:39:55.540	spid51	Zeroing c:\db\Dummy.mdf from page 0 to 392 (0x0 to 0x310000)
67	2013-09-01 13:39:55.540	spid51	Zeroing completed on c:\db\Dummy.mdf
68	2013-09-01 13:39:55.550	spid51	Zeroing c:\db\Dummy_log.ldf from page 0 to 98 (0x0 to 0xc4000)
69	2013-09-01 13:39:55.560	spid51	Zeroing completed on c:\db\Dummy_log.ldf
70	2013-09-01 13:39:55.610	spid51	Starting up database 'Dummy'.
71	2013-09-01 13:39:55.620	spid51	FixupLogTail(progress) zeroing c:\db\Dummy_log.ldf from 0x5000 to...
72	2013-09-01 13:39:55.620	spid51	Zeroing c:\db\Dummy_log.ldf from page 3 to 32 (0x6000 to 0x40000)
73	2013-09-01 13:39:55.620	spid51	Zeroing completed on c:\db\Dummy_log.ldf

Figure 1-5. *Checking whether Instant File Initialization is enabled–SQL Server error log*

Another important database option that controls database file sizes is *Auto Shrink*. When this option is enabled, SQL Server shrinks the database files every 30 minutes, reducing their size and releasing the space to the operating system. This operation is very resource intensive and is rarely useful, as the database files grow again when new data comes into the system. Moreover, it greatly increases index fragmentation in the database. **Auto Shrink should never be enabled.** Moreover, Microsoft will remove this option in future versions of SQL Server.

■ **Note** We will talk about index fragmentation in greater detail in Chapter 6, "Index Fragmentation."

Data Pages and Data Rows

The space in the database is divided into logical 8KB *pages*. These pages are continuously numbered starting with zero, and they can be referenced by specifying a file ID and page number. The page numbering is always continuous, such that when SQL Server grows the database file, new pages are numbered starting from the highest page number in the file plus one. Similarly, when SQL Server shrinks the file, it removes the highest-number pages from the file.

DATA STORAGE IN SQL SERVER

Generally speaking, there are three different ways, or technologies, in which SQL Server stores and works with the data in the database. With the classic *row-based storage*, the data is stored in data rows that combine the data from all columns together.

SQL Server 2012 introduced *columnstore indexes* and *column-based storage*. This technology stores the data on a per-column rather than a per-row basis. We will cover column-based storage in Part VII of this book.

Finally, there is the set of in-memory technologies introduced in SQL Server 2014 and further improved in SQL Server 2016. Even though they persist the data on disk for redundancy purposes, their storage format is very different from both row- and column-based storage. We will discuss in-memory technologies in Part VIII of this book.

This part of the book is focused on row-based storage and classic B-Tree indexes and heaps.

Figure 1-6 shows the structure of a data page.

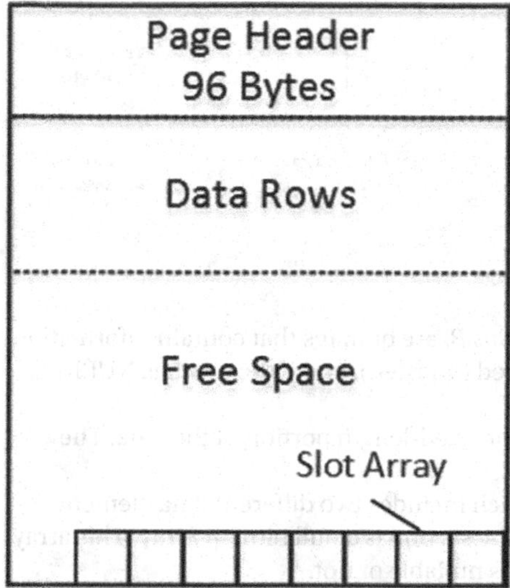

***Figure 1-6.** The data page structure*

A 96-byte page header contains various pieces of information about a page, such as the object to which the page belongs, the number of rows and amount of free space available on the page, links to the previous and next pages if the page is in an index-page chain, and so on.

Following the page header is the area where actual data is stored. This is followed by free space. Finally, there is a slot array, which is a block of two-byte entries indicating the offset at which the corresponding data rows begin on the page.

The *slot array* indicates the logical order of the data rows on the page. If data on a page needs to be sorted in the order of the index key, SQL Server does not physically sort the data rows on the page, but rather it populates the slot array based on the index sort order. Slot 0 (rightmost in Figure 1-6) stores the offset for the data row with the lowest key value on the page; slot 1, the second-lowest key value; and so forth. We will discuss indexes in greater depth in the next chapter.

SQL Server offers a rich set of system data types that can be logically separated into two different groups: fixed length and variable length. Fixed-length data types, such as `int`, `datetime`, `char`, and others, always use the same amount of storage space regardless of their value, *even when it is NULL*. For example, the `int` column always uses 4 bytes and an `nchar(10)` column always uses 20 bytes to store information.

In contrast, variable-length data types, such as `varchar`, `varbinary`, and a few others, use as much storage space as is required to store data, plus two extra bytes. For example, an `nvarchar(4000)` column would use only 12 bytes to store a five-character string and, in most cases, two bytes to store a NULL value. We will discuss the case where variable-length columns do not use storage space for NULL values later in this chapter.

Let's look at the structure of a data row, as shown in Figure 1-7.

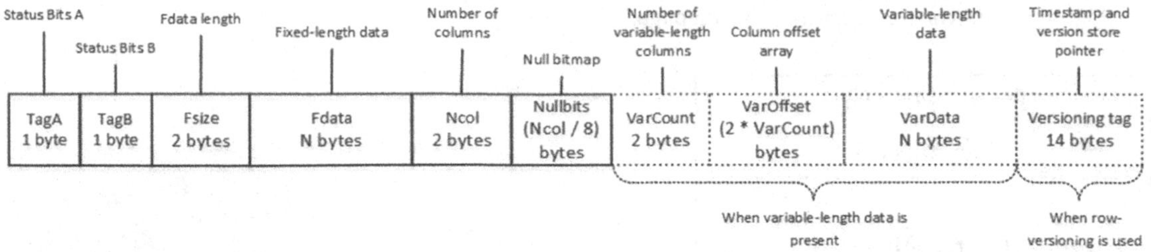

Figure 1-7. *Data row structure*

The first two bytes of the row, called *Status Bits A* and *Status Bits B*, are bitmaps that contain information about the row, such as row type, if the row has been logically deleted (ghosted), and if the row has NULL values, variable-length columns, and a versioning tag.

The next two bytes in the row are used to store the length of the fixed-length portion of the data. They are followed by the fixed-length data itself.

After the fixed-length data portion, there is a *null bitmap*, which includes two different data elements. The first two-byte element is the number of columns in the row. The second is a null bitmap array. This array uses one bit for each column of the table, regardless of whether it is nullable or not.

A null bitmap is always present in data rows in heap tables or clustered index leaf rows, even when the table does not have nullable columns. However, the null bitmap is not present in non-leaf index rows nor in leaf-level rows of nonclustered indexes when there are no nullable columns in the index.

Following the null bitmap, there is the variable-length data portion of the row. It starts with a two-byte number of variable-length columns in the row followed by a column-offset array. SQL Server stores a two-byte offset value for each variable-length column in the row, even when the value is NULL. It is followed by the actual variable-length portion of the data. Finally, there is an optional 14-byte versioning tag at the end of the row. This tag is used during operations that require row versioning, such as an online index rebuild, optimistic isolation levels, triggers, and a few others.

■ **Note** We will discuss index maintenance in Chapter 6, triggers in Chapter 9, and optimistic isolation levels in Chapter 21.

Let's create a table, populate it with some data, and look at the actual row data. The code is shown in Listing 1-4. The `Replicate` function repeats the character provided as the first parameter ten times.

Listing 1-4. The data row format: Table creation

```
create table dbo.DataRows
(
    ID int not null,
    Col1 varchar(255) null,
    Col2 varchar(255) null,
    Col3 varchar(255) null
);

insert into dbo.DataRows(ID, Col1, Col3)  values (1,replicate('a',10),replicate('c',10));
insert into dbo.DataRows(ID, Col2) values (2,replicate('b',10));
```

```
dbcc ind
(
    'SQLServerInternals' /*Database Name*/
    ,'dbo.DataRows' /*Table Name*/
    ,-1 /*Display information for all pages of all indexes*/
);
```

An undocumented but well-known DBCC IND command returns information about table page allocations. You can see the output of this command in Figure 1-8.

	PageFID	PagePID	IAMFID	IAMPID	ObjectID	IndexID	PartitionNum...	PartitionID	iam_chain_ty...	PageType	IndexLe
1	1	214644	NULL	NULL	750625717	0	1	72057594045005824	In-row data	10	NULL
2	1	214643	1	214644	750625717	0	1	72057594045005824	In-row data	1	0

Figure 1-8. *DBCC IND output*

There are two pages that belong to the table. The first one, with PageType=10, is a special type of page called an *IAM allocation map*. This page tracks the pages that belong to a particular object. Do not focus on that now, however, as we will cover allocation map pages later in this chapter.

■ **Note** SQL Server 2012 introduces another undocumented data-management function (DMF), sys.dm_db_database_page_allocations, which can be used as a replacement for the DBCC IND command. The output of this DMF provides more information when compared to DBCC IND, and it can be joined with other system DMVs and/or catalog views.

The page with PageType=1 is the actual data page that contains the data rows. The PageFID and PagePID columns show the actual file and page numbers for the page. You can use another undocumented command, DBCC PAGE, to examine its contents, as shown in Listing 1-5.

Listing 1-5. The data row format: DBCC PAGE call

```
-- Redirecting DBCC PAGE output to console
dbcc traceon(3604);
dbcc page
(
    'SqlServerInternals' /*Database Name*/
    ,1 /*File ID*/
    ,214643 /*Page ID*/
    ,3 /*Output mode: 3 - display page header and row details */
);
```

Listing 1-6 shows the output of the DBCC PAGE that corresponds to the first data row. SQL Server stores the data in byte-swapped order. For example, a two-byte value of 0001 would be stored as 0100.

Listing 1-6. DBCC PAGE output for the first row

```
Slot 0 Offset 0x60 Length 39

Record Type = PRIMARY_RECORD        Record Attributes =  NULL_BITMAP VARIABLE_COLUMNS
Record Size = 39
Memory Dump @0x000000000EABA060

0000000000000000:  30000800 01000000 04000403 001d001d 00270061  0...............'.a
0000000000000014:  61616161 61616161 61636363 63636363 636363    aaaaaaaaacccccccccc

Slot 0 Column 1 Offset 0x4 Length 4 Length (physical) 4
ID = 1

Slot 0 Column 2 Offset 0x13 Length 10 Length (physical) 10
Col1 = aaaaaaaaaa

Slot 0 Column 3 Offset 0x0 Length 0 Length (physical) 0
Col2 = [NULL]

Slot 0 Column 4 Offset 0x1d Length 10 Length (physical) 10
Col3 = cccccccccc
```

Let's look at the data row in more detail, as shown in Figure 1-9.

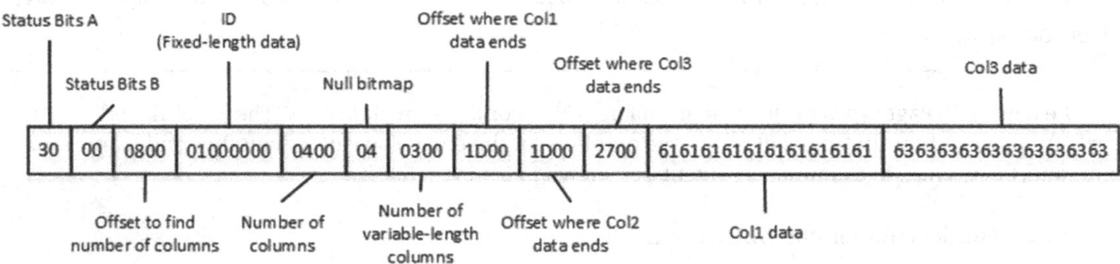

Figure 1-9. *First data row*

As you can see, the row starts with the two status bits followed by a two-byte value of 0800. This is the byte-swapped value of 0008, which is the offset for the `Number of Columns` attribute in the row. This offset tells SQL Server where the fixed-length data part of the row ends.

The next four bytes are used to store fixed-length data, which is the ID column in our case. After that, there is the two-byte value that shows that the data row has four columns, followed by a one-byte NULL bitmap. With just four columns, one byte in the bitmap is enough. It stores the value of 04, which is 00000100 in the binary format. It indicates that the third column in the row contains a NULL value.

The next two bytes store the number of variable-length columns in the row, which is 3 (0300 in byte-swapped order). It is followed by an offset array, in which every two bytes store the offset where the variable-length column data ends. As you can see, even though Col2 is NULL, it still uses the slot in the offset array. Finally, there is the actual data from the variable-length columns.

Now, let's look at the second data row. Listing 1-7 shows the `DBCC PAGE` output, and Figure 1-10 shows the row data.

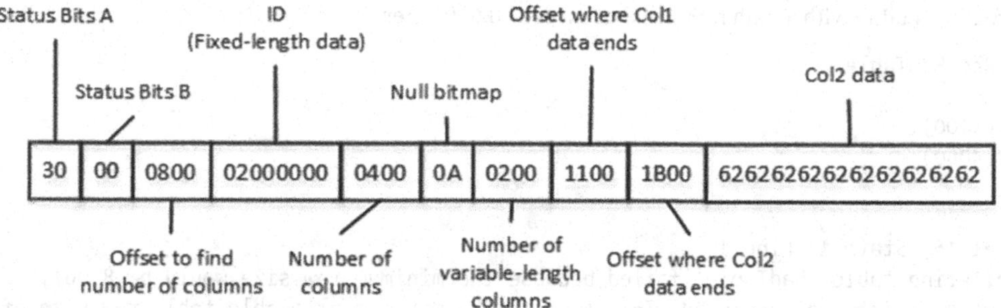

Figure 1-10. *Second data row data*

Listing 1-7. DBCC PAGE output for the second row

```
Slot 1 Offset 0x87 Length 27

Record Type = PRIMARY_RECORD         Record Attributes =  NULL_BITMAP VARIABLE_COLUMNS
Record Size = 27
Memory Dump @0x000000000EABA087

0000000000000000:   30000800 02000000 04000a02 0011001b 00626262  0.................bbb
0000000000000014:   62626262 626262                               bbbbbbb

Slot 1 Column 1 Offset 0x4 Length 4 Length (physical) 4
ID = 2

Slot 1 Column 2 Offset 0x0 Length 0 Length (physical) 0
Col1 = [NULL]

Slot 1 Column 3 Offset 0x11 Length 10 Length (physical) 10
Col2 = bbbbbbbbbb

Slot 1 Column 4 Offset 0x0 Length 0 Length (physical) 0
Col3 = [NULL]
```

The NULL bitmap in the second row represents a binary value of 00001010, which shows that `Col1` and `Col3` are NULL. Even though the table has three variable-length columns, the number of variable-length columns in the row indicates that there are just two columns/slots in the offset array. SQL Server does not maintain the information about the trailing NULL variable-length columns in the row.

■ **Tip** You can reduce the size of the data row by creating tables in a manner in which variable-length columns, which usually store null values, are defined as the last ones in the `CREATE TABLE` statement. This is the only case in which the order of columns in the `CREATE TABLE` statement matters.

The fixed-length data and internal attributes must fit into the 8,060 bytes available on the single data page. SQL Server does not let you create the table when this is not the case. For example, the code in Listing 1-8 produces an error.

Listing 1-8. Creating a table with a data row size that exceeds 8,060 bytes

```
create table dbo.BadTable
(
    Col1 char(4000),
    Col2 char(4060)
)

Msg 1701, Level 16, State 1, Line 1
Creating or altering table 'BadTable' failed because the minimum row size would be 8,067,
including 7 bytes of internal overhead. This exceeds the maximum allowable table row size of
8,060 bytes.
```

Large Objects Storage

Even though the fixed-length data and the internal attributes of a row must fit into a single page, SQL Server can store the variable-length data on different data pages. There are two different ways to store the data, depending on the data type and length.

Row-Overflow Storage

SQL Server stores variable-length column data that does not exceed 8,000 bytes on special pages called *row-overflow pages*. Let's create a table and populate it with the data shown in Listing 1-9.

Listing 1-9. Row-overflow data: Creating a table

```
create table dbo.RowOverflow
(
    ID int not null,
    Col1 varchar(8000) null,
    Col2 varchar(8000) null
);

insert into dbo.RowOverflow(ID, Col1, Col2) values
(1,replicate('a',8000),replicate('b',8000));
```

As you see, SQL Server creates the table and inserts the data row without any errors, even though the data-row size exceeds 8,060 bytes. Let's look at the table page allocation using the `DBCC IND` command. The results are shown in Figure 1-11.

	PageFID	PagePID	IAMFID	IAMPID	ObjectID	IndexID	PartitionNum...	PartitionID	iam_chain_type	PageType	IndexL
1	1	3039527	NULL	NULL	814625945	0	1	72057594045071360	In-row data	10	NULL
2	1	214647	1	3039527	814625945	0	1	72057594045071360	In-row data	1	0
3	1	214646	NULL	NULL	814625945	0	1	72057594045071360	Row-overflow data	10	NULL
4	1	214645	1	214646	814625945	0	1	72057594045071360	Row-overflow data	3	0

Figure 1-11. *Row-overflow data: DBCC IND results*

Now you can see two different sets of IAM and data pages. The data page with PageType=3 represents the data page that stores row-overflow data.

Let's look at data page 214647, which is the in-row data page that stores main row data. The partial output of the DBCC PAGE command for the page (1:214647) is shown in Listing 1-10.

Listing 1-10. Row-overflow data: DBCC PAGE results for IN_ROW data

```
Slot 0 Offset 0x60 Length 8041

Record Type = PRIMARY_RECORD        Record Attributes = NULL_BITMAP VARIABLE_COLUMNS
Record Size = 8041
Memory Dump @0x000000000FB7A060

0000000000000000:  30000800 01000000 03000002 00511f69 9f616161  0............Q.iŸaaa
0000000000000014:  61616161 61616161 61616161 61616161 61616161  aaaaaaaaaaaaaaaaaaaa
<Skipped>
0000000000001F40:  61616161 61616161 61616161 61616161 61020000  aaaaaaaaaaaaaaaaa...
0000000000001F54:  00010000 00290000 00401f00 00754603 00010000  .....)...@...uF.....
0000000000001F68:  00
```

As you can see, SQL Server stores Col1 data in-row. Col2 data, however, has been replaced with a 24-byte value. The first 16 bytes are used to store off-row storage metadata, such as type, length of the data, and a few other attributes. The last chunk of 8 bytes is the actual pointer to the row on the row-overflow page, which is made up by the file, page, and slot number. Figure 1-12 shows this in detail. Remember that all information is stored in byte-swapped order.

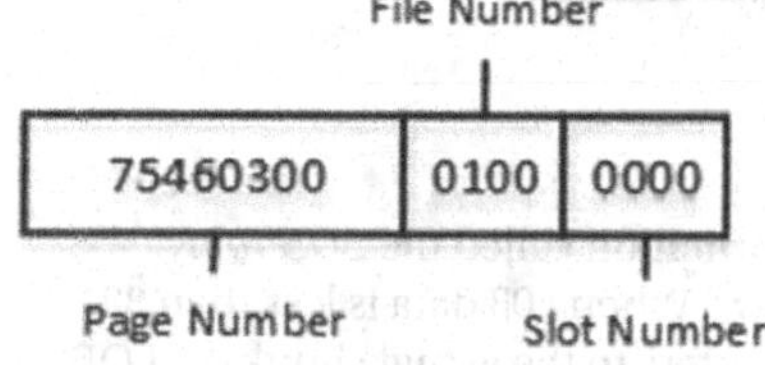

Figure 1-12. *Row-overflow data: Row-overflow page pointer structure*

As you can see, the slot number is 0, the file number is 1, and the page number is the hexadecimal value 0x00034675, which is decimal 214645. The page number matches the DBCC IND results shown in Figure 1-10.

The partial output of the DBCC PAGE command for the page (1:214645) is shown in Listing 1-11.

Listing 1-11. Row-overflow data: DBCC PAGE results for row-overflow data

```
Blob row at: Page (1:214645) Slot 0 Length: 8014 Type: 3 (DATA)
Blob Id:2686976

000000008E0A06E: 62626262  62626262  62626262  62626262 bbbbbbbbbbbbbbbb
000000008E0A07E: 62626262  62626262  62626262  62626262 bbbbbbbbbbbbbbbb
```

As you can see, Col2 data is stored in the first slot on the page.

LOB Storage

For the `text`, `ntext`, or `image` columns, SQL Server stores the data off-row by default. It uses another kind of pages called a *LOB data pages*.

■ **Note** You can control this behavior to a degree by using the "text in row" table option. For example, `exec sp_table_option dbo.MyTable, 'text in row', 200` forces SQL Server to store LOB data less than or equal to 200 bytes in-row. LOB data greater than 200 bytes would be stored in LOB pages.

The logical LOB data structure is shown in Figure 1-13.

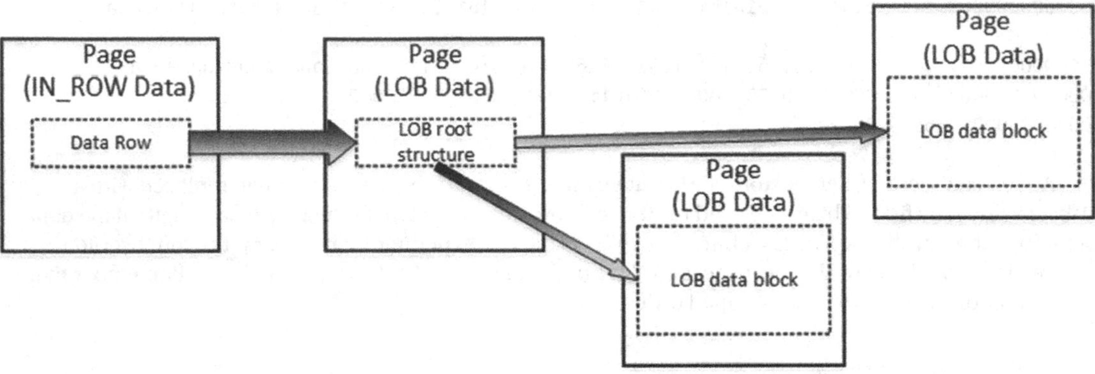

Figure 1-13. *LOB data: Logical structure*

As with row-overflow data, there is a pointer to another piece of information called the *LOB root structure*, which contains a set of the pointers to other data pages and rows. When LOB data is less than 32 KB and can fit into five data pages, the LOB root structure contains the pointers to the actual chunks of LOB data. Otherwise, the LOB tree starts to include additional intermediate levels of pointers, similar to the index B-Tree, which we will discuss in the next chapter.

Let's create the table and insert one row of data, as shown in Listing 1-12. We need to cast the first argument of the `replicate` function to `varchar(max)`. Otherwise, the result of the `replicate` function would be limited to 8,000 bytes.

Listing 1-12. LOB data: Table creation

```
create table dbo.TextData
(
    ID int not null,
    Col1 text null
);

insert into dbo.TextData(ID, Col1) values (1, replicate(convert(varchar(max),'a'),16000));
```

The page allocation for the table is shown in Figure 1-14.

	PageFID	PagePID	IAMFID	IAMPID	ObjectID	IndexID	PartitionNum...	PartitionID	iam_chain_ty...	PageType	Index
1	1	3046837	NULL	NULL	830626002	0	1	72057594045136896	In-row data	10	NULL
2	1	3046836	1	3046837	830626002	0	1	72057594045136896	In-row data	1	0
3	1	3046833	NULL	NULL	830626002	0	1	72057594045136896	LOB data	10	NULL
4	1	3046832	1	3046833	830626002	0	1	72057594045136896	LOB data	3	0
5	1	3046834	1	3046833	830626002	0	1	72057594045136896	LOB data	3	0
6	1	3046835	1	3046833	830626002	0	1	72057594045136896	LOB data	3	0

Figure 1-14. *LOB data: DBCC IND result*

As you can see, the table has one data page for in-row data and three data pages for `LOB` data. I am not going to examine the structure of the data row for in-row allocation; it is similar to the row-overflow allocation. However, with the LOB allocation, the table stores less metadata information in the pointer and uses 16 bytes rather than the 24 bytes required by the row-overflow pointer.

The result of the `DBCC PAGE` command for the page that stores the `LOB` root structure is shown in Listing 1-13.

Listing 1-13. LOB data: DBCC PAGE results for the LOB page with the LOB root structure

```
Blob row at: Page (1:3046835) Slot 0 Length: 84 Type: 5 (LARGE_ROOT_YUKON)

Blob Id: 131661824 Level: 0 MaxLinks: 5 CurLinks: 2

Child 0 at Page (1:3046834) Slot 0 Size: 8040 Offset: 8040
Child 1 at Page (1:3046832) Slot 0 Size: 7960 Offset: 16000
```

As you can see, there are two pointers to the other pages with `LOB` data blocks, which are similar to the blob data shown in Listing 1-11.

The format, in which SQL Server stores the data from the `(MAX)` columns, such as `varchar(max)`, `nvarchar(max)`, and `varbinary(max)`, depends on the actual data size. SQL Server stores it in-row when possible. When in-row allocation is impossible, and data size is less than or equal to 8,000 bytes, it is stored as row-overflow data. The data that exceeds 8,000 bytes is stored as `LOB` data.

■ **Important** `text`, `ntext`, and `image` data types are deprecated, and they will be removed in future versions of SQL Server. Use `varchar(max)`, `nvarchar(max)`, and `varbinary(max)` columns instead.

It is also worth mentioning that SQL Server always stores rows that fit into a single page using in-row allocations. When a page does not have enough free space to accommodate a row, SQL Server allocates a new page and places the row there rather than placing it on the half-full page and moving some of the data to row-overflow pages.

SELECT * and I/O

There are plenty of reasons why selecting all columns from a table with the `SELECT *` operator is not a good idea. It increases network traffic by transmitting columns that the client application does not need. It also makes query performance tuning more complicated, and it introduces side effects when the table schema changes.

It is recommended that you avoid such a pattern and instead explicitly specify the list of columns needed by the client application. This is especially important with row-overflow and LOB storage, when one row can have data stored in multiple data pages. SQL Server needs to read all of those pages, which can significantly decrease the performance of queries.

As an example, let's assume that we have table dbo.Employees, with one column storing employee pictures. Listing 1-14 creates the table and populates it with some data.

Listing 1-14. Select * and I/O: Table creation

```
create table dbo.Employees
(
    EmployeeId int not null,
    Name varchar(128) not null,
    Picture varbinary(max) null
);

;with N1(C) as (select 0 union all select 0) -- 2 rows
,N2(C) as (select 0 from N1 as T1 cross join N1 as T2) -- 4 rows
,N3(C) as (select 0 from N2 as T1 cross join N2 as T2) -- 16 rows
,N4(C) as (select 0 from N3 as T1 cross join N3 as T2) -- 256 rows
,N5(C) as (select 0 from N4 as T1 cross join N2 as T2) -- 1,024 rows
,IDs(ID) as (select row_number() over (order by (select null)) from N5)
insert into dbo.Employees(EmployeeId, Name, Picture)
    select
        ID, 'Employee ' + convert(varchar(5),ID),
        convert(varbinary(max),replicate(convert(varchar(max),'a'),120000))
    from Ids;
```

The table has 1,024 rows with binary data amounting to 120,000 bytes. Let's assume that we have code in the client application that needs the EmployeeId and Name to populate a drop-down menu. If a developer is not careful, he or she could write a select statement using the SELECT * pattern, even though a picture is not needed for this particular use case.

Let's compare the performance of two selects–one selecting all data columns and another that selects only EmployeeId and Name. The code to do this is shown in Listing 1-15. The execution time and number of reads on my computer is shown in Table 1-1.

Listing 1-15. Select * and I/O: Performance comparison

```
select * from dbo.Employees;
select EmployeeId, Name from dbo.Employees;
```

Table 1-1. *Execution Time of Two SELECT Operators*

	Number of Reads	Execution Time
select EmployeeID, Name from dbo.Employees	7	2 ms
select * from dbo.Employees	90,895	3,343 ms

As you can see, the first select, which reads the LOB data and transmits it to the client, is a few orders of magnitude slower than the second select. One case where this becomes extremely important is with client applications, which use Object Relational Mapping (ORM) frameworks. Developers tend to reuse the same entity objects in different parts of an application. As a result, an application may load all attributes/columns even though it does not need all of them in many cases.

It is better to define different entities with a minimum set of required attributes on an individual use-case basis. In our example, it would work best to create separate entities/classes, such as `EmployeeList` and `EmployeeProperties`. An `EmployeeList` entity would have two attributes: `EmployeeId` and `Name`. `EmployeeProperties` would include a `Picture` attribute in addition to the two mentioned. This approach can significantly improve the performance of systems.

Extents and Allocation Map Pages

SQL Server logically groups eight pages into 64 KB units called *extents*. There are two types of extents available: *mixed extents* store data that belongs to different objects, while *uniform extents* store the data for the same object.

By default, when a new object is created, SQL Server stores the first eight object pages in mixed extents. After that, all subsequent space allocation for that object is done with uniform extents.

SQL Server uses a special kind of pages, called *allocation maps,* to track extent and page usage in a file. There are several different types of allocation map pages in SQL Server.

Global allocation map (GAM) pages track if extents have been allocated by any objects. The data is represented as bitmaps, where each bit indicates the allocation status of an extent. Zero bits indicate that the corresponding extents are in use. The bits with a value of one indicate that the corresponding extents are free. Every GAM page covers about 64,000 extents, or almost 4 GB of data. This means that every database file has one GAM page for about 4 GB of file size.

Shared global allocation map (SGAM) pages track information about mixed extents. Similar to GAM pages, it is a bitmap with one bit per extent. The bit has a value of one if the corresponding extent is a mixed extent and has at least one free page available. Otherwise, the bit is set to zero. Like a GAM page, an SGAM page tracks about 64,000 extents, or almost 4 GB of data.

SQL Server can determine the allocation status of the extent by looking at the corresponding bits in the GAM and SGAM pages. Table 1-2 shows the possible combinations of the bits.

Table 1-2. *Allocation Status of the Extents*

Status	SGAM bit	GAM bit
Free, not in use	0	1
Mixed extent with at least one free page available	1	0
Uniform extent or full mixed extent	0	0

When SQL Server needs to allocate a new uniform extent, it can use any extent where a bit in the GAM page has the value of one. When SQL Server needs to find a page in a mixed extent, it searches both allocation maps looking for the extent with a bit value of one in an SGAM page and the corresponding zero bit in a GAM page. If there are no such extents available, SQL Server allocates the new free extent based on the GAM page, and it sets the corresponding bit to one in the SGAM page.

Even though mixed extents can save an insignificant amount of space in the database, they require SQL Server to perform more modifications of allocation map pages, which may become a source of contention in a busy system. It is especially critical for `tempdb` databases where small objects are usually created at a very fast rate.

SQL Server 2016 allows you to control mixed extents' space allocation on a per-database level by setting the `MIXED_PAGE_ALLOCATION` database option. By default, it is enabled for the user databases and disabled for `tempdb`. This configuration should be sufficient in a majority of the cases.

In SQL Server prior to 2016, you can disable mixed extents' space allocation on an entire instance by using trace flag `T1118`. Setting this flag can significantly reduce allocation map-pages contention on the busy OLTP servers, especially for the `tempdb` database. **I recommend you set this flag as a startup parameter on every SQL Server instance.**

Every database file has its own chain of `GAM` and `SGAM` pages. The first `GAM` page is always the third page in the data file (page number 2). The first `SGAM` page is always the fourth page in the data file (page number 3). The next `GAM` and `SGAM` pages appear every 511,230 pages in the data files, which allows SQL Server to navigate through them quickly when needed.

SQL Server tracks the pages and extents used by the different types of pages (`IN_ROW_DATA`, `ROW_OVERFLOW`, and `LOB` pages) that belong to the object with another set of the allocation map pages, called the *index allocation map (IAM)*. Every table/index has its own set of `IAM` pages, which are combined into separate linked lists called *IAM chains*. Each IAM chain covers its own *allocation unit*—`IN_ROW_DATA`, `ROW_OVERFLOW_DATA`, and `LOB_DATA`.

Each `IAM` page in the chain covers a particular `GAM` interval. The IAM page represents the bitmap, where each bit indicates if a corresponding extent stores the data that belongs to a particular allocation unit for a particular object. In addition, the first `IAM` page for the object stores the actual page addresses for the first eight object pages, which are stored in mixed extents.

Figure 1-15 shows a simplified version of the allocation map pages' bitmaps.

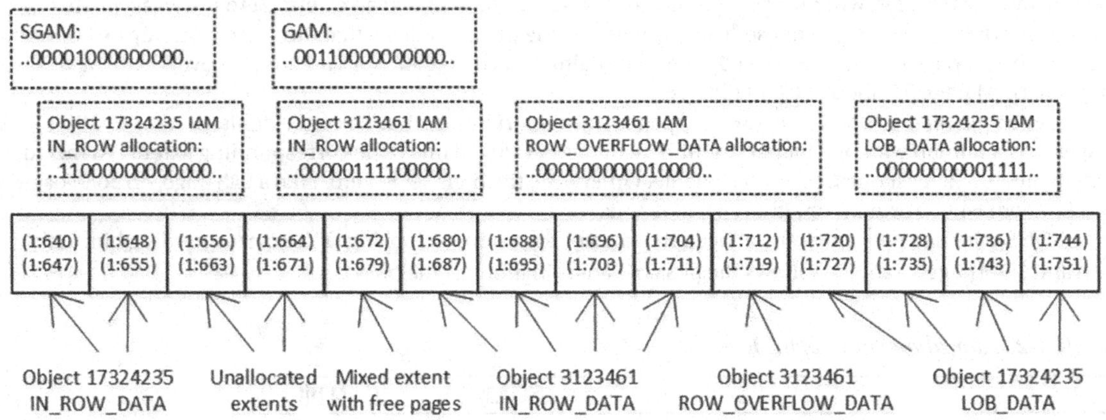

Figure 1-15. *Allocation map pages*

■ **Note** Partitioned tables and indexes have separate IAM chains for every partition. We will discuss partitioned tables in greater detail in Chapter 16, "Data Partitioning."

There is another type of allocation map page called *page free space (PFS)***.** Despite the name, `PFS` pages track a few different things. We can call `PFS` as a byte mask, where every byte stores information about a specific page, as shown in Figure 1-16.

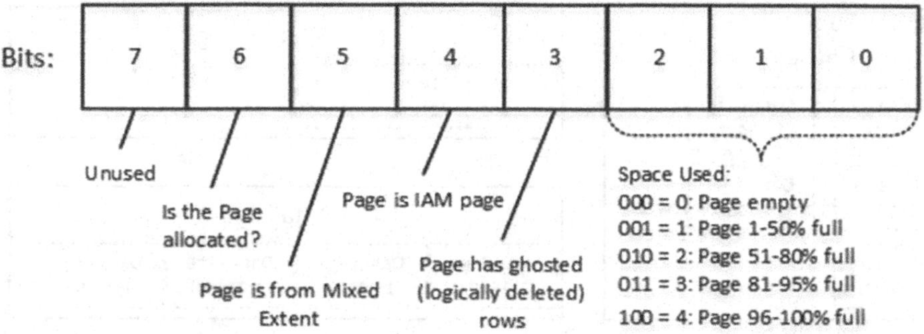

Figure 1-16. *Page status byte in PFS page*

The first three bits in the byte indicate the percentage of used space on the page. SQL Server tracks the used space for row-overflow and LOB data, as well as for in-row data in the heap tables, which we will discuss in the next chapter. These are the only cases in which the amount of free space on the page matters.

When you delete a data row from the table, SQL Server does not remove it from the data page, but rather marks the row as deleted. Bit 3 indicates whether the page has logically deleted (ghosted) rows. We will talk about the deletion process later in this chapter.

Bit 4 indicates if the page is an IAM page. Bit 5 indicates whether or not the page is in the mixed extent. Finally, bit 6 indicates if the page is allocated.

Every PFS page tracks 8,088 pages, or about 64 MB of data space. It is always the second page (page 1) in the file and every 8,088 pages thereafter.

There are two more types of allocation map pages. The seventh page (page 6) in the file is called a *differential changed map (DCM)*. These pages keep track of extents that have been modified since the last FULL database backup. SQL Server uses DCM pages when it performs DIFFERENTIAL backups.

The last allocation map is called a *bulk changed map (BCM)*. It is the eighth page (page 7) in the file, and it indicates which extents have been modified in minimally logged operations since the last transaction log backup. BCM pages are used only with a BULK-LOGGED database recovery model.

■ **Note** We will discuss different types of backups and recovery models in Part VI of this book.

Both DCM and BCM pages are bitmasks that cover 511,230 pages in the data file.

Data Modifications

SQL Server does not read or modify data rows directly on the disk. Every time you access data, SQL Server reads it into memory.

Let's look at what happens during data modifications. Figure 1-17 shows the initial state of the database before an update operation. There is a memory cache, called a *buffer pool*, that caches some of the data pages.

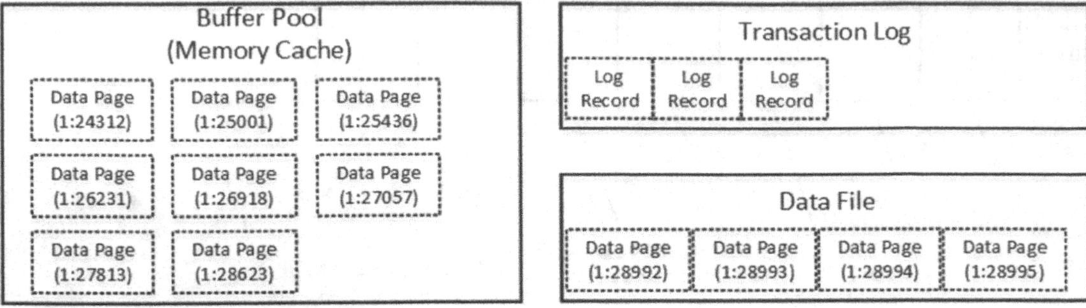

Figure 1-17. *Data modification: Initial stage*

Let's assume that you want to update the data row from the page (1:28992). This page is not in the buffer pool, and SQL Server needs to read the data page from the disk.

When the page is in memory, SQL Server updates the data row. This process includes two different steps. First, SQL Server generates a new transaction log record and *synchronously* writes it to the transaction log file. Next, it modifies the data row and marks the data page as modified (dirty). Figure 1-18 illustrates this point.

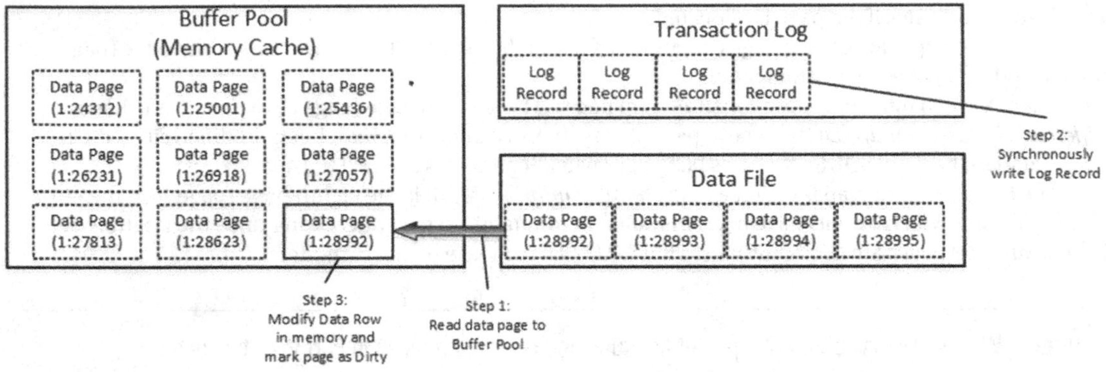

Figure 1-18. *Data modification: Modifying data*

Even though the new version of the data row is not yet saved in the data file, the transaction log record contains enough information to reconstruct (redo) the change if needed.

Finally, at some point, SQL Server *asynchronously* saves the dirty data pages into the data file and a special log record into the transaction log. This process is called a *checkpoint*. Figure 1-19 illustrates the checkpoint process.

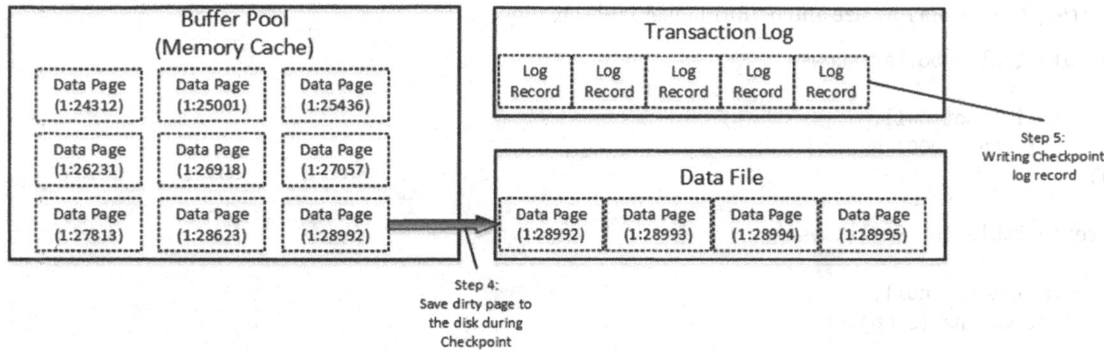

Figure 1-19. *Data modification: Checkpoint*

The insert process works in a similar manner. SQL Server reads the data page where the new data row needs to be inserted into the buffer pool, or it allocates a new extent/page if needed. After that, SQL Server synchronously saves the transaction log record, inserts a row into the page, and asynchronously saves the data page to the disk.

The same process transpires with deletions. As already mentioned, when you delete a row, SQL Server does not physically remove the row from the page. Rather, it flags deleted rows as ghosted (deleted) in the status bits. This speeds up deletion and allows SQL Server to undo it quickly if necessary.

The deletion process also sets a flag in the `PFS` page indicating that there is a ghosted row on the page. SQL Server removes ghosted rows in the background through a task called *ghost cleanup*.

There is another SQL Server process called *lazy writer* that can save dirty pages on disk. As the opposite to checkpoint, which saves dirty data pages by keeping them in the buffer pool, lazy writer processes the *least recently used* data pages (SQL Server tracks buffer pool page usage internally), releasing them from memory. It releases both dirty and clean pages, saving dirty data pages on disk during the process. As you can guess, lazy writer runs in case of memory pressure or when SQL Server needs to bring more data pages to the buffer pool.

There are two key points that you need to remember. First, when SQL Server processes DML queries (`SELECT`, `INSERT`, `UPDATE`, `DELETE`, and `MERGE`), it never works with the data without first loading the data pages into the buffer pool. Second, when you modify the data, SQL Server synchronously writes log records to the transaction log. The modified data pages are saved to the data files asynchronously in the background.

Much Ado about Data Row Size

As you already know, SQL Server is a very I/O-intensive application. SQL Server can generate an enormous amount of I/O activity, especially when it deals with large databases accessed by a large number of concurrent users.

There are many factors that affect the performance of queries, and the number of I/O operations involved is at the top of the list; that is, the more I/O operations a query needs to perform, the more data pages it needs to read, and the slower it gets.

The size of a data row affects how many rows will fit in a data page. Large data rows require more pages to store the data and, as a result, increase the number of I/O operations during scans. Moreover, objects will use more memory in the buffer pool.

Let's look at the following example and create two tables, as shown in Listing 1-16. The first table, `dbo.LargeRows`, uses a `char(2000)` fixed-length data type to store the data. As a result, you can fit only four rows per data page, regardless of the size of `Col` data. The second table, `dbo.SmallRows`, uses a `varchar(2000)` variable-length data type. Let's populate both of the tables with the same data.

Listing 1-16. Data row size and performance: Table creation

```
create table dbo.LargeRows
(
    ID int not null,
    Col char(2000) null
);

create table dbo.SmallRows
(
    ID int not null,
    Col varchar(2000) null
);

;with N1(C) as (select 0 union all select 0) -- 2 rows
,N2(C) as (select 0 from N1 as T1 cross join N1 as T2) -- 4 rows
,N3(C) as (select 0 from N2 as T1 cross join N2 as T2) -- 16 rows
,N4(C) as (select 0 from N3 as T1 cross join N3 as T2) -- 256 rows
,N5(C) as (select 0 from N4 as T1 cross join N4 as T2) - 65,536 rows
,IDs(ID) as (select row_number() over (order by (select null)) from N5)
insert into dbo.LargeRows(ID, Col)
    select ID, 'Placeholder' from Ids;

insert into dbo.SmallRows(ID, Col)
    select ID, 'Placeholder' from dbo.LargeRows;
```

Now, let's run the selects that scan the data and compare the number of I/O operations and execution times. You can see the code in Listing 1-17. The results I got on my computer are shown in Table 1-3.

Listing 1-17. Data row size and performance: SELECT statements

```
select count(*) from dbo.LargeRows;
select count(*) from dbo.SmallRows;
```

Table 1-3. *Number of Reads and Execution Times of the Queries*

	Number of Reads	Execution Time
`select count(*) from dbo.SmallRows`	227	5 ms
`select count(*) from dbo.LargeRows`	16,384	31 ms

As you can see, SQL Server needs to perform about 70 times more reads while scanning `dbo.LargeRows` data, which leads to the longer execution time.

You can improve the performance of the system by reducing the size of the data rows. One of the ways to do this is by using the smallest data type that covers the domain values when you create tables. For example:

- Use `bit` instead of `tinyint`, `smallint`, or `int` to store Boolean values. The `bit` data type uses one byte of storage space per eight columns.

- Use the appropriate date/time data type based on the precision you need. For example, an order-entry system can use `smalldatetime` (four bytes of storage space) or `datetime2(0)` (six bytes of storage space) rather than `datetime` (eight bytes of storage space) to store information on when an order was placed into the system when one-minute or one-second precision is enough.
- Use `decimal` or `real` rather than `float` whenever possible. Similarly, use `money` or `smallmoney` data types rather than `float` to store monetary values.
- Do not use large fixed-length char/binary data types unless the data is always populated and static in size.

As an example, let's look at Table 1-4, which shows two different designs for a table that collects location information.

Table 1-4. *Table That Collects Location Information*

`create table dbo.Locations`
`(`
`ATime datetime not null, -- 8 bytes`
`Latitude float not null, -- 8 bytes`
`Longitude float not null, -- 8 bytes`
`IsGps int not null, -- 4 bytes`
`IsStopped int not null, -- 4 bytes`
`NumberOfSatellites int not null, -- 4 bytes`
`)`
	`create table dbo.Locations2`
	`(`
	`ATime datetime2(0) not null, -- 6 bytes`
	`Latitude decimal(9,6) not null, -- 5 bytes`
	`Longitude decimal(9,6) not null, -- 5 bytes`
	`IsGps bit not null, -- 1 byte`
	`IsStopped bit not null, -- 0 bytes`
	`NumberOfSatellites tinyint not null, -- 1 byte`
	`)`

Total: 36 bytes	Total: 18 bytes

Table `dbo.Locations2` uses 18 bytes less storage space per data row. This does not appear particularly impressive in the scope of a single row; however, it quickly adds up. If a system collects 1,000,000 locations daily, 18 bytes per row produces about 18 MB of space savings per day–and 6.11 GB per year. In addition to the database space, it affects buffer pool memory usage, backup file size, network bandwidth, and a few other things.

It is especially important for databases in the cloud, where an excessive amount of data often forces you to use higher-tier virtual machines and cloud services and upgrade to premium storage. All of that can significantly increase your monthly service costs.

At the same time, you need to be careful with such an approach and not be too cheap. For example, choosing `smallint` as the data type for the `CustomerId` column is not a wise step. Even though 32,768 (or even 65,536) customers look good enough when you just start the development of a new system, the cost of code refactoring and changing the data type from `smallint` to `int` could be very high in the future.

Table Alteration

Let's look at what happens when you are altering a table. There are three different ways that SQL Server can proceed, as follows:

1. Alteration requires changing the metadata only. Examples of such an alteration include dropping a column, changing a not nullable column to a nullable one, or adding a nullable column to the table.

2. Alteration requires changing the metadata only, but SQL Server needs to scan the table data to make sure it conforms to the new definition. You can think about changing a nullable column to be not nullable, as an example. SQL Server needs to scan all data rows in the table to make sure that there are no null values stored in a particular column before changing the table metadata. Another example is changing a column data type to one with a smaller scope of domain values. If you change an `int` column to `smallint`, SQL Server needs to check if there are any rows with values outside of the `smallint` boundaries.

3. Alteration requires changing every data row in addition to the metadata. An example of such an operation is changing a column data type in a way that requires either a different storage format or a type conversion. For example, when you change a fixed-length `char` column to `varchar`, SQL Server needs to move the data from the fixed- to the variable-length section of the row. Another example is when changing `char` data type to `int`. This operation works as long as all `char` values can be converted to `int`, but SQL Server must physically update every data row in the table converting the data.

It is worth noting that table-locking behavior during alteration is version and edition specific. For example, the Enterprise Edition of SQL Server 2012 allows adding a new `NOT NULL` column, instantly storing the information at the metadata level without changing every row in the table. As another example, SQL Server 2016 adds the option of altering columns and adding and dropping primary-key and unique constraints online using the same technique as an online index rebuild under the hood.

■ **Note** We will discuss SQL Server locking and the concurrency model in greater detail in Part III of the book.

Unfortunately, table alteration never decreases the size of a data row. When you drop a column from a table, SQL Server does not reclaim the space that the column used.

When you change the data type to decrease the data length, for example from `int` to `smallint`, SQL Server continues to use same amount of storage space as before while checking that row values conform to the new data-type domain values.

When you change the data type to increase the data length, for example from `int` to `bigint`, SQL Server adds the new column under the hood and copies the original data to the new column in all data rows, leaving the space used by the old column intact.

Let's look at the following example. Listing 1-18 creates a table and checks the column offsets on the table.

Listing 1-18. Table alteration: Table creation and original column offsets check

```
create table dbo.AlterDemo
(
    ID int not null,
    Col1 int null,
    Col2 bigint null,
    Col3 char(10) null,
    Col4 tinyint null
);

select
    c.column_id, c.Name, ipc.leaf_offset as [Offset in Row]
    ,ipc.max_inrow_length as [Max Length], ipc.system_type_id as [Column Type]
```

```
from
    sys.system_internals_partition_columns ipc join sys.partitions p on
        ipc.partition_id = p.partition_id
    join sys.columns c on
        c.column_id = ipc.partition_column_id and
        c.object_id = p.object_id
where p.object_id = object_id(N'dbo.AlterDemo')
order by c.column_id;
```

Figure 1-20 shows the results of the query. All columns in the table are fixed length. The `Offset in Row` column indicates the starting offset of the data column in the row. The `Max Length` column specifies how many bytes of data the column uses. Finally, the `Column Type` column shows the system data type of the column.

	column_id	Name	Offset in Row	Max Length	Column Type
1	1	ID	4	4	56
2	2	Col1	8	4	56
3	3	Col2	12	8	127
4	4	Col3	20	10	175
5	5	Col4	30	1	48

Figure 1-20. *Table alteration: Column offsets before table alteration*

Now, let's perform a few alterations, as shown in Listing 1-19.

Listing 1-19. Table alteration: Altering the table

```
alter table dbo.AlterDemo drop column Col1;
alter table dbo.AlterDemo alter column Col2 tinyint;
alter table dbo.AlterDemo alter column Col3 char(1);
alter table dbo.AlterDemo alter column Col4 int;
```

If you check the column offsets again, you'll see the results shown in Figure 1-21.

	column_id	Name	Offset in Row	Max Length	Column Type
1	1	ID	4	4	56
2	3	Col2	12	1	48
3	4	Col3	20	1	175
4	5	Col4	31	4	56

Figure 1-21. *Table alteration: Column offsets after table alteration*

Even though we dropped the Col1 column, the offsets of the Col2 and Col3 columns have not been changed. Moreover, both the Col2 and Col3 columns require just one byte to store the data, although it does not affect the offsets of either.

Finally, the Col4 column offset has been changed. The column data length has been increased, and SQL Server created the new column to accommodate the new data type values.

Before the alterations, a row needed 27 bytes to store the data. Alteration increased the required storage space to 31 bytes even though the actual data size is just 10 bytes. 21 bytes of storage space per row are wasted.

The only way to reclaim the space is by rebuilding a heap table or clustered index, which we will discuss in Chapter 6.

If you rebuilt the table with the ALTER TABLE dbo.AlterDemo REBUILD command and checked the column offsets again, you would see the results shown in Figure 1-22.

	column_id	Name	Offset in R...	Max Length	Column Type
1	1	ID	4	4	56
2	3	Col2	8	1	48
3	4	Col3	9	1	175
4	5	Col4	10	4	56

Figure 1-22. *Table alteration: Column offsets after table rebuild*

As you can see, the table rebuild reclaims the unused space from the rows.

Finally, table alteration requires SQL Server to obtain a schema modification (SCH-M) lock on the table. It makes the table inaccessible by another session for the duration of the alteration. We will talk about schema locks in detail in Chapter 23, "Schema Locks."

Summary

SQL Server stores data in databases that consist of one or more transaction log files and one or more data files. Data files are combined into filegroups. Filegroups abstract the database file structure from database objects, which are logically stored in the filegroups rather than in database files. You should consider creating multiple data files for any filegroups that store volatile data.

SQL Server always zeros out transaction logs during a database restore and log file auto-growth. By default, it also zeros out data files unless instant file initialization is enabled. Instant file initialization significantly decreases database restore time and makes data file auto-growth instant. However, there is a small security risk associated with instant file initialization, as the uninitialized part of the database may contain data from previously deleted OS files. Nevertheless, it is recommended that you enable instant file initialization if such a risk is acceptable.

SQL Server stores information on 8,000 data pages combined into extents. There are two types of extents. Mixed extents store data from different objects. Uniform extents store data that belongs to a single object. SQL Server stores the first eight object pages in mixed extents. After that, only uniform extents are used during object space allocation. You should consider enabling trace flag T1118 to prevent mixed extents space allocation and reduce allocation map pages contention.

SQL Server uses special map pages to track allocations in the file. There are several allocation map types. GAM pages track which extents are allocated. SGAM pages track available mixed extents. IAM pages track extents that are used by the allocation units on the object (partition) level. PFS stores several page attributes, including free space available on the page, in heap tables and in row-overflow and LOB pages.

SQL Server stores actual data in data rows. There are two different kinds of data types available. Fixed-length data types always use the same storage space regardless of the value, even when it is NULL. Variable-length data storage uses the actual data value size.

The fixed-length part of the row and internal overhead must fit into a single data page. Variable-length data can be stored in separate data pages, such as row-overflow and LOB pages, depending on the actual data size and data type.

SQL Server reads the data pages into a memory cache called the buffer pool. When data is modified, SQL Server synchronously writes the log record into the transaction log. It saves the modified data pages asynchronously during the checkpoint and lazy writer processes.

SQL Server is a very I/O-intensive application, and reducing the number of I/O operations helps to improve the performance of systems. It is beneficial to reduce the size of data rows by using optimal data types. This allows you to put more rows in the data page and decreases the number of data pages to be processed during scan operations.

You need to be careful when altering tables. This process never decreases the size of rows. The unused space from the rows can be reclaimed by rebuilding a table or clustered index.

CHAPTER 2

Tables and Indexes: Internal Structure and Access Methods

SQL Server stores data in tables and indexes. They represent a collection of data pages with rows that belong to a single entity or object.

By default, the data in tables is unsorted. You can store it in sorted order by defining a clustered index on the table. Moreover, you can create nonclustered indexes that persist another copy of the data from the index columns sorted in a different order.

In this chapter, we will talk about the internal structure of the indexes, cover how SQL Server uses them, and discuss how to write queries in a way that efficiently utilizes them.

Heap Tables

Heap tables are tables without a clustered index. The data in heap tables is unsorted. SQL Server does not guarantee, nor does it maintain, a sorting order of the data in heap tables.

When you insert data into heap tables, SQL Server tries to fill pages as much as possible, although it does not analyze the actual free space available on a page. It uses the *page free space (PFS)* allocation map instead. SQL Server errs on the side of caution and uses the low value from the PFS free space percentage tier during the estimation.

For example, if a data page stores 4,100 bytes of data, and as result it has 3,960 bytes of free space available, PFS would indicate that the page is 51–80 percent full. SQL Server would not put a new row on the page if its size exceeds 20 percent (8,060 bytes * 0.2 = 1,612 bytes) of the page size. Let's examine that behavior and create the table with the code shown in Listing 2-1.

Listing 2-1. Inserting data into heap tables: Creating the table

```
create table dbo.Heap
(
    Val varchar(8000) not null
);

;with CTE(ID,Val)
as
(
    select 1, replicate('0',4089)
    union all
    select ID + 1, Val from CTE where ID < 20
```


D. Korotkevitch, *Pro SQL Server Internals*, DOI 10.1007/978-1-4842-1964-5_2

```
)
insert into dbo.Heap
    select Val from CTE;

select page_count, avg_record_size_in_bytes, avg_page_space_used_in_percent
from sys.dm_db_index_physical_stats(db_id(),object_id(N'dbo.Heap'),0,null,'DETAILED');
```

The following is the output of the code from Listing 2-1:

```
Result: 1 row per page. 4,100 bytes are used. 3,960 bytes are available per page

page_count          avg_record_size_in_bytes         avg_page_space_used_in_percent
-----------         -------------------------        -------------------------------
20                  4100                             50.6548060291574
```

At this point, the table stores 20 rows of 4,100 bytes each. SQL Server allocates 20 data pages—one page per row—with 3,960 bytes available. PFS would indicate that pages are 51-80 percent full.

The code shown in Listing 2-2 inserts a small 111-byte row, which is about 1.4 percent of the page size. As a result, SQL Server knows that the row would fit into one of the existing pages (they all have at least 20 percent of free space available), and a new page should not be allocated.

Listing 2-2. Inserting data into heap tables: Inserting a small row

```
insert into dbo.Heap(Val) values(replicate('1',100));

select page_count, avg_record_size_in_bytes, avg_page_space_used_in_percent
from sys.dm_db_index_physical_stats(db_id(),object_id(N'dbo.Heap'),0,null,'DETAILED');
```

The following is the output of the code from Listing 2-2:

```
Result: 100 bytes row has been inserted into one of existing pages (100 bytes = ~1.4% of
the page size)

page_count          avg_record_size_in_bytes         avg_page_space_used_in_percent
-----------         -------------------------        -------------------------------
20                  3910.047                         50.7246108228317
```

Lastly, a third insert statement, shown in Listing 2-3, needs 2,011 bytes for the row, which is about 25 percent of the page size. SQL Server does not know if any of the existing pages have enough free space to accommodate the row, and, as a result, it allocates a new page. You can see that SQL Server does not access existing pages by checking the actual free space, and it uses PFS data for the estimation.

Listing 2-3. Inserting data into heap tables: Inserting a large row

```
insert into dbo.Heap(Val) values(replicate('2',2000));

select page_count, avg_record_size_in_bytes, avg_page_space_used_in_percent
from sys.dm_db_index_physical_stats(db_id(),object_id(N'dbo.Heap'),0,null,'DETAILED');
```

The following is the output of the code from Listing 2-3:

```
Result: New page has been allocated for 2000 bytes row (2000 bytes = ~25% of the page size)

page_count          avg_record_size_in_bytes          avg_page_space_used_in_percent
-----------         -------------------------         ------------------------------
21                  3823.727                          49.4922782307882
```

This behavior leads to the situation where SQL Server unnecessarily allocates new data pages, leaving large amounts of free space unused. It is not always a problem when the size of rows vary—in those cases, SQL Server eventually fills empty spaces with the smaller rows. However, especially in cases when all rows are relatively large, you can end up with large amounts of unused space on the data pages.

When selecting data from the heap table, SQL Server uses an *index allocation map (IAM)* to find the pages and extents that need to be scanned. It analyzes what extents belong to the table and processes them based on their allocation order rather than on the order in which the data was inserted. Figure 2-1 illustrates this point.

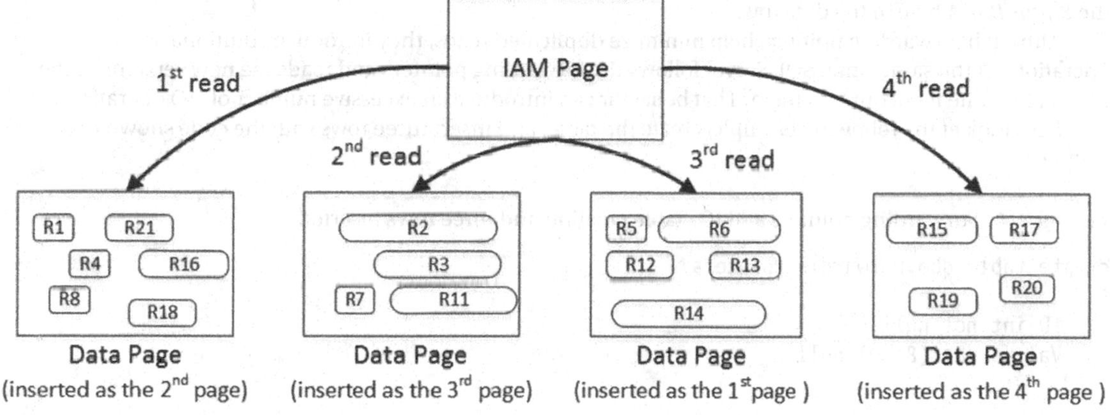

Figure 2-1. *Selecting data from the heap table*

When you update a row in the heap table, SQL Server tries to accommodate it on the same page. If there is no free space available, SQL Server moves the new version of the row to another page and replaces the old row with a special 16-byte row called a *forwarding pointer*. The new version of the row is called *forwarded row*. Figure 2-2 illustrates this point.

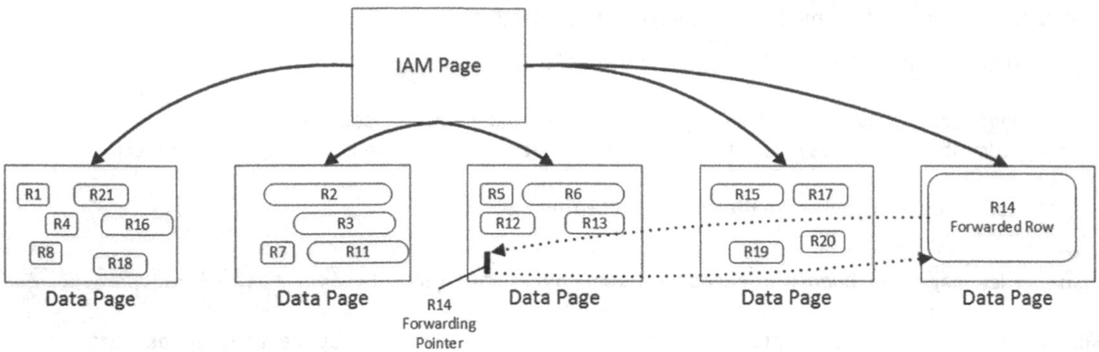

Figure 2-2. *Forwarding pointers*

There are two main reasons why forwarding pointers are used. First, they prevent updates of nonclustered index keys that reference the row. We will talk about nonclustered indexes in more detail later in this chapter.

In addition, forwarding pointers help minimize the number of duplicated reads; that is, situations in which a single row is read multiple times during a table scan. Let's look at Figure 2-2 as an example of this and assume that SQL Server scans the pages in left-to-right order. Let's further assume that the row in page 3 was modified after the page was read at the time when SQL Server was reading page 4. The new version of the row would be moved to page 5, which has yet to be processed. Without forwarding pointers, SQL Server would not know that the old version of the row had already been read, and it would read it again during the page 5 scan. With forwarding pointers, SQL Server would ignore the forwarded rows–they have a bit set in the *Status Bits A* byte in the data row.

Although forwarding pointers help minimize duplicated reads, they introduce additional read operations at the same time. SQL Server follows the forwarding pointers and reads the new versions of the rows at the time it encounters them. That behavior can introduce an excessive number of I/O operations.

Let's look at the following example, create the table, and insert three rows with the code shown in Listing 2-4.

Listing 2-4. Forwarding pointers and IO: Table creation and three rows inserted

```
create table dbo.ForwardingPointers
(
    ID int not null,
    Val varchar(8000) null
);

insert into dbo.ForwardingPointers(ID,Val)
values(1,null),(2,replicate('2',7800)),(3,null);

select page_count, avg_record_size_in_bytes, avg_page_space_used_in_percent
    ,forwarded_record_count
from sys.dm_db_index_physical_stats(db_id(),object_id(N'dbo.ForwardingPointers'),0
    ,null,'DETAILED');

set statistics io on
select count(*) from dbo.ForwardingPointers;
```

The following is the output of the code from Listing 2-4:

```
page_count    avg_record_size_in_bytes    avg_page_space_used_in_percent    forwarded_record_count
---------     ----------------------      ----------------------------      --------------------
1             2612.333                    98.8742278230788                  0

Table 'ForwardingPointers'. Scan count 1, logical reads 1
```

As you can see in Figure 2-3, all three rows fit into the single page, and SQL Server needs to read just that page when it scans the table.

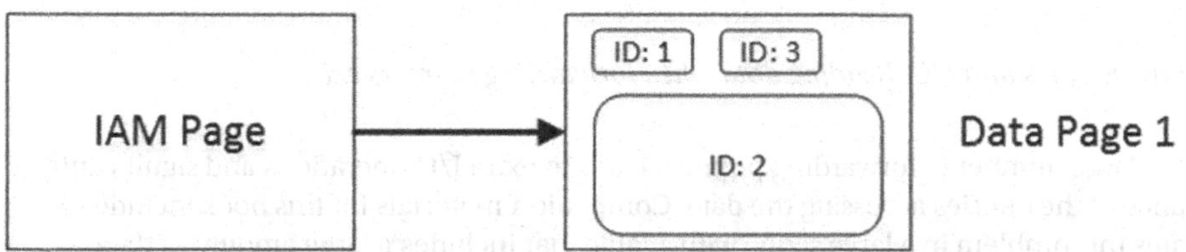

***Figure 2-3.** Forwarding pointers and I/O: Data pages after table creation*

Now, let's update two of the table rows by increasing their size. The new versions of the rows will not fit into the page anymore, which introduces the allocation of two new pages and two forwarding pointers. Listing 2-5 shows the code for this.

Listing 2-5. Forwarding pointers and I/O: Increasing size of the rows

```
update dbo.ForwardingPointers set Val = replicate('1',5000) where ID = 1;
update dbo.ForwardingPointers set Val = replicate('3',5000) where ID = 3;

select page_count, avg_record_size_in_bytes, avg_page_space_used_in_percent, forwarded_record_count
from sys.dm_db_index_physical_stats(db_id(),object_id(N'dbo.ForwardingPointers'),0,null
    ,'DETAILED');

set statistics io on
select count(*) from dbo.ForwardingPointers
```

The following is the output of the code from Listing 2-5:

```
page_count    avg_record_size_in_bytes    avg_page_space_used_in_percent    forwarded_record_count
---------     ---------------------       ----------------------------      --------------------
3             3577.4                      73.6800963676798                  2

Table 'ForwardingPointers'. Scan count 1, logical reads 5
```

When SQL Server reads the forwarding pointer rows from page 1, it follows them and reads pages 2 and 3 immediately. After that, SQL Server reads those pages one more time during the regular IAM scan process. As a result, we have five read operations, even though our table has just three data pages. Figure 2-4 illustrates this point.

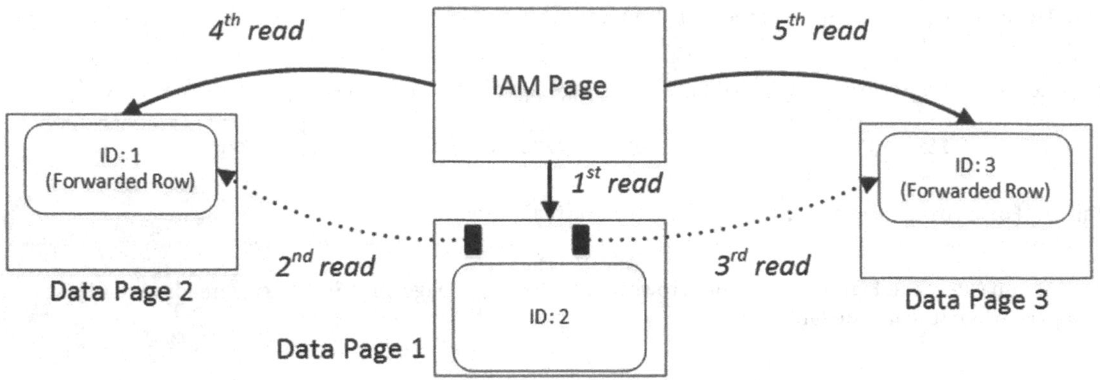

Figure 2-4. *Forwarding pointers and I/O: Reading data when forwarding pointers exist*

As you can see, the large number of forwarding pointers leads to extra I/O operations and significantly reduces the performance of the queries accessing the data. Companion materials for this book include the script that demonstrates this problem in a large scope with a table that includes a large amount of data.

When the size of the forwarded row is reduced by another update and the data page with forwarding pointer has enough space to accommodate the updated version of the row, SQL Server may move it back to its original data page and remove the forwarding pointer row. Nevertheless, the only reliable way to get rid of all of the forwarding pointers is by rebuilding the heap table. You can do that by using an `ALTER TABLE REBUILD` statement.

Heap tables can be useful in staging environments, where you want to import a large amount of data into the system as fast as possible. Inserting data into heap tables can often be faster than inserting it into tables with clustered indexes. Nevertheless, during a regular workload, tables with clustered indexes usually outperform heap tables, which have suboptimal space control and extra I/O operations introduced by forwarding pointers.

Clustered Indexes

A clustered index dictates the physical order of the data in a table, which is sorted according to the clustered index key. The table can have only one clustered index defined.

Let's assume that you want to create a clustered index on the heap table with the data. As a first step, which is shown in Figure 2-5, SQL Server creates another copy of the data that is then sorted based on the value of the clustered key. The data pages are linked in a double-linked list where every page contains pointers to the next and previous pages in the chain. This list is called the *leaf level* of the index, and it contains the actual table data.

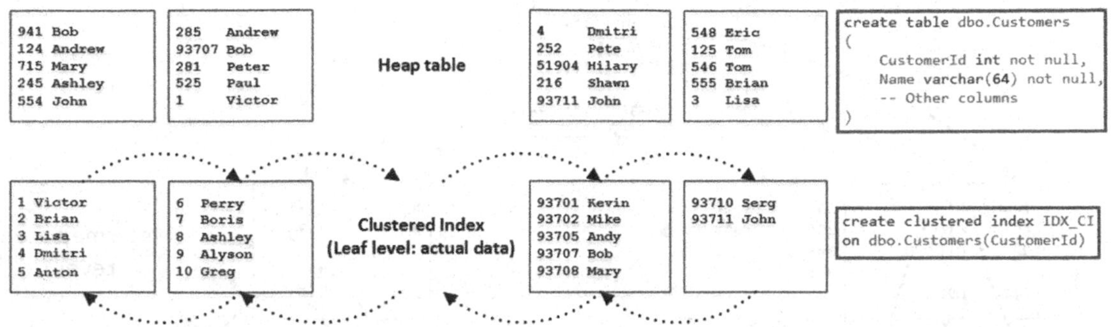

Figure 2-5. Clustered index structure: Leaf level

■ **Note** The sort order on the page is controlled by a slot array. Actual data on the page is unsorted.

When the leaf level consists of multiple pages, SQL Server starts to build an *intermediate level* of the index, as shown in Figure 2-6.

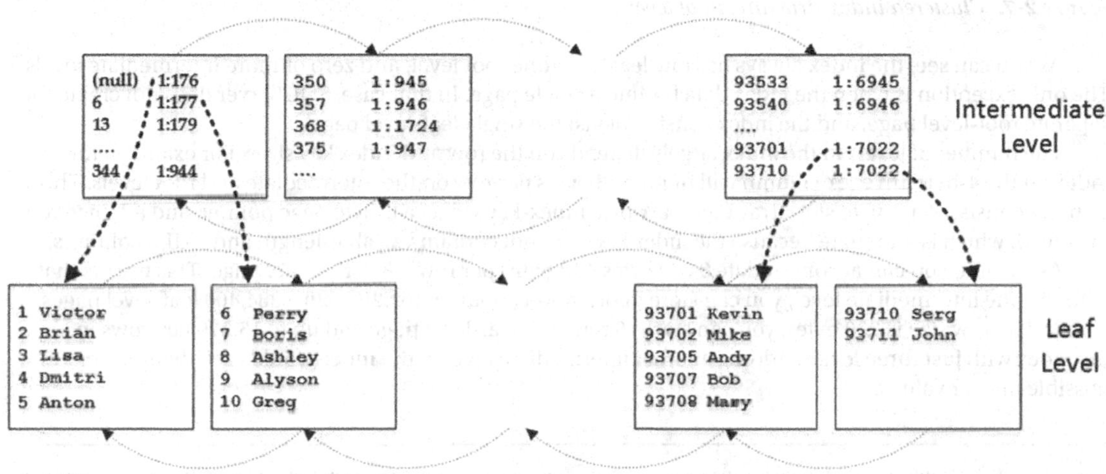

Figure 2-6. Clustered index structure: Intermediate and leaf levels

The intermediate level stores one row per leaf-level page. It stores two pieces of information: the physical address and the minimum value of the index key from the page it references. The only exception is the very first row on the first page, where SQL Server stores `NULL` rather than the minimum index key value. With such optimization, SQL Server does not need to update non-leaf-level rows when you insert the row with the lowest key value in the table.

The pages on the intermediate levels are also linked to the double-linked list. SQL Server adds more and more intermediate levels until there is a level that includes just the single page. This level is called the *root level*, and it becomes the entry point to the index, as shown in Figure 2-7.

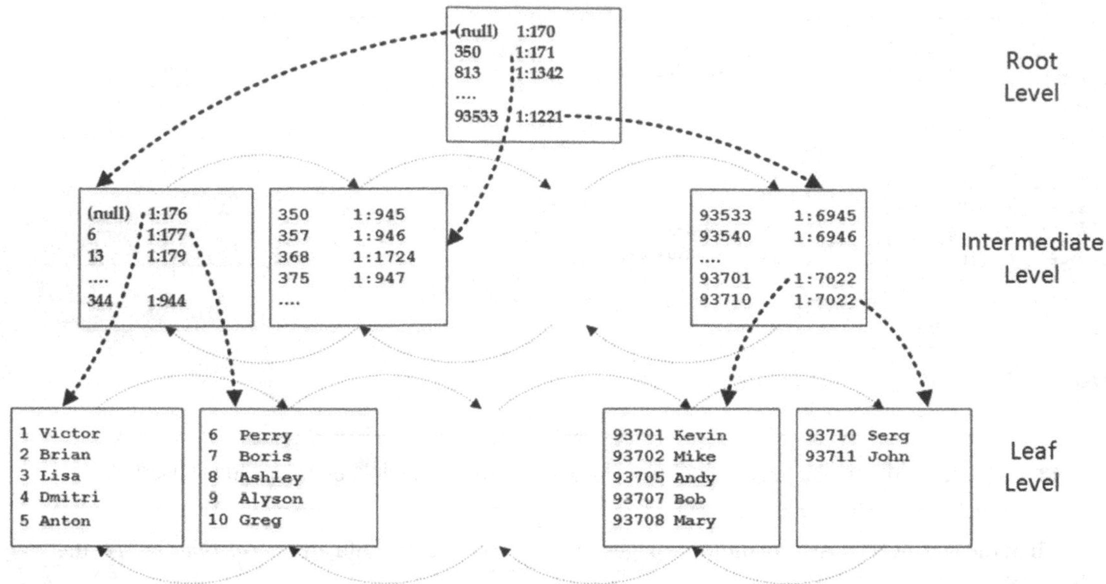

Figure 2-7. *Clustered index structure: Root level*

As you can see, the index always has one leaf level, one root level, and zero or more intermediate levels. The only exception is when the index data fits into a single page. In that case, SQL Server does not create the separate root-level page, and the index consists of just the single leaf-level page.

The number of levels in the index largely depends on the row and index key sizes. For example, the index on the 4-byte `integer` column will require 13 bytes per row on the intermediate and root levels. Those 13 bytes consist of a 2-byte slot-array entry, a 4-byte index-key value, a 6-byte page pointer, and a 1-byte row overhead, which is adequate because the index key does not contain variable-length and NULL columns.

As a result, you can accommodate 8,060 bytes / 13 bytes per row = 620 rows per page. This means that, with the one intermediate level, you can store information about up to 620 * 620 = 384,400 leaf-level pages. If your data row size is 200 bytes, you can store 40 rows per leaf-level page and up to 15,376,000 rows in the index with just three levels. Adding another intermediate level to the index would essentially cover all possible integer values.

■ **Note** In real life, index fragmentation would reduce those numbers. We will talk about index fragmentation in Chapter 6.

There are three different ways in which SQL Server can read data from the index. The first one is by an *ordered scan.* Let's assume that we want to run the `SELECT Name FROM dbo.Customers ORDER BY CustomerId` query. The data on the leaf level of the index is already sorted based on the `CustomerId` column value. As a result, SQL Server can scan the leaf level of the index from the first to the last page and return the rows in the order in which they were stored.

SQL Server starts with the root page of the index and reads the first row from there. That row references the intermediate page with the minimum key value from the table. SQL Server reads that page and repeats the process until it finds the first page on the leaf level. Then, SQL Server starts to read rows one by one, moving through the linked list of the pages until all rows have been read. Figure 2-8 illustrates this process.

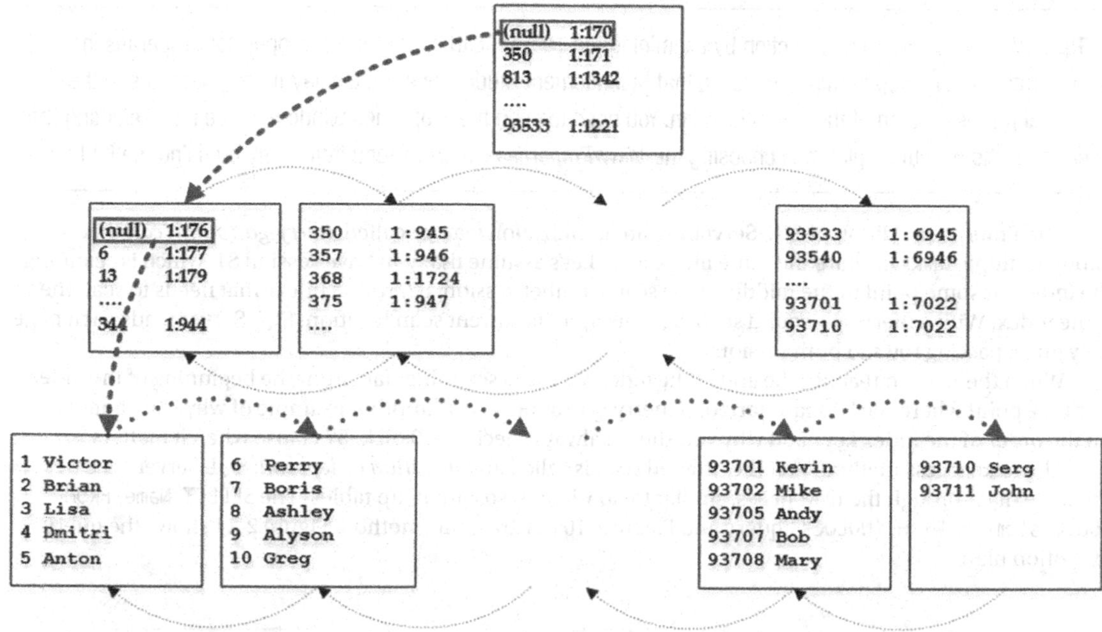

Figure 2-8. *Ordered index scan*

The execution plan for the preceding query shows the *Clustered Index Scan* operator with the *Ordered* property set to *true,* as shown in Figure 2-9.

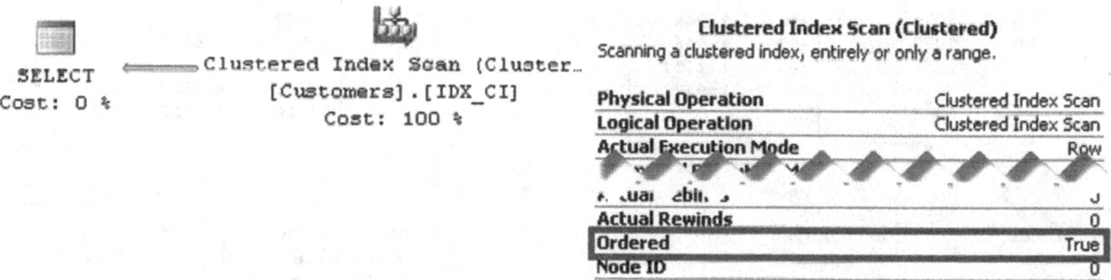

Figure 2-9. *Ordered index scan execution plan*

It is worth mentioning that the `order by` clause is not required for an ordered scan to be triggered. An ordered scan just means that SQL Server reads the data based on the order of the index key.

SQL Server can navigate through indexes in both directions, forward and backward. However, there is one important aspect that you must keep in mind: SQL Server does not use parallelism during backward index scans.

■ **Tip** You can check scan direction by examining the `INDEX SCAN` or `INDEX SEEK` operator properties in the execution plan. Keep in mind, however, that Management Studio does not display these properties in the graphical representation of the execution plan. You need to open the Properties window to see it by selecting the operator in the execution plan and choosing the *View/Properties Window* menu item or by pressing the F4 key.

The Enterprise Edition of SQL Server has an optimization feature called *merry-go-round scan* that allows multiple tasks to share the same index scan. Let's assume that you have session S1, which is scanning the index. At some point in the middle of the scan, another session, S2, runs a query that needs to scan the same index. With a merry-go-round scan, S2 joins S1 at its current scan location. SQL Server reads each page only once, passing rows to both sessions.

When the S1 scan reaches the end of the index, S2 starts scanning data from the beginning of the index until the point where the S2 scan started. A merry-go-round scan is another example of why you cannot rely on the order of the index keys and why you should always specify an `ORDER BY` clause when it matters.

The next access method after the ordered scan is called an *allocation order scan*. SQL Server accesses the table data through the IAM pages, similar to how it does so with heap tables. The `SELECT Name FROM dbo.Customers WITH (NOLOCK)` query and Figure 2-10 illustrate this method. Figure 2-11 shows the query execution plan.

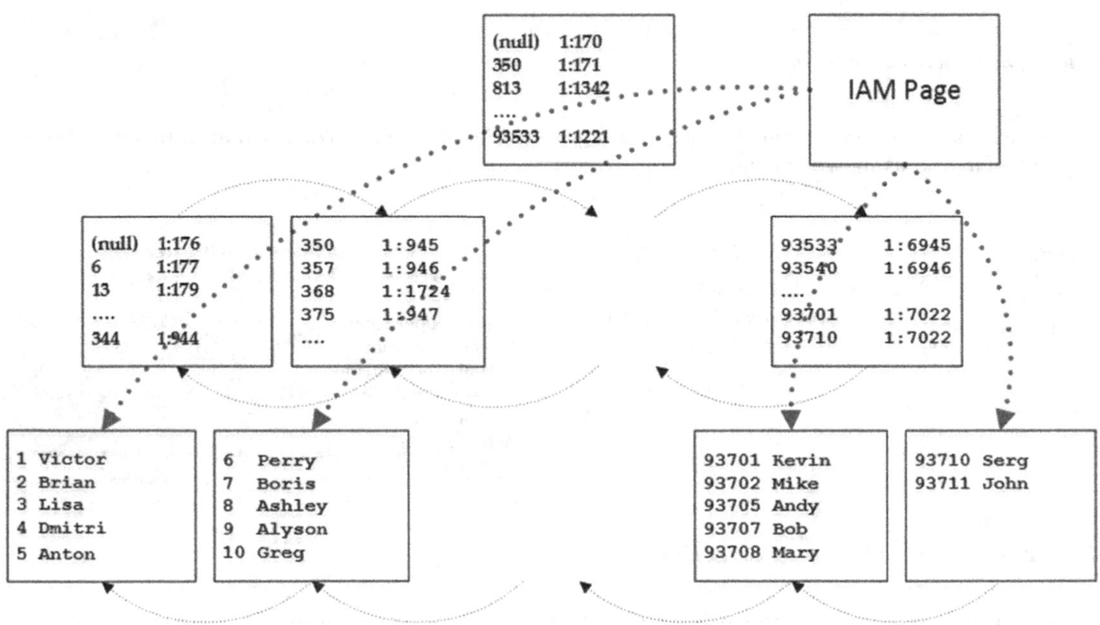

***Figure 2-10.** Allocation order scan*

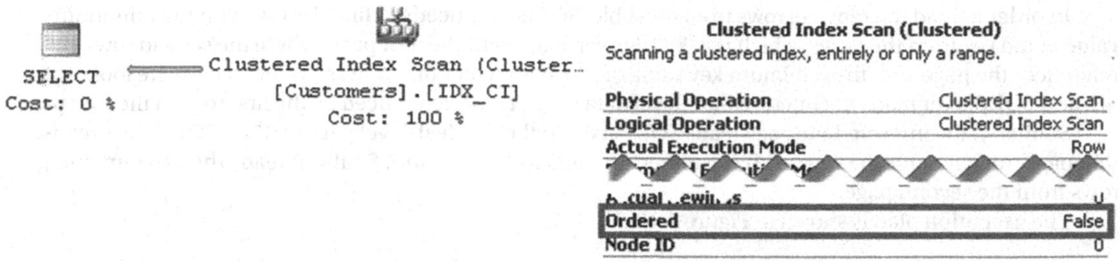

Figure 2-11. *Allocation order scan execution plan*

Unfortunately, it is not easy to detect when SQL Server uses an allocation order scan. Even though the `Ordered` property in the execution plan shows `false`, it indicates that SQL Server does not care whether the rows were read in the order of the index key, not that an allocation order scan was used.

An allocation order scan can be faster for scanning large tables, although it has a higher startup cost. SQL Server does not use this access method when the table is small. Another important consideration is data consistency. SQL Server does not use forwarding pointers in tables that have a clustered index, and an allocation order scan can produce inconsistent results. Rows can be skipped or read multiple times due to the data movement caused by page splits. As a result, SQL Server usually avoids using allocation order scans unless it reads the data in `READ UNCOMMITTED` or `SERIALIZABLE` transaction-isolation levels.

■ **Note** We will talk about page splits and fragmentation in Chapter 6, "Index Fragmentation," and discuss locking and data consistency in Part III, "Locking, Blocking, and Concurrency."

The last index access method is called *index seek*. The `SELECT Name FROM dbo.Customers WHERE CustomerId BETWEEN 4 AND 7` query and Figure 2-12 illustrate the operation.

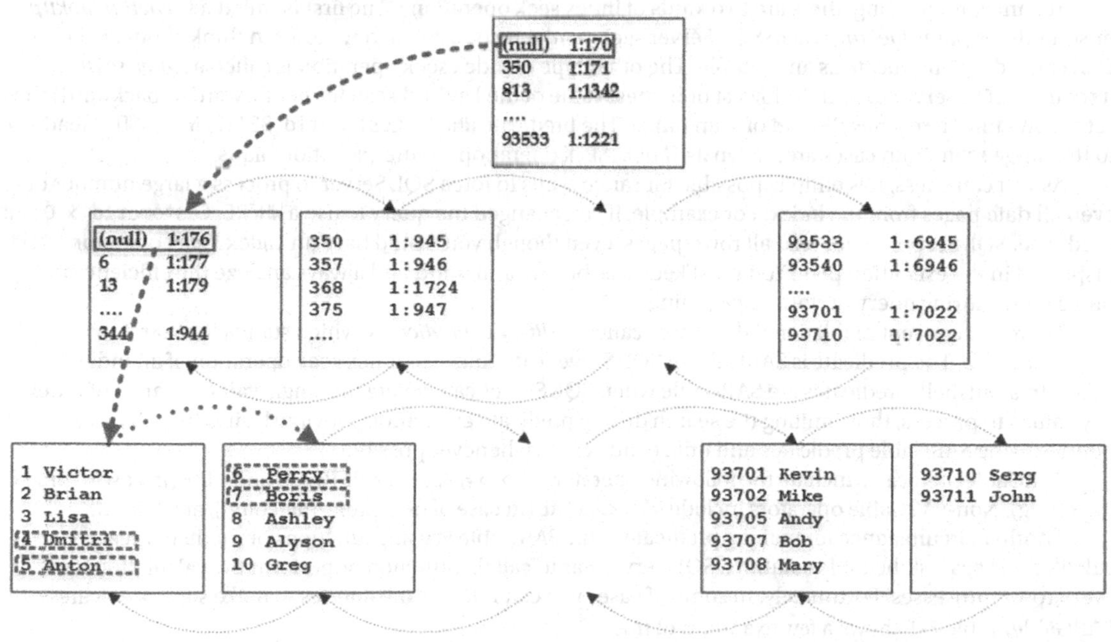

Figure 2-12. *Index seek*

In order to read the range of rows from the table, SQL Server needs to find the row with the minimum value of the key from the range, which is 4. SQL Server starts with the root page, where the second row references the page with the minimum key value of 350. It is greater than the key value that we are looking for (4), and SQL Server reads the intermediate-level data page (1:170) referenced by the first row on the root page.

Similarly, the intermediate page leads SQL Server to the first leaf-level page (1:176). SQL Server reads that page, then it reads the rows with CustomerIds equal to 4 and 5, and, finally, it reads the two remaining rows from the second page.

The execution plan is shown in Figure 2-13.

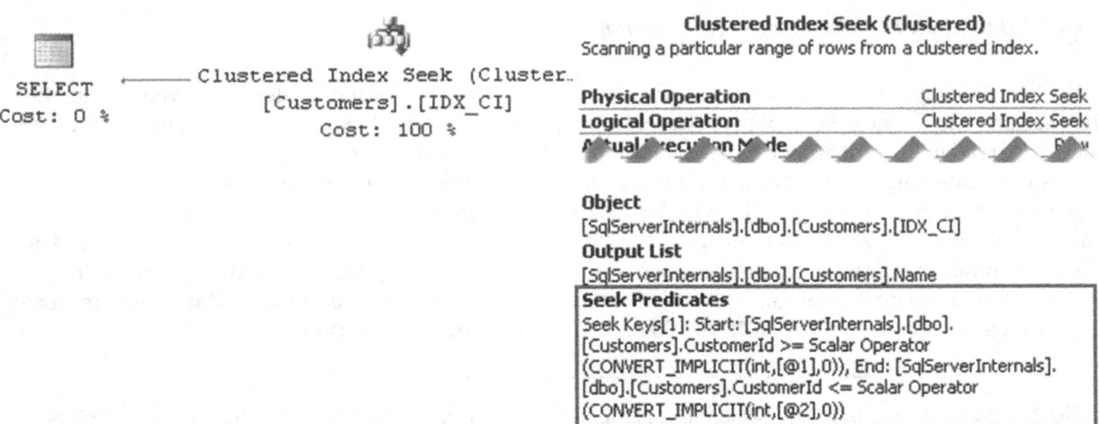

***Figure 2-13.** Index seek execution plan*

As you can guess, index seek is more efficient than index scan, because SQL Server processes just the subset of rows and data pages rather than scanning the entire table.

Technically speaking, there are two kinds of index seek operations. The first is called a *singleton lookup*, or sometimes *point-lookup*, where SQL Server seeks and returns a single row. You can think about `WHERE CustomerId = 2` predicate as an example. The other type of index seek operation is called a *range scan*, and it requires SQL Server to find the lowest or highest value of the key and scan (either forward or backward) the set of rows until it reaches the end of scan range. The predicate `WHERE CustomerId BETWEEN 4 AND 7` leads to the range scan. Both cases are shown as `INDEX SEEK` operations in the execution plans.

As you can guess, it is entirely possible for range scans to force SQL Server to process a large number or even all data pages from the index. For example, if you changed the query to use a `WHERE CustomerId > 0` predicate, SQL Server would read all rows/pages, even though you would have an `Index Seek` operator displayed in the execution plan. You must keep this behavior in mind and always analyze the efficiency of range scans during query performance tuning.

There is a concept in relational databases called *SARGable predicates*, which stands for Search *Argument able*. The predicate is SARGable if SQL Server can utilize an index seek operation, if an index exists. In a nutshell, predicates are SARGable when SQL Server can isolate the single value or range of index key values to process, thus limiting the search during predicate evaluation. Obviously, it is beneficial to write queries using SARGable predicates and utilize index seek whenever possible.

SARGable predicates include the following operators: =, >, >=, <, <=, `IN`, `BETWEEN`, and `LIKE` (in case of prefix matching). Non-SARGable operators include `NOT`, <>, `LIKE` (in case of non-prefix matching), and `NOT IN`.

Another circumstance for making predicates non-SARGable is using functions or mathematical calculations against the table columns. SQL Server has to call the function or perform the calculation for every row it processes. Fortunately, in some of cases you can refactor the queries to make such predicates SARGable. Table 2-1 shows a few examples of this.

Table 2-1. *Examples of Refactoring Non-SARGable Predicates into SARGable Ones*

Operation	Non-SARGable implementation	SARGable implementation
Mathematical calculations	`Column - 1 = @Value`	`Column = @Value + 1`
	`ABS(Column) = 1`	`Column IN (-1, 1)`
Date manipulation	`CAST(Column as date) = @Date (in SQL Server prior 2008)` `convert(datetime, convert (varchar(10),Column,121))`	`Column >= @Date and Column < DATEADD(day,1,@Date)`
	`DATEPART(year,Column) = @Year`	`Column >= @Year and Column < DATEADD(year,1,@Year)`
	`DATEADD(day,7,Column) > GETDATE()`	`Column > DATEADD(day,-7,GETDATE())`
Prefix search	`LEFT(Column,3) = 'ABC'`	`Column LIKE 'ABC%'`
Substring search	`Column LIKE '%ABC%'`	`Use Full-Text Search or other technologies`

Another important factor that you must keep in mind is *type conversion*. In some cases, you can make predicates non-SARGable by using incorrect data types. Let's create a table with a `varchar` column and populate it with some data, as shown in Listing 2-6.

Listing 2-6. SARG predicates and data types: Test table creation

```
create table dbo.Data
(
    VarcharKey varchar(10) not null,
    Placeholder char(200)
);

create unique clustered index IDX_Data_VarcharKey
on dbo.Data(VarcharKey);

;with N1(C) as (select 0 union all select 0) -- 2 rows
,N2(C) as (select 0 from N1 as T1 cross join N1 as T2) -- 4 rows
,N3(C) as (select 0 from N2 as T1 cross join N2 as T2) -- 16 rows
,N4(C) as (select 0 from N3 as T1 cross join N3 as T2) -- 256 rows
,N5(C) as (select 0 from N4 as T1 cross join N4 as T2) -- 65,536 rows
,IDs(ID) as (select row_number() over (order by (select null)) from N5)
insert into dbo.Data(VarcharKey)
    select convert(varchar(10),ID) from IDs;
```

The clustered index key column is defined as `varchar`, even though it stores integer values. Now, let's run two selects, as shown in Listing 2-7, and look at the execution plans.

Listing 2-7. SARG predicates and data types: Select with integer parameter

```
declare
    @IntParam int = '200'

select * from dbo.Data where VarcharKey = @IntParam;
select * from dbo.Data where VarcharKey = convert(varchar(10),@IntParam);
```

As you can see in Figure 2-14, in the case of the integer parameter, SQL Server scans the clustered index, converting varchar to an integer for every row. In the second case, SQL Server converts the integer parameter to a varchar at the beginning and utilizes a much more efficient *clustered index seek* operation.

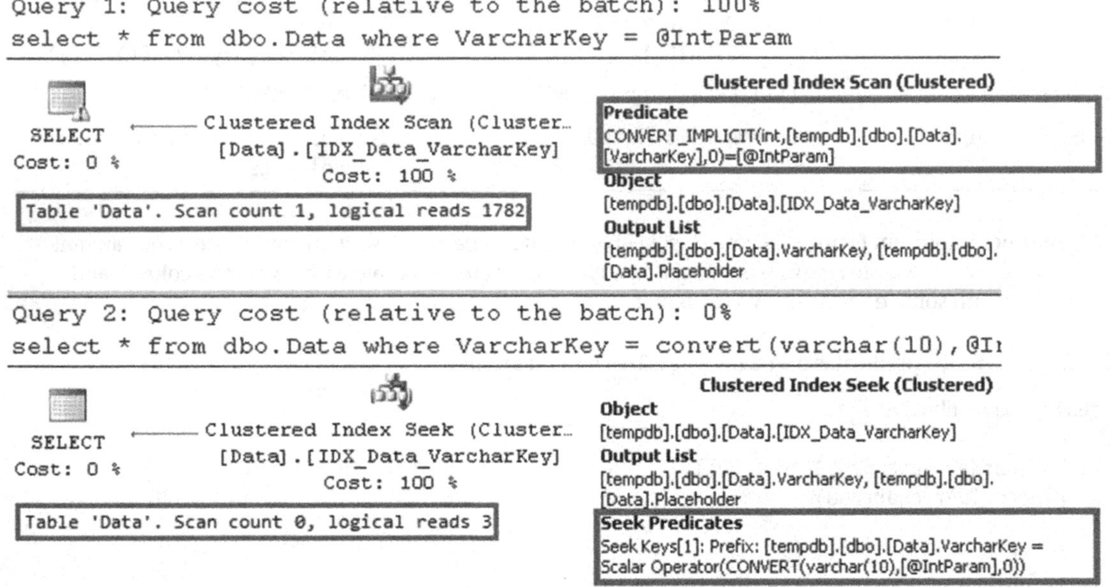

Figure 2-14. *SARG predicates and data types: Execution plans with integer parameter*

■ **Tip** Pay attention to the column data types in the join predicates. Implicit or explicit data type conversions can significantly decrease the performance of the queries.

You will observe very similar behavior in the case of unicode string parameters. Let's run the queries shown in Listing 2-8. Figure 2-15 shows the execution plans for the statements.

Listing 2-8. SARG predicates and data types: Select with string parameter

```
select * from dbo.Data where VarcharKey = '200';
select * from dbo.Data where VarcharKey = N'200'; -- unicode parameter
```

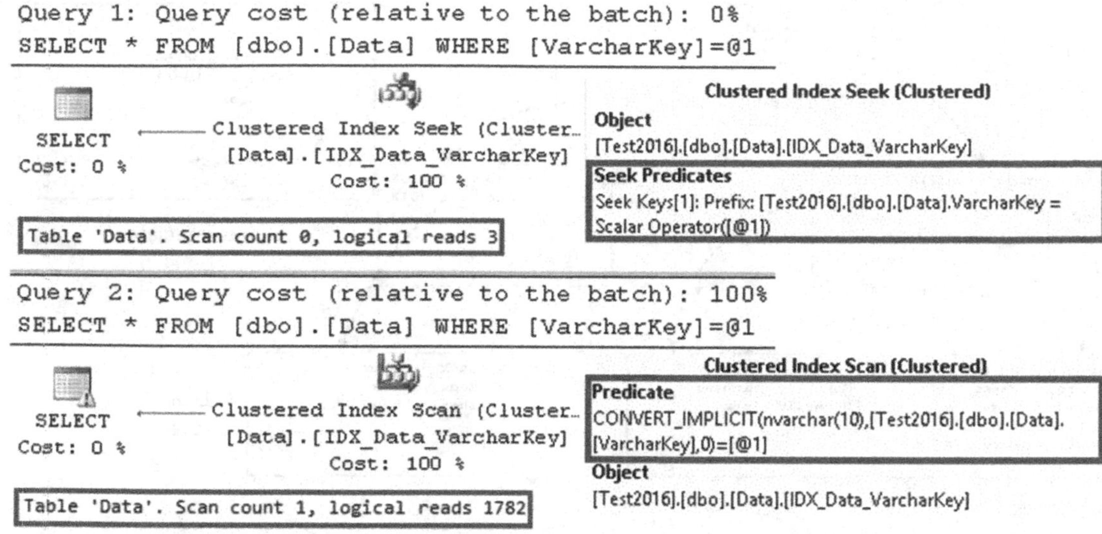

Figure 2-15. *SARG predicates and data types: Execution plans with string parameter*

As you can see, a unicode string parameter is non-SARGable for varchar columns. This is a much bigger issue than it appears to be. While you rarely write queries in this way, as shown in Listing 2-8, most application development environments nowadays treat strings as unicode. As a result, SQL Server client libraries generate unicode (nvarchar) parameters for string objects unless the parameter data type is explicitly specified as varchar. This makes the predicates non-SARGable, and it can lead to major performance hits due to unnecessary scans, even when varchar columns are indexed.

■ **Important** Always specify parameter data types in client applications. For example, in ADO.Net, use `Parameters.Add("@ParamName",SqlDbType.Varchar, <Size>).Value = stringVariable` instead of `Parameters.Add("@ParamName").Value = stringVariable` overload. Use mapping in ORM frameworks to explicitly specify non-unicode attributes in the classes.

It is also worth mentioning that varchar parameters are SARGable for nvarchar unicode data columns.

Composite Indexes

Indexes with multiple key columns are called *composite (or compound) indexes*. The data in the composite indexes is sorted on a per-column basis from leftmost to rightmost columns. Figure 2-16 shows the structure of a composite index.

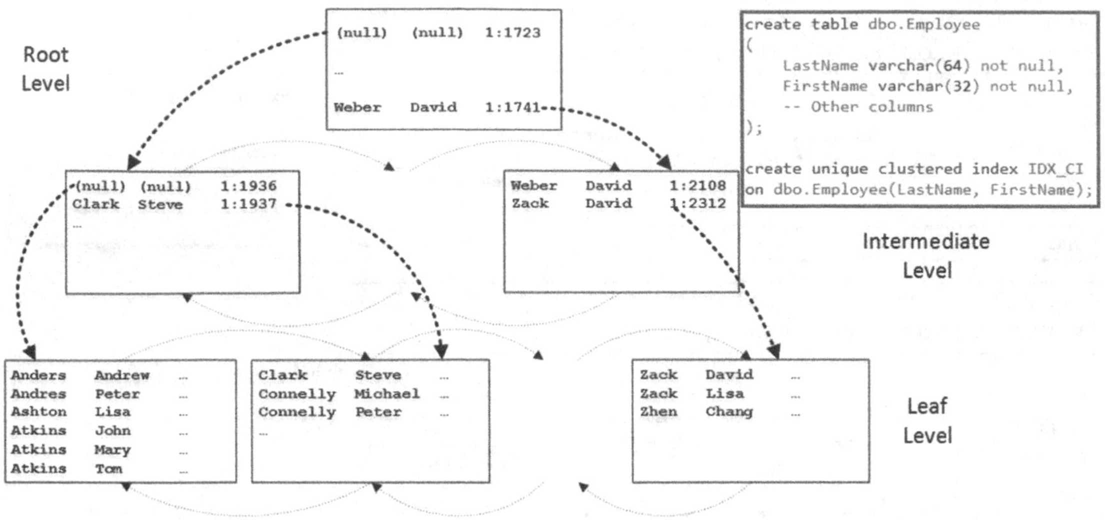

Figure 2-16. *Composite index structure*

The SARGability of a composite index depends on the SARGability of the predicates on the leftmost index columns. Table 2-2 shows examples of SARGable and non-SARGable predicates using the index from Figure 2-16 as the example.

Table 2-2. *SARGable and Non-SARGable Predicates on a Composite Index*

SARGable predicates	Non-SARGable predicates
`LastName = 'Clark' and FirstName = 'Steve'`	`LastName <> 'Clark' and FirstName = 'Steve'`
`LastName = 'Clark' and FirstName <> 'Steve'`	`LastName LIKE '%ar%' and FirstName = 'Steve'`
`LastName = 'Clark'`	`FirstName = 'Steve'`
`LastName LIKE 'Cl%'`	

Nonclustered Indexes

While a clustered index specifies how data rows are sorted in a table, nonclustered indexes define a separate sorting order for a column or set of columns and persist them as a separate data structure.

You can think about a book as an example. Page numbers would represent the book's *clustered index.* The index at the end of the book shows the list of terms from the book in alphabetical order. Each term references the page numbers where the term is mentioned. The index represents the *nonclustered index* of the terms.

When you need to find a term in the book, you can look it up in the index. It is a fast and efficient operation, because terms are sorted in alphabetical order. Next, you can quickly find the pages on which the terms are mentioned using the page numbers specified there. Without the index, the only choice would be reading all of the pages in the book one by one until all references to the term were found.

The nonclustered index structure is very similar to the clustered index structure. Let's create a nonclustered index on the `Name` column from the `Customers` table with a `CREATE NONCLUSTERED INDEX IDX_NCI ON dbo.Customers(Name)` statement. Figure 2-17 shows the structures of both indexes.

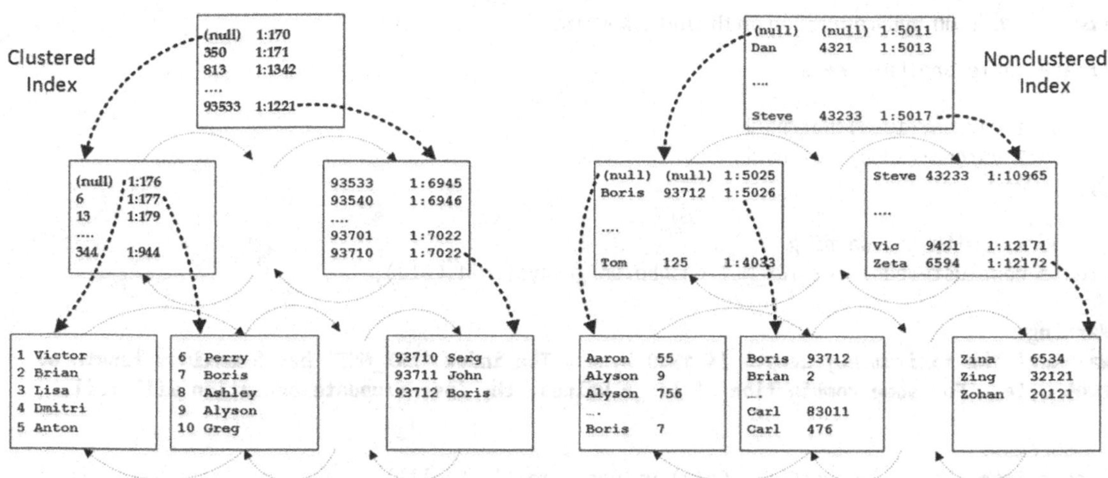

Figure 2-17. *Clustered and nonclustered index structures*

The leaf level of the nonclustered index is sorted based on the value of the index key—Name in our case. Every row on the leaf level includes the key value and *row-id*. For heap tables, *row-id* is the physical location of the row, defined as *file:page:slot*, and has the size of eight bytes.

■ **Note** Another reason why SQL Server uses forwarding pointers in heap tables is to prevent the updating of nonclustered index rows when the original row in the heap table has been moved to another data page after the update. Nonclustered indexes keep the old row-id, which references the forwarding pointer row.

For tables with a clustered index, *row-id* represents the value of the clustered index key of the row.

■ **Important** This is a very important point to remember. Nonclustered indexes do not store information about physical row location when a table has a clustered index. They store the value of the clustered index key instead.

Like clustered indexes, the intermediate and root levels of nonclustered indexes store one row per page from the level they reference. That row consists of the physical address and the minimum value of the key from the page. In addition, for non-unique indexes, it also stores the row-id of such a row.

■ **Note** It is important to define a nonclustered index as unique when the data is unique. Intermediate- and root-level rows of unique indexes are more compact, because SQL Server does not maintain the row-id there. Moreover, the uniqueness of the index helps Query Optimizer generate more efficient execution plans.

SQL Server 2016 allows you to define nonclustered indexes with a key size up to 1,700 bytes. Previous versions of SQL Server limit that to 900 bytes. The maximum clustered index key size is 900 bytes in all versions. SQL Server allows the creation of indexes with a key size that can potentially exceed this limit because of variable-length columns, although you would not be able to insert such rows into a table. Listing 2-9 shows an example of this (you need to use the 900-bytes threshold if you run it on SQL Server 2014 or below)

Listing 2-9. 1700-bytes limitation on the index key size

```
create table dbo.LargeKeys
(
    Col1 varchar(1000) not null,
    Col2 varchar(1000) not null
);

-- Success with the warning
create nonclustered index IDX_NCI on dbo.LargeKeys(Col1,Col2);
```

Warning:
Warning! The maximum key length is 1700 bytes. The index 'IDX_NCI' has a maximum length of 2000 bytes. For some combination of large values, the insert/update operation will fail.

```
-- Success:
insert into dbo.LargeKeys(Col1, Col2) values('Small','Small');

-- Failure:
insert into dbo.LargeKeys(Col1, Col2) values(replicate('A',900),replicate('B',900));
```

Error:
Msg 1946, Level 16, State 3, Line 4
Operation failed. The index entry of length 1800 bytes for the index 'IDX_NCI' exceeds the maximum length of 1700 bytes.

Let's look at how SQL Server uses nonclustered indexes, assuming that you run the following query: `SELECT * FROM dbo.Customers WHERE Name = 'Boris'`

As shown in the first step in Figure 2-18, SQL Server starts with the root page of the nonclustered index. The key value *Boris* is less than *Dan,* and SQL Server goes to the intermediate page referenced from the first row in the root-level page.

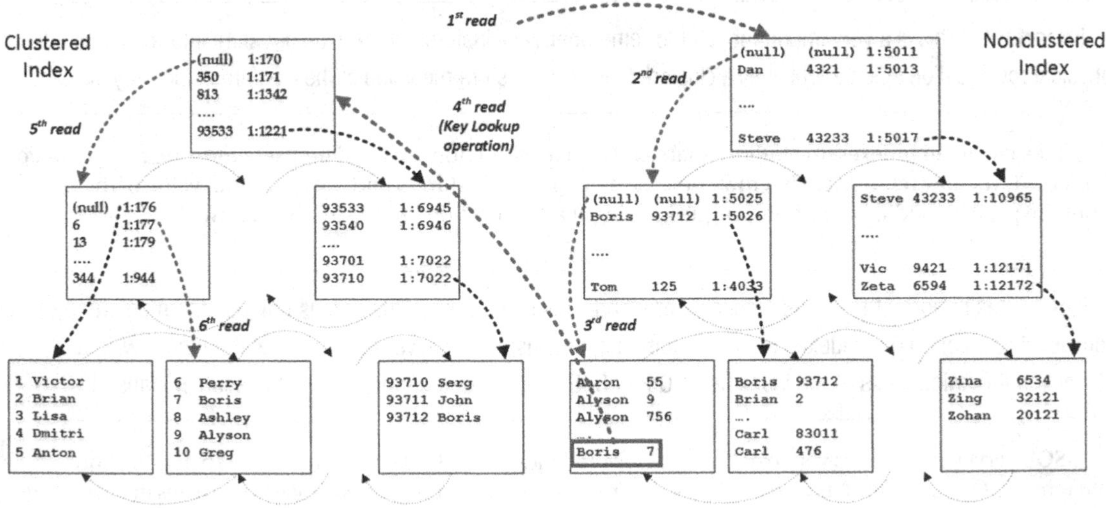

Figure 2-18. *Nonclustered index usage: Step 1*

The second row of the intermediate page indicates that the minimum key value on the page is *Boris*, although the index had not been defined as unique and SQL Server does not know if there are other *Boris* rows stored on the first page. As a result, it goes to the first leaf page of the index and finds the row with the key value *Boris* and a row-id equal to 7 there.

In our case, the nonclustered index does not have any data besides *CustomerId* and *Name*, and SQL Server needs to traverse the clustered index tree and obtain the data from other columns from there. This operation is called *key lookup*.

In the next step, shown in Figure 2-19, SQL Server comes back to the nonclustered index and reads the second page from the leaf level. It finds another row with the key value *Boris* and row-id 93712, and it performs a key lookup again.

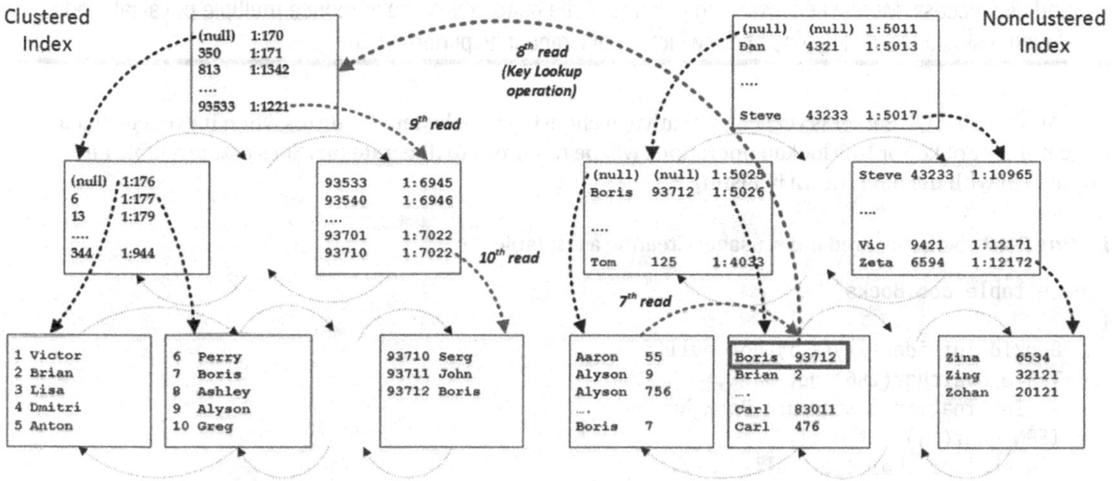

Figure 2-19. *Nonclustered index usage: Step 2*

As you can see, SQL Server had to read the data pages ten times, even though the query returned just two rows. The number of I/O operations can be calculated based on the following formula: `(number of levels in nonclustered index) + (number of pages read from the leaf level of nonclustered index) + (number of rows found) * (number of levels in clustered index)`. As you can guess, a large `number of rows found` and, therefore, a large number of key lookup operations, lead to a large number of I/O operations, which makes nonclustered index usage inefficient.

There is another important factor contributing to nonclustered index inefficiency. Key lookups read the data from different places in the data files. Even though data pages from root and intermediate index levels are often cached and introduce just logical reads, accessing leaf-level pages leads to random physical I/O activity. In contrast, index scans trigger sequential I/O activity, which is more efficient than random I/O, especially in the case of magnetic hard drives.

KEY LOOKUPS VS. RID LOOKUPS

Nonclustered indexes defined on heap tables reference the actual location of the rows in the data file. SQL Server uses the *RID lookup* operation to obtain the data row from the heap. In theory, RID lookup seems to be more efficient than key lookup, because it can read the row directly without traversing the root and intermediate levels of the clustered index.

In reality, however, the performance impact of reading non-leaf clustered index data pages is relatively small. Those pages are usually cached in the buffer pool and do not introduce physical I/O to access. Logical reads still introduce some overhead; however, it is usually insignificant compared to physical I/O and disk access. Moreover, forwarding pointers in the heap tables can introduce multiple physical reads during a single RID lookup operation, which would impact its performance.

As a result, SQL Server is very conservative in choosing nonclustered indexes when it expects that a large number of key or RID lookup operations will be required. To illustrate this, let's create a table and populate it with the data shown in Listing 2-10.

Listing 2-10. Nonclustered index usage: Creating a test table

```
create table dbo.Books
(
    BookId int identity(1,1) not null,
    Title nvarchar(256) not null,
    -- International Standard Book Number
    ISBN char(14) not null,
    Placeholder char(150) null
);

create unique clustered index IDX_Books_BookId on dbo.Books(BookId);

-- 1,252,000 rows
;with Prefix(Prefix)
as
(
    select 100
    union all
    select Prefix + 1
    from Prefix
    where Prefix < 600
)
,Postfix(Postfix)
as
(
    select 100000001
    union all
    select Postfix + 1
    from Postfix
    where Postfix < 100002500
)
```

```
insert into dbo.Books(ISBN, Title)
    select
        convert(char(3), Prefix) + '-0' + convert(char(9),Postfix)
        ,'Title for ISBN' + convert(char(3), Prefix) + '-0' + convert(char(9),Postfix)
    from Prefix cross join Postfix
option (maxrecursion 0);

create nonclustered index IDX_Books_ISBN on dbo.Books(ISBN);
```

At this point, the table has 1,252,000 rows. The ISBN column is populated with data in the following format: *<Prefix>-<Postfix>* with prefixes from 100 to 600 and 2,500 postfixes each.

Let's try to select the data for one of the prefixes, as shown in Listing 2-11.

Listing 2-11. Nonclustered index usage: Selecting data for a single prefix

```
-- 2,500 rows
select * from dbo.Books where ISBN like '210%'
```

As you can see in Figure 2-20, SQL Server decided to use a *nonclustered index seek* with a key lookup as the execution plan. Selecting 2,500 rows introduces 7,676 logical reads. The clustered index IDX_Books_BookId has three levels, which leads to 7,500 reads during key lookup operations. The remaining 176 reads were performed on the nonclustered index when SQL Server traversed the index tree and read pages during a range scan operation.

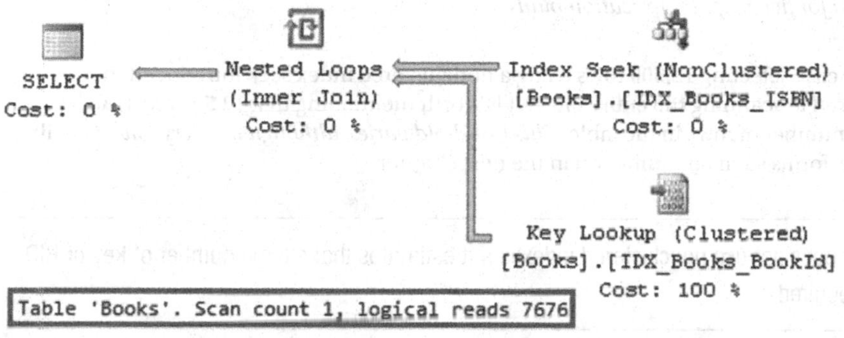

Figure 2-20. *Selecting data for the single prefix: Execution plan*

For the next step, let's select the data for five different prefixes. We will run two different selects. In the first one, we will give SQL Server the ability to choose the execution plan it wishes. In the second select, we will force the use of a nonclustered index with the index hint. The code to accomplish this is shown in Listing 2-12. Figure 2-21 shows the execution plans.

Listing 2-12. Nonclustered index usage: Selecting data for five prefixes

```
-- 12,500 rows
select * from dbo.Books where ISBN like '21[0-4]%'
select * from dbo.Books with (index = IDX_BOOKS_ISBN) where ISBN like '21[0-4]%'
```

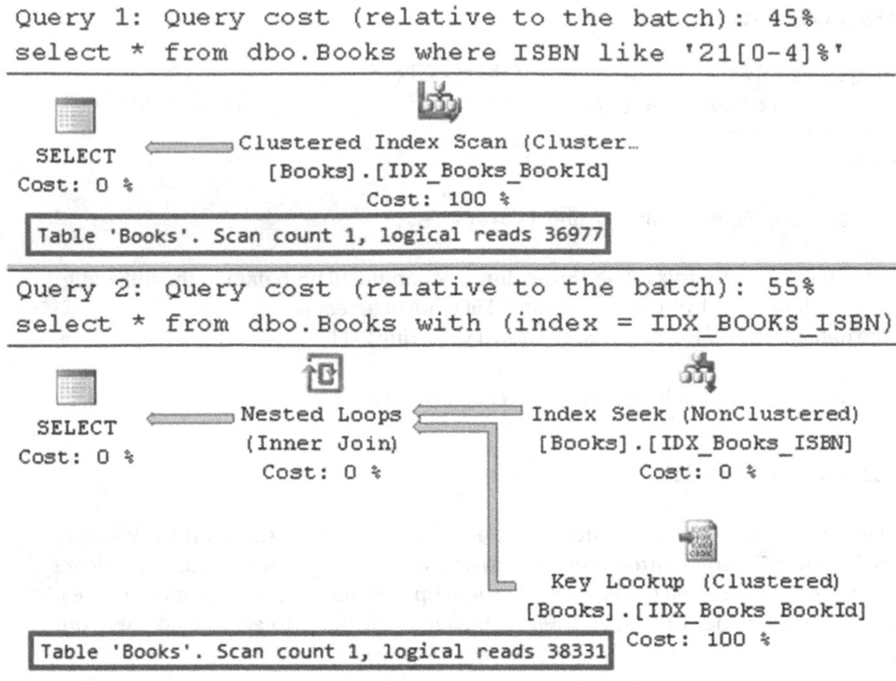

Figure 2-21. *Selecting data for five prefixes: Execution plans*

As you can see, in our case selecting 12,500 rows using a nonclustered index seek introduced more logical reads when compared to scanning the entire table. It is worth mentioning that 12,500 rows are less than 1 percent of the total number of rows in the table. *This threshold varies, although it is very low.* We will discuss how SQL Server performs such an estimation in the next chapter.

■ **Important** SQL Server does not use nonclustered indexes if it estimates that a large number of key or RID lookup operations will be required.

Nonclustered indexes help improve the performance of queries, although this comes at its own price. They maintain a copy of the data from the index columns. When columns are updated, SQL Server needs to update them in the every index in which they are included.

Even though SQL Server allows the creation of either 250 or 999 nonclustered indexes per table, depending on the version, it is not a good idea to create a lot of them. We will talk about indexing strategies in Chapter 7, "Designing and Tuning the Indexes."

Summary

Clustered indexes define the sorting order for data in a table. Nonclustered indexes store a copy of the data for a subset of table columns sorted in the order in which the key columns are defined.

Both clustered and nonclustered indexes are stored in a multiple-level tree-like structure called a *B-Tree*. Data pages on each level are linked in a double-linked list.

The leaf level of the clustered index stores the actual table data. The intermediate- and root-level pages store one row per page from the next level. Every row includes the physical address and minimum value of the key from the page that it references.

The leaf level of a nonclustered index stores the data from the index columns and row-id. For tables with a clustered index, row-id is the clustered key value of the row. Then intermediate and root levels of a nonclustered index are similar to those of a clustered index, although when the index is not unique, those rows store row-id in addition to the minimum index key value. It is beneficial to define indexes as unique, as it makes the intermediate and root levels more compact. Moreover, uniqueness helps Query Optimizer generate more efficient execution plans.

SQL Server needs to traverse the clustered index tree to obtain any data from the columns that are not part of the nonclustered index. Those operations, called *key lookups*, are expensive in terms of I/O. SQL Server does not use nonclustered indexes if it expects that a large number of key or RID lookup operations will be required.

Tables with a clustered index usually outperform heap tables. It is thus beneficial to define a clustered index on tables in most cases.

SQL Server can utilize indexes in two separate ways. The first way is an *index scan* operation, where it reads every page from the index. The second one is an *index seek* operation, where SQL Server processes just a subset of the index pages. It is beneficial to use SARGable predicates in queries, which allows SQL Server to perform index seek operations by exactly matching the row or range of rows in the index.

You should avoid calculations and/or function calls against data columns, because it makes predicates non-SARGable. You should also take care to use the correct data types for parameters, especially when dealing with unicode and non-unicode strings.

CHAPTER 3

Statistics

SQL Server Query Optimizer uses a cost-based model when choosing an execution plan for queries. It estimates the costs of the different execution plans and chooses the one with the lowest cost. Remember, however, that SQL Server does not search for the *best* execution plan available for the query, as evaluating all possible alternatives is time consuming and expensive in terms of the CPU. The goal of Query Optimizer is finding a *good enough* execution plan, *fast enough*.

Cardinality estimation (estimation of the number of rows that need to be processed at each step of query execution) is one of the most important factors in query optimization. This number affects the choice of join strategies, amount of memory (memory grant) required for query execution, and quite a few other things.

The choice of indexes to use while accessing the data is among those factors. As you will remember, key and RID lookup operations are expensive in terms of I/O, and SQL Server does not use nonclustered indexes when it estimates that a large number of these operations will be required. SQL Server maintains statistics on indexes–and in some cases on columns–which help in performing such estimations.

Introduction to SQL Server Statistics

SQL Server statistics are system objects that contain information about data distribution in the index key values and, sometimes, in regular column values. Statistics can be created on any data type that supports comparison operations, such as >, <, =, and so on.

Let's examine the `IDX_BOOKS_ISBN` index statistics from the `dbo.Books` table we created in Listing 2-15 in the previous chapter. You can do this by using the `DBCC SHOW_STATISTICS ('dbo.Books',IDX_BOOKS_ISBN)` command. The results are shown in Figure 3-1.

D. Korotkevitch, *Pro SQL Server Internals*, DOI 10.1007/978-1-4842-1964-5_3

	Name	Updated	Rows	Rows Sampled	Steps	Density
1	IDX_Books_ISBN	Aug 17 2013 2:29PM	1252500	1252500	183	1

Average key length	String Index	Filter Expression	Unfiltered Rows
18	YES	NULL	1252500

	All density	Average Len...	Columns
1	7.984032E-07	14	ISBN
2	7.984032E-07	18	ISBN, BookId

	RANGE_HI_KEY	RANGE_ROWS	EQ_ROWS	DISTINCT_RANGE_ROWS	AVG_RANGE_ROWS
1	100-0100000001	0	1	0	1
2	101-0100001796	4294	1	4294	1
3	104-0100002488	8191	1	8191	1
4	106-0100001584	4095	1	4095	1
5	109-0100002276	8191	1	8191	1
6	112-0100000920	6143	1	6143	1
7	114-0100000016	4095	1	4095	1
8	115-0100001812	4095	1	4095	1

Figure 3-1. *DBCC SHOW_STATISTICS output*

As you can see, the `DBCC SHOW_STATISTICS` command returns three result sets. The first one contains general metadata information about the statistics, such as name, update date, number of rows in the index at the time when the statistics were updated, and so on. The `Steps` column in the first result set indicates the number of steps/values in the histogram (more about this later). The `Density` value is not used by Query Optimizer and is displayed for backward-compatibility purposes only.

The second result set, called *density vector*, contains information about density for the combination of key values from the statistics (index). It is calculated based on a `1 / number of distinct values` formula, and it indicates how many rows, on average, each combination of key values has. Even though the `IDX_Books_ISBN` index has just one key column `ISBN` defined, it also includes a clustered index key as part of the index row. Our table has 1,252,500 unique ISBN values, and the density for the `ISBN` column is `1.0 / 1,252,500 = 7.984032E-07`. All combinations of the `(ISBN, BookId)` columns are also unique and have the same density.

The last result set is called the *histogram*. Every record in the histogram, called a *histogram step*, includes the sample key value in the leftmost column of the statistics (index) and information about the data distribution in the range of values from the preceding to the current `RANGE_HI_KEY` value. Let's examine histogram columns in greater depth.

> The `RANGE_HI_KEY` column stores the sample value of the key. This value is the upper-bound key value for the range defined by the histogram step. For example, record (step) #3 with `RANGE_HI_KEY = '104-0100002488'` in the histogram from Figure 3-1 stores information about the interval from `ISBN > '101-0100001796'` to `ISBN <= '104-0100002488'`.
>
> The `RANGE_ROWS` column estimates the number of rows within the interval. In our case, the interval defined by record (step) #3 has 8,191 rows.
>
> `EQ_ROWS` indicates how many rows have a key value equal to the `RANGE_HI_KEY` upper-bound value. In our case, there is only one row with `ISBN = '104-0100002488'`.
>
> `DISTINCT_RANGE_ROWS` indicates how many distinct values of the keys are within the interval. In our case, all of the values of the keys are unique, so `DISTINCT_RANGE_ROWS = RANGE_ROWS`.

`AVG_RANGE_ROWS` indicates the average number of rows per distinct key value in the interval. In our case, all of the values of the keys are unique, so `AVG_RANGE_ROWS = 1`.

Let's insert a set of duplicate `ISBN` values into the index with the code shown in Listing 3-1.

Listing 3-1. Inserting duplicate ISBN values into the index.

```
;with Prefix(Prefix)
as ( select Num from (values(104),(104),(104),(104),(104)) Num(Num) )
,Postfix(Postfix)
as
(
    select 100000001
    union all
    select Postfix + 1 from Postfix where Postfix < 100002500
)
insert into dbo.Books(ISBN, Title)
    select
        convert(char(3), Prefix) + '-0' + convert(char(9),Postfix)
        ,'Title for ISBN' + convert(char(3), Prefix) + '-0' + convert(char(9),Postfix)
    from Prefix cross join Postfix
option (maxrecursion 0);

-- Updating the statistics
update statistics dbo.Books IDX_Books_ISBN with fullscan;
```

Now, if you run the `DBCC SHOW_STATISTICS ('dbo.Books',IDX_BOOKS_ISBN)` command again, you will see the results shown in Figure 3-2.

	Name	Updated	Rows	Rows Sampled	Steps	Density
1	IDX_Books_ISBN	Sep 18 2013 3:23PM	1265000	1265000	184	0.8801289

Average key len...	String Index	Filter Expression	Unfiltered Rows
18	YES	NULL	1265000

	All density	Average Len...	Columns
1	7.984032E-07	14	ISBN
2	7.905138E-07	18	ISBN, BookId

	RANGE_HI_KEY	RANGE_ROWS	EQ_ROWS	DISTINCT_RANGE_ROWS	AVG_RANGE_ROWS
1	100-0100000001	0	1	0	1
2	100-0100002248	2246	1	2246	1
3	104-0100000001	7752	6	7752	1
4	104-0100000685	4098	6	683	6
5	104-0100001369	4098	6	683	6
6	105-0100000001	6786	1	1131	6
7	106-0100001597	4095	1	4095	1
8	109-0100002289	8191	1	8191	1
9	113-0100000481	8191	1	8191	1
10	116-0100001173	8191	1	8191	1
11	118-0100002317	8143	1	8143	1

Figure 3-2. *DBCC SHOW_STATISTICS output*

ISBN values with the prefix 104 now have duplicates, and this affects the histogram. It is also worth mentioning that the density information in the second result set is also changed. The density for ISBNs with duplicate values is higher than for the combination of (ISBN, BookId) columns, which is still unique.

Let's run the SELECT BookId, Title FROM dbo.Books WHERE ISBN LIKE '114%' statement and check the execution plan, as shown in Figure 3-3.

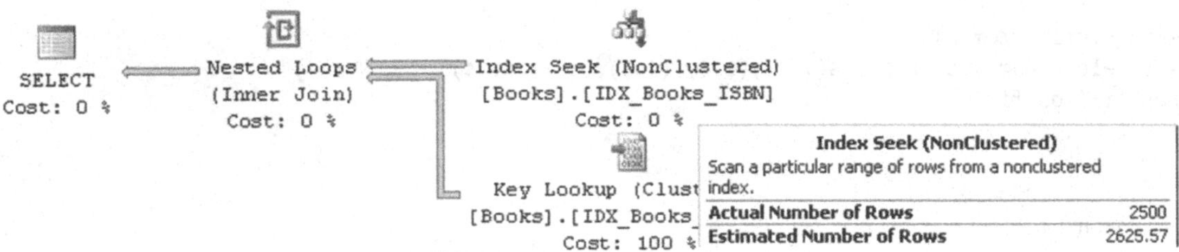

Figure 3-3. *Execution plan of the query*

There are two important properties that most execution plan operators have. *Actual Number of Rows* indicates how many rows were processed during operator execution. *Estimated Number of Rows* indicates the number of rows SQL Server estimated for that operator during the Query Optimization stage. In our case, SQL Server estimates that there are 2,625 rows with ISBNs starting with 114. If you look at the histogram shown in Figure 3-2, you will see that step 10 stores the information about data distribution for the ISBN interval that includes the values that you are selecting. Even with linear approximation, you can estimate the number of rows to be close to what SQL Server determined.

There are two very important things to remember about statistics.

1. The histogram stores information about data distribution for the leftmost statistics (index) column only. There is information about the multi-column density of the key values in statistics, but that is it. All other information in the histogram relates to data distribution for the leftmost statistics column only.

2. SQL Server retains at most 200 steps in the histogram, regardless of the size of the table and if the table is partitioned. The intervals covered by each histogram step increase as the table grows. This leads to less accurate statistics in the case of large tables.

In the case of composite indexes, when all columns from the index are used as predicates in all queries, it is beneficial to define a column with lower density/higher percentage of unique values as the leftmost column of the index. This will allow SQL Server to better utilize the data distribution information from the statistics. You should consider the SARGability of the predicates, however. For example, if all queries are using FirstName=@FirstName and LastName=@LastName predicates in the where clause, it is better to have LastName as the leftmost column in the index. Nonetheless, this is not the case for predicates like FirstName=@FirstName and LastName<>@LastName, where LastName is not SARGable.

Column-Level Statistics

In addition to index-level statistics, you can create separate column-level statistics. Moreover, in some cases SQL Server creates such statistics automatically.

Let's take a look at an example and create a table and populate it with the data shown in Listing 3-2.

Listing 3-2. Column-level statistics: Table creation

```
create table dbo.Customers
(
    CustomerId int not null identity(1,1),
    FirstName  nvarchar(64) not null,
    LastName nvarchar(128) not null,
    Phone varchar(32) null,
    Placeholder char(200) null
);

create unique clustered index IDX_Customers_CustomerId
on dbo.Customers(CustomerId)
go

-- Inserting cross-joined data for all first and last names 50 times
-- using GO 50 command in Management Studio
;with FirstNames(FirstName)
as
(
    select Names.Name
    from ( values('Andrew'),('Andy'),('Anton'),('Ashley'),('Boris'),('Brian'),
         ('Cristopher'),('Cathy')
        ,('Daniel'),('Donny'),('Edward'),('Eddy'),('Emy'),('Frank'),('George'),
         ('Harry'),('Henry')
        ,('Ida'),('John'),('Jimmy'),('Jenny'),('Jack'),('Kathy'),('Kim'),('Larry'),
         ('Mary'),('Max')
        ,('Nancy'),('Olivia'),('Olga'),('Peter'),('Patrick'),('Robert'),('Ron'),
         ('Steve'),('Shawn')
        ,('Tom'),('Timothy'),('Uri'),('Vincent') ) Names(Name)
)
,LastNames(LastName)
as
(
    select Names.Name
    from ( values('Smith'),('Johnson'),('Williams'),('Jones'),('Brown'),('Davis'),('Miller')
        ,('Wilson'), ('Moore'),('Taylor'),('Anderson'),('Jackson'),('White'),('Harris') )
Names(Name)
)
insert into dbo.Customers(LastName, FirstName)
    select LastName, FirstName from FirstNames cross join LastNames
go 50

insert into dbo.Customers(LastName, FirstName) values('Isakov','Victor')
go

create nonclustered index IDX_Customers_LastName_FirstName
on dbo.Customers(LastName, FirstName);
```

Every combination of first and last names specified in the first INSERT statement has been inserted into the table 50 times. In addition, there is one row, with the first name *Victor,* inserted by the second INSERT statement.

Now, let's assume that you want to run a query that selects the data based on the FirstName parameter only. That predicate is not SARGable for the IDX_Customers_LastName_FirstName index because there is no SARGable predicate on the LastName column, which is the leftmost column in the index.

SQL Server offers two different options on how to execute the query. The first option is to perform a *clustered index scan*. The second option is to use a *nonclustered index scan* while doing a *key lookup* for every row of the nonclustered index where the FirstName value matches the parameter.

The nonclustered index row size is much smaller than that of the clustered index. It uses fewer data pages, and a scan of the nonclustered index would be more efficient as compared to a clustered index scan, owing to the fewer I/O reads that it performs. At the same time, the plan with a nonclustered index scan would be less efficient than a clustered index scan when the table has a large number of rows with a particular FirstName and a large number of key lookups is required. Unfortunately, the histogram for the IDX_Customers_LastName_FirstName index stores the data distribution for the LastName column only, and SQL Server does not know about the FirstName data distribution.

Let's run the two selects shown in Listing 3-3 and examine the execution plans in Figure 3-4.

Listing 3-3. Column-level statistics: Querying data

```
select CustomerId, FirstName, LastName, Phone
from dbo.Customers
where FirstName = 'Brian';

select CustomerId, FirstName, LastName, Phone
from dbo.Customers
where FirstName = 'Victor';
```

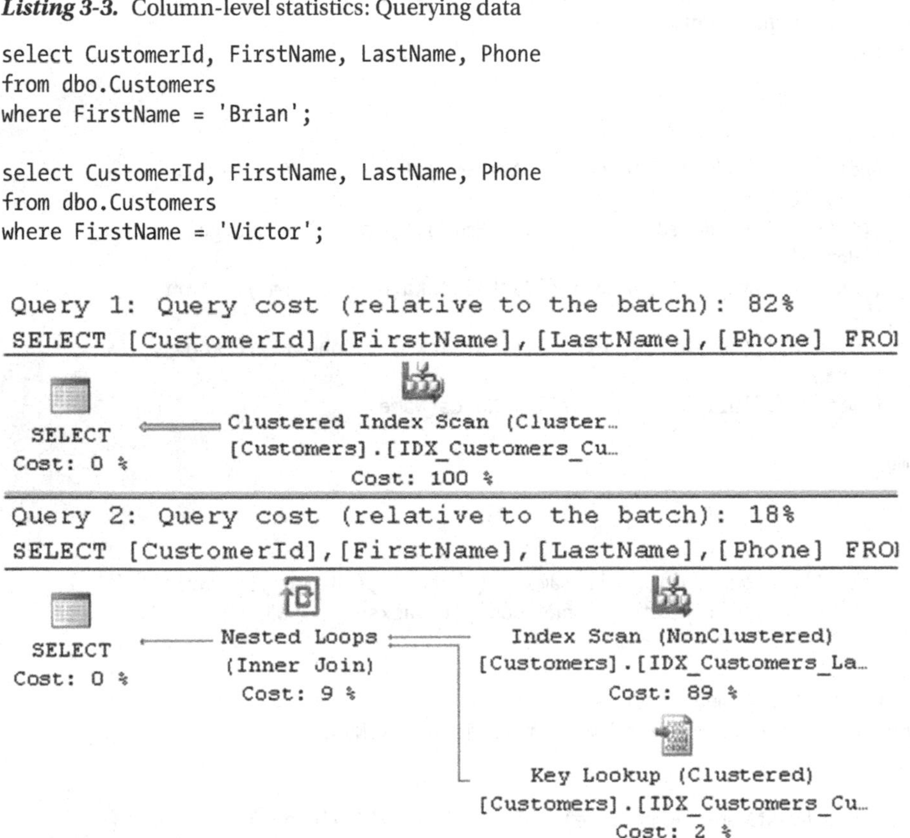

Figure 3-4. *Column-level statistics: Execution plans*

As you can see, SQL Server decides to use a clustered index scan for the first select, which returns 700 rows, and a nonclustered index scan for the second select, which returns a single row.

Now, let's query the sys.stats catalog view and check the table's statistics. The code for this is shown in Listing 3-4. Alternatively, you can explore the *Statistics* node of the dbo.Customers table in Management Studio.

Listing 3-4. Column-level statistics: Querying sys.stats view

```
select  stats_id, name, auto_created
from sys.stats
where object_id = object_id(N'dbo.Customers')
```

The query returned three rows, as shown in Figure 3-5.

	stats_id	name	auto_created
1	1	IDX_Customers_CustomerId	0
2	2	IDX_Customers_LastName_FirstName	0
3	3	_WA_Sys_00000002_276EDEB3	1

Figure 3-5. *Column-level statistics: Result of the query*

The first two rows correspond to the clustered and nonclustered indexes from the table. The last one, with the name that starts with the _WA prefix, displays column-level statistics, which were created automatically when SQL Server optimized our queries. It is worth noting that SQL Server does not drop those column-level statistics automatically after they are created.

■ **Tip** Consider renaming auto-created _WA statistics to simplify database management.

Let's examine it with the DBCC SHOW_STATISTICS ('dbo.Customers', _WA_Sys_00000002_276EDEB3) command. As you can see in Figure 3-6, it stores information about the data distribution for the FirstName column. As a result, SQL Server can estimate the number of rows for first names, which we used as parameters, and generate different execution plans for each parameter value.

	Name	Updated	Rows	Rows Sampled	Steps	Density	Average key len...	String Index	Filter Expressi...	Unfiltered Rows
1	_WA_Sys_00000002_276EDEB3	Oct 2 2013 9:03AM	28001	28001	41	0	9.900075	YES	NULL	28001

	All density	Average Len...	Columns
1	0.02439024	9.900075	FirstName

	RANGE_HI_KEY	RANGE_ROWS	EQ_ROWS	DISTINCT_RANGE_ROWS	AVG_RANGE_ROWS
32	Peter	0	700	0	1
33	Robert	0	700	0	1
39	Uri	0	700	0	1
40	Victor	0	1	0	1
41	Vincent	0	700	0	1

Figure 3-6. *Column-level statistics: Auto-created statistics on the FirstName column*

You can manually create statistics on a column or on multiple columns with the `CREATE STATISTICS` command. Statistics created on multiple columns are similar to statistics created on composite indexes. They include information about multi-column density, although the histogram retains data distribution information for the leftmost column only.

There is overhead associated with column-level statistics maintenance, although it is much smaller than that of an index, which needs to be updated every time data modifications occur. In some cases, when particular queries do not run very often, you can elect to create column-level statistics rather than an index. Column-level statistics help Query Optimizer find better execution plans, even though those execution plans are suboptimal due to the index scans involved. At the same time, statistics do not add overhead during data modification operations, and they help you avoid index maintenance. This approach works only for rarely executed queries, however. You need to create indexes to optimize queries that run often.

Finally, do not forget to re-evaluate and drop redundant column-level statistics when you add the new indexes to the table.

Statistics and Execution Plans

SQL Server creates and updates statistics automatically by default. There are two options on the database level that control such behavior:

1. *Auto Create Statistics* controls whether or not the optimizer creates column-level statistics automatically. This option does not affect index-level statistics, which are always created. The Auto Create Statistics database option is enabled by default.
2. When the *Auto Update Statistics* database option is enabled, SQL Server checks if statistics are outdated every time it compiles or executes a query and updates them if needed. The Auto Update Statistics database option is also enabled by default.

■ **Tip** You can control the auto update behavior of statistics on the index level by using the `STATISTICS_NORECOMPUTE` index option. By default, this option is set to OFF, which means that statistics are automatically updated. Another way to change auto update behavior at the index or table levels is by using the `sp_autostats` system stored procedure.

SQL Server determines if statistics are outdated based on the number of changes performed by the `INSERT`, `UPDATE`, `DELETE`, and `MERGE` statements that affect the statistics columns. SQL Server counts how many times the statistics columns were changed, rather than the number of changed rows. For example, if you change the same row 100 times, it would be counted as 100 changes rather than as 1 change.

There are three different scenarios, called *statistics update thresholds,* also sometimes known as *statistics recompilation thresholds,* in which SQL Server marks statistics as outdated.

1. When a table is empty, SQL Server outdates statistics when you add data to the table.
2. When a table has less than 500 rows, SQL Server outdates statistics after every 500 changes of the statistics columns.
3. **Prior to SQL Server 2016 and in SQL Server 2016 with database compatibility level < 130:** When a table has 500 or more rows, SQL Server outdates statistics after every 500 + (20% of total number of rows in the table) changes of the statistics columns.

In SQL Server 2016 with database compatibility level = 130: Statistics update threshold on large tables becomes dynamic and depends on the size of the table. The more rows the table has, the lower the threshold is. On large tables with millions or even billions of rows, the statistics update threshold can be just a fraction of a percentage of the total number of rows in the table. This behavior can also be enabled with the trace flag T2371 in SQL Server 2008R2 SP1 and above.

Table 3-1 summarizes statistics update threshold behavior in different versions of SQL Server.

Table 3-1. *Statistics Update Threshold and SQL Server Versions*

	Prior to SQL Server 2016	SQL Server 2016 with Database Compatibility Level < 130	SQL Server 2016 with Database Compatibility Level = 130
Default behavior	Static (~20%) threshold	Static (~20%) threshold	Dynamic threshold
T2371	Dynamic threshold in SQL Server 2008R2 SP1 and above	Dynamic threshold	Dynamic threshold (trace flag is ignored)

That leads us to a very important conclusion. With the static statistics update threshold, the number of changes to statistics columns required to trigger a statistics update is proportional to the table size. The larger the table, the less often statistics are automatically updated. For example, in the case of a table with 1 billion rows, you would need to perform about 200 million changes to statistics columns to make the statistics outdated. **It is recommended to use dynamic update threshold when possible.**

Let's look at how that behavior affects our systems and execution plans. At this point, the table dbo.Books has 1,265,000 rows. Let's add 250,000 rows to the table with the prefix 999, as shown in Listing 3-5. In this example, I am using SQL Server 2012 without T2371 enabled. You can see the different results if you run it with the dynamic statistics update threshold enabled. Moreover, the new cardinality estimator introduced in SQL Server 2014 can also change the behavior. We will discuss it later in the chapter.

Listing 3-5. Adding rows to dbo.Books

```
;with Postfix(Postfix)
as
(
    select 100000001
    union all
    select Postfix + 1
    from Postfix
    where Postfix < 100250000
)
insert into dbo.Books(ISBN, Title)
    select
        '999-0' + convert(char(9),Postfix)
        ,'Title for ISBN 999-0' + convert(char(9),Postfix)
    from Postfix
option (maxrecursion 0);
```

Now, let's run the SELECT * FROM dbo.Books WHERE ISBN LIKE '999%' query that selects all of the rows with such a prefix.

If you examine the execution plan of the query, shown in Figure 3-7, you will see nonclustered index seek and key lookup operations, even though they are inefficient in cases where you need to select almost 20 percent of the rows from the table.

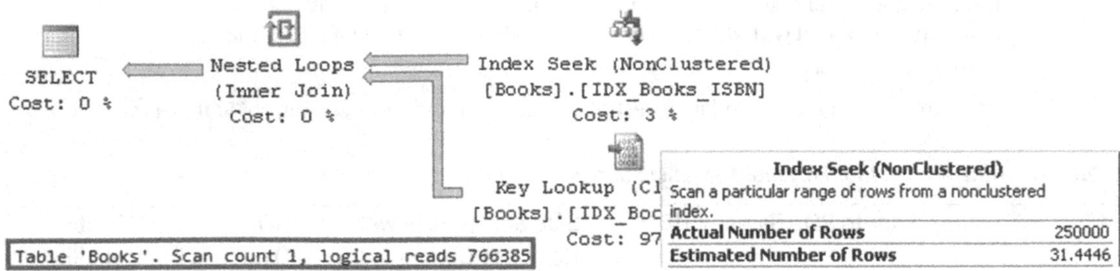

Figure 3-7. *Execution plan for the query selecting rows with the 999 prefix*

You will also notice in Figure 3-7 that there is a huge discrepancy between the estimated and actual number of rows for the Index Seek operator. SQL Server estimated that there are only 31.4 rows with prefix 999 in the table, even though there are 250,000 rows with such a prefix. As a result, a highly inefficient plan is generated.

Let's look at the IDX_BOOKS_ISBN statistics by running the DBCC SHOW_STATISTICS ('dbo.Books', IDX_BOOKS_ISBN) command. The output is shown in Figure 3-8. As you can see, even though we inserted 250,000 rows into the table, statistics were not updated, and there is no data in the histogram for the prefix 999. The number of rows in the first result set corresponds to the number of rows in the table during the last statistics update. It does not include the 250,000 rows just inserted.

	Name	Updated	Rows	Rows Sampled	Steps	Density	Average k
1	IDX_Books_ISBN	Oct 2 2013 10:42AM	1265000	1265000	184	0.9901289	18

	All density	Average Len...	Columns
1	7.984032E-07	14	ISBN
2	7.905138E-07	18	ISBN, BookId

	RANGE_HI_KEY	RANGE_ROWS	EQ_ROWS	DISTINCT_RANGE_ROWS	AVG_RANGE_ROWS
182	594-0100002205	8191	1	8191	1
183	598-0100000397	8191	1	8191	1
184	600-0100002500	7102	1	7102	1

Figure 3-8. *IDX_BOOKS_ISBN statistics*

Let's now update statistics using the UPDATE STATISTICS dbo.Books IDX_Books_ISBN WITH FULLSCAN command, and then run the SELECT * FROM dbo.Books WHERE ISBN LIKE '999%' query again. The execution plan for the query is shown in Figure 3-9. The estimated number of rows is now correct, and SQL Server ended up with a much more efficient execution plan that uses a clustered index scan with about 17 times fewer I/O reads than before.

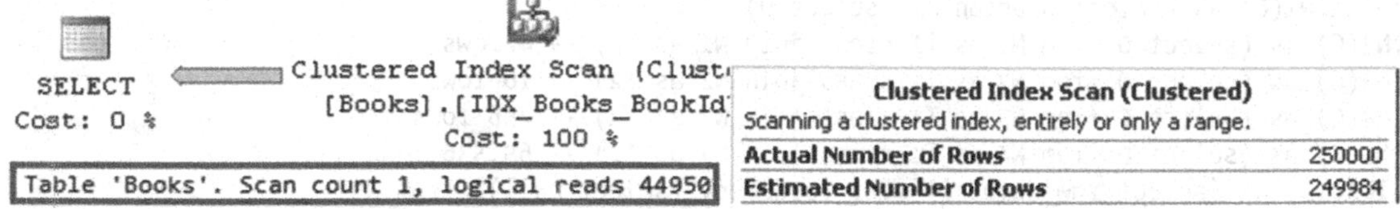

Figure 3-9. *Execution plan for the query selecting rows with the 999 prefix after a statistics update*

As you can see, incorrect cardinality estimations can lead to highly inefficient execution plans. Outdated statistics are, perhaps, one of the most common reasons for incorrect cardinality estimations. **You can pinpoint some of these cases by examining the estimated and actual number of rows in the execution plans. A big discrepancy between these two values often indicates that statistics are incorrect.** Updating statistics can solve this problem and generate more efficient execution plans.

Statistics and Query Memory Grants

SQL Server queries need memory for execution. Different operators in the execution plans have different memory requirements. For example, the Index Scan operator fetches rows one by one and does not need to store multiple rows in memory. Other operators–for example, the Sort operator–need access to the entire rowset before it starts execution.

SQL Server tries to estimate the amount of memory (memory grant) required for a query and its operators based on row size and cardinality estimation. It is important that the memory grant is correct. Underestimations and overestimations both introduce inefficiencies. Overestimations waste SQL Server memory. Moreover, it may take longer to allocate a large memory grant on busy servers.

Underestimations, on the other hand, can lead to a situation in which some operators in the execution plan do not have enough memory. If the Sort operator does not have enough memory for an in-memory sort, SQL Server spills the rowset to `tempdb` and sorts the data there. A similar situation occurs with hash tables. SQL Server uses `tempdb` if needed. In either case, using `tempdb` can significantly decrease the performance of an operation, and of a query in general.

Let's look at an example and create a table, populating it with some data. Listing 3-6 creates the table `dbo.MemoryGrantDemo` and populates it with 65,536 rows. The `Col` column stores values from 0 to 99, with either 655 or 656 rows per value. There is a nonclustered index on the `Col` column, which is created at the end of the script. As a result, statistics on that index are accurate, and SQL Server would be able to estimate correctly the number of rows per each `Col` value in the table.

Listing 3-6. Cardinality estimation and memory grants: Table creation

```
create table dbo.MemoryGrantDemo
(
    ID int not null,
    Col int not null,
    Placeholder char(8000)
);

create unique clustered index IDX_MemoryGrantDemo_ID
on dbo.MemoryGrantDemo(ID);
```

```
;with N1(C) as (select 0 union all select 0) -- 2 rows
,N2(C) as (select 0 from N1 as T1 cross join N1 as T2) -- 4 rows
,N3(C) as (select 0 from N2 as T1 cross join N2 as T2) -- 16 rows
,N4(C) as (select 0 from N3 as T1 cross join N3 as T2) -- 256 rows
,N5(C) as (select 0 from N4 as T1 cross join N4 as T2) -- 65,536 rows
,IDs(ID) as (select row_number() over (order by (select null)) from N5)
insert into dbo.MemoryGrantDemo(ID,Col,Placeholder)
    select ID, ID % 100, convert(char(100),ID) from IDs;

create nonclustered index IDX_MemoryGrantDemo_Col
on dbo.MemoryGrantDemo(Col);
```

As a next step, shown in Listing 3-7, we add 656 new rows to the table, with Col=1000. This is just 1 percent of the total table data, and, as a result, the statistics are not going to be outdated. As you already know, the histogram would not have any information about the Col=1000 value.

Listing 3-7. Cardinality estimation and memory grants: Adding 656 rows

```
;with N1(C) as (select 0 union all select 0) -- 2 rows
,N2(C) as (select 0 from N1 as T1 cross join N1 as T2) -- 4 rows
,N3(C) as (select 0 from N2 as T1 cross join N2 as T2) -- 16 rows
,N4(C) as (select 0 from N3 as T1 cross join N3 as T2) -- 256 rows
,N5(C) as (select 0 from N4 as T1 cross join N2 as T2) -- 1,024 rows
,IDs(ID) as (select row_number() over (order by (select null)) from N5)
insert into dbo.MemoryGrantDemo(ID,Col,Placeholder)
    select 100000 + ID, 1000, convert(char(100),ID)
    from IDs
    where ID <= 656;
```

Now, let's try to run two queries that select data with the predicate on the Col column using the execution plan with a Sort operator. The code for doing this is shown in Listing 3-8. I am using a variable as a way to suppress the result set from being returned to the client. I am running this code in SQL Server 2012. The new cardinality estimator introduced in SQL Server 2014 would lead to different estimations in this case, as we will discuss later in the chapter.

Listing 3-8. Cardinality estimation and memory grants: Selecting data

```
declare
    @Dummy int

set statistics time on
select @Dummy = ID from dbo.MemoryGrantDemo where Col = 1 order by Placeholder;
select @Dummy = ID from dbo.MemoryGrantDemo where Col = 1000 order by Placeholder;
set statistics time off
```

Query Optimizer will be able to correctly estimate the number of rows with Col=1. However, this is not the case for the Col=1000 predicate. Look at the execution plans shown in Figure 3-10.

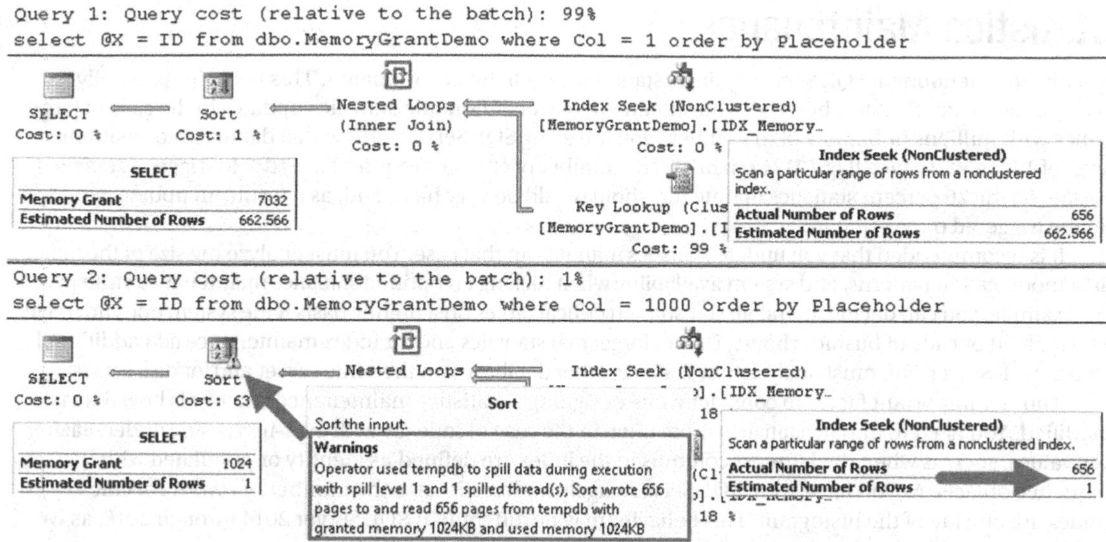

Figure 3-10. *Cardinality estimation and memory grants: Execution plans*

Even though the execution plans look very similar, the cardinality estimations and memory grants are different. Another difference is that the Sort operator icon in the second query has an exclamation mark. If you look at the operator properties, you will see a warning, which indicates that this operation spilled to `tempdb`.

The execution time of the queries on my computer is as follows:

```
SQL Server Execution Times:
   CPU time = 0 ms,  elapsed time = 17 ms.

SQL Server Execution Times:
   CPU time = 16 ms,  elapsed time = 88 ms.
```

As you can see, the second query with the incorrect memory grant and `tempdb` spill is about five times slower than the first one, which performs an in-memory sort.

You can also monitor `tempdb` spills with Extended Events and SQL Profiler by capturing the Sort Warning and Hash Warning events. Moreover, SQL Server 2016, SQL Server 2014 SP2, and SQL Server 2012 SP3 display additional information related to spills in the execution plans. It includes the number of data pages involved in the spill and number of spilled threads in parallel execution plans, along with memory grant information. This is extremely useful when you need to estimate the performance impact that spills introduce.

■ **Note** We will discuss memory grants in more detail in Chapter 25, "Query Optimization and Execution," and Chapter 28, "System Troubleshooting."

Statistics Maintenance

As I already mentioned, SQL Server updates statistics automatically by default. This behavior is usually acceptable for small tables; however, you should not rely on automatic statistics updates in the case of large tables with millions or billions of rows unless you are using SQL Server 2016 with a database compatibility level of 130 or with trace flag T2371 enabled. The number of changes required in order to trigger a statistics update by the 20 percent statistics update threshold would be very high, and, as a result, an update would not be triggered often enough.

It is recommended that you update statistics manually in that case. You must analyze the size of the table, data modification patterns, and system availability when picking an optimal statistics maintenance strategy. For example, you can decide to update statistics on critical tables on a nightly basis if the system does not have a heavy load outside of business hours. Do not forget that statistics and/or index maintenance add additional load to SQL Server. You must analyze how it affects other databases on the same server and/or disk arrays.

Another important factor to consider while designing a statistics maintenance strategy is how data is modified. You need to update statistics more often in the case of indexes with ever-increasing or decreasing key values, such as when the leftmost columns in the index are defined as identity or populated with sequence objects. As you have seen, SQL Server hugely underestimates the number of rows if specific key values are outside of the histogram. This behavior may be different in SQL Server 2014 through 2016, as we will see later in this chapter.

You can update statistics by using the UPDATE STATISTICS command. When SQL Server updates statistics, it reads a sample of the data rather than scanning the entire index. You can change that behavior by using the FULLSCAN option, which forces SQL Server to read and analyze all of the data from the index. As you may guess, that option provides the most accurate results, although it can introduce heavy I/O activity in the case of large tables.

■ **Note** SQL Server updates statistics when you rebuild the index. We will talk about index maintenance in greater detail in Chapter 6, “Index Fragmentation.”

You can update all of the statistics in the database by using the sp_updatestats system stored procedure. It is recommended you use this stored procedure and update all of the statistics in the database after you upgrade it to a new version of SQL Server. You should run this along with the DBCC UPDATEUSAGE stored procedure, which corrects incorrect page- and row-count information in the catalog views.

There is a sys.dm_db_stats_properties DMV, which shows you the number of modifications made to statistics columns since the last statistics update. The code, which utilizes that DMV, is shown in Listing 3-9.

Listing 3-9. Using sys.dm_db_stats_properties

```
select
    s.stats_id as [Stat ID], sc.name + '.' + t.name as [Table], s.name as [Statistics]
    ,p.last_updated, p.rows, p.rows_sampled, p.modification_counter as [Mod Count]
from
    sys.stats s join sys.tables t on
        s.object_id = t.object_id
    join sys.schemas sc on
        t.schema_id = sc.schema_id
    outer apply
        sys.dm_db_stats_properties(t.object_id,s.stats_id) p
where
    sc.name = 'dbo' and t.name = 'Books';
```

The result of the query, shown in Figure 3-11, indicates that there were 250,000 modifications made to the statistics columns since the last statistics update. You can build a statistics maintenance routine that regularly checks the `sys.dm_db_stats_properties` DMV and rebuilds statistics with large `modification_counter` values.

	Stat ID	Table	Statistics	last_updated	rows	rows_sampl...	Mod Count
1	1	dbo.Books	IDX_Books_BookId	2013-10-02 11:44:40.1600000	1765000	1765000	0
2	2	dbo.Books	IDX_Books_ISBN	2013-10-02 11:10:01.0500000	1515000	1515000	250000

Figure 3-11. *Sys.dm_db_stats_properties output*

Another statistics-related database option is *Auto Update Statistics Asynchronously*. By default, when SQL Server detects that statistics are outdated, it pauses query execution, synchronously updates statistics, and generates a new execution plan after the statistics update is complete. With an asynchronous statistics update, SQL Server executes the query using the old execution plan, which is based on outdated statistics, while updating statistics in the background asynchronously. It is recommended that you keep to the synchronous statistics update unless the system has a very short query timeout, in which case a synchronous statistics update can timeout the queries.

Finally, SQL Server does not drop column-level statistics automatically when you create new indexes. You should drop redundant column-level statistics objects manually.

New Cardinality Estimator (SQL Server 2014–2016)

As you already know, the quality of query optimization depends on accurate cardinality estimations. SQL Server must correctly estimate the number of rows in each step of query execution in order to generate an efficient execution plan. The cardinality estimation model used in SQL Server 2005-2012 was initially developed for SQL Server 7.0 and released in 1998. Obviously, there were some minor improvements and changes in the newer versions of SQL Server; however, conceptually, the model remains the same.

There are four major assumptions used in the model, including:

> *Uniformity*: This model assumes uniform data distribution in the absence of statistical information. For example, inside histogram steps, it is assumed that all key values are to be distributed evenly and uniformly.
>
> *Independence*: This model assumes that attributes in the entities are independent of each other. For example, when a query has several predicates against different columns of the same table, it assumes that the columns are not related in any way.
>
> *Simple Containment*: This model assumes that users query for the data that exists in the tables. For example, when you join two tables, in the absence of statistical information, the model assumes that all distinct values from one table exist in the other. The selectivity of the join operator in this model is based on the selectivity of the join predicates.
>
> *Inclusion*: This model assumes that when an attribute is compared to a constant, there is always a match.

Even though such assumptions provide acceptable results in many cases, they are not always correct. Unfortunately, the original implementation of the model makes it very hard to refactor, which led to a decision to redesign it in SQL Server 2014. The new cardinality estimator uses a different code set that is much easier to support and has several different assumptions in the model, including:

> *Correlation*: The new model assumes a correlation between the predicates in the queries; this resembles more cases in real-life querying as compared to the Independence assumption model.
>
> *Base Containment*: This model assumes that users may query for data that does not exist in the tables. It factors the base table's histograms into join operations in addition to the selectivity of join predicates.

In SQL Server 2014 and 2016, you can choose the cardinality estimation model on a per-database level with the setting for database compatibility level, or on a server, session, or even query level with the use of trace flags. Moreover, the new cardinality estimator in SQL Server 2016 allows you to choose between SQL Server 2014 and 2016 implementations.

■ **Note** You can see the version of the cardinality estimation model by analyzing the `CardinalityEstimationModelVersion` property of the root element in the execution plan. It can have the values of 70, 120, and 130, which correspond to legacy, SQL Server 2014, and 2016 implementations.

Table 3-2 illustrates the cardinality estimator model choice in SQL Server 2014 and 2016 based on the database compatibility level and trace flags `T2312`/`T9481`. These trace flags can be used on both the server and query levels. As a reminder, database compatibility models of 120 and 130 correspond to SQL Server 2014 and 2016 respectively.

***Table 3-2.** Cardinality Estimator Model Choice in SQL Server 2014-2016*

	Database Compatibility Level < 120	Database Compatibility Level = 120	Database Compatibility Level = 130
Default behavior	70	120 in both SQL Server 2014 and 2016	130
`T2312`	120 in both SQL Server 2014 and 2016	120 in both SQL Server 2014 and 2016	130
`T9481`	70	70	70

A new feature of SQL Server 2016, *database scoped configuration*, allows you to override the cardinality estimator model's choice based on the database compatibility level. You can enable the legacy estimator by using the `ALTER DATABASE SCOPED CONFIGURATION SET LEGACY_CARDINALITY_ESTIMATION = ON` statement. Table 3-3 shows the choice of the model when the `LEGACY_CARDINALITY_ESTIMATION` database scoped configuration is enabled.

Table 3-3. *Cardinality Estimator Model Choice in SQL Server 2016 When LEGACY_CARDINALITY_ESTIMATION=ON*

	Database Compatibility Level < 120	Database Compatibility Level = 120	Database Compatibility Level = 130
Default behavior	70	70	70
T2312	70	120	130
T9481	70	70	70

One of the key difference between legacy and new cardinality estimators is how they handle multi-statement table-valued functions. The legacy cardinality estimator always expects a function to return a single row. Both the 120 and 130 estimators expect 100 rows. Neither of the models are correct; however, in many cases an estimation of 100 rows would work better when multi-statement table-valued functions return a large amount of data. We will discuss user-defined functions in detail in Chapter 11.

Let's examine a few different examples and compare the behavior of the legacy and new cardinality estimators.

Comparing Cardinality Estimators: Up-to-Date Statistics

As a first test, let's check out how both models perform estimations when statistics are up to date. Listing 3-10 constructs a test table, populates it with some data, and creates clustered and nonclustered indexes on the table.

Listing 3-10. Comparing cardinality estimators: Test table creation

```
create table dbo.CETest
(
    ID int not null,
    ADate date not null,
    Placeholder char(10)
);

;with N1(C) as (select 0 union all select 0) -- 2 rows
,N2(C) as (select 0 from N1 as T1 cross join N1 as T2) -- 4 rows
,N3(C) as (select 0 from N2 as T1 cross join N2 as T2) -- 16 rows
,N4(C) as (select 0 from N3 as T1 cross join N3 as T2) -- 256 rows
,N5(C) as (select 0 from N4 as T1 cross join N4 as T2) -- 65,536 rows
,IDs(ID) as (select row_number() over (order by (select null)) from N5)
insert into dbo.CETest(ID,ADate)
    select ID,dateadd(day,abs(checksum(newid())) % 365,'2016-06-01') from IDs;

create unique clustered index IDX_CETest_ID on dbo.CETest(ID);
create nonclustered index IDX_CETest_ADate on dbo.CETest(ADate);
```

If you examined nonclustered index statistics with the `DBCC SHOW_STATISTICS('dbo.CETest', IDX_CETest_ADate)` command, you would see results similar to those shown in Figure 3-12. Actual histogram values may be different when you run the script, because the `ADate` values were generated randomly. Ignore the highlights in the figure for now, though I will refer to them later.

	Name	Updated	Rows	Rows Sampled	Steps	Density
1	IDX_CETest_ADate	Jun 10 2016 1:53PM	65536	65536	200	0.005546964

Average key length	String Index	Filter Expression	Unfiltered Rows
7	NO	NULL	65536

	All density	Average Length	Columns
1	0.002739726	3	ADate
2	1.525879E-05	7	ADate, ID

	RANGE_HI_KEY	RANGE_ROWS	EQ_ROWS	DISTINCT_RANGE_ROWS	AVG_RANGE_ROWS
1	2016-06-01	0	177	0	1
2	2016-06-02	0	178	0	1
3	2016-06-04	193	189	1	193
4	2016-06-05	0	178	0	1
5	2016-06-07	171	174	1	171
6	2016-06-08	0	169	0	1
7	2016-06-10	195	190	1	195
8	2016-06-13	349	165	2	174.5
9	[illegible]	[illegible]	[illegible]	[illegible]	[illegible]

Figure 3-12. *IDX_CETest_AData statistics*

As you can see, the table has 65,536 rows. Let's test cardinality estimations in cases where we use a predicate for a value that is a key in one of the histogram's steps. The query is shown in Listing 3-11. I will run it in compatibility levels of 110, 120, and 130 and compare the results of all models.

Listing 3-11. Up-to-date statistics: Selecting data for a value that is a key in the histogram step

```
alter database SQLServerInternals set compatibility_level = 110 /* 120; 130 */
go

select ID, ADate, Placeholder
from dbo.CETest with (index=IDX_CETest_ADate)
where ADate = '2016-06-07';
```

As you can see in Figure 3-13, the results are the same in all cases. SQL Server uses a value from the EQ_ROWS column from the fifth histogram step for the estimation.

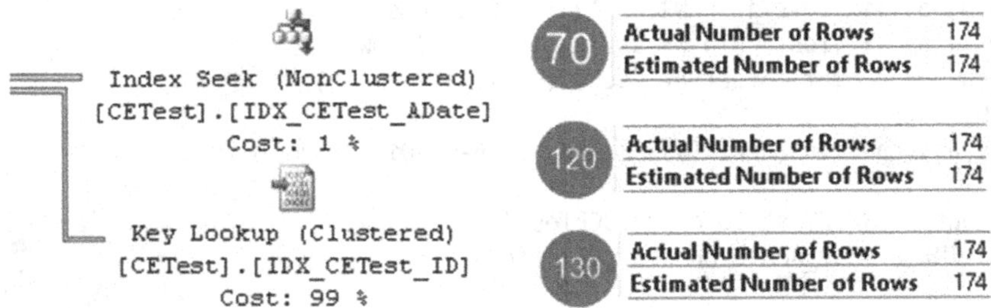

Figure 3-13. *Up-to-date statistics: Cardinality estimations for a value that is a key in the histogram step*

Now, let's run a query that selects data for `ADate = '2016-06-11'`, which is not present in the histogram as a key. The results shown in Figure 3-14 are the same for all models. SQL Server uses the `AVG_RANGE_ROWS` column value from the eighth histogram step for the estimation.

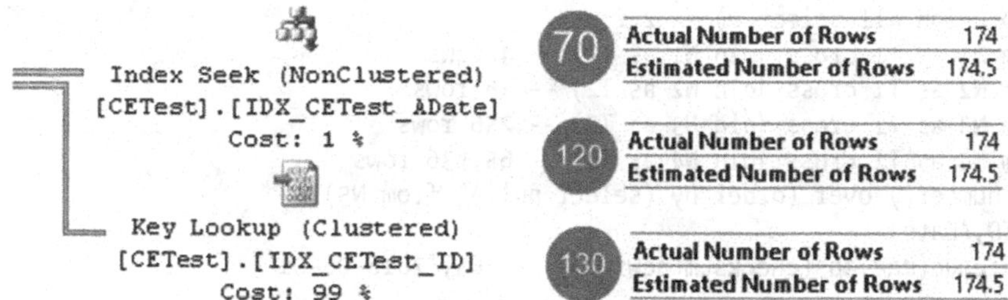

Figure 3-14. *Up-to-date statistics: Cardinality estimations for a value that is not a key in the histogram step.*

Finally, let's run a parameterized query, as shown in Listing 3-12, using a local variable as the predicate. In this case, SQL Server uses average selectivity in the index and estimates the number of rows by multiplying the density of the key by the total number of rows in the index: `0.002739726 * 65536 = 179.551`. All models produce the same result, as shown in Figure 3-15.

Listing 3-12. Up-to-date statistics: Selecting data for unknown value

```
declare
    @D date = '2016-06-07';

select ID, ADate, Placeholder
from dbo.CETest with (index=IDX_CETest_ADate)
where ADate = @D;
```

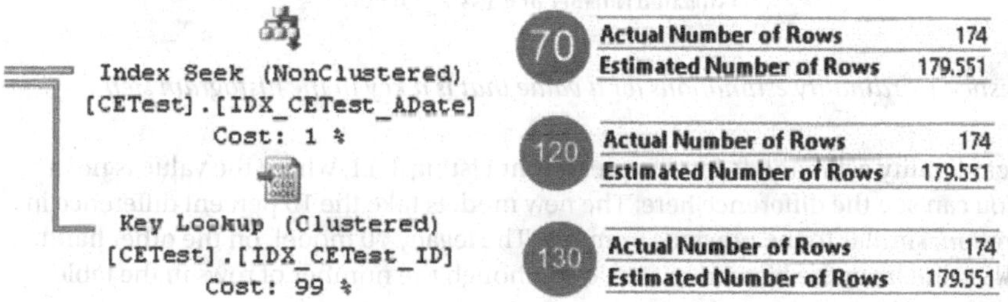

Figure 3-15. *Up-to-date statistics: Cardinality estimations for an unknown value*

As you can see, when the statistics are up to date, all models provide the same results.

Comparing Cardinality Estimators: Outdated Statistics

Unfortunately, in systems with non-static data, data modifications always outdate the statistics. Let's look at how this affects cardinality estimations by inserting 6,554 new rows in the table, which is 10 percent of the total number of rows. Listing 3-13 shows the code for achieving this. I am also disabling the automatic statistics update option in the database to avoid a statistics update resulting from the dynamic statistics update threshold being met in compatibility level 130. Do not forget to re-enable it later when you are working with other demo scripts from the companion materials of this book.

Listing 3-13. Comparing cardinality estimators: Adding new rows

```
alter database SQLServerInternals set auto_update_statistics off
go

;with N1(C) as (select 0 union all select 0) -- 2 rows
,N2(C) as (select 0 from N1 as T1 cross join N1 as T2) -- 4 rows
,N3(C) as (select 0 from N2 as T1 cross join N2 as T2) -- 16 rows
,N4(C) as (select 0 from N3 as T1 cross join N3 as T2) -- 256 rows
,N5(C) as (select 0 from N4 as T1 cross join N4 as T2) -- 65,536 rows
,IDs(ID) as (select row_number() over (order by (select null)) from N5)
insert into dbo.CETest(ID,ADate)
    select ID + 65536,dateadd(day,abs(checksum(newid())) % 365,'2016-06-01')
    from IDs
    where ID <= 6554;
```

Now, let's repeat our tests. Figure 3-16 illustrates the cardinality estimation for the query from Listing 3-11, where the value is present as a key in the histogram step. As you can see, all models estimated 191.401 rows, which is 10 percent more than previously. SQL Server compares the number of rows in the table with the original Rows value in the statistics and adjusts the value from the EQ_ROWS column in the fifth histogram step accordingly.

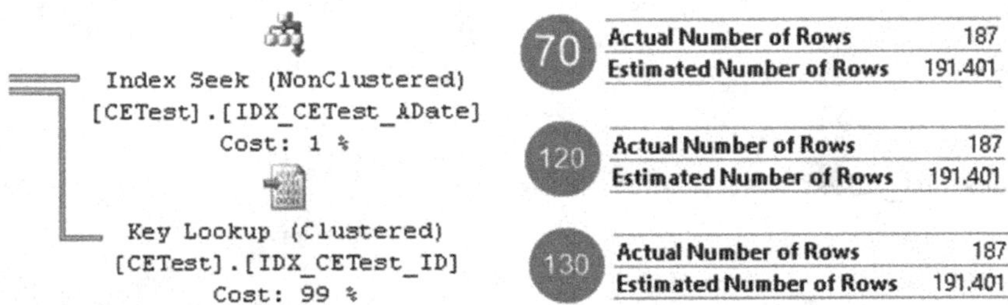

Figure 3-16. *Outdated statistics: Cardinality estimations for a value that is a key in the histogram step*

Figure 3-17 shows the cardinality estimations for the query from Listing 3-11, where the value is not a key in the histogram step. You can see the difference here. The new models take the 10 percent difference in the row count into consideration, similar to the previous example. The legacy 70 model, on the other hand, still uses the AVG_RANGE_ROWS value from the histogram step, even though the number of rows in the table does not match the number of rows kept in the statistics.

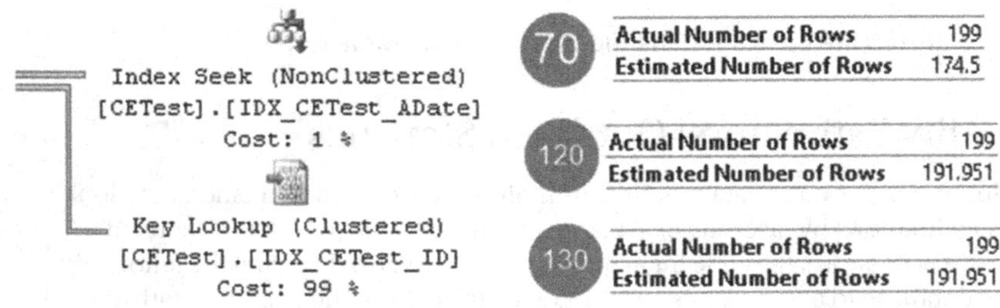

Figure 3-17. *Outdated statistics: Cardinality estimations for a value that is not a key in the histogram step*

The same thing happens with the parameterized query from Listing 3-12. The new models adjust the estimation based on the row-count differences, while the legacy model ignores them. Figure 3-18 illustrates these estimations.

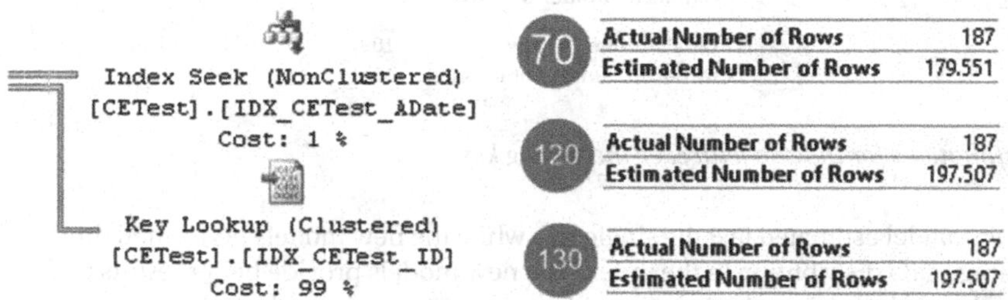

Figure 3-18. *Outdated statistics: Cardinality estimations for an unknown value*

Both approaches have their pros and cons. The new models produce better results when new data has been evenly distributed in the index. This is exactly what happened in our case when `ADate` values were randomly generated. Alternatively, the legacy model works better in cases of uneven distribution of new values when the distribution of old values did not change. You can think about indexes with ever-increasing key values as an example.

Comparing Cardinality Estimators: Indexes with Ever-Increasing Key Values

The next test compares the behavior of cardinality estimators when the value is outside of the histogram range. This often happens in cases of indexes with ever-increasing key values, such as those on the identity or sequence columns. Right now, we have such a situation with the `IDX_CETest_ID` index. Index statistics were not updated after we inserted new rows, as shown in Figure 3-19.

	Name	Updated	Rows	Rows Sampled	Steps	Density	Average key length
1	IDX_CETest_ID	Jun 10 2016 1:53PM	65536	65536	2	1	4

	All density	Average Length	Columns
1	1.525879E-05	4	ID

	RANGE_HI_KEY	RANGE_ROWS	EQ_ROWS	DISTINCT_RANGE_ROWS	AVG_RANGE_ROWS
1	1	0	1	0	1
2	65536	65534	1	65534	1

Figure 3-19. *Indexes with ever-increasing keys: Histogram*

Listing 3-14 shows the queries that select data for certain parameters, which are not present in the histogram. Figure 3-20 shows the cardinality estimations.

Listing 3-14. Indexes with ever-increasing key values: Test query

```
select top 10 ID, ADate
from dbo.CETest
where ID between 66000 and 67000
order by PlaceHolder;
```

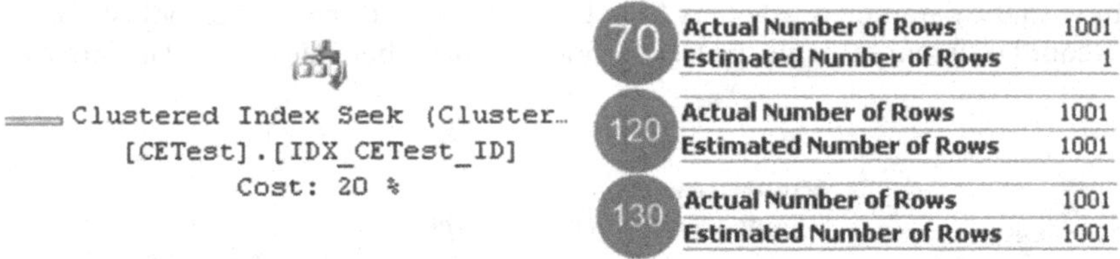

Figure 3-20. *Cardinality estimations for indexes with ever-increasing keys*

As you can see, the legacy model estimated just the single row while the new models performed the estimation based on the average data distribution in the index. The new models provide better results and let you avoid frequent manual statistics updates for indexes with ever-increasing key values.

Comparing Cardinality Estimators: Joins

Let's look at how both models handle joins and create another table, as shown in Listing 3-15. The table has a single ID column populated with data from the dbo.CETest table, referencing it with a foreign key constraint, which we will discuss in greater depth in Chapter 8.

Listing 3-15. Cardinality estimators and joins: Creating another table

```
create table dbo.CETestRef
(
    ID int not null
        constraint FK_CTTestRef_CTTest foreign key references dbo.CETest(ID)
);

insert into dbo.CETestRef(ID) -- 72,090 rows
    select ID from dbo.CETest;

create unique clustered index IDX_CETestRef_ID on dbo.CETestRef(ID);
```

As a first step, let's run the query with a join, as shown in Listing 3-16. This query returns data from the dbo.CETestRef table only. A foreign key constraint guarantees that every row in the dbo.CETestRef table has a corresponding row in the dbo.CETest table; therefore, SQL Server can eliminate the join from the execution plan. We will discuss join elimination in detail in Chapter 10.

Listing 3-16. Cardinality estimators and joins: Test query 1

```
select d.ID
from dbo.CETestRef d join dbo.CETest m on
    d.ID = m.ID
```

Figure 3-21 shows the cardinality estimations for the query. As you can see, both models work the same, correctly estimating the number of rows.

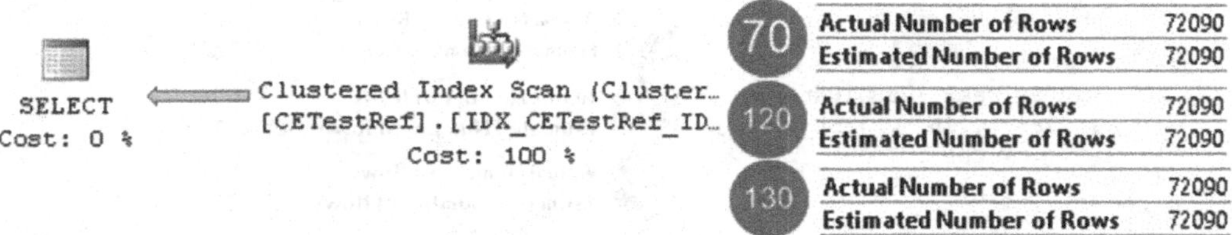

Figure 3-21. *Cardinality estimations with join elimination*

Let's change our query and add a column from the referenced table to the result set. The code for doing this is shown in Listing 3-17.

Listing 3-17. Cardinality estimators and joins: Test query 2

```
select d.ID, m.ID
from dbo.CETestRef d join dbo.CETest m on
    d.ID = m.ID
```

Even though a foreign key constraint guarantees that the number of rows in the result set will match the number of rows in the CETestRef table, the legacy cardinality estimator does not take it into consideration and therefore underestimates the number of rows. The new cardinality estimators do a better job, providing the correct result. Figure 3-22 illustrates the latter, showing the estimations for the *Join* operator.

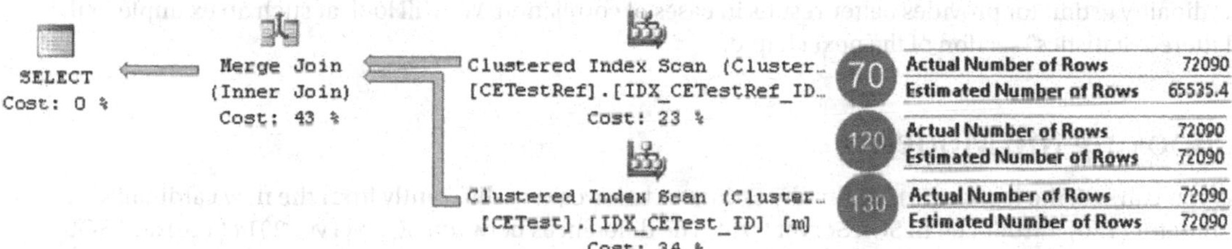

Figure 3-22. *Cardinality estimations with join*

It is worth mentioning that the new models do not always provide a 100 percent correct estimation when joins are involved. Nevertheless, the results are generally better than with the legacy model.

Comparing Cardinality Estimators: Multiple Predicates

The new cardinality estimation model removes the Independence assumption, and it expects some level of correlation between entities' attributes. It performs estimations differently when queries have multiple predicates that involve multiple columns in the table. Listing 3-18 shows an example of such a query. Figure 3-23 shows the cardinality estimations for both models.

Listing 3-18. Query with multiple predicates

```
select ID, ADate
from dbo.CETest
where
    ID between 20000 and 30000 and
    ADate between '2017-01-01' and '2017-02-01';
```

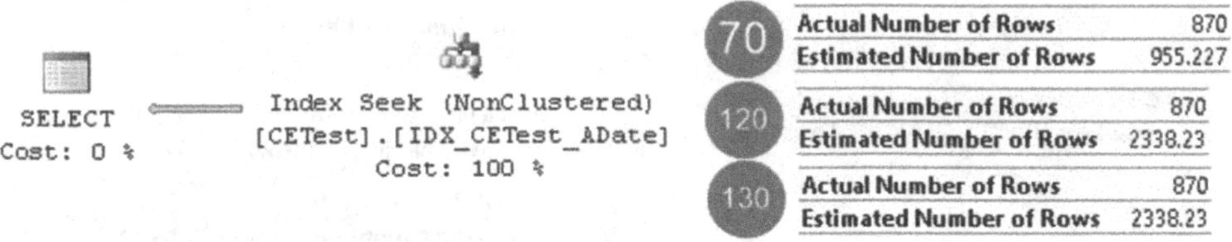

Figure 3-23. *Cardinality estimations with multiple predicates*

The legacy cardinality estimator assumes the independence of predicates and uses the following formula:

```
(Selectivity of first predicate * Selectivity of second predicate) * (Total number of rows
in table) = (Estimated number of rows for first predicate * Estimated number of rows for
second predicate) / (Total number of rows in the table).
```

The new cardinality estimator expects some correlation between predicates, and it uses another approach called an *exponential backoff algorithm*, which is as follows:

```
(Selectivity of most selective predicate) * SQRT(Selectivity of next most selective
predicate) * (Total number of rows in table).
```

This change fits entirely into the "It depends" category. The legacy cardinality estimator works better when there is no correlation between attributes/predicates, as demonstrated in our example. The new cardinality estimator provides better results in cases of correlation. We will look at such an example in the "Filtered Statistics" section of the next chapter.

Choosing the Model

As you can see, the legacy (70) cardinality estimator behaves very differently from the new cardinality estimator (120) introduced in SQL Server 2014. The differences between SQL Server 2014 (120) and SQL Server 2016 (130) models are less noticeable. There are several areas where SQL Server 2016 has some enhancements. Most notably, it better handles the estimations for ever-increasing indexes and better utilizes density information from multi-column statistics. However, you should consider the 130 model as an enhancement over the 120 model rather than an entirely new implementation.

As a general rule, you should always choose the most recent model for a new development. Upgrades, on the other hand, are more complicated. Even though the new cardinality estimation model could provide better results in systems with modern workloads, there is always the possibility of performance regression resulting from the different execution plans. It is impossible to build a model that covers all possible workloads and data distributions, and you should carefully test the system after upgrading.

In SQL Server 2016, you can utilize a new component called *Query Store*, which captures and persists execution statistics and plans in the system. This can dramatically simplify the testing process, allowing you to quickly pinpoint performance regressions. Obviously, you need to have a representative workload and data distribution during testing. We will discuss Query Store in greater depth in Chapter 29.

Of course, nothing prevents you from using the legacy cardinality estimator after the upgrade. However, you should expect that the majority of future enhancements and improvements in the product will belong to the new model. The legacy cardinality estimator would not disappear from SQL Server; however, I seriously doubt that Microsoft will continue to invest a significant amount of time and resources into the old model.

Query Optimizer Hotfixes and Trace Flag T4199

The complexity of Query Optimizer and the massive customer base of the product introduce supportability issues. It is impossible to test hotfixes and improvements in every possible scenario and workload, and, therefore, there is always the possibility of performance issues introduced by any changes in query optimization algorithms.

The situation is changing along with the adoption of the Clouds. SQL databases in Microsoft Azure share a code base with the boxed version. SQL Server, along with other Microsoft products, follows a *cloud-first* model where features are deployed to the Clouds long before they appear in the boxed products. It allows Microsoft to test the function across millions of SQL databases, collecting telemetry from various production workloads and fixing any issues before RTM release. All of this greatly improves the quality of and reduces the number of bugs in the product.

Historically, Microsoft has been very cautious about shipping hotfixes and changes in Query Optimizer. They had been disabled by default and had to be enabled by using the individual trace flags associated with them. Another trace flag, `T4199`, combines many of those hotfixes–which were recommended to be enabled in most systems–under a single flag. Nevertheless, the majority of installations do not have those trace flags enabled and would not benefit from all improvements in the product.

As of SQL Server 2016, hotfix-distribution policy is controlled by the database compatibility level rather than by trace flags. Setting the database compatibility level to 130 enables all Query Optimizer hotfixes and enhancements similar to trace flag `T4199`. That flag, in turn, enables the hotfixes introduced after the SQL Server 2016 RTM release, as is illustrated in Table 3-4.

***Table 3-4.** Database Compatibility Level and Hotfixes in SQL Server 2016*

Compatibility Level	TF4199	Hotfixes Released Before SQL Server 2016 RTM	Hotfixes Released After SQL Server 2016 RTM
<= 120	Off	Disabled	Disabled
<= 120	On	Enabled	Disabled
130	Off	Enabled	Disabled
130	On	Enabled	Enabled

You should rely on the same behavior in future releases of SQL Server. Setting the database compatibility level to the product version will enable all hotfixes and enhancements from the previous versions of SQL Server. Trace flag `T4199` would enable all hotfixes introduced in the current SQL Server version after the RTM release.

This behavior would lead to a situation in which trace flag `T4199` would control different sets of hotfixes in different versions of SQL Server in the future. It can be safer to rely on database compatibility level rather than on the trace flag after you perform the SQL Server 2016 upgrade, switching to the legacy cardinality estimator using the `LEGACY_CARDINALITY_ESTIMATOR` database setting if needed.

■ **Note** You can read more about the Query Optimizing Servicing Model at `https://support.microsoft.com/en-us/kb/974006`.

Summary

Correct cardinality estimation is one of the most important factors that allows the Query Optimizer to generate efficient execution plans. Cardinality estimation affects the choice of indexes, join strategies, and other parameters.

SQL Server uses statistics to perform cardinality estimations. The vital part of statistics is the histogram, which stores information about data distribution in the leftmost statistics column. Every step in the histogram contains a sample statistics-column value and information about what happens in the histogram step, such as how many rows are in the interval, how many unique key values there are, and so on.

SQL Server creates statistics for every index defined in the system. In addition, you can create column-level statistics on individual or multiple columns in the table. SQL Server creates column-level statistics automatically if the database has the Auto Create Statistics option enabled.

Statistics have a few limitations. There are at most 200 steps (key value intervals) stored in the histogram. As a result, the histogram's steps cover larger key value intervals as the table grows. This leads to larger approximations within the intervals and less accurate cardinality estimations on tables with millions or billions of rows. Moreover, the histogram stores information about data distribution for the leftmost statistics column only. There is no information about other columns in the statistics or index aside from multi-column density.

SQL Server tracks the number of changes made in statistics columns. By default, SQL Server outdates and updates statistics after that number exceeds about 20 percent of the total number of rows in the table. As a result, statistics are rarely updated automatically on large tables. You need to consider updating statistics on large tables manually based on a schedule.

In SQL Server 2016, with database compatibility level 130, the statistics update threshold is dynamic and based on the size of the table, which makes statistics on large tables more accurate. You can use trace flag `T2371` in previous versions of SQL Server, or with database compatibility level lower than 130. It is recommended that you set this trace flag in the majority of systems.

You should also update statistics on ever-increasing or ever-decreasing indexes more often, as SQL Server tends to underestimate the number of rows when the parameters are outside of the histogram, unless you are using the new cardinality estimation model introduced in SQL Server 2014.

The new cardinality estimation model is enabled in SQL Server 2014 and 2016 for databases with a compatibility level of 120 or 130. This model addresses a few common issues, such as estimations for ever-increasing indexes when statistics are not up to date; however, it may introduce plan regressions in some cases. You should carefully test existing systems before enabling the new cardinality estimation model after upgrading SQL Server.

CHAPTER 4

Special Indexing and Storage Features

This chapter discusses several storage- and indexing-related features available in SQL Server. It covers indexes with included columns, filtered indexes and statistics, data compression, and sparse columns.

Indexes with Included Columns

As you already know, SQL Server rarely uses nonclustered indexes when it expects that a large number of *Key* or *RID lookups* is required. Those operations usually lead to a large number of reads, both logical and physical.

With key lookup operations, SQL Server accesses multiple data pages from different levels in a clustered index every time it needs to obtain a single row. Even though root and intermediate index levels are usually cached in the buffer pool, access to leaf-level pages produces random, and often physical, I/O reads, which are slow, especially in the case of magnetic disk drives.

This is also true for heap tables. Even though the row-id in a nonclustered index stores the physical location of the row from the heap table, and RID lookup operations do not need to traverse the clustered index tree, they still introduce random I/O. Moreover, forwarding pointers can lead to extra reads if a row has been updated and moved to another page.

The existence of key or RID lookups is the crucial factor here. Rows in a nonclustered index are smaller than those in a clustered index. Nonclustered indexes use fewer data pages and, therefore, are more efficient. SQL Server uses nonclustered indexes even when it expects that a large number of rows need to be selected, as long as key or RID lookups are not required.

As you will recall, nonclustered indexes store data from the index key columns and row-id. For tables with clustered indexes, the row-id is the clustered key value of the index row. The values in all indexes are the same: when you update the row, SQL Server synchronously updates all indexes.

SQL Server does not need to perform key or RID lookups when all of the data a query needs exists in a nonclustered index. Those indexes are called *covering indexes* as they provide all of the information that a query needs, and they are essentially covering the query.

Making nonclustered indexes covering ones is one of the most commonly used query optimization techniques. In the past, the only way to achieve this was to add columns, referenced by the queries, as the rightmost index key columns. Even though this method generally worked, it had a few disadvantages.

First, SQL Server stores sorted index rows based on index key values. An update of the index key columns can lead to a situation where a row needs to be moved to a different place in the index, which increases the I/O and transaction log load, as well as fragmentation.

Second, new columns increase the size of the index key, which can potentially increase the number of levels in the index, making it less efficient.

D. Korotkevitch, *Pro SQL Server Internals*, DOI 10.1007/978-1-4842-1964-5_4

Finally, a nonclustered index key cannot exceed 900 or 1,700 bytes, depending on the SQL Server version. As a result, you cannot add a large amount of data or LOB columns to the index. Even though making a large index row is not necessarily a good idea, it could be helpful in some cases.

SQL Server 2005 introduced a new way of making covering indexes by storing columns in the index without adding them to the index key. The data from these columns are stored on the leaf level only and do not affect the sorting order of the index rows. As a result, SQL Server does not need to move rows to different places in the index when included columns are modified. Included columns are not counted toward the 900/1,700 bytes index key size limit, and you can even store LOB columns if absolutely needed.

Figure 4-1 illustrates the structure of an index with included columns, defined as `CREATE INDEX IDX_Customers_Name ON dbo.Customers(Name) INCLUDE(DateOfBirth)` on the table, which has `CustomerId` as the clustered index.

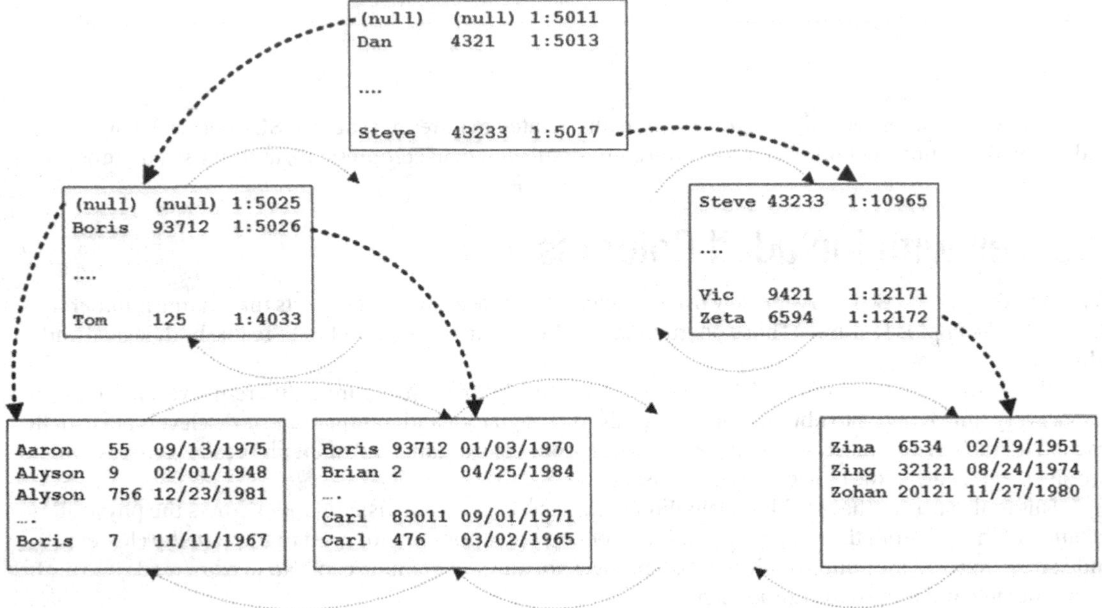

Figure 4-1. *Structure of an index with included columns*

Let's look at how an index with included columns can help us with query optimization. We will use table `dbo.Customers`, which we created and populated with data in Listing 3-3 in the previous chapter. That table has a clustered index on the `CustomerId` column and a composite nonclustered index on the `(LastName, FirstName)` columns.

Let's select data for a customer with last name *Smith*. We will run two queries. In the first case, we will allow SQL Server to choose the execution plan by itself. In the second case, we will force SQL Server to use a nonclustered index via an index hint. The code to do this is shown in Listing 4-1. Figure 4-2 shows the execution plans for the queries.

Listing 4-1. Selecting data for a customer with the last name 'Smith'

```
select CustomerId, LastName, FirstName, Phone
from dbo.Customers
where LastName = 'Smith';
```

```
select CustomerId, LastName, FirstName, Phone
from dbo.Customers with (Index=IDX_Customers_LastName_FirstName)
where LastName = 'Smith';
```

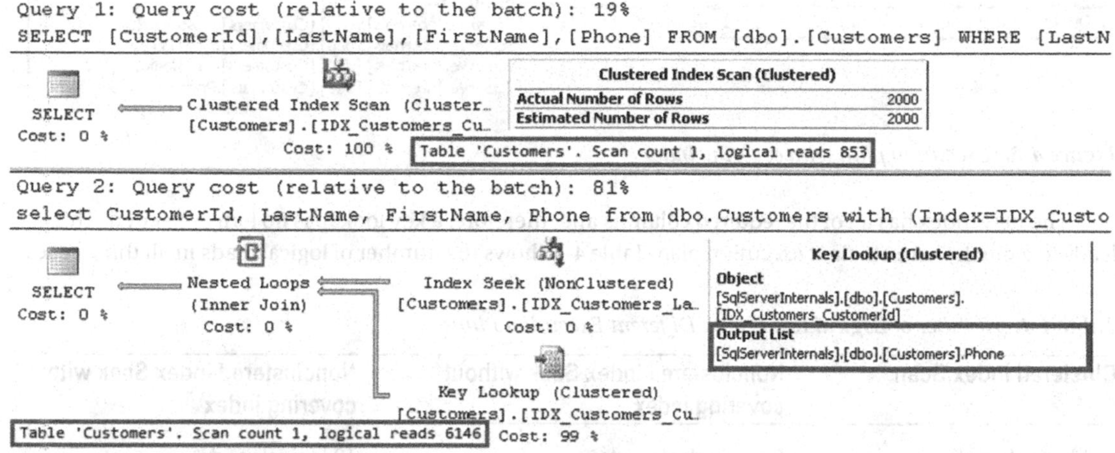

Figure 4-2. *Execution plans for the queries*

As you can see, SQL Server correctly estimated the number of rows with `LastName = 'Smith'`, and it decided to use a clustered index scan instead of a nonclustered index seek. A *nonclustered index seek* and key lookups introduce seven times more reads to obtain the data.

The query selects four columns from the table: `CustomerId`, `LastName`, `FirstName`, and `Phone`. `LastName` and `FirstName` are key columns in the nonclustered index key. `CustomerId` is the clustered index key, which makes it the row-id in the nonclustered index. The only column that is not present in the nonclustered index is `Phone`. You can confirm it by looking at the output list in the key lookup operator properties in the execution plan.

Let's make our index a covering one by including the `Phone` column there and then seeing how it affects the execution plan. The code to achieve this is shown in Listing 4-2. Figure 4-3 shows the new execution plan.

Listing 4-2. Creating a covering index and running the query a second time

```
create nonclustered index IDX_Customers_LastName_FirstName_PhoneIncluded
on dbo.Customers(LastName, FirstName)
include(Phone);

select CustomerId, LastName, FirstName, Phone
from dbo.Customers
where LastName = 'Smith';
```

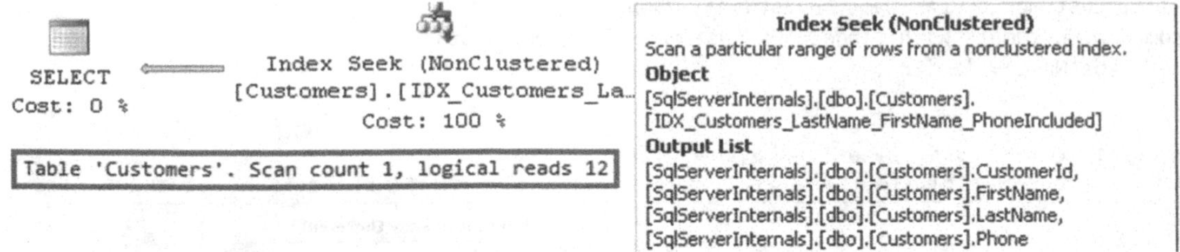

Figure 4-3. *Execution plan with covering index*

The new index has all of the required columns and, therefore, a key lookup is no longer needed. This leads to a much more efficient execution plan. Table 4-1 shows the number of logical reads in all three cases.

Table 4-1. *Number of Logical Reads with Different Execution Plans*

Clustered Index Scan	Nonclustered Index Seek without covering index	Nonclustered Index Seek with covering index
853 logical reads	6,146 logical reads	12 logical reads

■ **Note** The new covering index, `IDX_LastName_FirstName_PhoneIncluded`, makes the original nonclustered index, `IDX_LastName_FirstName`, redundant. We will discuss index consolidation in greater detail in Chapter 7, "Designing and Tuning the Indexes."

Although covering indexes are a great tool that can help optimize queries, they come at a cost. Every column in the index increases its leaf-level row size and the number of data pages it uses on disk and in memory. That introduces additional overhead during index maintenance and increases the database size. Moreover, queries need to read more pages when scanning all or part of the index. Covering indexes do not necessarily introduce a noticeable performance impact during small range scans, when reading a few extra pages is far more efficient as compared to using key lookups. However, they could negatively affect the performance of queries that scan a large number of data pages or the entire index.

By adding a column to nonclustered indexes, you store the data in multiple places. This improves the performance of queries that select the data. However, during updates, SQL Server needs to change the rows in every index where updated columns are present.

Let's look at the example and run two `UPDATE` statements, as shown in Listing 4-3. The first statement modifies the `Placeholder` column, which is not included in any nonclustered index. The second statement modifies the `Phone` column, which is included in the `IDX_Customers_LastName_FirstName_PhoneIncluded` index.

Listing 4-3. Updating data in dbo.Customers table

```
update dbo.Customers set Placeholder = 'Placeholder' where CustomerId = 1;
update dbo.Customers set Phone = '505-123-4567' where CustomerId = 1;
```

As you can see in Figure 4-4, the execution plan of the second `UPDATE` statement requires SQL Server to update data in both the clustered and nonclustered indexes.

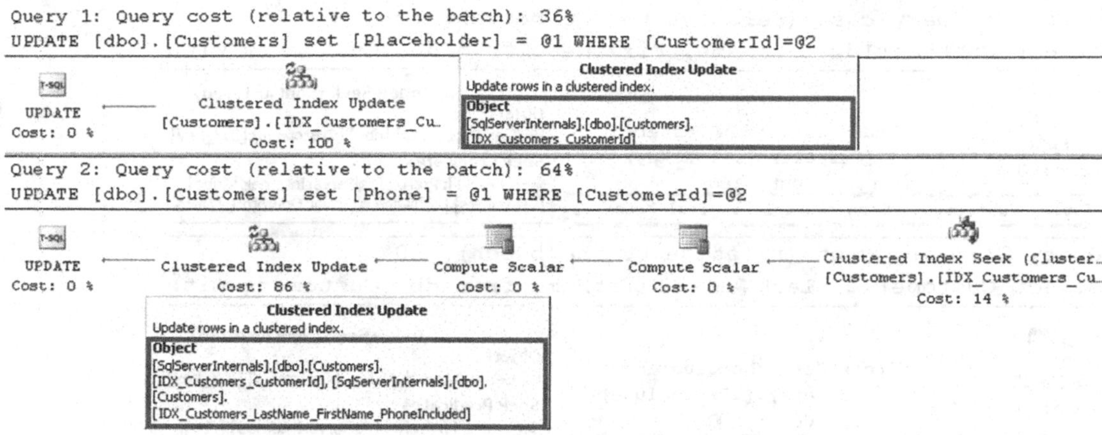

Figure 4-4. *Execution plans for UPDATE statements*

That behavior reduces the performance of data-modification queries, introducing additional locking in the system and contributing to index fragmentation. You need to be careful and consider the pros and cons of making an index a covering one on a case-by-case basis.

■ **Note** We will discuss locking in detail in Part III, "Locking, Blocking, and Concurrency."

It is important to know when to add a column to the index key and when to make it an included column. While in both cases the column is present on the leaf level of the index, predicates on included columns are not SARGable. Let's compare two indexes, as shown in Listing 4-4.

Listing 4-4. Included versus key columns: Index creation

```
drop index IDX_Customers_LastName_FirstName_PhoneIncluded on dbo.Customers;
drop index IDX_Customers_LastName_FirstName on dbo.Customers;

create index IDX_Key on dbo.Customers(LastName, FirstName);
create index IDX_Include on dbo.Customers(LastName) include(FirstName);
```

The data in the `IDX_Key` index is sorted based first on `LastName` and then on `FirstName`. The data in `IDX_Include` is sorted based on `LastName` only. `FirstName` does not affect the sorting order in the index at all.

`LastName` is SARGable in both indexes. Both indexes support *Index Seek* while searching for a particular `LastName` value. There is no difference in performance when `LastName` is the only predicate in the query. Listing 4-5 and Figure 4-5 illustrate this point.

Listing 4-5. Included versus key columns: Selecting by LastName only

```
select CustomerId, LastName, FirstName
from dbo.Customers with (index = IDX_Key)
where LastName = 'Smith';

select CustomerId, LastName, FirstName
from dbo.Customers with (index = IDX_Include)
where LastName = 'Smith';
```

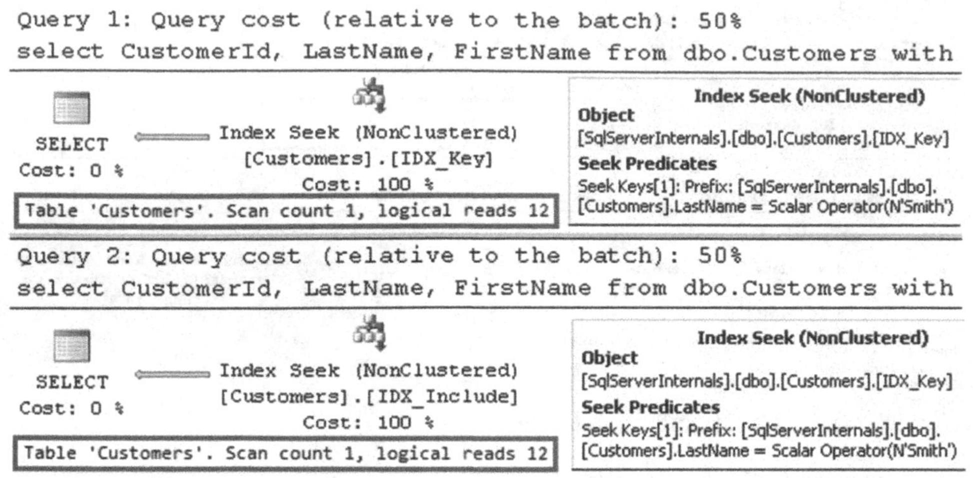

Figure 4-5. *Included versus key columns: Selecting by LastName only*

Nonetheless, the situation changes when you add the `FirstName` predicate to the queries. With the `IDX_Key` index, a query is able to do an *index seek* using both `LastName` and `FirstName` as seek predicates. This would not be possible with the `IDX_Include` index. SQL Server needs to scan all rows with a specific `LastName` and check the predicate on the `FirstName` column. Listing 4-6 and Figure 4-6 illustrate this point.

Listing 4-6. Included versus key columns: Selecting by LastName and FirstName

```
select CustomerId, LastName, FirstName
from dbo.Customers  with (index = IDX_Key)
where LastName = 'Smith' and FirstName = 'Andrew';

select CustomerId, LastName, FirstName
from dbo.Customers  with (index = IDX_Include)
where LastName = 'Smith' and FirstName = 'Andrew';
```

Query 1: Query cost (relative to the batch): 22%
select CustomerId, LastName, FirstNam ... dex
SELECT
Cost: 0 %
Index Seek (NonClustered)
[Customers].[IDX_Key]
Cost: 100 %
Table 'Customers'. Scan count 1, logical reads 3
Index Seek (NonClustered)
Object
[SqlServerInternals].[dbo].[Customers].[IDX_Key]
Seek Predicates
Seek Keys[1]: Prefix: [SqlServerInternals].[dbo].[Customers].LastName, [SqlServerInternals].[dbo].[Customers].FirstName = Scalar Operator(N'Smith'), Scalar Operator(N'Andrew')
Query 2: Query cost (relative to the
select CustomerId, LastName, FirstNam ... index
SELECT
Cost: 0 %
Index Seek (NonClustered)
[Customers].[IDX_Include]
Cost: 100 %
Table 'Customers'. Scan count 1, logical reads 12
Index Seek (NonClustered)
Predicate
[SqlServerInternals].[dbo].[Customers].[FirstName] =N'Andrew'
Object
[SqlServerInternals].[dbo].[Customers].[IDX_Include]
Seek Predicates
Seek Keys[1]: Prefix: [SqlServerInternals].[dbo].[Customers].LastName = Scalar Operator(N'Smith')

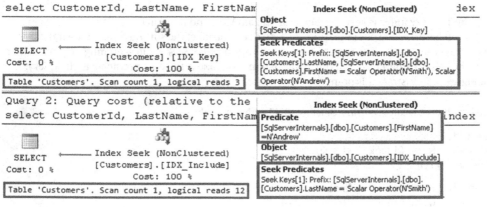

Figure 4-6. *Included versus key columns: Selecting by LastName and FirstName*

As you can see, it is better to add a column as the key column if you expect to use SARGable predicates against that column. Otherwise, it is better to add a column as an included column, make the non-leaf index levels smaller, and avoid the overhead of maintaining the sorting on extra columns.

Finally, it is impossible to avoid mentioning the SELECT * pattern when we talk about covering indexes. SELECT * returns the data for all columns in the table, which essentially prevents you from creating covering indexes to optimize it. You should not use SELECT * in the code.

Filtered Indexes

Filtered indexes, introduced in SQL Server 2008, allow you to index only a subset of the data. That reduces the index size and the maintenance overhead.

Consider a table with some data that needs to be processed. This table can have a Processed bit column, which indicates the row status. Listing 4-7 shows a possible table structure.

Listing 4-7. Filtered indexes: Table creation

```
create table dbo.Data
(
        RecId int not null,
        Processed bit not null,
        /* Other Columns */
);

create unique clustered index IDX_Data_RecId on dbo.Data(RecId);
```

Let's assume that you have a backend process that loads unprocessed data based on the query shown in Listing 4-8.

Listing 4-8. Filtered indexes: Query that reads unprocessed data

```
select top 1000 RecId, /* Other Columns */
from dbo.Data
where Processed = 0
order by RecId;
```

This query can benefit from the following index: CREATE NONCLUSTERED INDEX IDX_Data_Processed_RecId ON dbo.Data(Processed, RecId). However, all index rows with a key value of Processed=1 would be useless. They will increase the index's size, waste storage space, and introduce additional overhead during index maintenance.

Filtered indexes solve that problem by allowing you to index just unprocessed rows, making the index small and efficient. Listing 4-9 illustrates this concept.

Listing 4-9. Filtered indexes: Filtered index

```
create nonclustered index IDX_Data_Unprocessed_Filtered
on dbo.Data(RecId)
include(Processed)
where Processed = 0;
```

■ **Important** The SQL Server Query Optimizer has a design limitation that can lead to suboptimal execution plans when columns from the filter are not present in leaf-level index rows. Always add all columns from the filter to the index, as either key or included columns.

Filtered indexes have a few limitations. Only simple filters are supported. You cannot use a logical `OR` operator, and you cannot reference functions and calculated columns.

Another important limitation of filtered indexes relates to plan caching. SQL Server could not use a filtered index when the execution plan needs to be cached and the index cannot be used with some combination of parameter values. For example, the `IDX_Data_Unprocessed_Filtered` index could not be used with the parameterized query shown in Listing 4-10, even if `@Processed=0` at the time of compilation.

Listing 4-10. Filtered indexes: Parameterized query

```
select top 1000 RecId, /* Other Columns */
from dbo.Data
where Processed = @Processed
order by RecId;
```

SQL Server cannot cache the plan, which is using a filtered index, because this plan would be incorrect for the calls with `@Processed=1`. The solution here is to use a statement-level recompile with `option (recompile)`, use dynamic SQL, or add an `IF` statement, as shown in Listing 4-11.

Listing 4-11. Filtered indexes: Rewriting a parameterized query with an IF statement

```
if @Processed = 0
        select top 1000 RecId, /* Other Columns */
        from dbo.Data
        where Processed = 0
        order by RecId;
else
        select top 1000 RecId, /* Other Columns */
        from dbo.Data
        where Processed = 1
        order by RecId;
```

■ **Note** We will discuss plan caching in greater depth in Chapter 26, "Plan Caching."

Another very important aspect that you need to remember when dealing with filtered indexes is how SQL Server updates statistics on them. Unfortunately, SQL Server does not count the modifications of columns from the filter toward the statistics update threshold. As an example, let's populate the dbo.Data table with some data and then update statistics after that. The code for doing this is shown in Listing 4-12.

Listing 4-12. Filtered indexes: Inserting data and updating statistics

```
;with N1(C) as (select 0 union all select 0) -- 2 rows
,N2(C) as (select 0 from N1 as T1 CROSS JOIN N1 as T2) -- 4 rows
,N3(C) as (select 0 from N2 as T1 CROSS JOIN N2 as T2) -- 16 rows
,N4(C) as (select 0 from N3 as T1 CROSS JOIN N3 as T2) -- 256 rows
,N5(C) as (select 0 from N4 as T1 CROSS JOIN N4 as T2) -- 65,536 rows
,IDs(ID) as (select row_number() over (order by (select NULL)) from N5)
insert into dbo.Data(RecId, Processed)
        select ID, 0 from Ids;

update statistics dbo.Data;
```

At this point, the dbo.Data table has 65,536 rows. Let's update all of the data in the table and set Processed = 1. After that, we will look at the statistics' column modification count. The code to do this is shown in Listing 4-13.

Listing 4-13. Filtered indexes: Updating data

```
update dbo.Data set Processed = 1;

select
        s.stats_id as [Stat ID], sc.name + '.' + t.name as [Table], s.name as [Statistics]
        ,p.last_updated, p.rows,p .rows_sampled, p.modification_counter as [Mod Count]
from
        sys.stats s join sys.tables t on
                s.object_id = t.object_id
        join sys.schemas sc on
                t.schema_id = sc.schema_id
        outer apply
                sys.dm_db_stats_properties(t.object_id,s.stats_id) p
where
        sc.name = 'dbo' and t.name = 'Data'
```

As you can see in Figure 4-7, the modification count for the filtered index column shows zero. Moreover, the number of rows in the index is still 65,536, even though all rows in the table are now processed.

	Stat ID	Table	Statistics	last_updated	rows	rows_sampled	Mod Count
1	1	dbo.Data	IDX_Data_RecId	2016-06-11 13:31:11.9500000	65536	65536	0
2	2	dbo.Data	IDX_Data_Unprocessed_Filtered	2016-06-11 13:31:11.9666667	65536	65536	0

Figure 4-7. *Filtered indexes: Statistics information*

If you look at the histogram shown in Figure 4-8, you will see that it contains the old data distribution information.

	RANGE_HI_KEY	RANGE_ROWS	EQ_ROWS	DISTINCT_RANGE_ROWS	AVG_RANGE_ROWS
1	1	0	1	0	1
2	65535	65533	1	65533	1
3	65536	0	1	0	1

Figure 4-8. *Filtered indexes: Statistics histogram*

This behavior can lead to incorrect cardinality estimation and suboptimal execution plans. You should regularly update statistics on filtered indexes when the filter columns are volatile and are not included in the index key. On the positive side, filtered indexes are usually small, and index maintenance introduces less overhead than with regular indexes.

Another area where filtered indexes are very useful is in supporting uniqueness on a subset of values. As a practical example, think about a table with SSN (Social Security Number) as the optional nullable column. This scenario usually requires you to maintain the uniqueness of the provided SSN values. You cannot use a unique nonclustered index for such a purpose, however. SQL Server treats NULL as the regular value and does not allow you to store more than one row with a non-specified SSN. Fortunately, a unique filtered index does the trick. Listing 4-14 shows such an approach.

Listing 4-14. Supporting uniqueness on a subset of values

```
create table dbo.Customers
(
        CustomerId int not null,
        SSN varchar(11) null,
        /* Other Columns */
);

create unique index IDX_Customers_SSN on dbo.Customers(SSN)
where SSN is not null;
```

Filtered Statistics

One of the assumptions with the legacy cardinality estimator (70) is the independence of query predicates from each other. To illustrate this concept, let's look at the code shown in Listing 4-15. This table stores information about articles, and it has a few attributes, such as Color and Size.

Listing 4-15. Cardinality estimation with multiple predicates

```
create table dbo.Articles
(
        ArticleId int not null,
        Name nvarchar(64) not null,
        Description nvarchar(max) null,
        Color nvarchar(32) null,
        Size smallint null
);

select ArticleId, Name from dbo.Articles where Color = 'Red' and Size = 3
```

When you filter data based on both attributes, Query Optimizer correctly assumes that only a subset of the rows will be red in color. Moreover, only some of the red articles will have a size equal to three. As a result, it expects that the total number of rows with both predicates applied will be lower than with either of the single predicates applied.

While this approach works fine in some cases, it would introduce an incorrect cardinality estimation in the case of highly correlated predicates. Let's look at another example and create a table that stores information about cars, including their make and model. Listing 4-16 creates this table and populates it with some data. As a final step, it creates column-level statistics on both columns.

Listing 4-16. Correlated predicates: Table creation

```
create table dbo.Cars
(
       ID int not null identity(1,1),
       Make varchar(32) not null,
       Model varchar(32) not null
);

;with N1(C) as (select 0 union all select 0) -- 2 rows
,N2(C) as (select 0 from N1 as T1 cross join N1 as T2) -- 4 rows
,N3(C) as (select 0 from N2 as T1 cross join N2 as T2) -- 16 rows
,N4(C) as (select 0 from N3 as T1 cross join N3 as T2) -- 256 rows
,IDs(ID) as (select row_number() over (order by (select null)) from N4)
,Models(Model)
as
(
    select Models.Model
    from ( values('Yaris'),('Corolla'),('Matrix'),('Camry'),('Avalon'),('Sienna')
        ,('Tacoma'),('Tundra'),('RAV4'),('Venza'),('Highlander'),('FJ Cruiser'),('4Runner')
        ,('Sequoia'),('Land Cruiser'),('Prius') ) Models(Model)
)
insert into dbo.Cars(Make,Model)
    select 'Toyota', Model from Models cross join IDs;

;with N1(C) as (select 0 union all select 0) -- 2 rows
,N2(C) as (select 0 from N1 as T1 cross join N1 as T2) -- 4 rows
,N3(C) as (select 0 from N2 as T1 cross join N2 as T2) -- 16 rows
,N4(C) as (select 0 from N3 as T1 cross join N3 as T2) -- 256 rows
,IDs(ID) as (select row_number() over (order by (select null)) from N4)
,Models(Model)
as
(
    select Models.Model
    from (  values('Accord'),('Civic'),('CR-V'),('Crosstour'),('CR-Z'),('FCX Clarity')
        ,('Fit'),('Insight'),('Odyssey'),('Pilot'),('Ridgeline') ) Models(Model)
)
insert into dbo.Cars(Make,Model)
    select 'Honda', Model from Models cross join IDs;

create statistics stat_Cars_Make on dbo.Cars(Make);
create statistics stat_Cars_Model on dbo.Cars(Model);
```

SQL Server correctly estimates cardinality when you run queries with a single predicate, as shown in Listing 4-17 and Figure 4-9.

Listing 4-17. Correlated predicates: Cardinality estimations with single predicates

```
select count(*) from dbo.Cars where Make = 'Toyota';
select count(*) from dbo.Cars where Model = 'Corolla';
```

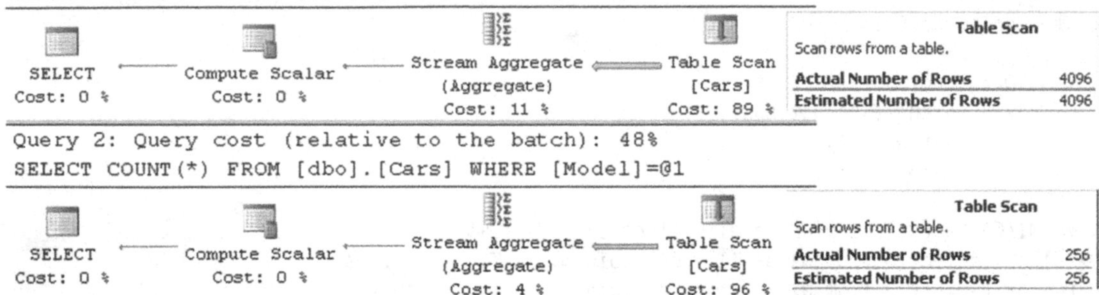

Figure 4-9. *Cardinality estimations with a single predicate*

However, cardinality estimations would be incorrect when both predicates are specified. Figure 4-10 illustrates cardinality estimation for the query: `SELECT COUNT(*) FROM dbo.Cars WHERE Make='Toyota' and Model='Corolla'` when the legacy cardinality estimator is used.

Query 1: Query cost (relative to the batch): 100%
select count(*) from dbo.Cars where Make = 'Toyota' and Model = 'Corolla'
SELECT
Cost: 0 %
Compute Scalar
Cost: 0 %
Stream Aggregate
(Aggregate)
Cost: 4 %
Table Scan
[Cars]
Cost: 96 %
Table Scan
Scan rows from a table.
Actual Number of Rows 256
Estimated Number of Rows 151.704

Figure 4-10. *Cardinality estimation with correlated predicates (legacy cardinality estimator)*

The legacy cardinality estimator (70) assumes the independence of predicates and uses the following formula:

```
(Selectivity of first predicate * Selectivity of second predicate) * (Total number of rows
in table) = (Estimated number of rows for first predicate * Estimated number of rows for
second predicate) / (Total number of rows in the table) = (4096 * 256) / 6912 = 151.704
```

The new cardinality estimator (120), introduced in SQL Server 2014, takes a different approach and assumes some correlation between predicates. It uses the following formula:

```
(Selectivity of most selective predicate) * SQRT(selectivity of next most selective
predicate) = (256 / 6912) * SQRT(4096 / 6912) * 6912 = 256 * SQRT(4096 / 6912) = 197.069
```

Even though this formula provides better results in this case, it is still incorrect, as shown in Figure 4-11.

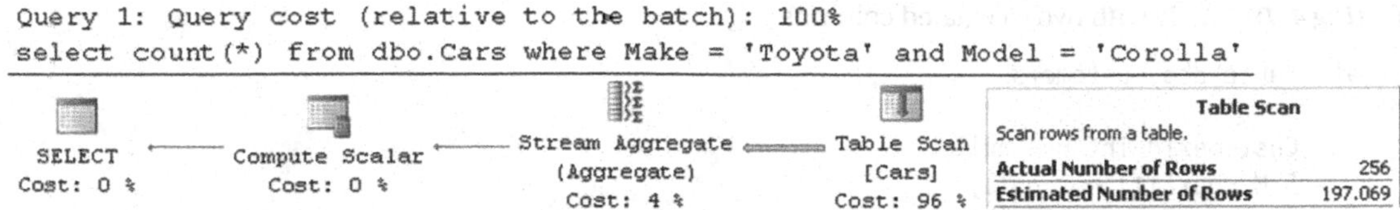

Figure 4-11. *Cardinality estimation with correlated predicates (new cardinality estimator)*

One solution to this problem is the use of filtered column-level statistics. These could improve cardinality estimation in the case of correlated predicates. Listing 4-18 creates filtered statistics on the Model column for all cars made by Toyota.

Listing 4-18. Correlated predicates: Creating filtered statistics

```
create statistics stat_Cars_Toyota_Models
on dbo.Cars(Model)
where Make='Toyota'
```

Now, if you run the SELECT statement again, you will get a correct cardinality estimation, as shown in Figure 4-12.

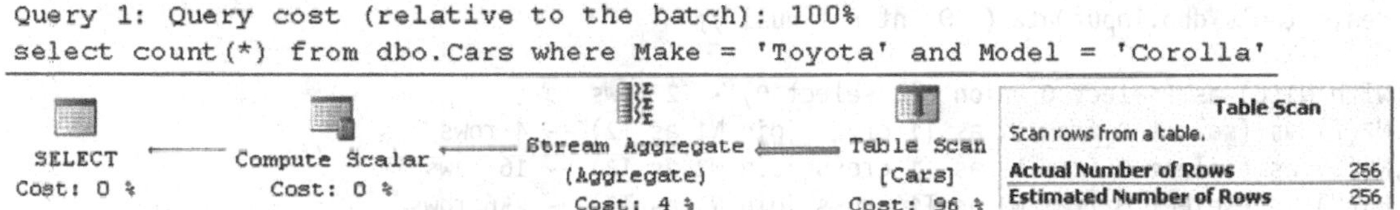

Figure 4-12. *Cardinality estimation with filtered statistics*

The limitations of filtered statistics are similar to those of filtered indexes. SQL Server would not use this feature for cardinality estimation in the case of cached plans when there is the possibility that filtered statistics would not be applicable for all possible parameter choices. One of the cases where this happens is autoparameterization, which is when SQL Server replaces constant values in the WHERE clause of a query with parameters; that is, SQL Server would not use statistics if it autoparameterizes the predicate on the Model column in the preceding query. A statement-level recompile can help you to avoid such a situation. Moreover, SQL Server does not count the modifications of filter columns toward the statistics-modification threshold, which thus requires you to update statistics manually in some cases.

Calculated Columns

SQL Server allows you to define calculated columns in a table using expressions or system and scalar user-defined functions. Listing 4-19 shows an example of a table with two calculated columns.

Listing 4-19. Table with two calculated columns

```
create table dbo.Customers
(
        CustomerId int not null,
        SSN char(11) not null,
        Phone varchar(32) null,
        SSNLastFour as (right(SSN,4)),
        PhoneAreaCode as (dbo.ExtractAreaCode(Phone)),
        /* Other Columns */
);
```

SQL Server calculates the value of the calculated column when queries reference it. This can introduce some performance impact in the case of complex calculations, especially when a calculated column is referenced in the `WHERE` clause of a query. You can avoid this by making the calculated columns `PERSISTED`. In that case, SQL Server persists the calculated values, storing them in data rows similar to regular columns. While this approach improves the performance of queries that read data by removing any on-the-fly calculations, it reduces the performance of data modifications and increases the size of the rows.

User-defined functions (UDF) allow the implementation of very complex calculations. However, they can significantly reduce the performance of queries. Let's look at an example and create a table with 65,536 rows, as shown in Listing 4-20. We will use this table as the source of the data.

Listing 4-20. Calculated columns and UDF: Creating a table with data

```
create table dbo.InputData ( ID int not null );

;with N1(C) as (select 0 union all select 0) -- 2 rows
,N2(C) as (select 0 from N1 as T1 cross join N1 as T2) -- 4 rows
,N3(C) as (select 0 from N2 as T1 cross join N2 as T2) -- 16 rows
,N4(C) as (select 0 from N3 as T1 cross join N3 as T2) -- 256 rows
,N5(C) as (select 0 from N4 as T1 cross join N4 as T2 ) -- 65,536 rows
,Nums(Num) as (select row_number() over (order by (select null)) from N5)
insert into dbo.InputData(ID)
        select Num from Nums;
```

For the next step, let's create two other tables with calculated columns. One of the tables persists calculated column data while the other table does not. The code to accomplish this is shown in Listing 4-21.

Listing 4-21. Calculated columns and UDF: Creating test tables

```
create function dbo.SameWithID(@ID int)
returns int
with schemabinding
as
begin
        return @ID;
end
go
```

```
create table dbo.NonPersistedColumn
(
	ID int not null,
	NonPersistedColumn as (dbo.SameWithID(ID))
);

create table dbo.PersistedColumn
(
	ID int not null,
	PersistedColumn as (dbo.SameWithID(ID)) persisted
);
```

In the first test, let's measure the performance impact of the persisted calculated column during a batch-insert operation. The code for this is shown in Listing 4-22.

Listing 4-22. Calculated columns and UDF: Comparing the performance of batch-insert operations

```
insert into dbo.NonPersistedColumn(ID)
	select ID from dbo.InputData;

insert into dbo.PersistedColumn(ID)
	select ID from dbo.InputData;
```

The execution time on my computer is shown in Table 4-2.

Table 4-2. *Batch-Insert Performance*

dbo.NonPersistedColumn	dbo.PersistedColumn
100 ms	449ms

As a next step, let's compare the performance of the queries, which reference the persisted and non-persisted calculated columns during the SELECT operation, using the code shown in Listing 4-23.

Listing 4-23. Calculated columns and UDF: Comparing the performance of SELECT operations

```
select count(*)
from dbo.NonPersistedColumn
where NonPersistedColumn = 42;

select count(*)
from dbo.PersistedColumn
where PersistedColumn = 42;
```

In the case of the non-persisted calculated column, SQL Server calls the user-defined function to evaluate the predicate on every row, which significantly increases the execution time, as shown in Table 4-3.

Table 4-3. *Select Performance with Warm Cache*

dbo.PersistedColumn	dbo.NonPersistedColumn
7 ms	218ms

The noticeable performance impact is mainly related to the user-defined function call's overhead. However, you would still have a performance impact because of the calculations, granted of a smaller scope, even if user-defined functions were not used.

■ **Note** We will discuss user-defined functions and their performance implications in greater depth in Chapter 11, "User-Defined Functions."

Calculated columns that use user-defined functions prevent Query Optimizer from generating parallel execution plans even when queries do not reference them. This is one of the design limitations of Query Optimizer. We can see this behavior if we run the query shown in Listing 4-24. The code uses undocumented trace flag T8649, which forces SQL Server to produce a parallel execution plan if it is possible. As usual, be careful with undocumented trace flags and do not use them in production.

Listing 4-24. Calculated columns and parallel execution plans

```
select count(*) from dbo.NonPersistedColumn option (querytraceon 8649);
select count(*) from dbo.PersistedColumn option (querytraceon 8649);
select count(*) from dbo.InputData option (querytraceon 8649);
```

As you can see in Figure 4-13, the only time SQL Server is able to generate a parallel execution plan is in the table without a calculated column. It is worth mentioning that SQL Server is able to generate parallel execution plans for tables with calculated columns, as long as they are not calculated with user-defined functions.

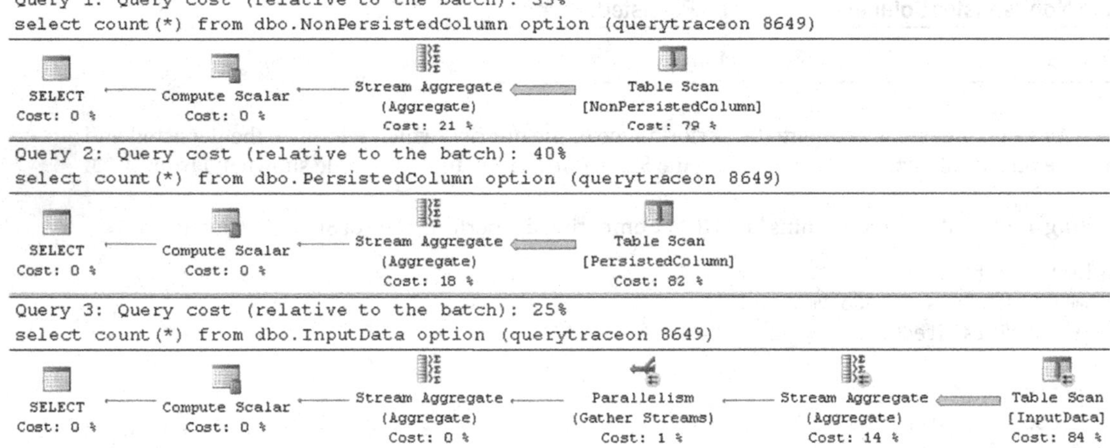

Figure 4-13. *Calculated columns and parallel execution plans*

You can create indexes on calculated columns even when those columns are not persisted. This is a great option when the main use case for a calculated column is to support index seek operations. One such example is searching by the last four digits in an SSN. You can create a nonclustered index on the SSNLastFour calculated column in the dbo.Customers table (shown in Listing 4-19) without making the calculated column persisted. Such an approach saves storage space for data.

The code shown in Listing 4-25 creates an index on a non-persisted calculated column and references this column in the query.

Listing 4-25. Indexing a non-persisted calculated column

```
create unique nonclustered index IDX_Customers_SSNLastFour
on dbo.Customers(SSNLastFour);

select CustomerId, SSN
from dbo.Customers
where SSNLastFour = '1234';
```

Figure 4-14 shows the execution plan for the SELECT statement. As you can see, SQL Server is able to use the nonclustered index.

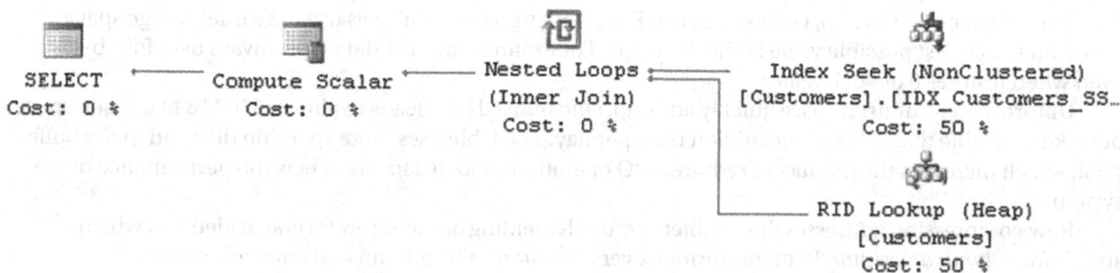

Figure 4-14. *Execution plan that utilizes a nonclustered index on a non-persisted calculated column*

It is important to decide where to calculate data. Even though calculated columns are convenient for developers, they add load to SQL Server during calculations. This decision is even more important in cases where applications use ORM frameworks and load calculated columns as attributes of the entities. This scenario increases the chance that calculated columns will be referenced and calculated, even when they are not needed for some of the use cases.

You also need to remember that a typical system includes multiple application servers with only one active database server serving all of the data. It is usually simpler and cheaper to scale out application servers than it is to upgrade the database server.

Calculating data at the application server or client level reduces the load on SQL Server. However, if the system does not have dedicated data-access and/or business-logic tiers, it could lead to supportability issues when a calculation needs to be done in multiple places in the code. As usual, the decision falls into the "It Depends" category, and you need to evaluate the pros and cons of every approach.

Data Compression

The Enterprise Edition of SQL Server 2008 and above allows you to reduce the size of tables by implementing data compression. There are two types of data compression available: *row* and *page*. *Row compression* reduces the size of rows by using a different row format, which eliminates the unused storage space from fixed-length data. *Page compression* works on the data-page scope, and it removes duplicated byte sequences from a page.

Data pages in the buffer pool store data in the same format as data is stored on disk. Compression is implemented transparently to other SQL Server features; that is, SQL Server components that access data do not know if compression is used or not.

Even though data compression allows you to put more rows into data pages, it does not increase the amount of data that a row can store. The 8,060 bytes maximum row size limitation still applies, regardless of the compression settings. SQL Server guarantees that the disabling of data compression will always succeed and, therefore, an uncompressed row must always fit on a data page.

Let's examine how both compression types are implemented.

Row Compression

As you should remember, the regular row format, called *FixedVar*, stores fixed- and variable-length data in different sections of the row. The benefit of such an approach is fast access to column data. Fixed-length columns always have the same in-row offset. The offset of variable-length column data can also be easily obtained based on the offset array information.

This fast access, however, comes at a cost. Fixed-length columns always use the same storage space based on the largest possible value of the data type. For example, the `int` data type always uses four bytes, even when it stores 0 or `NULL` values.

Unfortunately, unused space quickly adds up. One unused byte leads to almost 350 MB of unused space per year in a table that collects one million rows per day. The table uses more space on disk and in the buffer pool, which increases the number of required I/O operations and negatively affects the performance of the system.

Row compression addresses this problem by implementing another row format, called *CD*, which stands for *column descriptor*. With this format, every row stores the column and data description information for the row using the exact amount of storage space required for the value. Figure 4-15 illustrates the CD row format.

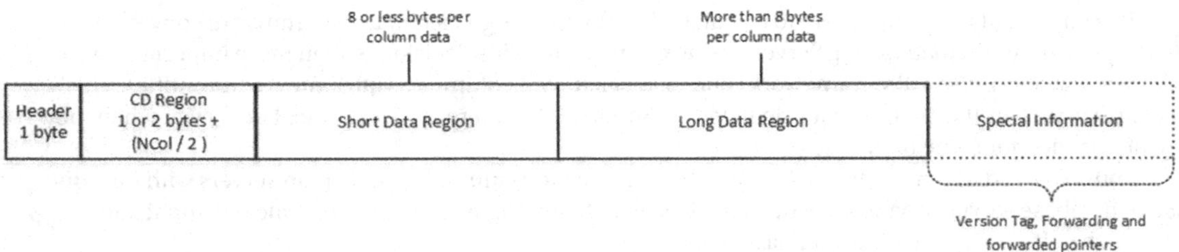

Figure 4-15. *CD row format*

Similar to the FixedVar row format, data in the CD format is separated into two different sections: *Short Data Region* and *Long Data Region*. However, the separation is based on the size of the data rather than on the data type. The Short Data Region stores data up to 8 bytes in size. Larger values are stored in the Long Data Region. Let's look at the row format in depth.

The *Header* byte is a bitmask, which is similar to the *Status Bits A* byte in the FixedVar row format. It consists of various bits representing the properties of the row, such as if it is an index row, if it has a versioning tag, if the row was deleted, and a few other attributes.

The *CD region* stores information about the column data in the row. It starts with either one or two bytes indicating the number of columns in the CD array. The first bit in the first byte indicates if there are more than 127 columns, in which case two bytes are needed to store the number of columns. It is followed by the *CD array* itself. Each element in the array stores information about one of the columns, and it uses four bits to store one of the following values:

0 (0x0) indicates that the corresponding column is `NULL`

1 (0x1) indicates that the corresponding column stores an empty value for the data type. For example, an empty value for `int` columns would be 0. Empty columns do not use space in either the Short or the Long Data Region sections.

2 (0x2) indicates that the corresponding column is a 1-byte short value.

3 (0x3) indicates that the corresponding column is a 2-byte short value.

4 (0x4) indicates that the corresponding column is a 3-byte short value.

5 (0x5) indicates that the corresponding column is a 4-byte short value.

6 (0x6) indicates that the corresponding column is a 5-byte short value.

7 (0x7) indicates that the corresponding column is a 6-byte short value.

8 (0x8) indicates that the corresponding column is a 7-byte short value.

9 (0x9) indicates that the corresponding column is an 8-byte short value.

10 (0xA) indicates that the corresponding column has more than an 8-byte value and is stored in Long Data Region.

11 (0xB) indicates that the corresponding column is a `bit` column with the value of one. Such a column does not space in the Short Data Region.

Offsets for column data in the Short Data Region can be calculated based on the CD region information. However, that calculation could be expensive when there is a large number of columns. SQL Server optimizes it by storing a series of 30-column clusters at the beginning of the Short Column Data region. For example, if the Short Data Region has 70 columns, SQL Server stores an array with two one-byte elements. The first element/byte stores the size of the first 30-column cluster. The second element/byte stores the size of the second 30-column cluster. An array is not stored if the row has less than 30 columns.

Figure 4-16 illustrates such an example. The value 10 (0xA) in the CD array indicates that the column stores long data, and therefore the actual Short Data Region column cluster can include less than 30 values—18, 16, and 4 in this example.

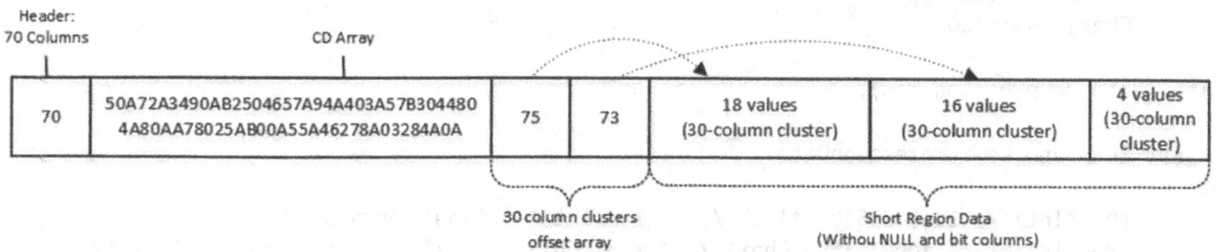

Figure 4-16. *Example of CD and Short Data Regions data*

The Long Data Region starts with an offset array, which is similar to a variable-length offset array in the FixedVar row format.

The first byte is a bitmask with two meaningful bits. The first one is always 1, which tells SQL Server that the offset array uses two-byte values. The second bit indicates if the row has any complex columns that store data off-row.

The next two bytes store the number of columns in the array to follow.

The most significant bit in the first byte of each element in the offset array indicates if it is a complex column. Other bits store the ending offset of the column.

Similar to the Short Data Region, SQL Server optimizes access to the trailing columns by storing an array with a number of long data columns in each 30-column cluster. Figure 4-17 illustrates the Long Data Region for the same row shown in Figure 4-16.

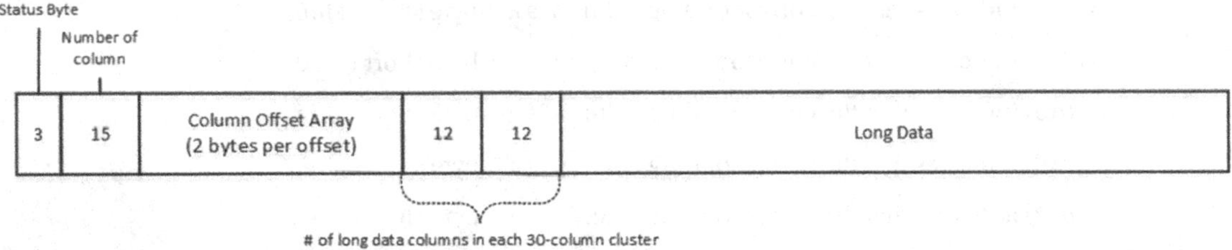

Figure 4-17. *Example of Long Data Region data*

Let's examine the actual row data and create a table, as shown in Listing 4-26.

Listing 4-26. Row compression: Creating a table

```
create table dbo.RowCompressionData
(
        Int1 int,
        Int2 int,
        Int3 int,
        VarChar1 varchar(1000),
        VarChar2 varchar(1000),
        Bit1 bit,
        Bit2 bit,
        Char1 char(1000),
        Char2 char(1000),
        Char3 char(1000)
)
with (data_compression=row);

insert into dbo.RowCompressionData
values
        (0 /*Int1*/, 2147483647 /*Int2*/, null /*Int3*/, 'aaa'/*VarChar1*/
        ,replicate('b',1000) /*VarChar2*/, 0 /*BitCol1*/, 1 /*BitCol2*/, null /*Char1*/
        ,replicate('c',1000) /*Char2*/, 'dddddddddd' /*Char3*/);
```

Listing 4-27 shows the partial DBCC PAGE command results. You can use the same technique, described in Chapter 1, to obtain a page number for the row.

Listing 4-27. Row compression: DBCC PAGE results

```
Slot 0 Offset 0x60 Length 2033
Record Type = (COMPRESSED) PRIMARY_RECORD
Record attributes = LONG DATA REGION
Record size = 2033
CD Array
CD array entry=Column 1 (cluster 0, CD array offset 0): 0x01 (EMPTY)
CD array entry=Column 2 (cluster 0, CD array offset 0): 0x05 (FOUR_BYTE_SHORT)
CD array entry=Column 3 (cluster 0, CD array offset 1): 0x00 (NULL)
CD array entry=Column 4 (cluster 0, CD array offset 1): 0x04 (THREE_BYTE_SHORT)
CD array entry=Column 5 (cluster 0, CD array offset 2): 0x0a (LONG)
CD array entry=Column 6 (cluster 0, CD array offset 2): 0x01 (EMPTY)
CD array entry=Column 7 (cluster 0, CD array offset 3): 0x0b (BIT_COLUMN)
CD array entry=Column 8 (cluster 0, CD array offset 3): 0x00 (NULL)
CD array entry=Column 9 (cluster 0, CD array offset 4): 0x0a (LONG)
CD array entry=Column 10 (cluster 0, CD array offset 4): 0x0a (LONG)

Record Memory Dump
0EA4A060:   210a5140 1a0baaff ffffff61 61610103 00e803d0  !.Q@..ªÿÿÿaaa…è.Ð
0EA4A074:   07da0762 62626262 62626262 62626262 62626262  .Ú.bbbbbbbbbbbbbbbb
<SKIPPED>
0EA4A448:   62626262 62626262 62626262 62626262 62626262  bbbbbbbbbbbbbbbbbbb
0EA4A45C:   62626263 63636363 63636363 63636363 63636363  bbbccccccccccccccccc
0EA4A470:   63636363 63636363 63636363 63636363 63636363  ccccccccccccccccccc
<SKIPPED>
0EA4A830:   63636363 63636363 63636363 63636363 63636363  ccccccccccccccccccc
0EA4A844:   63636364 64646464 64646464 64                 cccdddddddddd

Slot 0 Column 1 Offset 0x0 Length 4 Length (physical) 0
Int1 = 0
Slot 0 Column 2 Offset 0x7 Length 4 Length (physical) 4
Int2 = 2147483647
Slot 0 Column 3 Offset 0x0 Length 0 Length (physical) 0
Int3 = [NULL]
Slot 0 Column 4 Offset 0xb Length 3 Length (physical) 3
VarChar1 = aaa
Slot 0 Column 5 Offset 0x17 Length 1000 Length (physical) 1000
VarChar2 = bbbbbbbbbbbbbbbbbbbbbbbbbbbbbb <SKIPPED>
Slot 0 Column 6 Offset (see CD array entry) Length 1
Bit1 = 0
Slot 0 Column 7 Offset (see CD array entry) Length 1
Bit2 = 1
Slot 0 Column 8 Offset 0x0 Length 0 Length (physical) 0
Char1 = [NULL]
Slot 0 Column 9 Offset 0x3ff Length 1000 Length (physical) 1000
Char2 = cccccccccccccccccccccccccccccccc <SKIPPED>
Slot 0 Column 10 Offset 0x7e7 Length 1000 Length (physical) 10
Char3 = dddddddddd
```

Figure 4-18 illustrates the data in the row. Keep in mind that multi-byte values are stored in byte-swapped order, similar to with the FixedVar format. Moreover, four-bit sections in the CD array are also swapped within each byte.

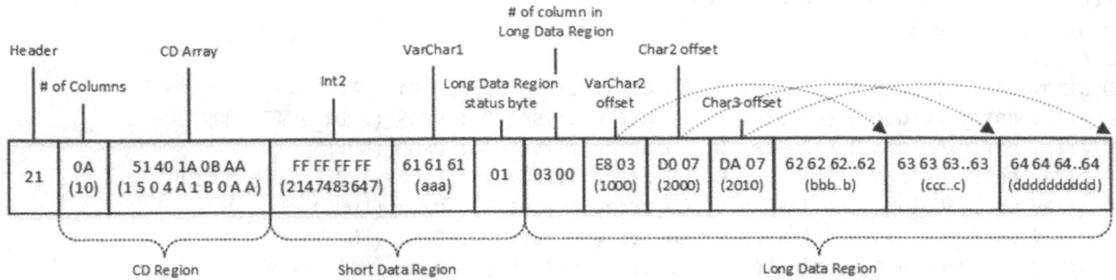

Figure 4-18. *Row compression: Row data*

There is one very important catch, however. In some cases, compression can increase the size of the row. Consider a situation where you have a table with multiple fixed-length columns that utilize all storage space according to the data type. Consider `tinyint` columns that store non-zero values, `smallint` columns that store two-byte values, or `datetime` columns that always use eight bytes. Those columns would not benefit from row compression, and, in fact, row compression would use an extra four bits per column in the CD array, which you do not have with the FixedVar format. Fortunately, those cases are relatively rare, and row compression usually introduces significant space savings.

Finally, it is worth repeating that default type values—for example, zeroes for `int` and `bit` data types—do not use storage space outside of the four bits in the CD region.

Page Compression

Page compression works differently than row compression does. It is applied to the entire page, but only after the page is full and only when the compression saves a significant amount of space on the page. Moreover, SQL Server does not use page compression on non-leaf index levels—those are compressed with row compression when page compression is used.

Page compression consists of three different stages. First, SQL Server performs row compression on the rows. Next, it performs *prefix compression* on the column level by locating and reusing the most common prefix, which reduces the data size for values in that column. Finally, SQL Server does a *dictionary compression* by removing all of the duplicates in the data across all columns. Let's examine prefix and dictionary compressions in depth.

As a first step, SQL Server detects the most common prefix in a column's data and finds the longest value that is using such a prefix. This value is called the *anchor value*. All other rows on the page store the difference between their values and the anchor values, rather than the actual values.

Let's look at an example, assuming that we have a four-column table with the data shown in Table 4-4.

Table 4-4. *Page Compression: Original Data*

Column 1	Column 2	Column 3	Column 4
PALETTE	CAN	NULL	PONY
PAL	BALL	MILL	HORSE
POX	BILL	MALL	TIGER
PILL	BOX	MAN	BUNNY

For the first column, the most common prefix is *P*; therefore *PALETTE* is the anchor value. SQL Server stores the anchor value as an empty not null string (`<><>` is used to indicate anchor values in the tables that follow). All other values are stored based on the prefix. For example, the value *PILL* is stored as `<1><ILL>`, indicating that it should use one letter from the anchor value as the prefix followed by *ILL*. The value *PAL* is stored as `<3><>`, indicating that it uses three letters from the anchor value only. If no usable prefix is found, SQL Server does not store the anchor value and all data is stored as is.

Table 4-5 illustrates page data after prefix compression has been applied.

Table 4-5. *Page Compression: Data After Prefix Compression*

	Column 1	Column 2	Column 3	Column 4
Anchor value	PALETTE	BALL	MALL	NULL
	<><>	<><CAN>	NULL	PONY
	<3><>	<><>	<1><ILL>	HORSE
	<1><OX>	<1><ILL>	<><>	TIGER
	<1><ILL>	<1><OX>	<2><N>	BUNNY

During dictionary compression, SQL Server detects the same patterns across all data on the page and replaces them with dictionary entries, as shown in Table 4-6. This process is type-agnostic and works with byte sequences. The row is still using the CD data format. The CD array stores a value of 13 (0xC) to indicate that the row value has been replaced with a dictionary entry.

Table 4-6. *Page Compression: Data After Dictionary Compression*

Column 1	Column 2	Column 3	Column 4
Dictionary Entities: [D1]: <1><OX>; [D2]:<1><ILL>			
<><>	<><CAN>	NULL	PONY
<3><>	<><>	[D2]	HORSE
[D1]	[D2]	<><>	TIGER
[D2]	[D1]	<2><N>	BUNNY

Both anchor and dictionary values are optional. SQL Server does not create either or both of them if the data patterns do not repeat often enough.

When a page is compressed, SQL Server adds another hidden row, called the *compression information (CI) record*, right after the page header. Figure 4-19 illustrates its format.

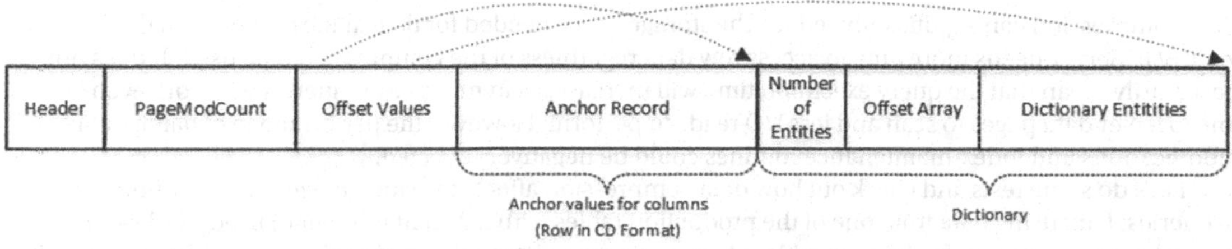

Figure 4-19. *Compression information record format*

A *Header* is a bitmask that indicates the CI record version and if it has an anchor record and/or dictionary entry present.

The *PageModCount* indicates the number of changes on the page after it has been compressed. SQL Server tries to recompress the page and rebuild the CI records either after 25 modifications or when the number of modifications exceeds 25 percent of the number of rows on the page.

Offsets is an array that stores the beginning and ending offsets of the anchor record and/or dictionary entry in the CI record.

The *Anchor* Record is another row in CD format, with each column representing the anchor value for a particular table column.

The *Dictionary* stores an array of dictionary entries and consists of three parts: number of entries, their offsets, and actual values.

As already mentioned, SQL Server stores the data in page-compressed format only when the page is full and compression leads to significant space savings. When a page is full, SQL Server performs compression and evaluates if the newly compressed page can store either five more rows or 25 percent more rows than before the compression. If that is the case, then page compression is retained and SQL Server stores the data in page-compressed format. Otherwise, the page compression is discarded and data is stored in row-compressed format.

The same process occurs when `PageModCount` in the CI record exceeds the threshold. SQL Server tries to recompress a page, evaluating the space savings and either keeping or discarding results.

■ **Note** You can see page-compression statistics in the `page_compression_attempt_count` and `page_compression_success_count` columns in the `sys.dm_db_index_operational_stats` DMF.

Finally, neither transaction log records for data modifications nor the version store in `tempdb` supports page compression. SQL Server needs to decompress the page and remove anchor and dictionary records every time a row needs to be placed in the version store or written to the transaction log. This can introduce an additional performance impact when optimistic isolation levels or `AFTER` triggers are used, or when compressed data is frequently modified.

■ **Note** We will discuss the version store in more detail in Chapter 9, "Triggers," and Chapter 21, "Optimistic Isolation Levels." Transaction log internals are covered in Chapter 30, "Transaction Log Internals."

Performance Considerations

Data compression can significantly reduce the storage space needed for data at the cost of extra CPU load. SQL Server needs more time to access row data regardless of the compression type used. It does not necessarily mean that the query execution time will increase, as in many cases queries will work even faster due to fewer data pages to scan and less I/O reads to perform. However, the performance of batch data modifications and index-maintenance routines could be negatively affected.

Let's do some tests and check out how data compression affects the storage size and execution time of queries. I am using data from one of the production tables with a decent number of fixed- and variable-length columns. Obviously, different table schema and data distribution will lead to slightly different results. However, in most cases, you would see similar patterns.

To begin the tests, I created three different heap tables and inserted one million rows into each of them. After that, I created clustered indexes with different compression settings and `FILLFACTOR=100`. This workflow led to fully populated data pages and zero index fragmentation.

During the first test, I ran `SELECT` statements to scan all of the clustered indexes accessing some row data. The second test updated every row in the tables, changing the value of the fixed-length column in a way that did not increase the row size. The third test inserted another batch of one million rows into the tables. Finally, I rebuilt all of the clustered indexes.

You can see the execution statistics in Table 4-7. All tests ran with a warm cache, with the data pages cached in the buffer pool. Cold cache could reduce the difference in execution times for the queries against compressed and non-compressed data, because queries against compressed data perform less physical I/O.

Table 4-7. *Data Compression, Storage Space, and Performance*

	Size (MB)	Avg. Row Size (bytes)	SELECT Elapsed Time (ms)	UPDATE Elapsed Time (ms)	INSERT Elapsed Time (ms)	INDEX REBUILD Elapsed Time (ms)
No Compression	285	287	298	3,745	12,596	21,537
Row Compression	181	183	224	12,618	17,808	33,074
Page Compression	94	81	267	36,690	39,121	76,694

All statements were forced to run on a single CPU by using a `MAXDOP 1` query hint. Using parallelism would decrease the query execution times; however, it would also add the overhead of parallelism management during query execution. We will discuss such overhead later in this book.

As you can see, data compression improved the performance of the queries that read and scan the data, even without physical I/O involved. This leads us to conclude that reading compressed data adds very little overhead to the system. However, compression decreased the performance of data modifications; therefore, it is expensive to compress data, especially when using page compression.

CPU overhead, however, is not the only factor to consider. Compression reduces the size of rows and the number of data pages required to store them. Compressed indexes use less space in the buffer pool, which allows you to cache more data in the system. Compression can significantly reduce the amount of physical I/O and improve system performance as a result of such caching, even with all the data modification overhead involved. Furthermore, data compression reduces the size of the database and thus the size of backup files and their storage costs.

Obviously, it is impossible to provide generic advice when it comes to using data compression. In some cases, especially with heavily CPU-bound servers, compression can degrade system performance. However, in most cases, compression will benefit the systems. Row compression is usually a good choice when the data is volatile. Page compression, on the other hand, is better suited for static data. You should analyze each case individually, however, taking CPU and I/O load, data-modification patterns, and various other factors into account.

You should also estimate how much space compression actually saves you. There is no reason to be compressing the data if the space savings is minimal. Row compression reduces the storage space used by fixed-length data. It does not help much with variable-length data storage space. The results of page compression depend on the data itself rather than on data types. Finally, both data compression methods work with in-row data only, and they will not compress data stored in row-overflow and LOB pages.

As a rule of thumb, I usually enable row compression for all volatile indexes when it introduces space savings, and page compression for indexes with static data. I also consider enabling page compression even when data is volatile when the size of the active data in the system exceeds the amount of available memory. As I already mentioned, compression allows SQL Server to cache more data in the buffer pool, thus reducing physical I/O activity and improving the performance of the system even with all the data modification overhead involved.

■ **Tip** Data compression can be useful when you deal with third-party systems with an excessive use of fixed-length data types. For example, some independent software vendors use the fixed-length `char` data type to store text information. Implementing data compression here significantly reduces table storage space and improves system performance transparently to the applications.

You can estimate the space savings of row and page compression by using the `sp_estimate_data_compression_savings` stored procedure. This procedure copies a sample of the data to `tempdb` and applies the desired data compression method, estimating the space savings. Obviously, it can produce incorrect results if data is distributed unevenly. I am including the script that estimates the compression space saving for all indexes in the database to the companion materials for the book.

You can apply different data compression methods on a per-index basis. In the case of partitioned tables, compression can be applied on a per-partition basis. For example, you may decide to use row compression or no compression at all for partitions with volatile operational data and page compression for static archived data.

■ **Note** We will talk about partitioned tables and other data-partition techniques in Chapter 16, "Data Partitioning."

Sparse Columns

Sparse columns, introduced in SQL Server 2008, have a special storage format optimized for the storage of `NULL` values. As you will remember, without data compression, fixed-length columns always use the same storage space, even when they store `NULL` values. Variable-length columns use an amount of space based on the size of the value, along with an extra two bytes found in the variable-length offset array.

When a column is defined as *sparse*, it does not use any storage space when it is `NULL`, at the cost of extra storage overhead in cases of `NOT NULL` values. This storage overhead is four bytes for fixed-length data types and two bytes for variable-length data types.

■ **Caution** Even though `NULL` fixed-length data types do not use storage space when defined as sparse, you should not interchange them with variable-length data types. A sparse `char` column would be stored in-row when it is `NOT NULL` and contribute toward the 8,060 maximum row size limit. Alternatively, a sparse `varchar` column could be stored in a row-overflow page if needed.

Sparse column data is stored in a special part of the row called the *sparse vector*. I am not going to dive into the sparse vector internal storage format, but I want to mention that it is located after the variable-length portion of the row. Moreover, the sparse vector adds extra storage overhead, which increases size of the row and counts toward the 8,060-byte limit.

Table 4-8 shows the required storage space used by data types for a regular nonsparse column and for a sparse column that stores a `NOT NULL` value. It also shows the minimum percentage of rows that must have `NULL` values to achieve a net space savings of 40 percent.

Table 4-8. Space Used by Nonsparse and Sparse Columns

Data Type	Nonsparse storage space (bytes)	Sparse storage space when not null (bytes)	NULL percentage
Bit	0.125	4.125	98%
Tinyint	1	5	86%
Smallint	2	6	76%
Date	3	7	69%
time(0)	3	7	69%
Int	4	8	64%
Real	4	8	64%
Smallmoney	4	8	64%
Smalldatetime	4	8	64%
time(7)	5	9	60%
decimal/numeric(1,s)	5	9	60%
datetime2(0)	6	10	57%
Bigint	8	12	52%
Float	8	12	52%
Money	8	12	52%
Datetime	8	12	52%
datetime2(7)	8	12	52%
datetimeoffset(0)	8	12	52%
datetimeoffset(7)	10	14	49%
Uniqueidentifier	16	20	43%
decimal/numeric(38,s)	17	21	42%
Variable-length types	2 + avg data size	4 + avg data size	60%

Sparse columns allow the creation of wide tables with up to 30,000 columns. Some systems—for example, Microsoft SharePoint—use wide tables to store semistructured data.

Think about a table that stores different types of documents, as an example. Each document type has its own set of attributes/columns defined. Some attributes, such as *Document Number* and *Creation Date,* exist in every document type, while other are unique for a specific type.

If you decided to keep all documents in a single table, you could define common attributes as regular nonsparse columns and document-type-related attributes as sparse columns. That approach can significantly reduce table row size in cases where a large number of attributes store NULL values.

It is worth mentioning that you can choose other design solutions besides wide tables in such situations. You may consider storing different document types in separate tables, with another table used to store common document attributes. Alternatively, you could use XML to store some of the attributes or unpivot them into another name/value pairs table. Every approach has its pros and cons based on business and functional requirements.

There is still a limitation of a maximum of 1,024 nonsparse columns per table. Moreover, the in-row part of the row must not exceed 8,060 bytes.

Managing a large number of sparse columns in the code can become cumbersome. As a workaround, SQL Server allows you to define a designated column called COLUMN_SET. Think about the COLUMN_SET column as an untyped, calculated XML column that contains information about NOT NULL sparse columns from a row.

The COLUMN_SET column changes the behavior of the SELECT * operation. When it is specified, SQL Server does not include individual sparse columns in the result set, returning a COLUMN_SET column instead. Moreover, if you add new sparse columns to a table, they would appear in the result set.

Listing 4-28 illustrates an example of this. The code creates two tables with sparse columns—one with COLUMN_SET—and it populates them with the same data.

Listing 4-28. Sparse columns: COLUMN_SET—tables creation

```
create table dbo.SparseDemo
(
        ID int not null,
        Col1 int sparse,
        Col2 varchar(32) sparse,
        Col3 int sparse
);

create table dbo.ColumnSetDemo
(
        ID int not null,
        Col1 int sparse,
        Col2 varchar(32) sparse,
        Col3 int sparse,
        SparseColumns xml column_set for all_sparse_columns
);

insert into dbo.SparseDemo(ID,Col1) values(1,1);
insert into dbo.SparseDemo(ID,Col3) values(2,2);
insert into dbo.SparseDemo(ID,Col1,Col2) values(3,3,'Col2');

insert into dbo.ColumnSetDemo(ID,Col1,Col2,Col3)
        select ID,Col1,Col2,Col3 from dbo.SparseDemo;
```

As a next step, let's select data from those tables using the SELECT * operator, as shown in Listing 4-29.

Listing 4-29. Sparse columns: COLUMN_SET—select *

```
select 'SparseDemo' as [Table], * from dbo.SparseDemo;
select 'ColumnSetDemo' as [Table], * from dbo.ColumnSetDemo;
```

Figure 4-20 shows the results. As you can see, when you select data from the second table, there are no individual sparse columns in the result set.

	Table	ID	Col1	Col2	Col3
1	SparseDemo	1	1	NULL	NULL
2	SparseDemo	2	NULL	NULL	2
3	SparseDemo	3	3	Col2	NULL

	Table	ID	SparseColumns
1	ColumnSetDemo	1	<Col1>1</Col1>
2	ColumnSetDemo	2	<Col3>2</Col3>
3	ColumnSetDemo	3	<Col1>3</Col1><Col2>Col2</Col2>

Figure 4-20. *Sparse columns: COLUMN_SET and select **

You can insert or update sparse columns through the `COLUMN_SET` column. Listing 4-30 shows an example of this, and Figure 4-21 shows the result of the execution.

Listing 4-30. Sparse columns: Using COLUMN_SET to manipulate data

```
insert into dbo.ColumnSetDemo(ID, SparseColumns)
values(4, '<col1>4</col1><col2>Insert data through column_set</col2>');

update dbo.ColumnSetDemo
set SparseColumns = '<col2>Update data through column_set</col2>'
where ID = 3;

select ID, Col1, Col2, Col3 from dbo.ColumnSetDemo where ID in (3,4);
```

	ID	Col1	Col2	Col3
1	3	NULL	Update data through column_set	NULL
2	4	4	Insert data through column_set	NULL

Figure 4-21. *Sparse columns: Using COLUMN_SET to manipulate data*

Working with sparse columns through `COLUMN_SET` can simplify development and database administration, especially when the table schema is changing due to business or functional requirements.

■ **Note** There is a set of restrictions related to the `COLUMN_SET` column. Read this document for more details: `http://technet.microsoft.com/en-us/library/cc280521.aspx`.

Regular indexes are inefficient with sparse columns due to the large number of `NULL` values. You should use filtered indexes instead. Even a large number of filtered indexes might be acceptable and would not introduce noticeable data-modification and -maintenance overhead in cases where a very small subset of the rows is being indexed.

Microsoft suggests implementing sparse columns in cases where the net space savings would be at least 20 to 40 percent as compared to a nonsparse implementation. Sparse columns, however, have a cost. Some SQL features, such as replication, change tracking, and change data capture, are limited when dealing with sparse columns and/or column sets. Moreover, tables with sparse columns cannot be compressed.

You need to monitor the data when dealing with sparse columns. The percentage of NULL values in the columns could change over time, which makes sparse columns inefficient.

With the Enterprise Edition of SQL Server, I prefer to use data compression rather than sparse columns when the goal is to reduce the amount of storage space used by fixed-length columns that store mostly NULL values. Data compression decreases storage space like sparse columns in that use case and, at the same time, is transparent to other SQL Server features.

Summary

SQL Server does not use nonclustered indexes in cases where it expects a large number of key or RID lookup operations to be required. You can eliminate these operations by adding columns to the index and making it covering for the queries. This approach is a great optimization technique that can dramatically improve the performance of the system.

Adding included columns to the index, however, increases the size of leaf-level rows, which would negatively affect the performance of the queries that scan data. It would also introduce additional index-maintenance overhead, slow down data-modification operations, and increase locking in the system.

Filtered indexes allow you to reduce index storage size and maintenance costs by indexing just a subset of the data. SQL Server has a few design limitations associated with filtered indexes. Even though it is not a requirement, you should make all columns from the filters part of the leaf-level index rows so as to prevent the generation of suboptimal execution plans.

Modifications of the columns from the filter do not increment the statistics' column modification counter, which can make the statistics inaccurate. You need to factor that behavior into your statistics maintenance strategy for the system.

Filtered statistics allow you to improve cardinality estimations in the case of highly correlated predicates in the queries. They have all of the limitations of filtered indexes, however.

The Enterprise Edition of SQL Server supports two different data compression methods. Row compression reduces data row size by removing unused storage space from rows. Page compression removes duplicated sequences of bytes from data pages.

Data compression can significantly reduce table storage space at the cost of extra CPU load, especially when data is modified. However, compressed data uses less space in the buffer pool and requires fewer I/O operations, which can improve the performance of the system. Row compression could be a good choice even with volatile data on non-heavily-CPU-bound systems. Page compression is a good choice for static data.

Sparse columns allow you to reduce row size when some columns store primarily NULL values. Sparse columns do not use storage space while storing NULL values at the cost of the extra storage space required for NOT NULL values.

Although sparse columns allow the creation of wide tables with thousands of columns, you should be careful with them. There is still the 8,060-byte in-row data size limit, which can prevent you from inserting or updating some rows. Moreover, wide tables usually introduce development and administrative overhead when frequent schema alteration is required.

Finally, you should monitor the data stored in sparse columns, making sure that the percentage of NOT NULL data is not increasing, which would make sparse storage less efficient than nonsparse storage.

CHAPTER 5

SQL Server 2016 Features

Dmitri Korotkevitch with Thomas Grohser

This chapter provides an overview of several new SQL Server 2016 features, such as temporal tables, stretch databases, row-level security, dynamic data masking, and Always Encrypted.

Temporal Tables

The majority of systems nowadays deal with data that changes over time. New data is collected and inserted into the system, old data is purged, and catalog entities are modified.

There are two requirements that often exist in systems. The first is keeping an audit trail of any data changes, providing information on *who* changed *what* and *when* it happened. There are many ways to build this solution based on existing technologies, such as SQL Audit, change tracking, and change data capture. It is also very common to see custom implementations based on triggers.

Unfortunately, in some cases, keeping an audit trail of the changes is not enough. Some systems–for example, inventory management or financial portfolio management solutions–need to be able to access a *snapshot* of the data at any given point in time. It is possible to reconstruct such snapshots from audit trail tables; however, it is a complex task prone to errors, especially if multiple related tables are involved.

System-versioned temporal tables are the new type of user table that helps to implement those requirements. They are designed to keep a full history of data changes and allow easy point-in-time analysis.

SYSTEM-VERSIONED AND APPLICATION-VERSIONED TEMPORAL TABLES

ANSI SQL 2011 defines two types of temporal tables. *System-versioned temporal tables* keep a history of data changes based on the time when those changes occurred in the system. They provide you with a snapshot of the data that existed in the database at a particular time. *Application-versioned temporal tables*, on the other hand, provide you with a data snapshot that is valid from a business standpoint.

Consider the insurance system as an example. Each insurance policy has effective dates that define when the policy started and expired, or will expire. Application-versioned temporal tables could help to identify the policies that were active at a particular time. System-versioned temporal tables could help to find the policy data rows that were present in the database at a particular time, regardless of whether those policies were active or not.

Unfortunately, SQL Server 2016 RTM does not support application-versioned temporal tables.

D. Korotkevitch, *Pro SQL Server Internals*, DOI 10.1007/978-1-4842-1964-5_5

In a nutshell, each system-versioned temporal table consists of two tables–the *current table* with the current data, and a *history table* that stores old versions of the rows. Every time you modify or delete data in the current table, SQL Server adds an original version of those rows to the history table.

A current table should always have a primary key defined. Moreover, both current and history tables should have two datetime2 columns, called *period columns*, that indicate the lifetime of the row. SQL Server populates these columns automatically based on transaction start time when the new versions of the rows were created. When a row has been modified several times in one transaction, SQL Server does not preserve uncommitted intermediary row versions in the history table.

It is worth repeating that period columns always store transaction start time rather than time of the actual DML operation. This provides you point-in-time consistency when a transaction modifies several related entities; for example, *Orders* and *OrderLineItems*. It opens the door to another phenomenon, however, which we will discuss later in the chapter.

There are three ways in which you can create history tables. First, you can allow SQL Server to generate an anonymous history table by omitting its name during temporal table creation. SQL Server then creates a history table, auto-generating its name. Alternatively, you can specify the history table's name and schema and allow SQL Server to create the corresponding table.

In both of those cases, SQL Server places the history tables in a default filegroup, creating non-unique clustered indexes on the two datetime2 columns that control row lifetime . It does not create any other indexes on the table.

■ **Important** In both the Enterprise and Developer Editions, history tables use page compression by default. You will be unable to restore the database in lower editions of SQL Server unless you rebuild the index removing the data compression.

Lastly, you can assign an existing table to become a history table for the temporal table, assuming that table schemas are compatible. As you can guess, this approach provides you with the most flexibility in configuration.

Listing 5-1 shows the code that creates a temporal table by specifying the *history* table schema and table name. It has new temporal table-related language constructs in bold-face font.

Listing 5-1. Creating a temporal table

```
create table dbo.Employees
(
    EmployeeId int not null,
    FullName nvarchar(128) not null,
    Position nvarchar(128) not null,
    Salary money not null,
    SysStartTime datetime2 generated always as row start not null,
    SysEndTime datetime2 generated always as row end not null,
    constraint PK_Employees
    primary key clustered(EmployeeId)
    period for system_time(SysStartTime, SysEndTime)
)
with
(
    system_versioning = on (history_table = dbo.EmployeesHistory)
);

create nonclustered index IDX_Employees_FullName
on dbo.Employees(FullName);
```

Figure 5-1 illustrates both current and history tables in SSMS and also shows the properties of the clustered index defined on the history table.

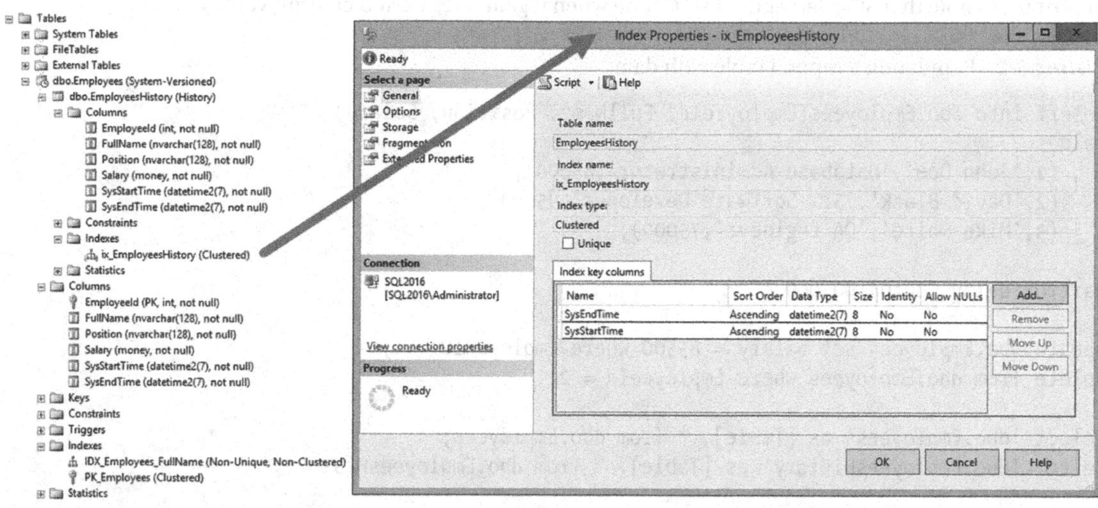

***Figure 5-1.** Temporal table in SSMS*

Current and history tables are, obviously, *logically* linked to each other and would have a matching set of columns. There are no dependencies, however, on the *physical* storage and indexing . The tables can each have a different set of indexes, being located in separate filegroups and even using different storage technologies. For example, it is possible to use a clustered columnstore index for the history data while keeping row-based storage in the current table.

History tables, however, cannot have unique indexes or foreign key and table constraints, nor can they participate in change tracking, change data capture, or transactional or merge replications. You should treat history tables the same way as you treat regular tables during index and statistics maintenance, which we will discuss in the next chapter.

When you alter the schema of the current table, the changes are propagated to the history table. You cannot drop the temporal table, however, until you stop system versioning with `ALTER TABLE SET (SYSTEM_VERSIONING = OFF)` command. This command converts a temporal table to two regular tables in the database.

When you update or delete data in the current table, SQL Server copies the affected rows to the history table. Figure 5-2 illustrates the execution plan of the `DELETE FROM dbo.Employees WHERE EmployeeId = @EmployeeId` statement with a *clustered index insert* to the history table. On a side note, SQL Server does not store the current version of the row in the history table, and, therefore, the `INSERT` statement does not insert data there.

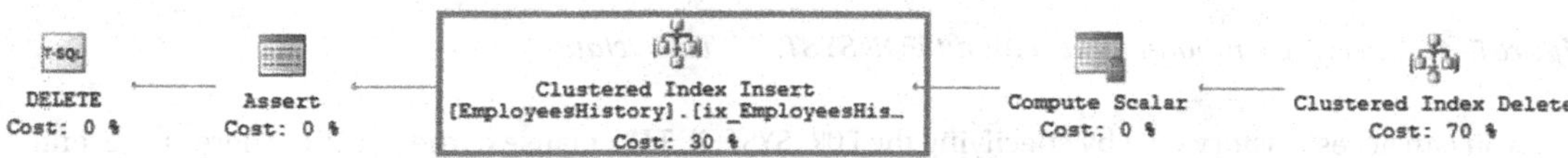

***Figure 5-2.** Execution plan of DELETE statement*

When you select the data from temporal table, SQL Server accesses either one or both tables depending on the query. Let's look at a few examples, and as a first step, let's populate the dbo.Employees table with some data, as shown in Listing 5-2. Figure 5-3 shows the output of the SELECT statements from the code. It is important to note that SQL Server uses UTC time when it generates period column values.

Listing 5-2. Populating temporal table with data

```
insert into dbo.Employees(EmployeeId, FullName, Position, Salary)
values
    (1,'John Doe','Database Administrator',85000),
    (2,'David Black','Sr. Software Developer',95000),
    (3,'Mike White','QA Engineer',75000);

waitfor delay '00:01:00.000';

update dbo.Employees set Salary = 85500 where EmployeeID = 1;
delete from dbo.Employees where EmployeeId = 2;

select 'dbo.Employees' as [Table], * from dbo.Employees;
select 'dbo.EmployeesHistory' as [Table], * from dbo.EmployeesHistory;
```

You can query the history data directly; however, you should remember that it does not contain the *current* version of the rows. Figure 5-3 just illustrated that–there was just one old row for *John Doe* and no data for *Mike White* in the dbo.EmployeesHistory table.

	Table	EmployeeId	FullName	Position	Salary	SysStartTime	SysEndTime
1	dbo.Employees	1	John Doe	Database Administrator	85500.00	2016-07-09 17:57:20.9770748	9999-12-31 23:59:59.9999999
2	dbo.Employees	3	Mike White	QA Engineer	75000.00	2016-07-09 17:56:20.9561164	9999-12-31 23:59:59.9999999

	Table	EmployeeId	FullName	Position	Salary	SysStartTime	SysEndTime
1	dbo.EmployeesHistory	1	John Doe	Database Administrator	85000.00	2016-07-09 17:56:20.9561164	2016-07-09 17:57:20.9770748
2	dbo.EmployeesHistory	2	David Black	Sr. Software Developer	95000.00	2016-07-09 17:56:20.9561164	2016-07-09 17:57:21.0082704

Figure 5-3. *The data in the tables*

By default, when you query the current table, the query works with the current snapshot of the data, similar to how regular tables work, and it does not access history data. Figure 5-4 illustrates that.

```
Query 1: Query cost (relative to the batch): 100%
select * from dbo.Employees

SELECT          Clustered Index Scan (Clustered)
Cost: 0 %       [Employees].[PK_Employees]
                Cost: 100 %
```

	EmployeeId	FullName	Position	Salary	SysStartTime	SysEndTime
1	1	John Doe	Database Administrator	85500.00	2016-07-09 17:57:20.9770748	9999-12-31 23:59:59.9999999
2	3	Mike White	QA Engineer	75000.00	2016-07-09 17:56:20.9561164	9999-12-31 23:59:59.9999999

Figure 5-4. *Querying temporal table without FOR SYSTEM_TIME clause*

You can access history data by specifying the FOR SYSTEM_TIME clause of the SELECT. There are several possible options.

The `FOR SYSTEM_TIME AS OF <time>` option returns a snapshot of the data that corresponds to a particular point in time in the system. SQL Server combines data from both tables when it executes the `SELECT`. Figure 5-5 illustrates the output and execution plan of the `SELECT * FROM dbo.Employees FOR SYSTEM_TIME AS OF '2016-07-09T17:57:00'` statement. As you can see, the data represents the state after the initial insert and before the data modifications seen in Listing 5-2.

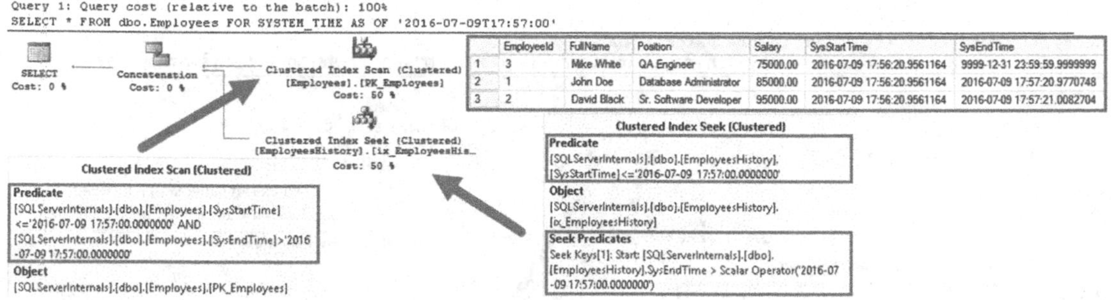

	EmployeeId	FullName	Position	Salary	SysStartTime	SysEndTime
1	3	Mike White	QA Engineer	75000.00	2016-07-09 17:56:20.9561164	9999-12-31 23:59:59.9999999
2	1	John Doe	Database Administrator	85000.00	2016-07-09 17:56:20.9561164	2016-07-09 17:57:20.9770748
3	2	David Black	Sr. Software Developer	95000.00	2016-07-09 17:56:20.9561164	2016-07-09 17:57:21.0082704

***Figure 5-5.** Querying temporal table: FOR SYSTEM_TIME AS OF*

As you can see in Figure 5-5, SQL Server adds the predicates on period columns in both tables. You should add indexes on these columns when you use the `FOR SYSTEM_TIME` option in the queries.

`FOR SYSTEM_TIME FROM <starttime> TO <endtime>` and `FOR SYSTEM_TIME BETWEEN <starttime> AND <endtime>` clauses return you all versions of the rows that existed in a specific time interval. The difference between them is that `FOR SYSTEM_TIME FROM` excludes the `<endtime>` from the output while `FOR SYSTEM_TIME BETWEEN` includes it. Figure 5-6 illustrates that.

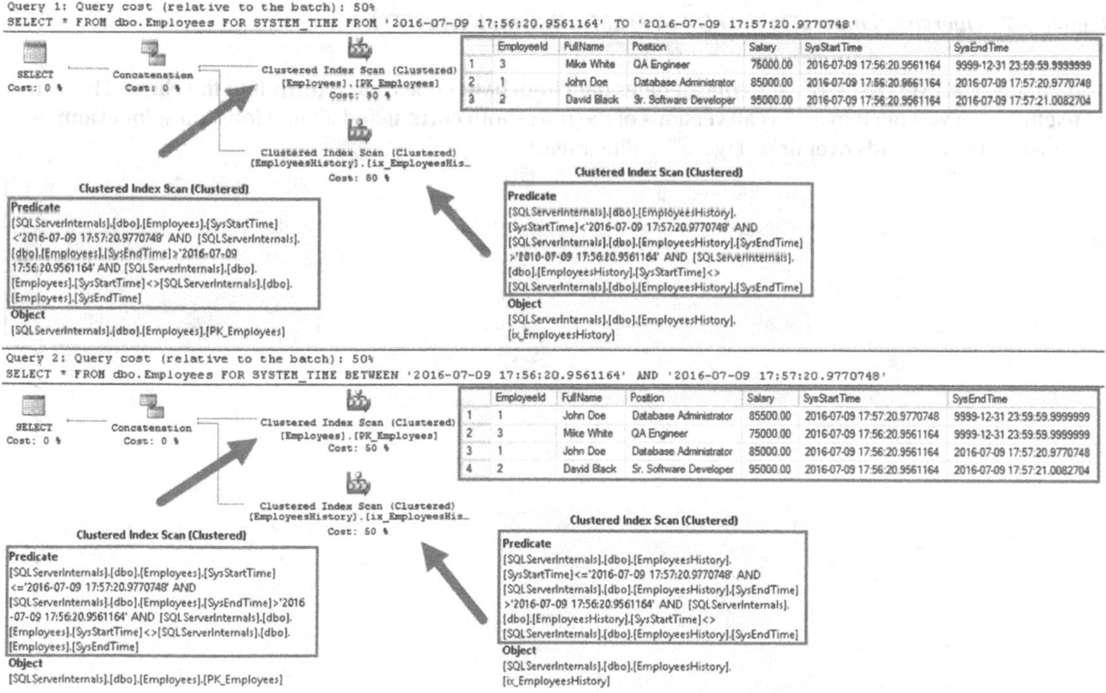

	EmployeeId	FullName	Position	Salary	SysStartTime	SysEndTime
1	3	Mike White	QA Engineer	75000.00	2016-07-09 17:56:20.9561164	9999-12-31 23:59:59.9999999
2	1	John Doe	Database Administrator	85000.00	2016-07-09 17:56:20.9561164	2016-07-09 17:57:20.9770748
3	2	David Black	Sr. Software Developer	95000.00	2016-07-09 17:56:20.9561164	2016-07-09 17:57:21.0082704

	EmployeeId	FullName	Position	Salary	SysStartTime	SysEndTime
1	1	John Doe	Database Administrator	85500.00	2016-07-09 17:57:20.9770748	9999-12-31 23:59:59.9999999
2	3	Mike White	QA Engineer	75000.00	2016-07-09 17:56:20.9561164	9999-12-31 23:59:59.9999999
3	1	John Doe	Database Administrator	85000.00	2016-07-09 17:56:20.9561164	2016-07-09 17:57:20.9770748
4	2	David Black	Sr. Software Developer	95000.00	2016-07-09 17:56:20.9561164	2016-07-09 17:57:21.0082704

***Figure 5-6.** Querying temporal table: FOR SYSTEM_TIME FROM and FOR SYSTEM_TIME BETWEEN*

The FOR SYSTEM_TIME CONTAINED IN option returns you all versions of the rows that were valid in a specific time interval. It does not include any current versions and should work only with the history table.

Figure 5-7 illustrates the execution plan of a query with the FOR SYSTEM_TIME CONTAINED IN clause. Even though it includes a clustered index scan operator on the current table, the filter operator prevents it from being executed.

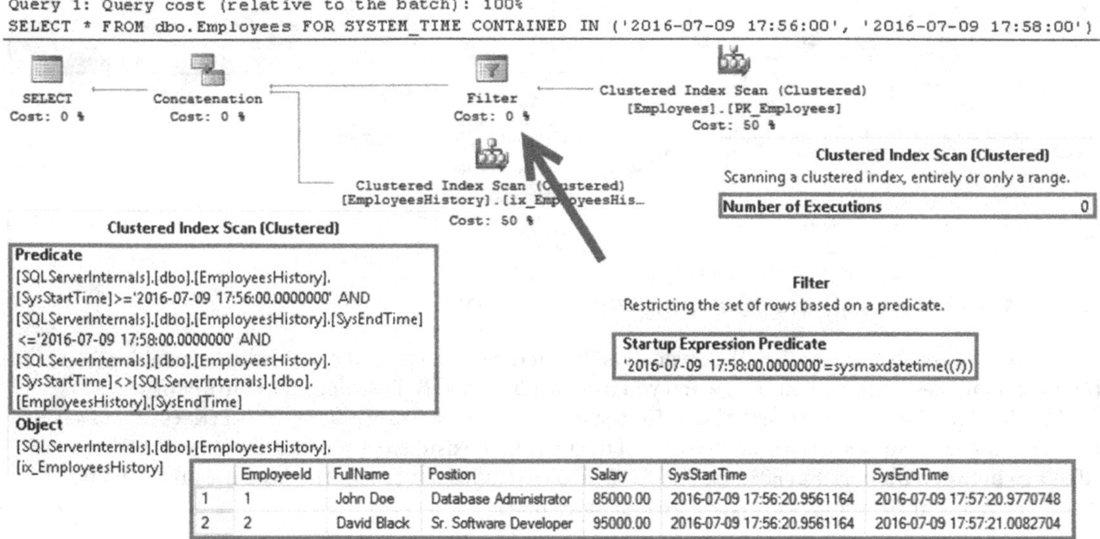

	EmployeeId	FullName	Position	Salary	SysStartTime	SysEndTime
1	1	John Doe	Database Administrator	85000.00	2016-07-09 17:56:20.9561164	2016-07-09 17:57:20.9770748
2	2	David Black	Sr. Software Developer	95000.00	2016-07-09 17:56:20.9561164	2016-07-09 17:57:21.0082704

***Figure 5-7.** Querying temporal table: FOR SYSTEM_TIME CONTAINED IN*

Finally, FOR SYSTEM_TIME ALL concatenates data from both tables and returns it to the client. This can be useful when you need to access all versions of the rows–both current and all previous ones; for example, when you analyze trends over time. Figure 5-8 illustrates that.

Query 1: Query cost (relative to the batch): 100%
SELECT * FROM dbo.Employees FOR SYSTEM_TIME ALL ORDER BY EmployeeId

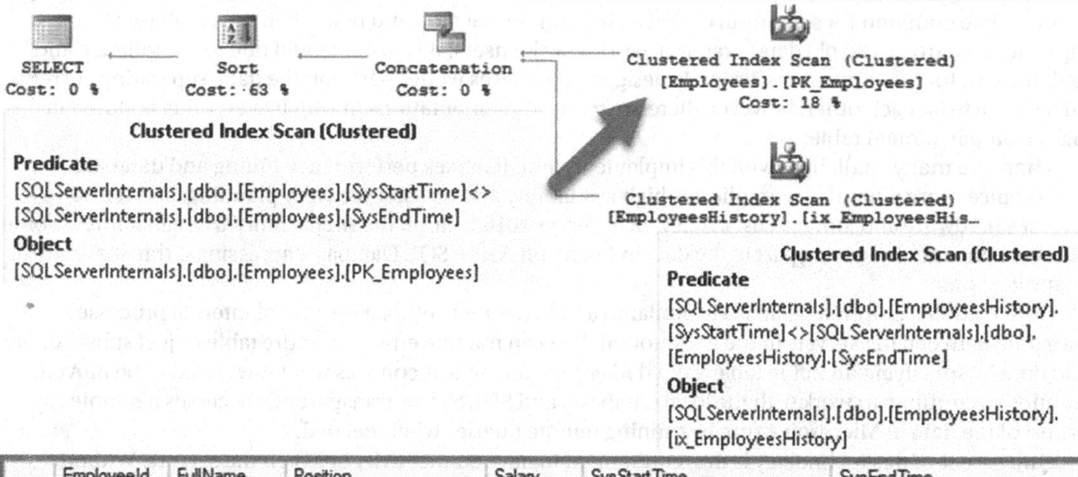

	EmployeeId	FullName	Position	Salary	SysStartTime	SysEndTime
1	1	John Doe	Database Administrator	85500.00	2016-07-09 17:57:20.9770748	9999-12-31 23:59:59.9999999
2	1	John Doe	Database Administrator	85000.00	2016-07-09 17:56:20.9561164	2016-07-09 17:57:20.9770748
3	2	David Black	Sr. Software Developer	95000.00	2016-07-09 17:56:20.9561164	2016-07-09 17:57:21.0082704
4	3	Mike White	QA Engineer	75000.00	2016-07-09 17:56:20.9561164	9999-12-31 23:59:59.9999999

***Figure 5-8.** Querying temporal table: FOR SYSTEM_TIME ALL*

I would like to reiterate one very important point. Accessing temporal data with the `FOR SYSTEM_TIME` clause adds predicates on the period columns in both the current and history tables. You need to factor that into the indexing strategy for the system.

There is another phenomenon you need to be aware of when dealing with queries that access temporal data. As I already mentioned, SQL Server populates period columns with a time that corresponds to the start time of the transaction that inserted, updated, or deleted the data. Therefore, temporal queries can return data that have not yet been committed at a specific point in time.

Consider a situation in which you have a transaction that started at time `TStart` and committed at time `TEnd`. The data modifications done by this transaction will be invisible to other sessions unless they are using the `READ UNCOMMITTED` transaction isolation level. Depending on the isolation level, those sessions will either be blocked or read snapshot of the data at the `TStart` time.

However, if you query temporal data using the `FOR SYSTEM_TIME` clause, SQL Server filters data based on period columns, which contain the `TStart` rather than the `TEnd` timestamp, which can lead to incorrect results.

■ **Note** We will discuss transaction isolation level and concurrency in Part V of the book.

You can read more about temporal tables at `https://msdn.microsoft.com/en-us/library/dn935015.aspx`

Stretch Databases

It has become common for systems to collect a large amount of data and retain it in the database for a long time. In many cases, old data is rarely accessed by the users; it is just retained due to compliance and regulations or for other purposes. Properly designed databases would partition the data, separating current and old data from each other; however, there are many implementations in which everything is stored in a single, non-partitioned table.

There are many challenges with this implementation. It makes performance tuning and database maintenance more difficult. It complicates high availability and disaster recovery planning, and it also increases hardware and storage costs. A new SQL Server 2016 feature, the *stretch database*, can address some of these challenges by storing part of the data in Microsoft Azure SQL Database, accessing it transparently to the applications.

Conceptually, a stretch database is similar to a linked server setup, with a set of internal processes that move data between the servers in the background. You can migrate either an entire table or just subset of the table data by specifying an inline table-valued *filter function*, which controls what rows need to be moved. The queries continue to work with the local database, and SQL Server transparently accesses a remote portion of the data in Microsoft Azure by running remote queries when needed.

One caveat of this technology is the requirement to have connectivity between the servers. Without connectivity, the queries–which access remote data–would fail. You should remember this behavior when you choose to use the feature.

Figure 5-9 provides a high-level overview of stretch database implementation. When data is migrated, SQL Server temporarily retains a copy of migrated rows in the local internal-staging tables, ensuring that the data can be reconciled if you restore local or Azure SQL database backups. By default, the data is retained for eight hours, which corresponds to SQL Azure's automatic backup schedule. You can increase this time with the `sys.sp_rda_set_rpo_duration` stored procedure. Keep in mind, however, that a longer retention time increases the size of the staging tables in the local database.

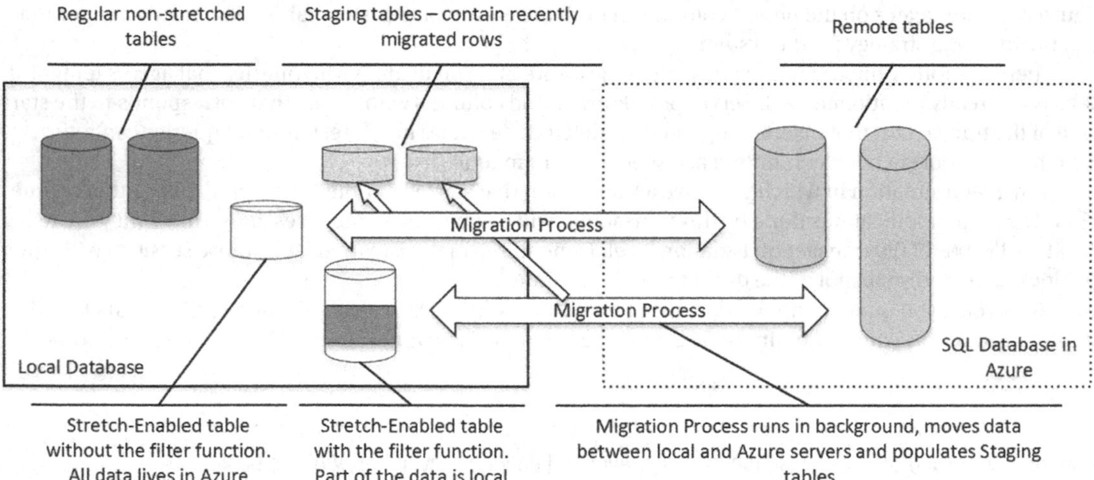

Figure 5-9. *Stretch database overview*

When you back up the stretch-enabled database, SQL Server creates a *shallow backup*. It only contains the local data and rows eligible for the migration at the time when the backup runs. The remote portion of the data in Azure SQL Database is protected by automatic, geo-redundant storage snapshot backups that run every eight hours and are retained for seven days, providing you with a range of restore points. We will discuss Azure storage snapshot backups in Chapter 31.

After you restore the stretch-enabled database, you need to re-establish the connection between the local and Azure databases with the `sys.sp_rda_reauthorize_db` stored procedure. You can perform a point-in-time restoration of the SQL database from the Azure portal, where storage backups are maintained for seven days.

Configuring Stretch Database

Before you can start using stretching, it has to be enabled on both the server and database levels. Perhaps the easiest way to perform the initial setup is using the *Enable Database for Stretch* wizard in SSMS. This wizard configures both server- and database-level stretching and also allows you to choose the tables to stretch.

Alternatively, you can use T-SQL to configure it. You can enable stretching on the server level by running the `EXEC SP_CONFIGURE 'remote data archive', '1'` command, which requires `sysadmin` or `serveradmin` permissions.

Listing 5-3 illustrates how you can enable stretching on the database using the existing Microsoft Azure SQL Server as the target. This action requires `CONTROL DATABASE` permission to execute.

Listing 5-3. Enable stretch database on the database level

```
-- Creating the Master Key
create master key encryption by password='Strong Password';

-- Creating the Database Scoped Credentials with SQL Server Login Info
create database scoped credential SQLServerLoginInfo
with
    identity = 'my_azure_sql_server_login_name'
    ,secret = 'my_password';

-- Enabling Stretching for the database
alter database MyDatabase
set remote_data_archive = on
(
    server = 'myserver.database.windows.net'
    ,credential = SQLServerLoginInfo
);
```

After the feature is enabled, you can choose the tables to stretch. The *Stretch Database Advisor* tool, which is included in *SQL Server 2016 Upgrade Advisor*, can help you to identify the tables that can most benefit from the technology, along with any blocking issues that can prevent stretching.

There are quite a few such blocking issues in SQL Server 2016 RTM. For example, a table cannot have `DEFAULT` and `CHECK` constraints nor be referenced by foreign keys. The table cannot use `XML`, `text`, `ntext`, `image`, `timestamp`, `sql_variant`, or `CLR` data types, nor be included in the indexed views.

There are other limitations after stretch is enabled. The most notable is that SQL Server does not enforce `UNIQUE` and `PRIMARY KEY` constraints nor allow you to `UPDATE` and `DELETE` migrated data.

■ **Note** You can read about the Stretch Database Advisor tool at `https://msdn.microsoft.com/en-us/library/dn935004.aspx`. The full list of limitations is available at `https://msdn.microsoft.com/en-us/library/mt605114.aspx`

When a table is stretch-compatible, you can stretch it by using the `ALTER TABLE SET (REMOTE_DATA_ARCHIVE = ON)` command or through the *Stretch* task in SSMS. As I already mentioned, you can migrate either the entire table or a subset of the table data. The latter case requires you to specify the filter function that controls which rows need to be migrated. When the filter function is provided, SQL Server applies it to the rows in the table using the `CROSS APPLY` operator. The row is eligible for migration when the function returns a non-empty result set.

Listing 5-4 illustrates both methods. It shows `ALTER TABLE` statements that migrate the entire `dbo.AppLogs` table and a subset of the data from the `dbo.Orders` table. The `migration_state` option controls the direction of migration. It can have one of three values: `OUTBOUND` (data is moved from the local database to Azure), `INBOUND` (data is moved back from Azure to the local database), and `PAUSED`.

Listing 5-4. Enable stretch for the tables

```
alter table dbo.AppLogs
set (remote_data_archive = on (migration_state = outbound));

create function dbo.fnOrdersOlderThanJan2016(@OrderDate datetime2(0))
returns table
with schemabinding
as
return
(
    select 1 as is_migrating
    where @OrderDate < convert(datetime2(0), '1/1/2016', 101)
)
go

alter table dbo.Orders set
(
    remote_data_archive = on
    (
        filter_predicate = dbo.fnOrdersOlderThanJan2016(OrderDate),
        migration_state = outbound
    )
);
```

As you can guess, the filter functions should be *deterministic* and should not depend on the data outside of the row it is evaluating. You cannot perform any data access from there. Moreover, only the primitive predicates and conditions, such as `AND` and `OR` predicates, `IN`, `IS NULL`, `IS NOT NULL`, and comparison operators are supported. All of this guarantees that a function always returns the same result for the same set of parameter values.

You can change the filter function by altering the table. However, the new function should provide *less restrictive* results and allow you to migrate more rows than before.

Listing 5-5 illustrates the function `dbo.fnOrdersOlderThanFeb2016`, which can replace the `dbo.fnOrdersOlderThanJan2016` function defined in Listing 5-4. It also shows the `ALTER TABLE` statement that replaces the filter function. This code shows an example of the sliding window scenario implementation with stretch databases.

Listing 5-5. Replacing the filter function

```
create function dbo.fnOrdersOlderThanFeb2016(@OrderDate datetime2(0))
returns table
with schemabinding
as
return
(
    select 1 as is_migrating
    where @OrderDate < convert(datetime2(0), '2/1/2016', 101)
)
go

alter table dbo.Orders set
(
    remote_data_archive = on
    (
        filter_predicate = dbo.fnOrdersOlderThanFeb2016(OrderDate),
        migration_state = outbound
    )
);
```

As another example, Listing 5-6 illustrates a function that cannot be used as replacement of the original filter function. It adds the predicate @Completed parameter and, therefore, is more restrictive than the original. Thus, some of the rows that have already been migrated are not eligible for migration anymore, which is not allowed.

Listing 5-6. More restrictive filter function

```
create function dbo.fnInvalid(@OrderDate datetime2(0), @Completed bit)
returns table
with schemabinding
as
return
(
    select 1 as is_migrating
    where
        (@Completed = 1) and
        @OrderDate < convert(datetime2(0), '2/1/2016', 101)
)
```

Querying Stretch Databases

Even though stretch databases are transparent to client applications, they do not guarantee that query performance will remain the same. In some cases, stretching can improve performance by reducing the amount of data to scan locally and/or running scans in parallel on both servers. In other cases, they could hurt performance due to network latency and cross-server joins.

If you have ever worked with linked servers, you should be aware of potential performance issues with the technology. The distributed queries work great when predicates can be evaluated remotely and servers do not need to push a large amount of data over the network. Otherwise, the large amount of network traffic and remote calls can greatly affect performance. There is also the connectivity aspect of the technology. The distributed queries would fail if there were no connectivity between the servers.

All of that remains true for stretch databases. Let's look at several examples related to performance and data access.

Listing 5-7 shows the code that creates the dbo.Customers and dbo.Orders tables and populates them with some data. It also assumes that we enabled stretching for the dbo.Orders table by running the code from Listing 5-5 and migrated all orders older than February 2016 to Microsoft Azure.

Listing 5-7. Querying stretch databases: Table creation

```
create table dbo.Customers
(
    CustomerId int identity(1,1) not null,
    Name nvarchar(32) not null,
    PostalCode char(5) not null,
    constraint PK_Customers primary key clustered(CustomerId)
);

create table dbo.Orders
(
    OrderId int not null,
    CustomerID int not null,
    OrderDate datetime2(0) not null,
    Amount money not null,
    Completed bit not null,
    constraint PK_Orders primary key clustered(OrderId)
);

create nonclustered index IDX_Orders_CustomerId on dbo.Orders(CustomerId);
create nonclustered index IDX_Orders_OrderDate on dbo.Orders(OrderDate);

-- 65,536 customers total. 256 customers per Postal Code
;with N1(C) as (select 0 union all select 0) -- 2 rows
,N2(C) as (select 0 from N1 as T1 cross join N1 as T2) -- 4 rows
,N3(C) as (select 0 from N2 as T1 cross join N2 as T2) -- 16 rows
,N4(C) as (select 0 from N3 as T1 cross join N3 as T2) -- 256 rows
,IDs(ID) as (select row_number() over (order by (select null)) from N4)
insert into dbo.Customers(Name, PostalCode)
    select 'Customer ' + convert(varchar(32),i1.ID * i2.Id)
            ,convert(char(5),10000 + i2.ID)
    from IDs i1 cross join IDs i2;

declare
    @StartDate datetime2(0) = '2016-09-01';

;with N1(C) as (select 0 union all select 0) -- 2 rows
,N2(C) as (select 0 from N1 as T1 cross join N1 as T2) -- 4 rows
,N3(C) as (select 0 from N2 as T1 cross join N2 as T2) -- 16 rows
,N4(C) as (select 0 from N3 as T1 cross join N3 as T2) -- 256 rows
,N5(C) as (select 0 from N4 as T1 cross join N4 as T2) -- 65,536 rows
,N6(C) as (select 0 from N5 as T1 cross join N3 as T2) -- 1,048,576 rows
,IDs(ID) as (select row_number() over (order by (select null)) from N6)
```

```
insert into dbo.Orders(OrderId, CustomerId, Amount, OrderDate, Completed)
    select ID, ID % 65536 + 1, Id % 50, dateadd(day,-ID % 365, getDate()), 0
    from IDs;

/* Enable Stretching for dbo.Orders table with Listing 5-5 code */
```

First, let's run a query that calculates how many orders were submitted in January and February of 2016. That code is shown in Listing 5-8.

Listing 5-8. Querying stretch databases: Counting total number of orders

```
select count(*) as [Order Count]
from dbo.Orders o
where o.OrderDate >= '2016-01-01' and o.OrderDate < '2016-03-01';
```

Figure 5-10 illustrates a partial execution plan for the query. As you can see, SQL Server performed COUNT() aggregation remotely, and the remote query returned just a single row to the local server.

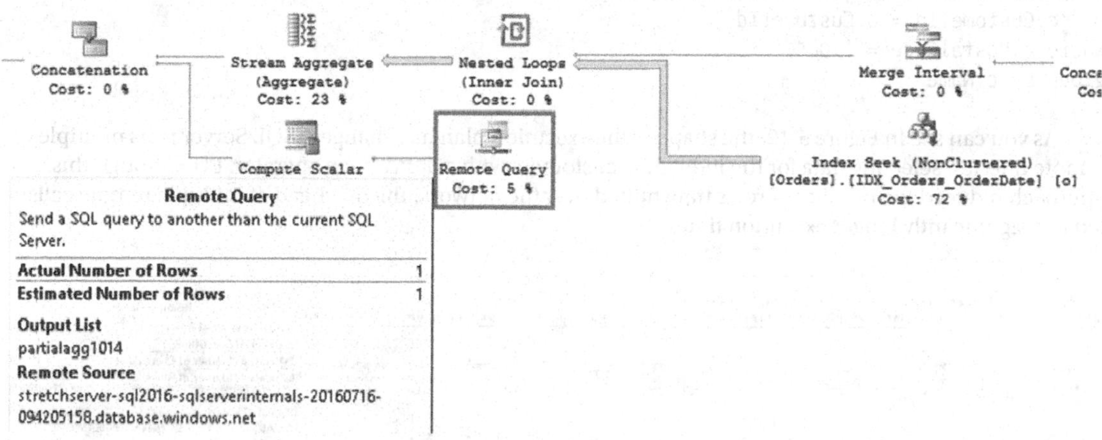

Figure 5-10. *Execution plan: Counting total number of orders*

Now, let's run a query that calculates the total sales on a per-customer basis, as shown in Listing 5-9.

Listing 5-9. Querying stretch databases: Total sales on per-customer basis

```
select c.Name, sum(o.Amount) as [Total Sales]
from dbo.Customers c join dbo.Orders o on
    c.CustomerId = o.CustomerId
group by c.Name
```

Figure 5-11 shows the execution plan and execution time of the query. As you can see, SQL Server decides to bring all the remote data over the network and perform aggregation locally. You can also see a cardinality estimation error, even though statistics were up to date on both servers. It happened because of the extra internal predicates which remote SQL Server added to the query.

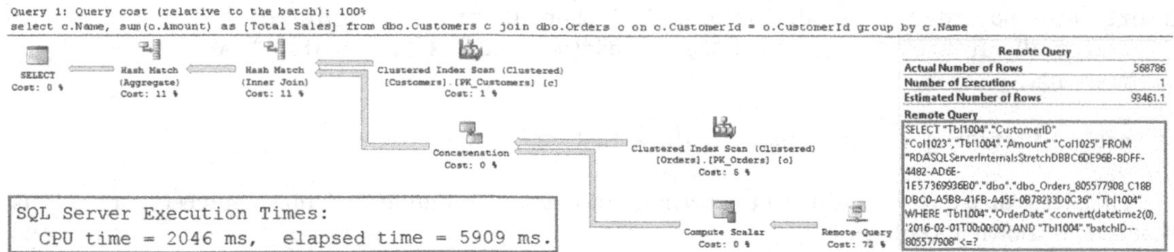

Figure 5-11. *Execution plan: Total sales on per-customer basis*

Finally, let's add the predicate to the previous query, filtering customers by the postal code. This query is shown in Listing 5-10.

Listing 5-10. Querying stretch databases: Filter by PostalCode

```
select c.Name, sum(o.Amount) as [Total Sales]
from dbo.Customers c join dbo.Orders o on
    c.CustomerId = o.CustomerId
where c.PostalCode = '10050'
group by c.Name
```

As you can see in Figure 5-12, the shape of the execution plan has changed. SQL Server runs multiple remote queries, selecting data for the individual customers with a *nested loop* operator. Even though this approach reduced the number of rows transmitted over the network, the overhead of multiple remote calls led to a significantly longer execution time.

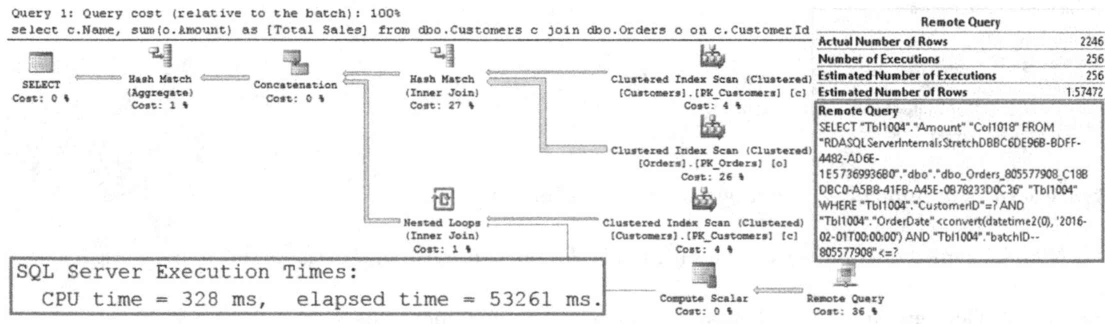

Figure 5-12. *Execution plan: Filtering by PostalCode*

All of these queries did not have the predicate on the `OrderDate` column, and, therefore, SQL Server had to access both local and remote data. Adding such a predicate would allow SQL Server to eliminate unnecessary remote-server access. For example, if you run the `SELECT COUNT(*) FROM dbo.Orders WHERE OrderDate >= '2016-05-01'` statement, you would have the execution plan, which does not access the remote server, shown in Figure 5-13.

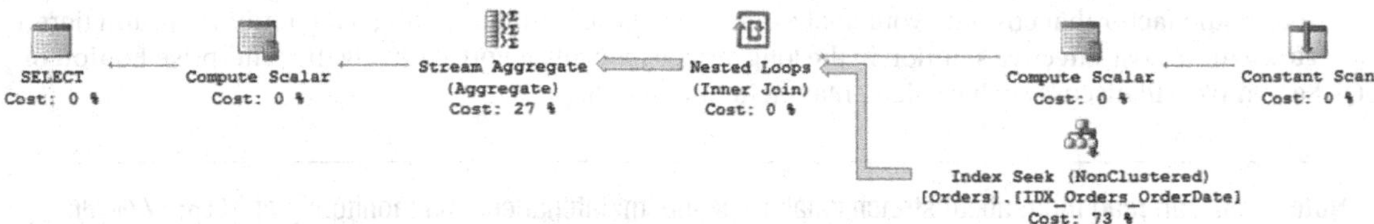

***Figure 5-13.** Execution plan: Predicate on OrderDate column*

Parameterization and autoparameterization, however, can still lead to a situation in which the query has to access the remote server when the plan is cached. While it would not necessarily introduce a huge performance impact–the remote query could just evaluate the predicate value without performing any data access–the query would fail if there were no connectivity between the servers.

You should keep these performance and connectivity implications in mind when you decide to stretch the data. In many cases, it is safer to partition the data to separate tables, stretching the entire *History* table rather than migrating a subset of data from the single table. This approach, however, requires code changes and defeats purpose of the transparency of the technology to client applications.

■ **Note** We will discuss data partitioning in more detail in Chapter 16 and plan caching in Chapter 26.

Finally, it is worth repeating that, by default, SQL Server does not allow you to specify the data location when you query stretch-enabled table. Nor does it allow you to update or delete remote data after rows have been migrated. There is the table hint–`WITH (REMOTE_DATA_ARCHIVE_OVERRIDE)`–which allows the members of the `db_owner` role to change the scope of the queries. This hint can have one of the three values:

`LOCAL_ONLY` - runs the query against local data only

`REMOTE_ONLY` - runs the query against remote data only

`STAGE_ONLY` - runs the query against staged data (the rows that temporarily persisted in the local database after they were migrated to Azure)

This hint can be used with `SELECT`, `UPDATE`, and `DELETE` queries and allows you to modify and delete remote data. Be careful, however, if you need to modify remote data in the scope of the active transaction. This operation can take a considerable amount of time, and can even fail if SQL Server cannot access the remote database. It is better to implement data modifications asynchronously using Service Broker or other queue-based technologies.

Stretch Database Pricing

Stretch database is an exciting feature that can be helpful in many scenarios. Unfortunately, it is expensive.

The cost of using stretch database consists of two parts–compute and storage. Essentially, you are choosing the performance tier of Microsoft Azure SQL Database and also paying for the storage of the database files and backups.

The pricing in Microsoft Azure can change at any time, but as of September 2016, the lowest compute tier with 100 DSU (Database Stretch Units) is priced at $1,860 per month. The storage cost is $164 per 1TB of storage per month. In reality, it means that you have to pay more than $2,000 per month to store 1 TB of data remotely using the lowest compute tier.

You should factor that cost into your analysis. In many cases, implementing data partitioning and tiered storage is a more cost-effective solution in the long term, especially if you are using the Enterprise Edition of SQL Server. We will discuss such implementation in Chapter 16.

■ **Note** You can read more about stretch database setup, maintenance, and monitoring at `https://msdn.microsoft.com/en-us/library/dn935011.aspx`

Row-Level Security

Row-level security limits read and write access to some of the rows in tables on a per-user basis. As the opposite to regular SELECT, INSERT, UPDATE, and DELETE permissions that work on the scope of entire table, row-level security helps to implement a security model that takes row data into consideration. For example, in client-management systems, you can use row-level security to limit regular users' access to a subset of the clients while allowing the regional managers to see all clients from the region. Another common use case is security in a multi-tenant setup when tenants' data should be invisible to the other tenants in the system.

To implement row-level security, you have to write an inline table-valued function, which is called a *policy function*. This function returns a single-row result set for the rows that should be visible to the user. As the next step, you should create a *security policy* that binds that function to the table.

Let's look at an example and assume that we want to implement a simple client-management system. The code shown in Listing 5-11 creates several users in the database and a table with a few rows.

Listing 5-11. Row-level security: Set up users and table for row-level security

```
create user ClientManager1 without login;
create user RegionalManager without login;
create schema Client;
go

create table Client.Client1
(
    ClientID int not null,
    ClientManager sysname not null,
    Revenue money not null,
    OtherInfo nvarchar(100) not null
);

grant select on Client.Client1 to ClientManager1, RegionalManager;

insert into Client.Client1 values
    (1, 'ClientManager1', 100000, 'abc')
    ,(2, 'ClientManager1', 200000, 'def')
    ,(3, 'ClientManager2', 300000, 'ghi')
    ,(4, 'ClientManager2', 400000, 'jkl')
    ,(5, 'ClientManager3', 500000, 'mno');
```

With the current implementation, every user can see all data in the table. You can test it by impersonating the users with the EXECUTE AS command, as shown in Listing 5-12.

Listing 5-12. Row-level security: Select data impersonating user

```
execute as user = 'ClientManager1';
select * from Client.Client1;
revert;
```

As you can see in Figure 5-14, the query returns all rows, which is expected at this point. The execution plan is a simple full *table scan.*

	ClientID	ClientManager	Revenue	OtherInfo
1	1	ClientManager1	100000.00	abc
2	2	ClientManager1	200000.00	def
3	3	ClientManager2	300000.00	ghi
4	4	ClientManager2	400000.00	jkl
5	5	ClientManager3	500000.00	mno

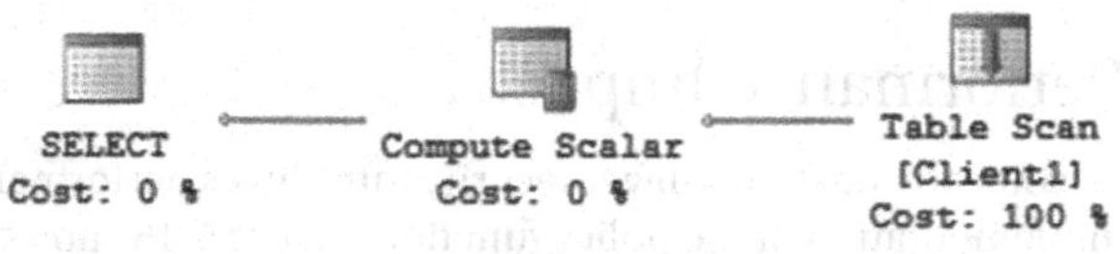

SELECT Cost: 0 % — Compute Scalar Cost: 0 % — Table Scan [Client1] Cost: 100 %

Figure 5-14. *Row-level security: Data and execution plan without RLS applied*

Let's set up row-level security and, as the first step, create a policy function that determines if a row can be seen by a user. In the example shown in Listing 5-13, the function is very simple. It takes one argument–the manager name—and compares it to the user that executes the query. Obviously, in a real-world scenario, it would be better to check Active Directory group memberships instead.

The function must return a row (the value and column name do not matter) if a table row should be made visible to the current user. It is also worth noting that the security function defined with the SCHEMABINDING clause does not require users to have SELECT permissions for the tables accessed from within the function. Alternatively, functions defined without the SCHEMABINDING clause will require the user to have those permissions.

Listing 5-13. Row-level security: Security policy function

```
create function Client.fn_LimitToManager(@Manager as sysname)
returns table
with schemabinding
as
return
( select 1 AS fn_LimitToManagerResult
  where @Manager = user_name() or user_name() = 'RegionalManager' )
```

The final step is creating the security policy that ties the function and the table together. You can see the syntax of the command in Listing 5-14. The FILTER predicate in the security policy specifies the function that is responsible for the read access to the data. The BLOCK predicate, which we will discuss later in the chapter, controls write access to the data.

Listing 5-14. Row-level security: Security policy

```
create security policy LimitMgrFilter
add filter predicate Client.fn_LimitToManager(ClientManager)
on Client.Client1
with (state = on)
```

If you run the code from Listing 5-12 again, you should see that the query returns just two rows that are managed by *ClientManager1*, as shown in Figure 5-15.

	ClientID	ClientManager	Revenue	OtherInfo
1	1	ClientManager1	100000.00	abc
2	2	ClientManager1	200000.00	def

Figure 5-15. *Row-level security: Data after RLS has been applied*

Performance Impact

As you can guess, row-level security introduces performance overhead, which depends on the implementation of the policy function. Figure 5-16 shows the execution plan of the query from Listing 5-12 after the security policy has been applied. You can see an additional *Filter* operator that corresponds to the policy function.

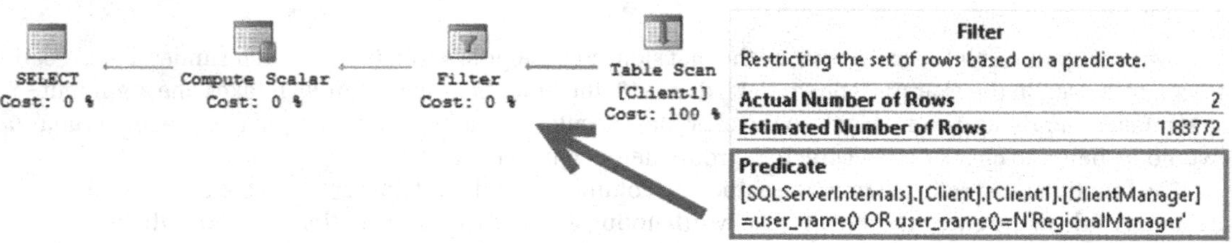

Figure 5-16. *Execution plan with row-level security applied*

Let's change our example to use a lookup table that stores client/manager relations, as shown in Listing 5-15. As the last step, the code will run a SELECT statement impersonating the user, similar to in Listing 5-12.

Listing 5-15. Row-level security: Reference table in security policy function

```
create table Client.ClientManager
(
    ID int not null
        constraint PK_ClientManager primary key clustered,
    ManagerName nvarchar(100) not null,
    isRegionalManager bit not null
);

insert into Client.ClientManager values
    (1,'ClientManager1',0), (2,'ClientManager2',0)
    ,(3,'ClientManager3',0), (4,'RegionalManager',1);

create table Client.Client2
(
    ClientID int not null,
    ClientManagerID int not null
        constraint FK_Client2_ClientManager
```

```
        foreign key references Client.CLientManager(ID),
    ClientName nvarchar(64) not null,
    CreditLimit money not null,
    IsVIP bit not null
        constraint DEF_Client2_IsVIP default 0
);

grant select on Client.Client2 to ClientManager1, RegionalManager;

;with N1(C) as (select 0 union all select 0) -- 2 rows
,N2(C) as (select 0 from N1 as T1 cross join N1 as T2) -- 4 rows
,N3(C) as (select 0 from N2 as T1 cross join N2 as T2) -- 16 rows
,N4(C) as (select 0 from N3 as T1 cross join N3 as T2) -- 256 rows
,N5(C) as (select 0 from N4 as T1 cross join N4 as T2) -- 65,536 rows
,IDs(ID) as (select ROW_NUMBER() over (order by (select null)) from N5)
insert into Client.Client2(ClientID, ClientManagerID, ClientName, CreditLimit, IsVip)
    select ID, ID % 3 + 1, convert(nvarchar(6),ID), 100000, abs(sign(ID % 10) - 1)
    from IDS
go

create function Client.fn_LimitToManager2(@ManagerID AS int)
returns table
with schemabinding
as
return
( select 1 as fn_LimitToManagerResult
  from Client.ClientManager
  where ManagerName = user_name()
    and ((ID = @ManagerID) or (isRegionalManager = 1)) )
go

create security policy LimitMgrFilter2
add filter predicate Client.fn_LimitToManager2(ClientManagerID)
on Client.Client2
with (state = on);
go

-- Getting data while impersonating the user
execute as user = 'ClientManager1';
select * from Client.Client2;
revert;
```

As you can see in the execution plan shown in Figure 5-17, row-level security added the nested loop join to the execution plan, performing a clustered index scan on each execution. As you can guess, this would significantly affect the performance of the query.

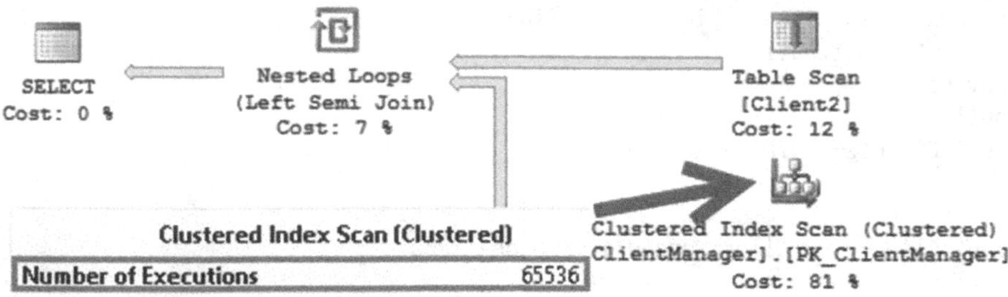

Figure 5-17. *Execution plan with lookup table*

The performance impact of row-level security depends on the complexity of the policy function, which is applied to every row in the result set. You should make policy functions as simple as possible, limiting data access whenever it is possible. In cases where data access is required, you need to make sure that it is optimized. For example, adding the index with `CREATE INDEX IDX_ClientManager_ManagerName ON Client.ClientManager(ManagerName) INCLUDE(IsRegionalManager)` would eliminate the clustered index scan and would lead to the execution plan shown in Figure 5-18.

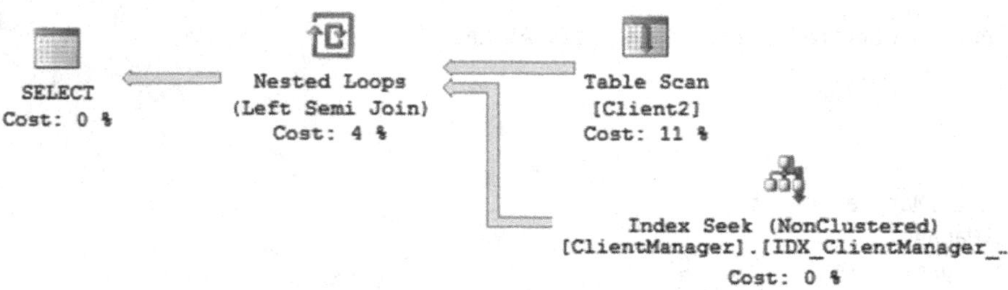

Figure 5-18. *Execution plan with lookup table after index creation*

In some cases, when the security model is relatively static, you can consider storing some information in the session context, populating it on the login phase. A policy function could get the information from there using the `session_context()` function rather than performing data access. You will see an example of how to use session context in Chapter 9.

Other useful functions that can help you to eliminate data access are the following: `user_name()`, `suser_name()`, `suser_sname()`, `original_login()`, `is_member('domain\group')`, `is_rolemember('rolename', original_login())`, `is_srvrolemember('serverrolename', original_login()`, `app_name()`, `program_name()`, `platform()`, `session_user()`, `sessionproperty()`, `database_principal_id()`, and `@@SPID`.

Blocking Modifications

Row-level security can be used to prevent users from modifying data on the row level. In this case, the security policy should have the `BLOCK` predicate instead of or in addition to a `FILTER` predicate. The predicates work together–the rows filtered out by the `FILTER` predicate are invisible to the user and, therefore, it is impossible to update or delete those rows, with or without the `BLOCK` predicate specified. The `FILTER` predicate, however, would not prevent users from inserting data that violates the predicate condition, and you need to use the `BLOCK` predicate to avoid it.

You can specify BLOCK predicates for BEFORE INSERT, AFTER INSERT, BEFORE UPDATE, AFTER UPDATE, and BEFORE DELETE operations. BEFORE predicates are useful when you want to prevent data modifications for some rows. AFTER predicates help to block operations when the values violate the predicate.

Listing 5-16 shows such an example. The BEFORE UPDATE predicate prevents the update of VIP clients (IsVIP=1) for non-regional managers. The AFTER UPDATE predicate disallows non-regional managers to set the CreditLimit value above 100,000. The script also grants UPDATE permission on the table and denies the right to update the ClientManagerId value to both users.

Listing 5-16. Row-level security: BLOCK predicates

```
/* Checking if user is the Regional Manager */
create function Client.fn_CurrentUserIsRegionalManager()
returns table
with schemabinding
as
return
(
    select 1 as Result
    from Client.ClientManager
    where ManagerName = user_name() and IsRegionalManager = 1
)
go

create function Client.fn_checkCanUpdateVIP(@IsVIP bit)
returns table
with schemabinding
as
return
(
    select 1 as CanUpdateClient
    where
        case
            when @IsVip = 0 then 1
            else (select Result from Client.fn_CurrentUserIsRegionalManager())
        end = 1
)
go

create function Client.fn_checkCanUpdateCreditLimit(@CreditLimit money)
returns table
with schemabinding
as
return
(
    select 1 as CanUpdateClient
    where
        case
            when @CreditLimit <= 100000 then 1
            else (select Result from Client.fn_CurrentUserIsRegionalManager())
        end = 1
)
go
```

```
alter security policy LimitMgrFilter2
add block predicate Client.fn_checkCanUpdateVIP(IsVip) on Client.Client2 before update,
add block predicate Client.fn_checkCanUpdateCreditLimit(CreditLimit) on Client.Client2 after update;

grant update on Client.Client2 to ClientManager1, RegionalManager;
deny update Client.Client2(ClientManager) to ClientManager1, RegionalManager;
```

As you have probably noticed, the predicates in Listing 5-15 do not validate the client ownership for non-regional manager users. That validation is done by the `FILTER` predicate, which will make those rows invisible and, therefore, exclude them from the update.

Finally, there is one other important thing to remember about `BEFORE UPDATE` and `AFTER UPDATE BLOCK` predicates. SQL Server does not evaluate them unless you update the columns that are used as parameters in the policy function. For example, the implementation in Listing 5-15 would not prevent non-regional manager users from updating the `ClientName` of VIP clients. You can either add extra parameters to the function, as shown in Listing 5-17, or rely on triggers to address the problem.

Listing 5-17. Row-level security: Adding extra columns to BLOCK predicates (partial)

```
create function Client.fn_checkCanUpdateVIP(@IsVIP bit, @ClientName nvarchar(64))
returns table
with schemabinding
as
return
(
    select 1 as CanUpdateClient
    where
        case
            when @IsVip = 0 then 1
            else (select Result from Client.fn_CurrentUserIsRegionalManager())
        end = 1
)
go

alter security policy LimitMgrFilter2
add block predicate Client.fn_checkCanUpdateVIP(IsVip,ClientName) on Client.Client2 before update,
```

■ **Note** You can read more about row-level security at `https://msdn.microsoft.com/en-us/library/dn765131.aspx`

Always Encrypted

Always Encrypted is the new SQL Server 2016 Enterprise Edition feature that allows you to encrypt both *data-at-rest* and *data-in-transit* in the system on a per-column basis. Always Encrypted has two key differences when compared to other similar technologies.

First, it performs encryption and decryption of the data *almost* transparently to the client applications, and data-in-transit encryption does not rely on transport security, such as SSL or TLS. Second, and more important, it allows you to implement a true *separation of duties* between security administrators, who manage security keys in the key store, and database administrators, who manage metadata about security keys in the database. With this separation, neither role would be able to decrypt sensitive data in the system.

Always Encrypted Overview

Always Encrypted uses two types of keys to protect data. The *column encryption key* (CEK) encrypts the data in the database. The *column master key* (CMK) encrypts the column encryption keys. The encrypted CEKs are stored in the database, while the CMKs are stored in a trusted key store, such as Windows Certificate Store, Azure Key Vault, or Hardware Security Modules. It is also possible to implement a custom key store, if necessary.

The data in the database is always stored encrypted using the `AEAD_AES_256_CBC_HMAC_SHA_256` algorithm, and it is never decrypted by SQL Server. All decryption is done by the client application, which needs to use an Always Encrypted-enabled client driver. As of August 2016, Always Encrypted is supported by the Microsoft .Net 4.6, Microsoft JDBC 6.0, and Windows ODBC 13.1 SQL Server drivers. This list may change in the future.

The application needs to specify that it can handle Always Encrypted in the connection string using the `Column Encryption Setting` property. When SQL Server sends encrypted data back to such applications, it attaches an encrypted CEK and the location of the CMK to the result set. The client driver communicates with the key store and gets the CMK, which is used to decrypt the CEK and column data.

A similar process happens with parameterized queries. The driver collaborates with SQL Server in determining what parameters should be encrypted. It obtains the CEK and the location of the CMK from SQL Server, gets the CMK from the key store, and encrypts the parameter values before sending a query to SQL Server. All encryption and decryption is done transparently to the client applications, and data is never transmitted over the wire unencrypted. It is also worth noting that the driver uses the local cache to store decrypted column encryption keys so as to reduce the number of round trips made to the key store.

Figure 5-19 illustrates the Always Encrypted components.

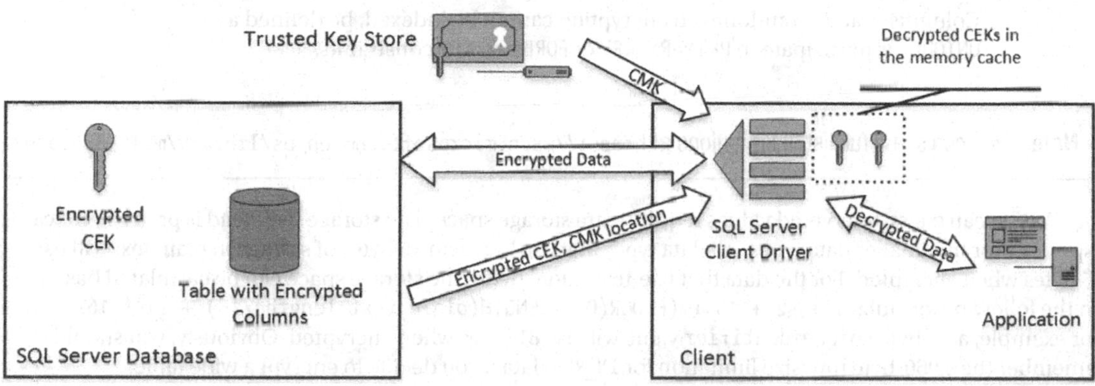

Figure 5-19. *Always Encrypted workflow*

Communication with the server adds extra round trips and network traffic. Figure 5-20 shows the calls performed by a client application while running the query against a table with an encrypted `ClientName` column. As you can see, the driver called the `sp_describe_parameter_encryption` stored procedure, which provides the information about the encrypted column.

timestamp	statement
2016-08-19 00:44:38.504	exec sp_describe_parameter_encryption N'select ClientId, ClientName from dbo.ClientsEncrypted where ClientName = @ClientName',N'@ClientName varchar(64)'
2016-08-19 00:44:38.520	exec sp_executesql N'select ClientId, ClientName from dbo.ClientsEncrypted where ClientName = @ClientName',N'@ClientName varchar(64)',@ClientName=0x01F2BB840E8A9FD98F3...

Figure 5-20. *Client/SQL Server communication with Always Encrypted enabled*

Always Encrypted supports two different types of encryption. *Deterministic encryption* always generates the same encrypted value for any given unencrypted value, which allows you to create indexes on encrypted columns and utilize them for point-lookup searches, equality joins, and grouping. However, deterministic encryption increases security risks by allowing unauthorized users to examine patterns in encrypted data and guess their values. Deterministic encryption is not the best choice if the number of possible encrypted values is relatively small.

The second type of encryption, *randomized encryption*, generates random values during each encryption. It is more secure than deterministic encryption; however, it prevents searching, grouping, and joining on encrypted columns.

There are several other limitations associated with Always Encrypted. The most notable are:

- The following data types cannot be encrypted: `xml`, `timestamp/rowversion`, `image`, `(n)text`, `sql_variant`, `hierarchyid`, `geography`, `geometry` and user-defined types

- Text columns (`(n)char` and `(n)varchar`) must have binary `BIN2` collation in order to be encrypted.

- Encrypted columns cannot have `DEFAULT` or `CHECK` constraints.

- Columns that use randomized encryption cannot be indexed, be defined as `UNIQUE`, or participate in `PRIMARY KEY` or `FOREIGN KEY` constraints.

■ **Note** You can see a full list of limitations at `https://msdn.microsoft.com/en-us/library/mt163865.aspx`

As you can guess, encrypted values require extra storage space. The storage overhead is pretty significant, especially for the smaller data types. All data types that use less than 16 bytes of storage in plain text will use 65 bytes when encrypted. For the data that use 16 or more bytes, the storage space can be calculated based on the following formula: `1 + 32 + 16 + (FLOOR(DATALENGTH(plain_text_length)/16) + 1) * 16`. For example, a 16-byte `uniqueidentifier` value will use 81 bytes when encrypted. Obviously, you should remember the 8,060-byte row-size limitation for `IN_ROW` data if you decide to encrypt a wide table.

Programmability

As I already mentioned, Always Encrypted works *almost* transparently to the application. All encryption and decryption is done by the driver, and you just need to enable Always Encrypted by setting the `Column Encryption Setting=enabled` property in the connection string.

There is a catch, however. Once data is encrypted, SQL Server is unable to decrypt it to perform any operations that require decrypted data. Consider the `dbo.Employees` table with an encrypted `Salary` column as an example. SQL Server would be unable to execute the `SELECT * FROM dbo.Employees WHERE Salary >= @Salary` statement because it is unable to decrypt the `Salary` column's data to evaluate the predicate. Similarly, SQL Server would be unable to perform a substring search using the `LIKE` operator or calculate the length of an encrypted string column with the `LEN` function. All of these queries would fail, and you would need to change the client application and implement all of the logic there after the data is decrypted. In many cases, this will also require the client application to bring more data over the network.

The columns encrypted with randomized encryption cannot be used in any predicates, join conditions, or grouping. Randomized encryption generates different values for the same input and, therefore, SQL Server cannot compare the data without decrypting it. Deterministic encryption, on the other hand, guarantees the same encrypted value for the same input, and SQL Server can perform equality comparisons of encrypted data, which allows you to reference columns with deterministic encryption in point-lookup searches, equality joins, and grouping. You can also index columns with deterministic encryption to optimize those use cases.

Equality comparison is the only operation supported by deterministic encryption. For example, the query with the `Salary = @Salary` predicate would work with deterministic encryption, while the `Salary >= @Salary` predicate would fail the query regardless of encryption type.

Always Encrypted does not support ad-hoc non-parameterized queries, and it also requires you to use parameters when inserting data or updating encrypted columns. You should also use parameters in equality search predicates against columns with deterministic encryption. Even though these requirements look like limitations, removing ad-hoc workload reduces the plan's cache-memory consumption and could improve the performance of the system. Nevertheless, it may require code changes in the client application.

Security Considerations and Key Management

It is always important to choose the right tool for the job, and Always Encrypted has one key difference when compared to other SQL Server encryption technologies. It is the only technology that allows you to implement the *separation of duties* security concept, separating the roles of security and database administrators in a business. When this separation is not required, it is entirely possible that other SQL Server technologies would be the better solution. For example, it can be easier to encrypt data-at-rest with *transparent data encryption* (TDE) and/or *column-level encryption* using SSL/TLS for transport security.

Moreover, implementing a separation of duties is never limited to the technical implementation. It requires businesses to define and adopt formal policies and processes, with technology just supporting them. For example, one of the prerequisites to Always Encrypted implementation is defining the key management process, which outlines how security keys need to be generated, stored, backed up, and rotated.

As a general rule, security administrators should generate CMK and CEK on a computer separate from SQL Server. This will prevent a rogue administrator of a computer that is hosting Always Encrypted data from accessing the keys on disk or in computer memory. It is also important to back up the keys after they are generated and store those backups in a safe physical location.

Key rotation is another important factor in security. Always Encrypted allows you to rotate both CMK and CEK, either in SSMS or with T-SQL. Rotation of CMK decrypts all CEK with the old key and encrypts them with the new key. This is a very fast operation. Rotation of CEK, on the other hand, will require you to decrypt and encrypt all table data, which can be very time consuming on large tables.

Finally, it is important to remember that with Always Encrypted, the data is decrypted on the driver level and is stored in memory in plain text. Some security standards and regulations require the application to keep certain data encrypted even in memory. For example, *payment card industry* (PCI) standards require you to keep all credit card numbers encrypted all the time. You should combine Always Encrypted with other technologies when this is the case.

■ **Note** You can see read more about Always Encrypted and how to configure and use it at `https://msdn.microsoft.com/en-us/library/mt163865.aspx`

Dynamic Data Masking

Dynamic data masking allows you to hide the content of sensitive columns by masking it in the result sets. It allows you to obfuscate either entire column data or just part of the value; for example, allowing users to see the last four digits of a credit card number or Social Security number.

Dynamic data masking works on a per-column level and is controlled by the `UNMASK` permission. Users with such permission will see unmasked data in the result set, while users without that permission will see obfuscated data. For example, you can grant `UNMASK` permission on the `CreditCardNumber` column to the *Accounting* group, who will see the unmasked value. The *Call Center* group, on the other hand, should not have this permission and would see the masked value instead.

The masking rule is controlled by the *masking function*. SQL Server 2016 RTM supports four masking functions, specified next. It is worth noting that `NULL` values will always be displayed as `NULL`.

> `default()` returns the default value for the data type. For example, the function uses *0* for numeric data types and *1900-01-01* for date and time information. For the text data, it replaces the text with *XXXX* characters.
>
> `email()` masks the value of the email address by showing the first actual letter from the email, replacing everything else with *xxx@XXXX.com*. For example, a *tg@grohser.at* email address will be replaced with a *txxx@XXXX.com* value.
>
> `random()` works only with numeric datatypes (`int`, `float`, `money`, ...) and replaces data with a random value from the interval specified as a parameter of the function.
>
> `partial()` is the most flexible function, allowing you to define a custom string that is used for masking. It takes three parameters, such as `prefix`, `padding`, and `suffix`. `Prefix` and `suffix` are integer values that define the number of characters at the beginning and end of the text that are populated from the original value. The optional `padding` value controls the masking pattern.

Listing 5-18 shows dynamic data masking in action. The code creates a table with several columns masked with different masking functions. Then, it performs two `SELECT` queries in context of the users both with and without `UNMASK` permissions.

Listing 5-18. Dynamic data masking in action

```
create table dbo.Consultants
(
    ID int not null,
    FirstName varchar(32)
        masked with (function='partial(1,"XXXXXXXX",0)') not null,
    LastName varchar(32) not null,
    DateOfBirth date
        masked with (function='default()') not null,
    SSN char(12)
        masked with (function='partial(0,"XXX-XXX-",4)') not null,
    EMail nvarchar(255)
        masked with (function='email()') not null,
    SpendingLimit money
    masked with (function='random(500,1000)') not null
);
```

```
insert into dbo.Consultants(ID,FirstName,LastName,DateOfBirth,SSN,Email,SpendingLimit)
values
    (1,'Thomas','Grohser','1/1/1980','123-456-7890','tg@grohser.com',10000)
    ,(2,'Dmitri','Korotkevitch','1/1/2010','234-567-8901','dk@aboutsqlserver.com',10000);

create user NonPrivUser without login;
grant select on dbo.Consultants to NonPrivUser;
go

-- Running as db_owner who can UNMASK the data
select * from dbo.Consultants;

-- Running as non-privilege user without UNMASK permission
execute as user = 'NonPrivUser';
select * from dbo.Consultants
revert;
```

Figure 5-21 shows the output of both queries. The result sets represent unmasked and masked data respectively.

	ID	FirstName	LastName	DateOfBirth	SSN	EMail	SpendingLimit
1	1	Thomas	Grohser	1980-01-01	123-456-7890	tg@grohser.com	10000.00
2	2	Dmitri	Korotkevitch	2010-01-01	234-567-8901	dk@aboutsqlserver.com	10000.00

	ID	FirstName	LastName	DateOfBirth	SSN	EMail	SpendingLimit
1	1	TXXXXXXXX	Grohser	1900-01-01	XXX-XXX-7890	tXXX@XXXX.com	634.7006
2	2	DXXXXXXXX	Korotkevitch	1900-01-01	XXX-XXX-8901	dXXX@XXXX.com	801.5957

Figure 5-21. *Dynamic data masking in action*

Performance and Security Considerations

When data needs to be obfuscated, SQL Server applies the masking after the data-access operators, usually using *compute scalar*. Figure 5-22 shows the execution plan of the SELECT query from Listing 5-16.

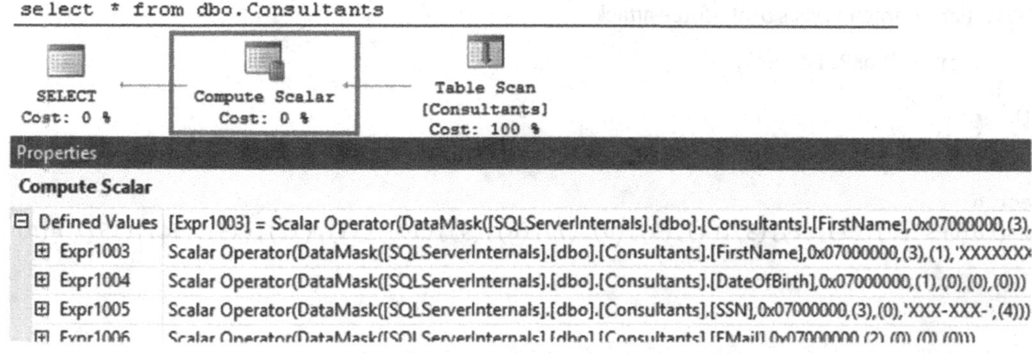

Figure 5-22. *Execution plan of the query with dynamic data masking*

As you can guess, this implementation introduces relatively little performance impact; however, it leads to security issues. The predicates are evaluated against non-masked data, and a malicious person who has the ability to execute queries against the table could obtain the values by performing a brute-force attack.

Listing 5-19 demonstrates how an attacker could guess the value of the `SpendingLimit` column in the `dbo.Consultants` table. SQL Server performs the join based on the unmasked value, which allows the attacker to capture them. Figure 5-23 shows the output from the attack.

Listing 5-19. Brute-force attack on the masked data

```
execute as user = 'NonPrivUser';

;with N1(C) as (select 0 union all select 0) -- 2 rows
,N2(C) as (select 0 from N1 as T1 cross join N1 as T2) -- 4 rows
,N3(C) as (select 0 from N2 as T1 cross join N2 as T2) -- 16 rows
,N4(C) as (select 0 from N3 as T1 cross join N3 as T2) -- 256 rows
,N5(C) as (select 0 from N4 as T1 cross join N4 as T2) -- 65,536 rows
,PossibleValues(SpendingLimit)
as (select row_number() over (order by (select null)) from N5)
select c.ID, p.SpendingLimit, c.SpendingLimit as MaskedLimit
from dbo.Consultants c join PossibleValues p on
    c.SpendingLimit >= p.SpendingLimit - 1 and
    c.SpendingLimit < p.SpendingLimit;

revert;
```

	ID	SpendingLimit	MaskedLimit
1	1	10000.00	918.3721
2	2	10000.00	575.5607

Figure 5-23. *Result of the attack*

Unfortunately, a similar approach can be taken with any data types that can be casted to text. The attack can be implemented on a per-character basis, as shown in Listing 5-20. The code splits the data from the masked columns into individual characters and joins them with a result set that represents all possible ASCII characters. The query in Listing 5-20 reveals the `DateOfBirth` and first 24 characters of the `Email` columns; however, it could easily be adopted to deal with longer strings. Figure 5-24 shows the result of the query.

Listing 5-20. Per-character basis brute-force attack

```
execute as user = 'NonPrivUser';

;with N(n)
as
(
    select n
    from (values (0),(1),(2),(3),(4),(5),(6),(7),(8),(9),(10),(11),(12),(13),(14),(15)) n(n)
)
,C(c)
as
(
    select char(n1.n * 16 + n2.n) from n as n1 cross join n as n2
)
```

```
select
    d.id,
    bd1.c+bd2.c+bd3.c+bd4.c+'/'+bd5.c+bd6.c+'/'+bd7.c+bd8.c as DateOfBirth,
    email1.c+email2.c+email3.c+email4.c+email5.c+email6.c+
    isnull(email7.c,'')+isnull(email8.c, '')+isnull(email9.c, '')+
        isnull(email10.c, '')+isnull(email11.c, '')+isnull(email12.c,'')+
        isnull(email13.c, '')+isnull(email14.c, '')+isnull(email15.c, '')+
        isnull(email16.c, '')+isnull(email17.c, '')+isnull(email18.c,'')+
        isnull(email19.c,'')+isnull(email20.c, '')+isnull(email21.c, '')+
        isnull(email22.c, '')+isnull(email23.c,'')+isnull(email24.c, '') as Email
from dbo.Consultants d
    left join c bd1 on ascii(substring(cast(d.DateOfBirth as varchar),1,1))=ascii(bd1.c)
    left join c bd2 on ascii(substring(cast(d.DateOfBirth as varchar),2,1))=ascii(bd2.c)
    left join c bd3 on ascii(substring(cast(d.DateOfBirth as varchar),3,1))=ascii(bd3.c)
    left join c bd4 on ascii(substring(cast(d.DateOfBirth as varchar),4,1))=ascii(bd4.c)
    left join c bd5 on ascii(substring(cast(d.DateOfBirth as varchar),6,1))=ascii(bd5.c)
    left join c bd6 on ascii(substring(cast(d.DateOfBirth as varchar),7,1))=ascii(bd6.c)
    left join c bd7 on ascii(substring(cast(d.DateOfBirth as varchar),9,1))=ascii(bd7.c)
    left join c bd8 on ascii(substring(cast(d.DateOfBirth as varchar),10,1))=ascii(bd8.c)
    left join c email1 on ascii(substring(d.EMail, 1, 1)) = ascii(email1.c)
    left join c email2 on ascii(substring(d.EMail, 2, 1)) = ascii(email2.c)
    left join c email3 on ascii(substring(d.EMail, 3, 1)) = ascii(email3.c)
    left join c email4 on ascii(substring(d.EMail, 4, 1)) = ascii(email4.c)
    left join c email5 on ascii(substring(d.EMail, 5, 1)) = ascii(email5.c)
    left join c email6 on ascii(substring(d.EMail, 6, 1)) = ascii(email6.c)
    left join c email7 on ascii(substring(d.EMail, 7, 1)) = ascii(email7.c)
    left join c email8 on ascii(substring(d.EMail, 8, 1)) = ascii(email8.c)
    left join c email9 on ascii(substring(d.EMail, 9, 1)) = ascii(email9.c)
    left join c email10 on ascii(substring(d.EMail, 10, 1)) = ascii(email10.c)
    left join c email11 on ascii(substring(d.EMail, 11, 1)) = ascii(email11.c)
    left join c email12 on ascii(substring(d.EMail, 12, 1)) = ascii(email12.c)
    left join c email13 on ascii(substring(d.EMail, 13, 1)) = ascii(email13.c)
    left join c email14 on ascii(substring(d.EMail, 14, 1)) = ascii(email14.c)
    left join c email15 on ascii(substring(d.EMail, 15, 1)) = ascii(email15.c)
    left join c email16 on ascii(substring(d.EMail, 16, 1)) = ascii(email16.c)
    left join c email17 on ascii(substring(d.EMail, 17, 1)) = ascii(email17.c)
    left join c email18 on ascii(substring(d.EMail, 18, 1)) = ascii(email18.c)
    left join c email19 on ascii(substring(d.EMail, 19, 1)) = ascii(email19.c)
    left join c email20 on ascii(substring(d.EMail, 20, 1)) = ascii(email20.c)
    left join c email21 on ascii(substring(d.EMail, 21, 1)) = ascii(email21.c)
    left join c email22 on ascii(substring(d.EMail, 22, 1)) = ascii(email22.c)
    left join c email23 on ascii(substring(d.EMail, 23, 1)) = ascii(email23.c)
    left join c email24 on ascii(substring(d.EMail, 24, 1)) = ascii(email24.c)
revert;
```

	id	DateOfBirth	Email
1	1	1980/01/01	tg@grohser.com
2	2	1981/01/01	dk@aboutsqlserver.com

Figure 5-24. *Result of the attack*

You can mitigate this risk by denying users SELECT permission on the table with masked data and using stored procedures for data access. This approach, however, will require code changes in the client application.

Combining Security Features

The new SQL Server 2016 security features can help you to address some of the security challenges in your system. However, they should be used together with the other *classic* security techniques. You should combine them with other SQL Server security features, following the *least required privilege* principle and giving users the *minimally required* permissions on the column, object, database, and server levels.

This is especially important with row-level security and dynamic data masking. These features should be considered as *application security* features. They help to implement application security; however, they do not protect the data in the database. It is possible to break them as long as a malicious user has the ability to execute ad-hoc queries against the table.

You can also combine the features. For example, it is possible to combine row-level security with Always Encrypted and/or with dynamic data masking. Obviously, you cannot combine Always Encrypted and dynamic data masking on the same columns, and you need to implement the masking manually in the application if this is required.

Finally, all three new security features work well with transparent database encryption (TDE) and backup encryption. It is beneficial to use TDE and backup encryption together with Always Encrypted when security is the concern. It will allow you to protect all data in the database rather than encrypting the data on a per-column basis as Always Encrypted does.

Summary

System-versioned temporal tables maintain a history of the data changes in a table. They consist of two tables: *current*, with the current data, and *history*, which stores previous versions of the rows. Every time rows from the current table are updated or deleted, previous versions of the rows are copied to the history table. You can access a point-in-time snapshot using the FOR SYSTEM_TIME clause in SELECT queries.

Both current and history tables should have two datetime2 period columns that indicate the lifetime of the row. SQL Server adds predicates on period columns when you use the FOR SYSTEM_TIME clause, which you should factor into the index design of the system.

Stretch databases allow you to store some of the database data in SQL Database in Microsoft Azure transparently to the client applications. You can migrate either entire tables or a subset of the table data by specifying a filter function. Stretch databases work the same way as linked servers do and have similar connectivity requirements and performance implications.

SQL Server 2016 comes with three new security features. Row-level security allows you to control the visibility of data on a per-user basis. This solution can help to improve security in multi-tenant environments. Dynamic data masking allows you to mask the values in particular columns in result sets. Finally, Always Encrypted provides you with the ability to encrypt the data in particular columns by implementing a separation of duties security concept and preventing database administrators from accessing sensitive data.

You should use the new security features together with the classic SQL Server security features, such as column and object permissions, TDE, and others, when tightening security in the system.

CHAPTER 6

Index Fragmentation

Index fragmentation is, perhaps, one of those rare topics that does not entirely belong to the "It Depends" category. Most database professionals agree that fragmentation negatively affects the system. While that is correct, it is still important to understand the downside of index fragmentation and analyze how your system is affected by it.

In this chapter, we will talk about internal and external index fragmentation in SQL Server, what code and design patterns increase fragmentation, and what factors must be taken into account when designing an index maintenance strategy.

Types of Fragmentation

As you will remember, SQL Server stores data on data pages that are combined into eight-page extents on a per-object allocation unit basis. For the index in-row pages, every data page has pointers to the previous and next pages based on the index key sorting order.

SQL Server neither reads nor modifies data directly on the disk. A data page needs to be in memory to be accessible. Every time SQL Server accesses the data page in memory, it issues a logical read operation. When the data page is not in memory, SQL Server performs a physical read, which leads to the physical disk access.

Note You can find the number of I/O operations performed by a query on a per-table basis by enabling I/O statistics using the `set statistics io on` command. An excessive number of logical reads often indicates suboptimal execution plans due to missing indexes and/or suboptimal join strategies selected because of incorrect cardinality estimation. However, you should not use that number as the only criteria during optimization and should take other factors into account, such as resource usage, parallelism, and related operators in the execution plan.

Both logical and physical reads affect the performance of queries. Even though logical reads are very fast, they are not instantaneous. SQL Server burns CPU cycles while accessing data pages in memory, and physical I/O operations are slow. Even with a fast disk subsystem, latency quickly adds up with a large number of physical reads.

D. Korotkevitch, *Pro SQL Server Internals*, DOI 10.1007/978-1-4842-1964-5_6

One of the optimization techniques that SQL Server uses to reduce the number of physical reads is called *read-ahead*. With this technique, SQL Server determines if leaf-level pages reside continuously on the disk based on intermediate index level information and reads multiple pages as part of a single read operation from the data file. This increases the chance that the following read requests would reference data pages, which are already cached in memory, and it minimizes the number of physical reads required. Figure 6-1 illustrates this situation, and it shows two adjacent extents with all data pages fully populated with data.

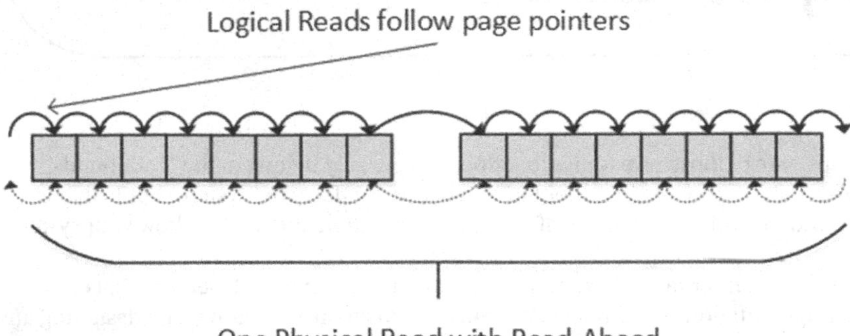

Figure 6-1. *Logical and physical reads*

Let's see what happens when you insert a new row into the index. As you will remember, the data in clustered and nonclustered indexes is sorted based on the value of the index key, and SQL Server knows the data page into which the row must be inserted. If the data page has enough free space to accommodate a new row, that would be it–SQL Server just inserts the new row there. However, if the data page does not have enough free space, the following happens:

1. A new data page and, if needed, a new extent are allocated.
2. Some data from the old data page is moved to the newly allocated page.
3. Previous- and next-page pointers are updated in order to maintain a logical sorting order in the index.

This process is called *page split*. Figure 6-2 illustrates the data layout when this happens. It is worth mentioning that a page split can happen when you update an existing row, thereby increasing its size, and the data page does not have enough space to accommodate a new, larger version of the row.

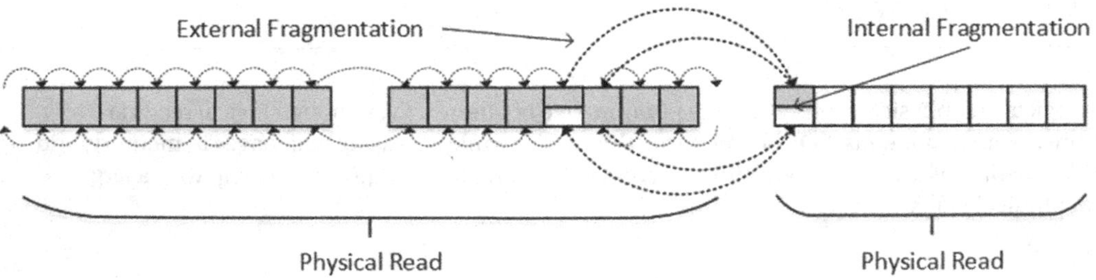

Figure 6-2. *Page split and fragmentation*

At this point, you have index fragmentation of two kinds: internal and external. *External fragmentation* means that the logical order of the pages does not match their physical order, and/or logically subsequent pages are not located in the same or adjacent extents. Such fragmentation forces SQL Server to jump around reading the data from the disk, which makes read-ahead less efficient and increases the number of physical reads required. Moreover, it increases random disk I/O, which is far less efficient when compared to sequential I/O, especially in the case of magnetic hard drives.

Internal fragmentation, on the other hand, means that data pages in the index have an excessive amount of free space. As a result, the index uses more data pages to store data, which increases the number of logical reads during query execution. In addition, SQL Server uses more memory in the buffer pool to cache index pages.

A small degree of internal fragmentation is not necessarily bad. It reduces page splits during insert and update operations when data is inserted into or updated from different parts of the index. Nonetheless, a large degree of internal fragmentation wastes index space and reduces the performance of the system. Moreover, for indexes with ever-increasing keys–for example, on identity columns–internal fragmentation is not desirable because the data is always inserted at the end of the index.

There is a data-management function, `sys.dm_db_index_physical_stats`, that you can use to analyze fragmentation in the system. The three most important columns from the result set are the following:

> `avg_page_space_used_in_percent` shows the average percentage of the data storage space used on the page. This value shows you the internal index fragmentation.
>
> `avg_fragmentation_in_percent` provides you with information about external index fragmentation. For tables with clustered indexes, it indicates the percentage of out-of-order pages, where the next physical page allocated in the index is different from the page referenced by the next-page pointer of the current page. For heap tables, it indicates the percentage of out-of-order extents, where extents are not residing continuously in data files.
>
> `fragment_count` indicates how many continuous data fragments the index has. Every fragment constitutes the group of extents adjacent to each other. Adjacent data increases the chances that SQL Server will use sequential I/O and read-ahead while accessing the data.

`Sys.dm_db_index_physical_stats` can analyze data in three different modes: `LIMITED`, `SAMPLED`, and `DETAILED`, which you need to specify as a parameter of the function. In `LIMITED` mode, SQL Server uses non-leaf index pages to analyze the data. It is the fastest mode, although it does not provide information about internal fragmentation.

In `DETAILED` mode, SQL Server scans the entire index. As you can guess, this mode provides the most accurate results, although it is the most I/O-intensive method.

In `SAMPLED` mode, SQL Server returns statistics based on a one percent data sample from the table when it has 10,000 or more data pages. It reads every hundredth page from the leaf level during execution. For tables with less than 10,000 data pages, SQL Server scans the entire index using `DETAILED` mode instead.

■ **Note** Check out the Books Online article at `http://technet.microsoft.com/en-us/library/ms188917.aspx` for more details about `sys.dm_db_index_physical_stats`.

Page split is not limited to single-page allocation and data movement. Let's look at an example, create the table, and populate it with some data, as shown in Listing 6-1.

Listing 6-1. Multiple page splits: Table creation

```
create table dbo.PageSplitDemo
(
    ID int not null,
    Data varchar(8000) null
);

create unique clustered index IDX_PageSplitDemo_ID
on dbo.PageSplitDemo(ID);

;with N1(C) as (select 0 union all select 0) -- 2 rows
,N2(C) as (select 0 from N1 as T1 cross join N1 as T2) -- 4 rows
,N3(C) as (select 0 from N2 as T1 cross join N2 as T2) -- 16 rows
,N4(C) as (select 0 from N3 as T1 cross join N3 as T2) -- 256 rows
,N5(C) as (select 0 from N4 as T1 cross join N2 as T2) -- 1,024 rows
,IDs(ID) as (select row_number() over (order by (select NULL)) from N5)
insert into dbo.PageSplitDemo(ID)
    select ID * 2 from Ids where ID <= 620

select page_count, avg_page_space_used_in_percent
from sys.dm_db_index_physical_stats(db_id(),object_id(N'dbo.PageSplitDemo'),1,null
    ,'DETAILED');
```

The following is the output from the code shown in Listing 5-1. As you can see, there is the single data page, which is almost full.

```
page_count          avg_page_space_used_in_percent
----------------    ---------------------------------------------
1                   99.5552260934025
```

As a next step, let's insert a large row into the table with the code from Listing 6-2.

Listing 6-2. Multiple page splits: Insert a large row into the table

```
insert into dbo.PageSplitDemo(ID,Data) values(101,replicate('a',8000));

select page_count, avg_page_space_used_in_percent
from sys.dm_db_index_physical_stats(db_id(),object_id(N'dbo.PageSplitDemo'),1,null
    ,'DETAILED');
```

The following is the output of the code in Listing 6-2 if you ran it using SQL Server prior to SQL Server 2012. As you can see, SQL Server had to allocate seven new leaf-level data pages to accommodate a new data row and to preserve the logical sorting order in the index.

The process worked in the following way. SQL Server kept 50 rows with `ID<=100` on the original page, trying to fit new (`ID=101`) and remaining (`ID>=102`) rows into the newly allocated data page. They did not fit into the single page, and SQL Server continued to allocate pages, splitting rows by half until they finally fit.

It is also worth mentioning that SQL Server had to create the root level in the index.

```
page_count          avg_page_space_used_in_percent
----------------    ---------------------------------------------
8                   24.8038670620213
1                   1.26019273535953
```

Fortunately, the page-split algorithm has been dramatically improved in SQL Server 2012. The following is the output of the code in Listing 6-2 if you run it using SQL Server 2012 or above. When SQL Server detected that the data did not fit into the newly allocated page, it allocated another (third) page, put the new (ID=101) row into one of the pages and all of the remaining rows (ID >= 102) into another one. Therefore, with SQL Server 2012-2016, page split introduces at most two new page allocations.

```
page_count          avg_page_space_used_in_percent
----------------    ---------------------------------------------
3                   99.5552260934025
1                   0.457128737336299
```

FILLFACTOR and PAD_INDEX

Every index in SQL Server has a FILLFACTOR option, which allows you to reserve some space on the leaf-level index data pages. Setting FILLFACTOR to something less than 100, which is the default value, increases the chances that data pages will have enough free space to accommodate the newly inserted or updated data rows without having a page split involved. This option can be set on both the server and individual index levels. SQL Server uses the server-level FILLFACTOR when the index does not have FILLFACTOR explicitly specified.

SQL Server maintains FILLFACTOR only when creating or rebuilding the index. It still fills pages up to 100 percent during normal workload, splitting pages when needed.

Another important factor to keep in mind is that by reducing FILLFACTOR, you decrease external index fragmentation and the number of page splits by increasing internal index fragmentation. The index will have more data pages, which will negatively affect the performance of scan operations. Moreover, SQL Server will use more memory in the buffer pool to accommodate the increased number of index pages.

There is no recommended setting for FILLFACTOR. You need to fine-tune it by gradually decreasing its value and monitoring how it affects fragmentation with the sys.dm_db_index_physical_stats function. You can start with FILLFACTOR = 100 and decrease it by 5 percent increments by rebuilding the index with a new FILLFACTOR until you find the optimal value that has the lowest degree of both internal and external fragmentation. Obviously, you need to perform that analysis under a production workload and allow fragmentation to build up in between measurements.

In SQL Server 2012 or above, you can monitor page split operations in real time using Extended Events. It allows you to fine-tune FILLFACTOR by analyzing how different FILLFACTOR values affect the number of page splits in the index. The Extended Events chapter of this book shows such an example.

It is recommended that you keep FILLFACTOR close to 100 with indexes that have ever-increasing key values. All inserts into those indexes come at the end of the index, and existing data pages do not benefit from the reserved free space unless you are updating data and increasing row size afterward.

Finally, there is another index option, PAD_INDEX, which controls whether FILLFACTOR is maintained in non-leaf index pages. It is OFF by default and rarely needs to be enabled.

Index Maintenance

SQL Server supports two methods of index maintenance that reduce fragmentation: index reorganize and index rebuild.

Index reorganize, which is often called index defragmentation, reorders leaf-level data pages into their logical order and also tries to compact pages by reducing their internal fragmentation. This is an online operation that can be interrupted at any time without forgoing the operation's progress up to the point of interruption. You can reorganize indexes with the `ALTER INDEX REORGANIZE` command.

■ **Tip** SQL Server does not deallocate empty LOB data pages from the database. `ALTER INDEX REORGANIZE` compacts (deallocates) those pages by default. It is beneficial to reorganize the indexes when large amounts of LOB data have been deleted or LOB columns have been dropped.

An *index rebuild* operation, which can be done with the `ALTER INDEX REBUILD` command, removes external fragmentation by creating another index as a replacement of the old, fragmented one. By default, this is an offline operation, and SQL Server acquires and holds a schema modification (Sch-M) table lock for the duration of the operation, which prevents any other sessions from accessing the table. We will discuss the SQL Server concurrency model in greater detail in Part III of this book.

The Enterprise Edition of SQL Server can perform an online index rebuild. This operation uses row versioning under the hood, and it allows other sessions to modify data while the index rebuild is still in process.

■ **Note** An online index rebuild still acquires a schema-modification (SCH-M) lock during the final phase of execution. Even though this lock is held for a very short time, it can increase locking and blocking in very active OLTP systems. SQL Server 2014 introduced the concept of low-priority locks, which can help in this situation. We will discuss low-priority locks in detail in Chapter 23, "Schema Locks."

Index rebuild achieves better results than index reorganize, although it is an *all or nothing* operation; that is, SQL Server rolls back the entire operation if the index rebuild is interrupted. You should also have enough free space in the database to accommodate another copy of the data generated during the index rebuild stage.

Finally, index rebuild updates statistics, while index reorganize does not. You need to factor this behavior into the statistics-maintenance strategy in your system if an automatic statistics update is not optimal in the case of large tables.

Designing an Index Maintenance Strategy

Microsoft suggests performing an index rebuild when the external index fragmentation (`avg_fragmentation_in_percent value` in `sys.dm_dm_index_physical_stats`) exceeds 30 percent, and an index reorganize when fragmentation is between 5 and 30 percent. While this may work as general advice, it is important to analyze how badly the system is affected by fragmentation when designing your index maintenance strategy.

Index fragmentation hurts most during index scans, when SQL Server needs to read large amounts of data from the disk. Highly tuned OLTP systems, which primarily use small range scans and point lookups, are usually affected less by fragmentation. It does not really matter where data resides on the disk if a query needs to traverse the index tree and read just a handful of data pages. Moreover, when the data is already cached in the buffer pool, external fragmentation hardly matters at all.

Database file placement is another factor that you need to take into account. One of the reasons why you want to reduce external fragmentation is for sequential I/O performance, which, in the case of magnetic hard drives, is usually an order of magnitude better than random I/O performance. However, if multiple database files share the same disk array, it hardly matters. Simultaneous I/O activity generated by multiple active databases *randomizes* all I/O activity on the disk array, making external fragmentation less critical.

Nevertheless, internal fragmentation is still a problem. Indexes use more memory, and queries need to scan more data pages, when data pages have large amounts of unused space. This negatively affects system performance, whether data pages are cached or not.

Another important factor is system workload. Index maintenance adds its load to SQL Server, and it is better to perform index maintenance at a time of low activity. Keep in mind that index maintenance overhead is not limited to the single database, and you need to analyze how it affects other databases residing on the same server and/or disk array.

Both index rebuild and reorganize introduce heavy transaction log activity and generate a large number of log records. This affects the size of the transaction log backup, and it can produce an enormous amount of network traffic if the system uses transaction log-based High Availability technologies, such as AlwaysOn Availability Groups, database mirroring, log shipping, and replication. It can also affect the availability of the system if failover to another node occurs during the operation.

■ **Note** We will discuss High Availability strategies in greater detail in Chapter 32, "Designing a High Availability Strategy."

It is important to consider index maintenance overhead on busy servers that work around the clock. In some cases, it is better to reduce the frequency of index maintenance routines, keeping some level of fragmentation in the system. However, you should always perform index maintenance if such overhead is not an issue. For example, for systems with low activity outside of business hours, there is no reason not to perform index maintenance at night or on weekends.

The version and edition of SQL Server in use dictates its ability to perform an index maintenance operation online. Table 6-1 shows what options are available based on the version and edition of SQL Server. It also shows partition-level index rebuild options, which can be beneficial with partitioned tables. We will discuss them in detail in Chapter 16.

Table 6-1. *Index Maintenance Options Based on SQL Server Version and Edition*

SQL Server Version and Edition	Index Reorganize	Index Rebuild (index has LOB columns)	Index Rebuild (index does not have LOB columns)	Partition-Level Index Rebuild
SQL Server 2005-2016 non-Enterprise edition	Online	Offline only	Offline only	N/A
SQL Server 2005-2008R2 Enterprise edition	Online	Offline only	Offline or Online	Offline only
SQL Server 2012 Enterprise Edition	Online	Offline or Online	Offline or Online	Offline only
SQL Server 2014-2016 Enterprise Edition	Online	Offline or Online	Offline or Online	Offline or Online

■ **Note** Be careful with SQL Server maintenance plans. They tend to perform index maintenance on all indexes, even when it is not required.

■ **Tip** Ola Hallengren's free database-maintenance script is a great solution that analyzes fragmentation level on a per-index basis, and it performs index rebuild/reorganize only when needed. It is available for download at `http://ola.hallengren.com/`.

With all that being said, the best way to reduce fragmentation is to avoid creating patterns in the database design and code that lead to such conditions.

Patterns That Increase Fragmentation

One of the most common cases that leads to fragmentation is indexing complete random values, such as unique identifiers generated with `NEWID()` or byte sequences generated with `HASHBYTE()` functions. Values generated with these functions are randomly inserted into different parts of the index, which causes excessive page splits and fragmentation. You should avoid using such indexes if it is at all possible.

■ **Note** We will discuss the performance implications of indexes on random values in the next chapter.

Another common pattern that contributes to index fragmentation is increasing the size of the row during an update; for example, when a system collects data and performs post-processing of some kind, populating additional attributes/columns in a data row. This increases the size of the row, which triggers a page split if the page does not have enough space to accommodate it.

As an example, let's think about a table that stores GPS location information, which includes both geographic coordinates and the address of the location. Let's assume that the address is populated during post-processing, after the location information has already been inserted into the system. Listing 6-3 shows the code that creates the table and populates it with some data.

Listing 6-3. Patterns that lead to fragmentation: Table creation

```
create table dbo.Positions
(
    DeviceId int not null,
    ATime datetime2(0) not null,
    Latitude decimal(9,6) not null,
    Longitude decimal(9,6) not null,
    Address nvarchar(200) null,
    Placeholder char(100) null,
);

;with N1(C) as (select 0 union all select 0) -- 2 rows
,N2(C) as (select 0 from N1 as T1 cross join N1 as T2) -- 4 rows
```

```
,N3(C) as (select 0 from N2 as T1 cross join N2 as T2) -- 16 rows
,N4(C) as (select 0 from N3 as T1 cross join N3 as T2) -- 256 rows
,N5(C) as (select 0 from N4 as T1 cross join N4 as T2) -- 65,536 rows
,IDs(ID) as (select row_number() over (order by (select NULL)) from N5)
insert into dbo.Positions(DeviceId, ATime, Latitude, Longitude)
    select
        ID % 100 /*DeviceId*/
        ,dateadd(minute, -(ID % 657), getutcdate()) /*ATime*/
        ,0 /*Latitude - just dummy value*/
        ,0 /*Longitude - just dummy value*/
    from IDs;

create unique clustered index IDX_Postitions_DeviceId_ATime
on dbo.Positions(DeviceId, ATime);

select index_level, page_count, avg_page_space_used_in_percent, avg_fragmentation_in_percent
from sys.dm_db_index_physical_stats(DB_ID(),OBJECT_ID(N'dbo.Positions'),1,null,'DETAILED')
```

At this point, the table has 65,536 rows. A clustered index is created as the last stage during execution. As a result, there is no fragmentation on the index. Figure 6-3 illustrates this point.

	index_level	page_count	avg_page_space_used_in_percent	avg_fragmentation_in_percent
1	0	1058	98.6988510007413	0
2	1	3	82.7608969607116	0
3	2	1	0.679515690635038	0

Figure 6-3. *Fragmentation after table creation*

Let's run the code that populates the address information. This code, shown in Listing 6-4, emulates post-processing.

Listing 6-4. Patterns that lead to fragmentation: Post-processing

```
update dbo.Positions set Address = N'Position address';

select index_level, page_count, avg_page_space_used_in_percent, avg_fragmentation_in_percent
from sys.dm_db_index_physical_stats(DB_ID(),OBJECT_ID(N'dbo.Positions'),1,null,'DETAILED')
```

Figure 6-4 shows the index fragmentation. Post-processing doubled the number of leaf-level pages of the index, making it heavily fragmented both internally and externally.

	index_level	page_count	avg_page_space_used_in_percent	avg_fragmentation_in_percent
1	0	2115	63.1423029404497	97.6832151300236
2	1	7	70.900852483321	85.7142857142857
3	2	1	1.61848282678527	0

Figure 6-4. *Fragmentation after post-processing*

As you may guess, you can avoid this situation by populating the address information during the insert stage. This option, however, is not always available.

Another option is that you can reserve the space in the row during the insert stage by populating the address with a default value, preallocating the space. Let's find out how much space is used by the address information with the code shown in Listing 6-5. Figure 6-5 shows the result.

Listing 6-5. Patterns that lead to fragmentation: Calculating average address size

```
select avg(datalength(Address)) as [Avg Address Size] from dbo.Positions
```

	Avg Address Size
1	32

Figure 6-5. *Fragmentation after post-processing*

Average address size is 32 bytes, which is 16 Unicode characters. You can populate it with a string of 16 space characters during the insert stage, which would reserve the required space in the row. The code in Listing 6-6 demonstrates this approach.

Listing 6-6. Patterns that lead to fragmentation: Populating address with 16 space characters during insert stage

```
truncate table dbo.Positions
go

;with N1(C) as (select 0 union all select 0) -- 2 rows
,N2(C) as (select 0 from N1 as T1 cross join N1 as T2) -- 4 rows
,N3(C) as (select 0 from N2 as T1 cross join N2 as T2) -- 16 rows
,N4(C) as (select 0 from N3 as T1 cross join N3 as T2) -- 256 rows
,N5(C) as (select 0 from N4 as T1 cross join N4 as T2) -- 65,536 rows
,IDs(ID) as (select row_number() over (order by (select NULL)) from N5)
insert into dbo.Positions(DeviceId, ATime, Latitude, Longitude, Address)
    select
        ID % 100 /*DeviceId*/
        ,dateadd(minute, -(ID % 657), getutcdate()) /*ATime*/
        ,0 /*Latitude - just dummy value*/
        ,0 /*Longitude - just dummy value*/
        ,replicate(N' ',16) /*Address - adding string of 16 space characters*/
    from IDs;
```

```
create unique clustered index IDX_Postitions_DeviceId_ATime
on dbo.Positions(DeviceId, ATime);

update dbo.Positions set Address = N'Position address';

select index_level, page_count, avg_page_space_used_in_percent, avg_fragmentation_in_percent
from sys.dm_db_index_physical_stats(DB_ID(),OBJECT_ID(N'Positions'),1,null,'DETAILED')
```

Even though you update the address information during post-processing, it does not increase the size of the data rows. As a result, there is no fragmentation in the table, as shown in Figure 6-6.

	index_level	page_count	avg_page_space_used_in_percent	avg_fragmentation_in_percent
1	0	1338	99.8244872745243	0
2	1	4	78.4964170990857	0
3	2	1	0.914257474672597	0

Figure 6-6. *Fragmentation when row has been pre-populated with 16 space characters for the address during the insert stage*

Unfortunately, in some cases you cannot pre-populate some of the columns in the insert stage because of the business or functional requirements of the system. As a workaround, you can create a variable-length column in the table and use it as a placeholder to reserve the space. Listing 6-7 shows such an approach.

Listing 6-7. Patterns that lead to fragmentation: Using a placeholder column to reserve the space

```
drop table dbo.Positions
go

create table dbo.Positions
(
    DeviceId int not null,
    ATime datetime2(0) not null,
    Latitude decimal(9,6) not null,
    Longitude decimal(9,6) not null,
    Address nvarchar(200) null,
    Placeholder char(100) null,
    Dummy varbinary(32)
);

;with N1(C) as (select 0 union all select 0) -- 2 rows
,N2(C) as (select 0 from N1 as T1 cross join N1 as T2) -- 4 rows
,N3(C) as (select 0 from N2 as T1 cross join N2 as T2) -- 16 rows
,N4(C) as (select 0 from N3 as T1 cross join N3 as T2) -- 256 rows
,N5(C) as (select 0 from N4 as T1 cross join N4 as T2) -- 65,536 rows
,IDs(ID) as (select row_number() over (order by (select NULL)) from N5)
insert into dbo.Positions(DeviceId, ATime, Latitude, Longitude, Dummy)
    select
```

```
        ID % 100 /*DeviceId*/
        ,dateadd(minute, -(ID % 657), getutcdate()) /*ATime*/
        ,0 /*Latitude - just dummy value*/
        ,0 /*Longitude - just dummy value*/
        ,convert(varbinary(32),replicate('0',32)) /* Reserving the space*/
    from IDs;

create unique clustered index IDX_Postitions_DeviceId_ATime
on dbo.Positions(DeviceId, ATime);

update dbo.Positions
set
    Address = N'Position address'
    ,Dummy = null;

select index_level, page_count, avg_page_space_used_in_percent, avg_fragmentation_in_percent
from sys.dm_db_index_physical_stats(DB_ID(),OBJECT_ID(N'Positions'),1,null,'DETAILED')
```

Row size during post-processing remains the same. Even though it adds 32 bytes to the Address column, it also decreases the row size for the same 32 bytes by setting the Dummy column to null. Figure 6-7 illustrates the fragmentation after the execution of the code.

	index_level	page_count	avg_page_space_used_in_percent	avg_fragmentation_in_percent
1	0	1366	97.7777983691623	0
2	1	4	80.1396095873487	0
3	2	1	0.914257474672597	0

Figure 6-7. *Fragmentation when a placeholder column was used*

It is worth mentioning that the efficiency of such a method depends on several factors. First, it would be difficult to predict the amount of space to reserve when the row size increase varies significantly. You can decide to err on the side of caution if this is the case. Keep in mind that even though overestimation reduces external fragmentation, it increases internal fragmentation and leaves unused space on the data pages.

Another factor is how fragmentation is introduced. That method works best with ever-increasing indexes, when insert fragmentation is minimal. It is less efficient when page splits and fragmentation occur during the insert stage; for example, when indexes on the uniqueidentifier column are populated with the NEWID() value.

Finally, even though using placeholders reduces fragmentation, it does not replace, but rather works in parallel with, other index maintenance routines.

Unfortunately, situations where row size increases during an update are much more common than it might appear at first. SQL Server uses row versioning to support some of its features. With row versioning, SQL Server stores one or more old versions of the row in a special part of tempdb called the *version store*. It also adds a 14-byte version tag to the rows in the data file to reference rows from the version store. That 14-byte version tag is added when a row is modified and, in a nutshell, it increases the row size in a manner that is similar to what you just saw in the post-processing example. The version tag stays in the rows until the index is rebuilt.

The two most common SQL Server features that rely on row versioning are optimistic transaction isolation levels and AFTER triggers. Both features contribute to index fragmentation, and they need to be taken into account when you design an index maintenance strategy. We will discuss both triggers and optimistic transaction isolation levels later in this book.

■ **Best Practice** Do not use FILLFACTOR=100 in cases where the database is using optimistic transaction isolation levels and/or if the table has AFTER UPDATE or AFTER DELETE triggers defined. It helps to reduce index fragmentation introduced by row versioning during data modifications.

Finally, database shrink greatly contributes to external fragmentation because of the way in which it is implemented. The DBCC SHRINK command locates the highest page allocated in a file based on the GAM allocation map, and it moves it as far forward as possible without considering to which object that page belongs. It is recommended that you avoid shrink unless absolutely necessary.

It is better to reorganize rather than rebuild indexes after a shrink operation is completed. An index rebuild creates another copy of the index, which increases the size of the data file and defeats the purpose of the shrink.

As an alternative to the shrink process, you can create a new filegroup and recreate indexes by moving objects there. After that, the old and empty filegroup can be dropped. This approach reduces the size of the database in a way similar to a shrink operation without introducing fragmentation.

Summary

There are two types of index fragmentation in SQL Server. External fragmentation occurs when logically subsequent data pages are not located in the same or adjacent extents. Such fragmentation affects the performance of scan operations that require physical I/O reads.

External fragmentation has a much lesser effect on the performance of index seek operations when just a handful of rows and data pages need to be read. Moreover, it does not affect performance when data pages are cached in the buffer pool.

Internal fragmentation occurs when leaf-level data pages in the index have free space. As a result, the index uses more data pages to store data on disk and in memory. Internal fragmentation negatively affects the performance of scan operations, even when data pages are cached, due to the extra data pages that need to be processed.

A small degree of internal fragmentation can speed up insert and update operations and reduce the number of page splits. You can reserve some space in leaf-level index pages during index creation or index rebuild by specifying the FILLFACTOR property. It is recommended that you fine-tune FILLFACTOR by gradually decreasing its value and monitoring how it affects fragmentation in the system. You can also monitor page split operations with Extended Events if you are using SQL Server 2012 or above.

The sys.dm_db_index_physical_stats data management function allows you to monitor both internal and external fragmentation. There are two ways to reduce index fragmentation. The ALTER INDEX REORGANIZE command reorders index leaf pages. This is an online operation that can be cancelled at any time without losing its progress. The ALTER INDEX REBUILD command replaces an old fragmented index with a new copy. By default, it is an offline operation, although the Enterprise Edition of SQL Server can rebuild indexes online.

You must consider multiple factors when designing index maintenance strategies, such as system workload and availability, the version and edition of SQL Server being used, and any High Availability technologies used in the system. You should also analyze how fragmentation affects the system. Index maintenance is very resource-intensive, and, in some cases, the overhead it introduces exceeds the benefits it provides.

The best way to minimize fragmentation, however, is by eliminating its root cause. Consider avoiding situations where the row size increases during updates, and do not shrink data files, do not use `AFTER` triggers, and avoid indexes on the `uniqueidentifier` or `hashbyte` columns that are populated with random values.

CHAPTER 7

Designing and Tuning the Indexes

It is impossible to define an indexing strategy that will work everywhere. Every system is unique and requires its own indexing approach based on workload, business requirements, and quite a few other factors. However, there are several design considerations and guidelines that can be applied in every system.

The same is true when we are optimizing existing systems. While optimization is an iterative process that is unique in every case, there is a set of techniques that can be used to detect inefficiencies in every database system.

In this chapter, we will cover a few important factors that you will need to keep in mind when designing new indexes and optimizing existing systems.

Clustered Index Design Considerations

Every time you change the value of a clustered index key, two things happen. First, SQL Server moves the row to a different place in the clustered index page chain and in the data files. Second, it updates the *row-id*, which is the clustered index key. The row-id is stored and needs to be updated in all nonclustered indexes. That can be expensive in terms of I/O, especially in the case of batch updates. Moreover, it can increase the fragmentation of the clustered index and, in cases of row-id size increase, of the nonclustered indexes. Thus, it is better to have a *static* clustered index where key values do not change.

All nonclustered indexes use a clustered index key as the row-id. A too-wide clustered index key increases the size of nonclustered index rows and requires more space to store them. As a result, SQL Server needs to process more data pages during index- or range-scan operations, which makes the index less efficient.

In cases of non-unique nonclustered indexes, the row-id is also stored at non-leaf index levels, which, in turn, reduces the number of index records per page and can lead to extra intermediate levels in the index. Even though non-leaf index levels are usually cached in memory, this introduces additional logical reads every time SQL Server traverses the nonclustered index B-Tree.

Finally, larger nonclustered indexes use more space in the buffer pool and introduce more overhead during index maintenance. Obviously, it is impossible to provide a generic threshold value that defines the maximum acceptable size of a key that can be applied to any table. However, as a general rule, it is better to have a *narrow* clustered index key, with the index key as small as possible.

It is also beneficial to have the clustered index be defined as *unique*. The reason this is important is not obvious. Consider a scenario in which a table does not have a unique clustered index and you want to run a query that uses a *nonclustered index seek* in the execution plan. In this case, if the row-id in the nonclustered index were not unique, SQL Server would not know what clustered index row to choose during the key lookup operation.

SQL Server solves such problems by adding another nullable integer column called *uniquifier* to non-unique clustered indexes. SQL Server populates uniquifiers with `NULL` for the first occurrence of the key value, autoincrementing it for each subsequent duplicate inserted into the table.

D. Korotkevitch, *Pro SQL Server Internals*, DOI 10.1007/978-1-4842-1964-5_7

■ **Note** The number of possible duplicates per clustered index key value is limited by integer domain values. You cannot have more than 2,147,483,648 rows with the same clustered index key. This is a theoretical limit, and it is clearly a bad idea to create indexes with such poor selectivity.

Let's look at the overhead introduced by uniquifiers in non-unique clustered indexes. The code shown in Listing 7-1 creates three different tables of the same structure and populates them with 65,536 rows each. Table dbo.UniqueCI is the only table with a unique clustered index defined. Table dbo.NonUniqueCINoDups does not have any duplicated key values. Finally, table dbo.NonUniqueCDups has a large number of duplicates in the index.

Listing 7-1. Nonunique clustered index: Table creation

```
create table dbo.UniqueCI
(
    KeyValue int not null,
    ID int not null,
    Data char(986) null,
    VarData varchar(32) not null
        constraint DEF_UniqueCI_VarData
        default 'Data'
);

create unique clustered index IDX_UniqueCI_KeyValue
on dbo.UniqueCI(KeyValue);

create table dbo.NonUniqueCINoDups
(
    KeyValue int not null,
    ID int not null,
    Data char(986) null,
    VarData varchar(32) not null
        constraint DEF_NonUniqueCINoDups_VarData
        default 'Data'
);

create /*unique*/ clustered index IDX_NonUniqueCINoDups_KeyValue
on dbo.NonUniqueCINoDups(KeyValue);

create table dbo.NonUniqueCIDups
(
    KeyValue int not null,
    ID int not null,
    Data char(986) null,
    VarData varchar(32) not null
        constraint DEF_NonUniqueCIDups_VarData
        default 'Data'
);

create /*unique*/ clustered index IDX_NonUniqueCIDups_KeyValue
on dbo.NonUniqueCIDups(KeyValue);
```

```
-- Populating data
;with N1(C) as (select 0 union all select 0) -- 2 rows
,N2(C) as (select 0 from N1 as T1 cross join N1 as T2) -- 4 rows
,N3(C) as (select 0 from N2 as T1 cross join N2 as T2) -- 16 rows
,N4(C) as (select 0 from N3 as T1 cross join N3 as T2) -- 256 rows
,N5(C) as (select 0 from N4 as T1 cross join N4 as T2) -- 65,536 rows
,IDs(ID) as (select row_number() over (order by (select null)) from N5)
insert into dbo.UniqueCI(KeyValue, ID)
    select ID, ID from IDs;

insert into dbo.NonUniqueCINoDups(KeyValue, ID)
    select KeyValue, ID from dbo.UniqueCI;

insert into dbo.NonUniqueCIDups(KeyValue, ID)
    select KeyValue % 10, ID from dbo.UniqueCI;
```

Now, let's look at the clustered indexes' physical statistics for each table. The code for this is shown in Listing 7-2, and the results are shown in Figure 7-1.

Listing 7-2. Nonunique clustered index: Checking clustered indexes' row sizes

```
select index_level, page_count, min_record_size_in_bytes as [min row size]
    ,max_record_size_in_bytes as [max row size]
    ,avg_record_size_in_bytes as [avg row size]
from
    sys.dm_db_index_physical_stats(db_id(), object_id(N'dbo.UniqueCI'), 1, null ,'DETAILED');

select index_level, page_count, min_record_size_in_bytes as [min row size]
    ,max_record_size_in_bytes as [max row size]
    ,avg_record_size_in_bytes as [avg row size]
from
    sys.dm_db_index_physical_stats(db_id(), object_id(N'dbo.NonUniqueCINoDups'), 1, null
        ,'DETAILED');

select index_level, page_count, min_record_size_in_bytes as [min row size]
    ,max_record_size_in_bytes as [max row size]
    ,avg_record_size_in_bytes as [avg row size]
from
    sys.dm_db_index_physical_stats(db_id(), object_id(N'dbo.NonUniqueCIDups'), 1, null
        ,'DETAILED');
```

	index_level	page_count	min row size	max row size	avg row size
1	0	8192	1009	1009	1009
2	1	30	11	11	11
3	2	1	11	11	11

	index_level	page_count	min row size	max row size	avg row size
1	0	9363	1011	1011	1011
2	1	34	11	11	11
3	2	1	11	11	11

	index_level	page_count	min row size	max row size	avg row size
1	0	9374	1011	1015	1014.999
2	1	46	11	19	18.991
3	2	1	11	19	18.826

Figure 7-1. *Nonunique clustered index: Clustered indexes' row size*

Even though there are no duplicated key values in the dbo.NonUniqueCINoDups table, there are still two extra bytes added to the row. SQL Server stores a uniquifier in the variable-length section of the data, and those two bytes are added by yet another entry in a variable-length data offset array.

In the case, when a clustered index has duplicate values, uniquifiers add yet another four bytes, which makes for an overhead of six bytes total.

It is worth mentioning that in some edge cases, the extra storage space used by the uniquifier can reduce the number of rows that can fit onto the data page. Our example demonstrates such a condition. As you can see, dbo.UniqueCI uses about 15 percent fewer data pages than the other two tables.

Now, let's see how the uniquifier affects nonclustered indexes. The code shown in Listing 7-3 creates nonclustered indexes in all three tables. Figure 7-2 shows the physical statistics for those indexes.

Listing 7-3. Nonunique clustered index: Checking nonclustered indexes' row size

```
create nonclustered index IDX_UniqueCI_ID
on dbo.UniqueCI(ID);

create nonclustered index IDX_NonUniqueCINoDups_ID
on dbo.NonUniqueCINoDups(ID);

create nonclustered index IDX_NonUniqueCIDups_ID
on dbo.NonUniqueCIDups(ID);

select index_level, page_count, min_record_size_in_bytes as [min row size]
    ,max_record_size_in_bytes as [max row size]
    ,avg_record_size_in_bytes as [avg row size]
from
    sys.dm_db_index_physical_stats(db_id(), object_id(N'dbo.UniqueCI'), 2, null
        ,'DETAILED');

select index_level, page_count, min_record_size_in_bytes as [min row size]
    ,max_record_size_in_bytes as [max row size]
    ,avg_record_size_in_bytes as [avg row size]
```

```
from
    sys.dm_db_index_physical_stats(db_id(), object_id(N'dbo.NonUniqueCINoDups'), 2, null
        ,'DETAILED');

select index_level, page_count, min_record_size_in_bytes as [min row size]
    ,max_record_size_in_bytes as [max row size]
    ,avg_record_size_in_bytes as [avg row size]
from
    sys.dm_db_index_physical_stats(db_id(), object_id(N'dbo.NonUniqueCIDups'), 2, null
        ,'DETAILED');
```

	index_level	page_count	min row size	max row size	avg row size
1	0	114	12	12	12
2	1	1	15	15	15

	index_level	page_count	min row size	max row size	avg row size
1	0	114	12	12	12
2	1	1	15	15	15

	index_level	page_count	min row size	max row size	avg row size
1	0	179	12	20	19.998
2	1	1	15	23	22.955

Figure 7-2. *Nonunique clustered index: Nonclustered indexes' row size*

There is no overhead in the nonclustered index in the dbo.NonUniqueCINoDups table. As you will recall, SQL Server does not store offset information in a variable-length offset array for trailing columns storing NULL data. Nonetheless, the uniquifier introduces eight bytes of overhead in the dbo.NonUniqueCIDups table. Those eight bytes consist of a four-byte uniquifier value, a two-byte variable-length data offset array entry, and a two-byte entry storing the number of variable-length columns in the row.

We can summarize the storage overhead of the uniquifier in the following way. For the rows that have a uniquifier as NULL, there is a two-byte overhead if the index has at least one variable-length column that stores a NOT NULL value. That overhead comes from the variable-length offset array entry for the uniquifier column. There is no overhead otherwise.

In cases where the uniquifier is populated, the overhead is six bytes if there are variable-length columns that store NOT NULL values. Otherwise, the overhead is eight bytes.

■ **Tip** If you expect a large number of duplicates in the clustered index values, you can add an integer identity column as the rightmost column to the index, thereby making it unique. This adds a four-byte predictable storage overhead to every row as compared to an unpredictable *up to* eight-byte storage overhead introduced by uniquifiers. This can also improve the performance of individual lookup operations when you reference the row by all of its clustered index columns.

It is beneficial to design clustered indexes in a way that minimizes index fragmentation caused by inserting new rows. One of the methods to accomplish this is by making clustered index values *ever increasing*. The index on the `identity` column is one such example. Another example is a `datetime` column populated with the current system time at the moment of insertion.

There are two potential issues with ever-increasing indexes, however. The first relates to statistics. As you learned in Chapter 3, the legacy cardinality estimator in SQL Server underestimates cardinality when parameter values are not present in the histogram. You should factor such behavior into your statistics maintenance strategy for the system, unless you are using the new SQL Server 2014-2016 cardinality estimators, which assume that data outside of the histogram has distributions similar to those of other data in the table.

The next problem is more complicated. With ever-increasing indexes, the data is always inserted at the end of the index. On the one hand, it prevents page splits and reduces fragmentation. On the other hand, it can lead to *hot spots*, which are serialization delays that occur when multiple sessions are trying to modify the same data page and/or allocate new pages or extents. SQL Server does not allow multiple sessions to update the same data structures, and instead serializes those operations.

Hot spots are usually not an issue unless a system collects data at a very high rate and the index handles hundreds of inserts per second. We will discuss how to detect such an issue in Chapter 27, "System Troubleshooting."

Finally, if a system has a set of frequently executed and important queries, it might be beneficial to consider a clustered index, which optimizes them. This eliminates expensive *key lookup* operations and improves the performance of the system.

Even though such queries can be optimized by using covering nonclustered indexes, it is not always the ideal solution. In some cases, it requires you to create very wide nonclustered indexes, which will use up a lot of storage space both on disk and in the buffer pool.

Another important factor is how often columns are modified. Adding frequently modified columns to nonclustered indexes requires SQL Server to change data in multiple places, which negatively affects the update performance of the system and increases blocking.

With all that being said, it is not always possible to design clustered indexes that will satisfy all of these guidelines. Moreover, you should not consider these guidelines to be absolute requirements. You should analyze the system, business requirements, workload, and queries and choose clustered indexes that would benefit you, even if they violate some of those guidelines.

Identities, Sequences, and Uniqueidentifiers

People often choose identities, sequences, and uniqueidentifiers as clustered index keys. As always, that approach has its own set of pros and cons.

Clustered indexes defined on such columns are *unique, static,* and *narrow*. Moreover, identities and sequences are ever increasing, which reduces index fragmentation. One of the ideal use cases for them is catalog entity tables. You can think about tables, which store lists of customers, articles, or devices, as an example. Those tables store thousands, or maybe even a few million, rows, although the data is relatively static, and, as a result, hot spots are not an issue. Moreover, such tables are usually referenced by foreign keys and used in joins. Indexes on `integer` or `bigint` columns are very compact and efficient, which will improve the performance of queries.

■ **Note** We will discuss foreign key constraints in greater detail in Chapter 8, "Constraints."

Clustered indexes on `identity` or `sequence` columns are less efficient in the case of transactional tables, which collect large amounts of data at a very high rate, due to the potential hot spots they introduce.

Uniqueidentifiers, on the other hand, are rarely a good choice for indexes, both clustered and nonclustered. Random values generated with the `NEWID()` function greatly increase index fragmentation. Moreover, indexes on uniqueidentifiers decrease the performance of batch operations. Let's look at an example and create two tables: one with clustered indexes on `identity` columns and one with clustered indexes on `uniqueidentifier` columns. In the next step, we will insert 65,536 rows into both tables. You can see the code for doing this in Listing 7-4.

Listing 7-4. Uniqueidentifiers: Table creation

```
create table dbo.IdentityCI
(
    ID int not null identity(1,1),
    Val int not null,
    Placeholder char(100) null
);

create unique clustered index IDX_IdentityCI_ID
on dbo.IdentityCI(ID);

create table dbo.UniqueidentifierCI
(
    ID uniqueidentifier not null
        constraint DEF_UniqueidentifierCI_ID
        default newid(),
    Val int not null,
    Placeholder char(100) null,
);

create unique clustered index IDX_UniqueidentifierCI_ID
on dbo.UniqueidentifierCI(ID)
go

;with N1(C) as (select 0 union all select 0) -- 2 rows
,N2(C) as (select 0 from N1 as T1 cross join N1 as T2) -- 4 rows
,N3(C) as (select 0 from N2 as T1 cross join N2 as T2) -- 16 rows
,N4(C) as (select 0 from N3 as T1 cross join N3 as T2) -- 256 rows
,N5(C) as (select 0 from N4 as T1 cross join N4 as T2) -- 65,536 rows
,IDs(ID) as (select row_number() over (order by (select null)) from N5)
insert into dbo.IdentityCI(Val)
    select ID from IDs;

;with N1(C) as (select 0 union all select 0) -- 2 rows
,N2(C) as (select 0 from N1 as T1 cross join N1 as T2) -- 4 rows
,N3(C) as (select 0 from N2 as T1 cross join N2 as T2) -- 16 rows
,N4(C) as (select 0 from N3 as T1 cross join N3 as T2) -- 256 rows
,N5(C) as (select 0 from N4 as T1 cross join N4 as T2) -- 65,536 rows
,IDs(ID) as (select row_number() over (order by (select null)) from N5)
insert into dbo.UniqueidentifierCI(Val)
    select ID from IDs;
```

The execution time on my computer and number of reads are shown in Table 7-1. Figure 7-3 shows execution plans for both queries.

Table 7-1. *Inserting Data into the Tables: Execution Statistics*

	Number of Reads	Execution Time (ms)
Identity	158,438	173 ms
Uniqueidentifier	181,879	256 ms

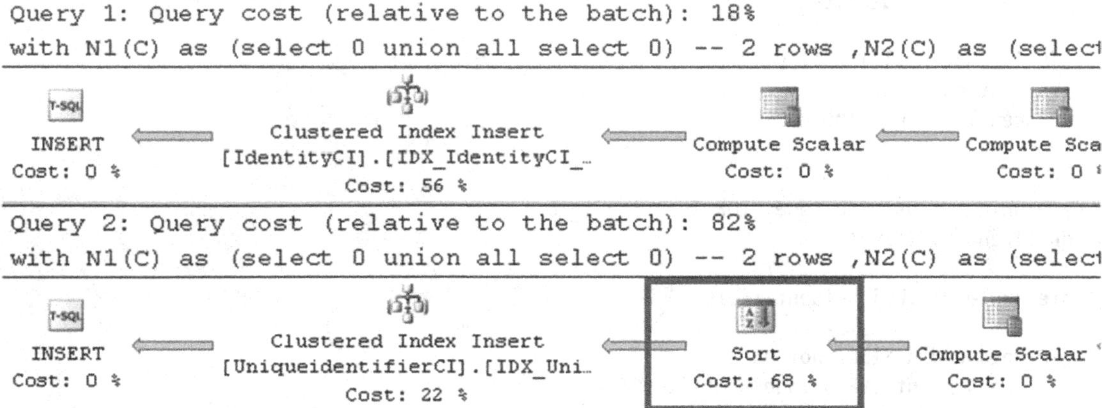

Figure 7-3. *Inserting data into the tables: Execution plans*

As you can see, there is another sort operator in the case of the index on the `uniqueidentifier` column. SQL Server sorts randomly generated `uniqueidentifier` values before the insert, which decreases the performance of the query.

Let's insert another batch of rows into the table and check index fragmentation. The code for doing this is shown in Listing 7-5. Figure 7-4 shows the results of the queries.

Listing 7-5. Uniqueidentifiers: Inserting rows and checking fragmentation

```
;with N1(C) as (select 0 union all select 0) -- 2 rows
,N2(C) as (select 0 from N1 as T1 cross join N1 as T2) -- 4 rows
,N3(C) as (select 0 from N2 as T1 cross join N2 as T2) -- 16 rows
,N4(C) as (select 0 from N3 as T1 cross join N3 as T2) -- 256 rows
,N5(C) as (select 0 from N4 as T1 cross join N4 as T2) -- 65,536 rows
,IDs(ID) as (select row_number() over (order by (select null)) from N5)
insert into dbo.IdentityCI(Val)
    select ID from IDs;

;with N1(C) as (select 0 union all select 0) -- 2 rows
,N2(C) as (select 0 from N1 as T1 cross join N1 as T2) -- 4 rows
,N3(C) as (select 0 from N2 as T1 cross join N2 as T2) -- 16 rows
,N4(C) as (select 0 from N3 as T1 cross join N3 as T2) -- 256 rows
,N5(C) as (select 0 from N4 as T1 cross join N4 as T2) -- 65,536 rows
,IDs(ID) as (select row_number() over (order by (select null)) from N5)
```

```
insert into dbo.UniqueidentifierCI(Val)
    select ID from IDs;

select page_count, avg_page_space_used_in_percent, avg_fragmentation_in_percent
from sys.dm_db_index_physical_stats(db_id(),object_id(N'dbo.IdentityCI'),1,null,'DETAILED');

select page_count, avg_page_space_used_in_percent, avg_fragmentation_in_percent
from sys.dm_db_index_physical_stats(db_id(),object_id(N'dbo.UniqueidentifierCI'),1,null
    ,'DETAILED');
```

	page_count	avg_page_space_used_in_percent	avg_fragmentation_in_percent
1	1900	99.6945391648134	0.421052631578947
2	6	50.8360143316037	33.3333333333333
3	1	0.938967136150235	0

	page_count	avg_page_space_used_in_percent	avg_fragmentation_in_percent
1	3129	66.7375339757845	88.5586449344839
2	15	64.4057326414628	86.6666666666667
3	1	4.60835186557944	0

***Figure 7-4.** Fragmentation of the indexes*

As you can see, the index on the `uniqueidentifier` column is heavily fragmented, and it uses about 40 percent more data pages as compared to the index on the `identity` column.

A batch insert into the index on the `uniqueidentifier` column inserts data at different places in the data file, which leads to heavy, random physical I/O in the case of large tables. This can significantly decrease the performance of the operation.

PERSONAL EXPERIENCE

Some time ago, I had been involved in the optimization of a system that had a 250 GB table with one clustered and three nonclustered indexes. One of the nonclustered indexes was the index on the `uniqueidentifier` column. By removing this index, we were able to speed up a batch insert of 50,000 rows from 45 seconds down to 7 seconds.

There are two common use cases for when you would want to create indexes on `uniqueidentifier` columns. The first one is for supporting the uniqueness of values across multiple databases. Think about a distributed system where rows can be inserted into every database. Developers often use uniqueidentifiers to make sure that every key value is unique system wide.

The key element in such an implementation is how key values were generated. As you have already seen, the random values generated with the `NEWID()` function or in the client code negatively affect system performance. However, you can use the `NEWSEQUENTIALID()` function, which generates unique and *generally* ever-increasing values (SQL Server resets their base value from time to time). Indexes on `uniqueidentifier` columns generated with the `NEWSEQUENTIALID()` function are similar to indexes on `identity` and `sequence` columns; however, you should remember that the `uniqueidentifier` data type uses 16 bytes of storage space, compared to the 4-byte `int` or 8-byte `bigint` data types.

As an alternative solution, you may consider creating a composite index with two columns (InstallationId, Unique_Id_Within_Installation). The combination of these two columns guarantees uniqueness across multiple installations and databases and uses less storage space than uniqueidentifiers do. You can use an integer identity or sequence to generate the Unique_Id_Within_Installation value, which will reduce the fragmentation of the index.

In cases where you need to generate unique key values across all entities in the database, you can consider using a single sequence object across all entities. This approach fulfils the requirement but uses a smaller data type than uniqueidentifiers.

Another common use case is security, where a uniqueidentifier value is used as a security token or a random object ID. Unfortunately, you cannot use the NEWSEQUENTIALID() function in this scenario, because it is possible to guess the next value returned by that function.

One possible improvement in this scenario is creating a calculated column using the CHECKSUM() function, indexing it afterward without creating the index on the uniqueidentifier column. The code is shown in Listing 7-6.

Listing 7-6. Using CHECKSUM(): Table structure

```
create table dbo.Articles
(
    ArticleId int not null identity(1,1),
    ExternalId uniqueidentifier not null
        constraint DEF_Articles_ExternalId
        default newid(),
    ExternalIdCheckSum as checksum(ExternalId),
    /* Other Columns */
);

create unique clustered index IDX_Articles_ArticleId
on dbo.Articles(ArticleId);

create nonclustered index IDX_Articles_ExternalIdCheckSum
on dbo.Articles(ExternalIdCheckSum);
```

■ **Tip** You can index a calculated column without persisting it.

Even though the IDX_Articles_ExternalIdCheckSum index is going to be heavily fragmented, it will be more compact as compared to the index on the uniqueidentifier column (a 4-byte key versus 16 bytes). It also improves the performance of batch operations because of faster sorting, which also requires less memory to proceed.

One thing that you must keep in mind is that the result of the CHECKSUM() function is not guaranteed to be unique. You should include both predicates to the queries, as shown in Listing 7-7.

Listing 7-7. Using CHECKSUM(): Selecting data

```
select ArticleId /* Other Columns */
from dbo.Articles
where checksum(@ExternalId) = ExternalIdCheckSum and ExternalId = @ExternalId
```

■ **Tip** You can use the same technique in cases where you need to index string columns larger than 900/1,700 bytes, which is the maximum size of a nonclustered index key. Even though such an index would not support *range scan* operations, it could be used for *point lookups*.

Nonclustered Index Design Considerations

It is hard to find the tipping point where joining multiple nonclustered indexes is more efficient than using single nonclustered *index seek* and *key lookup* operations. When index selectivity is high and SQL Server estimates a small number of rows will be returned by the index seek operation, the key lookup cost would be relatively low. In such cases, there is no reason to use another nonclustered index. Alternatively, when index selectivity is low, index seek returns a large number of rows, and SQL Server typically would not use it because it is not efficient.

Let's look at an example where we will create a table and populate it with 1,048,576 rows. `Col1` stores 50 different values in the column, `Col2` stores 150 values, and `Col3` stores 200 values. Finally, we will create three different nonclustered indexes on the table. The code for doing this is shown in Listing 7-8.

Listing 7-8. Multiple nonclustered indexes: Table creation

```
create table dbo.IndexIntersection
(
    Id int not null,
    Placeholder char(100),
    Col1 int not null,
    Col2 int not null,
    Col3 int not null
);

create unique clustered index IDX_IndexIntersection_ID
on dbo.IndexIntersection(ID);

;with N1(C) as (select 0 union all select 0) -- 2 rows
,N2(C) as (select 0 from N1 as T1 cross join N1 as T2) -- 4 rows
,N3(C) as (select 0 from N2 as T1 cross join N2 as T2) -- 16 rows
,N4(C) as (select 0 from N3 as T1 cross join N3 as T2) -- 256 rows
,N5(C) as (select 0 from N4 as T1 cross join N4 as T2) -- 65,536 rows
,N6(C) as (select 0 from N3 as T1 cross join N5 as T2) -- 1,048,576 rows
,IDs(ID) as (select row_number() over (order by (select null)) from N6)
insert into dbo.IndexIntersection(ID, Col1, Col2, Col3)
    select ID, ID % 50, ID % 150, ID % 200 from IDs;

create nonclustered index IDX_IndexIntersection_Col1
on dbo.IndexIntersection(Col1);
create nonclustered index IDX_IndexIntersection_Col2
on dbo.IndexIntersection(Col2);
create nonclustered index IDX_IndexIntersection_Col3
on dbo.IndexIntersection(Col3);
```

For the next step, let's look at the execution plan of a query that selects data from the table using three predicates in the where clause. Each predicate can use an index seek operation on an individual index. The code for doing this is shown in Listing 7-9, and the execution plan is shown in Figure 7-5. As a side note, you might see a different execution plan and cardinality estimations in your environment based on the SQL Server version and service pack you have installed.

Listing 7-9. Multiple nonclustered indexes: Selecting data

```
select ID
from dbo.IndexIntersection
where Col1 = 42 and Col2 = 43 and Col3 = 44;
```

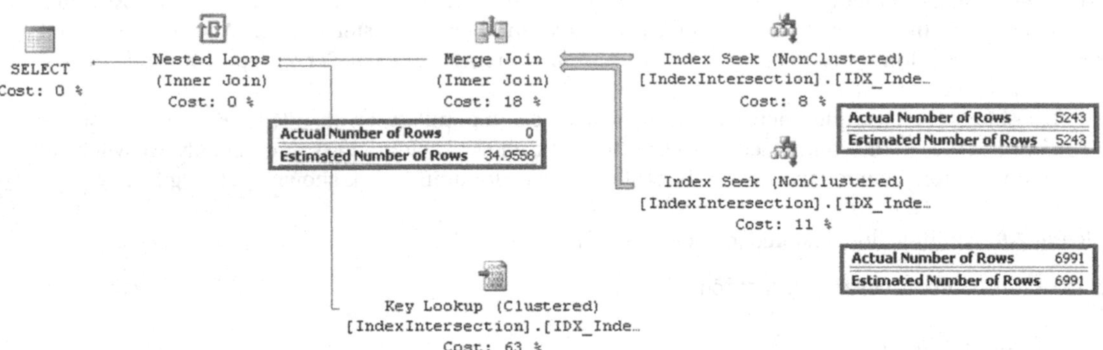

Figure 7-5. *Multiple nonclustered indexes: Execution plan with index intersection*

There are a couple of things worth mentioning here. Even though there is another nonclustered index on Col1, and all indexes include an ID column, which is row-id, SQL Server elects to use a key lookup rather than perform a third index seek operation. There are 20,971 rows in the table with Col1=42, which makes a key lookup the better choice.

Another important factor is the cardinality estimations. Even though SQL Server correctly estimates cardinality for both index seek operations, the estimation after the join operator is incorrect. SQL Server does not have any data about the correlation of column values in the table, which can lead to cardinality estimation errors and, potentially, suboptimal execution plans.

Let's add another covering index, which will include all three columns from the where clause, and run the query from Listing 7-9 again. The code creates the index shown in Listing 7-10. The execution plan is shown in Figure 7-6.

■ **Note** The new index with the two included columns makes the IDX_IndexIntersection_Col1 index redundant. We will discuss this situation later in this chapter.

Listing 7-10. Multiple nonclustered indexes: Adding a covering index

```
create nonclustered index IDX_IndexIntersection_Col3_Included
on dbo.IndexIntersection(Col3)
include (Col1, Col2)
```

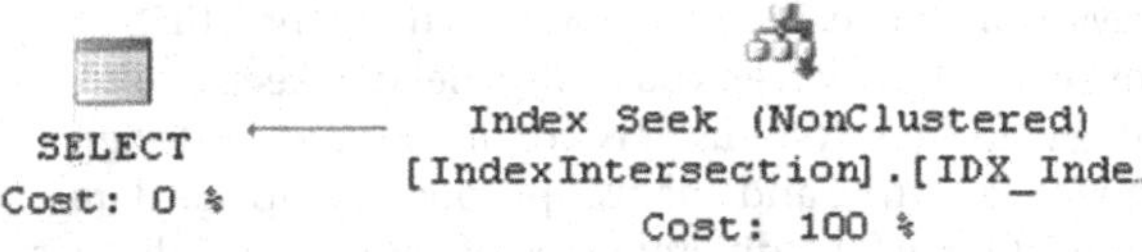

***Figure 7-6.** Multiple nonclustered indexes: Execution plan with covering index*

The CPU time and the number of reads are shown in Table 7-2.

***Table 7-2.** Index Intersection Versus Covering Index*

	Number of Reads	CPU Time (ms)
Index Intersection	29	9 ms
Covering Index	18	1 ms

Even though the number of reads is not very different in both cases, the CPU time of the query with index intersection is much higher than that for the query with a covering index.

A design with multiple narrow, nonclustered indexes, which lead to index intersection, can still help, especially in the case of a data warehouse workload where queries need to scan and aggregate a large amount of data. They are less efficient, however, when compared to covering indexes. It is usually better to create a small set of wide indexes with multiple columns included rather than a large number of narrow, perhaps single-column, indexes.

While ideal indexes would cover the queries, it is not a requirement. A small number of key lookup operations is perfectly acceptable. Ideally, SQL Server would perform a nonclustered index seek, filtering out rows even further by evaluating other predicates against included columns from the index. This would reduce the number of key lookups required. The key here is evaluating the query predicates against the data from nonclustered indexes rather than after the key lookup stage. You can achieve this by including predicate columns in the index.

It is impossible to advise you about how many indexes per table you should create. Moreover, it is different for systems with OLTP, data warehouse, or mixed workloads. In any case, that number fits into the "It Depends" category.

In OLTP systems, where data is highly volatile, you should have the *minimally required* set of indexes. While it is important to have enough indexes to provide sufficient query performance in the system, you must consider the data modification overhead introduced by them. In some cases, it is preferable to live with suboptimal performance of rarely executed queries rather than live with the overhead during every data modification operation.

In data warehouse environments, you can create a large number of indexes and/or indexed views, especially when data is relatively static and is refreshed based on a given schedule. In some cases, you can achieve better update performance by dropping indexes before and recreating them after the update. It is also worth mentioning that in dedicated data warehouse systems, you will usually get significantly better performance by using columnstore indexes.

■ **Note** We will discuss indexed views in Chapter 9, "Views." Columnstore indexes are covered in Part VIII of the book.

Working in mixed-workload environments is always a challenge. I tend to optimize them for OLTP activity, which is usually customer facing and thus more critical. However, you always need to keep reporting/data warehouse aspects in mind when dealing with such systems. It is not uncommon to design a set of tables to store aggregated data and then use them for reporting and analysis purposes, or to use data partitioning that combines row-based and column-based storage for a different type of data. We will discuss the latter scenario in Chapter 16 of this book.

Finally, remember to define indexes as unique whenever possible. Unique nonclustered indexes are more compact because they do not store row-id on non-leaf levels. Moreover, uniqueness helps the Query Optimizer to generate more efficient execution plans.

Optimizing and Tuning Indexes

System optimization and performance tuning is an iterative, never-ending process, especially in cases where a system is in development. New features and functions often require you to re-evaluate and refactor the code and change the indexes in the system.

While index tuning is an essential part of system optimization, it is hardly the only area on which you must focus. There are plenty of other factors besides bad or missing indexes that can lead to suboptimal performance. You must analyze the entire stack, which includes the hardware, operating system, SQL Server, and database configurations, when troubleshooting your systems.

■ **Note** We will talk about system troubleshooting in greater detail in Chapter 27, "System Troubleshooting."

Index tuning of existing systems may require a slightly different approach as compared to the development of new systems. With new development, it often makes sense to postpone index tuning until the later stages when the database schema and queries are more or less finalized. This approach helps to avoid spending time on optimizations that become obsolete due to code refactoring. This is especially true in the case of agile development environments, where such refactoring is routinely done at every iteration.

You should still create the minimally required set of indexes at the very beginning of new development. This includes primary key constraints and indexes and/or constraints to support uniqueness and referential integrity in the system. However, all further index tuning can be postponed until the later development stages.

There are two *must have* elements during the index tuning of new systems. First, the database should store enough data, ideally with data distribution similar to that expected in production. Second, you should be able to simulate workload, which helps to pinpoint the most common queries and inefficiencies in the system.

Optimization of existing systems requires a slightly different approach. Obviously, in some cases you must fix critical production issues, and there is no alternative but to add or adjust indexes quickly. However, as a general rule, you should perform index analysis and consolidation, remove unused and inefficient indexes, and sometimes refactor the queries before adding new indexes to the system. Let's look at all these steps in detail.

Detecting Unused and Inefficient Indexes

Indexes improve the performance of read operations. The term *read* is a bit confusing in the database world, however. Every DML query, such as `SELECT`, `INSERT`, `UPDATE`, `DELETE`, or `MERGE`, reads the data. For example, when you delete a row from a table, SQL Server reads a handful of pages, locating that row in every index.

■ **Note** Every database system, including the ones with highly volatile data, handles many more reads than writes.

At the same time, indexes introduce overhead during data modifications. Rows need to be inserted into or deleted from every index. Columns must be updated in every index where they are present. Obviously, we want to reduce such overhead and drop indexes that are not used very often.

SQL Server tracks index usage statistics internally and exposes it through the `sys.dm_db_index_usage_stats` and `sys.dm_db_index_operation_stats` DMOs.

The first data management view–`sys.dm_db_index_usage_stats`–provides information about different types of index operations and the time when such an operation was last performed. Let's look at an example and create a table, populate it with some data, and look at index usage statistics. The code for doing this is shown in Listing 7-11.

Listing 7-11. Index-usage statistics: Table creation

```
create table dbo.UsageDemo
(
    ID int not null,
    Col1 int not null,
    Col2 int not null,
    Placeholder char(8000) null
);

create unique clustered index IDX_CI on dbo.UsageDemo(ID);
create unique nonclustered index IDX_NCI1 on dbo.UsageDemo(Col1);
create unique nonclustered index IDX_NCI2 on dbo.UsageDemo(Col2);

;with N1(C) as (select 0 union all select 0) -- 2 rows
,N2(C) as (select 0 from N1 as T1 cross join N1 as T2) -- 4 rows
,N3(C) as (select 0 from N2 as T1 cross join N2 as T2) -- 16 rows
,IDs(ID) as (select row_number() over (order by (select null)) from N3)
insert into dbo.UsageDemo(ID, Col1, Col2)
    select ID, ID, ID from IDs;

select
    s.Name + N'.' + t.name as [Table] ,i.name as [Index]
    ,ius.user_seeks as [Seeks], ius.user_scans as [Scans]
    ,ius.user_lookups as [Lookups]
    ,ius.user_seeks + ius.user_scans + ius.user_lookups as [Reads]
    ,ius.user_updates as [Updates], ius.last_user_seek as [Last Seek]
    ,ius.last_user_scan as [Last Scan], ius.last_user_lookup as [Last Lookup]
    ,ius.last_user_update as [Last Update]
from
```

```
    sys.tables t join sys.indexes i on
        t.object_id = i.object_id
    join sys.schemas s on
        t.schema_id = s.schema_id
    left outer join sys.dm_db_index_usage_stats ius on
        ius.database_id = db_id() and
        ius.object_id = i.object_id and
        ius.index_id = i.index_id
where
    s.name = N'dbo' and t.name = N'UsageDemo'
order by
    s.name, t.name, i.index_id
```

The `user_seeks`, `user_scans`, and `user_lookups` columns in `sys.dm_db_index_usage_stats` indicate how many times the index was used for index seek, index scan, and key lookup operations respectively. `User_updates` indicates the number of inserts, updates, and deletes the index handled. The `sys.dm_index_usage_stats` DMV also returns statistics about index usage by the system as well as the last time the operation occurred.

As you can see in Figure 7-7, both clustered and nonclustered indexes were updated once, which is the `INSERT` statement in our case. Neither of the indexes were used for any type of read activity.

	Table	Index	Seeks	Scans	Lookups	Reads	Updates	Last Seek	Last Scan	Last Lookup	Las
1	dbo.UsageDemo	IDX_CI	0	0	0	0	1	NULL	NULL	NULL	20
2	dbo.UsageDemo	IDX_NCI1	0	0	0	0	1	NULL	NULL	NULL	20
3	dbo.UsageDemo	IDX_NCI2	0	0	0	0	1	NULL	NULL	NULL	20

***Figure 7-7.** Index usage statistics after table creation*

One thing worth mentioning is that we are using an outer join in the select. The `sys.dm_db_index_usage_stats` and `sys.dm_index_operation_stats` DMOs do not return any information about the index if it has not been used since statistics counters were reset.

■ **Important** Index usage statistics reset on SQL Server restarts. Moreover, they clear whenever the database is detached or shut down when the `AUTO_CLOSE` database property is enabled. Moreover, SQL Server 2012 and 2014 have a bug that resets statistics when the index is rebuilt. This bug is fixed in SQL Server 2012 SP3 CU3, SQL Server 2014 SP2, and SQL Server 2016.

You must keep this behavior in mind during index analysis. It is not uncommon to have indexes to support queries that execute on a given schedule. As an example, you can think about an index that supports a payroll process running on a bi-weekly or monthly basis. Index statistics information could indicate that the index has not been used for reads if SQL Server was recently restarted or, in the case of SQL Server 2012 RTM-SP3 CU2 and SQL Server 2014 RTM and SP1, if the index was recently rebuilt.

■ **Tip** You can consider creating and dropping such an index on a schedule in order to avoid update overhead in between-process executions.

Now, let's run a few queries against the dbo.UsageDemo table, as shown in Listing 7-12.

Listing 7-12. Index usage statistics: Queries

```
-- Query 1: CI Seek (Point lookup)
select Placeholder from dbo.UsageDemo where ID = 5;

-- Query 2: CI Seek (Range Scan)
select count(*)
from dbo.UsageDemo with (index=IDX_CI)
where ID between 2 and 6;

-- Query 3: CI Scan
select count(*) from dbo.UsageDemo with (index=IDX_CI);

-- Query 4: NCI Seek (Point Lookup + Key Lookup)
select Placeholder from dbo.UsageDemo where Col1 = 5;

-- Query 5: NCI Seek (Range Scan - all data from the table)
select count(*) from dbo.UsageDemo where Col1 > -1;

-- Query 6: NCI Seek (Range Scan + Key Lookup)
select sum(Col2)
from dbo.UsageDemo with (index = IDX_NCI1)
where Col1 between 1 and 5;

-- Queries 7-8: Updates
update dbo.UsageDemo set Col2 = -3 where Col1 = 3;
update dbo.UsageDemo set Col2 = -4 where Col1 = 4;
```

If you run the SELECT, which displays index usage statistics, again, you would see the results shown in Figure 7-8.

	Table	Index	Seeks	Scans	Lookups	Reads	Updates	Last	
1	dbo.UsageDemo	IDX_CI	2	1	4	7	3	201	'1.900
2	dbo.UsageDemo	IDX_NCI1	5	0	0	5	1	201	.4.897
3	dbo.UsageDemo	IDX_NCI2	0	0	0	0	3	NUL	'1.900

Figure 7-8. *Index usage statistics after several queries*

There are a couple of important things to note here. First, sys.dm_db_index_usage_stats returns how many times the corresponding operations appear in the execution plan. For example, there are only four lookup operations returned for the IDX_CI index, which indicates that there were four queries with the key lookup operation in the execution plan, regardless of how many key lookups were actually performed during query execution.

Second, the sys.dm_db_index_usage_stats DMV counts both point lookups and range scans as seeks, which corresponds to the index seek operator. This could mask a situation in which an index seek performs range scans on a large number of rows. For example, the fifth query in our example scanned all rows from the IDX_NCI1 index, although it was counted as *Seek* rather than *Scan*.

When you do such an analysis in production systems, you can consider removing indexes that handle more updates than reads, similar to IDX_NCI2 from our example. In some cases, it is also beneficial not to count scan operations toward reads, especially in OLTP environments, where queries that perform index scans should usually be optimized.

While sys.dm_db_index_usage provides a good high-level overview of index usage based on operations from the execution plan, sys.dm_db_index_operation_stats dives deeper and provides detailed level I/O, access methods, and locking statistics for the indexes.

The key difference between two DMOs is how they collect data. Sys.dm_db_index_usage_stats tracks how many times an operation appeared in the execution plan. Alternatively, sys.dm_db_index_operation_stats tracks operations at the row level. In our key lookup example, sys.dm_db_index_operation_stats would report eight operations rather than four.

Even though sys.dm_db_index_operation_stats provides very detailed information about index usage, I/O, and locking overhead, it could become overwhelming, especially during the initial performance-tuning stage. It is usually easier to do an initial analysis with sys.dm_db_index_usage_stats and then use sys.dm_db_index_operation_stats later when fine-tuning the system.

■ **Note** You can read more about sys.dm_db_index_operation_stats DMF at Books Online: http://technet.microsoft.com/en-us/library/ms174281.aspx

■ **Important** Make sure that usage statistics collect enough information representing typical system workload before performing an analysis.

Index Consolidation

As we discussed in Chapter 2, "Tables and Indexes: Internal Structure and Access Methods," SQL Server can use a composite index for an index seek operation as long as a query has a SARGable predicate on the leftmost query column.

Let's look at the table shown in Listing 7-13. There are two nonclustered indexes, IDX_Employee_LastName_FirstName and IDX_Employee_LastName, which each have a LastName column defined as the leftmost column. The first index, IDX_Employee_LastName_FirstName, can be used for an index seek operation as long as there is a SARGable predicate on the LastName column, even when a query does not have a predicate on the FirstName column. Thus, the IDX_Employee_LastName index is redundant.

Listing 7-13. Example of redundant indexes

```
create table dbo.Employee
(
    EmployeeId int not null,
    LastName nvarchar(64) not null,
    FirstName nvarchar(64) not null,
    DateOfBirth date not null,
    Phone varchar(20) nul
);
```

```
create unique clustered index IDX_Employee_EmployeeId
on dbo.Employee(EmployeeId);

create nonclustered index IDX_Employee_LastName_FirstName
on dbo.Employee(LastName, FirstName);

create nonclustered index IDX_Employee_LastName
on dbo.Employee(LastName);
```

As a general rule, you can remove redundant indexes from the system. Although such indexes can be slightly more efficient during scans due to their compact size, update overhead usually outweighs this benefit.

Obviously, there are always exceptions to the rule. Consider a Shopping Cart system that allows for searching for products by part of their name. There are several ways to implement this feature, though when the table is small enough, an index scan operation performed on the nonclustered index on the Name column may provide acceptable performance. In such a scenario, you want to have the index be as compact as possible to reduce its size and the number of reads required during a scan operation. Thus, you might consider keeping a separate nonclustered index on the Name column, even when this index can be consolidated with other ones.

The script shown in Listing 7-14 returns information about potentially redundant indexes with the same leftmost column defined. Figure 7-9 shows the result of the execution.

Listing 7-14. Detecting potentially redundant indexes

```
select
    s.Name + N'.' + t.name as [Table]
    ,i1.index_id as [Index1 ID], i1.name as [Index1 Name]
    ,dupIdx.index_id as [Index2 ID], dupIdx.name as [Index2 Name]
    ,c.name as [Column]
from
    sys.tables t join sys.indexes i1 on
        t.object_id = i1.object_id
    join sys.index_columns ic1 on
        ic1.object_id = i1.object_id and
        ic1.index_id = i1.index_id and
        ic1.index_column_id = 1
    join sys.columns c on
        c.object_id = ic1.object_id and
        c.column_id = ic1.column_id
    join sys.schemas s on
        t.schema_id = s.schema_id
        cross apply
        (
            select i2.index_id, i2.name
            from
```

```
                sys.indexes i2 join sys.index_columns ic2 on
                    ic2.object_id = i2.object_id and
                    ic2.index_id = i2.index_id and
                    ic2.index_column_id = 1
            where
                i2.object_id = i1.object_id and
                i2.index_id > i1.index_id and
                ic2.column_id = ic1.column_id
        ) dupIdx
order by
    s.name, t.name, i1.index_id
```

	Table	Index1 ID	Index1 Name	Index2 ID	Index2 Name	Column
1	dbo.Employee	2	IDX_Employee_LastName_FirstName	3	IDX_Employee_LastName	LastName

Figure 7-9. *Potentially redundant indexes*

After you detect potentially redundant indexes, you should analyze all of them on a case-by-case basis. In some instances, consolidation is trivial. For example, if a system has two indexes, `IDX1(LastName, FirstName) include (Phone)` and `IDX2(LastName) include(DateOfBirth)`, you can consolidate them as `IDX3(LastName, FirstName) include(DateOfBirth, Phone)`.

In the other cases, consolidation requires further analysis. For example, if a system has two indexes, `IDX1(OrderDate, WarehouseId)` and `IDX2(OrderDate, OrderStatus)`, you have three options. You can consolidate it as `IDX3(OrderDate, WarehouseId) include(OrderStatus)` or as `IDX4(OrderDate, OrderStatus) include(WarehouseId)`. Finally, you can leave both indexes in place. The decision primarily depends on the selectivity of the leftmost column and index usage statistics.

■ **Tip** The `sys.dm_db_index_operation_stats` function provides information about index usage at the row level. Moreover, it tracks the number of point lookups separately from range scans. It is beneficial to use this function when analyzing index consolidation options.

Finally, you should remember that the goal of index consolidation is removing *redundant* and *unnecessary* indexes. While reducing index update overhead is important, it is safer to keep an unnecessary index than it is to drop a *necessary* one. You should always err on the side of caution during this process.

Detecting Suboptimal Queries

There are plenty of ways to detect suboptimal queries using both standard SQL Server and third-party tools. There are two main metrics to analyze when detecting suboptimal queries: number of I/O operations and CPU time of the query.

Having a large number of I/O operations is often a sign of suboptimal or missing indexes, especially in OLTP systems. It also affects query CPU time—the more data that needs to be processed, the more CPU time that needs to be consumed doing it. However, the opposite is not always true. There are plenty of factors besides I/O that can contribute to high CPU time. The most common ones are multi-statement user-defined functions; imperative code; and calculations.

■ **Note** We will discuss user-defined functions in more detail in Chapter 10, "Functions."

SQL Profiler is, perhaps, the most commonly used tool to detect suboptimal queries. You can set up a SQL trace to capture a `SQL:Stmt Completed` event and filter it by the `Reads`, `CPU`, or `Duration` columns.

There is a difference between CPU time and duration, however. The `CPU` column indicates how much CPU time a query uses. The `Duration` column stores total query execution time. With parallel execution plans, the CPU time consists of the time spent by all CPUs and could exceed the duration. High duration, however, does not necessarily indicate high CPU time, as blocking and I/O latency affect the execution time of the query.

Starting with SQL Server 2008, it is better to use Extended Events rather than SQL Profiler. Extended Events are more flexible and introduce less overhead as compared to SQL traces.

■ **Note** We will discuss Extended Events in greater detail in Chapter 28, "Extended Events."

SQL Server tracks execution statistics for queries and exposes them via the `sys.dm_exec_query_stats` DMV. Querying this DMV is, perhaps, the easiest way to find the most expensive queries in the system. Listing 7-15 shows an example of a query that returns information about the fifty most expensive queries in a system in terms of the average I/O per execution.

Listing 7-15. Using sys.dm_exec_query_stats

```
select top 50
    substring(qt.text, (qs.statement_start_offset/2)+1,
     ((
        case qs.statement_end_offset
            when -1 then datalength(qt.text)
            else qs.statement_end_offset
        end - qs.statement_start_offset)/2)+1) as [Sql]
    ,qs.execution_count as [Exec Cnt]
    ,(qs.total_logical_reads + qs.total_logical_writes)
            / qs.execution_count as [Avg IO]
    ,qp.query_plan as [Plan]
    ,qs.total_logical_reads as [Total Reads]
    ,qs.last_logical_reads as [Last Reads]
    ,qs.total_logical_writes as [Total Writes]
    ,qs.last_logical_writes as [Last Writes]
    ,qs.total_worker_time as [Total Worker Time]
    ,qs.last_worker_time as [Last Worker Time]
    ,qs.total_elapsed_time/1000 as [Total Elps Time]
    ,qs.last_elapsed_time/1000 as [Last Elps Time]
    ,qs.creation_time as [Compile Time]
    ,qs.last_execution_time as [Last Exec Time]
from
    sys.dm_exec_query_stats qs with (nolock)
        cross apply sys.dm_exec_sql_text(qs.sql_handle) qt
        cross apply sys.dm_exec_query_plan(qs.plan_handle) qp
order by
     [Avg IO] desc
option (recompile)
```

The query result, shown in Figure 7-10, helps you quickly identify optimization targets in the system. In our example, the second query in the result set executes very often, which makes it an ideal candidate for optimization, even though it is not the most expensive query in the system. Obviously, you can sort the results by other criteria, such as the number of executions, execution time, and so on.

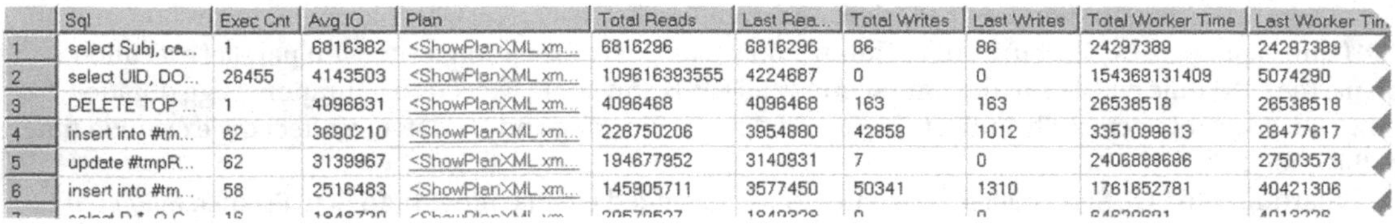

	Sql	Exec Cnt	Avg IO	Plan	Total Reads	Last Rea...	Total Writes	Last Writes	Total Worker Time	Last Worker Tim
1	select Subj, ca...	1	6816382	<ShowPlanXML xm...	6816296	6816296	86	86	24297389	24297389
2	select UID, DO...	26455	4143503	<ShowPlanXML xm...	109616393555	4224687	0	0	154369131409	5074290
3	DELETE TOP ...	1	4096631	<ShowPlanXML xm...	4096468	4096468	163	163	26538518	26538518
4	insert into #tm...	62	3690210	<ShowPlanXML xm...	228750206	3954880	42859	1012	3351099613	28477617
5	update #tmpR...	62	3139967	<ShowPlanXML xm...	194677952	3140931	7	0	2406888686	27503573
6	insert into #tm...	58	2516483	<ShowPlanXML xm...	145905711	3577450	50341	1310	1761652781	40421306
7	[illegible]	[illegible]	[illegible]	[illegible]	[illegible]	[illegible]	[illegible]	[illegible]	[illegible]	[illegible]

Figure 7-10. *Sys.dm_exec_query_stats results*

Unfortunately, `sys.dm_exec_query_stats` returns information only about queries with execution plans cached. As a result, there are no statistics for those statements that use a statement-level recompile with `option (recompile)`. Moreover, `execution_count` data can be misleading if a query was recently recompiled. You can correlate the `execution_count` and `creation_time` columns to detect the most frequently executed queries.

■ **Note** We will discuss plan caches in greater detail in Chapter 26, "Plan Caching."

Starting with SQL Server 2008, there is another DMV, `sys.dm_exec_procedure_stats`, which returns similar information about stored procedures that have execution plans cached. Listing 7-16 shows a query that returns a list of the fifty most I/O-intensive procedures. Figure 7-11 shows the results of this query on one of the production servers.

Listing 7-16. Using sys.dm_exec_procedure_stats

```
select top 50
    s.name + '.' + p.name as [Procedure]
    ,qp.query_plan as [Plan]
    ,(ps.total_logical_reads + ps.total_logical_writes) /
            ps.execution_count as [Avg IO]
    ,ps.execution_count as [Exec Cnt]
    ,ps.cached_time as [Cached]
    ,ps.last_execution_time as [Last Exec Time]
    ,ps.total_logical_reads as [Total Reads]
    ,ps.last_logical_reads as [Last Reads]
    ,ps.total_logical_writes as [Total Writes]
    ,ps.last_logical_writes as [Last Writes]
    ,ps.total_worker_time as [Total Worker Time]
    ,ps.last_worker_time as [Last Worker Time]
    ,ps.total_elapsed_time as [Total Elapsed Time]
    ,ps.last_elapsed_time as [Last Elapsed Time]
from
```

```
    sys.procedures as p with (nolock) join sys.schemas s with (nolock) on
        p.schema_id = s.schema_id
    join sys.dm_exec_procedure_stats as ps with (nolock) on
        p.object_id = ps.object_id
    outer apply sys.dm_exec_query_plan(ps.plan_handle) qp
order by
     [Avg IO] desc
option (recompile);
```

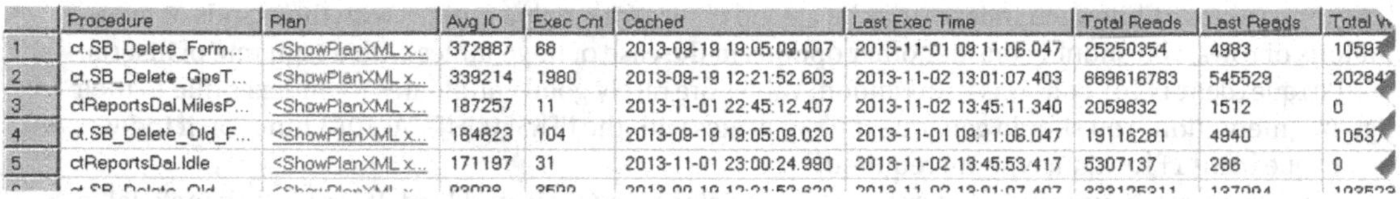

	Procedure	Plan	Avg IO	Exec Cnt	Cached	Last Exec Time	Total Reads	Last Reads	Total W...
1	ct.SB_Delete_Form...	<ShowPlanXML x...	372887	68	2013-09-19 19:05:09.007	2013-11-01 09:11:06.047	25250354	4983	1059
2	ct.SB_Delete_GpsT...	<ShowPlanXML x...	339214	1980	2013-09-19 12:21:52.603	2013-11-02 13:01:07.403	669616783	545529	20284
3	ctReportsDal.MilesP...	<ShowPlanXML x...	187257	11	2013-11-01 22:45:12.407	2013-11-02 13:45:11.340	2059832	1512	0
4	ct.SB_Delete_Old_F...	<ShowPlanXML x...	184823	104	2013-09-19 19:05:09.020	2013-11-01 09:11:06.047	19116281	4940	1053
5	ctReportsDal.Idle	<ShowPlanXML x...	171197	31	2013-11-01 23:00:24.990	2013-11-02 13:45:53.417	5307137	286	0

Figure 7-11. *Sys.dm_exec_procedure_stats results*

■ **Note** We will discuss the `sys.dm_exec_query_stats` and `sys.dm_exec_procedure_stats` views in greater detail in Chapter 28, "System Troubleshooting."

SQL Server collects information about missing indexes in the system and exposes it via a set of DMVs with names starting at `sys.dm_db_missing_index`. Moreover, you can see suggestions for creating such indexes in the execution plans displayed in Management Studio.

There are two caveats when dealing with suggestions about missing indexes. First, SQL Server suggests the index, which only helps the particular query you are executing. It does not take update overhead, other queries, and existing indexes into consideration. For example, if a table already has an index that covers the query with the exception of one column, SQL Server suggests creating a new index rather than changing an existing one.

Moreover, suggested indexes help to improve the performance of a specific execution plan. SQL Server does not consider indexes that can change the execution plan shape and, for example, use a more efficient join type for the query.

■ **Important** Creating indexes strictly based on suggestions from missing indexes DMVs will lead to a large number of redundant and inefficient indexes in the system.

The quality of Database Engine Tuning Advisor (DTA) results greatly depends on the quality of the workload used for analysis. Good and representative workload data leads to decent results, which is much better than the suggestions provided by missing indexes DMVs. Make sure to capture the workload, which includes data modification queries in addition to select queries, if you use DTA.

Regardless of the quality of the tools, all of them have the same limitation: they are analyzing and tuning indexes based on existing database schema and code. You can often achieve much better results by performing database schema and code refactoring in addition to index tuning.

Summary

An ideal clustered index is narrow, static, and unique. Moreover, it optimizes the most important queries against the table and reduces fragmentation. It is often impossible to design a clustered index that satisfies all of the five design guidelines provided in this chapter. You should analyze the system, business requirements, and workload and choose the most efficient clustered indexes—even when they violate some of those guidelines.

Ever-increasing clustered indexes usually have low fragmentation because the data is inserted at the end of the table. A good example of such indexes are identities, sequences, and ever-incrementing date/time values. While such indexes may be a good choice for catalog entities with thousands or even millions of rows, you should consider other options in the case of huge tables with a high rate of inserts.

`Uniqueidentifier` columns with random values are rarely good candidates for indexes due to their high fragmentation. You should generate the key values with the `NEWSEQUENTIALID()` function if indexes on the `uniqueidentifier` data type are required.

SQL Server rarely uses index intersection, especially in an OLTP workload. It is usually beneficial to have a small set of wide, composite, nonclustered indexes with included columns rather than a large set of narrow one-column indexes.

In OLTP systems, you should create a minimally required set of indexes to avoid index update overhead. In data warehouse systems, the number of indexes greatly depends on the data-refresh strategy. You should also consider using columnstore indexes in dedicated data warehouse databases.

It is important to drop unused and inefficient indexes and perform index consolidation before adding new indexes to the system. This simplifies the optimization process and reduces data modification overhead. SQL Server provides index usage statistics with the `sys.dm_db_index_usage_stats` and `sys.dm_db_index_operation_stats` DMOs.

You can use SQL Server Profiler, Extended Events, and DMVs, such as `sys.dm_exec_query_stats` and `sys.dm_exec_procedure_stats`, to detect inefficient queries. Moreover, there are plenty of tools that can help with monitoring and index tuning. With all that being said, you should always consider query and database schema refactoring as an option. It often leads to much better performance improvements when compared to index tuning by itself.

PART II

Other Things That Matter

CHAPTER 8

Constraints

It is important to design databases in a way that makes efficient processing and querying of the data possible. That by itself, however, is not enough. We must make sure that the data we get from the database can be trusted. Think about an Order Entry system, for example. We can query the `OrderLineItems` table to get the information about products we sold, but we cannot trust the results unless we know that the table has no orphaned rows that do not belong to any orders in our system.

Constraints allow us to declare the data integrity and business rules for the database and have SQL Server enforce them. They ensure that data is *logically* correct, help us to catch bugs in the early stages of development, and improve the supportability and performance of the system. Let's look at the different types of constraints in more detail.

Primary Key Constraints

Conceptually, database design can be separated into logical and physical design stages. During the logical database design stage, we identify the entities in systems based on business requirements, and we define the attributes and relations between them. After that, during the physical database design stage, we map those entities to the database tables, defining data access strategies through the indexes and design the physical data placement across different filegroups and storage arrays.

Even though the logical and physical database design stages are often mixed together, conceptually they are separate from each other and can even be performed by different teams, especially on large projects.

Primary key constraints define the attribute or set of attributes that uniquely identify an object in an entity or in the physical database design scope; that is, a row in a table. Internally, primary key constraints are implemented as unique indexes. By default, SQL Server creates a primary key as a unique clustered index, although it is not a requirement. We can have nonclustered primary keys, or we can even have tables with no primary keys at all.

As you have probably already noticed, the first part of this book did not mention primary keys, and it routinely used *clustered indexes* instead. This was done on purpose. Primary keys conceptually belong to the logical database design domain, while clustered and nonclustered indexes are the part of the physical database design.

Database professionals, however, often mix the two by defining the clustered indexes as primary keys, even though, in some cases, it is incorrect from a logical design standpoint. For example, consider an Order Entry system with an `Orders` table with an `OrderId` identity column. This column uniquely identifies the order row, and it would be a perfect candidate for a primary key constraint. Whether it is a clustered or nonclustered primary key depends on the other factors, mainly on how we query and work with the data. In the end, we would have something similar to the code shown in Listing 8-1.

D. Korotkevitch, *Pro SQL Server Internals*, DOI 10.1007/978-1-4842-1964-5_8

Listing 8-1. Orders table

```
create table dbo.Orders
(
    OrderId int not null identity(1,1),
    -- other columns
    constraint PK_Orders
    primary key clustered(OrderId)
)
```

The `OrderLineItems` table could have two key columns: `OrderId`, which references the row from the `Orders` table, and the `OrderLineItemId` identity column. In most cases, we will work with `OrderLineItems` in the context of the specific `Order` and will have `OrderId` as the predicate in our queries. Therefore, the natural candidate for the clustered index in this table would be `(OrderId, OrderLineItemId)`. It would be *logically* incorrect, however, to define that clustered index as the primary key—the row can be uniquely identified by the single `OrderLineItemId` identity column, and we do not need `OrderId` for this purpose.

The question of whether we want to define a nonclustered primary key on `OrderLineItemId` depends on the other factors. From the logical design standpoint, it would be the right thing to do, especially if the table is referenced by the other tables with foreign key constraints, which we will discuss later in this chapter. This would introduce another nonclustered index, however, which we need to store and maintain. The final implementation might be similar to the code shown in Listing 8-2.

Listing 8-2. OrderLineItems table

```
create table dbo.OrderLineItems
(
    OrderId int not null,
    OrderLineItemId int not null identity(1,1),
    -- other columns

    constraint PK_OrderLineItems
    primary key nonclustered(OrderLineItemId)
);

create unique clustered index IDX_OrderLineItems_OrderId_OrderLineItemId
on dbo.OrderLineItems(OrderId,OrderLineItemId);
```

While primary keys can be represented as unique indexes from the physical implementation standpoint, there is the minor difference between them. No primary key columns can be nullable. On the other hand, unique indexes can be created on the nullable columns and would treat `NULL` as the regular value.

One very important thing to remember is that we cannot change the definition of the primary key or, in fact, change the definition of any constraint without dropping and recreating it. As a result, if a primary key constraint is clustered, it will lead to two table rebuilds. Dropping the constraint would remove the clustered index and convert the table to a heap table. Adding a clustered primary key creates a clustered index on the heap table. Alternatively, changing the definition of the clustered index would lead to the single index rebuild.

■ **Tip** Disable nonclustered indexes in case you need to drop and recreate a clustered primary key constraint. Enable (rebuild) them after both operations are done. This will speed up the process, because nonclustered indexes will be rebuilt only once after the operation is completed rather than during each step.

Primary keys usually benefit the system. They provide better data integrity and improve the supportability of the system. I would recommend defining the primary keys when you can afford to have the additional index on the primary key columns.

■ **Note** Some SQL Server features, such as transactional replication, require that tables have primary keys defined. Defining a clustered index without a primary key is not sufficient.

Because primary keys are implemented as regular indexes, there is no special catalog view for them. You can look at the `is_primary_key` column in the `sys.indexes` catalog view to determine if the index is defined as the primary key.

■ **Note** SQL Server Catalog Views allow us to obtain information about database and server metadata programmatically. See `http://technet.microsoft.com/en-us/library/ms174365.aspx` for more details.

Unique Constraints

Unique constraints enforce the uniqueness of the values from one or multiple attributes in the entity or, in the physical world, columns in the table. Similar to primary keys, unique constraints uniquely identify rows in a table, although they can be created on the nullable columns and would thus treat `NULL` as one of the possible values. Like primary keys, unique constraints belong to the logical database design and are implemented as unique, nonclustered indexes on the physical level.

The code in Listing 8-3 shows a table with two unique constraints defined: one constraint defined on the `SSN` column and another one on the combination of the `DepartmentCode` and `IntraDepartmentCode` columns.

Listing 8-3. Defining unique constraints

```
create table dbo.Employees
(
    EmployeeId int not null
        constraint PK_Employees primary key clustered,
    Name nvarchar(64) not null,
    SSN char(9) not null
        constraint UQ_Employees_SSN unique,
    DepartmentCode varchar(32) not null,
    IntraDepartmentCode varchar(32) not null,

    constraint UQ_Employees_Codes
    unique(DepartmentCode, IntraDepartmentCode)
)
```

As you can see in Figure 8-1, SQL Server Management Studio lists unique (and primary key) constraints in two different places: under both the *Key* and *Indexes* nodes.

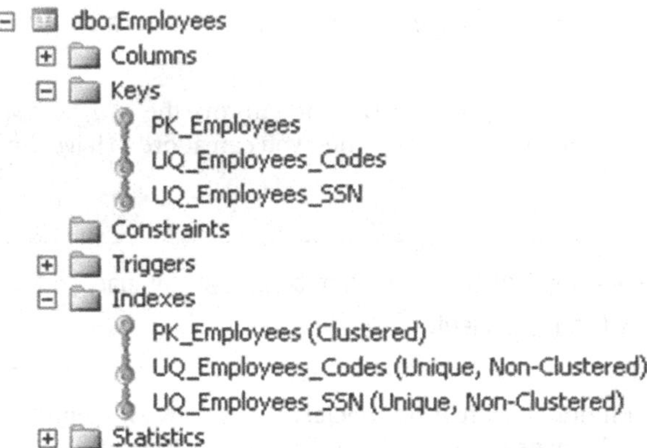

Figure 8-1. *Unique constraints in SQL Server Management Studio*

Generally, it is a good idea to have uniqueness enforced when data is unique. This helps to keep the data clean and avoids data integrity issues. Unique constraints can also help Query Optimizer to generate more efficient execution plans. The downside is that you will have to maintain another nonclustered index for every uniqueness condition you define. You need to consider the data modification and index maintenance overhead that are introduced when choosing to implement constraints.

Whether to choose a unique constraint or a unique index largely depends on personal preferences. Uniqueness usually comes in the form of a business requirement, and enforcing uniqueness with constraints can contribute to system supportability. On the other hand, unique indexes are more flexible. You can include columns and use those indexes for query optimization purposes in addition to uniqueness enforcement. You can also specify the sorting order, which can help in some rare cases.

It is also impossible to alter a unique constraint definition without dropping and recreating it. Even though dropping a constraint is a metadata operation, which does not introduce data movement, there is a possibility that a uniqueness rule will be violated when a constraint is dropped. Alternatively, you can change the unique index definition in atomary operation by using the `CREATE INDEX .. WITH (DROP_EXISTING=ON)` statement.

Like primary key constraints, there is no special catalog view for unique constraints. There is the column `is_unique_constraint` in the `sys.indexes` catalog view, which shows if an index is created as a unique constraint.

Foreign Key Constraints

Foreign key constraints identify and enforce relations between entities/tables. Think about our `Orders` and `OrderLineItems` tables example. Every `OrderLineItems` row belongs to a corresponding `Orders` row and cannot exist by itself. These kinds of relations are enforced with foreign key constraints.

Like other constraints, foreign keys enforce data integrity. It is always easier to deal with clean and correct data rather than cleaning up data on the fly. In addition, during the development and testing stages, foreign keys help catch a good number of bugs related to incorrect data processing.

However, foreign keys come with a price. Every time you insert data into the *referencing* table, you need to check to see if there are corresponding rows in the *referenced* table. Let's look at the example using the same `Orders` and `OrderLineItems` tables we created earlier in this chapter. When you insert a row into the `OrderLineItems` table without any foreign keys defined, the query needs to perform only one clustered index insert operation, as shown in Figure 8-2.

***Figure 8-2.** Inserting a row into the referencing table with no foreign key constraint defined*

Now, let's add a foreign key constraint to the table. Listing 8-4 shows the `ALTER TABLE` statement, which performs this task.

Listing 8-4. Adding a foreign key constraint to the OrderLineItems table

```
alter table dbo.OrderLineItems with check
add constraint FK_OrderLineItems_Orders
foreign key(OrderId)
references dbo.Orders(OrderId)
```

When you run the insert again, you will see that the execution plan changes, as shown in Figure 8-3.

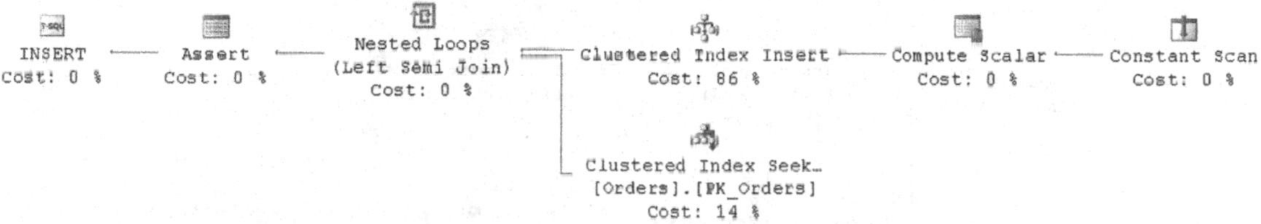

***Figure 8-3.** Inserting a row into the referencing table with a foreign key constraint defined*

As you can see, the plan now includes a clustered index seek operation on the *referenced* (`Orders`) table. SQL Server needs to validate the foreign key constraint and make sure that there is a corresponding order row for the line item that you are inserting.

Now, let's see what happens when you delete the row from the `Orders` table. As you see in Figure 8-4, our execution plan now includes a clustered index seek on the *referencing* (`OrderLineItems`) table. SQL Server needs to check to see if there are any line-item rows that reference the row you are deleting. If there are any such line-item rows, SQL Server either aborts the deletion or performs some cascade actions, depending on the rules of the foreign key constraint.

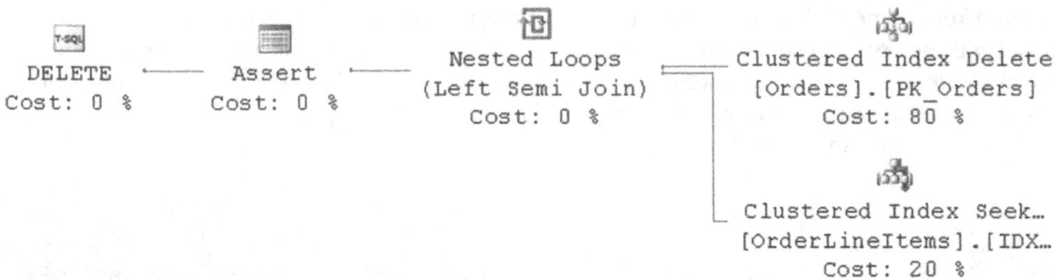

Figure 8-4. *Deleting a row from the referenced table (no cascade actions)*

Let's add an `ON DELETE CASCADE` action to the foreign-key constraint, as shown in Listing 8-5. Now when you delete the row from the `Orders` table, SQL Server needs to find and delete the referencing rows from the `OrderLineItems` table. The execution plan is shown in Figure 8-5.

Listing 8-5. Replacing the constraint with ON DELETE CASCADE action

```
alter table dbo.OrderLineItems drop constraint FK_OrderLineItems_Orders;

alter table dbo.OrderLineItems with check
add constraint FK_OrderLineItems_Orders
foreign key(OrderId)
references dbo.Orders(OrderId)
on delete cascade;
```

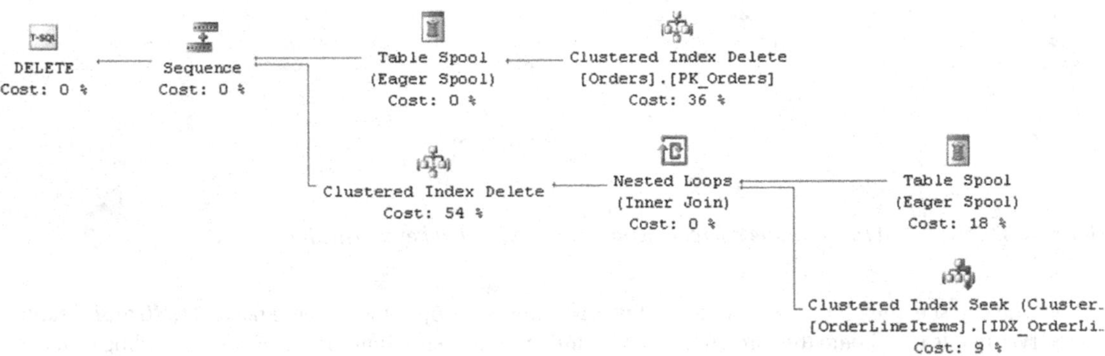

Figure 8-5. *Deleting a row from the referenced table (ON DELETE CASCADE action)*

There is one very important thing to remember: when you create the foreign key constraint, SQL Server requires you to have a unique index on the *referenced* (`OrderId`) column in the *referenced* (`Orders`) table. However, there is no requirement to have a similar index on the *referencing* (`OrderLineItems`) table. If you do not have such an index, any referential integrity checks on the referencing tables will introduce the scan operation. In order to prove this, let's drop the clustered index on the `OrderLineItems` table using the `DROP INDEX IDX_OrderLineItems_OrderId_OrderLineItemId ON dbo.OrderLineItems` statement.

Now, when you run the deletion again, you will see the execution plan, as shown in Figure 8-6.

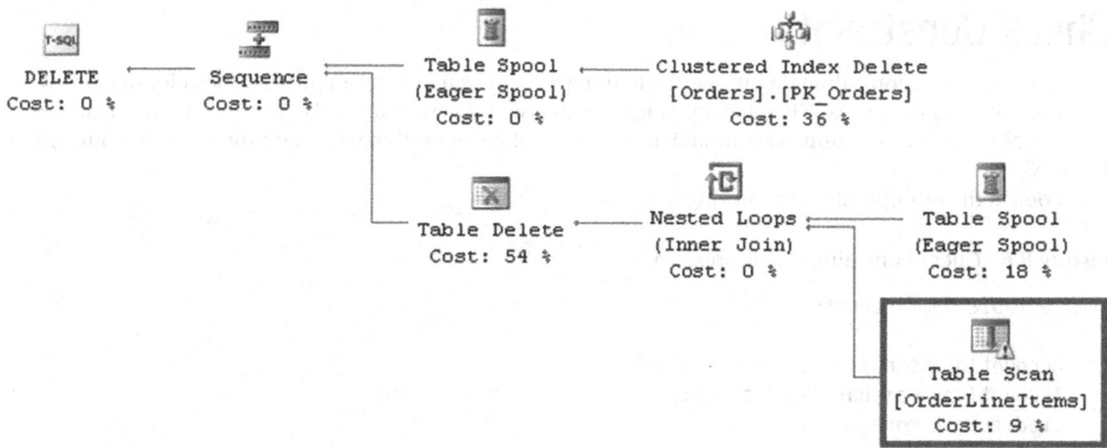

Figure 8-6. *Deleting the row from the referenced table without an index specified on the referencing column*

Missing indexes on the referencing columns could have a huge performance impact in the case of large tables. This would introduce excessive and unnecessary I/O load and contribute to blocking. Also, besides referential integrity support, those indexes can be helpful during join operations between the tables. With very rare exceptions, you should create those indexes when you create the foreign key constraints.

In some cases, foreign key constraints can help the Query Optimizer. They can help eliminate unnecessary joins, especially when views are involved, as well as improve the performance of some queries in data warehouse environments.

■ **Note** We will discuss join elimination in greater detail in Chapter 10, "Views."

Unfortunately, foreign keys are incompatible with some SQL Server features. For example, when a table is partitioned and referenced by a foreign key, you cannot alter the table and switch the partition to another table. You can still have the table partitioned, however, if a partition switch is not involved. Another example is table truncation. You cannot truncate a table when it is referenced by foreign keys.

Defining foreign key constraints is usually a good thing, assuming, of course, that you are OK with the extra indexes and that the system can handle the slight performance overhead introduced by index seek operations during referential integrity checks. In OLTP systems, I recommend that you always create foreign keys when referencing catalog entities where the amount of data is relatively small and static. For example, an order-entry system's catalog entities would include *Articles, Customers, Warehouses,* and so forth. You need to be careful, however, when dealing with transactional entities that store billions of rows and handle thousands of inserts per second. I would still use foreign keys whenever possible, though I would analyze the performance implications on a case-by-case basis.

There are a couple of catalog views, `sys.foreign_keys` and `sys.foreign_key_columns`, that provide information concerning any foreign key constraints that are defined in the database.

Check Constraints

Check constraints enforce domain integrity by limiting the values that you can put into the column or into multiple columns in the row. They specify a logical expression that is evaluated every time a row is inserted or when corresponding columns are modified, and they fail the operation when an expression is evaluated as *FALSE*.

Look at the example shown in Listing 8-6.

Listing 8-6. Check constaints: Table creation

```
create table dbo.Accounts
(
    AccountId int not null identity(1,1),
    AccountType varchar(32) not null,
    CreditLimit money null,

    constraint CHK_Accounts_AccountType
    check (AccountType in ('Checking','Saving','Credit Card')),

    constraint CHK_Accounts_CreditLimit_For_CC
    check ((AccountType <> 'Credit Card') or (CreditLimit > 0))
)
```

There are two check constraints specified. The first one, `CHK_Accounts_AccountType`, enforces the rule that `AccountType` needs to belong to one of three values. The second one is more complex. It enforces the rule that, for credit card accounts, there should be a positive `CreditLimit` provided. One key point to remember is that data is rejected only when a constraint expression is evaluated as *FALSE*. `NULL` results are accepted. For example, the `INSERT` statement shown in Listing 8-7 works just fine.

Listing 8-7. Check constaints: Inserting a NULL value

```
insert into dbo.Accounts(AccountType, CreditLimit)
values('Credit Card',null)
```

The main purpose of check constraints is to enforce data integrity, although they can, in some cases, help Query Optimizer and simplify execution plans. Assume that you have two tables: one that contains positive numbers and another one that contains negative numbers, as shown in Listing 8-8.

Listing 8-8. Check constaints: PositiveNumbers and NegativeNumbers tables creation

```
create table dbo.PositiveNumbers
( PositiveNumber int not null );

create table dbo.NegativeNumbers
( NegativeNumber int not null );

insert into dbo.PositiveNumbers(PositiveNumber) values(1);
insert into dbo.NegativeNumbers(NegativeNumber) values(-1);
```

Now, let's run a `SELECT` that joins the data from those two tables. You can see the `SELECT` statement in Listing 8-9 and the execution plan in Figure 8-7.

Listing 8-9. Check constaints: Two tables joined without check constraints created

```
select *
from dbo.PositiveNumbers e join dbo.NegativeNumbers o on
        e.PositiveNumber = o.NegativeNumber
```

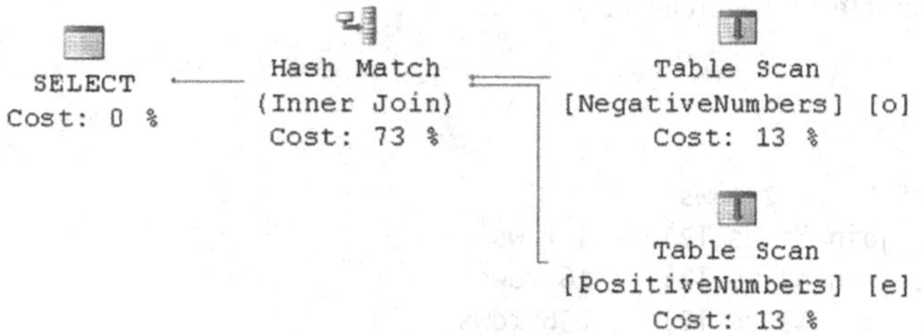

Figure 8-7. *Execution plan without check constraints*

As you can see, SQL Server scans and joins the two tables. That makes sense. Even if we had named our tables in a very specific way, nothing would prevent us from inserting positive values into the NegativeNumbers table and vice versa. Now, let's add the check constraints that enforce the rules. You can see the ALTER TABLE statements in Listing 8-10.

Listing 8-10. Check constaints: Adding check constraints to the table

```
alter table dbo.PositiveNumbers
add constraint CHK_IsNumberPositive
check (PositiveNumber > 0);

alter table dbo.NegativeNumbers
add constraint CHK_IsNumberNegative
check (NegativeNumber < 0);
```

If you run the select again, you will see a different execution plan, as shown in Figure 8-8.

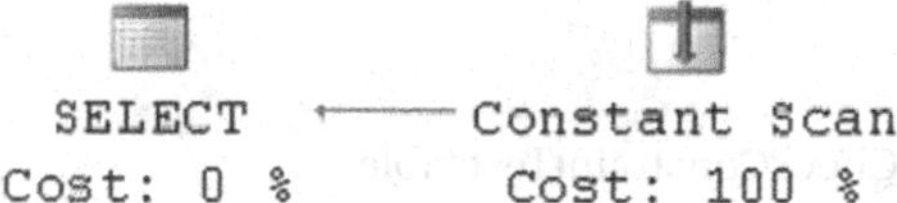

Figure 8-8. *Execution plan with check constraints*

SQL Server evaluated the check constraints, determined that they were mutually exclusive, and removed any unnecessary joins.

■ **Note** One very important situation where you must define check constraints is in the case of partitioned views. Check constraints prevent access to unnecessary tables and greatly improve the performance of queries. We will discuss partitioning views in greater detail in Chapter 16, "Data Partitioning."

Obviously, check constraints introduce overhead during data modifications, especially when you are calling the functions from the constraints. They can significantly decrease the performance of batch operations that insert or update data.

Let's create a table and insert 65,536 rows into it without using check constraints. The code is shown in Listing 8-11.

Listing 8-11. Check constaints: CheckConstraintTest table creation

```
create table dbo.CheckConstraintTest
( Value varchar(32) not null );

with N1(C) as (select 0 union all select 0) -- 2 rows
,N2(C) as (select 0 from N1 as T1 cross join N1 as T2) -- 4 rows
,N3(C) as (select 0 from N2 as T1 cross join N2 as T2) -- 16 rows
,N4(C) as (select 0 from N3 as T1 cross join N3 as T2) -- 256 rows
,N5(C) as (select 0 from N4 as T1 cross join N4 as T2) -- 65,536 rows
,IDs(ID) as (select row_number() over (order by (select null)) from N5)
insert into dbo.CheckConstraintTest(Value)
    select 'ABC' from IDs;
```

You can see the part of the execution plan that inserts data into the table in Figure 8-9.

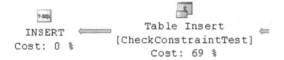

Figure 8-9. *Part of the execution plan: Insert without check constraints*

On my computer, the execution time is as follows:

```
SQL Server Execution Times:
   CPU time = 78 ms,  elapsed time = 87 ms.
```

Let's add a check constraint to the table and see how it affects the performance of the INSERT operation. The code is shown in Listing 8-12.

Listing 8-12. Check constaints: Adding a check constraint to the CheckConstraintTest table

```
alter table dbo.CheckConstraintTest with check
add constraint CHK_CheckConstraintTest_Value
check (Value = 'ABC')
```

As you can see in Figure 8-10, there are two additional operations in the plan introduced by the check constraint, which leads to a longer execution time.

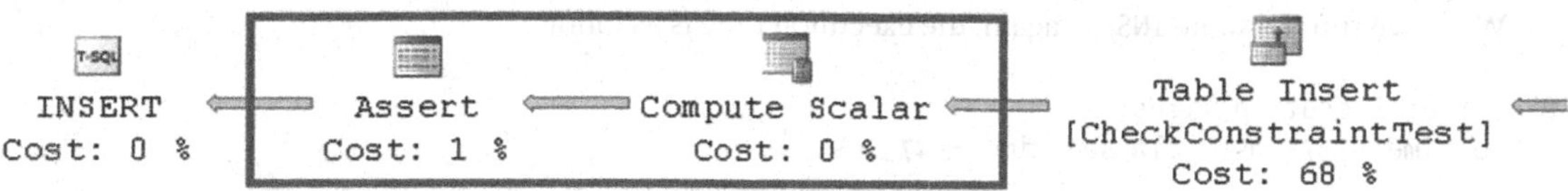

Figure 8-10. *Part of the execution plan: insert with check constraint*

On my computer, the execution time is as follows:

```
SQL Server Execution Times:
   CPU time = 93 ms,  elapsed time = 118 ms.
```

Now, let's see what happens when we call a system function from the check constraint. Let's change the constraint definition, as shown in Listing 8-13.

Listing 8-13. Check constaints: Replacing check constraints with one that calls a system function

```
alter table dbo.CheckConstraintTest
drop constraint CHK_CheckConstraintTest_Value;

alter table dbo.CheckConstraintTest with check
add constraint CHK_CheckConstraintTest_Value
check (Right(Value, 1) = 'C');
```

After we run our insert again, the execution time is as follows:

```
SQL Server Execution Times:
   CPU time = 109 ms,  elapsed time = 131 ms.
```

While system functions do not necessarily introduce huge overhead in terms of CPU load and execution time, user-defined functions (UDFs) are a different story. Let's create a simple UDF and see how it affects performance. The code is shown in Listing 8-14.

Listing 8-14. Check constaints: Replacing a check constraint with one that calls a UDF function

```
create function dbo.DummyCheck(@Value varchar(32))
returns bit
with schemabinding
as
    return (1);
go

alter table dbo.CheckConstraintTest
drop constraint CHK_CheckConstraintTest_Value;

alter table dbo.CheckConstraintTest
add constraint CHK_CheckConstraintTest_Value
check (dbo.DummyCheck(Value) = 1);
```

When we run the same INSERT again, the execution time is as follows:

```
SQL Server Execution Times:
   CPU time = 375 ms,  elapsed time = 475 ms.
```

As you can see, it now takes five times as long to run as when the table did not have a check constraint specified.

■ **Note** We will discuss the performance implications of user-defined functions in greater detail in Chapter 11, "Functions."

As with other constraint types, check constraints help us to enforce data integrity and, in some cases, lead to better execution plans. It is a good idea to use them as long as you can live with the overhead that they introduce during data modification. You can get information about check constraints from the `sys.check_constraints` catalog view.

Wrapping Up

One other important thing that you need to keep in mind when dealing with foreign key and check constraints is whether the constraints are trusted. When a constraint is not trusted, SQL Server will not guarantee that all data in the table complies with the constraint rule. Moreover, SQL Server does not take untrusted constraints into consideration during the query optimization stage. You can see if a constraint is trusted by examining the `is_not_trusted` column in the corresponding catalog view.

SQL Server validates constraints during data modifications regardless of whether they are trusted or not. Having an untrusted constraint does not mean that SQL Server permits violations of it. It means that old data was not validated at the moment the constraint was created.

■ **Note** In some cases, SQL Server can still benefit from untrusted foreign key constraints. They can trigger the Query Optimizer to explore additional join strategies (star join extensions) when the table structure belongs to a star or snowflake schema in data warehouse environments.

You can control if a constraint is created as trusted by using the `WITH CHECK` / `WITH NOCHECK` parameters of the `ALTER TABLE` statement. By using the `WITH CHECK` condition, you force SQL Server to validate whether existing data complies with a constraint rule, which would lead to a table scan. The problem here is that such an operation requires a schema modification (Sch-M) lock, which makes the table inaccessible to other sessions. Such a scan can be very time consuming on large tables. Alternatively, creating untrusted constraints with the `WITH NOCHECK` condition is a metadata operation.

■ **Note** We will talk about schema locks in greater detail in Chapter 23, "Schema Locks."

Finally, you always need to name constraints explicitly, even if it is not a requirement, as it is inconvenient to deal with auto-generated names. With auto-generated names, you need to query the catalog views every time you access constraints programmatically. The use of auto-generated names also reduces the supportability of a system. For example, it is very hard to know what a constraint with the name `CK__A__3E52440B` does without diving deeper into the details.

I recommend that you choose a naming convention that works best for you and use it across the system. Details do not really matter, as long as it is consistent and ideally provides information about the rules for which the constraints are responsible. In my systems, I am using DEF_<Table>_<Column> for the default constraints, CHK_<Table>_<Column_Or_Description> for the check constraints, UQ_<TableName>_<ColNames> for the unique constraints, and <FK>_<ReferencingTable>_<ReferencedTable> for the foreign key constraints. This notation helps me to understand what constraints are doing simply by glancing at their names.

Constraints are a very powerful tool that helps to keep the data clean and improves the supportability and performance of the system. Use them wisely.

Summary

Primary key constraints define the column or set of columns that uniquely identify a row in a table. Internally, primary key constraints are implemented as unique indexes and can be either clustered or nonclustered.

Foreign key constraints define the relationships between tables in the system. They help to improve data quality in the database; however, they introduce some overhead during referential integrity checks. It is important to define the index on the referencing column in the referencing table whenever it is possible.

Check constraints enforce domain integrity by limiting the values that you can put into the column or into multiple columns in the row. As with foreign key constraints, they help to improve data quality in the system at the cost of validation overhead during data modifications. You should consider this overhead, especially in cases when you are using user-defined functions to validate the constraint.

Foreign key and check constraints can be either trusted or untrusted. SQL Server does not validate untrusted constraints at the creation stage; however, it performs validation after the constraint has been created. In most cases, Query Optimizer does not rely on untrusted constraints during query optimization.

Summary

CHAPTER 9

Triggers

Triggers define the code that runs in response to specific events. There are three types of triggers available in SQL Server, as follows:

1. DML triggers fire when data modification occurs. You can use DML triggers in cases where you need to enforce specific business rules during data modifications and the system does not have a dedicated data access tier implemented. You can think about audit-trail functional, which captures who changed the data in the table, as an example. When a system has multiple applications working with the database directly, an audit-trail implementation based on triggers is the simplest one.
2. DDL triggers fire in response to events that change database and server objects. You can use DDL triggers to prevent or audit those changes; for example, dropping tables, altering stored procedures, or creating new logins.
3. Logon triggers fire during the user login process. You can use triggers for audit purposes, as well as to prevent users from logging in to the system when needed.

DML Triggers

DML triggers allow you to define the code that will be executed during data modification operations, such as `INSERT`, `UPDATE`, `DELETE`, or `MERGE`. There are two types of DML triggers: `INSTEAD OF` and `AFTER` triggers. `INSTEAD OF` triggers run as a *replacement* of the actual data modification operation on a table or view. With these types of triggers, you can evaluate and/or implement business rules. You also need to issue the actual DML statement against a table if you want the data to be modified. `AFTER` triggers fire following a data modification operation, when the data in the table has been changed.

D. Korotkevitch, *Pro SQL Server Internals*, DOI 10.1007/978-1-4842-1964-5_9

Let's see what happens when we insert data into a table that has triggers and constraints defined. First, let's create a table using the code shown in Listing 9-1.

Listing 9-1. Inserting data into the table: Table and two triggers creation

```
create table dbo.OrderLineItems
(
    OrderId int not null,
    OrderLineItemId int identity(1,1) not null,
    ProductId int not null,
    ProductName nvarchar(64) not null,
    CreationDate smalldatetime not null,
        constraint DEF_OrderLineItems_CreationDate
        default GetUtcDate(),
    Quantity decimal(9,3) not null,
    Price smallmoney not null,

    constraint PK_OrderLineItems
    primary key clustered(OrderId, OrderLineItemId),

    constraint CHK_OrderLineItems_PositiveQuantity
    check (Quantity > 0),

    constraint FK_OrderLineItems_Orders
    foreign key(OrderId)
    references dbo.Orders(OrderId),

    constraint FK_OrderLineItems_Products
    foreign key(ProductId)
    references dbo.Products(ProductId)
)
go

create trigger trg_OrderLineItems_InsteadOfInsert on dbo.OrderLineItems
instead of insert
as
begin
    if @@rowcount = 0
        return;
    set nocount on
    if not exists(select * from inserted)
        return;

    insert into dbo.OrderLineItems(OrderId, ProductId, ProductName, Quantity, Price)
        select i.OrderId, i.ProductId, p.ProductName, i.Quantity, i.Price
        from inserted i join dbo.Products p on
                i.ProductId = p.ProductId;
end
go
```

```
create trigger trg_OrderLineItems_AfterInsert on dbo.OrderLineItems
after insert
as
begin
    if @@rowcount = 0
        return;
    set nocount on
    if not exists(select * from inserted)
        return;

    if exists
    (
        select *
        from inserted i join dbo.Orders o on
                i.OrderId = o.OrderId
        where o.Status = 'CLOSED'
    )
    begin
        raiserror('Cannot change the closed order',16,1);
        rollback tran;
        return;
    end
end
```

The table has both primary and foreign keys as well as default and check constraints. INSTEAD OF and AFTER triggers are also defined. Let's take a look at what happens when we run an INSERT statement against the table, as shown in Listing 9-2.

Listing 9-2. Inserting data into the table: Insert statement

```
insert into dbo.OrderLineItems(OrderId, ProductId, ProductName, Quantity, Price)
values(@OrderId, @ProductId, @ProductName, @Quantity, @Price)
```

In the first step, SQL Server creates and populates inserted and deleted virtual tables that contain information about the new and old versions of the rows affected by the DML statement. These tables will be accessible in the INSTEAD OF trigger. In our case, the inserted table would have one row with the values that we provided in the INSERT statement and the deleted table would be empty, because there is no "old" version of the row when we insert it. We will talk about these tables later in this chapter, but for now let us remember one very important thing: *DML triggers have a statement scope and would be fired just once regardless of how many rows were affected. The virtual tables could have more than one row, and the implementation needs to handle that correctly.*

In the next step, SQL Server fires the trg_OrderLineItems_InsteadOfInsert INSTEAD OF trigger. In the trigger, we are implementing the business logic and executing an INSERT statement against the actual table. Our implementation of the trigger ignores the ProductName value provided by the original INSERT statement and replaces it with the actual product name from the Products table. An inner join also filters out the rows that do not have corresponding products in the system. Even if we enforce the same rule by foreign key constraint, such an implementation behaves differently. Violation of the foreign key constraint terminates the entire batch without inserting any rows, while a join in the trigger just filters out incorrect rows and inserts the correct ones.

■ **Tip** Whether you should use such an approach, ignoring the incorrect rows rather than terminating the batch, depends on the business requirements. Although it can help in some cases, it complicates system troubleshooting. At a bare minimum, I suggest that you log information about the skipped rows somewhere in the system.

When the `INSTEAD OF` trigger runs the `INSERT` statement, SQL Server performs the following tasks in the sequence:

1. It assigns the default constraint value to the `CreationDate` column.
2. It validates the not null, primary key, unique, check constraints, and unique indexes in the table, and it terminates the statement in the case of constraint or uniqueness violations.
3. It checks referential integrity and terminates the statement in case of foreign key constraint violations. Otherwise, it inserts the new rows into the table.

■ **Note** `AFTER` triggers do not fire in the case of constraint or index-uniqueness violations.

Finally, we have the new `inserted` and `deleted` tables created, and the `AFTER` triggers are fired. At this point, the new row has already been inserted into the table and, if we needed to roll back the changes, SQL Server would undo the `INSERT` operation. In the preceding example, it would be more efficient to have the order-status check being implemented as part of `INSTEAD OF` rather than as an `AFTER` trigger.

As I already mentioned, triggers run on a per-statement rather than a per-row basis. Our implementation needs to work correctly when `inserted` and `deleted` tables have more than one row. For example, the implementation in Listing 9-3 would fail with the exception that the subquery used in the `set` operator returns more than one row if multiple rows are being updated.

Listing 9-3. Triggers implementation: Incorrect implementation

```
create trigger Trg_OrderLineItems_AfterUpdate_Incorrect on dbo.OrderLineItems
after update
as
begin
    -- Some code here
    declare
        @OrderId int;

    set @OrderId = (select OrderId from inserted);
    -- Some code here
end

Error Message:
Msg 512, Level 16, State 1, Procedure Trg_OrderLineItems_AfterUpdate_Incorrect, Line 9
Subquery returned more than 1 value. This is not permitted when the subquery
follows =, !=, <, <= , >, >= or when the subquery is used as an expression.
```

Alternatively, triggers would fire even if the DML statement did not change (insert, update, or delete) any data. In that case, both the inserted and the deleted tables would be empty. In order to create an efficient implementation, you need to have a few checks in the beginning of the trigger to prevent unnecessary code from being executed. Let's look at our implementation again, as shown in Listing 9-4.

Listing 9-4. Trigger implementation: Preventing unnecessary code from being executed

```
create trigger trg_OrderLineItems_InsteadOfInsert on dbo.OrderLineItems
instead of insert
as
begin
    if @@rowcount = 0
        return;
    set nocount on
    if not exists(select * from inserted)
        return;
    -- Some code here
end
```

The first statement in the trigger—`if @@rowcount = 0`—checks if the `INSERT` statement did, in fact, insert any rows. As an example, you can think about the insert/select pattern when the `SELECT` query did not return any data. You would like to avoid having a trigger code be executed in such cases.

The second statement—`set nocount on`—stops SQL Server from returning the message that displays the number of rows affected by the code in the trigger. Some client libraries do not handle multiple messages correctly.

The last statement—`if not exists(select * from inserted)`—is trickier. While `@@rowcount` can help you detect when there are no rows affected by `INSERT`, `UPDATE`, or `DELETE` statements, it would not work very well with `MERGE`. That operator, introduced in SQL Server 2008, allows you to combine all three actions into the single statement. Triggers would fire even if there were no corresponding actions. `@@rowcount` in the trigger represents the total number of rows affected by the `MERGE` statement.

Let's create a simple table with three triggers that displays the value of `@@rowcount` and the number of rows in the `inserted` and `deleted` tables. You can see this code in Listing 9-5. It is also worth mentioning that it is very bad practice to return any result sets from triggers, because it could easily break client applications.

Listing 9-5. Triggers and MERGE statement: Table and three triggers creation

```
create table dbo.Data(Col int not null);

create trigger trg_Data_AI on dbo.Data
after insert
as
    select
        'After Insert' as [Trigger]
        ,@@RowCount as [RowCount]
        ,(select count(*) from inserted) as [Inserted Cnt]
        ,(select count(*) from deleted) as [Deleted Cnt];
```

```
create trigger trg_Data_AU on dbo.Data
after update
as
    select
        'After Update' as [Trigger]
        ,@@RowCount as [RowCount]
        ,(select count(*) from inserted) as [Inserted Cnt]
        ,(select count(*) from deleted) as [Deleted Cnt];

create trigger trg_Data_AD on dbo.Data
after delete
as
    select
        'After Delete' as [Trigger]
        ,@@RowCount as [RowCount]
        ,(select count(*) from inserted) as [Inserted Cnt]
        ,(select count(*) from deleted) as [Deleted Cnt];
```

Now, let's run the MERGE statement, as shown in Listing 9-6.

Listing 9-6. Triggers and MERGE statement: MERGE

```
merge into dbo.Data as Target
using (select 1 as [Value]) as Source
on Target.Col = Source.Value
when not matched by target then
        insert(Col) values(Source.Value)
when not matched by source then
        delete
when matched then
        update set Col = Source.Value;
```

Because the dbo.Data table is empty, the MERGE statement would insert one row there. Let's look at the output from the triggers, as shown in Figure 9-1.

Trigger	RowCount	Inserted Cnt	Deleted Cnt
After Insert	1	1	0

Trigger	RowCount	Inserted Cnt	Deleted Cnt
After Update	1	0	0

Trigger	RowCount	Inserted Cnt	Deleted Cnt
After Delete	1	0	0

Figure 9-1. *@@rowcount, inserted and deleted tables with MERGE operator*

As you can see, all three triggers were fired. In each of them, @@rowcount represented the number of rows affected by the MERGE. However, with the AFTER UPDATE and AFTER DELETE triggers, the inserted and deleted tables were empty. You need to check the content of these tables in order to prevent the code in the trigger from being executed if they are empty.

As you can guess, there is overhead associated with the triggers. At a bare minimum, SQL Server needs to create inserted and deleted virtual tables when triggers are present. SQL Server does not analyze whether there is any logic that references those tables within the trigger, and simply always creates them. While the overhead associated with INSTEAD OF triggers is not particularly large, this is not the case with AFTER triggers. AFTER triggers store the data from those tables in the special part of tempdb called the *version store*, keeping it until after the transaction completes.

■ **Note** SQL Server uses the version store to maintain multiple versions of the rows, and it supports several features, such as optimistic transaction isolation levels, online indexing, multiple active result sets (MARS), and triggers. We will talk about it in greater detail in Chapter 21, "Optimistic Isolation Levels."

While version store usage introduces additional tempdb load, there is another important factor that you need to keep in mind. In order to maintain the links between the new and old versions of the rows, AFTER UPDATE and AFTER DELETE triggers add a 14-byte versioning tag pointer to the rows they modified or deleted, which will stay until the index has been rebuilt. That could increase the row size and introduce fragmentation similar to that in the insert/update pattern discussed in Chapter 6, "Index Fragmentation." Let's look at an example and create a table with some data, as shown in Listing 9-7.

Listing 9-7. Triggers and fragmentation: Table creation

```
create table dbo.Data
(
    ID int not null identity(1,1),
    Value int not null,
    LobColumn varchar(max) null,
    constraint PK_Data
    primary key clustered(ID)
);

;with N1(C) as (select 0 union all select 0) -- 2 rows
,N2(C) as (select 0 from N1 as T1 cross join N1 as T2) -- 4 rows
,N3(C) as (select 0 from N2 as T1 cross join N2 as T2) -- 16 rows
,N4(C) as (select 0 from N3 as T1 cross join N3 as T2) -- 256 rows
,N5(C) as (select 0 from N4 as T1 cross join N4 as T2 ) -- 65,536 rows
,Numbers(Num) as (select row_number() over (order by (select null)) from N5)
insert into dbo.Data(Value)
    select Num from Numbers;
```

Now, let's delete every other row in the table, looking at the index's physical statistics before and after the deletion. The code is found in Listing 9-8, and the results are shown in Figure 9-2.

Listing 9-8. Triggers and fragmentation: Physical index stats before and after deletion

```
select
    alloc_unit_type_desc as [AllocUnit], index_level,page_count,
    ,avg_page_space_used_in_percent as [SpaceUsed]
    ,avg_fragmentation_in_percent as [Frag %]
from sys.dm_db_index_physical_stats(DB_ID(),OBJECT_ID(N'dbo.Data'),1,null,'DETAILED');

delete from dbo.Data where ID % 2 = 0;

select
    alloc_unit_type_desc as [AllocUnit], index_level,page_count,
    ,avg_page_space_used_in_percent as [SpaceUsed]
    ,avg_fragmentation_in_percent as [Frag %]
from sys.dm_db_index_physical_stats(DB_ID(),OBJECT_ID(N'dbo.Data'),1,null,'DETAILED');
```

	AllocUnit	index_level	page_count	SpaceUsed	Frag %
1	IN_ROW_DATA	0	138	99.7192488262911	1.44927536231884
2	IN_ROW_DATA	1	1	22.1398566839634	0

	AllocUnit	index_level	page_count	SpaceUsed	Frag %
1	IN_ROW_DATA	0	138	59.3169755374351	1.44927536231884
2	IN_ROW_DATA	1	1	22.1398566839634	0

Figure 9-2. *Clustered index physical statistics after DELETE statement without AFTER DELETE trigger*

As you should remember, the DELETE operation does not physically remove the row from the page; it just marks it as a ghost row. In our example, the only thing that was changed is the amount of free space on the pages.

Now, let's truncate the table and populate it with the same data as before with the code shown in Listing 9-9.

Listing 9-9. Triggers and fragmentation: Populating table with data

```
truncate table dbo.Data;

;with N1(C) as (select 0 union all select 0) -- 2 rows
,N2(C) as (select 0 from N1 as T1 cross join N1 as T2) -- 4 rows
,N3(C) as (select 0 from N2 as T1 cross join N2 as T2) -- 16 rows
,N4(C) as (select 0 from N3 as T1 cross join N3 as T2) -- 256 rows
,N5(C) as (select 0 from N4 as T1 cross join N4 as T2 ) -- 65,536 rows
,Numbers(Num) as (select row_number() over (order by (select null)) from N5)
insert into dbo.Data(Value)
    select Num from Numbers;
```

Next, let's create the empty AFTER DELETE trigger on the table, as shown in Listing 9-10.

Listing 9-10. Triggers and fragmentation: Trigger creation

```
create trigger trg_Data_AfterDelete
on dbo.data
after delete
as
    return;
```

If you run the same deletion statement as you did previously, you will see the results shown in Figure 9-3.

	AllocUnit	index_level	page_count	SpaceUsed	Frag %
1	IN_ROW_DATA	0	138	99.7192488262911	1.44927536231884
2	IN_ROW_DATA	1	1	22.1398566839634	0

	AllocUnit	index_level	page_count	SpaceUsed	Frag %
1	IN_ROW_DATA	0	275	70.6388188781814	99.6363636363636
2	IN_ROW_DATA	1	1	44.1438102297999	0

Figure 9-3. *Clustered index physical statistics after DELETE statement with AFTER DELETE trigger*

Versioning tags increased the size of the rows and led to massive page splits and fragmentation during `DELETE` operations. Moreover, in the end, we almost doubled the number of pages in the index.

■ **Note** In some cases, when there is only in-row allocation involved (for example, when a table does not have either LOB columns or variable-length columns, which can potentially require it to store data in the row-overflow pages), SQL Server optimizes that behavior and does not add 14 bytes of versioning tags to the rows.

Triggers are always running during the same transaction as the statement that fired them. We need to make trigger execution time as short as possible to minimize the duration of locks being held. In the event a trigger contains complex logic that can be executed outside of the transaction, you can consider implementing that logic using Service Broker. The trigger can send Service Broker a message, and Service Broker in turn can execute an activation procedure that implements the logic.

■ **Note** Coverage of Service Broker is outside of the scope of this book. You can read about it at `https://msdn.microsoft.com/en-us/library/bb522893.aspx`.

DDL Triggers

DDL triggers allow you to define the code that executes in response to various DDL events, such as the creation, alteration, or deletion of database objects; changing permissions; and updating statistics. You can use these triggers for audit purposes, as well as to restrict some operations on database schemas. For example, the trigger shown in Listing 9-11 would prevent the accidental altering or dropping of a table, and it could be used as a safety feature in a production environment.

Listing 9-11. DDL Triggers: Preventing the altering and dropping of tables in production

```
create trigger trg_PreventAlterDropTable on database
for alter_table, drop_table
as
begin
    print 'Table cannot be altered or dropped with trgPreventAlterDropTable trigger enabled' ;
    rollback;
end
```

While this approach helps with keeping tables and their schemas intact, it introduces one potential problem. DDL triggers fire *after* an operation is completed. As a result, using our example, if you have the session altering the table, SQL Server would perform the alteration before the trigger fires and then would roll back all of the changes.

Let's prove it now. As a first step, let's alter the trigger to capture information about the table structure during execution and then display a list of the columns in the table when it fires. You can see the code that does this in Listing 9-12.

Listing 9-12. DDL triggers: Trigger code

```
alter trigger trg_PreventAlterDropTable on database
for alter_table
as
begin
    declare
        @objName nvarchar(257) =
            eventdata().value('/EVENT_INSTANCE[1]/SchemaName[1]','nvarchar(128)') +
                '.' + eventdata().value('/EVENT_INSTANCE[1]/ObjectName[1]','nvarchar(128)');

    select column_id, name
    from sys.columns
    where object_id = object_id(@objName);

    print 'Table cannot be altered or dropped with trgPreventAlterDropTable trigger enabled'
    rollback;
end
```

Now, let's run the ALTER TABLE statement that adds a persistent computed column to the table, capturing I/O statistics during the execution. You can see the code for doing this in Listing 9-13.

Listing 9-13. DDL triggers: ALTER TABLE statement

```
set statistics io on;
alter table Delivery.Addresses add NewColumn as AddressId persisted;
```

This alteration adds another column to every data row in the table. We can see the results in Figure 9-4.

	column_id	name
1	1	AddressId
2	2	CustomerId
3	3	Address
4	4	City
5	5	State
6	6	Zip
7	7	Direction
8	8	NewColumn

```
Table 'Addresses'. Scan count 1, logical reads 1255, physical reads 3, read-ahead reads 1035,
Table 'syscolpars'. Scan count 1, logical reads 2, physical reads 0, read-ahead reads 0, lob

Table cannot be altered or dropped until trgPreventAlterDropTable trigger is disabled !
Msg 3609, Level 16, State 2, Line 2
The transaction ended in the trigger. The batch has been aborted.
```

Figure 9-4. *Table structure in DDL trigger with I/O statistics of the operation*

As you can see, when the trigger fires, the table has already been altered and a new column called NewColumn has been created. As a result, when the trigger rolls back the transaction, SQL Server needs to undo the table alteration. This process can be very inefficient, especially with large tables.

As you have already seen, we are using the EVENTDATA() function from within the trigger to get information about the DDL event. This function returns an xml value that contains information about the type of event, session and DDL command, affected object, as well as other attributes. For instance, in our example, you would get the following XML code:

```
<EVENT_INSTANCE>
    <EventType>ALTER_TABLE</EventType>
    <PostTime>2015-11-28T12:26:44.453</PostTime>
    <SPID>54</SPID>
    <ServerName>SQL2016</ServerName>
    <LoginName>SQL2016\Administrator</LoginName>
    <UserName>dbo</UserName>
    <DatabaseName>SqlServerInternals</DatabaseName>
    <SchemaName>Delivery</SchemaName>
    <ObjectName>Addresses</ObjectName>
    <ObjectType>TABLE</ObjectType>
    <AlterTableActionList>
        <Create>
            <Columns>
```

```
                <Name>NewColumn</Name>
            </Columns>
        </Create>
    </AlterTableActionList>
    <TSQLCommand>
        <SetOptions ANSI_NULLS="ON" ANSI_NULL_DEFAULT="ON"
                ANSI_PADDING="ON" QUOTED_IDENTIFIER="ON" ENCRYPTED="FALSE" />
        <CommandText>alter table Delivery.Addresses add NewColumn as AddressId persisted</
CommandText>
    </TSQLCommand>
</EVENT_INSTANCE>
```

DDL triggers can be created on either the server or database scope. Some of the DDL events–`CREATE_DATABASE`, for example–would require the trigger to have a server scope. Other events–`ALTER_TABLE`, for example–could use either of them. When such a trigger is created on the server scope, it would fire in the instance of the corresponding event in any database on the server.

In SQL Server Management Studio, database-level DDL triggers can be found under the *Programmability* node in the database. Server-level DDL triggers are displayed under the *Server Objects* node. You can also use `sys.triggers` and `sys.server_triggers` catalog views to find them with T-SQL.

Logon Triggers

Logon triggers fire after a user is successfully authenticated on the server, but before the session has been established. Some of the scenarios in which you can use logon triggers are to prevent the same user from opening multiple database connections or to restrict access to the system based on some custom criteria. The trigger in Listing 9-14 prevents the *HRLogin* login from accessing the system outside of business hours.

Listing 9-14. Logon trigger

```
create trigger trg_Logon_BusinessHoursOnly
on all server
for logon
as
begin
    declare
        @currTime datetime = current_timestamp;

    if original_login() = 'HRLogin' and
         (    -- Check if today is weekend
                    ((@@datefirst + datepart(dw, @currTime)) % 7 in (0,1)) or
                    (cast(@currTime as time) >= '18:00:00') or
                    (cast(@currTime as time) < '8:00:00')
        )
            rollback;
end
```

Like DDL triggers, there is an EVENTDATA function that returns XML with additional information about a logon event. An example of this XML code follows here:

```
<EVENT_INSTANCE>
    <EventType>LOGON</EventType>
    <PostTime>2016-11-18T17:55:40.090</PostTime>
    <SPID>55</SPID>
    <ServerName>SQL2016</ServerName>
    <LoginName>SQL2016\Administrator</LoginName>
    <LoginType>Windows (NT) Login</LoginType>
    <SID>sid</SID>
    <ClientHost>&lt;local machine&gt;</ClientHost>
    <IsPooled>0</IsPooled>
</EVENT_INSTANCE>
```

You need to make sure that the logon trigger executes as fast as possible to prevent possible connection timeouts. You need to be very careful if the trigger is accessing external resources where response time is not guaranteed. Think about a CLR function that performs additional authentication against a corporate Active Directory, as an example. That function needs to set a short timeout for AD queries and correctly handle possible exceptions. Otherwise, nobody would be able to log in to SQL Server.

UPDATE() and COLUMNS_UPDATED() Functions

The UPDATE and COLUMNS_UPDATED functions allow you to check if specific columns were affected by INSERT or UPDATE operations.

The UPDATE function accepts a column name as the parameter and returns a Boolean value that shows if the column was affected by the statement that fired the trigger. For INSERT operations, it always returns TRUE. For UPDATE operations, it would return TRUE if an attempt was made or, more specifically, if a column were present in the list of columns that needed to be updated, **regardless of whether it changed the value or not.** For example, in Listing 9-15, the UPDATE statement does not change the value of column C in the row. However, the UPDATE(C) function in the trigger returns TRUE because column C was included in the list of the columns in the UPDATE statement.

Listing 9-15. UPDATE() function behavior

```
create trigger trg_T_AU
on dbo.T
after update
as
begin
    -- Some code here
    if update(C)
        -- Some code here
end
go

declare @V int = null;
update T set C = IsNull(@V, C) where ID = 1;
```

Listing 9-16 shows an example of a trigger that recalculates the order total when a line-item price or quantity changes.

Listing 9-16. UPDATE() function implementation example

```
create trigger trg_OrderLineItems_AfterUpdate
on dbo.OrderLineItems
after update
as
begin
    -- Some code here
    if update(Quantity) or update(Price)
    begin
        -- recalculating order total
        update o
        set
            o.Total =
                    (   select sum(li.Price * li.Quantity)
                        from dbo.OrderLineItems li
                        where li.OrderId = o.OrderId  )
        from dbo.Orders o
        where o.OrderId in (select OrderId from inserted);
    end;
    -- Some code here
end
```

The `COLUMNS_UPDATED` function returns the `varbinary` value, which represents a bitmask where each bit is set to 1 in case the column was affected by the statement. The order of the bits, from least significant to the most significant, corresponds to the `column_id` value from the `sys.columns` catalog view.

Assuming that the `column_id` for the `Quantity` column is 4 and the `column_id` for the `Price` column is 5, we can replace the `if` operator with the following bitmask comparison: `if columns_updated() & 24 <> 0`.

The integer value 24 represents the binary value 11000. The result of the bitwise & (and) operator would not be equal to 0 if either of the corresponding bits returned by the `columns_updated` function were set to 1.

Nested and Recursive Triggers

Both DDL and DML triggers are nested when their actions fire triggers in other tables. For example, you can have an `AFTER UPDATE` trigger on Table A that updates Table B, which has its own `AFTER UPDATE` trigger defined. When nested triggers are enabled, the trigger on Table B would be fired. You can control that behavior by setting the `nested trigger` server configuration option. The code in Listing 9-17 disables the nested triggers execution.

Listing 9-17. Disabling nested triggers

```
EXEC sp_configure 'show advanced options', 1;
GO
RECONFIGURE ;
GO
EXEC sp_configure 'nested triggers', 0 ;
GO
RECONFIGURE;
GO
```

By default, nested triggers execution is enabled. In the case of infinite loops, SQL Server terminates the execution and rolls back the transaction when the nesting level exceeds 32.

Another database option, `recursive_triggers`, controls if an `AFTER` trigger can fire itself. There are two types of recursion. With *direct recursion*, the trigger fires itself by performing the same action against the table where it has been defined; for example, when an `AFTER UPDATE` trigger updates the same table. By default, direct recursion is disabled. *Indirect recursion*, on the other hand, happens when Table A performs the action that fires the trigger in Table B, and the trigger on Table B performs the action that fires the same trigger on Table A. To prevent indirect recursion from happening, we need to disable the `nested triggers` configuration option on the server level.

■ **Caution** You need to be careful about changing the nested triggers or recursive triggers options. Developers often rely on default trigger behavior, and you can break existing systems by changing those options.

First and Last Triggers

In a situation where a table has multiple `AFTER` triggers, you can specify what triggers are firing first and last by using the `sp_settriggerorder` system stored procedure. For example, the code in Listing 9-18 makes `trg_Data_AUAudit` the first trigger in the execution.

Listing 9-18. Specifying triggers' execution order

```
sp_settriggerorder @triggername = ' trg_Data_AUAudit', @order = 'first'
    ,@stmttype = 'UPDATE'
```

Each action—`INSERT`, `UPDATE`, and `DELETE`—can have its own first and last triggers specified. The value will be cleared when the trigger is altered.

You cannot control the order in which triggers fire in any other way.

CONTEXT_INFO and SESSION_CONTEXT

Every session has up to 128 bytes of binary data value, called context information, associated with it. That value has the session scope, and it can be used when you need to pass some parameters to or from triggers. You can set the value with the `SET CONTEXT_INFO` statement and retrieve it with the `CONTEXT_INFO` function.

As an example, let's modify the DDL trigger `trg_PreventAlterDropTable` to allow table alteration when the context information contains the string `ALLOW_TABLE_ALTERATION`. The code for doing this is shown in Listing 9-19.

Listing 9-19. CONTEXT_INFO: Trigger code

```
create trigger trg_PreventAlterDropTable on database
for alter_table
as
begin
    if isnull(convert(varchar(22),context_info()),'') <> 'ALLOW_TABLE_ALTERATION'
    begin
        print 'Table alteration is not allowed in such context';
        rollback;
    end
end
```

To be able to alter the table, the session needs to set `CONTEXT_INFO`, as shown in Listing 9-20.

Listing 9-20. CONTEXT_INFO: Setting CONTEXT_INFO value

```
declare
        @CI varbinary(128) = convert(varbinary(22),'ALLOW_TABLE_ALTERATION');
set context_info @CI

alter table Delivery.Addresses add NewColumn int null
```

Context binary data is also exposed through the `CONTEXT_INFO` column in the `sys.dm_exec_request`, `sys.dm_exec_sessions`, and `sys.processes` system views.

SQL Server 2016 introduced the concept of session-specific storage called *session context*, which allows each session to store up to 256 KB of data in key-value pairs. As you can guess, session context is much more flexible and easier to work with compared to context information.

Listing 9-21 illustrates an example of a DDL trigger that allows table alterations based on the session-context data.

Listing 9-21. Session context: Trigger code

```
create table dbo.AlterationEvents
(
    OnDate datetime2(7) not null
        constraint DEF_AlterationEvents_OnDate
        default sysutcdatetime(),
    Succeed bit not null,
    RequestedBy varchar(255) not null,
    Description varchar(8000) not null,

    constraint PK_AlterationEvents
    primary key clustered(OnDate)
)
go
```

```
create trigger trg_PreventAlterDropTable_WithAudit on database
for alter_table
as
begin
    set nocount on
    declare
        @AlterationAllowed bit = 1
        ,@RequestedBy varchar(255)
        ,@Description varchar(8000)

    select
        @AlterationAllowed = convert(bit,session_context(N'AlterationAllowed'))
        ,@RequestedBy = convert(varchar(255),session_context(N'RequestedBy'))
        ,@Description = convert(varchar(255),session_context(N'Description'));

    if (@AlterationAllowed != 1) or (IsNull(@RequestedBy,'') = '') or
        (IsNull(@Description,'') = '')
    begin
        set @AlterationAllowed = 0;
        print 'Table alteration is not allowed in such context';
        rollback;
    end;

    insert into dbo.AlterationEvents(Succeed,RequestedBy,Description)
    values(@AlterationAllowed,IsNull(@RequestedBy,'Not Provided')
        ,IsNull(@Description,'Not Provided'));
end
```

Listing 9-22 shows the code that populates the session context with values that allow for performing the alteration.

Listing 9-22. Session context: Populating session-context data

```
exec sp_set_session_context @key = N'AlterationAllowed', @value = 1, @read_only = 0
exec sp_set_session_context @key = N'RequestedBy', @value = 'Developers', @read_only = 0
exec sp_set_session_context @key = N'Description', @value = 'Client App v1.0.1 Support'
    ,@read_only = 0

alter table dbo.Config add SyncURL nvarchar(1024) not null;
```

■ **Note** You can read more about session context at `https://msdn.microsoft.com/en-us/library/mt605113.aspx`

Summary

Triggers can help in certain scenarios. DDL triggers can validate and prevent unwanted metadata changes in the system. Logon triggers can help implement custom authentication. DML triggers can help centralize some logic in the code, especially when there is no dedicated data access tier in the system. One example is the implementation of an audit-trail function when you want to capture information about users who change data. While there are other approaches to implementing such tasks, trigger-based implementation can be the simplest.

Unfortunately, triggers come at a high cost. `AFTER` DML triggers introduce overhead related to the maintenance of `inserted` and `deleted` virtual tables. This leads to extra `tempdb` load and index fragmentation. `INSTEAD OF` triggers could lead to system supportability issues. It is easy to forget or overlook the logic implemented in such triggers.

DDL triggers run after schema changes are done. While you can roll back those changes from within the triggers, such operations can be very expensive in terms of I/O, CPU, and transaction log activity, especially with large tables.

Finally, logon triggers can prevent users from logging into the system when incorrectly implemented due to bugs in the logic or connection timeouts introduced by long execution times, especially when those triggers access external resources.

Triggers always run in the context of a transaction. Any active locks–that is, data and schema–will be held while a trigger is running and until the transaction is completed. You need to make your triggers as quick and efficient as possible and avoid any actions that could potentially take a long time. For example, it is a bad idea to implement an audit-trail function that uses an external (linked) server for the logging. If that server goes down, it will take a long time for a connection attempt to timeout. In addition, if you did not handle the exception properly, it would roll back the original transaction.

Keeping all of these implications in mind, you need to be very careful when dealing with triggers. It is better to avoid them unless absolutely necessary.

CHAPTER 10

Views

Views represent virtual tables defined by underlying queries, and they add another layer of abstraction to the system. Views hide implementation details and can present queries with complex joins and aggregation as a single table. Moreover, views can be used to restrict access to the data and provide just a subset of the rows and columns to users.

There are two different kinds of views available in SQL Server: regular views and indexed (materialized) views. Let's look at them in detail.

Views

Regular views are just the metadata. When you reference a view in your queries, SQL Server replaces it with the query from the view definition, then optimizes and executes the statement, as the view is not actually present. Views work in a way similar to the `#define` macro in the C programming language, where a pre-processor replaces the macro with its definition during compilation.

There are two main benefits provided by views. First, they simplify security administration in the system. You can use views as another security layer and grant users permissions on the views rather than on the actual tables. Moreover, views can provide users with only a subset of the data, filtering out of some rows and columns from the original tables.

Consider a situation where you have a table that contains information about a company's employees, which has both private and public attributes. The code that creates this table is shown in Listing 10-1.

Listing 10-1. Views and security: Table creation

```
create table dbo.Employees
(
    EmployeeId int not null,
    Name nvarchar(100) not null,
    Position nvarchar(100) not null,
    Email nvarchar(256) not null,
    DateOfBirth date not null,
    SSN varchar(10) not null,
    Salary money not null,
    -- specifies if employee info needs to be listed in the intranet
    PublishProfile bit not null,

    constraint PK_Employee
    primary key clustered(EmployeeID)
)
```


D. Korotkevitch, *Pro SQL Server Internals*, DOI 10.1007/978-1-4842-1964-5_10

Let's assume that you have a system that displays the company directory on the company intranet. You can define the view that selects public information from the table, filtering out the employees who do not want their profiles to be published, and then grant users SELECT permission on the view rather than on the table. You can see this code in Listing 10-2.

Listing 10-2. Views and security: View creation

```
create view dbo.vPublicEmployeeProfiles(EmployeeId, Name, Position, Email)
as
    select EmployeeId, Name, Position, Email
    from dbo.Employees
    where PublishProfile = 1
go

grant select on object::dbo.vPublicEmployeeProfiles to [IntranetUsers];
```

While you can accomplish this task without a view by using column-level permissions and an additional filter in the queries, the view approach is simpler to develop and maintain.

■ **Note** In SQL Server 2016, you can use row-level security to exclude rows from result sets.

Another benefit of views is that they abstract the database schema from the client applications. You can alter the database schema, keeping it transparent to the applications, by altering the views and changing the underlying queries. It is then transparent to the client applications as long as the view's interface remains the same.

In addition, you can hide complex implementation details and table joins and use views as a simple interface to client applications. This approach is a bit dangerous, however. It could lead to unnecessary and unexpected performance overhead in the system. You should also avoid creating nested views that reference other views in underlying queries because of optimization challenges and performance issues they could introduce.

Let's look at a few examples and assume that we have an order-entry system with two tables: dbo.Orders and dbo.Clients. The code to create these tables is shown in Listing 10-3.

Listing 10-3. Views and joins: Tables creation

```
create table dbo.Clients
(
    ClientId int not null,
    ClientName varchar(32),
    constraint PK_Clients
    primary key clustered(ClientId)
);
```

```
create table dbo.Orders
(
    OrderId int not null identity(1,1),
    Clientid int not null,
    OrderDate datetime not null,
    OrderNumber varchar(32) not null,
    Amount smallmoney not null,
    constraint PK_Orders
    primary key clustered(OrderId)
);
```

Let's create a view that returns order information, including client names, as shown in Listing 10-4.

Listing 10-4. Views and joins: vOrders view creation

```
create view dbo.vOrders(OrderId, Clientid, OrderDate, OrderNumber, Amount, ClientName)
as
    select o.OrderId, o.ClientId, o.OrderDate, o.OrderNumber, o.Amount, c.ClientName
    from dbo.Orders o join dbo.Clients c on
            o.Clientid = c.ClientId;
```

This implementation is very convenient for developers. By referencing the view, they have complete information about the orders without worrying about the underlying join. When a client application wants to select a specific order, it could issue a SELECT, as shown in Listing 10-5, and get an execution plan, as shown in Figure 10-1.

Listing 10-5. Views and joins: Selecting all columns from vOrders view

```
select OrderId, Clientid, ClientName, OrderDate, OrderNumber, Amount
from dbo.vOrders
where OrderId = @OrderId
```

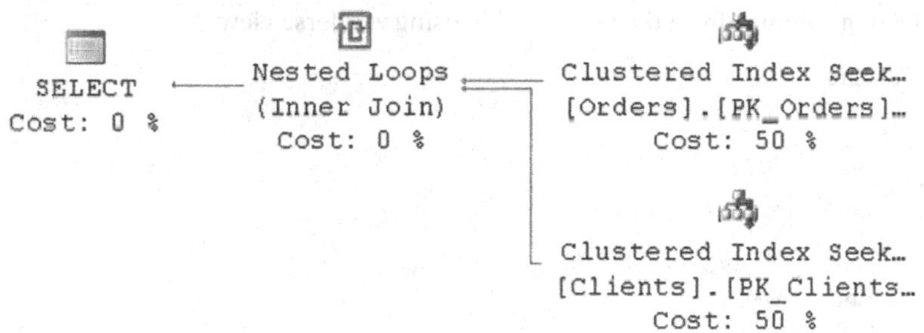

Figure 10-1. *Execution plan when selecting all columns from the view*

This is exactly what you were expecting. SQL Server replaces the view with an underlying query that selects data from the dbo.Orders table, joining it with the data from the dbo.Clients table. However, if you run a query that returns columns only from the dbo.Orders table, as shown in Listing 10-6, you would have an unexpected execution plan, as shown in Figure 10-2.

Listing 10-6. Views and joins: Selecting columns from the Orders table using vOrders view

```
select OrderId, OrderNumber, Amount
from dbo.vOrders
where OrderId = @OrderId
```

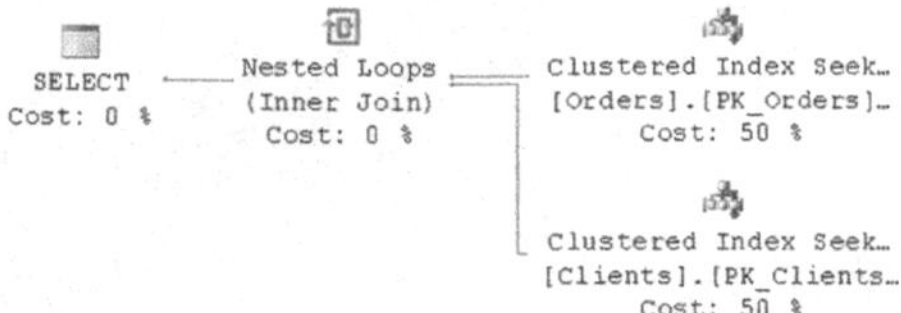

Figure 10-2. *Execution plan when selecting columns that belong to the Orders table only*

As you can see, SQL Server still does the join, even if you do not need ClientName column data. It makes sense; you are using an inner join in the view, and SQL Server needs to exclude the rows from the dbo.Orders table that do not have corresponding rows in the dbo.Clients table.

There are two options for how you can address this and eliminate the unnecessary join from the execution plan. The first is to use an outer join rather than the inner one, as shown in Listing 10-7.

Listing 10-7. Views and joins: vOrders2 view creation

```
create view dbo.vOrders2(OrderId, Clientid, OrderDate, OrderNumber, Amount, ClientName)
as
    select o.OrderId, o.ClientId, o.OrderDate, o.OrderNumber, o.Amount, c.ClientName
    from dbo.Orders o left outer join dbo.Clients c on
            o.Clientid = c.ClientId;
```

Now, if you run the SELECT statement, as shown in Listing 10-8, you would have an execution plan without an inner join, as shown in Figure 10-3.

Listing 10-8. Views and joins: Selecting columns from the Orders table using vOrders2 view

```
select OrderId, OrderNumber, Amount
from dbo.vOrders2
where OrderId = @OrderId
```

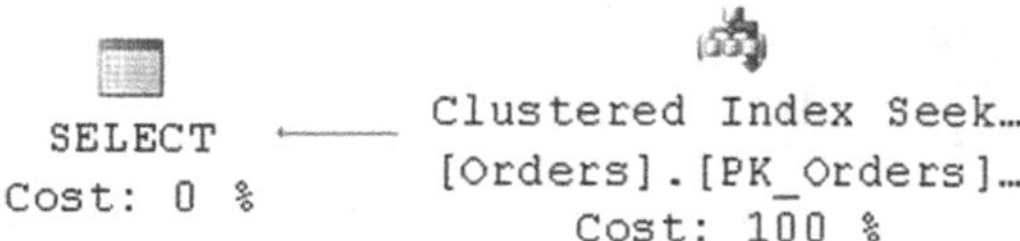

Figure 10-3. *Execution plan with left outer join*

While it does the trick, outer joins restrict the choices available to the Query Optimizer when generating execution plans. Another thing to keep in mind is that you changed the behavior of the view. If you can now have orders that do not belong to clients in the system, then the new implementation would not exclude them from the result set. This can introduce side effects and break other code that references the view and relies on the old behavior of the inner join. You must analyze the data and subject area before implementing join elimination using outer joins.

A better option is adding a foreign key constraint to the `dbo.Orders` table, as shown in Listing 10-9.

Listing 10-9. Views and joins: Adding a foreign-key constraint

```
alter table dbo.Orders with check
add constraint FK_Orders_Clients
foreign key(ClientId)
references dbo.Clients(ClientId)
```

A trusted foreign key constraint guarantees that every order has a corresponding client row. As a result, SQL Server can eliminate the join from the plan. Figure 10-4 shows the execution plan if you query the `dbo.vOrders` view using the code from Listing 10-6, which selects data from the `dbo.Orders` table only.

```
SELECT      ←——    Clustered Index Seek…
Cost: 0 %          [Orders].[PK_Orders]…
                        Cost: 100 %
```

Figure 10-4. *Execution plan with inner join when foreign-key constraint is present*

Unfortunately, there is no guarantee that SQL Server will eliminate all unnecessary joins, especially in very complex cases with many tables involved. Moreover, SQL Server does not eliminate joins if the foreign key constraints include more than one column.

Now, let's review a situation where a system collects location information for devices that belong to multiple companies. The code that creates the tables is shown in Listing 10-10.

Listing 10-10. Join elimination and multi-column foreign key constraints: Table creation

```
create table dbo.Devices
(
    CompanyId int not null,
    DeviceId int not null,
    DeviceName nvarchar(64) not null,
);

create unique clustered index IDX_Devices_CompanyId_DeviceId
on dbo.Devices(CompanyId, DeviceId);

create table dbo.Positions
(
    CompanyId int not null,
    OnTime datetime2(0) not null,
    RecId bigint not null,
    DeviceId int not null,
    Latitude decimal(9,6) not null,
    Longitute decimal(9,6) not null,
```

```
    constraint FK_Positions_Devices
    foreign key(CompanyId, DeviceId)
    references dbo.Devices(CompanyId, DeviceId)
);

create unique clustered index IDX_Positions_CompanyId_OnTime_RecId
on dbo.Positions(CompanyId, OnTime, RecId);

create nonclustered index IDX_Positions_CompanyId_DeviceId_OnTime
on dbo.Positions(CompanyId, DeviceId, OnTime);
```

Let's create a view that joins these tables, as shown in Listing 10-11.

Listing 10-11. Join elimination and multi-column foreign key constraints: View creation

```
create view dbo.vPositions(CompanyId, OnTime, RecId, DeviceId, DeviceName, Latitude,
Longitude)
as
    select p.CompanyId, p.OnTime, p.RecId, p.DeviceId, d.DeviceName, p.Latitude, p.Longitude
    from dbo.Positions p join dbo.Devices d on
            p.CompanyId = d.CompanyId and p.DeviceId = d.DeviceId;
```

Now, let's run the SELECT shown in Listing 10-12. This returns the columns from the dbo.Positions table only and produces the execution plan shown in Figure 10-5.

Listing 10-12. Join elimination and multi-column foreign key constraints: Select from vPositions view

```
select OnTime, DeviceId, Latitude, Longitude
from dbo.vPositions
where CompanyId = @CompanyId and OnTime between @StartTime and @StopTime
```

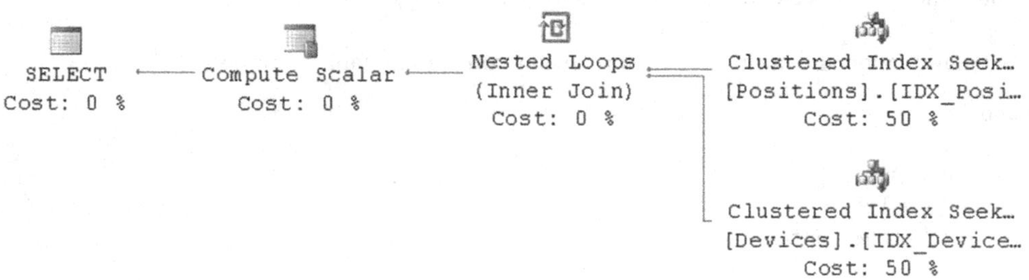

Figure 10-5. *Execution plan with multi-column foreign key constraints*

Even with a foreign key constraint in place, you still have the join. SQL Server does not perform join elimination when a foreign key constraint has more than one column. Unfortunately, there is very little you can do in such a situation to perform join elimination. You can use the approach with the outer join, although it is worth considering querying the tables directly rather than using views in such a scenario.

Finally, SQL Server does not perform join elimination, even with single-column foreign key constraints, when tables are created in tempdb. You need to keep this in mind if you use tempdb as the staging area for the ETL processes when you load data from external sources and do some processing and data transformation before inserting the data into a user database.

Indexed (Materialized) Views

As opposed to views, which are just metadata, *indexed views* materialize the data from the view queries, storing it in the database in a way similar to tables. Then, every time the base tables are updated, SQL Server synchronously refreshes the data in the indexed views, thus keeping them up to date.

In order to define an indexed view, you need to create a regular view using the *schemabinding* option. This option *binds* the view and underlying tables, and it prevents any alteration of the tables that affects the view.

Next, you need to create a unique clustered index on the view. At this point, SQL Server *materializes* the view data in the database. You can also create nonclustered indexes if needed, after the clustered index has been created. When indexes are defined as unique, SQL Server enforces the rule and fails any modification of the base tables if there is a uniqueness violation. You can rely on this behavior to support uniqueness on a subset of the values in SQL Server 2005, or in complex cases, which are not supported by filtered indexes. One such example is the filter that includes OR conditions.

There are plenty of requirements and restrictions in order for a view to be indexable. To name just a few, a view cannot have subqueries, semi or outer joins, reference LOB columns, or have UNION, DISTINCT, or TOP specified. There are also restrictions on the aggregate functions that can be used with a view. Finally, a view needs to be created with specific SET options, and it can reference only deterministic functions, which always return the same result when they are called with a specific set of parameter values.

■ **Note** Look at Books Online at http://technet.microsoft.com/en-us/library/ms191432.aspx for a complete list of requirements and restrictions.

■ **Tip** You can use the function OBJECTPROPERTY with parameter IsIndexable to determine if you can create a clustered index on the view. The following select returns 1 if the view vPositions is indexable:

```
SELECT OBJECTPROPERTY (OBJECT_ID(N'dbo.vPositions','IsIndexable')
```

One instance where an indexed view is useful is for the optimization of queries that include joins and aggregations on large tables. Let's look at this situation, assuming that you have the dbo.OrderLineItems and dbo.Products tables in the system. The code that creates these tables is shown in Listing 10-13.

Listing 10-13. Indexed views: Table creation

```
create table dbo.Products
(
    ProductID int not null identity(1,1),
    Name nvarchar(100) not null,
    constraint PK_Product
    primary key clustered(ProductID)
);
```

```
create table dbo.OrderLineItems
(
    OrderId int not null,
    OrderLineItemId int not null identity(1,1),
    Quantity decimal(9,3) not null,
    Price smallmoney not null,
    ProductId int not null,

    constraint PK_OrderLineItems
    primary key clustered(OrderId,OrderLineItemId),

    constraint FK_OrderLineItems_Products
    foreign key(ProductId)
    references dbo.Products(ProductId)
);

create index IDX_OrderLineItems_ProductId on dbo.OrderLineItems(ProductId);
```

Now, let's imagine a dashboard that displays information about the ten most popular products sold to date. The dashboard can use the query shown in Listing 10-14.

Listing 10-14. Indexed views: Dashboard query

```
select top 10 p.ProductId, p.name as ProductName, sum(o.Quantity) as TotalQuantity
from
    dbo.OrderLineItems o join dbo.Products p on
        o.ProductId = p.ProductId
group by
        p.ProductId, p.Name
order by
        TotalQuantity desc
```

If you were to run this dashboard query in the system, you would receive the execution plan shown in Figure 10-6.

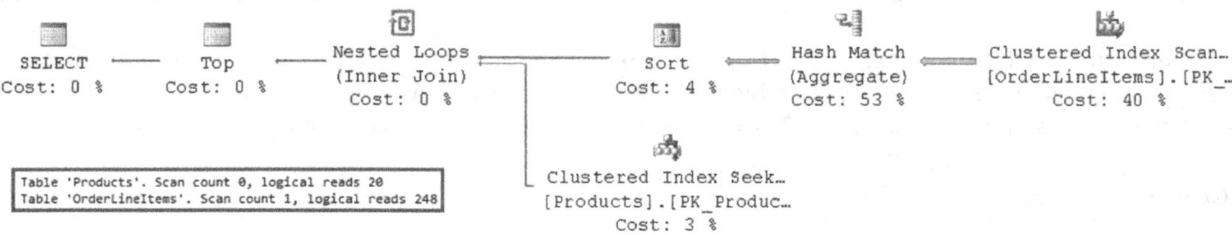

Figure 10-6. *Execution plan of a query that selects the top 10 most popular products*

As you can see, this plan scans and aggregates the data from the `dbo.OrderLineItems` table, which is expensive in terms of I/O and CPU. Alternatively, you can create an indexed view that does the same aggregation and materializes the results in the database. The code to create this view is shown in Listing 10-15. On a side note, one of the requirements for indexed views is the presence of a `COUNT_BIG(*)` aggregation when the `GROUP BY` clause is present.

Listing 10-15. Indexed views: Indexed view creation

```
create view dbo.vProductSaleStats(ProductId, ProductName, TotalQuantity, Cnt)
with schemabinding
as
    select p.ProductId, p.Name, sum(o.Quantity), count_big(*)
    from dbo.OrderLineItems o join dbo.Products p on
            o.ProductId = p.ProductId
    group by
            p.ProductId, p.Name
go

create unique clustered index IDX_vProductSaleStats_ProductId
on dbo.vProductSaleStats(ProductId);

create nonclustered index IDX_vClientOrderTotal_TotalQuantity
on dbo.vProductSaleStats(TotalQuantity desc)
include(ProductName);
```

The code in Listing 10-15 creates a unique clustered index on the `ProductId` column as well as a nonclustered index on the `TotalQuantity` column.

Now you can select data directly from the view, as shown in Listing 10-16.

Listing 10-16. Indexed views: Selecting data from the indexed view

```
select top 10 ProductId, ProductName, TotalQuantity
from dbo.vProductSaleStats
order by TotalQuantity desc
```

The execution plan shown in Figure 10-7 is much more efficient.

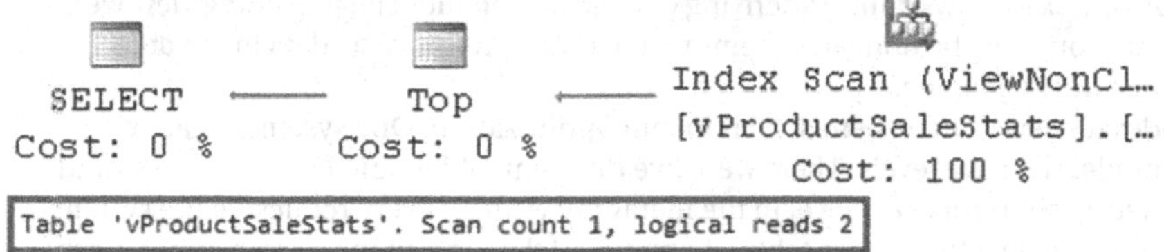

Figure 10-7. *Execution plan of a query that selects the top 10 most popular products utilizing an indexed view*

As always, "there ain't no such thing as a free lunch." Now, SQL Server needs to maintain the view. Each time you insert or delete the `dbo.OrderLineItem` row or, perhaps, modify the quantity or product there, SQL Server needs to update the data in the indexed view in addition to in the main table.

Let's look at the execution plan of the `INSERT` operation, as shown in Figure 10-8.

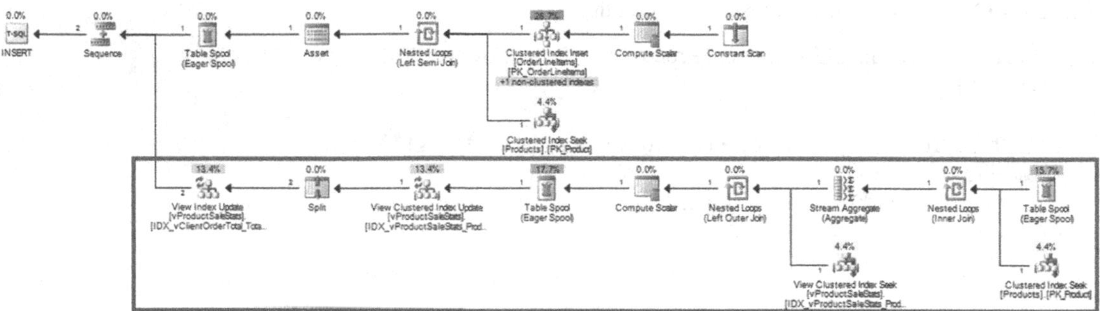

Figure 10-8. *Execution plan of a query that inserts data into OrderLineItems table*

The part of the plan in the highlighted area is responsible for indexed view maintenance. This portion of the plan could introduce a lot of overhead when data in the table is highly volatile, which leads us to a very important conclusion: *indexed views work best when the benefits we get while selecting the data exceed the overhead of maintaining the view during data modifications.* Simply said, indexed views are most beneficial when the underlying data is relatively static. Think about data warehouse systems where a typical workload requires a lot of joins and aggregations and the data is updating infrequently, perhaps based on some schedule, as an example.

■ **Tip** Always test the performance of the batch data update when there is an indexed view referencing a table. In some cases, it would be faster to drop and recreate the view rather than keeping it during such operations.

In an OLTP system, you need to consider carefully the pros and cons of indexed views on a case-by-case basis. It is better to avoid indexed views if the underlying data is too volatile. The preceding view we created is an example of what should *not* be done in systems where data—in this case, data in the `dbo.OrderLineItems` table–is constantly changing.

Another area where indexed views can be beneficial is in join optimization. One system I dealt with had a hierarchical security model with five levels. There were five different tables, and each of them stored information about specific permissions for every level in the hierarchy. Almost every request in the system checked permissions by joining the data from those tables. I optimized that part of the system by creating an indexed view that performed a five-table join so that every request performed just a single index seek operation against the indexed view. Even though it was an OLTP system, the data in the underlying tables was relatively static, and the benefits achieved exceeded the overhead of the indexed view maintenance.

While indexed views can be created in every edition of SQL Server, their behavior is indeed edition-specific. Non-Enterprise editions of SQL Server need to reference a view directly in queries using the WITH (NOEXPAND) hint in order to use data from the indexed view. Without the hint, SQL Server expands the indexed view definition and replaces it with an underlying query similar to regular views. Enterprise and Developer editions do not require such hints. SQL Server can utilize indexed views even when you do not reference them in the query.

Now, let's return to our previous example. In Enterprise Edition, when you run the query shown in Listing 10-17, you would still get an execution plan that utilizes it, as shown in Figure 10-9.

Listing 10-17. Indexed views: Dashboard query

```
select top 10 p.ProductId, p.name as ProductName, sum(o.Quantity) as TotalQuantity
from
    dbo.OrderLineItems o join dbo.Products p on
        o.ProductId = p.ProductId
group by
    p.ProductId, p.Name
order by
    TotalQuantity desc
```

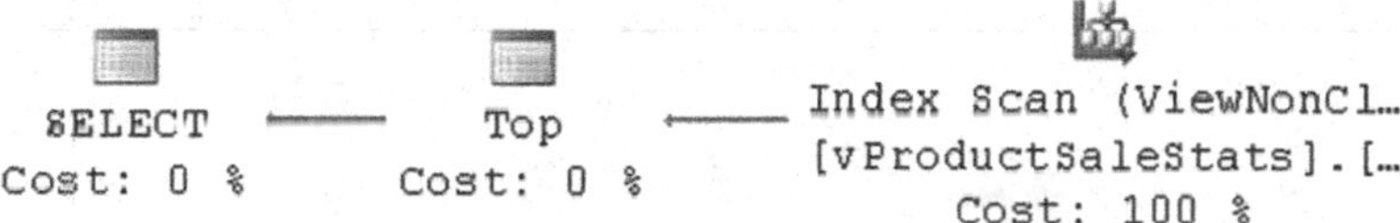

Figure 10-9. *Execution plan of a query that does not reference the indexed view (Enterprise or Developer editions)*

In fact, the Enterprise Edition of SQL Server can use indexed views for any queries, regardless of how close they are to the view definition. For example, let's run a query that selects a list of all of the products ever sold in the system. This query is shown in Listing 10-18.

Listing 10-18. Indexed views: Query that returns a list of all of the products ever sold in the system

```
select p.ProductId, p.Name
from dbo.Products p
where
        exists ( select *
                 from dbo.OrderLineItems o
                 where p.ProductId = o.ProductId )
```

SQL Server recognizes that it would be cheaper to scan the indexed view rather than perform the join between two tables, and it generates a plan, as shown in Figure 10-10.

SELECT
Cost: 0 %
Index Scan (ViewNonCl...
[vProductSaleStats].[...
Cost: 100 %

Figure 10-10. *Execution plan of the query (Enterprise or Developer editions)*

In some cases, you can use such behavior if you need to optimize systems where you cannot change the database schema and queries. If you are working with Enterprise Edition, you can create the indexed views, and the optimizer would start using them for some of the queries, even when those queries do not reference the views directly. Obviously, you need to carefully consider the indexed view maintenance overhead that you would introduce with such an approach.

Partitioned Views

Partitioned views combine data via a `UNION ALL` of multiple tables stored on the same or different database servers. One of the common use cases for such an implementation is data partitioning; that is, when you split data among multiple tables based on some criteria–for example, how recent it is–and then combine the data from all the tables via the partitioned view.

Another case is *data sharding*, which is when you separate (shard) data between multiple servers based on some criteria. For example, a large, Web-based shopping-cart system can shard data based on the geographic locations of the customers. In such cases, partitioned views can combine the data from all shards and use it for analysis and reporting purposes.

■ **Note** We will discuss partitioned views in greater detail in Chapter 16, "Data Partitioning."

Updatable Views

Client applications can modify data in underlying tables through a view. It can reference the view in DML statements, although there is a set of requirements to be met. To name just a few, all modifications must reference columns from only one base table. Those columns should be physical columns and should not participate in calculations and aggregations.

■ **Note** You can see the full list of requirements in Books Online at `http://technet.microsoft.com/en-us/library/ms187956.aspx`.

These restrictions are the biggest downside of this approach. One of the reasons we are using views is to add another layer of abstraction that hides the implementation details. By doing updates directly against views, we are limited in how we can alter them. If our changes violate some of the requirements for making the view updatable, the DML statements issued by the client applications would fail.

Another way to make a view updatable is by defining an `INSTEAD OF` trigger. While this gives us the flexibility to re-factor views in the manner we want, this approach is usually slower than directly updating the underlying tables. It also makes the system harder to support and maintain; you must remember that data in tables can be modified through views.

Finally, you can create the view with the `CHECK OPTION` parameter. When this option is specified, SQL Server checks if the data inserted or updated through the view conforms to criteria set in the view's `SELECT` statement. It guarantees that the rows will be visible through the view after the transaction is committed. For example, look at the table and view defined in Listing 10-19.

Listing 10-19. CHECK OPTION: Table and view creation

```
create table dbo.Numbers(Number int)
go

create view dbo.PositiveNumbers(Number)
as
    select Number
    from dbo.Numbers
    where Number > 0
with check option
go
```

Either of the statements shown in Listing 10-20 would fail because they violate the criteria `Number > 0` specified in the view query.

Listing 10-20. CHECK OPTION: Failed statements

```
insert into dbo.PositiveNumbers(Number) values(-1)
update dbo.PositiveNumbers set Number = -1 where Number = 1
```

You should consider creating a view with `CHECK OPTION` when the view is being used to prevent access to a subset of the data and when client applications update the data through the view. Client applications would not be able to modify data outside of the allowed scope.

Summary

Views are a powerful and useful tool that can help in several different situations. Regular views can provide a layer of abstraction from both the security and implementation standpoints. Indexed views can help with system optimization, and they reduce the number of joins and aggregations that need to be performed.

As with other SQL Server objects, views come at a cost. Regular views can negatively affect performance by introducing unnecessary joins. Indexed views introduce overhead during data modifications, and you need to maintain their indexes in a manner similar to that for those defined on regular tables. You need to keep these factors in mind when designing views.

Views are generally better suited to reading data. Updating data through views is a questionable practice. Using `INSTEAD OF` triggers is usually slower than directly updating the underlying tables. Without triggers, there are restrictions that you have to follow to make views updatable. Changing the implementation of the views could lead to side effects and break client applications.

As with the other database objects, you need to consider the pros and cons of views, especially when you design the dedicated data access tier. Another option you have at your disposal is using stored procedures. Even though views are generally simpler to use in client applications, you can add another filter predicate on the client side, for example, without changing anything in the view definition, and stored procedures provide more flexibility and control over implementation during the development and optimization stages.

CHAPTER 11

User-Defined Functions

This chapter discusses multi-statement and inline user-defined functions. It analyzes how SQL Server executes multi-statement functions and the performance impact they introduce. After that, this chapter demonstrates a technique that can help address those performance issues by converting multi-statement functions into inline ones.

Much Ado About Code Reuse

One of the first things that developers learn about in their career is the benefits of code reuse. Encapsulating and reusing code into separate libraries speeds up the development and testing process and reduces the number of bugs in the system.

Unfortunately, this approach does not always work well in the case of T-SQL. From a development and testing standpoint, code reuse definitely helps. However, from a performance standpoint, it could introduce unnecessary overhead when implemented incorrectly. One such example is a "one size fits all" approach where developers create a single stored procedure or function and then use it to support different use cases. For example, consider a system with two tables–dbo.Orders and dbo.Clients–as shown in Listing 11-1.

Listing 11-1. Code reuse: Table creation

```
create table dbo.Clients
(
    ClientId int not null,
    ClientName varchar(32),

    constraint PK_Clients
    primary key clustered(ClientId)
);

create table dbo.Orders
(
    OrderId int not null identity(1,1),
    Clientid int not null,
    OrderDate datetime not null,
    OrderNumber varchar(32) not null,
    Amount smallmoney not null,
    IsActive bit not null,
```


D. Korotkevitch, *Pro SQL Server Internals*, DOI 10.1007/978-1-4842-1964-5_11

```
    constraint PK_Orders
    primary key clustered(OrderId)
);

create index IDX_Orders_OrderNumber
on dbo.Orders(OrderNumber)
include(IsActive, Amount)
where IsActive = 1;
```

Let's assume that the system has a stored procedures-based data access tier, and one of these procedures provides information about all of the active orders in the system. The stored procedure code is shown in Listing 11-2.

Listing 11-2. Code reuse: Stored procedure that returns a list of active orders in the system

```
create proc dbo.usp_Orders_GetActiveOrders
as
    select o.OrderId, o.ClientId, c.ClientName, o.OrderDate, o.OrderNumber, o.Amount
    from dbo.Orders o join dbo.Clients c on
            o.Clientid = c.ClientId
    where IsActive = 1;
```

A client application can call this stored procedure whenever an order list is needed. For example, it can have a page that displays the list with all order attributes as well as a drop-down control that shows only order numbers and amounts. In both cases, the same stored procedure can be used–applications just need to ignore any unnecessary columns in the output while populating the drop-down list.

While this approach helps us to reuse the code, it also reuses the execution plan. When we run the stored procedure, we will get the plan, as shown in Figure 11-1.

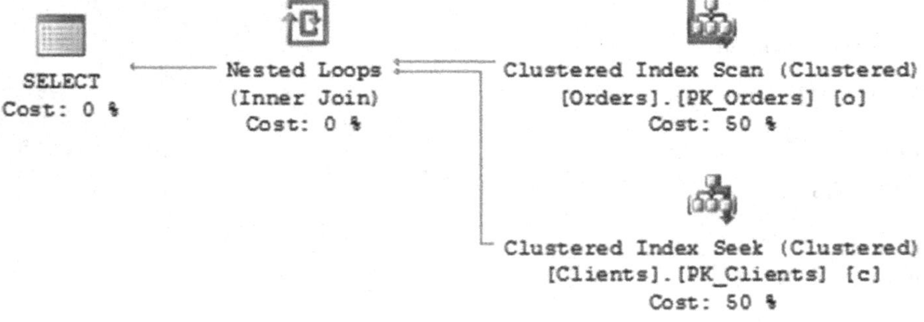

Figure 11-1. *Execution plan of the dbo.usp_Orders_GetActiveOrders stored procedure*

This execution plan would be used in both cases. However, the drop-down control does not need all of the order attributes or the client information, and it can get the required information with the query shown in Listing 11-3.

Listing 11-3. Code reuse: Select that returns the information required for drop-down control

```
select OrderId, OrderNumber, Amount
from dbo.Orders
where IsActive = 1
```

Such a query would have a much more efficient execution plan without the join operator, as shown in Figure 11-2.

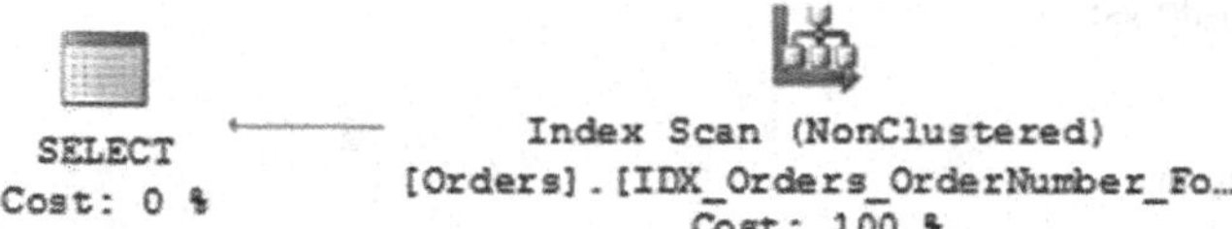

Figure 11-2. *Execution plan of query that returns order numbers and amounts for the drop-down control*

As you can see, by reusing the same stored procedure, we introduced a suboptimal execution plan with an unnecessary join and a *clustered index scan* as opposed to a filtered, nonclustered index scan for one of our use cases. We could also have very similar problems with user-defined functions, which we are going to discuss in this chapter.

There are three types of user-defined functions available in SQL Server: *scalar, multi-statement table-valued,* and *inline table-valued.* However, I would rather use a different classification based on their execution behavior and impact; that is, *multi-statement* and *inline* functions.

Multi-Statement Functions

The code in a *multi-statement function* starts with a BEGIN and ends with an END keyword. It does not matter how many statements they have; that is, functions with a single RETURN statement are considered multi-statement as long as the BEGIN and END keywords are present.

There are two different types of multi-statement functions. The first is the *scalar* function, which returns a single scalar value. The second type is the *table-valued* function, which builds and returns a table result set that can be used anywhere in the statement.

Unfortunately, multi-statement function calls are expensive and introduce significant CPU overhead. Let's populate the dbo.Orders table that we already defined with 100,000 rows and create a scalar function that truncates the time part of the OrderDate column. The function code is shown in Listing 11-4.

Listing 11-4. Multi-statement functions overhead: Scalar function creation

```
create function dbo.udfDateOnly(@Value datetime)
returns datetime
with schemabinding
as
begin
    return (convert(datetime,convert(varchar(10),@Value,121)));
end
```

This function accepts the datetime parameter and converts it to a varchar in a way that truncates the time part of the value. As a final step, it converts that varchar back to datetime, and it returns that value to the caller. This implementation is terribly inefficient. It introduces the overhead of both the function call and the type conversions. However, we often see it in various production systems.

Now, let's run the statement shown in Listing 11-5. This query counts the number of orders with an OrderDate of March 1, 2013.

Listing 11-5. Multi-statement functions overhead: Select that uses scalar function

```
select count(*)
from dbo.Orders
where dbo.udfDateOnly(OrderDate) =  '2013-03-01'
```

The execution time on my computer is as follows:

```
SQL Server Execution Times:
   CPU time = 468 ms,  elapsed time = 509 ms
```

For the next step, let's try to perform a type conversion without the scalar function, as shown in Listing 11-6.

Listing 11-6. Multi-statement functions overhead: Select without scalar function

```
select count(*)
from dbo.Orders
where convert(datetime,convert(varchar(10),OrderDate,121))) =  '2013-03-01'
```

The execution time for this query is as follows:

```
SQL Server Execution Times:
   CPU time = 75 ms,  elapsed time = 82 ms.
```

You can see that the statement runs six times faster without any multi-statement call overhead involved, although there is a better way to write this query. You can check if OrderDate is within the date interval, as shown in Listing 11-7.

Listing 11-7. Multi-statement functions overhead: Select without type conversion

```
select count(*)
from dbo.Orders
where OrderDate >=  '2013-03-01' and OrderDate < '2013-03-02'
```

This approach cuts execution time to the following:

```
SQL Server Execution Times:
   CPU time = 0 ms,  elapsed time = 5 ms.
```

As you can see, user-defined multi-statement function and type conversion operations, which can be considered as system functions, introduce huge overhead and significantly increase query execution time. However, you would hardly notice it in the execution plans. Figure 11-3 shows the execution plan for the queries that use user-defined functions (Listing 11-5) and date interval (Listing 11-7).

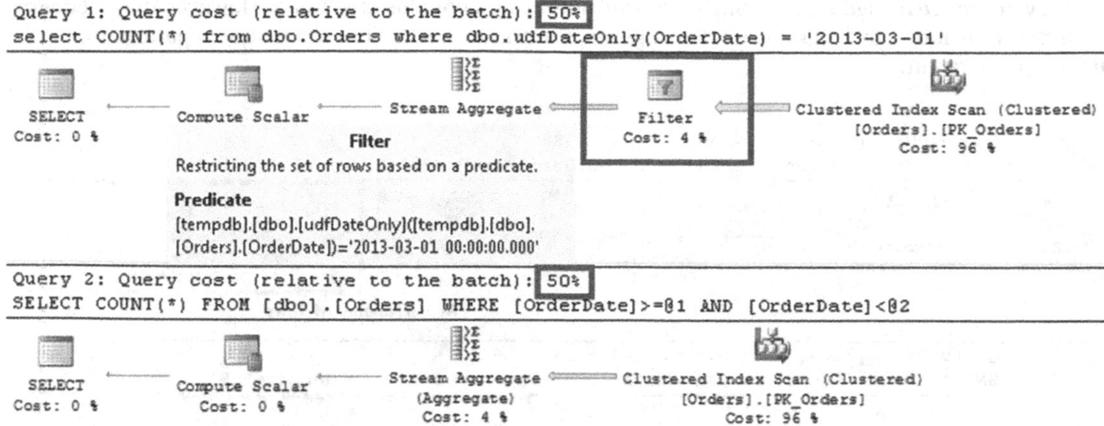

Figure 11-3. *Execution plans with and without a scalar user-defined function*

A user-defined function adds the *filter* operator to the execution plan. However, the costs for both operator and query are way off base.

If you run SQL Server Profiler and capture the *SP:Starting* event, you would see the screen shown in Figure 11-4. As you can see, SQL Server calls the function 100,000 times—once for every row.

Untitled - 2 (.\SQL2012)

EventClass	ObjectName	ObjectType	TextData
SP:Starting	udfDateOnly	20038 - FN	select COUNT(*) from dbo.Orders ...
SP:Starting	udfDateOnly	20038 - FN	select COUNT(*) from dbo.Orders ...
SP:Starting	udfDateOnly	20038 - FN	select COUNT(*) from dbo.Orders ...
SP:Starting	udfDateOnly	20038 - FN	select COUNT(*) from dbo.Orders ...
SP:Starting	udfDateOnly	20038 - FN	select COUNT(*) from dbo.Orders ...
SP:Starting	udfDateOnly	20038 - FN	select COUNT(*) from dbo.Orders ...
SP:Starting	udfDateOnly	20038 - FN	select COUNT(*) from dbo.Orders ...
SP:Starting	udfDateOnly	20038 - FN	select COUNT(*) from dbo.Orders ...

```
select COUNT(*)
from dbo.Orders
where dbo.udfDateOnly(OrderDate) = '2013-03-01'
```

Trace is running. | Ln 100000, Col 1 | Rows: 100000

Figure 11-4. *SQL trace with SP:Starting event*

Another important factor is that multi-statement functions make the predicates non-SARGable. Let's add an index on the `OrderDate` column with the `CREATE NONCLUSTERED INDEX IDX_Orders_OrderDate ON dbo.Orders(OrderDate)` statement and then check the execution plans of the queries.

As you can see in Figure 11-5, both queries are now using a nonclustered index. However, the first query scans the entire index and calls the function for every row within it, while the second query performs an *index seek* operation.

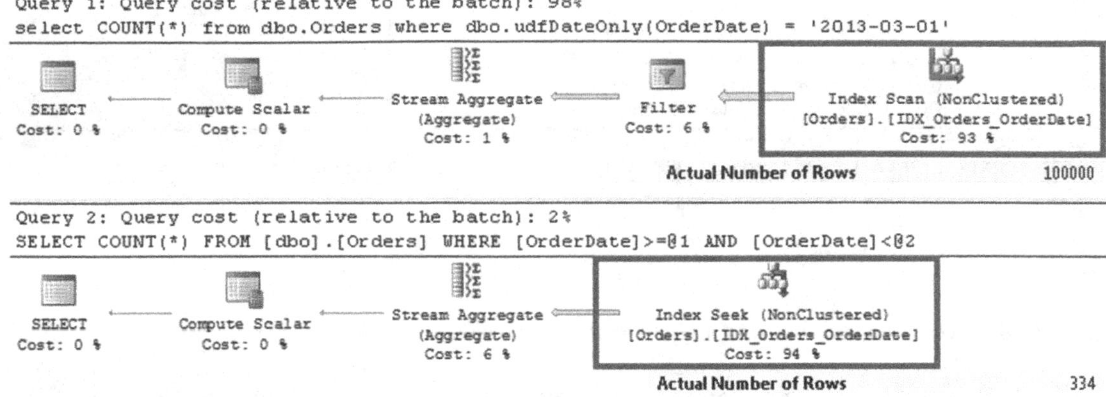

Figure 11-5. *Execution plans of the queries with a non-clustered index on the OrderDate column*

There are also some limitations on how the Query Optimizer works with multi-statement functions. First, it does not factor function-execution overhead into the plan. As you already saw in Figure 11-4, there is an additional filter operator in the execution plan, although SQL Server expects this operator to have a very low cost, which is not even close to the real overhead it introduces. Moreover, SQL Server does not factor the cost of the operators within the function into the execution plan cost of the calling query.

To illustrate this behavior, let's create a function that returns the number of orders for a specific client based on the `ClientId` provided as the parameter. This function is shown in Listing 11-8.

Listing 11-8. Multi-statement function costs and estimates: Function creation

```
create function dbo.ClientOrderCount(@ClientId int)
returns int
with schemabinding
as
begin
    return
    (
        select count(*)
        from dbo.Orders
        where ClientId = @ClientId
    )
end
```

Now, let's call this function with the `SELECT dbo.ClientOrderCount(1)` statement and look at the execution plan, shown in Figure 11-6.

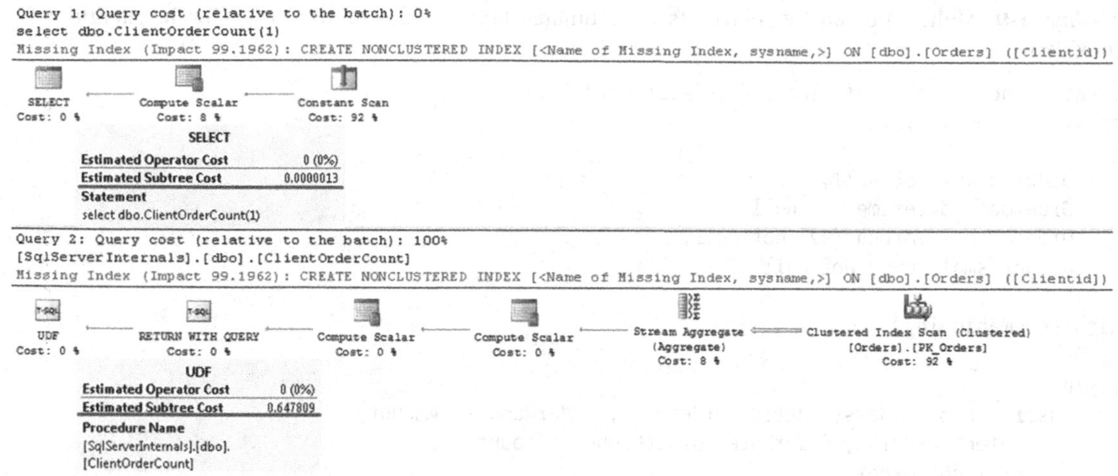

Figure 11-6. *Estimated execution plan for the multi-statement function*

As you can see, SQL Server displays the execution plans for two queries. There are no indexes on the `ClientId` column, and the function needs to perform a clustered index scan on the `dbo.Orders` table even though the Query Optimizer does not factor the estimated cost of the function into the outer query cost.

Another very important limitation is that with the legacy cardinality estimator (70) Query Optimizer always estimates that a multi-statement table-valued function returns just a single row, regardless of the statistics available. New cardinality estimator models (120 and 130) in SQL Server 2014 and 2016 always estimate that a multi-statement table-valued function returns 100 rows.

To demonstrate this, let's create a nonclustered index on the `ClientId` column with the `CREATE NONCLUSTERED INDEX IDX_Orders_ClientId ON dbo.Orders(ClientId)` statement in the database that uses the legacy cardinality estimator.

In this demo, we have 100 clients in the system with 1,000 orders per client. As you should remember, a statistics histogram retains 200 steps, so it would store information for every `ClientId`. You can confirm this by running the `DBCC SHOW_STATISTICS('dbo.Orders', 'IDX_Orders_ClientId')` command. The partial output is shown in Figure 11-7.

	RANGE_HI_KEY	RANGE_ROWS	EQ_ROWS	DISTINCT_RANGE_ROWS	AVG_RANGE_ROWS
1	0	0	1000	0	1
2	1	0	1000	0	1
3	2	0	1000	0	1
4	3	0	1000	0	1

Figure 11-7. *Index IDX_Orders_ClientId histogram*

Now, let's create a multi-statement table-valued function that returns the order information for a specific client and call it in the single-client scope. The code for accomplishing this is shown in Listing 11-9.

Listing 11-9. Multi-statement function costs and estimates: Function that returns orders for the clientid provided

```
create function dbo.udfClientOrders(@ClientId int)
returns @Orders table
(
    OrderId int not null,
    OrderDate datetime not null,
    OrderNumber varchar(32) not null,
    Amount smallmoney not null
)
with schemabinding
as
begin
    insert into @Orders(OrderId, OrderDate, OrderNumber, Amount)
        select OrderId, OrderDate, OrderNumber, Amount
        from dbo.Orders
        where ClientId = @ClientId
    return
end
go

select c.ClientName, o.OrderId, o.OrderDate, o.OrderNumber, o.Amount
from dbo.Clients c cross apply dbo.udfClientOrders(c.ClientId) o
where c.ClientId = 1
```

■ **Note** The `APPLY` operator invokes a table-valued function for every row from the outer table. The table-valued function can accept values from the row as parameters. SQL Server joins the row from the outer table with every row from the function output, similar to a two-table join. `CROSS APPLY` works in a manner similar to the inner join. Thus, if the function does not return any rows, the row from the outer table would be excluded from the output. `OUTER APPLY` works in a way similar to the outer join.

Even though there is enough statistical information to estimate the number of orders correctly for the client with `ClientId=1`, the estimated number of rows is incorrect. Figure 11-8 demonstrates this. This behavior can lead to a highly inefficient execution plan when functions return a large number of rows. It is also worth mentioning that the new cardinality estimator in SQL Server 2014 and 2016 would estimate 100 rows in this example, which is also incorrect.

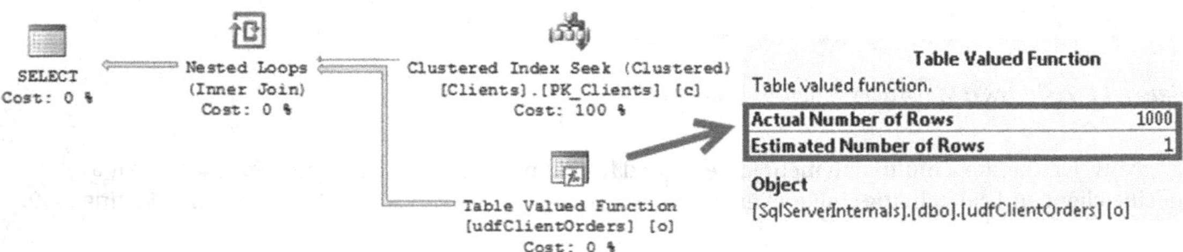

Figure 11-8. *Execution plan of query with multi-statement table-valued function (legacy cardinality estimator)*

You should remember this limitation and avoid using multi-statement table-valued functions when cardinality estimation errors can lead to inefficient plans. A common scenario is when functions are involved in joins. In many cases, you will get better results by storing the function result set in a temporary table, using that in the joins instead, as we will discuss in Chapter 13.

As you probably noticed, all of the functions were created with the *schemabinding* option. While it is not required, specifying this option can help in several ways. It *binds* the function with the objects they reference, and it prevents any metadata changes that could potentially break the code. Moreover, when the function does not access the data, *schemabinding* forces SQL Server to analyze the function body. SQL Server will know that the function does not access any data, which helps to generate more efficient execution plans. We will look at this situation in detail in Chapter 25, "Query Optimization and Execution."

Inline Table-Valued Functions

Inline table-valued functions work in a manner that is completely different from multi-statement functions. Sometimes, these functions are even named *parameterized views*. This definition makes a lot of sense. As opposed to multi-statement functions, which execute as separate code blocks, SQL Server expands and embeds inline table-valued functions into the actual queries, similar to regular views, and it optimizes their statements as part of the queries. As a result, there are no separate calls of the function and you don't have to deal with its associated overhead.

Let's rewrite our multi-statement table-valued function to be an inline table-valued function, as shown in Listing 11-10. Then we will examine the execution plan, shown in Figure 11-9.

Listing 11-10. Inline table-valued functions: Function that returns orders for the clientid provided

```
create function dbo.udfClientOrdersInline(@ClientId int)
returns table
as
return
(
    select OrderId, OrderDate, OrderNumber, Amount
    from dbo.Orders
    where ClientId = @ClientId
)
go

select c.ClientName, o.OrderId, o.OrderDate, o.OrderNumber, o.Amount
from dbo.Clients c cross apply dbo.udfClientOrdersInline(c.ClientId) o
where c.ClientId = 1;
```

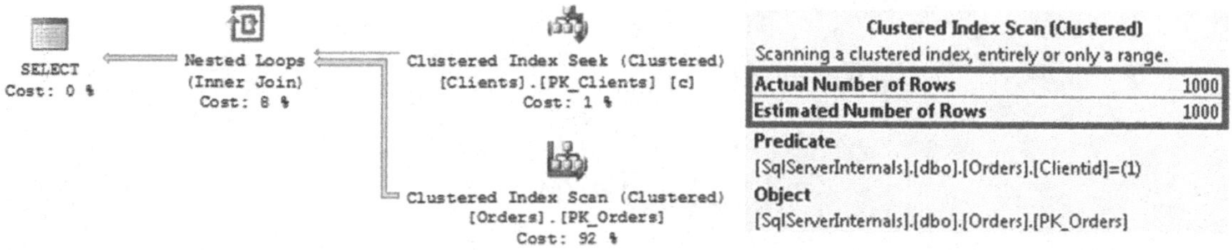

SELECT
Cost: 0 %
Nested Loops
(Inner Join)
Cost: 8 %
Clustered Index Seek (Clustered)
[Clients].[PK_Clients] [c]
Cost: 1 %
Clustered Index Scan (Clustered)
[Orders].[PK_Orders]
Cost: 92 %

Clustered Index Scan (Clustered)
Scanning a clustered index, entirely or only a range.

Actual Number of Rows	1000
Estimated Number of Rows	1000

Predicate
[SqlServerInternals].[dbo].[Orders].[Clientid]=(1)
Object
[SqlServerInternals].[dbo].[Orders].[PK_Orders]

Figure 11-9. *Execution plan of query with an inline table-valued function*

As you can see, there is no reference to the function in the execution plan, and now the estimated number of rows is correct. In fact, you will get exactly the same execution plan if you do not use the inline table-valued function at all. Listing 11-11 and Figure 11-10 illustrate this point.

Listing 11-11. Inline table-valued functions: Select statement without inline table-valued function

```
select c.ClientName, o.OrderId, o.OrderDate, o.OrderNumber, o.Amount
from dbo.Clients c join dbo.Orders o on
      c.ClientId = o.Clientid
where c.ClientId = 1
```

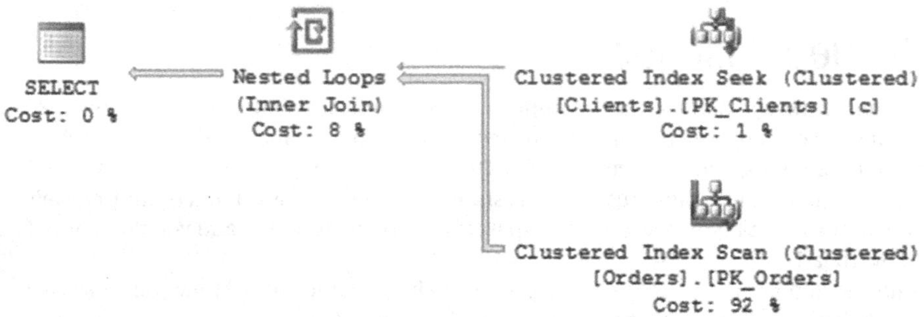

Figure 11-10. *Execution plan of query without an inline table-valued function*

■ **Note** Code reuse based on inline table-valued functions may be acceptable in some cases. SQL Server expands and optimizes those functions with outer statements and can eliminate unnecessary overhead and joins. Remember, however, the join elimination issues we discussed in the previous chapter.

While inline table-valued functions can help us encapsulate and reuse code without unnecessary side effects, they cannot include more than one statement. Fortunately, in some cases you can re-factor the code and convert multi-statement functions into inline table-valued functions.

As a general rule, scalar functions can be replaced with inline table-valued functions that return a one-row table with a single column. As an example, look at the implementation of the `dbo.udfDateOnly` function. You can convert it to an inline table-valued function, as shown in Table 11-1.

Table 11-1. *Converting Multi-Statement Scalar to Inline Table-Valued Function*

<table>
<tr><th>Multi-statement scalar function</th><th>Inline table-valued function</th></tr>
<tr><td><pre>create function dbo.udfDateOnly
  (@Value datetime)
returns datetime
with schemabinding
as
begin
  return
    convert(datetime,
      convert(varchar(10),@Value,121))
end

select count(*)
from dbo.Orders
where
  dbo.udfDateOnly(OrderDate) = '2013-03-01'</pre></td><td><pre>create function dbo.udfDateOnlyInline
  (@Value datetime)
returns table
as
return
(
  select
    convert(datetime,
      convert(varchar(10),@Value,121))
    as [OrderDate]
)
select count(*)
from dbo.Orders o cross apply
  dbo.udfDateOnlyInline(o.OrderDate) udf
where udf.OrderDate = '2013-03-01'</pre></td></tr>
</table>

If you run the SELECT with an inline table-valued function, the execution plan shown in Figure 11-11 would still use an index scan operator instead of an index seek. Even with an inline table-valued function, you cannot make the predicate SARGable due to the convert system function calls.

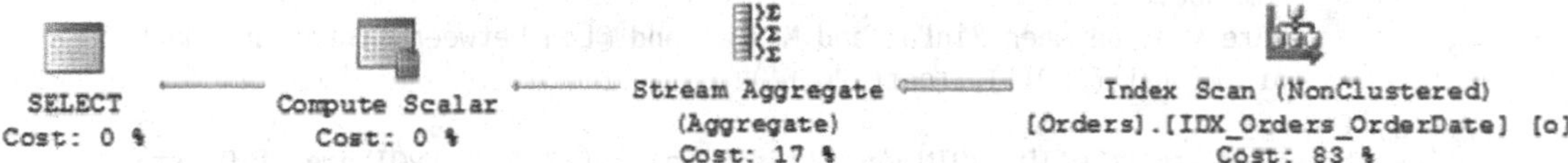

Figure 11-11. *Execution plan of query with inline table-valued function*

If you compare the execution plan shown in Figure 11-11 with the plan that uses a multi-statement scalar function, as shown in Figure 11-5, you will observe that there is no filter operator in Figure 11-11. SQL Server checks the predicate as part of the index scan operator. This behavior is the same in the query from Listing 11-6.

The execution time on my computer is as follows:

```
SQL Server Execution Times:
   CPU time = 78 ms,  elapsed time = 84 ms.
```

While it is still far from being optimal due to the scan performed, these numbers are much better than what we had with the multi-statement function call.

Of course, it is much trickier when the function consists of multiple statements. Fortunately, in some cases you can be creative and re-factor those functions to be inline ones. An IF statement can often be replaced with a CASE operator, and Common Table Expressions can sometimes take care of procedural style code.

As an example, let's look at a multi-statement function that accepts geographic location as the input parameter and returns a table with information about nearby points of interest (POI). This table includes information about the first POI in alphabetical order by name, as well as an optional XML column that contains the list of all POI IDs to which that location belongs. In the database, each POI is specified by a pair of min and max latitudes and longitudes. Listing 11-12 shows the implementation of the multi-statement table-valued function.

Listing 11-12. Converting multi-statement to inline functions: Multi-statement function implementation

```
create function dbo.GetPOIInfo(@Lat decimal(9,6), @Lon decimal(9,6), @ReturnList bit)
returns @Result table
(
    POIID int not null,
    POIName nvarchar(64) not null,
    IDList xml null
)
as
begin
    declare
        @POIID int, @POIName nvarchar(64), @IDList xml

    select top 1 @POIID = POIID, @POIName = Name
    from dbo.POI
    where @Lat between MinLat and MaxLat and @Lon between MinLon and MaxLon
    order by Name;

    if @@rowcount > 0
    begin
        if @ReturnList = 1
            select @IDList =
            (
                select POIID as [@POIID]
                from dbo.POI
                where @Lat between MinLat and MaxLat and @Lon between MinLon and MaxLon
                for xml path('POI'), root('POIS')
            );
        insert into @Result(POIID, POIName, IDList) values(@POIID, @POIName, @IDList);
    end
    return;
end
```

As you can see, there are two separate queries against the table in the implementation. If you want to convert this function to an inline table-valued function, you can run the queries as two CTEs, or as subselects and then cross-join their results. The `If @ReturnList = 1` statement can be replaced with the CASE operator, as you can see in the implementation shown in Listing 11-13.

Listing 11-13. Converting multi-statement to inline functions: Inline function implementation

```
create function dbo.GetPOIInfoInline(@Lat decimal(9,6), @Lon decimal(9,6), @ReturnList bit)
returns table
as
return
(
    with TopPOI(POIID, POIName)
    as
    (
        select top 1 POIID, Name
        from dbo.POI
```

```
        where @Lat between MinLat and MaxLat and @Lon between MinLon and MaxLon
        order by Name
    )
    ,IDList(IDList)
    as
    (
        select
            case
                when @ReturnList = 1
                then
                  ( select POIID as [@POIID]
                    from dbo.POI
                    where @Lat between MinLat and MaxLat and @Lon between MinLon and MaxLon
                    for xml path('POI'), root('POIS'), type )
                else null
            end
    )
    select TopPOI.POIID, TopPOI.POIName, IDList.IDList
    from TopPOI cross join IDList
)
```

There is a very important difference between the two implementations, however. The multi-statement function will not run the second SELECT, which generates the XML, when the first query does not return any rows. There is no reason for it to do so: location does not belong to any POI. Alternatively, inline implementation would always run the two queries. It could even degrade performance when the location does not belong to a POI, and the underlying query against the POI table is expensive. It would be better to split the function into two separate ones, GetPOINameInline and GetPOIIDListInline, and re-factor the outer queries in the manner shown in Listing 11-14.

Listing 11-14. Converting multi-statement to inline functions: Re-factoring of the outer query

```
from
    dbo.Locations l
        outer apply dbo.GetPOINameInline(l.Latitude, l.Longitude) pn
        outer apply
        (
            select
                case
                    when @ReturnList = 1 and pn.POIID is not null
                   then ( select IDList from dbo.GetPOIIDListInline(l.latitude,l.longitude) )
                    else null
                end
        ) pids
```

A CASE statement in the second OUTER APPLY operator guarantees that the second function will be executed only when the dbo.GetPOINameInline function returns the data (pn.POIID is not null); that is, there is at least one POI for the location.

■ **Note** You can see other examples of converting complex multi-statement functions to inline table-valued functions in Chapter 14, "CLR," and in the companion materials of the book.

Summary

While encapsulation and code reuse are great processes that can simplify and reduce the cost of development, they are not always well suited for T-SQL code. Generalization of an implementation in order to support multiple use cases within a single method can lead to suboptimal execution plans in some cases. This is especially true for multi-statement functions, both scalar and table-valued. There is large overhead associated with their calls, which in turn introduces serious performance issues when functions are called for a large number of rows. Moreover, SQL Server does not expand them to the referenced queries, and it always estimates that table-valued functions will return a single row when using the legacy cardinality estimator or 100 rows with the new cardinality estimator in SQL Server 2014 and 2016.

Predicates that include multi-statement functions are always non-SARGable, regardless of the indexes defined on the table. This can lead to suboptimal execution plans for the queries and extra CPU load due to the function calls. You need to keep all of these factors in mind when creating multi-statement functions.

On the other hand, inline table-valued functions are expanded to the outer queries, similar to regular views. They do not have the same overhead as multi-statement functions and are optimized as part of the queries. You should re-factor multi-statement functions to inline table-valued functions whenever possible.

CHAPTER 12

XML and JSON

We are living in a world full of information. Businesses are constantly collecting large amounts of data from multiple sources, processing it, and exchanging it with other systems. XML and its popular alternative JSON have become the de-facto standards for information exchange. They work across different platforms and are supported in every development platform that exists today.

Moreover, not all data easily fits into a structured relational data model. For example, we can think about an Internet of Things (IoT) system that collects metrics from different types of sensors. Some sensors might provide information about temperature, while others could supply humidity data. Although there are several ways to store such data in a database, XML and JSON are definitely options worth considering.

In this chapter, we will talk about the XML and JSON data types, system design considerations, and a few methods that can help to improve system performance while working with XML data in SQL Server.

To Use or Not to Use XML or JSON? That Is the Question!

One of the key questions you will need to answer when dealing with XML and JSON data in a database is what use cases you need to support. Although both technologies, XML and JSON, give you the flexibility to deal with semi-structured data, they come at a price. XQuery is CPU-intensive, and it does not provide performance on par with queries against relational data. You can overcome some of these limitations by creating XML indexes, which internally shred XML data into the relational format, but these indexes require a lot of storage space–often several times more than the XML data itself.

JSON, on the other hand, adds less overhead to CPU, but its support in SQL Server is rather limited. It is not supported in SQL Server prior 2016, and it requires a database compatibility level of 130 for all features to be enabled. Moreover, SQL Server does not support the native JSON data type, and you have to store it as a string. Nor does SQL Server allow you to index JSON data. You can create calculated persisted columns for some JSON properties and index them afterward; however, it is impossible to automatically shred JSON data into the relational format as XML indexes do.

In cases where the only requirement is keeping the XML data without any further processing, the best approach is to store it as regular BLOB in the `varbinary(max)` column. This allows reconstruction of the original document without any encoding-related issues being introduced by `varchar`/`nvarchar` data types. The XML data type is not a good choice, as it does not preserve the original document. Even when it is acceptable, there is overhead associated with parsing the XML data that you would prefer to avoid.

If you decide to store XML data in a binary format, consider putting it into a separate table with a one-to-one relationship to the main table. This helps to reduce the row size in the main table and would improve the performance of the system in many scenarios. You can also compress it either in the client code or by using the `COMPRESS` and `DECOMPRESS` functions in SQL Server 2016, or by building CLR-based compression in the earlier versions of SQL Server. Compression can also help to reduce the size of the large JSON fragments in the database.

D. Korotkevitch, *Pro SQL Server Internals*, DOI 10.1007/978-1-4842-1964-5_12

When you need to work with XML or JSON data in SQL Server, you have a few choices. If the data fits into a structured relational model, you will get the best performance by shredding and storing it in a relational table format. For example, you can shred and store XML or similar JSON data, as shown in Listing 12-1, into two tables, `Orders` and `OrderLineItems`.

Listing 12-1. XML that fits into a relation model

```
<Order OrderId="42" OrderTotal="49.96">
  <CustomerId>123</CustomerId>
  <OrderNum>10025</OrderNum>
  <OrderDate>2016-07-15T10:05:20</OrderDate>
  <OrderLineItems>
    <OrderLineItem>
      <ArticleId>250</ArticleId>
      <Quantity>3</Quantity>
      <Price>9.99</Price>
    </OrderLineItem>
    <OrderLineItem>
      <ArticleId>404</ArticleId>
      <Quantity>1</Quantity>
      <Price>19.99</Price>
    </OrderLineItem>
  </OrderLineItems>
</Order>
```

In some cases, when the data is semi-structured, you can shred the structured part into non-XML/non-JSON columns, retaining the semi-structured part as XML/JSON. Listing 12-2 shows an example of this. In this case, you can consider shredding and keeping location-related information in the non-XML columns and keeping `DeviceData` information as XML.

Listing 12-2. Semistructured XML

```
<Locations>
  <Location DeviceId="321432345" Timestamp="2016-07-10T09:01:03">
    <Latitude>47.609102</Latitude>
    <Longitude>-122.321503</Longitude>
    <DeviceData>
      <Ignition>1</Ignition>
      <Sensor1>0</Sensor1>
      <Sensor2>1</Sensor2>
    </DeviceData>
  </Location>
  <Location DeviceId="1563287" Timestamp="2016-07-10T09:02:00">
    <Latitude>47.610611</Latitude>
    <Longitude>-122.201202</Longitude>
    <DeviceData>
      <Speed>56</Speed>
      <Temperature>29</Temperature>
    </DeviceData>
  </Location>
</Locations>
```

Using sparse columns is another option. You can create a wide table with a large number of sparse columns that represent all possible attributes from the XML/JSON data without introducing the storage overhead associated with the storage of NULL values.

You can shred the XML/JSON in the code at the time that you insert or update the data. Alternatively, you can create a set of scalar user-defined functions that extract the data from XML/JSON and store it in the persisted calculated columns. Both approaches have their pros and cons. With the first approach, you need to shred the XML data and update the columns every time the XML/JSON data is updated, potentially in different places in the code. The second approach, on the other hand, can lead to some performance issues. User-defined functions, which shred the data into calculated columns, would prevent parallel execution plans for any queries that are referencing the table, even when calculated columns are not used. Moreover, in some cases, when you reference calculated columns, SQL Server recalculates their values rather than use persisted fields.

Although XML and JSON data add flexibility to our data model, they affect the performance of the system. You must always keep this in mind when designing solutions.

XML Data Type

An XML data type stores data in an internal format using UTF-16 encoding with some compression involved, and it does not preserve the original XML document. Listing 12-3 shows an example of this.

Listing 12-3. XML data type does not preserve original XML document

```
select cast(
N'<script>
<![CDATA[
function max(a,b)
{
    if (a <= b) then { return b; } else { return a; }
}]]>
</script>' as xml)
```

Result:

```
<script>


function max(a,b)
{
    if (a &lt;= b) then { return b; } else { return a; }
}

</script>
```

As you can see, there is no CDATA section in the output, and the < character has been replaced with character entity **<**.

The total storage space used by the XML data type varies. Even with compression, it can exceed the raw text size when the original text uses UTF-8 encoding. However, with UTF-16 data, XML could save some space compared to the text representation.

There are two types of XML data available in SQL Server: *untyped* and *typed*. Untyped XML can store data as long as it is in a valid format, while typed XML is bound by the XML schema. You can create an XML schema with a `CREATE XML SCHEMA COLLECTION` statement and assign it to a column, parameter, or variable of the XML data type.

Typed XML allows SQL Server to take advantage of the data-type information from the XML nodes. Although it improves XQuery performance, it also introduces overhead from schema validation when data is inserted or modified. Usually, you like to have XML typed in cases where the data conforms to a specific XML schema and you can afford such overhead.

The XML schema is stored in the system tables in an internal format. As with regular XML data, SQL Server does not persist the original schema definition. You need to store it separately, perhaps as a BLOB, in case you need to reconstruct it in the future.

As I already mentioned, you can create indexes on XML data. There are two kinds of XML indexes: *primary* and *secondary*. Primary XML indexes shred the XML data into a relational format, and they have either one or two rows for each XML node. Secondary XML indexes are nonclustered indexes defined in the relational table that stores the primary XML index data. They can help with the performance of some operations against XML data.

Now, let's create the table shown in Listing 12-4. We will insert one row of data using the XML from Listing 12-1.

Listing 12-4. Primary XML index on untyped XML

```
create table dbo.XmlDemo
(
    ID int not null identity(1,1),
    XMLData xml not null,
    constraint PK_XmlDemo primary key clustered(ID)
);

insert into dbo.XMLDemo(XMLData)
values(/*XML From Listing 12-1*/);

create primary xml index XML_Primary_XmlDemo
on dbo.XmlDemo(XMLData);
```

Next, let's look at the internal structure of the primary XML index. You can find the name of the internal table that stores the index by querying the `sys.internal_tables` view. You will see results similar to the ones shown in Figure 12-1.

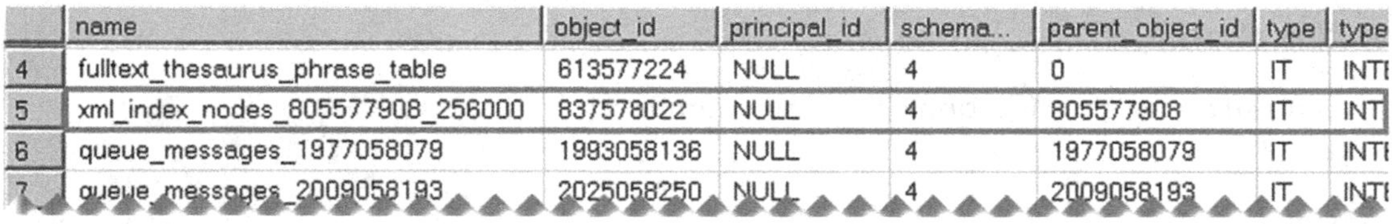

	name	object_id	principal_id	schema...	parent_object_id	type	type
4	fulltext_thesaurus_phrase_table	613577224	NULL	4	0	IT	INT
5	xml_index_nodes_805577908_256000	837578022	NULL	4	805577908	IT	INT
6	queue_messages_1977058079	1993058136	NULL	4	1977058079	IT	INT
7	queue_messages_2009058193	2025058250	NULL	4	2009058193	IT	INT

Figure 12-1. *Sys.internal_tables content*

Now, if you query the data from the primary XML index table, you will see the results shown in Figure 12-2. You need to connect through a dedicated admin connection to be able to do this.

	id	nid	tagname	taguri	tid	value	lvalue	lvalue...	hid	xsinil	xsitype	pk1
1	0x	9	NULL	NULL	NULL	NULL	NULL	NULL		0	0	1
2	0x58	65536	NULL	NULL	NULL	NULL	NULL	NULL	À€	0	0	1
3	0x586CF80003973260	-2147418111	NULL	NULL	NULL	42	NULL	NULL	á€À€	0	0	1
4	0x586EF800039732A0	-2147418110	NULL	NULL	NULL	49.96	NULL	NULL	â€À€	0	0	1
5	0x5B[illegible]0	655[illegible]9	NULL	NULL	NULL	NULL	NULL	NULL	[illegible]	0	0	1
24	0x5CAD78	65546	NULL	NULL	NULL	NULL	NULL	NULL	Ê€Ç€Æ€À€	0	0	1
25	0x5CAD7AC0	4	NULL	NULL	NULL	19.99	NULL	NULL	„€Ê€Ç€Æ€À€	0	0	1

***Figure 12-2.** Primary XML index data (untyped XML)*

As you can see, one row of data from the original table produced twenty-five rows in the primary XML index, with twelve columns each. The clustered index of the primary XML index consists of the primary key in the original table (`pk1` column in the output) and the internal node ID (`id` column in the output). The `HID` column, which stands for *hierarchy ID*, contains a reverse path to the node in the binary format.

It is also worth mentioning that the primary XML index requires tables to have a clustered primary key defined. Neither a unique clustered index nor a nonclustered primary key will work.

Now, let's create a schema collection and construct the table using typed XML. The code for accomplishing this is shown in Listing 12-5.

Listing 12-5. Primary XML index on typed XML

```
create xml schema collection XmlDemoCollection as
N'<xs:schema attributeFormDefault="unqualified" elementFormDefault="qualified"
xmlns:xs="http://www.w3.org/2001/XMLSchema">
  <xs:element name="Order">
    <xs:complexType>
      <xs:sequence>
        <xs:element type="xs:int" name="CustomerId"/>
        <xs:element type="xs:string" name="OrderNum"/>
        <xs:element type="xs:dateTime" name="OrderDate"/>
        <xs:element name="OrderLineItems">
          <xs:complexType>
            <xs:sequence>
              <xs:element name="OrderLineItem" maxOccurs="unbounded" minOccurs="0">
                <xs:complexType>
                  <xs:sequence>
                    <xs:element type="xs:short" name="ArticleId"/>
                    <xs:element type="xs:int" name="Quantity"/>
                    <xs:element type="xs:float" name="Price"/>
                  </xs:sequence>
                </xs:complexType>
              </xs:element>
            </xs:sequence>
          </xs:complexType>
        </xs:element>
      </xs:sequence>
      <xs:attribute type="xs:int" name="OrderId"/>
```

```
      <xs:attribute type="xs:float" name="OrderTotal"/>
    </xs:complexType>
  </xs:element>
</xs:schema>';

create table dbo.XmlTypedDemo
(
    ID int not null identity(1,1),
    XMLData xml (document xmldemocollection) not null,
    constraint PK_XmlTypedDemo primary key clustered(ID)
);

insert into dbo.XMLTypedDemo(XMLData)
values(/*XML From Listing 12-1*/);

create primary xml index XML_Primary_XmlTypedDemo
on dbo.XmlDemo(XMLData);
```

Now, let's look at the primary XML index for the typed XML, shown in Figure 12-3.

	id	nid	tagname	taguri	tid	value	lvalue	lvalue...	hid	xsinil	xsitype	pk1
1	0x	9	NULL	NULL	NULL	NULL	NULL	NULL		0	0	1
2	0x58	65536	NULL	NULL	65537	NULL	NULL	NULL	À€	0	0	1
3	0x586CF80003973260	-2147418111	NULL	NULL	318767217	42.0000000000	NULL	NULL	á€À€	0	0	1
4	0x586EF800039732A0	-2147418110	NULL	NULL	285212689	49.96	NULL	NULL	á€À€	0	0	1
5	0x5BC0	65539	NULL	NULL	318767217	123.0000000000	NULL	NULL	Ã€À€	0	0	1
[illegible]	[illegible]	[illegible]	[illegible]	[illegible]	[illegible]	[illegible]	[illegible]	[illegible]	[illegible]	[illegible]	[illegible]	1
15	0x5CAD68	65545	NULL	NULL	318767217	1.0000000000	NULL	NULL	É€Ç€Æ€À€	0	0	1
16	0x5CAD78	65546	NULL	NULL	285212689	19.99	NULL	NULL	Ê€Ç€Æ€À€	0	0	1

***Figure 12-3.** Primary XML index data (typed XML)*

As you can see, the primary XML index now has just sixteen rows–a single row for each XML node in the original data. It also has type information specified for every node (`tid` column).

Let's compare the storage space required for element- and attribute-centric XML for both the typed and untyped XML. Let's create two XML schema collections and four tables with primary XML indexes. Then, we will populate these tables with 65,536 rows of data. The code in Listing 12-6 shows all of these steps.

Listing 12-6. Comparing storage space required for both typed and untyped XML

```
create xml schema collection ElementCentricSchema as
'<xs:schema attributeFormDefault="unqualified" elementFormDefault="qualified"
        xmlns:xs="http://www.w3.org/2001/XMLSchema">
  <xs:element name="Order">
    <xs:complexType>
      <xs:sequence>
        <xs:element type="xs:int" name="OrderId"/>
        <xs:element type="xs:float" name="OrderTotal"/>
        <xs:element type="xs:int" name="CustomerId"/>
        <xs:element type="xs:string" name="OrderNum"/>
        <xs:element type="xs:dateTime" name="OrderDate"/>
        <xs:element name="OrderLineItems">
```

```
          <xs:complexType>
            <xs:sequence>
              <xs:element name="OrderLineItem" maxOccurs="unbounded" minOccurs="0">
                <xs:complexType>
                  <xs:sequence>
                    <xs:element type="xs:int" name="ArticleId"/>
                    <xs:element type="xs:int" name="Quantity"/>
                    <xs:element type="xs:float" name="Price"/>
                  </xs:sequence>
                </xs:complexType>
              </xs:element>
            </xs:sequence>
          </xs:complexType>
        </xs:element>
      </xs:sequence>
    </xs:complexType>
  </xs:element>
</xs:schema>';

create xml schema collection AttributeCentricSchema as
'<xs:schema attributeFormDefault="unqualified" elementFormDefault="qualified"
      xmlns:xs="http://www.w3.org/2001/XMLSchema">
  <xs:element name="Order">
    <xs:complexType>
      <xs:sequence>
        <xs:element name="OrderLineItem" maxOccurs="unbounded" minOccurs="0">
          <xs:complexType>
            <xs:simpleContent>
              <xs:extension base="xs:string">
                <xs:attribute type="xs:int" name="ArticleId" use="optional"/>
                <xs:attribute type="xs:int" name="Quantity" use="optional"/>
                <xs:attribute type="xs:float" name="Price" use="optional"/>
              </xs:extension>
            </xs:simpleContent>
          </xs:complexType>
        </xs:element>
      </xs:sequence>
      <xs:attribute type="xs:int" name="OrderId"/>
      <xs:attribute type="xs:float" name="OrderTotal"/>
      <xs:attribute type="xs:int" name="CustomerId"/>
      <xs:attribute type="xs:string" name="OrderNum"/>
      <xs:attribute type="xs:dateTime" name="OrderDate"/>
    </xs:complexType>
  </xs:element>
</xs:schema>';

create table dbo.ElementCentricUntyped
(
    ID int not null identity(1,1),
    XMLData xml not null,
    constraint PK_ElementCentricUntyped primary key clustered(ID)
);
```

```
create primary xml index XML_Primary_ElementCentricUntyped
on dbo.ElementCentricUntyped(XMLData);

create table dbo.ElementCentricTyped
(
    ID int not null identity(1,1),
    XMLData xml (document ElementCentricSchema) not null,
    constraint PK_ElementCentricTyped primary key clustered(ID)
);

create primary xml index XML_Primary_ElementCentricTyped
on dbo.ElementCentricTyped(XMLData);

create table dbo.AttributeCentricUntyped
(
    ID int not null identity(1,1),
    XMLData xml not null,
    constraint PK_AttributeCentricUntyped primary key clustered(ID)
);

create primary xml index XML_Primary_AttributeCentricUntyped
on dbo.AttributeCentricUntyped(XMLData);

create table dbo.AttributeCentricTyped
(
    ID int not null identity(1,1),
    XMLData xml (document AttributeCentricSchema) not null,
    constraint PK_AttributeCentricTyped primary key clustered(ID)
);

create primary xml index XML_Primary_AttributeCentricTyped
on dbo.AttributeCentricTyped(XMLData);

;with N1(C) as (select 0 union all select 0) -- 2 rows
,N2(C) as (select 0 from N1 as T1 CROSS JOIN N1 as T2) -- 4 rows
,N3(C) as (select 0 from N2 as T1 CROSS JOIN N2 as T2) -- 16 rows
,N4(C) as (select 0 from N3 as T1 CROSS JOIN N3 as T2) -- 256 rows
,N5(C) as (select 0 from N4 as T1 CROSS JOIN N4 as T2) -- 65,536 rows
,IDs(ID) as (select row_number() over (order by (select NULL)) from N5)
insert into dbo.ElementCentricUntyped(XMLData)
select '
<Order>
  <OrderId>42</OrderId>
  <OrderTotal>49.96</OrderTotal>
  <CustomerId>123</CustomerId>
  <OrderNum>10025</OrderNum>
  <OrderDate>2016-07-15T10:05:20</OrderDate>
  <OrderLineItems>
    <OrderLineItem>
      <ArticleId>250</ArticleId>
      <Quantity>3</Quantity>
```

```
      <Price>9.99</Price>
    </OrderLineItem>
    <OrderLineItem>
      <ArticleId>404</ArticleId>
      <Quantity>1</Quantity>
      <Price>19.99</Price>
    </OrderLineItem>
  </OrderLineItems>
</Order>'
from Ids;

insert into dbo.ElementCentricTyped(XMLData)
    select XMLData from dbo.ElementCentricUntyped;

with N1(C) as (select 0 union all select 0) -- 2 rows
,N2(C) as (select 0 from N1 as T1 CROSS JOIN N1 as T2) -- 4 rows
,N3(C) as (select 0 from N2 as T1 CROSS JOIN N2 as T2) -- 16 rows
,N4(C) as (select 0 from N3 as T1 CROSS JOIN N3 as T2) -- 256 rows
,N5(C) as (select 0 from N4 as T1 CROSS JOIN N4 as T2) -- 65,536 rows
,IDs(ID) as (select row_number() over (order by (select NULL)) from N5)
insert into dbo.AttributeCentricUntyped(XMLData)
select
N'<Order OrderId="42" OrderTotal="49.96" CustomerId="123"
      OrderNum="10025" OrderDate="2016-07-15T10:05:20">
  <OrderLineItem ArticleId="250" Quantity="3" Price="9.99"/>
  <OrderLineItem ArticleId="404" Quantity="1" Price="19.99"/>
</Order>'
from Ids;

insert into dbo.AttributeCentricTyped(XMLData)
    select XMLData from dbo.AttributeCentricUntyped;
```

When we compare the storage space used by all four tables, we see the results shown in Table 12-1.

Table 12-1. *Typed and Untyped XML Storage Requirements*

	Clustered Index Size (KB)	Primary XML Index Size (KB)	Total Size (KB)
Untyped Element-Centric XML	28,906	90,956	119,862
Typed Element-Centric XML	45,760	52,595	99,355
Untyped Attribute-Centric XML	26,021	57,390	83,411
Typed Attribute-Centric XML	36,338	54,105	90,443

As you can see, typed XML uses more space in the clustered index of the table because of the extra information stored in the XML data type column. At the same time, adding type information to element-centric XML can significantly reduce the size of the primary XML index. Unfortunately, even in a best-case scenario, XML indexes require a large amount of storage space that exceeds the storage space required by the XML data type itself.

■ **Note** The actual size of the primary XML index depends on the number of nodes and the data types in the XML data.

Secondary XML indexes are nonclustered indexes in a table and are represented by the primary XML index. Look at Table 12-2, which demonstrates a simplified version of some of the data from the primary XML index table from Figure 12-3.

Table 12-2. *Primary XML index simplified*

PK	ID	NodeId	Type	Value	HID
1	1	1 (Order)	Null	Null	
1	1.1	2 (OrderId)	xs:int	42	#@OrderId#Order
1	1.5	3 (OrderLineItems)	SectionT	Null	#OrderLineItems#Order
1	1.5.1	4 (OrderLineItem)	SectionT	Null	#OrderLineItem #OrderLineItems#Order
1	1.5.1.1	5 (ArticleId)	xs:int	250	#ArticleId #OrderLineItem #OrderLineItems#Order

The VALUE secondary XML index is a nonclustered index with two columns: Value and HID. As you can guess, the best use case for such indexes is when you want to locate rows based on the values and optional paths to the nodes. In our example, the VALUE secondary XML index would be beneficial if you wanted to find all of the orders that have a line item with a specific ArticleID.

The PATH secondary XML index has two columns: HID and Value. Like the VALUE index, the PATH index can be used to find all of the rows with a particular value in a particular path, although there are a couple of differences between these indexes. The VALUE index can be used to find an XML element or attribute with a specific value anywhere within the XML without referencing the path. The PATH index, on the other hand, is not a good choice for such a use case. The PATH index, however, is useful when you are checking the existence of an element based on a particular path. For instance, the PATH index is advantageous if you have an optional nullable node called Comments and you want to select all of the orders where that node is present. Moreover, the PATH index is useful when you are using the // shortcut in the path. For example, Order//ArticleId looks for an ArticleId element anywhere within the Order node. HID stores the inverted path and, as a result, SQL Server can perform a prefix lookup on the index when dealing with such queries.

The PROPERTY secondary XML index has three columns: PK, HID, and Value. This index is useful when you already know the row to which the XML belongs, and you want to get the value and potential node information for a specific path.

SQL Server 2012 and above supports selective XML indexes that allow you to index a subset of the XML nodes. These indexes help you to preserve the storage space when the majority of queries deal with a subset of the XML data. For more information about selective XML indexes, check out this link: http://msdn.microsoft.com/en-us/library/jj670108.aspx.

Working with XML Data

The XQuery implementation in SQL Server utilizes a relation engine. Although XQuery uses its own parser and performs its own algebrarization during the query compilation stage, the results are combined and optimized together with the DML portion of the query, then embedded into a single execution plan.

■ **Note** The algebrarization stage is responsible for name resolution, type derivation, and binding and converting XML operators into a relational-operators tree that can be further used by the Query Optimizer.

When XML indexes are present, SQL Server always retrieves the data from them. Otherwise, it uses table-valued functions to shred the XML data into a relational format. In both cases, the database engine works with a relational representation of the XML data while optimizing and executing the queries.

The XML data type in SQL Server supports five different methods. Four of them—`value`, `exist`, `query`, and `nodes`—can be used to access and transform the data. The last one, `modify`, uses XML DML to modify the data.

value() Method

The `value()` method returns a scalar value from the XML instance. XPath is an expression that defines the path to the value, and it should statically represent the singleton by referencing the single element or attribute from the XML.

The code shown in Listing 12-7 provides examples of singletons in untyped XML.

Listing 12-7. XPath referencing singletons in untyped XML

```
declare
    @X xml =
'<Order OrderId="42" OrderTotal="49.96">
  <Customer Id="123"/>
  <OrderLineItems>
    <OrderLineItem>
      <ArticleId>250</ArticleId>
      <Quantity>3</Quantity>
      <Price>9.99</Price>
    </OrderLineItem>
  </OrderLineItems>
</Order>'

-- SUCCESS: Get @Id from the first customer from first order
select @X.value('/Order[1]/Customer[1]/@Id','int')

-- ERROR: Not a singleton; XML can include information about multiple orders and/or customers
select @X.value('/Order/Customer/@Id','int')

-- SUCCESS: Get first ArticleId from the first order from the first line item
select @X.value('/Order[1]/OrderLineItems[1]/OrderLineItem[1]/ArticleId[1]','int')

-- ERROR: Not a singleton; SQL Server does not know that ArticleId is an element rather than
a section
select @X.value('/Order[1]/OrderLineItems[1]/OrderLineItem[1]/ArticleId','int')
```

■ **Note** The XML schema helps SQL Server detect if XPath references the singleton without specifying indexes/ordinals in the path expressions.

A key XQuery concept is called the *atomization of nodes*. When an XPath expression identifies an element in the untyped XML, XQuery does not know if that element is a section or if it has any child nodes. As a result, it tries to parse and concatenate the values from all XML child nodes from the section by adding another table-valued function to the execution plan. Doing so could introduce a noticeable performance hit to the query. As a workaround, use the XQuery function `text()`, which returns a text representation of the element and eliminates the table-valued function call.

Listing 12-8 shows an example of such behavior, and Figure 12-4 shows the execution plan of the two calls.

Listing 12-8. Atomization of nodes overhead

```
declare
    @X xml =
'<Order OrderId="42" OrderTotal="49.96">
  <CustomerId>123</CustomerId>
  <OrderNum>10025</OrderNum>
  <OrderDate>2016-07-15T10:05:20</OrderDate>
  <OrderLineItems>
    <OrderLineItem>
      <ArticleId>250</ArticleId>
      <Quantity>3</Quantity>
      <Price>9.99</Price>
    </OrderLineItem>
    <OrderLineItem>
      <ArticleId>404</ArticleId>
      <Quantity>1</Quantity>
      <Price>19.99</Price>
    </OrderLineItem>
  </OrderLineItems>
</Order>'

select @X.value('(/Order/CustomerId)[1]','int')
select @X.value('(/Order/CustomerId/text())[1]','int')
```

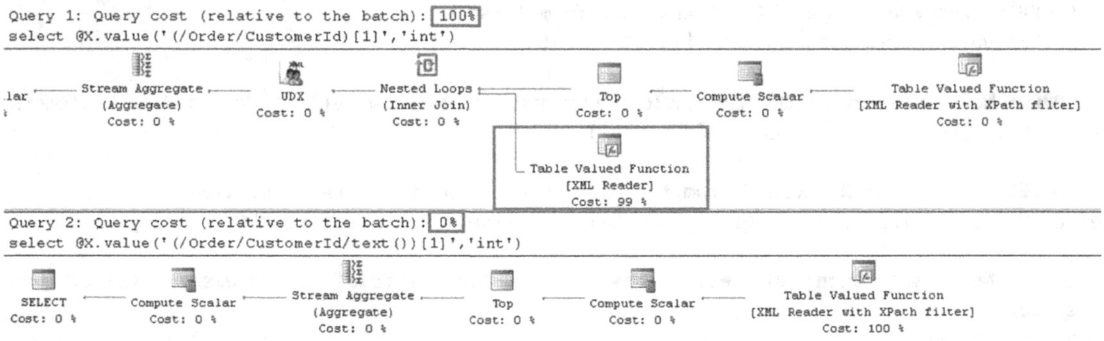

Figure 12-4. *Atomization of nodes overhead*

Atomization of nodes occurs only when an XML instance is untyped. Let's see what happens with typed XML data, as shown in Listing 12-9 and Figure 12-5.

Listing 12-9. Typed XML data and atomization of nodes

```
declare
    @X xml (document ElementCentricSchema) =
'<Order>
  <OrderId>42</OrderId>
  <OrderTotal>49.96</OrderTotal>
  <CustomerId>123</CustomerId>
  <OrderNum>10025</OrderNum>
  <OrderDate>2016-07-15T10:05:20</OrderDate>
  <OrderLineItems>
    <OrderLineItem>
      <ArticleId>250</ArticleId>
      <Quantity>3</Quantity>
      <Price>9.99</Price>
    </OrderLineItem>
    <OrderLineItem>
      <ArticleId>404</ArticleId>
      <Quantity>1</Quantity>
      <Price>19.99</Price>
    </OrderLineItem>
  </OrderLineItems>
</Order>'

select @X.value('(/Order/CustomerId)[1]','int')
```

Query 1: Query cost (relative to the batch): 100%
select @X.value('(/Order/CustomerId)[1]','int')

SELECT Cost: 0 % ← Compute Scalar Cost: 0 % ← Stream Aggregate (Aggregate) Cost: 0 % ← Top Cost: 0 % ← Compute Scalar Cost: 0 % ← Table Valued Function [XML Reader with XPath filter] Cost: 100 %

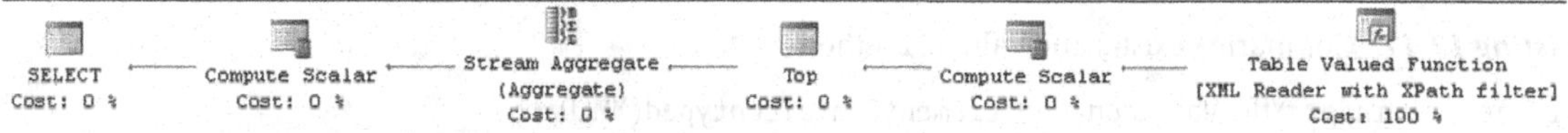

Figure 12-5. *Typed XML and atomization of nodes*

As you can see, there is no atomization of nodes overhead. SQL Server knows that `CustomerId` is an integer rather than a section. This is another benefit of preserving XML type information with XML schema collections.

Finally, let's check out what happens when we have a primary XML index defined and we run the same method against one of the rows from the `ElementCentricTyped` table, as shown in Listing 12-10. The execution plan is then shown in Figure 12-6.

Listing 12-10. Calling the XML data type method when XML index is present

```
select XmlData.value('(/Order/CustomerId)[1]','int')
from dbo.ElementCentricTyped
where ID = 1
```

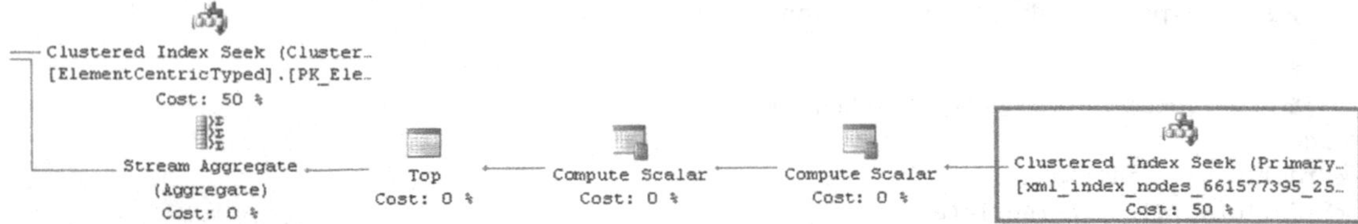

Figure 12-6. *Execution plan when the XML index is present*

As you can see, SQL Server retrieves the data from the primary XML index rather than using a table-valued function.

exists() Method

The `exist()` method returns 1 when XQuery/XPath returns non-empty results. Although you can use this method when you need to check for the existence of an XML node, the typical use case for such a method is to check for the existence of an element or attribute with a specific value.

This method usually outperforms the approach that shreds the XML using the `value()` method and compares the results afterward. This happens because you are evaluating the XPath predicate in the XML Reader rather than doing an evaluation after you shred the XML. You can also use the `sql:column()` and `sql:variable()` functions to pass the values from the variable or table column to the XPath predicate.

Another important factor is that the `exist()` method can utilize a secondary `FOR VALUE` XML index, while the `value()` method does not use it.

Now, let's create that index and compare the performance of the two methods. The code for accomplishing this is shown in Listing 12-11, and the execution plans are shown in Figure 12-7.

Listing 12-11. Comparing exist() and value() methods

```
create xml index XML_Value on dbo.ElementCentricUntyped(XMLData)
using xml index XML_Primary_ElementCentricUntyped for value;

select count(*)
from dbo.ElementCentricUntyped
where XmlData.exist('/Order/OrderNum/text()[.="10025"]') = 1;

select count(*)
from dbo.ElementCentricUntyped
where XmlData.value('(/Order/OrderNum/text())[1]','varchar(32)') = '10025';
```

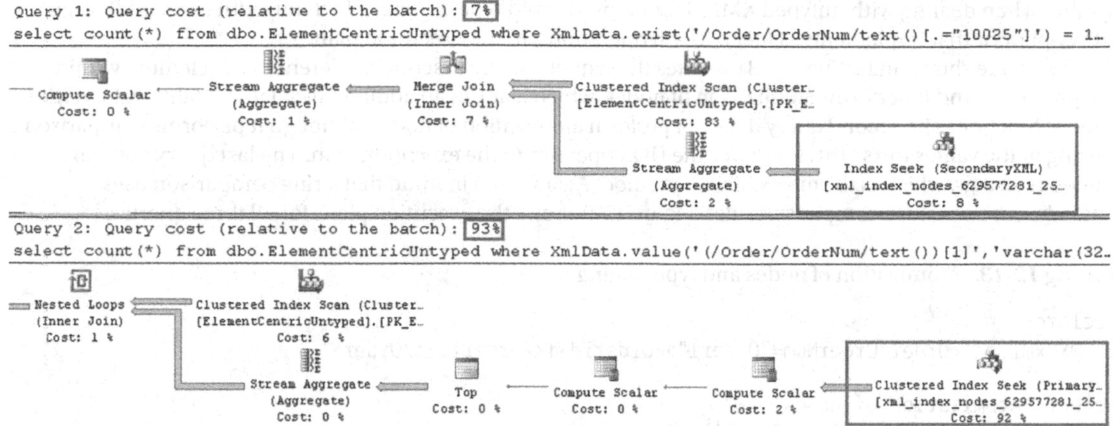

Figure 12-7. Comparing the exist() and value() methods

In cases where there is no FOR VALUE secondary XML index present, however, the value() method may be more efficient than the exist() method. There is one more caveat. XQuery compares string data as unicode case-sensitive strings, and it does not take database collation into consideration. Consequently, you can have different results when you perform a comparison within the XQuery value() method. The code shown in Listing 12-12 demonstrates an example of such behavior.

Listing 12-12. String comparison within XQuery

```
declare
  @X xml = '<Order OrderNum="Order1"><OrderId>1</OrderId></Order>'
  ,@V varchar(32) = 'ORDER1'

select 'exist(): found' as [Result]
where @X.exist('/Order/@OrderNum[.=sql:variable("@V")]') = 1

select 'value(): found' as [Result]
where @X.value('/Order[1]/@OrderNum','varchar(16)') = @V
```

As you can see in Figure 12-8, the exist() method compares the OrderNum attribute and the @V variable with case sensitivity, and it produces a different comparison result in T-SQL when case-insensitive collation is used.

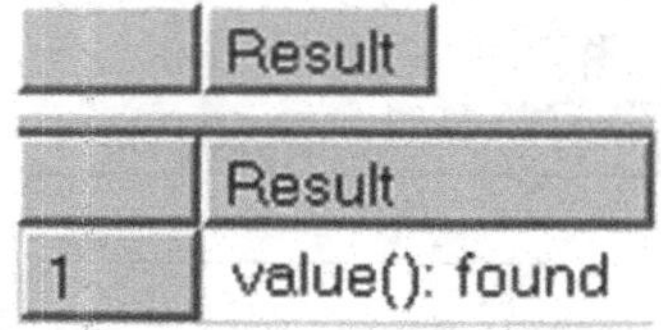

Figure 12-8. String comparison within XQuery

As with the value() method, the atomization of nodes rule applies to the exist() method. It is also better to move the node path to the outside of the predicate part, referencing it with the *current node* '.'

symbol when dealing with untyped XML. This helps to avoid type casting, which introduces an additional UDX operator that implements XQuery/XPath operations, to the execution plan.

The code shown in Listing 12-13 executes three queries. The first query references the element within the predicate, and it performs atomization of nodes, which leads to an additional call to the table-valued XML Reader function. The second query does not perform atomization of nodes, although it performs comparison casting of the values to `xs:int`. This adds the UDX operator to the execution plan. The last query compares values as strings, which is the most efficient method. Again, keep in mind that string comparison uses unicode, case-sensitive comparison rules. Figure 12-9 shows the execution plans for all three queries.

Listing 12-13. Atomization of nodes and type casting

```
declare
   @X xml = '<Order OrderNum="Order1"><OrderId>1</OrderId></Order>'

select 'Atomization of nodes'
where @X.exist('/Order[OrderId=1]') = 1;

select 'No text() function'
where @X.exist('/Order/OrderId[.=1]') = 1;

select 'With text() function'
where @X.exist('/Order/OrderId/text()[.=1]') = 1;
```

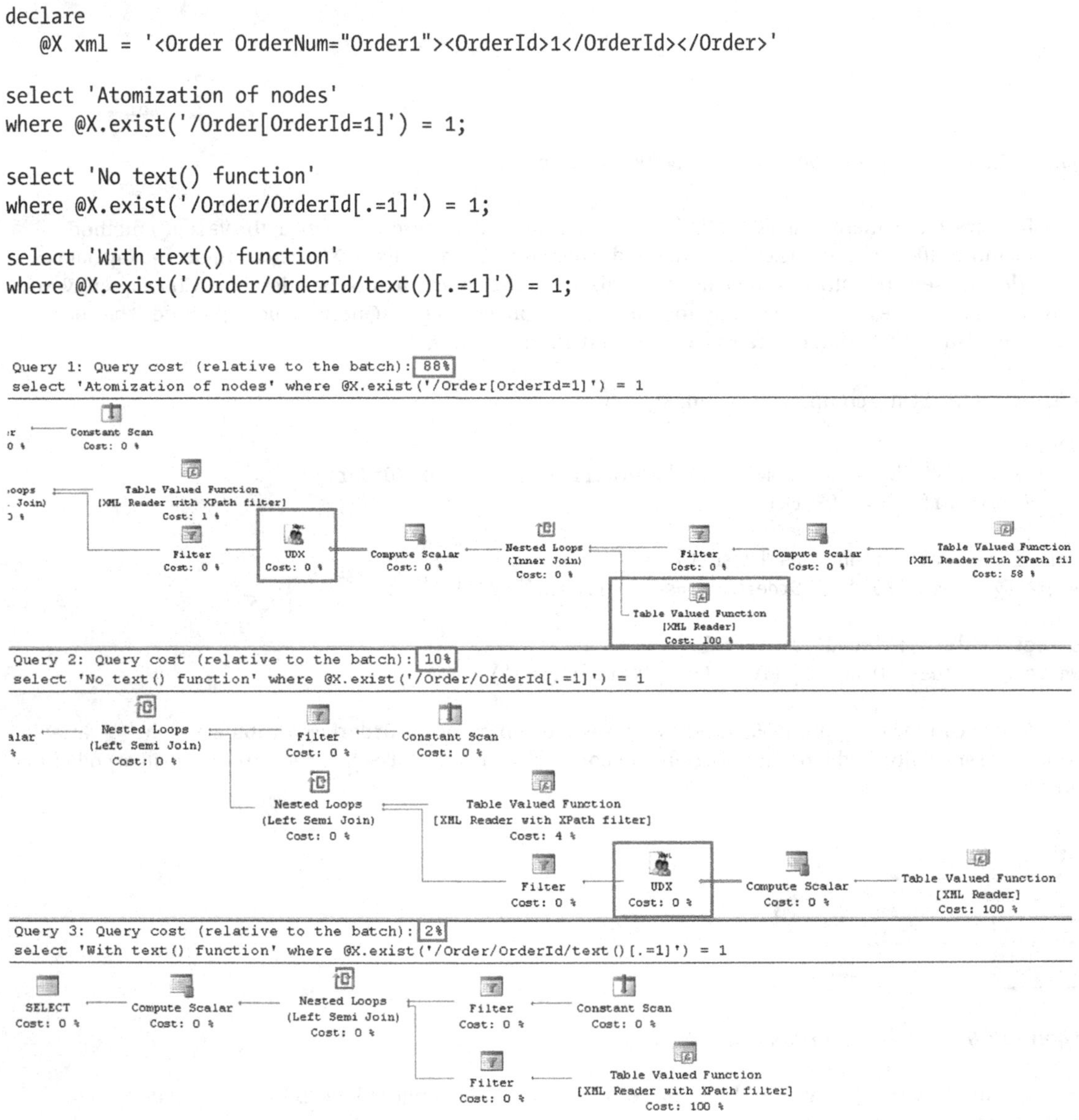

Figure 12-9. *Atomization of nodes and type casting*

query() Method

The query() method returns the untyped XML specified by that query. You can use this method to obtain part of the original XML or to transform it to another XML. The code shown in Listing 12-14 demonstrates both use cases. The results are shown in Figure 12-10.

Listing 12-14. The query() method

```
declare
    @X xml =
N'<Order OrderId="42" OrderTotal="49.96">
    <CustomerId>123</CustomerId>
    <OrderNum>10025</OrderNum>
</Order>'

select
    @X.query('/Order/CustomerId') as [Part of XML]
    ,@X.query('<Customer Id="{/Order/CustomerId/text()}"/>') as [Transform]
```

	Part of XML	Transform
1	<CustomerId>123</CustomerId>	<Customer Id="123" />

Figure 12-10. *The query() method*

nodes() Method

The nodes() method shreds XML into relational data. It returns a row set, with rows representing the nodes identified by the path expression. Furthermore, you can use other XML methods–value(), for example–to shred those rows into individual elements and attributes.

The code shown in Listing 12-15 shows how you can access the individual nodes from the row set and shred them into individual values. You can see the results in Figure 12-11.

Listing 12-15. The nodes() method

```
declare
    @X xml =
'<Order OrderId="42" OrderTotal="49.96">
  <CustomerId>123</CustomerId>
  <OrderNum>10025</OrderNum>
  <OrderDate>2016-07-15T10:05:20</OrderDate>
  <OrderLineItems>
    <OrderLineItem>
      <ArticleId>250</ArticleId>
      <Quantity>3</Quantity>
      <Price>9.99</Price>
    </OrderLineItem>
    <OrderLineItem>
      <ArticleId>404</ArticleId>
      <Quantity>1</Quantity>
```

```
      <Price>19.99</Price>
    </OrderLineItem>
  </OrderLineItems>
</Order>'

select
    t.c.query('.') as [Raw Node]
    ,t.c.value('(ArticleId/text())[1]','int') as [ArticleId]
from @X.nodes('/Order/OrderLineItems/OrderLineItem') as t(c)
```

	Raw Node	ArticleId
1	<OrderLineItem><ArticleId>250</ArticleId><Quantity>3</Quantity><Price>9.99</Price></OrderLineItem>	250
2	<OrderLineItem><ArticleId>404</ArticleId><Quantity>1</Quantity><Price>19.99</Price></OrderLineItem>	404

Figure 12-11. *The nodes() method*

When you use the nodes() method with the XML column from the table, you must use the APPLY operator. You can see an example of this in Listing 12-16.

Listing 12-16. Using the nodes() method with the APPLY operator

```
select
    t.ID
    ,sum(Items.Item.value('(Quantity/text())[1]','int') *
        Items.Item.value('(Price/text())[1]','float')) as [Total]
from
    dbo.ElementCentricUntyped t cross apply
        t.XMLData.nodes('/Order/OrderLineItems/OrderLineItem')
            as Items(Item)
group by
    t.ID
```

You should avoid referencing parent nodes with descendant axes in path expressions; rather, you should use a drill-down approach with multiple nodes() methods instead.

Now, let's compare the two approaches. Assume that you have XML that contains information about multiple orders, as shown in Listing 12-17.

Listing 12-17. Drill-down approach: XML

```
declare
    @X xml =
N'<Orders>
    <Order OrderId="42" CustomerId="123" OrderNum="10025">
        <OrderLineItem ArticleId="250" Quantity="3" Price="9.99"/>
        <OrderLineItem ArticleId="404" Quantity="1" Price="19.99"/>
    </Order>
    <Order OrderId="54" CustomerId="234" OrderNum="10025">
        <OrderLineItem ArticleId="15" Quantity="1" Price="14.99"/>
        <OrderLineItem ArticleId="121" Quantity="2" Price="6.99"/>
    </Order>
</Orders>'
```

Assume that you want to achieve a result set that includes OrderId, CustomerId, ArticleId, Quantity, and Price columns. The first approach uses the nodes() method to shred the OrderLineItems node, and it will access CustomerId and OrderId from there using descendant axes. The second approach will use two nodes() methods: one to shred the individual Order nodes and a second to shred OrderLineItems from those nodes. The code needed to accomplish both approaches is shown in Listing 12-18.

Listing 12-18. Drill-down approach: Queries

```
select
    LineItems.Item.value('../@OrderId','int') as [OrderId]
    ,LineItems.Item.value('../@OrderNum','varchar(32)') as [OrderNum]
    ,LineItems.Item.value('@ArticleId','int') as [ArticleId]
    ,LineItems.Item.value('@Quantity','int') as [Quantity]
    ,LineItems.Item.value('@Price','float') as [Price]
from
    @X.nodes('/Orders/Order/OrderLineItem') as LineItems(Item);

select
    Orders.Ord.value('@OrderId','int') as [OrderId]
    ,Orders.Ord.value('@OrderNum','varchar(32)') as [CustomerId]
    ,LineItems.Item.value('@ArticleId','int') as [ArticleId]
    ,LineItems.Item.value('@Quantity','int') as [Quantity]
    ,LineItems.Item.value('@Price','float') as [Price]
from
    @X.nodes('/Orders/Order') as Orders(Ord) cross apply
        Orders.Ord.nodes('OrderLineItem') as LineItems(Item)
```

Figure 12-12 shows the execution plans for the queries. Descendant axes introduce an additional pair of XML Readers in the execution plan, which significantly degrades the performance of the queries.

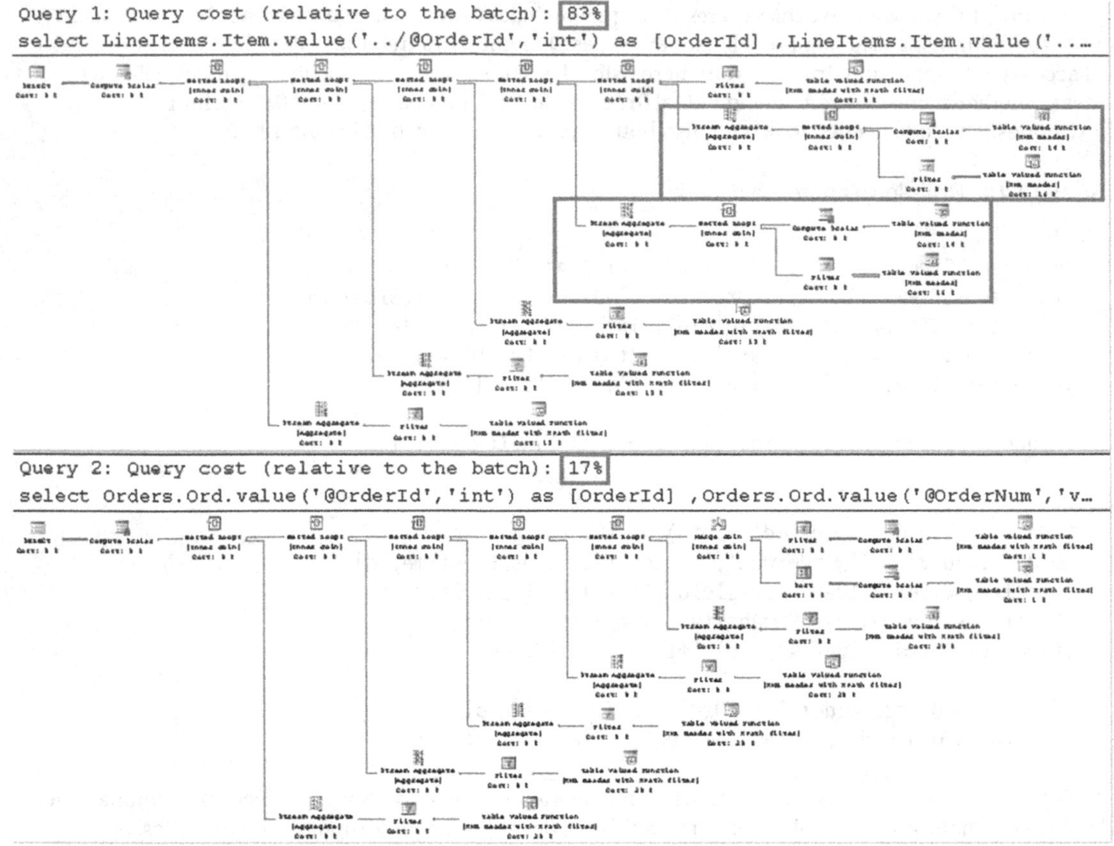
Query 1: Query cost (relative to the batch): 83%
select LineItems.Item.value('../@OrderId','int') as [OrderId] ,LineItems.Item.value('...
Query 2: Query cost (relative to the batch): 17%
select Orders.Ord.value('@OrderId','int') as [OrderId] ,Orders.Ord.value('@OrderNum','v...

Figure 12-12. *Drill-down approach: Execution plans*

modify() Method

Finally, the `modify()` method allows you to modify XML data by using the *XML data modification language (XML DML)*. I am not going to cover the DML XML syntax in depth. You can find detailed information about XML DML in Books Online at `http://msdn.microsoft.com/en-us/library/ms177454.aspx`.

All of the XQuery/XPath performance considerations discussed previously apply here as well.

OPENXML

OPENXML is another way of dealing with XML data in SQL Server. It utilizes the MSXML parser (`Msxmlsql.dll`), and it keeps documents in the memory cache, which can utilize up to one-eighth of SQL Server's memory.

All XML documents need to be parsed individually using the `sp_xml_preparedocument` stored procedure. As a result, you cannot use OPENXML to process XML data from multiple table rows. For single XML documents, OPENXML outperforms XQuery, although OPENXML's memory-usage pattern makes it a dangerous choice. You can lose a large amount of SQL Server memory if your code does not remove documents from the cache by using the `sp_xml_removedocument` stored procedure. I suggest avoiding OPENXML unless the performance of XQuery is insufficient for the task to be performed. For more information about OPENXML, read this article: `http://msdn.microsoft.com/en-us/library/ms186918.aspx`.

SELECT FOR XML

You can retrieve the results of the SELECT query in XML format by using the FOR XML clause. There are four modes that control the shape of the generated XML: RAW, AUTO, EXPLICIT, and PATH. I recommend that you use the PATH mode when you need to generate XML for a complex shape. The code shown in Listing 12-19 demonstrates using FOR XML PATH to accomplish this.

Listing 12-19. Using FOR XML PATH

```
declare
    @Orders table
    (
        OrderId int not null primary key,
        CustomerId int not null,
        OrderNum varchar(32) not null,
        OrderDate date not null
    )
declare
    @OrderLineItems table
    (
        OrderId int not null,
        ArticleId int not null,
        Quantity int not null,
        Price money not null,
        primary key(OrderId, ArticleId)
    )

insert into @Orders(OrderId, CustomerId, OrderNum, OrderDate)
values
    (42,123,'10025','2016-07-15T10:05:20'),
    (54,25,'10032','2016-07-15T11:21:00')

insert into @OrderLineItems(OrderId, ArticleId, Quantity, Price)
values
    (42,250,3,9.99), (42,404,1,19.99),
    (54,15,1,14.99), (54,121,2,6.99)

select
    o.OrderId as [@OrderId]
    ,o.OrderNum as [OrderNum]
    ,o.CustomerId as [CustomerId]
    ,o.OrderDate as [OrderDate]
    ,( select
            i.ArticleId as [@ArticleId]
            ,i.Quantity as [@Quantity]
            ,i.Price as [@Price]
        from @OrderLineItems i
        where i.OrderId = o.OrderId
        for xml path('OrderLineItem'),root('OrderLineItems'), type )
from @Orders o
for xml path('Order'),root('Orders');
```

```
-- RESULT:
<Orders>
  <Order OrderId="42">
    <OrderNum>10025</OrderNum>
    <CustomerId>123</CustomerId>
    <OrderDate>2016-07-15</OrderDate>
    <OrderLineItems>
      <OrderLineItem ArticleId="250" Quantity="3" Price="9.99" />
      <OrderLineItem ArticleId="404" Quantity="1" Price="19.99" />
    </OrderLineItems>
  </Order>
  <Order OrderId="54">
    <OrderNum>10032</OrderNum>
    <CustomerId>25</CustomerId>
    <OrderDate>2016-07-15</OrderDate>
    <OrderLineItems>
      <OrderLineItem ArticleId="15" Quantity="1" Price="14.99" />
      <OrderLineItem ArticleId="121" Quantity="2" Price="6.99" />
    </OrderLineItems>
  </Order>
</Orders>
```

You can use a `FOR XML PATH` clause to generate a delimiter-separated list of values. The code shown in Listing 12-20 generates a comma-separated list of `RecId` values from the table.

Listing 12-20. Generating comma-separated list of values with FOR XML PATH

```
select LEFT(Data,LEN(Data) - 1) -- removing right-most comma
from
    ( select convert(varchar(max),
        ( select RecId as [text()], ',' as [text()]
          from dbo.Data
          for XML PATH('') ) ) as Data
    ) List
```

This approach is very fast compared to using regular string concatenation in the code. You need to be careful, however, as SQL Server replaces characters with character entities when needed. For example, it would replace the < character with `<` if it is present.

For more information about the `FOR XML` clause and the shape of the XML it generates, read this article: `http://msdn.microsoft.com/en-us/library/ms178107.aspx`.

Working with JSON Data (SQL Server 2016)

SQL Server 2016 provides several methods that help when working with JSON data. There is no native JSON data type, and you need to store JSON data as text in the database. However, you can select data in JSON format using the `SELECT FOR JSON` operator, shred JSON data into row sets using the `OPENJSON` table-valued function, and manipulate JSON data with several built-in functions.

The choice between XML and JSON depends on many factors. Even though both technologies allow you to work with semi-structured data, they are different. XML, which stands for *eXtensive Markup Language*, is the *language* that allows you to describe, validate, and manipulate data. A properly constructed XML document is self-contained and self-explanatory, and it can be strongly typed through the XML schema. Finally, XQuery and XPath provide you with very powerful querying capabilities, and XLS allows you to transform one XML type to another.

JSON, on the other hand, stands for *JavaScript Object Notation*. It is not a language, but rather a data format optimized for data communication between the systems. It is easier to read, is lighter compared to XML, and is faster to shred and parse. It is not intended, however, for complex data manipulation and transformation.

XML support in SQL Server is much more robust. You can enforce strong typing with the XML schema and manipulate it with XQuery. You can also index it to improve the performance of the queries that deal with XML data. It is the better choice when you expect to query or modify semi-structured data in T-SQL and/or when you can benefit from XML indexes in the queries.

In contrast, SQL Server 2016 JSON support is rather limited. It is impossible to validate the JSON schema or index JSON data. It could be a good choice when you do not need to enforce a specific JSON schema nor expect to shred or parse a large amount of JSON data in the database.

Let's look at JSON support in SQL Server 2016.

SELECT FOR JSON

You can format query results in JSON format by using the `FOR JSON` clause and using either `AUTO` or `PATH` mode. In `AUTO` mode, the JSON output is formatted based on the structure of the `SELECT` statement. `PATH` mode, on the other hand, gives you full control over the output format.

There are three additional options that control the formatting, as follows:

> `ROOT` adds the top-level element to JSON output.
>
> `INCLUDE_NULL_VALUES` allows you to add `NULL` properties to the output. By default, `NULL` values are omitted.
>
> `WITHOUT_ARRAY_WRAPPER` removes array square brackets from enclosing the output.

Listing 12-21 shows an example of the `SELECT FOR JSON AUTO` operator. It is using the `@Orders` and `@OrderLineItems` table variables defined in Listing 12-19.

Listing 12-21. Using SELECT FOR JSON AUTO

```
select
    o.OrderId as [OrderId]
    ,o.OrderNum as [OrderNum]
    ,o.CustomerId as [CustomerId]
    ,o.OrderDate as [OrderDate]
    ,(
        select
            i.ArticleId as [ArticleId]
            ,i.Quantity as [Quantity]
            ,i.Price as [Price]
        from @OrderLineItems i
        where i.OrderId = o.OrderId
        for json auto
    ) as LineItems
from @Orders o
for json auto
```

```
-- Partial RESULT:
[
    {
        "OrderId":42,
        "OrderNum":"10025",
        "CustomerId":123,
        "OrderDate":"2016-07-15",
        "LineItems":
        [
            {
                "ArticleId":250,
                "Quantity":3,
                "Price":9.9900
            },
            {
                "ArticleId":404,
                "Quantity":1,
                "Price":19.9900
            }
        ]
    },
    {
        "OrderId":54,
        -- Skipped
    }
]
```

Similar to `SELECT FOR XML PATH`, `SELECT FOR JSON PATH` provides you with full control over the shape of the generated JSON. You can read more about it at `https://msdn.microsoft.com/en-us/library/dn921882.aspx`.

Built-In Functions

SQL Server 2016 provides several functions that work with JSON data, as follows:

> `ISJSON` tests whether a string contains valid JSON. You can use this function in the `CHECK` constraint if you need to enforce that the column stores valid JSON data.
>
> `JSON_VALUE` extracts a scalar value from a JSON string. You can use this function to extract JSON properties to persisted calculated columns and index them afterward.
>
> `JSON_QUERY` extracts an object or array from a JSON string.
>
> `JSON_MODIFY` updates the value of a property in a JSON string and returns a modified JSON string.

Listing 12-22 shows those functions in action.

Listing 12-22. Using built-in functions

```
declare
    @Data nvarchar(max) = N'
{
    "Book":{
        "Title":"Pro SQL Server Internals 2nd Edition",
        "ISBN":"978-1484219638",
        "Author": {
            "Name":"Dmitri Korotkevitch",
            "Blog":"http://aboutsqlserver.com"
        }
    }
}'

select
    isjson(@Data) as [Is JSON]
    ,json_value(@Data,'$.Book.Title') as [Title]
    ,json_query(@Data,'$.Book.Author') as [Author in JSON]
    ,json_modify(@Data,'$.Book.Year',2016) as [Modified JSON];
```

You can read more about this at `https://msdn.microsoft.com/en-us/library/dn921890.aspx`.

OPENJSON

The `OPENJSON` table-valued function allows you to shred JSON values into a row set. It is available only in databases that have a compatibility level of 130. You can call this function with or without an explicit schema definition for the output provided by the `WITH` clause.

Listing 12-23 shows an example that shreds the JSON data generated in Listing 12-20.

Listing 12-23. Using OPENJSON

```
declare
    @Data varchar(max) = '/* JSON FROM LISTING 12-20 */'

select
    Orders.OrderId, Orders.CustomerId, Orders.OrderNum
    ,Orders.OrderDate, Orders.LineItems
    ,sum(Items.Quantity * Items.Price) as Total
from
    openjson(@Data,'$')
    with
    (
        OrderId int '$.OrderId',
        CustomerId int '$.CustomerId',
        OrderNum varchar(32) '$.OrderNum',
        OrderDate date '$.OrderDate',
        LineItems nvarchar(max) '$.LineItems' as json
    ) as Orders
```

```
    cross apply
       openjson(Orders.LineItems,'$')
       with
       (
           Quantity int '$.Quantity',
           Price float '$.Price'
       ) as Items
group by
    Orders.OrderId, Orders.CustomerId, Orders.OrderNum
    ,Orders.OrderDate, Orders.LineItems
```

Figure 12-13 illustrates the output of this query. As you can see, the `LineItems` column from the first result set is in JSON format, which is then shredded by the second `OPENJSON` function.

	OrderId	CustomerId	OrderNum	OrderDate	LineItems	Total
1	42	123	10025	2016-07-15	[{"ArticleId":250,"Quantity":3,...	49.96
2	54	25	10032	2016-07-15	[{"ArticleId":15,"Quantity":1,"...	28.97

Figure 12-13. *OPENJSON: Output of the query*

Figure 12-14 shows a partial execution plan for the query. As you can see, SQL Server estimates fifty rows in the output for the `OPENJSON` function. This value is hardcoded, and it does not change, even if you enable the legacy cardinality estimator in the database. You should be aware of this behavior if you expect a large number of rows in the output.

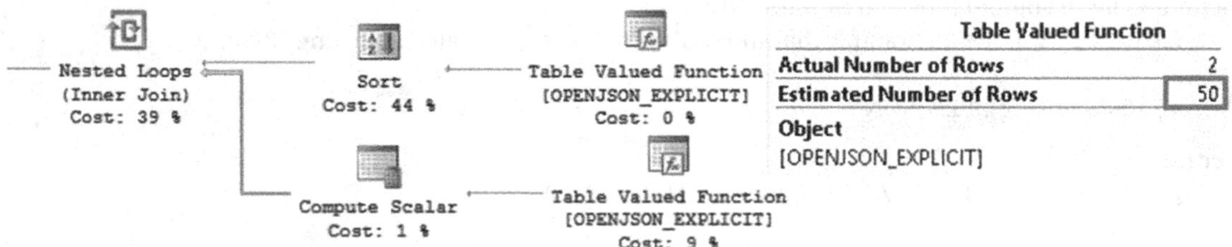

Figure 12-14. *OPENJSON: Execution plan of the query*

You can use JSON to pass a batch of rows from client applications, shredding it with the `OPENJSON` function afterward. It is less efficient as compared to table-valued parameters; however, it can be used if the SQL Client library does not support table-valued parameters. We will compare the performance of this approach with other methods in the next chapter.

You can read more about it at `https://msdn.microsoft.com/en-us/library/mt629158.aspx`.

Summary

While XML and JSON add flexibility to data models, it comes at a high cost. Queries against XML data are slower and more CPU-intensive than queries against relational data. You can improve XQuery performance with XML indexes, although they require a large amount of storage space—often several times larger than that of the XML data itself. JSON data manipulation adds less overhead to the CPU; however, it is supported in SQL Server 2016 only, and support is rather limited. SQL Server 2016 does not provide a native JSON data type nor allow the indexing of JSON data.

It is recommended that you create a primary XML index when the XML data is relatively static and index maintenance does not introduce a lot of overhead, XML data is queried often enough, and you will have enough storage space to accommodate the index. Secondary XML indexes, which are nonclustered indexes on the primary XML index's internal table, can be useful for optimizing specific query patterns in the code.

You can make XML typed by specifying that the XML conforms to a specific XML schema collection. Queries against typed XML are usually more efficient. Typed XML requires more storage space because the XML data type preserves type information, even though it reduces the size of the primary XML index, especially in the case of element-centric XML. You need to consider the overhead of the schema validation before making typed XML.

There are several rules that you must follow when designing efficient XQuery and XPath expressions. One of the biggest performance hits with untyped XML is the atomization of nodes. This introduces additional calls to the XML Reader's table-valued functions. Moreover, descendent axes in the path, expressions at the middle of the path, and type casts also negatively affect XQuery performance.

You must avoid property-container design patterns where you store name/value pairs, such as <props><name>color</name> <value>black</value></props>, unless they are absolutely needed. The reason for this is that property-container design patterns usually introduce expressions in the middle of the path when you access the data stored in the values elements of such XML.

The most important decisions are made during the design stage. You must evaluate whether XML or JSON needs to be used, and then you must define what data should be stored in the XML or JSON formats. When data conforms to a relational model, you will achieve better performance by shredding all or part of the data and retaining the separate elements and attributes as regular non-XML/non-JSON columns. While it is great to have flexibility in your system, you must remember that nothing is free, and flexibility comes at the cost of performance.

CHAPTER 13

Temporary Objects and TempDB

Temporary objects are an essential part of SQL Server. SQL Server will sometimes create them during query execution to store working tables and intermediate result sets. At other times, they are created by developers.

In this chapter, we will discuss a few different types of temporary objects that can be created by users: local and global temporary tables, table variables, user-defined table types, and table-valued parameters. We will also talk about tempdb and ways to optimize its performance.

Temporary Tables

We create *temporary tables* to store short-term information, such as intermediate results and temporary data during data processing. Temporary tables live in tempdb, and they behave very similarly to regular tables. There are a few minor differences, however, which we will discuss later in this chapter.

There are two kinds of temporary tables: local and global. *Local temporary tables* are named starting with the # symbol, and they are visible only in the session in which they were created and in the modules called from that session. When multiple sessions simultaneously create local temporary tables with the same name, each session will have its own instance of the table.

When you create a temporary table in a stored procedure, for example, you are able to access it in that specific stored procedure as well as in the stored procedures that you call from that stored procedure.

Caution You can access a temporary table created in a stored procedure from the triggers defined in some tables if the stored procedure performs the action that fires those triggers. However, this is clearly a bad idea, as the data modification operation will fail if a temporary table has not been created.

Listing 13-1 provides an example that demonstrates a temporary table scope.

Listing 13-1. Local temporary table scope and visibility

```
create table #SessionScope(C1 int not null)
go

create proc dbo.P1
as
begin
    -- Success: #SessionScope is visible because it's created
    -- in the session scope
    select * from #SessionScope
```


D. Korotkevitch, *Pro SQL Server Internals*, DOI 10.1007/978-1-4842-1964-5_13

```
    -- Results depends on how P1 is called
    select * from #P2Scope
end
go

create proc dbo.P2
as
begin
    create table #P2Scope(ID int)

    -- Success: #SessionScope is visible because it's created
    -- in the session scope
    select * from #SessionScope;

    -- Success - P1 is called from P2 so table #P2Scope is visible there
    exec dbo.P1;

    -- Success #P2Scope is visible from dynamic SQL called from within P2
    exec sp_executesql N'select * from #P2Scope';
end
go

-- Success: #SessionScope is visible because it's created in the session scope
select * from #SessionScope;

-- Success
exec dbo.P2;

-- Error: Invalid object name '#P2Scope'
exec dbo.P1;
```

The temporary table `#SessionScope` is created on the connection/session level. This table is visible and accessible from anywhere within the session. Another temporary table, `#P2Scope`, is created in the stored procedure `dbo.P2`. This table would be visible in the stored procedure (after it has been created) as well as in the other stored procedures and dynamic SQL called from `dbo.P2`. Finally, as you can see, stored procedure `dbo.P1` references both the `#SessionScope` and `#P2Scope` tables. As a result, that stored procedure works just fine when it is called from the `dbo.P2` stored procedure, although it would fail when called from anywhere else if the temporary table `#P2Scope` has not been created.

You can drop temporary tables using the `DROP TABLE` statement. Alternatively, SQL Server will drop them when the session has disconnected or after finishing the execution of the module in which they were created. In the preceding example, the `#SessionScope` table would be dropped when the session disconnected and `#P2Scope` would be dropped after the `dbo.P2` stored procedure finished execution.

Global temporary tables are created with names that start with ## symbols, and they are visible to all sessions. They are dropped after the session in which they were created disconnects *and* when other sessions stop referencing them.

Neither global nor local temporary tables can have triggers defined, nor can they participate in views. Nonetheless, like regular tables, you can create clustered and nonclustered indexes and define constraints in them.

SQL Server maintains statistics on the indexes defined in temporary tables in a manner similar to regular tables. Temporary tables have an additional statistics update threshold of six changes to the leftmost statistics column, which regular tables do not have. A `KEEP PLAN` query hint lets us prevent a statistics update based on that threshold and match a regular table's behavior.

Temporary tables are often used to simplify large and complex queries by splitting them into smaller and simpler ones. This helps the Query Optimizer find a better execution plan in a few ways. First, simpler queries usually have a smaller number of possible execution plans. This reduces the search area for Query Optimizer, and it improves the chances of finding a better execution plan. In addition, simpler queries usually have better cardinality estimations, because the number of errors tends to grow quickly when more and more operators appear in the plan. Moreover, statistics kept by temporary tables allow Query Optimizer to use actual cardinality data rather than relying on those often-incorrect estimates.

Let's look at one such example. In the first step, shown in Listing 13-2, we create a table and populate it with data.

Listing 13-2. Using temporary tables to optimize queries: Table creation

```
create table dbo.Orders
(
    OrderId int not null,
    CustomerId int not null,
    Amount money not null,
    Placeholder char(100),

    constraint PK_Orders
    primary key clustered(OrderId)
);

create index IDX_Orders_CustomerId on dbo.Orders(CustomerId);

;with N1(C) as (select 0 union all select 0) -- 2 rows
,N2(C) as (select 0 from N1 as T1 cross join N1 as T2) -- 4 rows
,N3(C) as (select 0 from N2 as T1 cross join N2 as T2) -- 16 rows
,N4(C) as (select 0 from N3 as T1 cross join N3 as T2) -- 256 rows
,N5(C) as (select 0 from N4 as T1 cross join N4 as T2) -- 65,536 rows
,IDs(ID) as (select row_number() over (order by (select null)) from N5)
insert into dbo.Orders(OrderId, CustomerId, Amount)
    select ID, ID % 250 + 1, Id % 50 from IDs;
```

At this point, the table has 65,536 order rows evenly distributed across 250 customers. In the next step, let's create a multi-statement table-valued function that accepts a comma-separated list of ID values as the parameter and returns a table with individual ID values in the rows. One possible implementation of such a function is shown in Listing 13-3.

Listing 13-3. Using temporary tables to optimize queries: Function creation

```
create function dbo.ParseIDList(@List varchar(8000))
returns @IDList table
(
    ID int
)
as
begin
    if (IsNull(@List,'') = '')
        return;
```

```
    if (right(@List,1) <> ',')
        select @List += ',';

    ;with CTE(F, L)
    as
    (
        select 1, charindex(',',@List)
        union all
        select L + 1, charindex(',',@List,L + 1)
        from CTE
        where charindex(',',@List,L + 1) <> 0
    )
    insert into @IDList(ID)
        select distinct convert(int,substring(@List,F,L-F))
    from CTE
    option (maxrecursion 0);

    return;
end
```

Now, let's run a SELECT statement that calculates the total amount for all orders for all customers. We will build a comma-separated list of values from 1 to 250 and use a dbo.ParseIDList function to parse it. We will join the dbo.Orders table with the function, as shown in Listing 13-4, and then examine the execution plan, shown in Figure 13-1.

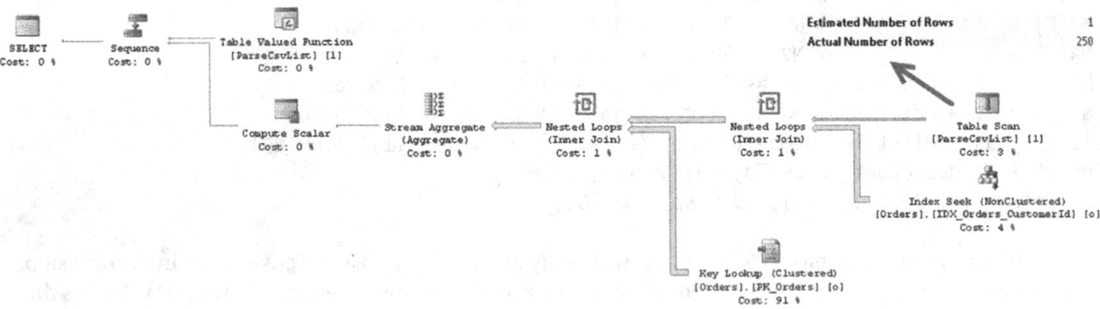

Figure 13-1. *Execution plan for the query that joins a table and a function (Legacy cardinality estimator)*

Listing 13-4. Using temporary tables to optimize queries: Joining the Orders table with a multi-statement table-valued function

```
declare
    @List varchar(8000)

-- Populate @List with comma-separated list of integers
-- from 1 to 250
;with N1(C) as (select 0 union all select 0) -- 2 rows
,N2(C) as (select 0 from N1 as T1 cross join N1 as T2) -- 4 rows
,N3(C) as (select 0 from N2 as T1 cross join N2 as T2) -- 16 rows
,N4(C) as (select 0 from N3 as T1 cross join N3 as T2) -- 256 rows
```

```
,IDs(ID) as (select row_number() over (order by (select null)) from N4)
select @List = convert(varchar(8000),
    ( select ID as [text()], ',' as [text()]
      from IDs
      where ID <= 250
      for xml path('')  ));

select sum(o.Amount)
from dbo.Orders o join dbo.ParseIDList(@List) l on
        o.CustomerID = l.ID;
```

As you know, legacy cardinality estimator always estimates that multi-statement table-valued functions return just one row. This would lead to a very inefficient execution plan in our example.

The I/O statistics and execution time on my computer produced the following results:

```
Table 'Orders'. Scan count 250, logical reads 201295
Table '#25869641'. Scan count 1, logical reads 1

 SQL Server Execution Times:
   CPU time = 249 ms,  elapsed time = 239 ms.
```

Now, let's change our approach and populate a temporary table with the values returned by the dbo.ParseIDList function, as shown in Listing 13-5.

Listing 13-5. Using temporary tables to optimize queries: Temporary table approach

```
declare
    @List varchar(8000)

-- Populate @List with comma-separated list of integers
-- from 1 to 250
;with N1(C) as (select 0 union all select 0) -- 2 rows
,N2(C) as (select 0 from N1 as T1 cross join N1 as T2) -- 4 rows
,N3(C) as (select 0 from N2 as T1 cross join N2 as T2) -- 16 rows
,N4(C) as (select 0 from N3 as T1 cross join N3 as T2) -- 256 rows
,IDs(ID) as (select row_number() over (order by (select null)) from N4)
select @List = convert(varchar(8000),
    ( select ID as [text()], ',' as [text()]
      from IDs
      where ID <= 250
      for xml path('')  ));

create table #Customers(ID int not null primary key);
insert into #Customers(ID)
    select ID from dbo.ParseIDList(@List);

select sum(o.Amount)
from dbo.Orders o join #Customers c on
        o.CustomerID = c.ID;

drop table #Customers;
```

As you can see in Figure 13-2, SQL Server estimates the number of IDs correctly, and, as a result, you end up with a much more efficient execution plan.

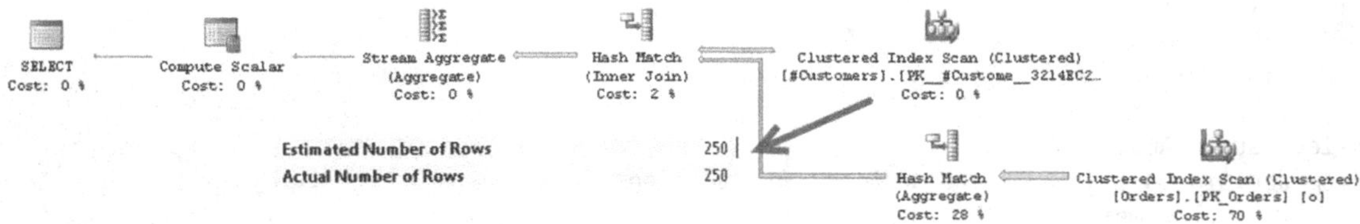

***Figure 13-2.** Execution plan for a query that uses temporary table*

The I/O statistics and execution time on my computer are as follows:

```
SQL Server Execution Times:
   CPU time = 0 ms,  elapsed time = 1 ms.
Table '#Customers__________00000000001D'. Scan count 0, logical reads 501
Table '#25869641'. Scan count 1, logical reads 1

 SQL Server Execution Times:
   CPU time = 0 ms,  elapsed time = 6 ms.
Table 'Orders'. Scan count 1, logical reads 1029
Table '#Customers__________00000000001D'. Scan count 1, logical reads 2
```

You can see that with the temporary table, our query is more than 30 times faster and uses two orders of magnitude less I/O compared to the query that used a multi-statement table-valued function.

Obviously, there is overhead associated with temporary tables, especially in cases when you insert a large amount of data. In some cases, such overhead would degrade the performance of the queries, even with the more efficient execution plans that were generated. For example, if in a majority of cases you calculated the total orders amount for a single or for very few customers, the approach with the temporary table would be slower than without it. You would end up with similar execution plans, but you would have to deal with the overhead from creating and populating the temporary table. On the other hand, you may decide to live with such overhead rather than having to deal with the poor performance that results on the rare occasions you run the query for a large list of customers.

Both the creation and the deletion of temporary tables require access to and modifications of the allocation map pages, such as IAM, SGAM, and PFS, as well as of the system tables. While the same actions occur during the creation of regular tables in users' databases, the system rarely creates and drops users' tables at a high rate. Temporary tables, on the other hand, can be created and dropped quite frequently. On busy systems, this can lead to contention when multiple sessions are trying to modify allocation map pages.

■ **Note** We will talk about how to detect such contention in Part V of this book, "Practical Troubleshooting."

In order to improve performance, SQL Server introduces the concept of *temporary objects caching*. This term is a bit confusing. It relates to temporary object allocation rather than data pages, which are cached in a buffer pool, similar to regular tables.

In a nutshell, with temporary objects caching, instead of dropping the table, SQL Server truncates it, keeping two pages per index pre-allocated: one IAM and one data page. The next time the table is created, SQL Server will reuse these pages, which helps reduce the number of modifications required in the allocation map pages.

Let's look at the example shown in Listing 13-6. In the first step, let's define the stored procedure that creates and drops the temporary table.

Listing 13-6. Temporary objects caching: Stored procedure

```
create proc dbo.TempTableCaching
as
    create table #T(C int not null primary key);
    drop table #T;
```

In the next step, let's run the stored procedure and examine the transaction log activity it generates. You can see the code for doing this in Listing 13-7.

Listing 13-7. Temporary objects caching: Running the stored procedure

```
checkpoint;
go
exec dbo.TempTableCaching;
go
select Operation, Context, AllocUnitName, [Transaction Name], [Description]
from sys.fn_dblog(null, null);
```

When you run this code for the first time, you will see results similar to those in Figure 13-3.

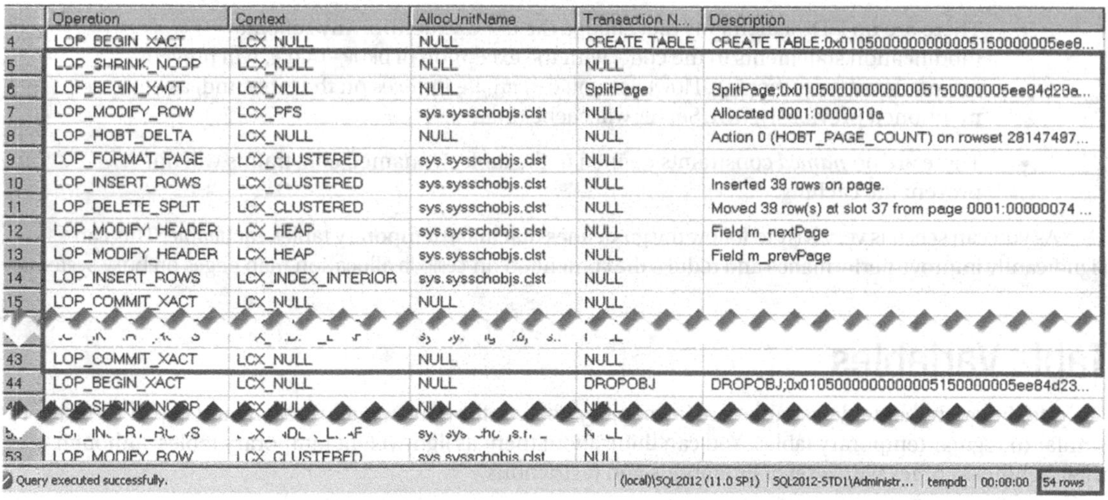

	Operation	Context	AllocUnitName	Transaction N...	Description
4	LOP_BEGIN_XACT	LCX_NULL	NULL	CREATE TABLE	CREATE TABLE;0x01050000000000051500000005ee8...
5	LOP_SHRINK_NOOP	LCX_NULL	NULL	NULL	
6	LOP_BEGIN_XACT	LCX_NULL	NULL	SplitPage	SplitPage;0x01050000000000051500000005ee84d23a...
7	LOP_MODIFY_ROW	LCX_PFS	sys.sysschobjs.clst	NULL	Allocated 0001:0000010a
8	LOP_HOBT_DELTA	LCX_NULL	NULL	NULL	Action 0 (HOBT_PAGE_COUNT) on rowset 28147497...
9	LOP_FORMAT_PAGE	LCX_CLUSTERED	sys.sysschobjs.clst	NULL	
10	LOP_INSERT_ROWS	LCX_CLUSTERED	sys.sysschobjs.clst	NULL	Inserted 39 rows on page.
11	LOP_DELETE_SPLIT	LCX_CLUSTERED	sys.sysschobjs.clst	NULL	Moved 39 row(s) at slot 37 from page 0001:00000074 ...
12	LOP_MODIFY_HEADER	LCX_HEAP	sys.sysschobjs.clst	NULL	Field m_nextPage
13	LOP_MODIFY_HEADER	LCX_HEAP	sys.sysschobjs.clst	NULL	Field m_prevPage
14	LOP_INSERT_ROWS	LCX_INDEX_INTERIOR	sys.sysschobjs.clst	NULL	
15	LOP_COMMIT_XACT	LCX_NULL	NULL	NULL	
[illegible]	[illegible]	[illegible]	[illegible]	[illegible]	
43	LOP_COMMIT_XACT	LCX_NULL	NULL	NULL	
44	LOP_BEGIN_XACT	LCX_NULL	NULL	DROPOBJ	DROPOBJ;0x01050000000000051500000005ee84d23...
[illegible]	LOP_SHRINK_NOOP	LCX_NULL	NULL	NULL	
[illegible]	[illegible]	[illegible]	[illegible]	[illegible]	
53	LOP_MODIFY_ROW	LCX_CLUSTERED	sys.sysschobjs.clst	NULL	

Query executed successfully. | (local)\SQL2012 (11.0 SP1) | SQL2012-STD1\Administr... | tempdb | 00:00:00 | 54 rows

Figure 13-3. *Log activity when a temporary table has not been cached*

As you can see, the first stored procedure call produced 51 log records. Forty of them (the highlighted portion) relate to the update of the allocation map pages and system tables during temporary table creation.

If you run the code from Listing 13-7 a second time, you will see a different picture, as shown in Figure 13-4.

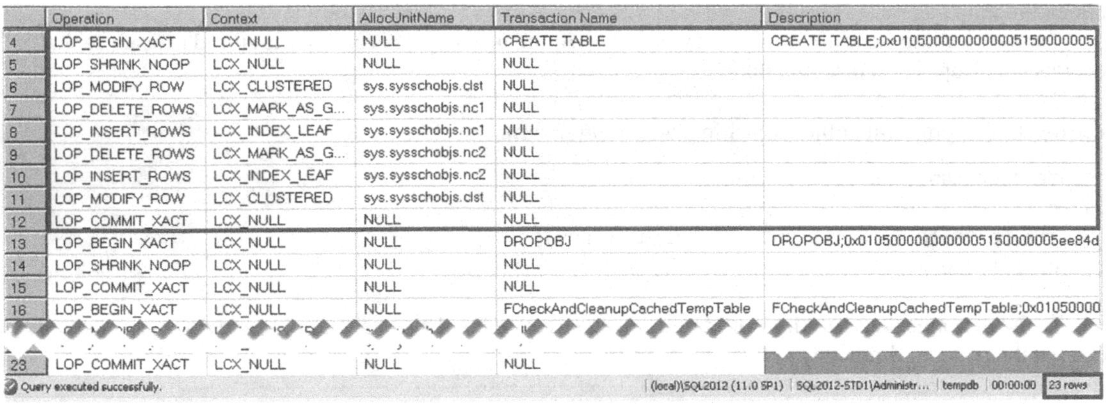

	Operation	Context	AllocUnitName	Transaction Name	Description
4	LOP_BEGIN_XACT	LCX_NULL	NULL	CREATE TABLE	CREATE TABLE;0x0105000000000005150000005
5	LOP_SHRINK_NOOP	LCX_NULL	NULL	NULL	
6	LOP_MODIFY_ROW	LCX_CLUSTERED	sys.sysschobjs.clst	NULL	
7	LOP_DELETE_ROWS	LCX_MARK_AS_G...	sys.sysschobjs.nc1	NULL	
8	LOP_INSERT_ROWS	LCX_INDEX_LEAF	sys.sysschobjs.nc1	NULL	
9	LOP_DELETE_ROWS	LCX_MARK_AS_G...	sys.sysschobjs.nc2	NULL	
10	LOP_INSERT_ROWS	LCX_INDEX_LEAF	sys.sysschobjs.nc2	NULL	
11	LOP_MODIFY_ROW	LCX_CLUSTERED	sys.sysschobjs.clst	NULL	
12	LOP_COMMIT_XACT	LCX_NULL	NULL	NULL	
13	LOP_BEGIN_XACT	LCX_NULL	NULL	DROPOBJ	DROPOBJ;0x0105000000000005150000005ee84d
14	LOP_SHRINK_NOOP	LCX_NULL	NULL	NULL	
15	LOP_COMMIT_XACT	LCX_NULL	NULL	NULL	
16	LOP_BEGIN_XACT	LCX_NULL	NULL	FCheckAndCleanupCachedTempTable	FCheckAndCleanupCachedTempTable;0x01050000
23	LOP_COMMIT_XACT	LCX_NULL	NULL	NULL	

Query executed successfully. | (local)\SQL2012 (11.0 SP1) | SQL2012-STD1\Administr... | tempdb | 00:00:00 | 23 rows

Figure 13-4. Log activity when the temporary table has been cached

This time, as the temporary table has been cached, table creation introduces just a few log records, all of which are against the system table with no allocation map pages involved.

SQL Server does not cache IAM or data pages for global temporary tables, nor does it cache local temporary tables created in the session scope. Only the temporary tables created within stored procedures and triggers are cached.

There are also a few requirements for the table and code, including the following:

- The table needs to be smaller than eight megabytes. Large tables are not cached.
- There are no DDL statements that change the table structure. Any schema modification statements in the code, with the exception of `DROP TABLE`, will prevent temporary objects caching. However, you can create indexes on the table and, as mentioned previously, SQL Server will cache them.
- There are no *named* constraints defined in the table. Unnamed constraints will not prevent the caching.

As you can see, it is very easy to follow the guidelines that make temporary tables cacheable. This can significantly improve performance and reduce the contention on `tempdb` allocation map pages on busy systems.

Table Variables

Despite the myth that table variables are in-memory objects, they are actually created and live in `tempdb`, similar to regular temporary tables. You can think about them as lightweight temporary tables, although their lightness comes with a set of limitations and restrictions.

■ **Note** In-Memory OLTP technology introduced in SQL Server 2014 allows you to create *memory-optimized table variables*. Those objects live only in memory and do not use `tempdb`. We will discuss In-Memory OLTP in Part VIII of this book.

The first major difference between temporary tables and table variables is the scope. Table variables live only within the batch in which they were created. They are not accessible from outside of the batch, as opposed to temporary tables. For example, when you define a table variable in a stored procedure, you are not able to reference it from the dynamic SQL nor from other stored procedures called from the original one.

You cannot create indexes on table variables, with the exception of primary key and unique constraints.

■ **Important** SQL Server does not maintain any statistics on table variables, and it always estimates that a table variable has just a single row, unless a statement-level recompile is used.

Look at the example shown in Listing 13-8. Here, we create a temporary table and table variable, populate it with some data, and check SQL Server's cardinality estimations.

Listing 13-8. Cardinality estimation for temporary tables and table variables

```
declare
    @TTV table(ID int not null primary key)

create table #TT(ID int not null primary key);

;with N1(C) as (select 0 union all select 0) -- 2 rows
,N2(C) as (select 0 from N1 as T1 cross join N1 as T2) -- 4 rows
,N3(C) as (select 0 from N2 as T1 cross join N2 as T2) -- 16 rows
,N4(C) as (select 0 from N3 as T1 cross join N3 as T2) -- 256 rows
,IDs(ID) as (select row_number() over (order by (select null)) from N4)
insert into #TT(ID)
    select ID from IDs;

insert into @TTV(ID)
    select ID from #TT;

select count(*) from #TT;
select count(*) from @TTV;
select count(*) from @TTV option (recompile);
```

As you can see in Figure 13-5, unless you are using a statement-level recompile, SQL Server estimates that a table variable has only one row. Cardinality estimation errors often progress quickly through the execution plan, and this can lead to highly inefficient plans when table variables are used. A statement-level recompile provides the Query Optimizer with information about the total number of rows, although no statistics are kept and the Query Optimizer knows nothing about data distribution in the table variable.

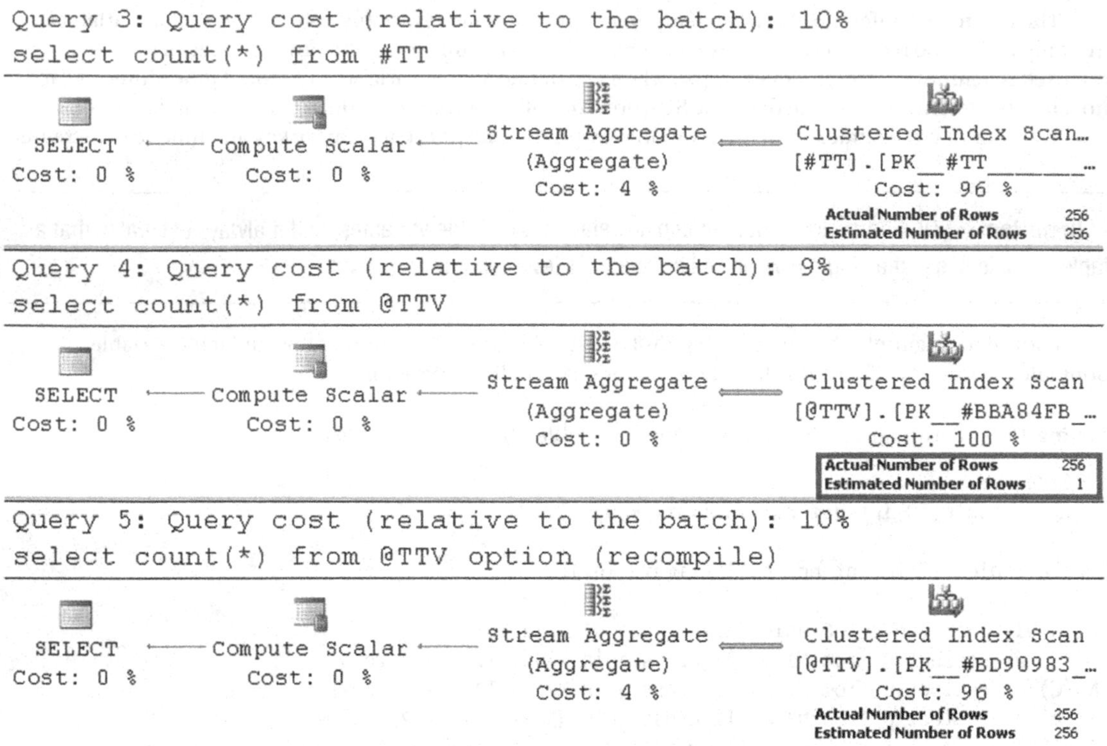

Query 3: Query cost (relative to the batch): 10%
select count(*) from #TT

SELECT Cost: 0 % ← Compute Scalar Cost: 0 % ← Stream Aggregate (Aggregate) Cost: 4 % ← Clustered Index Scan... [#TT].[PK__#TT________... Cost: 96 %

Actual Number of Rows 256
Estimated Number of Rows 256

Query 4: Query cost (relative to the batch): 9%
select count(*) from @TTV

SELECT Cost: 0 % ← Compute Scalar Cost: 0 % ← Stream Aggregate (Aggregate) Cost: 0 % ← Clustered Index Scan [@TTV].[PK__#BBA84FB_... Cost: 100 %

Actual Number of Rows 256
Estimated Number of Rows 1

Query 5: Query cost (relative to the batch): 10%
select count(*) from @TTV option (recompile)

SELECT Cost: 0 % ← Compute Scalar Cost: 0 % ← Stream Aggregate (Aggregate) Cost: 4 % ← Clustered Index Scan [@TTV].[PK__#BD90983_... Cost: 96 %

Actual Number of Rows 256
Estimated Number of Rows 256

Figure 13-5. *Cardinality estimation for temporary tables and table variables*

Now, let's change our previous example and add a `where ID > 0` clause to all three selects. All ID values in both tables are positive. When you run these queries, you will receive the cardinality estimations shown in Figure 13-6.

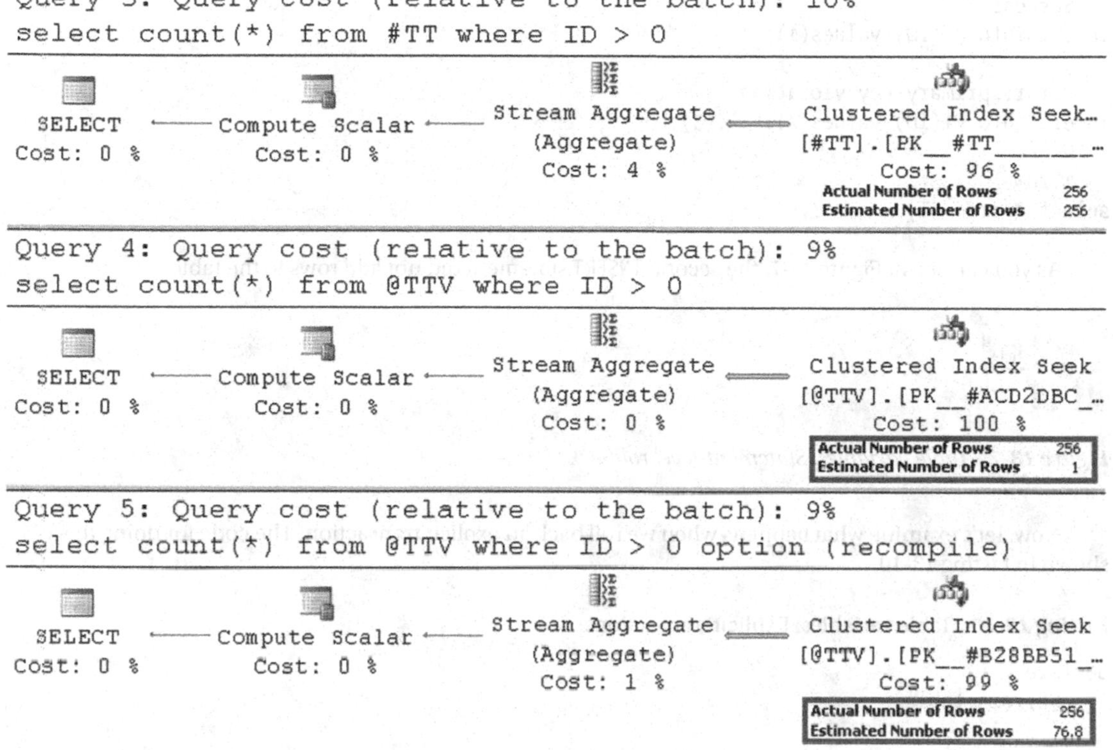

Figure 13-6. *Cardinality estimations for temporary tables and table variables*

Regular temporary tables maintain statistics on indexes, and, as a result, SQL Server was able to access the histogram and estimate the number of rows in the first `SELECT` correctly. As previously, without a statement-level recompile it is assumed that the table variable has only a single row. Nevertheless, even with a statement-level recompile, the estimations were way off. There are no statistics, and SQL Server assumes that the *greater* operator will return one-third of the rows from the table, which is incorrect in our case.

Another difference between temporary tables and table variables is how they handle transactions. Temporary tables are fully transaction-aware, similar to regular tables. Table variables, on the other hand, support only statement-level rollbacks. Any statement-level errors–for example, "key violation"–would roll back the statement, although explicit transaction rollback keeps the table variable data intact.

Let's look at a couple of examples. In the first example, we will produce a *primary key violation* error during the `INSERT` operation. The code for this is shown in Listing 13-9.

Listing 13-9. Temporary table variables: Statement-level rollback

```
declare
    @T table(ID int not null primary key)

-- Success
insert into @T(ID) values(1);

-- Error: primary key violation
insert into @T(ID) values(2),(3),(3);

-- 1 row
select * from @T;
```

As you can see in Figure 13-7, the second INSERT statement did not add rows to the table.

Figure 13-7. *Table variables: Statement-level rollback*

Now, let's examine what happens when we roll back an explicit transaction. The code for doing this is shown in Listing 13-10.

Listing 13-10. Table variables: Explicit transactions

```
declare
    @Errors table
    (
        RecId int not null primary key,
        [Error] nvarchar(512) not null
    )
begin tran
    -- Insert error information
    insert into @Errors(RecId, [Error])
    values
        (11,'Price mistake'),
        (42,'Insufficient stock');
rollback
/* Do something with errors */
select RecId, [Error] from @Errors;
```

As you can see in Figure 13-8, the explicit rollback statement did not affect the table variable data. You can benefit from such behavior when you need to collect some error or log information that you want to persist even after the transaction has been rolled back.

	RecId	Error
1	11	Price mistake
2	42	Insufficient stock

Figure 13-8. *Table variables: Explicit transactions*

■ **Caution** While table variables can outperform temporary tables in some cases because of their lower overhead, you need to be extremely careful with them, especially when you store large amounts of data in the table variable. The single-row cardinality estimation rule and missing statistics can produce highly inefficient plans with a large number of rows involved. A statement-level recompile can help address some cardinality estimation issues, although it will not help when the data distribution needs to be analyzed.

As a general rule of thumb, it is safer to use temporary tables than table variables when you need to join them with other tables. With single-row cardinality estimation, Query Optimizer usually chooses a *nested loop* when a table variable is present in the join. This join type is highly inefficient in cases where there is a large amount of data stored in both join inputs.

Table variables are a good choice when you need to deal with a large number of rows and no joins with other tables are involved. For example, you can think about a stored procedure where you stage the data, do some processing, and return the data to the client. If there is no other choice but to scan the entire table, you will have the same execution plan regardless of what object types are used. In these cases, table variables can outperform temporary tables. **Nevertheless, temporary tables are the safer choice in the majority of cases.**

Finally, table variables are cached in the same way as temporary tables are.

User-Defined Table Types and Table-Valued Parameters

You can define table types in the database. When you declare the variable of the table type in the code, it works the same way as with table variables.

Alternatively, you can pass the variables of the table types, called *table-valued parameters (TVPs)*, to T-SQL modules. While table-valued parameters are implemented as table variables under the hood, they are actually read-only. You cannot insert, update, or delete data in table-valued parameters.

The code in Listing 13-11 shows how you can use table-valued parameters. It creates the table type `dbo.tvpErrors`, a stored procedure with a table-valued parameter, and shows the examples how to pass that parameter to a stored procedure and dynamic SQL.

Listing 13-11. Table-valued parameters

```
create type dbo.tvpErrors as table
(
    RecId int not null primary key,
    [Error] nvarchar(512) not null,
)
go

create proc dbo.TvpDemo
(
    @Errors dbo.tvpErrors readonly
)
```

```
as
    select RecId, [Error] from @Errors;

    exec sp_executesql
        N'select RecId, [Error] from @Err'
        ,N'@Err dbo.tvpErrors readonly'
        ,@Err = @Errors;
go

declare
    @Errors dbo.tvpErrors

insert into @Errors(RecId, [Error])
values
    (11,'Price mistake'),
    (42,'Insufficient stock')

exec dbo.TvpDemo @Errors
```

As you can see, you need to mention explicitly that the table-valued parameter is read-only in both the stored procedure and the dynamic SQL parameter lists.

Table-valued parameters are one of the fastest ways to pass a batch of rows from a client application to a T-SQL routine. Table-valued parameters are an order of magnitude faster than separate DML statements, and, in some cases, they can even outperform bulk operations.

Now, let's run a few tests comparing the performance of inserting the data into the table using different methods and different batch sizes. As a first step, let's create a table to store the data, as shown in Listing 13-12. The actual table used in the tests has 21 data columns. A few data columns are omitted in the listings in order to save space. The actual test application and all the scripts are included in the book companion materials.

Listing 13-12. Inserting a batch of rows: Table creation

```
create table dbo.Data
(
    ID int not null,
    Col1 varchar(20) not null,
    Col2 varchar(20) not null,
    /* Seventeen more columns Col3 - Col19 */
    Col20 varchar(20) not null,

    constraint PK_DataRecords
    primary key clustered(ID)
)
```

The first method calls the separate `INSERT` statements from within the transaction. The .Net code to do this is shown in Listing 13-13. It is worth mentioning that the only purpose of this code is to generate dummy data and to test the performance of the different methods that insert data into the database.

Listing 13-13. Inserting a batch of rows: Using separate inserts

```
using (SqlConnection conn = GetConnection())
{
    /* Generating SqlCommand and parameters */
    SqlCommand cmd = new SqlCommand(
        @"insert into dbo.Data(ID,Col1,Col2,/*…*/Col20)
          values(@ID,@Col1,@Col2,/*…*/@Col20)",conn);
    cmd.Parameters.Add("@ID", SqlDbType.Int);
    for (int i = 1; i <= 20; i++)
        cmd.Parameters.Add("@Col" + i.ToString(), SqlDbType.VarChar, 20);
    /* Running individual insert statements in the loop
       within explicit transaction */
    using (SqlTransaction tran =
        conn.BeginTransaction(IsolationLevel.ReadCommitted))
    {
        try
        {
            cmd.Transaction = tran;
            for (int i = 0; i < packetSize; i++)
                cmd.Parameters[0].Value = i;
            for (int p = 1; p <= 20; p++)
                cmd.Parameters[p].Value = "Parameter: " + p.ToString();
            cmd.ExecuteNonQuery();
        }
        tran.Commit();
    }
    catch (Exception ex)
    {
        tran.Rollback();
    }
}
```

The second method sends the entire batch at once in an element-centric XML format, using a stored procedure to parse it. The .Net code is omitted, and the stored procedure is shown in Listing 13-14.

Listing 13-14. Inserting a batch of rows: Using element-centric XML

```
create proc dbo.InsertDataXmlElementCentric
(
    @Data xml
)
as
-- @Data is in the following format:
-- <Rows><R><ID>{0}</ID><C1>{1}</C1><C2>{2}</C2>..<C20>{20}</C20></R></Rows>
    insert into dbo.Data(ID,Col1,Col2,/*…*/ Col20)
        select
            rows.n.value('(ID/text())[1]', 'int')
            ,rows.n.value('(C1/text())[1]', 'varchar(20)')
            ,rows.n.value('(C2/text())[1]', 'varchar(20)')
```

```
            /* other 17 columns */
            ,rows.n.value('(C20/text())[1]', 'varchar(20)')
        from
            @Data.nodes('//Rows/R') rows(n)
```

The third method is very similar to the second, but it uses attribute-centric XML instead. The code for this is shown in Listing 13-15.

Listing 13-15. Inserting a batch of rows: Using attribute-centric XML

```
create proc dbo.InsertDataXmlAttributeCentric
(
    @Data xml
)
as
-- @Data is in the following format:
-- <Rows><R ID="{0}" C1="{1}" C2="{2}"..C20="{20}"/></Rows>
    insert into dbo.Data(ID,Col1,Col2,/*…*/Col20)
        select
            rows.n.value('@ID', 'int')
            ,rows.n.value('@C1', 'varchar(20)')
            ,rows.n.value('@C2', 'varchar(20)')
            /* other 17 columns */
            ,rows.n.value('@C20', 'varchar(20)')
        from
            @Data.nodes('//Rows/R') rows(n)
```

The fourth method uses a SqlBulkCopy .Net class with DataTable as the source using row-level locks. The code for this is shown in Listing 13-16.

Listing 13-16. Inserting a batch of rows: Using SqlBulkCopy .Net class

```
using (SqlConnection conn = GetConnection())
{
    /* Creating and populating DataTable object with dummy data */
    DataTable tbl = new DataTable();
    tbl.Columns.Add("ID", typeof(Int32));
    for (int i = 1; i <= 20; i++)
        tbl.Columns.Add("Col" + i.ToString(), typeof(string));
    for (int i = 0; i < packetSize; i++)
        tbl.Rows.Add(i, "Parameter: 1", /* Other columns */ "Parameter: 20");
    /* Saving data into the database */
    using (SqlBulkCopy bc = new SqlBulkCopy(conn))
    {
        bc.BatchSize = packetSize;
        bc.DestinationTableName = "dbo.Data";
        bc.WriteToServer(tbl);
    }
}
```

The next method uses table-valued parameters. Listing 13-17 shows the T-SQL code and Listing 13-18 shows the .Net part of the implementation.

Listing 13-17. Inserting a batch of rows: Table-valued parameters T-SQL code

```
create type dbo.tvpData as table
(
    ID int not null primary key,
    Col1 varchar(20) not null,
    Col2 varchar(20) not null,
    /* Seventeen more columns: Col3 - Col19 */
    Col20 varchar(20) not null
)
Go

create proc dbo.InsertDataTVP
(
    @Data dbo.tvpData readonly
)
as
    insert into dbo.Data(ID,Col1,Col2,/*…*/Col20)
        select ID,Col1,Col2,/*…*/Col20
        from @Data;
```

Listing 13-18. Inserting a batch of rows: Table-valued parameters .Net code

```
using (SqlConnection conn = GetConnection())
{
    DataTable tbl = new DataTable();
    tbl.Columns.Add("ID", typeof(Int32));
    for (int i = 1; i <= 20; i++)
        tbl.Columns.Add("Col" + i.ToString(), typeof(string));
    for (int i = 0; i < packetSize; i++)
        tbl.Rows.Add(i, "Parameter: 1", /* Other columns */ "Parameter: 20");
    /* Calling SP with TVP parameter */
    SqlCommand cmd = new SqlCommand("dbo.InsertDataTVP", conn);
    cmd.Parameters.Add("@Data", SqlDbType.Structured);
    cmd.Parameters[0].TypeName = "dbo.tvpData";
    cmd.Parameters[0].Value = table;
    cmd.ExecuteNonQuery();
}
```

Finally, the last method will pass the batch of rows in JSON format using the OPENJSON function to shred it. As you will remember, this method works only in SQL Server 2016 and requires the database to have a compatibility level of 130. Listing 13-19 illustrates the stored procedure that imports the data.

Listing 13-19. Inserting a batch of rows: Using JSON and the OPENJSON function

```
create proc dbo.InsertDataRecordsJSON
(
    @Data nvarchar(max)
)
as
    insert into dbo.Data(ID,Col1,Col2,/*…*/Col20)
        select ID,Col1,Col2,/*…*/Col20
        from openjson(@Data,'$')
        with (
            ID int '$.ID',
            Col1 varchar(20) '$.F1',
            Col2 varchar(20) '$.F2',
            /* Col3 - Col19 */
            Col20 varchar(20) '$.F20' );
```

I ran two series of tests measuring average execution time for the different methods and different batch sizes in SQL Server 2016 RTM. In the first test, the application ran on the same server as SQL Server. On the second test, the application connected to SQL Server over a network. You can see the execution time for these two tests in milliseconds in Tables 13-1 and 13-2.

Table 13-1. *Execution Time When the Application Was Run Locally (in Milliseconds)*

Rows	Separate inserts	Element-centric XML	Attribute-centric XML	SQLBulkCopy	Table-valued parameters	JSON
1,000	176	535	300	28	18	68
5,000	883	2,525	1,409	105	89	320
10,000	1,844	5,365	2,892	214	179	612
100,000	18,199	51,030	29,125	2,219	1,946	6,479

Table 13-2. *Execution Time When the Application Was Run Remotely (in Milliseconds)*

Rows	Separate inserts	Element-centric XML	Attribute-centric XML	SQLBulkCopy	Table-valued parameters	JSON
1,000	421	565	303	35	19	73
5,000	2,089	2,561	1,478	108	97	339
10,000	4,302	5,203	2,964	218	184	659
100,000	43,644	52,860	28,534	2,275	1,998	6,491

The performance of the separate INSERT statements greatly depends on network speed. This approach introduces a lot of network activity, and it does not perform well, especially with slow networks. The performance of the other methods do not depend greatly on the network.

As expected, the performance of attribute-centric XML is better than that of element-centric XML. It will also outperform separate inserts with the large batches—even with no network overhead involved. It is worth mentioning that the performance of XML implementations greatly depends on the data schema. Every XML element adds another operator to the execution plan, which slows XML parsing.

SQLBulkCopy and table-valued parameters are by far the fastest methods. Table-valued parameters were slightly more efficient in my test; however, the variation in performance is negligible and would depend on SQL Server version and tempdb performance.

Lastly, OPENJSON implementation in SQL Server 2016 outperforms individual INSERT statements and the XML approaches. Even though it is still slower as compared to table-valued parameters and SQLBulkCopy, it could be a good choice in some cases if SQL Client library does not support TVPs.

■ **Note** In-Memory OLTP allows you to use *memory-optimized table-valued parameters*, which are faster than their on-disk counterparts, especially with large batches of data. We will discuss them in Chapter 37, "In-Memory OLTP Programmability."

When you work with table-valued parameters in the client code, you need to assign a DataTable object to a corresponding SqlParameter object. The DataTable object should match the corresponding table-type definition from both the schema and data standpoints. The DataTable object should have the same number of columns, and these columns should have the same names and be in the same order as in the table type defined in the database. They also need to support type conversions between the corresponding .Net and SQL data types.

Data in the table needs to conform to the table type's primary and unique constraints, and it should not exceed the defined column sizes and T-SQL data type's domain values.

Finally, table types should not have sql_variant columns. Unfortunately, the .Net SQL client does not work with these correctly, and it raises exceptions during the call when the table-valued type has a sql_variant column defined.

Regular Tables in TempDB

You can create regular tables in tempdb, either directly or through the model database. User tables in tempdb are visible in all sessions.

Tempdb is recreated every time SQL Server restarts, and, because of this, it does not need to support crash recovery. As a result, tempdb uses the SIMPLE recovery model, and it has some additional logging optimizations, which make it more efficient than logging into the user's databases.

■ **Note** We will discuss recovery models and the differences in logging between tempdb and user databases in Chapter 30, "Transaction Log Internals."

Tempdb could be an option to be the staging area for ETL processes, where you need to load and process a large amount of data as fast as possible with minimum logging overhead. You can use temporary tables when the process is done as a single session; however, you need to use regular tables in more complex cases.

While tempdb can help with staging-area performance, client applications need to handle situations where tempdb is recreated and the tables with the data are gone. This may occur if SQL Server restarts or fails over to another node.

To make the situation even worse, this can happen transparently to the client applications in some cases. Applications need to handle these situations either by checking for the existence of the staging tables or, if you are creating tables automatically, persisting the state information somewhere else.

Let's assume that we have a table called dbo.ETLStatuses that contains information about the ETL process statuses. There are a couple of ways that you can create such a table. One is using a model database. All objects created in a model database are copied to tempdb during SQL Server startup.

■ **Caution** All objects created in a `model` database will be copied into the user databases that are created afterward.

Alternatively, you can create objects in `tempdb` using a stored procedure that executes upon SQL Server startup. Listing 13-20 shows such an example.

Listing 13-20. Creating a table in tempdb with a startup stored procedure

```
use master;
go

-- Enable scan for startup procs
exec sp_configure 'show advanced option', '1';
reconfigure;
exec sp_configure 'scan for startup procs', '1';
reconfigure;
go

create proc dbo.CreateETLStatusesTable
as
    create table tempdb.dbo.ETLStatuses
    (
        ProcessId int not null,
        ActivityTime datetime not null,
        StageNo smallint not null,
        [Status] varchar(16) not null,

        constraint PK_ETLStatuses
        primary key clustered (ProcessID)
    )
go

-- Mark procedure to run on SQL Server Startup
exec sp_procoption N'CreateETLStatusesTable', 'startup', 'on';
```

Listing 13-21 shows a possible implementation of the procedure that performs one of the stages of ETL processing by using the `dbo.ETLStatuses` table to validate process-state information.

Listing 13-21. Example of ETL stored procedure

```
-- Either defined in user db or in tempdb
create proc dbo.ETL_Process1Stage2
as
begin
-- Returns
-- 0: Success
-- -1: ETL tables do not exist - something is wrong
-- -2: ETLStatuses table does not have the record for the process
-- -3: Invalid stage
```

```
    set xact_abort on
    declare
        @StageNo smallint
        ,@Status varchar(16)

    if object_id(N'tempdb.dbo.ETLStatuses') is null or
        object_id(N'tempdb.dbo.ETLData') is null
            return -1;

    select @StageNo = StageNo, @Status = [Status]
    from tempdb.dbo.ETLStatuses
    where ProcessId = 1;
    if @@rowcount = 0
        return -2;

    if @StageNo <> 1 or @Status <> 'COMPLETED'
        return -3;

    -- This implementation rolls back all the changes in case of the error
    -- and throw the exception to the client application.
    begin tran
        update tempdb.dbo.ETLStatuses
        set ActivityTime = getutcdate(), StageNo = 2, [Status] = 'STARTED'
        where ProcessId = 1;

        /* Do Some Processing */

        update tempdb.dbo.ETLStatuses
        set ActivityTime = getutcdate(), [Status] = 'COMPLETED'
        where ProcessId = 1;
    commit
    return 0;
end
```

Of course, there are other ways to accomplish the same task. However, the key point here is the need to make your code aware of the situation when `tempdb` is recreated and the staged data is gone.

Optimizing TempDB Performance

`Tempdb` is usually one of the busiest databases on the server. In addition to temporary objects created by users, SQL Server uses this database to store internal result sets during query executions, version store, internal temporary tables for sorting, hashing, and database consistency checking, and so forth. `Tempdb` performance is a crucial component in overall server health and performance. Thus, in most cases, you should put `tempdb` on the fastest disk array that you have available.

In cases where you are using Standard Edition on the servers that have more memory that SQL Server can utilize, it is possible to create RAM drive and put `tempdb` there. Make sure that the RAM drive has enough space to accommodate `tempdb` growth in that case. In Enterprise Edition, however, it is better to leave the memory to SQL Server and place `tempdb` on the fastest disk array instead.

Redundancy of the array is another issue. On one hand, you do not need to worry much about the data that you are storing in tempdb. On the other hand, if the tempdb disk array goes down, SQL Server becomes unavailable. As a general rule then, you would like to have disk array redundancy.

Although, in some cases, when tempdb performance becomes a bottleneck and your High Availability strategy supports the simultaneous failure of two or more nodes, and furthermore there are spare parts available and there is a process in place that allows you to bring the failed node(s) online quickly, you could consider making the tempdb disk array non-redundant. This is a dangerous route, however, and you need to consider the pros and cons of this decision very carefully, avoiding unnecessary failovers whenever it is possible.

There is a trace flag, T1118, that prevents SQL Server from using mixed extents for space allocation. By allocating uniform extents only, you reduce the number of changes required in the allocation map pages during object creation. Moreover, even if temporary objects caching keeps only one data page cached, that page would belong to its own free uniform extent. As a result, SQL Server does not need to search, and potentially allocate, the mixed extents with free pages that are available during the allocation of pages two to eight of the table. Those pages can be stored in the same uniform extent in which the first cached data page belongs.

The bottom line is that trace flag T1118 can significantly reduce allocation map pages contention in tempdb. This trace flag should be enabled in every SQL Server instance prior to SQL Server 2016; that is, there is no downside to doing this.

SQL Server 2016, on the other hand, does not use mixed extents allocation in tempdb, even without T1118 enabled. Thus, this trace flag is not required in SQL Server 2016.

Another way to reduce contention is by creating multiple tempdb data files. Every data file has its own set of allocation map pages, and, as a result, allocations are spread across these files and pages. This reduces the chances of contention, because fewer threads are then competing simultaneously for access to the same allocation map pages.

There is no generic rule that defines the optimal number of tempdb data files—everything depends on the actual system workload and behavior. The old guidance–to have the number of data files equal the number of logical processors–is no longer the best advice. While that approach still works, an extremely large number of data files could degrade the performance of the system due to the file-management overhead.

Having multiple data files can also degrade the performance of tempdb spills when SQL Server uses tempdb to store internal record sets during *Sort* and *Hash* operations. As a general rule, you would need to perform query optimization to reduce spills in the system; however, if it is impossible, you can consider using the -E SQL Server startup parameter, which increases the number of extents allocated in each data file in a proportional fill algorithm. Use this startup parameter with care and as a last resort and validate how it affects your workload. We will discuss spills in detail in Chapter 25.

The Microsoft CSS team performed a stress test of tempdb performance using a server with 64 logical processors running under a heavy load with 500 connections that create, populate, and drop temporary tables into the loop. Table 13-3 displays the execution time based on the number of files in tempdb and a trace flag T1118 configuration.

Table 13-3. *Execution time based on the number of data files in tempdb*

	1 data file	8 data files	32 data files	64 data files
Without T1118	1,080 seconds	45 seconds	17 seconds	15 seconds
With T1118	525 seconds	38 seconds	15 seconds	15 seconds

As you can see, creating more than one data file dramatically improved tempdb performance, although it stabilized at some point. For instance, there was only a marginal difference in performance between the scenarios with 32 and 64 data file.

In general, you should start with a number of files equal to the number of logical processors in case the system has eight or fewer logical processors. Otherwise, start with eight data files and add them in groups of four in case there is still contention in the system. Make sure that the files are created with the same initial size and same auto-growth parameters, with growth size set in megabytes rather than by percentage. This helps you to avoid situations where files grow disproportionately, causing some files to process more allocations than others do.

SQL Server 2016 simultaneously grows all tempdb data files whenever any single data file needs to be grown. This reduces the chance that tempdb data files would grow unevenly and would have disproportional allocations. You should still make sure that all files have identical auto-growth parameters specified.

You can enable the same auto-growth behavior in previous versions of SQL Server by using trace flag T1117. Keep in mind, however, that this behavior will be applied server-wide and affect user databases. All data files in the filegroup will grow together at the time of an auto-growth event.

It is also beneficial to apply the latest SQL Server service packs and cumulative updates to the system. Microsoft constantly optimizes tempdb performance and reduces tempdb disk activity in the various use cases.

Of course, the best method of optimizing tempdb performance is to reduce unnecessary activity. You can re-factor your code to avoid the unnecessary usage of temporary tables, avoid sending extra load to the version store because of triggers or unnecessary optimistic transaction isolation levels, reduce the number of internal working tables created by SQL Server by optimizing the queries and simplifying execution plans, and so on. The less unnecessary activity tempdb has, the better it performs.

Summary

There are many different object types that can be created by users in tempdb. Temporary tables behave similarly to regular tables. They can be used to store intermediate data during processing. In some cases, you can split complex queries into smaller ones by keeping intermediate results in temporary tables. While this introduces the overhead of creating and populating the temporary tables, it can help Query Optimizer to generate simpler and more efficient execution plans.

Table variables are a lightweight version of temporary tables. While they can outperform temporary tables in some cases, they have a set of restrictions and limitations. These limitations can introduce suboptimal execution plans, especially when you join table variables with other tables.

Table-valued parameters allow you to pass row sets as parameters to stored procedures and functions. They are the one of the fastest ways to pass batches of rows from client applications to T-SQL routines.

The user's table in tempdb can be used as the staging area for data during ETL processes. This approach can outperform the staging tables in the user databases due to the more efficient logging in tempdb. However, client applications need to handle the situations when those tables and/or data disappear after a SQL Server restart or failover to another node.

As opposed to regular tables in the user's database, temporary objects can be created at a very high rate and can introduce allocation map page and system object contention in tempdb. You should create multiple tempdb data files and, in SQL Server 2014 and below, use trace flag T1118 to reduce contention.

Finally, you should utilize temporary objects caching, which reduces contention even further. You need to avoid named constraints in temporary tables, and do not alter them to make them cacheable.

CHAPTER 14

CLR

There are several different programming paradigms that exist nowadays. Some languages, such as SQL or XQuery, are *declarative*. They define *what* needs to be done without specifying *how* it needs to be achieved. Other languages, such as C# or Java, are *imperative*. This model requires specifying an exact, step-by-step control flow of the execution, defining *how* to achieve the results.

As an example, think about a scenario where you need to read all of the data that belongs to a specific customer. In the declarative model implemented in SQL, you would use the `where` clause with the predicate on the `CustomerId` column. In the imperative model, you would process all records, one by one, comparing `CustomerId` using the `IF` operator.

SQL is a declarative language, and it has been optimized for set-based declarative logic. Even though Transact SQL has a set of constructs that allows us to develop imperative code, the constructs are not very efficient. Moreover, the T-SQL language is very limited compared to modern imperative development languages. The Common Language Runtime (CLR) helps address some of these challenges by providing the execution environment for .Net code within SQL Server, and it allows us to develop various database objects using .Net programming languages.

Implementation of imperative, procedural-style code in CLR is usually more efficient than in T-SQL. Moreover, CLR outperforms T-SQL in computation-intensive areas, such as mathematical calculation, string manipulation, serialization, byte-level manipulation on large objects, and others.

Covering all aspects of CLR development easily merits a book by itself. This chapter provides an overview of CLR integration in SQL Server, discusses several security-related questions, and compares the performance of T-SQL and CLR routines in a few different areas.

CLR Integration Overview

SQL Server loads the .Net runtime environment inside its own process, and it manages memory and other resources there. It has full control over the environment, and it can shut down .Net application domains if needed.

Note *Application domain* is the key concept in .Net, and it represents the isolated environment where .Net code is executed. It provides a similar level of isolation for Windows processes in native Windows code.

CLR code is compiled into assembly DLLs, which are stored within the database. You can register and catalog assemblies there using the `CREATE ASSEMBLY` statement, specifying either the path to the file or a binary sequence of assembly bits that represent assembly code. SQL Server then loads the assembly into a separate application domain for validation and checks that the DLL or assembly bits represent compiled .Net code. In addition, SQL Server performs code verification to ensure that the assembly does not perform unauthorized actions.

D. Korotkevitch, *Pro SQL Server Internals*, DOI 10.1007/978-1-4842-1964-5_14

Assemblies belong to one of three different security categories, called *permission sets*. You need to specify the corresponding permission set as part of the CREATE ASSEMBLY statement. The categories are as follows:

> SAFE: This code is fully reliable, and it works in-process only. Only a subset of the standard .Net libraries and classes can be used here. This is the default permission set for assemblies and the only permission set supported in Microsoft Azure SQL databases.
>
> EXTERNAL_ACCESS: This code can perform some out-of-process calls that access external resources, such as the file system, registry, web services, and Windows event log. Similar to SAFE assemblies, only a subset of .Net libraries and classes can be used. The code is also guaranteed to be reliable.
>
> UNSAFE: There are no restrictions in unsafe CLR code. It can do out-of-process calls, utilize almost all .Net libraries, start its own threads, and perform other actions that can lead to unreliable code.

When you run CLR code, SQL Server creates a separate application domain on a database and assembly-owner basis. For example, if you have user *Mary* as the owner of assembly *A1* and user *Bob* as the owner of assemblies *A2* and *A3*, you would have two application domains where CLR code is running—one for Bob's and another for Mary's assemblies–regardless of how many users are calling CLR routines.

SQL Server can shut down an entire application domain when unhandled exceptions occur. This would affect the other sessions that are running CLR code in that domain. Conditions that can lead to this situation usually occur only with UNSAFE permission sets, and you need to be extremely careful when dealing with exception handling there.

You can troubleshoot CLR routine performance in a manner similar to that of T-SQL code. Profiler events (and corresponding Extended Events), such as *SQL:Batch Starting, Completed, SP:Starting, Completed, StmtStarting,* and *StmtCompleted,* monitor the execution of both T-SQL and CLR code.

Data-management views (DMVs), such as sys.dm_exec_query_stats, sys.dm_exec_requests, and sys.dm_os_memory_*, work the same way.

■ **Note** We will talk about performance troubleshooting with these DMVs in Part V of this book, "Practical Troubleshooting."

The performance counter *SQL Server:CLR\CLR Execution* shows the total time spent in CLR execution.

SQL Server T-SQL threads use cooperative non-preemptive scheduling and yields voluntarily. Managed CLR threads, on the other hand, use preemptive scheduling and rely on the host to interrupt them. Even if SQL Server had the ability to detect and interrupt non-yielding threads, runaway CLR code could affect the performance of the system to a much higher degree than T-SQL could. You must avoid such conditions and have CLR voluntarily yield from time to time by calling the System.Threading.Thread.Sleep(0) method in the CLR code.

You can identify the sessions that are running non-yielding CLR code with the sys.dm_clr_tasks DMV, as shown in Listing 14-1.

Listing 14-1. Identifying sessions with non-yielding CLR code

```
select
    er.session_id, ct.forced_yield_count,
    w.task_address, w.[state], w.last_wait_type, ct.state
from
    sys.dm_clr_tasks ct with (nolock) join
        sys.dm_os_workers w with (nolock) on
            ct.sos_task_address = w.task_address
    join sys.dm_exec_requests er with (nolock) on
            w.task_address = er.task_address
where
    ct.type = 'E_TYPE_USER'
```

The results shown in Figure 14-1 include information about currently running CLR tasks. The `forced_yield_count` column indicates how many times the scheduler forced CLR code to yield.

	session_id	forced_yield_count	task_address	state	last_wait_type	state
1	52	19	0x00000003E25FC558	RUNNING	SLEEP_TASK	E_TASK_ATTACHED_TO_CLR

Figure 14-1. *Identifying the sessions with non-yielding CLR code*

Security Considerations

SQL Server has CLR integration disabled by default. Although this would not prevent you from deploying the database with assemblies and CLR objects, you would not be able to call CLR routines until CLR is enabled on the server level. You can enable CLR with the code shown in Listing 14-2.

Listing 14-2. Enabling CLR integration

```
sp_configure 'show advanced options', 1;
reconfigure;
go
sp_configure 'clr enabled', 1;
reconfigure;
go
sp_configure 'show advanced options', 0;
reconfigure;
go
```

The requirement to have CLR enabled on the server level can lead to roadblocks for independent software vendors (ISV) who are trying to deploy their systems in Enterprise environments. Database and security administrators in such environments often oppose such requirements when dealing with ISVs.

It is also worth mentioning that system-level CLR code is always enabled. You can use system CLR types, such as `HierarchyId`, `Geometry`, and `Geography`, regardless of the configuration setting. We will discuss these types in detail in the next chapter.

CLR objects that access data break the ownership chaining in a manner similar to dynamic SQL. This leads to additional security-management overhead in the system. Let's look at the example shown in Listing 14-3 and Listing 14-4.

Listing 14-3. Ownership chaining: CLR part

```
[Microsoft.SqlServer.Server.SqlFunction(DataAccess = DataAccessKind.Read)]
public static SqlMoney GetOrderTotalCLR(SqlInt32 orderId)
{
      using (SqlConnection conn = new SqlConnection("context connection=true"))
      {
            conn.Open();
            SqlCommand cmd = new SqlCommand(
@"select @Result = sum(Quantity * Price)
from dbo.OrderLineItems
where OrderId = @OrderId", conn);

            cmd.Parameters.Add("@OrderId", SqlDbType.Int).Value = orderId;
            cmd.Parameters.Add("@Result", SqlDbType.Float).Direction = ParameterDirection.Output;
            cmd.ExecuteNonQuery();
            return new SqlMoney((double)cmd.Parameters[1].Value);
      }
}
```

Listing 14-4. Ownership chaining: T-SQL part

```
create function dbo.GetOrderTotal(@OrderId int)
returns money
as
      return
      (
            select sum(Quantity * Price) as Total
            from dbo.OrderLineItems
            where OrderId = @OrderId
      )
go

create view dbo.vOrdersTSQL(OrderId, OrderTotal)
as
      select o.OrderId, dbo.GetOrderTotal(o.OrderId)
      from dbo.Orders o
go

create view dbo.vOrdersCLR(OrderId, OrderTotal)
as
      select o.OrderId, dbo.GetOrderTotalCLR(o.OrderId)
      from dbo.Orders o
go

grant select on object::dbo.vOrdersTSQL to [Bob];
grant select on object::dbo.vOrdersCLR to [Bob];
go

execute as user='Bob';
```

```
-- Success
select * from dbo.vOrdersTSQL;

-- Failure - Bob needs to have SELECT permission on dbo.OrderLineItems table
select * from dbo.vOrdersCLR;
```

In Listing 14-4, we created two views, dbo.vOrdersTSQL and dbo.vOrdersCLR, which utilize T-SQL and CLR user-defined functions. Both functions select data from the dbo.OrderLineItems table.

When user *Bob* queries the dbo.vOrdersTSQL view, it works just fine. SQL Server does not require *Bob* to have SELECT permission on the tables referenced by the view as long as he has SELECT permission on the view itself, and both the view and the table have the same owner. This is an example of *ownership chaining*.

However, *Bob* would not be able to query the dbo.vOrdersCLR view, as ownership chaining would not work in the CLR routines, and he needs to have SELECT permission on the dbo.OrderLineItems table in order for the dbo.GetOrderTotalCLR method to work.

When CLR code accesses external resources, it is done in the context of a SQL Server startup account, and it could require that additional privileges be granted. You can work around such requirements by using impersonation in the .Net code, although it would work only when Windows Authentication is used.

Finally, EXTERNAL_ACCESS or UNSAFE assemblies must be signed with the same key as the SQL Server login, which has EXTERNAL ACCESS or UNSAFE permission granted. Let's look at how you can do that.

As a first step, as shown in Figure 14-2, you need to generate a *key pair* file. Visual Studio and Windows SDK have the utility *sn.exe* that you can use.

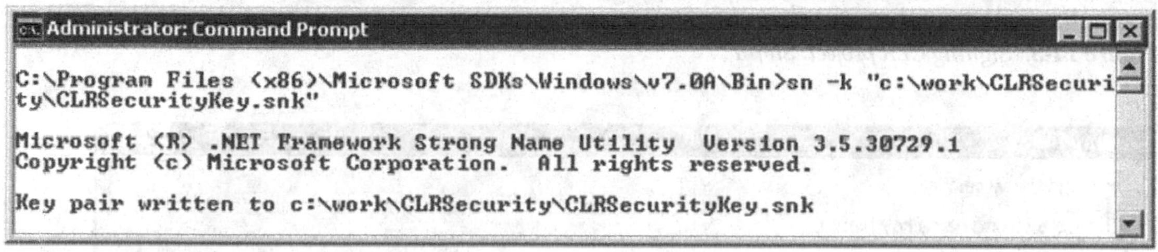

Figure 14-2. *Generating key pair file with sn.exe*

You should specify the generated file in the CLR project properties, as shown in Figures 14-3 and 14-4.

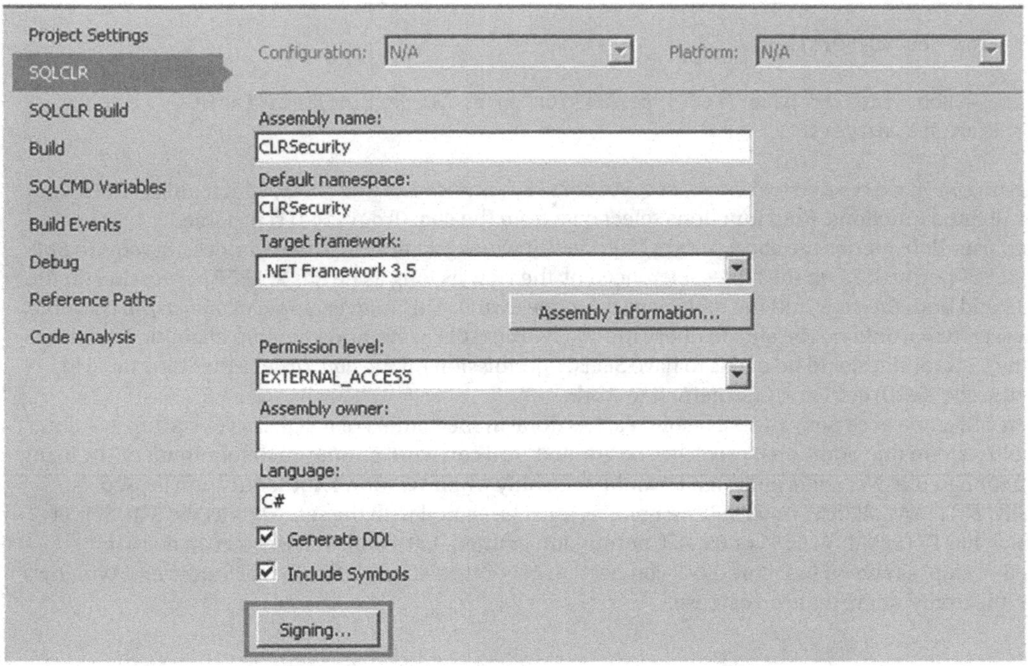

Figure 14-3. *Signing CLR project: Step 1*

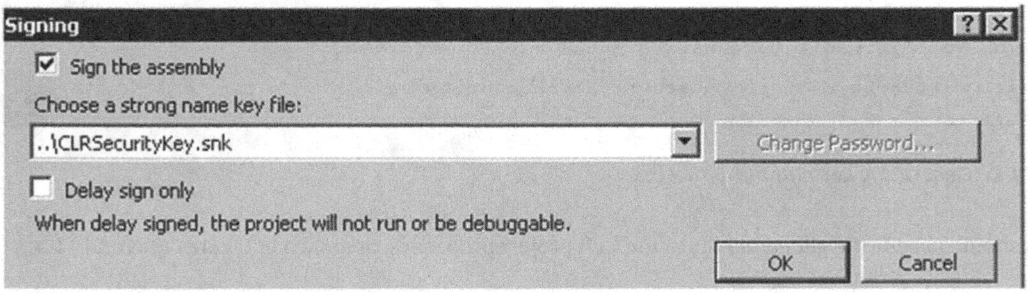

Figure 14-4. *Signing CLR project: Step 2*

After that, you can create an asymmetric key from the key pair file and create a login with corresponding permissions, as shown in Listing 14-5.

Listing 14-5. Creating a login with EXTERNAL ACCESS permissions from the key pair file

```
use master
go

-- Creating master key if it does not exist
if not exists
(
    select *
```

```
    from sys.symmetric_keys
    where name = '##MS_DatabaseMasterKey##'
)
    create master key encryption by password = '$trOngPas$word1';
go

create asymmetric key KeyExternalAccess from file = 'c:\SQL\CLRSecurity\CLRSecurityKey.snk';
create login CLRExtAccessLogin from asymmetric key KeyExternalAccess;
grant external access assembly to CLRExtAccessLogin;
```

You should now be able to successfully register the signed assembly that requires the EXTERNAL_ACCESS permission set.

■ **Note** An alternative option for registering the assembly with the EXTERNAL_ACCESS or UNSAFE permission set is to mark the hosting database as TRUSTWORTHY. However, this action violates security best practices.

All of these security requirements must be taken into consideration when you decide to start using CLR integration in your systems, especially if you are an independent software vendor (ISV) and you are planning to deploy the software to a large number of customers.

Performance Considerations

It is not easy to compare the performance of CLR and T-SQL routines. The technologies are different in nature, and they should be used for different tasks. T-SQL is an interpreted language, which is optimized for set-based logic and data access. CLR, on the other hand, produces compiled code that works best with imperative logic.

Even with imperative code, you need to decide if you want to implement it in CLR or on the client side, perhaps running on application servers. CLR works within the SQL Server process. While on one hand it eliminates network traffic and can provide you with the best performance due to its "closeness" to the data as compared to code running on the application server, on the other hand CLR adds to the load of SQL Server. It could be easier and cheaper to add more application servers rather than upgrading the SQL Server box.

There are some cases, however, where you must use CLR code. One example is on queries that perform RegEx (regular expression) evaluation as part of the where clause. It would be inefficient to move such an evaluation to the client code, and there is no regular expressions support in SQL Server. CLR is your only option in this instance. In other cases, however, when imperative logic can be moved to application servers, you should consider such an option, especially when those servers reside close to SQL Server and network latency and throughput is not an issue.

In this section, we will compare the performance of CLR and T-SQL in a few different areas. Similar to other SQL Server technologies, the choice between CLR and T-SQL fits into the "It depends" category.

Before we begin, let's look at Table 14-1 and compare the objects supported by both technologies.

Table 14-1. *CLR and T-SQL Object Types*

	T-SQL	CLR
Scalar user-defined functions	Yes	Yes
Multi-statement table-valued user-defined functions	Yes	Yes
Inline table-valued user defined functions	Yes	No
Stored procedures	Yes	Yes
Triggers	Yes	Yes
User-defined aggregates	No	Yes
User-defined types	No	Yes

■ **Note** Even though you can create T-SQL types with `CREATE TYPE` statements, T-SQL user-defined types are delivered from scalar T-SQL types. CLR user-defined types, on the other hand, are .Net classes that can have multiple attributes and/or methods. We will discuss T-SQL and CLR user-defined types in greater depth in Chapter 15, "CLR Types."

CLR lets you create user-defined aggregates and complex types, which cannot be done with T-SQL. User-defined aggregates are a great way to expand the standard SQL Server function library and, as you will see later in this chapter, can provide very good performance when compared to T-SQL code. User-defined types can also help in some cases.

Let's create a simple table and populate it with some data, as shown in Listing 14-6.

Listing 14-6. Test table creation

```
create table dbo.Numbers
(
    Num int not null,
    constraint PK_Numbers
    primary key clustered(Num)
);

;with N1(C) as (select 0 union all select 0)
,N2(C) as (select 0 from N1 as T1 cross join N1 as T2)
,N3(C) as (select 0 from N2 as T1 cross join N2 as T2)
,N4(C) as (select 0 from N3 as T1 cross join N3 as T2)
,N5(C) as (select 0 from N4 as T1 cross join N4 as T2)
,N6(C) as (select 0 from N4 as T1 cross join N4 as T2 cross join N2 as T3) -- 262,144 rows
,Nums(Num) as (select row_number() over (order by (select null)) from N6)
insert into dbo.Numbers(Num)
    select Num from Nums;
```

The invocation of the T-SQL scalar function introduces higher overhead when compared to its CLR counterpart. Let's prove that with a test where we will use functions that accept an integer value as a parameter and return 1 when this value is even. The CLR implementation is shown in Listing 14-7.

Listing 14-7. Invocation overhead: CLR functions

```
[Microsoft.SqlServer.Server.SqlFunction(
    IsDeterministic=true,
    IsPrecise=true,
    DataAccess=DataAccessKind.None) ]
public static SqlInt32 EvenNumberCLR(SqlInt32 num)
{  return new SqlInt32((num % 2 == 0) ? 1 : 0);  }

[Microsoft.SqlServer.Server.SqlFunction(
    IsDeterministic=true,
    IsPrecise=true,
    DataAccess=DataAccessKind.Read) ]
public static SqlInt32 EvenNumberCLRWithDataAccess(SqlInt32 num)
{  return new SqlInt32((num % 2 == 0) ? 1 : 0);   }
```

There is a set of attributes specified for each function. These attributes describe the function behavior, and they can help Query Optimizer generate a more efficient execution plan.

In our case, there are three attributes specified. `IsDeterministic` tells if the function is deterministic, and it always returns the same result for specific parameter values and database states. Our function is deterministic—even numbers are always even. As a counter example, you can think about the `getdate()` system function, which is not deterministic—results will be different every time it is called.

`IsPrecise` describes if functions involve imprecise calculations; for example, using floating-point operations.

Finally, the `DataAccess` attribute indicates if a function performs any data access. If this is the case, SQL Server calls the function in a different context that will allow it to access the data in the database. Setting up such a context introduces additional overhead during the function call, which you will see in our tests.

T-SQL implementation of those functions is shown in Listing 14-8.

Listing 14-8. Invocation overhead: T-SQL functions

```
create function dbo.EvenNumber(@Num int)
returns int
with schemabinding
as
    return (case when @Num % 2 = 0 then 1 else 0 end);

create function dbo.EvenNumberInline(@Num int)
returns table
as
return
(
    select (case when @Num % 2 = 0 then 1 else 0 end) as Result
);
```

Let's use scalar and inline table-valued functions in our test and measure average execution time for the statements shown in Listing 14-9. The results in my environment are shown in Table 14-2.

Listing 14-9. Invocation overhead: Test statements

```
-- CLR UDF - no data access context
select count(*)
from dbo.Numbers
where dbo.EvenNumberCLR(Num) = 1

-- CLR UDF - data access context
select count(*)
from dbo.Numbers
where dbo.EvenNumberCLRWithDataAccess(Num) = 1

-- TSQL - Scalar UDF
select count(*)
from dbo.Numbers
where dbo.EvenNumber(Num) = 1;

-- TSQL - Multi-statement UDF
select count(*)
from
    dbo.Numbers n cross apply
        dbo.EvenNumberInline(n.Num) e
where
    e.Result = 1;
```

Table 14-2. *Invocation Overhead of T-SQL and CLR Routines: Execution Time*

CLR UDF No data-access context	CLR UDF With data-access context	T-SQL Scalar UDF	T-SQL Inline Multi-statement
167 ms	246 ms	675 ms	18 ms

Each statement performs a *clustered index scan* of the dbo.Numbers table and checks if the Num column is even for every row of the table. For CLR and T-SQL scalar user-defined functions, that would introduce the function calls. Inline table-valued functions, on the other hand, perform the calculation inline.

As you can see, a CLR UDF without a data access context runs about four times faster when compared to the T-SQL scalar function. Even with data access context overhead, the CLR implementation is still faster than T-SQL scalar UDF, although in this particular example the best performance can be achieved if we stop using functions at all rather than converting them to CLR. The overhead of the function call is much higher than with inline calculations.

While you should always think about code re-factoring as an option, there are instances when CLR will outperform inline T-SQL implementation even with all of the overhead involved. The two most common areas for this are mathematical calculations and string manipulations.

Let's test the performance of a function that calculates the distance between two points defined by latitude and longitude coordinates. The CLR implementation is shown in Listing 14-10. The T-SQL implementation is shown in Listing 14-11. We will test two T-SQL approaches: scalar and inline table-valued functions.

Listing 14-10. Calculating the distance between two points: CLR function

```
[Microsoft.SqlServer.Server.SqlFunction(IsDeterministic=true, IsPrecise=false,
DataAccess=DataAccessKind.None) ]
public static SqlDouble CalcDistanceCLR
        (SqlDouble fromLat, SqlDouble fromLon, SqlDouble toLat, SqlDouble toLon)
{
    double fromLatR =  Math.PI / 180 * fromLat.Value;
    double fromLonR = Math.PI / 180 * fromLon.Value;
    double toLatR = Math.PI / 180 * toLat.Value;
    double toLonR = Math.PI / 180 * toLon.Value;

    return new SqlDouble(
        2 * Math.Asin(
            Math.Sqrt(
                Math.Pow(Math.Sin((fromLatR - toLatR) / 2.0),2) +
                    (Math.Cos(fromLatR) * Math.Cos(toLatR) * Math.Pow(Math.Sin((fromLonR -
                     toLonR) / 2.0),2) )
            )
        ) * 20001600.0 / Math.PI
    );
}
```

Listing 14-11. Calculating the distance between two points: T-SQL functions

```
create function dbo.CalcDistance
        (@FromLat decimal(9,6), @FromLon decimal(9,6),@ToLat decimal(9,6), @ToLon
decimal(9,6))
returns float
with schemabinding
as
    declare
        @Dist float
        ,@FromLatR float = radians(@FromLat)
        ,@FromLonR float = radians(@FromLon)
        ,@ToLatR float = radians(@ToLat)
        ,@ToLonR float = radians(@ToLon)

    set @Dist =
        2 * asin(
            sqrt(
                power(sin( (@FromLatR - @ToLatR) / 2.), 2) +
                    ( cos(@FromLatR) * cos(@ToLatR) * power(sin((@FromLonR - @ToLonR) / 2.0), 2))
            )
        ) * 20001600. / pi();
    return @Dist;

create function dbo.CalcDistanceInline
        (@FromLat decimal(9,6), @FromLon decimal(9,6),@ToLat decimal(9,6), @ToLon
decimal(9,6))
returns table
as
```

```
return
(
    with Rads(FromLatR, FromLonR, ToLatR, ToLonR)
    as
    (
        select radians(@FromLat), radians(@FromLon), radians(@ToLat), radians(@ToLon)
    )
    select
        2 * asin(
            sqrt(
                power(sin((FromLatR - ToLatR) / 2.), 2) +
                        (cos(FromLatR) * cos(ToLatR) * power(sin((FromLonR - ToLonR) /
                         2.0),2))
            )
        ) * 20001600. / pi() as Distance
    from Rads
);
```

When you compare the results of the calculations for 262,144 rows, as shown in Table 14-3, you can see that CLR UDF performs almost two times faster than the inline table-valued function and more than five times faster than the T-SQL scalar UDF.

Table 14-3. *Calculating Distance Between Two Points: Execution Time*

CLR UDF	TSQL Scalar UDF	TSQL Inline Table-Valued function
347 ms	1,955 ms	721 ms

Now, let's look at data access performance. The first test compares the execution time of the separate DML statements from the T-SQL and CLR stored procedures. In this test, I created procedures that calculate the number of rows in the `dbo.Numbers` table for a specific range of numbers. The T-SQL and CLR implementations are shown in Listings 14-12 and 14-13 respectively.

Listing 14-12. Data access performance: T-SQL procedure (individual statements)

```
create proc dbo.ExistInInterval(@MinNum int, @MaxNum int, @RowCount int output)
as
    set @RowCount = 0;
    while @MinNum <= @MaxNum
    begin
        if exists( select * from dbo.Numbers where Num = @MinNum )
            set @RowCount += 1
        set @MinNum += 1
    end;
```

Listing 14-13. Data access performance: CLR procedure (individual statements)

```
[Microsoft.SqlServer.Server.SqlProcedure]
public static void ExistInIntervalCLR(SqlInt32 minNum, SqlInt32 maxNum, out SqlInt32 rowCnt)
{
    int result = 0;
    using (SqlConnection conn = new SqlConnection("context connection=true"))
    {
        conn.Open();
        SqlCommand cmd = new SqlCommand
             ("select Num from dbo.Numbers where Num between @minNum and @maxNum", conn);
        cmd.Parameters.Add("@Result", SqlDbType.Int).Direction = ParameterDirection.Output;
        cmd.Parameters.Add("@Number", SqlDbType.Int);
        for (int i = minNum.Value; i <= maxNum.Value; i++)
        {
            cmd.Parameters[1].Value = i;
            cmd.ExecuteNonQuery();
            result += (int)cmd.Parameters[0].Value;
            System.Threading.Thread.Sleep(0);
        }
    }
    rowCnt = new SqlInt32(result);
}
```

Table 14-4 shows the average execution time for stored procedure calls that lead to 50,000 individual SELECT statements. As you can see, data access using CLR code works about five times slower than data access using T-SQL.

Table 14-4. *Data Access Performance (Individual Statements): Execution Time*

T-SQL Stored Procedure	CLR Stored Procedure
410 ms	2,330 ms

You need to keep this in mind when designing user-defined functions that need to access data from the database. While CLR is more efficient than T-SQL in terms of invocation, data access code will work significantly slower. You need to test both implementations to figure out which solution is more efficient for your purposes. Moreover, you need to consider code re-factoring and removing UDF from the queries as another possibility.

In the next step, let's look at the performance of the .Net SqlDataReader class and compare it to cursor implementation in T-SQL. You can see the CLR code in Listing 14-14 and the T-SQL implementation in Listing 14-15.

Listing 14-14. Data access performance: CLR procedure (SQL Reader)

```
[Microsoft.SqlServer.Server.SqlProcedure]
public static void ExistInIntervalReaderCLR
        ( SqlInt32 minNum, SqlInt32 maxNum, out SqlInt32 rowCnt )
{
    int result = 0;
    using (SqlConnection conn = new SqlConnection("context connection=true"))
```

```
    {
        conn.Open();
        SqlCommand cmd = new SqlCommand
             ("select Num from dbo.Numbers where Num between @MinNum and @MaxNum", conn);
        cmd.Parameters.Add("@MinNum", SqlDbType.Int).Value = minNum;
        cmd.Parameters.Add("@MaxNum", SqlDbType.Int).Value = maxNum;
        using (SqlDataReader reader = cmd.ExecuteReader())
        {
            while (reader.Read())
            {
                result++;
                // Yielding every 500 rows
                if (result % 500 == 0) System.Threading.Thread.Sleep(0);
            }
        }
    }
    rowCnt = new SqlInt32(result);
}
```

Listing 14-15. Data access performance: T-SQL procedure (Cursor)

```
create proc dbo.ExistInIntervalCursor(@MinNum int, @MaxNum int, @RowCount int output)
as
    declare
        @Num int
    declare
        curWork cursor fast_forward
        for
            select Num
            from dbo.Numbers
            where Num between @MinNum and @MaxNum

    set @RowCount = 0;
    open curWork;
    fetch next from curWork into @Num;
    while @@fetch_status = 0
    begin
        set @RowCount += 1;
        fetch next from curWork into @Num;
    end
    close curWork;
    deallocate curWork;
```

As you can see in Table 14-5, row-by-row processing using `SqlDataReader` is much more efficient than using the T-SQL cursor.

Table 14-5. *Data Access Performance (SQLReader Versus Cursor): Execution Time*

T-SQL Stored Procedure	CLR Stored Procedure
556 ms	116 ms

Finally, let's look at the performance of CLR aggregates. We will use an aggregate that concatenates the values into a comma-separated string. The code for doing this is shown in Listing 14-16.

Listing 14-16. CLR aggregate

```
[Serializable]
[SqlUserDefinedAggregate(
    Format.UserDefined, IsInvariantToNulls=true, IsInvariantToDuplicates=false,
    IsInvariantToOrder=false, MaxByteSize=-1) ]
public class Concatenate : IBinarySerialize
{
    // The buffer for the intermediate results
    private StringBuilder intermediateResult;

    // Initializes the buffer
    public void Init() { this.intermediateResult = new StringBuilder(); }

    // Accumulate the next value if not null
    public void Accumulate(SqlString value)
    {
        if (value.IsNull)
            return;
        this.intermediateResult.Append(value.Value).Append(',');
    }

    // Merges the partially completed aggregates
    public void Merge(Concatenate other)
    { this.intermediateResult.Append(other.intermediateResult); }

    // Called at the end of aggregation
    public SqlString Terminate()
    {
        string output = string.Empty;
        if (this.intermediateResult != null && this.intermediateResult.Length > 0)
        { // Deleting the trailing comma
            output = this.intermediateResult.ToString(0, this.intermediateResult.Length - 1);
        }
        return new SqlString(output);
    }

    // Deserializing data
    public void Read(BinaryReader r)
    { intermediateResult = new StringBuilder(r.ReadString()); }

    // Serializing data
    public void Write(BinaryWriter w)
    { w.Write(this.intermediateResult.ToString()); }
}
```

As with user-defined functions, it is extremely important to set the attributes that tell Query Optimizer about CLR aggregate behavior and implementation. This helps generate more efficient execution plans and prevents incorrect results due to optimization. It is also important to specify the MaxByteSize attribute that defines the maximum size of the aggregate output. In our case, we set it to -1, which means that the aggregate can hold up to 2 GB of data.

Let's compare the performance of two different T-SQL implementations. In the first one, I will use a SQL variable to hold intermediate results. This approach implements imperative row-by-row processing under the hood. The second method utilizes the FOR XML PATH technique that we discussed in Chapter 13. The code is shown in Listing 14-17.

Listing 14-17. String concatenation: T-SQL implementation

```
-- Using SQL Variable
declare
    @V nvarchar(max) = N''
    ,@MaxNum int -- test batch size

select @V = @V + convert(nvarchar(32), Num) + ','
from dbo.Numbers
where Num <= @MaxNum;

-- removing trailing comma
select @V = case when @V = '' then '' else left(@V,len(@V) - 1) end;

-- display results
select @v;

-- FOR XML PATH
select case when Result is null then '' else left(Result,len(Result) - 1) end
from
    (
        select convert(nvarchar(max),
            (
                select Num as [text()], ',' as [text()]
                from dbo.Numbers
                where Num <= @MaxNum
                for xml path('')
            )) as Result
    ) r
```

Table 14-6 shows the average execution time when we concatenate different numbers of rows.

Table 14-6. *String Concatenation: Execution Time*

	CLR Aggregate	SQL Variable	FOR XML PATH
1,000 rows	3 ms	1 ms	<1 ms
10,000 rows	12 ms	129 ms	3 ms
25,000 rows	33 ms	840 ms	6 ms
50,000 rows	63 ms	37,182 ms	21 ms
100,000 rows	146 ms	535,040 ms	43 ms

As you can see, CLR aggregate has a slightly higher startup cost when compared to the T-SQL variable approach, although that quickly disappears on larger row sets. The performance of both the CLR aggregate and the `FOR XML PATH` methods linearly depends on the number of rows, while the performance of the SQL variable approach degrades exponentially. SQL Server needs to initiate a new instance of the string every time it concatenates a new value, and it does not work efficiently, especially when the string becomes large. Finally, the `FOR XML PATH` approach is the most efficient regardless of the number of the rows concatenated.

The key point is that you always need to look at the options available to replace imperative code with declarative set-based logic. While CLR usually outperforms imperative T-SQL code, set-based logic outperforms both of them.

As you can see, each technology—T-SQL and CLR—has its own strengths and weaknesses. CLR is better at handling imperative code and complex calculations, and it has a much lower invocation cost for user-defined functions. T-SQL, on the other hand, outperforms CLR in the data-access area with the exception of row-by-row processing, where the .Net `SqlDataReader` class is faster than T-SQL cursors.

Summary

CLR code adds flexibility to SQL Server. It helps improve the performance of functions that require complex calculations and expands the standard function library by adding new methods. It lets you access external resources from within the database code.

CLR code, however, comes at a performance and security cost. CLR code runs within the SQL Server process, which adds an extra load and can introduce significant performance issues when coded incorrectly. Moreover, CLR introduces security challenges. It needs to be enabled on the server level, which violates security best practices. It also breaks ownership chaining, which will require using special care with permissions.

Keeping all of this in mind, you should always evaluate other options before using CLR code. You need to consider moving imperative logic to the client application and/or re-factoring your queries to use declarative set-based logic whenever possible.

As with the other technologies available within SQL Server, the question: "What is better: T-SQL or CLR?" has no right answer. Different use cases require different solutions, and it is always beneficial to evaluate and test all of the available options during the decision-making stage.

CHAPTER 15

CLR Types

CLR types make up another area of Common Language Runtime (CLR) integration with SQL Server. User-defined CLR types allow us to expand the standard type library by developing .Net classes and registering them in the database. Standard CLR types, such as `Geometry`, `Geography`, and `HierarchyId`, provide built-in support for spatial and hierarchical data. You will learn about both user-defined and system CLR types in this chapter.

User-Defined CLR Types

SQL Server has supported user-defined types (UDT) for years. Historically, T-SQL-based user-defined types were used to enforce type consistency. For example, when you needed to persist U.S. postal addresses in a several tables, you could create a user-defined type to store state information using the following statement: `CREATE TYPE dbo.PostalState FROM char(2) NOT NULL.`

Now you can use `dbo.PostalState` as a data type that defines table columns, parameters, and SQL variables. This guarantees that every reference to the postal state in the database has exactly the same format: a non-nullable, two-character string.

This approach has a few downsides, though. SQL Server does not permit the alteration of type definitions. If, at any point in time, you need to make `dbo.PostalState` nullable or, perhaps, allow full state names rather than abbreviations, the only option is to drop and recreate the type. Moreover, you must remove any references to that type in the database in order to do that.

Tip You can alter the type of the column to the base data type used by the UDT. This is a metadata-only operation.

T-SQL user-defined types are always delivered from a scalar T-SQL type. For example, you cannot create a T-SQL user-defined data type called *Address* that includes multiple attributes. Nor can you define check constraints on the type level. Constraints can still be defined individually on the column level, although such an approach is less convenient. Keeping all of this in mind, we can conclude that T-SQL user-defined types have very limited use in SQL Server.

Note You can perform validation on the type level by binding the rule object to the UDT. It is not recommended, however, as rules are deprecated and will be removed in a future version of SQL Server.

D. Korotkevitch, *Pro SQL Server Internals*, DOI 10.1007/978-1-4842-1964-5_15

CLR user-defined types, on the other hand, address some of these issues. They allow you to create complex types with multiple attributes/properties, define data-validation rules for the type, and implement methods that you can use to enhance the functionality of the type.

As an example, let's look at the implementation of a type that represents a simplified version of a U.S. postal address. The code for this is shown in Listing 15-1.

Listing 15-1. CLR user-defined type

```
[Serializable]
[Microsoft.SqlServer.Server.SqlUserDefinedType(
    Format.UserDefined,
    ValidationMethodName = "ValidateAddress",
    MaxByteSize=8000) ]
public struct USPostalAddress : INullable, IBinarySerialize
{
    // Needs to be sorted to support BinarySearch
    private static readonly List<string> _validStates = new List<string>
    {
        "AK","AL","AR","AZ","CA","CO","CT","DC","DE","FL","GA","HI","IA"
        ,"ID","IL","IN","KS","KY","LA","MA","MD","ME","MI","MN","MO","MS"
        ,"MT","NC","ND","NE","NH","NJ","NM","NV","NY","OH","OK","OR","PA"
        ,"PR","RI","SC","SD","TN","TX","UT","VA","VT","WA","WI","WV","WY"
    };

    private bool _null;
    private string _address;
    private string _city;
    private string _state;
    private string _zipCode;

    public bool IsNull { get { return _null; } }

    public string Address
    {
        [SqlMethod(IsDeterministic = true, IsPrecise = true)]
        get { return _address; }
    }

    public string City
    {
        [SqlMethod(IsDeterministic = true, IsPrecise = true)]
        get { return _city; }
    }

    public string State
    {
        [SqlMethod(IsDeterministic = true, IsPrecise=true)]
        get { return _state; }
    }
```

```
public string ZipCode
{
    [SqlMethod(IsDeterministic = true, IsPrecise = true)]
    get { return _zipCode; }
}

public override string ToString()
{ return String.Format("{0}, {1}, {2}, {3}", _address, _city, _state, _zipCode); }

// The static representation of Null object
public static USPostalAddress Null
{
    get
    {
        USPostalAddress h = new USPostalAddress();
        h._null = true;
        return h;
    }
}

// Validation that Address information is correct
private bool ValidateAddress()
{
    // Check that all attributes are specified and state is valid
    return
        !(  String.IsNullOrEmpty(_address) || String.IsNullOrEmpty(_city) ||
            String.IsNullOrEmpty(_state) || String.IsNullOrEmpty(_zipCode) ||
            _validStates.BinarySearch(_state.ToUpper()) == -1 );
}

// Creating object from the string
public static USPostalAddress Parse(SqlString s)
{
    if (s.IsNull) return Null;
    USPostalAddress u = new USPostalAddress();
    string[] parts = s.Value.Split(",".ToCharArray());
    if (parts.Length != 4)
        throw new ArgumentException("Incorrect format. Should be <Address>, <City>,
        <State>, <ZipCode>");
    u._address = parts[0].Trim();
    u._city = parts[1].Trim();
    u._state = parts[2].Trim();
    u._zipCode = parts[3].Trim();
    if (!u.ValidateAddress())
        throw new ArgumentException("Incorrect format. Attributes are empty or State is
        incorrect");
    return u;
}

// Example of the class method
 [SqlMethod(OnNullCall = false, IsDeterministic = true, DataAccess=DataAccessKind.None)]
```

```
    public double CalculateShippingCost(USPostalAddress destination)
    {
        // Calculating shipping cost between two addresses
        return (destination.State == this.State)?15.0:25.0;
    }

    // IBinarySerializer.Read
    public void Read(System.IO.BinaryReader r)
    {
        _address = r.ReadString();
        _city = r.ReadString();
        _state = r.ReadString();
        _zipCode = r.ReadString();
    }

    // IBinarySerializer.Write
    public void Write(System.IO.BinaryWriter w)
    {
        w.Write(_address);
        w.Write(_city);
        w.Write(_state);
        w.Write(_zipCode);
    }
}
```

As you can see, the type includes four different public attributes/properties (Street, City, State, and ZIPCode) and several methods. Some of the methods (ToString, Parse, Read, and Write) are required to support type creation and serialization. Another (CalculateShippingCost) is an example of a type functionality enhancement.

In the database, you can use this type when defining table columns, variables, and parameters. Listing 15-2 and Figure 15-1 show an example of this.

Listing 15-2. CLR user-defined type usage

```
declare
    @MicrosoftAddr dbo.USPostalAddress = 'One Microsoft Way, Redmond, WA, 98052'
    ,@GoogleAddr dbo.USPostalAddress = '1600 Amphitheatre Pkwy, Mountain View, CA, 94043'

select
    @MicrosoftAddr as [Raw Data]
    ,@MicrosoftAddr.ToString() as [Text Data]
    ,@MicrosoftAddr.Address as [Address]
    ,@MicrosoftAddr.CalculateShippingCost(@GoogleAddr) as [ShippingCost]
```

	Raw Data	Text Data	Address	ShippingCost
1	0x114F6E65204D6963726F736F...	One Microsoft Way, Redmond, WA, 98052	One Microsoft Way	25

Figure 15-1. *CLR user-defined type usage*

CLR user-defined types let you easily expand the SQL Server type library with your own types, developed and used in an object-oriented manner. It sounds too good to be true from a development standpoint, and, unfortunately, there are a few caveats about which you need to be aware.

As I already mentioned, SQL Server does not let you alter a type after you create it. You can redeploy a new version of the assembly with the `ALTER ASSEMBLY` command. This allows you to change the implementation of the methods and/or fix any bugs in the implementation, although you would not be able to change the interface of existing methods, nor would you be able to utilize new public methods unless you drop and re-create the type. This requires removing all type references from the database code.

All of this means that you must perform the following set of actions to re-deploy the type:

1. Remove all type references from the T-SQL code.
2. Persist all data from the columns of that type somewhere else, either by shredding type attributes to a relational format or casting them to `varbinary`. You need to be careful with the latter approach and make sure that the new version of the type object can be deserialized from the old object's binary data.
3. Drop all columns of that type.
4. Drop type, redeploy assembly, and create type again.
5. Recreate the columns and re-populate them with the data.
6. Rebuild the indexes, reclaiming the space from the old columns and reducing fragmentation.
7. Recreate T-SQL code that references the type.

As you can see, this introduces a large amount of maintenance overhead, and it can lead to prolonged system downtimes.

Performance is another very important aspect to consider. SQL Server stores CLR types in binary format. Every time you access attributes or methods of a CLR type, SQL Server deserializes the object and calls the CLR method, which leads to overhead similar to what you saw in Chapter 14.

Let's run some tests and create two tables with address information: one using regular T-SQL data types and another using a `dbo.USPostalAddress` CLR user-defined type. You can see the code for doing this in Listing 15-3.

Listing 15-3. UDT performance: Table creation

```
create table dbo.Addresses
(
    ID int not null identity(1,1),
    Address varchar(128) not null,
    City varchar(64) not null,
    State char(2) not null,
    ZipCode varchar(10) not null,

    constraint CHK_Address_State check
    (  State in ( 'AK','AL','AR','AZ','CA','CO','CT','DC','DE','FL','GA','HI','IA','ID'
        ,'IL','IN','KS','KY','LA','MA','MD','ME','MI','MN','MO','MS','MT','NC','ND','NE','NH'
        ,'NJ','NM','NV','NY','OH','OK','OR','PA','PR','RI','SC','SD','TN','TX','UT','VA'
        ,'VT','WA','WI','WV','WY') ),
    constraint PK_Addresses primary key clustered(ID)
);
```

```
create table dbo.AddressesCLR
(
    ID int not null identity(1,1),
    Address dbo.USPostalAddress not null,
    constraint PK_AddressesCLR primary key clustered(ID)
);

;with Streets(Street)
as
(
    select v.v
    from (values('Street 1'),('Street 2'),('Street 3'),('Street 4'),('Street 5')
                ,('Street 6'),('Street 7'),('Street 8'),('Street 9'),('Street 10')) v(v)
)
,Cities(City)
as
(
    select v.v
    from (values('City 1'),('City 2'),('City 3'),('City 4'),('City 5')
                ,('City 6'),('City 7'),('City 8'),('City 9'),('City 10')) v(v)
)
,ZipCodes(Zip)
as
(
    select v.v
    from (values('99991'),('99992'),('99993'),('99994'),('99995')
                ,('99996'),('99997'),('99998'),('99999'),('99990')) v(v)
)
,States(state)
as
(
    select v.v
    from (values('AL'),('AK'),('AZ'),('AR'),('CA'),('CO'),('CT'),('DE'),('FL'),('GA'),('HI')
     ,('ID'),('IL'),('IN'),('IA'),('KS'),('KY'),('LA'),('ME'),('MD'),('MA'),('MI'),('MN')
     ,('MS'),('MO'),('MT'),('NE'),('NV'),('NH'),('NJ'),('NM'),('NY'),('NC'),('ND'),('OH')
     ,('OK'),('OR'),('PA'),('RI'),('SC'),('SD'),('TN'),('TX'),('UT'),('VT'),('VA'),('WA')
     ,('WV'),('WI'),('WY'),('DC'),('PR')) v(v)
)
insert into dbo.Addresses(Address,City,State,ZipCode)
    select Street,City,State,Zip
    from Streets cross join Cities cross join States cross join ZipCodes;

insert into dbo.AddressesCLR(Address)
    select Address + ', ' + City + ', ' + State + ', ' + ZipCode from dbo.Addresses;
```

Now, let's run a test and look at the performance of the queries against both tables. We will use the queries shown in Listing 15-4.

Listing 15-4. UDT performance: Querying the data

```
select State, count(*)
from dbo.Addresses
group by State

select Address.State, count(*)
from dbo.AddressesCLR
group by Address.State
```

As you can see in Figure 15-2, the second SELECT introduces a CLR method call for every row, and this significantly affects the performance of the query. You can see information about the call in the *compute scalar* operator properties, as shown in Figure 15-3.

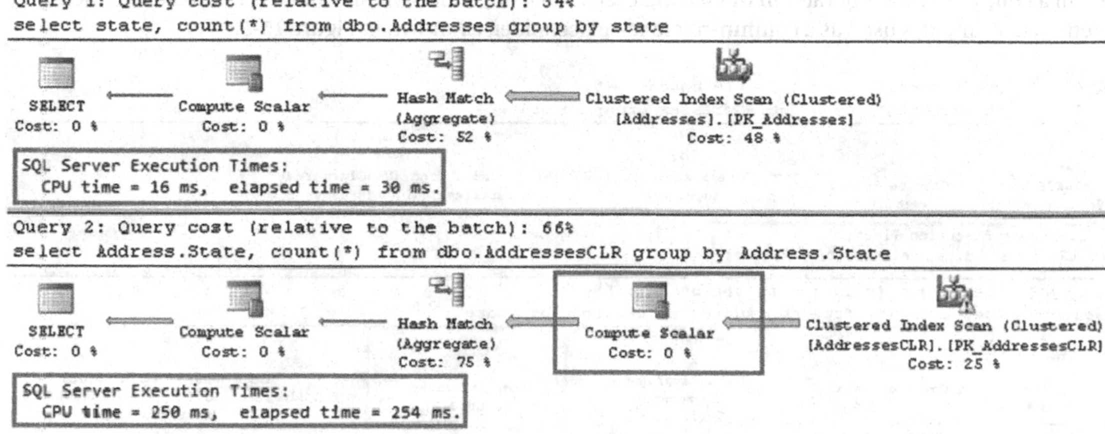

Figure 15-2. *UDT performance: Querying the data*

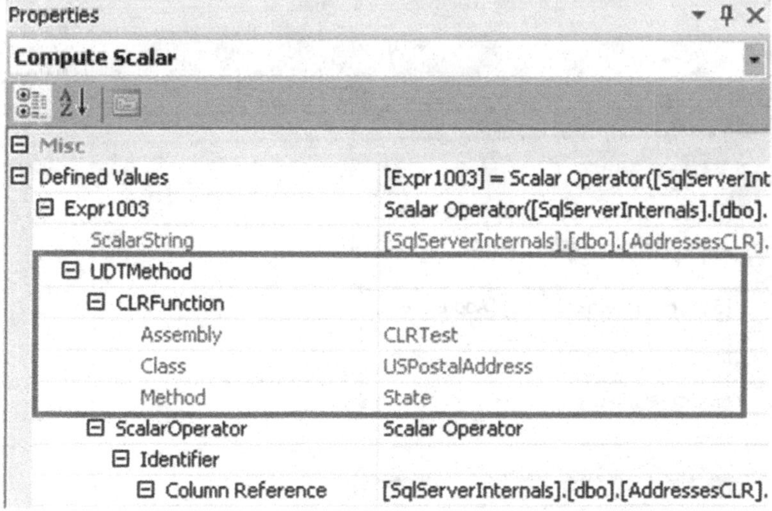

Figure 15-3. *UDT performance: Computer scalar operator properties*

Some of the performance issues can be addressed with persisted calculated columns, which can even be indexed if needed. Let's test this by adding a State column to the dbo.AddressesCLR table and creating indexes in both tables. The code for doing this is shown in Listing 15-5.

Listing 15-5. UDT performance: Adding a persisted calculated column

```
alter table dbo.AddressesCLR add State as Address.State persisted;
-- Rebuild the index to reduce the fragmentation caused by alteration
alter index PK_AddressesCLR on dbo.AddressesCLR rebuild;

create index IDX_AddressesCLR_State on dbo.AddressesCLR(State);
create index IDX_Addresses_State on dbo.Addresses(State);
```

Now, if you run the queries from Listing 15-4 again, you will see the results shown in Figure 15-4. There is still a compute scalar operator in the second execution plan, although this time it is not related to the CLR method call, and it is used as a column-reference placeholder, as shown in Figure 15-5.

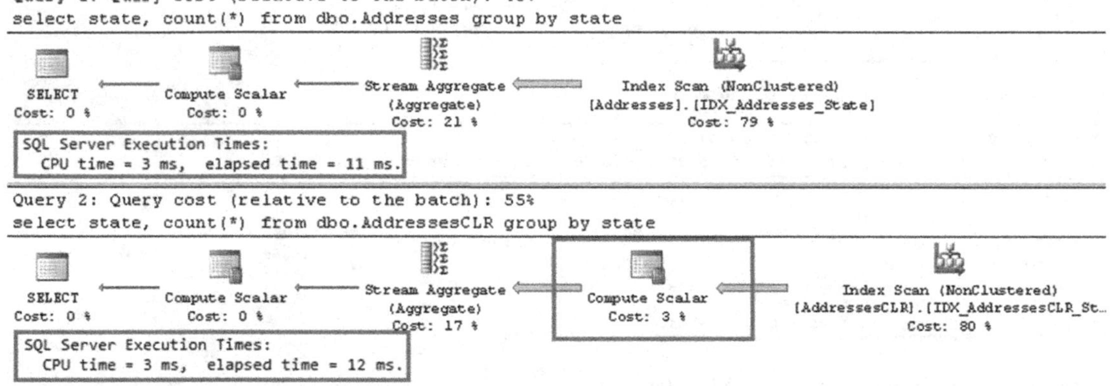

Figure 15-4. *UDT performance: Persisted calculated column*

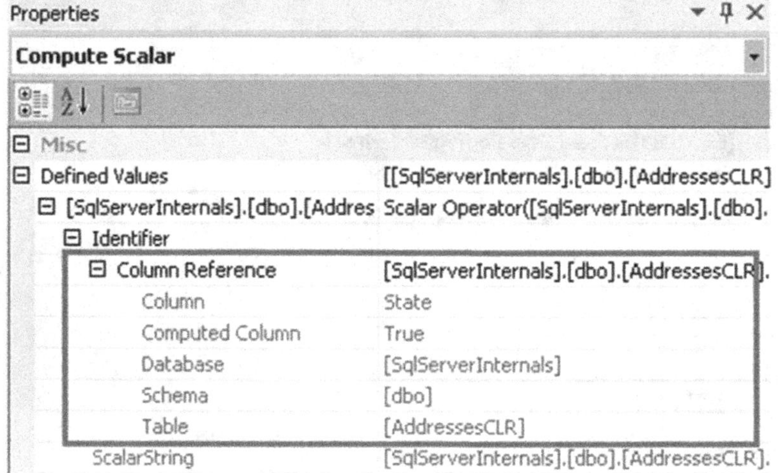

Figure 15-5. *UDT performance: Computer scalar operator with calculated column*

Although persisted calculated columns can help with performance, they increase the size of the rows. You are storing the same information several times, once as part of a UDT binary value and also in clustered and potentially nonclustered indexes. These columns also introduce additional overhead for maintaining calculated columns when UDT data is frequently modified.

Keeping supportability and performance aspects in mind, you should be very careful when introducing CLR user-defined types in your systems. The public methods of the type should be finalized before initial deployment, and the code must be carefully tested. This will help you to avoid situations where the type needs to be redeployed.

In addition, you need to minimize the number of CLR calls by creating and possibly indexing persisted calculated columns, which store the values of UDT properties and methods that are frequently called from the queries.

Spatial Data Types

SQL Server supports two data types to store spatial information: `geometry` and `geography`. `Geometry` supports planar, or Euclidean, flat-earth data. `Geography` supports ellipsoidal round-earth surfaces. Both data types can be used to store location information, such as GPS latitude and longitude coordinates. The `geography` data type considers the Earth's roundness and provides slightly better accuracy, although it has stricter requirements for the data. For example, data must fit in a single hemisphere, and polygons must be defined in a specific ring orientation. Client applications need to be aware of these requirements and handle them correctly in the code.

Storing location information in a `geometry` data type introduces its own class of problems. It works fine and often has better performance than a `geography` data type when you need to find out if a location belongs to a specific area or if areas are intersecting. However, you cannot calculate the distance between points: the unit of measure for the result is in decimal degrees, which are useless on a non-flat surface.

■ **Note** Coverage of spatial data type methods is outside of the scope of this book. If you are interested in learning more about this, check out this site for more details: `http://msdn.microsoft.com/en-us/library/bb933790.aspx`.

Although spatial data types provide a rich set of methods with which to work with data, you must consider performance aspects when dealing with them. Spatial data types are CLR-based; however, SQL Server 2012 SP3, SQL Server 2014 SP2, and SQL Server 2016 RTM allow you to use native implementation for some spatial methods, which can significantly improve performance in some scenarios. You should use the trace flags `T6533` and `T6534` to enable native implementation in SQL Server 2012 SP3 and SQL Server 2014 SP2. In SQL Server 2016, native implementation is enabled by default.

Let's compare the performance of the methods that calculate the distance between two points. A typical use case for such a scenario is a search for a point of interest (POI) close to a specific location. As a first step, let's create three different tables that store POI information.

The first table, `dbo.Locations`, stores coordinates using the `decimal(9,6)` data type. The two other tables use a `geography` data type. Finally, the table `dbo.LocationsGeoIndexed` has a `Location` column indexed with a special type of index called a *spatial index*. These indexes help improve the performance of some operations, such as distance calculations or ones that check to see if objects intersect. The code is shown in Listing 15-6.

Listing 15-6. POI Lookup: Creating test tables

```
create table dbo.Locations
(
    Id int not null identity(1,1),
    Latitude decimal(9,6) not null,
    Longitude decimal(9,6) not null,
    constraint PK_Locations primary key clustered(Id)
);

create table dbo.LocationsGeo
(
    Id int not null identity(1,1),
    Location geography not null,
    constraint PK_LocationsGeo primary key clustered(Id)
);

create table dbo.LocationsGeoIndexed
(
    Id int not null identity(1,1),
    Location geography not null,
    constraint PK_LocationsGeoIndexed primary key clustered(Id)
);

-- 241,402 rows
;with Latitudes(Lat)
as
(
    select convert(float,40.0)
    union all
    select convert(float,Lat + 0.01)
    from Latitudes
    where Lat < 48
)
,Longitudes(Lon)
as
(
    select convert(float,-120.0)
    union all
    select Lon - 0.01
    from Longitudes
    where Lon > -123
)
insert into dbo.Locations(Latitude, Longitude)
    select Latitudes.Lat, Longitudes.Lon
    from Latitudes cross join Longitudes
option (maxrecursion 0);

insert into dbo.LocationsGeo(Location)
    select geography::Point(Latitude, Longitude, 4326)
    from dbo.Locations;
```

```
insert into dbo.LocationsGeoIndexed(Location)
    select Location
    from dbo.LocationsGeo;

create spatial index Idx_LocationsGeoIndexed_Spatial
on dbo.LocationsGeoIndexed(Location);
```

■ **Tip** We store location information in relational format using the `decimal(9,6)` data type rather than `float`. Decimal data types use six bytes less storage space per pair of values, and they provide accuracy that exceeds that of commercial-grade GPS receivers.

The storage space used by the tables from Listing 15-6 is shown in Table 15-1.

Table 15-1. *Storage Space Used by the Tables in Listing 15-6*

dbo.Locations	dbo.LocationsGeo	dbo.LocationsGeoIndexed
5,488 KB	9,368 KB	13,936 KB

As you can see, the binary representation of the spatial type uses more space than the relational format. As expected, the spatial index requires additional space, although the overhead is not nearly as much as the overhead produced by the XML indexes that you saw in Chapter 12, "XML and JSON."

Let's run tests that measure the performance of queries that calculate the number of locations within one mile of Seattle's city center. In the `dbo.Locations` table, we will use the `dbo.CalcDistanceCLR` function, which was defined in Chapter 14. For the two other tables, we will call the spatial method `STDistance`, both with and without native implementation enabled via trace flags. The test code to accomplish this is shown in Listing 15-7. The query execution plans are shown in Figure 15-6.

Listing 15-7. POI Lookup: Test queries

```
/* In SQL Server 2012 SP3 and SQL Server 2014 SP2 use T6533 and T6534 to enable native
implementation */
declare
    @Lat decimal(9,6) = 47.620309
    ,@Lon decimal(9,6) = -122.349563

declare
    @G geography = geography::Point(@Lat,@Lon,4326)

select ID
from dbo.Locations
where dbo.CalcDistanceCLR(Latitude, Longitude, @Lat, @Lon) < 1609;

select ID
from dbo.LocationsGeo
where Location.STDistance(@G) < 1609;

select ID
from dbo.LocationsGeoIndexed
where Location.STDistance(@G) < 1609;
```

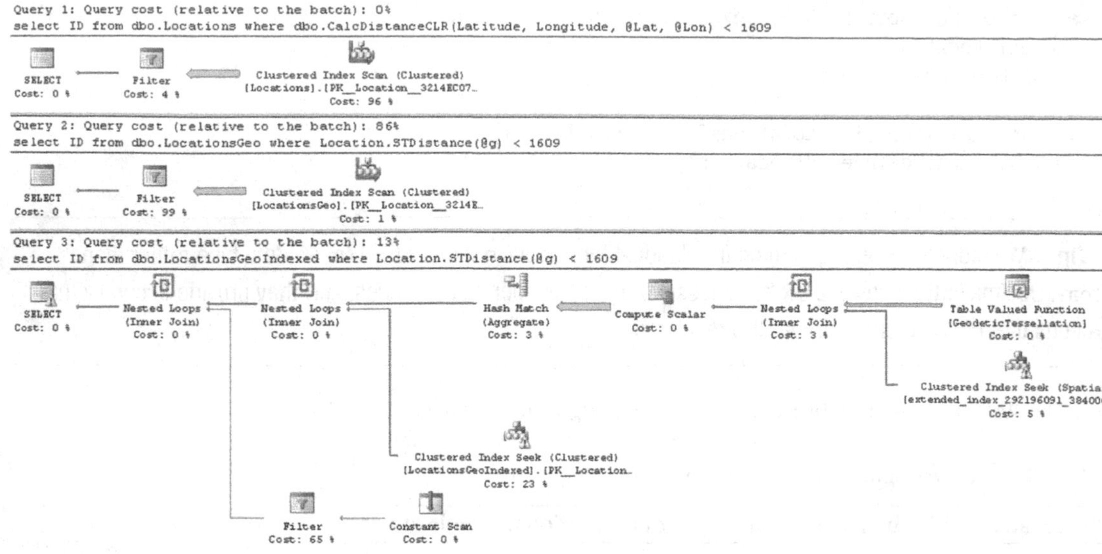

Figure 15-6. *POI Lookup: Execution plans*

The first and second queries perform *clustered index scans* and calculate the distance for every row of the tables. The last query uses a spatial index to look up such rows. You can see the execution times for the queries in my environment in Table 15-2.

Table 15-2. *POI Lookup: Execution Time*

	dbo.Locations	dbo.LocationsGeo	dbo.LocationsGeoIndexed
SQL Server 2014 SP1	245 ms	9,477 ms	42 ms
SQL Server 2014 SP2 without T6533 and T6534	245 ms	9,652 ms	15 ms
SQL Server 2014 SP2 with T6533 and T6534	245 ms	224 ms	15 ms
SQL Server 2016	241 ms	222 ms	12 ms

As you can see, the spatial index greatly benefits the query. It is also worth mentioning that without the index, the performance of the `CalcDistanceCLR` method is significantly better compared to the `STDistance` method when native implementation is not enabled.

Although the spatial index greatly improves performance, it has its own limitations. It works within the scope of the entire table, and all other predicates are evaluated after spatial index operations. This can introduce suboptimal plans in some cases.

As an example, let's look at a use case for when we store POI information on a customer-by-customer basis, as shown in Listing 15-8. It is worth noting that this code will take a significant amount of time to execute and will produce a large amount of transaction log records.

Listing 15-8. Customer-based POI lookup: Table creation

```
create table dbo.LocationsGeo2
(
    CompanyId int not null,
    Id int not null identity(1,1),
    Location geography not null,
    constraint PK_LocationsGeo2
    primary key clustered(CompanyId,Id)
);

-- 12,070,100 rows; 50 companies; 241,402 rows per company
;with Companies(CID)
as
(
    select 1
    union all
    select CID + 1 from Companies where CID < 50
)
insert into dbo.LocationsGeo2(CompanyId,Location)
    select c.CID, l.Location
    from dbo.LocationsGeo l cross join Companies c;

create spatial index Idx_LocationsGeo2_Spatial
on dbo.LocationsGeo2(Location);
```

In this case, when we perform a POI lookup for a specific company, the CompanyId column must be included as the predicate to the queries. SQL Server has two choices on how to proceed. The first choice is a *clustered index seek* based on the CompanyId value's calling the STDistance method for every POI that belongs to the company. The second choice is to use a spatial index, find all POIs within the specified distance regardless of the company to which they belong, and, finally, join it with the clustered index data. Let's run the queries shown in Listing 15-9.

Listing 15-9. Customer-based POI lookup: Test queries

```
declare
    @Lat decimal(9,6) = 47.620309
    ,@Lon decimal(9,6) = -122.349563
    ,@CompanyId int = 15

declare
    @g geography = geography::Point(@Lat,@Lon,4326)

select count(*)
from dbo.LocationsGeo2 with (index= PK_LocationsGeo2)
where Location.STDistance(@g) < 1609 and CompanyId = @CompanyId;

select count(*)
from dbo.LocationsGeo2 with (index=Idx_LocationsGeo2_Spatial)
where Location.STDistance(@g) < 1609 and CompanyId = @CompanyId;
```

Neither method is efficient when a table stores a large amount of data for a sizable number of companies. The execution plan of the first query utilizing a clustered index seek shows that it performed the `STDistance` call 241,402 times, or once for every company POI. The execution plan is shown in Figure 15-7.

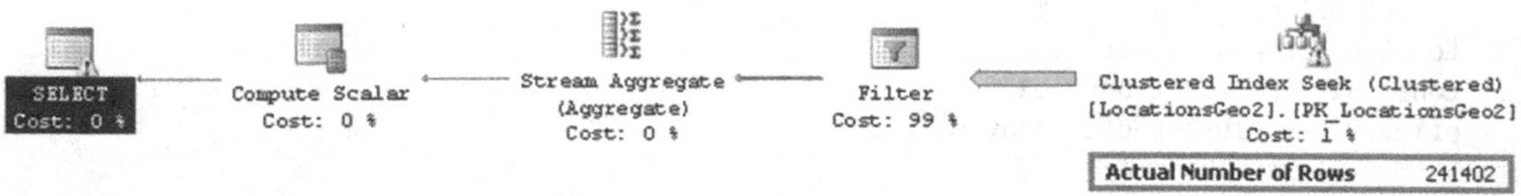

Figure 15-7. *Customer-based POI lookup: Execution plan for the first query*

The execution plan for the second query, which is shown in Figure 15-8, indicates that the spatial index lookup returned 550 rows; that is, all POI in the area, regardless of to which company they belong. SQL Server then had to join the rows with the clustered index before evaluating the `CompanyId` predicate.

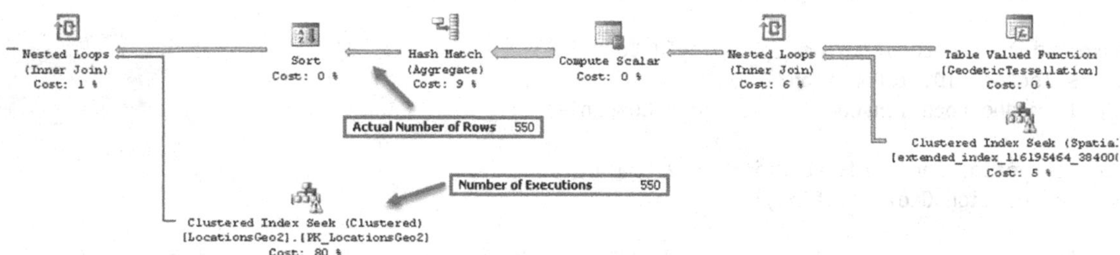

Figure 15-8. *Customer-based POI 'ookup: Execution plan for the second query*

One of the ways to solve such a problem is called the *bounding box* approach. This method lets us minimize the number of calculations by filtering out POIs that are outside of the area of interest.

As you can see in Figure 15-9, all points that we need to select reside in the circle, with the location at the center point and radius specified by the distance. The only points that we need to evaluate reside within the box that surrounds the circle.

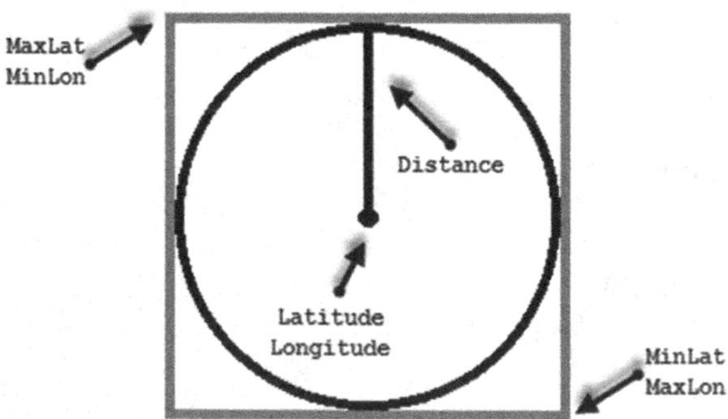

Figure 15-9. *Customer-based POI lookup: Bounding box*

We can calculate the coordinates of the corner points of the box, persist them in the table, and use a regular nonclustered index to pre-filter the data. This lets us minimize the number of expensive distance calculations to be performed.

The calculation of the bounding box's corner points can be done with a CLR table-valued function, as shown in Listing 15-10. Listing 15-11 shows the T-SQL code that alters the table and creates a nonclustered index there.

Listing 15-10. Customer-based POI lookup: Calculating bounding-box coordinates

```
private struct BoundingBox
{
    public double minLat;
    public double maxLat;
    public double minLon;
    public double maxLon;
}

private static void CircleBoundingBox_FillValues(
    object obj, out SqlDouble MinLat, out SqlDouble MaxLat,
    out SqlDouble MinLon, out SqlDouble MaxLon)
{
    BoundingBox box = (BoundingBox)obj;
    MinLat = new SqlDouble(box.minLat);
    MaxLat = new SqlDouble(box.maxLat);
    MinLon = new SqlDouble(box.minLon);
    MaxLon = new SqlDouble(box.maxLon);
}

[Microsoft.SqlServer.Server.SqlFunction(
    DataAccess = DataAccessKind.None, IsDeterministic = true, IsPrecise = false,
    SystemDataAccess = SystemDataAccessKind.None,
    FillRowMethodName = "CircleBoundingBox_FillValues",
    TableDefinition = "MinLat float, MaxLat float, MinLon float, MaxLon float") ]
public static IEnumerable CalcCircleBoundingBox(SqlDouble lat, SqlDouble lon, SqlInt32
distance)
{
    if (lat.IsNull || lon.IsNull || distance.IsNull) return null;

    BoundingBox[] box = new BoundingBox[1];
    double latR =  Math.PI / 180 * lat.Value;
    double lonR = Math.PI / 180 * lon.Value;
    double rad45 = 0.785398163397448300;  // RADIANS(45.)
    double rad135 = 2.356194490192344800; // RADIANS(135.)
    double rad225 = 3.926990816987241400; // RADIANS(225.)
    double rad315 = 5.497787143782137900; // RADIANS(315.)
    double distR = distance.Value * 1.4142135623731 * Math.PI / 20001600.0;
    double latR45 = Math.Asin(Math.Sin(latR) * Math.Cos(distR) + Math.Cos(latR) *
            Math.Sin(distR) * Math.Cos(rad45));
    double latR135 = Math.Asin(Math.Sin(latR) * Math.Cos(distR) + Math.Cos(latR) *
            Math.Sin(distR) * Math.Cos(rad135));
    double latR225 = Math.Asin(Math.Sin(latR) * Math.Cos(distR) + Math.Cos(latR) *
            Math.Sin(distR) * Math.Cos(rad225));
```

```
    double latR315 = Math.Asin(Math.Sin(latR) * Math.Cos(distR) + Math.Cos(latR) *
            Math.Sin(distR) * Math.Cos(rad315));
    double dLonR45 = Math.Atan2(Math.Sin(rad45) * Math.Sin(distR) * Math.Cos(latR),
            Math.Cos(distR) - Math.Sin(latR) * Math.Sin(latR45));
    double dLonR135 = Math.Atan2(Math.Sin(rad135) * Math.Sin(distR) * Math.Cos(latR),
            Math.Cos(distR) - Math.Sin(latR) * Math.Sin(latR135));
    double dLonR225 = Math.Atan2(Math.Sin(rad225) * Math.Sin(distR) * Math.Cos(latR),
            Math.Cos(distR) - Math.Sin(latR) * Math.Sin(latR225));
    double dLonR315 = Math.Atan2(Math.Sin(rad315) * Math.Sin(distR) * Math.Cos(latR),
            Math.Cos(distR) - Math.Sin(latR) * Math.Sin(latR315));
    double lat45 = latR45 * 180.0 / Math.PI;
    double lat225 = latR225 * 180.0 / Math.PI;
    double lon45 = (((lonR - dLonR45 + Math.PI) % (2 * Math.PI)) - Math.PI) * 180.0 / Math.PI;
    double lon135 = (((lonR - dLonR135 + Math.PI) % (2 * Math.PI)) - Math.PI) *180.0 / Math.PI;
    double lon225 = (((lonR - dLonR225 + Math.PI) % (2 * Math.PI)) - Math.PI) *180.0 / Math.PI;
    double lon315 = (((lonR - dLonR315 + Math.PI) % (2 * Math.PI)) - Math.PI) *180.0 / Math.PI;

    box[0].minLat = Math.Min(lat45, lat225);
    box[0].maxLat = Math.Max(lat45, lat225);
    box[0].minLon = Math.Min(Math.Min(lon45, lon135), Math.Min(lon225,lon315));
    box[0].maxLon = Math.Max(Math.Max(lon45, lon135), Math.Max(lon225, lon315));
    return box;
}
```

Listing 15-11. Customer-based POI lookup: Altering the table

```
alter table dbo.LocationsGeo2 add MinLat decimal(9,6);
alter table dbo.LocationsGeo2 add MaxLat decimal(9,6);
alter table dbo.LocationsGeo2 add MinLon decimal(9,6);
alter table dbo.LocationsGeo2 add MaxLon decimal(9,6);

update t
set
    t.MinLat = b.MinLat
    ,t.MinLon = b.MinLon
    ,t.MaxLat = b.MaxLat
    ,t.MaxLon = b.MaxLon
from
    dbo.LocationsGeo2 t cross apply
        dbo.CalcCircleBoundingBox(t.Location.Lat,t.Location.Long,1609) b;

create index IDX_LocationsGeo2_BoundingBox
on dbo.LocationsGeo2(CompanyId, MinLon, MaxLon)
include (MinLat, MaxLat);
```

Now, you can change the query to utilize the bounding box. This query is shown in Listing 15-12. The corresponding execution plan is shown in Figure 15-10.

Listing 15-12. Customer-based POI lookup: Query utilizing bounding box

```
declare
    @Lat decimal(9,6) = 47.620309
    ,@Lon decimal(9,6) = -122.349563
    ,@CompanyId int = 15

declare
    @g geography = geography::Point(@Lat,@Lon,4326)

select count(*)
from dbo.LocationsGeo2
where
    Location.STDistance(@g) < 1609 and
    CompanyId = @CompanyId and
    @Lat between MinLat and MaxLat and
    @Lon between MinLon and MaxLon;
```

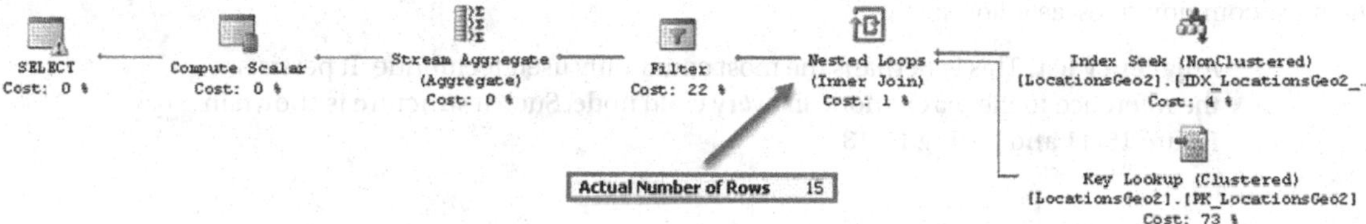

Figure 15-10. *Customer-based POI lookup: Execution plan (bounding-box approach)*

As you can see, the last query calculated the distance 15 times. This is a significant improvement over the 241,402 calculations in the original query. The execution times in my environment are shown in Table 15-3.

Table 15-3. *Customer-Based POI Lookup: Execution Times*

	Clustered Index Seek	Spatial Index	Bounding Box
SQL Server 2014 SP1	9,923 ms	55 ms	13 ms
SQL Server 2014 SP2 without T6533 and T6534	10,337 ms	19 ms	10 ms
SQL Server 2014 SP2 with T6533 and T6534	231 ms	18 ms	10 ms
SQL Server 2016	222 ms	16 ms	5 ms

As you can see, the bounding box outperforms both the clustered index seek and the spatial index lookup, even with native implementation enabled. Obviously, this would be the case only when the bounding box reduced the number of the calculations to a degree that offset the overhead of the *nonclustered index seek* and *key lookup* operations. It is also worth mentioning that you do not need a spatial index with such an approach.

You can also use a bounding box for other use cases; for example, when you are checking to see if a position belongs to the area defined by a polygon. The bounding box corner coordinates should store the minimum and maximum latitude and longitude coordinates of the polygon's corner points. Like the distance calculation, you would filter out the locations outside of the box before performing an expensive spatial method call that validates whether the point is within the polygon area.

HierarchyId

The `HierarchyId` data type helps you work with hierarchical data structures. It is optimized to represent trees, which are the most common type of hierarchical data.

■ **Note** Coverage of `HierarchyId` data-type methods is beyond the scope of this book. You can learn more about the `HierarchyId` data type at `http://technet.microsoft.com/en-us/library/bb677173.aspx`.

There are several techniques that allow us to store hierarchical information in a database. Let's look at the most common ones, as follows:

> **Adjacency list.** This is perhaps the most commonly used technique. It persists the reference to the parent node in every child node. Such a structure is shown in Figure 15-11 and Listing 15-13.

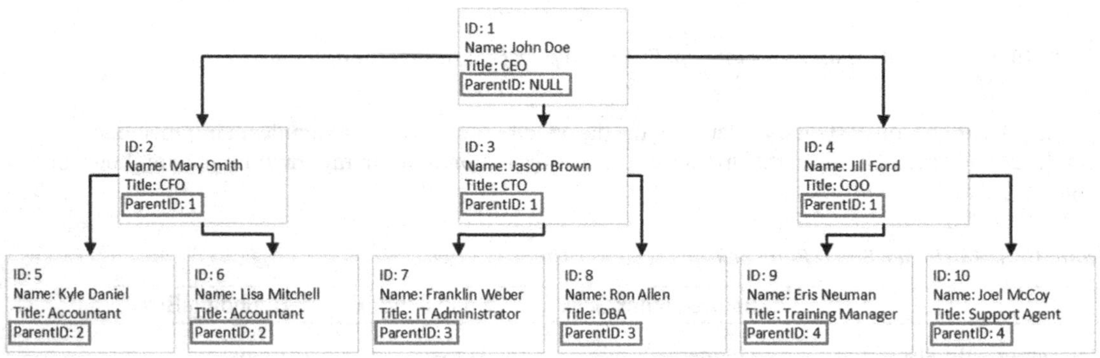

Figure 15-11. *Adjacency list*

Listing 15-13. Adjancency list DDL

```
create table dbo.OrgChart
(
    ID int not null,
    Name nvarchar(64) not null,
    Title nvarchar(64) not null,
    ParentID int null,

    constraint PK_OrgChart primary key clustered(ID),
```

```
    constraint FK_OrgChart_OrgChart
    foreign key(ParentId)
    references dbo.OrgChart(ID)
)
```

Closure table. This is similar to an adjacency list; however, the parent-child relationship is stored separately. Figure 15-12 and Listing 15-14 show an example of a Closure Table.

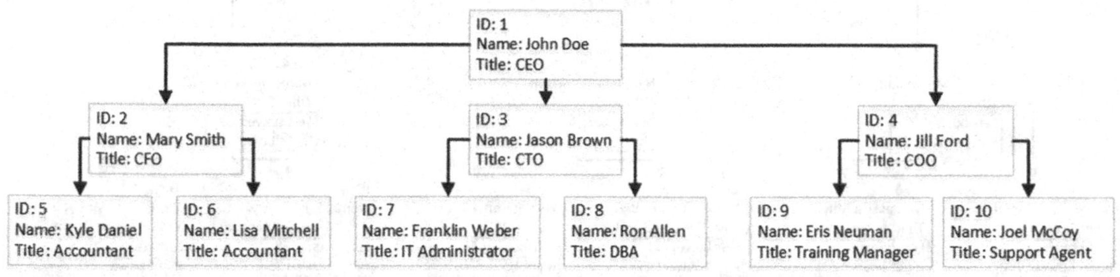

Figure 15-12. *Closure table*

Listing 15-14. Closure table DDL

```
create table dbo.OrgChart
(
    ID int not null,
    Name nvarchar(64) not null,
    Title nvarchar(64) not null,

    constraint PK_OrgChart primary key clustered(ID),
);

create table dbo.OrgTree
(
    ParentId int not null,
    ChildId int not null,

    constraint PK_OrgTree primary key clustered(ParentId, ChildId),

    constraint FK_OrgTree_OrgChart_Parent
    foreign key(ParentId)
    references dbo.OrgChart(ID),

    constraint FK_OrgTree_OrgChart_Child
    foreign key(ChildId)
    references dbo.OrgChart(ID)
);
```

Nested sets. With nested sets, every node contains two values, called *left* and *right bowers*. Child node bower values are within the interval of the parent node bowers. As a result, when you need to find all of the children of the parent, you can select all nodes with left and right bower values in between the parent values. Figure 15-13 and Listing 15-15 show an example of nested sets.

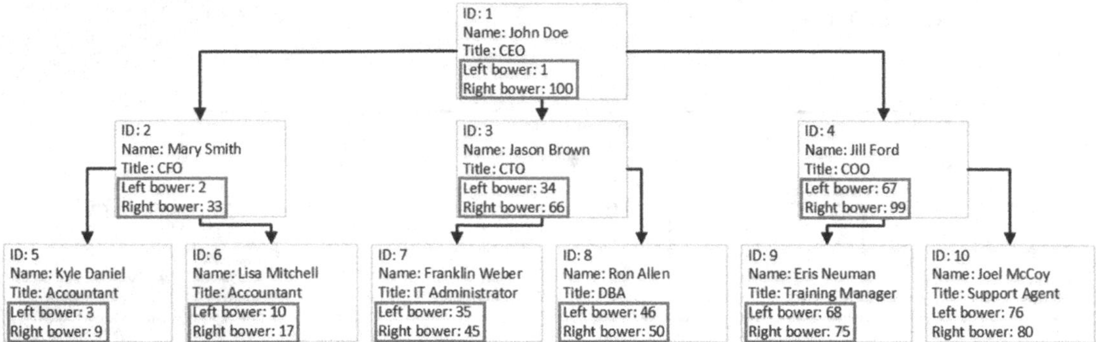

Figure 15-13. *Nested sets*

Listing 15-15. Nested sets DDL

```
create table dbo.OrgChart
(
    ID int not null,
    Name nvarchar(64) not null,
    Title nvarchar(64) not null,
    LeftBower float not null,
    RightBower float not null,

    constraint PK_OrgChart primary key clustered(ID),
);
```

Materialized path. This persists the hierarchical path in every node by concatenating information about the parents up to the root of the hierarchy. As a result, you can find all child nodes by performing a prefix lookup based on the parent path. Some implementations store actual key values of the nodes in the path, while others store the relative position of the node in the hierarchy. Figure 15-14 shows an example of the latter. Listing 15-16 shows one possible implementation of such a method.

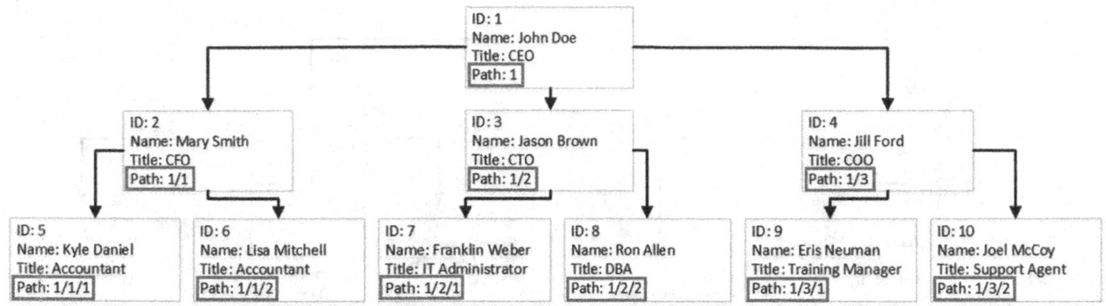

Figure 15-14. *Materialized (hierarchical) path*

Listing 15-16. Materialized path DDL

```
create table dbo.OrgChart
(
    ID int not null,
    Name nvarchar(64) not null,
    Title nvarchar(64) not null,
    Path varchar(256) not null,

    constraint PK_OrgChart primary key clustered(ID),
);
```

Each hierarchy approach has its own strengths and weaknesses. Adjacency lists and closure tables are easy to maintain; adding new members to or removing them from the hierarchy, as well as subtree movement, affects a single or very small number of the nodes. However, querying those structures often requires recursive or imperative code.

In contrast, nested sets and materialized paths are very easy to query, although hierarchy maintenance is expensive. For example, if you move the subtree to a different parent, you must update the corresponding bower or path values for each child in the subtree.

The HierarchyId type uses the materialized path technique, persisting relative path information in a way similar to the example shown in Figure 15-14. The path information is stored in binary format. The actual storage space varies and depends on a few factors. For starters, each level in the hierarchy adds an additional node to the path and increases its size.

Another important factor is how a new HierarchyId value is generated. As already mentioned, HierarchyId stores the relative positions of the nodes rather than their absolute key values. As a result, if you need to add a new child node at the node rightmost to the parent, you can increment the value from the former rightmost node. However, if you need to add the node in between two existing nodes, that would require persisting additional information in the path. Figure 15-15 shows an example of this.

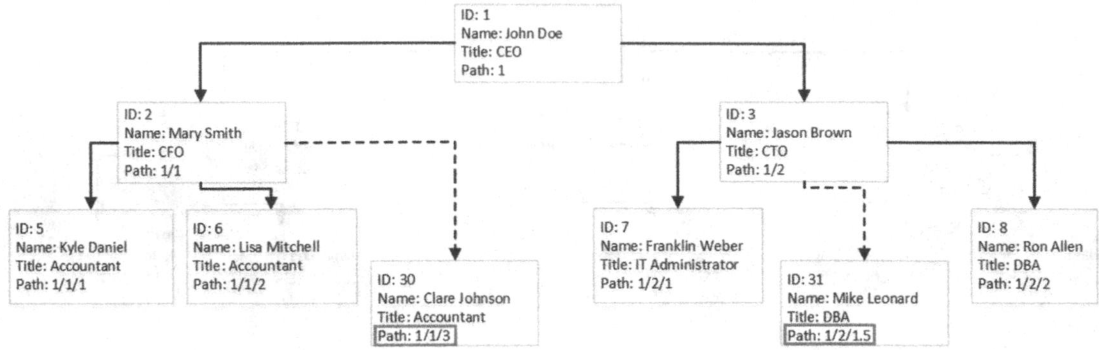

Figure 15-15. *Inserting data*

Let's test how HierarchyId generation affects the path size by creating the table shown in Listing 15-17.

Listing 15-17. HierarchyId: Test table

```
create table dbo.HierarchyTest
(
    ID hierarchyid not null,
    Level tinyint not null
)
```

The code shown in Listings 15-18 and 15-19 creates an eight-level hierarchy with eight children per node. We will compare the average data size of HierarchyId data when children nodes are inserted as the rightmost nodes (Listing 15-18) and when they are inserted in between existing nodes (Listing 15-19).

Listing 15-18. HierarchyId: Adding children nodes as rightmost nodes

```
declare
    @MaxLevels int = 8
    ,@ItemPerLevel int = 8
    ,@Level int = 2

insert into dbo.HierarchyTest(ID, Level) values(hierarchyid::GetRoot(), 1);

while @Level <= @MaxLevels
begin
    ;with CTE(ID, Child, Num)
    as
     (
        select ID, ID.GetDescendant(null,null), 1
        from dbo.HierarchyTest
        where Level = @Level - 1
        union all
        select ID, ID.GetDescendant(Child,null), Num + 1
        from CTE
        where Num < @ItemPerLevel
    )
```

```
    insert into dbo.HierarchyTest(ID, Level)
        select Child, @Level from CTE
    option (maxrecursion 0);
    set @Level += 1;
end;

select avg(datalength(ID)) from dbo.HierarchyTest;
```

```
Result:
-----------
5
```

Listing 15-19. HierarchyId: Adding children nodes in between existing nodes

```
truncate table dbo.HierarchyTest
go

declare
    @MaxLevels int = 8
    ,@ItemPerLevel int = 8
    ,@Level int = 2

insert into dbo.HierarchyTest(ID, Level) values(hierarchyid::GetRoot(), 1);

while @Level <= @MaxLevels
begin
    ;with CTE(ID, Child, PrevChild, Num)
    as
    (
        select ID, ID.GetDescendant(null,null), convert(hierarchyid,null), 1
        from dbo.HierarchyTest
        where Level = @Level - 1
        union all
        select ID,
            case
                when PrevChild < Child
                then ID.GetDescendant(PrevChild, Child)
                else ID.GetDescendant(Child, PrevChild)
            end, Child, Num + 1
        from CTE
        where Num < @ItemPerLevel
    )
    insert into dbo.HierarchyTest(ID, Level)
        select Child, @Level from CTE
    option (maxrecursion 0);
    set @Level += 1;
end;

select avg(datalength(ID)) from dbo.HierarchyTest;
```

```
Result:
----------
11
```

As you can see, adding children in between existing nodes in the hierarchy more than doubled the size of the path stored.

■ **Note** The `HierarchyId` data type has an additional two bytes of overhead stored in the variable-length offset array in every row.

The key point that you need to remember is that the `HierarchyId` data type persists a hierarchical path, and it provides a set of methods that help when working with hierarchical data. *It does not enforce the correctness of the hierarchy stored in a table, nor the uniqueness of the values. It is your responsibility to enforce it in the code.*

The maintenance of hierarchical data is expensive. Changing the path for the node with the children requires an update of the path in every child node. This leads to the update of multiple rows in the table. Moreover, the `HierarchyId` column is usually indexed, which introduces physical data movement and additional index fragmentation, especially when the `HierarchyId` column is part of a clustered index. You need to keep this in mind when designing an index maintenance strategy for tables with `HierarchyId` columns when the data is volatile.

Summary

User-defined CLR data types allow us to expand the standard SQL Server type library. Unfortunately, this flexibility has a price. CLR data types are stored in the database in binary format, and accessing the object properties and methods leads to deserialization and CLR method calls. This can introduce serious performance issues when those calls are done for a large number of rows.

You can reduce the number of CLR calls by adding persisted calculated columns that store the results of frequently accessed properties and methods. At the same time, this increases the size of the rows and introduces overhead when data is modified.

Another important aspect is maintainability. SQL Server does not support the `ALTER TYPE` operation. It is impossible to change the interface of existing methods or utilize new methods of the type until it is dropped and recreated.

`Geometry` and `geography` types help us work with spatial data. They provide a rich set of methods used to manipulate the data, although these methods are usually expensive and can lead to poor performance when called for a large number of rows. SQL Server 2012 SP3, SQL Server 2014 SP2, and SQL Server 2016 allow you to use the native implementation for some of the methods, which can significantly improve the performance of spatial calls. It is enabled by default in SQL Server 2016. In SQL Server 2012 SP3 and SQL Server 2014 SP2, you can enable it with trace flags `T6533` and `T6534`.

Spatial indexes can address some performance issues, although they work within the scope of the entire table. All further predicate evaluation is done at later execution stages. This leads to suboptimal performance when spatial operations are done on subsets of the data. You can use a bounding-box approach to address this issue, filtering out the unneeded rows prior to calling spatial methods.

`HierarchyId` types provide built-in support for hierarchical data. Although it has excellent query performance, hierarchy maintenance is expensive. Every change in the hierarchy requires an update of the hierarchical path in every child node. You must consider such overhead when data is volatile.

`HierarchyId` types do not enforce the correctness of the hierarchical structure. That must be done in the code. You should also avoid inserting new nodes in between existing ones, as this increases the size of the path stored.

Finally, support of system- and user-defined CLR types is not consistent across different development platforms. You need to make sure that client applications can utilize them before making the decision to use them. Alternatively, you can hide those types behind the data-access tier with T-SQL stored procedures when it is possible and feasible.

CHAPTER 16

Data Partitioning

The amount of data stored in relational databases is growing exponentially every year. Customers are collecting more data, and they are processing and retaining it for a longer amount of time. We, as database professionals, are working with databases that have become larger over time.

From a development standpoint, database size is not that critical. Non-optimized queries time out regardless of the database size. However, from a database-administration standpoint, the management of large databases introduces additional challenges. Data partitioning helps to address some of these challenges.

In this chapter, we will discuss the reasons we want to partition data, and we will cover the different techniques of data partitioning what are available in SQL Server. We will focus on practical implementation scenarios and typical data partitioning use cases in SQL Server.

Reasons to Partition Data

Let's assume that our system stores data in a large non-partitioned table. This approach dramatically simplifies development. All data is in the same place, and you can read the data from and write the data to the same table. With such a design, however, all of the data is stored in the same location. The table resides in a single filegroup, which consists of one or multiple files stored on the same disk array. Even though, technically speaking, you could spread indexes across different filegroups or data files across different disk arrays, it introduces additional database management challenges, reduces the recoverability of data in case of a disaster, and rarely helps with performance.

At the same time, in almost every system, data, which is stored in large tables, can be separated into two different categories: *operational* and *historical*. The first category consists of the data for the current operational period of the company and handles most of the customers' requests in the table. Historical data, on the other hand, belongs to the older operational periods, which the system must retain for various reasons, such as regulations and business requirements, among others.

Most activity in the table is performed against operational data, even though it can be very small compared to the total table size. Obviously, it would be beneficial to store operational data on a fast and expensive disk array. Historical data, on the other hand, does not need such I/O performance.

When data is not partitioned, you cannot separate it between disk arrays. You either have to pay extra for the fast storage you do not need or compromise and buy larger but slower storage.

It is also common for operational and historical data to have different workloads. Operational data usually supports OLTP transactions from the customer-facing part of the system. Historical data is mainly used for analysis and reporting. These two workloads produce different sets of queries, which would benefit from a different set of indexes and, sometimes, even from different storage formats. For example, operational data can benefit from In-Memory OLTP while historical data can utilize columnstore indexes.

D. Korotkevitch, *Pro SQL Server Internals*, DOI 10.1007/978-1-4842-1964-5_16

Unfortunately, it is almost impossible to index a subset of the data in a table. Even though you can use filtered indexes and/or indexed views, both approaches have several limitations. In most cases, you have to create a set of indexes covering both workloads in the table scope. This requires additional storage space and introduces update overhead for operational activity in the system. Moreover, volatile operational data requires different and more frequent index maintenance as compared to static historical data, which is impossible to implement in such a case.

■ **Note** SQL Server 2016 allows you to create filtered columnstore indexes that help speed up analysis and reporting queries against historical data. We will discuss them in detail in Part VII of the book.

Data compression is another important factor to consider. Static historical data would usually benefit from, page compression, which can significantly reduce the storage space required. Moreover, it could improve the performance of queries against historical data in non-CPU-bound systems by reducing the number of I/O operations required to read the data. At the same time, page compression introduces unnecessary CPU overhead when the data is volatile.

■ **Tip** In some cases, it is beneficial to use page compression even with volatile operational data when it saves a significant amount of space and the system works under a heavy I/O load. As usual, you should test and monitor how it affects the system.

Unfortunately, it is impossible to compress only part of the data in a table. You would either have to compress the entire table, which would introduce CPU overhead on operational data, or keep the historical data uncompressed at additional storage and I/O cost.

In cases of read-only historical data, it could be beneficial to exclude it from full database backups. This would reduce the size of the backup file, I/O, and network load during backup operations. Regrettably, partial database backups work on the filegroup level, which makes it impossible when the data is not partitioned.

The Enterprise Edition of SQL Server supports piecemeal restore, which allows you to restore the database and bring it online on a filegroup-by-filegroup basis. It is great to have a Disaster Recovery strategy that allows you to restore operational data and make it available to customers separately from the historical data. This could significantly reduce the disaster recovery time for large databases.

Unfortunately, such a design requires the separation of operational and historical data between different filegroups, which is impossible when the data is not partitioned.

■ **Note** We will discuss backup and disaster-recovery strategies in greater detail in Chapter 31, "Designing a Backup Strategy."

Another important factor is statistics. As you will remember, the statistics histogram stores a maximum of 200 steps, regardless of the table size. As a result, the histogram steps on large tables must cover a bigger interval of key values. It makes the statistics and cardinality estimation less accurate, and it can lead to suboptimal execution plans, in the case of large tables. Moreover, unless you are using databases with a compatibility level of 130 in SQL Server 2016 or have trace flag `T2371` enabled, SQL Server does not outdate statistics unless you have changed statistics columns in about 20 percent of the total number of rows in the table.

That list is by no means complete, and there are other factors as to why data partitioning is beneficial, although any of the aforementioned reasons is enough to start considering it.

When to Partition?

Database professionals often assume that data partitioning is required only for very large databases (VLDB). Even though database size definitely matters, it is hardly the only factor to consider.

Service Level Agreement (SLA) is one of the key elements in the decision to partition or not. When a system has an availability-based SLA clause, data partitioning becomes essential. The duration of possible downtime depends on how quickly you can recover a database and restore it from a backup after disaster. That time depends on the total size of the essential filegroups that need to be online for the system to be functional. Data partitioning is the only approach that allows you to separate data between different filegroups and use a piecemeal restore to minimize downtime.

A performance-based SLA clause is another important factor. Data partitioning can help address some of the challenges of performance tuning. For example, by partitioning data between multiple tables, you will improve the accuracy of statistics and can use different indexing strategies for historical and operational data. Moreover, data partitioning allows you to implement a *tiered storage* approach and put the operational part of the data on faster disks, which improves the performance of the system. We will discuss tiered storage in greater detail later in this chapter.

The key point to remember is that you should not rely on database size as the only criteria for partitioning. Consider data partitioning merely to be a tool that helps you address some of the challenges. This tool can be useful regardless of database size.

Nevertheless, data partitioning comes at a cost. It changes the execution plans of queries and often requires code re-factoring. You need to keep this in mind, especially in the case of new development. When you expect a system to collect a large amount of data in the future, it is often better to implement data partitioning at a very early development stage. Even though data partitioning introduces development overhead, such overhead may be much smaller than that which is involved in code re-factoring and the re-testing of a production system with large amount of data.

Finally, it is often very hard if not impossible to partition the data while keeping the database online and available to users. Moving large amount of data around can be time consuming and can lead to long downtime. This is another argument for implementing data partitioning during the initial stage of development.

Data Partitioning Techniques

There are two data partitioning techniques available in SQL Server: *partitioned tables* and *partitioned views*. We will look at them in detail in this section.

It is impossible to avoid mentioning SQL Server 2016's stretch databases in the context of data partitioning. Even though they allow us to address some of the VLDB administration challenges and reduce the storage cost and disaster recovery time, I would consider them to be a different technique than *classic* data partitioning. Stretch databases allow you to *transparently* build distributed database systems by moving part of the data into the Cloud rather than partition the data in one central place. As we already discussed in Chapter 5, this approach comes with a set of benefits and downsides, which you need to analyze when choosing the technology to use in your system.

■ **Note** In this chapter, we will use an order entry system that stores order information for two and a half years as our example. Let's assume that we want to partition the data on a monthly basis and that our operational period consists of two months: May and June 2016.

Partitioned Tables

Table partitioning is an Enterprise Edition feature that was introduced in SQL Server 2005. You can think of partitioned tables as logical tables that consist of multiple individual internal physical tables–partitions. This terminology—*logical* and *physical* table—is not standard, although it describes it perfectly.

Every table in SQL Server is partitioned. When a table is not partitioned by the user, SQL Server treats it as a single-partition table internally.

SQL Server tracks allocation units, such as IN-ROW, ROW-OVERFLOW, and LOB data, separately for each partition. For example, a table with 10 partitions would have 30 different IAM chains per data file—one per allocation unit per partition.

There are two additional database objects that are used together with table partitioning. A *partition function* specifies boundary values, which are the criteria on how data needs to be partitioned. A *partition scheme* specifies the filegroups in which physical partition tables are stored.

Listing 16-1 shows the code that creates partitioned table dbo.OrdersPT, with the data partitioned on a monthly basis. This code assumes that the database has four different filegroups: FG2014 and FG2015 store data for years 2014 and 2015, respectively. FG2016 stores data for the first four months of 2016. Finally, the FASTSTORAGE filegroup stores operational data starting from May 2016.

Listing 16-1. Creating a partitioned table

```
create partition function pfOrders(datetime2(0))
as range right for values
('2014-02-01', '2014-03-01','2014-04-01','2014-05-01','2014-06-01','2014-07-01'
,'2014-08-01','2014-09-01','2014-10-01','2014-11-01','2014-12-01','2015-01-01'
,'2015-02-01','2015-03-01','2015-04-01','2015-05-01','2015-06-01','2015-07-01'
,'2015-08-01','2015-09-01','2015-10-01','2015-11-01','2015-12-01','2016-01-01'
,'2016-02-01','2016-03-01','2016-04-01','2016-05-01','2016-06-01','2016-07-01');

create partition scheme psOrders
as partition pfOrders
to (FG2014 /* FileGroup to store data <'2014-02-01' */
,FG2014 /* FileGroup to store data >='2014-02-01' and <'2014-03-01' */
,FG2014,FG2014,FG2014,FG2014,FG2014
,FG2014,FG2014,FG2014,FG2014,FG2014
,FG2015 /* FileGroup to store data >='2015-01-01' and <'2015-02-01' */
,FG2015,FG2015,FG2015,FG2015,FG2015
,FG2015,FG2015,FG2015,FG2015,FG2015,FG2015
,FG2016 /* FileGroup to store data >='2016-01-01' and <'2016-02-01' */
,FG2016,FG2016,FG2016
,FASTSTORAGE /* FileGroup to store data >='2016-05-01' and <'2016-06-01' */
,FASTSTORAGE /* FileGroup to store data >='2016-06-01' and <'2016-07-01' */
,FASTSTORAGE /* FileGroup to store data >='2016-07-01' */ );

create table dbo.OrdersPT
(
    OrderId int not null,
    OrderDate datetime2(0) not null,
    OrderNum varchar(32) not null,
    OrderTotal money not null,
    CustomerId int not null,
    /* Other Columns */
);
```

```
create unique clustered index IDX_OrdersPT_OrderDate_OrderId
on dbo.OrdersPT(OrderDate, OrderId)
with
(
    data_compression = page on partitions(1 to 28),
    data_compression = row on partitions(29 to 31)
)
on psOrders(OrderDate);

create nonclustered index IDX_OrdersPT_CustomerId
on dbo.OrdersPT(CustomerId)
with
(
    data_compression = page on partitions(1 to 28),
    data_compression = row on partitions(29 to 31)
)
on psOrders(OrderDate);
```

You control how boundary values are stored by specifying either the `RANGE LEFT` or `RANGE RIGHT` parameter of the partition function. In our example, we are using the `RANGE RIGHT` parameter, which indicates that the boundary value is stored on the right partition. With this option, if 2014-02-01 is the first boundary value, the leftmost partition stores the data that is prior to that date. All values that are equal to the boundary value are stored in the partition that is second from the left. Alternatively, if we used the `RANGE LEFT` parameter, the boundary value data would be stored in the left partition.

Figure 16-1 shows the physical data layout of the `dbo.OrdersPT` table.

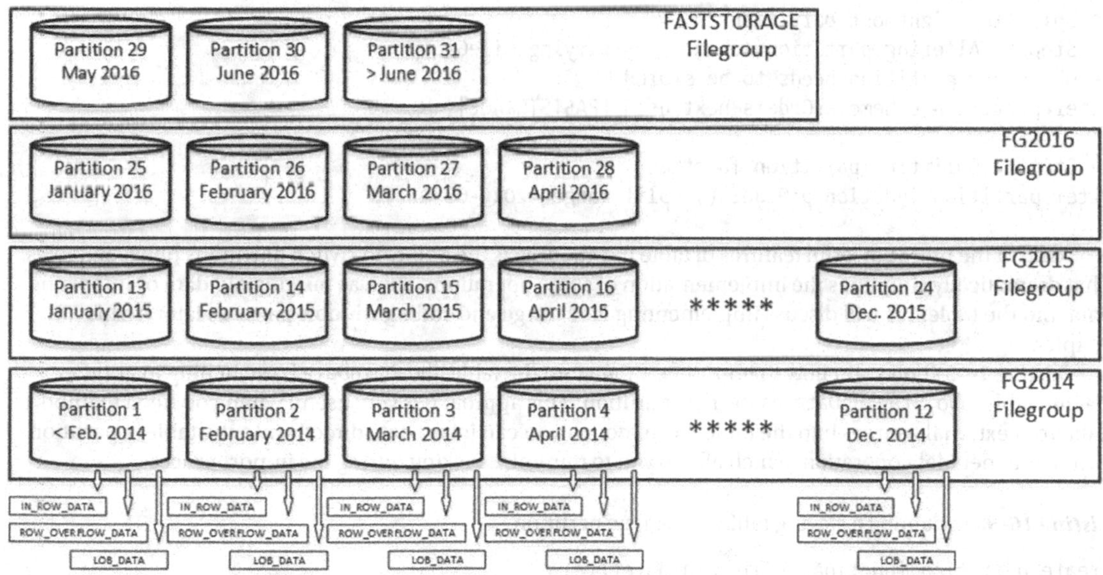

Figure 16-1. *Data layout of the dbo.OrdersPT table*

Each partition can reside in its own filegroup and have its own data compression method. However, all partitions have exactly the same schema and set of indexes that are controlled by the logical table. Moreover, SQL Server does not maintain individual statistics at the partition level. There is a single 200-step histogram on the index, regardless of whether it is partitioned or not.

SQL Server 2014 and 2016 introduce the concept of *incremental statistics*, which allows you to create per-partition statistics. When you enable it, SQL Server starts to track the number of statistics column updates at the partition level and marks statistics as outdates when it exceeds the threshold on an individual partition. Subsequent statistics updates would refresh statistics on the individual partition rather than on entire table. This behavior needs to be enabled with the `statistics_incremental` index and `incremental` statistics options respectively.

Even through incremental statistics improve statistics maintenance on partitioned tables, the histogram is still limited to 200 steps for the entire index, regardless of whether incremental statistics are enabled or not.

Table partitioning can be implemented in a transparent manner to the client applications. The code continues to reference the logical table while SQL Server manages the internal data layout under the hood. There are still some cases, however, when you need to reference individual partitions during the query-optimization stage. We will talk about these cases later in the chapter.

You can create new (*split*) or drop existing (*merge*) partitions by altering the partition scheme and functions. The code in Listing 16-2 merges the two leftmost and splits the rightmost partitions in the `dbo.OrdersPT` table. After the split, the leftmost partition will store the data with an `OrderDate` before March 1, 2014, and the two rightmost partitions of the table will store data with an `OrderDate` for July 2016, equal to or greater than 2016-08-01, respectively.

Listing 16-2. Splitting and merging partitions

```
/* Merging two leftmost partitions */
alter partition function pfOrders() merge range('2014-02-01');

/* Splitting rightmost partition */
-- Step 1: Altering partition scheme - specifying FileGroup
-- where new partition needs to be stored
alter partition scheme psOrders next used [FASTSTORAGE];

-- Step 2: Splitting partition function
alter partition function pfOrders() split range('2016-08-01');
```

One of the most powerful features of table partitioning is the ability to switch partitions between tables. That dramatically simplifies the implementation of some operations, such as purging old data or importing data into the table. We will discuss implementing data purge and sliding window patterns later in this chapter.

Listing 16-3 shows you how to import new data into the table `dbo.MainData` by switching in another staging table, `dbo.StagingData`, as the new partition. This approach is very useful when you need to import data from external sources into the table. Even though you can insert data directly into the table, a partition switch is a metadata operation, which allows you to minimize locking during the import process.

Listing 16-3. Switching a staging table as the new partition

```
create partition function pfMainData(datetime)
as range right for values
('2016-02-01', '2016-03-01','2016-04-01','2016-05-01','2016-06-01','2016-07-01'
,'2016-08-01','2016-09-01','2016-10-01','2016-11-01','2016-12-01');
```

```
create partition scheme psMainData
as partition pfMainData
all to (FG2016);

/* Even though we have 12 partitions - one per month, let's assume that only
January-April data is populated. E.g., we are in the middle of the year */
create table dbo.MainData
(
    ADate datetime not null,
    ID bigint not null,
    CustomerId int not null,
    /* Other Columns */
    constraint PK_MainData
    primary key clustered(ADate, ID)
    on psMainData(ADate)
);

create nonclustered index IDX_MainData_CustomerId
on dbo.MainData(CustomerId)
on psMainData(ADate);

create table dbo.StagingData
(
    ADate datetime not null,
    ID bigint not null,
    CustomerId int not null,
    /* Other Columns */
    constraint PK_StagingData
    primary key clustered(ADate, ID),

    constraint CHK_StagingData
    check(ADate >= '2016-05-01' and ADate < '2016-06-01')
) on [FG2016];

create nonclustered index IDX_StagingData_CustomerId
on dbo.StagingData(CustomerId)
on [FG2016];

/* Switching partition */
alter table dbo.StagingData
switch to dbo.MainData
partition 5;
```

Both tables must have exactly the same schema and indexes. The staging table should be placed in the same filegroup as the destination partition in the partitioned table. Finally, the staging table must have a CHECK constraint, which prevents values from outside of the partition boundaries.

As you probably noticed, all nonclustered indexes have been partitioned in the same way as clustered indexes. Such indexes are called *aligned indexes*. Even though there is no requirement to keep indexes aligned, SQL Server would not be able to switch partitions when a table has non-aligned, nonclustered indexes defined.

Finally, the partition switch operation does not work if a table is referenced by foreign key constraints defined in other tables. Nevertheless, a partition switch is allowed when the table itself has foreign key constraints referencing other tables.

Partitioned Views

Unlike partitioned tables, partitioned views work in every edition of SQL Server. In such schemas, you create individual tables and combine data from all of them via a partitioned view using the `union all` operator.

■ **Note** SQL Server allows you to define partitioned views by combining data from multiple databases or even SQL Server instances. The latter case is called a *distributed partitioned view.* The coverage of such scenarios is outside of the scope of this book. However, they behave similarly to partitioned views defined in a single-database scope.

Listing 16-4 shows an example of data partitioning of the *Orders* entity using a partitioned view approach.

Listing 16-4. Creating partitioned views

```
create table dbo.Orders2014_01
(
    OrderId int not null,
    OrderDate datetime2(0) not null,
    OrderNum varchar(32) not null,
    OrderTotal money not null,
    CustomerId int not null,
    /* Other Columns */
    constraint PK_Orders2014_01
    primary key clustered(OrderId),

    constraint CHK_Orders2014_01
    check (OrderDate >= '2014-01-01' and OrderDate < '2014-02-01')
) on [FG2014];

create nonclustered index IDX_Orders2014_01_CustomerId
on dbo.Orders2014_01(CustomerId)
on [FG2014];

create table dbo.Orders2014_02
(
    OrderId int not null,
    OrderDate datetime2(0) not null,
    OrderNum varchar(32) not null,
    OrderTotal money not null,
    CustomerId int not null,
    /* Other Columns */
    constraint PK_Orders2014_02
    primary key clustered(OrderId)
    with (data_compression=page),
```

```
    constraint CHK_Orders2014_02
    check (OrderDate >= '2014-02-01' and OrderDate < '2014-03-01')
) on [FG2014];

create nonclustered index IDX_Orders2014_02_CustomerId
on dbo.Orders2014_02(CustomerId)
with (data_compression=page)
on [FG2014];

/* Other tables */

create table dbo.Orders2016_06
(
    OrderId int not null,
    OrderDate datetime2(0) not null,
    OrderNum varchar(32) not null,
    OrderTotal money not null,
    CustomerId int not null,
    /* Other Columns */
    constraint PK_Orders2016_06
    primary key clustered(OrderId)
    with (data_compression=row),

    constraint CHK_Orders2016_06
    check (OrderDate >= '2016-06-01' and OrderDate < '2016-07-01')
) on [FASTSTORAGE];

create nonclustered index IDX_Orders2016_04_CustomerId
on dbo.Orders2016_06(CustomerId)
with (data_compression=row)
on [FASTSTORAGE]
go

create view dbo.Orders(OrderId, OrderDate, OrderNum, OrderTotal, CustomerId /*Other
Columns*/)
With schemabinding
as
    select OrderId, OrderDate, OrderNum, OrderTotal, CustomerId /*Other Columns*/
    from dbo.Orders2014_01
    union all
    select OrderId, OrderDate, OrderNum, OrderTotal, CustomerId /*Other Columns*/
    from dbo.Orders2014_02
    /* union all -- Other tables */
    union all
    select OrderId, OrderDate, OrderNum, OrderTotal, CustomerId /*Other Columns*/
    from dbo.Orders2016_06;
```

Figure 16-2 shows the physical data layout of the tables.

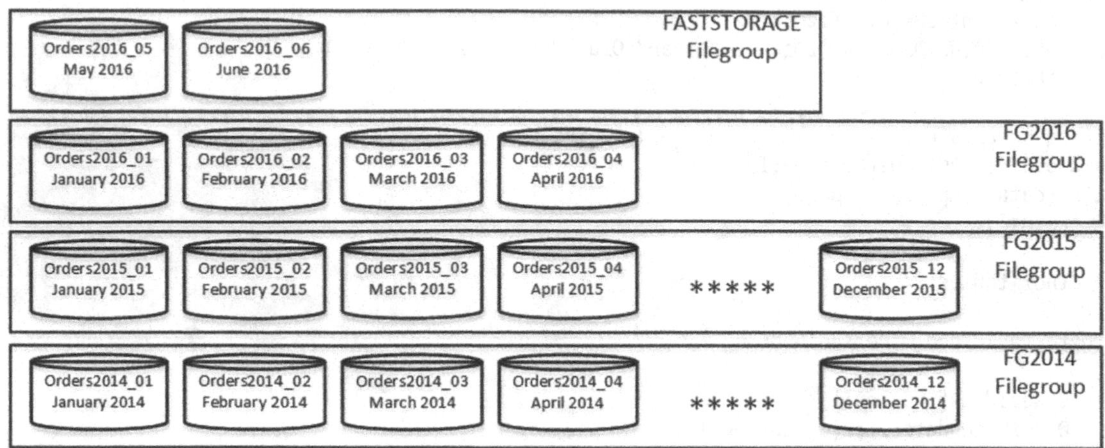

Figure 16-2. *Data layout with a partitioned-view approach*

As you can see, different tables can be placed into different filegroups, which can even be marked as read-only if needed. Each table can have its own set of indexes and maintain individual, more accurate statistics. Moreover, each table can have its own schema. This is beneficial if operational activities require tables to have additional columns–for data processing, for example–which you can drop afterward. The difference in schemas can be abstracted on the partitioned view level.

■ **Tip** You can combine In-Memory OLTP memory-optimized tables, columnstore-based tables, and regular on-disk B-Tree tables in the same partitioned view. This can help to improve the performance of the systems with the mixed workload.

It is extremely important to have CHECK constraints defined in each table. These constraints help SQL Server avoid accessing unnecessary tables while querying the data. Listing 16-5 shows an example of queries against a partitioned view.

Listing 16-5. Queries against partitioned view

```
select count(*) from dbo.Orders;
select count(*) from dbo.Orders where OrderDate = '2016-06-03'
```

As you can see in Figure 16-3, the first query requires SQL Server to access all of the tables from the partitioned view. Alternatively, the second query has `OrderDate` as a parameter, which allows SQL Server to pinpoint the single table that needs to be queried.

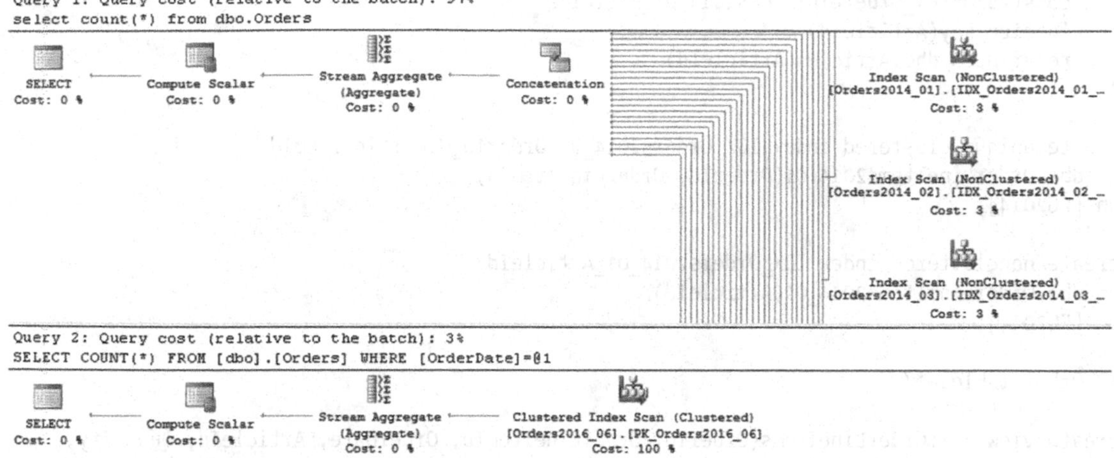

***Figure 16-3.** Execution plans of the queries against a partitioned view*

You should always add predicates, which reduce the number of tables to be processed by the queries. Let's look at a practical example and, as a first step, create another entity called *OrderLineItems*. Obviously, you would like to partition it in the same way as the *Orders* entity; that is, on a monthly basis.

■ **Tip** You should partition related entities and place them in filegroups in a way that supports piecemeal restore and that allows you to bring entities online together.

Listing 16-6 shows the code that creates the set of tables and the partitioned view. Even though the `OrderDate` column is redundant in the `OrderLineItems` tables, you need to add it to all of the tables in order to create a consistent partitioning layout with the `Orders` tables.

Listing 16-6. OrderLineItems partition view

```
create table dbo.OrderLineItems2014_01
(
    OrderId int not null,
    OrderLineItemId int not null,
    OrderDate datetime2(0) not null,
    ArticleId int not null,
    Quantity decimal(9,3) not null,
    Price money not null,
    /* Other Columns */

    constraint CHK_OrderLineItems2014_01
    check (OrderDate >= '2014-01-01' and OrderDate < '2014-02-01'),

    constraint FK_OrderLineItems_Orders_2014_01
    foreign key(OrderId)
    references dbo.Orders2014_01(OrderId),
```

```
    constraint FK_OrderLineItems2014_01_Articles
    foreign key(ArticleId)
    references dbo.Articles(ArticleId)
);

create unique clustered index IDX_Orders2014_01_OrderId_OrderLineItemId
on dbo.OrderLineItems2014_01(OrderId, OrderLineItemId)
on [FG2014];

create nonclustered index IDX_Orders2014_01_ArticleId
on dbo.OrderLineItems2014_01(ArticleId)
on [FG2014];

/* Other tables */

create view dbo.OrderLineItems(OrderId, OrderLineItemId, OrderDate, ArticleId, Quantity, 
Price)
with schemabinding
as
    select OrderId, OrderLineItemId, OrderDate, ArticleId, Quantity, Price
    from dbo.OrderLineItems2014_01
    /*union all other tables*/
    union all
    select OrderId, OrderLineItemId, OrderDate, ArticleId, Quantity, Price
    from dbo.OrderLineItems2016_06;
```

Let's assume that you have a query that returns a list of orders that includes a particular item bought by a specific customer in January 2016. The typical implementation of such a query is shown in Listing 16-7.

Listing 16-7. Selecting a list of customer orders with a specific item: Non-optimized version

```
select o.OrderId, o.OrderNum, o.OrderDate, i.Quantity, i.Price
from dbo.Orders o join dbo.OrderLineItems i on
        o.OrderId = i.OrderId
where
        o.OrderDate >= '2016-01-01' and
        o.OrderDate < '2016-02-01' and
        o.CustomerId = @CustomerId and
        i.ArticleId = @ArticleId
```

As you can see in Figure 16-4, SQL Server has to perform an *index seek* in every `OrderLineItems` table while searching for line-item records. Query Optimizer is not aware that all required rows are stored in the `dbo.OrderLineItems2016_01` table.

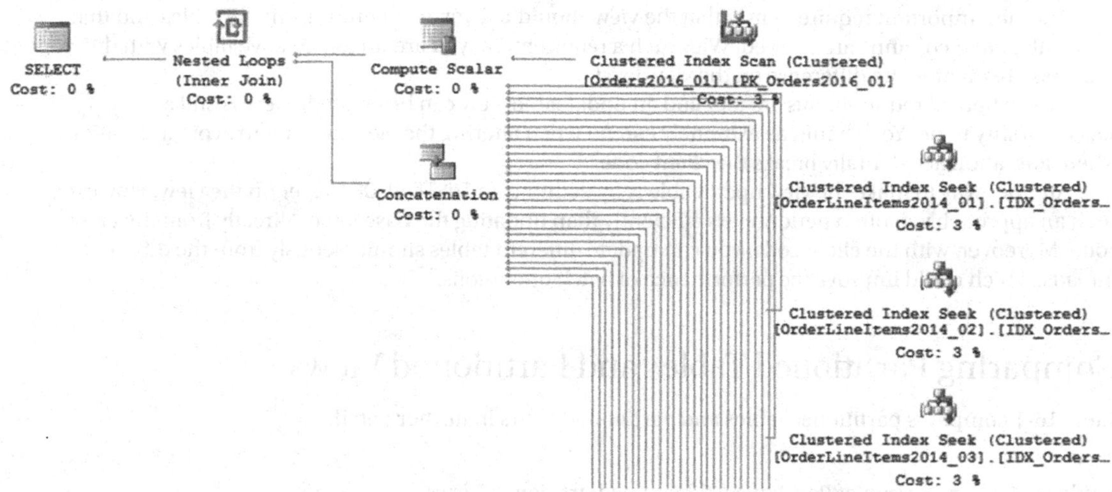

Figure 16-4. *Execution plan of a non-optimized query*

You can optimize this query by adding another join predicate on the OrderDate column, as shown in Listing 16-8. CHECK constraints allow Query Optimizer to eliminate access to tables that cannot store data for a particular month. The execution plan is shown in Figure 16-5.

Listing 16-8. Selecting a list of customer orders with a specific item: Optimized version

```
select o.OrderId, o.OrderNum, o.OrderDate, i.Quantity, i.Price
from dbo.Orders o join dbo.OrderLineItems i on
        o.OrderId = i.OrderId and o.OrderDate = i.OrderDate
where
        o.OrderDate >= '2016-01-01' and
        o.OrderDate < '2016-02-01' and
        o.CustomerId = @CustomerId and
        i.ArticleId = @ArticleId
```

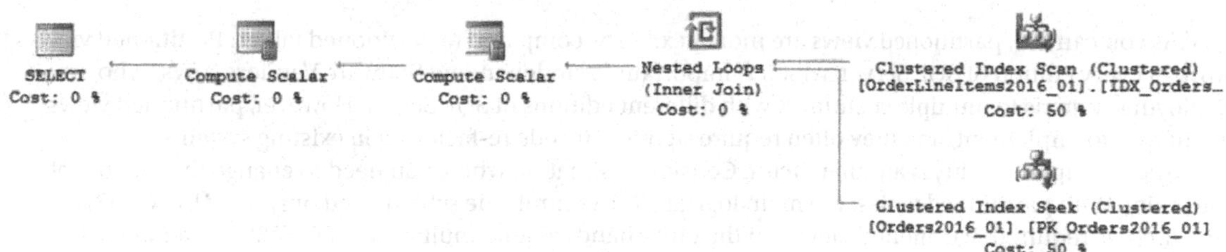

Figure 16-5. *Execution plan of an optimized query*

Unfortunately, in most cases using partitioned views requires modifications of the client code, especially when you update the data. In some cases, you can update the data directly through the view; however, partitioned views have a few restrictions in order to be updateable. For example, tables from the view should have a CHECK constraint that defines the partitioning criteria, and a column from that constraint must be part of the primary key.

Another important requirement is that the view should deliver all columns from the tables and that is it; no calculated columns are allowed. With such a requirement, you are unable to have tables with different schemas abstracting the difference on the view level.

Even when all requirements are met and an updateable view can be created, there is still a supportability issue. You should be extremely careful when altering the view in order to avoid a situation where alteration accidentally breaks the client code.

Another way to make the view updateable is by defining an `INSTEAD OF` trigger on the view. However, such an approach will often perform less efficiently than updating the base tables directly from the client code. Moreover, with the client code, you can update different tables simultaneously from the different threads, which could improve the performance of batch operations.

Comparing Partitioned Tables and Partitioned Views

Table 16-1 compares partitioned tables and partitioned views in further detail.

Table 16-1. *Comparison of Partitioned Tables and Partitioned Views*

Partitioned Tables	Partitioned Views
Enterprise and Developer editions only	All editions
Maximum 1,000 or 15,000 partitions depending on SQL Server version	Maximum 255 tables/partitions
Same table schema and indexes across all partitions	Every table/partition can have its own schema and set of indexes
Statistics kept at the table level	Separate statistics per table/partition
No partition-level online index rebuild prior to SQL Server 2014	Online index rebuild of the table/partition with Enterprise Edition of SQL Server
Transparent to client code (some query re-factoring may be required)	Usually requires changes in the client code
Transparent for replication	Requires changes in publications when a new table/partition is created and/or an existing table/partition is dropped

As you can see, partitioned views are more flexible as compared to partitioned tables. Partitioned views work in every edition of SQL Server, which is important for Independent Software Vendors (ISVs) who are deploying systems to multiple customers with different editions of SQL Server. However, partitioned views are harder to implement, and they often require significant code re-factoring in existing systems.

System supportability is another factor. Consider a situation where you need to change the schema of the entity. With partitioned tables, the main logical table controls the schema and only one `ALTER TABLE` statement is required. Partitioned views, on the other hand, require multiple `ALTER TABLE` statements—one per underlying table.

This is not necessarily a bad thing, though. With multiple `ALTER TABLE` statements, you acquire schema modification (SCH-M) locks at the individual table level, which can reduce the time the lock is held and access to the table is blocked. We will discuss schema locks in greater detail in Chapter 23, "Schema Locks."

Sometimes you can abstract schema changes at the partitioned view level, which allows you to avoid altering some tables. Think about adding a `NOT NULL` column with a default constraint, as an example. In SQL Server 2005-2008R2, this operation would modify every data row in the table and keep the schema modification (SCH-M) lock held for the duration of the operation. It also generates a large amount of transaction log activity.

In the case of partitioned views, you can alter only operational data tables by using a constant with historical data tables in the view. Listing 16-9 illustrates such an approach. Keep in mind that such an approach prevents a partitioned view from being updateable.

Listing 16-9. Abstracting schema changes in the partitioned view

```
alter table dbo.Orders2016_06
add IsReviewed bit not null
    constraint DEF_Orders2016_06_IsReviewed
    default 0;

alter view dbo.Orders(OrderId, OrderDate, OrderNum, OrderTotal, CustomerId, IsReviewed)
with schemabinding
as
    select OrderId, OrderDate, OrderNum, OrderTotal, CustomerId, 0 as [IsReviewed]
    from dbo.Orders2014_01
    /* union all -- Other tables */
    union all
    select OrderId, OrderDate, OrderNum, OrderTotal, CustomerId, IsReviewed
    from dbo.Orders2016_06;
```

Using Partitioned Tables and Views Together

You can improve the supportability of a system and reduce the number of required tables by using partitioned tables and partitioned views together. With such an approach, you are storing historical data in one or more partitioned tables and operational data in regular table(s), combining all of them into a partitioned view.

Listing 16-10 shows such an example. There are three partitioned tables, dbo.Orders2014, dbo.Orders2015, and dbo.Orders2016, which store historical data that is partitioned on a monthly basis. There are also two regular tables storing operational data: dbo.Orders2016_05 and dbo.Orders2016_06.

Listing 16-10. Using partitioned tables and views together

```
create partition function pfOrders2014(datetime2(0))
as range right for values
('2014-02-01', '2014-03-01','2014-04-01','2014-05-01','2014-06-01','2014-07-01'
,'2014-08-01','2014-09-01','2014-10-01','2014-11-01','2014-12-01');

create partition scheme psOrders2014
as partition pfOrders2014
all to ([FG2014]);

create table dbo.Orders2014
(
    OrderId int not null,
    OrderDate datetime2(0) not null,
    OrderNum varchar(32) not null,
    OrderTotal money not null,
    CustomerId int not null,
    /* Other Columns */
    constraint CHK_Orders2014
    check(OrderDate >= '2014-01-01' and OrderDate < '2015-01-01')
);
```

```
create unique clustered index IDX_Orders2014_OrderDate_OrderId
on dbo.Orders2014(OrderDate, OrderId)
with (data_compression = page)
on psOrders2014(OrderDate);

create nonclustered index IDX_Orders2014_CustomerId
on dbo.Orders2014(CustomerId)
with (data_compression = page)
on psOrders2014(OrderDate);
go

/* dbo.Orders2015 table definition - skipped */

create partition function pfOrders2016(datetime2(0))
as range right for values
('2016-02-01', '2016-03-01','2016-04-01','2016-05-01','2016-06-01','2016-07-01'
,'2016-08-01','2016-09-01','2016-10-01','2016-11-01','2016-12-01');

create partition scheme psOrders2016
as partition pfOrders2016
all to ([FG2016]);

create table dbo.Orders2016
(
    OrderId int not null,
    OrderDate datetime2(0) not null,
    OrderNum varchar(32) not null,
    OrderTotal money not null,
    CustomerId int not null,
    /* Other Columns */
    constraint CHK_Orders2016
    check(OrderDate >= '2016-01-01' and OrderDate < '2016-05-01')
);

create unique clustered index IDX_Orders2016_OrderDate_OrderId
on dbo.Orders2016(OrderDate, OrderId)
with (data_compression = page)
on psOrders2016(OrderDate);

create nonclustered index IDX_Orders2016_CustomerId
on dbo.Orders2016(CustomerId)
with (data_compression = page)
on psOrders2016(OrderDate);

create table dbo.Orders2016_05
(
    OrderId int not null,
    OrderDate datetime2(0) not null,
    OrderNum varchar(32) not null,
    OrderTotal money not null,
    CustomerId int not null,
```

```
    /* Other Columns */
    constraint CHK_Orders2016_05
    check(OrderDate >= '2016-05-01' and OrderDate < '2016-06-01')
);

create unique clustered index IDX_Orders2016_05_OrderDate_OrderId
on dbo.Orders2016_05(OrderDate, OrderId)
with (data_compression = row)
on [FASTSTORAGE];

create nonclustered index IDX_Orders2016_05_CustomerId
on dbo.Orders2016_05(CustomerId)
with (data_compression = row)
on [FASTSTORAGE]

/* dbo.Orders2016_06 table definition */

create view dbo.Orders(OrderId, OrderDate, OrderNum, OrderTotal, CustomerId /*Other
Columns*/)
with schemabinding
as
    select OrderId, OrderDate, OrderNum, OrderTotal, CustomerId /*Other Columns*/
    from dbo.Orders2014
    union all
    select OrderId, OrderDate, OrderNum, OrderTotal, CustomerId /*Other Columns*/
    from dbo.Orders2015
    union all
    select OrderId, OrderDate, OrderNum, OrderTotal, CustomerId /*Other Columns*/
    from dbo.Orders2016
    union all
    select OrderId, OrderDate, OrderNum, OrderTotal, CustomerId /*Other Columns*/
    from dbo.Orders2016_05
    union all
    select OrderId, OrderDate, OrderNum, OrderTotal, CustomerId /*Other Columns*/
    from dbo.Orders2016_06;
```

It is worth mentioning that table dbo.Orders2016 is partitioned on a monthly basis up to the end of the year, even though it stores data up to the operational period, which starts in May. CHECK constraints in that table indicate this.

The data layout is shown in Figure 16-6.

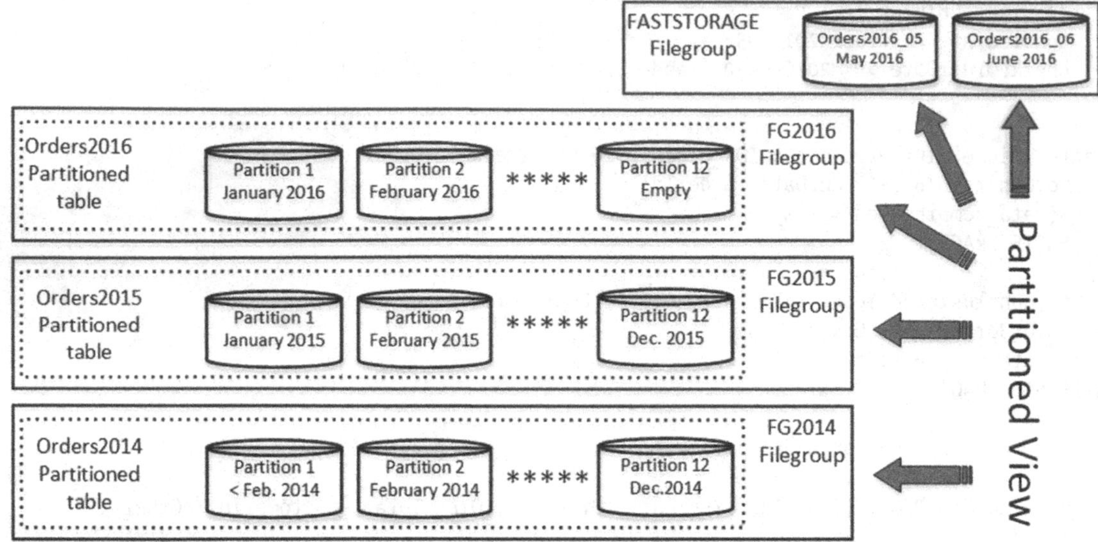

Figure 16-6. *Using partitioned tables and views together: Data layout*

As you can see, such an approach dramatically reduces the number of tables as compared to a partitioned views implementation, keeping the flexibility of partitioned views intact.

Tiered Storage

One of the key benefits of data partitioning is the reduction of storage costs in the system. You can achieve this in two different ways. First, you can reduce the size of the data by using data compression on the historical part of the data. Moreover, and more important, you can separate data between different storage arrays in the system.

It is very common to have different performance and availability requirements for different data in the system. In our example, it is possible to have 99.99 percent availability and 20 ms latency SLAs defined for operational data. However, for the older historical data, the requirements could be quite different. For example, orders from 2014 must be retained in the system without any performance requirements, and the availability SLA is much lower than it is for operational data.

You can design a data layout and storage subsystem based on these requirements. Figure 16-7 illustrates one possible solution. You can use a fast, SSD-based RAID-10 array for the `FASTSTORAGE` filegroup, which contains operational data. Data for January-April 2016 is relatively static, and it could be stored on the slower RAID-5 array using 15,000 RPM disks. Finally, you can use slow and cheap 5,400 RPM disks in the RAID-1 array for the data from the years 2015 and 2014.

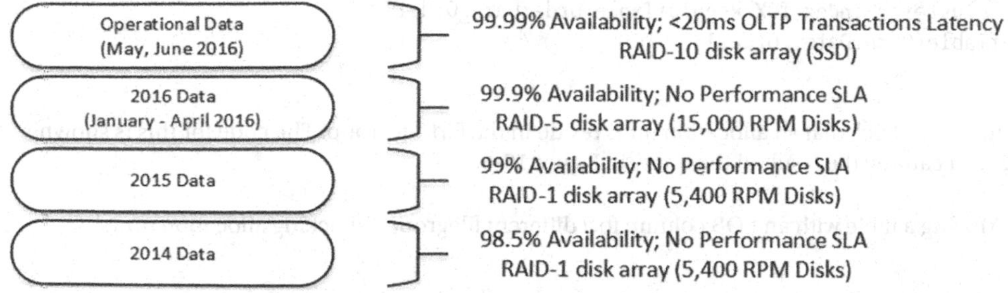

Figure 16-7. *Tiered storage*

Tiered storage can significantly reduce the storage costs of the system. Finally, it is also much easier to get an approved budget allocation to buy a lower capacity, faster disk array due to its lower cost.

The key question with tiered storage design is how to move data between different tiers when the operational period changes, all while keeping the system online and available to customers. Let's look at the available options in greater detail.

Moving Non-Partitioned Tables Between Filegroups

You can move a non-partitioned table to another filegroup by rebuilding all of the indexes, using the new filegroup as the destination. This operation can be done online in the Enterprise Edition of SQL Server with the `CREATE INDEX WITH (ONLINE=ON, DROP_EXISTING=ON)` command. Other sessions can access the table during the online index rebuild. Therefore, the system is available to customers.

■ **Note** Online index rebuild acquires schema modification (SCH-M) lock during the final phase of execution. Even though this lock is held for a very short time, It can increase locking and blocking in very active OLTP systems. SQL Server 2014 introduces the concept of low-priority locks, which can be used to improve system concurrency during online index rebuild operations. We will discuss them in detail in Chapter 23, "Schema Locks."

Unfortunately, there are two caveats associated with online index rebuilds. First, even with Enterprise Edition, SQL Server 2005-2008R2 does not support an online index rebuild if an index has large object (LOB) columns defined, such as `(n)text`, `image`, `(n)varchar(max)`, `varbinary(max)`, `xml`, and several others.

The second issue is more complicated. Index rebuild does not move `LOB_DATA` allocation units to the new filegroup. Let's look at an example and create a table that has an LOB column on the `FG1` filegroup. Listing 16-11 shows the code for this.

Listing 16-11. Moving a table with an LOB column to a different filegroup: Table creation

```
create table dbo.RegularTable
(
    OrderDate date not null,
    OrderId int not null identity(1,1),
    OrderNum varchar(32) not null,
    LobColumn varchar(max) null,
    Placeholder char(50) null,
) textimage_on [FG1];
```

```
create unique clustered index IDX_RegularTable_OrderDate_OrderId
on dbo.RegularTable(OrderDate, OrderId)
on [FG1];
```

As a next step, let's check that all allocation units reside in the FG1 filegroup. The code for this is shown in Listing 16-12. You can see the result of the query in Figure 16-8.

Listing 16-12. Moving a table with an LOB column to a different filegroup: Checking allocation units' placement

```
select
    p.partition_number as [Partition]
    ,object_name(p.object_id) as [Table]
    ,filegroup_name(a.data_space_id) as [FileGroup]
    ,a.type_desc as [Allocation Unit]
from
    sys.partitions p join sys.allocation_units a on
        p.partition_id = a.container_id
where
    p.object_id = object_id('dbo.RegularTable')
order by
    p.partition_number
```

	Partition	Table	FileGroup	Allocation Unit
1	1	RegularTable	FG1	IN_ROW_DATA
2	1	RegularTable	FG1	LOB_DATA
3	1	RegularTable	FG1	ROW_OVERFLOW_DATA

Figure 16-8. *Allocation units' placement after table creation*

Now, let's rebuild the clustered index, moving the data to the FG2 filegroup. The code for doing this is shown in Listing 16-13.

Listing 16-13. Rebuilding the index by moving data to a different filegroup

```
create unique clustered index IDX_RegularTable_OrderDate_OrderId
on dbo.RegularTable(OrderDate, OrderId)
with (drop_existing=on, online=on)
on [FG2]
```

Now, if you run the query from Listing 16-12 again, you will see the results shown in Figure 16-9. As you can see, the index rebuild moved IN_ROW_DATA and ROW_OVERFLOW_DATA allocation units to the new filegroup, keeping LOB_DATA intact.

	Partition	Table	FileGroup	Allocation Unit
1	1	RegularTable	FG2	IN_ROW_DATA
2	1	RegularTable	FG1	LOB_DATA
3	1	RegularTable	FG2	ROW_OVERFLOW_DATA

Figure 16-9. *Allocation units' placement after index rebuild*

Fortunately, there is a workaround available. You can move LOB_DATA allocation units to another filegroup by performing an online index rebuild that uses a partition scheme rather than a filegroup as the destination.

Listing 16-14 shows such an approach. As a first step, you need to create a partition function with one boundary value and two partitions in such a way that leaves one partition empty. After that, you need to create a partition scheme using a destination filegroup for both partitions and then perform an index rebuild into this partition scheme. Finally, you need to merge both partitions by altering the partition function. This is a quick metadata operation because one of the partitions is empty.

Listing 16-14. Rebuilding an index in a partition scheme

```
create partition function pfRegularTable(date)
as range right for values ('2100-01-01');

create partition scheme psRegularTable
as partition pfRegularTable
all to ([FG2]);

create unique clustered index IDX_RegularTable_OrderDate_OrderId
on dbo.RegularTable(OrderDate, OrderId)
with (drop_existing=on, online=on)
on psRegularTable(OrderDate);

alter partition function pfRegularTable()
merge range('2100-01-01');
```

Figure 16-10 shows the allocation units' placement after the index rebuild.

	Partition	Table	FileGroup	Allocation Unit
1	1	RegularTable	FG2	IN_ROW_DATA
2	1	RegularTable	FG2	LOB_DATA
3	1	RegularTable	FG2	ROW_OVERFLOW_DATA

Figure 16-10. *Allocation units' placement after rebuilding the index in a partition scheme*

Obviously, this method requires the Enterprise Edition of SQL Server. It also would require SQL Server 2012 or above to work as an online operation because of the LOB columns involved.

Without the Enterprise Edition of SQL Server, your only option for moving LOB_DATA allocation units is to create a new table in the destination filegroup and then copy the data to it from the original table.

Moving Partitions Between Filegroups

You can move a single partition from a partitioned table to another filegroup by altering the partition scheme and function. Altering the partition scheme marks the filegroup in which the newly created partition must be placed. Splitting and merging the partition function triggers the data movement.

The way that data is moved between partitions during SPLIT RANGE and MERGE RANGE operations depends on the RANGE LEFT and RANGE RIGHT parameters of the partition function. Let's look at an example that assumes you have a database with four filegroups: FG1, FG2, FG3, and FG4. You have a partition function in the database that uses RANGE LEFT values, as shown in Listing 16-15.

Listing 16-15. RANGE LEFT partition function

```
create partition function pfLeft(int) as range left for values (10,20);

create partition scheme psLeft
as partition pfLeft
to ([FG1],[FG2],[FG3]);

alter partition scheme psLeft next used [FG4];
```

In a RANGE LEFT partition function, the boundary values represent the highest value in a partition. When you split a RANGE LEFT partition, the new partition with the highest new boundary value is moved to the NEXT USED filegroup.

Table 16-2 shows a partition and filegroup layout for the various SPLIT operations.

Table 16-2. *RANGE LEFT Partition Function and SPLIT Operations*

	FG1	FG2	FG3	FG4
Original	{min..10}	{11..20}	{21..max}	
SPLIT RANGE(0)	{1..10}	{11..20}	{21..max}	{min..0}
SPLIT RANGE(15)	{min..10}	{16..20}	{21..max}	{11..15}
SPLIT RANGE(30)	{min..10}	{11..20}	{31..max}	{21..30}

Now, let's look at what happens when you have a RANGE RIGHT partition function with the same boundary values, as defined in Listing 16-16.

Listing 16-16. RANGE RIGHT partition function

```
create partition function pfRight(int) as range right for values (10,20);

create partition scheme psRight
as partition pfRight
to ([FG1],[FG2],[FG3]);

alter partition scheme psRight next used [FG4];
```

In a RANGE RIGHT partition function, the boundary values represent the lowest value in a partition. When you split a RANGE RIGHT partition, the new partition with the new lowest boundary value is moved to the NEXT USED filegroup.

Table 16-3 shows a partition and filegroup layout for the various SPLIT operations.

Table 16-3. RANGE RIGHT Partition Function and SPLIT Operations

	FG1	FG2	FG3	FG4
Original	{min..9}	{10..19}	{20..max}	
SPLIT RANGE(0)	{min.. -1}	{10..19}	{20..max}	{0..9}
SPLIT RANGE(15)	{min..9}	{10..14}	{20..max}	{15..19}
SPLIT RANGE(30)	{min..9}	{10..19}	{20..29}	{30..max}

Now, let's look at a MERGE operation that assumes you have partition functions with the boundary values of (10, 20, 30). For a RANGE RIGHT partition function, the data from the right partition is moved to the left partition filegroup. Table 16-4 illustrates this point.

Table 16-4. RANGE RIGHT Partition Function and MERGE Operations

	FG1	FG2	FG3	FG4
Original	{min..9}	{10..19}	{20..29}	{30..max}
MERGE RANGE(10)	{min.. 19}		{20..29}	{30..max}
MERGE RANGE(20)	{min..9}	{10..29}		{30..max}
MERGE RANGE(30)	{min..9}	{10..19}	{20..max}	

Conversely, with a RANGE LEFT partition function, the data from the left partition is moved to the right partition filegroup, as shown in Table 16-5.

Table 16-5. RANGE LEFT Partition Function and MERGE Operations

	FG1	FG2	FG3	FG4
Original	{min..10}	{11..20}	{21..30}	{31..max}
MERGE RANGE(10)		{min..20}	{21..30}	{31..max}
MERGE RANGE(20)	{min..10}		{11..30}	{31..max}
MERGE RANGE(30)	{min..10}	{11..20}		{21..max}

When you move a partition to a different filegroup, you should choose a boundary value at which to SPLIT and MERGE the partition function. For example, if you want to move a partition that stores May 2016 data in the dbo.OrdersPT table from the FASTSTORAGE to the FG2016 filegroup, you need to MERGE and SPLIT a boundary value of 2016-05-01. The partition function is defined as RANGE RIGHT, and, as a result, the MERGE operation moves May 2016 data to the partition containing the April 2016 data, which resides on the FG2016 filegroup. Afterward, the SPLIT operation would move the May 2016 data to the filegroup you specified as NEXT USED by altering the partition scheme.

You can see the code to accomplish this in Listing 16-17. As a reminder, the dbo.OrdersPT table was created in Listing 16-1.

Listing 16-17. Moving data for a single partition

```
-- Moving May 2016 partition data to April 2016 filegroup
alter partition function pfOrders() merge range ('2016-05-01');

-- Marking that next used filegroup
alter partition scheme psOrders next used [FG2016];

-- Creating new partition for May 2016 moving it to FG2016
alter partition function pfOrders() split range ('2016-05-01');
```

Even though the code is very simple, there are a couple of problems with such an approach. First, the data is moved twice when you MERGE and SPLIT a partition function. Another problem is that SQL Server acquires and holds a schema modification (SCH-M) lock for the duration of the data movement, which prevents other sessions from accessing the table.

There is no easy workaround for the problem of keeping the table online during data movement. One of the options, shown in Listing 16-18, is to rebuild the indexes using a different partition scheme. Even though this operation can be performed online, it introduces huge I/O and transaction log overhead because you are rebuilding indexes for the entire table rather than moving a single partition. Moreover, this operation will not work online in SQL Server 2005-2008R2 if the table has LOB columns.

Listing 16-18. Moving data for a single partition

```
create partition scheme psOrders2
as partition pfOrders
to (FG2014,FG2014,FG2014,FG2014,FG2014,FG2014,FG2014,FG2014,FG2014,FG2014
,FG2014,FG2014,FG2015,FG2015,FG2015,FG2015,FG2015,FG2015,FG2015,FG2015,FG2015
,FG2015,FG2015,FG2015,FG2016,FG2016,FG2016,FG2016,FASTSTORAGE,FASTSTORAGE);

create unique clustered index IDX_OrdersPT_OrderDate_OrderId
on dbo.OrdersPT(OrderDate, OrderId)
with
(
    data_compression = page on partitions(1 to 28),
    data_compression = none on partitions(29 to 31),
    drop_existing = on, online = on
)
on psOrders2(OrderDate);

create nonclustered index IDX_OrdersPT_CustomerId
on dbo.OrdersPT(CustomerId)
with
(
    data_compression = page on partitions(1 to 28),
    data_compression = none on partitions(29 to 31),
    drop_existing = on, online = on
)
on psOrders2(OrderDate);
```

Another workaround would be to switch the partition to a staging table, moving that table to a new filegroup with an online index rebuild, and then switching the table back to being the partition to the original table. This method requires some planning and additional code to make it transparent to the client applications.

Let's look more closely at this approach. One of the key elements here is the view, which works as another layer of abstraction for the client code, hiding the staging table during the data movement process.

Let's create a table that stores data for the year 2016 and is partitioned on a monthly basis. The table stores the data up to April in the FG1 filegroup, using FG2 afterward. You can see the code for doing this in Listing 16-19.

Listing 16-19. Using a temporary table to move partition data: Table and view creation

```
create partition function pfOrders(datetime2(0))
as range right for values
('2016-02-01','2016-03-01','2016-04-01','2016-05-01','2016-06-01','2016-07-01');

create partition scheme psOrders
as partition pfOrders
to (FG1,FG1,FG1,FG1,FG2,FG2,FG2);

create table dbo.tblOrders
(
    OrderId int not null,
    OrderDate datetime2(0) not null,
    OrderNum varchar(32) not null,
    OrderTotal money not null,
    CustomerId int not null,
    /* Other Columns */
);

create unique clustered index IDX_tblOrders_OrderDate_OrderId
on dbo.tblOrders(OrderDate, OrderId)
on psOrders(OrderDate);

create nonclustered index IDX_tblOrders_CustomerId
on dbo.tblOrders(CustomerId)
on psOrders(OrderDate);
go

create view dbo.Orders(OrderId, OrderDate, OrderNum, OrderTotal, CustomerId /*Other
Columns*/)
with schemabinding
as
    select OrderId, OrderDate, OrderNum, OrderTotal, CustomerId /*Other Columns*/
    from dbo.tblOrders;
```

As you can see, the script creates an updateable dbo.Orders view in addition to the table. All access to the data should be done through that view.

Let's assume that you want to move May 2016 data to the FG1 filegroup. As a first step, you need to create a staging table and switch May's partition to be located there. The table must reside in the FG2 filegroup and have a CHECK constraint defined. The code for accomplishing this is shown in Listing 16-20.

Listing 16-20. Using a temporary table to move partition data: Switching the partition to the staging table

```
create table dbo.tblOrdersStage
(
    OrderId int not null,
    OrderDate datetime2(0) not null,
    OrderNum varchar(32) not null,
    OrderTotal money not null,
    CustomerId int not null,
    /* Other Columns */
    constraint CHK_tblOrdersStage
    check(OrderDate >= '2016-05-01' and OrderDate < '2016-06-01')
);

create unique clustered index IDX_tblOrdersStage_OrderDate_OrderId
on dbo.tblOrdersStage(OrderDate, OrderId)
on [FG2];

create nonclustered index IDX_tblOrdersStage_CustomerId
on dbo.tblOrdersStage(CustomerId)
on [FG2];

alter table dbo.tblOrders switch partition 5 to dbo.tblOrdersStage;
```

Now you have data in two different tables, and you need to alter the view, making it partitioned. That change allows client applications to read the data transparently from both tables. However, it would prevent the view from being updateable. The simplest way to address this is to create INSTEAD OF triggers on the view.

You can see the code for doing this in Listing 16-21. It shows only one INSTEAD OF INSERT trigger statement in order to save space in this book.

Listing 16-21. Using a temporary table to move partition data: Altering the view

```
alter view dbo.Orders(OrderId, OrderDate, OrderNum, OrderTotal, CustomerId /*Other
Columns*/)
with schemabinding
as
    select OrderId, OrderDate, OrderNum, OrderTotal, CustomerId /*Other Columns*/
    from dbo.tblOrders
    union all
    select OrderId, OrderDate, OrderNum, OrderTotal, CustomerId /*Other Columns*/
    from dbo.tblOrdersStage
go

create trigger dbo.trgOrdersView_Ins
on dbo.Orders
instead of insert
as
    if @@rowcount = 0 return
    set nocount on
    if not exists(select * from inserted)
        return
```

```
    insert into dbo.tblOrders(OrderId, OrderDate, OrderNum, OrderTotal, CustomerId)
        select OrderId, OrderDate, OrderNum, OrderTotal, CustomerId
        from inserted
        where OrderDate < '2016-05-01' or OrderDate >= '2016-06-01';

    insert into dbo.tblOrdersStage(OrderId, OrderDate, OrderNum, OrderTotal, CustomerId)
        select OrderId, OrderDate, OrderNum, OrderTotal, CustomerId
        from inserted
        where OrderDate >= '2016-05-01' and OrderDate < '2016-06-01';
```

You can now move the staging table to the FG1 filegroup by performing an index rebuild, as shown in Listing 16-22. It is worth repeating that if the table has LOB columns, it cannot work as an online operation in SQL Server 2005-2008R2. Moreover, you will need to use a workaround and rebuild the indexes to the new partition scheme to move the LOB_DATA allocation units, as was shown earlier in Listing 16-14.

Listing 16-22. Using a temporary table to move partition data: Moving the staging table

```
create unique clustered index IDX_tblOrdersStage_OrderDate_OrderId
on dbo.tblOrdersStage(OrderDate, OrderId)
with (drop_existing=on, online=on)
on [FG1];

create nonclustered index IDX_tblOrdersStage_CustomerId
on dbo.tblOrdersStage(CustomerId)
with (drop_existing=on, online=on)
on [FG1];
```

As the final step, you need to move the dbo.tblOrders table's May data partition to the FG1 filegroup by merging and splitting the partition function. The partition is empty, and a schema modification (SCH-M) lock will not be held for a long time. After that, you can switch the staging table back to being a partition to the dbo.tblOrders table, drop the trigger, and alter the view again. The code for doing this is shown in Listing 16-23.

Listing 16-23. Using a temporary table to move partition data: Moving the staging table

```
alter partition function pfOrders() merge range ('2016-05-01');

alter partition scheme psOrders next used [FG1];

alter partition function pfOrders() split range ('2016-05-01');

alter table dbo.tblOrdersStage switch to dbo.tblOrders partition 5;

drop trigger dbo.trgOrdersView_Ins;

alter view dbo.Orders(OrderId, OrderDate, OrderNum, OrderTotal, CustomerId /*Other Columns*/)
with schemabinding
as
    select OrderId, OrderDate, OrderNum, OrderTotal, CustomerId /*Other Columns*/
    from dbo.tblOrders;
```

The same technique would work if you needed to archive data into another table. You could switch the staging table to be a partition there, as long as the table schemas and indexes were the same.

Moving Data Files Between Disk Arrays

As you can see, there are plenty of limitations that can prevent online cross-filegroup data movement, even in the Enterprise Edition of SQL Server. It is simply impossible to do this in the non-Enterprise editions, which do not support online index rebuilds at all.

Fortunately, there is still a workaround that allows you to build tiered storage, regardless of those limitations. You can keep the objects in the same filegroups by moving the filegroup database files to different disk arrays.

There are two ways to implement this. First, you can manually copy the data files and alter the database to specify their new locations. Unfortunately, this approach requires system downtime for the duration of the file copy operation, which can take a long time with large amount of data unless the system is using database mirroring as High Availability technology. When this is the case, you can move database files using the following set of actions:

1. Modify file paths using the `ALTER DATABASE MODIFY FILE (FILENAME=...)` commands on the secondary (mirror) server. This is a metadata operation, which changes files' locations in the system catalogs.
2. Shut down secondary (mirror) instance and copy database files to the new locations.
3. Start secondary (mirror) instance and perform failover, making it primary (principal) server.
4. Repeat the process on the former primary (principal) and now secondary (mirror) server.

Even though this approach is almost transparent to the client applications, it requires you to shut down entire SQL Server instances and perform failover operations. There is also the possibility of data loss if the primary (principal) server crashes when the secondary (mirror) server is offline.

There is another method that allows you to move the data online by adding new files to the filegroup and shrinking the original files with the `DBCC SHRINKFILE(EMPTYFILE)` command. SQL Server moves the data between files transparently to the client applications, keeping the system online, no matter the edition of SQL Server.

Listing 16-24 shows the code for moving data files from filegroup `FG2015` to disk `S:`. It assumes that the filegroup has two files with the logical names `Orders2015_01` and `Orders2015_02` before the execution.

Listing 16-24. Moving data files between disk arrays

```
use master
go

alter database OrderEntryDB
add file ( name = N'Orders2015_03', filename = N'S:\Orders2015_03.ndf' )
to filegroup [FG1];

alter database OrderEntryDB
add file ( name = N'Orders2015_04', filename = N'S:\Orders2015_04.ndf' )
to filegroup [FG1];
go

use OrderEntryDb
go
```

```
-- Preventing the second OLD file to grow
-- This stops movement of the data between OLD data files
declare
    @MaxFileSizeMB int
    ,@SQL nvarchar(max)

-- Obtaining the current file size
select @MaxFileSizeMB = size / 128 + 1
from sys.database_files
where name = 'Orders2015_02';

set @SQL = N'alter database OrderEntryDb
modify file(name=N''Orders2015_02'',maxsize=' +
    convert(nvarchar(32),@MaxFileSizeMB) + N'MB);';

exec sp_executesql @SQL;

-- Step 1: Shrinking and removing first old file
dbcc shrinkfile(Orders2015_01, emptyfile);
alter database OrderEntryDb remove file Orders2015_01;

-- Step 2: Shrinking and removing second old file
dbcc shrinkfile(Orders2015_02, emptyfile);
alter database OrderEntryDb remove file Orders2015_02;
```

■ **Important** Make sure to create new files with the same initial size and auto-growth parameters, with growth size specified in MB. This helps SQL Server evenly distribute data across data files.

When you empty a file with the DBCC SHRINKFILE command, it distributes the data across all other files in the filegroup, including files that you will empty and remove in the next steps. You can avoid this overhead by restricting maximum file size and preventing the auto-growth of the files you are going to remove, as was shown in Listing 16-24.

Unfortunately, this approach introduces index fragmentation. The data in the new data files would be heavily fragmented after the DBCC SHRINKFILE operation. You should perform index maintenance after the data has been moved.

■ **Tip** Index REORGANIZE could be a better choice than REBUILD in this case. REORGANIZE is an online operation, which would not block access to the table. Moreover, it would not increase the size of the data files.

Both DBCC SHRINKFILE and index maintenance introduce a huge amount of transaction log activity. You need to remember this behavior and perform regular log backups to allow the transaction log to truncate.

■ **Note** We will discuss transaction log management in greater depth in Chapter 30, "Transaction Log Internals."

Finally, it is worth noting that this technique would not work for the movement of the primary (MDF) data file in the database. SQL Server does not allow you to remove this file from the database. It is another reason why it is better to avoid storing any user objects in the **primary** filegroup.

■ **Tip** You can still run the `DBCC SHRINKFILE(EMPTYFILE)` command on the primary (MDF) data file. It would move the majority of the data to other files in the **primary** filegroup and fail during the final stage of the execution.

You can monitor the progress of the `SHRINK` operation by using the script shown in Listing 16-25. This script shows you the currently allocated file size and amount of free space for each of the database files.

Listing 16-25. Monitoring the size of the database files

```
select
    name as [FileName], physical_name as [Path], size / 128.0 as [CurrentSizeMB]
    ,size / 128.0 - convert(int,fileproperty(name,'SpaceUsed')) / 128.0 as [FreeSpaceMb]
from sys.database_files
```

Tiered Storage in Action

Table 16-6 shows the available online data movement options for different database objects based on the version and edition of SQL Server in use.

Table 16-6. *Online Data Movement of Database Objects Based on the SQL Server Version and Edition*

<table>
<tr><th></th><th>Moving Partition to Different Filegroup</th><th>Moving Table with LOB Columns to Different Filegroup</th><th>Moving Table without LOB Columns to Different Filegroup</th><th>Moving Data to Different Disk Array</th></tr>
<tr><td>SQL Server 2012-2016 Enterprise Edition</td><td rowspan="2">Straightforward approach held schema modification (SCH-M) lock. Can be implemented with staging table and partitioned view (Subject of LOB column offline index rebuild limitation in SQL Server 2005-2008R2)</td><td>Supported</td><td>Supported</td><td rowspan="3">Supported in every edition (Introduces fragmentation and overhead)</td></tr>
<tr><td>SQL Server 2005-2008R2 Enterprise Edition</td><td>Not Supported</td><td>Supported</td></tr>
<tr><td>Non-Enterprise Edition</td><td>N/A</td><td>Not Supported</td><td>Not Supported</td></tr>
</table>

As you can see, it is generally easier to implement online data movement using non-partitioned rather than partitioned tables. This makes the approach that we discussed in the "Using Partitioned Tables and Views Together" section of this chapter one of the most optimal solutions. With such an approach, you are using non-partitioned tables to store operational data, keeping the historical data in partitioned tables, as was shown in Figure 16-6.

Let's look at the process of changing the operational period in more depth, assuming that you need to archive May 2016 data and extend the operational period to July 2016.

In the first step shown in Figure 16-11, you move the dbo.Orders2016_05 table from FASTSTORAGE to the FG2016 filegroup.

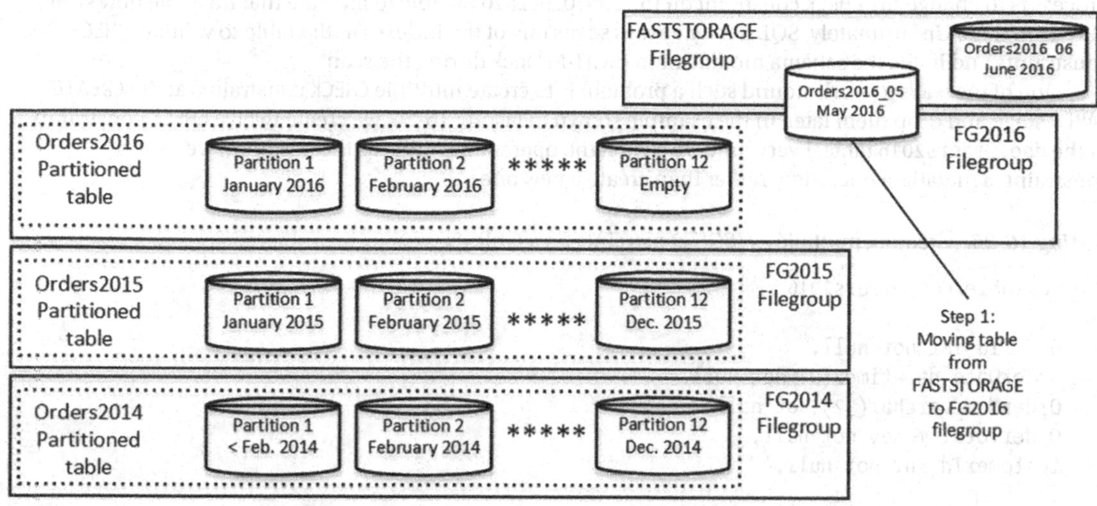

Figure 16-11. *Tiered storage in action: Moving the dbo.Orders2016_05 table*

After that, you switch the dbo.Orders2016_05 table into the partition of the dbo.Orders2016 table, creating a new dbo.Orders2016_07 table in the FASTSTORAGE filegroup and recreating the partitioned view. You can see these steps demonstrated in Figure 16-12.

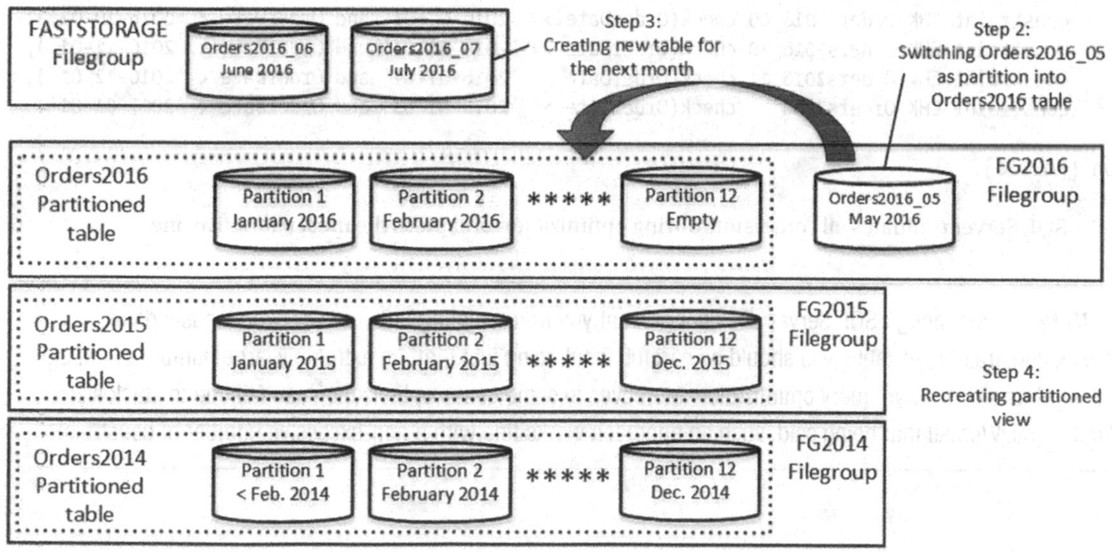

Figure 16-12. *Tiered storage in action: Further steps*

All of these operations can be done online with the Enterprise Edition of SQL Server 2012 and above. They can also be done online with SQL Server 2005-2008R2, as long as the tables do not contain LOB columns.

There is still the possibility of a lengthy hold of the schema modification (SCH-M) lock at the time when you switch `dbo.Orders2016_05` into the `dbo.Orders2016` table. One of the things you need to do during this process is to change the `CHECK` constraint on the `dbo.Orders2016` table to indicate that the table now stores May 2016 data. Unfortunately, SQL Server always scans one of the indexes in the table to validate `CHECK` constraints and holds the schema modification (SCH-M) lock during the scan.

One of the ways to work around such a problem is to create multiple `CHECK` constraints at the `CREATE TABLE` stage and drop them later. In the example shown in Listing 16-26, we create twelve `CHECK` constraints in the `dbo.Orders2016` table. Every time we switch the operational table as the partition, we drop a constraint, a metadata operation, rather than create a new one.

Listing 16-26. Creating multiple *CHECK* constraints on a table

```
create table dbo.Orders2016
(
    OrderId int not null,
    OrderDate datetime2(0) not null,
    OrderNum varchar(32) not null,
    OrderTotal money not null,
    CustomerId int not null,

    constraint CHK_Orders2016_01 check(OrderDate >= '2016-01-01' and OrderDate < '2016-02-01'),
    constraint CHK_Orders2016_02 check(OrderDate >= '2016-01-01' and OrderDate < '2016-03-01'),
    constraint CHK_Orders2016_03 check(OrderDate >= '2016-01-01' and OrderDate < '2016-04-01'),
    constraint CHK_Orders2016_04 check(OrderDate >= '2016-01-01' and OrderDate < '2016-05-01'),
    constraint CHK_Orders2016_05 check(OrderDate >= '2016-01-01' and OrderDate < '2016-06-01'),
    constraint CHK_Orders2016_06 check(OrderDate >= '2016-01-01' and OrderDate < '2016-07-01'),
    constraint CHK_Orders2016_07 check(OrderDate >= '2016-01-01' and OrderDate < '2016-08-01'),
    constraint CHK_Orders2016_08 check(OrderDate >= '2016-01-01' and OrderDate < '2016-09-01'),
    constraint CHK_Orders2016_09 check(OrderDate >= '2016-01-01' and OrderDate < '2016-10-01'),
    constraint CHK_Orders2016_10 check(OrderDate >= '2016-01-01' and OrderDate < '2016-11-01'),
    constraint CHK_Orders2016_11 check(OrderDate >= '2016-01-01' and OrderDate < '2016-12-01'),
    constraint CHK_Orders2016    check(OrderDate >= '2016-01-01' and OrderDate < '2017-01-01')
)
on [FG2016]
```

SQL Server evaluates all constraints during optimization and picks the most restrictive one.

■ **Note** Even though SQL Server does not prevent you from creating hundreds or even thousands of `CHECK` constraints per table, you should be careful about doing just that. An extremely large number of `CHECK` constraints slows down query optimization. Moreover, in some cases optimization can fail due to stack size limitations. With all that being said, such an approach works fine with a non-excessive number of constraints.

Tiered Storage and High Availability Technologies

Even though we will discuss High Availability (HA) technologies in greater depth in Chapter 32, it is important to mention their compatibility with tiered storage and data movement in this chapter. There are two different factors to consider: database files and filegroups management, and data movement overhead. Neither of them affects the SQL Server failover cluster, where you have a single copy of the database. However, such is not the case for transaction log–based HA technologies, such as AlwaysOn Availability Groups, database mirroring, and log shipping.

Neither of the High Availability technologies prevents you from creating database files. However, with transaction log–based HA technologies, you should maintain exactly the same folder and disk structure on all nodes, and SQL Server must be able to create new files in the same path everywhere. Otherwise, HA data flow would be suspended.

Another important factor is the overhead introduced by the index rebuild or `DBCC SHRINKFILE` commands. They are very I/O intensive and generate a huge amount of transaction log records. All of these records need to be transmitted to secondary nodes, which could saturate the network.

There is one lesser-known problem, though. Transaction log–based HA technologies work with transaction log records only. There is a set of threads, called *REDO threads*, which *asynchronously* replay transaction log records and apply changes in the data files on the secondary nodes. Even with synchronous synchronization, available in AlwaysOn Availability Groups and database mirroring, SQL Server *synchronously* saves (hardens) the log record in transaction logs only. The REDO threads apply changes in the database files *asynchronously*.

The performance of REDO threads is the limiting factor here. Data movement could generate transaction log records faster than REDO threads can apply the changes in the data files. It is not uncommon for the REDO process to require minutes or even hours to catch up. This could lead to extended system downtimes in the case of failover, because the database in the new primary node stays in a recovery state until the REDO stage is done.

You should also be careful if you are using readable secondaries with AlwaysOn Availability Groups. Even though the data is available during the REDO process, it is not up to date, and queries against primary and secondary nodes will return different results.

■ **Note** Any type of heavy transaction log activity can introduce such a problem with readable secondaries.

You should be careful implementing tiered storage when transaction log–based HA technologies are in use. You should factor potential downtime during failover into availability SLA and minimize it by moving data on an index-by-index basis, allowing the secondaries to catch up in between operations. You should also prevent read-only access to secondaries during data movement.

Implementing Sliding Window Scenario and Data Purge

OLTP systems are often required to keep data for a specific length of time. For example, an order entry system could keep orders for a year and have a process that is run the first day of every month to delete older orders. With this implementation, called a *sliding window* scenario, you have a window on the data that *slides* and purges the oldest data based on a given schedule.

The only way to implement a sliding window scenario with non-partitioned data is by purging the data with `DELETE` statements. This approach introduces huge I/O and transaction log overhead. Moreover, it could contribute to concurrency and blocking issues in the system. Fortunately, data partitioning dramatically simplifies this task, making the purge a metadata-only operation.

When you implement a sliding window scenario, you usually partition the data based on the purge interval. Even though it is not a requirement, it helps you to keep the purge process on a metadata level. As an example, in the order entry system just described you could partition the data on a monthly basis.

In the case of partitioned views, the purge process is simple. You need to drop the oldest table, create another table for the *next partition period* data, and then recreate the partitioned view. It is essential to have the next partition period table predefined to make sure that there is always a place where the data can be inserted.

Partitioned table implementation is similar. You can purge old data by switching the corresponding partition to a temporary table, which you can truncate afterward. For the next month's data, you need to use the split partition function.

There is a catch, though. In order to keep the operation on a metadata level and reduce the time that the schema modification (SCH-M) lock is held, you should keep the rightmost partition empty. This prevents SQL Server from moving data during the split process, which can be very time consuming in case with large tables.

■ **Note** Even a metadata-level partition switch can lead to locking and blocking in very active OLTP systems. SQL Server 2014 introduces the concept of low-priority locks, which can be used to improve system concurrency during such operations. We will discuss them in detail in Chapter 23, "Schema Locks."

Let's look at an example, assuming that it is now June 2016 and the purge process will run on July 1st. As you can see in Listing 16-27, the partition function `pfOrderData` has boundary values of 2016-07-01 and 2016-08-01. These values predefine two partitions: one for the July 2016 data and an empty rightmost partition that you would split during the purge process.

It is important to have both partitions predefined. The data will be inserted into the July 2016 partition as of midnight of July 1st, before the purge process is running. The empty rightmost partition guarantees that the partition split during the purge process will be done at the metadata level.

There is also a `dbo.OrderDataTmp` table created in the script, which we will use as the destination for the partition switch and purge. That table must reside in the same filegroup with the leftmost partition and have the same schema and indexes defined.

Listing 16-27. Sliding window scenario: Object creation

```
create partition function pfOrderData(datetime2(0))
as range right for values
('2015-07-01','2015-08-01','2015-09-01','2015-10-01','2015-11-01','2015-12-01'
,'2016-01-01','2016-02-01','2016-03-01','2016-04-01','2016-05-01','2016-06-01'
,'2016-07-01','2016-08-01' /* One extra empty partition */ );

create partition scheme psOrderData as partition pfOrderData all to ([FG1]);

create table dbo.OrderData
(
    OrderId int not null,
    OrderDate datetime2(0) not null,
    OrderNum varchar(32) not null,
    OrderTotal money not null,
    CustomerId int not null,
    /* Other Columns */
);
```

```
create unique clustered index IDX_OrderData_OrderDate_OrderId
on dbo.OrderData(OrderDate, OrderId)
on psOrderData(OrderDate);

create nonclustered index IDX_OrderData_CustomerId
on dbo.OrderData(CustomerId)
on psOrderData(OrderDate);

create table dbo.OrderDataTmp
(
    OrderId int not null,
    OrderDate datetime2(0) not null,
    OrderNum varchar(32) not null,
    OrderTotal money not null,
    CustomerId int not null,
    /* Other Columns */
);

create unique clustered index IDX_OrderDataTmp_OrderDate_OrderId
on dbo.OrderDataTmp(OrderDate, OrderId)
on [FG1];

create nonclustered index IDX_OrderDataTmp_CustomerId
on dbo.OrderDataTmp(CustomerId)
on [FG1];
```

The purge process is shown in Listing 16-28. It switches the leftmost partition to the temporary table and splits the rightmost partition, creating a new empty partition for next month's run.

Listing 16-28. Sliding window scenario: Purge process

```
-- Purging old partition
alter table dbo.OrderData switch partition 1 to dbo.OrderDataTmp;
truncate table dbo.OrderDataTmp;

-- Creating new partition
alter partition scheme psOrderData next used [FG1];
alter partition function pfOrderData() split range('2016-09-01');
```

Potential Issues

Despite all of the benefits that data partitioning delivers, they do come at a cost. First, SQL Server requires a partitioned column to be a part of the clustered index key in the partitioned table. This, in turn, adds that column to the row-id and increases the row size in every nonclustered index. For example, in a table that stores 365 million rows, a `datetime`-partitioned column adds 2.7 GB per nonclustered index, not counting fragmentation overhead and non-leaf-level storage space.

■ **Tip** Always choose the most storage-efficient data type based on the business requirements. In the previous example, you can use `smalldatetime` (four bytes) or `datetime2(0)` (six bytes) instead of `datetime` (eight bytes) if one-minute or one-second precisions are acceptable.

Even though you can mitigate this space increase in some cases by implementing data compression on the historical data, the row-id size increase can add new non-leaf levels to the indexes as well as extra reads when SQL Server traverses index B-trees.

Uniqueness support is another issue. You cannot create a unique constraint or index on a partitioned view. With partitioned tables, SQL Server requires a partitioned column to be part of aligned unique nonclustered indexes. This enforces uniqueness only in the single-partition scope. Although you could define non-aligned unique indexes, it would prevent you from using a partition switch, which is one of the greatest benefits of partitioned tables.

Unfortunately, there is no easy solution for this problem. In cases where you need to support uniqueness across multiple data partitions, you have to implement complex code, often using a `SERIALIZEABLE` transaction isolation level, and this can introduce blocking issues in the system. We will discuss transaction isolation levels in greater depth in Chapter 17, "Lock Types."

Ultimately, the biggest problem with data partitioning is that it changes the execution plans of the queries. It can introduce suboptimal performance for some queries, which worked just fine when the data had not been partitioned.

Let's look at one such example and create a non-partitioned table, then populate it with some random data, as shown in Listing 16-29.

Listing 16-29. Potential issues with data partitioning: Creating a non-partitioned table

```
create table dbo.Data
(
    Id int not null,
    DateCreated datetime not null
        constraint DEF_Data_DateCreated default getutcdate(),
    DateModified datetime not null
        constraint DEF_Data_DateModified default getutcdate(),
    Placeholder char(500) null
);

create unique clustered index IDX_Data_Id
on dbo.Data(DateCreated, Id);

create unique nonclustered index IDX_Data_DateModified_Id
on dbo.Data(DateModified, Id);

declare @StartDate datetime = '2016-01-01';

;with N1(C) as (select 0 union all select 0) -- 2 rows
,N2(C) as (select 0 from N1 as T1 cross join N1 as T2) -- 4 rows
,N3(C) as (select 0 from N2 as T1 cross join N2 as T2) -- 16 rows
,N4(C) as (select 0 from N3 as T1 cross join N3 as T2) -- 256 rows
,N5(C) as (select 0 from N4 as T1 cross join N4 as T2) -- 65,536 rows
,N6(C) as (select 0 from N5 as T1 cross join N2 as T2 cross join N1 as T3) -- 524,288 rows
,IDs(ID) as (select row_number() over (order by (select NULL)) from N6)
insert into dbo.Data(ID, DateCreated, DateModified)
```

```
select ID, dateadd(second,35 * Id,@StartDate),
    case
        when ID % 10 = 0
        then dateadd(second, 24 * 60 * 60 * (ID % 31) + 11200 + ID % 59 + 35 * ID,
            @StartDate)
        else dateadd(second,35 * ID,@StartDate)
    end
from IDs;
```

Let's assume that we have a process that reads modified data from the table and exports it somewhere. While there are a few different ways to implement such a task, perhaps the simplest method is to use a query, as shown in Listing 16-30, with the `@DateModified` parameter representing the most recent `DateModified` value from the previous record set read.

Listing 16-30. Potential issues with data partitioning: Reading modified data

```
select top (@Top) Id, DateCreated, DateModified, PlaceHolder
from dbo.Data
where DateModified > @LastDateModified
order by DateModified, Id
```

The execution plan of the query, which selects 100 rows, is shown in Figure 16-13. The plan is very efficient, and it utilizes a *nonclustered index seek* with a range scan. SQL Server finds the first row with a `DateModified` value that exceeds `@LastDateModified` and then scans the index, selecting the first 100 rows from there.

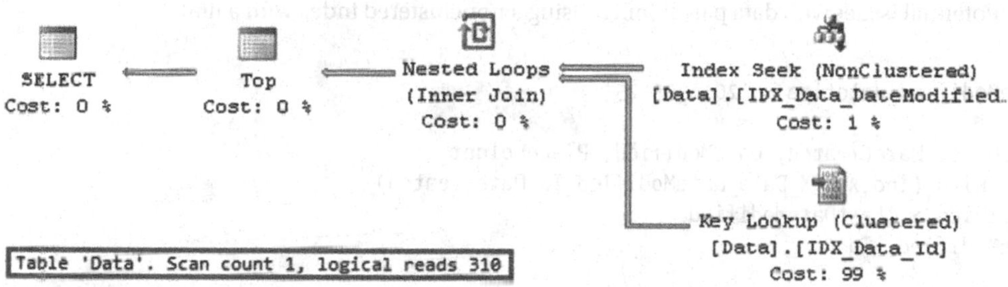

Figure 16-13. *Execution plan with non-partitioned table*

Now, let's partition the table on a monthly basis, as shown in Listing 16-31.

Listing 16-31. Potential issues with data partitioning: Partitioning the table

```
create partition function pfData(datetime)
as range right for values
('2016-02-01', '2016-03-01','2016-04-01','2016-05-01','2016-06-01','2016-07-01','2016-08-01');

create partition scheme psData as partition pfData all to ([FG1]);

create unique clustered index IDX_Data_DateCreated_Id
on dbo.Data(DateCreated,ID)
on psData(DateCreated);
```

```
create unique nonclustered index IDX_Data_DateModified_Id_DateCreated
on dbo.Data(DateModified, ID, DateCreated)
on psData(DateCreated);
```

If you run the code from Listing 16-30 again, the execution plan would change, as shown in Figure 16-14. As you can see, SQL Server decides to use a *clustered index scan*, which dramatically decreases the performance of the query.

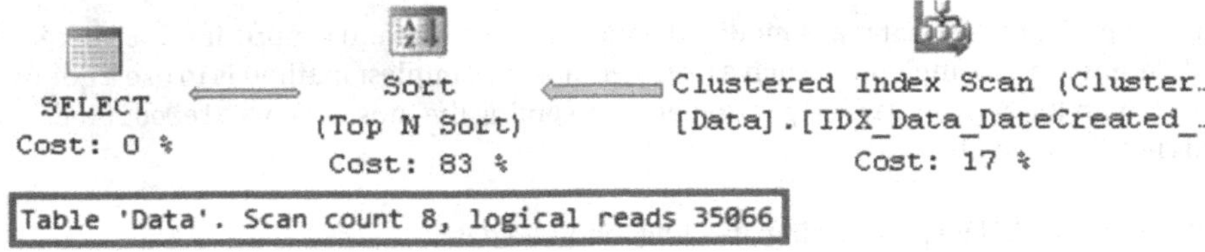

Figure 16-14. *Execution plan with partitioned table*

The root cause of the problem is related to the fact that the data in clustered and nonclustered indexes are now sorted on a partition-by-partition basis rather than across the entire table. You can think about each partition as an individual table with its own set of data and indexes. SQL Server decides that, in such a situation, a clustered index scan is the cheapest option with which to proceed.

Let's look at what happens if you force SQL Server to use a nonclustered index with an index hint, as shown in Listing 16-32.

Listing 16-32. Potential issues with data partitioning: Using a nonclustered index with a hint

```
declare
    @LastDateModified datetime = '2016-05-25'

select top 100 Id, DateCreated, DateModified, PlaceHolder
from dbo.Data with (index=IDX_Data_DateModified_Id_DateCreated)
where DateModified > @LastDateModified
order by DateModified, Id
```

As you can see in Figure 16-15, the execution plan is even less efficient than before. SQL Server located and read all of the rows with a DateModified greater than @LastDateModified from every partition, and it performed a *key lookup* operation for all of them, sorting the data afterward.

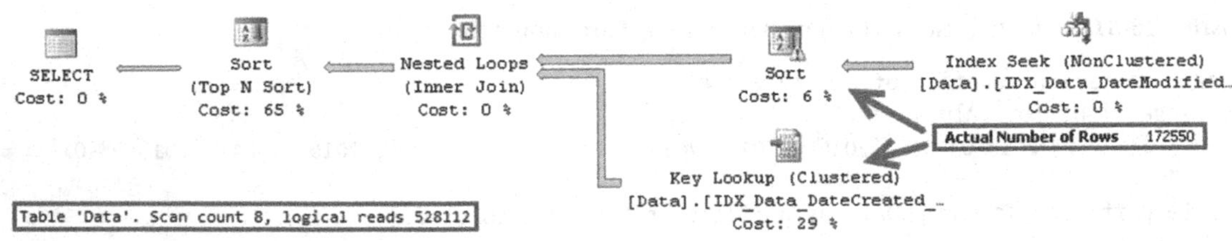

Figure 16-15. *Execution plan with index hint*

There is no easy way to fix the problem. You can use non-aligned nonclustered indexes, which are not partitioned. Unfortunately, you cannot use a partition switch in such cases, nor perform a piecemeal database restore, making subsets of the data available to customers. Thus, the only option you have is code re-factoring.

■ **Tip** You can drop a non-aligned nonclustered index before a partition switch and recreate it after the switch is done.

The `$PARTITION` system function returns a partition number for the value provided as a parameter. You can use this function in a `where` clause in the query, which eliminates other partitions and produces execution plans similar to the queries against non-partitioned tables. You can see the query, which reads modified rows from partition 5, in Listing 16-33.

Listing 16-33. Potential issues with data partitioning: Selecting data from a single partition

```
declare
    @LastDateModified datetime = '2016-05-25'

select top 100 Id, DateCreated, DateModified, PlaceHolder
from dbo.Data with (index=IDX_Data_DateModified_Id_DateCreated)
where
    DateModified > @LastDateModified and
    $partition.pfData(DateCreated) = 5
order by DateModified, Id
```

As you can see in Figure 16-16, the execution plan is very similar to the query that read modified data from the non-partitioned table.

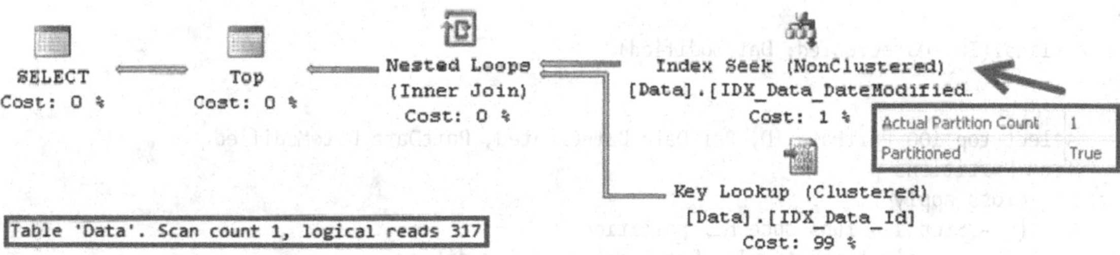

Figure 16-16. *Execution plan for the query: Selecting data from a single partition*

In some cases, you can use this behavior to optimize queries against partitioned tables. In our case, you can have the following algorithm:

1. Read the top 100 modified rows from every partition using the `$PARTITION` function, limiting execution to the single-partition scope.

2. Sort the rows read in the previous step and select the top 100 rows across all partitions.

3. Select data from the clustered index for the 100 rows returned by the previous step.

The first step of the algorithm requires you to know the number of partitions in the table. You can use `sys.partition_range_values` DMV to find the number of boundary values in the partition function, which is one less than the number of partitions in the table.

The code in Listing 16-34 shows an optimized version of the query. `Partitions` CTE returns the numbers that correspond to the partition numbers in the table, which are used as filters in the `CROSS APPLY` operator of the `Steps1and2` CTE. The `CROSS APPLY` operator implements the first step of the algorithm. The `SELECT` in the `CROSS APPLY` executes once per partition.

The outer select statement in the `Steps1and2` CTE sorts the data returned by the `CROSS APPLY` operator across all partitions, which is the second step in the algorithm.

Finally, the last `SELECT` outside of the CTE is the third step in the algorithm.

Listing 16-34. Potential issues with data partitioning: Optimized query

```
declare
    @LastDateModified datetime = '2016-05-25'
    ,@BoundaryValuesCount int

-- Getting number of boundary values in partition function
select @BoundaryValuesCount = max(boundary_id)
from sys.partition_functions pf join sys.partition_range_values prf on
        pf.function_id = prf.function_id
where pf.name = 'pfData'

;with Partitions(PartitionNum)
as
(
    select 1
    union all
    select PartitionNum + 1
    from Partitions
    where PartitionNum <= @BoundaryValuesCount
)
,Steps1and2(Id, DateCreated, DateModified)
as
(
    select top 100 PartData.ID, PartData.DateCreated, PartData.DateModified
    from Partitions p
        cross apply
        ( -- Step 1 - runs once per partition
                select top 100 Id, DateCreated, DateModified
                from dbo.Data
                where
                    DateModified > @LastDateModified and
                    $Partition.pfData(DateCreated) = p.PartitionNum
                order by DateModified, ID
        ) PartData
    order by PartData.DateModified, PartData.Id
)
-- Step 3 - CI seek as Key Lookup operation
select s.Id, s.DateCreated, s.DateModified, d.Placeholder
from Steps1and2 s join dbo.Data d on
        d.Id = s.Id and s.DateCreated = d.DateCreated
order by s.DateModified, s.Id
```

You can see the execution plan of this query in Figure 16-17. The plan is almost as efficient as the one against non-partitioned tables.

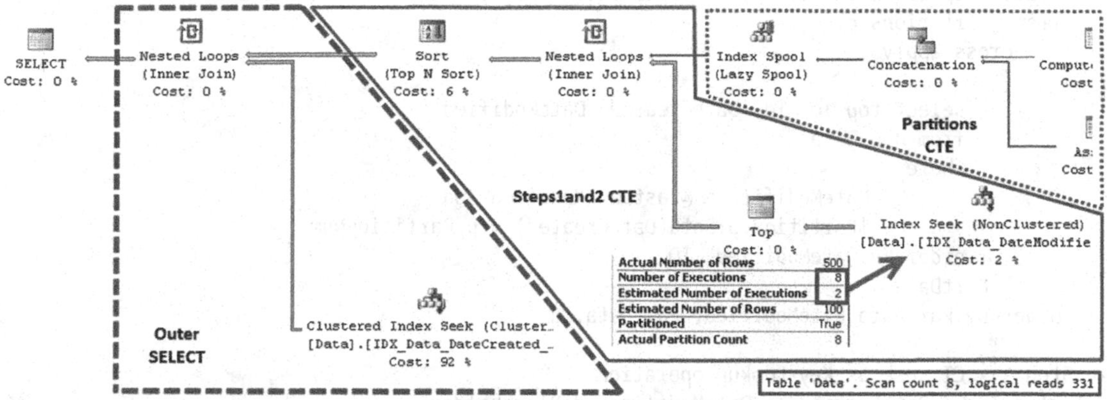

Figure 16-17. *Execution plan of the optimized query*

Unfortunately, SQL Server underestimates the number of executions and rows returned by recursive CTE. It can lead to further cardinality estimation errors and subefficient execution plans in some cases. You can avoid this error by using a temporary table to store partition numbers, as shown in Listing 16-35.

Listing 16-35. Storing partition numbers in a temporary table

```
declare
    @LastDateModified datetime = '2016-05-25',
    @BoundaryValuesCount int

create table #Partitions(PartitionNum smallint not null primary key);

-- Getting number of boundary values in partition function
select @BoundaryValuesCount = max(boundary_id)
from sys.partition_functions pf join  sys.partition_range_values prf on
        pf.function_id = prf.function_id
where pf.name = 'pfData';

;with Partitions(PartitionNum)
as
(
    select 1
    union all
    select PartitionNum + 1
    from Partitions
    where PartitionNum <= @BoundaryValuesCount
)
insert into #Partitions(PartitionNum)
    select PartitionNum from Partitions;
```

```
;with Steps1and2(Id, DateCreated, DateModified)
as
(
    select top 100 PartData.ID, PartData.DateCreated, PartData.DateModified
    from #Partitions p
        cross apply
        (
            select top 100 Id, DateCreated, DateModified
            from dbo.Data
            where
                    DateModified > @LastDateModified and
                    $Partition.pfData(DateCreated) = p.PartitionNum
            order by DateModified, ID
        ) PartData
    order by PartData.DateModified, PartData.Id
)
-- Step 3 - CI seek as Key Lookup operation
select s.Id, s.DateCreated, s.DateModified, d.Placeholder
from Steps1and2 s join dbo.Data d on
        d.Id = s.Id and s.DateCreated = d.DateCreated
order by s.DateModified, s.Id
```

Alternatively, if the number of partitions is static and predefined, you can hardcode it in the `Partitions` CTE, as shown in Listing 16-36.

Listing 16-36. Hardcoding partition numbers

```
declare
    @LastDateModified datetime = '2016-05-25'

;with Partitions(PartitionNum)
as
(
    select v.V from (values(1),(2),(3),(4),(5),(6),(7),(8)) v(V)
)
,Steps1and2(Id, DateCreated, DateModified)
as
(
    select top 100 PartData.ID, PartData.DateCreated, PartData.DateModified
    from Partitions p
        cross apply
        (
            select top 100 Id, DateCreated, DateModified
            from dbo.Data
            where
                    DateModified > @LastDateModified and
                    $Partition.pfData(DateCreated) = p.PartitionNum
            order by DateModified, ID
        ) PartData
    order by PartData.DateModified, PartData.Id
)
```

```
-- Step 3 - CI seek as Key Lookup operation
select s.Id, s.DateCreated, s.DateModified, d.Placeholder
from Steps1and2 s join dbo.Data d on
        d.Id = s.Id and s.DateCreated = d.DateCreated
order by s.DateModified, s.Id
```

To review, data partitioning changes the execution plans of the queries. You should carefully test systems in a staging environment using databases of a size and data distribution similar to that of production. This will help to avoid unpleasant surprises when changes are implemented on production servers.

Summary

Management of a large amount of data is a challenging task, especially when the data is not partitioned. Keeping a large amount of data in the same place is not efficient for several different reasons. It increases storage costs and introduces overhead due to the different workload and index management requirements for the various parts of the data. Moreover, it prevents piecemeal database restore, which complicates availability SLA compliance.

There are two main data partitioning techniques available in SQL Server. Partitioned tables are available in the Enterprise Edition of SQL Server. They allow you to partition table data into separate internal tables/partitions, which are transparent to client applications. Each partition can be placed in its own filegroup and have its own data compression. However, the database schema, indexes, and statistics are the same across all partitions.

Alternatively, you can partition the data by separating it between multiple tables, combining all of them through a partitioned view using the `union all` operator. Every table can have its own schema and set of indexes and maintain its own statistics. Partitioned views are supported in all editions of SQL Server.

Although partitioned views are more flexible, such an implementation requires code re-factoring and increases the system maintenance cost because of the large number of tables involved. You can reduce that cost by combining partitioned tables and views together.

Data partitioning helps reduce storage subsystem cost by implementing tiered storage. With such an approach, you can place active operational data on a fast disk array while keeping old, rarely accessed historical data on cheaper disks. You should design a strategy that allows you to move data between different disk arrays when needed. Different versions and editions of SQL Server require different implementation approaches for this task.

You should be careful moving a large amount of data when transaction log-based High Availability technologies are in use. A large amount of transaction log records leads to a REDO process backlog on secondary nodes and can increase system downtime in case of a failover. Moreover, you should prevent queries from accessing readable secondaries in case of a backlog.

You can use data partitioning to improve the performance and concurrency of data import and purge operations. Make sure to keep the rightmost partition empty when you are implementing a sliding window scenario in the system.

Finally, data partitioning comes at a cost. In the case of partitioned tables, a partition column must be included in the clustered index, which increases the size of nonclustered index rows. Moreover, indexes are sorted within individual partitions. This can lead to suboptimal execution plans and regressions after partitioning has been implemented. The `$PARTITION` function can be used to access data in individual partitions, and this can help with optimization.

PART III

Locking, Blocking, and Concurrency

CHAPTER 17

Lock Types and Transaction Isolation Levels

The concurrency model is, perhaps, the least understood part of SQL Server internals. It can often be confusing; you can encounter hard-to-explain blocking issues in almost every SQL Server installation. Internally, however, the SQL Server concurrency model is based on several well-defined principles, which we are going to discuss in this part of the book.

This chapter starts with the key concept of SQL Server concurrency–*locks*. It will provide an overview of the major lock types in SQL Server, explain their compatibility, and, finally, demonstrate how different transaction isolation levels affect the lifetime of the locks in the system.

PART III CODE

All of the code examples in Part III of this book will rely on the `Delivery.Orders` table defined here. This table has a clustered primary key on the `OrderId` column with no nonclustered indexes defined.

```
create table Delivery.Orders
(
    OrderId int not null identity(1,1),
    OrderDate smalldatetime not null,
    OrderNum varchar(20) not null,
    Reference varchar(64) null,
    CustomerId int not null,
    PickupAddressId int not null,
    DeliveryAddressId int not null,
    Amount smallmoney not null,
    ModTime datetime2(0) not null,
    Placeholder char(100) not null

    constraint PK_Orders
    primary key clustered(OrderId)
)
```


D. Korotkevitch, *Pro SQL Server Internals*, DOI 10.1007/978-1-4842-1964-5_17

Transactions and ACID

Transactions are the units of work that read and modify data in a database and help to enforce the consistency and durability of the data in a system. Every transaction in a properly implemented transaction-management system has four different characteristics known as *atomicity, consistency, isolation,* and *durability,* often referenced as *ACID.*

- *Atomicity* guarantees that each transaction executes as an "all or nothing" approach. All changes done within a transaction are either committed or rolled back in full. Consider the classic example of transferring money between checking and savings bank accounts. That action consists of two separate operations: decreasing the balance of the checking account and increasing the balance of the savings account. Transaction atomicity guarantees that both operations either succeed or fail together, and a system will never be in the situation where money was deducted from the checking account but was never added to the savings account.
- *Consistency* ensures that any database transaction brings the database from one consistent state to another and that none of the defined database rules and constraints are violated.
- *Isolation* ensures that the changes done in the transaction are isolated and invisible to other transactions until the transaction is committed.
- *Durability* guarantees that after a transaction is committed, all changes done by the transaction stay permanent and will survive a system crash. SQL Server achieves durability by flushing transaction log records to disk at the commit stage.

Isolation is, perhaps, the most complex requirement to implement. By the book, transaction isolation should guarantee that the concurrent execution of multiple transactions brings the system to the same state as if those transactions were executed serially. However, in most database systems such a rule is often relaxed and is controlled by *transaction isolation levels.*

Historically, SQL Server supports six isolation levels, which can be separated into two different categories. *Pessimistic isolation levels,* such as `READ UNCOMMITTED`, `READ COMMITTED`, `REPEATABLE READ`, and `SERIALIZABLE` rely strictly on locking. *Optimistic isolation levels*–`READ COMMITTED SNAPSHOT` and `SNAPSHOT`–utilize row versioning in addition to locking.

We will discuss pessimistic isolation levels in detail in this chapter and will cover optimistic isolation levels in Chapter 21 of this book.

Major Lock Types

SQL Server uses locking to support the isolation requirement of the transaction. The locks are acquired and held on the *resources,* such as data rows, pages, tables (objects), databases, and others. By default, SQL Server uses row-level locking when acquiring locks on data rows, which minimizes possible concurrency issues in the system. You should remember, however, that the only guarantee SQL Server provides is enforcing data isolation and consistency based on transaction isolation levels. The locking behavior is not documented, and in some cases SQL Server can choose to use a lower locking granularity than row-level locking. Nevertheless, lock compatibility rules are always enforced, and an understanding of the locking model is enough to troubleshoot and address the majority of concurrency issues in the system.

Internally, SQL Server uses more than 20 different lock types. However, they can be grouped into several major categories based on their type and usage.

Exclusive (X) Locks

Exclusive (X) locks are acquired by *writers*–INSERT, UPDATE, DELETE, and MERGE statements that modify data. These queries acquire an exclusive (X) lock on the affected rows and hold them until the end of the transaction. As you can guess by the name—*exclusive* means *exclusive*—only one session can hold an exclusive (X) lock on the resource at any given point in time. This behavior enforces the most important concurrency rule in the system–multiple sessions cannot modify the same data simultaneously. That's it. Other sessions are unable to acquire exclusive (X) locks on the row until the first transaction is completed and exclusive (X) lock on the modified row is released.

Transaction isolation levels do not affect exclusive (X) lock behavior. Exclusive (X) locks are acquired and held until the end of the transaction, even in READ UNCOMMITTED mode. The longer a transaction you have, the longer the exclusive (X) locks would be held.

Intent (I*) Locks

Even though row-level locking improves consistency, keeping the locks on only the row level would be bad from a performance standpoint. Consider a situation where a session needs to have exclusive access to the table–for example, during the table alteration. In this case, if only row-level locking existed, the session would have to scan the entire table, checking whether any row-level locks were held there. As you can imagine, this would be an extremely inefficient process, especially on large tables.

SQL Server addresses this situation by introducing the concept of *intent (I*) locks*. Intent locks are held on the data page and table levels, and they indicate the existence of locks on the child objects. Let's run the code from Listing 17-1 and check what locks were held after we updated one row in the table. The code uses sys.dm_tran_locks dynamic management view (DMV), which returns information about current lock requests in the system.

Listing 17-1. Updating a row and checking the locks held

```
set transaction isolation level read uncommitted
begin tran
    update Delivery.Orders
    set Reference = 'New Reference'
    where OrderId = 100;

    select resource_type, resource_description,
        request_type, request_mode, request_status
     from sys.dm_tran_locks
    where request_session_id = @@spid;
commit
```

Figure 17-1 illustrates the output from this SELECT statement. As you can see, SQL Server held an exclusive (X) lock on the row (key) and two intent exclusive (IX) locks–one each on the page and on the object (table). Those intent exclusive (IX) locks indicate the existence of the exclusive (X) row-level lock held. Finally, there is also the shared (S) lock on the database, which we will cover later in this chapter.

	resource_type	resource_description	request_type	request_mode	request_status
1	DATABASE		LOCK	S	GRANT
2	PAGE	1:944	LOCK	IX	GRANT
3	KEY	(931e04457546)	LOCK	X	GRANT
4	OBJECT		LOCK	IX	GRANT

Figure 17-1. *Exclusive (X) and intent exclusive (IX) locks*

The `resource_description` column indicates the resources on which those locks are acquired. For the page, it indicates its physical location (page 944 in database file 1) and for the row (key) it indicates the hash value of the index key.

When a session needs to obtain object- or page-level locks, it could check the lock compatibility with the other locks (intent or full) held on the table or page rather than scanning the table/page and checking row-level locks there.

Update (U) Locks

SQL Server uses another lock type, *update (U) locks*, during data modifications, acquiring them while searching for the rows that need to be updated. After an update (U) lock is acquired, SQL Server reads the row and *evaluates* if the row needs to be updated by checking the row data against query predicates. If this is the case, SQL Server converts update (U) to an exclusive (X) lock and performs the data modification. Otherwise, the update (U) lock is released.

Let's look at the example and run the code seen in Listing 17-2.

Listing 17-2. Updating multiple rows using a clustered index key as the predicate

```
begin tran
    update Delivery.Orders
    set Reference = 'New Reference'
    where OrderId in (1000, 5000);
commit
```

Figure 17-2 illustrates how locks were acquired and released during query execution. SQL Server acquired an intent exclusive (IX) lock on the table and then intent update (IU) locks on the pages and update (U) locks on the rows, converting them to intent exclusive (IX) and exclusive (X) locks afterward. The locks were held until the end of the transactions and were released at the time of `COMMIT`.

name	mode	resource_descri...	resource_type
lock_acquired	IX		OBJECT
lock_acquired	IU	1:4581	PAGE
lock_acquired	U	(1f00de11a529)	KEY
lock_acquired	IX	1:4581	PAGE
lock_acquired	X	(1f00de11a529)	KEY
lock_acquired	IU	1:4665	PAGE
lock_acquired	U	(086dba16bcf4)	KEY
lock_acquired	IX	1:4665	PAGE
lock_acquired	X	(086dba16bcf4)	KEY
lock_released	X	(086dba16bcf4)	KEY
lock_released	IX	1:4665	PAGE
lock_released	X	(1f00de11a529)	KEY
lock_released	IX	1:4581	PAGE
lock_released	IX		OBJECT

***Figure 17-2.** Update (U) and exclusive (X) locks*

Update (U) locks' behavior depends on the execution plan. In some cases, SQL Server acquires update (U) locks on all rows first, converting them to exclusive (X) locks afterward. In other cases–when, for example, you update only one row based on the clustered index value–SQL Server can acquire an exclusive (X) lock without an update (U) lock being used at all.

The number of locks to acquire also greatly depends on the execution plan. Let's run the `UPDATE Delivery.Orders SET Reference = 'Ref' WHERE OrderNum='1000'` statement, filtering data based on the `OrderNum` column. Figure 17-3 illustrates the locks that were acquired and released along with the total number of locks processed.

name	mode	resource_descri...	resource_type
lock_acquired	IU	1:4746	PAGE
lock_acquired	U	(c03154f3046a)	KEY
lock_released	U	(c03154f3046a)	KEY
lock_acquired	U	(20057a7cc0d6)	KEY
lock_released	U	(20057a7cc0d6)	KEY
lock_acquired	U	(d94911eb25da)	KEY
lock_released	U	(d94911eb25da)	KEY
lock_acquired	U	(e16c266249af)	KEY
lock_released	U	(e16c266249af)	KEY

package_name	event_name	count
sqlserver	lock_acquired	1070885
sqlserver	lock_released	1070885

Figure 17-3. *Locks during query execution*

There are no indexes on the `OrderNum` column, and SQL Server needs to perform a *clustered index scan*, acquiring an update (U) lock on every row from the table. More than one million locks have been acquired, even though the statement updated just a single row.

This behavior illustrates one of the typical blocking scenarios. Consider a situation where one of the sessions held an exclusive (X) lock on a single row. If another session tried to update a different row by running a nonoptimized `UPDATE` statement, SQL Server would acquire an update (U) lock on every row it is scanning and eventually would be blocked from reading the row with the exclusive (X) lock held on it. It does not matter that the second session does not need to update that row; SQL Server still needs to acquire an update (U) lock to evaluate if the row needs to be updated.

Shared (S) Locks

Shared (S) locks are acquired by the readers–`SELECT` queries–in the system. As you can guess by the name, shared (S) locks are compatible with each other, and multiple sessions can hold shared (S) locks on the same resource.

Let's run the code from Table 17-1 to illustrate that.

Table 17-1. *Shared (S) Locks*

Session 1 (SPID=53)	Session 2 (SPID=55)

`set transaction isolation level repeatable read`
`begin tran`
`    select OrderNum`
`    from Delivery.Orders`
`    where OrderId = 500;`
	`set transaction isolation level repeatable read`
	`begin tran`
	`    select OrderNum`
	`    from Delivery.Orders`
	`    where OrderId = 500;`

`select request_session_id, resource_type`
`    ,resource_description, request_type`
`    ,request_mode, request_status`
`from sys.dm_tran_locks;`
`commit;`
	`commit`

Figure 17-4 illustrates the output from the `sys.dm_tran_locks` view. As you can see, both sessions acquired shared (S) locks on the database, intent shared (IS) locks on the table and page (1:955), and shared (S) locks on the row, all without blocking each other.

	request_session_id	resource_type	resource_description	request_type	request_mode	request_status
1	53	DATABASE		LOCK	S	GRANT
2	55	DATABASE		LOCK	S	GRANT
3	53	PAGE	1:955	LOCK	IS	GRANT
4	55	PAGE	1:955	LOCK	IS	GRANT
5	53	KEY	(c07b8c04b989)	LOCK	S	GRANT
6	55	KEY	(c07b8c04b989)	LOCK	S	GRANT
7	53	OBJECT		LOCK	IS	GRANT
8	55	OBJECT		LOCK	IS	GRANT

***Figure 17-4.** Locks acquired by the sessions*

Lock Compatibility, Behavior, and Lifetime

Table 17-2 shows the lock compatibility matrix.

***Table 17-2.** Lock Compatibility Matrix (I*, S, U, X locks)*

	(IS)	(S)	(IU)	(U)	(IX)	(X)
(IS)	Yes	Yes	Yes	Yes	Yes	No
(S)	Yes	**Yes**	Yes	**Yes**	No	**No**
(IU)	Yes	Yes	Yes	No	Yes	No
(U)	Yes	**Yes**	No	**No**	No	**No**
(IX)	Yes	No	Yes	No	Yes	No
(X)	No	**No**	No	**No**	No	**No**

The key lock compatibility rules are as follows:

- Intent (IS/IU/IX) locks are compatible with each other. Intent locks indicate the existence of locks on the child objects, and multiple sessions can hold intent locks on the object and page levels simultaneously.
- Exclusive (X) locks are incompatible with each other and any other lock types. Multiple sessions cannot update the same row simultaneously. Moreover, readers that acquire shared (S) locks cannot read uncommitted rows with exclusive (X) locks held on them.
- Update (U) locks are incompatible with each other as well as with exclusive (X) locks. Writers cannot evaluate if the row needs to be updated simultaneously nor access a row that has an exclusive (X) lock held.
- Update (U) locks are compatible with shared (S) locks. Writers can evaluate if the row needs to be updated without a block or being blocked by the readers. It is worth noting that (S)/(U) lock compatibility is the main reason why SQL Server uses update (U) locks internally. They reduce the blocking between readers and writers.

As you already know, exclusive (X) lock behavior does not depend on transaction isolation level. **Writers always acquire exclusive (X) locks and hold them until the end of the transaction.** With the exception of the SNAPSHOT isolation level, the same is true for update (U) locks; writers use them when evaluating if rows need to be updated.

The shared (S) locks' behavior, on the other hand, depends on transaction isolation level.

■ **Note** SQL Server always works with the data in transaction context. In this case, when applications do not start explicit transactions with BEGIN TRAN/COMMIT statements, SQL Server uses implicit transactions for the duration of the statements. Even SELECT statements run within their own lightweight transactions. SQL Server does not write them to the transaction log, although all locking and concurrency rules still apply.

In the READ UNCOMMITTED isolation level, shared (S) locks are not acquired. Therefore, readers can read the rows that have been modified by other sessions and have exclusive (X) locks held on them. This isolation level reduces the blocking in the system by eliminating conflicts between readers and writers at the cost of the data consistency. Readers would read the current (modified) version of the row regardless of what happens next–if changes would be rolled back, or if a row is modified multiple times. This explains why this isolation level is often called a *dirty read*.

The code in Table 17-3 illustrates this. The first session runs a DELETE statement, acquiring an exclusive (X) lock on the row. The second session runs a SELECT statement in READ UNCOMMITTED mode.

Table 17-3. *Transaction Isolation Levels and Concurrency*

Session 1	Session 2

`begin tran`
`    delete from Delivery.Orders`
`    where OrderId = 95;`	

	`-- Success / No Blocking`
	`set transaction isolation level read uncommitted;`
	`select OrderId, Amount`
	`from Delivery.Orders`
	`where OrderId between 94 and 96;`

`rollback;`	

In the READ UNCOMMITTED isolation level, readers do not acquire shared (S) locks. Session 2 would not be blocked and would return the result set shown in Figure 17-5. It does not include the row with OrderId=95, which has been deleted in the uncommitted transaction in the first session, even though the transaction is rolled back afterward.

	OrderId	Amount
1	94	30.00
2	96	10.00

Figure 17-5. *READ UNCOMMITTED and shared (S) lock behavior*

It is worth noting again that exclusive (X) and update (U) locks' behavior is not affected by transaction isolation level. You will have writers/writers blocking even in READ UNCOMMITTED mode.

In the READ COMMITTED isolation level, SQL Server acquires and releases shared (S) locks immediately after the row has been read. This guarantees that transactions cannot read uncommitted data from the other sessions. Let's run the code from Listing 17-3.

Listing 17-3. Reading data in READ COMMITTED isolation level

```
set transaction isolation level read committed;
select OrderId, Amount
from Delivery.Orders
where OrderId in (90,91);
```

Figure 17-6 illustrates how SQL Server acquires and releases the locks. As you can see, row-level locks are acquired and released immediately.

name	mode	resource_descri...	resource_type
lock_acquired	IS		OBJECT
lock_acquired	IS	1:386	PAGE
lock_acquired	S	(bbd62f3afb44)	KEY
lock_released	S	(bbd62f3afb44)	KEY
lock_acquired	S	(a2ae6a22daf4)	KEY
lock_released	S	(a2ae6a22daf4)	KEY
lock_released	IS	1:386	PAGE
lock_released	IS		OBJECT

Figure 17-6. *Shared (S) locks' behavior in READ COMMITTED mode*

It is worth noting that in some cases, in READ COMMITTED mode, SQL Server can hold shared (S) locks for the duration of the SELECT statement. One such example is a query that reads LOB data from the table.

In the REPEATABLE READ isolation level, SQL Server acquires shared (S) locks and holds them until the end of transaction. This guarantees that other sessions cannot modify the data after it is read. You can see that behavior if you run the code from Listing 17-3, changing the isolation level to REPEATABLE READ.

Figure 17-7 illustrates how SQL Server acquires and releases the locks. As you can see, SQL Server acquires both shared (S) locks first, releasing them at the end of transaction.

name	mode	resource_descri...	resource_type
lock_acquired	IS		OBJECT
lock_acquired	IS	1:386	PAGE
lock_acquired	S	(bbd62f3afb44)	KEY
lock_acquired	S	(a2ae6a22daf4)	KEY
lock_released	S	(a2ae6a22daf4)	KEY
lock_released	S	(bbd62f3afb44)	KEY
lock_released	IS	1:386	PAGE
lock_released	IS		OBJECT

Figure 17-7. *Shared (S) locks' behavior in REPEATABLE READ mode*

In the SERIALIZABLE isolation level, shared (S) locks are also held until the end of transaction. However, SQL Server uses another variation of the locks called *range locks*. Range locks (both shared and exclusive) protect index key ranges rather than individual rows.

Consider a situation where a Delivery.Orders table has just two rows, with OrderId values of 1 and 10. In the REPEATABLE READ isolation level, a SELECT statement would acquire two row-level locks. Other sessions would not be able to modify those rows, but they could still insert the new row in between those values. In the SERIALIZABLE isolation level, a SELECT statement would acquire a range shared (RangeS-S) lock, preventing other sessions from inserting any rows in between OrderId of 1 and 10.

Figure 17-8 illustrates how SQL Server acquires and releases locks in the SERIALIZABLE isolation level.

name	mode	resource_descri...	resource_type
lock_acquired	IS		OBJECT
lock_acquired	IS	1:386	PAGE
lock_acquired	RS_S	(bbd62f3afb44)	KEY
lock_acquired	RS_S	(a2ae6a22daf4)	KEY
lock_released	RS_S	(a2ae6a22daf4)	KEY
lock_released	RS_S	(bbd62f3afb44)	KEY
lock_released	IS	1:386	PAGE
lock_released	IS		OBJECT

Figure 17-8. *Shared (S) locks' behavior in the SERIALIZABLE isolation level*

Table 17-4 summarizes how SQL Server works with shared (S) locks in pessimistic isolation levels.

Table 17-4. Pessimistic Transaction Isolation Levels and Shared (S) Locks' Behavior

Transaction isolation level	Table hint	Shared lock behavior
READ UNCOMMITTED	(NOLOCK)	(S) locks not acquired
READ COMMITTED (default)	(READCOMMITTED)	(S) locks acquired and released immediately
REPEATABLE READ	(REPEATABLEREAD)	(S) locks acquired and held till end of transaction
SERIALIZABLE	(SERIALIZABLE) or (XLOCK)	Range locks acquired and held till end of transaction

You can control isolation levels and locking behavior on the transaction level by using the SET TRANSACTION ISOLATION LEVEL statement, or on the table level with the table locking hint. It is also possible to use different isolation levels in the same query on a per-table basis, as it is shown in Listing 17-4.

Listing 17-4. Controlling locking behavior with table hints

```
select c.CustomerName, sum(o.Total) as [Total]
from dbo.Customers c with (READCOMMITTED)
    join dbo.Orders o with (SERIALIZABLE) on
        o.CustomerId = c.CustomerId
group by
    c.CustomerName;
```

You can control the type of locks acquired by readers with the (UPDLOCK) and (XLOCK) table hints. Those hints force SELECT queries to use update (U) and exclusive (X) locks, respectively, rather than shared (S) locks. This can be useful when you need to prevent multiple SELECT queries from accessing the data simultaneously.

Listing 17-5 demonstrates how you can implement custom counters in the system. The SELECT statement uses an exclusive (X) lock, which will block other sessions from reading the same counter row until the transaction is committed.

■ **Note** This code is shown for demonstration only, and it does not handle the situation where a specific counter does not exist in the table. It is better to use a SEQUENCE object instead.

Listing 17-5. Counters table management

```
begin tran
    select @Value = Value
    from dbo.Counters with (XLOCK)
    where CounterName = @CounterName;

    update dbo.Counters
    set Value += @ReserveCount
    where CounterName = @CounterName;
commit
```

Another locking hint (READPAST) allows sessions to skip rows with incompatible locks held rather than being blocked. You will see an example of when such a hint is useful in Chapter 22 of this book.

■ **Note** For more information about table hints, go to http://msdn.microsoft.com/en-us/library/ms187373.aspx.

Transaction Isolation Levels and Data Consistency

Finally, let's analyze common data inconsistency issues that exist in multi-user environments.

Dirty Reads: This issue arises when a transaction reads uncommitted (dirty) data from other uncommitted transactions. It is unknown if those active transactions would be committed or rolled back or if data is logically consistent. Think about the example where a user transfers money from a checking to a savings account. There are two physical operations with the data, decreasing checking and increasing savings account balances, logically combined in one transaction. If another session reads account balances in between the two updates, the results would be incorrect.

From the locking prospective, this phenomenon could occur in the READ UNCOMMITTED isolation level when sessions do not acquire shared (S) locks, ignoring exclusive (X) locks from the other sessions. All other pessimistic isolation levels use shared (S) locks and are protected from dirty reads.

Non-Repeatable Reads: Subsequent attempts to read the same data from within the same transaction return different results. This data inconsistency issue arises when the other transactions modified or even deleted data between the reads. Consider a situation where you render a report that displays a list of orders for a specific customer along with some aggregated information (for example, total amount spent by customer on a monthly basis). If another session modifies or, perhaps, deletes the orders in between those queries, the result sets will be inconsistent.

From the locking standpoint, such a phenomenon could occur when sessions don't protect/lock the data in between reads. This could happen in the READ UNCOMMITTED isolation level that does not use shared (S) locks, as well as in the READ COMMITTED isolation level, where sessions acquire and release shared (S) locks immediately. REPEATABLE READ and SERIALIZABLE isolation levels hold the shared (S) locks until the end of the transaction, which prevents data modifications once data is read.

Phantom Reads: This phenomenon occurs when subsequent reads within the same transaction return new rows (the ones that the transaction did not read before). Think about the previous example where another session inserted a new order in between the queries' execution. Only the SERIALIZABLE isolation level with range locks is free from such phenomenon.

Two other phenomena are related to data movement due to a change of the index key value:

Duplicated Reads: This issue occurs when a query returns the same row multiple times. Think about the query that returns the list of the orders for the specific time interval, scanning the index on the OrderDate column during the execution. If another query changes the OrderDate value, moving the row from the processed (scanned) to the non-processed part of the index, such a row will be read twice.

This condition is similar to non-repeatable reads and can occur when readers do not hold shared (S) locks after rows were read in `READ UNCOMMITTED` and `READ COMMITTED` isolation levels.

Skipped Rows: This phenomenon occurs when queries do not return some of the rows. It could occur in a situation similar to the duplicated reads just described, where rows have been moved from the non-processed to the processed part of the index. Only the `SERIALIZABLE` isolation level, which locks the index key range interval, is free from such phenomenon.

Table 17-5 summarizes data inconsistency issues within different transaction isolation levels.

Table 17-5. *Transaction Isolation Levels and Data Inconsistency Anomalies*

	Dirty Reads	Non-Repeatable Reads	Duplicated Reads	Phantom Reads	Skipped Rows
`READ UNCOMMITTED`	Yes	Yes	Yes	Yes	Yes
`READ COMMITTED`	No	Yes	Yes	Yes	Yes
`REPEATABLE READ`	No	No	No	Yes	Yes
`SERIALIZABLE`	No	No	No	No	No

`SERIALIZABLE` is the only pessimistic transaction isolation level that protects you from data inconsistency issues. However, this isolation level introduces major concurrency issues due to excessive locking in systems with volatile data. Fortunately, optimistic isolation levels, which we will discuss in Chapter 21, could address inconsistency phenomena without introducing excessive blocking in the system.

Summary

SQL Server uses locking to support data-isolation and -consistency rules, using row-level locking as the highest degree of granularity.

Exclusive (X) locks are acquired by writers when data is modified. Exclusive (X) locks are always acquired and held until the end of transactions, regardless of the isolation level. Update (U) locks are acquired when writers evaluate if data needs to be modified. These locks are converted into exclusive (X) locks if rows need to be updated. Intent (I*) locks are acquired on the object and page levels, and they indicate the existence of child row-level locks of the same type.

With the exception of the `READ UNCOMMITED` isolation level, SQL Server acquires shared (S) locks while reading data in pessimistic isolation levels. Transaction isolation level controls when shared (S) locks are released. In the `READ COMMITTED` isolation level, these locks are released immediately after the row has been read. In `REPEATABLE READ` and `SERIALIZABLE` isolation levels, shared (S) locks are held until the end of the transaction. Moreover, in the `SERIALIZABLE` isolation level, SQL Server uses range locks, locking the ranges of the index keys rather than individual rows.

You can control transaction isolation levels with the `SET TRANSACTION ISOLATION LEVEL` statement on the transaction level or with table locking hints on the per-table level in the individual queries.

CHAPTER 18

Troubleshooting Blocking Issues

Blocking is one of the most common problems encountered in systems. When blocking occurs, multiple queries block each other, which increases the execution time of queries and introduces timeouts. All of this negatively affects the user's experience with the system.

This chapter provides an overview of how you can troubleshoot blocking issues in a system.

General Troubleshooting Approach

Blocking occurs when multiple sessions compete for the same resource. Even though in some cases this is the correct and expected behavior (for example, multiple sessions cannot update the same row simultaneously), more often than not it happens because of unnecessary scans due to nonoptimized queries.

Some degree of blocking always exists in systems, and it is completely normal. What is not normal, however, is excessive blocking. From the end user's standpoint, excessive blocking masks itself as a general performance problem. The system is slow, queries are timing out, and there are deadlocks. With the exception of deadlocks, slow performance is not necessarily a sign of blocking issues; there could easily be nonoptimized queries by themselves. However, blocking issues can definitely contribute to a general system slowdown.

Note One of the easiest ways to find out if the system suffers from blocking is by looking at the lock waits in the wait statistics, which we will discuss in Part V of this book.

In a nutshell, to troubleshoot blocking issues you must follow these steps:

1. Detect the queries involved in the blocking.
2. Find out why blocking occurs.
3. Fix the root cause of the issue.

SQL Server provides you with several tools that can help you troubleshoot blocking issues in a system. These tools can be separated into two different categories. The first category consists of dynamic management views (DMVs) that you can use to troubleshoot what is happening in the system at present. These tools are useful when you have access to the system at the time of blocking, and you want to perform real-time troubleshooting.

The second category of tools allows you to collect information about blocking problems in the system and retain it for further analysis. Let's look at both categories in detail.

D. Korotkevitch, *Pro SQL Server Internals*, DOI 10.1007/978-1-4842-1964-5_18

Troubleshooting Blocking Issues in Real Time

The key tool for troubleshooting real-time blocking is the `sys.dm_tran_locks` dynamic management view, which provides information about currently active requests to the Lock Manager. It returns you a list of lock requests and their status, such as `GRANT` or `WAIT`, information about resources on which locks were requested, and several other useful attributes.

Table 18-1 shows you the code that leads to the blocking conditions.

Table 18-1. *Code That Leads to the Blocking Conditions*

Session 1 (SPID=52)	Session 2 (SPID=53)	Comments
`set transaction isolation level read uncommitted begin tran delete from Delivery.Orders where OrderId = 95`		Session 1 acquires exclusive (X) lock on the row with OrderId=95
	`select OrderId, Amount from Delivery.Orders with (readcommitted) where OrderNum = '1000'`	Session 2 is blocked trying to acquire shared (S) lock on the row with OrderId=95
`rollback`		

Figure 18-1 shows the partial output from the `sys.dm_tran_locks`, `sys.dm_os_waiting_tasks`, and `sys.dm_exec_requests` views at the time the blocking occurred. As you can see, Session 53 is waiting for a shared (S) lock on the row with the exclusive (X) lock held by Session 52. The `LCK_M_S` wait type in the output indicates the shared (S) lock wait. We will discuss wait types in more detail in Part V of this book.

	request_session_id	resource_type	resource_description	request_mode	request_type	request_status
1	53	DATABASE		S	LOCK	GRANT
2	52	DATABASE		S	LOCK	GRANT
3	53	PAGE	1:377	IS	LOCK	GRANT
4	52	PAGE	1:377	IX	LOCK	GRANT
5	52	KEY	(5be201b53ff8)	X	LOCK	GRANT
6	53	KEY	(5be201b53ff8)	S	LOCK	WAIT
7	53	OBJECT		IS	LOCK	GRANT
8	52	OBJECT		IX	LOCK	GRANT

	session_id	wait_duration_ms	wait_type	blocking_session_id	resource_description
1	53	157064	LCK_M_S	52	keylock hobtid=72057594067025920 dbi...

	session_id	status	wait_type	wait_time	wait_resource	command
1	53	suspended	LCK_M_S	157064	KEY: 13:72057594067025920 (5be201b53ff8)	SELECT

Figure 18-1. *Output from the system views at time of blocking*

The information provided by the `sys.dm_tran_locks` view is a bit too cryptic to troubleshoot, and you need to join it with other dynamic management views, such as `sys.dm_exec_requests` and `sys.dm_os_waiting_tasks`, to gain a clearer picture. Listing 18-1 provides the required code.

Listing 18-1. Getting more information about blocked and blocking sessions

```
select
    tl.resource_type as [Resource Type]
    ,db_name(tl.resource_database_id) as [DB Name]
    ,case tl.resource_type
        when 'OBJECT' then object_name(tl.resource_associated_entity_id
            ,tl.resource_database_id)
        when 'DATABASE' then 'DB'
        else
            case when tl.resource_database_id = db_id()
                then
                     (  select object_name(object_id, tl.resource_database_id)
                        from sys.partitions
                        where hobt_id = tl.resource_associated_entity_id )
                else '(Run under DB context)'
            end
    end as [Object]
    ,tl.resource_description as [Resource]
    ,tl.request_session_id as [Session]
    ,tl.request_mode as [Mode]
    ,tl.request_status as [Status]
    ,wt.wait_duration_ms as [Wait (ms)]
    ,qi.sql
    ,qi.query_plan
from
    sys.dm_tran_locks tl with (nolock) left outer join
        sys.dm_os_waiting_tasks wt with (nolock) on
            tl.lock_owner_address = wt.resource_address and tl.request_status = 'WAIT'
    outer apply
    (
        select
            substring(s.text, (er.statement_start_offset / 2) + 1,
                 ((  case er.statement_end_offset
                          when -1
                          then datalength(s.text)
                          else er.statement_end_offset
                     end - er.statement_start_offset) / 2) + 1) as sql
            , qp.query_plan
        from
            sys.dm_exec_requests er with (nolock)
                cross apply sys.dm_exec_sql_text(er.sql_handle) s
                outer apply sys.dm_exec_query_plan(er.plan_handle) qp
        where
            tl.request_session_id = er.session_id
    ) qi
where
    tl.request_session_id <> @@spid
order by
    tl.request_session_id
option (recompile)
```

Figure 18-2 shows the results of the query. As you can see, it is much easier to understand, and it provides you with more-useful information, including currently running batches and their execution plans. Keep in mind that the execution plans obtained from the DMVs in this chapter do not include the actual execution statistics metrics, such as the actual number of rows returned by operators and the number of their execution.

	Resource Type	DB Name	Object	Resource	Session	Mode	Status	Wait (ms)	sql	query_plan
1	DATABASE	SQLServerInternals	DB		52	S	GRANT	NULL	NULL	NULL
2	OBJECT	SQLServerInternals	Orders		52	IX	GRANT	NULL	NULL	NULL
3	PAGE	SQLServerInternals	Orders	1:377	52	IX	GRANT	NULL	NULL	NULL
4	KEY	SQLServerInternals	Orders	(5be201b53ff8)	52	X	GRANT	NULL	NULL	NULL
5	KEY	SQLServerInternals	Orders	(5be201b53ff8)	53	S	WAIT	486032	select OrderId, Amount fro...	<ShowPlanXML xmlns="h...
6	DATABASE	SQLServerInternals	DB		53	S	GRANT	NULL	select OrderId, Amount fro...	<ShowPlanXML xmlns="h...
7	PAGE	SQLServerInternals	Orders	1:377	53	IS	GRANT	NULL	select OrderId, Amount fro...	<ShowPlanXML xmlns="h...
8	OBJECT	SQLServerInternals	Orders		53	IS	GRANT	NULL	select OrderId, Amount fro...	<ShowPlanXML xmlns="h...

***Figure 18-2.** Joining sys.dm_os_tran_locks with other DMVs*

■ **Note** You need to run the query in the context of the database involved in the blocking to correctly resolve the object names. Also of importance is that, for the sessions in which lock requests were granted, SQL and Query Plan represent the currently executed batch, rather than the batch that triggered the original locking request.

The `sys.dm_tran_locks` view returns one row for each active lock request in the system, which can lead to very large result sets when you run it on busy servers. You can reduce the amount of information and perform a self-join of this view based on the `resource_description` and `resource_associated_entity_id` columns, and you can identify the sessions that compete for the same resources. Such an approach allows you to filter the results and only see the sessions that are involved in the blocking chains.

Listing 18-2 and Figure 18-3 illustrate the code and query results.

Listing 18-2. Filtering out blocked and blocking session information

```
select
    tl1.resource_type as [Resource Type]
    ,db_name(tl1.resource_database_id) as [DB Name]
    ,case tl1.resource_type
        when 'OBJECT' then object_name(tl1.resource_associated_entity_id
            ,tl1.resource_database_id)
        when 'DATABASE' then 'DB'
        else
            case when tl1.resource_database_id = db_id()
                then
                    (  select object_name(object_id, tl1.resource_database_id)
                       from sys.partitions
                       where hobt_id = tl1.resource_associated_entity_id )
                else '(Run under DB context)'
            end
    end as [Object]
    ,tl1.resource_description as [Resource]
    ,tl1.request_session_id as [Session]
    ,tl1.request_mode as [Mode]
    ,tl1.request_status as [Status]
    ,wt.wait_duration_ms as [Wait (ms)]
```

```
        ,qi.sql
        ,qi.query_plan
from
    sys.dm_tran_locks tl1 with (nolock) join sys.dm_tran_locks tl2 with (nolock) on
        tl1.resource_associated_entity_id = tl2.resource_associated_entity_id
    left outer join sys.dm_os_waiting_tasks wt with (nolock) on
        tl1.lock_owner_address = wt.resource_address and tl1.request_status = 'WAIT'
    outer apply
    (
        select
            substring(s.text, (er.statement_start_offset / 2) + 1,
                ((  case er.statement_end_offset
                        when -1
                        then datalength(s.text)
                        else er.statement_end_offset
                    end - er.statement_start_offset) / 2) + 1) as sql
            , qp.query_plan
        from
            sys.dm_exec_requests er with (nolock)
                cross apply sys.dm_exec_sql_text(er.sql_handle) s
                outer apply sys.dm_exec_query_plan(er.plan_handle) qp
        where
            tl1.request_session_id = er.session_id
    ) qi
where
    tl1.request_status <> tl2.request_status and
    (
        tl1.resource_description = tl2.resource_description or
        ( tl1.resource_description is null and tl2.resource_description is null )
    )
option (recompile)
```

	Resource Type	DB Name	Object	Resource	Session	Mode	Status	Wait (ms)	sql	query_plan
1	KEY	SQLServerInternals	Orders	(5be201b53ff8)	52	X	GRANT	NULL	NULL	NULL
2	KEY	SQLServerInternals	Orders	(5be201b53ff8)	53	S	WAIT	486154	select OrderId, Amount fr...	<ShowPlanXML xmlns="htt...

***Figure 18-3.** Blocked and blocking sessions*

As you already know, blocking occurs when two or more sessions are competing for the same resource. You need to answer two questions during troubleshooting:

Why does the *blocking* session hold the lock on the resource?

Why does the *blocked* session acquire the lock on the resource?

It is usually easier to start troubleshooting by looking at the *blocked* session, where you have the blocked statement and its execution plan available. In many cases, you can identify the root cause of the blocking by analyzing its execution plan, which you can obtain from the dynamic management views (as was just demonstrated) or by re-running the query.

Figure 18-4 shows the execution plan of the blocked query from our example.

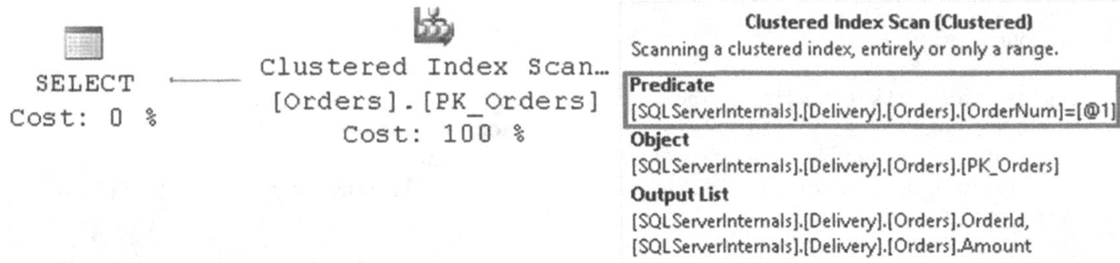

Figure 18-4. *Execution plan for the blocked query*

As you can see from the execution plan, the blocked query is scanning the entire table looking for orders with the predicate on the `OrderNum` column. The query uses a `READ COMMITTED` transaction isolation level, and it acquires a shared (S) lock on every row in the table. As a result, at some point the query is blocked by the first `DELETE` query that holds an exclusive (X) lock on one of the rows. It is worth noting that the query would be blocked even if the row with the exclusive (X) lock held did not have `OrderNum='1000'`. SQL Server cannot evaluate the predicate until the shared (S) lock is acquired and the row is read.

You can resolve the problem by optimizing the query and adding an index on the `OrderNum` column, which will replace the *clustered index scan* with a *nonclustered index seek* operator in the execution plan. This will eliminate lock collision and blocking as long as the queries do not delete and select the same rows.

Even though in many instances you can detect and resolve the root cause of the blocking by analyzing and optimizing the *blocked* query, this is not always the case. Consider a situation where you have a session that updated a large number of rows in a table and thus acquired and held a large number of exclusive (X) locks on those rows. Other sessions that need to access those rows would be blocked, even in the case of efficient execution plans that do not perform unnecessary scans. The root cause of the blocking in this case is the *blocking* rather than the *blocked* session.

Unfortunately, it is much harder to detect the statement that acquired the locks. The queries from Listings 18-1 and 18-2 provide you with information about currently running statements in *blocking* sessions, rather than intelligence about the statement that caused the blocking condition. Moreover, in some cases where a client application has an error and keeps an uncommitted transaction idle, queries do not return any information at all. You can see such a condition in Figures 18-2 and 18-3, where both SQL statements and execution plans were `NULL`. In such cases, you need to analyze what code in the blocking session has caused the blocking. You can use the `sys.dm_exec_sessions` view to obtain information about the host and application of the blocking session. When you know which statement the blocking session is currently executing, you can analyze the client and T-SQL code to locate the transaction to which this statement belongs. One of the previously executed statements in that transaction would be the one that caused the blocking condition.

A *blocked process report*, which we are about to discuss, can also help during such troubleshooting.

Collecting Blocking Information for Further Analysis

Although DMVs can be very useful in providing information about the current state of the system, they would not help much if you did not run them at the exact same time the blocking occurred. Fortunately, SQL Server helps capture blocking information automatically via the *blocked process report*. This report provides information about the blocking condition, which you may retain for further analysis.

There is a configuration setting called *blocked process threshold* that specifies how often SQL Server checks for blocking in the system and generates a report. Listing 18-3 shows the code that sets the threshold to ten seconds.

Listing 18-3. Specifying blocking process threshold

```
sp_configure 'show advanced options', 1;
go
reconfigure;
go
sp_configure 'blocked process threshold', 10; -- in seconds
go
reconfigure;
go
```

You need to fine-tune the value of the blocked process threshold in production. It is important to avoid false positives and, at the same time, capture the problems. Microsoft suggests not going below five seconds as the minimum value, and you obviously need to set the value to less than query timeout.

There are a few ways to capture that report in the system. You can use SQL Trace–there is a "Blocked Process Report" event in the "Errors and Warnings" section, as shown in Figure 18-5.

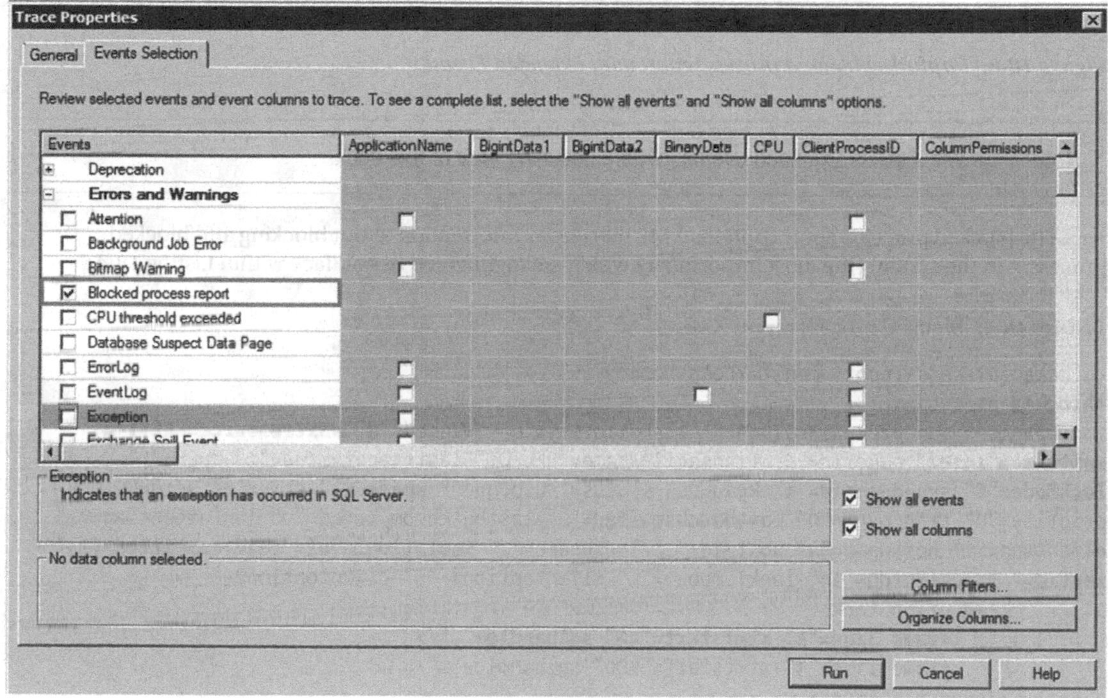

Figure 18-5. *Blocked process report event in SQL Trace*

Alternatively, you can create an Extended Event Session using the `blocked_process_report` event, as shown in Figure 18-6. This session will provide you with several additional attributes other than what is provided by SQL Trace.

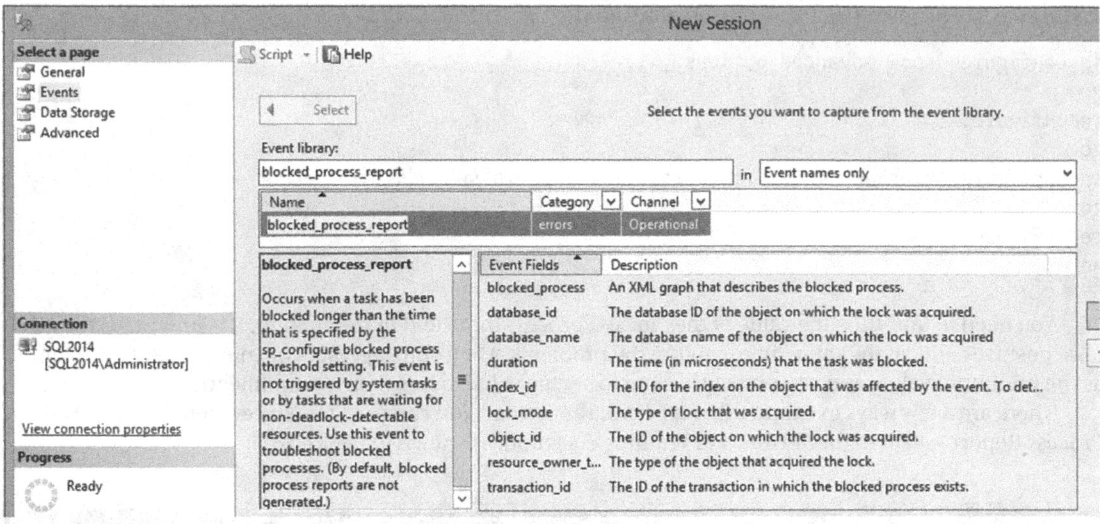

Figure 18-6. *Capturing blocked process report with Extended Events*

■ **Note** We will discuss Extended Events in more detail in Part V of this book.

The blocked process report contains XML that shows information about blocking and blocked processes in the system (the most important of which are highlighted in boldface within Listing 18-4).

Listing 18-4. Blocked process report XML

```
<blocked-process-report monitorLoop="224">
<blocked-process>
    <process id="process3e576c928" taskpriority="0" logused="0" waitresource="KEY: …"
waittime="14102" ownerId="…" transactionname="SELECT" lasttranstarted="…" XDES="…"
lockMode="S" schedulerid="1" kpid="…" status="suspended" spid="53" sbid="0" ecid="0"
priority="0" trancount="0" lastbatchstarted="…" lastbatchcompleted="…" lastattention="…"
clientapp="…" hostname="…" hostpid="…" loginname="…" isolationlevel="read committed (2)"
xactid="…" currentdb="14" lockTimeout="…" clientoption1="…" clientoption2="…">
        <executionStack>
            <frame line="3" stmtstart="46" sqlhandle="…"/>
            <frame line="3" stmtstart="100" sqlhandle="…"/>
        </executionStack>
        <inputbuf>
set transaction isolation level read committed
select OrderId, Amount
from Delivery.Orders
where OrderNum = '1000'
        </inputbuf>
    </process>
</blocked-process>
<blocking-process>
```

```
    <process status="sleeping" spid="54" sbid="0" ecid="0" priority="0" trancount="1"
lastbatchstarted="..." lastbatchcompleted="..." lastattention="..." clientapp="..."
hostname="..." hostpid="..." loginname="..." isolationlevel="read uncommitted (1)"
xactid="..." currentdb="14" lockTimeout="..." clientoption1="..." clientoption2="...">
        <executionStack/>
        <inputbuf>
set transaction isolation level read uncommitted
begin tran
        delete from Delivery.Orders
        where OrderId = 95
        </inputbuf>
    </process>
</blocking-process>
</blocked-process-report>
```

As with real-time troubleshooting, you should analyze both blocking and blocked processes and find the root cause of the problem. From the blocked-process standpoint, the most important information is the following:

waittime: The length of time the query is waiting, in milliseconds

lockMode: The type of lock being waited for

isolationlevel: The transaction isolation level

executionStack and *inputBuf*: The query and/or the execution stack. You will see how to obtain the actual SQL statement involved in blocking in Listing 18-5.

From the blocking-process standpoint, you must look at the following:

status: Status is whether the process is *running*, *sleeping*, or *suspended*. In a situation in which the process is sleeping, there is an uncommitted transaction. When the process is suspended, that process either waits for the resource (for example, page from the disk) or there is a blocking chain involved. We will talk more about the SQL Server execution model in Part V of this book.

trancount: A `trancount` value greater than 1 indicates nested transactions. If the process status is *sleeping* at the same time, then there is a good chance that the client did not commit the nested transactions correctly (for example, the number of `commit` statements is less than the number of `begin tran` statements in the code).

executionStack and *inputBuf*: As we already discussed, in some cases you need to analyze what happens in the blocking process. Some common issues include runaway transactions (for example, missing `commit` statements in the nested transactions); long-running transactions with, perhaps, some UI involved; or excessive scans (for example, a missing index on the referencing column in the detail table leads to scans during a referential integrity check). Information about queries from the blocking session could be useful here. Remember that in cases of a blocked process, *executionStack* and *inputBuf* would correspond to the queries that were running at the moment when the blocked process report was generated rather than at the time of the blocking.

Nevertheless, in a large number of cases, blocking occurs because of unnecessary scans due to nonoptimized queries, and you can detect it by analyzing blocked queries. So, the next logical step is to look at the blocked query execution plan and detect inefficiencies. You can either run the query and check the execution plan or use DMVs and obtain an execution plan from `sys.dm_exec_query_stats` based on the `sql_handle`, `stmtStart`, and `stmtEnd` elements from the execution stack. Listing 18-5 and Figure 18-7 show the code and query output for this strategy.

Listing 18-5. Obtaining query text and execution plan

```
declare
    @H varbinary(max) = /* Insert sql_handle from the top line of the execution stack */
    ,@S int =  /* Insert stmtStart from the top line of the execution stack */
    ,@E int = /* Insert stmtEnd from the top line of the execution stack */

select
    substring(qt.text, (qs.statement_start_offset / 2) + 1,
        (( case qs.statement_end_offset
                when -1 then datalength(qt.text)
                else qs.statement_end_offset
            end - qs.statement_start_offset) / 2) + 1) as sql
    ,qp.query_plan
    ,qs.creation_time
    ,qs.last_execution_time
from
    sys.dm_exec_query_stats qs with (nolock)
        cross apply sys.dm_exec_sql_text(qs.sql_handle) qt
        outer apply sys.dm_exec_query_plan(qs.plan_handle) qp
where
    qs.sql_handle = @H and
    qs.statement_start_offset = @S
    and qs.statement_end_offset = @E
option (recompile)
```

	SQL	query_plan
1	SELECT [OrderId],[Amount] FR...	<ShowPlanXML xmlns="http://schema...

Figure 18-7. *Getting information from sys.dm_exec_query_stats*

There are a couple of potential problems with the `sys.dm_exec_query_stats` view that you should be aware of. First, this view relies on the execution plan cache. You would not be able to get the execution plan if it is not in the cache; for example, if the query used a statement-level recompile with an `option (recompile)` clause.

Second, there is a chance that you will have more than one cached plan returned. In some cases, SQL Server keeps the execution statistics even after recompilation occurs, which could produce multiple rows in the result set. Moreover, you may have multiple cached plans when sessions use different `SET` options. There are two columns—`creation_time` and `last_execution_time`—that can help you pinpoint the right plan.

This dependency on the plan cache during troubleshooting is the biggest downside of the blocked process report. SQL Server eventually removes old plans from the plan cache after queries are recompiled and/or plans are not reused. Therefore, the longer you wait with the troubleshooting, the less chance you have that the plan would be present in the cache.

One of the ways to address this issue is by building a monitoring solution based on Extended Events and/or Event Notifications. This allows you to parse the blocked process report at the time of the blocking and increases the chance that you will capture the right execution plan, compared to starting analysis later. I have included an example showing how to set up monitoring with Event Notifications in the companion materials of the book.

SQL Server 2016 allows you to collect and persist information about running queries and their execution plans and statistics in a new component called *Query Store*. The Query Store does not rely on the plan cache, and it is extremely useful during system troubleshooting. We will discuss Query Store in greater depth in Part V of this book.

Summary

The process of troubleshooting blocking issues in a system requires you to detect the queries involved in the blocking, find the root cause of the problem, and address the issue.

The `sys.dm_tran_locks` data management view provides you with information about all of the active lock requests in the system. It can help you detect blocking situations in real time. You can join this view with other DMVs, such as `sys.dm_exec_requests`, `sys.dm_exec_query_stats`, `sys.dm_exec_sessions`, and `sys.dm_os_waiting_tasks`, to obtain more information about the sessions and queries involved in the blocking conditions.

SQL Server can generate a *blocking process report* that provides you with information about blocking, which you can collect and retain for further analysis. You can use SQL Traces, Extended Events, and Event Notifications to capture it.

In a large number of cases, blocking occurs due to excessive scans introduced by nonoptimized queries. You should analyze the execution plans of both blocking and blocked queries in order to detect and optimize inefficiencies.

Another common issue that results in blocking is incorrect transaction management in the code, which includes runaway transactions and interaction with users in the middle of open transactions, among other things.

CHAPTER 19

Deadlocks

A *deadlock* is a special blocking case when multiple sessions, or sometimes multiple execution threads within a single session, block each other. When it happens, SQL Server terminates one of the sessions, thus allowing others to continue.

This chapter demonstrates why deadlocks occur in the system and explains how to troubleshoot and resolve them.

Classic Deadlock

A classic deadlock occurs when two or more sessions are competing for the same set of resources. Let's look at a by-the-book example and assume that you have two sessions updating two rows in the table in the opposite order.

As the first step, session 1 updates the row *R1* and session 2 updates the row *R2*. You know that at this point both sessions acquire and hold exclusive (X) locks on the rows. You can see this happening in Figure 19-1.

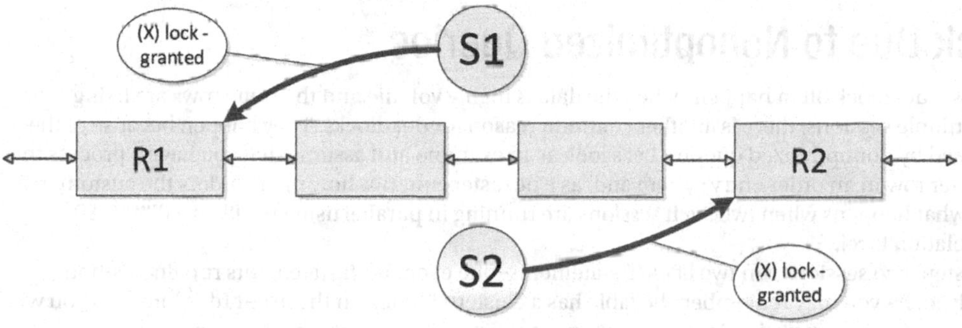

***Figure 19-1.** Classic deadlock, step 1*

Next, let's assume that session 1 wants to update the row *R2*. It will try to acquire an exclusive (X) lock on *R2* and will be blocked because of the exclusive (X) lock already held by session 2. If session 2 wants to update *R1*, the same thing will happen–it will be blocked because of the exclusive (X) lock held by session 1. As you can see, at this point both sessions wait on each other and cannot continue the execution. This represents the classic deadlock, shown in Figure 19-2.

D. Korotkevitch, *Pro SQL Server Internals*, DOI 10.1007/978-1-4842-1964-5_19

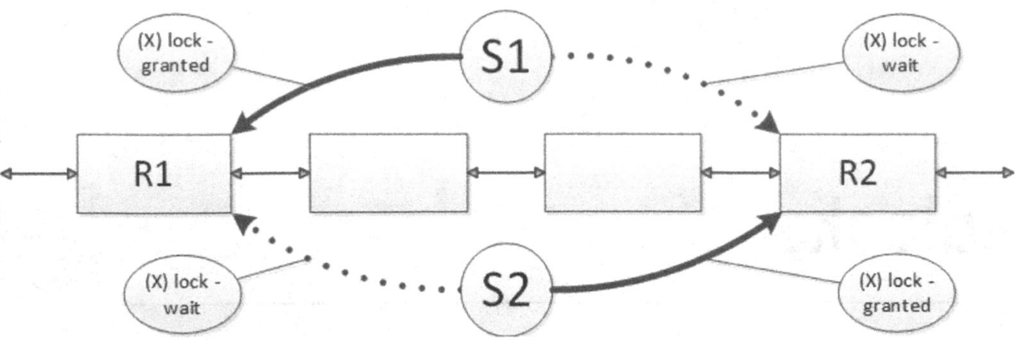

Figure 19-2. *Classic deadlock, step 2*

There is the system task *Deadlock Monitor* that wakes up every five seconds and checks if there are any deadlocks in the system. When a deadlock is detected, SQL Server rolls back one of the transactions. That releases all locks held in that transaction and allows other sessions to continue.

■ **Note** The Deadlock Monitor wake-up interval goes down if there are deadlocks in the system. In some cases, it could wake up as often as ten times per second.

The choice of which session is chosen as the deadlock victim depends on a few things. By default, SQL Server rolls back the session that uses less log space for the transaction. You can control it, up to a degree, by setting deadlock priority for the session with the `SET DEADLOCK_PRIORITY` command.

Deadlock Due to Nonoptimized Queries

While the classic deadlock often happens when the data is highly volatile and the same rows are being updated by multiple sessions, there is another common reason for deadlocks. They happen because of the scans introduced by nonoptimized queries. Let's look at an example and assume that you have a process that updates an order row in an order entry system and, as a next step, queries how many orders the customer has. Let's see what happens when two such sessions are running in parallel using the `READ COMMITTED` transaction isolation level.

As a first step, two sessions run two `UPDATE` statements–one each. Both statements run fine without blocking involved. As you may remember, the table has a clustered index on the `OrderId` column, so you will have a *clustered index seek* operation in the execution plan. Figure 19-3 illustrates this step.

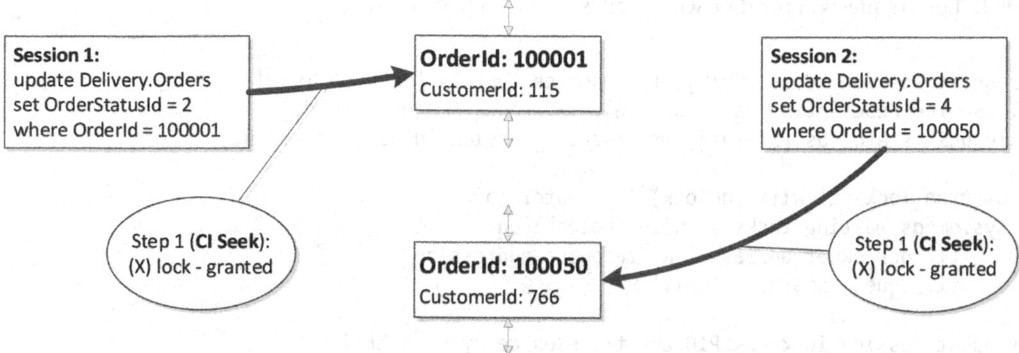

***Figure 19-3.** Deadlock due to scans, step 1*

At this point, both sessions hold exclusive (X) locks on their respective updated rows. For the second step, the sessions each run `SELECT` statements based on the `CustomerId` filter. There are no nonclustered indexes on the table, so the execution plan will have a *clustered index scan* operation. In the `READ COMMITTED` isolation level, SQL Server acquires shared (S) locks when reading data, and, as a result, each session would be blocked as soon as it tried to read the row with an exclusive (X) lock held. Figure 19-4 illustrates this.

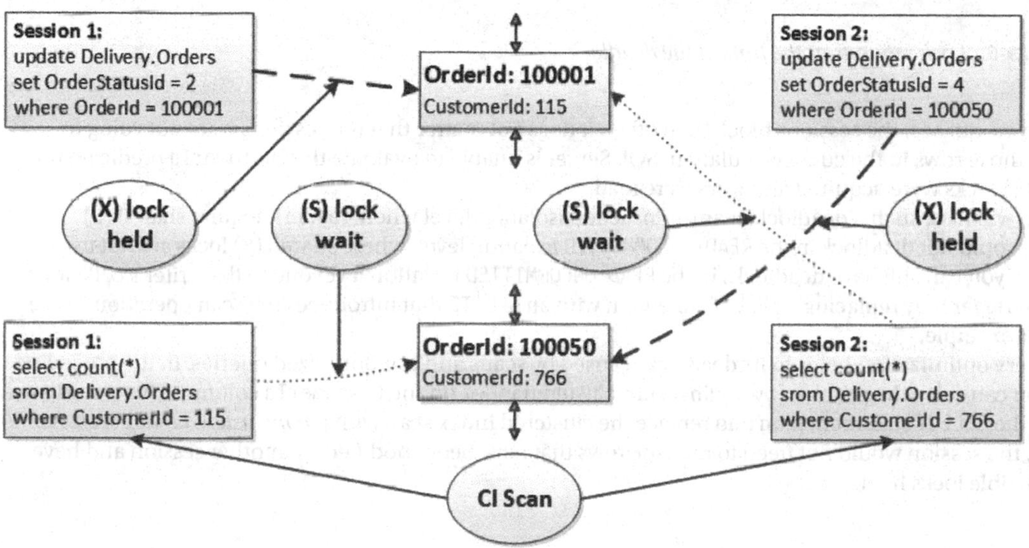

***Figure 19-4.** Deadlock due to scans, step 2*

If you ran the query shown in Listing 19-1 at the time when both sessions were blocked and before the Deadlock Monitor task woke up, you would see the results shown in Figure 19-5.

Listing 19-1. Lock requests at the time when both sessions were blocked

```
select
    tl.request_session_id as [SPID], tl.resource_type as [Resouce Type]
    ,tl.resource_description as [Resource], tl.request_mode as [Mode]
    ,tl.request_status as [Status], wt.blocking_session_id as [Blocked By]
from
    sys.dm_tran_locks tl with (nolock) left outer join
        sys.dm_os_waiting_tasks wt with (nolock) on
            tl.lock_owner_address = wt.resource_address and
            tl.request_status = 'WAIT'
where
    tl.request_session_id <> @@SPID and tl.resource_type = 'KEY'
order by
    tl.request_session_id
```

	SPID	Resouce Type	Resource	Mode	Status	Blocked By
1	51	KEY	(2fe59e02884b)	S	WAIT	52
2	51	KEY	(74a07545ba5b)	X	GRANT	NULL
3	52	KEY	(74a07545ba5b)	S	WAIT	51
4	52	KEY	(2fe59e02884b)	X	GRANT	NULL

Figure 19-5. *Lock requests at the time of the deadlock*

As you can see, the sessions block each other. It does not matter that the sessions were not going to include those rows in the count calculation. SQL Server is unable to evaluate the `CustomerId` predicate until shared (S) locks were acquired and rows were read.

You will have such a deadlock in any transaction isolation level where readers acquire shared (S) locks. It would not deadlock in the `READ UNCOMMITTED` isolation level, where shared (S) locks are not used. However, you can still have deadlocks in the `READ UNCOMMITTED` isolation level due to the writer's collision. You can trigger it by replacing a `SELECT` statement with an `UPDATE` that introduces the scan operation in the previous example.

Query optimization helps to fix deadlocks caused by scans and nonoptimized queries. In the preceding case, you can solve the problem by adding a nonclustered index on the `CustomerId` column. This would change the `SELECT` statement plan and replace the clustered index scan with a *nonclustered index seek*. As a result, the session would not need to read the rows that have been modified by another session and have incompatible locks held.

Key Lookup Deadlock

In some cases, you can have a deadlock when multiple sessions are trying to read and update the same row simultaneously.

Let's assume that you have a nonclustered index on the table, and one session wants to read the row using this index. If the index is not covering and the session needs some data from the clustered index, you would have an execution plan with the *nonclustered index seek* and *key lookup* operations. The session would acquire shared (S) locks on the nonclustered index row first and on the clustered index row after that.

Meanwhile, if you have another session that updates one of the columns that is part of the nonclustered index based on the clustered key value, that session would acquire exclusive (X) locks in the opposite order; that is, on the clustered index row first and on the nonclustered index row after that.

Figure 19-6 shows what happens after the first step. Both sessions successfully acquired locks on the rows in the clustered and nonclustered indexes.

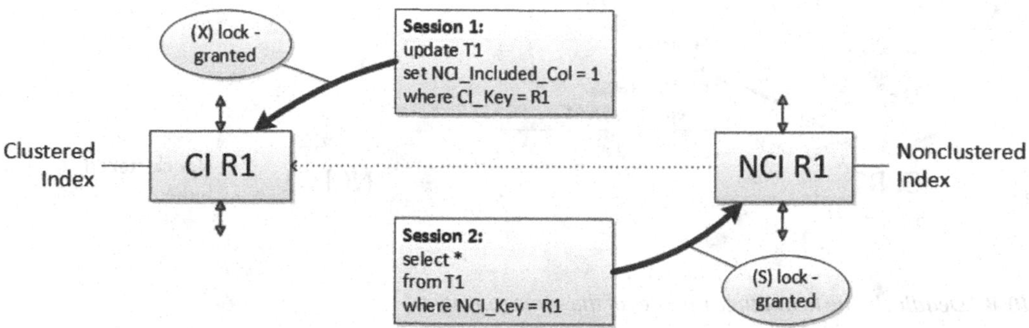

Figure 19-6. Key lookup deadlock, step 1

In the next step, each session is trying to acquire a lock on the row in the other index, which would be blocked, as shown in Figure 19-7.

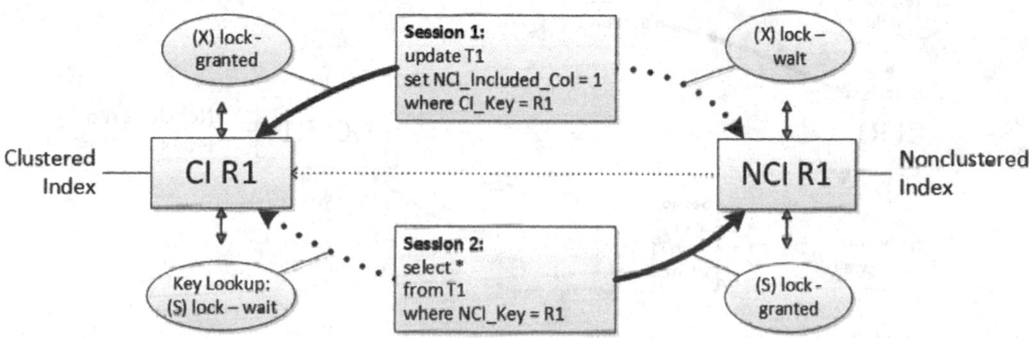

Figure 19-7. Key lookup deadlock, step 2

If it happens in exactly the same moment, you would have a deadlock, and the session that reads the data would be chosen as the deadlock victim. A solution here is to make the nonclustered index covering and avoid the key lookup operation.

Unfortunately, that solution would increase the size of the leaf rows in the nonclustered index and introduce additional overhead during data modification and index maintenance. Alternatively, you can use optimistic isolation levels and switch to READ COMMITTED SNAPSHOT mode. We will cover this approach in greater detail in Chapter 21, "Optimistic Isolation Levels."

Deadlock Due to Multiple Updates of the Same Row

Another, similar, deadlock pattern can be introduced by multiple updates of the same row if the subsequent update accesses or changes columns in the different nonclustered indexes. This could lead to a deadlock situation similar to what you already saw where another session places a lock on the nonclustered index row in between updates. A common scenario is when an AFTER UPDATE trigger updates the same row.

Let's look at a situation where you have a table with clustered and nonclustered indexes and the AFTER UPDATE trigger defined. Let's have session 1 update a column that does not belong to the nonclustered index. This step is shown in Figure 19-8. It acquires an exclusive (X) lock on the row for the clustered index only.

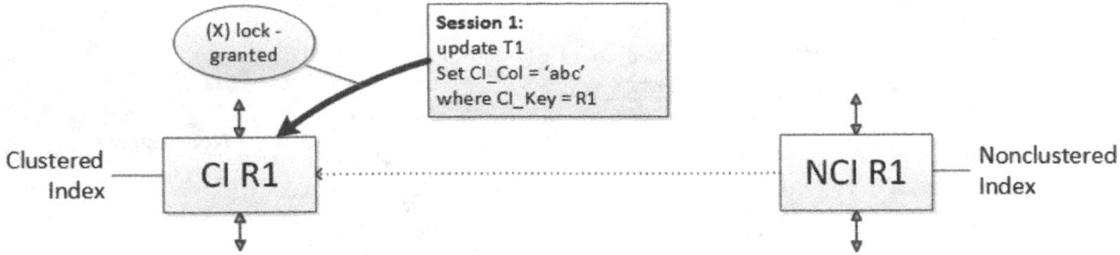

Figure 19-8. *Deadlock due to multiple updates of the same row, step 1*

The update fires the AFTER UPDATE trigger. Meanwhile, let's assume that another session is trying to select the same row using the nonclustered index. This session successfully acquires a shared (S) lock on the nonclustered index row during the nonclustered index seek operation. However, it would be blocked when trying to obtain a shared (S) lock on the clustered index row during the key lookup, as shown in Figure 19-9.

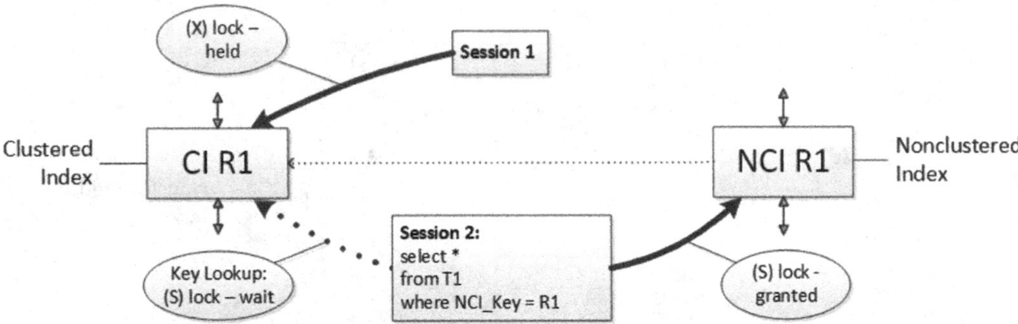

Figure 19-9. *Deadlock due to multiple updates of the same row, step 2*

Finally, if the session 1 trigger tries to update the same row again, modifying the column that exists in the nonclustered index, it would be blocked by the shared (S) lock held by session 2. Figure 19-10 illustrates this situation.

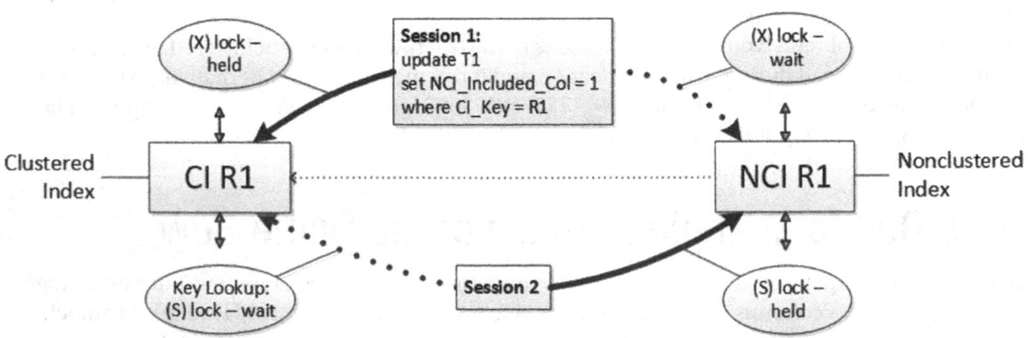

Figure 19-10. *Deadlock due to multiple updates of the same row, step 3*

Let's prove this with the code shown in Listing 19-2.

Listing 19-2. Multiple updates of the same row

```
create table dbo.T1
(
    CI_Key int not null,
    NCI_Key int not null,
    CI_Col varchar(32),
    NCI_Included_Col int
);

create unique clustered index IDX_T1_CI on dbo.T1(CI_Key);

create nonclustered index IDX_T1_NCI
on dbo.T1(NCI_Key)
include (NCI_Included_Col);

insert into dbo.T1(CI_Key,NCI_Key,CI_Col,NCI_Included_Col)
values(1,1,'a',0), (2,2,'b',0), (3,3,'c',0), (4,4,'d',0);

begin tran
    update dbo.T1 set CI_Col = 'abc' where CI_Key = 1;

    select
        l.request_session_id as [SPID], object_name(p.object_id) as [Object]
            ,i.name as [Index]
            ,l.resource_type as [Lock Type], l.resource_description as [Resource]
            ,l.request_mode as [Mode], l.request_status as [Status]
            ,wt.blocking_session_id as [Blocked By]
    from
        sys.dm_tran_locks l join sys.partitions p on
            p.hobt_id = l.resource_associated_entity_id
        join sys.indexes i on
            p.object_id = i.object_id and p.index_id = i.index_id
        left outer join sys.dm_os_waiting_tasks wt with (nolock) on
            l.lock_owner_address = wt.resource_address and
            l.request_status = 'WAIT'
    where
        resource_type = 'KEY' and request_session_id = @@SPID;

    update dbo.T1 set NCI_Included_Col = 1 where NCI_Key = 1

    select
        l.request_session_id as [SPID], object_name(p.object_id) as [Object]
            ,i.name as [Index]
            ,l.resource_type as [Lock Type], l.resource_description as [Resource]
            ,l.request_mode as [Mode], l.request_status as [Status]
            ,wt.blocking_session_id as [Blocked By]
    from
        sys.dm_tran_locks l join sys.partitions p on
            p.hobt_id = l.resource_associated_entity_id
```

```
        join sys.indexes i on
            p.object_id = i.object_id and p.index_id = i.index_id
        left outer join sys.dm_os_waiting_tasks wt with (nolock) on
            l.lock_owner_address = wt.resource_address and
            l.request_status = 'WAIT'
    where
        resource_type = 'KEY' and request_session_id = @@SPID;
commit
```

The code in Listing 19-2 updates the row twice. If you looked at the row-level locks held after first update, you would see only one lock held on the clustered index, as shown in Figure 19-11.

	SPID	Object	Index	Lock Type	Resource	Mode	Status	Blocked By
1	56	T1	IDX_T1_CI	KEY	(8194443284a0)	X	GRANT	NULL

Figure 19-11. *Row-level locks after the first update*

The second update, which updates the column that exists in the nonclustered index, places another exclusive (X) there, as shown in Figure 19-12. This proves that the lock on the nonclustered index row is not acquired until the index column is actually updated.

	SPID	Object	Index	Lock Type	Resource	Mode	Status	Blocked By
1	56	T1	IDX_T1_CI	KEY	(8194443284a0)	X	GRANT	NULL
2	56	T1	IDX_T1_NCI	KEY	(e2338e2f4a9f)	X	GRANT	NULL

Figure 19-12. *Row-level locks after the second update*

Now, let's look at another session with SPID = 55 running the SELECT shown in Listing 19-3 in between two updates, at a time when you have just one row-level lock held.

Listing 19-3. The code that leads to the deadlock

```
select CI_Key, CI_Col
from dbo.T1 with (index = IDX_T1_NCI)
where NCI_Key = 1
```

As you can see in Figure 19-13, the query successfully acquires the shared (S) lock on the nonclustered index row and is blocked from trying to acquire the lock on the clustered index row.

	SPID	Object	Index	Lock Ty...	Resource	Mode	Status	Blocked By
1	56	T1	IDX_T1_CI	KEY	(8194443284a0)	X	GRANT	NULL
2	55	T1	IDX_T1_CI	KEY	(8194443284a0)	S	WAIT	56
3	55	T1	IDX_T1_NCI	KEY	(e2338e2f4a9f)	S	GRANT	NULL

Figure 19-13. *Row-level locks when SELECT query is blocked*

If you now ran the second update in the original session with SPID = 56, it would try to acquire an exclusive (X) lock on the nonclustered index, and it would be blocked by the second (SELECT) session, as shown in Figure 19-14. This leads to the deadlock condition.

	SPID	Object	Index	Lock Ty...	Resource	Mode	Status	Blocked By
1	56	T1	IDX_T1_CI	KEY	(8194443284a0)	X	GRANT	NULL
2	55	T1	IDX_T1_CI	KEY	(8194443284a0)	S	WAIT	56
3	55	T1	IDX_T1_NCI	KEY	(e2338e2f4a9f)	S	GRANT	NULL
4	56	T1	IDX_T1_NCI	KEY	(e2338e2f4a9f)	X	WAIT	55

Figure 19-14. *Row-level locks when second update is running (deadlock)*

The best method to avoid such problems is to eliminate multiple updates of the same rows. You can use variables or temporary tables to store preliminary data and run the single UPDATE statement close to the end of the transaction. Alternatively, you can change the code and assign some temporary value to NCI_Included_Col as part of the first UPDATE statement, which would acquire exclusive (X) locks on both of the indexes. SELECT from the second session would be unable to acquire the lock on the nonclustered index, and the second update would run just fine.

As a last resort, you could read the row using a plan that utilizes both indexes using an XLOCK locking hint, which will place exclusive (X) locks on both rows, as shown in Listing 19-4 and Figure 19-15. Obviously, you need to consider the overhead this introduces.

Listing 19-4. Obtaining exclusive (X) locks on the rows in both indexes

```
begin tran
    declare
        @Dummy varchar(32)

    select @Dummy = CI_Col
    from dbo.T1 with (XLOCK index=IDX_T1_NCI)
    where NCI_Key = 1;

    select
        l.request_session_id as [SPID], object_name(p.object_id) as [Object]
            ,i.name as [Index]
            ,l.resource_type as [Lock Type], l.resource_description as [Resource]
            ,l.request_mode as [Mode], l.request_status as [Status]
            ,wt.blocking_session_id as [Blocked By]
    from
        sys.dm_tran_locks l join sys.partitions p on
            p.hobt_id = l.resource_associated_entity_id
        join sys.indexes i on
            p.object_id = i.object_id and p.index_id = i.index_id
        left outer join sys.dm_os_waiting_tasks wt with (nolock) on
            l.lock_owner_address = wt.resource_address and
            l.request_status = 'WAIT'
    where
        resource_type = 'KEY' and request_session_id = @@SPID;

    update dbo.T1 set CI_Col = 'abc' where CI_Key = 1;
```

```
    /* some code */

    update dbo.T1 set NCI_Included_Col = 1 where NCI_Key = 1;
commit
```

	SPID	Object	Index	Lock Type	Resource	Mode	Status
1	56	T1	IDX_T1_CI	KEY	(8194443284a0)	X	GRANT
2	56	T1	IDX_T1_NCI	KEY	(e2338e2f4a9f)	X	GRANT

Figure 19-15. *Row-level locks after SELECT statement with (XLOCK) hint*

Deadlock Troubleshooting

In a nutshell, deadlock troubleshooting is very similar to the blocking problems troubleshooting. You need to analyze the processes and queries involved in the deadlock, identify the root cause of the problem, and, finally, fix it.

Similar to the *blocking process report*, there is the *deadlock graph*, which provides you with the information about deadlock in an XML format. There are plenty of ways to obtain the deadlock graph, as follows:

- Trace Flag 1222: This trace flag saves deadlock information to the SQL Server error log. You can enable it for all sessions with the `DBCC TRACEON(1222,-1)` command or by using startup *parameter -T1222*. It is a perfectly safe method to use in production.
- `xml_deadlock_report` Extended Event
- `Deadlock graph` SQL Trace event. It is worth noting that SQL Profiler displays the graphic representation of the deadlock. The *Extract Event Data* action from the event context menu (right mouse click) allows you to extract an XML deadlock graph.
- You can create an event notification that fires when deadlock occurs.

Starting with SQL Server 2008, every system has the `system_health` Extended Event session enabled by default. This session captures basic server health information including the `xml_deadlock_report` event. This could be a great place to start troubleshooting if no other collection methods were enabled.

In SQL Server 2012 and above, you can access `system_health` session data from the *Management* node in Management Studio, as shown in Figure 19-16. You could analyze the target data by searching for the `xml_deadlock_report` event.

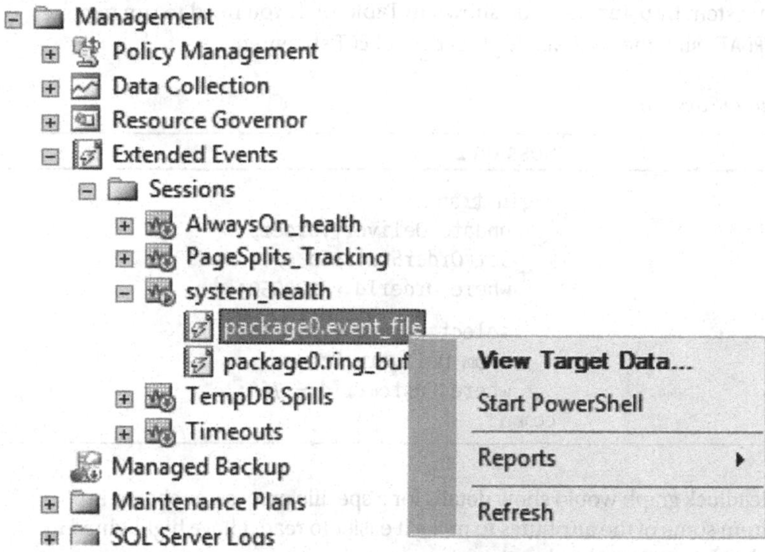

Figure 19-16. *Accessing system_health Extended Events session*

■ **Note** We will discuss Extended Events in more detail in Chapter 27.

An XML representation of the deadlock graph contains two different sections, as shown in Listing 19-5. The sections `<process-list>` and `<resource-list>` contain information about the processes and resources involved in the deadlock.

Listing 19-5. Deadlock graph format

```
<deadlock-list>
        <deadlock victim="...">
                <process-list>
                        <process id="...">
                                ...
                        </process>
                        <process id="...">
                                ...
                        </process>
                </process-list>
                <resource-list>
                        <information about resource involved in the deadlock>
                                ...
                        </ information about resource involved in the deadlock>
                        <information about resource involved in the deadlock>
                                ...
                        </ information about resource involved in the deadlock>
                </resource-list>
        </deadlock>
</deadlock-list>
```

Let's trigger a deadlock in the system by using the code shown in Table 19-1. You need to run two sessions in parallel, running the UPDATE statements first and then the SELECT statements.

Table 19-1. *Triggering Deadlock in the System*

Session 1	Session 2

begin tran
    update Delivery.Orders
    set OrderStatusId = 1
    where OrderId = 100001;
 	
    select count(*) as [Cnt]
    from Delivery.Orders
    where CustomerId = 317;
commit
	begin tran
	    update Delivery.Orders
	    set OrderStatusId = 1
	    where OrderId = 100050;
	
	    select count(*) as [Cnt]
	    from Delivery.Orders
	    where CustomerId = 766;
	commit

Each <process> node in the deadlock graph would show details for a specific process, as shown in Listing 19-6. I removed the values from some of the attributes to make it easier to read. I have highlighted in bold the ones that are especially helpful during troubleshooting.

Listing 19-6. Deadlock graph: <Process> node

```
<process id="process3e4b29868" taskpriority="0" logused="264" waitresource="KEY: ..."
waittime="..." ownerId="..." transactionname="... " lasttranstarted="..." XDES="..."
lockMode="S" schedulerid="..." kpid="..." status="suspended" spid="55" sbid="..."
ecid="..." priority="0" trancount="1" lastbatchstarted="..." lastbatchcompleted="..."
lastattention="..." clientapp="..." hostname="..." hostpid="..." loginname="..."
isolationlevel="read committed (2)" xactid="..." currentdb="..." lockTimeout="..."
clientoption1="..." clientoption2="...">
    <executionStack>
        <frame procname="adhoc" line="1" stmtstart="26" sqlhandle="...">
            SELECT COUNT(*) [Cnt] FROM [Delivery].[Orders] WHERE [CustomerId]=@1
        </frame>
    </executionStack>
    <inputbuf>
                select count(*) as [Cnt]
                from Delivery.Orders
                where CustomerId = 766
            commit
    </inputbuf>
</process>
```

The id attribute uniquely identifies the process. Waitresource and lockMode provide information about the lock type and the resource for which the process is waiting. In our example, you can see that the process is waiting for the shared (S) lock on one of the rows (keys).

The Isolationlevel attribute shows you the current transaction isolation level. Finally, executionStack and inputBuf allow you to find the SQL statement that was executed when the deadlock occurred. In some cases, especially when stored procedures are involved, you would need to use the sys.dm_exec_sql_text function to get the SQL statements in the same way as we did in Listing 18-5 in the previous chapter.

The <resource-list> section of deadlock graph contains information about the resources involved in the deadlock. It is shown in Listing 19-7.

Listing 19-7. Deadlock graph: <Resource-list> node

```
<resource-list>
    <keylock hobtid="72057594039500800" dbid="14" objectname="SqlServerInternals.
Delivery.Orders" indexname="PK_Orders" id="lock3e98b5d00" mode="X"
associatedObjectId="72057594039500800">
        <owner-list>
            <owner id="process3e6a890c8" mode="X"/>
        </owner-list>
        <waiter-list>
            <waiter id="process3e4b29868" mode="S" requestType="wait"/>
        </waiter-list>
    </keylock>
    <keylock hobtid="72057594039500800" dbid="14" objectname="SqlServerInternals.
Delivery.Orders" indexname="PK_Orders" id="lock3e98ba500" mode="X"
associatedObjectId="72057594039500800">
        <owner-list>
            <owner id="process3e4b29868" mode="X"/>
        </owner-list>
        <waiter-list>
            <waiter id="process3e6a890c8" mode="S" requestType="wait"/>
        </waiter-list>
    </keylock>
</resource-list>
```

The name of the XML element identifies the type of resource. `Keylock`, `pagelock`, and `objectlock` stand for the row-level, page, and object locks, respectively. You can also see to which objects and indexes those locks belong. Finally, the `owner-list` and `waiter-list` nodes provide information about the processes that own and wait for the locks, along with the type of locks acquired and requested. You can correlate this information with the data from the `process-list` section of the graph.

As you have probably already guessed, the next steps are very similar to the blocked process troubleshooting; that is, you need to pinpoint the queries involved in the deadlock and find out why deadlock occurred.

There is one important factor to consider, however. In most cases, deadlock involves more than one statement per session running in the same transaction. The deadlock graph provides you with information about the last statement only—the one that triggered the deadlock.

You can see the *signs* of the other statements in the `resource-list` node. It shows you that processes held exclusive (X) locks on the rows, but it does not tell you about the statements that acquired them. It is very useful to identify the statements involved in the deadlock while analyzing the root cause of the problem.

In our example, when you look at the listing shown in Table 19-1, you would see the two statements. The `UPDATE` statement updates the single row—it acquires and holds an exclusive (X) lock there. You can see that both processes own those exclusive (X) locks in the `resource-list` node of the deadlock graph.

In the next step, you need to understand why `SELECT` queries are trying to obtain shared (S) locks on the rows with exclusive (X) locks already held. You can look at the execution plans for the `SELECT` statements from the `process` nodes by either running the queries or using the `sys.dm_exec_query_stats` DMV, as was shown in Listing 18-5 in the previous chapter. As a result, you will get the execution plan shown in Figure 19-17. The figure also shows the number of locks acquired during query execution.

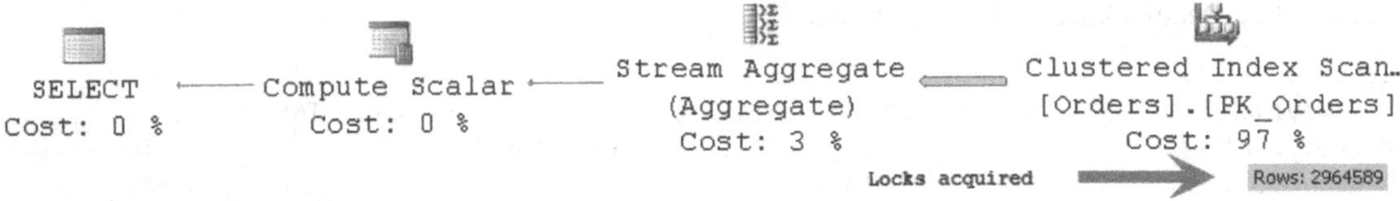

Figure 19-17. Execution plan for the query

As you can see, there is a clustered index scan in the plan, which gives you enough data for analysis. SELECT queries scanned the entire table. Because both processes were using the READ COMMITTED isolation level, the queries tried to acquire a shared (S) lock on every row from the table and were blocked by the exclusive (X) locks held by another session. It did not matter that those rows did not have the CustomerId that the queries were looking for. In order to evaluate this predicate, queries had to read those rows, which required acquiring shared (S) locks on them.

You can solve this deadlock situation by adding a nonclustered index on the CustomerID column. This would eliminate the clustered index scan and replace it with an *index seek* operator, as shown in Figure 19-18.

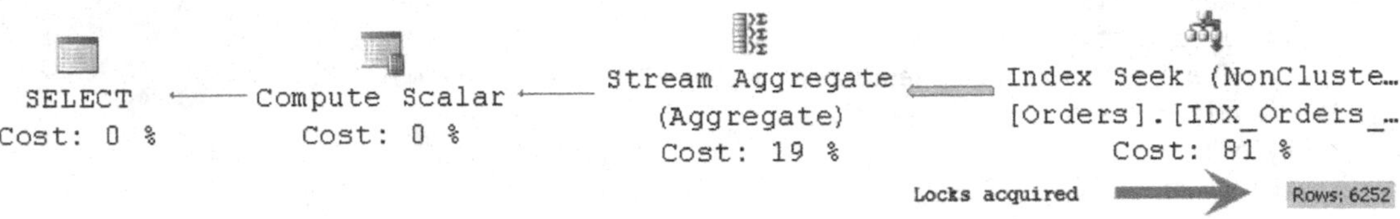

Figure 19-18. Execution plan for query with nonclustered index

Instead of acquiring a shared (S) lock on every row of the table, the query would read only the rows that belong to a specific customer. This would dramatically reduce the number of shared (S) locks to be acquired, and it would prevent the query from being blocked by exclusive (X) locks on the rows that belong to different customers.

In some cases, you can have intra-query parallelism deadlocks–when the query with a parallel execution plan deadlocks itself. Fortunately, these cases are rare and are usually introduced by a bug in SQL Server rather than by application or database issues. You can detect these cases when a deadlock graph has more than two processes with the same SPID and when resource-list has an exchangeEvent and/or threadPoll listed as resource(s) without any lock resources associated with them. When this happens, you can work around the problem by reducing the degree of parallelism for the query with a MAXDOP hint. There is also the chance that the issue has already been fixed in the latest service pack or cumulative update.

Reducing the Chance of Deadlocks

Finally, there are several practical bits of advice I can provide to help you to reduce the chance of deadlocks in the system, as follows:

1. **Optimize the queries.** Scans introduced by nonoptimized queries are the most common causes of deadlocks. Correct indexes not only improve the performance of the queries, but also reduce the number of rows that need to be read and locks that need to be acquired, thus reducing the chance of lock collisions with other sessions.

2. **Keep locks as short as possible.** As you will recall, all exclusive (X) locks are held until the end of the transaction. Make transactions short and try to update data as close to the end of the transaction as possible to reduce the chance of lock collision. In our example, you can change the code and swap around the `SELECT` and `UPDATE` statements. This would solve the particular deadlock problem, because the transactions would not have any statements that could be blocked after exclusive (X) locks were acquired.

3. **Use the lowest transaction isolation level that provides the required data consistency.** This reduces the time that shared (S) locks are held. Even if you swapped `SELECT` and `UPDATE` statements in our example, you could still have a deadlock in the `REPEATABLE READ` or `SERIALIZABLE` isolation levels. With those isolation levels, you would have shared (S) locks held until the end of the transaction, and they would block `UPDATE` statements. In `READ COMMITTED` mode, shared (S) locks are released after a row is read and `UPDATE` statements would not be blocked. In some cases, you can switch to optimistic isolation levels, which we will discuss in Chapter 22.

4. **Avoid updating the row multiple times within the same transaction when multiple indexes are involved.** As you saw earlier in this chapter, SQL Server does not place exclusive (X) locks on nonclustered index rows when index columns are not updated. Other sessions can place incompatible locks there and block subsequent updates, which would lead to deadlocks.

5. **Use retry logic.** Wrap critical code into `TRY..CATCH` blocks and retry the action if deadlock occurs. The error number for the exception caused by the deadlock is 1205. The code in Listing 19-8 shows how you can implement that.

Listing 19-8. Using TRY..CATCH block to retry the operation in case of deadlock

```
-- Declare and set variable to track number of retries to try before exiting.
declare
     @retry int = 5

-- Keep trying to update table if this task is selected as the deadlock victim.
while (@retry > 0)
begin
     begin try
          begin tran
               -- some code that can lead to the deadlock
           commit
     end try
     begin catch
          -- Check error number. If deadlock victim error, then reduce retry count
          -- for next update retry. If some other error occurred, then exit WHILE loop.
               if (error_number() = 1205)
                    set @retry = @retry - 1;
               else
                    set @retry = 0;

               if xact_state() <> 0
                    rollback;
     end catch
end
```

Summary

With the exception of intra-query parallelism deadlocks, which are considered to be a bug in the SQL Server code, deadlocks occur when multiple sessions compete for the same set of resources.

The key element in deadlock troubleshooting is the deadlock graph, which provides information about the processes and resources involved in the deadlock. You can collect the deadlock graph by enabling trace flag `T1222`, capturing the `xml_deadlock_report` Extended Event and `Deadlock graph` SQL Trace event, or setting up deadlock event notification in the system. In SQL Server 2008 and above, the `xml_deadlock_report` event is included in the `system_health` Extended Event session, which is enabled by default in every SQL Server installation.

The deadlock graph will provide you with information about the queries that triggered the deadlock. You should remember, however, that in the majority of cases deadlock involves multiple statements that acquired and held locks within the same transaction.

Even though deadlocks can happen for many reasons, more often than not they happen due to excessive locking during scans in nonoptimized queries. Query optimization can help to address them.

CHAPTER 20

Lock Escalation

Although row-level locking is great from a concurrency standpoint, it is expensive. In memory, a lock structure uses 64 bytes in 32-bit and 128 bytes in 64-bit operating systems. Keeping information about millions of row- and page-level locks would require SQL Server to allocate gigabytes of RAM to storing them.

SQL Server reduces the number of locks held in memory with a technique called *lock escalation*, which we will discuss in this chapter.

Lock Escalation Overview

Once a statement acquires at least 5,000 row- and page-level locks on the same object, SQL Server tries to escalate, or perhaps better said, replace, those locks with a single table- or, in some cases, partition-level lock. The operation would succeed if no other sessions held incompatible locks on the object or partition.

When such an operation succeeds, SQL Server releases all row- and page-level locks held by the transaction on the object (or partition), keeping the object- (or partition-) level lock only. If the operation fails, SQL Server continues to use row-level locking and repeats escalation attempts after about every 1,250 new locks acquired. In addition to the number of locks taken, SQL Server can escalate locks when the total number of locks in the instance exceeds memory or configuration thresholds.

Note The thresholds for number of locks, 5,000/1,250, is an approximation. The actual number of acquired locks that triggers lock escalation vary.

Let's look at an example. The first session starts a transaction in the `REPEATABLE READ` transaction isolation level and runs a `SELECT` statement that counts the number of rows in the `Delivery.Orders` table. As you will remember, in this isolation level, SQL Server keeps shared (S) locks until the end of the transaction.

Let's disable lock escalation for this table with the `ALTER TABLE SET (LOCK_ESCALATION=DISABLE)` command (more about this later) and look at the number of locks SQL Server acquires as well as at the memory required to store them. We will use a `WITH (ROWLOCK)` hint to prevent the situation in which SQL Server *optimizes* the locking by acquiring page-level shared (S) locks instead of row-level locks. In addition, while the transaction is still active, let's insert another row from a different session to demonstrate how lock escalation affects concurrency in the system.

Table 20-1 shows the code of both sessions along with the output from the dynamic management views (DMVs). Figure 20-1 shows the *Lock Memory (KB)* system performance counter while the transaction is active.

D. Korotkevitch, *Pro SQL Server Internals*, DOI 10.1007/978-1-4842-1964-5_20

Table 20-1. *Test Code with Lock Escalation Disabled*

Session 1	Session 2

alter table Delivery.Orders set
   (lock_escalation=disable);
set transaction isolation level repeatable read
begin tran
    select count(*) from Delivery.Orders with (rowlock);	

	-- Success insert into Delivery.Orders (OrderDate,OrderNum,CustomerId) values(getUTCDate(),'99999',100);

-- Result: 10,212,326
    select count(*) as [Lock Count]
    from sys.dm_tran_locks;
 	
    -- Result: 1,940,272 KB
    select sum(pages_kb) as [Memory, KB]
    from sys.dm_os_memory_clerks
    where type = 'OBJECTSTORE_LOCK_MANAGER';
commit	

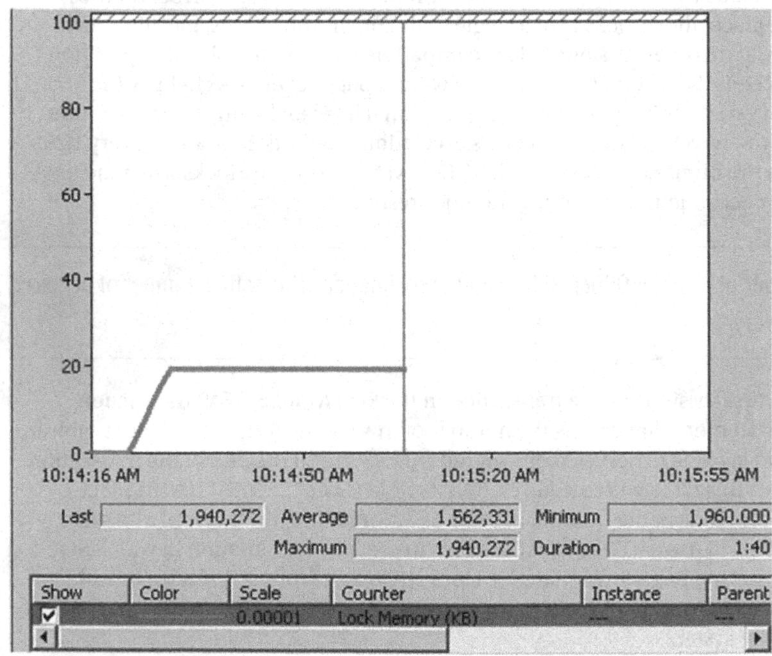

Figure 20-1. *Lock Memory (KB) system performance counter*

As you can see, from a concurrency standpoint, the row-level locking is perfect. Sessions do not block each other as long as they do not compete for the same rows. At the same time, keeping a large number of locks is memory intensive, and memory is one of the most precious resources in SQL Server. This is especially important for non-Enterprise editions in which there is a limitation on the amount of memory that can be utilized. In our example, SQL Server needs to keep millions of lock structures utilizing almost two gigabytes of RAM. This number includes the row-level shared (S) locks as well as the page-level intent shared (IS) locks. Moreover, there is the overhead of maintaining the locking information and the large number of lock structures in the system.

Let's see what happens if we enable lock escalation with the `ALTER TABLE SET (LOCK_ESCALATION=TABLE)` command and run the code shown in Table 20-2. Figure 20-2 shows the output from the `sys.dm_tran_locks` view.

***Table 20-2.** Test Code with Lock Escalation Enabled*

Session 1	Session 2

`alter table Delivery.Orders set (lock_escalation=table);`
`set transaction isolation level repeatable read`
`begin tran`
`    select count(*) from Delivery.Orders with (rowlock);`	

	`-- The session is blocked`
	`insert into Delivery.Orders`
	`(OrderDate,OrderNum,CustomerId)`
	`values(getUTCDate(),'100000',100);`

`    select`
`        request_session_id as [SPID]`
`        ,resource_type as [Resource]`
`        ,request_mode as [Lock Mode]`
`        ,request_status as [Status]`
`    from sys.dm_tran_locks;`
`commit`	

	SPID	Resource	Lock Mo...	Status
1	57	DATABASE	S	GRANT
2	58	DATABASE	S	GRANT
3	57	OBJECT	S	GRANT
4	58	OBJECT	IX	WAIT

***Figure 20-2.** Sys.dm_tran_locks output with lock escalation enabled*

SQL Server replaces the row- and page-level locks with an object-level shared (S) lock. Although this is great from a memory-usage standpoint—there is just a single lock to maintain—it affects concurrency. As you can see, the second session is blocked; it cannot acquire an intent exclusive (IX) lock on the table because it is incompatible with the full shared (S) lock held by the first session. It is also worth mentioning that the `WITH (ROWLOCK)` hint does not affect lock escalation behavior.

Lock escalation is enabled by default and could introduce the blocking issues, which can be confusing for developers and database administrators. Let's talk about a few typical cases.

The first case is reporting using the `REPEATABLE READ` or `SERIALIZABLE` isolation levels for data consistency purposes. If reporting queries are reading large amounts of data when there are no sessions updating the data, those queries can escalate shared (S) locks to the table level. Afterward, all writers would be blocked, even when trying to insert new data or modify data not read by reporting queries, as you saw earlier in this chapter. One of the ways to address this issue is by switching to *optimistic transaction isolation levels*, which we will discuss in the next chapter.

The second case is the implementation of the purge process. Let's assume that you need to purge a large amount of data using a DELETE statement. If the implementation deletes a large number of rows at once, you could have an exclusive (X) lock escalated to the table level. This blocks access to the table for all writers, as well as for the readers in the READ COMMITTED, REPEATABLE READ, or SERIALIZABLE isolation levels, even when those queries are working with a completely different set of data than the one you are purging.

Finally, you can think about the process that inserts a large batch of rows with a single INSERT statement. Similar to the purge process, it could escalate an exclusive (X) lock to the table level and block the other sessions from accessing it.

All of these patterns have one thing in common: they acquire and hold a large number of row- and page-level locks as part of a single statement. This triggers lock escalation, which would succeed if there were no other sessions holding incompatible locks on the table (or partition) level. This would then block other sessions from acquiring incompatible intent or full locks on the table (or partition) until the first session completes the transaction, regardless of whether the blocked sessions are trying to access the data affected by the first session or not.

It is worth repeating that lock escalation is triggered by the number of locks acquired by the statement, rather than by the transaction. If the separate statements acquire less than 5,000 row- and page-level locks each, lock escalation is not triggered, regardless of the total number of locks the transaction holds. Listing 20-1 shows an example where multiple update statements run in a loop within a single transaction.

Listing 20-1. Lock escalation and multiple statements

```
declare
    @id int = 1

begin tran
    while @id < 100000
    begin
        update Delivery.Orders
        set OrderStatusId = 1
        where OrderId between @id and @id + 4998;

        select @id += 4999
    end

    select count(*) as [Lock Count]
    from sys.dm_tran_locks
    where request_session_id = @@SPID;
commit
```

Figure 20-3 shows the output of the SELECT statement from Listing 20-1. Even when the total number of locks the transaction holds is far more than the threshold, lock escalation is not triggered.

	Total Lock Count
1	133870

Figure 20-3. *Number of locks held by the transaction*

Lock Escalation Troubleshooting

There are a few ways to troubleshoot blocking problems that occur because of lock escalation. One sign of potential problems is a high percentage of intent lock waits in the wait statistics.

You can monitor and capture lock escalations with Extended Events. Figure 20-4 illustrates the `lock_escalation` Extended Event and some of the available event fields.

■ **Note** We will talk about wait statistics analysis and Extended Events in Part V of this book.

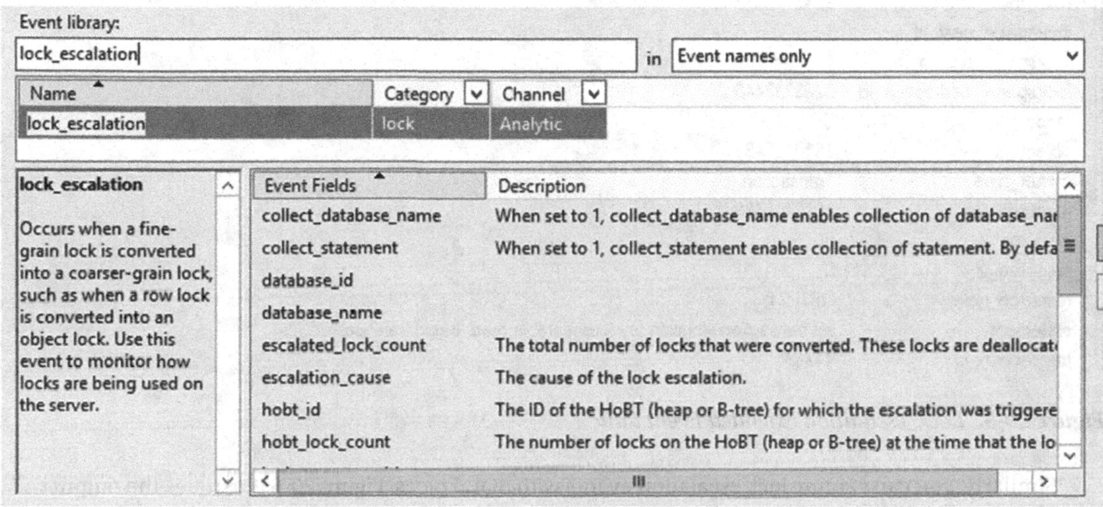

Figure 20-4. *Lock_escalation Extended Event*

Figure 20-5 illustrates the data captured by the event.

name	timestamp
lock_escalation	2016-01-28 06:31:36.8237675

Details

Field	Value
database_id	13
database_name	SQLServerInternals
escalated_lock_count	6249
escalation_cause	Lock threshold
hobt_id	72057594067222528
hobt_lock_count	6248
lockspace_nest_id	1
lockspace_sub_id	1
lockspace_workspace_id	5288332448
mode	S
object_id	1810105489
owner_type	Transaction
resource_0	1810105489
resource_1	0
resource_2	0
resource_type	OBJECT
statement	set transaction isolation level repeatable read begin tran select ...
transaction_id	443696

Figure 20-5. *Lock_escalation Extended Event data*

Similarly, you can capture lock escalation events with SQL Traces. Figure 20-6 illustrates the output from this event in the *SQL Profiler* application.

EventClass	EventSubClass	IntegerData	IntegerData2	LineNumber	Mode	Offset	ObjectID	ObjectID2	Type	TextData
Lock:Escalation	0 - LOCK_THRESHOLD	6248	6249	3	3 - S	124	1810...	7205...	5 - OBJECT	set tra...

```
set transaction isolation level repeatable read
begin tran
        select count(*)
        from Delivery.Orders with (rowlock)
commit
```

Figure 20-6. *Lock-escalation event in SQL Server Profiler*

SQL Trace provides the following attributes:

- *EventSubClass* indicates what triggered the lock escalation—number of locks or memory threshold.
- *IntegerData* and *IntegerData2* show the number of locks that existed at the time of the escalation and how many locks were converted during the escalation process. It is worth noting that in our example lock escalation occurred when the statement acquired 6,248 rather than 5,000 locks.
- *Mode* tells what kind of lock was escalated.

- *ObjectID* is the object_id of the table for which lock escalation was triggered.
- *ObjectID2* is the *HoBT* ID for which lock escalation was triggered.
- *Type* represents lock escalation granularity.
- *TextData, LineNumber,* and *Offset* provide the information on the batch and statement that triggered lock escalation.

There is also the *Table Lock Escalations/sec* performance counter in the "SQL Server Access Methods" section, which can be useful for baselining the system.

From the blocked-session standpoint, if you run the code shown in Listing 18-2 (Chapter 18), you will see the results shown in Figure 20-7.

	Resource Type	DB Name	Object	Resource	Session	Mode	Status	Wait (ms)	sql	query_plan
1	OBJECT	SqlServerInternals	Orders		62	S	GRANT	NULL	NULL	NULL
2	OBJECT	SqlServerInternals	Orders		63	IX	WAIT	3455	INSERT INTO [Deli...	<ShowPlan...

Figure 20-7. *Blocked and blocking sessions due to lock escalation*

The key point here is that you have two object-level locks. The blocked session is trying to acquire an intent lock on the object level while the blocking session holds an incompatible full lock.

If you look at the blocked process report, you can see that the blocked process is waiting on the intent lock on the object, as shown in Listing 20-2.

Listing 20-2. Blocked process report (partial)

```
<blocked-process-report>
 <blocked-process>
  <process id="..." taskpriority="0" logused="0" waitresource="OBJECT: ..." waittime="..."
ownerId="..." transactionname="user_transaction" lasttranstarted="..." XDES="..."
lockMode="IX" schedulerid="..." ...>
```

Keep in mind that there could be other reasons for the sessions to acquire full object locks or be blocked waiting for an intent lock on the table. You must correlate the information from the other venues (Extended Events, SQL Traces, and so on) to be sure blocking occurs because of lock escalation.

Although lock escalation can introduce blocking issues, it helps to preserve SQL Server memory. Without lock escalation, the large number of locks held by the instance reduces the size of the buffer pool. As a result, you have fewer data pages in the cache, which could lead to a higher number of physical I/O operations and degrade the performance of the queries. In addition, SQL Server could terminate the queries with error 1204 when there is no available memory to store the lock information. Figure 20-8 shows just such an error message.

Results | Messages

```
Msg 1204, Level 19, State 4, Line 4
The instance of the SQL Server Database Engine cannot obtain a LOCK resource at this time.
Rerun your statement when there are fewer active users. Ask the database administrator to
check the lock and memory configuration for this instance, or to check for long-running
transactions.
```

Figure 20-8. *Error 1204*

In SQL Server 2008 and above, you can control escalation behavior at the table level by using the ALTER TABLE SET LOCK_ESCALATION statement. This option affects lock escalation behavior for all clustered and nonclustered indexes defined on the table. Three options are available:

> DISABLE: This option disables lock escalation for a specific table.
>
> TABLE: SQL Server escalates locks to the table level. This is the default option.
>
> AUTO: SQL Server escalates locks to the partition level when the table is partitioned or to the table level when the table is not partitioned. Use this option with large partitioned tables, especially when there are large reporting queries running on the old data.

Unfortunately, SQL Server 2005 does not support this option, and the only way to disable lock escalation in this version is by using documented trace flags T1211 or T1224 at the instance or session level. Keep in mind that you need to have sysadmin rights to call the DBCC TRACEON command and set trace flags at the session level.

> T1211 disables lock escalation, regardless of the memory conditions.
>
> T1224 disables lock escalation based on the number of locks threshold, although lock escalation can still be triggered in cases of memory pressure.

■ **Note** You can read more about trace flags T1211 and T1224 in Books Online at http://technet.microsoft.com/en-us/library/ms188396.aspx.

As with the other blocking issues, you should find the root cause of why lock escalation occurs. You should also think about the pros and cons of disabling lock escalation on particular objects in the system. Although it could reduce the blocking in the system, SQL Server would use more memory to store lock information. And, of course, you can consider code re-factoring as another option.

In case lock escalation is triggered by the writers, you can reduce the batches to the point at which they are acquiring less than 5,000 row- and page-level locks per object. You can still process multiple batches in the same transaction–the 5,000 locks threshold is per statement. At the same time, you should remember that smaller batches are usually less effective than large ones. You need to fine-tune the batch sizes and find the optimal values. It is normal to have lock escalation triggered as long as object-level locks are not held for an excessive period of time and/or it does not affect the other sessions.

As for lock escalations triggered by readers, you should avoid situations in which many shared (S) locks are held. One example is scans due to nonoptimized or reporting queries in the REPEATABLE READ or SERIALIZABLE transaction isolation levels when queries hold shared (S) locks until the end of the transaction. The example shown in Listing 20-3 runs the SELECT from the Delivery.Orders table using the REPEATABLE READ isolation level. Figure 20-9 shows the output of the query.

Listing 20-3. Lock escalation triggered by nonoptimized query

```
set transaction isolation level repeatable read
begin tran
    select OrderId, OrderDate, Amount
    from Delivery.Orders
    where OrderNum = '1';

    select
        resource_type as [Resource Type]
        ,case resource_type
```

```
            when 'OBJECT' then object_name(resource_associated_entity_id,resource_database_id)
            when 'DATABASE' then 'DB'
            else
                ( select object_name(object_id, resource_database_id)
                        from sys.partitions
                        where hobt_id = resource_associated_entity_id )
        end as [Object]
        ,request_mode as [Mode]
        ,request_status as [Status]
    from sys.dm_tran_locks
    where request_session_id = @@SPID;
commit
```

	OrderId	OrderDate	Amount
1	1	2013-04-07 13:07:00	20.00

	Resource Type	Object	Mode	Status
1	DATABASE	DB	S	GRANT
2	OBJECT	Orders	S	GRANT

***Figure 20-9.** Selecting data in the REPEATABLE READ isolation level*

Even if the query returned just a single row, you can see that shared (S) locks have been escalated to the table level. Let's take a look at the execution plan shown in Figure 20-10.

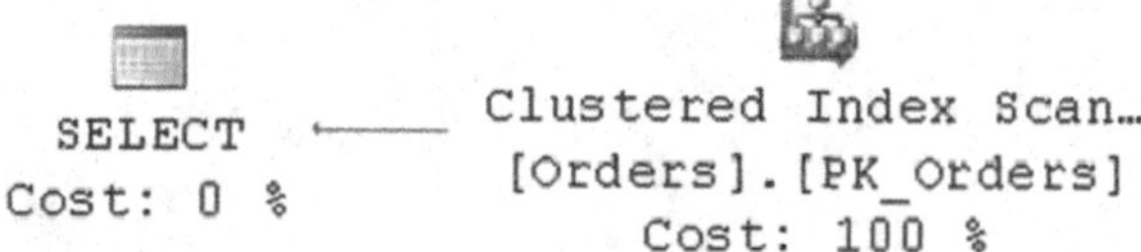

***Figure 20-10.** Execution plan of the query*

There are no indexes on the `OrderNum` column, and SQL Server uses the *clustered index scan* operator. Even if the query returns just a single row, it acquires and holds shared (S) locks on all the rows it read. As a result, lock escalation is triggered. If you add an index on the `OrderNum` column, it changes the execution plan to a *nonclustered index seek*. Only one row is read, very few row- and page-level locks are acquired and held, and lock escalation is not needed.

In some cases, you may consider partitioning the tables and setting the lock escalation option to use partition-level escalation, rather than table level, using the `ALTER TABLE SET (LOCK_ESCALATION=AUTO)` statement. This could help in scenarios in which you must purge old data using the `DELETE` statement or run reporting queries against old data in the `REPEATABLE READ` or `SERIALIZABLE` isolation levels. In those cases, statements escalate the locks to partitions, rather than to tables, and queries that are not accessing those partitions would not be blocked.

In other cases, you can switch to optimistic isolation levels, which will be discussed in Chapter 21. Finally, you would not have any reader-related blocking issues in the `READ UNCOMMITTED` transaction isolation level, where shared (S) locks are not acquired, although this method is not recommended because of all the other data consistency issues it introduces.

Summary

SQL Server escalates locks to the object level after the statement acquires and holds about 5,000 row- and page-level locks. When escalation succeeds, SQL Server keeps the single object-level lock, blocking other sessions with incompatible lock types from accessing the table. If escalation fails, SQL Server repeats escalation attempts after about every 1,250 new locks are acquired.

Lock escalation fits perfectly into the “It Depends” category. It reduces the SQL Server Lock Manager memory usage and the overhead of maintaining a large number of locks. At the same time, it could increase blocking in the system because of the object- or partition-level locks held.

You should keep lock escalation enabled unless you find that it introduces noticeable blocking issues in the system. Even in those cases, however, you should perform root-cause analysis as to why blocking due to lock escalation occurs and evaluate the pros and cons of disabling it. You should also look at the other options available, such as code and database schema re-factoring, query tuning, or switching to optimistic transaction isolation levels. Any of these options might be the better choice to solve blocking problems, rather than disabling lock escalation.

CHAPTER 21

Optimistic Isolation Levels

Optimistic transaction isolation levels were introduced in SQL Server 2005 as a new way to deal with blocking problems and to address data consistency issues. With optimistic transaction isolation levels, queries read "old" committed versions of rows while accessing the data modified by the other sessions, rather than being blocked by the incompatibility of shared (S) and exclusive (X) locks.

This chapter explains how optimistic isolation levels are implemented and how they affect the locking behavior of the system.

Row Versioning Overview

With optimistic transaction isolation levels, when updates occur, SQL Server stores the old versions of the rows in a special part of `tempdb` called *version store*. The original rows in the database are also modified with 14-byte pointers that reference the old versions of the rows. Depending on the situation, you can have more than one version record stored in the version store for the row. Figure 21-1 illustrates this behavior.

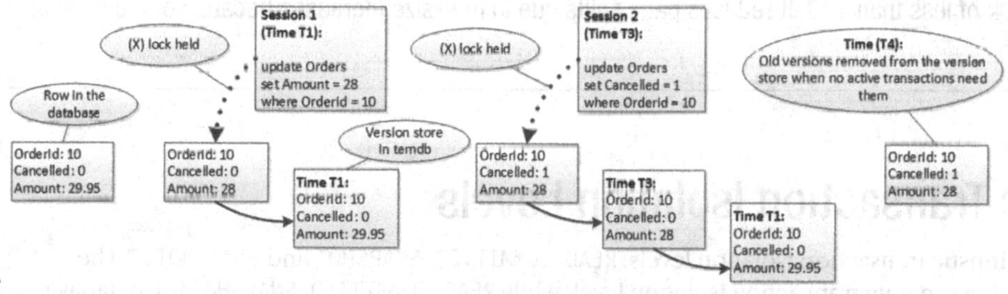

***Figure 21-1.** Version store*

Now, when readers (and sometimes writers) access the row that holds an exclusive (X) lock, they read the old version from the version store rather than being blocked, as shown in Figure 21-2.

D. Korotkevitch, *Pro SQL Server Internals*, DOI 10.1007/978-1-4842-1964-5_21

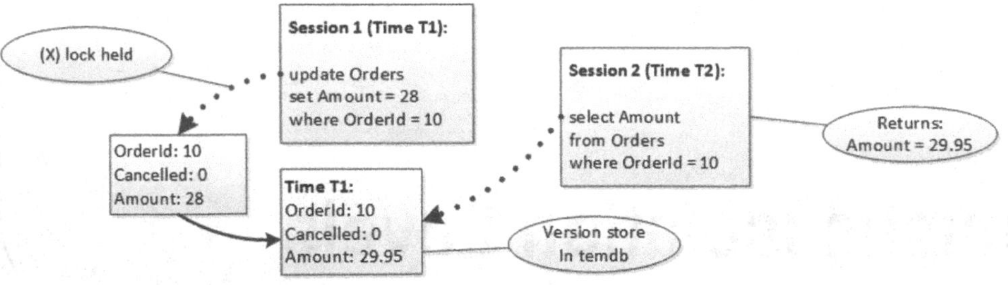

Figure 21-2. *Readers and version store*

As you can guess, while optimistic isolation levels help reduce blocking, there are some tradeoffs. Most significant among these is that they contribute to `tempdb` load. Using optimistic isolation levels on highly volatile systems can lead to very heavy `tempdb` activity and can significantly increase `tempdb` size. We will look at this issue in greater detail later in this chapter.

There is overhead during data modification and retrieval. SQL Server needs to copy the data to `tempdb` as well as maintain a linked list of the version records. Similarly, it needs to traverse that list when reading data. This adds additional CPU and I/O load. You need remember these tradeoffs, especially when you host the system in the Cloud, where I/O performance can quickly become a bottleneck in the system.

Finally, optimistic isolation levels contribute to index fragmentation. When a row is modified, SQL Server increases the row size by 14 bytes due to the versioning tag pointer. If a page is tightly packed and a new version of the row does not fit into the page, it will lead to a page split and further fragmentation. This is very similar to the insert/update pattern we discussed in Chapter 6, "Index Fragmentation." Those 14 bytes will stay in the row, even after records are removed from the version store, until the index is rebuilt.

■ **Tip** If optimistic isolation levels are used, it is recommended that you reserve some space on the pages by using a `FILLFACTOR` of less than 100. It reduces page splits due to row-size increases because of the version store pointers.

Optimistic Transaction Isolation Levels

There are two optimistic transaction isolation levels: `READ COMMITTED SNAPSHOT` and `SNAPSHOT`. To be precise, `SNAPSHOT` is a separate transaction isolation level, while `READ COMMITTED SNAPSHOT` is a database option that changes the behavior of the readers in the `READ COMMITTED` transaction isolation level.

Let's examine these levels in depth.

READ COMMITTED SNAPSHOT Isolation Level

Both optimistic isolation levels need to be enabled on the database level. You can enable `READ COMMITTED SNAPSHOT (RCSI)` with the `ALTER DATABASE SET READ_COMMITTED_SNAPSHOT ON` command. This statement needs to acquire an exclusive (X) database lock in order to change the database option, and it will be blocked if there are other users connected to the database. You can address this by running the `ALTER DATABASE SET READ_COMMITTED_SNAPSHOT ON WITH ROLLBACK AFTER X SECONDS` command. This will roll back all active transactions and terminate existing database connections, which allows the changing of the database option.

As already mentioned, RCSI changes the behavior of the readers in READ COMMITTED mode. It does not affect the behavior of the writers, however.

As you can see in Figure 21-3, instead of acquiring shared (S) locks and being blocked by exclusive (X) locks held on the row, readers use the old version of the row from the version store. Writers still acquire update (U) and exclusive (X) locks in the same way as in pessimistic isolation levels. Again, as you can see, blocking between writers from different sessions still exists, although writers do not block readers, in a similar manner to the READ UNCOMMITTED mode.

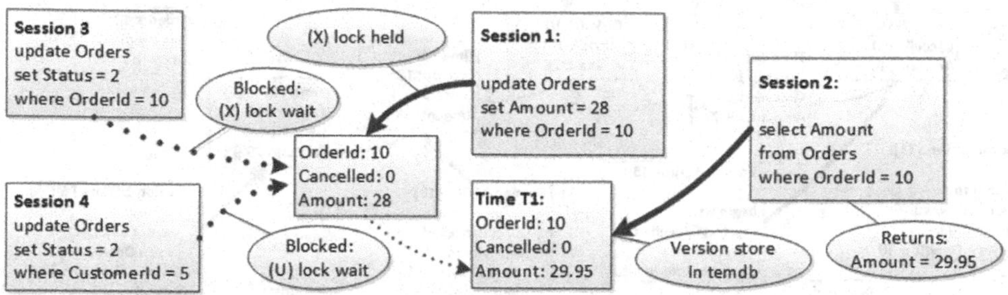

Figure 21-3. *Read Committed Snapshot isolation level behavior*

There is a major difference between the READ UNCOMMITTED and READ COMMITTED SNAPSHOT isolation levels, however. READ UNCOMMITTED removes the blocking at the expense of data consistency. Many consistency anomalies are possible, including reading uncommitted data, duplicated reads, and missed rows. On the other hand, the READ COMMITTED SNAPSHOT isolation level provides you with full statement-level consistency. Statements running in this isolation level do not access uncommitted data nor the data committed after the statement started.

As the obvious conclusion, you should avoid using the NOLOCK hint in queries that use the READ COMMITTED SNAPSHOT isolation level. While using NOLOCK with READ UNCOMMITTED is a bad practice by itself, it is completely useless in READ COMMITTED SNAPSHOT mode, which provides you with the same blocking behavior without losing data consistency for the queries.

■ **Tip** Switching a database to the READ COMMITTED SNAPSHOT isolation level can be a great emergency technique when the system is suffering from blocking issues. It removes writers/readers blocking without any code changes, assuming that readers are running in the READ COMMITTED isolation level. Obviously, this is only a temporary solution, and you need to detect and eliminate the root cause of the problem.

SNAPSHOT Isolation Level

SNAPSHOT is a separate transaction isolation level, and it needs to be set explicitly in the code with a SET TRANSACTION ISOLATION LEVEL SNAPSHOT statement or by using a WITH (SNAPSHOT) table hint.

By default, using the SNAPSHOT isolation level is prohibited. You must enable it with an ALTER DATABASE SET ALLOW_SNAPSHOT_ISOLATION ON statement. This statement does not require an exclusive database lock, and it can be executed with other users connected to the database.

A SNAPSHOT isolation level provides transaction-level consistency. Transactions will see a *snapshot* of the data at the moment when the transaction started, regardless of how long the transaction was active and how many data changes were made via other transactions during that time.

In the example shown in Figure 21-4, we have session 1, which starts the transaction and reads the row at time *T1*. At time *T2*, we have session 2, which modifies the row in the implicit transaction. At this moment, the old (original) version of the row is moved to the version store in `tempdb`.

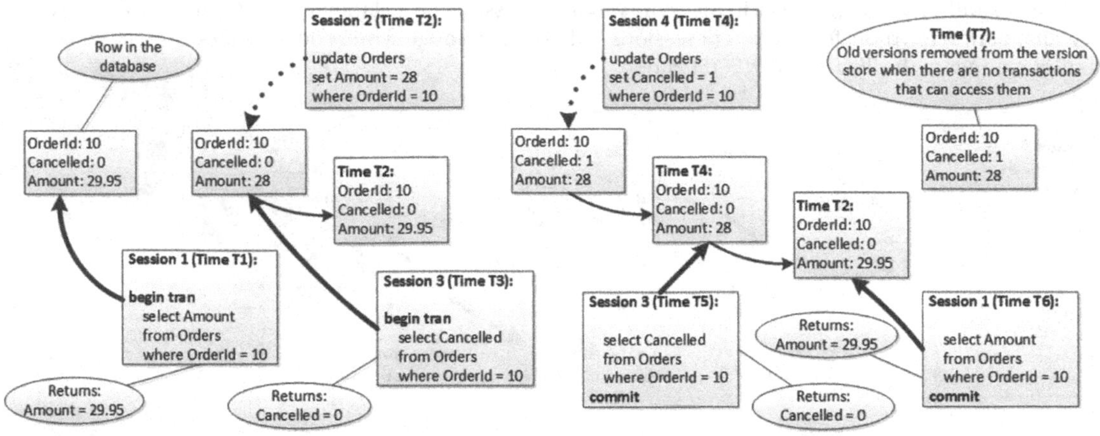

Figure 21-4. *Snapshot isolation level and readers behavior*

In the next step, we have session 3, which starts another transaction and reads the same row at time *T3*. It sees the version of the row as modified and committed by session 2 (at time *T2*). At time *T4*, we have session 4, which modifies the row in the implicit transaction again. At this time, we have two versions of the rows in the version store—one that existed between *T2* and *T4* and the original version that existed before *T2*. Now, if session 3 runs the `SELECT` again, it would use the version that existed between *T2* and *T4*, because this version was committed at the time the session 3 transaction started. Similarly, session 1 would use the original version of the row that existed before *T2*. At some point after session 1 and session 3 are committed, the version store clean-up task would remove both records from the version store–assuming, of course, that there are no other transactions that need them.

The `SERIALIZABLE` and `SNAPSHOT` isolation levels provide the same level of protection against data inconsistency issues; however, there is a subtle difference in their behavior. A `SNAPSHOT` isolation level transaction sees data as of the beginning of a transaction. With the `SERIALIZABLE` isolation level, the transaction sees data as of the time when the data was accessed for the first time. Consider a situation where a session is reading data from a table in the middle of a transaction. If another session changed the data in that table after the transaction started but before data was read, the transaction in the `SERIALIZABLE` isolation level would see the changes while the `SNAPSHOT` transaction would not.

A `SNAPSHOT` isolation level provides transaction-level data consistency with no blocking involved, although it could generate an enormous amount of data in `tempdb`. If you have a session that deletes millions of rows from the table, all of those rows need to be copied to the version store, even if the original `DELETE` statement is running in a non-`SNAPSHOT` isolation mode, just to preserve the state of the data for possible `SNAPSHOT` or `RCSI` transactions.

Now, let's examine the writer's behavior. Let's assume that session 1 starts the transaction and updates one of the rows. That session holds an exclusive (X) lock there, as shown in Figure 21-5.

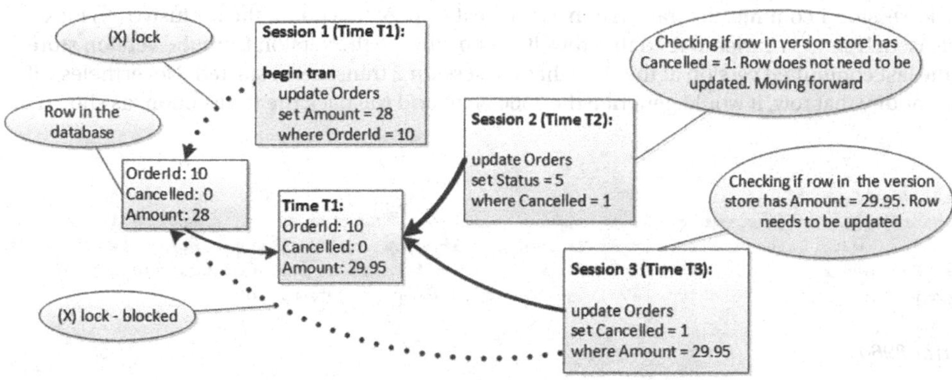

***Figure 21-5.** Snapshot isolation level and writer's behavior (1)*

Session 2 wants to update all rows where `Cancelled = 1`. It starts to scan the table, and when it needs to read the data for `OrderId = 10`, it reads the row from the version store; that is, the last committed version before the session 2 transaction started. This version is the original (non-updated) version of the row, and it has `Cancelled = 0`, so session 2 does not need to update it. Session 2 continues scanning the rows without being blocked by update (U) and exclusive (X) lock incompatibility.

Similarly, session 3 wants to update all rows with `Amount = 29.95`. When it reads the version of the row from the version store, it determines that the row needs to be updated. Again, it does not matter that session 1 also changes the amount for the same row. At this point, a "new version" of the row has not been committed and it is invisible to the other sessions. Now, session 3 wants to update the row in the database, tries to acquire an exclusive (X) lock, and is blocked because session 1 already has an exclusive (X) lock there.

There is another possibility, however. Let's consider the following scenario, keeping in mind the transaction consistency that a `SNAPSHOT` isolation level guarantees.

In the example shown in Figure 21-6, session 1 starts a transaction and updates one of the rows. In the next step, session 2 starts another transaction. In fact, it does not really matter what session starts the transaction first, as long as a new version of the row with `OrderId = 10` is not committed.

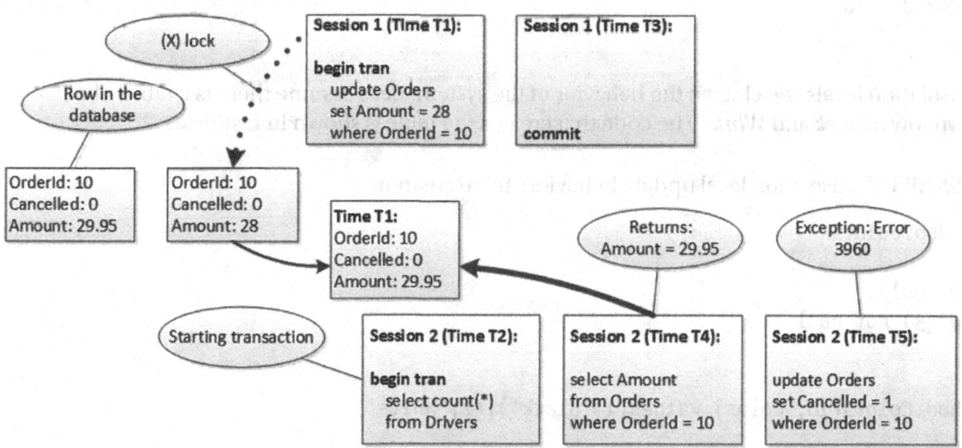

***Figure 21-6.** Snapshot isolation level and writer's behavior (2)*

In either case, session 1 commits the transaction as the next step. At this point, the exclusive (X) lock on the row is released. If session 2 tries to read that row, it would still use the version from the version store, because it was the last committed version at the time that the session 2 transaction started. Nevertheless, if session 2 tries to modify that row, it would generate the 3960 error and roll back the transaction, as shown in Figure 21-7.

```
Msg 3960, Level 16, State 2, Line 1
Snapshot isolation transaction aborted due to update conflict. You cannot use snapshot isolation
to access table 'Delivery.Orders' directly or indirectly in database 'SqlServerInternals' to
update, delete, or insert the row that has been modified or deleted by another transaction. Retry
the transaction or change the isolation level for the update/delete statement.
```

Figure 21-7. *Error 3960*

■ **Tip** You can implement retry logic with `TRY/CATCH` statements to handle the 3960 error if business requirements allow that.

You need to keep this behavior in mind when you are updating the data in the `SNAPSHOT` isolation level in a system with volatile data. If other sessions update the rows that you are modifying after the transaction is started, you would end up with this error, even if you did not access those rows before the update. One of the possible workarounds is using `READCOMMITTED` or other non-optimistic isolation level table hints as part of the `UPDATE` statement, as shown in Listing 21-1.

Listing 21-1. Using READCOMMITTED hint to prevent 3960 error

```
set transaction isolation level snapshotxs
begin tran
    select count(*) from Delivery.Drivers;

    update Delivery.Orders with (readcommitted)
    set Cancelled = 1
    where OrderId = 10;
commit
```

`SNAPSHOT` isolation levels can change the behavior of the system. Let's assume there is a table, `dbo.Colors`, with two rows: *Black* and *White*. The code that creates the table is shown in Listing 21-2.

Listing 21-2. SNAPSHOT isolation level update behavior: Table creation

```
create table dbo.Colors
(
    Id int not null,
    Color char(5) not null
);

insert into dbo.Colors(Id, Color) values(1,'Black'),(2,'White')
```

Now, let's run two sessions simultaneously. In the first session, we run the update that sets the color to white for the rows where the color is currently black by using the `UPDATE dbo.Colors SET Color='White' WHERE Color='Black'` statement. In the second session, let's perform the opposite operation by using the `UPDATE dbo.Colors SET Color='Black' WHERE Color='White'` statement.

Let's run both sessions simultaneously in READ COMMITTED or any other pessimistic transaction isolation level. In the first step, as shown in Figure 21-8, we have the race condition. One of the sessions places exclusive (X) locks on the row it updated while the other session will be blocked when trying to acquire an update (U) lock on the same row.

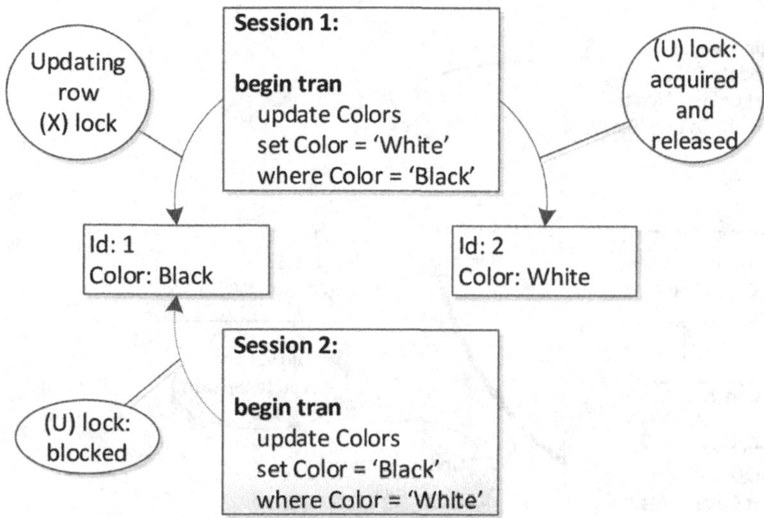

Figure 21-8. *Pessimistic locking behavior: Step 1*

Once the first session commits the transaction, the exclusive (X) lock will be released. At this point, the row will have a *Color* value updated by the first session so that the second session updates two rows rather than one, as shown in Figure 21-9. In the end, both rows in the table will be either *Black* or *White* depending on which session acquires the lock first.

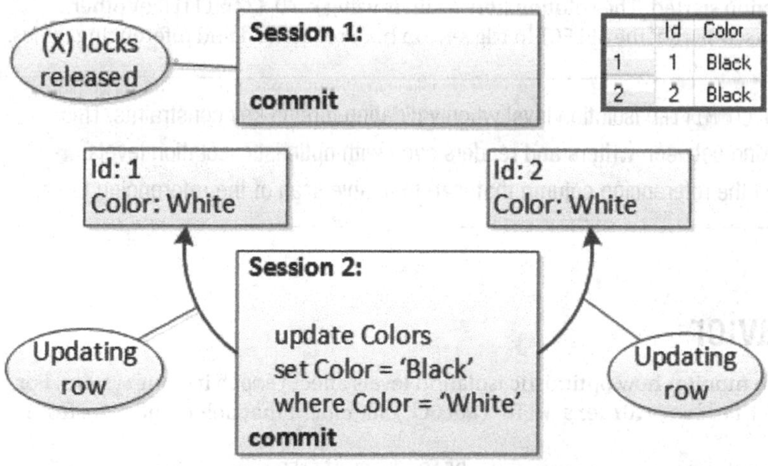

Figure 21-9. *Pessimistic locking behavior: Step 2*

With the SNAPSHOT isolation level, however, this works a bit differently, as shown in Figure 21-10. When the first session updates the row, it moves the old version of the row to the version store. The second session will read the row from there, rather than being blocked, and vice versa. As a result, the colors will be swapped.

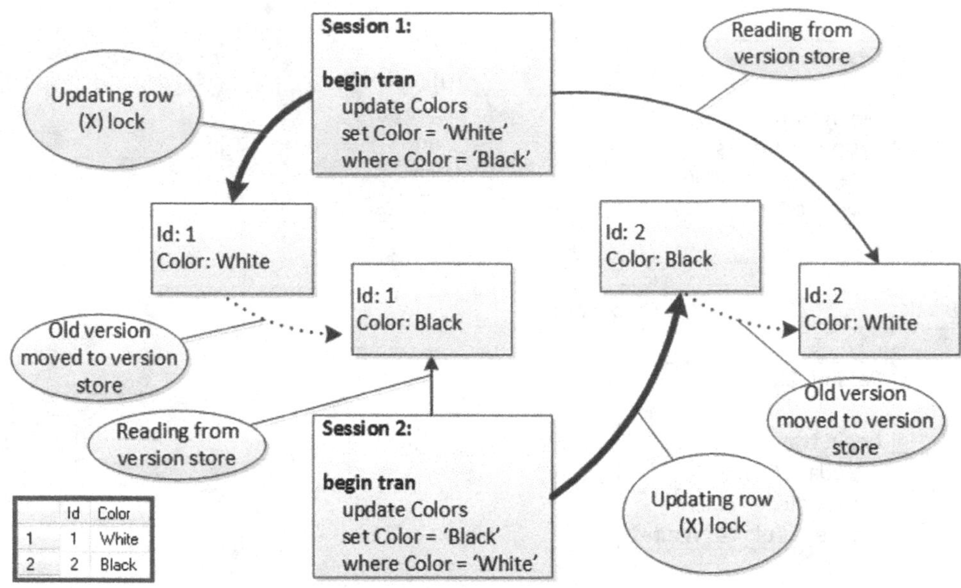

Figure 21-10. *Snapshot isolation level locking behavior*

You need to be aware of RCSI and SNASPSHOT isolation level behavior, especially if you have code that relies on blocking. One example is trigger-based implementation of referential integrity. You can have an ON DELETE trigger on the referenced table, where you are running a SELECT statement, to check if there are any rows in another table referencing deleted rows. With an optimistic isolation level, the trigger can skip the rows that were inserted after the transaction started. The solution here again is using READ COMMITTED or other pessimistic isolation level table hints as part of the SELECT in triggers on both referenced and referencing tables.

■ **Note** SQL Server uses a READ COMMITTED isolation level when validating foreign key constraints. This means that you can still have blocking between writers and readers even with optimistic isolation levels, especially if there are no indexes on the referencing column that lead to a table scan of the referencing table.

Version Store Behavior

As already mentioned, you need to monitor how optimistic isolation levels affect tempdb in your system. For example, let's run the DELETE FROM Delivery.Orders WITH (NOLOCK) statement that deletes all rows from the Delivery.Orders table.

The WITH (NOLOCK) hint forces the statement to run in the READ UNCOMMITTED transaction isolation level. Even if there are no other transactions using optimistic isolation levels, there is still a possibility that they will start before the DELETE transaction commits. As a result, SQL Server needs to maintain the version store, regardless of whether there are any active transactions that use optimistic isolation levels.

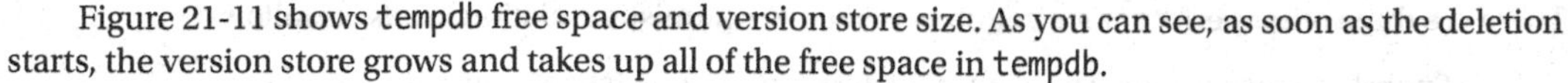

Figure 21-11 shows tempdb free space and version store size. As you can see, as soon as the deletion starts, the version store grows and takes up all of the free space in tempdb.

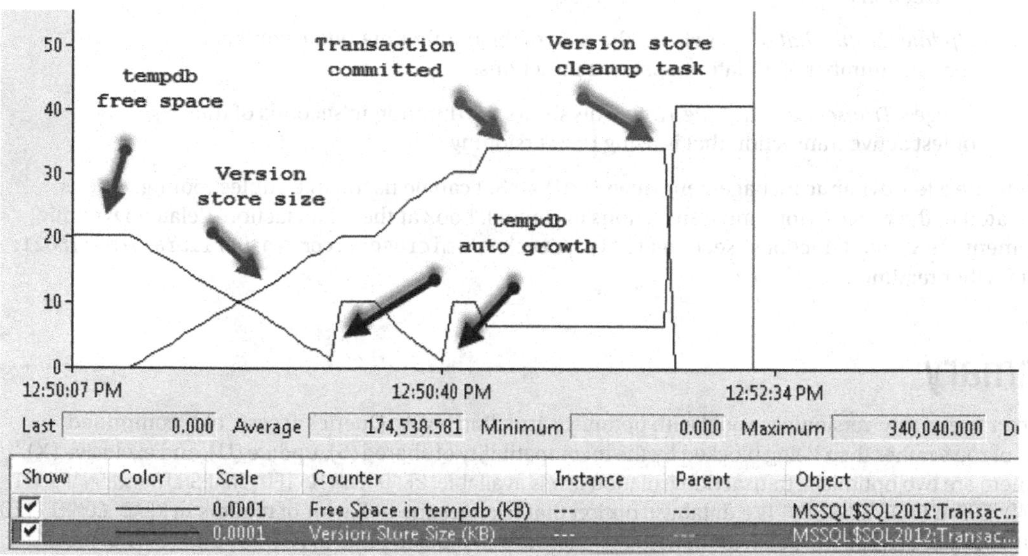

Figure 21-11. *Tempdb free space and version store size*

In Figure 21-12, you can see the version store generation and cleanup rate. The generation rate remained more or less the same during execution, while the cleanup task cleaned the version store after the transaction was committed. By default, the cleanup task runs once per minute as well as before an auto-growth event, in case tempdb is full.

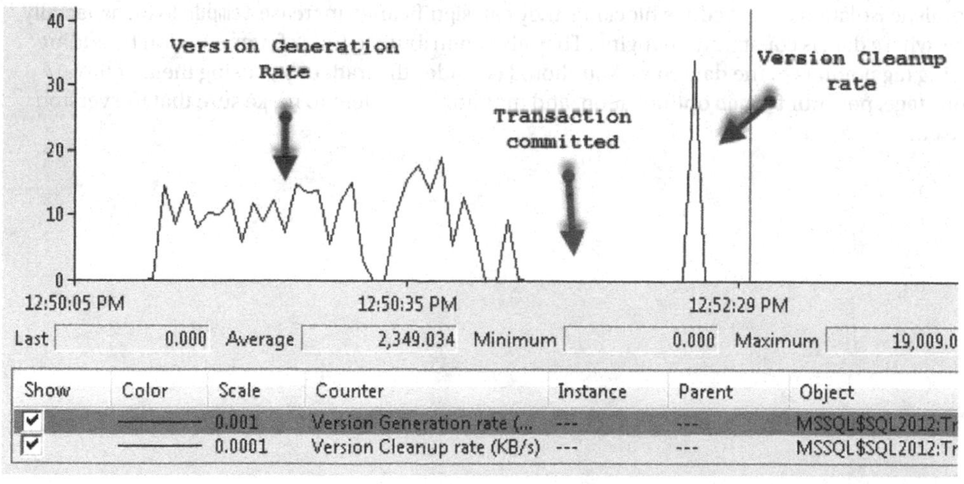

Figure 21-12. *Version generation and cleanup rates*

There are three other performance counters related to optimistic isolation levels, as follows:

1. *Snapshot Transactions*. This shows the total number of active snapshot transactions.
2. *Update Conflict Ratio*. This shows the ratio of the number of update conflicts to the total number of update snapshot transactions.
3. *Longest Transaction Running Time*. This shows the duration in seconds of the oldest active transaction that is using row versioning.

There are a few dynamic management views (DMVs) that can be useful in troubleshooting various issues related to the version store and transactions in general. Look at the "Transaction-Related Dynamic Management Views and Functions" section at `http://technet.microsoft.com/en-us/library/ms178621.aspx` for further reading.

Summary

SQL Server uses a row-versioning model with optimistic isolation levels. Queries access "old" committed versions of rows rather than being blocked by the incompatibility of shared (S), update (U), and exclusive (X) locks. There are two optimistic transaction isolation levels available: `READ COMMITTED SNAPSHOT` and `SNAPSHOT`.

`READ COMMITTED SNAPSHOT` is a database option that changes the behavior of readers in `READ COMMITTED` mode. It does not change the behavior of writers—there is still blocking due to (U)/(U) and (U)/(X) locks' incompatibility. `READ COMMITTED SNAPSHOT` does not require any code changes, and it can be used as an emergency technique when a system is experiencing blocking issues.

`READ COMMITTED SNAPSHOT` provides statement-level consistency; that is, the query reads a snapshot of the data at the time the statement started.

The `SNAPSHOT` isolation level is a separate transaction isolation level that needs to be explicitly specified in the code. This level provides transaction-level consistency; that is, the query accesses a snapshot of the data at the time the transaction started.

With the `SNAPSHOT` isolation level, writers do not block each other, with the exception of a situation where both sessions are updating the same rows. Such a situation leads either to blocking or to a 3960 error.

While optimistic isolation levels reduce blocking, they can significantly increase `tempdb` load, especially in OLTP systems where data is constantly changing. They also contribute to index fragmentation by adding 14-byte versioning tag pointers to the data rows. You should consider the tradeoffs of using them at the implementation stage, perform `tempdb` optimization, and monitor the system to make sure that the version store is not abused.

CHAPTER 22

Application Locks

This chapter discusses another SQL Server locking feature called *application locks*, which allow you to place locks on an application's resources as identified by name. One of the most common scenarios where application locks are beneficial is serializing access to T-SQL code in the client application, similar to critical sections and mutexes.

Application Locks Overview

Application locks allow an application to place a lock on an *application resource*, which is not related to database objects and is identified by name only. The lock would follow the regular rules in terms of lock compatibility, and it can be one of the following types: shared (S), update (U), exclusive (X), intent shared (IS), and intent exclusive (IX).

An application needs to call the `sp_getapplock` stored procedure to acquire the lock, using the following parameters:

`@Resource`: Specifies the name of the application lock

`@LockMode`: Specifies the lock type

`@LockOwner`: Should be one of two values—*Transaction* or *Session*—and control the owner (and scope) of the lock.

`@LockTimeout`: Specifies the timeout in milliseconds. If stored procedure cannot acquire the lock within this interval, it would return an error.

`@DbPrincipal`: Specifies security context (the caller needs to be a member of *database_principal*, *dbo*, or *db_owner* roles)

This procedure returns a value greater than or equal to zero in the case of success, and a negative value in the case of failure. As with regular locks, there is the possibility of deadlocks, although this would not roll back the transaction of the session that is chosen as the victim, but would rather return an error code that indicates the deadlock condition.

An application needs to call the `sp_releaseapplock` stored procedure to release the application lock. Alternatively, in cases where the `@LockOwner` of the lock is a transaction, the lock would be automatically released when the transaction commits or rolls back. This is similar to regular locks.

Application Locks Usage

There is a concept in computer science called *mutual execution*. It signifies that multiple threads or processes cannot execute specific code at the same time. As an example, think about a multi-threaded application in which threads use shared objects. In those systems, you often need to serialize the code that accesses those objects, preventing the race conditions where multiple threads read and update them simultaneously.

D. Korotkevitch, *Pro SQL Server Internals*, DOI 10.1007/978-1-4842-1964-5_22

Every development language has a set of synchronization primitives that can accomplish such tasks (for example, mutexes and critical sections). Application locks do the same trick when you need to serialize some part of the T-SQL code.

As an example, let's think about a system that collects some data, saves it into the database, and has a set of application servers for data processing. Each application server reads the package of data, processes it, and finally deletes processed data from the original table. Obviously, you do not want different application servers processing the same rows, and serializing the data loading process is one of the available options. An exclusive (X) table lock would not work, because it blocks any table access, rather than just the data loading. Implementing serialization on the application server level is not a trivial task either. Fortunately, application locks could help to solve the problem.

Let's assume that you have the table shown in Listing 22-1. For simplicity's sake, there is a column called `Attributes` that represents all of the row data.

Listing 22-1. Table structure

```
create table dbo.RawData
(
    ID int not null,
    Attributes char(100) not null
        constraint DEF_RawData_Attributes default 'Row Data',
    ProcessingTime datetime not null
        constraint DEF_RawData_ProcessingTime default '2000-01-01',
    constraint PK_RawData
    primary key clustered(ID)
)
```

There are two important columns: ID, which is the primary key, and `ProcessingTime`, which represents the time at which the row was loaded for processing. You should use UTC rather than local time to support situations in which application servers are residing in different time zones, as well as to prevent issues when the clock is adjusted to Daylight Saving Time. This column also helps to prevent other sessions from re-reading the data while it is still processing. It is better to avoid Boolean (bit) columns for such purposes, because if the application server crashes the row would remain in the table forever. With the time column, the system can read it again after some length of timeout.

Now, let's create the stored procedure that reads the data, as shown in Listing 22-2.

Listing 22-2. Stored procedure that reads the data

```
create proc dbo.LoadRawData(@PacketSize int)
as
    set nocount, xact_abort on

    declare
        @EarliestProcessingTime datetime
        ,@ResCode int

    declare
        @Data table
          (
                ID int not null primary key,
                Attributes char(100) not null
            )
```

```
begin tran
    exec @ResCode = sp_getapplock
        @Resource = 'LoadRowDataLock'
        ,@LockMode = 'Exclusive'
        ,@LockOwner = 'Transaction'
        ,@LockTimeout = 15000; -- 15 seconds
    if @ResCode >= 0 -- success
    begin
        -- We assume that app server processes the packet within 1 minute unless crashed
        select @EarliestProcessingTime = dateadd(minute,-1,getutcdate());
        ;with DataPacket(ID, Attributes, ProcessingTime)
        as
        (
            select top (@PacketSize) ID, Attributes, ProcessingTime
            from dbo.RawData
            where ProcessingTime <= @EarliestProcessingTime
            order by ID
        )
        update DataPacket
        set ProcessingTime = getutcdate()
        output inserted.ID, inserted.Attributes into @Data(ID, Attributes);
    end
    -- we don't need to explicitly release application lock because @LockOwner is
    -- Transaction
commit
select ID, Attributes from @Data;
```

The stored procedure obtains an exclusive (X) application lock at the beginning of the transaction. As a result, all other sessions calling the stored procedure will be blocked until the transaction is committed and the application lock is released. It guarantees that only one session can update and read the data simultaneously from within the stored procedure. At the same time, other sessions can still work with the table (for example, insert new rows or delete processed rows). Application locks are separate from data locks, and sessions would not be blocked unless they were trying to obtain an application lock for the same `@Resource` with the `sp_getapplock` call.

Figure 22-1 demonstrates the output from the `sys.dm_tran_locks` data management view at the time when two sessions were calling the `dbo.LoadRawData` stored procedure simultaneously. The session with `SPID=58` successfully obtained an application lock, while the other session, with `SPID=63`, is blocked. A `resource_type` value of `APPLICATION` indicates an application lock.

	request_session_id	resource_type	resource_description	request_type	request_status	request_owner_type
1	58	APPLICATION	0:[LoadRowDataLock]:(039ad780)	LOCK	GRANT	TRANSACTION
2	63	APPLICATION	0:[LoadRowDataLock]:(039ad780)	LOCK	WAIT	TRANSACTION

Figure 22-1. *Sys.dm_tran_locks output*

It is worth mentioning that, if our goal is to simply guarantee that multiple sessions cannot read the same rows simultaneously, rather than serializing the entire read process, there is another, simpler, solution. You can use locking table hints, as shown in Listing 22-3.

Listing 22-3. Serializing access to the data with table locking hints

```
;with DataPacket(ID, Attributes, ProcessingTime)
as
(
    select top (@PacketSize) ID, Attributes, ProcessingTime
    from dbo.RawData with (updlock, readpast)
    where ProcessingTime <= @EarliestProcessingTime
    order by ID
)
update DataPacket
set ProcessingTime = getutcdate()
output inserted.ID, inserted.Attributes into @Data(ID, Attributes)
```

The UPDLOCK hint forces SQL Server to use update (U) rather than shared (S) locks during SELECT operations. This prevents other sessions from reading the same rows simultaneously. At the same time, the READPAST hint forces the sessions to skip the rows with incompatible locks held rather than being blocked.

Although both implementations accomplish the same goal, they use different approaches. The latter serializes access to the same rows by using data (row level) locks. Application locks serialize access to the code and prevent multiple sessions from running the statement simultaneously. This can be very useful in cases where you want to prevent some code from being executed in parallel.

Summary

Application locks allow an application to place a lock on an application resource; it is not related to database objects and is identified by name. It is a useful tool that helps you to implement *mutual execution* code patterns, serializing access to T-SQL code similar to critical sections and mutexes in the client applications.

You can create application locks using the sp_getapplock stored procedure and release them using the sp_releaseapplock stored procedure. Application locks can have either session or transaction scope, and they follow regular lock compatibility rules as the data locks.

CHAPTER 23

Schema Locks

SQL Server uses two additional lock types, called *schema locks*, to prevent table and metadata alteration during query execution. This chapter discusses schema locks in depth, along with other topics such as lock partitioning, which occurs in systems with more than 16 CPUs, and low-priority locks, which were introduced in SQL Server 2014 to reduce blocking during online index rebuilds and partition switch operations.

Schema Modification Locks

SQL Server needs to protect database metadata in order to prevent situations where the table structure is changed in the middle of query execution. The problem is more complicated than it seems, however. Even though exclusive (X) table locks can, in theory, block access to a table during an `ALTER TABLE` operation, they would not work in a `READ UNCOMMITTED` isolation level where readers do not acquire intent shared (IS) table locks.

SQL Server uses two additional lock types to address the problem: schema stability (Sch-S) and schema modification (Sch-M) locks. Schema modification (Sch-M) locks are acquired before any metadata changes and during the execution of a `TRUNCATE TABLE` statement. You can think about this lock type as a "super lock." It is incompatible with any other lock types, and it completely blocks access to the object.

Similar to exclusive (X) locks, schema modification (Sch-M) locks are held until the end of the transaction. You need to keep this in mind when you run DDL statements within explicit transactions. While explicit transaction allows you to roll back all of the schema changes in case of an error, it also prevents any access to the affected objects until the transaction is committed.

Important Many database schema-comparison tools use explicit transactions in the alteration script. This could introduce serious blocking when you run the script on live servers while other users are accessing the system.

SQL Server also uses schema modification (Sch-M) locks while altering the partition function. This can seriously affect the availability of the system when such alterations introduce data movement or scans. Access to the entire partitioned table is then blocked until the operation is completed.

Schema stability (Sch-S) locks are used during DML query compilation and execution. SQL Server acquires them regardless of the transaction isolation level, even in `READ UNCOMMITTED` mode. Schema stability (Sch-S) locks are compatible with any lock type other than schema modification (Sch-M) locks.

SQL Server can perform some optimizations to reduce the number of locks acquired. While a schema stability (Sch-S) lock is always used during query compilation, SQL Server can replace it with an intent object lock during query execution. Let's look at the example shown in Table 23-1.

The first session starts the transaction and alters the table, acquiring a schema modification (Sch-M) lock there. In the next step, two other sessions run a `SELECT` statement in the `READ UNCOMMITTED` isolation level and a `DELETE` statement, respectively.

D. Korotkevitch, *Pro SQL Server Internals*, DOI 10.1007/978-1-4842-1964-5_23

Table 23-1. Schema Locks: Query Compilation

Session 1 (SPID=64)	Session 2 (SPID=65)	Session 3 (SPID=66)

`begin tran`
`alter table Delivery.Orders`
`add Dummy int;`		

	`select count(*)`
	`from Delivery.Orders`
	`with (nolock);`
		`delete from Delivery.Orders`
		`where OrderId = 1;`

`select request_session_id`
`,resource_type, request_type`
`,request_mode, request_status`
`from sys.dm_tran_locks`
`where resource_type = 'OBJECT';`
`rollback`		

As you can see in Figure 23-1, sessions 2 and 3 were blocked while waiting for schema stability (Sch-S) locks that were required for query compilation.

	request_session_id	resource_type	request_type	request_mode	request_status
1	64	OBJECT	LOCK	Sch-M	GRANT
2	65	OBJECT	LOCK	Sch-S	WAIT
3	66	OBJECT	LOCK	Sch-S	WAIT

***Figure 23-1.** Schema locks during query compilation*

If you run that example a second time, when queries are compiled and plans are in the cache, you would see a slightly different picture, as shown in Figure 23-2.

	request_session_id	resource_type	request_type	request_mode	request_status
1	64	OBJECT	LOCK	Sch-M	GRANT
2	65	OBJECT	LOCK	Sch-S	WAIT
3	66	OBJECT	LOCK	IX	WAIT

***Figure 23-2.** Schema locks when execution plans are cached*

The second session would still wait for the schema stability (Sch-S) lock. There are no shared (S) locks in the READ UNCOMMITTED mode, and the schema stability (Sch-S) lock is the only way to keep a schema stable during execution. However, the session with the DELETE statement would wait for an intent exclusive (IX) lock instead. That lock type needs to be acquired anyway, and it can replace a schema stability (Sch-S) lock because it is also incompatible with schema modification (Sch-M) locks and prevents the schema from being altered.

Mixing schema modification locks with other lock types in the same transaction increases the possibility of deadlocks. Let's assume that we have two sessions. The first one starts the transaction and updates the row in the table. At this point, it holds an exclusive (X) lock on the row and two intent exclusive (IX) locks, one each on the page and the table. If another session tries to read (or update) the same row, it will be blocked. At this point, it will wait for the shared (S) lock on the row and then will have the intent shared (IS) locks held on the page and the table. That stage is illustrated in Figure 23-3. (Page-level intent locks are omitted.)

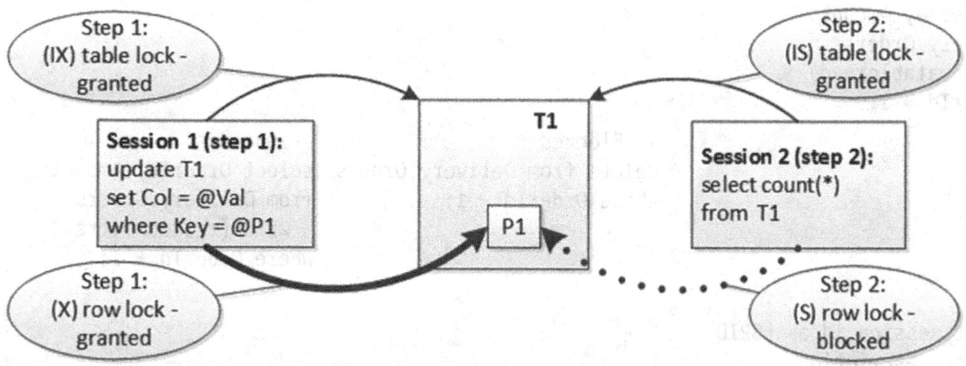

***Figure 23-3.** Deadlock due to mixed DDL and DML statements: Step 1*

If at this point the first session wants to alter the table, it will need to acquire a schema modification (Sch-M) lock. This lock type is incompatible with any other lock type, and the session will be blocked by the intent shared (IS) lock held by the second session, which leads to a deadlock condition, as shown in Figure 23-4.

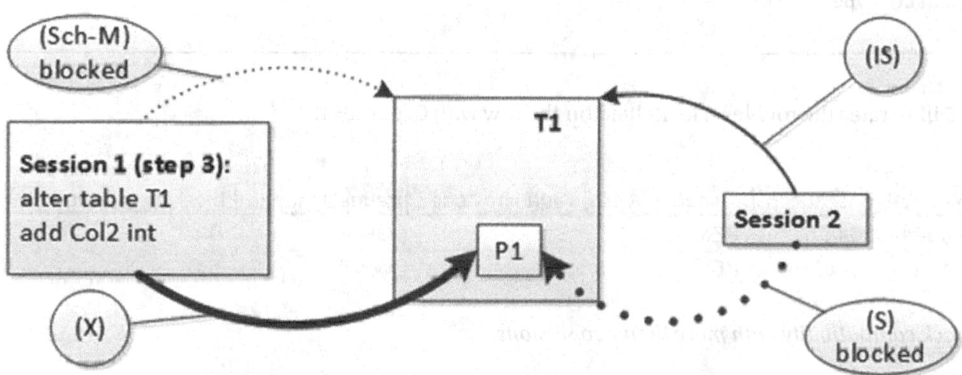

***Figure 23-4.** Deadlock due to mixed DDL and DML statements: Step 2*

Multiple Sessions and Lock Compatibility

One important point we have yet to cover is lock compatibility when more than two sessions are competing for the same resource. Let's look at a couple of examples.

As you can see in Table 23-2, the first session (`SPID=55`) holds a shared (S) lock on the row. The second session (`SPID=54`) is trying to acquire an exclusive (X) lock on the same row, and it is being blocked due to lock incompatibility. The third session (`SPID=53`) is reading the same row in the `READ COMMITTED` transaction isolation level. This session has not been blocked.

Table 23-2. *Multiple Sessions and Lock Compatibility (READ COMMITTED Isolation Level)*

Session 1 (SPID=55)	Session 2 (SPID=54)	Session 3 (SPID=53)

begin tran
  select OrderId, Amount
  from Delivery.Orders
    with (repeatableread)
  where OrderId = 1;		

	-- Blocked delete from Delivery.Orders where OrderId = 1;	-- Success select OrderId, Amount from Delivery.Orders with (readcommitted) where OrderId = 1;

select
    l.request_session_id as [SPID],
    l.resource_description,
    l.resource_type, l.request_mode,
    l.request_status,
    r.blocking_session_id
  from
    sys.dm_tran_locks l join
      sys.dm_exec_requests r on
        l.request_session_id =
           r.session_id
  where l.resource_type = 'KEY';
rollback		

Figure 23-5 illustrates the row-level locks held on the row with OrderId=1.

	SPID	resource_description	resource_type	request_mode	request_status	blocking_session_id
1	55	(8194443284a0)	KEY	S	GRANT	0
2	54	(8194443284a0)	KEY	X	WAIT	55

Figure 23-5. *Lock compatibility with more than two sessions*

As you can see in Figure 23-6, the third session did not even try to acquire the shared (S) lock on the row. There is already a shared (S) lock on the row held by the first session (SPID=55), which guarantees that the row has not been modified by uncommitted transactions. In a READ COMMITTED isolation level, a shared (S) lock releases immediately after a row is read. As a result, session 3 (SPID=53) does not need to hold its own shared (S) lock after reading the row, and it can rely on the lock from session 1.

EventClass	EventSequence	SPID	Mode	Type	TextData
Lock:Acquired	34	55	6 - IS	5 - OBJECT	
Lock:Acquired	35	55	6 - IS	6 - PAGE	1:323
Lock:Acquired	36	55	3 - S	7 - KEY	(8194443284a0)
Lock:Acquired	37	54	8 - IX	5 - OBJECT	
Lock:Acquired	38	54	8 - IX	6 - PAGE	1:323
Lock:Acquired	39	53	6 - IS	5 - OBJECT	
Lock:Acquired	40	53	6 - IS	6 - PAGE	1:323

***Figure 23-6.** Locks acquired during the operation*

Let's change our example and see what happens if the third session tries to read the row in a REPEATABLE READ isolation level, where a shared (S) lock needs to be held until the end of the transaction, as shown in Table 23-3. In this case, the third session will need to acquire its own shared (S) lock, and it will be blocked because of an incompatible exclusive (X) lock from the second session in the queue.

***Table 23-3.** Multiple Sessions and Lock Compatibility (REPEATABLE READ Isolation Level)*

Session 1 (SPID=55)	Session 2 (SPID=54)	Session 3 (SPID=53)

```
begin tran
  select OrderId, Amount
  from Delivery.Orders
    with (repeatableread)
  where OrderId = 1;
                                          -- Blocked                     -- Blocked
                                          delete from Delivery.Orders  select OrderId, Amount
                                          where OrderId = 1;           from Delivery.Orders
                                                                         with (repeatableread)
                                                                       where OrderId = 1;
  select
    l.request_session_id as [SPID],
    l.resource_description,
    l.resource_type, l.request_mode,
    l.request_status,
    r.blocking_session_id
  from
    sys.dm_tran_locks l join
      sys.dm_exec_requests r on
        l.request_session_id =
          r.session_id
  where l.resource_type = 'KEY';
rollback
```

Figure 23-7 illustrates the row-level locks requests at this point.

	SPID	resource_description	resource_type	request_mode	request_status	blocking_session_id
1	55	(8194443284a0)	KEY	S	GRANT	0
2	54	(8194443284a0)	KEY	X	WAIT	55
3	53	(8194443284a0)	KEY	S	WAIT	54

Figure 23-7. *Lock compatibility with more than two sessions*

This leads as to a very important conclusion: **In order to be granted, a lock needs to be compatible with all of the lock requests on that resource, granted or not**.

It is also worth noting that the first scenario, where the third session ran in the `READ COMMITTED` isolation level and did not acquire a lock on the resource, can be considered an internal optimization, which you should not rely upon. In some cases, SQL Server still acquires another shared (S) lock on the resource in `READ COMMITTED` mode, even if there is another shared (S) lock already held. In such a case, the query would be blocked, similar to the `REPEATABLE READ` isolation level example.

Lock Partitioning

The behavior we just observed means that lock requests are serialized, and thus requests on the same object should not deadlock each other. Unfortunately, there is another factor that complicates matters. When a system has 16 or more logical processors, SQL Server starts to use a technique called *lock partitioning*. This term is a bit confusing, as it has nothing to do with table partitioning or lock escalation. When lock partitioning is enabled, SQL Server starts to store the information about locks on a per-scheduler (logical CPU) basis. In this mode, intent shared (IS), intent exclusive (IX), and schema stability (Sch-S) locks are acquired and stored on a single partition based on the CPU (scheduler) where the batch is executing. All other lock types need to be acquired on all of the partitions. This does not change anything from a lock compatibility standpoint. When a session needs to acquire an exclusive (X) table lock, for example, it would go through all of the lock partitions and be blocked if any partition held an incompatible intent lock on the table.

However, there are two consequences about which you need to be aware. First, SQL Server needs more memory to store lock information. Non-partitioned locks are stored separately in every partition, and if, for example, a system has 20 CPUs, it would maintain 20 lock structures instead of just one. All lock types that can be acquired on the row level are non-partitioned.

The second issue is more complicated. Lock partitioning increases the chances of deadlocks when object-level locks are involved.

Let's look at an example and assume that the first session updates a row in a system that uses lock partitioning. If this batch is executing on CPU 2, the session acquires an intent exclusive (IX) table lock, which is partitioned and stored on CPU 2 only. It also acquires a row-level exclusive (X) lock, which is not partitioned and is stored across all CPUs. (I am omitting page-level intent locks again for simplicity's sake.)

The second session is trying to alter the table, and it needs to acquire a schema modification (Sch-M) lock. This lock type is non-partitioned, so the session needs to acquire it on every CPU. It successfully acquires and holds the locks on CPUs 0 and 1, and it is blocked on CPU 2 due the lock's incompatibility with the intent exclusive (IX) lock held there. Figure 23-8 illustrates this condition.

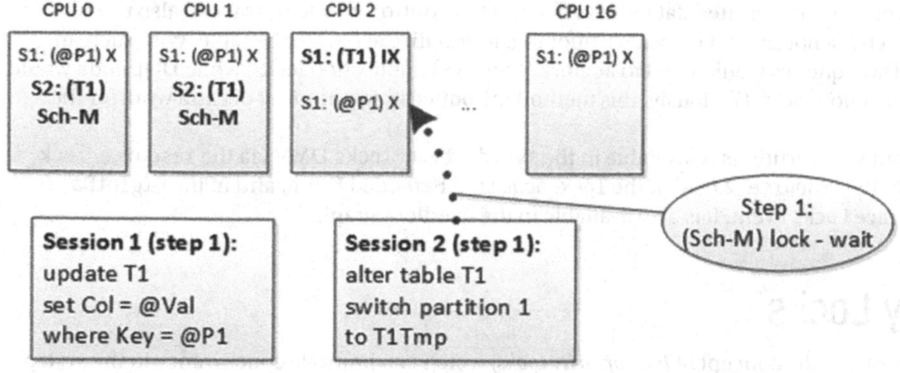

Figure 23-8. *Deadlock due to lock partitioning: Step 1*

If the first session now tries to acquire another intent table lock on CPUs 0 or 1, it would be blocked because the second session already holds a schema modification (Sch-M) lock there. We again have a deadlock, as shown in Figure 23-9.

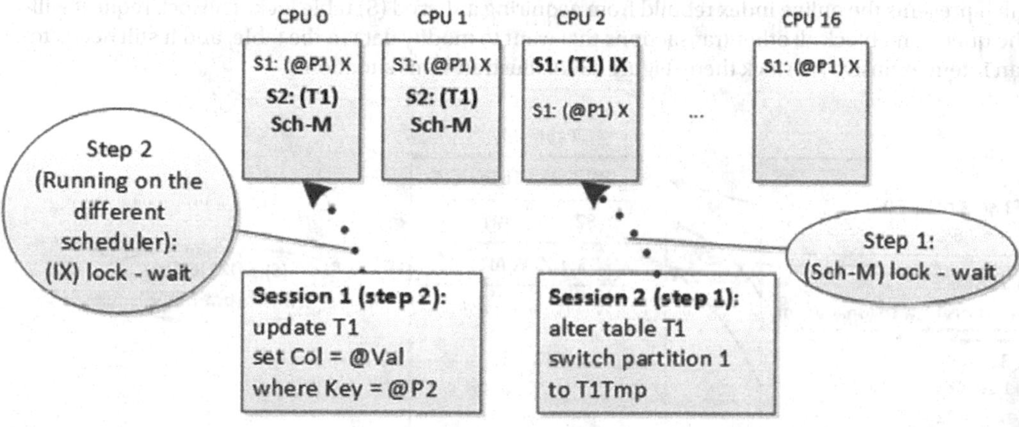

Figure 23-9. *Deadlock due to lock partitioning: Step 2*

While this could happen with any object-level, non-intent lock type, one of the most common scenarios happens with partitioned table-related operations, such as a partition switch or a partition function alteration. These operations require schema modification (Sch-M) locks, which can often lead to deadlocks on busy systems when many sessions are accessing the same object.

Unfortunately, there is very little you can do about it. Lock partitioning cannot be disabled through documented approaches. The undocumented trace flag `T1229` does the trick; however, using undocumented trace flags is not recommended in production. Moreover, in those systems with a large number of CPUs, disabling lock partitioning can lead to performance issues resulting from excessive serialization during lock structures management.

With lock partitioning in place, the best option that you have is to implement retry logic using `TRY/CATCH` around DDL statements. A `SET DEADLOCK_PRIORITY` boost could also help reduce the chance that a DDL session will be chosen as the deadlock victim.

In cases where you have a dedicated data access tier and full control around it, you can also use application locks, which are not subject to lock partitioning, to serialize access to the table. With such an implementation, all DML queries would need to acquire shared (S) application locks, while DDL code would use exclusive (X) application locks. Obviously, this method introduces a fair amount of extra work for the implementation.

Information about lock partitions is available in the `sys.dm_tran_locks` DMV via the `resource_lock_partition` column, in the `resource_2` field of the `lock_acquired` Extended Event, and in the `BigIntData1` column in the SQL Trace `Locks` event. It is also available in the deadlock graph.

Low-Priority Locks

SQL Server 2014 introduced the concept of *low-priority locks*, which can improve concurrency in the system during online index rebuilds and partition switch operations. You already know that a partition switch acquires a schema modification (Sch-M) lock. The same is also true with an online index rebuild. Even though it holds an intent shared (IS) table lock during the rebuild process, it needs to acquire a shared (S) table lock at the beginning and a schema modification (Sch-M) lock in the final phase of execution. Both locks are held for a very short time; however, they can introduce blocking issues in busy OLTP environments.

Consider a situation where you start an online index rebuild at a time when you have another active transaction modifying data in a table. That initial transaction will hold an intent exclusive (IX) lock on the table, which prevents the online index rebuild from acquiring a shared (S) table lock. The lock request will wait in the queue and block all other transactions that want to modify data in the table, and it still needs to acquire an intent exclusive (IX) lock there. Figure 23-10 illustrates this situation.

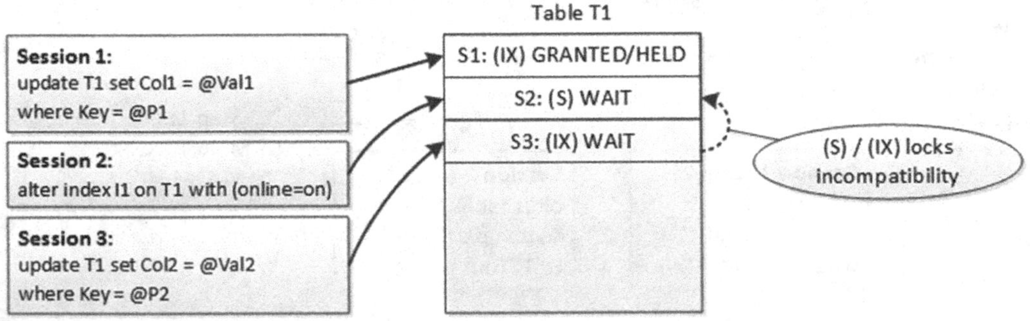

Figure 23-10. *Blocking during the initial stage of an index rebuild*

This blocking condition clears only after the first transaction is completed and the online index rebuild acquires and releases a shared (S) table lock. A similar blocking condition could occur in the final stage of an online index rebuild when it needs to acquire a schema modification (Sch-M) lock to replace an index reference in the metadata. Both readers and writers will be blocked while the index rebuild waits for the schema modification (Sch-M) lock to be granted.

While this behavior occurs in every version of SQL Server, you can mitigate blocking issues in SQL Server 2014 and 2016 by using low-priority locks. Low-priority locks do not block other sessions that want to acquire incompatible lock types while they are waiting for such locks to be acquired. Conceptually, you can think of low-priority locks as staying in a different locking queue than regular locks. Figure 23-11 illustrates this concept.

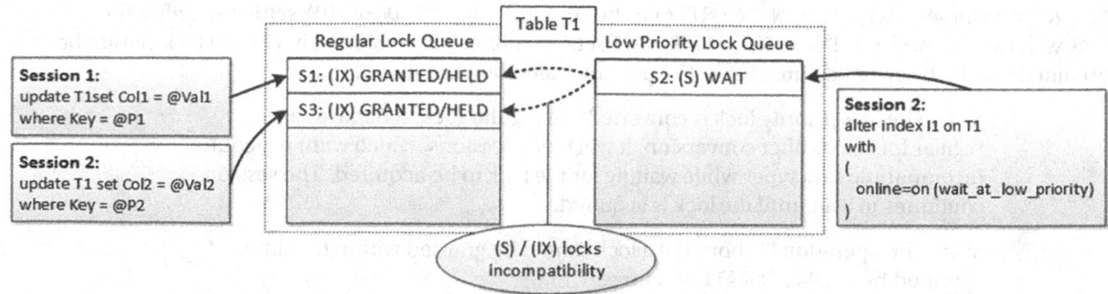

Figure 23-11. Low-priority locks

■ **Important** It is essential to remember that as soon as a low-priority lock is acquired it will then behave the same as a regular lock, preventing other sessions from acquiring incompatible locks on the resource.

Figure 23-12 shows the output of the query from Listing 18-1 in Chapter 18. It demonstrates how low-priority locks are shown in the `sys.dm_tran_locks` data management view output. It is worth noting that the view does not provide the wait time of those locks.

	Resource Type	DB Name	Object	Resource	Session	Mode	Status	Wait (ms)	sql
1	OBJECT	Dummy2	Customers		61	IX	GRANT	NULL	update Delivery.Customers set Name = 'Customer' ...
2	OBJECT	Dummy2	Customers		62	S	LOW_PRIORITY_WAIT	NULL	alter index PK_Customers on Delivery.Customers re...
3	OBJECT	Dummy2	PK_Customers		62	Sch-S	GRANT	NULL	alter index PK_Customers on Delivery.Customers re...
4	OBJECT	Dummy2	Customers		62	IS	GRANT	NULL	alter index PK_Customers on Delivery.Customers re...

Figure 23-12. Low-priority locks in the sys.dm_tran_locks data management view

You can specify lock priority with a `WAIT_AT_LOW_PRIORITY` clause in the `ALTER INDEX` and `ALTER TABLE` statements, as shown in Listing 23-1.

Listing 23-1. Specifying lock priority

```
alter index PK_Customers on Delivery.Customers rebuild
with
(
    online=on
    (
        wait_at_low_priority( max_duration=10 minutes, abort_after_wait=blockers )
    )
);

alter table Delivery.Orders
switch partition 1 to Delivery.OrdersTmp
with
(
    wait_at_low_priority ( max_duration=60 minutes, abort_after_wait=self )
)
```

As you can see, WAIT_AT_LOW_PRIORITY has two options. The MAX_DURATION setting specifies the lock wait time in minutes. The ABORT_AFTER_WAIT setting defines the session behavior if a lock cannot be obtained within the specified time limit. The possible values are as follows:

> NONE: The low-priority lock is converted to a regular lock. It behaves as a regular lock does after conversion. It will block sessions, which want to acquire incompatible lock types while waiting for the lock to be acquired. The session continues to wait until the lock is acquired.
>
> SELF: The operation is aborted if a lock cannot be granted within the time specified by the MAX_DURATION setting.
>
> BLOCKERS: All sessions that held locks on the resource are aborted, and the session that is waiting for a low-priority lock is able to acquire it.

■ **Note** Omitting the WAIT_AT_LOW_PRIORITY clause works the same way as specifying WAIT_AT_LOW_PRIORITY(MAX_DURATION=0 MINUTES, ABORT_AFTER_WAIT=NONE).

Very active OLTP tables always have a large number of concurrent sessions accessing them. Therefore, there is always the possibility that a session will not be able to acquire a low-priority lock even with a prolonged MAX_DURATION specified. You may consider using the ABORT_AFTER_WAIT=BLOCKERS option, which will allow the operation to complete, especially when client applications have proper exception handling and retry logic implemented.

Summary

SQL Server uses schema locks to protect metadata from alteration during query compilation and execution. There are two types of schema locks in SQL Server: schema stability (Sch-S) and schema modification (Sch-M) locks.

Schema stability (Sch-S) locks are acquired on objects referenced by queries during query compilation and execution. In some cases, however, SQL Server can replace schema stability (Sch-S) locks with intent table locks, which also protect the table schema. Schema stability (Sch-S) locks are compatible with any other lock type, with the exception of schema modification (Sch-M) locks.

Schema modification (Sch-M) locks are incompatible with any other lock type. SQL Server uses them during DDL operations. If a DDL operation needs to scan or modify the data (for example, adding a trusted foreign key constraint to the table or altering a partition function on a non-empty partition), the schema modification (Sch-M) lock would be held for the duration of the operation. This can take a long time on large tables and can cause severe blocking issues in the system. You need to keep this in mind when designing systems with DDL and DML operations running in parallel.

SQL Server uses lock partitioning on systems that have 16 or more logical processors. With lock partitioning, SQL Server maintains separate lock structures on a per-processor basis. Intent and schema stability locks are held within a single lock partition, while other lock types are acquired and held across all partitions. This increases the amount of memory required to store lock information, and it can increase the chances of deadlocks occurring when DDL and DML statements are running in parallel.

SQL Server 2014 and 2016 support low-priority locks, which can be used to reduce blocking during online index rebuild and partition switch operations. These locks do not block other sessions that are requesting incompatible lock types at the time when the low-priority lock is waiting for the lock to be acquired.

CHAPTER 24

Designing Transaction Strategies

This rather short chapter provides a set of generic guidelines for how you can design transaction strategies and improve concurrency in the systems.

Considerations and Code Patterns

Blocking occurs when multiple sessions compete for the same set of resources. Sessions are trying to acquire incompatible locks on them, which leads to lock collision and blocking.

As you already know, SQL Server acquires the locks when it *processes* data. It does not matter how many rows need to be modified or returned to the client. What matters is how many rows SQL Server accesses during the statement execution. It is entirely possible that a query that selected or updated just a single row acquired thousands or even millions of locks because of an *index scan* operator in the execution plan.

Proper query optimization and index tuning reduce the number of rows SQL Server needs to access during query executions. This, in turn, reduces the number of locks to acquire and the chance that lock collisions will occur.

Tip Optimize the queries. It will help to improve concurrency, performance, and user experience in the system.

Another method for reducing the chance of lock collision is reducing the length of time locks are held. Exclusive (X) locks are always held until the end of the transaction. The same is true for shared (S) locks in the `REPEATABLE READ` and `SERIALIZABLE` isolation levels. The longer locks are held, the bigger the chance is that lock collision and blocking will occur.

You need to make transactions as short as possible and avoid any long-time operations or interactions with users through the UI while a transaction is active. You also need to be careful when dealing with external resources using CLR or linked servers. For example, when a linked server is down, it can take a long time before a connection timeout occurs, and you want to avoid a situation where locks are kept all that time.

Tip Make transactions as short as possible.

Update the data as close to the end of the transaction as possible. This reduces the time that exclusive (X) locks are held. In some cases, it might make sense to use temporary tables as the staging place, inserting data there and updating the actual tables at the very end of the transaction.

D. Korotkevitch, *Pro SQL Server Internals*, DOI 10.1007/978-1-4842-1964-5_24

One particular instance when this technique is useful is an UPDATE statement that is impossible or unpractical to optimize. Consider a situation where the statement scans a large number of rows but updates just a handful of them. You can change the code, storing the clustered index key values of the rows that need to be updated in a temporary table, later running an UPDATE based on those collected key values.

Listing 24-1 shows an example of a statement that could lead to a *clustered index scan* during execution. SQL Server will need to acquire an update (U) lock on every row of the table.

Listing 24-1. Reducing blocking with temporary table: Original statement

```
update dbo.Orders
set
    Cancelled = 1
where
    (PendingCancellation = 1) or
    (Paid = 0 and OrderDate < @MinUnpaidDate) or
    (Status = 'BackOrdered' and EstimatedStockDate > @StockDate)
```

You can change the code to be similar to that shown in Listing 24-2. The SELECT statement either acquires shared (S) locks or does not acquire row-level locks at all, depending on the isolation level. The UPDATE statement is optimized, and it acquires just a handful of update (U) and exclusive (X) locks.

Listing 24-2. Reducing blocking with a temporary table: Using a temporary table to stage key values for the update

```
create table #OrdersToBeCancelled
( OrderId int not null primary key );

insert into #OrdersToBeCancelled(OrderId)
    select OrderId
    from dbo.Orders
    where
        (PendingCancellation = 1) or
        (Paid = 0 and OrderDate < @MinUnpaidDate) or
        (Status = 'BackOrdered' and EstimatedStockDate > @StockDate);

update dbo.Orders
set Cancelled = 1
where OrderId in (select OrderId from #OrdersToBeCancelled);
```

You need to remember that while this approach helps to reduce blocking, creating and populating temporary tables can introduce significant I/O overhead, especially when there is a large amount of data involved. This method should be considered as the last resort; creating the correct indexes is the better option in most cases.

■ **Tip** Modify data as close to the end of the transaction as possible.

You should avoid updating a row multiple times within the same transaction, especially when UPDATE statements modify data in the different nonclustered indexes. Remember that SQL Server acquires locks on a per-index basis when index rows are updated. Having multiple updates increases the chances of a deadlock occurring when other sessions are accessing the updated rows.

■ **Tip** Do not update data rows multiple times in a single transaction.

You need to understand whether lock escalation affects your system, especially in cases of OLTP workload. You can monitor object-level blocking conditions and locking waits and correlate it with *lock escalation* Extended and Trace Events. Remember that lock escalation helps to reduce memory consumption and improve performance in the system. You should analyze why lock escalation occurs and how it affects the system before making any decisions. In many cases, it is better to change the code and workflows rather than disable it.

■ **Tip** Monitor lock escalation in the system.

You should avoid mixing statements that can lead to row- and object-level locks in the same transaction in general, and mixing DML and DDL statements in particular. This pattern can lead to deadlock conditions as well as to blocking between intent and full object-level locks. This is especially important when servers have 16 or more logical CPUs, which enables lock partitioning.

■ **Tip** Do not mix DDL and DML statements in one transaction.

You need to analyze the root cause of deadlocks if you have them in your system. In most cases, query optimization and code re-factoring would help to address them. However, in some cases, especially if lock partitioning is involved, you can consider implementing retry logic around critical use cases in the system.

■ **Tip** Find the root cause of deadlocks. Implement retry logic if query optimization and code re-factoring do not address them.

Choosing Transaction Isolation Level

Choosing the right transaction isolation level is not a trivial task. You should find the right balance between blocking and `tempdb` overhead, and between the required level of data consistency and the isolation in the system. The system must provide reliable data to the customers, and you should not compromise by choosing an isolation level that cannot guarantee it just because you want to reduce blocking.

You should choose the *minimally required* isolation level that provides the required data consistency. In many cases, the default `READ COMMITTED` isolation level is *good enough*, especially if queries are optimized and do not perform unnecessary scans. Avoid using `REPEATABLE READ` or `SERIALIZABLE` isolation levels in OLTP systems unless you have legitimate reasons to do so. These isolation levels hold shared (S) locks until the end of the transaction, which can lead to severe blocking issues with volatile data. They can also trigger shared (S) lock escalation during the scans.

As a general rule, it is better to avoid the `READ UNCOMMITTED` isolation level. Even though many database professionals are trying to reduce blocking by switching to this isolation level, either explicitly or with `NOLOCK` hints, this is rarely the right choice. First, `READ UNCOMMITTED` does not address the blocking issues introduced by writers. They still acquire update (U) locks during scans. Most important, however, is that by using `READ UNCOMMITTED`, you are stating that data consistency is not required at all, and that it is not only about reading uncommitted data. SQL Server can choose execution plans that use *allocation map scans* on large tables, which can lead to missing rows and duplicated reads resulting from page splits, especially in busy systems with volatile data.

In a majority of the cases, optimistic isolation levels, especially `READ COMMITTED SNAPSHOT`, are a better choice than `READ UNCOMMITTED`, `REPEATABLE READ`, or `SERIALIZABLE`, even in OLTP systems. It provides statement-level data consistency without readers/writers blocking involved. Historically, I have been very cautious suggesting `RCSI` in OLTP systems due to its `tempdb` overhead; however, nowadays it becomes a lesser issue with modern hardware and solid state-based disk arrays. You should still factor additional index fragmentation and `tempdb` overhead into your analysis though. It is also worth noting that `READ COMMITTED SNAPSHOT` is enabled in Microsoft Azure SQL Databases.

As a general rule, I recommend you do not use the `SNAPSHOT` isolation level in OLTP systems due to its excessive `tempdb` usage unless transaction-level consistency is absolutely required. It could be a good choice for data warehouse and reporting systems where data is static most of the time.

You should be very careful with transaction management if you enable the `SNAPSHOT` isolation level in the database. Bugs and uncommitted transactions can prevent `tempdb` version store clean up and lead to the excessive growth of `tempdb` data files. It can happen even if you do not use `SNAPSHOT` transactions in the system, as long as the `ALLOW_SNAPSHOT_ISOLATION` database setting is enabled.

Optimistic isolation levels, however, often *mask* poorly optimized queries in the system. Even though those queries contribute to the bad system performance, they are not involved in the blocking conditions and are often ignored. It is not uncommon to see cases where people *solve* the readers/writers blocking by enabling `READ COMMITTED SNAPSHOT` and do not address the root cause of the blocking afterward. You should remember it and perform query optimization regardless of whether you have blocking in the system or not.

For data warehouse systems, transaction strategy greatly depends on how data is updated. For static read-only data, any isolation level will work, because readers do not block other readers. You can even switch the database to read-only mode so as to reduce the locking overhead. Otherwise, optimistic isolation levels are a good choice. They provide either transaction- or statement-level consistency for report queries, and they eliminate possible blocking with the writers involved.

Last but not least, it is completely normal to use different isolation levels in a system and even within the same transaction. You need to analyze the use cases and choose the right transaction strategy on case-by-case basis.

Summary

Query optimization helps to improve concurrency in a majority of the cases. Properly optimized queries acquire fewer locks, which reduces the chance of lock collisions and blocking in the system. You should also keep transactions as short as possible and modify data close to the end of the transaction to reduce the length of time locks are held.

Business requirements should dictate the data consistency and isolation rules in the system. You should choose the *minimally required* isolation level that satisfies them. Do not use `READ UNCOMMITTED` unless it is absolutely necessary in order to avoid the consistency issues it introduces.

Optimistic isolation levels could be acceptable even with an OLTP workload as long as the system can handle additional `tempdb` overhead. It is better to use `READ COMMITTED SNAPSHOT` unless transactional-level consistency is required.

Every system is unique, and it is impossible to provide generic advice that can be applied everywhere. However, a good understanding of SQL Server concurrency models will help you to design the right transaction strategies and address any blocking issues in the systems.

PART IV

Query Life Cycle

CHAPTER 25

Query Optimization and Execution

SQL Server Query Processor is perhaps the least visible and least well-known part of SQL Server. It does not expose a large set of public features, and it allows very limited control in a documented and supported way. It accepts a query as input, compiles and optimizes it to generate the execution plan, and finally executes it.

This chapter discusses the query life cycle and provides a high-level overview of the query optimization process. It explains how SQL Server executes queries, discusses several commonly used operators, and addresses query and table hints that you can use to fine-tune some aspects of query optimization.

Query Life Cycle

Every query submitted to SQL Server goes through a process of compilation and execution. That process consists of the steps shown in Figure 25-1.

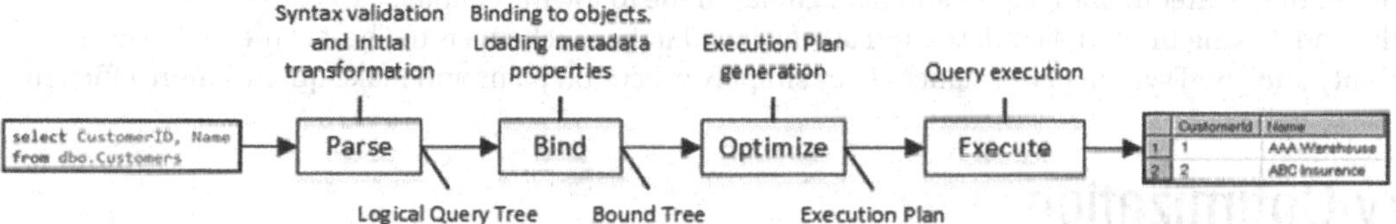

Figure 25-1. *Query life cycle*

When SQL Server receives a query, it goes through the *parsing* stage. SQL Server compiles and validates the query's syntax and transforms it into a structure called a *logical query tree.* That tree consists of various *logical* relational algebraic operators, such as inner and outer joins, aggregations, and others.

In the next step, called *binding*, SQL Server binds logical tree nodes to the actual database objects, converting the logical tree to a *bound tree.* It validates that all objects referenced in the query are valid, that they exist in the database, and that all columns are correct. Finally, SQL Server loads various metadata properties associated with tables and columns; for example, `CHECK` and `NOT NULL` constraints.

Query Optimizer uses the bound tree as input during the *optimization* stage when the actual *execution plan* is generated. The execution plan is also a tree-like structure and is comprised of *physical* operators; it is used by SQL Server to execute a query. Physical operators perform the actual work during query execution, and they are different from logical operators. For example, a logical inner join can be transformed to one of three physical joins, such as a nested loop, merge, or hash join.

One of the key elements that you need to remember is that Query Optimizer is not looking for the *best execution plan* that exists for the query. Query optimization is a complex and expensive process, and it is often impossible to evaluate all possible execution strategies.

D. Korotkevitch, *Pro SQL Server Internals*, DOI 10.1007/978-1-4842-1964-5_25

For example, inner joins are commutative, and thus the result of `(A join B)` is equal to result of `(B join A)`. Therefore, there are two possible ways that SQL Server can perform a two-table join; six ways that it can do three-table joins, and `N!`, which is `(N * (N - 1) * (N - 2) * ..)`, combinations for an *N*-table join. For a ten-table join, the number of possible combinations is 3,628,800, which is impossible to evaluate in a reasonable time period. Moreover, there are multiple physical join operators, which increases that number even further.

Optimization time is another important factor. For example, it is impractical to spend an extra ten seconds on optimization only to find an execution plan that saves just a fraction of a second during execution.

■ **Important** The goal of query optimization is to find a *good enough* execution plan, *quickly enough*.

SQL is a declarative language in which you should focus on what *needs to be done* rather than *how* to achieve it. As a general rule, you should not expect that the way you write a query will affect the execution plan. SQL Server applies various heuristics that transform the query internally by removing contradicting parts, changing join orders, and performing other re-factoring steps.

As with other general rules, they are correct only up to a point. It is often possible to improve the performance of a query by re-factoring and simplifying it, removing correlated subqueries, or splitting a complex query down into a few simple ones. As you know, cardinality estimation errors quickly progress and grow through the execution plan, which can lead to suboptimal performance, especially with very complex queries.

Moreover, you should not expect an execution plan for a particular query to always be the same and to rely on it as such. Query Optimizer algorithms change with every version of SQL Server, and even with service pack releases. Even when this is not the case, statistics and data distribution changes lead to recompilation and potentially different execution plans.

You can control the execution plan's shape with query and table hints and plan guides. We will discuss hints in more detail later in this chapter and plan guides in the following chapter.

In the end, having the correct indexes and an efficient database schema is the best way to achieve predictability and good system performance. They simplify execution plans and make queries more efficient.

Query Optimization

The query optimization process consists of multiple phases, as shown in Figure 25-2.

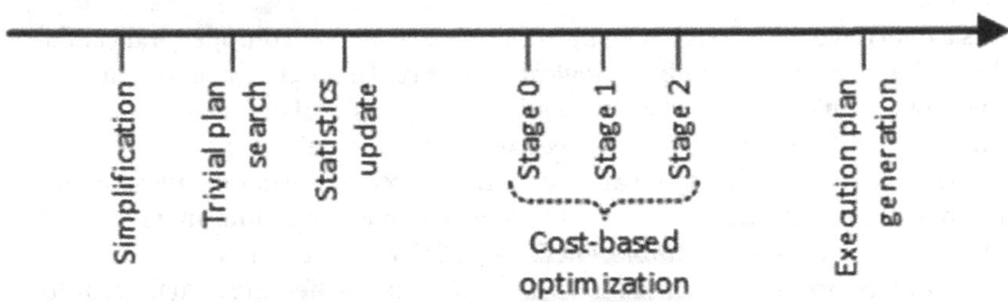

***Figure 25-2.** Query optimization phases*

During the *simplification* stage, SQL Server transforms the query tree in a way that simplifies the optimization process further. Query Optimizer removes contradictions in the queries, performs computed column matching, and works with joins, picking an initial join order based on the statistics and cardinality data.

Listing 25-1 provides an example of removing contradicting parts in a query. Both tables, dbo.NegativeNumbers and dbo.PositiveNumbers, have CHECK constraints that dictate the domain scope for the values. SQL Server can detect domain-value contradictions, and it understands that an inner join operation will not return any data. It generates the execution plan, which does not access tables at all, as shown in Figure 25-3.

Listing 25-1. Removing contradicting parts from the execution plan

```
create table dbo.PositiveNumbers
(
    PositiveNumber int not null
        constraint CHK_PositiveNumbers check (PositiveNumber > 0)
);

create table dbo.NegativeNumbers
(
    NegativeNumber int not null
        constraint CHK_NegativeNumbers check (NegativeNumber < 0)
);

select *
from dbo.PositiveNumbers e join dbo.NegativeNumbers o on
    e.PositiveNumber = o.NegativeNumber
```

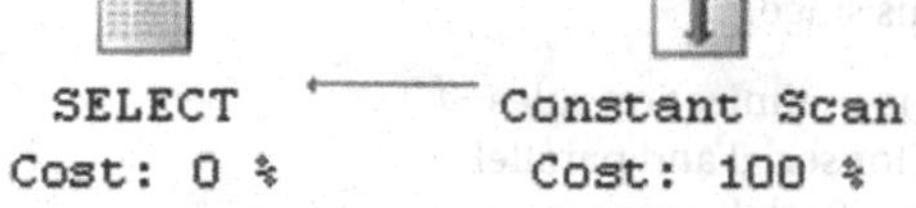

SELECT ← Constant Scan
Cost: 0 % Cost: 100 %

Figure 25-3. *Execution plan for the query*

After the simplification phase is completed, Query Optimizer checks if there is a *trivial plan* available for the query. This happens either when a query has only one plan available to execute or when the choice of plan is obvious. Listing 25-2 shows such an example.

Listing 25-2. Query with trivial execution plan

```
create table dbo.Data
(
    ID int not null,
    Col1 int not null,
    Col2 int not null,
    constraint PK_Data primary key clustered(ID)
);

select ID, Col1, Col2 from dbo.Data where ID = 11111;
```

SQL Server generates the trivial execution plan, which uses a *clustered index seek* operator, as shown in Figure 25-4.

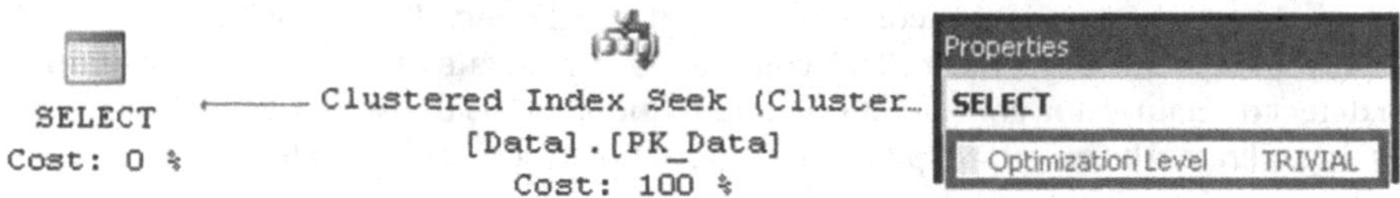

Figure 25-4. *Trivial execution plan*

Even though there are technically two different execution plan choices, clustered index seek and *clustered index scan,* Query Optimizer does not consider the scan option because it is clearly more expensive. Moreover, adding nonclustered indexes on `Col1` or `Col2` would introduce additional, non-optimal execution plan choices. Nevertheless, Query Optimizer is still able to detect it and generates a trivial execution plan instead. You can check if an execution plan is trivial in the properties of the root operator or in the XML representation of the plan.

If a trivial plan was not found, SQL Server checks whether any auto-updated statistics are outdated and triggers a statistics update if needed. If the statistics need to be updated synchronously, which is the default option, Query Optimizer waits until the statistics update is finished. Otherwise, an optimization is done based on old, outdated statistics while statistics are updated asynchronously in another thread. After that, SQL Server starts a cost-based optimization, which includes a few different stages. Each stage explores more rules, and, as a consequence, it can take a longer time to execute.

> **Stage 0** is called *Transaction Processing,* and it is targeted at scenarios that have an OLTP workload with multiple (at least three) table joins selecting a relatively small number of rows using indexes. This stage usually uses nested loop joins, although in some cases it may consider a hash join instead. Only a limited number of optimization rules are explored during this stage.
>
> **Stage 1** is called *Quick Plan,* and it applies most of the optimization rules available in SQL Server. It may be run twice, looking for serial and parallel execution plans, if needed. Most queries in SQL Server find the execution plan during this stage.
>
> **Stage 2** is called *Full Optimization,* and it performs the most comprehensive and, therefore, longest-running analysis, exploring all of the optimization rules available.

Each stage has its own entry and termination conditions. For example, Stage 0 requires a query to have at least three-table joins; otherwise, it will not be executed. Alternatively, if the cost of the plan exceeds some threshold during optimization, the stage is terminated and Query Optimizer moves on to the next, more comprehensive, stage. Optimization can be completed at any stage, as soon as a *"good enough"* plan is found.

You can examine the details of the optimization process by using undocumented trace flag `T8675`. The usual disclaimer about undocumented trace flags applies here: be careful, and do not use them in production. You will also need to use trace flag `T3604` to redirect output to the console.

Figure 25-5 illustrates the optimization statistics for one of the queries. As you can see, SQL Server performed Stage 0 and Stage 1 optimizations, generating the execution plan after Stage 1.

```
End of simplification, time: 0.002 net: 0.002 total: 0.002 net: 0.002

end exploration, tasks: 116 no total cost time: 0.004 net: 0.004 total: 0.007 net: 0.007

end search(0),  cost: 8.0054 tasks: 422 time: 0.002 net: 0.002 total: 0.01 net: 0.01

end exploration, tasks: 660 Cost = 8.0054 time: 0.001 net: 0.001 total: 0.011 net: 0.011

end search(1),  cost: 4.18091 tasks: 992 time: 0.004 net: 0.004 total: 0.016 net: 0.016

End of post optimization rewrite, time: 0 net: 0 total: 0.017 net: 0.017

End of query plan compilation, time: 0.001 net: 0.001 total: 0.018 net: 0.018
```

***Figure 25-5.** Optimization statistics returned by trace flag 8675*

■ **Note** The documented data management view (DMV) `sys.dm_exec_query_optimizer_info` allows you to retrieve Query Optimizer–related statistics. While this DMV provides a great overview in the server scope, it does not allow you to filter information for the specific session, which makes it very hard to use in busy environments. You can get more information about this DMV at `http://technet.microsoft.com/en-us/library/ms175002.aspx`.

Finally, when Query Optimizer is satisfied with the optimization results, it generates the execution plan.

As you can guess, SQL Server analyzes and explores a large number of alternative execution strategies during the query optimization stage. Those alternatives, which are part of the query tree, are stored in the part of Query Optimizer called *Memo*. SQL Server performs a cost estimation for every group in Memo, which allows it to locate the least expensive alternative when generating an execution plan.

The cost calculation is based on a complex mathematical model that considers various factors, such as cardinality, row size, expected memory usage, number of sequential and random I/O operations, parallelism overhead, and others. The costing numbers and plan cost are meaningless by themselves; they should be used for comparison only.

There are quite a few assumptions in the costing model that help to make it more consistent, as follows:

Random I/O is anticipated to be evenly distributed across the database files. For example, if an execution plan requires performing ten *RID lookup* operations in a heap table, the costing model would expect that ten random physical I/O operations would be required. In reality, the data might reside on the same data pages, which could lead to a situation where Query Optimizer overcosts some operators in the plan.

Query Optimizer expects all queries to start with cold cache and perform physical I/O when accessing the data. This may be incorrect in production systems where data pages are often cached in the buffer pool. In some rare cases, this assumption could lead to a situation where SQL Server chooses a less efficient plan that requires less I/O at the cost of higher CPU or memory usage.

Query Optimizer assumes that sequential I/O performance is significantly faster than random I/O performance. While this is usually true for magnetic hard drives, it is not exactly the case with solid-state media, where random I/O performance is much closer to sequential I/O, as compared to magnetic hard drives. SQL Server does not take drive type into account and overcosts random I/O operations in the case of solid-state-based disk arrays. It can generate execution plans with a clustered index scan instead of a *nonclustered index seek* and *key lookup*, which could be less efficient with SSD-based disk subsystems for some of the queries. It is also worth noting that the same thing could happen with modern high-performance disk arrays with a large number of drives and very good random I/O performance.

With all that being said, the costing model in SQL Server *generally* produces correct and consistent results. However, as with any mathematical model, the quality of the output highly depends on the quality of the input data. For example, it is impossible to provide correct cost estimations when the cardinality estimations are incorrect due to outdated statistics. Keeping statistics up to date helps SQL Server generate efficient execution plans.

Query Execution

SQL Server generates an execution plan in the final stage of query optimization. The execution plan is then passed to the *query executor*, which, as you can guess by its name, executes the query.

The execution plan is a tree-like structure that includes a set of *operators*, sometimes called *iterators*. Typically, SQL Server uses a *row-based* execution model where each operator generates a single row by requesting the row from one or more children and passing the generated row to its parent.

■ **Note** SQL Server 2012 introduced a new batch mode execution model, which is used with some data warehouse queries. We will talk about this execution model in Part VIII of this book.

Let's look at an example that illustrates a row-based execution model, assuming that you have the query shown in Listing 25-3.

Listing 25-3. Row-based execution: Sample query

```
select top 10 c.CustomerId, c.Name, a.Street, a.City, a.State, a.ZipCode
from dbo.Customers c join dbo.Addresses a on
    c.PrimaryAddressId = a.AddressId
order by c.Name
```

This query would produce the execution plan shown in Figure 25-6. SQL Server selects all of the data from the `dbo.Customers` table, sorts it based on the `Name` column, getting the first ten rows, joins it with the `dbo.Addresses` data, and returns it to the client.

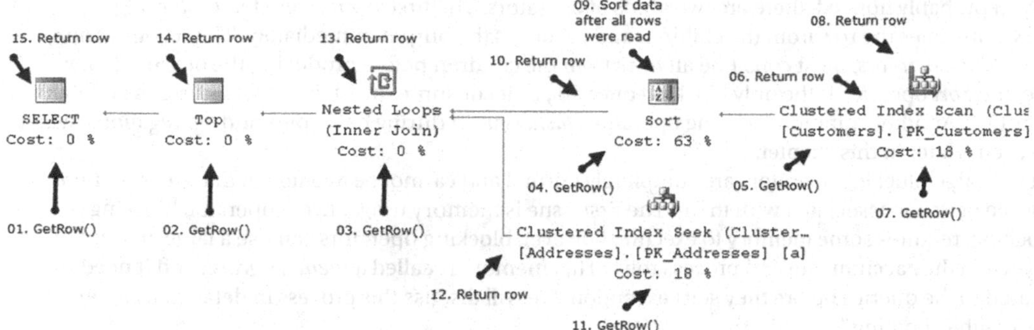

Figure 25-6. *Row-based model: Getting the first row in the output*

Let's look at how SQL Server executes such a query on an operator-by-operator basis. The *SELECT* operator, which is the parent operator in the execution plan, calls the `GetRow()` method of the *Top* operator. The *Top* operator, in turn, calls the `GetRow()` method of the *nested loop join.*

As you know, a join needs to get data from two different sources to produce output. As a first step, it calls the `GetRow()` method of the *Sort* operator. In order to do sorting, SQL Server needs to read all of the rows first; therefore, the *Sort* operator calls the `GetRow()` method of the *Clustered Index Scan* operator multiple times, accumulating the results. The *Scan* operator, which is the lowest operator in the execution plan tree, returns one row from the `dbo.Customers` table per call. Figure 25-6 shows just two `GetRow()` calls for simplicity's sake.

When all of the data from the `dbo.Customers` table has been read, the *Sort* operator performs the sorting and returns the first row back to the *Join* operator, which then calls the `GetRow()` method of the *Clustered Index Seek* operator on the `dbo.Addresses` table. If there is a match, the *Join* operator concatenates data from both inputs and passes the resulting row back to the *Top* operator, which, in turn, passes it to *SELECT*.

The *SELECT* operator returns a row to the client and requests the next row by calling the `GetRow()` method of the *Top* operator again. The process repeats until the first ten rows are selected. It is worth mentioning that the operators kept their state, and the *Sort* operator preserves the sorted data and can return all subsequent rows without accessing the *Clustered Index Scan* operator again, as shown in Figure 25-7.

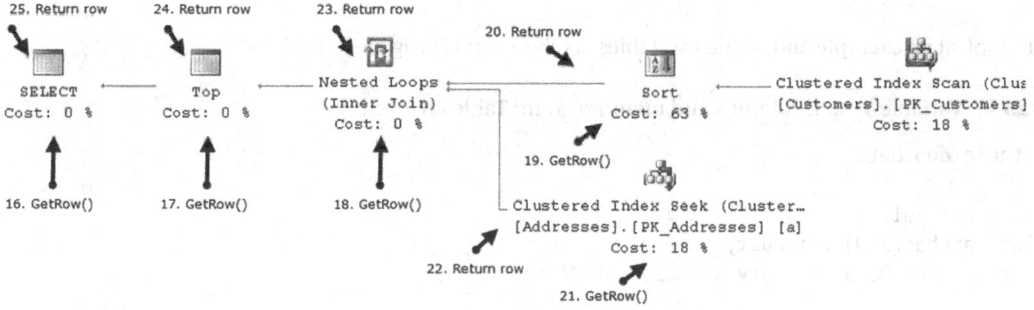

Figure 25-7. *Row-based model: Getting the subsequent row*

■ **Note** There are two other methods, `Open()` and `Close()`, called for each operator during execution. The `Open()` method initializes the operator before the first `GetRow()` call. The `Close()` method performs clean up at the end of the execution.

As you probably noticed, there are two kinds of operators. The first group, called *non-blocking operators*, consumes the row from the children and produces the output immediately. The second group, called *blocking operators*, must consume all rows from the children before producing the output. In our example, the *Sort* operator is the only blocking operator, as it consumes all of the `dbo.Customers` table's rows before sorting. Another common blocking operator, *Hash*, is used during hash joins and aggregations, which we will discuss later in this chapter.

Even though blocking operators are completely normal and cannot be avoided in many cases, there are a couple of issues associated with them. The first issue is memory usage. Every operator, blocking or non-blocking, requires some memory to execute; however, blocking operators can use a large amount of memory when they accumulate and process rows. That memory is called a *memory grant*, and it needs to be allocated to the queries before they start execution. We will discuss this process in detail in Chapter 28, "System Troubleshooting."

Correct memory grant size estimation is very important. Overestimation and underestimation both negatively affect the system. Overestimation wastes server memory, and it can increase how long a query waits for a memory grant. Underestimation, on the other hand, can force SQL Server to perform sorting or hashing operations in `tempdb` rather than in memory, which is significantly slower. This condition is called *tempdb spill*.

Memory estimation for an operator depends on the cardinality and average row size estimation. Either error leads to an incorrect memory grant request. The typical sources of cardinality estimation errors are inaccurate statistics, non-SARGable predicates and functions in `where` clauses and join conditions, and Query Optimizer model limitations. They can often be addressed by statistics maintenance and query simplification and optimization. However, dealing with row-size estimation errors is a bit trickier.

SQL Server knows the size of the fixed-length data portion of the row. For variable-length columns, however, it estimates that data populates, on average, 50 percent of the defined column size. For example, if you had two columns defined as `varchar(100)` and `nvarchar(200)`, SQL Server would estimate that every data row stores 50 and 200 bytes in those columns, respectively. For `(n)varchar(max)` and `varbinary(max)` columns, SQL Server uses 4,000 bytes as the base figure.

■ **Tip** You can improve row-size estimation by defining variable-length columns to be two times larger than the average size of the data stored there.

Let's look at an example and create two tables, as shown in Listing 25-4.

Listing 25-4. Variable-length columns and memory grant: Table creation

```
create table dbo.Data1
(
    ID int not null,
    Value varchar(100) not null,
    constraint PK_Data1 primary key clustered(ID)
);

create table dbo.Data2
(
    ID int not null,
    Value varchar(200) not null,
    constraint PK_Data2 primary key clustered(ID)
);
```

```
;with N1(C) as (select 0 union all select 0) -- 2 rows
,N2(C) as (select 0 from N1 as T1 cross join N1 as T2) -- 4 rows
,N3(C) as (select 0 from N2 as T1 cross join N2 as T2) -- 16 rows
,N4(C) as (select 0 from N3 as T1 cross join N3 as T2) -- 256 rows
,N5(C) as (select 0 from N4 as T1 cross join N4 as T2 ) -- 65,536 rows
,Nums(Num) as (select row_number() over (order by (select null)) from N5)
insert into dbo.Data1(ID, Value)
    select Num, replicate('0',100) from Nums;

insert into dbo.Data2(ID, Value)
    select ID, Value from dbo.Data1;
```

In the next step, let's run two identical queries against those tables, as shown in Listing 25-5. I am using the variable as a way to discard the result set.

Listing 25-5. Variable-length columns and memory grant: Queries

```
declare
        @V varchar(200)

select @V = Value from dbo.Data1 where ID < 42000 order by Value, ID desc;
select @V = Value from dbo.Data2 where ID < 42000 order by Value, ID desc;
```

As you can see in Figure 25-8, an incorrect memory grant forced SQL Server to spill data to `tempdb`, which increased the execution time.

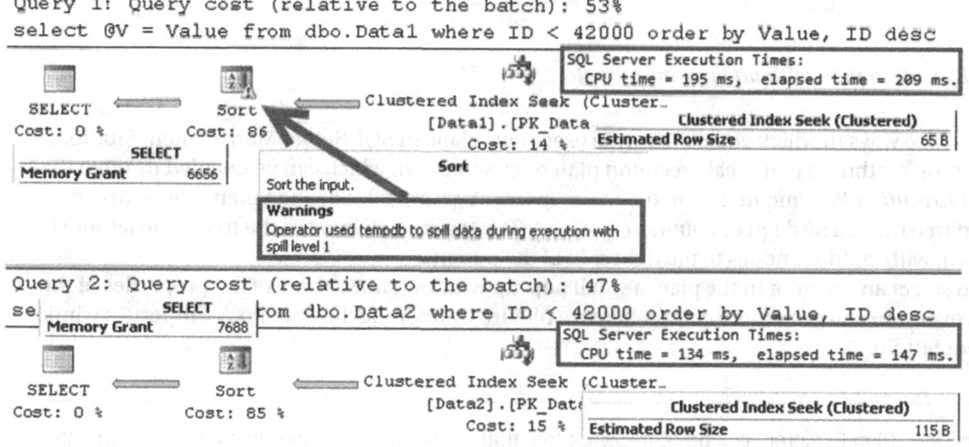

Figure 25-8. *Variable-length columns and memory grant: Execution plan*

■ **Tip** You can monitor data spills to `tempdb` with Sort and Hash Warnings in SQL Trace and Extended Events. You can also specify the minimum and maximum sizes of the memory grant with the `MIN_GRANT_PERCENT` and `MAX_GRANT_PERCENT` query hints if you are using SQL Server 2012 SP3, SQL Server 2014 SP2, or SQL Server 2016.

Blocking operators can negatively affect the performance of queries when they are present in parallel sections of the execution plan. The *Parallelism* operator, which merges data from parallel executing threads, would wait until all threads were finished with their execution. Thus, the execution time would depend on the slowest thread. Blocking operators can contribute to delays, especially in the case of `tempdb` spills. Such conditions often happen when a parallel thread workload has been unevenly distributed due to cardinality estimation errors.

■ **Tip** You can see the distribution of workload between threads when you open the Properties window for the operators in the parallel section of the graphical execution plan in SQL Server Management Studio.

In some cases, adding indexes can remove blocking operators from execution plans. For example, if you added the index `CREATE INDEX IDX_Customers_Name ON dbo.Customers(Name)`, SQL Server would not need to sort customer data anymore, and the query from Listing 25-3 would end up with an execution plan without blocking operators, as shown in Figure 25-9.

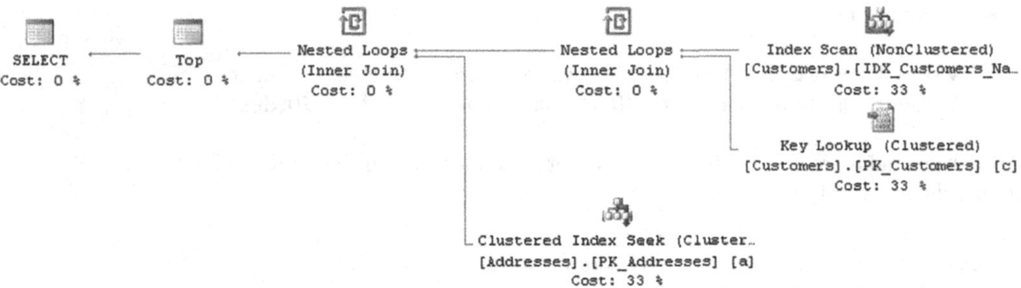

Figure 25-9. *Execution plan without blocking operators*

There are three ways in which you can analyze execution plans in SQL Server Management Studio. The most common method is graphical execution plan representation, which can be enabled through the *Include Actual Execution Plan* menu item in the *Query* menu. A graphical execution plan represents an execution plan tree rotated 90 degrees counter-clockwise. The top root element of the tree is the leftmost icon on the plan, with children nodes to the right side of the parents.

When you select an operator in the plan, a small pop-up window shows some of the properties of the operator. However, you can get a more comprehensive picture by opening the operator's Properties window in Management Studio.

■ **Tip** SentryOne "Plan Explorer" is a great freeware tool that simplifies execution-plan analysis. You can download it from: `http://sentryone.com`.

In addition to a graphical representation of the execution plan, SQL Server can display it as text or as XML. A text representation places each operator onto individual lines that display parent–child relationships with indents and | symbols. A text execution plan may be useful when you need to share a compact and easy-to-understand representation of the execution plan without worrying about image size and the scale of the graphical execution plan.

An XML execution plan represents operators as XML nodes, with child operator nodes nested in parent nodes. It is the most complete representation of the execution plan and includes a large set of attributes that are omitted in other modes. However, an XML execution plan is complex and requires some time and practice before it becomes easy to understand.

In addition to the actual execution plan, SQL Server can provide an *estimated execution plan* without running the actual query. This allows you to obtain the execution plan shape quickly for analysis. However, it does not include actual row and execution counts, which are very helpful during query performance tuning.

Table 25-1 shows different commands that generate estimated and actual execution plans in graphical, text, and XML modes.

Table 25-1. *Commands That Generate Actual and Estimated Execution Plans*

Plan Type	Command / Menu Item	Execute a query	Include Estimated Row and Execution Count	Include Actual Row and Execution Count
Graphical	Display Estimated Execution Plan	No	Yes	No
	Include Actual Execution Plan	Yes	Yes	Yes
Text	SET SHOWPLAN_TEXT ON	No	No	No
	SET SHOWPLAN_ALL ON	No	Yes	No
	SET STATISTICS PROFILE ON	Yes	Yes	Yes
XML	SET SHOWPLAN_XML ON	No	Yes	No
	SET STATISTICS PROFILE XML	Yes	Yes	Yes

■ **Important** You should always pay attention to the difference between actual and estimated row counts in execution plans. A large discrepancy between these two values is often a sign of cardinality estimation errors resulting from inaccurate statistics.

Operators

SQL Server uses two types of operators: *logical* and *physical*. These operators are used during the different stages of the query life cycle in different types of query trees. SQL Server uses logical operators during the parsing and binding stages and replaces them with physical operators during optimization. For example, an *inner join* logical operator can be replaced with one of three physical join operators in the execution plan.

It is impossible to cover all physical operators in this chapter; however, we will discuss a few common ones that you will often encounter in execution plans.

Joins

There are multiple variations of physical join operators in SQL Server that dictate how join predicates are matched and what is included in the resulting row. However, in terms of algorithms, there are just three join types: *nested loop*, *merge*, and *hash* joins.

Nested Loop Join

A *nested loop join* is the simplest join algorithm. As with any join type, it accepts two inputs, which are called *outer* and *inner* tables. The algorithm for an inner nested loop join is shown in Listing 25-6, and the algorithm for an outer nested loop join is shown in Listing 25-7.

Listing 25-6. Inner nested loop join algorithm

```
for each row R1 in outer table
        for each row R2 in inner table
                if R1 joins with R2
                        return join (R1, R2)
```

Listing 25-7. Outer nested loop join algorithm

```
for each row R1 in outer table
        for each row R2 in inner table
                if R1 joins with R2
                        return join (R1, R2)
                else
                        return join (R1, NULL)
```

As you can see, the cost of the algorithm depends on the size of the inputs, and it is proportional to its multiplication; that is, the size of the outer input multiplied by the size of the inner input. The cost grows quickly with the size of the inputs; therefore, a nested loop join is efficient when at least one of the inputs is small. In cases of an equality join predicate, it is also beneficial to have the predicate column(s) in the inner table indexed. This helps to avoid an *index scan* operation during execution.

A nested loop join does not require join keys to have an equality predicate. SQL Server evaluates the join predicate between every row from both inputs. In fact, it does not require a join predicate at all. For example, the CROSS JOIN logical operator would lead to a nested loop physical join where all rows from both inputs are joined together.

Merge Join

The *merge join* works with two sorted inputs. It compares two rows, one at time, and returns their join to the client if they are equal. Otherwise, it discards the lesser value and moves on to the next row in the input.

Contrary to nested loop joins, a merge join requires at least one equality predicate on the join keys. Listing 25-8 shows the algorithm for the inner merge join.

Listing 25-8. Inner merge join algorithm

```
/* Pre-requirements: Inputs I1 and I2 are sorted */
get first row R1 from input I1
get first row R2 from input I2
while not end of either input
begin
```

```
        if R1 joins with R2
        begin
                return join (R1, R2)
                get next row R2 from I2
        end
        else if R1 < R2
                get next row R1 from I1
        else /* R1 > R2 */
                get next row R2 from I2
end
```

The cost of the merge join algorithm is proportional to the sum of the sizes of both inputs, which makes it more efficient on large inputs as compared to a nested loop join. However, a merge join requires both inputs to be sorted, which is often the case when inputs are indexed on the join-key column.

In some cases, SQL Server may decide to sort input(s) using the *Sort* operator before a merge join. The cost of the sort obviously needs to be factored in along with the cost of the join operator during the analysis. You can also consider creating indexes to pre-sort the data.

Hash Join

Unlike the nested loop join, which works best on small inputs, and the merge join, which excels on sorted inputs, a *hash join* is designed to handle large, unsorted inputs. The hash join algorithm consists of two different phases.

During the first, or *build,* phase, a hash join scans one of the inputs (usually the smaller one), calculates the hash values of the join keys, and places them into the hash table. Next, in the second, or *probe,* phase, the hash join scans the second input and checks, or *probes,* if the hash value of the join key from the second input exists in the hash table. When this is the case, SQL Server evaluates the join predicate for the row from the second input and all rows from the first input that belong to the same hash bucket.

This comparison must be done, because the algorithm that calculates the hash values does not guarantee the uniqueness of the hash value of individual keys, which leads to *hash collision* when multiple keys generate the same hash. Even though there is the possibility of additional overhead from the extra comparison operations due to hash collisions, such situations are relatively rare.

Listing 25-9 shows the algorithm of an inner hash join.

Listing 25-9. Inner hash join algorithm

```
/* Build Phase */
for each row R1 in input I1
begin
        calculate hash value on R1 join key
        insert hash value to appropriate bucket in hash table
end
/* Probe Phase */
for each row R2 in input I2
begin
        calculate hash value on R2 join key
        for each row R1 in hash table bucket
                if R1 joins with R2
                        return join (R1, R2)
end
```

As you can guess, a hash join requires memory to store the hash table. The performance of a hash join greatly depends on correct memory grant estimation. When the memory estimation is incorrect, the hash join stores some hash table buckets in `tempdb`, which can greatly reduce the performance of the operator.

When this happens, SQL Server tracks where the buckets are located: either in memory or on disk. For each row from the second input, it checks where the hash bucket is located. If it is in memory, SQL Server processes the row immediately. Otherwise, it stores the row in another internal temporary table in `tempdb`.

After the first pass is done, SQL Server discards in-memory buckets, replacing them with the buckets from disk, and repeats the probe phase for all of the remaining rows from the second input that were stored in the internal temporary table. If there still wasn't enough memory to accommodate all hash buckets, some of them would be spilled on-disk again.

The number of times this happens is called the *recursion level*. SQL Server tracks it and eventually switches to a special *bailout* algorithm, which is less efficient, although it's guaranteed to complete at some point.

■ **Tip** You can monitor hash table spills to `tempdb` with *Hash Warnings* in SQL Trace and Extended Events.

Similar to a merge join, hash joins require at least one equality predicate in the join condition.

Comparing Join Types

As usual, the choice of join operator fits into the "It Depends" category. Each join type has its own pros and cons, which makes it good for some use cases and not so good for others.

Table 25-2 compares different join types in various scenarios.

Table 25-2. *Join type comparison*

	Nested Loop Join	Merge Join	Hash Join
Best use case	Small inputs. Preferable with index on join key in inner table.	Medium-to-large inputs sorted on index key.	Medium-to-large inputs.
Requires sorted input	No	Yes	No
Requires equality predicate	No	Yes	Yes
Blocking operator	No	No	Yes (Build phase only)
Uses memory	No	No	Yes
Uses tempdb	No	No (with exception of many-to-many joins)	Yes, in case of spills
Preserves order	Yes (outer input)	Yes	No

One of the common mistakes people make during performance tuning is relying strictly on the number of logical reads produced by the query. Even though that number is a great performance characteristic, it could be misleading in the case of joins. For example, it is entirely possible that a hash join produces fewer reads as compared to a nested loop. However, it would not factor in CPU usage and memory overhead or the performance implications of `tempdb` spills and bailouts.

The merge join is another great example. While it is more efficient than a nested loop on sorted inputs, it is easy to overlook the overhead of the *Sort* operation, which often prepares input for the merge join.

As usual, you should keep join behaviors and the pros and cons of each join type in mind, factoring this into your analysis.

Aggregates

Aggregates perform a calculation on a set of values and return a single value. A typical example of aggregates in SQL is the `MIN()` function, which returns the minimal value from the group of values it processes.

SQL Server supports two types of aggregate operators: *stream* and *hash* aggregates.

Stream Aggregate

A *stream aggregate* performs the aggregation based on sorted input; for example, when data is sorted on a column that is specified in a group by clause. Listing 25-10 shows the stream aggregate algorithm.

Listing 25-10. Stream aggregate algorithm

```
/* Pre-requirement: input is sorted */
for each row R1 from input
begin
        if R1 does not match current group by criteria
        begin
                return current aggregate results (if any)
                clear current aggregate results
                set current group criteria to match R1
        end
        update aggregate results with R1 data
end
return current aggregate results (if any)
```

Because of the sorted-input requirement, SQL Server often uses a stream aggregate together with the *Sort* operator. Let's look at an example and create a table with some sales information for a company. After that, let's run the query, which calculates the total amount of sales for each customer. The code to perform this is shown in Listing 25-11.

Listing 25-11. Query that uses stream aggregate

```
create table dbo.Orders
(
    OrderID int not null,
    CustomerId int not null,
    Total money not null,
    constraint PK_Orders primary key clustered(OrderID)
);

;with N1(C) as (select 0 union all select 0) -- 2 rows
,N2(C) as (select 0 from N1 as T1 cross join N1 as T2) -- 4 rows
,N3(C) as (select 0 from N2 as T1 cross join N2 as T2) -- 16 rows
,N4(C) as (select 0 from N3 as T1 cross join N3 as T2) -- 256 rows
```

```
,Nums(Num) as (select row_number() over (order by (select null)) from N4)
insert into dbo.Orders(OrderId, CustomerId, Total)
    select Num, Num % 10 + 1, Num from Nums;

select Customerid, sum(Total) as [Total Sales]
from dbo.Orders
group by CustomerId;
```

You can see the execution plan of the query in Figure 25-10. There is no index on the CustomerId column, and SQL Server needs to add a *Sort* operator to guarantee sorted input for the *Stream Aggregate* operator.

Figure 25-10. *Execution plan of the query with stream aggregate*

Hash Aggregate

A *hash aggregate* is very similar to a hash join. It is targeted toward large input and requires memory to store the hash table. The hash aggregate algorithm is shown in Listing 25-12.

Listing 25-12. Hash aggregate algorithm

```
for each row R1 from input
begin
        calculate hash value of R1 group columns
        check for a matching row in hash table
        if matching row exists
                update aggregate results of matching row
        else
                insert new row into hash table
end
return all rows from hash table with aggregate results
```

Similar to a hash join, a hash table can be spilled to tempdb, which negatively affects the performance of the aggregate.

Comparing Aggregates

As with joins, stream and hash aggregates are targeted toward different use cases. A stream aggregate works best with sorted input—either because of existing indexes or when the amount of data is small and can be easily sorted. A hash aggregate, on the other hand, is targeted toward large, unsorted inputs.

Table 25-3 compares hash and stream aggregates.

Table 25-3. Aggregate Comparison

	Stream Aggregate	Hash Aggregate
Best use case	Small-size input where data can be sorted with the *Sort* operator or pre-sorted input	Medium-to-large unsorted input
Requires sorted input	Yes	No
Blocking	No. However, it often requires a blocking *Sort* operator.	Yes
Uses memory	No	Yes
Uses tempdb	No	Yes, in case of spills

You should consider the cost of the *Sort* operator during performance tuning if it is used only to support a stream aggregate pre-requirement. The cost of sorting usually exceeds the cost of stream aggregation itself. You can often remove it by creating indexes, which would sort the data in the order required for a stream aggregate.

Spools

Spool operators, in a nutshell, are internal in-memory or in-tempdb caches/temporary tables. SQL Server often uses spools for performance reasons to cache the results of complex subexpressions that need to be used several times during query execution.

Let's look at an example and use the table we created in Listing 25-11. We will run a query that returns information about all of the orders, together with the total amount of sales on a per-customer basis, as shown in Listing 25-13.

Listing 25-13. Table Spool example

```
select OrderId, CustomerID, Total, sum(Total) over(partition by CustomerID) as [Customer
Sales]
from dbo.Orders
```

The execution plan for the query is shown in Figure 25-11. As you can see, SQL Server scans the table, sorts the data based on the CustomerID order, and uses a *Table Spool* operator to cache the results. This allows SQL Server to access the cached data and avoid an expensive sorting operation later.

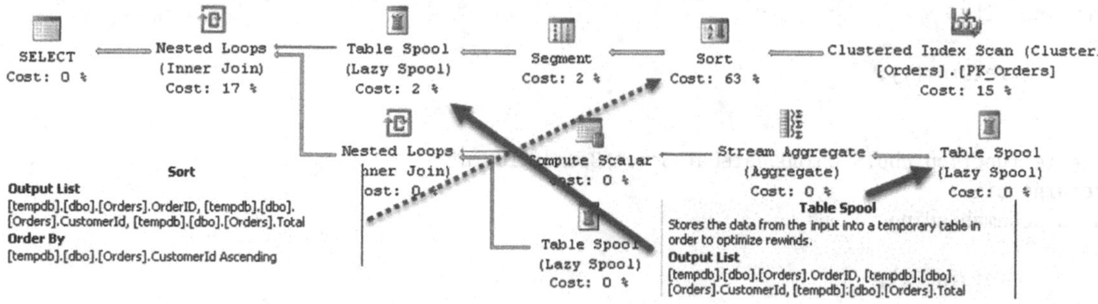

Figure 25-11. *Execution plan of the query*

Even though a *Table Spool* operator is shown in the execution plan several times, it is essentially the same spool/cache. SQL Server builds it the first time and uses its data later.

SQL Server uses spools for *Halloween Protection* when modifying the data. Halloween Protection helps you avoid situations where data modifications affect what data need to be updated. The classic example of such a situation is shown in Listing 25-14. Without Halloween Protection, the INSERT statement would fall into an infinite loop, reading the rows it has been inserting.

Listing 25-14. Halloween Protection

```
create table dbo.HalloweenProtection
(
    Id int not null identity(1,1),
    Data int not null
);

insert into dbo.HalloweenProtection(Data)
    select Data from dbo.HalloweenProtection;
```

The execution plan of the INSERT statement is shown in Figure 25-12. SQL Server uses the *Table Spool* operator to cache the data from the table prior to the INSERT to avoid an infinite loop during execution.

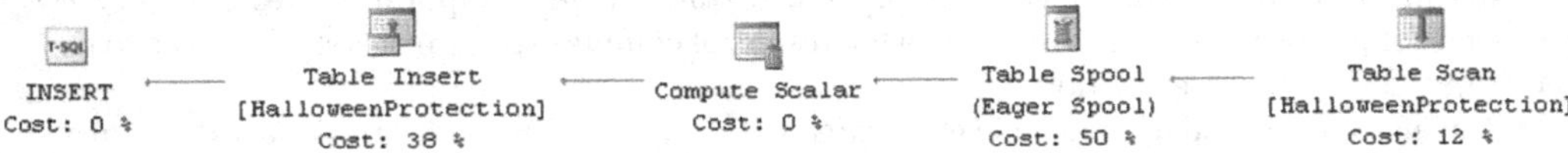

Figure 25-12. *Halloween Protection execution plan*

As I mentioned in Chapter 11, "User-Defined Functions," it is important to use the WITH SCHEMABINDING option when you define scalar user-defined functions. This option forces SQL Server to analyze if a user-defined function performs data access and avoids extra Halloween Protection–related *Spool* operators in the execution plan.

Listing 25-15 shows an example of code that creates two user-defined functions, using them in the where clause of UPDATE statements.

Listing 25-15. Halloween Protection and user-defined functions

```
create function dbo.ShouldUpdateData(@Id int)
returns bit
as
        return (1);
go

create function dbo.ShouldUpdateDataSchemaBound(@Id int)
returns bit
with schemabinding
as
        return (1);
go

update dbo.HalloweenProtection set Data = 0 where dbo.ShouldUpdateData(ID) = 1;
update dbo.HalloweenProtection set Data = 0 where dbo.ShouldUpdateDataSchemaBound(ID) = 1;
```

Neither of these functions accesses the data, and therefore cannot introduce the Halloween effect. However, SQL Server does not know that in the case of non-schema-bound functions, and it adds a *Spool* operator to execution plan, as shown in Figure 25-13.

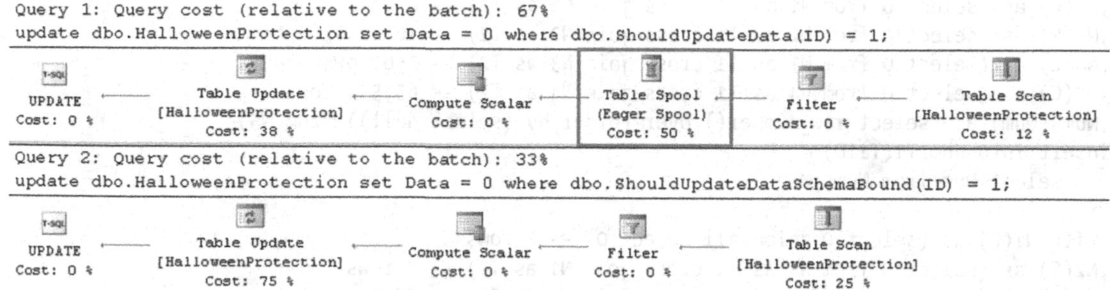

Figure 25-13. *Halloween Protection and user-defined functions: Execution plans*

Spool temporary tables are usually referenced as *worktables* in the I/O statistics for the queries. You should analyze table spool–related reads during query performance tuning. While spools can improve the performance of queries, there is the management and `tempdb` overhead introduced by the unnecessary spools. You can often remove them by creating appropriate indexes on the tables.

SQL Server 2016 introduced the new query hint `NO_PERFORMANCE_SPOOL`, which can prevent *Spool* operators from being added to the execution plan. This could be helpful in some cases, especially in systems with a very heavy `tempdb` load, when the overhead of creating an internal spool temporary table is unacceptable. However, this hint changes the execution plan's shape and can degrade the performance of queries in other cases. Use it with great care, and always analyze how it affects the execution plans and performance of the queries.

Parallelism

SQL Server can execute queries using multiple CPUs simultaneously. Even though parallel query execution can reduce the response time of queries, it comes at a cost. Parallelism always introduces the overhead of managing multiple execution threads.

Let's look at an example and create two tables, as shown in Listing 25-16. The script inserts 65,536 rows into table `dbo.T1` and 1,048,576 rows into table `dbo.T2`.

Listing 25-16. Parallelism: Table creation

```
create table dbo.T1
(
    T1ID int not null,
    Placeholder char(100),
    constraint PK_T1 primary key clustered(T1ID)
);

create table dbo.T2
(
    T1ID int not null,
    T2ID int not null,
    Placeholder char(100)
);
```

```
create unique clustered index IDX_T2_T1ID_T2ID
on dbo.T2(T1ID, T2ID);

;with N1(C) as (select 0 union all select 0) -- 2 rows
,N2(C) as (select 0 from N1 as T1 cross join N1 as T2) -- 4 rows
,N3(C) as (select 0 from N2 as T1 cross join N2 as T2) -- 16 rows
,N4(C) as (select 0 from N3 as T1 cross join N3 as T2) -- 256 rows
,N5(C) as (select 0 from N4 as T1 cross join N4 as T2) -- 65,536 rows
,Nums(Num) as (select row_number() over (order by (select null)) from N5)
insert into dbo.T1(T1ID)
    select Num from Nums;

;with N1(C) as (select 0 union all select 0) -- 2 rows
,N2(C) as (select 0 from N1 as T1 cross join N1 as T2) -- 4 rows
,N3(C) as (select 0 from N2 as T1 cross join N2 as T2) -- 16 rows
,Nums(Num) as (select row_number() over (order by (select null)) from N3)
insert into dbo.T2(T1ID, T2ID)
    select T1ID, Num from dbo.T1 cross join Nums;
```

In the next step, let's run two SELECT statements, as shown in Listing 25-17.

Listing 25-17. Parallelism: Test queries

```
select count(*)
from
    (
        select t1.T1ID, count(*) as Cnt
        from dbo.T1 t1 join dbo.T2 t2 on
            t1.T1ID = t2.T1ID
        group by t1.T1ID
    ) s
option (maxdop 1);

select count(*)
from
    (
        select t1.T1ID, count(*) as Cnt
        from dbo.T1 t1 join dbo.T2 t2 on
            t1.T1ID = t2.T1ID
        group by t1.T1ID
    ) s;
```

We force a serial execution plan for the first query using MAXDOP 1 as a query hint. The second query has a parallel execution plan. Figure 25-14 illustrates this scenario.

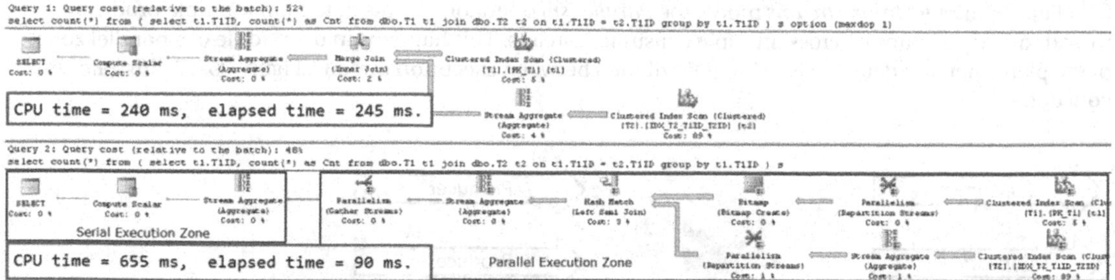

Figure 25-14. *Parallel execution: Query plans*

As you can see, the response (elapsed) time of the first query is much slower than that of the second query: 245 milliseconds versus 90 milliseconds. However, the total CPU time of the first query is much lower compared to second query: 240 milliseconds versus 655 milliseconds. We are using CPU resources for parallelism management.

A parallel execution plan does not necessarily mean that all operators are executing in parallel. An execution plan can have both parallel and serial execution zones. The parallel plan shown in Figure 25-14 runs a subquery in a parallel zone and an outer COUNT(*) calculation serially.

The *Parallelism* operator, sometimes called *Exchange,* manages parallelism during query execution. It accepts the input data from one or more *producer* threads and distributes it across one or more *consumer* threads, and it can run in three different modes.

In *distribute streams* mode, the *Parallelism* operator accepts data from one producer thread and distributes it across multiple consumer threads. This mode is usually the entry point to the parallel execution zone in the plan. Figure 25-15 illustrates this concept.

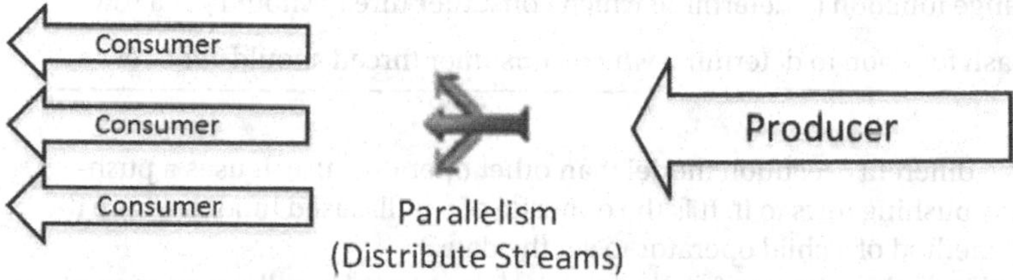

Figure 25-15. *Parallelism: Distribute streams mode*

In *gather streams* mode, the *Parallelism* operator merges the data from multiple producer threads and passes it to a single consumer thread. This mode is usually the exit point from the parallel execution zone in the plan. Figure 25-16 illustrates this idea.

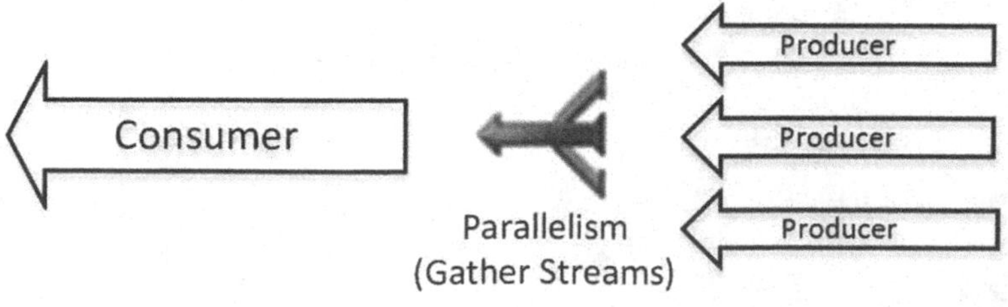

Figure 25-16. *Parallelism: Gather streams mode*

Finally, in *repartition streams* mode, the *Parallelism* operator accepts data from multiple producer threads and distributes it across multiple consumer threads. This happens in the middle of a parallel zone of the plan when the data needs to be redistributed between execution threads. Figure 25-17 illustrates this concept.

Figure 25-17. *Parallelism: Repartition streams mode*

There are several different ways that data can be distributed between consumer threads. Table 25-4 summarizes these methods.

Table 25-4. *Data Redistribution Methods in Parallelism*

Redistribution Method	Description
Broadcast	Send row to all consumer threads
Round Robin	Send row to the next consumer thread in sequence
Demand	Send row to the next consumer thread that requests the row
Range	Use range function to determine which consumer thread should get a row
Hash	Use hash function to determine which consumer thread should get a row

The *Parallelism* operator uses a different execution model than other operators use. It uses a push-based model, with producer threads pushing rows to it. It is the opposite of a pull-based model, where the parent operator calls the `GetRow()` method of a child operator to get the data.

An evenly distributed workload is the key element for the good performance of parallel execution plans. You can see the number of rows processed by each thread in the "Actual Number of Rows" section of the operator's Properties window in Management Studio. That information is not displayed in a tool-tip in the graphical execution plans. Thread 0 is the parallelism-management thread, which always shows zero as the number of rows.

Uneven data distribution and outdated statistics are common causes of uneven workload distribution between threads. Figure 25-18 shows how workload distribution changes after a statistics update on one of the tables. The left side shows the distribution before the statistics update, and the right side shows it after the update.

Actual Number of Rows	798758	Actual Number of Rows	798763
Thread 0	0	Thread 0	0
Thread 1	137706	Thread 1	103534
Thread 2	118506	Thread 2	94323
Thread 3	90571	Thread 3	100914
Thread 4	72024	Thread 4	97662
Thread 5	70814	Thread 5	101151
Thread 6	185179	Thread 6	101396
Thread 7	57607	Thread 7	101168
Thread 8	66351	Thread 8	98615

Figure 25-18. *Workload distribution before and after a statistics update*

Query and Table Hints

Query Optimizer usually does a good job of generating decent execution plans. However, in some cases you can decide to fine-tune the shape of the execution plan with query and table hints. For example, query and table hints allow you to force Query Optimizer to choose specific indexes or join types for the query.

Query hints are a great, but very dangerous, tool. They can help you improve the quality of execution plans; however, they could also significantly decrease the performance of the system when applied incorrectly. You should have a very good understanding of how SQL Server works and know your system and data before using them.

The supportability of the system is another very important factor. You should document cases where hints are used and periodically re-evaluate if they are still required. The amount of data and data-distribution changes can lead to situations where plans forced by hints become suboptimal. For example, consider a situation where a hint forces Query Optimizer to use a nested loop join. This join type will work more inefficiently as the amount of data and the size of inputs grows.

Forcing Query Optimizer to use a specific index is another example. The choice of index can become inefficient in the case of data selectivity changes, and it would prevent Query Optimizer from using other indexes that were created later. Moreover, the code would be broken and queries would error out if you ever dropped or renamed the index referenced by the hint.

As a general rule, you should only use hints as a last resort. If you do, make sure that the statistics are up to date and that the query cannot be optimized, simplified, or re-factored before applying them.

In cases of parameter sniffing, it is usually better to use the `OPTIMIZE FOR` hint or statement-level recompile rather than force specific index usage with an index hint. We will discuss these approaches in greater depth in the next chapter.

INDEX Table Hint

`INDEX` is, perhaps, one of the most commonly used table hints. It forces Query Optimizer to use a specific index for data access. It requires you to specify either the name or ID of the index as a parameter. In most cases, the name of the index is the better choice for supportability reasons. There are two exceptions, however, where index ID is the better option: forcing a clustered index or heap table scan. You can consider using 1 and 0 respectively as the ID in those cases.

SQL Server can use either *Scan* or *Seek* access methods with an index. Listing 25-18 shows an example of `INDEX` hint usage, which forces SQL Server to use the `IDX_Orders_OrderDate` index in the query.

Listing 25-18. INDEX query hint

```
select OrderId, OrderDate, CustomerID, Total
from dbo.Orders with (Index = IDX_Orders_OrderDate)
where OrderDate between @StartDate and @EndDate
```

One of the legitimate use cases for an INDEX query hint is to force SQL Server to use one of the composite indexes in those cases where correct cardinality estimation is impossible. Consider a case where a table stores location information for multiple devices that belong to different accounts, as shown in Listing 25-19. Let's assume that DeviceId is unique only within a single account.

Listing 25-19. Composite indexes and uneven data distribution: Table creation

```
create table dbo.Locations
(
    AccountId int not null,
    DeviceId int not null,
    UtcTimeTag datetime2(0) not null,
    /* Other Columns */
);

create unique clustered index IDX_Locations_AccountId_UtcTimeTag_DeviceId
on dbo.Locations(AccountId, UtcTimeTag, DeviceId);

create unique nonclustered index IDX_Locations_AccountId_DeviceId_UtcTimeTag
on dbo.Locations(AccountId, DeviceId, UtcTimeTag);
```

It is common to have data distributed very unevenly in multi-tenant systems where some accounts have hundreds or even thousands of devices while others have just a few of them. Let's assume that we would like to select the data that belongs to a subset of devices for a specific time frame, as shown in Listing 25-20.

Listing 25-20. Composite indexes and uneven data distribution: Query

```
select DeviceId, UtcTimeTag /* Other Columns */
from dbo.Locations
where
    AccountId = @AccountID and
    UtcTimeTag between @StartTime and @StopTime and
    DeviceID in (select DeviceID from #ListOfDevices);
```

SQL Server has two different choices for the execution plan. The first choice uses a *nonclustered index seek* and a *key lookup*, which is better when you need to select data for a very small percentage of the devices in the account. In all other cases, it is more efficient to use a *clustered index seek* with AccountId and UtcTimeTag as seek predicates, and to perform a range scan for all devices that belong to the account.

Unfortunately, SQL Server would not have enough data to perform a correct cardinality estimation in either case. It can estimate the selectivity of particular AccountID data based on the histogram from either index; however, it is not enough to estimate cardinality for the list of devices.

One possible solution is to write code that calculates the number of devices in the #ListOfDevices table and compare it to the total number of devices per account, forcing SQL Server to use a specific index with an INDEX hint based on the comparison results.

It is worth mentioning that such a system design is not optimal. It would be better to make DeviceId unique system-wide rather than just in the account scope. This would allow you to make DeviceId the leftmost column in the nonclustered index, which would help SQL Server with cardinality estimations based on the list of devices. This approach, however, would still not factor time parameters into such estimations.

FORCE ORDER Hint

A FORCE ORDER query hint preserves the join order in the query. When this hint is specified, SQL Server always joins tables in the order in which joins are listed in the from clause of the query. However, SQL Server would choose the least expensive join type in each case.

Listing 25-21 shows an example of such a hint. SQL Server will perform joins in the following order: ((TableA join TableB) join TableC).

Listing 25-21. FORCE ORDER hint

```
select /* Columns */
from
    TableA join TableB on TableA.ID = TableB.AID
    join TableC on TableB.ID = TableC.BID
option (force order)
```

LOOP, MERGE, and HASH JOIN Hints

You can specify join types with LOOP, MERGE, and HASH hints on both query and individual join levels. It is possible to specify more than one join type in the query hint and allow SQL Server to choose the least expensive one. A join operator hint takes precedence over a query hint if both are specified. Finally, a join type hint forces join orders in a way similar to a FORCE ORDER hint.

Listing 25-22 shows an example of using join type hints. SQL Server will perform joins in the following order: ((TableA join TableB) join TableC). It will use a nested loop join to join TableA and TableB, and either a nested loop or merge join for the TableC join.

Listing 25-22. Join type hints

```
select /* Columns */
from
    TableA inner loop join TableB on TableA.ID = TableB.AID
    join TableC on TableB.ID = TableC.BID
option (loop join, merge join)
```

FORCESEEK/FORCESCAN Hints

A FORCESEEK hint prevents SQL Server from using *index scan* operators. It can be used on both query and individual table levels and can be combined with an INDEX hint if needed. SQL Server would generate an error if an execution plan without index scans cannot be created. You can also specify an optional list of columns for SEEK predicates.

The opposite hint, FORCESCAN, prevents SQL Server from using *index seek* operators and forces it to scan data. Both of these hints were introduced in SQL Server 2008 SP1.

NOEXPAND/EXPAND VIEWS Hints

NOEXPAND and EXPAND VIEWS hints control how SQL Server handles indexed views. This behavior is edition-specific. By default, non-Enterprise editions of SQL Server expand indexed views to their definition and do not use data from them, even when views are referenced in the queries. You should specify a NOEXPAND hint to avoid this.

■ **Tip** Always specify a NOEXPAND hint when you reference an indexed view in the query if there is a possibility that the database might be moved to a non-Enterprise edition of SQL Server.

Listing 25-23 shows an example of NOEXPAND and INDEX hints, which force SQL Server to use the nonclustered index created on the indexed view.

Listing 25-23. NOEXPAND and INDEX hints

```
select CustomerID, ArticleId, TotalSales
from dbo.vArticleSalesPerCustomer
    with (NOEXPAND, Index=IDX_vArticleSalesPerCustomer_CustomerID)
where CustomerID = @CustomerID
```

Alternatively, the EXPAND VIEWS hint allows SQL Server to expand an indexed view to its definition in the Enterprise Edition. To be honest, I cannot think of use cases when such behavior is beneficial.

FAST N Hints

A FAST N hint tells SQL Server to generate an execution plan with the goal of quickly returning the number of rows specified as a parameter. This can generate an execution plan with non-blocking operators, even when such a plan is more expensive compared to one that uses blocking operators.

One possible use case for such a hint is an application that is loading a large amount of data in the background (perhaps caching it) and wants to display the first page of the data to the user as quickly as possible. Listing 25-24 shows an example of a query that uses such a hint.

Listing 25-24. FAST N hint

```
select o.OrderId, OrderNumber, OrderData, CustomerId, CustomerName, OrderTotal
from dbo.vOrders
where OrderDate > @StartDate
order by OrderDate desc
option (FAST 50)
```

■ **Note** You can see full list of query and table hints at http://technet.microsoft.com/en-us/library/ms181714.aspx.

Summary

The query life cycle consists of four different stages: parsing, binding, optimization, and execution. A query is transformed numerous times using tree-like structures, starting with a logical query tree at the parsing stage and finishing with the execution plan after optimization.

Query optimization is done in several phases. With the exception of the trivial plans search, SQL Server uses a cost-based model, evaluating the cost of access methods, resource usage, and a few other factors.

The quality of execution plans greatly depends on the correctness of input data. Accurate and up-to-date statistics are a key factor that improves cardinality estimations and allows SQL Server to generate efficient execution plans. However, as with any model, there are limitations. In some cases, you need to re-factor, split, and simplify queries to overcome such restrictions.

An execution plan consists of physical operators, which, with the exception of *Parallelism*, use a poll-based, row-based model. Each parent operator requests data from its children on a row-by-row basis. Starting with SQL Server 2012, there is another batch mode execution model available, which is used with columnstore indexes and some data warehouse queries.

There are two types of operators: blocking and non-blocking. Non-blocking operators serve rows back to parents as soon as they get them. Blocking operators acquire and cache all rows from children before returning rows to parents.

Blocking operators require memory to store data. In cases where the memory estimation is incorrect, data is spilled to `tempdb`. Such spills reduce the performance of queries and can be monitored with Sort and Hash Warnings in SQL Trace and Extended Events.

The two most common cases of incorrect memory grant sizes are incorrect cardinality and row-size estimates. You can improve these by keeping statistics up to date and defining variable-length data columns to be about twice as big as the actual data stored there. You should also avoid non-SARGable predicates in the join conditions, especially when a query joins a large number of tables.

You can control some aspects of query optimization by using query and table hints. However, you should be very careful when using them, documenting and periodically re-evaluating their usage. This helps to avoid subefficient execution plans due to data size or distribution changes, which invalidate the correctness of the hints' use.

CHAPTER 26

Plan Caching

Query optimization is a resource-intensive process that could introduce a significant CPU load on busy servers. SQL Server tries to minimize such load by caching plans in a special part of the process memory called the *plan cache.*

This chapter talks about *plan caching* in detail and consists of two parts. The first part provides a high-level overview of plan caching and discusses several issues associated with it. The second part dives deeper into plan cache internals and discusses the various data management views (DMVs) that you can use for plan cache monitoring.

Plan Caching Overview

SQL Server prevents unnecessary recompilations of queries by caching plans in a special area of the memory called the *plan cache.* In addition to prepared parameterized queries and ad-hoc queries and batches, it caches plans of various objects, such as stored procedures, triggers, user-defined functions, and a few others.

SQL Server does not cache actual execution plans, but rather caches a set of other plan-related entities, mainly *compiled plans.* Every time a query needs to be executed, SQL Server generates an actual execution plan from the compiled plan, which is an inexpensive operation as compared to compiled plan creation. Execution plans are run-time structures and are unique for each query execution; that is, if multiple sessions need to execute the same compiled plan, multiple execution plans would be generated, at one per session.

Note SQL Server documentation and other resources often ignore the difference between compiled and execution plans. They often refer to plan cache as the memory area that caches execution plans. This is completely normal, and you should not be confused by this description.

A compiled plan is generated for the entire batch and includes plans for individual statements from the batch. In this chapter, I typically reference query- or statement-level plans; however, plans for multi-statement batches behave in the same way.

In addition to compiled plans, SQL Server caches other structures, such as *compiled plan stubs, shell queries,* and a couple of others. We will talk about all of them in detail later in this chapter.

The number of cached plans does not directly affect the performance of SQL Server. However, plan cache uses memory and, therefore, can reduce the size of the buffer pool, which, in turn, can increase the number of physical reads and decrease system performance.

SQL Server uses different algorithms to determine which plans should be removed from the cache in case of memory pressure. For ad-hoc queries, this selection is based strictly on how often a plan is reused. For other types of plans, the cost of plan generation is also factored into the decision. We will talk about plan cache memory management later in this chapter.

D. Korotkevitch, *Pro SQL Server Internals*, DOI 10.1007/978-1-4842-1964-5_26

SQL Server recompiles queries when it suspects that currently cached plans are no longer valid. One such case is when the schema of the objects referenced by the plan changes. This could include the creation or dropping of columns, indexes, constraints, triggers, and statistics defined in a table.

Another case relates to stale statistics. SQL Server checks to see if the statistics are outdated when it looks up a plan from the cache, and it recompiles the query if they are. That recompilation, in turn, triggers a statistics update.

Temporary tables can increase the number of recompilations triggered by outdated statistics. As you will remember, SQL Server outdates statistics based on the number of modifications of the statistics (and index) columns. For regular tables, the statistics update thresholds are as follows:

When a table is empty, SQL Server outdates statistics when you add data to it.

When a table has less than 500 rows, SQL Server outdates statistics after every 500 changes to the statistics columns.

When a table has 500 or more rows, SQL Server outdates statistics after every 500+ changes (or 20 percent of the total number of rows in the table) to the statistics columns in cases where the database compatibility level is less than 130 (SQL Server 2016). For databases with a compatibility level of 130 or when trace flag `T2371` is enabled, that threshold is dynamic and is based on the total number of rows in the table.

However, for temporary tables there is another threshold value of six changes, which can lead to unnecessary recompilations in some cases. The `KEEP PLAN` query hint eliminates that threshold, and it makes the behavior of the temporary tables the same as the regular ones.

Another query hint, `KEEPFIXED PLAN`, prevents query recompilation in cases of outdated statistics. Queries would be recompiled only when the schemas of the underlying tables are changed or the recompilation is forced; for example, when a stored procedure is called using the `WITH RECOMPILE` clause.

The plan cache can store multiple plans for the same queries, batches, or T-SQL objects. Some of the `SET` options, such as `ANSI_NULL_DLFT_OFF`, `ANSI_NULL_DLFT_ON`, `ANSI_NULL`, `ANSI_PADDING`, `ANSI_WARNING`, `ARITHABORT`, `CONCAT_NULL_YELDS_NULL`, `DATEFIRST`, `DATEFORMAT`, `FORCEPLAN`, `DATEFORMAT`, `LANGUAGE`, `NO_BROWSETABLE`, `NUMERIC_ROUNDABORT`, and `QUOTED_IDENTIFIER`, affect plan reuse. Plans generated with one set of `SET` options cannot be reused by sessions that use a different set of `SET` options.

Unfortunately, different client libraries and development environments have different default `SET` options. For example, by default `ARITHABORT` is OFF in ADO.Net and `ON` in Management Studio. Remember this when you troubleshoot inefficient queries submitted by client applications. You could get different execution plans when you run those queries in Management Studio. When your database works with multiple client applications developed in different languages, you should consider specifying `SET` options in the same way at the session level after establishing the connection to SQL Server.

■ **Tip** You can change the default `SET` options for queries running in Management Studio to match the client applications via the *Options* menu item in the *Tools* menu.

Another common reason for duplicated plans in cache is using unqualified object names without specifying the object's schema. In that case, SQL Server resolves objects based on the default schema of the database's users, and, therefore, statements like `SELECT * FROM Orders` could reference completely different tables for different users, which prevents plan reuse. Alternatively, `SELECT * FROM Sales.Orders` always references the same table regardless of the default database schema for the user.

■ **Important** Always specify the schema when you reference tables and stored procedures. It reduces the size of the plan cache and speeds up the compilation process.

Finally, SQL Server does not cache plans if the batch or object includes string literals greater than 8 KB in size. For example, the plan for the following query is not going to be cached when a constant used in the WHERE clause has more than 8,192 characters:

```
SELECT * FROM Table1 WHERE Col='<insert more than 8,192 characters here>'
```

We will dive deeper into plan cache internals later in this chapter after discussing a few practical questions related to plan caching.

Parameter Sniffing

Plan caching can significantly reduce CPU load on systems by eliminating unnecessary query compilations. However, it also introduces a few problems. The most widely known problem is called *parameter sniffing*. SQL Server *sniffs* parameter values at the time of optimization and generates and caches a plan that is optimal for those values. Nothing is wrong with this behavior. However, in some cases, when data is unevenly distributed, it leads to a situation where the generated and *cached* plan is optimal only for atypical, rarely used parameter values. These cached plans could be suboptimal for further calls that use more common values as parameters.

Most database professionals have experienced a situation where some queries or stored procedures suddenly took a much longer time to complete than before, even though there were no recent deployments to production. In most cases, these situations happened due to parameter sniffing when queries were recompiled because of a statistics update.

Let's look at an example and create the table shown in Listing 26-1. We will populate it with data in such a way that most rows have the Country value set to 'USA'. Then, we will create a nonclustered index on the Country column.

Listing 26-1. Parameter sniffing: Table creation

```
create table dbo.Employees
(
        ID int not null,
        Number varchar(32) not null,
        Name varchar(100) not null,
        Salary money not null,
        Country varchar(64) not null,
        constraint PK_Employees primary key clustered(ID)
);

;with N1(C) as (select 0 union all select 0) -- 2 rows
,N2(C) as (select 0 from N1 as T1 cross join N1 as T2) -- 4 rows
,N3(C) as (select 0 from N2 as T1 cross join N2 as T2) -- 16 rows
,N4(C) as (select 0 from N3 as T1 cross join N3 as T2) -- 256 rows
,N5(C) as (select 0 from N4 as T1 cross join N4 as T2 ) -- 65,536 rows
,Nums(Num) as (select row_number() over (order by (select null)) from N5)
insert into dbo.Employees(ID, Number, Name, Salary, Country)
        select Num, convert(varchar(5),Num)
                ,'USA Employee: ' + convert(varchar(5),Num), 40000, 'USA'
        from Nums;
```

```
;with N1(C) as (select 0 union all select 0) -- 2 rows
,N2(C) as (select 0 from N1 as T1 cross join N1 as T2) -- 4 rows
,N3(C) as (select 0 from N2 as T1 cross join N2 as T2) -- 16 rows
,Nums(Num) as (select row_number() over (order by (select null)) from N3)
insert into dbo.Employees(ID, Number, Name, Salary, Country)
        select 65536 + Num, convert(varchar(5),65536 + Num)
                ,'Canada Employee: ' + convert(varchar(5),Num), 40000, 'Canada'
        from Nums;

create nonclustered index IDX_Employees_Country
on dbo.Employees(Country);
```

As the next step, let's create a stored procedure that calculates the average salary for employees in a specific country. The code to do this is shown in Listing 26-2. Even though we are using a stored procedure in this example, the same situation could happen with parameterized queries called from client applications.

Listing 26-2. Parameter sniffing: Stored procedure

```
create proc dbo.GetAverageSalary @Country varchar(64)
as
        select Avg(Salary) as [Avg Salary]
        from dbo.Employees
        where Country = @Country;
```

With the current data distribution, when the stored procedure is called with `@Country='USA'`, the optimal execution plan is a *clustered index scan*. However, for `@Country='Canada'`, the better execution plan is a *nonclustered index seek* with *key lookup* operations.

Let's call the stored procedure twice: the first time with `@Country='USA'` and the second time with `@Country='Canada'`, as shown in Listing 26-3.

Listing 26-3. Parameter sniffing: Calling a stored procedure

```
exec dbo.GetAverageSalary @Country='USA';
exec dbo.GetAverageSalary @Country='Canada';
```

As you can see in Figure 26-1, SQL Server compiles the stored procedure and caches the plan with the first call, then reuses it later. Even though such a plan is less efficient with the `@Country='Canada'` parameter value, it may be acceptable when those calls are rare, which is expected with such a data distribution.

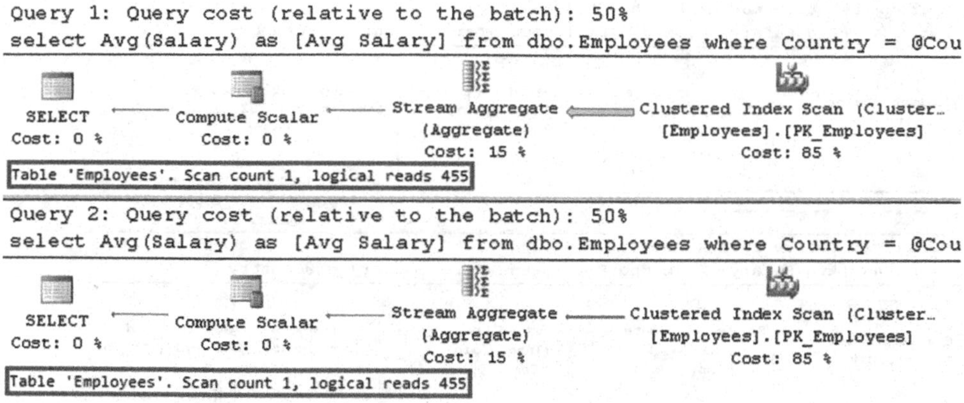

Query 1: Query cost (relative to the batch): 50%
select Avg(Salary) as [Avg Salary] from dbo.Employees where Country = @Cou

SELECT Cost: 0 % ← Compute Scalar Cost: 0 % ← Stream Aggregate (Aggregate) Cost: 15 % ← Clustered Index Scan (Cluster... [Employees].[PK_Employees] Cost: 85 %

Table 'Employees'. Scan count 1, logical reads 455

Query 2: Query cost (relative to the batch): 50%
select Avg(Salary) as [Avg Salary] from dbo.Employees where Country = @Cou

SELECT Cost: 0 % ← Compute Scalar Cost: 0 % ← Stream Aggregate (Aggregate) Cost: 15 % ← Clustered Index Scan (Cluster... [Employees].[PK_Employees] Cost: 85 %

Table 'Employees'. Scan count 1, logical reads 455

Figure 26-1. *Parameter sniffing: Cached plan for @Country='USA'*

Now, let's take a look at what happens if we swap those calls when the plan is not cached. Listing 26-4 shows the code for achieving this. We will use the `DBCC FREEPROCCACHE` command, which clears the plan cache. Another instance when this might happen is with a statistics update that forces a query to recompile.

■ **Important** Do not use the `DBCC FREEPROCCACHE` command in production.

Listing 26-4. Parameter sniffing: Calling a stored procedure with a different order of parameters

```
dbcc freeproccache
go
exec dbo.GetAverageSalary @Country='Canada';
exec dbo.GetAverageSalary @Country='USA';
```

As you can see in Figure 26-2, SQL Server now compiles and caches the plan based on the `@Country='Canada'` parameter value. Even though this plan is more efficient when the stored procedure is called with `@Country='Canada'`, it is highly inefficient for `@Country='USA'` calls.

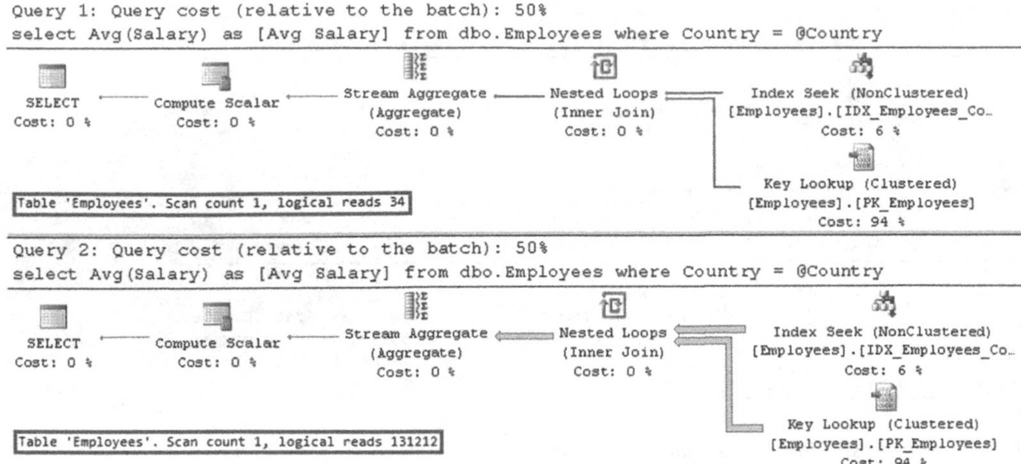

Figure 26-2. *Parameter sniffing: Cached plan for* `@Country='Canada'`

There are a few ways to address the issue. You can force the recompilation of either stored procedure using `EXECUTE WITH RECOMPILE` or a statement-level recompile with the `OPTION (RECOMPILE)` clause. Obviously, a statement-level recompile is better, because it performs the recompilation on a smaller scope. SQL Server *sniffs* the parameter values at the time of the recompilation, generating the optimal execution plan for each parameter value. Listing 26-5 shows the statement-level recompile approach.

Listing 26-5. Parameter sniffing: Statement-level recompile

```
alter proc dbo.GetAverageSalary @Country varchar(64)
as
    select Avg(Salary) as [Avg Salary]
    from dbo.Employees
    where Country = @Country
    option (recompile);
go
exec dbo.GetAverageSalary @Country='Canada';
exec dbo.GetAverageSalary @Country='USA';
```

As you can see in Figure 26-3, SQL Server does not cache the execution plan and instead recompiles the statement on every call, generating the most efficient execution plan for every parameter value.

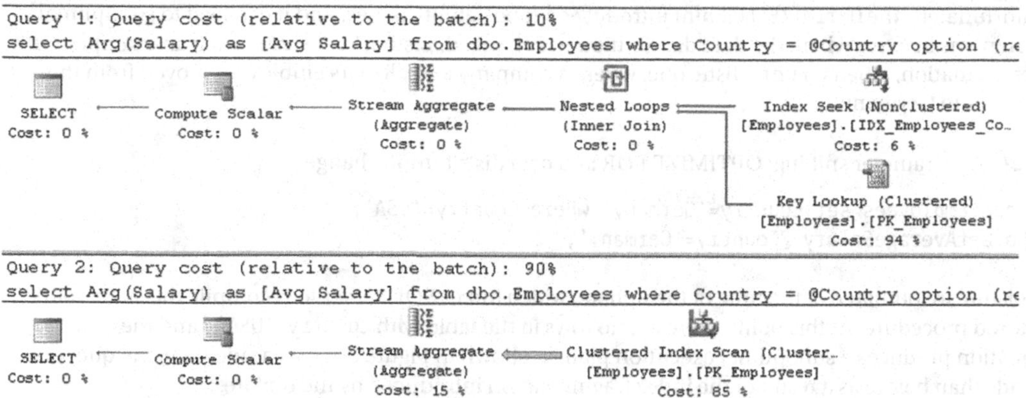

Figure 26-3. *Parameter sniffing: Statement-level recompile*

The statement-level recompile may be a good option to use when the queries do not execute very often or, in the case of complex queries, when the compilation time is just a fraction of the total execution time. However, it is hardly the best approach for frequently executed OLTP queries due to the extra CPU load that recompilation introduces.

Another option is using an `OPTIMIZE FOR` hint, which forces SQL Server to optimize a query for the specific parameter values provided in the hint. Listing 26-6 illustrates such an approach.

Listing 26-6. Parameter sniffing: OPTIMIZE FOR hint

```
alter proc dbo.GetAverageSalary @Country varchar(64)
as
    select Avg(Salary) as [Avg Salary]
    from dbo.Employees
    where Country = @Country
    option (optimize for(@Country='USA'));
go
exec dbo.GetAverageSalary @Country='Canada';
exec dbo.GetAverageSalary @Country='USA';
```

As you can see in Figure 26-4, SQL Server ignores the parameter value during compilation and optimizes the query, then caches the execution plan for the `@Country='USA'` value.

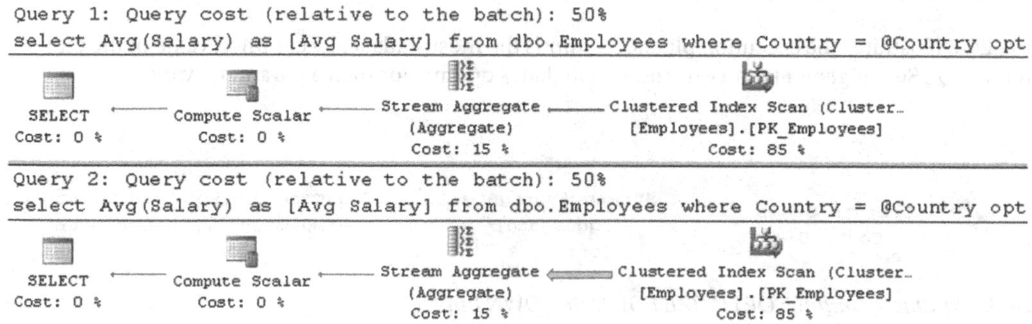

Figure 26-4. *Parameter Sniffing: OPTIMIZE FOR hint*

Unfortunately, the OPTIMIZE FOR hint introduces supportability issues, and it can lead to suboptimal execution plans in cases where the data distribution has changed. Listing 26-7 shows such an example. Let's consider a situation, albeit an unrealistic one, where a company and all of its employees moved from the United States to Germany.

Listing 26-7. Parameter sniffing: OPTIMIZE FOR and data distribution change

```
update dbo.Employees set Country='Germany' where Country='USA';
exec dbo.GetAverageSalary @Country='Germany';
```

Statistics are outdated at the time of the update, which forces SQL Server to recompile the statement in the stored procedure. At this point, there are no rows in the table with Country='USA', and the recompilation produces a suboptimal execution plan, as shown in Figure 26-5. As a side note, the query uses more reads than before as a result of the index fragmentation introduced by the update.

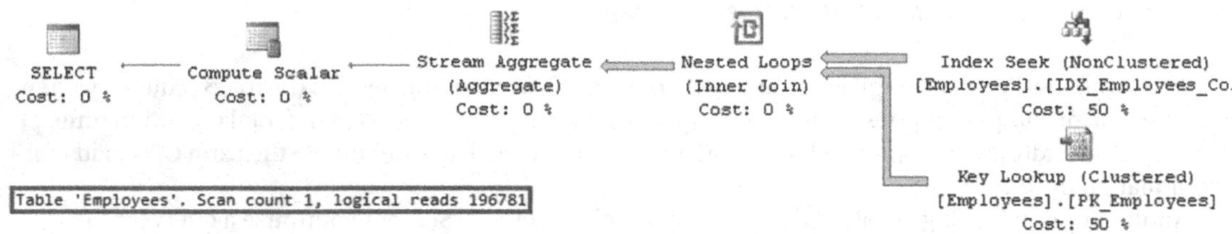

Figure 26-5. *Parameter sniffing: OPTIMIZE FOR and data-distribution change*

SQL Server 2008 introduced another optimization hint, OPTIMIZE FOR UNKNOWN, which helps to address such situations. With this hint, SQL Server performs an optimization based on the most statistically common value in the table. Listing 26-8 shows the code involved in doing this.

Listing 26-8. Parameter sniffing: OPTIMIZE FOR UNKNOWN hint

```
alter proc dbo.GetAverageSalary @Country varchar(64)
as
    select Avg(Salary) as [Avg Salary]
    from dbo.Employees
    where Country = @Country
    option (optimize for(@Country UNKNOWN));
go
exec dbo.GetAverageSalary @Country='Canada';
```

Figure 26-6 illustrates the execution plan. *Germany* is the most statistically common value in the table, and therefore SQL Server generates an execution plan that is optimal for such a parameter value.

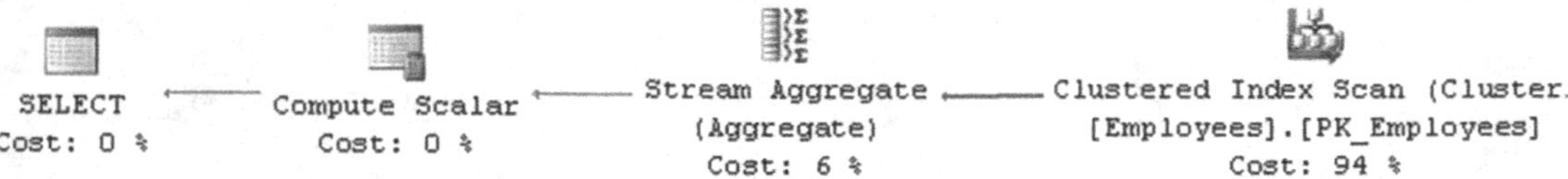

Figure 26-6. *Parameter sniffing: OPTIMIZE FOR UNKNOWN hint*

You can achieve the same results as an OPTIMIZE FOR UNKNOWN hint by using local variables instead of parameters. This method also works with SQL Server 2005, where the OPTIMIZE FOR UNKNOWN hint is not supported. Listing 26-9 illustrates this approach. It introduces the same execution plan as that in Figure 26-6–one with a *clustered index scan*.

Listing 26-9. Parameter sniffing: Using local variables

```
alter proc dbo.GetAverageSalary @Country varchar(64)
as
    declare
        @CountryTmp varchar(64) = @Country;
    select Avg(Salary) as [Avg Salary]
    from dbo.Employees
    where Country = @CountryTmp;
```

SQL Server 2016 allows you to control parameter sniffing on the database level through database scoped configuration by using the ALTER DATABASE SCOPED CONFIGURATION SET PARAMETER_SNIFFING command. Disabling parameter sniffing is equivalent to use the OPTIMIZE FOR UNKNOWN hint with all queries. Another command, ALTER DATABASE SCOPED CONFIGURATION CLEAR PROCEDURE_CACHE, allows you to clear the procedure plan cache for the database.

You can troubleshoot issues introduced by parameter sniffing by analyzing cached plans with the sys.dm_exec_query_stats view and the sys.dm_exec_query_plan function. We will discuss this in more detail, including how to obtain execution plans for currently running statements, both later in this chapter and in Chapter 28.

SQL Server 2016 introduces the new component called *Query Store*, which allows you to capture execution plans and runtime statistics of the queries in the system. Moreover, it helps you to avoid parameter sniffing issues by permitting you to force specific execution plans for queries. We will discuss the Query Store in detail in Chapter 29 of this book.

Plan Reuse

Plans cached by SQL Server must be valid for any combination of parameters during future calls that reuse the plan. In some cases, this can lead to situations where a cached plan is suboptimal for a specific set of parameter values.

One of the code patterns that often leads to such situations is the implementation of stored procedures that search for data based on a set of optional parameters. A typical implementation of such a stored procedure is shown in Listing 26-10. This code also creates two nonclustered indexes on the dbo.Employees table.

Listing 26-10. Plan reuse: Creation of stored procedure and indexes

```
create proc dbo.SearchEmployee
( @Number varchar(32) = null, @Name varchar(100) = null )
as
    select Id, Number, Name, Salary, Country
    from dbo.Employees
    where
        ((@Number is null) or (Number=@Number)) and
        ((@Name is null) or (Name=@Name));
go
```

```
create unique nonclustered index IDX_Employees_Number
on dbo.Employees(Number);
create nonclustered index IDX_Employees_Name
on dbo.Employees(Name);
```

A plan cached by SQL Server should work with any combination of input parameters, regardless of their values at the time when the query was compiled. If you were to call stored procedures multiple times using the code from Listing 26-11, SQL Server would decide to generate and cache a plan with an IDX_Employees_Number *index scan* and *key lookup* operations.

Listing 26-11. Plan reuse: Stored procedure calls

```
exec dbo.SearchEmployee @Number = '10000';
exec dbo.SearchEmployee @Name = 'Canada Employee: 1';
exec dbo.SearchEmployee @Number = '10000', @Name = 'Canada Employee: 1';
exec dbo.SearchEmployee @Number = NULL, @Name = NULL;
```

Figure 26-7 demonstrates Listing 26-11's execution plan for the stored procedure calls. As you can see, the query does not use the IDX_Employees_Number *nonclustered index seek* operation, even when the @Number parameter has a NOT NULL value, because this plan would not be valid when @Number is NULL. Moreover, when @Number is not provided, SQL Server has to perform a *key lookup* operation for every row in the table, which is highly inefficient.

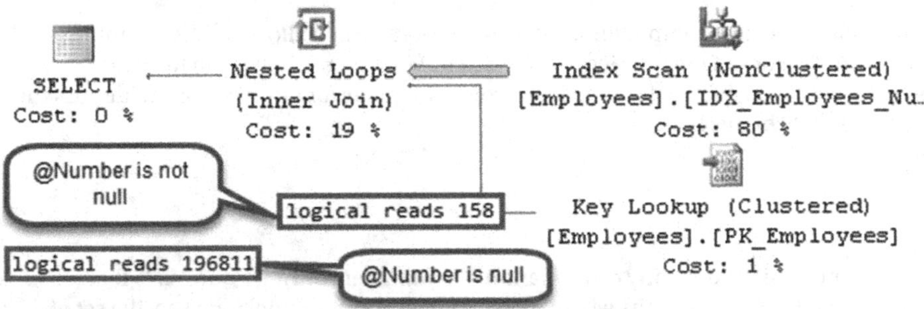

Figure 26-7. *Plan reuse: Execution plans for the stored procedure calls*

Similar to with parameter sniffing issues, you can address this problem with statement-level recompilation using the OPTION (RECOMPILE) clause. Figure 26-8 shows the execution plans in that case.

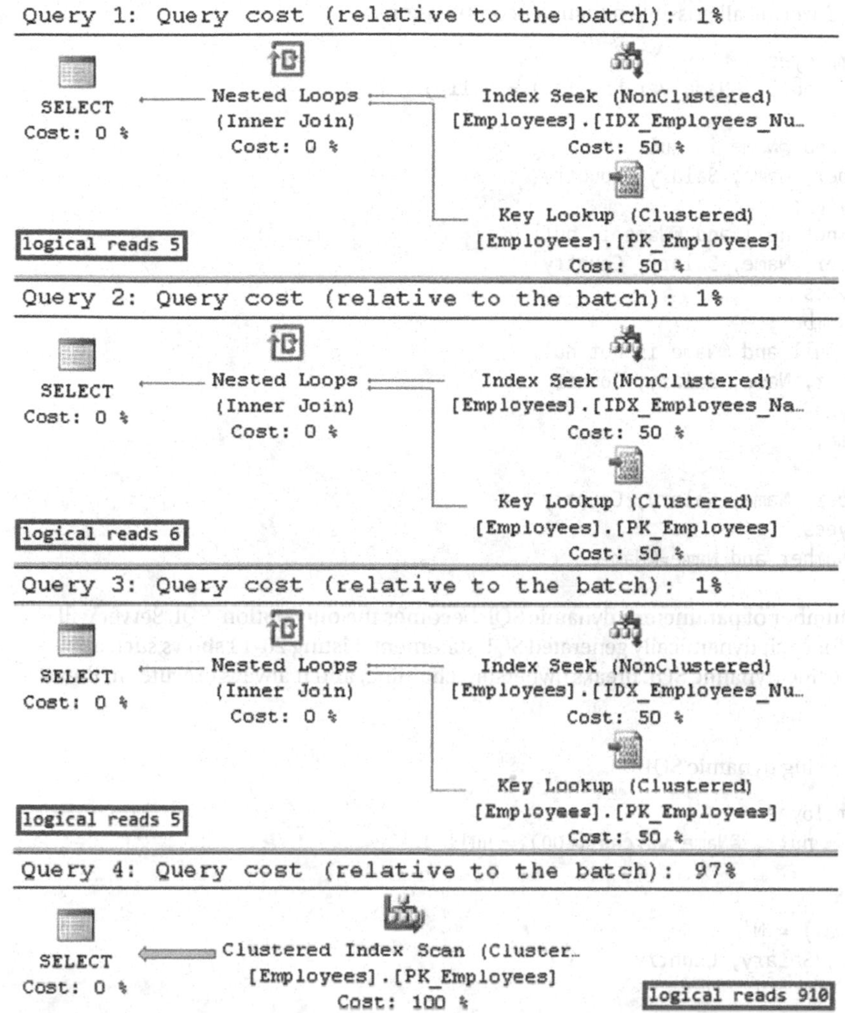

***Figure 26-8.** Plan reuse: Execution plans with statement-level recompile*

As you can see, SQL Server recompiles the query on every call, and therefore it can choose the most beneficial execution plan for every parameter set. It is worth mentioning again that plans are not cached in cases where a statement-level recompile is used.

Even though a statement-level recompile solves the problem, it introduces the overhead of constant recompilations, which you would like to avoid when stored procedures are called very often. One of the options that you have available is to write multiple queries using IF statements that cover all possible combinations of parameters. SQL Server would cache the plan for each statement in that case.

Listing 26-12 shows such an approach; however, it quickly becomes unmanageable with a large number of parameters. The number of combinations to cover is equal to the number of parameters squared.

Listing 26-12. Plan reuse: Covering all possible parameter combinations

```
alter proc dbo.SearchEmployee
(  @Number varchar(32) = null, @Name varchar(100) = null )
as
    if @Number is null and @Name is null
        select Id, Number, Name, Salary, Country
        from dbo.Employees;
    else if @Number is not null and @Name is null
        select Id, Number, Name, Salary, Country
        from dbo.Employees
        where Number=@Number;
    else if @Number is null and @Name is not null
        select Id, Number, Name, Salary, Country
        from dbo.Employees
        where Name=@Name;
    else
        select Id, Number, Name, Salary, Country
        from dbo.Employees
        where Number=@Number and Name=@Name;
```

In the case of a large number of parameters, dynamic SQL becomes the only option. SQL Server will cache the execution plans for each dynamically generated SQL statement. Listing 26-13 shows such an approach. Remember that using dynamic SQL breaks ownership chaining, and it always executes in the security context of `CALLER`.

Listing 26-13. Plan reuse: Using dynamic SQL

```
alter proc dbo.SearchEmployee
(  @Number varchar(32) = null, @Name varchar(100) = null )
as
    declare
        @SQL nvarchar(max) = N'
select Id, Number, Name, Salary, Country
from dbo.Employees
where 1=1' +
        case when @Number is not null then N' and Number=@Number' else N‘’ end +
        case when @Name is not null then N' and Name=@Name' else N” end;

    exec sp_executesql @Sql, N'@Number varchar(32), @Name varchar(100)'
        ,@Number=@Number, @Name=@Name;
```

■ **Important** Always use parameters with the sp_executesql procedure to avoid SQL Injection.

Remember this behavior when you are using filtered indexes. SQL Server will not generate and cache a plan that uses a filtered index in cases where that index cannot be used with some combination of parameter values. Listing 26-14 shows an example. SQL Server will not generate a plan, which is using the `IDX_Data_UnprocessedData` index, when the `@Processed` parameter is set to zero, because this plan would not be valid for a non-zero `@Processed` parameter value.

Listing 26-14. Plan reuse: Filtered indexes (non-functional demo)

```
create unique nonclustered index IDX_Data_UnprocessedData
on dbo.RawData(ID)
include(Processed)
where Processed = 0;

-- Cached Plan for the query would not use filtered index
select top 100 *
from dbo.RawData
where ID > @ID and Processed = @Processed
order by ID;
```

Plan Caching for Ad-Hoc Queries

SQL Server caches plans for ad-hoc queries (and batches), which use constants rather than parameters in the WHERE clause. Listing 26-15 shows an example of ad-hoc queries.

Listing 26-15. Ad-hoc queries

```
select * from dbo.Customers where LastName='Smith'
go
select * from dbo.Customers where LastName='Smith'
go
SELECT * FROM dbo.Customers WHERE LastName='Smith'
go
select * from dbo.Customers where LastName   =  'Smith'
go
```

SQL Server reuses plans for ad-hoc queries only in cases where the queries are exactly the same and a complete character-for-character match with each other. For example, the four queries from Listing 26-15 would introduce three different plans. The first and second queries are identical and share a plan. The two other queries would not reuse that plan due to the keywords' upper- and lowercase mismatch and the extra space characters around the equality operator in the WHERE clause.

Because of the nature of ad-hoc queries, they do not reuse plans very often. Unfortunately, cached plans for ad-hoc queries can consume a large amount of memory. Let's look at an example and run 1,000 simple ad-hoc batches, as shown in Listing 26-16, checking the plan cache state afterward. The script clears the content of the cache with the DBCC FREEPROCCACHE command; do not run this on a production server.

Listing 26-16. Ad-hoc queries' memory usage: Running ad-hoc queries

```
dbcc freeproccache
go

declare
    @SQL nvarchar(max)
    ,@I int = 0
while @I < 1000
```

```
begin
    select @SQL =
        N'declare @C int;select @C=ID from dbo.Employees where ID='
        + convert(nvarchar(10),@I);
    exec(@SQL);
    select @I += 1;
end
go

select
    p.usecounts, p.cacheobjtype, p.objtype, p.size_in_bytes, t.[text]
from
    sys.dm_exec_cached_plans p cross apply
        sys.dm_exec_sql_text(p.plan_handle) t
where
    p.cacheobjtype like 'Compiled Plan%' and
    t.[text] like '%Employees%'
order by
    p.objtype desc;
```

As you can see in Figure 26-9, there are 1,000 plans cached, each of which uses 32 KB of memory, or 32 MB total. As you can guess, ad-hoc queries in busy systems can lead to excessive plan cache memory usage.

	usecounts	cacheobjtype	objtype	size_in_bytes	text
1	1	Compiled Plan	Adhoc	32768	declare @C int;select @C=ID from dbo.Employees where ID=999
2	1	Compiled Plan	Adhoc	32768	declare @C int;select @C=ID from dbo.Employees where ID=998
41	1	Compiled Plan	Adhoc	32768	declare @C int;select @C=ID from dbo.Employees where ID=959

Query executed successfully. | (local)\SQL2012 (11.0 SP1) | SQL2012-STD1\Administr... | tempdb | 00:00:00 | 1000 rows

Figure 26-9. *Plan cache content after query execution*

SQL Server 2008 introduced a server-side configuration setting called *Optimize for ad-hoc workloads*. When this setting is enabled, SQL Server caches small, less-than-300-byte structures, called *compiled plan stubs*, instead of actual compiled plans. A compiled plan stub is a placeholder that is used to keep track of which ad-hoc queries were executed. When the same query runs a second time, SQL Server replaces the compiled plan stub with the actual compiled plan and reuses it going forward.

The *Optimize for ad-hoc workloads* setting is disabled by default. However, it should be enabled in most systems. Even though it introduces slight CPU overhead on the second ad-hoc query recompilation, it could significantly decrease plan cache memory usage on systems with heavy ad-hoc activity. That memory would be available for the buffer pool, which could reduce the number of physical I/O operations and improve system performance.

You can enable this setting with the code shown in Listing 26-17. In addition, it can be enabled in the Advanced tab of the Server Properties window in Management Studio.

Listing 26-17. Enabling Optimize for ad-hoc activity setting

```
exec sys.sp_configure N'optimize for ad hoc workloads', N'1';
reconfigure with override;
```

If you ran the code from Listing 26-16 with the *Optimize for ad-hoc workloads* setting enabled, you would see the plan cache content shown in Figure 26-10. As you can see, it now uses just 272 KB of memory rather than the 32 MB it used to before.

	usecounts	cacheobjtype	objtype	size_in_bytes	text
1	1	Compiled Plan Stub	Adhoc	272	declare @C int;select @C=ID from dbo.Employees where ID=999
2	1	Compiled Plan Stub	Adhoc	272	declare @C int;select @C=ID from dbo.Employees where ID=998
42	1	Compiled Plan Stub	Adhoc	272	declare @C int;select @C=ID from dbo.Employees where ID=958

Query executed successfully. | (local)\SQL2012 (11.0 SP1) | SQL2012-STD1\Administr... | tempdb | 00:00:00 | 1000 rows

Figure 26-10. *Plan cache content when Optimize for ad-hoc workload is enabled*

Auto-Parameterization

In some cases, SQL Server may decide to replace some constants in ad-hoc queries with parameters and cache compiled plans as if the queries were parameterized. When this happens, similar ad-hoc queries that use different constants can reuse cached plans.

Listing 26-18 shows two queries that could be parameterized and will share a compiled plan.

Listing 26-18. Parameterization

```
select ID, Number, Name from dbo.Employees where ID = 5
go
select ID, Number, Name from dbo.Employees where ID = 10
go
```

Internally, SQL Server stores the compiled plan as shown below:

```
(@1 tinyint)SELECT [ID],[Number],[Name] FROM [dbo].[Employees] WHERE [ID]=@1
```

By default, SQL Server defines a parameter data type based on a constant value, choosing the smallest data type where the value fits. For example, the query `SELECT ID, Number, Name FROM dbo.Employees WHERE ID = 10000` would introduce another cached plan, as shown below:

```
(@1 smallint)SELECT [ID],[Number],[Name] FROM [dbo].[Employees] WHERE [ID]=@1
```

When parameterization occurs, SQL Server stores another structure in the plan cache, called a *shell query*, in addition to the compiled plan of the parameterized query. The shell query uses about 16 KB of memory and stores information about the original query, linking it to the compiled plan.

In Figure 26-11, you can see the content of plan cache after we run the queries from Listing 26-18. As you can see, it stores the compiled plan and two shell queries.

	usecounts	cacheobjtype	objtype	size_in_bytes	text
1	2	Compiled Plan	Prepared	32768	(@1 tinyint)SELECT [ID],[Number],[Name] FROM [dbo].[Employees] WHERE [ID]=@1
2	1	Compiled Plan	Adhoc	16384	select ID, Number, Name from dbo.Employees where ID = 10
3	1	Compiled Plan	Adhoc	16384	select ID, Number, Name from dbo.Employees where ID = 5

Figure 26-11. *Plan cache content after parameterization occurred*

By default, SQL Server uses *simple parameterization,* and it is very conservative in parameterizing queries. Simple parameterization only happens when a cached plan is considered *safe to parameterize,* which means that the plan would be the same in terms of plan shape and cardinality estimations, even when constant/parameter values have changed. For example, a plan with a *nonclustered index seek* and *key lookup* on a unique index is safe because it would never return more than one row, regardless of the parameter value. Conversely, the same operation on a non-unique index is not safe. Different parameter values lead to different cardinality estimations, which makes a *clustered index scan* the better choice for some of them. Moreover, there are many language constructs that prevent simple parameterization, such as `IN`, `TOP`, `DISTINCT`, `JOIN`, `UNION`, subqueries, and quite a few others.

Alternatively, SQL Server can use *forced parameterization,* which can be enabled at the database level with the `ALTER DATABASE SET PARAMETERIZATION FORCED` command or on the query level with a `PARAMETERIZATION FORCED` hint. In this mode, SQL Server auto-parameterizes most ad-hoc queries, with very few exceptions.

As might be expected, forced parameterization comes with a set of benefits and drawbacks. While on one hand it can significantly reduce the size of the plan cache and CPU load, it also increases the chance of suboptimal execution plans due to parameter sniffing issues.

Another problem with forced parameterization is that SQL Server replaces constants with parameters without giving you any control about the constants you want to parameterize. This is especially critical for filtered indexes, where parameterization can prevent SQL Server from generating and caching a plan that utilizes them by replacing constant values in the statements with parameters. I am including one such example in the companion materials of the book.

One of the good use cases for forced parameterization is the complex ad-hoc queries submitted by a client application in cases where the choice of execution plan does not depend on constant values. While it is better to change the client application and parameterize queries, it is not always possible.

Listing 26-19 shows an example of such a query. Every query execution leads to a compilation, and it adds an entry to the plan cache. Such a query benefits from forced parameterization, because the most optimal execution plan for the query is a *clustered index seek,* and it does not change based on the constant/parameter value.

Listing 26-19. Example of a query that benefits from forced parameterization

```
select top 100 RecId, /* Other Columns */
from dbo.RawData
where RecID > 432312 -- Client application uses different values at every call
order by RecId
```

With all that being said, you should be careful with forced parameterization when you enable it at the database level. It is safer to enable it on the individual query level if needed.

Plan Guides

Query hints can be extremely useful in helping to resolve various plan caching-related issues. Unfortunately, in some cases you are unable to modify the query text, either because you do not have access to the application code or because the recompilation and redeployment is impossible or impractical.

You can solve such problems by using plan guides, which allow you to add hints to the queries or even force specific execution plans without changing a query's text. You can create them with the `sp_create_plan_guide` stored procedure and manage them with the `sp_control_plan_guide` stored procedure.

There are three types of plan guides available, as follows:

> An *Object* plan guide allows you to specify a hint for a query that exists in a T-SQL object, such as a stored procedure, trigger, or user-defined function.
>
> A *SQL* plan guide allows you to specify a hint for a particular SQL query, either standalone or as part of a batch.
>
> A *Template* plan guide allows you to specify a type of parameterization—forced or simple—for a particular query template, overriding the database setting.

The code in Listing 26-20 removes the query hint from the `dbo.GetAverageSalary` stored procedure and creates a plan guide with an `OPTIMIZE FOR UNKNOWN` hint. The `@Stmt` parameter should specify a query where a hint needs to be added, and `@module_or_batch` should specify the name of the object.

Listing 26-20. Object plan guide

```
alter proc dbo.GetAverageSalary @Country varchar(64)
as
    select Avg(Salary) as [Avg Salary]
    from dbo.Employees
    where Country = @Country;
go

exec sp_create_plan_guide
    @type = N'OBJECT'
    ,@name = N'object_plan_guide_demo'
    ,@stmt = N'select Avg(Salary) as [Avg Salary]
from dbo.Employees
where Country = @Country'
    ,@module_or_batch = N'dbo.GetAverageSalary'
    ,@params = null
    ,@hints = N'OPTION (OPTIMIZE FOR (@Country UNKNOWN))';
```

Now, if you ran the stored procedure for `@Country = 'Canada'`, you would get the execution plan shown in Figure 26-12. It is similar to what you had with the query hint within the stored procedure. You can see in the properties of the top operator in the graphical plan, as well as in its XML representation, that a plan guide was used during optimization.

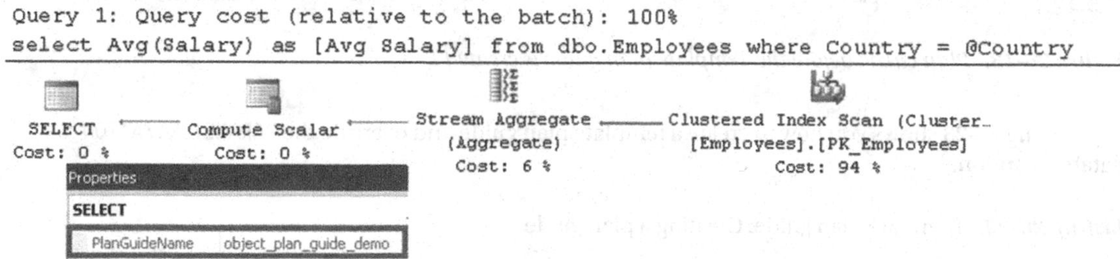

Figure 26-12. *Execution plan with Object plan guide*

Listing 26-21 shows an example of a SQL plan guide, which set the MAXDOP option for the query. In this mode, the @module_or_batch parameter should be set to null.

Listing 26-21. SQL plan guide

```
exec sp_create_plan_guide
    @type = N'SQL'
    ,@name = N'SQL_plan_guide_demo'
    ,@stmt = N'select Country, count(*) as [Count]
from dbo.Employees
group by Country'
    ,@module_or_batch = NULL
    ,@params = null
    ,@hints = N'OPTION (MAXDOP 2)' ;
```

Working with Template plan guides is a bit more complex. Unlike SQL and Object plan guides, where the @stmt parameter should be a character-for-character match with the queries, a Template plan guide requires you to provide the template for the query. Fortunately, you can use another system stored procedure, sp_get_query_template, to prepare it.

Let's look at an example and assume that we want SQL Server to auto-parameterize the query from Listing 26-22. Even though the execution plan for the query is safe—a clustered index seek on a unique index would always return one row–the TOP clause prevents SQL Server from parameterizing it. You can see the ad-hoc cached plan in Figure 26-13.

Listing 26-22. Template plan guide: Sample query

```
select top 1 ID, Number, Name from dbo.Employees where ID = 5;
go

select p.usecounts, p.cacheobjtype, p.objtype, p.size_in_bytes, t.[text]
from sys.dm_exec_cached_plans p cross apply
        sys.dm_exec_sql_text(p.plan_handle) t
where t.[text] like '%Employees%'
order by p.objtype desc
option (recompile);
```

	usecounts	cacheobjtype	objtype	size_in_bytes	text
1	1	Compiled Plan	Adhoc	24576	select top 1 ID, Number, Name from dbo.Employees where ID = 5;

Figure 26-13. *Plan cache before the Template plan guide is created*

Listing 26-23 shows you how to create a template plan guide and override the PARAMETERIZATION database option.

Listing 26-23. Template plan guide: Creating a plan guide

```
declare
    @stmt nvarchar(max)
    ,@params nvarchar(max)
```

```
-- Getting template for the query
exec sp_get_query_template
    @querytext = N'select top 1 ID, Number, Name from dbo.Employees where ID = 5;'
    ,@templatetext = @stmt output
    ,@params = @params output;

-- Creating plan guide
exec sp_create_plan_guide
    @type = N'TEMPLATE'
    ,@name = N'template_plan_guide_demo'
    ,@stmt = @stmt
    ,@module_or_batch = null
    ,@params = @params
    ,@hints = N'OPTION (PARAMETERIZATION FORCED)'
```

Now, if you ran the code from Listing 26-22, the statement would be parameterized, as shown in Figure 26-14.

	usecounts	cacheobjtype	objtype	size_in_bytes	text
1	1	Compiled Plan	Prepared	24576	(@0 int)select top 1 ID , Number , Name from dbo . Employees where ID = @0
2	1	Compiled Plan	Adhoc	16384	select top 1 ID, Number, Name from dbo.Employees where ID = 5;

***Figure 26-14.** Plan cache after Template plan guide is created*

As a final option, you can force SQL Server to use a specific execution plan by specifying it in the plan guide or using the `USE PLAN` query hint. Listing 26-24 shows an example of both approaches. The full XML plan is omitted to conserve space in the book.

Listing 26-24. Forcing XML query plan

```
-- Using USE PLAN query hint
select Avg(Salary) as [Avg Salary]
from dbo.Employees
where Country = 'Germany'
option (use plan N'<?xml version="1.0"?>
<ShowPlanXML><!-- Actual execution plan here --></ShowPlanXML>');
go

-- Using Plan Guide
declare
    @Xml xml = N'<?xml version="1.0"?>
<ShowPlanXML><!-- Actual execution plan here --> </ShowPlanXML>';

declare
    @XmlAsNVarchar nvarchar(max) = convert(nvarchar(max),@Xml)
```

```
exec sp_create_plan_guide
    @type = N'SQL'
    ,@name = N'xml_plan_guide_demo'
    ,@stmt = N'select Avg(Salary) as [Avg Salary]
from dbo.Employees
where Country = ''Germany'''
    ,@module_or_batch = NULL
    ,@params = null
    ,@hints = @XmlAsNVarchar;
```

While both the query hint and the plan guide force SQL Server to use a specific execution plan, in SQL Server 2008 and above, they exhibit different behaviors when the plan becomes incorrect. Query Optimizer will ignore an incorrect plan guide and generate a plan as if the plan guide has not been specified. A query with a USE PLAN hint, on the other hand, would generate an error. An example of such an error is shown here. SQL Server 2005, however, simply fails the query if an invalid plan guide is specified.

```
Msg 8712, Level 16, State 0, Line 1
Index 'tempdb.dbo.Employees.IDX_Employees_Country', specified in the USE PLAN hint, does not
exist. Specify an existing index, or create an index with the specified name.
```

You need to be careful when you change the schemas of the objects referenced in plan guides and USE PLAN hints. It is entirely possible to invalidate plans, even when your changes do not directly affect the indexes and columns used by a query. For example, unique indexes or constraints can eliminate some of the assertions in the plan and, therefore, invalidate a plan when you drop them. Another common example is changes in partition schemas and functions.

Starting with SQL Server 2008, you can use the sys.fn_validate_plan_guide system function to check if a plan guide is still valid. The code in Listing 26-25 shows an example of this.

Listing 26-25. Validating plan guides

```
select pg.plan_guide_id, pg.name, pg.scope_type_desc, pg.is_disabled, vpg.message
from sys.plan_guides pg cross apply
    ( select message from sys.fn_validate_plan_guide(pg.plan_guide_id) ) vpg;
```

The sys.fn_validate_plan_guide function returns a row if the plan guide is incorrect. You can see an example of its output in Figure 26-15.

	plan_guide_id	name	scope_type_desc	is_disabled	message
1	65545	xml_plan_guide_demo	SQL	0	Index 'tempdb.dbo.Employees.IDX_Empl...

Figure 26-15. *Validating plan guides*

As a final note, plan guides are only supported in the Standard, Enterprise, and Developer editions of SQL Server. You can still create plan guides in the unsupported editions, but Query Optimizer will ignore them.

Plan Cache Internals

SQL Server separates plan cache into four different memory areas called *cache stores*. Each cache store caches different entities and plans, as follows:

The *SQL Plans* cache store (internal name CACHESTORE_SQLCP) stores plans for parameterized and ad-hoc queries and batches, as well as for auto-parameterized plans.

The *Object Plans* cache store (CACHESTORE_OBJCP) stores plans for T-SQL objects, such as stored procedures, triggers, and user-defined functions.

The *Extended Stored Procedures* cache store (CACHESTORE_XPROC) stores plans for extended stored procedures.

The *Bound Trees* cache store (CACHESTORE_PHDR) stores bound trees generated during the query optimization stage.

■ **Note** SQL Server uses other cache stores that are not associated with plan cache. You can examine their content by using the `sys.dm_os_memory_cache_counters` data management view.

You can monitor the size of each cache store with a SELECT statement, as shown in Listing 26-26.

Listing 26-26. Checking a cache store's size

```
select type as [Cache Store], sum(pages_in_bytes) / 1024.0 as [Size in KB]
from sys.dm_os_memory_objects
where type in ( 'MEMOBJ_CACHESTORESQLCP','MEMOBJ_CACHESTOREOBJCP'
    ,'MEMOBJ_CACHESTOREXPROC','MEMOBJ_SQLMGR' )
group by type ;
```

Each cache store uses a hash table in which hash buckets keep zero or more plans. There are about 40,000 buckets in both the Object Plan store and the SQL Plan store in 64-bit instances, and about 10,000 buckets in 32-bit instances of SQL Server. The size of the Bound Trees cache store is about 1/10th of that number, and the number of buckets in the Extended Stored Procedures store is always 127. You can examine the cache store properties with the `sys.dm_os_memory_cache_hash_tables` view.

SQL Server uses a very simple algorithm to calculate the hash value for a plan based on the following formula: `(object_id * database_id) mod hash_table_size`.

For parameterized and ad-hoc queries, `object_id` is the internal hash of the query or batch. It is entirely possible that one bucket stores multiple plans for the same object or query. As we have already discussed, different SET options, database users, and quite a few other factors can prevent plan reuse. SQL Server compares multiple plan attributes when looking for the right plan in the cache. We will discuss how to analyze plan attributes later in this chapter.

Compiled plans cached for multi-statement batches are basically the arrays of individual statement-level plans. When a statement from a batch needs to be recompiled, SQL Server recompiles the individual statement rather than the entire batch.

SQL Server treats a cached batch plan as a single unit. The entire batch must be a character-for-character match with original batch that produced the cached plan in order for that plan to be reused. SQL Server generates an execution plan from the compiled plan for the entire batch.

The amount of memory that can be used by the plan cache depends on the version of SQL Server being used (see Table 26-1).

Table 26-1. *Plan Cache Pressure Limit Calculation Formula*

SQL Server Version	Cache Pressure Limit
SQL Server 2005 RTM, SP1	75% of visible target memory from 0-8 GB + 50% of visible target memory from 8 GB-64 GB + 25% of visible target memory > 64 GB
SQL Server 2005 SP2+, SQL Server 2008/2008R2, SQL Server 2012 - 2016	75% of visible target memory from 0-4 GB + 10% of visible target memory from 8 GB-64 GB + 5% of visible target memory > 64 GB

Visible memory is different in 32-bit and 64-bit instances of SQL Server. 32-bit instances of SQL Server have at most 2 GB or 3 GB of visible memory, depending on the presence of a /3GB switch in the `boot.ini` file. Even when AWE (Address Windows Extension) memory is in use, memory above 4 GB can be used for the buffer pool only. No such limitation exists on 64-bit instances of SQL Server.

SQL Server starts to remove plans from the cache in cases of memory pressure. There are two kinds of memory pressure: *local* and *global*. Local memory pressure happens when one of the cache stores grows too big and starts using too much SQL Server process memory. Global memory pressure happens when Windows forces SQL Server to reduce its physical memory usage, or when the size of all cache stores combined reaches 80 percent of the plan cache pressure limit.

Local memory pressure is triggered when one of the cache stores starts to use too much memory. In SQL Server 2005-2008R2, where single-page and multi-page allocations are treated separately, memory pressure occurs when a cache store reaches 75 percent of the plan cache pressure limit in a single-page allocation or 50 percent in a multi-page allocation. In SQL Server 2012 and above, there is only one memory allocator, called the *any-size page allocator*, and memory pressure is triggered when a cache store grows to 62.5 percent of the plan cache pressure limit.

Local memory pressure can also be triggered based on the number of plans in the SQL and Object Plan cache stores. That number is about four times the hash table size, which is 40,000 or 160,000 plans on 32-bit and 64-bit instances respectively.

Both local and global memory pressure remove plans from the cache using an algorithm called *eviction policy*, which is based on plan cost. For ad-hoc plans, the cost starts with zero and increments by one with every plan reuse. Other types of plans measure the cost of resources required to produce them. It is based on I/O, memory, and context switches in the units, called *ticks*, as shown here:

I/O: Each I/O operation costs 1 tick, with a maximum of 19.

Memory: Each 16 pages of memory costs 1 tick, with a maximum of 4.

Context Switches: Each switch costs 1 tick, with a maximum of 8.

When not under memory pressure, costs are not decreased until the total size of all cached plans reaches 50 percent of the buffer pool size. At that point, the *Lazy Writer* process starts periodically scanning plan caches, decrementing the cost of each plan by one on each scan, removing plans with zero cost. Alternatively, each plan reuse increments its cost by one for ad-hoc queries, or by the original plan generation cost for other types of plans.

Listing 26-27 shows you how to examine the current and original costs of cached entries in SQL and Object Plan cache stores.

Listing 26-27. Examining original and current costs of cache entries

```
select
    q.Text as [SQL], p.objtype, p.usecounts, p.size_in_bytes, mce.Type as [Cache Store]
    ,mce.original_cost, mce.current_cost, mce.disk_ios_count
    ,mce.pages_kb  /* Use pages_allocation_count in SQL Server prior 2012 */
    ,mce.context_switches_count, qp.query_plan
```

```
from
    sys.dm_exec_cached_plans p with (nolock) join
        sys.dm_os_memory_cache_entries mce with (nolock) on
            p.memory_object_address = mce.memory_object_address
    cross apply sys.dm_exec_sql_text(p.plan_handle) q
    cross apply sys.dm_exec_query_plan(p.plan_handle) qp
where
    p.cacheobjtype = 'Compiled plan' and
    mce.type in (N'CACHESTORE_SQLCP',N'CACHESTORE_OBJCP')
order by
    p.usecounts desc
```

Examining Plan Cache

There are several data management views that provide plan cache-related information. Let's look at some of them in depth.

As you already saw, the `sys.dm_exec_cached_plans` view provides information about every plan stored in the SQL and Object Plan cache stores. The key column in the view is `plan_handle`, which uniquely identifies the plan. In the case of a batch, that value remains the same even when some statements from the batch are recompiled. In addition to `plan_handle`, this view provides information about the type of plan (Compiled Plan, Compiled Plan Stub, and so forth) in the `cacheobjtype` column, type of object (Proc, Ad-Hoc query, Prepared, Trigger, and so on) in the `objtype` column, reference and use counts, memory size, and a few other attributes.

The data management function `sys.dm_exec_plan_attributes` accepts `plan_handle` as a parameter and returns a set of attributes for a particular plan. Those attributes include references to the database and object to which the plan belongs, the `user_id` of the session that submits the batch, and quite a few other attributes.

One of the attributes, `sql_handle`, links the plan to the batch for which the plan has been compiled. You can use it together with the `sys.dm_exec_sql_text` function to obtain its SQL text.

Each attribute has a flag if it is included in the *cache key*. SQL Server reuses plans only when both the `sql_handle` and cache key of the cached plan match the values from the submitted batch. Think about the `set_option` attribute as an example. It is included in the cache key; therefore, different SET options would lead to different cache key values, which would prevent plan reuse.

One SQL batch, identified by `sql_handle`, can have multiple plans, identified by `plan_handle`—one for each cache key attribute's value. Listing 26-28 illustrates an example of this.

Listing 26-28. `SQL_Handle` and `plan_handle` relations

```
set quoted_identifier off
go
select top 1 ID from dbo.Employees where Salary > 40000;
go
set quoted_identifier on
go
select top 1 ID from dbo.Employees where Salary > 40000
go
;with PlanInfo(sql_handle, plan_handle, set_options)
as
(
```

```
    select pvt.sql_handle, pvt.plan_handle, pvt.set_options
    from
     (  select p.plan_handle, pa.attribute, pa.value
        from sys.dm_exec_cached_plans p with (nolock) outer apply
                sys.dm_exec_plan_attributes(p.plan_handle) pa
        where cacheobjtype = 'Compiled Plan' ) as pc
    pivot (max(pc.value) for pc.attribute
        in ("set_options", "sql_handle")) as pvt
)
select pi.sql_handle, pi.plan_handle, pi.set_options, b.text
from
    PlanInfo pi cross apply
        sys.dm_exec_sql_text(convert(varbinary(64),pi.sql_handle)) b
```

Figure 26-16 shows two different plans for the same SQL batch, resulting from the difference in SET options.

	sql_handle	plan_handle	set_options	text
1	0x020000005D8A8628859FF7E07D00B8...	0x060002005D8A8628109198ED03...	4345	select top 1 ID from dbo.Employees ...
2	0x020000005D8A8628859FF7E07D00B8...	0x060002005D8A8628908298ED03...	4281	select top 1 ID from dbo.Employees ...

Figure 26-16. `Plan_handle` *and* `sql_handle`

You can obtain an XML representation of the execution plan with the `sys.dm_exec_query_plan` function, which accepts `plan_handle` as a parameter. However, it does not return a query plan if the XML plan has more than 128 nested levels, because of XML data-type limitations. In that case, you can use the `sys.dm_exec_text_query_plan` function, which returns a text representation of the XML plan instead.

You can retrieve information about currently executed requests by using the `sys.dm_exec_requests` view. Listing 26-29 shows the query, which returns the data on currently running requests from user sessions, sorted by their running time in descending order.

Listing 26-29. Using `sys.dm_exec_requests`

```
select
    er.session_id, er.user_id, er.status, er.database_id, er.start_time
    ,er.total_elapsed_time, er.logical_reads, er.writes
    ,substring(qt.text, (er.statement_start_offset/2)+1,
        ( ( case er.statement_end_offset
                when -1 then datalength(qt.text)
                else er.statement_end_offset
            end - er.statement_start_offset ) /2 ) +1 ) as [SQL]
    ,qp.query_plan, er.*
from
    sys.dm_exec_requests er with (nolock)
        cross apply sys.dm_exec_sql_text(er.sql_handle) qt
        cross apply sys.dm_exec_query_plan(er.plan_handle) qp
where
    er.session_id > 50 and /* Excluding system processes */
    er.session_id <> @@SPID
order by
    er.total_elapsed_time desc
```

The `sys.dm_exec_query_stats`, `sys.dm_exec_procedure_stats`, and `sys.dm_exec_trigger_stats` views provide aggregated performance statistics for queries, procedures, and triggers that have cached plans. They return one row for every cached plan per object, as long as the plan stays in the cache. These views are extremely useful during performance troubleshooting. We will discuss their use in depth in Chapter 28.

`Sys.dm_exec_query_stats` is supported in SQL Server 2005 and above. `Sys.dm_exec_procedure_stats` and `sys.dm_exec_trigger_stats` were introduced in SQL Server 2008.

■ **Note** You can find more information about execution-related DMOs at `http://technet.microsoft.com/en-us/library/ms188068.aspx`.

Summary

Query optimization is an expensive process that increases CPU load on busy systems. SQL Server reduces such load by caching plans in a special part of memory called the plan cache. It includes plans for T-SQL objects, such as stored procedures, triggers, and user-defined functions; ad-hoc queries and batches; and a few other plan-related entities.

SQL Server reuses plans for ad-hoc queries and batches only when there is a character-for-character match of the query/batch texts. Moreover, different `SET` options and/or references to unqualified objects could prevent plan reuse.

Caching plans for ad-hoc queries can significantly increase plan cache memory usage. It is recommended that you enable the server-side *Optimize for ad-hoc workloads* configuration setting if you are using SQL Server 2008 and above.

SQL Server *sniffs parameters* and generates and caches plans that are optimal for the parameter values at the time of compilation. In cases of uneven data distribution, this could lead to performance issues when cached plans are not optimal for the typically submitted parameter values. You can address such issues with a statement-level recompile, `OPTIMIZE FOR` query hints, or, in SQL Server 2016, with Query Store.

You can specify hints directly in queries. Alternatively, you can use plan guides, which allow you to apply hints or force specific execution plans without changing the query text.

Cached plans should be valid for every possible combination of parameters. This can lead to suboptimal plans when a query has `OR` conditions to support optional parameter values. You can address such issues with a statement-level recompile, or by building SQL dynamically and omitting `OR` conditions.

PART V

Practical Troubleshooting

CHAPTER 27

Extended Events

Extended Events is a highly scalable performance monitoring and troubleshooting solution introduced in SQL Server 2008. It is targeted as a replacement for SQL Traces, which was deprecated in SQL Server 2012. Extended Events are lightweight, and they have the flexibility to allow for troubleshooting of some scenarios that were not possible with SQL Traces.

This chapter provides an overview of the Extended Events framework and shows you how to work with them.

Extended Events Overview

Even though SQL Traces events are extremely easy to set up, they have serious limitations. All event types generate output in the same format. The same columns in the output could provide different data for different SQL Traces events. For example, in the `SQL:Batch Completed` event, the `TextData` column contains the text of the SQL batch. Alternatively, in the `Lock:Acquired` event, the same column shows a resource where a lock was acquired. It is complicated to analyze the output of the traces that collect different events.

Performance is another important factor. A SQL Server component called *Trace Controller* manages SQL Traces defined by all *trace consumers*. It keeps an internal bitmap that shows event types that are consumed by currently active traces and, therefore, need to be collected. Other SQL Server components, which in this context are called *trace producers*, analyze that bitmap and fire corresponding events when needed.

Trace producers do not know what data columns are included in the trace. Data for all of the columns is collected and passed to the controller, which evaluates trace filters and discards unneeded events and data columns.

This architecture introduces unnecessary overhead. Consider a situation where you want to capture long-running SQL statements from a specific session. SQL Traces would have very few columns defined and collect just a handful of events. Trace producers, however, would fire events for each SQL statement that comes to the system. The trace controller would do all further filtering and column removal.

The Extended Events framework has been designed with the goal of addressing these limitations in mind. Similar to SQL Traces, it includes *event sessions* that define the boundaries for event collection. They specify event types and data that needs to be collected, predicates that are used in filters, and targets where the data is stored. SQL Server can write events to targets either synchronously, in the same thread where the event occurs, or asynchronously, buffering data in the memory reserved for each event session.

Extended Events uses an XML format. Each event type has its own set of data columns. For example, the `sql_statement_completed` event provides the number of reads and writes, CPU time, duration, and other execution statistics for a query. You can collect additional attributes–for example, the tsql stack–by executing operators called *actions*. In contrast to SQL Traces, Extended Events does not collect unnecessary data; that is, only a small set of event data columns and specified actions are collected.

D. Korotkevitch, *Pro SQL Server Internals*, DOI 10.1007/978-1-4842-1964-5_27

When SQL Server triggers an *event*, it checks for any active event sessions that consume such an event. When such sessions exist, SQL Server collects the event data columns and, if predicates were defined, collects the information needed for their evaluation. If predicate evaluation succeeds and the event needs to be fired, SQL Server collects all of the actions, passes data to synchronous targets, and buffers data for asynchronous targets. Figure 27-1 illustrates this process.

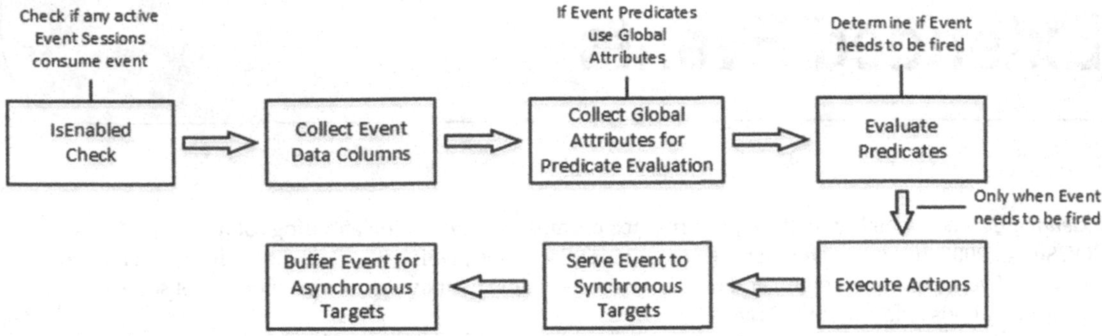

Figure 27-1. *Extended Events life cycle*

Finally, it is worth noting that Extended Events support in SQL Server 2008 is rather limited, and it does not include all of the events that exist in SQL Traces. Moreover, Management Studio in SQL Server 2008 does not include a UI to work with Extended Events. Fortunately, those limitations have been addressed in SQL Server 2012 and above, where all SQL Traces events have corresponding Extended Events, and Management Studio provides the tools to manage and analyze Extended Events data.

■ **Note** You can download the SQL Server 2008 Extended Events Management Studio Add-In developed by Jonathan Kehayias from the SqlSkills.com website at `http://www.sqlskills.com/free-tools/`, or from CodePlex. Moreover, Jonathan wrote an excellent tutorial on Extended Events called "An XEvent a Day," which is available at `http://www.sqlskills.com/blogs/jonathan/category/xevent-a-day-series/`.

Extended Events Objects

The Extended Events framework consists of several different objects. Let's examine them in detail.

Packages

SQL Server combines Extended Events objects into *packages*. You can think of packages as containers for metadata information. Each Extended Events object is referenced by a two-part name, which includes package and object names. Packages do not define a functional boundary for the events. It is completely normal to use objects from different packages together.

Different versions of SQL Server have a different number of packages available and expose them with the `sys.dm_xe_packages` view. You can examine them with the code shown in Listing 27-1. The `Capabilities` column is a bitmask that describes the properties of the package. The leftmost bit indicates if the package is private, and thus if objects from that package are used by SQL Server internally and are not accessible to users. For example, the `SecAudit` package is private and is used by SQL Server for audit functions. This package cannot be referenced in any user-defined Extended Events session.

Listing 27-1. Examining Extended Events packages

```
select
    dxp.guid, dxp.name, dxp.description, dxp.capabilities
    ,dxp.capabilities_desc, os.name as [Module]
from
    sys.dm_xe_packages dxp join sys.dm_os_loaded_modules os on
        dxp.module_address = os.base_address
```

Figure 27-2 shows the output of this query in SQL Server 2016.

	guid	name	description	capabilities	capa...	Module
1	03FDA7D0-91B...	sqlserver	Extended events for Microsoft SQL Server	NULL	NULL	C:\Program
2	655FD93F-336...	sqlserver	Extended events for Microsoft SQL Server	NULL	NULL	C:\Program
3	F235752A-D5C...	SecAudit	Security Audit Events	1	private	C:\Program
4	C0AB75C5-B1E...	ucs	Extended events for Unified Communications Stack	NULL	NULL	C:\Program
5	1E99FE90-A4F...	sqlclr	Extended events for SQL CLR	NULL	NULL	C:\Program
6	B086C2F3-273...	filestream	Extended events for SQL Server FILESTREAM and FileTable	NULL	NULL	C:\Program
7	A7A93404-1BD...	SQLSatellite	Extended events for SQL Satellite	NULL	NULL	C:\Program
8	E3CCBF2F-CD...	sqlsni	Extended events for Microsoft SQL Server	NULL	NULL	C:\Program
9	3078EA7F-9B2...	sqlserver	Extended events for Microsoft SQL Server	NULL	NULL	C:\Program
10	60AA9FBF-673...	package0	Default package. Contains all standard types, maps, compare operators, actions and targets	256	utility	C:\Program
11	BD97CC63-3F3...	sqlos	Extended events for SQL Operating System	NULL	NULL	C:\Program
12	8F5C6497-A27...	qds	Extended events for Query Store	NULL	NULL	C:\Program
13	741DF03F-54B...	XtpRuntime	Extended events for the XTP Runtime	NULL	NULL	C:\Program
14	4F6BDDD7-25...	XtpCompile	Extended events for the XTP Compile	NULL	NULL	C:\Program
15	E2FC7CCD-B0...	XtpEngine	Extended events for the XTP Engine	NULL	NULL	C:\Program

Figure 27-2. *Extended Events packages in SQL Server 2016*

Events

Events correspond to specific points in SQL Server code; for example, completion of a SQL statement, acquiring and releasing a lock, deadlock conditions, and others.

Different versions of SQL Server expose a different number of events. Moreover, the number of events may increase with service pack releases. For example, SQL Server 2008 SP2 exposes 253 events, SQL Server 2012 RTM exposes 617 events, SQL Server 2012 SP1 exposes 625 events, SQL Server 2014 RTM exposes 870 events, and SQL Server 2016 RTM exposes 1,301 events.

In SQL Server 2012 and above, every SQL Traces event has a corresponding Extended Event. The opposite, however, is not true. SQL Traces is deprecated in SQL Server 2012, and the new SQL Server features do not expose troubleshooting capabilities through SQL Traces, using Extended Events instead.

You can analyze available events with the `sys.dm_xe_objects` view, as shown in Listing 27-2. Figure 27-3 shows the partial output of a query from SQL Server 2016.

Listing 27-2. Examining Extended Events

```
select xp.name as [Package], xo.name as [Event], xo.Description
from sys.dm_xe_packages xp join sys.dm_xe_objects xo on
    xp.guid = xo.package_guid
where
    (xp.capabilities is null or xp.capabilities & 1 = 0) and -- exclude private packages
    (xo.capabilities is null or xo.capabilities & 1 = 0) and -- exclude private objects
    xo.object_type = 'event'
order by
    xp.name, xo.name
```

	Package	Event	Description
55	qds	query_store_loaded	Fired when Query Store is loaded
56	qds	query_store_notify_force_failure_failed	Fired when Query Store failed to notify force failure
57	qds	query_store_persist_task_init_failed	Fired when persist task fails during initialization
58	qds	query_store_plan_forcing_failed	Occurs when forcing of plan from Query Store fail
59	qds	query_store_plan_persistence_failure	Fired if there's a failure to persist plan
60	qds	query_store_plan_removal	Fired when plan is removed
61	qds	query_store_query_persistence_failure	Fired if there's a failure to persist query
62	qds	query_store_read_write_failed	Fired if the read/write to Query Store internal tables failed

Figure 27-3. *Extended Events events in SQL Server 2016*

Each event has a set of associated columns that belong to one of three categories, as follows:

> *Read Only* columns contain static information about an event, such as the event GUID, schema version, and other static information.
>
> *Data* columns contain run-time event data. For example, `sql_statement_completed` events expose various execution statistics- related data columns, such as the number of I/O operations, CPU time, and other run-time event data.
>
> *Customizable* columns allow you to change their values during event session creation, and they control the behavior of the event. For example, the `collect_statement` column of `sql_statement_completed` events controls if a SQL statement is collected when an event is fired. It is enabled by default; however, you can change its value and disable statement collection on busy servers. Alternatively, the `collect_parameterized_plan_handle` column is disabled by default, but it could be enabled if needed.

You can examine event columns with the `sys.dm_xe_object_columns` view. Listing 27-3 shows you how to obtain column information for the `sql_statement_completed` event.

Listing 27-3. Examining Extended Events columns

```
select
    dxoc.column_id, dxoc.name, dxoc.type_name as [Data Type]
    ,dxoc.column_type as [Column Type], dxoc.column_value as [Value], dxoc.description
from
    sys.dm_xe_object_columns dxoc
where
    dxoc.object_name = 'sql_statement_completed'
```

The set of available columns changes based on the SQL Server version in use. Figure 27-4 shows the output of the preceding query in SQL Server 2008, and Figure 27-5 shows it in SQL Server 2012 and above. It is worth noting that the `VERSION` column value in the event data is different in those cases.

	column_id	name	Data Type	Column Type	Value	description
1	0	ID	uint16	readonly	60	Numeric ID
2	1	UUID	guid_ptr	readonly	CDFD84F9-18...	Globally Unique ID
3	2	VERSION	uint8	readonly	1	Event schema version
4	3	CHANNEL	etw_channel	readonly	2	ETW Channel
5	4	KEYWORD	keyword_map	readonly	128	Associated Keyword
6	0	source_database_id	uint16	data	NULL	NULL
7	1	object_id	uint32	data	NULL	NULL
8	2	object_type	uint16	data	NULL	NULL
9	3	cpu	uint32	data	NULL	NULL
10	4	duration	int64	data	NULL	NULL
11	5	reads	uint64	data	NULL	NULL
12	6	writes	uint64	data	NULL	NULL

***Figure 27-4.** sql_statement_completed event columns in SQL Server 2008*

	column_id	name	Data Type	Column Type	Value	description
1	0	UUID	guid_ptr	readonly	CDFD8...	Globally Unique ID
2	1	VERSION	uint8	readonly	2	Event schema version
3	2	CHANNEL	etw_channel	readonly	2	ETW Channel
4	3	KEYWORD	keyword_map	readonly	64	Associated Keyword
5	0	collect_statement	boolean	customizable	true	When set to 0, collect_statement disables collection of statement. By default the statement column is generated.
6	1	collect_parameterized_plan_handle	boolean	customizable	false	When set to 1, collect_parameterized_plan_handle enables collection of parameterized_plan_handle. By defau...
7	0	duration	int64	data	NULL	The time (in microseconds) that it took to execute the statement.
8	1	cpu_time	uint64	data	NULL	Indicates the CPU time (in microseconds) that is consumed by the statement.
9	2	physical_reads	uint64	data	NULL	The number of physical page reads that were issued by the statement.
10	3	logical_reads	uint64	data	NULL	The number of logical page reads that were issued by the statement.
11	4	writes	uint64	data	NULL	The number of page writes that were issued by the statement
12	5	row_count	uint64	data	NULL	The number of rows that were touched by the statement.
13	6	last_row_count	uint64	data	NULL	The last row count for this statement.
14	7	line_number	int32	data	NULL	The statement line number, in relation to the beginning of the batch.
15	8	offset	int32	data	NULL	The statement start offset, in relation to the beginning of the batch.
16	9	offset_end	int32	data	NULL	The statement end offset, in relation to the beginning of the batch. The value will be -1 for the last statement.
17	10	statement	unicode_string	data	NULL	The text of the statement that triggered the event.
18	11	parameterized_plan_handle	binary_data	data	NULL	The plan handle of the cache entry of the parameterised query plan.

***Figure 27-5.** sql_statement_completed event columns in SQL Server 2012 and above*

Predicates

Predicates define Boolean conditions for when an event needs to be fired. For example, if you want to collect information about CPU-intensive queries, you can define a predicate on the `cpu_time` column of the `sql_statement_completed` event, capturing only the statements with CPU time that exceeds some predefined threshold.

Even though predicates look very similar to column filters in SQL Traces, there is a subtle difference between them. SQL Traces evaluates column filters after an event is collected and passed to the trace controller. In contrast, Extended Events collects the minimally required amount of data to evaluate predicates and does not execute actions or fire events if the predicates were evaluated as `False`.

Predicates can be defined against either the event data columns or global attributes, such as `session_id`, `database_id`, and many others. You can see a list of the available global attributes by using the query shown in Listing 27-4. Figure 27-6 shows the partial output of this query in SQL Server 2016.

Listing 27-4. Examining global attributes

```
select xp.name as [Package], xo.name as [Predicate], xo.Description
from sys.dm_xe_packages xp join sys.dm_xe_objects xo on
    xp.guid = xo.package_guid
where
    (xp.capabilities is null or xp.capabilities & 1 = 0) and -- exclude private packages
    (xo.capabilities is null or xo.capabilities & 1 = 0) and -- exclude private objects
    xo.object_type = 'pred_source'
order by
    xp.name, xo.name
```

	Package	Predicate	Description
16	sqlserver	client_app_name	Get the current client application name
17	sqlserver	client_connection_id	Get the optional identifier provided at connection time by a client
18	sqlserver	client_hostname	Get the current client hostname
19	sqlserver	client_pid	Get the current client process ID
20	sqlserver	context_info	Get the same value as the CONTEXT_INFO() function.
21	sqlserver	database_id	Get the current database ID
22	sqlserver	database_name	Get the current database name
23	sqlserver	is_system	Get whether current session is system
24	sqlserver	nt_domain	Get the current NT domain

Figure 27-6. *Global attributes that can be used in predicates*

Predicates can use the basic arithmetic operations and comparison functions provided by the Extended Events framework. You can examine the list of available functions by using the query shown in Listing 27-5. Figure 27-7 shows the partial output of this query in SQL Server 2016.

Listing 27-5. Examining comparison functions

```
select xp.name as [Package], xo.name as [Comparison Function], xo.Description
from sys.dm_xe_packages xp join sys.dm_xe_objects xo on
    xp.guid = xo.package_guid
where
    (xp.capabilities is null or xp.capabilities & 1 = 0) and -- exclude private packages
    (xo.capabilities is null or xo.capabilities & 1 = 0) and -- exclude private objects
    xo.object_type = 'pred_compare'
order by
    xp.name, xo.name
```

	Package	Comparison Function	Description
1	package0	divides_by_uint64	Whether a uint64 divides another with no remainder
2	package0	equal_ansi_string	Equality operator between two ANSI string values
3	package0	equal_binary_data	Equality operator between two Binary values
4	package0	equal_boolean	Equality operator between two Boolean values
5	package0	equal_float64	Equality operator between two 64-bit double values
6	package0	equal_guid	Equality operator between two GUID values

Figure 27-7. *Comparison functions that can be used in predicates*

In contrast to Transact SQL, Extended Events supports short-circuit predicate evaluation, similar to development languages like C# or Java. When you have multiple predicates defined with logical OR and AND conditions, SQL Server stops the evaluation as soon as the result is definitive. For example, if you have two predicates using the logical AND operator, and the first predicate is evaluated as `False`, SQL Server does not evaluate the second predicate.

■ **Tip** Collecting global attributes data adds slight overhead to predicate evaluation. It is helpful to write multiple predicates in such a way that the event data columns are evaluated prior to the global attributes, thus preventing global attribute data collection due to short-circuiting.

SQL Server maintains the predicate state within an event session. For example, the `package0.counter` attribute stores the number of times the predicate was evaluated. You can rely on the predicate state if you want to create event sessions that sample the data; for example, collecting data for every one hundredth or, perhaps, the first ten occurrences of the event.

Actions

Actions provide you with the ability to collect additional information with the events. Available actions include `session_id`, `client_app_name`, `query_plan_hash`, and many others. Actions are executed after predicates are evaluated, and only if an event is going to be fired.

SQL Server executes actions synchronously in the same thread as the events, which adds overhead to event collection. The amount of overhead depends on the action. Some of them–for example, `session_id` or `cpu_id`–are relatively lightweight. Others, such as `sql_text` or `callstack`, can add significant overhead to SQL Server when they are collected with frequently fired events. The same applies to execution plan-related events and actions. They can add considerable overhead to the server.

■ **Important** Even though individual Extended Events are lightweight compared to SQL Traces events, they can still add considerable overhead to the server when used incorrectly. Do not add unnecessary load to SQL Server, and collect only those events and actions that are required for troubleshooting.

You can examine the list of available actions by using the query shown in Listing 27-6. Figure 27-8 shows the partial output of the query when run in SQL Server 2016.

Listing 27-6. Examining actions

```
select xp.name as [Package], xo.name as [Action], xo.Description
from sys.dm_xe_packages xp join sys.dm_xe_objects xo on
    xp.guid = xo.package_guid
where
    (xp.capabilities is null or xp.capabilities & 1 = 0) and -- exclude private packages
    (xo.capabilities is null or xo.capabilities & 1 = 0) and -- exclude private objects
    xo.object_type = 'action'
order by
    xp.name, xo.name
```

	Package	Action	Description
1	package0	callstack	Collect the current call stack
2	package0	collect_cpu_cycle_time	Collect the current CPU's cycle count
3	package0	collect_current_thread_id	Collect the current Windows thread ID
4	package0	collect_system_time	Collect the current system time with 100 microsecon...
5	package0	debug_break	Break the process in the default debugger
19	sqlos	worker_address	Collect current worker address
20	sqlserver	client_app_name	Collect client application name
21	sqlserver	client_connection_id	Collects the optional identifier provided at connectio...

Figure 27-8. *Extended Events actions*

Types and Maps

In the Extended Events framework, data attributes are strongly typed with either types or maps. *Types* represent scalar data types, such as integer, character, or GUID. *Maps*, on the other hand, are enumerators that convert integer keys into a human-readable representation.

You can think of wait types as an example of Extended Events maps. The list of available wait types is pre-defined, and SQL Server can return an integer wait type key with events. The `wait_types` map allows you to convert this code into an easy-to-understand wait type definition.

You can see the list of available types and maps by using the query shown in Listing 27-7. Figure 27-9 shows the partial output of the query when run in SQL Server 2016.

Listing 27-7. Examining types and maps

```
select xo.object_type as [Object], xo.name, xo.description, xo.type_name, xo.type_size
from sys.dm_xe_objects xo
where xo.object_type in ('type','map')
```

	Object	name	description	type_name	type_size
5	type	int8	Signed 8-bit integer	int8	1
6	type	int16	Signed 16-bit integer	int16	2
31	type	xml	Well formed XML fragment	xml	0
32	map	keyword_map	Event grouping keywords	uint32	4
33	map	event_opcode	Event pair	uint32	4

Figure 27-9. *Extended Events types and maps*

You can examine the list of map values for a type with the `sys.dm_xe_map_values` view. Listing 27-8 shows you how to obtain values for the `wait_types` map. Figure 27-10 shows the partial output of the query.

Listing 27-8. Examining wait_types map

```
select name, map_key, map_value
from sys.dm_xe_map_values
where name = 'wait_types'
order by map_key
```

	name	map_key	map_value
20	wait_types	19	LCK_M_RX_S
21	wait_types	20	LCK_M_RX_U
22	wait_types	21	LCK_M_RX_X
23	wait_types	32	LATCH_NL
24	wait_types	33	LATCH_KP

Figure 27-10. *wait_types map keys values*

Targets

When all event data is collected and the event is fired, it goes to the *targets*, which allow you to store and retain raw event data or perform some data analysis and aggregation.

Similar to packages, some targets are private and cannot be used in an Extended Events session's definition. You can examine the list of public targets by using the code shown in Listing 27-9.

Listing 27-9. Examining public targets

```
select
    xp.name as [Package], xo.name as [Action], xo.Description
    ,xo.capabilities_desc as [Capabilities]
from
    sys.dm_xe_packages xp join sys.dm_xe_objects xo on
        xp.guid = xo.package_guid
where
    (xp.capabilities is null or xp.capabilities & 1 = 0) and -- exclude private packages
    (xo.capabilities is null or xo.capabilities & 1 = 0) and -- exclude private objects
    xo.object_type = 'target'
order by
    xp.name, xo.name
```

The set of available targets is pretty much the same in different versions of SQL Server. Target names, however, are different between SQL Server 2008/2008R2 and subsequent versions. Figure 27-11 shows the list of available targets in SQL Server 2012-2016.

	Package	Action	Description	Capabilities
1	package0	etw_classic_sync_target	Event Tracing for Windows (ETW) Synchronous Target	singleton synchronous
2	package0	event_counter	Use the event_counter target to count the number of occurrences of each event in the event session.	synchronous
3	package0	event_file	Use the event_file target to save the event data to an XEL file, which can be archived and used for later analysis and revie...	process_whole_buffers
4	package0	histogram	Use the histogram target to aggregate event data based on a specific event data field or action associated with the event. ...	NULL
5	package0	pair_matching	Pairing target	process_whole_buffers
6	package0	ring_buffer	Asynchronous ring buffer target.	process_whole_buffers

Figure 27-11. *SQL Server 2012-2016 Extended Events targets*

Now, let's look at targets in greater depth. Some of the most useful are listed here:

The ring_buffer target stores data in an in-memory ring buffer of a predefined size. When it is full, new events override the oldest ones in the buffer. Therefore, events can be consumed indefinitely. However, only the newest events are retained. This target is most useful when you need to perform troubleshooting and do not need to retain event data afterward. This is an asynchronous target (more about this later) and is supported in all versions of SQL Server.

The asynchronous_file_target (SQL Server 2008/2008R2) and event_file (SQL Server 2012-2016) targets store events in the file using a proprietary binary format. These targets are most useful when you want to retain raw event data collected by a session. These targets are asynchronous.

The etw_classic_sync_target is a file-based target that writes data in a format that can be used by ETW-enabled readers. This target is used when you need to correlate SQL Server events with event-tracing events that are generated by Windows Kernel and other non-SQL Server components. (These scenarios are outside of the scope of this book.) This is a synchronous target and is supported in all versions of SQL Server.

The synchronous_event_counter (SQL Server 2008/2008R2) and the event_counter (SQL Server 2012-2016) targets count the number of occurrences of each event in an event session. This target is useful when you need to analyze the particular metrics from a workload without introducing the overhead of full event collection. You can think about counting the number of queries in the system as an example. These targets are synchronous.

The synchronous_bucketizer (SQL Server 2008/2008R2), asynchronous_bucketizer (SQL Server 2008/2008R2), and histogram (SQL Server 2012-2016) targets allow you to count the number of specific events, grouping the results based on a specified event data column or action. For example, you can count the number of queries in the system on a per-database basis. The bucketizer targets in SQL Server 2008/2008R2 can be either synchronous or asynchronous, while the histogram target is asynchronous.

The pair_matching target helps you to troubleshoot situations in which one of the expected events does not occur for some reason. One such example is troubleshooting orphaned transactions by looking for database_transaction_begin events without corresponding database_transaction_end events. The pair_matching target discards all matching event pairs, keeping only events that do not match. This is an asynchronous target and is supported in all versions of SQL Server.

Each target has its own set of properties that need to be configured with event sessions. For example, the ring_buffer target requires you to specify the amount of memory and/or number of events to keep as well as the maximum number of occurrences of each event type in the buffer. Listing 27-10 shows you how to examine the configuration parameters of a target, using the event_file target as an example. Figure 27-12 shows the output of this query.

Listing 27-10. Examining target configuration parameters

```
select
    oc.column_id, oc.name as [Column], oc.type_name
    ,oc.Description, oc.capabilities_desc as [Capabilities]
from
    sys.dm_xe_objects xo join sys.dm_xe_object_columns oc on
        xo.package_guid = oc.object_package_guid and
        xo.name = oc.object_name
where
    xo.object_type = 'target' and
    xo.name = 'event_file'
order by
    oc.column_id
```

	column_id	Column	type_name	Description	Capabilities
1	0	filename	unicode_string_ptr	Specifies the location and file name of the log	mandatory
2	1	max_file_size	uint64	Maximum file size in MB	
3	2	max_rollover_files	uint32	Maximum number of files to retain	
4	3	increment	uint64	Size in MB to grow the file	
5	4	metadatafile	unicode_string_ptr	Not used	

Figure 27-12. *Event_file target configuration settings*

■ **Note** You can read more about targets and their configuration settings at `http://technet.microsoft.com/en-us/library/bb630339.aspx`. Remember that configuration settings vary in different versions of SQL Server.

You can use multiple event targets in one event session. For example, you can combine the `event_file` target with the `ring_buffer`, using the latter for real-time troubleshooting while retaining events in the file.

As you have already seen, targets can be either synchronous or asynchronous. SQL Server writes data to synchronous targets in the execution thread that fires an event. For asynchronous targets, SQL Server buffers events in the memory, periodically flushing them out to the targets. The `EVENT_RETENTION_MODE` event session configuration setting controls what happens with new events when buffers are full, as follows:

> The `NO_EVENT_LOSS` option indicates that all events must be retained and event loss is unacceptable. SQL Server execution threads wait until buffers are flushed and have the free space to accommodate the new events. As you can guess, this option can introduce a major performance impact on SQL Server. Think about an event session that collects information about acquired and released locks, using the `event_file` target as an example. That event session can collect an enormous amount of events, and I/O throughput quickly becomes a bottleneck when the event data is saved.

> The `ALLOW_SINGLE_EVENT_LOSS` option allows a session to lose a single event when the buffers are full. This option reduces the performance impact on SQL Server while minimizing the loss of event data collected.

> The `ALLOW_MULTIPLE_EVENT_LOSS` option allows a session to lose multiple events when the buffers are full. This option minimizes the performance impact on SQL Server at the cost of the potential loss of a large number of events.

Creating Events Sessions

Now, it is time to bring everything together and look at Extended Events sessions. We will focus on a T-SQL implementation; however, you can use Management Studio with SQL Server 2012 and above, or Jonathan Kehayias' SSMS Add-In with SQL Server 2008 if you prefer to work through the UI.

Each Extended Events session specifies the events to collect, targets for collected data, and several configuration properties. Listing 27-11 shows a statement that creates an Extended Events session that collects information about tempdb spills using the hash_warning and sort_warning events. This code works in SQL Server 2012 and above, as SQL Server 2008/2008R2 does not support hash_warning or sort_warning events. However, the syntax of the CREATE EVENT SESSION command is the same in every version of SQL Server.

Listing 27-11. Creating an event session

```
create event session [TempDB Spills]
on server
add event sqlserver.hash_warning
(
    action ( sqlserver.session_id, sqlserver.plan_handle, sqlserver.sql_text )
    where ( sqlserver.is_system=0 )
),
add event sqlserver.sort_warning
(
    action ( sqlserver.session_id, sqlserver.plan_handle, sqlserver.sql_text )
    where ( sqlserver.is_system=0 )
)
add target package0.event_file
( set filename='c:\ExtEvents\TempDB_Spiils.xel', max_file_size=25 ),
add target package0.ring_buffer
( set max_memory=4096 )
with  -- Extended Events session properties
(
    max_memory=4096KB
    ,event_retention_mode=allow_single_event_loss
    ,max_dispatch_latency=15 seconds
    ,track_causality=off
    ,memory_partition_mode=none
    ,startup_state=off
);
```

As already mentioned, for asynchronous targets, SQL Server stores collected events in a set of memory buffers, using multiple buffers to separate the collection and processing of events. The number of buffers and their size depends on the max_memory and memory_partition_mode settings. SQL Server uses the following algorithm, rounding the buffer size up to the next 64 KB boundary:

> memory_partition_mode = none: SQL Server uses three central buffers with the size of max_memory / 3 rounded up to next 64 KB boundary. For example, a max_memory of 4000 KB would create three buffers of 1344 KB each, regardless of the server configuration.

memory_partition_mode = per_node: SQL Server creates a separate set of three buffers each per NUMA node. For example, on a server with two NUMA nodes, a max_memory of 4000 KB would create six buffers, three per node, at a size of 704 KB per buffer.

memory_partition_mode = per_cpu: SQL Server creates the number of buffers based on this formula, 2.5 * (number of CPUs), and partitions them on a per-CPU basis. For example, on a server with 20 CPUs, a max_memory of 4000 KB would create 50 buffers of 128 KB each.

Partitioning by NUMA node or CPU allows multiple CPUs to store events in a separate set of buffers, which helps reduce contentions and, therefore, the performance impact of Extended Events sessions that collect a very large number of events. There is a caveat, however. An event needs to be able to fit into the buffer in order to be collected. As you may have noticed, buffer partitioning increases the number of buffers, and this reduces their size. This is usually not a problem, because most of the events are relatively small. However, it is also possible to define a very large event that would not fit into the buffer. Make sure that you increase max_memory when you partition events on a server with a large number of NUMA nodes and/or CPUs.

■ **Note** You can examine the largest_event_dropped_size column of the sys.dm_xe_sessions view to check if the buffers are big enough to fit the events.

SQL Server flushes the event session data to asynchronous targets when the buffers are full and/or based on a time interval specified by the max_dispatch_latency setting, which is 30 seconds by default.

The startup_state option controls whether an event session should start automatically on SQL Server startup.

Finally, the track_causality option allows you to track the sequence of events and see how different events lead to each other. An example of such a scenario is a SQL statement that triggers a file read event, which in turn triggers a wait event with PAGELATCHIO wait, and so forth. When this option is enabled, SQL Server adds a unique activity ID that is a combination of the GUID value, which remains the same for the task, and the event sequence number.

After an event session is created, you can start or stop it with the ALTER EVENT SESSION command, or drop it with the DROP EVENT SESSION command, as shown in Listing 27-12.

Listing 27-12. Working with an event session

```
-- Starting Event Session
alter event session [TempDB Spills] on server state=start;
-- Stopping Event Session
alter event session [TempDB Spills] on server state=stop;
-- Dropping Event Session
drop event session [TempDB Spills] on server;
```

Working with Event Data

Management Studio 2012 and above provides you with a UI to monitor a live stream of event data or to examine data already collected in the targets. This UI is very convenient and flexible, and it allows you to customize the layout of a grid that shows events, letting you group and aggregate event data and export it into the database table, event, or CSV files. You should be careful, however, when connecting to a live stream of events, because event sessions can generate events faster than Management Studio can consume them. When this happens, Management Studio disconnects from the live stream of data to avoid a negative impact on server performance.

In this section, I will not discuss how to work with the Management Studio UI, but rather will focus on T-SQL implementation. I would encourage you, however, to experiment with Management Studio. Even though the Extended Events management UI has some limitations, it is more than sufficient in a large number of cases.

The key Extended Events data management views that can be used to examine event sessions and data include the following:

The `sys.dm_xe_sessions` view provides information about active event sessions. It shows the configuration parameters of the sessions as well as execution statistics, such as the number of dropped events or the amount of time that event collection contributed to blocking if the `NO_EVENT_LOSS` option was used.

The `sys.dm_xe_session_targets` view returns information about targets. One of the key columns of the view is `event_data`. Some targets–for example, `ring_buffer` or `histogram`–expose collected event data in this column. For other targets, such as `event_file`, the `event_data` column contains metadata information, such as the file name and session statistics.

The `sys.dm_xe_sessions_object_columns` view exposes configuration values for objects bound to the session. You can use this view to obtain the configuration properties for the targets; for example, the event file path.

■ **Note** You can find more information about Extended Events DMVs at `http://technet.microsoft.com/en-us/library/bb677293.aspx`.

Now, let's look at how to access data collected in different targets.

Working with the ring_buffer Target

`Ring_buffer` event data is exposed through the `event_data` column in the `sys.dm_xe_session_targets` view. Listing 27-13 shows how to parse data collected by the `TempDB Spill` event session, which we defined in Listing 27-11.

Listing 27-13. Examining ring_buffer target data

```
;with TargetData(Data)
as
(
    select convert(xml,st.target_data) as Data
    from sys.dm_xe_sessions s join sys.dm_xe_session_targets st on
        s.address = st.event_session_address
    where s.name = 'TempDB Spills' and st.target_name = 'ring_buffer'
)
,EventInfo([Event Time],[Event],SPID,[SQL],PlanHandle)
as
(
```

```
    select
        t.e.value('@timestamp','datetime') as [Event Time]
        ,t.e.value('@name','sysname') as [Event]
        ,t.e.value('(action[@name="session_id"]/value)[1]','smallint') as [SPID]
        ,t.e.value('(action[@name="sql_text"]/value)[1]','nvarchar(max)') as [SQL]
        ,t.e.value('xs:hexBinary((action[@name="plan_handle"]/value)[1])'
                ,'varbinary(64)') as [PlanHandle]
    from
        TargetData cross apply
            TargetData.Data.nodes('/RingBufferTarget/event') as t(e)
)
select
    ei.[Event Time], ei.[Event], ei.SPID, ei.SQL, qp.Query_Plan
from
    EventInfo ei outer apply
        sys.dm_exec_query_plan(ei.PlanHandle) qp
```

If you forced a tempdb spill with the code from Listings 3-6, 3-7, and 3-8 in Chapter 3, you would see results similar to what is shown in Figure 27-13.

	Event Time	Event	SPID	SQL	Query_Plan
1	2016-06-11 18:11:52.530	sort_warning	61	declare @Dummy ...	<ShowPlanXML xmlns="http...
2	2016-06-11 18:12:05.943	sort_warning	61	declare @Dummy ...	<ShowPlanXML xmlns="http...
3	2016-06-11 18:12:11.320	sort_warning	61	declare @Dummy ...	<ShowPlanXML xmlns="http...

Figure 27-13. *Examining ring_buffer target data*

Unfortunately, the `sys.dm_xe_session_targets` view has a limitation that limits the size of the `target_data` column XML output to 4 MB. This can lead to a situation where some of the events from the `ring_buffer` target are not present in the view. This could happen even when the configured size of the `ring_buffer` is less than 4 MB; events are stored in binary format internally, and XML serialization can significantly increase the output size, making it larger than 4 MB. It is safer to use file-based targets to avoid this "missing events" situation.

Working with event_file and asynchronous_file_target Targets

The `sys.fn_xe_file_target_read_file` table-valued function allows you to read the content of the `asynchronous_file_target` and `event_file` targets.

Similar to SQL Traces, Extended Events' file-based targets can generate multiple rollover files. You can read data from an individual file by specifying the exact file name in the first parameter of the function, `@path`. Alternatively, you can read data from all of the files by using `@path` with wildcards.

The SQL Server 2008/2008R2 `asynchronous_file_target` creates another file type called a *metadata file*. You should provide the path to this file as the second parameter of the function, `@mdpath`. Though SQL Server 2012-2016 does not use metadata files, this function still has such a parameter for backward-compatibility reasons. You can use `NULL` instead.

Finally, the third and fourth parameters allow you to specify the point at which to start reading. The third parameter, `@initial_file_name`, is the first file to read. The fourth parameter, `@initial_offset`, is the starting offset in the file. This function skips all of the data from the file up to the offset value. Both the file name and offsets are included in the result set, which allows you to implement code that reads only the newly collected data.

Listing 27-14 illustrates how you can read data from the `event_file` target generated by a TempDB Spills session in SQL Server 2016.

Listing 27-14. Reading data from the event_file target

```
;with TargetData(Data, File_Name, File_Offset)
as
(
    select convert(xml,event_data) as Data, file_name, file_offset
    from sys.fn_xe_file_target_read_file('c:\extevents\TempDB_Spiils*.xel', null, null
        ,null)
)
,EventInfo([Event Time], [Event], SPID, [SQL], PlanHandle, File_Name, File_Offset)
as
(
    select
        Data.value('/event[1]/@timestamp','datetime') as [Event Time]
        ,Data.value('/event[1]/@name','sysname') as [Event]
        ,Data.value('(/event[1]/action[@name="session_id"]/value)[1]','smallint') as [SPID]
        ,Data.value('(/event[1]/action[@name="sql_text"]/value)[1]','nvarchar(max)')
            as [SQL]
        ,Data.value('xs:hexBinary((/event[1]/action[@name="plan_handle"]/value)[1])'
            ,'varbinary(64)') as [PlanHandle]
        ,File_Name, File_Offset
    from TargetData
)
select ei.[Event Time], ei.File_Name, ei.File_Offset, ei.[Event], ei.SPID, ei.SQL
    ,qp_Query_Plan
from EventInfo ei outer apply sys.dm_exec_query_plan(ei.PlanHandle) qp
```

For active sessions, you can obtain the path to the target file from the `sys.dm_xe_session_object_columns` view. However, this path does not include rollover information, which SQL Server appends to the file name when it is created. You need to transform it by adding a wildcard to the path. Listing 27-15 shows how you can do this with SQL Server 2012-2016.

Listing 27-15. Reading the path to the event_file target file in SQL Server 2012-2016

```
declare
    @dataFile nvarchar(260)

-- Get path to event data file
select
    @dataFile = left(column_value,len(column_value ) - charindex('.',reverse(column_value)))
      + '*.' + right(column_value, charindex('.',reverse(column_value))-1)
from
    sys.dm_xe_session_object_columns oc join sys.dm_xe_sessions s on
        oc.event_session_address = s.address
where
    s.name = 'TempDB Spills' and
    oc.object_name = 'event_file' and
    oc.column_name = 'filename';
```

You can use a similar approach to obtain the path to the metadata file in SQL Server 2008/2008R2. The metadatafile path, however, could be NULL in the sys.dm_xe_session_object_columns view if you did not specify it as a parameter of the target, and you will need to use the same file name as that of the event file, replacing the extension with xem if this is the case.

Working with event_counter and synchronous_event_counter Targets

The synchronous_event_counter (SQL Server 2008/2008R2) and event_counter (SQL Server 2012-2016) targets allow you to count the number of occurrences of specific events. Both targets provide data in a very simple XML format, which can be accessed through the event_data column in the sys.dm_xe_session_targets view.

Listing 27-16 creates an event session that counts the number of reads from and writes to tempdb files; this will work in SQL Server 2012-2016. This same code will work in SQL Server 2008/2008R2 if you replace the target name with synchronous_event_counter.

Listing 27-16. Creating a session that counts number of reads and writes to/from tempdb files

```
create event session [FileStats]
on server
add event sqlserver.file_read_completed ( where(sqlserver.database_id = 2) ),
add event sqlserver.file_write_completed ( where(sqlserver.database_id = 2) )
add target package0.event_counter
with
(
    event_retention_mode=allow_single_event_loss
    ,max_dispatch_latency=5 seconds
);
```

After you start the session, you can examine the data collected with the code shown in Listing 27-17. You should change the target name to synchronous_event_counter in the TargetData CTE if you are working with SQL Server 2008/2008R2.

Listing 27-17. Examining session data

```
;with TargetData(Data)
as
(
    select convert(xml,st.target_data) as Data
    from sys.dm_xe_sessions s join sys.dm_xe_session_targets st on
        s.address = st.event_session_address
    where s.name = 'FileStats' and st.target_name = 'event_counter'
)
,EventInfo([Event],[Count])
as
(
    select t.e.value('@name','sysname') as [Event], t.e.value('@count','bigint') as [Count]
    from
        TargetData cross apply
            TargetData.Data.nodes
                ('/CounterTarget/Packages/Package[@name="sqlserver"]/Event') as t(e)
)
select [Event], [Count] from EventInfo;
```

Working with histogram, synchronous_ bucketizer, and asynchronous_ bucketizer Targets

Histogram or bucketizer targets group occurrences of specific event types based on event data. Let's consider a scenario where you have a SQL Server instance with a large number of databases, and you want to find out which databases are not in use. You could analyze the index usage statistics; however, that method is not bulletproof and can provide incorrect results for rarely used databases if the statistics were unloaded due to a SQL Server restart, index rebuild, or for other reasons.

Extended Events can help you in this scenario. There are two simple ways to achieve your goal. You can analyze the activity against different databases by capturing the sql_statement_starting and rpc_starting events. Alternatively, you can look at database-level shared (S) locks, which are acquired by any sessions accessing a database. With either approach, histogram or bucketizer targets allow you to count the occurrences of these events, grouping them by database_id.

Let's look at the second approach and implement an event session that tracks database-level locks. As a first step, let's analyze the data columns of the lock_acquired event with the query shown in Listing 27-18. Figure 27-14 shows partial results of the query.

Listing 27-18. Examining lock_acquired event data columns

```
select column_id, name, type_name
from sys.dm_xe_object_columns
where column_type = 'data' and object_name = 'lock_acquired'
```

	column_id	name	type_name
1	0	resource_type	lock_resource_type
2	1	mode	lock_mode
3	2	owner_type	lock_owner_type
4	3	transaction_id	int64
5	4	database_id	uint32
6	5	lockspace_workspace_id	ptr

Figure 27-14. *Lock_acquired event data columns*

As you can see, the resource_type and owner_type columns' data types are maps. You can examine all possible values with the queries shown in Listing 27-19. Figure 27-15 shows partial results of the queries.

Listing 27-19. Examining lock_resource_type and lock_owner_type maps

```
select name, map_key, map_value
from sys.dm_xe_map_values
where name = 'lock_resource_type'
order by map_key;

select name, map_key, map_value
from sys.dm_xe_map_values
where name = 'lock_owner_type'
order by map_key;
```

	name	map_key	map_value
1	lock_resource_type	0	UNKNOWN_LOCK_RESOURCE
2	lock_resource_type	1	NULL_RESOURCE
3	lock_resource_type	2	DATABASE
4	lock_resource_type	3	FILE
5	lock_resource_type	4	UNUSED1
6	lock_resource_type	5	OBJECT

	name	map_key	map_value
1	lock_owner_type	1	Transaction
2	lock_owner_type	2	Cursor
3	lock_owner_type	3	Session
4	lock_owner_type	4	SharedXactWorkspace
5	lock_owner_type	5	ExclusiveXactWorkspace
6	lock_owner_type	6	LockConflictNotificationObject

Figure 27-15. *lock_resource_types and lock_owner_types values*

`Lock_acquired` events with an `owner_type` of `DATABASE` and `resource_type` of `SharedXActWorkspace` would fire every time that a session accesses a database. Listing 27-20 creates an event session that captures these events using SQL Server 2012-2016. This approach works in SQL Server 2008/2008R2 if you change the target name.

Listing 27-20. Creating an event session

```
create event session DBUsage
on server
add event sqlserver.lock_acquired
(
    where
        database_id > 4 and -- Users DB
        owner_type = 4 and -- SharedXactWorkspace
        resource_type = 2 and -- DB-level lock
        sqlserver.is_system = 0
)
add target package0.histogram
(
    set
        slots = 32 -- Based on # of DB
        ,filtering_event_name = 'sqlserver.lock_acquired'
        ,source_type = 0 -- event data column
        ,source = 'database_id' -- grouping column
)
with
(
    event_retention_mode=allow_single_event_loss
    ,max_dispatch_latency=30 seconds
);
```

`Histogram` and/or `bucketizer` targets, have four different parameters, as follows:

> `slots` indicates the maximum number of different values (groups) to retain. SQL Server ignores all new values (groups) as soon as that number is reached. You should be careful and always reserve enough slots to keep information for all groups that might be present in the data. In our example, you should have a slot value that exceeds the number of databases in the instance. SQL Server rounds the provided value to the next power of two in order to improve performance.
>
> `source` contains the name of the event column or action that provides data for grouping.

source_type is the type of the object by which you are grouping, and it can be either 0 or 1, which indicate a grouping by event data column or action, respectively. The default value is 1, which is action.

filtering_event_name is an optional value that specifies the event from an event session that you are using as the data source for grouping. It should be specified if you group by event data column, and it could be omitted when grouping by action. In the latter case, grouping can be done based on actions from multiple events.

You can access histogram or bucketizer event data through the event_data column in the sys.dm_xe_session_targets view. Listing 27-21 shows the code that analyzes the results of the DBUsage event, session.

Listing 27-21. Examining histogram data

```
;with TargetData(Data)
as
(
    select convert(xml,st.target_data) as Data
    from sys.dm_xe_sessions s join sys.dm_xe_session_targets st on
        s.address = st.event_session_address
    where s.name = 'DBUsage' and st.target_name = 'histogram'
)
,EventInfo([Count],[DBID])
as
(
    select t.e.value('@count','int'), t.e.value('((./value)/text())[1]','smallint')
    from
        TargetData cross apply
            TargetData.Data.nodes('/HistogramTarget/Slot') as t(e)
)
select e.dbid, d.name, e.[Count]
from sys.databases d left outer join EventInfo e on
        e.DBID = d.database_id
where d.database_id > 4
order by e.Count
```

Finally, it is worth noting that this approach can result in *false positives* by counting the locks acquired by various maintenance tasks, such as CHECKDB, backups, and others, as well as by SQL Server Management Studio.

Working with the pair_matching Target

The pair_matching target maintains information about unmatched events when a *begin* event does not have a corresponding *end* event, dropping out events from the target when they have a match. Think of orphaned transactions where database_transaction_begin events do not have corresponding database_transaction_end events, as an example. Another case is a query timeout when the sql_statement_starting event does not have a corresponding sql_statement_completed event.

Let's look at the latter example and create an event session, as shown in Listing 27-22. The pair_matching target requires you to specify matching criteria based on the event data column and/or actions. It is also worth noting that in some cases–for example, with ADO.Net SQL Client library–you also need to capture rpc_starting and rpc_completed events during troubleshooting.

Listing 27-22. Creating an event session with a pair_matching target

```
create event session [Timeouts]
on server
add event sqlserver.sql_statement_starting ( action (sqlserver.session_id) ),
add event sqlserver.sql_statement_completed ( action (sqlserver.session_id) )
add target package0.pair_matching
(
    set
        begin_event = 'sqlserver.sql_statement_starting'
        ,begin_matching_columns = 'statement'
        ,begin_matching_actions = 'sqlserver.session_id'
        ,end_event = 'sqlserver.sql_statement_completed'
        ,end_matching_columns = 'statement'
        ,end_matching_actions = 'sqlserver.session_id'
        ,respond_to_memory_pressure = 0
)
with
(
    max_dispatch_latency=10 seconds
    ,track_causality=on
);
```

You can examine pair_matching data through the event_data column in the sys.dm_xe_session_targets view. Listing 27-23 illustrates such an approach.

Listing 27-23. Examining pair_matching target data

```
;with TargetData(Data)
as
(
    select convert(xml,st.target_data) as Data
    from sys.dm_xe_sessions s join sys.dm_xe_session_targets st on
        s.address = st.event_session_address
    where s.name = 'Timeouts' and st.target_name = 'pair_matching'
)
select
    t.e.value('@timestamp','datetime') as [Event Time]
    ,t.e.value('@name','sysname') as [Event]
    ,t.e.value('(action[@name="session_id"]/value/text())[1]','smallint') as [SPID]
    ,t.e.value('(data[@name="statement"]/value/text())[1]','nvarchar(max)') as [SQL]
from
    TargetData cross apply TargetData.Data.nodes('/PairingTarget/event') as t(e)
```

System_health and AlwaysOn_Health Sessions

One of the great features of the Extended Events framework is the system_health event session, which is created and is running on every SQL Server installation by default. This session captures various types of information about the status and resource usage of SQL Server components, high severity and internal errors, excessive waits for resources or locks, and quite a few other events. The session uses ring_buffer and event_file targets to store the data.

The system_health session is started on SQL Server startup by default. It gives you an idea of what recently happened in a SQL Server instance as you begin troubleshooting. Moreover, recent critical events have already been collected without requiring you to set up any monitoring routines.

One such example is deadlock troubleshooting. The system_health session collects the xml_deadlock_report event. Therefore, when customers complain about deadlocks, you can analyze already-collected data without waiting for the next deadlock to occur.

The Enterprise Edition of SQL Server 2012-2016 and Standard Edition of SQL Server 2016 introduced another default Extended Events session called AlwaysOn_health. As you can guess by the name, this session collects information about AlwaysOn Availability Groups–related events, such as errors and failovers. This session is enabled only when SQL Server participates in an AlwaysOn Availability Group.

Finally, SQL Server 2016 has another event session called telemetry_xevents that collect various telemetry data, storing it in a ring_buffer target. The majority of the information belongs to the new SQL Server 2016 features, such as row-level security, stretch databases, and temporal tables; however, some of the information is related to regular operations, such as database creation, missing statistics and join predicates, and others.

You can examine events collected by system_health, AlwaysOn_health, and telemetry_xevents sessions by scripting them in SQL Server Management Studio. You can even modify session definitions if needed. Be careful, however, because those changes can be overwritten during SQL Server upgrades or service pack installations.

Using Extended Events

Let's look at a couple of practical examples of how you can use Extended Events during troubleshooting.

Detecting Expensive Queries

You can detect expensive queries in the system by capturing sql_statement_completed and rpc_completed events that have execution metrics that exceed some thresholds. This approach allows you to capture queries that do not have an execution plan cached and that are not exposed by the sys.dm_exec_query_stats view. However, you will need to perform additional work aggregating and analyzing the collected data afterward when choosing what queries need to be optimized.

It is very important to find the right threshold values that define expensive queries in your system. Even though you do not want to capture an excessive amount of information, it is important to collect the *right* information. Optimization of relatively inexpensive, but very frequently executed, queries can provide much better results when compared to the optimization of expensive but rarely executed queries. Analysis of the sys.dm_exec_query_stats view data can help you detect some of those queries, and it should be used in parallel with Extended Events.

Listing 27-24 shows an event session that captures queries that use more than five seconds of CPU time or that issued more than 10,000 logical reads or writes. Obviously, you need to fine-tune filters based on your system workload, avoiding the collection of excessive amounts of data.

Listing 27-24. Capturing expensive queries

```
create event session [Expensive Queries]
on server
add event sqlserver.sql_statement_completed
(
    action ( sqlserver.plan_handle )
    where
    (
```

```
        (
            cpu_time >= 5000000 or -- Time in microseconds
            logical_reads >= 10000 or writes >= 10000
        ) and sqlserver.is_system = 0
    )
),
add event sqlserver.rpc_completed
(
    where
    (
        (
            cpu_time >= 5000000 or -- Time in microseconds
            logical_reads >= 10000 or writes >= 10000
        ) and sqlserver.is_system = 0
    )
)
add target package0.event_file
( set filename = 'c:\ExtEvents\Expensive Queries.xel' )
with
( event_retention_mode=allow_single_event_loss );
```

Listing 27-25 shows the query that extracts the data from the event_file target.

Listing 27-25. Extracting expensive queries information

```
;with TargetData(Data, File_Name, File_Offset)
as
(
    select convert(xml,event_data) as Data, file_name, file_offset
    from sys.fn_xe_file_target_read_file('c:\extevents\Expensive*.xel',null, null, null)
)
,EventInfo([Event], [Event Time], [CPU Time], [Duration], [Logical Reads], [Physical Reads]
    ,[Writes], [Rows], [Statement], [PlanHandle], File_Name, File_Offset)
as
(
    select
        Data.value('/event[1]/@name','sysname') as [Event]
        ,Data.value('/event[1]/@timestamp','datetime') as [Event Time]
        ,Data.value('((/event[1]/data[@name="cpu_time"]/value/text())[1])','bigint')
            as [CPU Time]
        ,Data.value('((/event[1]/data[@name="duration"]/value/text())[1])','bigint')
            as [Duration]
        ,Data.value('((/event[1]/data[@name="logical_reads"]/value/text())[1])'
            ,'int') as [Logical Reads]
        ,Data.value('((/event[1]/data[@name="physical_reads"]/value/text())[1])'
            ,'int') as [Physical Reads]
        ,Data.value('((/event[1]/data[@name="writes"]/value/text())[1])','int') as [Writes]
        ,Data.value('((/event[1]/data[@name="row_count"]/value/text())[1])','int') as [Rows]
        ,Data.value('((/event[1]/data[@name="statement"]/value/text())[1])','nvarchar(max)')
            as [Statement]
```

```
        ,Data.value('xs:hexBinary(((/event[1]/action[@name="plan_handle"]/value/text())[1]))'
            ,'varbinary(64)') as [PlanHandle]
        ,File_Name, File_Offset
    from TargetData
)
select
    ei.[Event], ei.[Event Time]
    ,ei.[CPU Time] / 1000 as [CPU Time (ms)]
    ,ei.[Duration] / 1000 as [Duration (ms)]
    ,ei.[Logical Reads], ei.[Physical Reads], ei.[Writes], ei.[Rows], ei.[Statement]
    ,ei.[PlanHandle], ei.File_Name, ei.File_Offset, qp.Query_Plan
from EventInfo ei outer apply sys.dm_exec_query_plan(ei.PlanHandle) qp
```

Further steps depend on your objectives. In some cases, you can see the obvious optimization targets when you analyze raw event data. In other situations, you will need to perform additional analysis and look at the frequency of executions, aggregating data based on query_hash or query_plan_hash actions data.

You may also consider creating a process that runs based on a schedule, extracting newly collected data and persisting it in a table. This approach increases the chances of capturing query plans if they are still in the plan cache. You can use ring_buffer rather than event_file as the target in such an implementation.

Monitoring Page Split Events

Extended Events can help you to address problems that were hard and sometimes even impossible to troubleshoot with other methods. One such example is the monitoring of *page split* events, which allows you to identify indexes that suffer from page splits and fragmentation.

Capturing actual page splits is a tricky process. Even though SQL Server 2012 exposes the page_split event, it does not differentiate between page splits that occur during new page allocations in ever-increasing indexes and *regular* page splits. Fortunately, you can use the LOP_DELETE_SPLIT operation of the transaction_log event instead. This operation marks the deletion of the rows on the original page at the time of the split event.

Listing 27-26 shows the code that creates the Extended Events session that captures page split information in one of the databases. The session uses the histogram target, counting events on a per-index bases.

Listing 27-26. Capturing page-split events

```
create event session PageSplits_Tracking
on server
add event sqlserver.transaction_log
(
    where operation = 11  -- lop_delete_split
        and database_id = 17
)
add target package0.histogram
(
    set
        filtering_event_name = 'sqlserver.transaction_log',
        source_type = 0, -- event column
        source = 'alloc_unit_id'
)
```

The code in Listing 27-27 shows how to extract the data from the target.

Listing 27-27. Analyzing page-split information

```
;with Data(alloc_unit_id, splits)
as
(
    select c.n.value('(value)[1]', 'bigint') as alloc_unit_id, c.n.value('(@count)[1]'
        ,'bigint') as splits
    from
    (
        select convert(xml,target_data) target_data
        from sys.dm_xe_sessions s with (nolock) join sys.dm_xe_session_targets t on
            s.address = t.event_session_address
        where s.name = 'PageSplits_Tracking' and t.target_name = 'histogram'
    ) as d cross apply
        target_data.nodes('HistogramTarget/Slot') as c(n)
)
select
    s.name + '.' + o.name as [Table], i.index_id, i.name as [Index]
    ,d.Splits, i.fill_factor as [Fill Factor]
from
    Data d join sys.allocation_units au with (nolock) on
        d.alloc_unit_id = au.allocation_unit_id
    join sys.partitions p with (nolock) on
        au.container_id = p.partition_id
    join sys.indexes i with (nolock) on
        p.object_id = i.object_id and p.index_id = i.index_id
    join sys.objects o with (nolock) on
        i.object_id = o.object_id
    join sys.schemas s on
        o.schema_id = s.schema_id
```

You can also use this technique during index FILLFACTOR tuning when analyzing how different values affect page splits in real time.

Extended Events in Azure SQL Databases

Extended Events are also supported in Microsoft Azure SQL Databases v12. Even though the list of exposed events is relatively small, it supports the events that are helpful during the troubleshooting of common performance problems, such as detecting inefficient queries, blocking issues, tempdb spills, excessive memory grants, and a few others.

At the time when this book was written, SQL Azure supported three event targets: such as `ring_buffer`, `event_counter`, and `event_file`. You can analyze the list of supported Extended Events objects by querying the catalog views using the queries from this chapter.

You can create Extended Events sessions in SQL Databases and query targets, as with the regular SQL Server. There are a couple of minor differences in the syntax, however. First, you have to use the `CREATE EVENT SESSION ON DATABASE` rather than the `ON SERVER` clause. SQL Databases scope events to the database rather than to the server level. The naming convention for database management views is also different. You should add `_database` to the name; for example, use the `sys.dm_xe_database_sessions` view instead of the `sys.dm_xe_sessions` view.

■ **Note** You can read about Extended Events support in Azure SQL Databases at `https://azure.microsoft.com/en-us/documentation/articles/sql-database-xevent-db-diff-from-svr/`

Summary

Extended Events is a lightweight and highly scalable monitoring and debugging infrastructure that will replace SQL Traces in future versions of SQL Server. It addresses the usability limitations of SQL Traces, and it places less overhead on SQL Server by collecting only the information required and by performing predicate analysis at a very early stage of event execution.

SQL Server exposes new Extended Events with every new release. Starting with SQL Server 2012, all SQL Traces events have corresponding Extended Events. Moreover, new SQL Server features do not provide any SQL Traces support, relying on Extended Events instead.

Extended Events provides data in XML format. Every event type has its own schema, which includes specific data columns for that event type. You can add additional information to event data with a global set of available actions, and you can apply predicates to event data, filtering out events that you do not need.

Event data can be stored in multiple in-memory and on-disk targets, which allows you to collect raw event data or perform some analysis and aggregation, such as counting and grouping events or tracking an unmatched pair of events.

The `system_health` event session provides information about general SQL Server component health, resource usage, and high severity errors. This session is created and is running by default on every instance of SQL Server. One of the collected events is `xml_deadlock_report`, which allows you to obtain a deadlock graph for recent deadlocks without needing to set up a SQL Traces event or a `T1222` trace flag.

Extended Events is a great technology that allows you to troubleshoot very complex scenarios that are impossible to troubleshoot using other methods. Even though the learning curve is steep, it is very beneficial to learn and use Extended Events.

CHAPTER 28

System Troubleshooting

Things do not always work as expected. System performance can degrade over time when the amount of data and load increases, or sometimes a server can become unresponsive and stop accepting any connections at all. In either case, you need to find and fix such problems quickly while working under pressure and stress.

In this chapter, we will talk about the SQL Server execution model and discuss system troubleshooting based on wait statistics analysis. I will show you how to detect common issues frequently encountered in systems.

Looking at the Big Picture

Even though this chapter focuses on the troubleshooting of database-related issues, you need to remember that databases and SQL Server never live in a vacuum. There are always customers who use client applications. Those applications work with single or multiple databases from one or more instances of SQL Server. SQL Server, in turn, runs on physical or virtual hardware, with data stored on disks often shared with other customers and database systems. Finally, all system components use the network for communication and network-based storage access.

From the customers' standpoint, most problems present themselves as general performance issues. Client applications feel slow and unresponsive, queries time out, and, in some cases, applications cannot even connect to the database. Nevertheless, the root cause of the problem could be anywhere. Hardware could be malfunctioning or incorrectly configured; the database might have inefficient schemas, indexing, or code; SQL Server could be overloaded; or client applications could have bugs or design issues.

Important You should always look at all of the components of a system during troubleshooting to identify the root cause of the problem.

The performance of a system depends on its slowest component. For example, if SQL Server uses SAN storage, you should look at the performance of both the storage subsystem and the network. If network throughput is not sufficient to transmit data, improving SAN performance wouldn't help much. You could achieve better results by optimizing network throughput or by reducing the amount of network traffic with extra indexes or database schema changes.

Another example is client-side data processing when a large amount of data needs to be transmitted to client applications. While you could improve application performance by upgrading the network, you could obtain much better results by moving the data processing to SQL and/or application servers, thereby reducing the amount of data travelling over the wire.

D. Korotkevitch, *Pro SQL Server Internals*, DOI 10.1007/978-1-4842-1964-5_28

In this chapter, we will focus on troubleshooting the database portion of the system. However, I would still like to mention the various components and configuration settings that you should analyze during the initial stage of performance troubleshooting. Do not consider this list to be a comprehensive guide on hardware and software configuration. Be sure to do further research using Microsoft MSDN documentation, white papers, and other resources, especially when you need to deploy, configure, or troubleshoot complex infrastructures.

Hardware and Network

As a first step in troubleshooting, it is beneficial to look at the SQL Server hardware and network configuration. There are several aspects of this involved. First, it makes sense to analyze if the server is powerful enough to handle the load. Obviously, this is a very subjective question that often cannot be answered based solely on the server specifications. However, in some cases you will see that the hardware is clearly underpowered.

One example of when this happens is with systems developed by independent software vendors (ISV) and deployed in an Enterprise environment. Such deployments usually happen in stages. Decision makers evaluate system functionality under a light load during the trial/pilot phase. It is entirely possible that the database has been placed into second-grade hardware or an underprovisioned virtual machine during trials and stayed there even after full deployment.

SQL Server is a very I/O-intensive application, and a slow or misconfigured I/O subsystem often becomes a performance bottleneck. One very important setting that is often overlooked is partition alignment. Old versions of Windows created partitions right after 63 hidden sectors on a disk, which striped the disk allocation unit across multiple stripe units in RAID arrays. With such configurations, a single I/O request to a disk controller leads to multiple I/O operations in order to access data from the different RAID stripes.

Fortunately, partitions created in Windows Server 2008 and above are aligned by default. However, Windows does not realign existing partitions created in older versions of Windows when you upgrade operating systems or attach disks to servers. It is possible to achieve a 20 to 40 percent I/O performance improvement by fixing an incorrect partition alignment without making any other changes to the system.

Windows allocation unit size also comes into play. Most SQL Server instances would benefit from 64 KB units; however, you should take the RAID stripe size into account. Use the RAID stripe size recommended by the manufacturer; however, make sure that the Windows allocation unit resides on a single RAID stripe. For example, a 1 MB RAID stripe size works fine with 64 KB Windows allocation units, hosting 16 allocation units per stripe when disk partitions are aligned.

■ **Tip** You can read more about partition alignments at `http://technet.microsoft.com/en-us/library/dd758814.aspx`.

Finally, you need to analyze network throughput. Network performance depends on the slowest link in the topology. For example, if one of the network switches in the path between SQL Server and a SAN has two-gigabit uplink, the network throughput would be limited to two gigabits, even when all other network components in the topology are faster than that. This is especially important in cases of network-based storage, when every physical I/O operation utilizes the network and, as a general rule, you would like to have network throughput be faster than disk performance. Moreover, always remember to factor in the distance information travels over a network. Accessing remote data adds extra latency and slows down communication.

Operating System Configuration

You should look at the operating system configuration as the next step. It is especially important in the case of a 32-bit OS where the amount of user memory available to processes is limited. It is crucial that you check that 32-bit version of SQL Server can use extended memory, that the "Use AWE Memory" setting is enabled, and that the SQL Server startup account has *Lock Pages in Memory* permission. Nevertheless, the 32-bit version of SQL Server can use extended memory for the buffer pool only. This limits the amount of memory that can be utilized by other components, such as the plan cache and lock manager. **It is always beneficial to upgrade to a 64-bit version of SQL Server, especially because Microsoft dropped support of the 32-bit SQL Server version starting with SQL Server 2016.**

You should check which software is installed and which processes are running on the server. Non-essential processes use memory and contribute to server CPU load. Think about antivirus software, as an example. It is better to protect the server from viruses by restricting user access and revoking administrator permissions than to have antivirus software constantly running on the server. If company policy requires that you have antivirus up and running, make sure that the system and user databases are excluded from the scan. You should also exclude the folders with `FILESTREAM` and `FILETABLES` data from the scan if you use those technologies in the system.

Using development and troubleshooting tools locally on the server is another commonly encountered mistake. Developers and database administrators often run Management Studio, SQL Profiler, and other tools on a server during deployment and troubleshooting. These tools reduce the amount of memory available to SQL Server and contribute to unnecessary load. It is always better to access SQL Server remotely whenever possible.

Also, check if SQL Server is virtualized. Virtualization helps reduce IT costs, improves the availability of the system, and simplifies management. However, virtualization adds another layer of complexity during performance troubleshooting. Work with system administrators or use third-party tools to make sure that the host is not overloaded, even when performance metrics in a guest virtual machine appear normal.

Another common problem related to virtualization is resource overallocation. As an example, it is possible to configure a host in such a way that the total amount of memory allocated for all guest virtual machines exceeds the amount of physical memory installed on the host. That configuration leads to artificial memory pressure and introduces performance issues for a virtualized SQL Server. Again, you should work with system administrators to address such situations.

SQL Server Configuration

It is typical to have multiple databases hosted on a SQL Server instance. Database consolidation helps lower IT costs by reducing the number of servers that you must license and maintain. All those databases, however, use the same pool of SQL Server resources, contribute to its load, and affect each other. Heavy SQL Server workload from one system can negatively impact the performance of other systems.

You can analyze such conditions by examining resource-intensive and frequently executed queries on the server scope. If you detect a large number of such queries coming from different databases, you may consider optimizing all of them or to separate the databases onto different servers. We will discuss how to detect such queries later in this chapter.

You should also check if multiple SQL Server instances are running on the same server and how they affect the performance of each other. This condition is a bit trickier to detect and requires you to analyze various performance counters and DMOs from multiple instances. One of the most common problems in this situation happens when multiple SQL Server instances compete for memory, introducing memory pressure on each other. It might be beneficial to set and fine-tune the minimum and maximum memory settings for each instance based on requirements and load.

It is also worth noting that various Microsoft and third-party products often install separate SQL Server instances without your knowledge. Always check to see if this is the case on non-dedicated servers.

Finally, check the tempdb configuration and make sure that it is optimal, as we have already discussed in Chapter 13, "Temporary Objects and TempDb."

DATABASE CONSOLIDATION

It is impossible to avoid a discussion of the database consolidation process when we talk about SQL Server installations hosting multiple databases. Even though it is not directly related to the topic of this chapter, I would like to review several aspects of the database consolidation process here.

There is no universal consolidation strategy that can be used with every project. You should analyze the amount of data, load, hardware configuration, and business and security requirements when making this decision. However, as a general rule, you should avoid consolidating OLTP and data warehouse/reporting databases onto the same server when they are working under a heavy load. Data warehouse queries usually process large amounts of data, which leads to heavy I/O activity and flushes the content of the buffer pool. Taken together, this negatively affects the performance of other systems.

Listing 28-1 shows you how to get information about buffer pool usage on a per-database basis. Similarly, you can get information about I/O activity for each database file with the sys.dm_io_virtual_file_stats function. We will discuss this function in greater detail later in this chapter.

Listing 28-1. Buffer-pool usage on a per-database basis

```
select database_id as [DB ID], db_name(database_id) as [DB Name]
    ,convert(decimal(11,3),count(*) * 8 / 1024.0) as [Buffer Pool Size (MB)]
from sys.dm_os_buffer_descriptors with (nolock)
group by database_id
order by [Buffer Pool Size (MB)] desc;
```

You should also analyze the security requirements when consolidating databases. Some security features, such as Audit, work on the server scope and add performance overhead for all of the databases on the server. Transparent Data Encryption (TDE) is another example. Even though it is a database-level feature, SQL Server encrypts tempdb when either of the databases has TDE enabled, which also introduces performance overhead for other systems.

As a general rule, you should avoid consolidating databases with different security requirements on the same instance of SQL Server. Using multiple instances of SQL Server, perhaps virtualizing them, is a better choice, even when such instances or virtual machines run on the same server/host.

Database Options

Every *production* database should have the *Auto Shrink* option disabled. As we have already discussed, Auto Shrink periodically triggers the database shrink process, which introduces unnecessary I/O load and heavy index fragmentation. Moreover, this operation is practically useless, because further data modifications and index maintenance make database files grow yet again.

The *Auto Close* option forces SQL Server to remove any database-related objects from memory when the database does not have any connected users. As you can guess, it leads to extra physical I/O and query compilations as users reconnect to the database afterward. With the rare exception of very infrequently accessed databases, the Auto Close setting should be disabled.

It is better to have multiple data files in filegroups with volatile data. This helps avoid allocation map contention, similar to what happens in the case of `tempdb`. We will discuss the symptoms of such contention later in this chapter.

MY FIVE-MINUTE CONFIGURATION CHECKLIST

There are several items that I usually check during the initial system analysis stage. These allow me to quickly locate some of the SQL Server and database configuration issues.

OS Version and Edition. The big red flags are the use of old (Windows Server 2003/2008) and/or 32-bit editions of the OS.

SQL Server Version and Edition. As with the OS, I'd check if the system is using 64-bit SQL Server. I would also validate service pack and CU level. I do not advocate upgrading to the latest CU immediately; however, it is important to find out if the system is running on a supported version of the product/service pack and what the known issues are of that build.

Is *Instant File Initialization* enabled? It needs to be enabled in most systems.

What trace flags are in use? In a majority of the systems prior to SQL Server 2016, I would enable `T1118` (disabling mixed extent allocation) and `T2371` (make statistics update threshold dynamic). I would also suggest you enable `T4199` (enable Query Optimizer hotfixes), even though it could require regression testing and system monitoring. As you will remember, in SQL Server 2016, `T2371` and `T4199` are not required for databases with a compatibility level of 130. Another useful trace flag is `T3226`, which prevents SQL Server from storing successful backup information in the log, ballooning its size.

SQL Server memory configuration. More on this later.

Is the *Optimize for ad-hoc workload* setting enabled? It needs to be enabled in most systems.

High-level configuration of the disk subsystem, which includes raid level, stripe size, and partition alignment. In reality, in the majority of cases, I analyze this configuration at the same time as I look at I/O subsystem latency, throughput, and redundancy. It is also impossible to avoid a discussion about data and log files placement. As you know, separation of data and log files to different disk arrays is good practice, and it provides better data recoverability in the event of a disaster. However, you should also consider I/O system performance and throughput. In some cases, when the storage subsystem does not have enough spindles, you can get better performance by placing all files onto a single drive rather than spreading spindles across multiple drives. Nevertheless, you need to consider the increased risk of data loss with this approach.

Number of `tempdb` data files, and data/log files' auto-growth parameters.

User database options. It includes Auto Shrink and Auto Close, which both should be disabled, and `Page Verify`, which should be set to `CHECKSUM`. I'd look at statistics update parameters, correlating them with the statistics maintenance plan in the future. I also check if the *Allow Snapshot Isolation* option is enabled. The key is avoiding unnecessary `tempdb` overhead by enabling and not using it. Obviously, the database recovery model also needs to be analyzed at the time of Disaster Recovery strategy analysis.

Database files' auto-growth parameters and number of VLFs (virtual log files) in the transaction log. Data files in the same filegroup should have the same initial sizes and auto-growth parameters specified in MB rather than percentage. The number of VLFs should be manageable, which we will discuss in Chapter 30, "Transaction Log Internals." In some cases, I would consider enabling trace flag `T1117` to guarantee that all files in the filegroup would auto-grow at same time. In SQL Server 2016, this behavior is controlled by the `AUTOGROW_ALL_FILES` filegroup setting rather than by the trace flag.

This list is just the starting point of analysis and does not cover anything beyond basic configuration issues, nor does it provide you with any information about bottlenecks and system health. Nevertheless, it is useful as an initial stage of system troubleshooting.

Resource Governor Overview

The Enterprise Edition of SQL Server comes with another useful feature called *Resource Governor*. It allows you to separate different workload patterns and sessions into separate *workload groups*. The classification is done through a user-defined function called a *classifier function*, which SQL Server calls at the login stage. The classifier function performs classification based on user-defined criteria; for example, login, host, or application name.

Workload groups allow you to specify several parameters, such as `MAXDOP`, maximum number of concurrent requests to execute, percentage of the workspace memory available for query memory grant (more on this later), and a couple of others. Moreover, each workload group is associated with the *resource pool*, which allows you to customize or throttle resource usage for associated workgroups.

SQL Server documentation refers to resource pools as the virtual SQL Server instances inside the main one. I do not think it is accurate though. Resource pools do not provide enough isolation from each other; they, however, do allow you to configure some parameters, such as setting affinity, limiting CPU bandwidth, and controlling workspace memory for memory grants. In SQL Server 2014 and 2016, you can also control disk throughput. **Resource Governor, however, does not allow you to control buffer pool usage; it is shared across all pools.**

There are two system workload groups and resource pools: *internal* and *default*. As you can guess by the names, the first one handles internal workload. The second one is responsible for all non-classified workload. In reality, you can change the parameters of the default workload group—for example, reducing the size of the maximum memory grant–without creating other user-defined workload groups and pools.

Figure 28-1 illustrates an example of Resource Governor configuration. It represents a scenario that separates customer-facing OLTP and internal reporting activity, thus preventing a situation where reporting queries saturate disk throughput and CPU. Another common example is creating a separate workload and resource pool for maintenance activity, thereby mitigating the impact of index maintenance or database consistency checks by limiting disk throughput for those operations.

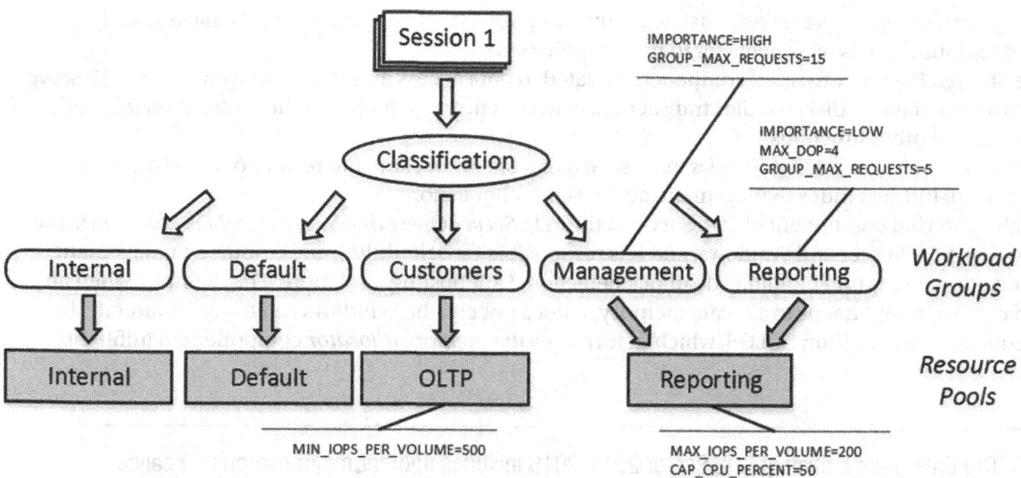

Figure 28-1. *Example of Resource Governor configuration*

Resource Governor configuration is a complex topic that is outside of the scope of this book. You can read more about it at `http://msdn.microsoft.com/en-us/library/bb933866.aspx`.

SQL Server Execution Model

From a high level, the architecture of SQL Server includes five different components, as shown in Figure 28-2.

<table>
<tr><td colspan="2">Protocol Layer (Client Communication)</td><td rowspan="5">Utilities (DBCC, Backup, Restore, BCP, etc)</td></tr>
<tr><td colspan="2">Query Processor</td></tr>
<tr><td>Query Optimization
(Plan Generation, Costing, Statistics, etc)</td><td>Query Execution
(Parallelism, Memory Grants, etc)</td></tr>
<tr><td colspan="2">Storage Engine
(Data Access, Locking Manager, Transaction Log Management, etc)</td></tr>
<tr><td colspan="2">SQLOS
(Scheduling, Resource Management, Deadlock Detection, etc)</td></tr>
</table>

Figure 28-2. *High-level SQL Server architecture*

The *Protocol* layer handles communications between SQL Server and client applications. The data is transmitted in an internal format called *Tabular Data Stream (TDS)* using one of the standard network communication protocols, such as TCP/IP or Named Pipes. Another communication protocol, called *shared memory*, can be used when both SQL Server and the client application run locally on the same server. The shared memory protocol does not utilize the network and is more efficient than the others.

Different editions of SQL Server have different protocols enabled after installation. For example, the SQL Server Express Edition has all network protocols disabled by default, and it would not be able to serve network requests until you enable them. You can enable and disable protocols in the SQL Server Configuration Manager utility.

The *Query Processor* layer is responsible for query optimization and execution. We have already discussed various aspects of its behavior in previous chapters.

The *Storage Engine* consists of components related to data access and data management in SQL Server. It works with the data on disk, handles transactions and concurrency, manages the transaction log, and performs several other functions.

SQL Server includes a set of *Utilities* that are responsible for backup and restore operations, bulk loading of data, full-text index management, and several other actions.

Finally, the vital component of SQL Server is the *SQL Server Operating System (SQLOS)*. SQLOS is the layer between SQL Server and Windows, and it is responsible for scheduling and resource management, synchronization, exception handling, deadlock detection, CLR hosting, and more. For example, when any SQL Server component needs to allocate memory, it does not call the Windows API function directly, but rather requests memory from SQLOS, which in turn uses the *memory allocator* component to fulfill the request.

■ **Note** The Enterprise Edition of SQL Server 2014-2016 includes another major component called *In-Memory OLTP Engine*. We will discuss this component in more detail in Part VIII, "In-Memory OLTP."

SQLOS was initially introduced in SQL Server 7.0 to improve the efficiency of scheduling in SQL Server and to minimize context and kernel mode switching. The major difference between Windows and SQLOS is the scheduling model. Windows is a general-purpose operating system that uses preemptive scheduling. It controls what processes are currently running, suspending and resuming them as needed. Alternatively, with the exception of CLR code, SQLOS uses cooperative scheduling, where processes yield voluntarily on a regular basis.

SQLOS creates a set of *schedulers* when it starts. The number of schedulers is equal to the number of logical CPUs in the system, plus one extra scheduler for the Dedicated Admin Connection, which we will discuss later in this chapter. For example, if a server has two quad-core CPUs with hyper-threading enabled, SQL Server creates 17 schedulers. Each scheduler can be in either an ONLINE or OFFLINE stage based on the process affinity settings and core-based licensing model.

Even though the number of schedulers matches the number of CPUs in the system, there is no strict one-to-one relationship between them unless the process affinity is set. In some cases, and under heavy load, it is possible to have more than one scheduler running on the same CPU. Alternatively, when process affinity is set, schedulers are bound to CPUs in a strict one-to-one relationship.

Each scheduler is responsible for managing working threads called *workers*. The maximum number of workers in a system is specified by the *Max Worker Thread* configuration option. The default value of *zero* indicates that SQL Server calculates the maximum number of worker threads based on the number of schedulers in the system. In a majority of cases, you do not need to change this default value.

Each time there is a task to execute, it is assigned to a worker in an idle state. When there are no idle workers, the scheduler creates a new one. It also destroys idle workers after 15 minutes of inactivity or in case of memory pressure. It is also worth noting that each worker would use 512 KB of RAM in 32-bit and 2 MB of RAM in 64-bit SQL Server for the thread stack.

Workers do not move between schedulers. Moreover, a task is never moved between workers. SQLOS, however, can create child tasks and assign them to different workers; for example, in the case of parallel execution plans.

Each task can be in one of six different states:

Pending: Task is waiting for an available worker.

Done: Task is completed.

Running: Task is currently executing on the scheduler.

Runnable: Task is waiting for the scheduler to be executed.

Suspended: Task is waiting for external event or resource.

Spinloop: Task is processing a spinlock. We will discuss spinlocks later in this chapter.

Each scheduler has at most one task in a running state. In addition, it has two different queues—one for runnable tasks and one for suspended tasks. When the running task needs some resources—a data page from a disk, for example—it submits an I/O request and changes its state to *suspended*. It stays in the *suspended* queue until the request is fulfilled and the page is read. After that, the task is moved to the *runnable* queue, where it is ready to resume execution.

A grocery store is, perhaps, the closest real-life analogy to the SQL Server execution model. Think of cashiers as representing schedulers. Customers in checkout lines are similar to tasks in the runnable queue. A customer who is currently checking out is similar to a task in the running state.

If an item is missing a UPC code, a cashier sends a store worker to do a price check. The cashier suspends the checkout process for the current customer, asking her or him to step aside (to the suspended queue). When the worker comes back with the price information, the customer who had stepped aside moves to the end of the checkout line (end of the runnable queue).

It is worth mentioning that the SQL Server process is much more efficient than real life, where others wait patiently in line during a price check. However, a customer who is forced to move to the end of the runnable queue would probably disagree with such a conclusion.

Figure 28-3 illustrates the typical task life cycle of the SQL Server execution model. The total task execution time can be calculated as a summary of the time the task spent in the running state (when it ran on the scheduler), in the runnable state (when it waited for an available scheduler), and in the suspended state (when it waited for a resource or external event).

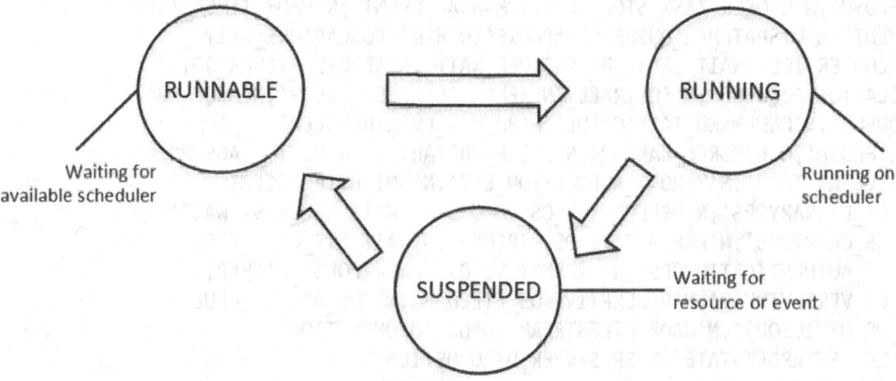

Figure 28-3. *Task life cycle*

SQL Server tracks the cumulative time tasks spend in a suspended state for different types of waits and exposes this through the `sys.dm_os_wait_stats` view. This information is collected as of the time of the last SQL Server restart or since it was cleared with the `DBCC SQLPERF('sys.dm_os_wait_stats', CLEAR)` command.

Listing 28-2 shows how to find the top *wait types* in a system, which are the wait types for which workers spent the most time waiting. It filters out some nonessential wait types mainly related to internal SQL Server processes. Even though it is beneficial to analyze some of them during advanced performance tuning, you rarely focus on them during the initial stage of system troubleshooting.

■ **Note** Every new version of SQL Server introduces new wait types. You can see a list of wait types at `http://msdn.microsoft.com/en-us/library/ms179984.aspx`. Make sure to select the appropriate version of SQL Server.

Listing 28-2. Detecting top wait types in the system

```
;with Waits
as
(
    select
            wait_type, wait_time_ms, waiting_tasks_count,signal_wait_time_ms
            ,wait_time_ms - signal_wait_time_ms as resource_wait_time_ms
            ,100. * wait_time_ms / SUM(wait_time_ms) over() as Pct
            ,row_number() over(order by wait_time_ms desc) AS RowNum
    from sys.dm_os_wait_stats with (nolock)
    where
        wait_time_ms > 0 and
            wait_type not in /* Filtering out non-essential system waits */
    (N'CLR_SEMAPHORE',N'LAZYWRITER_SLEEP',N'RESOURCE_QUEUE', N'DBMIRROR_DBM_EVENT'
    ,N'SLEEP_TASK',N'SLEEP_SYSTEMTASK',N'SQLTRACE_BUFFER_FLUSH',N'FSAGENT'
    ,N'DBMIRROR_EVENTS_QUEUE', N'DBMIRRORING_CMD', N'DBMIRROR_WORKER_QUEUE'
    ,N'WAITFOR',N'LOGMGR_QUEUE',N'CHECKPOINT_QUEUE',N'FT_IFTSHC_MUTEX'
    ,N'REQUEST_FOR_DEADLOCK_SEARCH',N'HADR_CLUSAPI_CALL',N'XE_TIMER_EVENT'
    ,N'BROKER_TO_FLUSH',N'BROKER_TASK_STOP',N'CLR_MANUAL_EVENT',N'HADR_TIMER_TASK'
    ,N'CLR_AUTO_EVENT',N'DISPATCHER_QUEUE_SEMAPHORE',N'HADR_LOGCAPTURE_WAIT'
    ,N'FT_IFTS_SCHEDULER_IDLE_WAIT',N'XE_DISPATCHER_WAIT',N'XE_DISPATCHER_JOIN'
    ,N'HADR_NOTIFICATION_DEQUEUE',N'SQLTRACE_INCREMENTAL_FLUSH_SLEEP',N'MSQL_XP'
    ,N'HADR_WORK_QUEUE',N'ONDEMAND_TASK_QUEUE',N'BROKER_EVENTHANDLER'
    ,N'SLEEP_BPOOL_FLUSH',N'KSOURCE_WAKEUP',N'SLEEP_DBSTARTUP',N'DIRTY_PAGE_POLL'
    ,N'BROKER_RECEIVE_WAITFOR',N'MEMORY_ALLOCATION_EXT',N'SNI_HTTP_ACCEPT'
    ,N'PREEMPTIVE_OS_LIBRARYOPS',N'PREEMPTIVE_OS_COMOPS',N'WAIT_XTP_HOST_WAIT'
    ,N'PREEMPTIVE_OS_CRYPTOPS',N'PREEMPTIVE_OS_PIPEOPS',N'WAIT_XTP_CKPT_CLOSE'
    ,N'PREEMPTIVE_OS_AUTHENTICATIONOPS',N'PREEMPTIVE_OS_GENERICOPS',N'CHKPT'
    ,N'PREEMPTIVE_OS_VERIFYTRUST',N'PREEMPTIVE_OS_FILEOPS',N'QDS_ASYNC_QUEUE'
    ,N'PREEMPTIVE_OS_DEVICEOPS',N'HADR_FILESTREAM_IOMGR_IOCOMPLETION'
    ,N'PREEMPTIVE_XE_GETTARGETSTATE',N'SP_SERVER_DIAGNOSTICS_SLEEP'
    ,N'BROKER_TRANSMITTER',N'PWAIT_ALL_COMPONENTS_INITIALIZED'
    ,N'QDS_PERSIST_TASK_MAIN_LOOP_SLEEP',N'PWAIT_DIRECTLOGCONSUMER_GETNEXT'
    ,N'QDS_CLEANUP_STALE_QUERIES_TASK_MAIN_LOOP_SLEEP',N'SERVER_IDLE_CHECK'
    ,N'SLEEP_DCOMSTARTUP',N'SQLTRACE_WAIT_ENTRIES',N'SLEEP_MASTERDBREADY'
    ,N'SLEEP_MASTERMDREADY',N'SLEEP_TEMPDBSTARTUP',N'XE_LIVE_TARGET_TVF'
    ,N'WAIT_FOR_RESULTS',N'WAITFOR_TASKSHUTDOWN',N'PARALLEL_REDO_WORKER_SYNC'
    ,N'PARALLEL_REDO_WORKER_WAIT_WORK',N'SLEEP_MASTERUPGRADED'
    ,N'SLEEP_MSDBSTARTUP',N'WAIT_XTP_OFFLINE_CKPT_NEW_LOG')
)
select
    w1.wait_type as [Wait Type]
    ,w1.waiting_tasks_count as [Wait Count]
```

```
    ,convert(decimal(12,3), w1.wait_time_ms / 1000.0) as [Wait Time]
    ,convert(decimal(12,1), w1.wait_time_ms / w1.waiting_tasks_count)
        as [Avg Wait Time]
    ,convert(decimal(12,3), w1.signal_wait_time_ms / 1000.0)
        as [Signal Wait Time]
    ,convert(decimal(12,1), w1.signal_wait_time_ms / w1.waiting_tasks_count)
        as [Avg Signal Wait Time]
    ,convert(decimal(12,3), w1.resource_wait_time_ms / 1000.0)
        as [Resource Wait Time]
    ,convert(decimal(12,1), w1.resource_wait_time_ms / w1.waiting_tasks_count)
        as [Avg Resource Wait Time]
    ,convert(decimal(6,3), w1.Pct) as [Percent]
    ,convert(decimal(6,3), w1.Pct + IsNull(w2.Pct,0)) as [Running Percent]
from
    Waits w1 cross apply
    (
            select sum(w2.Pct) as Pct
            from Waits w2
            where w2.RowNum < w1.RowNum
    ) w2
where
    w1.RowNum = 1 or w2.Pct <= 99
order by
    w1.RowNum
option (recompile);
```

Figure 28-4 illustrates the output of a script from a production server at the beginning of the troubleshooting process. We will talk about wait types from output later in this chapter.

	Wait Type	Wait Count	Wait Time	Avg Wait Time	Signal Wait Time	Avg ...	Resource Wai...	Avg Res...	Percent	Running P...
1	BACKUPBUFFER	107368907	888614.416	8.0	64402.065	0.0	824212.351	7.0	30.719	30.719
2	BACKUPIO	95095235	678922.496	7.0	17227.066	0.0	661695.430	6.0	23.470	54.188
3	CXPACKET	43228324	261312.352	6.0	20174.908	0.0	241137.444	5.0	9.033	63.222
4	WRITELOG	118895762	187905.027	1.0	12761.249	0.0	175143.778	1.0	6.496	69.717
5	PAGEIOLATCH_EX	94728055	156663.344	1.0	3599.205	0.0	153064.139	1.0	5.416	75.133
6	PAGEIOLATCH_SH	83334090	152310.870	1.0	2224.455	0.0	150086.415	1.0	5.265	80.398
7	ASYNC_IO_COMPLETION	164	124082.565	756601.0	0.130	0.0	124082.435	756600.0	4.289	84.688
8	ASYNC_NETWORK_IO	108082332	91240.442	0.0	5025.154	0.0	86215.288	0.0	3.154	87.842
[illegible]	IO_COMPLETION	[illegible]	[illegible]	[illegible]	[illegible]	[illegible]	[illegible]	[illegible]	[illegible]	[illegible]

Figure 28-4. *Output of the script on a production server*

There are other useful SQLOS-related data management views, as follows:

> `sys.dm_os_waiting_tasks` returns a list of currently suspended tasks, including wait type, waiting time, and the resource for which it is waiting. It also includes the ID of the blocking session, if any.

The `sys.dm_exec_requests` view provides a list of requests currently executing on SQL Server. This includes information about the session that submits the request; the current status of request; information about the current wait type if a task is suspended; SQL and plan handles; execution statistics; and several other attributes. In SQL Server 2016, you can use it together with the new function, `sys.dm_exec_input_buffer`, to obtain information about currently running SQL statements. In earlier versions of SQL Server, you can use the `sys.dm_exec_sql_text` function for such a purpose.

The `sys.dm_exec_session_wait_stats` view, introduced in SQL Server 2016, provides the aggregated wait statistics on a per-session level. Keep in mind that information is updated after the wait has ended, and you need to analyze data from `sys.dm_os_waiting_tasks` and/or `sys.dm_exec_requests` views when you troubleshoot waits from currently running sessions. You can also use the `sqlos.wait_info` Extended Event in earlier versions of SQL Server to track session waits.

The `sys.dm_os_schedulers` view returns information about schedulers, including their status, workers, and task information.

The `sys.dm_os_threads` view provides information about workers.

The `sys.dm_os_tasks` view provides information about tasks, including their state and some execution statistics.

Wait Statistics Analysis and Troubleshooting

The process of analyzing the top waits in the system is called *wait statistics analysis*. This is one of the frequently used troubleshooting and performance-tuning techniques in SQL Server. Figure 28-5 illustrates a typical wait statistics analysis troubleshooting cycle.

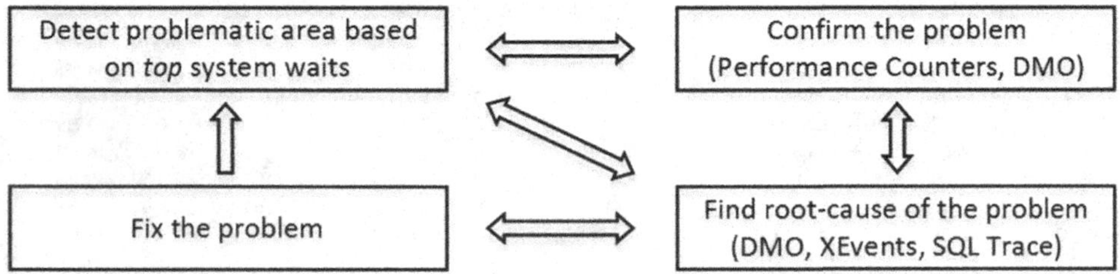

Figure 28-5. *Wait statistics analysis troubleshooting cycle*

As a first step, look at the wait statistics, which detect the top waits in the system. This narrows down the area of concern for further analysis. After that, you confirm the problem using other tools, such as DMV, Windows Performance Monitor, SQL Traces, and Extended Events, and detect the root cause of the problem. When the root cause is confirmed, you fix it and analyze the wait statistics again, choosing a new target for analysis and improvement.

This is a never-ending process. Waits always exist in systems, and there is always space for improvement. However, a generic 80/20 Pareto principle can be applied to almost any troubleshooting and optimization process. You achieve an 80 percent effect or improvement by spending 20 percent of your time. At some point, further optimization does not provide a sufficient return on investment, and it is better to spend your time and resources elsewhere.

Even though wait statistics can help you detect problematic areas in a system, it is not always easy to find the root cause of a problem. Different issues affect and often mask each other.

Figure 28-6 illustrates such a situation. Bad system performance due to a slow and unresponsive I/O subsystem often occurs due to missing indexes and nonoptimized queries that overload it. Those queries require SQL Server to scan a large amount of data, which flushes the content of the buffer pool and contributes to CPU load. Moreover, missing indexes introduce locking and blocking in the system.

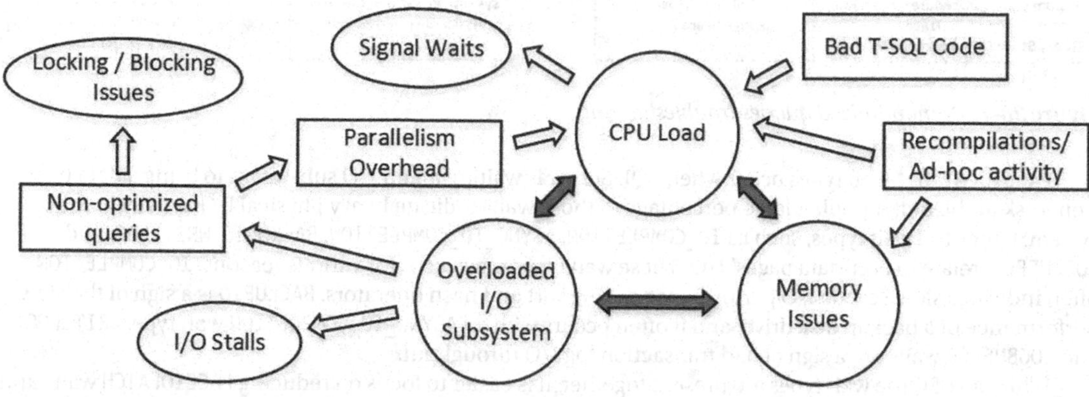

Figure 28-6. *Everything is related*

Ad-hoc queries and recompilations contribute to CPU load and increase plan cache size, which in turn leaves less memory for the buffer pool. It also increases I/O subsystem load due to the extra physical I/O required.

Let's look at different issues frequently encountered in systems and discuss how we can detect and troubleshoot them.

I/O Subsystem and Nonoptimized Queries

The most common root cause of issues related to a slow and/or overloaded I/O subsystem is nonoptimized queries, which require SQL Server to scan a large amount of data. When SQL Server does not have enough physical memory to cache all of the required data in the buffer pool, which is typically the case for large systems, physical I/O occurs and constantly replaces data in the buffer pool.

■ **Tip** You can add or allocate more physical memory to the server that hosts SQL Server when an I/O subsystem is overloaded. Extra memory increases the size of the buffer pool and the amount of data SQL Server can cache. It reduces the physical I/O required to scan the data. While it does not fix the root cause of the problem, it can work as an emergency fix and buy you some time. Remember that non-Enterprise editions of SQL Server have limitations in the amount of memory that they can utilize. Lastly, data compression in Enterprise Edition can also reduce the size of the data that needs to be cached.

Figure 28-7 illustrates a situation with nonoptimized queries, and it shows the metrics and tools that can be used to diagnose and fix these problems.

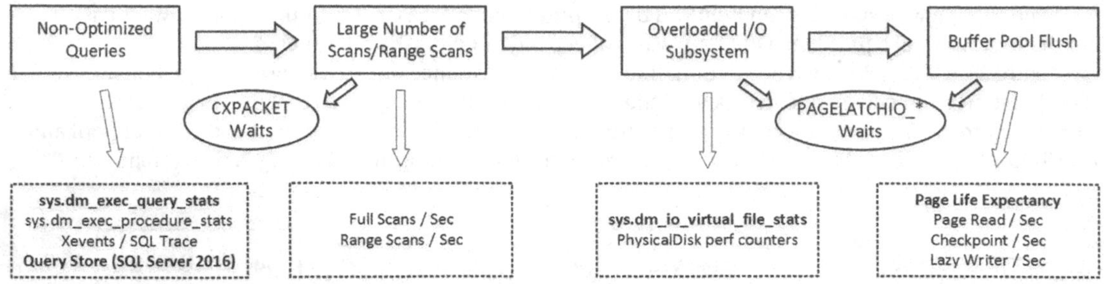

Figure 28-7. *Nonoptimized queries troubleshooting*

PAGEIOLATCH_* wait types occur when SQL Server is waiting for an I/O subsystem to bring a data page from disk to the buffer pool. A large percentage of those waits indicate heavy physical I/O activity in the system. Other I/O wait types, such as IO_COMPLETION, ASYNC_IO_COMPLETION, BACKUPIO, WRITELOG, and LOGBUFFER, relate to non-data pages' I/O. These wait types may occur for various reasons. IO_COMPLETION often indicates slow tempdb I/O performance during sort and hash operators. BACKUPIO is a sign of the slow performance of a backup disk drive, and it often occurs with an ASYNC_IO_COMPLETION wait type. WRITELOG and LOGBUFFER waits are a sign of bad transaction log I/O throughput.

When all of these wait types are present together, it is easier to focus on reducing PAGEIOLATCH waits and data-related I/O. This will reduce the load on the I/O subsystem and, in turn, can improve the performance of non-data-related I/O operations.

It has become common nowadays for servers to have enough physical memory to cache an entire active data set in the buffer pool. Such systems usually have a relatively low percentage of PAGEIOLATCH waits present. Queries in these systems introduce a low amount of physical I/O activity, and even nonoptimized queries can have acceptable execution times. One sign of such a condition in OLTP systems is having a significant amount of parallelism CXPACKET waits and a low percentage of PAGEIOLATCH waits, with or without non-data page I/O-related waits present. You will need to confirm the situation by looking at query execution statistics, which we will discuss later in this chapter.

Nonoptimized queries without physical disk activity do not necessarily introduce a visible performance impact on the system. There is a hidden danger in this situation, however: the amount of data growth. It can reach the tipping point when data does not fit into memory anymore and the system starts to experience performance issues because of the excessive disk activity that the situation introduced. Moreover, nonoptimized queries can contribute to concurrency issues even without physical I/O being involved. Nevertheless, you should analyze whether optimizing such queries would provide you with sufficient ROI for your efforts.

The sys.dm_io_virtual_file_stats function provides you with I/O statistics for data and log files, including information about a number of I/O operations, the amount of data processed, and I/O stalls, which is the time that SQL Server waited for I/O operations to complete. This can help you detect most I/O-intensive databases and data files, which is especially useful when a SQL Server instance hosts a large number of databases. This view is also useful when you work on database consolidation projects.

Listing 28-3 shows you a query that obtains information about I/O statistics for all of the databases on a server. Figure 28-8 illustrates the partial output of this query when run against one of the production servers.

Listing 28-3. Using sys.dm_io_virtual_file_stats

```
select
    fs.database_id as [DB ID], fs.file_id as [File Id], mf.name as [File Name]
    ,mf.physical_name as [File Path], mf.type_desc as [Type], fs.sample_ms as [Time]
    ,fs.num_of_reads as [Reads], fs.num_of_bytes_read as [Read Bytes]
    ,fs.num_of_writes as [Writes], fs.num_of_bytes_written as [Written Bytes]
```

```
    ,fs.num_of_reads + fs.num_of_writes as [IO Count]
    ,convert(decimal(5,2),100.0 * fs.num_of_bytes_read /
        (fs.num_of_bytes_read + fs.num_of_bytes_written)) as [Read %]
    ,convert(decimal(5,2),100.0 * fs.num_of_bytes_written /
        (fs.num_of_bytes_read + fs.num_of_bytes_written)) as [Write %]
    ,fs.io_stall_read_ms as [Read Stall], fs.io_stall_write_ms as [Write Stall]
    ,case when fs.num_of_reads = 0
        then 0.000
        else convert(decimal(12,3),1.0 * fs.io_stall_read_ms / fs.num_of_reads)
    end as [Avg Read Stall]
    ,case when fs.num_of_writes = 0
        then 0.000
        else convert(decimal(12,3),1.0 * fs.io_stall_write_ms / fs.num_of_writes)
    end as [Avg Write Stall]
from
    sys.dm_io_virtual_file_stats(null,null) fs join
        sys.master_files mf with (nolock) on
            fs.database_id = mf.database_id and fs.file_id = mf.file_id
        join sys.databases d with (nolock) on
            d.database_id = fs.database_id
where
    fs.num_of_reads + fs.num_of_writes > 0;
```

	DB ID	File Id	File Name	File Path	Type	Time	Reads	Read Bytes
1	5	1	CTCloud_Primary_file	F:\Databas...	ROWS	2082125133	28640	634617856
2	5	2	CTCloud_Log_file	F:\Databas...	LOG	2082125133	5786691	4856755533312
3	5	3	CTCloud_Entities_file1	F:\Databas...	ROWS	2082125133	3836810	213045534720
4	5	4	CTCloud_Entities_file2	F:\Databas...	ROWS	2082125133	3606346	164764073984
5	5	5	CTCloud_Entities_file3	F:\Databas...	ROWS	2082125133	3707361	131695001600

Writes	Written Bytes	IO Count	Read %	Write %	Read Stall	Write Stall	Avg Read St...	Avg Write Stall
5777438	74420396032	5806078	0.85	99.15	234236	20120804	0.179	3.483
255007793	11700852344320	260794484	29.33	70.67	18821891	511247441	3.253	2.005
65903077	792104493056	69739887	21.20	78.80	25738654	307697614	6.708	4.669
45587023	547723214848	49193369	23.13	76.87	24074753	100938420	6.676	2.214
89880283	1003102298112	93587644	11.61	88.39	19261189	144064060	5.195	1.603

Figure 28-8. *Sys_dm_io_virtual_file_stats output*

Unfortunately, sys.dm_io_virtual_file_stats provides cumulative statistics as of the time of a SQL Server restart, without any way to clear it. If you need to get a snapshot of the current load in the system, you should run this function several times and compare how the results changed between calls. I'm including the code that implements such an approach in the companion materials of this book.

You can analyze various system performance counters using the *PhysicalDisk* object to obtain information about current I/O activity, such as the number of requests and the amount of data being read and written. These counters, however, are most useful when compared against the baseline, which we will discuss later in this chapter.

Performance counters from the *SQL Server:Buffer Manager* object provide various metrics related to the buffer pool and data-page I/O. One of the most useful counters is *page life expectancy*, which indicates the average time a data page stays in the buffer pool. Historically, Microsoft suggested that values above 300 seconds were acceptable and *good enough*; however, this is hardly the case with modern servers, which use large amounts of memory. One approach to defining the lowest acceptable value for the counter is by multiplying 300 seconds by every 4 GB of buffer pool memory. For example, a server that uses 56 GB of memory for the buffer pool should have a page life expectancy greater than 4,200 seconds (56/4*300). However, as with other counters, it is better to compare the current value against a baseline than to rely on a statically defined threshold.

The *page read/sec* and *page write/sec* counters show the number of physical data pages that were read and written, respectively. *Checkpoint pages/sec* and *lazy writer/sec* indicate the activity of the checkpoint and lazy writer processes that save dirty pages to disks. High numbers in those counters and a low value for page life expectancy could be a sign of memory pressure. However, a high number of checkpoints could transpire because of a large number of transactions in the system, and you should include the *transactions/sec* counter in the analysis.

In a scenario where servers have enough physical memory to cache the active data set in memory, you would notice the high value of the page life expectancy and low value of the page read/sec counters. The values of page write/sec and checkpoint pages/sec would depend on the volatility of the data in the system.

The *buffer cache hit ratio* indicates the percentage of pages that are found in the buffer pool without the requirement of performing a physical read operation. A low value for this counter indicates a constant buffer pool flush and is a sign of a large amount of physical I/O. However, a high value in the counter is meaningless. Read-ahead reads often bring data pages to memory, increasing the buffer cache hit ratio value and masking the problem. In the end, page life expectancy is a more reliable counter for this analysis.

■ **Note** You can read more about performance counters from the buffer manager object at `http://technet.microsoft.com/en-us/library/ms189628.aspx`.

The *full scans/sec* and *range scan/sec* performance counters from the *SQL Server:Access Methods* object provide you with information about the scan activity in the system. Their values, however, can be misleading. While scanning a large amount of data negatively affects performance, small range scans or full scans of small temporary tables are completely acceptable. As with other performance counters, it is better to compare counter values against a baseline rather than relying on absolute values.

There are several ways to detect I/O-intensive queries using standard SQL Server tools. One of the most common approaches is by capturing system activity using SQL Traces or Extended Events, filtering the data by the number of reads and/or writes. You can also analyze query duration; however, you should be careful with such an approach. The longest-running queries are not necessarily the most I/O-intensive ones. There are other factors that can increase query execution time. Think about locking and blocking, as an example.

This approach, however, requires you to perform additional analysis after the data is collected. You should check how frequently queries are executed when determining targets for optimization.

Another very simple and powerful method of detecting resource intensive queries is the `sys.dm_exec_query_stats` data management view. SQL Server tracks various statistics, including the number of executions and I/O operations and elapsed and CPU times, and exposes them through that view. Furthermore, you can join it with other data management objects and obtain the SQL text and execution plans for those queries. This simplifies the analysis, and it can be helpful during the troubleshooting of various performance and plan cache issues in the system.

Listing 28-4 shows a query that returns the 50 most I/O-intensive queries, which have been plan cached at the moment of execution. It is worth noting that `sys.dm_exec_query_stats` has slightly different columns in the result set in different versions of SQL Server. The query in Listing 28-5 works in SQL Server 2008R2 and above. You can remove the last four columns from the `SELECT` list to make it compatible with SQL Server 2005-2008.

Listing 28-4. Using `sys.dm_exec_query_stats`

```
select top 50
    substring(qt.text, (qs.statement_start_offset/2)+1,
    ((
        case qs.statement_end_offset
            when -1 then datalength(qt.text)
            else qs.statement_end_offset
        end - qs.statement_start_offset)/2)+1) as SQL
    ,qp.query_plan as [Query Plan]
    ,qs.execution_count as [Exec Cnt]
    ,(qs.total_logical_reads + qs.total_logical_writes) / qs.execution_count as [Avg IO]
    ,qs.total_logical_reads as [Total Reads], qs.last_logical_reads as [Last Reads]
    ,qs.total_logical_writes as [Total Writes], qs.last_logical_writes as [Last Writes]
    ,qs.total_worker_time as [Total Worker Time], qs.last_worker_time as [Last Worker Time]
    ,qs.total_elapsed_time / 1000 as [Total Elapsed Time]
    ,qs.last_elapsed_time / 1000 as [Last Elapsed Time]
    ,qs.last_execution_time as [Last Exec Time]
    ,qs.total_rows as [Total Rows], qs.last_rows as [Last Rows]
    ,qs.min_rows as [Min Rows], qs.max_rows as [Max Rows]
from
    sys.dm_exec_query_stats qs with (nolock)
        cross apply sys.dm_exec_sql_text(qs.sql_handle) qt
        cross apply sys.dm_exec_query_plan(qs.plan_handle) qp
order by
    [Avg IO] desc
```

As you can see in Figure 28-9, it allows you to easily define optimization targets based on resource usage and the number of executions. For example, the second query in the result set is the best candidate for optimization because of how frequently it runs.

	SQL	Query Plan	Exec Cnt	Avg IO	Total Reads	Last Reads	Total Writes	Last Writes	Total Worker Time	Last Worker T...
1	select Subj, cast(ReceiverUID ...	<ShowPlanXML xmlns="http...	1	6816382	6816298	6816286	86	86	24297389	24297389
2	select UID, DOCTYPE_ID, REG...	<ShowPlanXML xmlns="http...	26455	4143503	109616393555	4224687	0	0	164369131409	5074290
3	DELETE TOP (@delete_batch...	<ShowPlanXML xmlns="http...	1	4096631	4096468	4096468	163	163	26538518	26538518
4	insert into #tmpReportIncoming...	<ShowPlanXML xmlns="http...	62	3690210	228750206	3954880	42859	1012	3351099813	28477617
5	update #tmpReportIncomingCo...	<ShowPlanXML xmlns="http...	62	3139967	194677952	3140931	7	0	2406888688	27503573

Figure 28-9. *Sys.dm_exec_query_stats results*

Unfortunately, `sys.dm_exec_query_stats` does not return any information for queries that do not have compiled plans cached. Usually this is not an issue, because our optimization targets are not only resource intensive, but are also frequently executed queries. Plans of these queries usually stay in the cache because of their frequent reuse. However, SQL Server does not cache plans in cases of statement-level recompiles, and therefore `sys.dm_exec_query_stats` misses such queries. You should use Extended Events and/or SQL Traces to capture them. I usually start with queries from the `sys.dm_exec_query_stats` function output and crosscheck the optimization targets with Extended Events later.

The new SQL Server 2016 component called Query Store addresses such an issue. It captures and persists execution statistics and execution plans for those queries without any dependencies on the plan cache. We will discuss Query Store in depth in the next chapter.

Query plans can be removed from the cache, and therefore they are not included in the `sys.dm_exec_query_stats` results in cases of a SQL Server restart, memory pressure, or recompilations due to a statistics update, as well as in a few other cases. It is beneficial to analyze the `creation_time` and `last_execution_time` columns in addition to the number of executions.

SQL Server 2008 and above provide stored procedure–level execution statistics with the sys.dm_exec_procedure_stats view. It provides similar metrics as sys.dm_exec_query_stats, and it can be used to determine the most resource intensive stored procedures in the system. Listing 28-5 shows a query that returns the 50 most I/O-intensive stored procedures, which have plan cached at the moment of execution.

Listing 28-5. Using sys.dm_exec_procedure_stats

```
select top 50
    db_name(ps.database_id) as [DB]
    ,object_name(ps.object_id, ps.database_id) as [Proc Name]
    ,ps.type_desc as [Type]
    ,qp.query_plan as  [Plan]
    ,ps.execution_count as [Exec Count]
    ,(ps.total_logical_reads + ps.total_logical_writes) / ps.execution_count as [Avg IO]
    ,ps.total_logical_reads as [Total Reads], ps.last_logical_reads as [Last Reads]
    ,ps.total_logical_writes as [Total Writes], ps.last_logical_writes as [Last Writes]
    ,ps.total_worker_time as [Total Worker Time], ps.last_worker_time as [Last Worker Time]
    ,ps.total_elapsed_time / 1000 as [Total Elapsed Time]
    ,ps.last_elapsed_time / 1000 as [Last Elapsed Time]
    ,ps.last_execution_time as [Last Exec Time]
from
    sys.dm_exec_procedure_stats ps with (nolock)
        cross apply sys.dm_exec_query_plan(ps.plan_handle) qp
order by
     [Avg IO] desc
```

SQL Server 2016 introduces another view, sys.dm_exec_function_stats, which allows you to track execution statistics of scalar user-defined functions. It works with T-SQL, CLR, and In-Memory OLTP scalar functions; however, it does not capture table-valued functions' execution statistics.

The sys.dm_exec_function_stats view returns information similar to that returned by sys.dm_exec_procedure_stats. In fact, the code from Listing 28-5 would work as long as you replaced the DMV name there.

There are plenty of tools available on the market to help you automate the data collection and analysis process, including the SQL Server Management Data Warehouse. All of them help you to achieve the same goal and find optimization targets in the system.

Finally, it is worth mentioning that the data warehouse and reporting systems usually play by different rules. In those systems, it is typical to have I/O-intensive queries that scan large amounts of data. Performance tuning of such systems can require different approaches than those found in OLTP environments, and they often lead to database schema changes rather than index tuning.

Parallelism

Parallelism is perhaps one of the most confusing aspects of troubleshooting. It exposes itself with the CXPACKET wait type, which often can be seen in the list of top waits in the system. The CXPACKET wait type, which stands for *Class eXchange*, occurs when parallel threads are waiting for other threads to complete their execution.

Let's consider a simple example and assume that we have a parallel plan with two threads followed by the *exchange/repartition streams* operator. When one parallel thread finishes its work, it waits for the other thread to complete. The waiting thread does not consume any CPU resources; it just waits, generating the CXPACKET wait type.

The CXPACKET wait type merely indicates that there is parallelism in the system, and, as usual, this fits into the "It Depends" category. It is beneficial when large and complex queries utilize parallelism, because it can dramatically reduce their execution time. However, there is always overhead associated with parallelism management and exchange operators. For example, if a serial plan finishes in one second on a single CPU, the execution time of the parallel plan that uses two CPUs would always exceed 0.5 seconds. There is always extra CPU time required for parallelism management. Even though the response (elapsed) time of the parallel plan would be smaller, the CPU time would always be greater than in the case of the serial plan. You want to avoid such overhead when a large number of OLTP queries are waiting for the available CPU to execute. Having a high percentage of SOS_SCHEDULER_YIELD and CXPACKET waits is a sign of such a situation.

One common misconception suggests that you should completely disable parallelism in cases where you have a large percentage of CXPACKET waits in an OLTP system and then set the server-level MAXDOP setting to 1. However, this is not the right way to deal with parallelism waits. You need to investigate the root cause of the parallelism in the OLTP system and analyze why SQL Server has generated parallel execution plans. In most cases, it occurs due to complex and/or nonoptimized queries. Query optimization simplifies execution plans and removes parallelism.

Moreover, any OLTP system has some legitimate complex queries that would benefit from parallelism. It is better to increase the *Cost Threshold for Parallelism* configuration option rather than to disable parallelism by setting the MAXDOP setting to 1. This would allow you to utilize parallelism with complex and expensive queries while keeping low-cost OLTP queries running serially.

There is no generic advice for how the *Cost Threshold for Parallelism* value needs to be set. By default, it is set to five, which is very low nowadays. You should analyze the activity and cost of the queries in your system to find the optimal value for this setting. Check the cost of the queries that you want to run serially and in parallel, and adjust the threshold value accordingly. You can see that cost in the properties of the root (top) operator in the execution plan.

Speaking of the MAXDOP setting, in general it should not exceed the number of logical CPUs per hardware NUMA node. However, in some data warehouse systems, you can consider using a MAXDOP setting that exceeds this number. Again, you should analyze and test your workload to find the optimal value for this setting.

Memory-Related Wait Types

SQL Server allocates query memory grants from a special part of the buffer pool called *workspace memory*. The maximum size of workspace memory is limited to 75 percent of the buffer pool size. By default, the maximum query memory grant size cannot exceed 25 percent of workspace memory; however, you can control it through the REQUEST_MAX_MEMORY_GRANT_PERCENT setting in the Resource Governor workload group.

As you already know, every query uses a small amount of memory to execute. In addition, *sort* and *hash* operators require additional memory to run, which can be separated into two groups, as follows:

Required memory is needed to store internal data structures that are required for the operation. The query would not run without this memory available.

Additional memory is used to store the data rows in memory during the operation. The amount of additional memory is based on row size and cardinality estimations. The query could run if the amount of additional memory is insufficient, spilling the data to tempdb when needed.

The amount of required memory is also affected by parallelism. Each worker needs to create its own set of internal data structures for *sort* or *hash* operators. Moreover, exchange operators will need some memory to buffer the rows.

After the size of the memory grant is calculated, SQL Server checks if it exceeds the maximum size limit and reduces it if needed. After that, it requests memory from the MEMORYCLERK_SQLQERESERVATIONS memory clerk, which uses a thread synchronization object called *Resource Semaphore* to allocate the memory. We will talk about memory clerks and SQL Server memory allocation later in this chapter.

When memory cannot be allocated, Resource Semaphore puts the queries in the wait queues, which leads to RESOURCE_SEMAPHORE waits. Internally, Resource Semaphore uses two wait queues, ranking queries based on the memory grant size and query cost. One queue, called *Small-query Resource Semaphore,* stores the queries that require less than 5 MB and cost less than 3 cost units. The second queue stores all other queries.

When Resource Semaphore receives the new request, it first checks if any query is waiting, then processes requests based on the first come, first served principle. It favors the small-query queue over the regular one, which reduces the waiting time for the small queries that do not require a large amount of memory.

Large memory grants consume system memory and can prevent queries from being immediately executed. Unfortunately, sometimes SQL Server overestimates the size of the memory grants required for the queries, usually because of cardinality overestimations. A common case for such an error is a complex query with a large number of joins and non-SARGable predicates, and/or functions in join conditions and the WHERE clause. SQL Server has to apply heuristics during the cardinality estimations, which may produce incorrect results for the actual data.

You should monitor the situation of the memory grants in the system. Even a small percentage of RESOURCE_SEMAPHORE waits can indicate serious performance issues. This can be a sign of memory pressure and poorly optimized and extremely inefficient queries.

You can confirm the problem by looking at the *memory grants pending* performance counter in the *SQL Server:Memory Manager* object. This counter shows the number of queries waiting for memory grants. Ideally, the counter value should be zero all the time.

The sys.dm_exec_query_resource_semaphores view shows the statistics for both Resource Semaphore queues, including granted and available workspace memory, number of queries in the waiting queue, and a few other parameters. You can also look at the sys.dm_exec_query_memory_grants view, which provides information about memory grant requests, both pending and outstanding. Listing 28-6 illustrates how you can obtain information about them, along with the query text and execution plan.

Listing 28-6. Obtaining query information from the sys.dm_exec_query_memory_grants view

```
select
    mg.session_id, t.text as [SQL], qp.query_plan as [Plan], mg.is_small, mg.dop
    ,mg.query_cost, mg.request_time, mg.required_memory_kb, mg.requested_memory_kb
    ,mg.wait_time_ms, mg.grant_time, mg.granted_memory_kb, mg.used_memory_kb
    ,mg.max_used_memory_kb
from
    sys.dm_exec_query_memory_grants mg with (nolock)
        cross apply sys.dm_exec_sql_text(mg.sql_handle) t
        cross apply sys.dm_exec_query_plan(mg.plan_handle) as qp
```

SQL Server 2012 SP3, SQL Server 2014 SP2, and SQL Server 2016 have several enhancements that simplify memory grant troubleshooting. The sys.dm_exec_query_stats view provides memory grant-related statistics in the output columns. There is also the query_memory_grant_usage Extended Event, which you can use to track memory allocation in real time. Finally, Query Store in SQL Server 2016 collects memory grant metrics along with other parameters.

If you run older builds of SQL Server, you can obtain information about memory grants from the cached execution plans. As with other metrics, memory grant information there lacks actual execution statistics, and it also shows information about memory grant requests that are required for the serial execution plans, without parallelism overhead involved.

Listing 28-7 shows how you can obtain memory grant information from the cached execution plans using the sys.dm_exec_cached_plans view. Alternatively, you can obtain similar information by using the sys.dm_exec_query_stats view and the sys.dm_exec_query_plan function.

Listing 28-7. Getting memory grant information from the cached plans

```
;with xmlnamespaces(default 'http://schemas.microsoft.com/sqlserver/2004/07/showplan')
,Statements(PlanHandle, ObjType, UseCount, StmtSimple)
as
(
    select cp.plan_handle, cp.objtype, cp.usecounts, nodes.stmt.query('.')
    from sys.dm_exec_cached_plans cp with (nolock)
        cross apply sys.dm_exec_query_plan(cp.plan_handle) qp
        cross apply qp.query_plan.nodes('//StmtSimple') nodes(stmt)
)
select top 50
    s.PlanHandle, s.ObjType, s.UseCount
    ,p.qp.value('@CachedPlanSize','int') as CachedPlanSize
    ,mg.mg.value('@SerialRequiredMemory','int') as [SerialRequiredMemory KB]
    ,mg.mg.value('@SerialDesiredMemory','int') as [SerialDesiredMemory KB]
from Statements s
    cross apply s.StmtSimple.nodes('.//QueryPlan') p(qp)
    cross apply p.qp.nodes('.//MemoryGrantInfo') mg(mg)
order by
    mg.mg.value('@SerialRequiredMemory','int') desc
```

You can restrict the maximum size of the memory grant by using the `MAX_GRANT_PERCENT` query hint, which is supported in SQL Server 2012 SP3, SQL Server 2014 SP2, and SQL Server 2016, or by restricting the `REQUEST_MAX_MEMORY_GRANT_PERCENT` setting in the Resource Governor workload group. However, the best approach is simplifying and optimizing the queries in a way that removes memory-intensive operators, such as hashes, sorts, and sometimes parallelism, from the execution plan. You can often achieve it by index tuning and query re-factoring.

`CXMEMTHREAD` is another memory-related wait type that you can encounter in systems. These waits occur when multiple threads are trying to allocate memory from unallocated memory HEAP simultaneously. You can often observe a high percentage of these waits in systems with a large number of ad-hoc queries, where SQL Server constantly allocates and de-allocates plan cache memory. Enabling the *Optimize for Ad-hoc Workloads* configuration setting can help address this problem if plan cache memory allocation is the root cause.

SQL Server has three categories of memory objects. Some of them are created globally on the server scope. Others are partitioned on a per-NUMA node or per-CPU basis. In SQL Server prior to 2016, you can use startup trace flag `T8048` to switch per-NUMA node to per-CPU partitioning, which can help reduce `CXMEMTHREAD` waits at the cost of extra memory usage. SQL Server 2016, on the other hand, promotes such partitioning to the per-NUMA level and then to the per-CPU level automatically when it detects contention, and therefore `T8048` is not required.

■ **Note** You can read more about Non-Uniform Memory Access (NUMA) architecture at `http://technet.microsoft.com/en-us/library/ms178144.aspx`.

Listing 28-8 shows you how to analyze the memory allocations of memory objects. You may consider applying the `T8048` trace flag if top memory consumers are per-NUMA node partitioned and you can see a large percentage of `CXMEMTHREAD` waits in the system. This is especially important in scenarios with servers that have more than eight CPUs per NUMA node, where older versions of SQL Server have known issues of per-NUMA node memory object scalability. As I already mentioned, this trace flag is not required in SQL Server 2016.

Listing 28-8. Analyzing memory-object partitioning and memory usage

```
select type, pages_in_bytes
    ,case
        when (creation_options & 0x20 = 0x20)
            then 'Global PMO. Cannot be partitioned by CPU/NUMA Node. T8048 not applicable.'
        when (creation_options & 0x40 = 0x40)
            then 'Partitioned by CPU. T8048 not applicable.'
        when (creation_options & 0x80 = 0x80)
            then 'Partitioned by Node. Use T8048 to further partition by CPU.'
        else 'Unknown'
    end as [Partitioning Type]
from sys.dm_os_memory_objects
order by pages_in_bytes desc
```

■ **Note** You can read an article published by the Microsoft CSS Team that explains how to debug `CXMEMTHREAD` wait types at `http://blogs.msdn.com/b/psssql/archive/2012/12/20/how-it-works-cmemthread-and-debugging-them.aspx`.

High CPU Load

As strange as it sounds, low CPU load on a server is not necessarily a good sign. It indicates that the server is under-utilized. Even though under-utilization leaves systems with room to grow, it increases the IT infrastructure and operational costs; there are more servers to host and maintain. Obviously, high CPU load is not good either. Constant CPU pressure on SQL Server makes systems unresponsive and slow.

There are several indicators that can help you detect that a server is working under CPU pressure. These include a high percentage of `SOS_SCHEDULER_YIELD` waits, which occur when a worker is waiting in a runnable state. You can analyze the *% processor time* and *processor queue length* performance counters and compare the signal and resource wait times in the `sys.dm_os_wait_stats` view, as shown in Listing 28-9. Signal waits indicate the waiting times for the CPU, while resource waits indicate the waiting times for resources, such as for pages from disk. Although Microsoft recommends that the signal wait type should not exceed 25 percent, I believe that 15 to 20 percent is a better target on busy systems.

Listing 28-9. Comparing signal and resource waits

```
select
    sum(signal_wait_time_ms) as [Signal Wait Time (ms)]
    ,convert(decimal(7,4), 100.0 * sum(signal_wait_time_ms) /
        sum (wait_time_ms)) as [% Signal waits]
    ,sum(wait_time_ms - signal_wait_time_ms) as [Resource Wait Time (ms)]
    ,convert(decimal(7,4), 100.0 * sum(wait_time_ms - signal_wait_time_ms) /
        sum (wait_time_ms)) as [% Resource waits]
from
    sys.dm_os_wait_stats with (nolock)
```

Plenty of factors can contribute to CPU load in a system, and bad T-SQL code is at the top of the list. Imperative processing, cursors, XQuery, multi-statement user-defined functions, and complex calculations are especially CPU-intensive.

The process of detecting the most CPU-intensive queries is very similar to that for detecting nonoptimized queries. You can use the sys.dm_exec_query_stats view, as was shown in Listing 28-4. You can sort the data by the total_worker_time column, which detects the most CPU-intensive queries with plans currently cached. Alternatively, you can use Extended Events, filtering data by CPU time rather than by I/O metrics.

Constant recompilation is another source of CPU load. You can check the *batch requests/sec, SQL compilations/sec,* and *SQL recompilations/sec* performance counters and calculate plan reuse with the following formula:

```
Plan Reuse = (Batch Requests/Sec - (SQL Compilations/Sec - SQL Recompilations/Sec)) / Batch
Requests/Sec
```

Low plan reuse in OLTP systems indicates heavy ad-hoc activity and often requires code re-factoring and the parameterization of queries. However, nonoptimized queries are still the major contributor to CPU load. With nonoptimized queries, SQL Server processes a large amount of data, which burns CPU cycles regardless of other factors. In most cases, query optimization reduces the CPU load in the system.

Obviously, the same is true for bad T-SQL code. You should reduce the amount of imperative data processing, avoid multi-statement functions, and move calculations and XML processing to the application side if at all possible.

Locking and Blocking

Excessive locking and blocking issues in a system presents various LCK_M_* wait types. Each lock type has its own corresponding wait type. For example, LCK_M_U indicates update (U) lock waits, which can be a sign of nonoptimized data modification queries.

We have already covered how to troubleshoot locking and blocking issues in a system. You need to detect which processes participated in the blocking chain with the *blocked process report, deadlock graph* events, and sys.dm_tran_locks view and find the root cause of the blocking. In most cases, it happens due to nonoptimized queries.

Worker Thread Starvation

In rare cases, SQL Server can experience *worker thread starvation,* a situation where there are no available workers to assign to new tasks. One scenario where this can happen is when a task acquires and holds a lock on a critical resource that is blocking a large number of other tasks/workers, which stays in a suspended state. When the number of workers in the system reaches the limit defined by the *Maximum Worker Thread* threshold, SQL Server is not able to create new workers, and new tasks remain unassigned, generating THREADPOOL waits.

Blocking is not the only reason why this situation could occur. It is also possible to reach the limit of worker threads in systems when the server is under memory pressure and/or does not have enough memory available. In those cases, workers stay assigned for a longer time, waiting for memory grants (check RESOURCE_SEMAPHORE waits) or performing a large number of physical I/O operations. Finally, heavy concurrent workload from a large number of users can also exhaust the workers pool.

As usual, you need to find the root cause of the problem. While it is possible to increase the Maximum Worker Thread number in the SQL Server configuration, this may or may not help. For example, in the blocking scenario just described, there is a good chance that newly created workers will be blocked in the same way as existing ones are. It is better to investigate the root cause of the blocking problem and address it instead.

You can check a blocking condition and locate the blocking session by analyzing the results of the sys.dm_os_waiting_tasks or sys.dm_exec_requests views. Listing 28-10 demonstrates the first approach. Keep in mind that the sys.dm_exec_requests view does not show tasks that do not have workers assigned and waiting with the THREADPOOL wait type. It is also worth noting that worker thread starvation may prevent any connections to the server. In that case, you need to use a *Dedicated Admin Connection (DAC)* for troubleshooting. We will discuss DAC later in this chapter.

Listing 28-10. Using sys.dm_os_waiting_tasks

```
select session_id, wait_type, wait_duration_ms, blocking_session_id, resource_description
from sys.dm_os_waiting_tasks with (nolock)
order by wait_duration_ms desc
```

As you can see in Figure 28-10, the ID of the blocking session is 51.

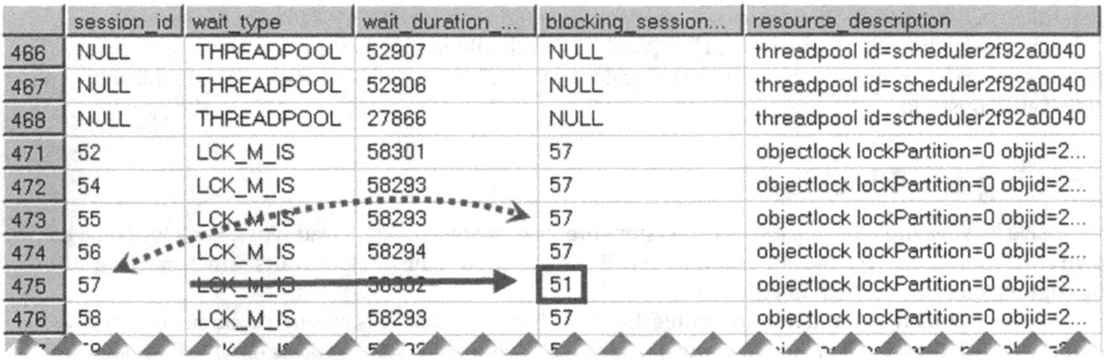

	session_id	wait_type	wait_duration_...	blocking_session...	resource_description
466	NULL	THREADPOOL	52907	NULL	threadpool id=scheduler2f92a0040
467	NULL	THREADPOOL	52906	NULL	threadpool id=scheduler2f92a0040
468	NULL	THREADPOOL	27866	NULL	threadpool id=scheduler2f92a0040
471	52	LCK_M_IS	58301	57	objectlock lockPartition=0 objid=2...
472	54	LCK_M_IS	58293	57	objectlock lockPartition=0 objid=2...
473	55	LCK_M_IS	58293	57	objectlock lockPartition=0 objid=2...
474	56	LCK_M_IS	58294	57	objectlock lockPartition=0 objid=2...
475	57	LCK_M_IS	58302	51	objectlock lockPartition=0 objid=2...
476	58	LCK_M_IS	58293	57	objectlock lockPartition=0 objid=2...

Figure 28-10. *Sys.dm_os_waiting_tasks result*

For the next step, you can use the sys.dm_exec_sessions and sys.dm_exec_connections views to get information about the blocking session, as shown in Listing 28-11. You can troubleshoot why the lock is held and/or terminate the session with the KILL command if needed.

Listing 28-11. Getting information about a blocking session

```
select
    ec.session_id, s.login_time, s.host_name, s.program_name, s.login_name
    ,s.original_login_name, ec.connect_time, qt.text as [SQL]
from
    sys.dm_exec_connections ec with (nolock)
        join sys.dm_exec_sessions s with (nolock) on
            ec.session_id = s.session_id
    cross apply sys.dm_exec_sql_text(ec.most_recent_sql_handle) qt
where
    ec.session_id = 51 -- session id of the blocking session
```

It is worth mentioning that even though increasing the Maximum Worker Thread setting does not necessarily solve the problem, it is always worth upgrading to a 64-bit version of Windows and SQL Server. A 64-bit version of SQL Server has more worker threads available by default, and it can utilize more memory for query grants and other components. It reduces memory grant waits and makes SQL Server more efficient, and therefore allows tasks to complete execution and frees up workers faster.

Workers, however, consume memory, which reduces the amount of memory available to other SQL Server components. This is not usually an issue, unless SQL Server is running on a server with very little physical memory available. You should consider adding more memory to the server if this is the case. After all, it is a cheap solution nowadays.

ASYNC_NETWORK_IO Waits

The ASYNC_NETWORK_IO wait type occurs when SQL Server generates data faster than the client application consumes it. While this could be a sign of insufficient network throughput, in a large number of cases ASYNC_NETWORK_IO waits accumulate because of incorrect or inefficient client code.

One such example is reading an excessive amount of data from the server. The client application reads unnecessary data or, perhaps, performs client-side filtering, which adds extra load and exceeds network throughput.

Another pattern includes reading and simultaneously processing the data, as shown in Listing 28-12. The client application consumes and processes rows one by one, keeping SqlDataReader open. Therefore, the worker waits for the client to consume all rows, generating the ASYNC_NETWORK_IO wait type.

Listing 28-12. Reading and processing of the data: Incorrect implementation

```
using (SqlConnection connection = new SqlConnection(connectionString))
{
    SqlCommand command = new SqlCommand(cmdText, connection);
    connection.Open();
    using (SqlDataReader reader = command.ExecuteReader())
    {
        while (reader.Read())
            ProcessRow((IDataRecord)reader);
    }
}
```

The correct way of handling such a situation is by reading all rows first as fast as possible and processing them after all rows have been read. Listing 28-13 illustrates this approach.

Listing 28-13. Reading and processing of the data: Correct implementation

```
List<Orders> orderRows = new List<Orders>();
using (SqlConnection connection = new SqlConnection(connectionString))
{
    SqlCommand command = new SqlCommand(cmdText, connection);
    connection.Open();
    using (SqlDataReader reader = command.ExecuteReader())
    {
        while (reader.Read())
            orderRows.Add(ReadOrderRow((IDataRecord)reader));
    }
}
ProcessAllOrderRows(orderRows);
```

You could easily duplicate such behavior by running a test in Management Studio, connecting to a SQL Server instance locally. It would use the shared memory protocol without any network traffic being involved. You could clear wait statistics on the server using the DBCC SQLPERF ('sys.dm_os_wait_stats', CLEAR) command, and run a SELECT statement that reads a large amount of data, displaying it in the result grid. If you checked the wait statistics after execution, you would see a large number of ASYNC_NETWORK_IO waits due to the slow grid performance, even though Management Studio was running locally on a SQL Server box. After that, you should repeat the test with the *Discard Results After Execution* configuration setting enabled. You should see the ASYNC_NETWORK_IO waits disappear.

You should check network performance and analyze the client code if you see a large percentage of ASYNC_NETWORK_IO waits in the system.

Latches and Spinlocks

Latches are lightweight synchronization objects that protect the consistency of SQL Server internal data structures. As the opposite of locks, which protect transactional data consistency, latches prevent the corruption of the data structures in memory.

Consider a situation where multiple sessions need to update different rows on the same data page. Those sessions would not block each other, because they don't acquire incompatible locks on the same objects. SQL Server, however, must prevent the situation where multiple sessions simultaneously update a data page structure in-memory, making it inconsistent and corrupting it. Moreover, SQL Server needs to prevent other sessions from accessing the data page structure at the time of modification. SQL Server uses latches to achieve this.

There are five different latch types in SQL Server, as follows:

> **KP** - Keep latch ensures that the referenced structure cannot be destroyed. It is compatible with any other latch type, with the exception of the Destroy (DT) latch.
>
> **SH** - Shared latch is required when thread needs to read the data structure. Shared latches are compatible with each other, along with the Keep (KP) and Update (UP) latches.
>
> **UP** - Update latch allows other threads to read the structure but prevents the updating of the structure. SQL Server uses them in some scenarios to improve concurrency, similar to update (U) locks. Update latches are compatible with Keep (KP) and Shared (SH) latches and incompatible with any other type.
>
> **EX** - Exclusive latch is required when a thread modifies the data structure. Conceptually, Exclusive (EX) latches are similar to exclusive (X) locks, and they are incompatible with other latch types, with the exception of Keep (KP) latches.
>
> **DT** - Destroy latch is required to destroy the data structure. For example, a Destroy latch is acquired at the time the *lazy writer* process removes a data page from the buffer pool. These latches are incompatible with any other latch type.

When the thread cannot obtain a latch on the data structure, it is placed into the FIFO queue, where it stays suspended, generating one of the latch-related wait types, until a latch can be obtained. We will discuss those types shortly.

In systems with 32 or more logical processors, SQL Server can partition some of the latches on a per-CPU basis. These partitioned latches are called *superlatches*, or sometimes *sub-latches*. In this scenario, each logical CPU maintains its own state and waiters list for the latch object, which improves the performance of acquiring shared (SH) latches on the referenced structures. Acquiring exclusive (EX) latches, on the other hand, requires synchronization across all superlatch partitions and, therefore, is more expensive compared to regular latches.

SQL Server dynamically promotes and demotes latches to/from superlatches based on activity. Latches on frequently read data structures–for example, root pages of the indexes–are quickly promoted to superlatches. Heavy modifications, such as page splits, could demote those superlatches back to regular latches.

The wait types generated by latches can belong to three different classes. Moreover, in each class, SQL Server uses different wait types based on latch type. You can determine latch type by the postfix on the wait type name. For example, PAGELATCH_EX wait type indicates exclusive (EX) latch on the data page structure, while PAGELATCH_SH indicates shared (SH) latch.

The three wait type classes are the following:

> PAGEIOLATCH - indicates I/O-related latches. SQL Server uses these latches/wait types while waiting for data pages to be read from disk to the buffer pool. A large percentage of such wait types could indicate a large amount of nonoptimized queries and/or a suboptimal disk system. We have already covered how to troubleshoot those conditions in this chapter.
>
> PAGELATCH - indicates buffer pool-related latches, which occur when threads need to access or modify data and allocation map pages in the buffer pool.
>
> LATCH - all other latches not related to the buffer pool

There are two main scenarios that can lead to PAGELATCH waits. The first is allocation map contention, which most often happens in tempdb, or sometimes in user tables with highly volatile data. As we already discussed in this book, you can address it by increasing the number of data files in tempdb and/or affected filegroups and, in SQL Server prior 2016, by enabling trace flag T1118, which prevents mixed extents allocation.

The second scenario involves ever-increasing or ever-decreasing indexes on the data, with very high concurrent insert activity. Consider a situation where you have a table that has an index on the identity column and accepts hundreds or thousands of inserts per second. While this design greatly reduces index fragmentation, all sessions insert data to the same data pages, acquiring exclusive PAGELATCH_EX latches and blocking each other. This condition is called *hot spots*, and the only way to address it is by changing the database schema and removing ever-increasing/ever-decreasing indexes.

When you see a large percentage of PAGELATCH waits, you should locate the resources where contention occurs. You can monitor the wait_resource column in the sys.dm_exec_requests view or the resource_description columns in the sys.dm_os_waiting_tasks view for corresponding wait types. The information in those columns includes the database ID, file ID, and page number, which will allow you to identify the root cause of the issue. For example, allocation map contention in tempdb often occurs on PFS (2:1:1) and SGAM (2:1:3) pages.

As a general rule, you do not need to focus on LATCH wait types during wait statistics analysis unless you see a high percentage of such wait types. In those cases, you can look at latch statistics in the system by using the sys.dm_os_latch_stats view, as shown in Listing 28-14. Figure 28-11 illustrates the output from one of the servers.

As a side note, you can clear latch statistics on your server with the DBCC SQLPERF('sys.dm_os_latch_stats', CLEAR) command.

Listing 28-14. Analyzing latch statistics

```
;with Latches
as
(
    select latch_class, wait_time_ms, waiting_requests_count
        ,100. * wait_time_ms / SUM(wait_time_ms) over() as Pct
        ,row_number() over(order by wait_time_ms desc) AS RowNum
    from sys.dm_os_latch_stats with (nolock)
    where latch_class not in (N'BUFFER',N'SLEEP_TASK') and wait_time_ms > 0
)
```

```
select
    l1.latch_class as [Latch Type]
    ,l1.waiting_requests_count as [Wait Count]
    ,convert(decimal(12,3), l1.wait_time_ms / 1000.0) as [Wait Time]
    ,convert(decimal(12,1), l1.wait_time_ms /
        l1.waiting_requests_count) as [Avg Wait Time]
    ,convert(decimal(6,3), l1.Pct) as [Percent]
    ,convert(decimal(6,3), l1.Pct + IsNull(l2.Pct,0))
        as [Running Percent]
from
    Latches l1 cross apply
        (
            select sum(l2.Pct) as Pct
            from Latches l2
            where l2.RowNum < l1.RowNum
        ) l2
where
        l1.RowNum = 1 or l2.Pct < 99
option (recompile);
```

	Latch Type	Wait Count	Wait Time	Avg Wait Time	Percent	Running Percent
1	ACCESS_METHODS_DATASET_PARENT	25546519	51728.454	2.0	92.530	92.530
2	LOG_MANAGER	938	2805.912	2991.0	5.019	97.550

***Figure 28-11.** Latch statistics*

Unfortunately, latch types are poorly documented. Even though they are listed at `https://msdn.microsoft.com/en-us/library/ms175066.aspx`, many of them are documented as *Internal Use Only*. I outline several common latch types in Table 28-1.

You can read more about latches and latch-contention troubleshooting at `http://www.microsoft.com/en-us/download/details.aspx?id=26665`.

Table 28-1. *Common Latch Types*

Latch Type	Description
`LOG_MANAGER`	Access to internal transaction log manager structures, usually when log is growing. Analyze why transaction log is not truncated. We will discuss transaction log internals and troubleshooting in Chapter 30.

`ACCESS_METHODS_DATASET_PARENT`
`ACCESS_METHODS_SCAN_RANGE_GENERATOR`
`ACCESS_METHODS_SCAN_KEY_GENERATOR`
`NESTING_TRANSACTION_FULL`
	Parallelism-related latches. Troubleshoot unnecessary parallelism.

`ACCESS_METHODS_HOBT_VIRTUAL_ROOT`	Access to the root index page. Can indicate a large amount of page splits in the index.
`ACCESS_METHODS_HOBT_COUNT`	Update of page/row count information in metadata tables. Can indicate heavy data modifications on individual table(s) from multiple sessions.
`FGCB_ADD_REMOVE`	Occurs during adding, removing, growing, and shrinking files in the filegroup. Check if *Instant File Initialization* is enabled and *Auto Shrink* database option is disabled.
`TRACE_CONTROLLER`	SQL Traces-related latches. Reduce the number of trace events running on the server and switch to Extended Events if possible.

Lastly, SQL Server uses another type of synchronization object–*spinlocks*. These are used when access to the data structure needs to be held for a very short amount of time. SQL Server uses spinlocks in a manner similar to latches while protecting internal data structures. The main difference between them is that when a thread is unable to acquire the spinlock, it spins constantly through a loop, periodically checking if the resource is available rather than giving the CPU to another thread, as latches do. This helps to avoid thread context switching, which is a relatively expensive operation.

Usually, you do not need to worry about spinlocks during system troubleshooting unless you experience a rare case of spinlock collision, which can occur on very busy systems with a large number of CPUs. Such a condition can present itself as a disproportional increase of CPU utilization as compared to the system throughput. For example, a 10 percent increase in transaction throughput led to 50 percent more load to the CPU. As you can guess, there are other cases that can lead to such conditions, and the best way to confirm that the system is suffering from spinlock collision is by comparing the system state to the baseline. You can obtain that baseline from the undocumented `sys.dm_os_spinlock_stats` view along with the `spinlock_backoff` Extended Event.

Troubleshooting of spinlock collision is a very advanced topic, which is outside of the scope of this book. You can read about it in the following white paper: `https://www.microsoft.com/en-us/download/details.aspx?id=26666`.

Wait Statistics: Wrapping Up

Table 28-2 shows symptoms of the most common problems you will encounter in systems, and it illustrates the steps you can take to address these problems.

Table 28-2. *Common Problems, Symptoms, and Solutions*

Problem	Symptoms / Monitoring Targets	Further Actions
Overloaded I/O Subsystem	PAGEIOLATCH, IO_COMPLETION, WRITELOG, LOGBUFFER, BACKUPIO waits. sys.dm_io_virtual_file_stats stalls. Low *page life expectancy*, High *page read/sec, page write/sec* performance counters	Check I/O subsystem configuration and throughput, especially in cases of non-data page I/O waits. Detect and optimize I/O-intensive queries using Query Store, sys.dm_exec_query_stats, SQL Traces, and Extended Events.
CPU Load	High CPU load, SOS_SCHEDULER_YIELD waits, high percentage of signal waits	Possible non-efficient T-SQL code. Detect and optimize CPU-intensive queries using Query Store, sys.dm_exec_query_stats, SQL Traces, and Extended Events. Check recompilation and plan reuse in OLTP systems.
Query Memory Grants	RESOURCE_SEMAPHORE waits. Non-zero *Memory Grants Pending* value. Pending requests in sys.dm_exec_memory_grants.	Detect and optimize queries that require large memory grants. Perform general query tuning.
HEAP Memory Allocation Contention	CXMEMTHREAD waits	Enable the *Optimize for Ad-hoc Workloads* configuration setting. Analyze which memory objects consume the most memory, and switch to per-CPU partitioning with the T8048 trace flag if appropriate. Apply the latest service pack.
Parallelism in OLTP Systems	CXPACKET waits	Find the root cause of parallelism; most likely nonoptimized or reporting queries. Perform query optimization for the nonoptimized queries that should not have parallel plans. Tune and increase *Cost Threshold for Parallelism* value.
Locking and Blocking	LCK_M_* waits. Deadlocks.	Detect queries involved in blocking with sys.dm_tran_locks, *blocking process report*, and *deadlock graph*. Eliminate root cause of blocking, most likely nonoptimized queries or client-code issues.
ASYNC_NETWORK_IO Waits	ASYNC_NETWORK_IO waits, Network performance counters	Check network performance. Review and re-factor client code (loading excessive amount of data and/or loading and processing data simultaneously).
Worker Thread Starvation	THREADPOOL waits	Detect and address root cause of the problem (blocking and/or load). Upgrade to 64-bit version of SQL Server. Increasing *Maximum Working Thread* value may or may not help.
Allocation-Map Contention	PAGELATCH waits	Detect resource that lead to contention using sys.dm_os_waiting_tasks and sys.dm_exec_requests. Add more data files. In the case of tempdb, use T1118 (not required in SQL Server 2016) and utilize temporary object caching.

This list is by no means complete; however, it should serve as a good starting point.

■ **Note** Read "SQL Server 2005 Performance Tuning using the Waits and Queues" white paper for more details about wait statistics-based performance troubleshooting methodology. It is available for download at `http://technet.microsoft.com/en-us/library/cc966413.aspx`. Even though this white paper was written to address SQL Server 2005, the information within it applies to any newer version of SQL Server as well.

Memory Management and Configuration

It is impossible to discuss system troubleshooting and SQLOS without covering how SQL Server works with the memory. Let's start with memory configuration.

Memory Configuration

As you know, SQL Server tries to allocate and use as much memory as is possible and required for operations. It does not allocate all the memory at start time; the allocation occurs on *as needed* basis–for example, when SQL Server reads data pages to the buffer pool or stores compiled plans in the cache. It is common to see instances that consume hundreds of gigabytes or even terabytes of memory. This is completely normal and, in a nutshell, is a good thing–it reduces the amount of physical I/O and recompilations and improves the performance of the system. **In reality, adding more memory to the servers is often the fastest and cheapest way to improve performance of the system.**

Non-Enterprise editions of SQL Server have a limit on the amount of memory they can utilize. Standard edition can use at most 128 GB of RAM in SQL Server 2014-2016 or 64 GB of RAM in earlier versions. Express edition is limited to 1 GB.

You can check SQL Server memory usage by analyzing performance counters from the *SQL Server: Memory Manager* object. *Total Server Memory (KB)* indicates how much memory SQL Server is consuming. *Target Server Memory (KB)* indicates the ideal amount of memory SQL Server wants to consume. A situation where *Total Server Memory (KB)* is significantly less than *Target Server Memory (KB)* can indicate memory pressure. Alternatively, you can use the `sys.dm_os_process_memory` view to obtain this information.

It is recommended you set the *Maximum Server Memory* setting in the SQL Server configuration. In SQL Server 2012 and above, this setting applies to all SQL Server internal components. In SQL Server prior to 2012, this setting controls the size of the buffer pool, and you need to reduce it to factor in the memory usage of the other components. In a majority of cases, those components will require an extra 1 to 2 GB of RAM reserved.

The *Maximum Server Memory* value should leave enough memory for the OS and applications running on the server. It is best to fine-tune it on each individual server. As a rule of thumb, you can start by reserving 4 GB for the first 16 GB of RAM and 1 GB per every 8 GB thereafter. For example, a server with 128 GB of RAM would lead to (128-16) / 8 + 4 = 110 GB of RAM to start with. Obviously, reduce this number, reserving memory for other applications, in case of non-dedicated SQL Server instances.

After the initial *Maximum Server Memory* value is set, you should monitor the *memory/available mbytes* performance counter, fine-tuning the *Maximum Server Memory* value as needed. You should always keep at least 500 MB of available memory (and even more on servers with a large amount of RAM installed) to avoid memory pressure situations.

It is also beneficial to give the SQL Server startup account the *Lock Pages in Memory* permission to prevent a situation where SQL Server memory is paged to disk. You can set it up in *Group Policy* (gpedit.msc) editor. *Lock Pages in Memory* is supported in both Enterprise and Standard editions; however, in Standard Edition of SQL Server 2005 and 2008 it requires a certain service pack level to work.

The 32-bit edition of SQL Server requires you to enable the *Lock Pages in Memory* privilege and the *AWE Enable* setting to utilize the extended memory of about 4 GB. However, I purposefully do not dive into memory configuration in 32-bit editions; there is absolutely no reason nowadays to use 32-bit OS and SQL Server. The 64-bit edition provides better performance, and it is beneficial to upgrade. It is worth mentioning again that SQL Server 2016 does not even come with a 32-bit edition.

Memory Allocation

All memory allocations in SQL Server are done through SQLOS. Internally, SQLOS partitions the memory into memory nodes based on the server's NUMA configuration. For example, a server with four NUMA nodes will have four memory nodes. A server without NUMA hardware will have just a single memory node.

Each memory node has a *memory allocator* component that is responsible for memory allocations, performing them by calling various Windows API methods. Prior to SQL Server 2012, memory nodes used different memory allocators for single- and multi-page allocations, called *single-page allocator* and *multi-page allocator*. Starting with SQL Server 2012, there is just one memory allocator called *any size page allocator*, which handles both types of allocations. You can track memory usage and allocations on a per-memory node basis with the `sys.dm_os_memory_nodes` view.

There is another key element of SQL Server memory architecture called *memory clerks*. Each major component of SQL Server has its own memory clerk, which works as the proxy between the component and the memory allocator. When the component needs the memory, it requests the corresponding memory clerk, which in turn gets the memory from the memory allocator. Each memory clerk tracks the allocation statistics, which allows you to determine memory usage by the individual components.

Listing 28-15 shows the code that returns the ten largest memory consumers on the server. Figure 28-12 shows the output from one of the production servers. In SQL Server prior to 2012, you should replace the `pages_kb` column with the summary of the `single_page_kb` and `multi_pages_kb` columns due to the different memory allocators SQL Server uses.

Listing 28-15. Analyzing memory clerks (SQL Server 2012 and above)

```
select top 10
    [type] as [Memory Clerk]
    ,convert(decimal(16,3),sum(pages_kb) / 1024.0) as [Memory Usage(MB)]
from sys.dm_os_memory_clerks with (nolock)
group by [type]
order by sum(pages_kb) desc
```

	Memory Clerk	Memory Usage(MB)
1	MEMORYCLERK_SQLBUFFERPOOL	442148.258
2	CACHESTORE_SQLCP	13894.266
3	OBJECTSTORE_LOCK_MANAGER	10886.336
4	USERSTORE_SCHEMAMGR	1313.797
5	MEMORYCLERK_HADR	1027.586
6	CACHESTORE_OBJCP	693.227
7	OBJECTSTORE_XACT_CACHE	427.570
8	MEMORYCLERK_SOSNODE	371.492
9	MEMORYCLERK_SQLSTORENG	202.430
10	MEMORYCLERK_SQLCLR	163.250

Figure 28-12. *Latch statistics*

Some of the common memory clerks are the following:

- `MEMORYCLERCK_SQLBUFFERPOOL` clerk shows the memory usage of the buffer pool. It is normal to have high memory usage by this clerk.
- `CACHESTORE_SQLCP` clerk displays memory usage of ad-hoc, auto-parameterized, and prepared plans. High memory usage by this clerk often indicates a large amount of ad-hoc queries in the system. Check if *Optimize for Ad-hoc Workload* setting is enabled and then parameterize the queries.
- `CACHESTORE_OBJCP` clerk is responsible for memory usage of compiled execution plans for stored procedures, functions, and triggers.
- `CACHESTORE_PHDR` clerk indicates memory usage of bound trees, the structures created by Query Optimizer.
- `USERSTORE_TOKENPERM` clerk shows memory usage of security token store. Some SQL Server versions have known bugs related to `USERSTORE_TOKENPERM` growth. Apply the latest service pack if you experience large memory usage by this clerk. As a temporary solution, you can clear the token store by using the `DBCC FREESYSTEMCACHE('TokenAndPermUserStore')` command.
- `OBJECTSTORE_LOCK_MANAGER` clerk displays the memory usage of the Lock Manager. A large amount of memory consumed by the Lock Manager can indicate a suboptimal transaction strategy in the system; for example, the use of large batch updates in long-running transactions.
- `MEMORYCLERK_SQLQERESERVATIONS` clerk is responsible for query memory grants reservation. A large amount of memory consumed by this clerk indicates excessive memory grants that reduce the size of the buffer pool. It is beneficial to analyze why queries require such memory grants if it happens.

Finally, the `DBCC MEMORYSTATUS` command provides information about SQL Server memory usage along with memory node and memory clerk statistics. Even though this information is very detailed, in many cases it is easier to use the `sys.dm_os_memory_clerks` and `sys.dm_os_memory_nodes` views to perform the filtering, grouping, and aggregation in the queries.

What to Do When the Server Is Not Responding

Situations where SQL Server stops responding, or where it is not accepting user requests, do not happen very often. Nevertheless, they do sometimes happen, and the first and most important rule is to not panic. SQL Server always treats data consistency as its top priority, and it is highly unlikely that something will happen to the data.

As a first step, you should validate that the problem is not an infrastructure-related one. You should check that the server and network are up and running and that the problem is not isolated to a particular client workstation or subset of the network. It is entirely possible that the problem is not related to SQL Server at all. For example, changes in a firewall configuration or a network switch malfunction could block communication between SQL Server and client applications.

Next, you should check the SQL Server error log. Some conditions, such as prolonged worker thread starvation, leave error messages in the log, notifying the system administrator about the problem. Moreover, such conditions could introduce unhandled internal exceptions and mini-dumps. Unfortunately, there is no guarantee that SQL Server will recover after such exceptions, and in some cases you will need to restart it. The key point of a restart, however, is performing a root-cause analysis of the problem. You need to analyze the error logs and default trace, do the research, and, in some cases, open a support case with Microsoft to make sure that the problem is detected and addressed.

■ **Note** Unhandled exceptions often occur because of bugs in SQL Server, which may already be fixed in the most recent service packs and cumulative updates. Consider applying them, and then open a support case with Microsoft CSS if this does not help.

You might need to connect to SQL Server for further troubleshooting. Fortunately, SQL Server 2005 introduced a special connection called *Dedicated Admin Connection (DAC)* that can be used for such a purpose. SQL Server reserves a private scheduler and a small amount of memory for DAC, which will allow you to connect even when SQL Server does not accept regular connections.

By default, DAC is available only locally. In some cases, when a server is completely overloaded, the operating system does not have adequate resources to handle user sessions, which prevents you from using DAC in local mode. You can change the configuration setting to allow a remote DAC connection with the code shown in Listing 28-16. Obviously, it is better to enable this setting during initial server configuration rather than waiting until problems occur.

Listing 28-16. Enabling remote admin connection

```
exec sp_configure 'remote admin connections', 1
go
reconfigure
go
```

You can connect to SQL Server with DAC by using the `ADMIN:` server-name prefix in the Management Studio connection box or with the `-A` option in `sqlcmd`. Only members of the `sysadmin` server role are allowed to connect, and only one session can use a DAC connection at any point in time.

■ **Important** You should use the connection dialog initiated from the Query window when you use DAC from Management Studio. Object Explorer uses multiple database connections by design, and therefore it cannot use DAC. Make sure that Intellisense and other Management Studio plugins are disabled before you attempt this connection.

A DAC connection can utilize a limited amount of resources, and it has a few restrictions on what operations can be done. For example, DAC does not support parallel query execution or backup/restore functions. It is designed for troubleshooting, and you should use DAC only for such a purpose.

We have already discussed worker thread starvation as one reason SQL Server may become unresponsive. Another possibility is *run-away queries*, which consume a major part of the resources on the server. You can detect such queries via the `sys.dm_exec_requests` view, as shown in Listing 28-17.

Listing 28-17. Detecting run-away queries

```
select top 10
    er.session_id, er.start_time, er.cpu_time, er.status, er.command, er.blocking_session_id
    ,er.wait_time, er.wait_type, er.last_wait_type, er.logical_reads
    ,substring(qt.text, (er.statement_start_offset/2)+1,
        (( case er.statement_end_offset
                when -1 then datalength(qt.text)
                else er.statement_end_offset
            end - er.statement_start_offset)/2)+1) as SQL
```

```
from
    sys.dm_exec_requests er with (nolock)
        cross apply sys.dm_exec_sql_text(er.sql_handle) qt
order by cpu_time desc
```

You can terminate a session with a run-away query using the `KILL` command. You should be careful, however, and analyze what the session is doing. SQL Server rolls back the active session transaction when you terminate it, which could be time- and resource-consuming in the case of heavy data modifications. It is entirely possible that allowing a session to finish a task is a faster and better option.

You can also consider using Resource Governor to prevent tasks from consuming all SQL Server resources. This could be especially useful if a server hosts multiple databases that belong to multiple systems. You can separate connections to different systems between resource pools, configured in such a way that leaves some resources available for every system.

Working with Baseline

As you have already observed, I regularly mention the *baseline* in this chapter. Creating a baseline is an essential task for any database and IT professional. It allows you to be proactive and detect problems in the early stages before they become visible and impact system health and performance.

Many performance counters and metrics have very limited use by themselves. Some of them have a threshold or *bad* value that indicates a problem; however, a *good* value does not always guarantee that a system is healthy. It is always beneficial to look at dynamics and trends and monitor how values are changing.

Consider the *page life expectancy* counter. The value of 10,000 is perfectly healthy for a server with 64 GB of memory. However, if it were 50,000 last week, this would indicate that something has changed. Perhaps the last deployment dropped some indexes or introduced nonoptimized queries that triggered a heavy I/O load. Monitoring the page life expectancy value over time allows you to be proactive and to start investigating and addressing the problem before it starts affecting other parts of the system.

Another good example is I/O subsystem performance. Every I/O subsystem has some breaking point where performance starts to drop exponentially with load increase. It is always beneficial to determine the limits before the initial deployment and to monitor how I/O load changes over time, making sure that there is still room to grow. The baseline will help you with monitoring and analysis.

■ **Tip** You can use the DiskSpd utility for stress testing the I/O subsystem before the initial deployment. You can download it from `https://gallery.technet.microsoft.com/DiskSpd-a-robust-storage-6cd2f223`.

There are plenty of tools on the market that can help you automate baseline creation and monitoring. However, you can easily implement it manually by collecting and persisting metrics on a regular basis using various data management objects and Windows performance counters exposed through the `sys.dm_os_performance_counters` view. We have already discussed quite a few of them, and obviously you can expand upon these with other information as needed.

It is very important to capture information for the system workload, which includes the number of connections, number of batches and transactions per second, size of the database, and other similar metrics. This will help you analyze trends, correlate workload with system load, and perform capacity analysis when needed.

It is also very beneficial to capture information about the performance of the system-critical parts of the code. Application developers can collect and persist the response time of the most critical queries and/or stored procedures, which will allow you to monitor trends, making sure that critical code performs satisfactorily all of the time.

Finally, creating a baseline is a very helpful first step in system troubleshooting. It helps you evaluate that you achieved desirable results, and you can then demonstrate them to management or customers.

Summary

Databases do not live in a vacuum. They are a part of a large ecosystem that includes various hardware and software components. The slowness and unresponsiveness of client applications are not necessarily database- or SQL Server–related. The root cause of the problem can be anywhere in the system, from hardware misconfiguration to incorrect application code.

It is important to check the entire system infrastructure as an initial step in the troubleshooting process. This includes the performance characteristics of the hardware, network topology and throughput, operating system and SQL Server configuration, processes, and databases running on the server.

SQL Server consists of several major components, including the protocol layer, query processor, storage engine, utilities, and SQL Server Operating System (SQLOS). SQLOS is the layer between Windows and all other SQL Server components, and it is responsible for scheduling, resource management, and several other low-level tasks.

SQLOS creates a number of schedulers equal to the number of logical processors in the system. Every scheduler is responsible for managing a set of workers that perform a job. Every task is assigned to one or more workers for the duration of the execution.

Tasks stay in one of three major states during execution: *running* (currently executing on scheduler), *runnable* (waiting for scheduler to execute), and *suspended* (waiting for the resource). SQL Server tracks the cumulative waiting time for the different types of waits and exposes this information to the users. Wait statistics analysis is a common performance troubleshooting technique that analyzes top system wait types and eliminates the root causes of waits.

It is essential that you create a baseline by collecting and monitoring various performance and load metrics in the system. A baseline helps you to be proactive in detecting and resolving problems in the early stages before they start affecting the users. It shows how system behavior and load changes over time, which helps in capacity analysis and prevents situations where a system outgrows the hardware.

CHAPTER 29

Query Store

Query Store is a new SQL Server 2016 component that collects execution plans and runtime statistics for the queries in the system. It helps you to detect suboptimal queries, shows how execution plans evolve over time, and allows you to force specific plans in order to address parameter sniffing–related issues.

This chapter provides an overview of the Query Store, explains how it is integrated into the query processing pipeline, and demonstrates how you can use it during system monitoring and performance troubleshooting.

Why Query Store?

Even though every database system is unique, there are several common tasks and problems each database professional has to deal with. Performance tuning is, perhaps, the most common one.

Performance tuning is a complex process. It covers many topics, such as hardware, OS and SQL Server setup and configuration, and application and database design, among other things. Query optimization is one of the top tasks in the list. The key challenge here is choosing what queries to optimize. It is neither possible nor feasible to optimize all queries in the system, and you need to focus on those that will provide you with the best return on investment. In reality, this means frequently executed queries that introduce heavy I/O activity and/or consume a large amount of CPU power and memory.

It is not always easy to detect such queries. Even though SQL Server keeps runtime execution statistics for cached execution plans, it has a few limitations. Plans can be removed from the cache for various reasons or not be cached at all; for example; when statement-level recompile is used. Finally, plan cache runtime statistics are not persisted in the database and will be cleared upon SQL Server restart.

You can address some of those limitations by capturing query runtime statistics with Extended Events; however, it will require complex analysis afterward and can also introduce performance overhead on already busy servers.

The second common type of problem database professionals have to address is performance regression introduced by parameter sniffing. As you will remember from Chapter 26, SQL Server recompiles queries because of statistics updates, and atypical parameter values at recompilation can lead to inefficient execution plans being cached and reused.

It is possible to proactively protect critical queries from such issues. However, this usually requires index or query hints, plan guides, or code changes. Any of these approaches has downsides, especially in the maintainability arena. In reality, database professionals usually deal with these problems reactively, after they have occurred in the system and users have reported performance issues.

Fortunately, the Query Store helps to address both of these challenges. You can consider it to be the *SQL Server flight data recorder*; when the Query Store is enabled, SQL Server captures and persists the runtime statistics and execution plans of the queries in the database. It shows you how execution plans evolve over time and allows you to force a specific execution plan for the query.

D. Korotkevitch, *Pro SQL Server Internals*, DOI 10.1007/978-1-4842-1964-5_29

Query Store is available in every edition of SQL Server 2016 and in Microsoft Azure SQL Databases. It introduces some overhead to SQL Server when it is enabled; however, such overhead is relatively small. We will discuss how to monitor such overhead later in the chapter.

Query Store Configuration

Query Store is a database-level feature and is disabled by default. You can enable it in SQL Server Management Studio (SSMS) or in T-SQL with the `ALTER DATABASE SET QUERY_STORE = ON` command.

Query Store can run in two operation modes. In the default, `READ_WRITE` mode, SQL Server collects and persists execution plans and runtime statistics in the Query Store and allows you to work with it. In `READ_ONLY` mode, you can query the data from the Query Store; however, SQL Server does not collect any new information there. You can set the operation mode using the `ALTER DATABASE SET QUERY_STORE (OPERATION_MODE = mode)` command.

The SSMS interface is a bit confusing. You can access the Query Store configuration through *Query Store* page of the *Database Properties* window. There are two Operation Mode settings available within the *General* group, as shown in Figure 29-1. *Operational Mode (Actual)* shows whether the Query Store is enabled as well as its current mode. *Operational Mode (Requested)* allows you to choose the new value or disable the Query Store, which will take effect after you apply the changes.

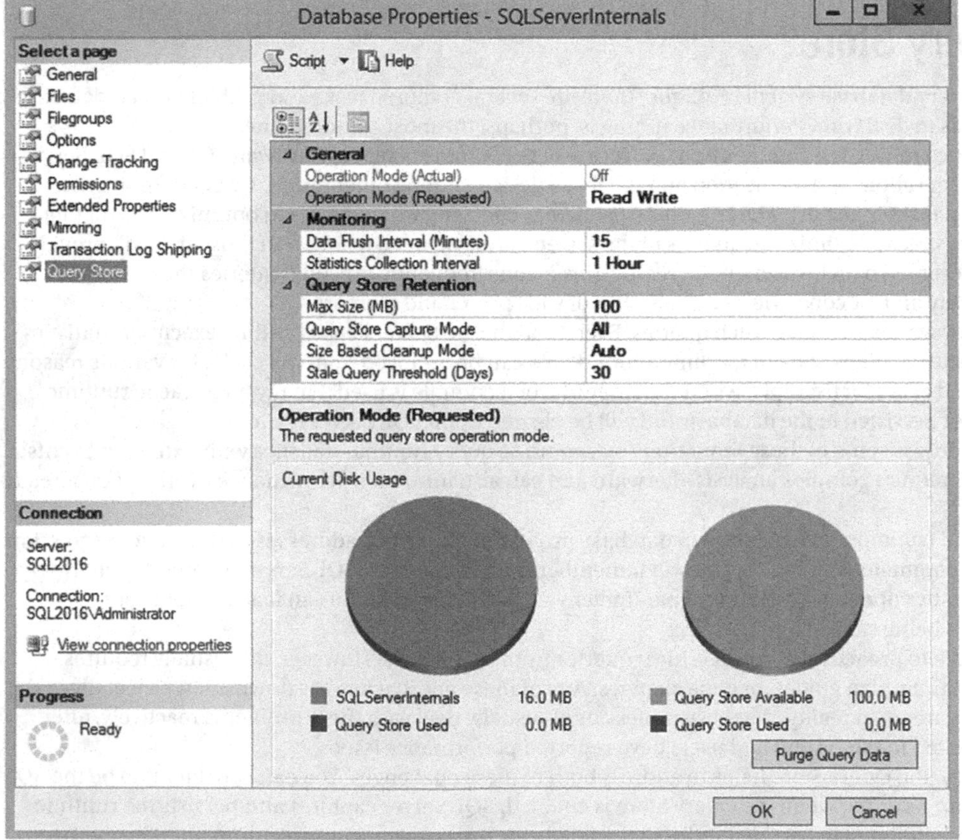

Figure 29-1. *Query Store configuration in SSMS*

In order to reduce the overhead, the Query Store keeps recently captured information in the in-memory cache, flushing it to disk based on the schedule defined by the DATA_FLUSH_INTERVAL_SECONDS setting (*Data Flush Interval (Minutes)* in SSMS), with a default value of 15 minutes. In a nutshell, this value controls the amount of captured data, which will be lost in the event of a SQL Server crash.

The Query Store aggregates runtime statistics over a fixed time interval controlled by the INTERVAL_LENGTH_MINUTES setting (*Statistics Collection Interval* in SSMS), with a default value of 60 minutes. Reducing this interval provides you with better granularity; however, it could increase the disk space required to store the information. Unfortunately, SQL Server does not allow you to specify an arbitrary value and you should choose one of the following: 1, 5, 10, 15, 30, 60, or 1440 minutes.

You can control the size of Query Store's on-disk tables with the MAX_STORAGE_SIZE_MB (*Max Size (MB)* in SSMS) setting. Once the size is reached, the Query Store becomes read-only. By default, SQL Server 2016 RTM allows Query Store to use up to 100 MB of disk space. You should remember that Query Store tables are placed into the primary filegroup and take this into consideration when you design database layout and your Disaster Recovery strategy.

The Query Store cleanup policy can be configured with STALE_QUERY_THRESHOLD_DAYS (*Stale Query Threshold (Days)* in SSMS) and SIZE_BASED_CLEANUP_POLICY (*Size Based Cleanup Mode* in SSMS) settings. The first one specifies how long information is retained in the Query Store. The second controls the automatic cleanup process, which runs when the Query Store is about 80 percent full and removes information about the least expensive queries.

■ **Important** SQL Server 2016 RTM has a bug that prevents automatic data cleanup in editions other than Enterprise and Developer. You should disable it in the affected editions by using the ALTER DATABASE SET QUERY_STORE (CLEANUP_POLICY = (STALE_QUERY_THRESHOLD_DAYS = 0), SIZE_BASED_CLEANUP_MODE = OFF) command and implement manual cleanup, as we will discuss later in this chapter. The bug is fixed in CU1.

The QUERY_CAPTURE_MODE setting (*Query Store Capture Mode* in SSMS) controls which queries are captured. It has one of three values: ALL, NONE, or AUTO. The first two values are self-explanatory. The last one triggers an internal algorithm that filters out insignificant queries.

Finally, the MAX_PLAN_PER_QUERY setting sets a limit on the number of plans maintained for each query. This setting is unavailable in SSMS.

The sys.database_query_store_options view provides you with information about current Query Store configuration settings and its size.

Query Store Internals

Internally, the Query Store consists of two related parts: *plan store* and *runtime statistics store*. SQL Server interacts with them during both query compilation and execution stages. When a query is compiling, SQL Server works with the plan store, updating its data and checking if there is a forced plan available. During query execution, SQL Server updates its execution statistics in the runtime statistics store.

As you already know, each store consists of both an in-memory cache and disk data. The new information is placed into the cache and asynchronously written to disk based on a schedule defined by the DATA_FLUSH_INTERVAL_SECONDS setting. In-memory cache can be also flushed manually with the sys.sp_query_store_flush_db stored procedure. SQL Server combines the data from both sources when you query the data from the Query Store.

Figure 29-2 illustrates a high-level SQL Server Query Store workflow.

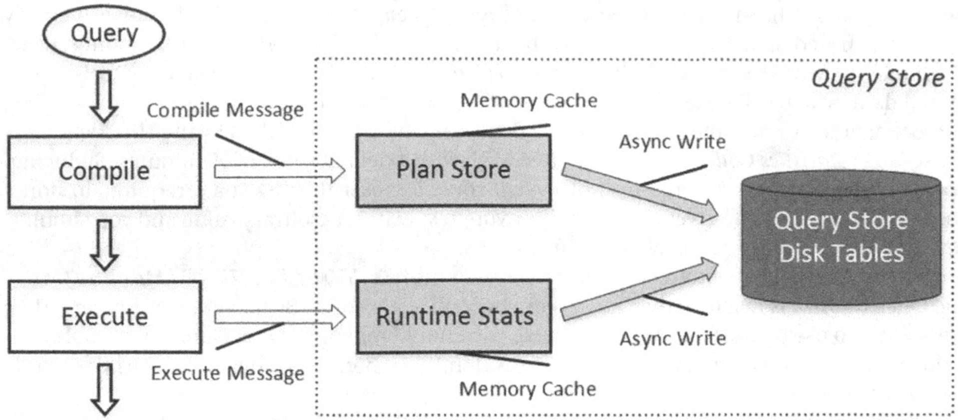

Figure 29-2. *High-level SQL Server Query Store workflow*

The Query Store is fully integrated into the query processing pipeline, as shown in Figure 29-3.

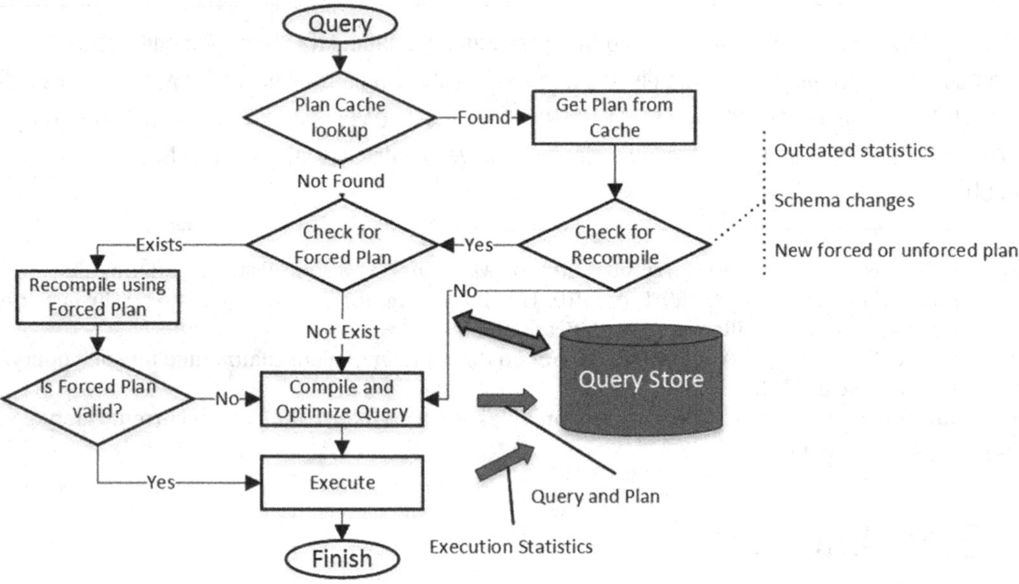

Figure 29-3. *Query-processing pipeline*

When a query needs to be executed, SQL Server looks up the execution plan in the plan cache. If a plan is found, SQL Server checks if the query needs to be recompiled due to a statistics update or other factors, or if there is a new forced plan created or old forced plan dropped from the Query Store.

During compilation, SQL Server checks if the query has a forced plan available. When that happens, the query essentially gets compiled with the forced plan, similar to when the `USE PLAN` hint is used. If the resulting plan is valid, it is cached in the plan cache and reused afterward.

If the forced plan is no longer valid—for example, when the user has dropped an index referenced in the forced plan—SQL Server does not fail the query, but rather compiles it again without the forced plan and caches the new plan afterward. The Query Store, on the other hand, persists both plans, marking the forced plan as invalid. All of this happens transparently to the applications.

You can access the Query Store data through several views, as shown in Figure 29-4.

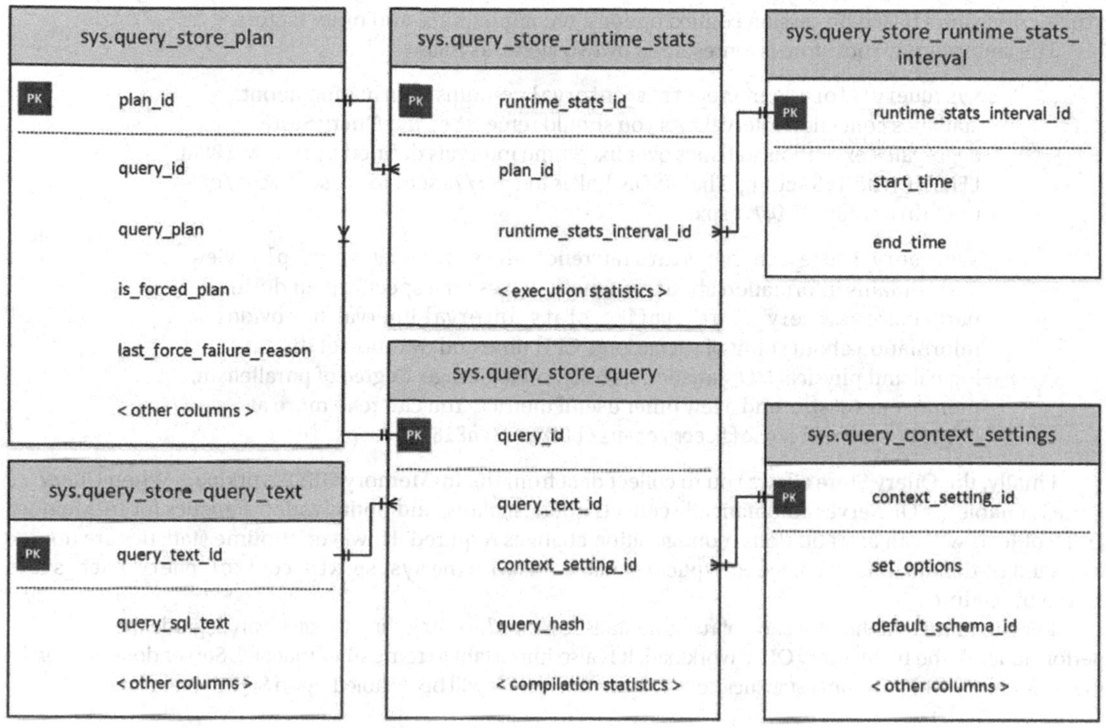

Figure 29-4. *Query Store views*

The plan store-related views include the following:

> `sys.query_store_query` provides information about queries, their compilation statistics, and last execution time. You can read about this view at `https://msdn.microsoft.com/en-us/library/dn818156.aspx`.

> `sys.query_store_query_text` shows information about query text. More information about this view is available at `https://msdn.microsoft.com/en-us/library/dn818159.aspx`.

> `sys.query_context_setting` contains information about context settings associated with the query. It includes `SET` options, default schema for the session, language, and other attributes. As you will remember from Chapter 26, SQL Server generates and caches separate execution plans based on these settings. This level of detail helps you to diagnose cases where the plan cache contains a large number of plans for the same query. The documentation is available at `https://msdn.microsoft.com/en-us/library/dn818148.aspx`.

`sys.query_store_plan` provides information about query execution plans. The `is_forced_plan` column indicates if the plan is forced. `Last_force_failure_reason` provides the reason why the forced plan was not applied to the query. You can read about this view at `https://msdn.microsoft.com/en-us/library/dn818155.aspx`.

As you can see, each query can have multiple entries in the `sys.query_store_query` and `sys.query_store_plan` views based on session context options, recompilations, and other factors.

The runtime statistics store is represented by two views, as follows:

`sys.query_store_runtime_stats_interval` contains information about statistics collection intervals. As you should remember, the Query Store aggregates execution statistics over fixed time intervals defined by the `INTERVAL_LENGTH_MINUTES` setting. The MSDN link is `https://msdn.microsoft.com/en-us/library/dn818147.aspx`.

`sys.query_store_runtime_stats` references the `sys.query_store_plan` view and contains information about runtime statistics for a specific plan during a particular `sys.query_store_runtime_stats_interval` interval. It provides information about count of executions, CPU time and duration of the calls, logical and physical I/O statistics, transaction log usage, degree of parallelism, memory grant size, and a few other useful metrics. You can read more at `https://msdn.microsoft.com/en-us/library/dn818158.aspx`.

Finally, the Query Store allows you to collect data from the In-Memory OLTP workload. When Query Store is enabled, SQL Server automatically collects queries, plans, and optimization statistics for In-Memory OLTP objects without any additional configuration changes required. However, runtime statistics are not collected by default, and you need to explicitly enable this with the `sys.sp_xtp_control_query_exec_stats` stored procedure.

Keep in mind that the collection of runtime statistics introduces overhead, which can degrade the performance of the In-Memory OLTP workload. It is also important to remember that SQL Server does not persist the In-Memory OLTP runtime statistics collection setting, and it will be disabled upon SQL Server restart.

■ **Note** We will discuss In-Memory OLTP in detail in Part VIII of this book.

Usage Scenarios

SQL Server provides you with a rich set of tools with which to work with Query Store in both SSMS and T-SQL. Let's look at them in detail.

As a first step, let's collect some data and emulate performance regression resulting from parameter sniffing. I will use the table and stored procedure defined in Listings 26-1 and 26-2 in Chapter 26, calling them in two sessions, as shown in Listing 29-1.

Listing 29-1. Emulating peformance regression resulting from parameter sniffing

```
-- Session 1
while 1 = 1
begin
    exec dbo.GetAverageSalary @Country='USA';
    waitfor delay '0:00:01.000';
end;

-- Session 2
dbcc freeproccache;
exec dbo.GetAverageSalary @Country='CANADA';
```

Working with Query Store in SSMS

After you have enabled Query Store in the database, you can see the *Query Store* folder in the Object Explorer, as shown in Figure 29-5. This folder contains four interactive reports that allow you to analyze collected data, force execution plans for the queries, and perform several other actions.

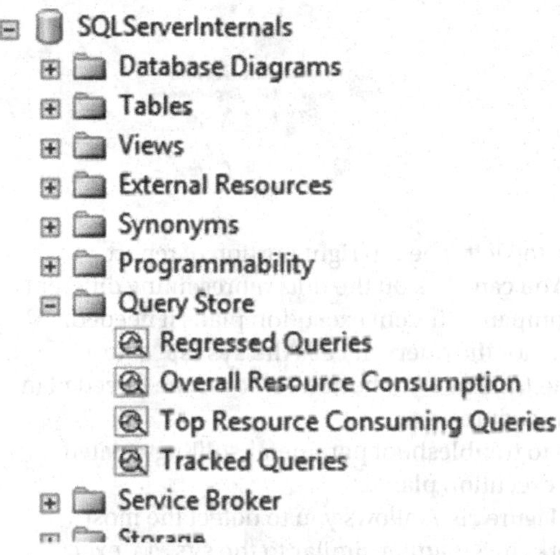

Figure 29-5. *Query Store folder in Object Explorer*

The *Regressed Queries* report, shown in Figure 29-6, displays the queries that have performance regressed over time. You can configure regression criteria and a time frame for the analysis, along with several other parameters.

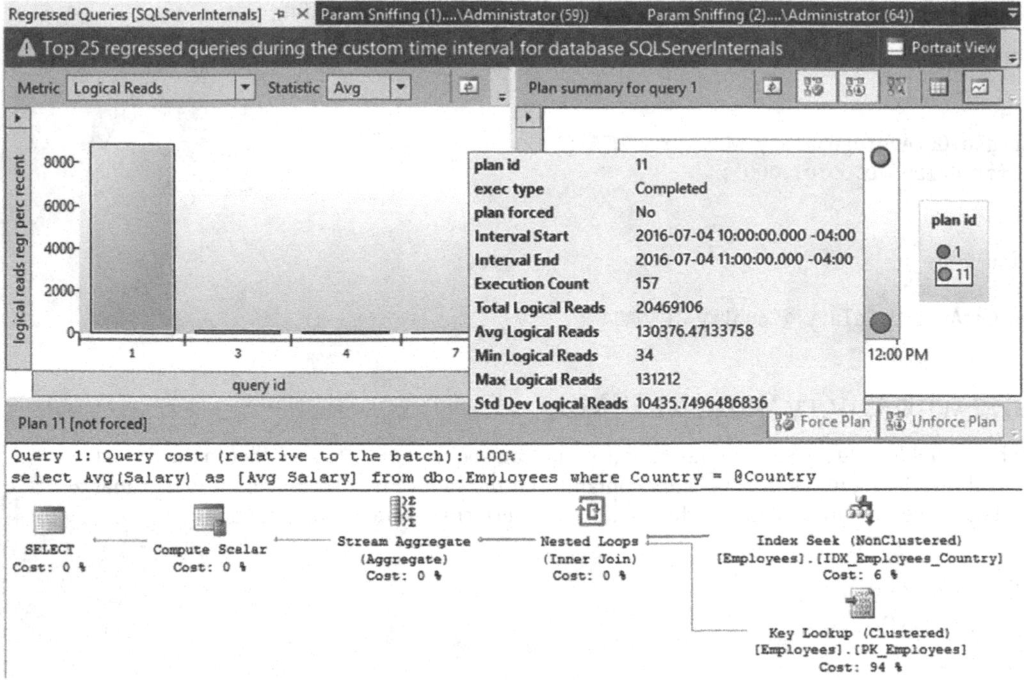

Figure 29-6. *Regressed Queries report*

You can choose the query to display in the graph on the top left. The top right portion of report illustrates collected execution plans for the selected query. You can click on the dots representing different execution plans and see them at the bottom. You can also compare different execution plans if needed.

The *Force Plan* button allows you to force a selected plan for the query. It calls the `sys.sp_query_store_force_plan` stored procedure internally. Similarly, the *Unforce Plan* button removes the forced plan by calling the `sys.sp_query_store_unforce_plan` stored procedure.

The Regressed Queries report is a great tool with which to troubleshoot parameter sniffing-related issues in the system and quickly fix them by forcing specific execution plans.

The *Top Resource Consuming Queries* report, shown in Figure 29-7, allows you to detect the most resource intensive queries in the system. In a nutshell, it works in a manner similar to the `sys.dm_exec_query_stats` view; however, it does not have that view's limitations, such as dependency on the plan cache. This report is a great tool that helps you to quickly identify optimization targets in the system.

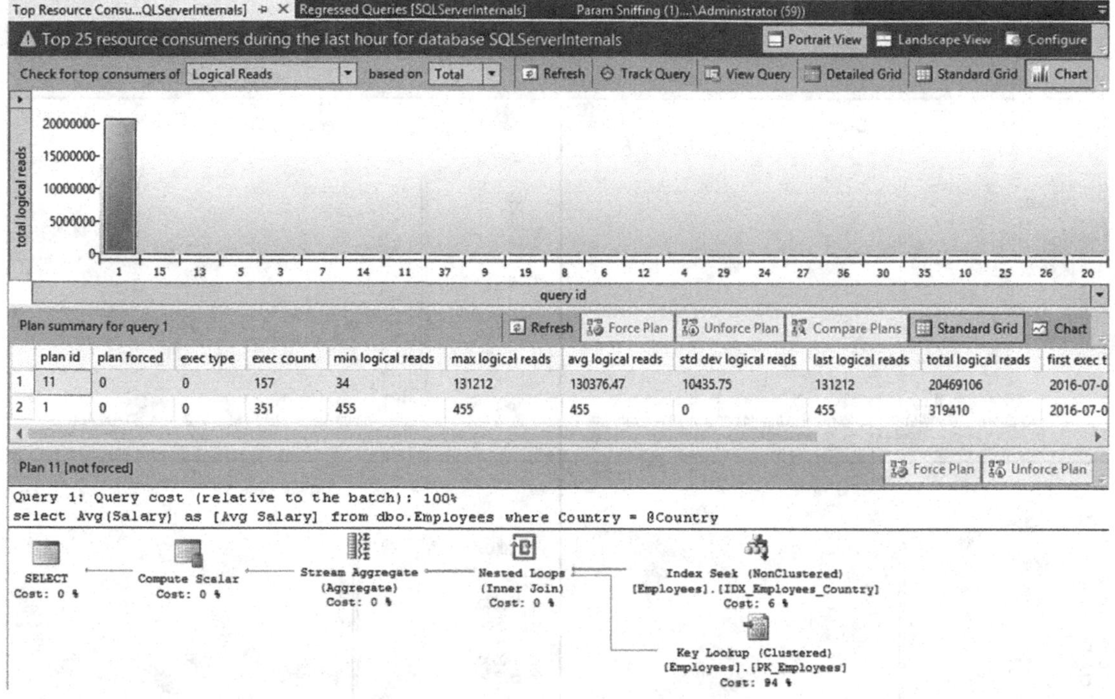

Figure 29-7. *Top Resource Consuming Queries report*

The *Overall Resource Consumption* report shows you statistics and resource usage of the workload over time intervals. It allows you to detect and analyze spikes in resource usage and drill down to the queries that introduce such spikes. Figure 29-8 illustrates the output of the report.

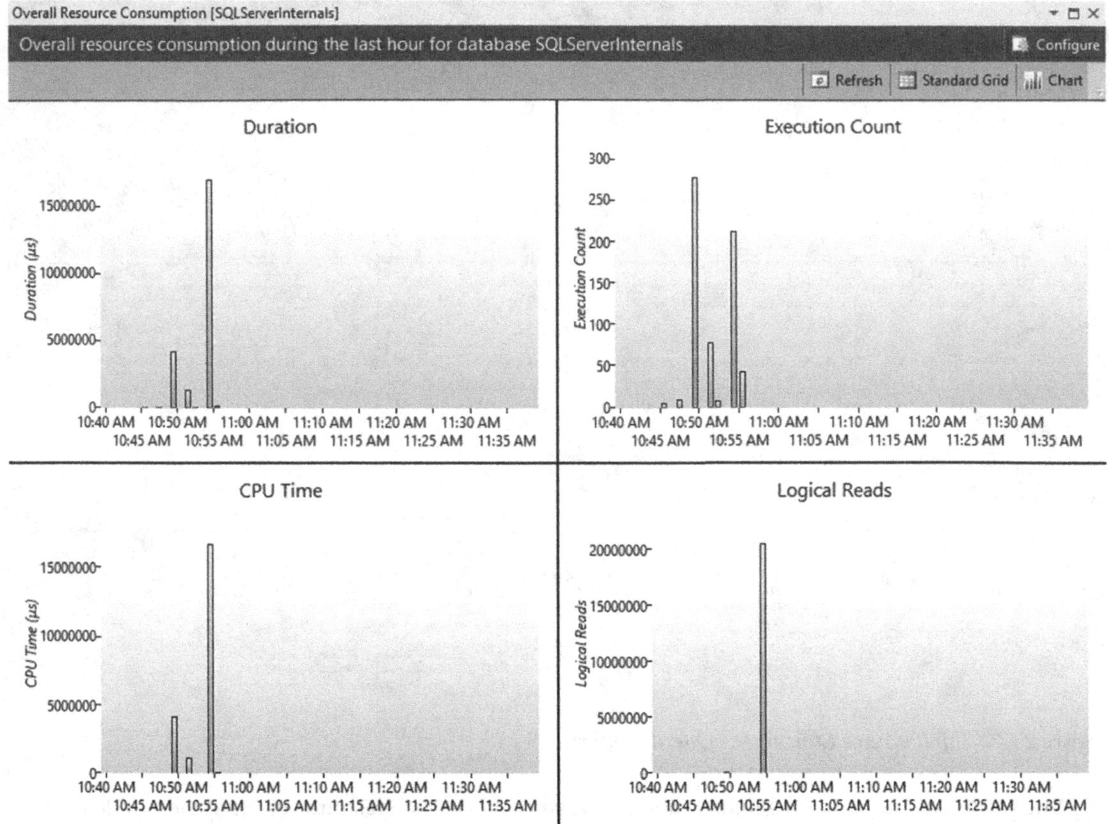

***Figure 29-8.** Overall Resource Consumption report*

The *Tracked Queries* report allows you to monitor execution plans and statistics for individual queries. It provides similar information as the *Regressed Queries* and *Top Resource Consuming Queries* reports but in the scope of individual queries. Figure 29-9 illustrates this.

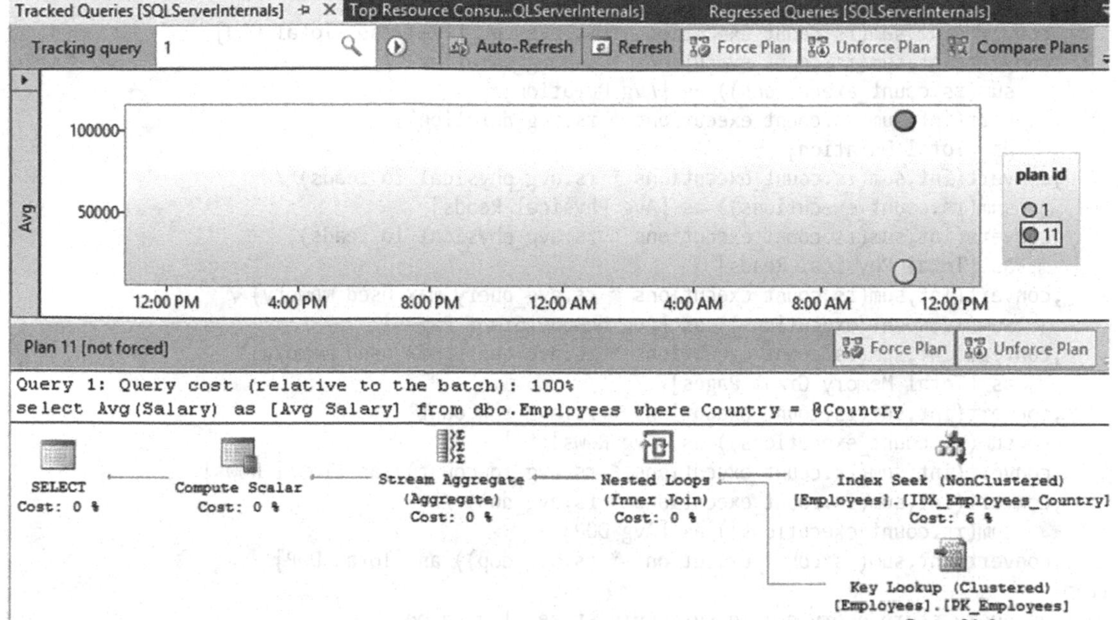

Figure 29-9. *Tracked Queries report*

Working with Query Store from T-SQL

Even though SSMS provides a rich set of tools with which to work with the Query Store, in some cases it is beneficial to use T-SQL and work with the Query Store data directly. Let's look at several common scenarios in which this is helpful.

The first very common task is searching for the most resource intensive queries while choosing targets for further performance optimizations. You already saw how to get execution statistics from the `sys.dm_exec_query_stats` view in the previous chapter. As you remember, this view depends on the plan cache, and you often need to cross-check the data with Extended Events during analysis. Query Store can provide you with similar information without any plan cache dependencies, which dramatically simplify the process.

Listing 29-2 illustrates the code that returns information for 50 recent, most I/O-intensive queries in the system. As you already know, the Query Store aggregates execution statistics over time intervals, and therefore you need to aggregate data from multiple `sys.query_store_runtime_stats` rows. The output will include data for all intervals that ended within the last 24 hours, grouping it by queries and their execution plans.

Listing 29-2. Getting information about most expensive queries

```
select top 50
    q.query_id, qt.query_sql_text, qp.plan_id, qp.query_plan
    ,sum(rs.count_executions) as [Execution Cnt]
    ,convert(int,sum(rs.count_executions *
        (rs.avg_logical_io_reads + avg_logical_io_writes)) /
            sum(rs.count_executions)) as [Avg IO]
    ,convert(int,sum(rs.count_executions *
        (rs.avg_logical_io_reads + avg_logical_io_writes))) as [Total IO]
    ,convert(int,sum(rs.count_executions * rs.avg_cpu_time) /
```

```
        sum(rs.count_executions)) as [Avg CPU]
    ,convert(int,sum(rs.count_executions * rs.avg_cpu_time)) as [Total CPU]
    ,convert(int,sum(rs.count_executions * rs.avg_duration) /
        sum(rs.count_executions)) as [Avg Duration]
    ,convert(int,sum(rs.count_executions * rs.avg_duration))
        as [Total Duration]
    ,convert(int,sum(rs.count_executions * rs.avg_physical_io_reads) /
        sum(rs.count_executions)) as [Avg Physical Reads]
    ,convert(int,sum(rs.count_executions * rs.avg_physical_io_reads))
        as [Total Physical Reads]
    ,convert(int,sum(rs.count_executions * rs.avg_query_max_used_memory) /
        sum(rs.count_executions)) as [Avg Memory Grant Pages]
    ,convert(int,sum(rs.count_executions * rs.avg_query_max_used_memory))
        as [Total Memory Grant Pages]
    ,convert(int,sum(rs.count_executions * rs.avg_rowcount) /
        sum(rs.count_executions)) as [Avg Rows]
    ,convert(int,sum(rs.count_executions * rs.avg_rowcount)) as [Total Rows]
    ,convert(int,sum(rs.count_executions * rs.avg_dop) /
        sum(rs.count_executions)) as [Avg DOP]
    ,convert(int,sum(rs.count_executions * rs.avg_dop)) as [Total DOP]
from
    sys.query_store_query q join sys.query_store_plan qp on
        q.query_id = qp.query_id
    join sys.query_store_query_text qt on
        q.query_text_id = qt.query_text_id
    join sys.query_store_runtime_stats rs on
        qp.plan_id = rs.plan_id
    join sys.query_store_runtime_stats_interval rsi on
        rs.runtime_stats_interval_id = rsi.runtime_stats_interval_id
where
    rsi.end_time >= dateadd(day,-1,getdate())
group by
    q.query_id, qt.query_sql_text, qp.plan_id, qp.query_plan
order by
    [Avg IO] desc;
```

Obviously, you can choose different criteria than average I/O. You can also add predicates to the WHERE and/or HAVING clauses of the query to narrow down the results. For example, you can add the filter by DOP if you want to detect queries that use parallelism in OLTP environments, then optimize them or fine-tune the *Cost Threshold for Parallelism* value.

■ **Important** SQL Server 2016 RTM has a bug that sometimes corrupts the text representation of the execution plan returned by the sys.query_store_plan view when it is joined with the other views in the same statement. You can implement a workaround by obtaining the plan_id first and then querying the sys.query_store_plan view, without any joins involved. The bug is fixed in one of the CU releases.

Listing 29-3 returns information about query regressions that occurred in the last 72 hours. It uses a two-times increase of the average query duration as the regression criteria and returns one row per query with the plans that have the lowest and highest average durations. You can use query_id from the output to perform further analysis of the regression.

Listing 29-3. Getting information about regressions

```
;with Regressions(query_id, query_text_id, plan1_id, plan2_id, plan1
    ,plan2, dur1, dur2, row_num)
as
(
    select
        q.query_id, q.query_text_id, qp1.plan_id, q2.plan_id
        ,qp1.query_plan, q2.query_plan, rs1.avg_duration, q2.avg_duration
        ,row_number() over (partition by qp1.plan_id order by rs1.avg_duration)
    from
        sys.query_store_query q join sys.query_store_plan qp1 on
            q.query_id = qp1.query_id
        join sys.query_store_runtime_stats rs1 on
            qp1.plan_id = rs1.plan_id
        join sys.query_store_runtime_stats_interval rsi1 on
            rs1.runtime_stats_interval_id = rsi1.runtime_stats_interval_id
        cross apply
        (
            select top 1
                qp2.query_plan, qp2.plan_id, rs2.avg_duration
            from
                sys.query_store_plan qp2
                    join sys.query_store_runtime_stats rs2 on
                        qp2.plan_id = rs2.plan_id
                join sys.query_store_runtime_stats_interval rsi2 on
                        rs2.runtime_stats_interval_id =
                            rsi2.runtime_stats_interval_id
            where
                q.query_id = qp2.query_id and
                qp1.plan_id <> qp2.plan_id and
                rsi1.start_time < rsi2.start_time and
                rs1.avg_duration * 2 <= rs2.avg_duration
            order by
                rs2.avg_duration desc
        ) q2
    where
        rsi1.start_time >= dateadd(day,-3,getdate())
)
select
    r.query_id, qt.query_sql_text, r.plan1_id, r.plan1, r.plan2_id, r.plan2
    ,r.dur1, r.dur2
from
    Regressions r join sys.query_store_query_text qt  on
        r.query_text_id = qt.query_text_id
where
    r.row_num = 1
order by
    r.dur2 / r.dur1 desc;
```

You can also use the Query Store to detect queries that pollute the plan cache. Listing 29-4 illustrates how you can get information about queries that generate multiple execution plans because of different context settings. The two most common conditions when it happens are sessions that use different SET options and queries that reference objects without schema names.

Listing 29-4. Queries with multiple context settings

```
select
    q.query_id, qt.query_sql_text
    ,count(distinct q.context_settings_id) as [Context Setting Cnt]
    ,count(distinct qp.plan_id) as [Plan Count]
from
    sys.query_store_query q join sys.query_store_query_text qt on
        q.query_text_id = qt.query_text_id
    join sys.query_store_plan qp on
        q.query_id = qp.query_id
group by
    q.query_id, qt.query_sql_text
having
    count(distinct q.context_settings_id) > 1
order by
    count(distinct q.context_settings_id);
```

Listing 29-5 shows how to find similar queries that have duplicated query_hash values and a low execution count. Usually, these queries belong to a non-parameterized ad-hoc workload in the system. You should parameterize these queries in the code, or, if that is impossible, you can consider forcing parameterization on the database level or with plan guides, as we discussed in Chapter 26.

Listing 29-5. Detecting queries with the same hash

```
select top 100
    q.query_hash
    ,count(*) as [Query Count]
    ,avg(rs.count_executions) as [Avg Exec Count]
from
    sys.query_store_query q join sys.query_store_plan qp on
        q.query_id = qp.query_id
    join sys.query_store_runtime_stats rs on
        qp.plan_id = rs.plan_id
group by
    q.query_hash
having
    count(*) > 1
order by
    [Avg Exec Count] asc, [Query Count] desc
```

As you can see, the information from Query Store provides you with endless possibilities for analysis and performance tuning in your system.

Managing and Monitoring Query Store

Even though Query Store should not introduce noticeable performance overhead to the system, it is important to monitor its health and performance impact. This will allow you to fine-tune Query Store parameters in a way that minimizes performance overhead and provides you with granular enough data for analysis.

The Query Store size depends on the data retention policy, which is controlled by the STALE_QUERY_THRESHOLD_DAYS and SIZE_BASED_CLEANUP_POLICY settings, and the collection mode, which is specified by the QUERY_CAPTURE_MODE and MAX_PLAN_PER_QUERY settings. Moreover, the size of the runtime statistics store greatly depends on the aggregation interval, which is defined by the INTERVAL_LENGTH_MINUTES value. The shorter the aggregation interval is, the more data there will be saved to the store.

It is important to define the aggregation interval in the way that fits your needs. Keeping the INTERVAL_LENGTH_MINUTES value unnecessarily small generates an excessive amount of data, which makes analysis more complicated. For example, if you want to create a general baseline of your system, an aggregation interval of one day would suffice. However, if you need a detailed analysis of how the workload changes during the day, you should use one hour, or even lower intervals. As usual, the key is avoiding the collection of unnecessary information in the system.

You can analyze the size of the Query Store and its state by using the sys.database_query_store_options view, as shown in Listing 29-6. You should monitor the Query Store's free space by analyzing the current_storage_size_mb and max_storage_size_mb values. Remember: Query Store will switch to read-only mode when it is full.

Listing 29-6. Analyzing Query Store state

```
select actual_state_desc, desired_state_desc, current_storage_size_mb
    ,max_storage_size_mb, readonly_reason, interval_length_minutes
    ,stale_query_threshold_days, size_based_cleanup_mode_desc
    ,query_capture_mode_desc
from sys.database_query_store_options
```

You can purge data from the Query Store by using the ALTER DATABASE SET QUERY_STORE CLEAR statement, or in Management Studio. Alternatively, you can clear the Query Store on a per-query basis by using the sys.sp_query_store_remove_query stored procedure, as shown in Listing 29-7. This code clears all queries that are older than three days and were executed only once. On a side note, the sys.sp_query_store_remove_plan stored procedure allows you to remove an individual plan from the Query Store.

Listing 29-7. Removing queries from the Query Store

```
declare
    @RecId int = -1
    ,@QueryId int
declare
    @Queries table
    (
        RecId int not null identity(1,1) primary key,
        QueryId int not null
    )
```

```
insert into @Queries(QueryId)
    select p.query_id
    from sys.query_store_plan p join sys.query_store_runtime_stats rs on
        p.plan_id = rs.plan_id
    group by
        p.query_id
    having
        sum(rs.count_executions) < 2 and
        max(rs.last_execution_time) < dateadd(day,-72,getdate());

while 1 = 1
begin
    select top 1 @RecId = RecId, @QueryID = QueryId
    from @Queries
    where RecId > @RecId
    order by RecID;

    if @@rowcount = 0
        break;
    exec sys.sp_query_store_remove_query @QueryID;
end;
```

There are several ways in which you can monitor Query Store performance. There are several performance counters in the *SQL Server:Query Store* object that allow you to track Query Store CPU usage and disk activity.

The Query Store exposes a large number of Extended Events. One of them, `query_store_plan_forcing_failed`, fires in situations where a forced plan cannot be applied. An instance where it could happen is when changing the database name. SQL Server keeps execution plans using a three-part object reference, and renaming the database would invalidate the plans.

Finally, SQL Server 2016 RTM exposes 19 Query Store-related wait types, which you can identify by the `QDS` prefix in the name. These waits should not be present in the system in a large amount, with the exception of `QDS_PERSIST_TASK_MAIN_LOOP_SLEEP` and `QDS_ASYNC_QUEUE` waits. These waits are normal, and you should filter them out as non-essential waits during wait statistics analysis.

Summary

The Query Store is SQL Server 2016's "flight data recorder" that captures execution plans and statistics for the queries in the system. It is fully integrated into the query processing pipeline and does not depend on the plan cache.

Internally, the Query Store consists of two stores: the plan store, which contains information about execution plans, and the runtime statistics store, which collects runtime execution statistics aggregated by specific time intervals. Both stores consist of in-memory cache and disk tables. The newly collected data is stored in-memory and flushed to disk based on a schedule. The Query Store disk tables are stored in the `primary` filegroup.

The Query Store is extremely helpful when you need to address parameter sniffing-related performance issues. It shows you how plans evolve over time and allows you to force a specific execution plan to a query. You can work with the Query Store through the set of interactive reports available in Management Studio or though the set of database views from T-SQL.

The Query Store should not introduce noticeable performance overhead to the system. You could monitor its impact through the set of performance counters and Extended Events. You should also prevent the Query Store from reaching its maximum size and becoming read-only, which can happen if automatic cleanup tasks are disabled.

PART VI

Inside the Transaction Log

CHAPTER 30

Transaction Log Internals

As you already know, every database in SQL Server has one or more transaction log files in addition to data files. The transaction log stores information about all of the changes made in the database, and it allows SQL Server to recover databases to transactionally consistent states in case of an unexpected shutdown or crash.

In this chapter, we will examine the internal structure of the transaction log, discuss how SQL Server logs data modifications, and review how it performs database crash recovery. We will also cover how to diagnose excessive transaction log growth and discuss a few best practices related to log management and I/O file placement.

Data Modifications, Logging, and Recovery

SQL Server always keeps databases in a transactionally consistent state. Data modifications done from within transactions must either be committed or be rolled back in full. SQL Server never allows data to be transactionally inconsistent by applying just a subset of the changes from uncommitted transactions.

This is true even when SQL Server shuts down unexpectedly. Every time SQL Server restarts, it runs a recovery process on every database in the instance. SQL Server rolls back (*undo*) all changes from uncommitted transactions and re-applies (*redo*) all changes done by committed transactions if they had not been saved into data files at the time of the shutdown or crash.

The same process happens when you restore a database from the backup. There is no guarantee that all transactions had been completed at the time the backup was run. Therefore, SQL Server needs to recover the database as the final step of the restore process.

The transaction log guarantees the transactional consistency of the data in the database. It consists of the stream of *log records* generated by data modification operations. Every log record has a unique, auto-incrementing *log sequence number (LSN)*, and it also describes the data change. The log record includes information about the operation and affected row; the old and new version of the data; the transaction that performed the modification; and so forth. Moreover, some internal operations, such as `CHECKPOINT`, generate their own log records.

Every data page keeps the LSN of the last log record that modified it. At the recovery stage, SQL Server can compare the LSNs of the log records from both the log and the data pages and find out if the most recent changes were saved to the data files. There is enough information stored in a log record to undo or redo the operation if needed.

SQL Server uses *write-ahead logging*, which guarantees that log records are written to the log file before dirty data pages are saved to the database. In Chapter 1, I mentioned that log records are saved synchronously with data modifications, while data pages are saved asynchronously during the `CHECKPOINT` process. That is not 100 percent accurate, however. SQL Server caches log records in a small memory cache called the *log buffer*, saving multiple log records at once. This helps reduce the number of physical I/O operations required.

Internally, the log buffer consists of 128 60KB structures called *log blocks*. SQL Server writes the log block to the transaction log file in a single I/O operation. This does not mean, however, that SQL Server waits

D. Korotkevitch, *Pro SQL Server Internals*, DOI 10.1007/978-1-4842-1964-5_30

until the entire log block is full; the size of the data in the write request may vary from 512 bytes to 60 KB. Moreover, SQL Server can have multiple outstanding log write requests in the queue. The maximum number of allowed requests depends on the SQL Server version.

Unfortunately, SQL Server documentation is a bit confusing and often references log blocks as log buffers, stating that every database has many of them. In the end, what matters is that every database caches log records in memory before flushing them to disk in batches of up to 60 KB.

Now, let's look at how data modifications work in greater detail. Let's assume that we have a system with an empty log buffer, and the last LSN in the transaction log is 7213, as shown in Figure 30-1. Let's also assume that there are two active transactions: `T1` and `T2`. Each of these transactions has `BEGIN TRAN` log records already saved in the transaction log.

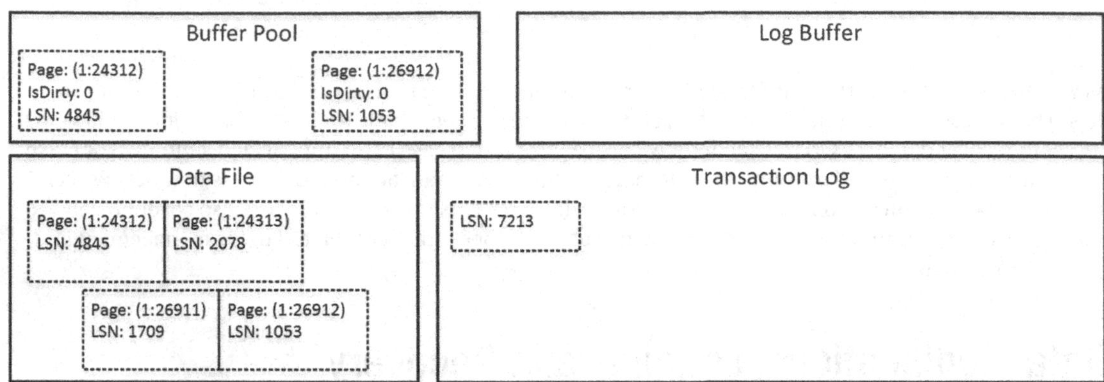

Figure 30-1. *Data modifications: Initial state*

As a first step, let's assume that transaction `T1` updates one of the rows from page (1:24312). As you can see in Figure 30-2, this operation generates a new log record, which has been placed into the log buffer. In addition, it modifies the data page, marking it as dirty, updating the LSN in the page header, and changing the data row. While the log record has not yet been saved (*hardened*) to the log file, it is not critical as long as the data page has not been saved in the data file. Both log record and modifications on the data page will be gone if there is a SQL Server crash, which is fine, because the transaction has not been committed.

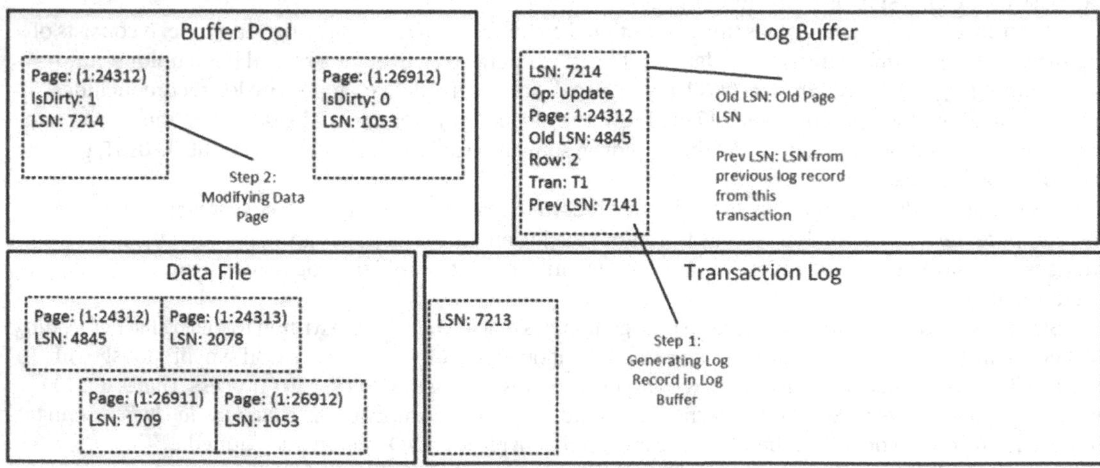

Figure 30-2. *Data modifications: T1 updates one of the rows*

Next, let's assume that transaction T2 inserts a new row into page (1:26912) and transaction T1 deletes another row on the same page. These operations generate two log records, which are placed into the log buffer, as shown in Figure 30-3.

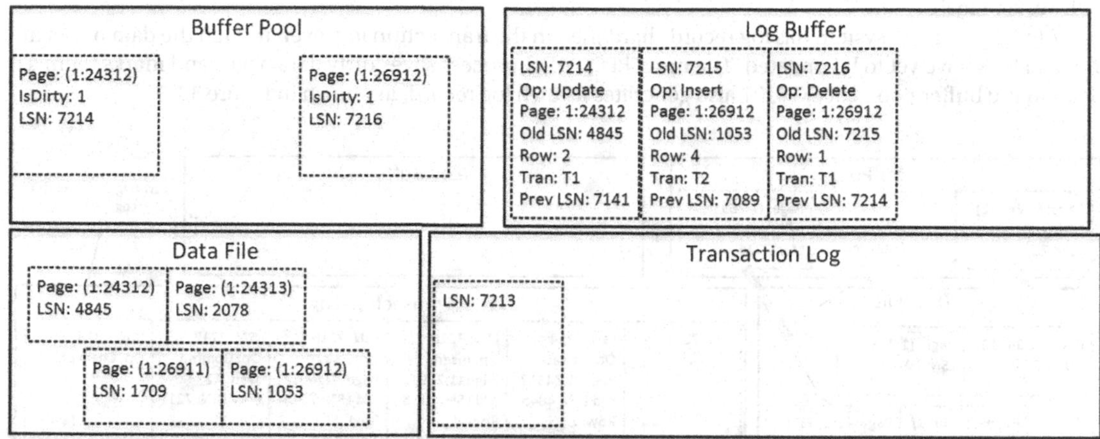

Figure 30-3. *Data modifications: T1 and T2 change data on another page*

As you can see, all log records are still in the log buffer. Now, let's assume that transaction `T2` wants to commit. This action generates another log record and forces SQL Server to flush the content of the log block to the disk, as shown in Figure 30-4. SQL Server hardens `COMMIT` and all preceding log records from the log buffer into the transaction log, regardless of the transactions that generated them.

■ **Note** To be exact, the `COMMIT` operation marks the part of the log buffer that includes `COMMIT` and all preceding log records as "Ready to Flush." Another SQL Server Process, *log writer*, continuously scans the log buffers and flushes "Ready to Flush" regions to the transaction log.

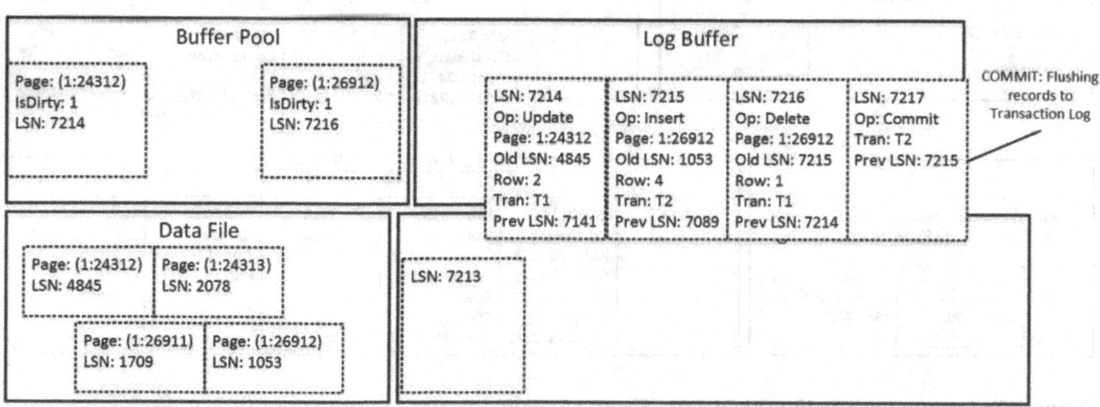

Figure 30-4. *Data modifications: Commit*

Client applications would receive confirmation that the transaction was committed only after all log records were hardened. Even though the data page (1:26912) would still be dirty and would not have been saved into the data file, hardened log records on the disk would have enough information to re-apply (redo) all of the changes done by the committed T2 transaction. Thus, it guarantees no data loss if there were to be a SQL Server crash.

At this point, the system has log records hardened in the transaction log, even though the data pages in the data files have yet to be updated. The next CHECKPOINT process saves dirty data pages and marks them as clean in the buffer pool. CHECKPOINT also generates its own log record, as shown in Figure 30-5.

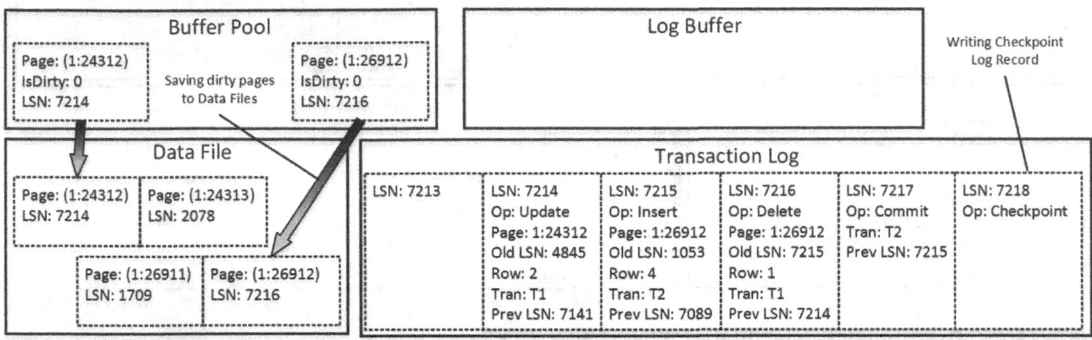

Figure 30-5. *Data modifications: CHECKPOINT*

At this time, pages in the data file store data from uncommitted transaction T1. However, log records in the transaction log have enough information to undo the changes if needed. When this is the case, SQL Server performs *compensation operations*, which execute the opposite actions of the original data modifications and generate *compensation log records.*

Figure 30-6 shows such an example. SQL Server performed a compensation update, generating a compensation log record with an LSN of 7219, to reverse the changes made by the original update operation with an LSN of 7214. It also generated a compensation insert with an LSN of 7920 to compensate for the delete operation with an LSN of 7216.

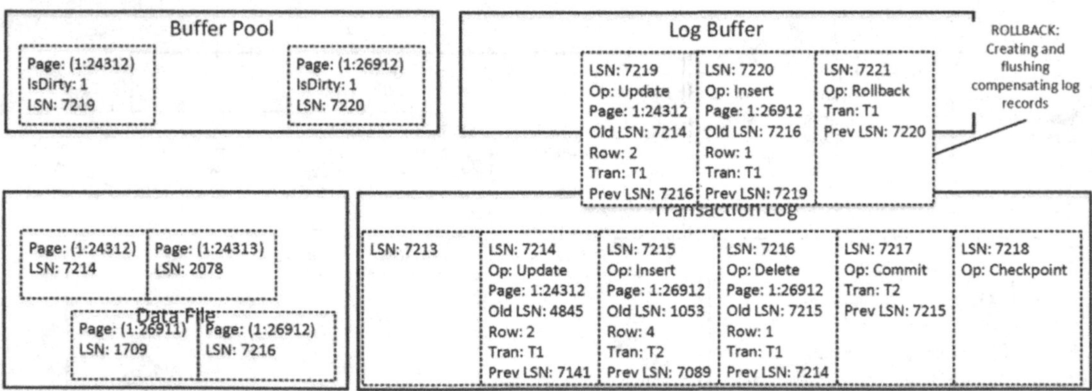

Figure 30-6. *Data modifications: ROLLBACK*

A write-ahead logging mechanism guarantees that dirty data pages are never saved into the data files until the corresponding log records are hardened in the transaction log. The opposite, however, is not true. The CHECKPOINT process is asynchronous, and there is a delay in between when log records are hardened and when pages in the data files are updated. Moreover, CHECKPOINT does not analyze whether the transactions that modified data pages were actually committed. Therefore, some pages in the data files reflect changes from uncommitted transactions.

The goal of the recovery process is to make the database transactionally consistent. SQL Server analyzes the transaction log, making sure that all changes from committed transactions are saved into the data files and all changes from uncommitted transactions are rolled back.

The recovery process consists of three different phases, as follows:

1. During the *analysis* phase, SQL Server locates the last CHECKPOINT operation in the log file, which is the last time dirty pages were saved into the data file. SQL Server builds a list of pages that were modified after CHECKPOINT as well as a list of transactions that were uncommitted at the time SQL Server stopped.
2. During the *redo* phase, SQL Server analyzes the transaction log from the initial LSN of the oldest active transaction at the moment of the crash, which is stored in the database boot page, and applies the changes to the data. Even though some of the changes could already be saved to the data files, SQL Server acquires locks on the modified rows, similar to with a regular workload. At the end of the redo phase, the database is in the state that it was in at the time when SQL Server shut down unexpectedly.
3. Finally, during the *undo* phase, SQL Server rolls back all active, uncommitted transactions.

Figure 30-7 shows an example of a recovery scenario for the database. SQL Server will redo and commit transactions T2 and T3 and roll back transaction T4.

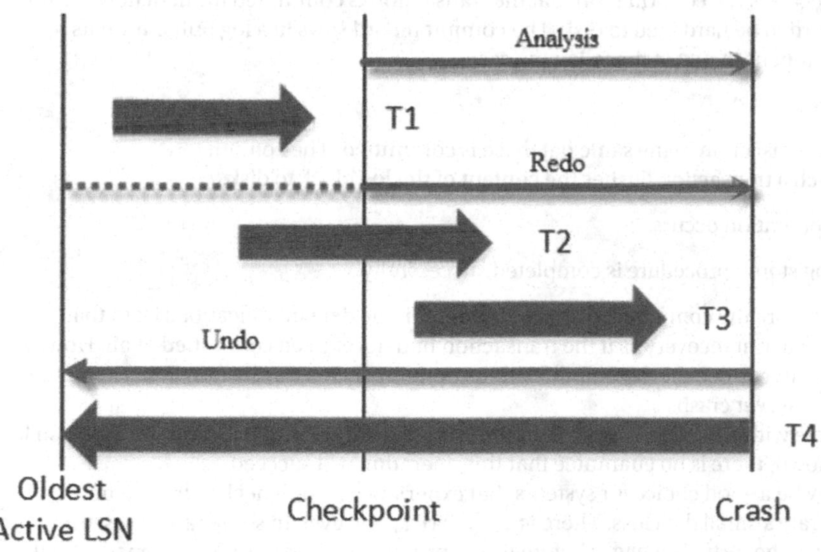

Figure 30-7. Database recovery

The recovery process uses a single thread per database. The Enterprise Edition of SQL Server supports *fast recovery*, which makes the database available to users after the redo stage.

There are two transaction log-related wait types you need to monitor in the system. WRITELOG waits occur when SQL Server flushes log blocks to the disk that is waiting for them to be hardened. An excessive amount of such waits indicate that the log drive does not have enough throughput to handle the log generation rate.

LOGBUFFER waits occur when SQL Server is waiting for the space in the log buffer to save the record. Even though it could happen shortly after database startup when SQL Server constructs a log buffer, usually these waits indicate that the log buffer is full and SQL Server is waiting until records are flushed to the disk that is generating WRITELOG waits in parallel.

You should analyze transaction log drive performance and throughput when you have these waits in the system. You can also look at data from `sys.dm_io_virtual_file_stats` and disk-related performance counters during analysis.

You could improve transaction log throughput by reducing the amount of generated log records and write operations. In many cases, it can be done by improving transaction management in the client application. An excessive amount of data modifications in the implicit individual transactions would generate an enormous amount of log records and force SQL Server to flush the log buffer on each commit. Changing the code to perform data modifications in a single explicit transaction would address this issue. Alternatively, if you are using SQL Server 2014-2016 and can tolerate the small amount of data loss, you can switch to delayed durability for transactions, which we are about to discuss.

Delayed Durability

Delayed durability, also known as *lazy commit*, was introduced in SQL Server 2014. As already discussed, by default a commit operation is synchronous. SQL Server flushes the content of the log buffer, hardening log records into a log file at the time of commit, and it sends a confirmation to the client only after a commit record is written to disk. Delayed durability changes this behavior by making the commit operation asynchronous. The client receives the confirmation that the transaction is committed immediately, without waiting for the commit record to be hardened to disk. The commit record stays in a log buffer until its content is flushed, which happens in one of the following cases:

- The log block is full.
- A fully durable transaction in the same database is committed. The commit record from such a transaction flushes the content of the log block to disk.
- A CHECKPOINT operation occurs.
- A `sp_flush_log` stored procedure is completed successfully.

If SQL Server crashed before the commit record were hardened, the data modifications from that transaction would be rolled back at recovery as if the transaction had never been committed at all. However, other transactions would be able to see the data modifications done by such a transaction in between the time of commit and the SQL Server crash.

Data loss is also possible with a regular SQL Server shutdown. Even though SQL Server tries to flush log buffers at the time of shutdown, there is no guarantee that this operation will succeed.

Delayed durability may be a good choice for systems that experience a bottleneck in transaction log writes and that can tolerate a small data loss. There is a small risk, however. In some rare cases, the CHECKPOINT process can flush the dirty data pages before the transaction log records are hardened. If SQL Server crashed at exactly the same moment, it would bring the database to a corrupted and transactionally inconsistent state after restart. You should evaluate that risk if you decided to use delayed durability.

One database option, DELAYED_DURABILITY, controls the behavior of delayed durability in the database scope. It may have one of these three options:

> DISABLED: This option disables delayed durability for database transactions regardless of the transaction durability mode. All transactions in the database are always fully durable. This is the default option and matches the behavior of previous versions of SQL Server.
>
> FORCED: This option forces delayed durability for database transactions regardless of the transaction durability mode.
>
> ALLOWED: Delayed durability is controlled at the transaction level. Transactions are fully durable unless delayed durability is specified.

It is worth noting that in the case of cross-database or distributed transactions, all transactions are fully durable regardless of their settings. The same applies to Change Tracking and Change Data Capture technologies. Any transaction that updates tables that are enabled for either of these technologies will be fully durable. Delayed durability is also not supported with transactional replication.

You can control transaction durability by specifying the durability mode in the COMMIT operator. Listing 30-1 shows an example of a transaction that uses delayed durability. As was already mentioned, the DELAYED_DURABILITY database option can override that setting.

Listing 30-1. Transaction with delayed durability

```
begin tran
        /* Do something */
commit with (delayed_durability=on)
```

Any other SQL Server technologies that work with the transaction log would see and process commit records from transactions with delayed durability only after those records were hardened in the log and, therefore, became durable in the database. For example, if a database backup finished in between a transaction commit and log buffer flush, the commit log record would not be included in the backup, and, therefore, the transaction would be rolled back at the time of a restore.

Another example is AlwaysOn Availability Groups. Secondary nodes would receive commit records only after those records were hardened in the log on the primary node and were transmitted over the network.

Virtual Log Files

Even though a transaction log can have multiple files, SQL Server works with it in a sequential manner while writing and reading a stream of log records. As a result, SQL Server does not benefit from the multiple physical log files.

■ **Note** You can benefit from the multiple log files in some edge cases. For example, placing multiple log files onto separate disk arrays will allow SQL Server to zero-initialize log files in parallel during database creation or restore operation.

Internally, SQL Server divides every physical log file into smaller sections called *virtual log files (VLF)*. SQL Server uses virtual log files as a unit of management; they can be either active or inactive.

A VLF is active when it stores the *active portion of the transaction log,* which contains the stream of log records required to keep the database transactionally consistent in the event of a transaction rollback or unexpected SQL Server shutdown. For now, do not focus on what keeps a log active; we will examine this later in this chapter. An inactive VLF contains the *truncated* (inactive) and unused parts of the transaction log.

Figure 30-8 shows an example of a transaction log and virtual log files.

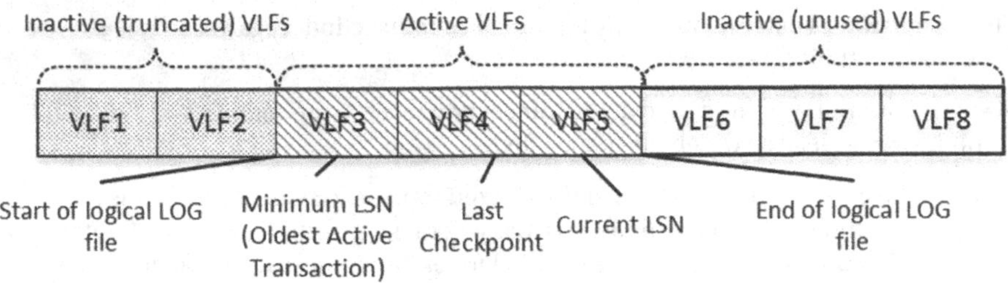

Figure 30-8. *Transaction log and virtual log files*

Transaction log truncation does not reduce the size of the log file on disk. Truncation means that parts of transaction log (one or more VLFs) are marked as inactive and ready for reuse. It clears up the internal space in the log, keeping log file size intact.

A transaction log is a wraparound file. When the end of the logical log file reaches the end of the physical file, the log wraps around it, as shown in Figure 30-9.

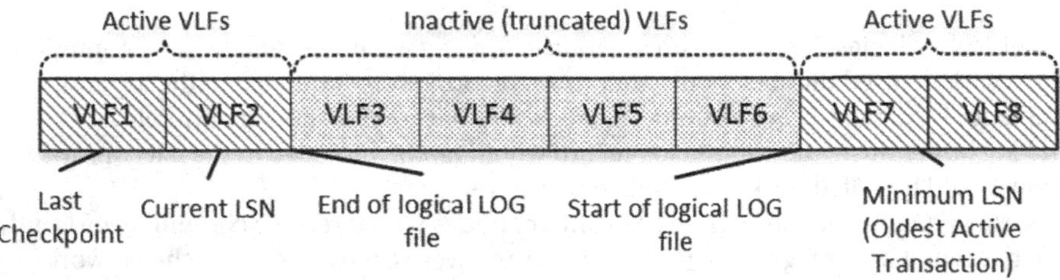

Figure 30-9. *A transaction log is a wraparound file*

SQL Server creates new virtual log files every time the log grows. The number of VLFs depends on the newly allocated space size and SQL Server version. The algorithm for SQL Server prior to 2014 is shown in Table 30-1.

Table 30-1. *Allocation Size and Number of VLFs Created (Prior to SQL Server 2014)*

Allocation Size	Number of VLFs Created
< 64 MB	4 VLFs
64 MB - 1 GB	8 VLFs
> 1 GB	16 VLFs

In SQL Server 2014 and 2016, the algorithm has changed a bit. It analyzes the current size of the log file, and if the growth is less than 1/8th the size of the current log size, it generates one VLF file. Otherwise, it uses the old algorithm.

You can examine virtual log files with the DBCC LOGINFO command. Figure 30-10 illustrates the output of such a command running against the master database on one SQL Server instance. It shows that the database has one physical log file with FileId = 2 and three virtual log files. Other columns indicate the following:

- Status is the status of the VLF. Values of 0 and 2 indicate inactive and active VLFs, respectively.
- FileSize is the size of the VLF in bytes.
- StartOffset is the starting offset of the VLF in the file.
- CreateLSN is the LSN at the moment when the VLF was created. Zero means that the VLF was created at database creation time.
- FSeqNo is the order of usage of the VLFs. The VLF with the highest FSeqNo is the file where the current log records are written.
- Parity can be one of two possible values: 64 and 128. SQL Server switches the parity value every time a VLF is reused. SQL Server uses the parity value to detect where to stop processing log records during a crash recovery.

	RecoveryUnitId	FileId	FileSize	StartOffset	FSeqNo	Status	Parity	CreateLSN
1	0	2	253952	8192	651	0	64	0
2	0	2	262144	262144	652	0	64	0
3	0	2	262144	524288	653	2	128	205000000044800004

Figure 30-10. *DBCC LOGINFO output*

Database Recovery Models

There are three database recovery models that affect transaction log management and truncation behavior: SIMPLE, FULL, and BULK LOGGED. While SQL Server logs enough information to roll back transactions and/or perform crash recovery regardless of the recovery model, such models control when a log is truncated and when VLFs become inactive. You cannot access and redo any actions from the inactive part of the log, and therefore truncation affects the amount of potential work loss if data files are unavailable.

It is again worth mentioning that transaction log truncation does not reduce the size of the log file, but rather marks VLFs as inactive and ready for reuse.

In the SIMPLE recovery model, SQL Server truncates the transaction log at CHECKPOINT. Let's assume that you have a system with three active VLFs, as shown in Figure 30-11. The oldest active LSN is in VLF4. Therefore, there is the possibility that SQL Server will need to access log records from VLF4 and VLF5 in case of transaction rollbacks, which requires SQL Server to keep VLF4 and VLF5 active.

There are no log records from the active transactions in VLF3, although some of the dirty data pages in the buffer pool may have corresponding log records stored there. SQL Server needs to access those records in case of a crash recovery to be able to redo the changes; therefore, VLF3 should also be kept active.

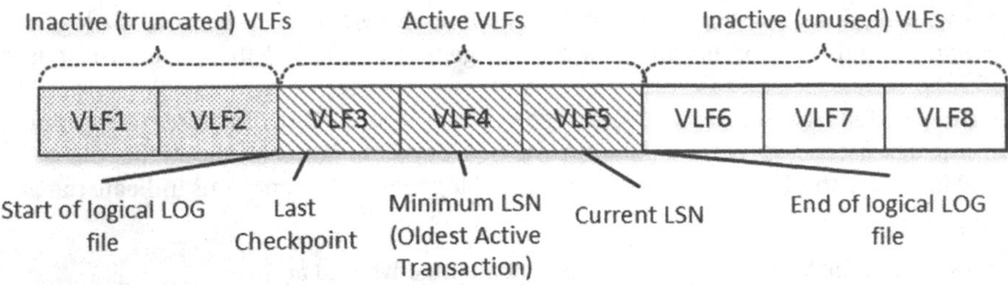

Figure 30-11. *SIMPLE recovery model: Initial stage*

When SQL Server performs a `CHECKPOINT`, all of the dirty data pages are saved into the data file. As a result, crash recovery does not need to redo any changes related to log records from `VLF3`, and it can be truncated and marked as inactive. However, `VLF4` must be kept active to support the rollback of the transactions that have corresponding log records stored in `VLF4`. Figure 30-12 illustrates this point.

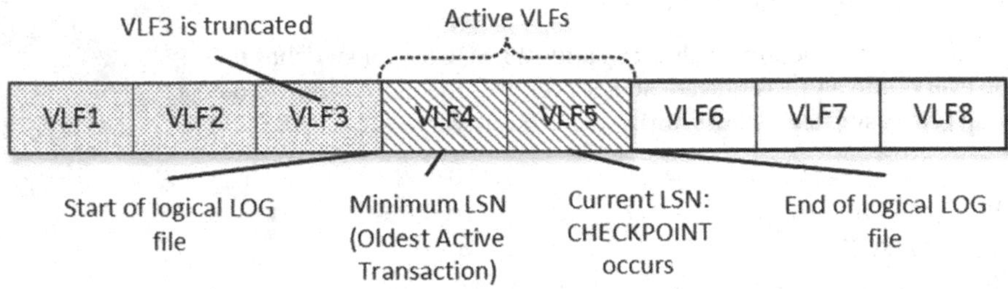

Figure 30-12. *SIMPLE recovery model: Log truncation after CHECKPOINT*

Thus, in the `SIMPLE` recovery model, the active part of transaction log starts with VLF, which contains the oldest LSN of the oldest active transaction or the last `CHECKPOINT`. It is also worth noting that if transaction replication is enabled, VLFs can be truncated only after the Replication Log Reader has processed transactions from there.

■ Note An active database backup defers transaction log truncation until it is completed.

As you can guess, even though SQL Server supports crash recovery in the `SIMPLE` model, you should keep both data and log files intact to avoid data loss and to keep the database transactionally consistent.

Alternatively, with the `FULL` or `BULK LOGGED` recovery models SQL Server supports transaction log backups, which allow you to recover the database and avoid data loss regardless of the state of the data files, as long as the transaction log is intact. This assumes, of course, that a proper set of backups is available. We will discuss the backup and recovery process in greater detail in the next chapter.

In the `FULL` and `BULK LOGGED` recovery models, SQL Server requires you to perform a transaction log backup in order to trigger log truncation. Moreover, truncation can be delayed if you have other processes that need to read the transaction log records. Think about transactional replication, database mirroring, and AlwaysOn Availability Groups as examples of such processes.

Figure 30-13 shows one example. Both minimum and current LSNs are in `VLF5`, although the LSN of the last transaction log backup is in `VLF3`. Therefore, the active portion of the transaction log includes `VLF3`, `VLF4`, and `VLF5`.

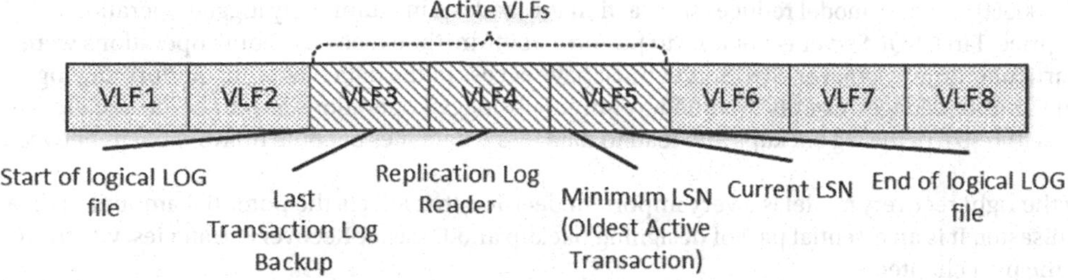

Figure 30-13. *FULL and BULK LOGGED recovery models: Initial stage*

After another transaction log backup, SQL Server can truncate `VLF3`. However, `VLF4` must remain active, as the Replication Log Reader has yet to process some of the log records from `VLF4`. Figure 30-14 illustrates this point.

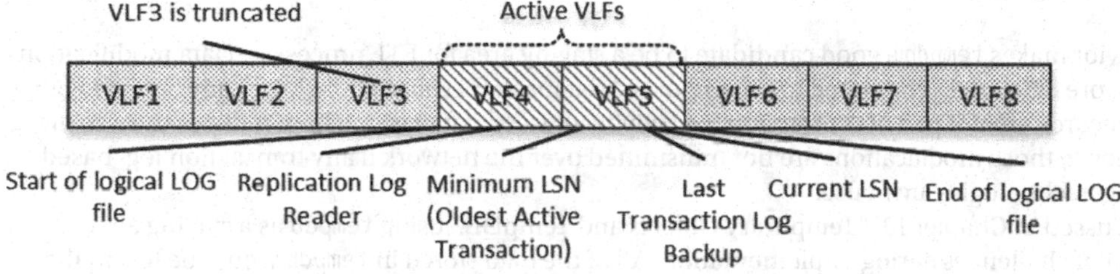

Figure 30-14. *FULL and BULK LOGGED recovery models: Log truncation*

As you can see, in the `FULL` or `BULK LOGGED` recovery models, the active part of transaction log starts with VLF, which contains the oldest of the following:

LSN of the last log backup

LSN of the oldest active transaction

LSN of the process that reads transaction log records

■ **Important** `FULL` database backup does not truncate the transaction log. You must perform a transaction log backup in order to do so.

The difference between the `FULL` and `BULK LOGGED` recovery models is in how SQL Server logs minimally logged operations, such as `CREATE INDEX`, `ALTER INDEX REBUILD`, `BULK INSERT`, `INSERT INTO`, `INSERT SELECT`, and a couple of others. In the `FULL` recovery model, those operations are fully logged. SQL Server writes log records for every data row affected by the operation. Alternatively, in the `BULK LOGGED` recovery model, SQL Server does not log minimally logged operations on a row-by-row basis; rather, it logs the extents allocation instead. All minimally logged operations generate new (or a copy of existing) objects, and extents deallocation rolls back the changes. The non-minimally logged operations are always fully logged in the `BULK LOGGED` model, like they are in the `FULL` recovery model. It is also worth noting that the `SIMPLE` recovery model logs minimally logged operations in a manner similar to the `BULK LOGGED` recovery model.

The BULK LOGGED recovery model reduces transaction log load during minimally logged operations, but it comes at price. First, SQL Server is not able to perform point-in-time recovery if bulk operations were running at a particular time. Moreover, SQL Server must have access to the data files while performing log backups, and it stores data pages/extents modified by minimally logged operations as part of the backup file. This can increase the size of the log backups and lead to data loss if data files become unavailable in between log backups.

Choosing the right recovery model is a very important decision that affects the potential amount of data loss in case of disaster. It is an essential part of designing Backup and Disaster Recovery strategies, which we will discuss in the next chapter.

TempDB Logging

All user objects in tempdb must be transactionally consistent. SQL Server must be able to roll back transactions that change data in tempdb in the same way as in the users' databases. However, tempdb is always recreated at SQL Server startup. Therefore, logging in tempdb does not need to support the redo stage of crash recovery. Log records in tempdb store just the *old values* from the modified data rows, omitting *new values*.

This behavior makes tempdb a good candidate to be a staging area for ETL processes. Data modifications in tempdb are more efficient as compared to ones in users' databases because of the lower amount of logging involved. Log records are not part of transaction log activity in users' databases, which reduces the size of log backups. Moreover, those modifications are not transmitted over the network if any transaction log-based High Availability technologies are in use.

As we discussed in Chapter 13, "Temporary Objects and TempDB," using tempdb as a staging area introduces a set of challenges during implementation. All of the data stored in tempdb would be lost in the case of a SQL Server restart or failover to another node. The code must be aware of such a possibility and handle it accordingly.

Excessive Transaction Log Growth

Excessive transaction log growth is a common problem that junior or accidental database administrators have to handle. It happens when SQL Server is unable to truncate the transaction log and reuse the space in the log file. In such a case, the log file continues to grow until it fills the entire disk, switching the database to read-only mode with this 9002 error: *"Transaction log full."*

There are plenty of reasons why SQL Server is unable to truncate the transaction log. You can examine the log_reuse_wait_desc column in the sys.databases view to discover the reason why the transaction log cannot be reused. You can see the query, which checks log_reuse_wait_desc for the users' databases, in Listing 30-2. The output of the query is shown in Figure 30-15.

Listing 30-2. Check log_reuse_wait_desc for users' databases

```
select database_id, name, recovery_model_desc, log_reuse_wait_desc
from sys.databases
where database_id >= 5
```

	database_id	name	recovery_model_desc	log_reuse_wait_desc
1	5	Utility	SIMPLE	NOTHING
2	6	Analysis	FULL	NOTHING
3	7	OrdersDb	FULL	LOG_BACKUP
4	8	Reporting	FULL	ACTIVE_TRANSACTION

Figure 30-15. *Log_reuse_wait_desc output*

For databases in the FULL or BULK LOGGED recovery models, one of the most common reasons the transaction log is not truncated is the lack of log backups. It is a common misconception that a FULL database backup truncates the transaction log. It is not true, and you must perform a log backup in order to do so. The Log_reuse_wait_desc value of LOG_BACKUP indicates that you need to perform a log backup in order to truncate the transaction log.

The Log_reuse_wait_desc value of ACTIVE_TRANSACTION indicates that there are long and/or uncommitted transactions in the system. SQL Server is unable to truncate the transaction log past the LSN of the oldest uncommitted transaction, regardless of the database recovery model in use.

The query in Listing 30-3 returns a list of the five oldest uncommitted transactions in the current database. It returns the time when the transaction was started, information about the session, and log usage statistics. On a side note, you can use the same query and change the order by clause to the Log Used column if you need to locate transactions that consume the most log space.

Listing 30-3. Finding five oldest active transactions in the system

```
select top 5
    ses_tran.session_id as [Session Id], es.login_name as [Login], es.host_name as [Host]
    ,es.program_name as [Program], es.login_time as [Login Time]
    ,db_tran.database_transaction_begin_time as [Tran Begin Time]
    ,db_tran.database_transaction_log_record_count as [Log Records]
    ,db_tran.[database_transaction_log_bytes_used] as [Log Used]
    ,db_tran.[database_transaction_log_bytes_reserved] as [Log Rsrvd]
    ,sqlText.text as [SQL], qp.query_plan as [Plan]
from
    sys.dm_tran_database_transactions db_tran join
        sys.dm_tran_session_transactions ses_tran on
            db_tran.transaction_id = ses_tran.transaction_id
    join sys.dm_exec_sessions es on
            es.[session_id] = ses_tran.[session_id]
    left outer join sys.dm_exec_requests er on
            er.session_id = ses_tran.session_id
    join sys.dm_exec_connections ec on
            ec.session_id = ses_tran.session_id
    cross apply
            sys.dm_exec_sql_text (ec.most_recent_sql_handle) sqlText
    cross apply
            sys.dm_exec_query_plan (er.plan_handle) qp
where
        db_tran.database_id = DB_ID()
order by
        db_tran.database_transaction_begin_time;
```

As I already mentioned, SQL Server has many processes that read the transaction log, such as transactional replication, change data capture, database mirroring, AlwaysOn Availability Groups, and others. Any of these processes can prevent transaction log truncation when there is a backlog. While it rarely happens when everything is working as expected, you may experience this issue if there is an error.

A common example of this situation is an unreachable secondary node in an Availability Group or database mirroring session. Log records, which have not been sent to the secondaries, will remain part of the active transaction log. This prevents its truncation. The `Log_reuse_wait_desc` column value would indicate this condition.

■ **Note** You can see the list of possible `log_reuse_wait_desc` values at `http://technet.microsoft.com/en-us/library/ms178534.aspx`.

If you experience a 9002 *Transaction log full* error, the key point is to not panic. The worst thing you can do is to perform an action that makes the database transactionally inconsistent. For example, shutting down SQL Server or detaching the database and deleting the transaction log file afterward will do just that. If the database has not been shut down cleanly, SQL Server may not be able to recover it, because the transaction log would be missing.

Creating another log file could be the fastest and simplest way to address this issue; however, it is hardly the best option in the long run. Multiple log files complicate database management. Moreover, it is hard to drop log files. SQL Server does not allow you to drop log files if they store an active portion of the log.

You must understand why the transaction log cannot be truncated and react accordingly. You can perform a log backup, identify and kill sessions that keep uncommitted active transactions, or remove an unreachable secondary node from the availability group depending on the root cause of the problem.

Transaction Log Management

It is better to manage transaction log size manually than to allow SQL Server to auto-grow it. Unfortunately, it is not always easy to determine optimal log size. On one hand, you want the transaction log to be big enough to avoid auto-growth events. On the other hand, you would like to keep the log small, saving disk space and reducing the time required to zero-initialize the log when the database is restored from a backup.

You should also keep some space reserved in the log file if you are using any High Availability or other technologies that rely on transaction log records. SQL Server is not able to truncate transaction log during log backups if something goes wrong with those processes. Moreover, you should implement a monitoring and notification framework that alerts you to such conditions and gives you time to react before the transaction log becomes full.

Another important factor is the number of VLFs in the log files. You should avoid situations where the transaction log becomes overly fragmented and has a large number of small VLFs. Similarly, you should avoid situations where the log has too few but very large VLFs.

For databases that require a large transaction log, you can pre-allocate space using 4,000 MB chunks, which generates 16 VLFs of 250 MB each. If a database does not require a large (more than 4,000 MB) transaction log, you can pre-allocate log space in one operation based on the size requirements.

■ **Note** There is a bug in SQL Server 2005–2008R2 that incorrectly grows the transaction log if its size is in multiples of 4 GB. You can use multiples of 4,000 MB instead. This bug has been fixed in SQL Server 2012 and in cumulative updates/service packs for older versions of SQL Server.

You should still allow SQL Server to auto-grow the transaction log in case of an emergency. However, choosing the right auto-growth size is tricky. For databases with large transaction logs, it is wise to use 4,000 MB so as to reduce the number of VLFs. However, zeroing out 4,000 MB of newly allocated space can be time consuming. Remember that SQL Server always zeroes out transaction logs, even when Instant File Initialization is enabled. All database activities that write to the log file are blocked during the auto-growth process. This is another argument for manual transaction log size management.

■ **Tip** The decision of what auto-growth size should be used depends on the performance of the I/O subsystem. You should analyze how long zero-initialization takes and find a sweet spot where the auto-growth time and the size of the generated VLFs are acceptable. 1 GB for auto-growth could work in many cases.

It is also worth noting that the Management Studio database creation dialog uses inefficient default transaction log auto-growth parameters, which leads to an excessive number of VLFs in the database. You need to change these parameters when you create the new database through Management Studio. Fortunately, this problem has been addressed in SQL Server 2016.

SQL Server writes to the transaction log synchronously in the case of data modifications. OLTP systems with volatile data and heavy transaction log activity should have the transaction log stored on a disk array with good write performance and low latency. Transaction log I/O performance is less important when the data is static; for example, in data warehouse systems. However, you should consider how it affects the performance and duration of the processes that refresh data there.

Best practices suggest you store the transaction log on a dedicated disk array optimized for sequential write performance. This is great advice for situations where an underlying I/O subsystem has enough power to accommodate multiple high-performance disk arrays. In some cases, however, when faced with budget constraints and not enough disk drives, you can achieve better I/O performance by storing data and log files on a single disk array. You should remember, however, that keeping data and log files on the same disk array could lead to data loss in case of a disk array failure.

Another important factor is the number of databases. When you place transaction logs from multiple active databases onto a single disk array, log I/O access becomes random rather than sequential. You should factor in such behavior when testing your I/O subsystem and then choose test scenarios that represent the workload that you expect to have in production.

Most important, you should store the transaction log to a highly redundant disk array. It is impossible to recover the database in a transactionally consistent state if the transaction log has been corrupted.

Summary

SQL Server uses a transaction log to store information about all data modifications made to the database. It allows SQL Server to keep the database transactionally consistent, even in the event of an unexpected shutdown or crash.

SQL Server uses a write-ahead logging mechanism, which guarantees that log records are always saved into the log file before the updated data pages are saved to the data files. SQL Server uses a small buffer to cache log records in memory, saving all of them at once when needed.

The transaction log is a wraparound file, which internally consists of multiple virtual log files. Every virtual log file can either be active or inactive. Transaction log truncation marks some VLFs as inactive, making them ready for reuse. In the `SIMPLE` recovery model, SQL Server truncates the transaction log at the `CHECKPOINT`. In the `FULL` and `BULK LOGGED` recovery models, SQL Server truncates the transaction log during log backups.

There are a number of issues that can prevent transaction log truncation. The most common ones are lack of transaction log backups in the `FULL` and `BULK LOGGED` recovery models, or long-running uncommitted transactions. You can examine what prevents log truncation by analyzing the `log_reuse_wait_desc` column in the `sys.databases` view.

You should avoid situations where the transaction log has too many or too few VLFs. Either circumstance negatively affects system performance. For databases that require large transaction log files, you can pre-allocate the transaction log with 4,000 MB chunks, which makes 16 VLFs of about 250 MB each.

It is recommended that you manage the transaction log size manually to avoid log auto-growth. However, you should still keep auto-growth enabled to avoid a *"9002: Transaction Log Full"* error. Auto-growth size should be specified in MB rather than as a percentage. You need to fine-tune the size based on the I/O performance of the system.

Fast transaction log throughput is essential for good performance, especially with OLTP systems. You must store the transaction log on a fast disk array, minimizing writing latency. Most important, that array must be redundant. It is impossible to recover the database in a transactionally consistent state if the transaction log is corrupted.

CHAPTER 31

Backup and Restore

In the technology world, it is just a matter of time before disaster happens. A database could become corrupted due to a user error, hardware malfunction, or software bug. A disk array could fail, making databases unavailable to users. An engineer could accidentally change the LUN configuration in a SAN array and affect the database it stores. A natural disaster could affect the availability of a datacenter. In any of these instances, it is essential to recover the database and bring the system online with minimal data loss and downtime.

This chapter discusses how SQL Server performs database backup and restore and covers several important use cases that can be used during the database recovery process. It also provides several ideas on how to design backup strategies in a way that minimizes system downtime and data loss.

Database Backup Types

There are three different types of database backups available in SQL Server.

A *full* database backup backs up the whole database. SQL Server performs a CHECKPOINT as the first step of database backup, backs up all allocated extents from the data files, and, finally, backs up the portion of the transaction log required in order to recover the database after a restore. That portion includes all log records, starting from the oldest of these events:

- The last CHECKPOINT.
- The beginning of the oldest active transaction.
- The beginning of the unscanned portion of the log if there are any processes that rely on the transaction log scan, such as transactional replication, database mirroring, AlwaysOn Availability Groups, and others.

A full database backup represents the database at the time when the backup operation was finished. It is supported in every recovery model.

A *differential* backup backs up those extents that have been modified since the last full backup. SQL Server tracks which extents have been changed with a set of allocation map pages called a *differential changed map (DCM)*. SQL Server clears these map pages only during a full database backup. Therefore, differential backups are cumulative, and each of them stores all extents that have been modified since the last full, rather than last differential, backup. Like a full database backup, differential backups work in every recovery model.

A *log* backup backs up the active portion of the transaction log, starting with the LSN of the last full or log backup. This backup type is only supported in the FULL or BULK LOGGED recovery models. It is an essential part of transaction log management and is required in order to trigger log truncation. It is worth reiterating that the full database backup does not truncate the transaction log in the FULL or BULK LOGGED recovery models. You should perform a log backup to truncate the transaction log.

If a log backup were running at the same time as a full database backup, log truncation would be deferred until the full backup was complete.

D. Korotkevitch, *Pro SQL Server Internals*, DOI 10.1007/978-1-4842-1964-5_31

For a database in the BULK LOGGED recovery model, log backups also store data from extents that were allocated during minimally logged bulk-copy operations, such as CREATE INDEX, ALTER INDEX REBUILD, BULK INSERT, INSERT INTO, INSERT SELECT, and a few others. These extents are tracked with another set of allocation map pages called a *bulk changed map (BCM)*. SQL Server must be able to access data files with those extents in order for the log backup to succeed.

In contrast to differential backups, log backups are incremental. Each subsequent log backup stores the portion of the transaction log starting at the point where the previous log backup finished. You must apply all log backups one by one during the restore process.

The sequence of log backups contains log records for all operations performed by SQL Server since last full backup. This allows you to redo the work and recover the database, even when database files are corrupted or unavailable. Moreover, it supports point-in-time recovery and allows you to recover the database up to a particular time. One case where this is beneficial is upon the accidental deletion of data or a database object. We will talk about such a situation later in this chapter.

■ **Important** The database in the BULK LOGGED recovery model does not support point-in-time recovery if the transaction log contains bulk logged operations running at the same time.

A special kind of log backup, called *tail-log backup*, is used when you need to recover a database after a disaster. It backs up log records that have not been backed up since the last log backup, and it prevents potential data loss during recovery. We will talk about tail-log backups in detail later in this chapter.

A continuous sequence of backups is called a *backup chain*. A backup chain starts with a full database backup, and it is required in order to restore the database up to the point of failure and/or a point in time.

Figure 31-1 shows an example of a backup chain and a tail-log backup.

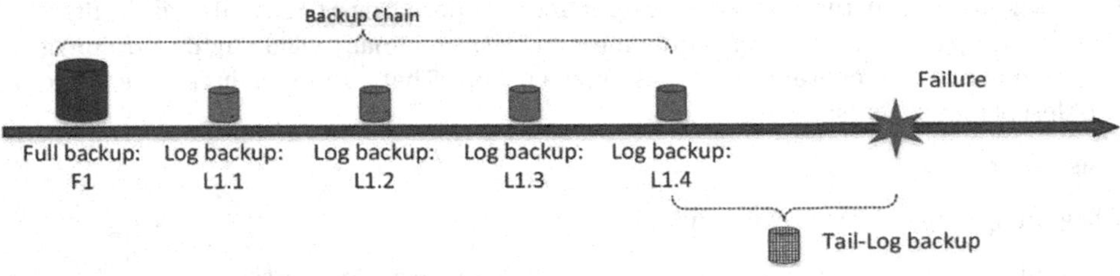

Figure 31-1. *Backup chain and tail-log backup*

Backing Up the Database

You can backup and restore the database using Management Studio UI, T-SQL, and PowerShell, as well as with third-party tools. In this chapter, we will focus on the T-SQL implementation.

Listing 31-1 shows the T-SQL statements that perform a full database backup using the BACKUP DATABASE command with a disk as the destination.

Listing 31-1. Performing a full database backup

```
backup database OrderEntryDb
to disk = N'e:\backups\OrderEntry.bak'
with format, init,
name = N'OrderEntryDb-Full Database Backup',
stats = 5, checksum, compression;
```

SQL Server allows you to store multiple backups in a single file. You should be extremely careful with this approach, however. While it reduces the number of files on the disk and simplifies their management, it is possible to override existing backups and invalidate the backup chain.

You should design your backup placement in a way that reduces the amount of data that needs to be copied over the network in case of disaster. Do not store backups from different log chains in the same file. Moreover, do not store differential backups together with other, redundant differential and/or log backups. This reduces both the size of the backup file and the time it takes to copy the file over a network in case of disaster.

The `FORMAT` and `INIT` options tell SQL Server to override all existing backups in the backup file.

The `CHECKSUM` option forces SQL Server to validate the checksum on the data pages and generate a checksum of the backup file. This helps to validate that the data pages have not been corrupted by the I/O subsystem after they were saved to disk. This option, however, should not be used as a replacement for a regular database consistency check with the `DBCC CHECKDB` command. `BACKUP WITH CHECKSUM` does not test the integrity of the database objects and allocation map pages, nor does it test pages that do not have a `CHECKSUM` generated.

Finally, the `COMPRESSION` option forces SQL Server to compress the backup. Backup compression can significantly reduce the size of the backup file, although it uses more CPU resources during the backup and restore processes. It is recommended that you use backup compression unless the system is heavily CPU-bound or the database is encrypted. In the latter case, backup compression does not introduce any space savings.

Backup compression is available in the Enterprise and Standard editions of SQL Server 2008R2 and above as well as in the Enterprise Edition of SQL Server 2008. It is worth mentioning that every edition of SQL Server can restore a compressed backup.

■ **Note** You can look at all of the available `BACKUP` command options at `http://technet.microsoft.com/en-us/library/ms186865.aspx`.

You can perform a differential backup using the `DIFFERENTIAL` option, as shown in Listing 31-2.

Listing 31-2. Performing a differential database backup

```
backup database OrderEntryDb
to disk = N'e:\backups\OrderEntry.bak'
with differential, noformat, noinit,
name = N'OrderEntryDb-Differential Database Backup',
stats = 5, checksum, compression;
```

Now, our backup file `OrderEntry.bak` has two backups: one `FULL` and another `DIFFERENTIAL`. Finally, Listing 31-3 shows you how to perform a transaction log backup by placing it into another file.

Listing 31-3. Performing a transaction log backup

```
backup log OrderEntryDb
to disk = N'e:\backups\OrderEntry.trn'
with format, init,
name = N'OrderEntryDb-Transaction Log Backup',
stats = 5, checksum, compression;
```

You must have `BACKUP DATABASE` and `BACKUP LOG` permissions granted in order to perform the backups. By default, those permissions are granted to the members of the `sysadmin` server role, `db_owner`, and `db_backupoperator` database roles. Moreover, the SQL Server startup account should have adequate permissions to write a backup file to the designated location.

You can specify multiple destination backup files and allow SQL Server to stripe backup across all of them. This can improve the performance of backup and subsequent restore operations if the I/O performance of the backup drive becomes a bottleneck.

The COPY_ONLY option allows you to perform a backup without breaking the log chain. One possible use case for such option is a situation where you need to bring a copy of the database to a development environment.

SQL Server stores the information about every backup and restore operation on a server instance in a set of tables defined in the msdb database. A description of these tables is outside of the scope of this book. You can read the Books Online article "Backup History and Header Information" at http://msdn.microsoft.com/en-us/library/ms188653.aspx for more details.

Finally, SQL Server writes information about every backup to the error log file. This could quickly balloon the size of the log file if backups are running frequently. You can disable this behavior with trace flag T3226. This makes error logs more compact at the cost of requiring a query against msdb to obtain a backup history.

Restoring the Database

You can restore a database with the RESTORE DATABASE command. You can see an example of this command in action in Listing 31-4. It restores the OrderEntryDB database at a new destination (the MOVE option controls this), and it applies differential and transaction log backups after that.

Listing 31-4. Restoring the database

```
-- Initial FULL backup
restore database OrderEntryDbDev
from disk = N'C:\Backups\OrderEntry.bak' with file = 1,
move N'OrderEntryDB' to N'c:\backups\OrderEntryDB.mdf',
move N'OrderEntryDB_log' to N'c:\backups\OrderEntryDB_log.ldf',
norecovery, nounload, stats = 5;

-- Differential backup
restore database OrderEntryDbDev
from disk = N'C:\Backups\OrderEntry.bak' with file = 2,
norecovery, nounload, stats = 5;

-- Transaction Log backup
restore log OrderEntryDbDev
from disk = N'C:\Backups\OrderEntry.trn'
with nounload, norecovery, stats = 10;

restore database OrderEntryDbDev with recovery;
```

When the backup file stores multiple backups, you should specify a file number by using the WITH FILE option. As I noted earlier, be careful with this approach and make sure that your backup routine does not accidentally override existing backups in the file.

Each RESTORE operation should have a database recovery option specified. When a backup is restored with the RECOVERY option, SQL Server recovers the database by performing both the redo and undo recovery stages, and it makes the database available to the users. No further backups can be restored. Alternatively, the NORECOVERY option performs only the redo stage of database recovery, and it leaves the database in the RESTORING state. It allows you to restore further backups from the log chain.

■ **Important** The UI interface in Management Studio uses the RECOVERY option by default. Always pay attention to this setting when using the Database Restore UI in Management Studio.

Accidental use of the RECOVERY option would require you to repeat the restore process from the beginning, which could be very time consuming in the case of large databases. It is safer to restore all backups with the T-SQL RESTORE command using the NORECOVERY option all of the time. Finally, you can recover the database and bring it online with the RESTORE DATABASE WITH RECOVERY command, as was shown in Listing 31-4.

We will discuss how to restore the database after a disaster later in this chapter. Now, let's cover a couple of useful options that you can use during a restore.

Restore to a Point in Time

You can restore the database to a point in time using the STOPAT option. This option accepts a date/time value or a variable as a parameter and restores the database to its state as of that time. Alternatively, you can use the STOPATMARK and STOPBEFOREMARK options, which allow you to restore the database by stopping at a particular LSN or named transaction.

One common use case for these options is the recovery of an accidentally dropped object. Let's look at the example shown in Listing 31-5 and create the database with table dbo.Invoices, populate it with some data, and perform a full database backup.

Listing 31-5. Point-in-time restore: Database creation

```
create database MyDB
go

create table MyDB.dbo.Invoices(InvoiceId int not null);
insert into MyDB.dbo.Invoices values(1),(2),(3) ;
go

backup database MyDB
to disk = N'c:\backups\MyDB.bak'
with noformat, init,
name = N'MyDB-Full Database Backup', stats = 5;
```

Now, let's assume that somebody accidentally dropped the dbo.Invoices table using the DROP TABLE dbo.Invoices command. If the database is active and other data has been modified over time, the best course of action would be to restore another copy of the database from the backup to the point in time when the table was dropped and then copy the data from the newly restored to the original database.

As a first step in the recovery process, let's make a backup of the transaction log, as shown in Listing 31-6. Obviously, in a real system, it is possible that you already have the log backup that covers the time when the table was dropped.

Listing 31-6. Point-in-time restore: Backing up the log

```
backup log MyDB
to disk = N'c:\backups\MyDB.trn'
with noformat, init,
name = N'MyDB-Transaction Log Backup', stats = 5;
```

The tricky part is finding the time when the table was dropped. One of the options that you have is analyzing the system default trace, which captures such events. You can use the fn_trace_gettable system function, as shown in Listing 31-7.

Listing 31-7. Point-in-time restore: Analyzing the system trace

```
declare
    @TraceFilePath nvarchar(2000)

select @TraceFilePath  = convert(nvarchar(2000),value)
from ::fn_trace_getinfo(0)
where traceid = 1 and property = 2;

select
    StartTime, EventClass
    ,case EventSubClass
        when 0 then 'DROP'
        when 1 then 'COMMIT'
        when 2 then 'ROLLBACK'
    end as SubClass
    ,ObjectID, ObjectName, TransactionID
from ::fn_trace_gettable(@TraceFilePath, default)
where EventClass = 47 and DatabaseName = 'MyDB'
order by StartTime desc
```

As you can see in Figure 31-2, there are two rows in the output. One of them corresponds to the time when the object was dropped. The other one relates to the time when the transaction was committed.

	StartTime	EventClass	SubClass	ObjectID	ObjectName	TransactionID
1	2016-03-10 06:21:27.707	47	COMMIT	565577053	Invoices	6394737
2	2016-03-10 06:21:27.697	47	DROP	565577053	Invoices	6394737

Figure 31-2. *Output from the default system trace*

You can use the time from the output to specify the STOPAT parameter of the RESTORE command, as shown in Listing 31-8. It is also possible to perform a point-in-time restore in the Management Studio Database Restore UI. However, that option does not allow you to specify milliseconds in the STOPAT value.

Listing 31-8. Point-in-time restore: Using the STOPAT parameter

```
restore database MyDBCopy
from disk = N'C:\Backups\MyDB.bak' with file = 1,
move N'MyDB' to N'c:\db\MyDBCopy.mdf',
move N'MyDB_log' to N'c:\db\MyDBCopy.ldf',
norecovery, stats = 5;

restore log MyDBCopy
from disk = N'C:\Backups\MyDB.trn' with file = 1,
norecovery, stats = 5,
stopat = N'2016-03-10T06:21:27.697';

restore database MyDBCopy with recovery;
```

While the system default trace is a very simple option, there is a downside. The time of the event in the trace is not precise enough, and it could be a few milliseconds apart from the time that you need to specify as the STOPAT value. Therefore, there is no guarantee that you would restore the most recent table data at the time of deletion. Moreover, there is a chance that the DROP OBJECT event has been overwritten or that the trace is disabled on the server.

One of the workarounds available for this is to use an undocumented system function, fn_dump_dblog, which returns the content of the transaction log backup file. You need to find the LSN that belongs to the DROP TABLE statement and restore a copy of the database using the STOPBEFOREMARK option. Listing 31-9 shows the code that calls the fn_dump_dblog function. Figure 31-3 shows the output of the query.

Listing 31-9. Point-in-time restore: Using the fn_dump_dblog function

```
select [Current LSN], [Begin Time], Operation,[Transaction Name], [Description]
from fn_dump_dblog
( default, default, default, default, 'C:\backups\mydb.trn',default, default, default
,default, default, default, default, default, default, default, default, default, default
,default, default, default, default, default, default, default, default, default, default
,default, default, default, default, default, default, default, default, default, default
,default, default, default, default, default, default, default, default, default, default
,default, default, default, default, default, default, default, default, default, default
,default, default, default, default, default, default, default, default, default, default )
where [Transaction Name] = 'DROPOBJ';
```

	Current LSN	Begin Time	Operation	Transaction Name	Description
1	00000024:00000178:0001	2016/03/10 06:21:27:693	LOP_BEGIN_XACT	DROPOBJ	DROPOBJ;0x010500000000000515

Figure 31-3. *Fn_dump_dblog output*

Listing 31-10 shows a RESTORE statement that uses the LSN from this output. You should specify the lsn:0x prefix in the STOPBEFOREMARK parameter. It tells SQL Server that you are using an LSN in hexadecimal format.

Listing 31-10. Point-in-time restore: Using the STOPBEFOREMARK parameter

```
restore log MyDBCopy
from disk = N'C:\Backups\MyDB.trn'
with file = 1,  norecovery, stats = 5,
stopbeforemark = 'lsn:0x 00000024:00000178:0001';
```

Analyzing transaction log records is a tedious and time consuming job. However, it provides the most accurate results. Moreover, you can use such a technique when data is accidentally deleted by the DELETE statement. Such an operation is not logged in the system default trace, and analyzing transaction log content is the only option available. Fortunately, there are third-party tools available that can simplify the process of searching for the LSN of the operation in the log.

Restore with STANDBY

When you finish a restore process using the NORECOVERY option, the database stays in the RESTORING state and it is unavailable to users. The STANDBY option allows you to access the database in read-only mode.

As mentioned previously, SQL Server performs the redo stage of recovery as the final step of the restore process. The undo stage of recovery is deferred until a restore is called with the RECOVERY option. The STANDBY option forces SQL Server to perform the undo stage using a temporary *undo file* to store the compensation log records generated during the undo process. The compensation log records do not become part of the database transaction log, and you can restore additional log backups or recover the database if needed.

Listing 31-11 illustrates the use of the RESTORE WITH STANDBY operator. It is worth mentioning that you should not specify RECOVERY/NORECOVERY options in this mode.

Listing 31-11. Restore with STANDBY option

```
restore log MyDBCopy
from disk = N'C:\Backups\MyDB.trn'
with file = 1, stats = 5,
standby = 'C:\Backups\undo.trn';
```

The STANDBY option can be used together with point-in-time restore. This can help you avoid unnecessary restores when you need to locate the LSN to use with the STOPBEFOREMARK option. Think about a situation where the log file has multiple DROP OBJECT transactions, and you do not know which one dropped the table that you wish to recover. In this case, you can perform multiple restores using both the STOPBEFOREMARK and STANDBY options, querying the database until you find the right spot for recovery.

Alternatively, you can use the STANDBY option together with STOPAT to analyze the database state at a specific time.

Designing a Backup Strategy

Every production system has two requirements that affect and shape backup strategy implementation. The first is the *Recovery Point Objective (RPO)*, which dictates how much data loss is acceptable in the case of disaster. The second requirement is the *Recovery Time Objective (RTO)*, which defines the acceptable downtime for the recovery process.

RPO and RTO metrics are usually included in the Service Level Agreements defined for the system. When RPO and RTO are not formally documented, you can determine them by interviewing stakeholders and gathering information about their expectations.

Non-technical stakeholders often have unrealistic expectations when defining RPO and RTO requirements. They often request zero data loss and zero system downtime. It is impossible to guarantee or achieve such goals in real life. Moreover, very small RPO/RTO adds additional load to the server and is often impractical and very expensive to implement. It is your job to educate stakeholders and work with them to define realistic RPO and RTO based on business requirements.

The RPO dictates the recovery model that the database should use. Table 31-1 shows possible data loss and recovery points for the different database recovery models, assuming that backup files are available and the backup chain is intact. Obviously, if both the data and log files are corrupted, restoring the last backup is the only option, regardless of the recovery model.

Table 31-1. *Data Loss Based on the Database Recovery Model*

Recovery Model	Description	Data Files Corruption	Log Corruption
SIMPLE	Log backups are not supported. The database can be restored to the point of the last full or differential backup.	Changes since the last full or differential backup must be redone.	
FULL	All operations are fully recorded in the transaction log.	No data loss	Changes since the last LOG backup must be redone.
BULK LOGGED	Bulk copy operations are minimally logged. All other operations are fully logged.	No data loss if bulk-copy operations did not occur since the last log backup. Otherwise, changes since the last LOG backup must be redone.	

In the `SIMPLE` recovery model, all changes since the last full or differential backup must be redone. Therefore, this model is not the best candidate for databases with volatile data that needs to be protected. However, the `SIMPLE` recovery model is perfectly acceptable when the data is static; for example, in data warehouse and/or reporting systems where the data is refreshed based on some schedule. You can use the `SIMPLE` recovery model by performing a full database backup after each data refresh.

Another possible use case for the `SIMPLE` recovery model is a database with data that can be easily and quickly reconstructed from other sources. In these cases, you might consider using this model to avoid transaction log maintenance. It is also worth noting that databases in the `SIMPLE` recovery model do not support features that rely on transaction log scans, such as database mirroring, AlwaysOn Availability Groups, log shipping, and others.

The `FULL` and `BULK LOGGED` recovery models log regular (non-bulk copy) operations in the same way as each other and have the same transaction log maintenance requirements. Even though the `BULK LOGGED` recovery model improves the performance of bulk-copy operations due to minimal logging, it is exposed to data loss in cases of data file corruption. You should avoid using the `BULK LOGGED` recovery model because of this. Nevertheless, you may consider switching the database from the `FULL` to the `BULK LOGGED` recovery model for the duration of bulk-copy operations (for example, during index rebuild) and then switching the database back to the `FULL` recovery model afterward.

■ **Important** You should perform a full or log backup immediately after you switch the database back to the `FULL` recovery model.

Neither of these recovery models would survive transaction log corruption and keep the database transactionally consistent. You should store the transaction log on a highly redundant disk array in order to minimize the chance of such situations. Neither solution, however, is 100 percent redundant. You should make regular log backups to minimize possible data loss. *The frequency of log backups helps control possible data loss and indicates how much work must be redone in instances of transaction log corruption.* For example, if you performed a log backup every hour, you would only lose up to one hour's work when restoring the last log backup.

■ **Important** The intervals between log backups should not exceed the time specified by the Recovery Point Objective requirement. You should also consider log backup duration when designing a backup strategy.

While it is relatively easy to define a backup strategy based on the RPO, it is much trickier with RTO, which specifies the maximum duration of the recovery process and therefore the system downtime. That time depends on a few factors, such as network throughput, which dictates how much time is required to transmit backup files over the network, as well as on the size and number of backup files. Moreover, this duration changes over time as the database and load grows. You should regularly test the database recovery process, making sure that it still meets RTO requirements.

Figure 31-4 shows a recovery scenario for a database that has multiple differentials and log backups. As a first step during recovery, you should make a tail-log backup, which backs up the portion of the transaction log that has not been backed up since the last log backup. After that, you should restore the last full backup, most recent differential backup, and all log backups taken afterward, including the tail-log backup.

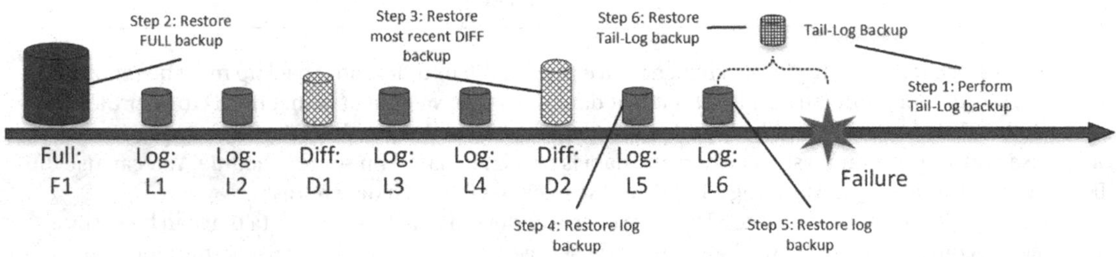

Figure 31-4. *Recovery sequence*

Let's assume that the example shown in Figure 31-4 represents a database with the primary filegroup residing on disk `M:`, secondary filegroup on disk `N:`, and transaction log on disk `L:`. All backup files are stored on disk `V:`. Listing 31-12 shows the script that recovers the database after a disaster when disk `N:` becomes corrupted and unavailable. The data files from the secondary filegroup are moved to disk `M:`. In this example, SQL Server must redo all data modifications that occurred in between the time of the differential backup `D2` and the time of failure.

Listing 31-12. Restoring the database after a disaster

```
-- Backing up Tail-Log. Database will be left in RESTORING stage
backup log RecoveryDemo
to disk = N'V:\RecoveryDemo-tail-log.trn'
with no_truncate, noformat, init,
name = N'RecoveryDemo-Tail-log backup',
norecovery, stats = 5;

-- Restoring FULL backup moving files from SECONDARY FG to M: drive
restore database RecoveryDemo
from disk = N'V:\RecoveryDemo-F1.bak' with file = 1,
move N'RecoveryDemo_Secondary' to N'M:\RecoveryDemo_Secondary.ndf',
norecovery, stats = 5;

-- Restoring DIFF backup
restore database RecoveryDemo
```

```
from disk = N'V:\RecoveryDemo-F2.bak' with file = 1,
norecovery, stats = 5;

-- Restoring L5 Log backup
restore log RecoveryDemo
from disk = N'V:\RecoveryDemo-L5.trn' with file = 1,
norecovery, stats = 5;

-- Restoring L6 Log backup
restore log RecoveryDemo
from disk = N'V:\RecoveryDemo-L6.trn' with file = 1,
norecovery, stats = 5;

-- Restoring tail-log backup
restore log RecoveryDemo
from disk = N'V:\RecoveryDemo-tail-log.trn' with file = 1,
norecovery, stats = 5;

-- Recovering database
restore database RecoveryDemo with recovery;
```

You can take multiple restore paths while recovering the database. In addition to the method just shown, you can also use differential backup D1, applying log backups L3-L7 and the tail-log backup. As another option, you can use only log backups after you have restored a full backup without using any differential backups at all. However, the time required for the restore process greatly depends on the amount of transaction log records that need to be replayed. Differential backups allow you to reduce the amount of time involved and speed up the restore process.

You should design a backup strategy and find the right combination of full, differential, and log backups that allows you to restore the database within the time defined by the RTO requirements. The key point here is to define the schedule of full and differential backups because the frequency of log backups depends on RPO and possible data loss.

■ **Tip** Remember to enable Instant File Initialization, which prevents the zeroing-out of data files during the database creation stage of restore.

You should create differential backups often enough to minimize the number of log backups that need to be restored and log records that need to be replayed in case of recovery. Differential backups are cumulative, though, and you should avoid the situation where they store a large amount of data modified since the last full backup. It would be better to perform full backups more often in that case.

As an example, consider a database that collects some data from external sources, keeping one week of the most recent data and purging it on a daily basis using a sliding window pattern implementation. In this schema, one-seventh of the data is changing on a daily basis.

Let's assume that a full backup is taken weekly and differential backups are taken daily. If the size of the full backup is 1 TB, the incremental backups would grow at a rate of 140–150 GB per day. In that case, if a disaster happened on the seventh day after the last full backup, you would need to restore 1 TB of full backup and about 850 GB of differential backups before applying log backups, which is very time consuming and redundant. It would be much more efficient to perform full backups on a daily basis in that case.

The location of backup files is another important factor that affects recovery time. It could be very time consuming to copy a large amount of data over the network. Consider keeping multiple copies of backup files when it is appropriate—off-site, on-site, and perhaps even locally on the server.

Make sure that you have enough free space on disk to store backup files and implement alerting in the system in case backup fails. Remember that failed log backups would prevent truncation of the transaction log and would force the transaction log to grow.

When fast system recovery is crucial, you can consider striping backup across multiple local DAS drives, copying backup files to other servers and offsite locations afterward. This will protect you from various types of failures and provide the best performance of backup and restore processes.

I/O subsystem and network performance are usually the biggest bottlenecks during backup and restore. Backup compression helps to reduce the size of the data that needs to be transmitted over the network or read from disk. Always use backup compression if the database is not encrypted and the server can handle the extra CPU load introduced by compression.

You should remember that backup compression affects the duration of backup and restore operations. SQL Server spends extra time compressing and decompressing data; however, this can be mitigated by a smaller backup file and thus a smaller amount of data being transmitted over the network and/or read from disk. You need to validate that you can still achieve RTO after you enable backup compression in the system.

One of the key elements of a good backup strategy is backup validation. It is not enough to back up the database. You should make sure that backup files are not corrupted and that the database can be restored from them. You can validate backup files by restoring them on another server.

■ **Tip** You can also perform database consistency checks by running `DBCC CHECKDB` after the backup is restored on another server. This helps reduce the load on the production server.

Another good practice that ensures the safety of a backup is storing a redundant set of backup files. Do not delete backup files with old differential and log backups after you make a new differential backup. Such a strategy may help you to recover the database when the most recent backup is corrupted.

Finally, databases do not live in a vacuum. It is not enough to recover a database after a disaster; it must also be available to the client applications. Backup and Disaster Recovery strategies should incorporate other elements from the database ecosystem and support database restore on another SQL Server. Those elements include server logins, SQL Jobs, Database Mail profiles, procedures in the `master` database, and a few others. They should be scripted and tested together with the backup strategy.

Partial Database Availability and Piecemeal Restore

Partial database availability is an Enterprise Edition feature that allows you to keep part of the database online during a disaster or to restore the database on a filegroup-by-filegroup basis, making these filegroups available to users one by one. Partial database availability works on per-filegroup basis and requires a `PRIMARY` filegroup and transaction log file to be available and online.

■ **Tip** Do not place user objects in the `PRIMARY` filegroup. This reduces the size of the `PRIMARY` filegroup and the time required to restore it in case of a disaster.

Partial database availability is especially beneficial in cases of data partitioning. Different data in the system may have different RTO requirements. For example, it is not uncommon to have the recovery time requirement for current critical operation data in minutes, while the recovery time for older, historical data is listed in hours or even days. Piecemeal restore allows you to perform a partial database restore and quickly bring operational data online without waiting for historical data to be restored.

Let's assume that we have the database OrderEntryDB with four filegroups: Primary, Entities, OperationalData, and HistoricalData. The Primary filegroup resides on the M: drive, Entities and OperationalData reside on the N: drive, and HistoricalData resides on the S: drive. Listing 31-13 shows the database layout for this.

Listing 31-13. Partial DB availability: Database layout

```
create database OrderEntryDB
on primary
(name = N'OrderEntryDB', filename = N'M:\OrderEntryDB.mdf'),
filegroup Entities
(name = N'OrderEntryDB_Entities', filename = N'N:\OrderEntryDB_Entities.ndf'),
filegroup OperationalData
(name = N'OrderEntryDB_Operational', filename = N'N:\OrderEntryDB_Operational.ndf'),
filegroup HistoricalData
(name = N'OrderEntryDB_Historical', filename = N'S:\OrderEntryDB_Historical.ndf')
log on
(name = N'OrderEntryDB_log', filename = N'L:\OrderEntryDB_log.ldf');
```

In the first example, let's assume that the S: drive is corrupted and the HistoricalData filegroup becomes unavailable. Let's see how you can recover the data from this filegroup and move the files to another drive.

As a first step, shown in Listing 31-14, you need to mark the corrupted file as being offline. This operation terminates all database connections, although users can reconnect to the database immediately afterward.

Listing 31-14. Partial DB availability: Mark file as offline

```
alter database OrderEntryDb modify file(name = OrderEntryDB_Historical, offline);
```

At this point, all of the data in the HistoricalData filegroup is unavailable to users. However, users can still work with the data from the other filegroups.

If you queried the sys.database_files view with the query shown in Listing 31-15, you would see that the data files from the HistoricalData filegroup have an OFFLINE state. Figure 31-5 shows this state.

Listing 31-15. Partial DB availability: Querying state of the files

```
select file_id, name, state_desc, physical_name
from sys.database_files
```

	file_id	name	state_desc	physical_name
1	1	OrderEntryDB	ONLINE	M:\OrderEntryDB.mdf
2	2	OrderEntryDB_log	ONLINE	L:\OrderEntryDB_log.ldf
3	3	OrderEntryDB_Entities	ONLINE	N:\OrderEntryDB_Entities.ndf
4	4	OrderEntryDB_Operational	ONLINE	N:\OrderEntryDB_Operational.ndf
5	5	OrderEntryDB_Historical	OFFLINE	S:\OrderEntryDB_Historical.ndf

Figure 31-5. *Partial DB availability: Data files' state after marking one file as offline*

In the next step, you should make a tail-log backup, as shown in Listing 31-16. It does not matter that the database is still online and that other sessions are generating log records. The `OrderEntryDB_Historical` file is offline, and therefore none of the newly generated log records would apply to the data in that file. It is worth mentioning that you should not use the `NORECOVERY` option when making a tail-log backup because `NORECOVERY` switches the database to a `RESTORING` state.

Listing 31-16. Partial DB availability: Making tail-log backup

```
backup log OrderEntryDB
to disk = N'V:\OrderEntryDB-tail-log.trn'
with no_truncate, init,
name = N'OrderEntryDB-Tail-log backup';
```

As a next step, you should restore a full backup from the current log chain, restoring individual files as shown in Listing 31-17.

Listing 31-17. Partial DB availability: Restoring a full backup

```
restore database OrderEntryDB
file = N'OrderEntryDB_Historical'
from disk = N'V:\OrderEntryDB.bak' with file = 1,
move  N'OrderEntryDB_Historical' to N'P:\OrderEntryDB_Historical.ndf',
norecovery, stats = 5;
```

If you ran the query that shows the state of the files from Listing 31-15 again, you would see the results shown in Figure 31-6. Only one file would be in the `RESTORING` stage, while all other files would be online and available to users.

	file_id	name	state_desc	physical_name
1	1	OrderEntryDB	ONLINE	M:\OrderEntryDB.mdf
2	2	OrderEntryDB_log	ONLINE	L:\OrderEntryDB_log.ldf
3	3	OrderEntryDB_Entities	ONLINE	N:\OrderEntryDB_Entities.ndf
4	4	OrderEntryDB_Operational	ONLINE	N:\OrderEntryDB_Operational.ndf
5	5	OrderEntryDB_Historical	RESTORING	P:\OrderEntryDB_Historical.ndf

Figure 31-6. *Partial DB availability: Data files' state after applying a full backup*

Finally, you should restore all other differential and log backup files, finishing with the tail-log backup. You do not need to specify each individual file here. SQL Server will restore only files that are in the `RESTORING` state. Review the code for doing this, shown in Listing 31-18.

Listing 31-18. Partial DB availability: Restoring other backup files

```
restore log OrderEntryDB
from disk = N'V:\OrderEntryDB.trn' with file = 1,
norecovery, stats = 5;
```

```
-- Restoring tail-log backup
restore log OrderEntryDB
from disk = N'V:\OrderEntryDB-tail-log.trn' with file = 1,
norecovery, stats = 5;

restore database OrderEntryDB with recovery;
```

The database is recovered, and all files are now online, as shown in Figure 31-7.

	file_id	name	state_desc	physical_name
1	1	OrderEntryDB	ONLINE	M:\OrderEntryDB.mdf
2	2	OrderEntryDB_log	ONLINE	L:\OrderEntryDB_log.ldf
3	3	OrderEntryDB_Entities	ONLINE	N:\OrderEntryDB_Entities.ndf
4	4	OrderEntryDB_Operational	ONLINE	N:\OrderEntryDB_Operational.ndf
5	5	OrderEntryDB_Historical	ONLINE	P:\OrderEntryDB_Historical.ndf

Figure 31-7. *Partial DB availability: Data files' state after restore*

You can use the same sequence of actions while recovering individual files in the non-Enterpise Editions of SQL Server, although the database switches to RESTORING state and would not be available to users during this process.

The same technique can be applied when you want to perform a piecemeal restore of the database, bringing it online on a filegroup-by-filegroup basis. You could use a RESTORE statement, specifying the list of the filegroups, and use the PARTIAL option. Listing 31-19 shows you how to perform a piecemeal restore of the Primary, Entities, and OperationalData filegroups.

Listing 31-19. Piecemeal filegroup restore: Restoring Primary, Entities, and OperationalData filegroups

```
restore database OrderEntryDB
filegroup='Primary', filegroup='Entities', filegroup='OperationalData'
from disk = N'V:\OrderEntryDB.bak' with file = 1,
move N'OrderEntryDB' to N'M:\OrderEntryDB.mdf',
move N'OrderEntryDB_Entities' to N'N:\OrderEntryDB_Entities.ndf',
move N'OrderEntryDB_Operational' to N'N:\OrderEntryDB_Operational.ndf',
move N'OrderEntryDB_log' to N'L:\OrderEntryDB_log.ldf',
norecovery, partial, stats= 5;

restore log OrderEntryDB
from disk = N'V:\OrderEntryDB.trn' with file = 1,
norecovery, stats = 5;

restore log OrderEntryDB
from disk = N'V:\OrderEntryDB-tail-log.trn' with file = 1,
norecovery, stats = 5;

restore database OrderEntryDB with recovery;
```

At this point, files from the restored filegroups are online, while the historical data file is in a RECOVERY_PENDING state. You can see the results of the query from Listing 31-15 in Figure 31-8.

	file_id	name	state_desc	physical_name
1	1	OrderEntryDB	ONLINE	M:\OrderEntryDB.mdf
2	2	OrderEntryDB_log	ONLINE	L:\OrderEntryDB_log.ldf
3	3	OrderEntryDB_Entities	ONLINE	N:\OrderEntryDB_Entities.ndf
4	4	OrderEntryDB_Operational	ONLINE	N:\OrderEntryDB_Operational.ndf
5	5	OrderEntryDB_Historical	RECOVERY_PENDING	S:\OrderEntryDB_Historical.ndf

Figure 31-8. *Piecemeal filegroup restore: Data files state after Primary, Entities, and OperationalData filegroups are restored*

Finally, you can bring the `HistoricalData` filegroup online by using the `RESTORE` statements shown in Listing 31-20.

Listing 31-20. Piecemeal filegroup restore: Restoring the HistoricalData filegroup

```
restore database OrderEntryDB
filegroup='HistoricalData'
from disk = N'V:\OrderEntryDB.bak' with file = 1,
move N'OrderEntryDB_Historical' to N'S:\OrderEntryDB_Historical.ndf',
norecovery, stats = 5;

restore log OrderEntryDB
from disk = N'V:\OrderEntryDB.trn' with file = 1,
norecovery, stats = 5;

restore log OrderEntryDB
from disk = N'V:\OrderEntryDB-tail-log.trn' with file = 1,
norecovery, stats = 5;

restore database OrderEntryDB with recovery;
```

A piecemeal restore greatly improves the availability of the system; however, you should design the data layout in such a way that allows you to utilize it. Usually, this implies the use of data partitioning techniques, which we discussed in Chapter 16, "Data Partitioning."

Partial Database Backup

SQL Server allows you to back up individual files and filegroups as well as exclude read-only filegroups from a backup. You can back up read-only filegroups separately and exclude them from regular full backups, which could dramatically reduce the size of backup files and backup time.

Listing 31-21 marks the `HistoricalData` filegroup as read-only, and it backs up the data from this filegroup. After that, it performs a full backup for read-write filegroups only using the `READ_WRITE_FILEGROUPS` option and log backup.

Listing 31-21. Partial backup: Performing backups

```
alter database OrderEntryDB modify filegroup HistoricalData readonly;

backup database OrderEntryDB
filegroup = N'HistoricalData'
```

```
to disk = N'V:\OrderEntryDB-hd.bak'
with noformat, init,
name = N'OrderEntryDB-HistoricalData Backup', stats = 5;

backup database OrderEntryDB read_write_filegroups
to disk = N'V:\OrderEntryDB-rw.bak'
with noformat, init,
name = N'OrderEntryDB-R/W FG Full', stats = 5;

backup log OrderEntryDB
to disk = N'V:\OrderEntryDB.trn'
with noformat, init,
name = N'OrderEntryDB-Transaction Log ', stats = 5;
```

You can exclude the HistoricalData filegroup from all further full backups as long as you keep the filegroup read-only.

If you need to restore the database after a disaster, you could perform a piecemeal restore of read-write filegroups, as shown in Listing 31-22.

Listing 31-22. Partial backup: Piecemeal restore of read-write filegroups

```
restore database OrderEntryDB
filegroup='Primary', filegroup='Entities', filegroup='OperationalData'
from disk = N'V:\OrderEntryDB-rw.bak' with file = 1,
move N'OrderEntryDB' to N'M:\OrderEntryDB.mdf',
move N'OrderEntryDB_Entities' to N'N:\OrderEntryDB_Entities.ndf',
move N'OrderEntryDB_Operational' to N'N:\OrderEntryDB_Operational.ndf',
move N'OrderEntryDB_log' to N'L:\OrderEntryDB_log.ldf',
norecovery, partial, stats = 5;

restore database OrderEntryDB
from disk = N'V:\OrderEntryDB-rw.bak' with file = 1,
norecovery,  stats = 5;

restore log OrderEntryDB
from disk = N'V:\OrderEntryDB.trn' with file = 1
norecovery,  stats = 5;

restore database OrderEntryDB with recovery;
```

The Primary, Entities, and OperationData filegroups are now online, and the HistoricalData filegroup is in the RECOVERY_PENDING state, as shown in Figure 31-9.

	file_id	name	state_desc	physical_name
1	1	OrderEntryDB	ONLINE	M:\OrderEntryDB.mdf
2	2	OrderEntryDB_log	ONLINE	L:\OrderEntryDB_log.ldf
3	3	OrderEntryDB_Entities	ONLINE	N:\OrderEntryDB_Entities.ndf
4	4	OrderEntryDB_Operational	ONLINE	N:\OrderEntryDB_Operational.ndf
5	5	OrderEntryDB_Historical	RECOVERY_PENDING	S:\OrderEntryDB_Historical.ndf

Figure 31-9. *Partial backup: Data files state after piecemeal restore of read-write filegroups*

You can bring the HistoricalData filegroup online by performing a restore of the original filegroup backup file, as shown in Listing 31-23.

Listing 31-23. Partial backup: Read-only filegroup restore

```
restore database OrderEntryDB
filegroup='HistoricalData'
from disk = N'V:\OrderEntryDB-hd.bak' with file = 1,
move N'OrderEntryDB_Historical' to N'S:\OrderEntryDB_Historical.ndf',
recovery, stats = 5;
```

Microsoft Azure Integration

SQL Server includes several backup-related features that are integrated with Microsoft Azure. Let's look at them in detail.

Backup to Microsoft Azure

Starting with SQL Server 2012 SP1 CU2, you can back up directly to or restore from Microsoft Azure Blob Storage by specifying the URL location as part of the BACKUP and RESTORE commands. Listing 31-24 shows an example of this process.

Listing 31-24. Backup to and restore from Windows Azure Blob Storage

```
create credential MyCredential
with identity = 'mystorageaccount', secret = '<Secret Key>';

backup database MyDb
to url = 'https://mystorageaccount.blob.core.windows.net/mycontainer/MyDb.bak'
with credential = 'MyCredential', stats = 5;

restore database MyDb
from url = 'https://mystorageaccount.blob.core.windows.net/mycontainer/MyDb.bak'
with credential = 'MyCredential', recovery, stats = 5;
```

Storing a database backup in Azure Blob Storage is a great option when you run SQL Server in a virtual machine in Microsoft Azure. However, for on-premises installations, you need to consider the upload and download bandwidth that you have available. Uploading and downloading large, multi-gigabyte backup files can take hours or even days, which makes it impractical and leads to prolonged downtime in case of disaster. With all that being said, storing backup files in Microsoft Azure can still be an option for small and non-mission critical databases with RTOs that allow prolonged downtime.

In addition to the BACKUP TO URL command, you can use the *Microsoft SQL Server Backup to Microsoft Windows Azure Tool*, which will work with any version and edition of SQL Server. This tool works separately from SQL Server. It intercepts backup files being written to the folders based on specified rules, and it uploads the files to Azure Blob Storage.

Unfortunately, the Microsoft SQL Server Backup to Microsoft Windows Azure Tool does not keep a local copy of backup files. You should consider the available bandwidth and RTO requirements if you decided to use it.

■ **Note** You can download the Microsoft SQL Server Backup to Microsoft Windows Azure Tool from `https://www.microsoft.com/en-us/download/details.aspx?id=40740`.

With all that being said, storing backup files in the Cloud can be a good option when you need a cost-effective, redundant solution for on-premises installations. Nonetheless, it is better to implement this separately from the SQL Server backup process, uploading a local copy of the backup files afterward. This approach allows you to quickly recover a database from a disaster by using the local copy of the backup files while keeping another copy of the files in the Cloud for redundancy purposes.

Managed Backup to Microsoft Azure

SQL Server 2014 introduced the concept of managed backup to Microsoft Azure Blob Storage. This can be enabled at the instance or database levels. SQL Server automatically performs full and transaction log backups based on the following criteria and retains them for up to 30 days:

Full backup is performed in any of the following situations: the last full backup was taken more than a week previously, there is log growth of 1 GB or more since the last full backup, or the backup chain is broken.

Transaction log backup is taken every two hours, when 5 MB of log space is used, or when transaction log backup is lagging behind the full backup.

SQL Server 2014 managed backup does not work with databases in the `SIMPLE` or `BULK LOGGED` recovery models, nor with system databases. These limitations have been removed in SQL Server 2016.

Managed backup backs up files to Microsoft Azure Blob Storage only. Local storage is not supported. All considerations that we discussed in the "Backup to Microsoft Azure" section also apply to managed backups.

■ **Note** You can read more about managed backups at `https://msdn.microsoft.com/en-us/library/dn449496.aspx`. Make sure to select the appropriate version of SQL Server. There are significant changes in the configuration between SQL Server 2014 and 2016.

File Snapshot Backup for Database Files in Azure

Starting with SQL Server 2014, you can store database files in Microsoft Azure Blob Storage with both on-premises and SQL Server in Azure VM installations. This provides you the option of using cheap and redundant storage in those systems that can tolerate lower I/O performance and higher latency of the Blob Storage.

As an additional enhancement, SQL Server 2016 allows you to utilize Azure Blob Snapshot capabilities as part of the database backup and restore processes. This approach works very differently from traditional backups. As the opposite of the regular backup files, which contain a copy of the data pages and log records, Blob Snapshots store a read-only copy of all database files at the time of snapshot creation.

Figure 31-10 illustrates the concept of file snapshot backups. Only full and log backups are supported. However, both of these types are very similar and contain a copy of all database files. The difference between them is that full backup initializes the backup chain while log backup truncates the log after the operation.

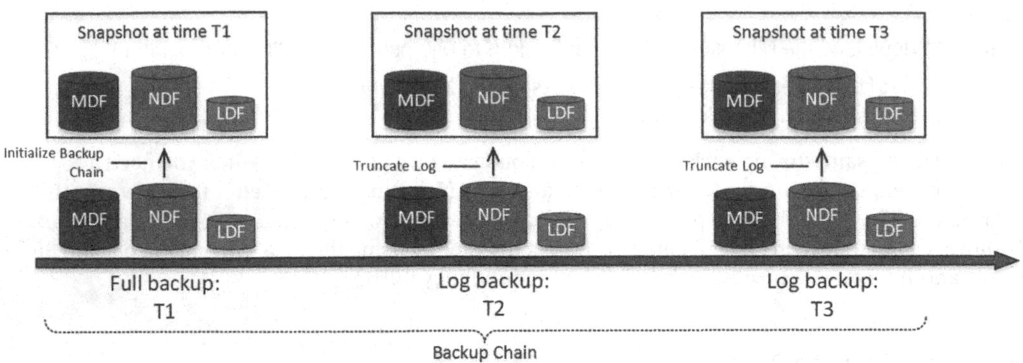

***Figure 31-10.** File snapshot backups*

The restore process copies database files from the snapshot, always creating a new copy of the database. As you can guess, this allows you to run the RESTORE DATABASE command using the log-backup snapshot as the source. It contains a copy of the database files, and you do not need to restore the full backup first.

For a point-in-time restore, you should use two adjacent backup sets performing two restore operations. First, you need to restore the database from the first backup set using the RESTORE DATABASE WITH NORECOVERY command. This command will create a new copy of the database as of the time of the backup set. Next, you need to restore the log from the second backup set using the RESTORE LOG WITH STOPAT statement. This command replays the portion of the transaction log starting from the previously restored backup set and up to the time specified in the STOPAT option. Figure 31-11 illustrates that.

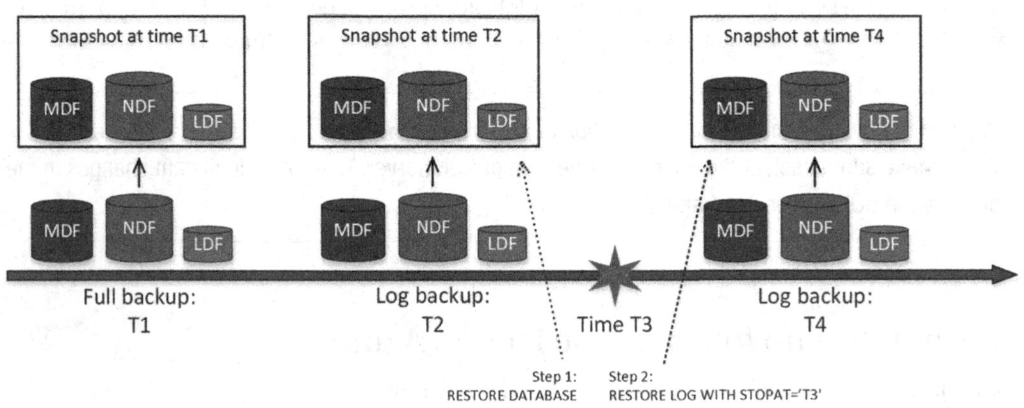

***Figure 31-11.** File snapshot point-in-time restore*

Listing 31-25 shows the code that implements this process.

Listing 31-25. File snapshot backup and point-in-time restore

```
-- Performing full and log database backups
backup database MyDb  /* T1 in Figure 31-11 */
to url = 'https://mystorageaccountname.blob.core.windows.net/mycontainername/MyDb.bak'
with file_snapshot;
```

```
backup log MyDb /* T2 in Figure 31-11 */
to url = 'https://mystorageaccountname.blob.core.windows.net/mycontainername/MyDb_2016-03-
11-08-00.trn'
with file_snapshot;

backup log MyDb /* T4 in Figure 31-11 */
to url = 'https://mystorageaccountname.blob.core.windows.net/mycontainername/MyDb_2016-03-
11-10-00.trn'
with file_snapshot;

-- Point in time restore at 10am /* T4 in Figure 31-11 */
restore database /* T2 in Figure 31-11 */
from url = 'https://mystorageaccountname.blob.core.windows.net/mycontainername/MyDb_2016-03-
11-08-00.trn'
with norecovery, replace;

restore log /* T4 in Figure 31-11 */
from url = 'https://mystorageaccountname.blob.core.windows.net/mycontainername/MyDb_2016-03-
11-11-00.trn'
with recovery, stopat = '2016-03-11T10:00:00.000';
```

As you can guess, the restore process utilizes file copy operations under the hood and needs to replay a very limited amount of transaction log records. This can provide a very significant time reduction as compared to the traditional restore process, and it simplifies the design of the backup strategy. You should add Azure storage costs into the equation, however. Even though Blob Storage is relatively cheap, its cost can be significant with a large number of snapshots, especially with large databases.

Finally, file snapshot backups require you to manage backup sets from within SQL Server. The manual deletion of snapshot files can invalidate the backup set. You should use the sys.sp_delete_backup and sys.sp_delete_backup_file_snapshot system stored procedures for such an action.

■ **Note** You can read more about file snapshot backups at `https://msdn.microsoft.com/en-us/library/mt169363.aspx`.

Summary

A full database backup stores a copy of the database that represents its state at the time when the backup finished. Differential backup stores extents that have been modified since the last full backup. Log backups store the portion of the transaction log starting from the last full or the end of the last log backup.

Full and differential backups are supported in every recovery model, while log backup is supported only in the `FULL` or `BULK LOGGED` recovery models.

Differential backups are cumulative. Every backup contains all of the extents modified since the last full backup. You can restore the latest differential backup when needed. Conversely, log backups are incremental and do not contain the part of the transaction log backed up by previous backups.

A full backup and a sequence of log backups make up a backup chain. You should restore all of the backups from a chain in the right order when restoring a database. You can use the `COPY_ONLY` option with full or log backups to keep the backup chain intact.

The frequency of log backups is dictated by the Recovery Point Objective (RPO) requirements. The log should be backed up in intervals that do not exceed the allowable data loss for a system.

A Recovery Time Objective (RTO) specifies the maximum acceptable duration of the recovery process, which affects full and differential backup schedules. You should also factor in the time required to transmit files over the network when designing a backup strategy. Backup compression can help reduce this time and improve the performance of backup and restore operations, but at a cost of extra CPU load and extra time as the compression and decompression of data takes place.

You should validate backup files and make sure that your backup strategy is valid and meets the RTO and RPO requirements. The duration of the backup and restore processes changes over time along with database size and load.

SQL Server Enterprise Edition supports piecemeal restore, which allows you to restore data on per-filegroup basis, keeping part of the database online. This feature greatly improves the availability of the system and helps to reduce the recovery time of critical operational data when the data is properly partitioned.

You can exclude read-only data from regular full backups, which can reduce backup time and the size of backup files. Consider putting read-only data into a separate filegroup and marking it as read-only when appropriate.

CHAPTER 32

High Availability Technologies

A High Availability (HA) strategy helps improve the availability of the system due to hardware, software, or network malfunctions. Even though it sounds similar to a backup and Disaster Recovery (DR) strategy, it is not the same. A High Availability strategy serves as the first level of defense, making a hardware failure or software crash transparent to users. Disaster recovery, on the other hand, deals with situations where a system needs to be recovered after a disaster that was not prevented by the High Availability strategy in use.

Think about a situation in which a system is hosted within a single datacenter. It may have a High Availability strategy that implements server redundancy within the datacenter, which keeps the system online in case of a server failure. However, it would not necessarily protect the system from a simultaneous malfunction of multiple servers, nor from datacenter-level disasters. A Disaster Recovery strategy will help you recover from the latter case, restoring or rebuilding the system on different hardware or in a different datacenter.

This chapter provides you with an overview of the different High Availability technologies available in SQL Server and explains the principles they were built upon. You should not view this chapter as a definitive guide on SQL Server High Availability implementations, which easily merit their own book.

This chapter does not cover High Availability technologies that are not SQL Server–based, such as SAN replication and virtualization technologies. You should research and evaluate those technologies if they are applicable to your environment.

SQL Server Failover Cluster

Perhaps the best-known High Availability technology in SQL Server is a *SQL Server failover cluster*. Until SQL Server 2005, a failover cluster was the only High Availability technology that supported automatic failover in case of a server failure.

Starting with SQL Server 2012, Microsoft changed the name of this technology, calling it an *AlwaysOn Failover Cluster*. However, I will continue to use the old name in this chapter to avoid confusion with *AlwaysOn Availability Groups*.

A SQL Server failover cluster is installed as a resource group of the Windows Server Failover Clustering (WSFC) cluster. WSFC should be installed and configured prior to SQL Server failover cluster installation.

With both WSFC and SQL Server failover clusters, the group of individual servers, called *nodes,* shares a set of resources, such as disks or databases in a SQL Server instance. However, only one node at time owns the resource. If a node fails, ownership is transferred to another node through a process called *failover*.

The simple installation of a failover cluster consists of two different nodes, each of which has a SQL Server instance installed. The nodes work with a single copy of the users' and system databases placed on shared storage. The cluster provides a virtual SQL Server name and IP address, which can be used by client applications. These resources are different from those assigned to a Windows Server Failover Clustering cluster. Figure 32-1 illustrates a simple failover cluster.

D. Korotkevitch, *Pro SQL Server Internals*, DOI 10.1007/978-1-4842-1964-5_32

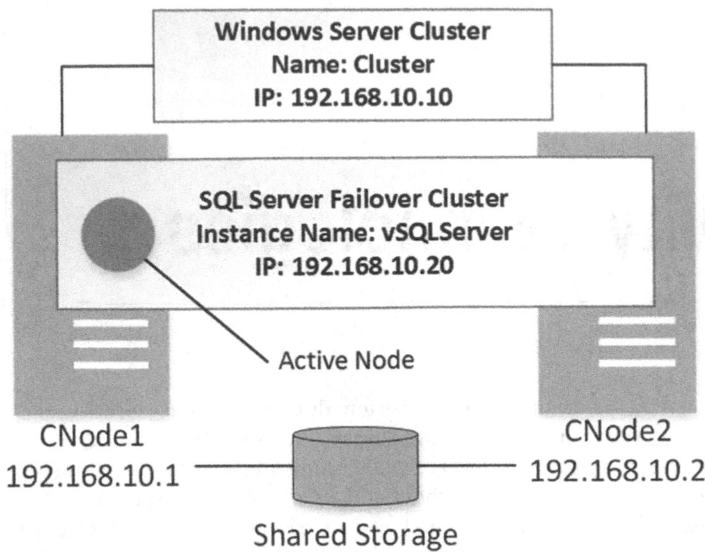

Figure 32-1. *Two-node WSFC with a single SQL Server failover cluster instance*

One of the SQL Server instances is active and handles all user requests. Another node provides hot standby. When something happens to the active node, the SQL Server cluster fails over to the second node, formerly the *passive* node, and starts from there. This process, in a nutshell, is a SQL Server instance restart. The new active node performs a crash recovery of all of the databases in the instance, preventing clients from connecting to the databases until this process is complete.

The duration of crash recovery and failover greatly depends on the amount of data modified by active transactions at the time of the failover. With short OLTP transactions, failover could be in the under-a-minute range. However, it is possible that failover can take much longer, as with active transactions that modified a large amount of data and need to be rolled back by a crash recovery process.

In-Memory OLTP, which we will discuss in Part VIII of this book, could also affect failover time. SQL Server loads all data from durable memory-optimized tables into the memory during database startup, which can be time consuming if there is a large amount of data.

A SQL Server failover cluster works on the instance level and protects the entire instance. It includes system and user databases, SQL Server configuration settings, logins and security, and SQL Agent jobs. Entire SQL Server instance fails over, it is impossible to have some databases running on a SQL Server instance installed on one node of the cluster and other databases running on another SQL Server instance installed on a different node.

Failover clustering requires that all databases be placed into shared storage. Starting with Windows Server 2012R2, you can use SMB shares to store the data. Nevertheless, storage becomes the single point of failure.

■ **Important** Always use highly redundant storage with failover clustering. Moreover, consider combining a SQL Server failover cluster with other High Availability technologies that allow you to store copies of the databases on a different storage devices. It increases the availability of the system and minimizes possible data loss in case of a storage failure.

The system databases also use shared storage. Fortunately, starting with SQL Server 2012, you can put tempdb onto the local drive, which can significantly improve the performance of the cluster, especially if you place it on the solid state-based storage.

While it is relatively easy to set up Windows clusters, which host a single SQL Server cluster instance, they double the number of servers that you will need. Even though you are generally not required to buy another SQL Server license if a passive node is used for High Availability only, there are still the hardware, electricity, and maintenance costs to consider.

■ **Note** Work with Microsoft licensing specialists to determine the exact licensing requirements for your High Availability configuration. Licensing requirements vary based on SQL Server version and existence of a Software Assurance agreement.

One of the ways to reduce the cost of a failover cluster solution is by using *multi-instance failover clusters*. In this configuration, one Windows cluster hosts multiple SQL Server failover cluster instances.

Figure 32-2 shows an example of a two-node multi-instance cluster. There are two cluster instances of SQL Server: vSales and vAccounting. The CNode1 cluster node is the active node for the vSales instance, and the CNode2 is the active node for the vAccounting instance.

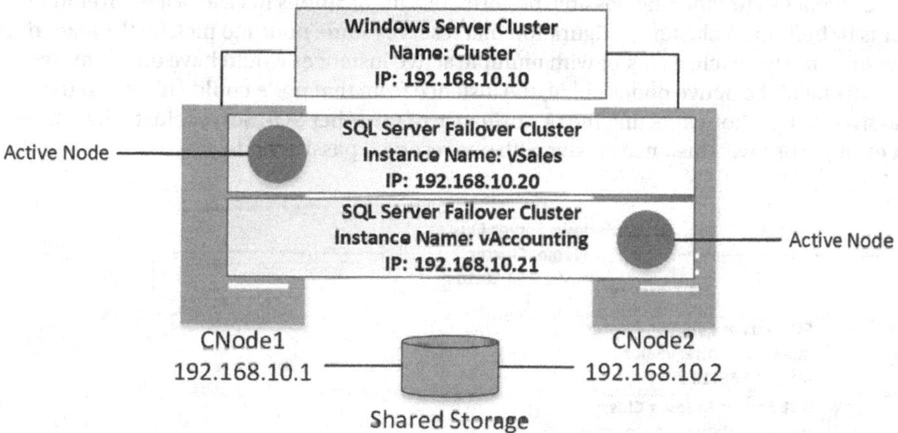

Figure 32-2. *Two-node multi-instance cluster*

In an ideal situation, when all cluster nodes are up and running, multiple SQL Server clusters would not affect each other's performance. Each SQL Server cluster instance is running on a separate node. Unfortunately, the situation becomes much more complex when one of the servers becomes unavailable, and the SQL Server instance fails over to another node, as shown in Figure 32-3. Both SQL Server cluster instances are running on the same server, competing for CPU and memory and affecting each other's performance.

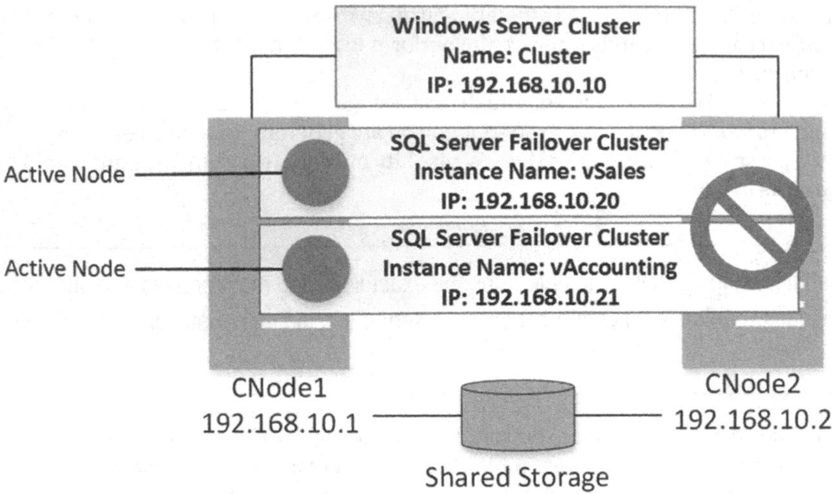

Figure 32-3. *Two-node multi-instance cluster: One-node failure*

One of the typical approaches to reducing possible performance implications in case of a failover in a multi-instance cluster is by building a cluster configuration that reserves some nodes to pick up the load in case of a failover. With such an approach, a cluster with multiple active instances would have one or more reserved passive nodes. If one of the active nodes failed, the instance from that node could fail over to the reserved, formerly passive node without affecting the performance of the other SQL Server cluster instances. Figure 32-4 shows an example of a two-instance cluster with one reserved passive node.

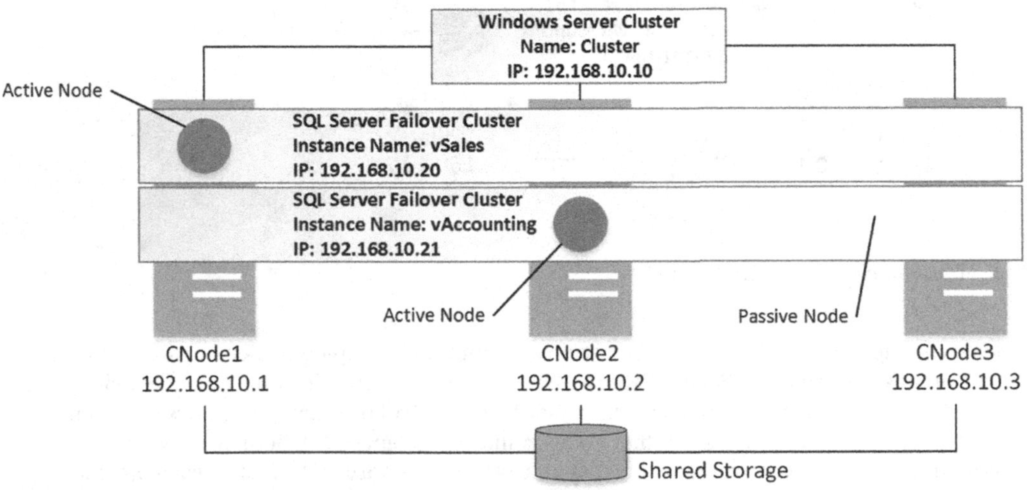

Figure 32-4. *Multi-instance cluster with one reserved passive node*

Unfortunately, you cannot implement configurations with reserved passive nodes in the Standard Edition of SQL Server, which supports two-node failover clusters only.

You should carefully plan multi-instance cluster configurations, assuming that multiple instances might end up running on the same node. You should buy hardware that can handle the load, then set up the minimum and maximum server memory for each instance on each node. It is better to set up the minimum server memory based on a worst-case scenario that assumes multiple instances are running simultaneously. The maximum server memory can be set up based on the best-case scenario, when there is only one instance running on the node.

Remember to keep some memory reserved for the OS when you set up the SQL Server *Maximum Server Memory* configuration option. We already discussed how to choose the right value for this setting in Chapter 28. Do not forget that in SQL Server versions prior to 2012, memory settings controlled the memory usage of the buffer pool only. You should factor in non-buffer pool memory when you set the memory settings.

Dealing with CPU configuration is more challenging. You can set up an affinity mask for the different instances, which restricts an instance from using some of the logical CPUs. However, this is not the best approach when you have only one instance running on a node and you would like to have as much CPU power available to the instance as possible. It is better to use the Windows System Resource Manager or Windows System Center and throttle CPU activity if needed.

You can monitor SQL Server cluster instances similar to how you monitor non-clustered ones. You should use a virtual SQL Server instance name, which ensures that the monitoring target always represents an active SQL Server instance, regardless of the cluster node where it is currently running.

■ **Note** You can read more about SQL Server failover clustering at `http://technet.microsoft.com/en-us/library/hh270278.aspx`.

Database Mirroring and AlwaysOn Availability Groups

The SQL Server failover cluster provides great instance-level protection. However, it does not protect against storage failure. Only one copy of the data is stored, and storage failure can lead to data loss.

That problem can be mitigated by another set of technologies, such as *database mirroring* and *AlwaysOn Availability Groups*, which allow you to persist a byte-by-byte copy of the databases on two or, in the case of AlwaysOn Availability Groups, several servers.

Database mirroring works on the database level. AlwaysOn Availability Groups work on the database group level, which may include one or more databases. Every database can participate in a single mirroring or AlwaysOn session. Each SQL Server instance, however, can host multiple mirrored databases or AlwaysOn Availability Groups.

The database scope is the key difference between these technologies and SQL Server failover clustering, which works on the SQL Server instance level. Only the database(s) are replicated between the nodes. While on the one hand this provides you with flexibility and allows you to replicate different databases to different servers, it also introduces administration overhead. You need to perform server configuration, set up logins and security, configure SQL Agent jobs, and perform other server-level actions individually on each server in the infrastructure.

Technologies Overview

Both mirroring and the AlwaysOn Availability Groups work by sending a stream of log records from *primary* to *secondary* servers, which are sometime called *nodes*. In database mirroring, these servers are called the *principal* and the *mirror*. All data modifications must be done on the primary server. With database mirroring, the database on the mirror server is inaccessible to the clients. With AlwaysOn Availability Groups, clients can access and read data from the secondary servers when it is enabled in the configuration.

The technology can work in either *synchronous* or *asynchronous* modes, which are also called *synchronous* and *asynchronous commits*. A synchronous commit guarantees no data loss for committed transactions as long as data replication is up to date and both servers can communicate with each other. With synchronous commits, the primary server does not send an acknowledgment that a transaction is committed to the client until the secondary server hardens a `COMMIT` log record in its transaction log. Figure 32-5 illustrates the step-by-step commit process in this mode.

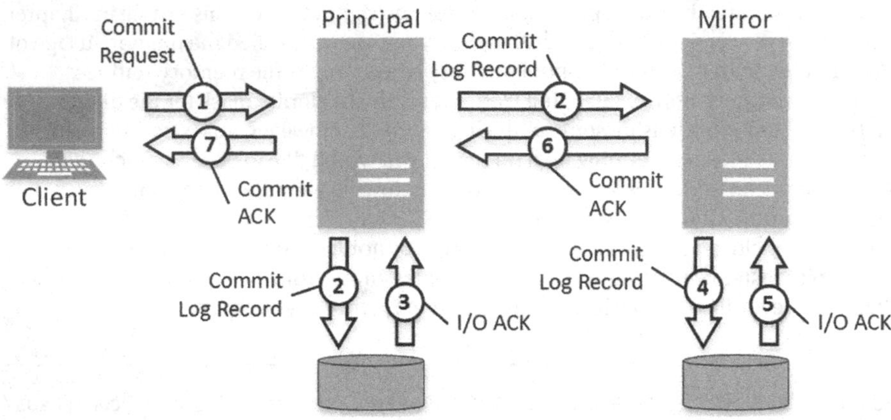

Figure 32-5. *Synchronous commit*

Let me reiterate that a synchronous commit *only* guarantees that there will be no data loss when both servers are online and the process is up to date. If, for example, the secondary server goes offline, the primary server continues to run and commit transactions, keeping the database on the secondary server in `SUSPENDED` state. It is building a *send queue* of the log records, which needs to be sent to the secondary server when it comes back online. If something happened with the primary server at this point, the data modifications since the time when the secondary server disconnected could be lost.

When the secondary server comes back online, synchronization switches to the `SYNCHRONIZING` state, and the primary server starts sending log records from the send queue to the secondary server. Data loss is still possible at this point. Only after all log records have been sent to the secondary server does the process switch to a `SYNCHRONIZED` state, which guarantees that no data loss will occur in synchronous commit mode.

The connectivity between the servers and the size of the send queue both affect transaction log truncation. SQL Server defers log truncation until all records from VLF are sent to the secondary servers. While in most cases this does not introduce any issues with log management, this is not the case when the secondary server is offline. The send queue will grow and the transaction log will not be able to truncate until the secondary server is online again and log records are transmitted over the network.

■ **Tip** Consider dropping database mirroring or removing the secondary server from the AlwaysOn Availability Group if you see prolonged secondary server downtime.

As you can see in Figure 32-5, steps 2, 4, 5, and 6 introduce extra latency, which depends on network and mirror server I/O performance. In some heavily loaded OLTP systems, such latency is unacceptable. You can avoid it by using asynchronous commit, which with database mirroring is called *high performance* mode. In this mode, the primary server sends log records to the secondary server, and it does not wait for acknowledgment before committing transactions, as illustrated in Figure 32-6.

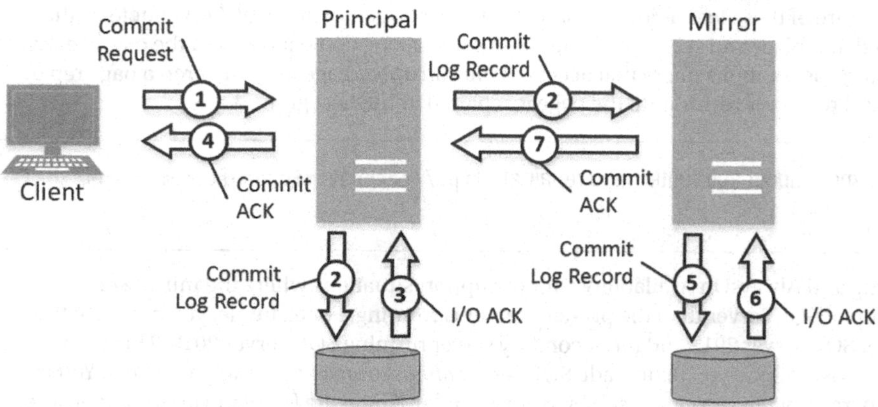

Figure 32-6. *Asynchronous commit*

Network latency with asynchronous commit does not affect the performance of the primary server, although there is a possibility of data loss based on log records that are in the send queue at the time when the primary server crashed.

Although both the primary and secondary server databases are byte-to-byte copies of each other, the process does not update the data files at the time when it hardens the log records in the transaction log. SQL Server applies the changes to the data files on the secondary server by replaying the log records asynchronously, regardless of the commit mode. **Synchronous commit only guarantees that log records are synchronously hardened in the transaction log. It does not guarantee or provide synchronous changes of the data files.**

On secondary servers, SQL Server uses the set of threads called *redo threads* to replay the log records and apply the changes to the data files. The number of active redo threads depends on technology, SQL Server version, number of worker threads in the system, and, most important, number of synchronized databases and their workload. A large number of mirrored or synchronized databases can exhaust the pool of worker threads and affect the performance of the system.

The portion of the transaction log that has yet to be replayed is called the *redo queue*. You should monitor the sizes of both the send queue on the primary server and the redo queue on the secondary server. The size of the send queue indicates possible data loss in cases of primary server failure. The size of the redo queue indicates how many log records must be replayed, and thus how long it could take to bring the mirrored database back online after failover.

The *SQLServer:Database Mirroring* performance counters provide information about database mirroring performance along with send and redo queue statistics. The *SQL Server:Availability Replica* and *SQL Server:Database Replica* counters provide AlwaysOn Availability Groups–related information.

You need to test how database maintenance affects the size of the redo queue. Some operations, such as an index rebuild or database shrink, can generate an enormous amount of log records, which in turn makes the redo queue very big. This can lead to a long crash recovery process in case of a failover, which could prevent you from meeting the availability requirements defined in the SLA.

■ **Tip** See `https://msdn.microsoft.com/en-us/library/ms190030.aspx` for more details about database mirroring monitoring. More information about AlwaysOn Availability Groups monitoring is available at `https://msdn.microsoft.com/en-us/library/ff877954.aspx`.

One very useful feature of these technologies is automatic page repair. When SQL Server detects that a data page is corrupted, it replaces this corrupted page with a fresh copy of the page from the other server. This is an asynchronous process, and a query that accessed the corrupted page and triggered a page repair could be interrupted and receive an error until the page is repaired in the background.

■ **Note** You can read more about automatic page repair at `http://technet.microsoft.com/en-us/library/bb677167.aspx`.

Database mirroring and AlwaysOn Availability Groups support situations where the mirror server is running a newer version of SQL Server than the primary server is running. For example, you can have the primary server running SQL Server 2012 and the secondary server running SQL Server 2016. This is an extremely useful feature, as it allows you to upgrade SQL Server *almost* transparently to your users. You can perform an in-place upgrade of the secondary server, failover, and upgrade the former primary server. Keep in mind that it is impossible to fail back to the older version of SQL Server after failover, and also remember to update all statistics in the database with the `sp_updatestats` stored procedure after an upgrade.

Database Mirroring: Automatic Failover and Client Connectivity

Synchronous database mirroring is available in two different modes: *high protection* and *high availability*. The only difference between these two modes is automatic failover support. SQL Server supports automatic failover in high availability mode; however, it requires you to have a third SQL Server instance, *witness*, which helps to support quorum in the configuration.

■ **Note** The quorum indicates that the servers that participated in the database mirroring session agreed on their roles; that is, which server worked as the principal and which worked as the mirror. In practice, quorum can be established as long as at least two servers (from principal, mirror, and witness) can communicate with each other. We will discuss what happens with mirroring when one or more servers are unavailable later in this chapter.

You can use any edition of SQL Server, including the Express Edition, as the witness. It is critical, however, that the witness instance be installed on another physical server to avoid the situation where a hardware malfunction of a single physical server kicks multiple SQL Server instances offline and prevents a quorum from being established.

Table 32-1 shows the similarities and differences among different database mirroring modes.

Table 32-1. *Database Mirroring Modes*

	High Performance	High Protection	High Availability
Commit	Asynchronous	Synchronous	
SQL Server edition	Enterprise Edition only	Enterprise and Standard editions	
Data loss	Possible	Not possible when DB is in SYNCHRONIZED state	
Automatic failover	Not supported	Not supported	Supported with witness server
Performance impact	None	Network and mirror I/O subsystem latency	

Let's look at a few possible failover scenarios in High Availability mode. The key point here is that, at any point in time, servers must have a quorum, and thus at least two servers must be able to connect to each other.

First, let's assume that the principal and witness servers lost the connection to the mirror server. The principal and witness servers still have a quorum, and the principal server continues to work on mirroring in SUSPENDED state. If at this stage the principal server lost its connection to the witness server, and therefore did not have a quorum, the principal server would shut down.

■ **Tip** Consider placing the witness instance close to the principal server to avoid connectivity issues between them and unnecessary failovers and shutdowns. It is also beneficial to fail back to a former principal server that is close to a witness instance, when the server is back online.

Now, let's assume that the principal server goes offline. In this case, the mirror and witness server can see each other and thus have a quorum, so automatic failover occurs and the mirror server becomes the new principal server. If the old principal server were to come back online and see both servers, it would become the mirror server and synchronize itself with the new principal server. Otherwise, it would shut itself down to avoid a *split brain* situation where two different servers allow clients to connect to different copies of the same database, changing the data simultaneously.

If the witness server goes offline, mirroring continues to work without the ability to perform automatic failover. This is similar to high protection mode, with the exception that if the principal server lost its connection to the mirror server without the witness server being available, the principal server would shut down to avoid a split brain situation.

In high protection mode, a loss of connectivity between the principal and mirror servers would not stop the principal server. If the principal goes down, you have to perform a manual failover to make the mirror server the new principal server. There is one caveat, though. If you performed a manual failover and at some point the principal server came back online without connectivity to the former mirror server, it would continue to behave as the principal server, which is a split brain situation.

The .Net SQL client automatically obtains and caches a mirror server name when it is connected to the principal server. If a failover happened *after* the mirror server name was cached, the client application would be able to reconnect to the mirror server, which would become the new principal server. However, if the failover occurred *before* the mirror server name was cached, the application would be unable to connect to the former principal server, which would now work as the mirror server and keep the database in RESTORING state. The application would be unable to obtain information about the new principal server and, therefore, would be unable to connect to the database.

You can avoid such situations by specifying the mirror server name in an additional connection string property, *Failover Partner*. The SQL client tries to connect to the server specified there only in cases when it is unable to connect to the principal server. When the principal server is online, the SQL client ignores the mirror server name specified in this property and caches the mirror server name as it was retrieved from the principal server.

You should be careful when removing database mirroring. The SQL client will be able to connect to the database after mirroring is removed only when it runs on the server specified in the *Server Name* property of the connection string. You will get a *"Database is not configured for database mirroring"* error if it runs on the server specified as a *Failover Partner*.

Database mirroring failover is usually faster than failover cluster failover. Contrary to a failover cluster, which restarts the entire SQL Server instance, database mirroring performs crash recovery on a single database. However, the actual duration of the failover process depends on the size of the redo queue and the number of log records that need to be replayed.

The PARTNER TIMEOUT database setting controls the database mirroring failover detection time, which is ten seconds by default. You can change this with the ALTER DATABASE SET PARTNER TIMEOUT command. It is beneficial to increase this setting if the network latency between the principal server and the mirror server is high; for example, when servers reside in different datacenters and/or in the Cloud.

Another example of when you should increase this setting is when you set up the database mirroring with a SQL Server failover cluster instance as one of the database mirroring partners. The cluster failover process usually takes longer than ten seconds, and keeping the default `PARTNER TIMEOUT` setting can trigger unnecessary database mirroring failovers. You should set the `PARTNER FAILOVER` value to be greater than the typical cluster failover time.

The database on the mirror server stays in `RESTORING` state; therefore, clients are unable to access it. However, it is possible to create a read-only database snapshot on the mirror server so you can access it for reporting purposes. This snapshot represents the database as of the last `CHECKPOINT` on the primary server.

■ **Note** Coverage of database snapshots is beyond the scope of this book. You can read more about this topic at `http://technet.microsoft.com/en-us/library/ms175158.aspx`.

Database mirroring has been deprecated in SQL Server 2012. AlwaysOn Availability Groups are a great replacement for database mirroring; however, in SQL Server 2012 and 2014, they included only to Enterprise Edition.

The Standard Edition of SQL Server 2016, on the other hand, supports *Basic Availability Groups*, which allow you to create a one-database, two-server replica similar to database mirroring. Basic Availability Groups, however, support asynchronous commit, which is not the case with database mirroring.

■ **Note** You can read more about database mirroring at `http://technet.microsoft.com/en-us/library/ms189852.aspx`.

AlwaysOn Availability Groups

As the opposite to database mirroring, AlwaysOn Availability Groups require and rely on the Windows Server Failover Clustering (WSFC) cluster. While this can make their infrastructure and setup more complicated as compared to database mirroring, it also simplifies the deployment of client applications. They can connect to the AlwaysOn Availability Group through the *listener*, which virtualizes a SQL Server instance in a way similar to the SQL Server failover cluster.

The AlwaysOn Availability Group consists of one primary node (or replica) with read/write access. In Enterprise Edition, you can have up to four secondary nodes with SQL Server 2012, and up to eight secondary nodes with SQL Server 2014–2016. The three nodes in the availability group can use synchronous commit. You need two nodes in order to support automatic failover. As I already mentioned, the Standard Edition of SQL Server 2016 supports two-node Basic Availability Groups.

Figure 32-7 shows an example of an AlwaysOn Availability Group configuration with three nodes.

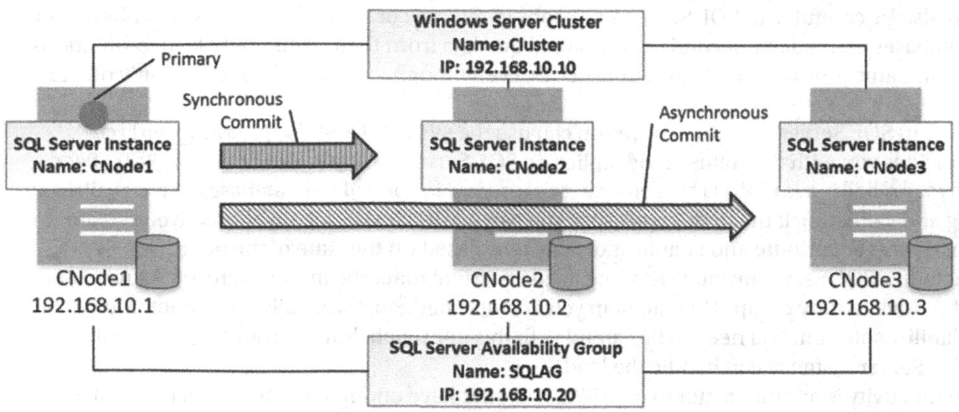

Figure 32-7. *AlwaysOn Availability Group*

In fact, the availability group can consist of a single primary node only. This behavior helps abstract the availability group infrastructure from applications. For example, you can set up a single-node availability group and create a listener, virtualizing a SQL Server instance during the initial stage of deployment. After that, system administrators can start changing connection strings using the listener as the server without having to worry about the availability group infrastructure's state while you are adding other nodes there.

Another useful example is changing database options that require single-user access, such as enabling the `READ COMMITTED SNAPSHOT` isolation level. It is impossible to switch the database to `SINGLE_USER` mode with database mirroring enabled. You can remove database mirroring and reestablish it later, although you will need to check all connection strings, making sure that the principal server is always specified as the *Server* rather than the *Failover Partner*. However, an AlwaysOn Availability Group allows you to remove all secondary nodes without having to worry about connection strings. While it is still not possible to switch a database that participates in an AlwaysOn Availability Group to `SINGLE_USER` mode, you can remove the database from availability group, change the database options, and add the database back to availability group in a matter of seconds with minimal impact on client applications.

Unlike database mirroring, which works on a single-database scope, AlwaysOn Availability Groups can include multiple databases. This guarantees that all of the databases in the group will be failed over together and will always have the same primary node. This behavior is helpful when a system requires multiple databases residing on the same server in order to be operational.

AlwaysOn Availability Groups allow read-only access to secondary nodes and also allow you to perform database backups from them. Moreover, an application can specify that it only needs read-only access in the connection string and the AlwaysOn Availability Group routes it to a readable secondary node automatically.

■ **Note** You can read about client connections to AlwaysOn Availability Groups at `http://technet.microsoft.com/en-us/library/hh510184.aspx`.

This behavior helps reduce the load on the primary server, although you should be careful and always monitor the size of the redo queue. It is entirely possible for the `REDO` process on secondaries to fall behind and serve clients data that is not up to date and is different from the database on the primary node. It is also important to remember that the failover process under such conditions can take a long time. Even though you would not have any data loss with a synchronous commit, the database would not be available until the crash recovery process finished.

You should also be careful with SQL Server Agent jobs in the case of readable secondaries. Jobs are able to access the databases on readable secondaries and read the data from there. This could lead to situations where you have the same jobs running on multiple nodes, even though you want them to run only on the primary node.

As a solution, in SQL Server 2014 and above you can use the `sys.fn_hadr_is_primary_replica` function that provides you with the status of the replica. In SQL Server 2012 you can check the `Role_Desc` column of the `sys.dm_hadr_availability_replica_states` view for one of the databases in the availability group, checking and validating if the node is primary. You can use it in every job or, alternatively, create another job that runs every minute and enable or disable jobs based on the state of the node.

You can include a SQL Server instance running inside a virtual machine in the Microsoft Azure Cloud as a member of the availability group. This can help you add another geographically redundant node to your High Availability solution. You need to be careful with this approach, however, and make sure that the Cloud-based SQL Server instance can handle the load.

Internet connectivity is another factor to consider. It should have enough bandwidth to transmit log records and be stable enough to keep the Microsoft Azure node online and connected most of the time. Remember that the transaction log will not be truncated when connectivity goes down, and some records were not transmitted to the secondary nodes.

AlwaysOn Availability Groups provide a great alternative to database mirroring. Unfortunately, this feature is not supported in the Standard Edition of SQL Server 2012–2014.

■ **Note** You can read about AlwaysOn Availability Groups at `http://technet.microsoft.com/en-us/library/hh510230.aspx`.

Log Shipping

Log shipping allows you to maintain a copy of the database on one or more secondary servers. In a nutshell, log shipping is a very simple process. You perform log backups based on some schedule, copy those backup files to a shared location, and restore them on one or more secondary servers. Optionally, you can have a separate server that monitors the log shipping process, retains information about backup and restore operations, and sends alerts if attention is required.

Figure 32-8 illustrates a log shipping configuration.

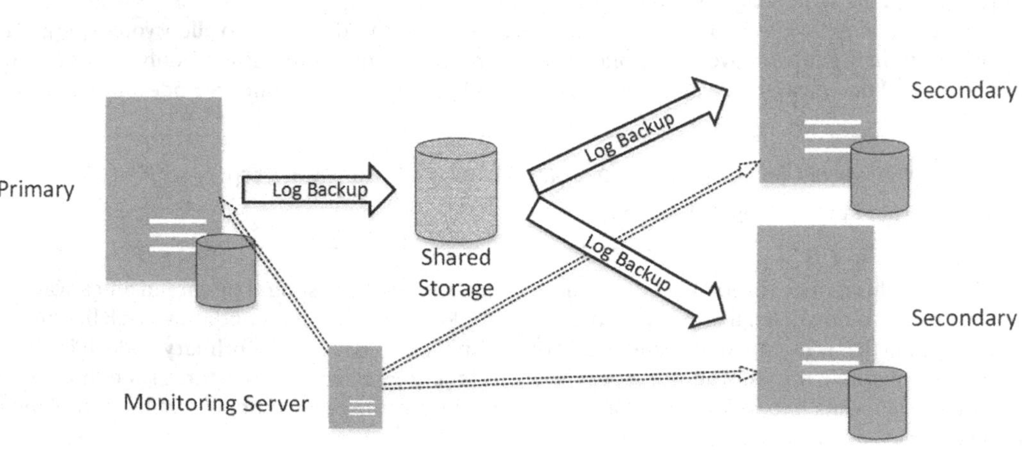

Figure 32-8. *Log shipping*

Log shipping does not protect against data loss. Log backups are done on a schedule, and if the transaction log on the primary server were corrupted you would lose all changes since the last log backup.

Log shipping is often used together with other High Availability technologies. One of the common scenarios is using it with a failover cluster instance, shipping the log to the secondary servers in remote off-site locations. This provides geo-redundancy for the data tier in the systems at a low implementation cost.

Log shipping is also useful in scenarios where you purposely do not want to have up-to-date data on the secondary servers. This could help you to recover data from accidental deletions on the primary server.

There is no automatic failover support with log shipping. Manual failover consists of a few steps. First, you need to disconnect users from the database and, perhaps, switch the database to `RESTRICTED_USER` or `SINGLE_USER` mode to avoid client connections during the failover process. Next, you need to back up the remaining part of the log that is on the primary server. It might be beneficial to use the `NORECOVERY` option during backup if you expect to fail back to the primary server later. Finally, you should apply all remaining log backups on the secondary server and recover the database to bring it online. Obviously, you should also change the connection strings to point to the new server.

Secondary servers keep the database in `RESTORING` state, preventing clients from accessing it. You can work around this by using the `STANDBY` option, which gives you read-only access to the database. However, clients will lose connectivity during the time it takes log backups to be restored. You should also consider the SQL Server licensing model, which requires you to purchase another license when the server is used for anything but supporting high availability.

You should design a log shipping strategy and backup schedule in a way that allows you to avoid a backlog when log backups are transmitted over the network and are restored more slowly than they were generated.

Make sure that the shared locations you use for backup storage have enough space to accommodate your backup files. You can reduce the storage size and transmission time and improve the performance of the backup and restore process by using backup compression if it is supported by your SQL Server version and edition, and if you have adequate CPU resources to handle the compression overhead.

Log shipping is, perhaps, the easiest solution to set up and maintain. It is also not uncommon to see custom *log shipping-like* implementations that allow you to implement additional business requirements and address the limitations of native SQL Server log shipping. Nevertheless, you should keep in mind possible data loss and consider combining it with other technologies if such data loss is unacceptable or if automatic failover is required.

■ **Note** You can read more about log shipping at `http://technet.microsoft.com/en-us/library/ms187103.aspx`.

Replication

In contrast to the technologies that we have already discussed in this chapter, *replication* is far more than a High Availability solution. The main goal of replication is to *copy* and *replicate* data across multiple databases. Even though it can be used as a High Availability technology, this is hardly its main purpose.

Replication works in the scope of *publications*, which are collections of database objects. Replication is a good choice if you want to protect just a subset of the data in the database; for example, a few critical tables. Another key difference between replication and other High Availability techniques is that replication allows you to implement a solution where data can be modified in multiple places. It could require the implementation of a complex conflict detection mechanism and, in some cases, have a negative performance impact, although this is a small price to pay in some scenarios.

There are three major types of replication available in SQL Server, as follows:

> *Snapshot replication* generates and distributes a snapshot of the data based on some schedule. One example when this could be useful is a set of tables that are updated based on a schedule, perhaps once per week. You may consider using snapshot replication to distribute the data from those tables after the update. Another example involves a small table with highly volatile data. In this case, when you do not need to have an up-to-date copy of the data on the secondary servers, snapshot replication would carry much less overhead as compared to other replication types.
>
> *Merge replication* allows you to replicate and merge changes across multiple servers, such as in scenarios where those servers are infrequently connected to each other. One possible example is a company with a central server and separate servers in branch offices. The data can be updated in every branch office and merged/distributed across the servers using merge replication. Unfortunately, merge replication requires changes in the database schema and the use of triggers, which can introduce performance issues.
>
> *Transactional replication* allows you to replicate changes between different servers with relatively low latency, usually in seconds. By default, secondary servers, called *subscribers*, are read-only, although you have the option to update data there. A special kind of transactional replication, called *peer-to-peer replication*, is available in the Enterprise Edition of SQL Server, and it allows you to build a solution with multiple updateable databases hosted on different servers and replicating data between each other.

Transaction replication is the most appropriate replication type to be used as a High Availability technology for updateable data. Figure 32-9 illustrates the components used in transactional replication. The primary server, called the *publisher*, is accessed by a special job known as the *Log Reader Agent*, which is constantly scanning the transaction log of the database configured for replication and harvesting log records that represent changes in the publications. Those log records are converted to logical operations (`INSERT`, `UPDATE`, `DELETE`) and are stored in another *distribution database*, usually on another server called *distributor*, which runs the Log Reader Agent job. Finally, the distributor either pushes those changes to subscribers or, alternatively, subscribers will pull them from the distributor based on the replication configuration.

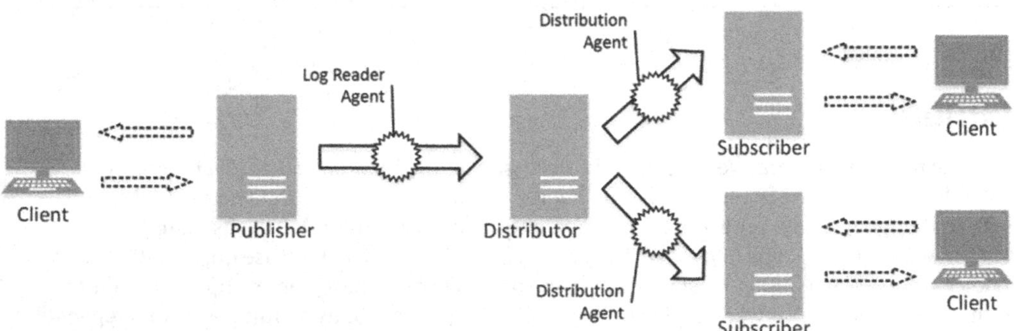

Figure 32-9. *Transactional replication with push subscriptions*

Peer-to-peer replication, shown in Figure 32-10, allows you to build a distributed and scalable solution with multiple updateable databases residing on different servers called *nodes*. It is an Enterprise Edition feature that is based on transaction replication, and therefore it has a very low latency to distribute the changes between nodes. One scenario where it is useful is with a system with multiple datacenters. You can host individual SQL Server instances in every datacenter and redirect clients to the nearest one. Peer-to-peer replication synchronizes data across all nodes and handles the situation when a node temporarily loses connectivity with other nodes.

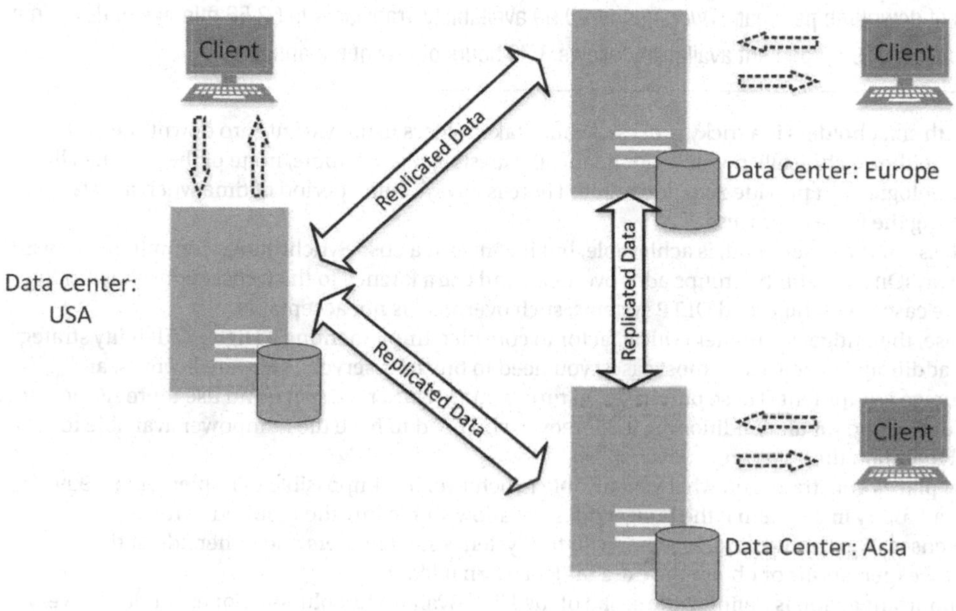

***Figure 32-10.** Peer-to-peer replication*

The biggest downside of replication is its complexity. Setting up and monitoring a complex replication topology is by far a more complex task than other High Availability solutions. Moreover, it often requires the implementation of a complex conflict resolution mechanism, and it can require changes in the application logic and database schema to minimize conflicts.

I would suggest avoiding the use of replication for High Availability purposes, unless you need to protect a very small subset of data in the database or have other use cases that would benefit from replication besides high availability.

■ **Note** You can read more about replication at `http://technet.microsoft.com/en-us/library/ms151198.aspx`

Designing a High Availability Strategy

The process of designing a High Availability strategy mixes art, science, and politics all together. It is an iterative process of collecting and often adjusting requirements, setting the right expectations, and building a solution that fits into the budget.

Requirements gathering is the first stage of the process. Like a backup strategy, you have to deal with RPO and RTO metrics. Usually, you can get them from the Service Level Agreement (SLA). Alternatively, if those metrics were not present in the SLA, you should work with the system's stakeholders to define them.

■ **Note** System availability requirements are usually measured in "groups of nines." For example, *five nines*, or 99.999 percent availability, means that system should be available 99.999 percent of time, which translates to 5.26 minutes of downtime per year. *Four nines*, or 99.99 availability, translates to 52.56 minutes of downtime per year. *Three nines*, or 99.9 percent availability, allows 8.76 hours of downtime annually.

Working with stakeholders is a tricky process. While stakeholders usually want zero downtime and zero data loss, this is neither technically possible nor financially feasible. For example, none of the existing High Availability technologies can provide zero downtime. There is always some period of time when a system is inaccessible during the failover process.

Zero data loss, on the other hand, is achievable, but it comes at a cost. Synchronous commit in database mirroring or AlwaysOn Availability Groups adds overhead and extra latency to the transactions that modify the data. In some cases, with high-end OLTP systems, such overhead is not acceptable.

In either case, the budget is another critical factor to consider. Implementing a High Availability strategy always leads to additional expenses. In most cases, you need to buy new servers, software licenses, and network and storage equipment. These purchases, in turn, require extra rack space and use more AC power for the new hardware and for air conditioning it. Moreover, you need to have the manpower available to implement and maintain the solution.

The budget places constraints on what you are able to achieve. It is impossible to implement 99.999 or even 99.99 availability in a system if the budget does not allow you to buy the required hardware and software licenses. You should work together with the system's stakeholders and either adjust the requirements and expectations or obtain the extra budget when needed.

Another important action is defining the scope of the High Availability solution. For example, it is very important to understand if the required availability level must be achieved around the clock, or just during business hours. Another important question to resolve is whether the solution should be geographically redundant. That requirement can dramatically increase the complexity and cost of the solution.

It is very important to not start the implementation until you have collected and analyzed all of the requirements, including budget constraints. Taken together, the requirements will dictate what technology or technologies you will be able to use for the implementation.

Table 32-2 compares the High Availability technologies available in different versions and editions of SQL Server.

Table 32-2. *Comparison of SQL Server High Availability Technologies*

	Failover Cluster	Log Shipping	Database Mirroring	AlwaysOn AG	Replication
SQL Server version	2005–2016	2005–2016	2005–2016 Deprecated in 2012–2016	2012–2016	2005–2016
Standard edition support	2 nodes only	Supported	Synchronous only	Not supported in 2012–2014. SQL Server 2016 supports basic AG.	Supported
Unit of protection	Instance	Database	Database	Group of databases. (One DB in basic AG)	Publication (Subset of data)
Data loss	No data loss but not protected against storage failure	Data loss based on log backup schedule	No data loss with synchronous mirroring	No data loss with synchronous commit	Data loss based on latency
Single point of failure	Storage	No	No	No	No
Failover	Automatic	Manual	Automatic (Requires witness)	Automatic	Manual
Failover time (best-case scenario)	Minutes (crash-recovery of all databases in the instance)	N/A	Seconds (crash recovery of a single database)	Seconds (crash recovery of all databases in AG)	N/A
Performance overhead	No overhead	No overhead	Overhead of synchronous commit	Overhead of synchronous commit	Additional load to transaction log

Obviously, you are not restricted to the use of a single High Availability technology. It is often beneficial to combine technologies, using a few of them together to be protected from different kinds of failures. For example, if an AlwaysOn Availability Group is not an option due to SQL Server version or edition incompatibility, you can use a failover cluster together with database mirroring or log shipping. A failover cluster will protect you from a server malfunction, while the second technology protects you against a storage system failure.

In cases where data loss is not allowed, the choices are limited to either database mirroring or AlwaysOn Availability Groups with synchronous commit. Even though a failover cluster uses a single copy of the database, and therefore you cannot lose data due to replication (or synchronization) latency, it is not protected against storage failure. Unfortunately, synchronous commit could introduce unacceptable latency in some of the edge cases.

This is an example of a situation where you need to work with the stakeholders and reach a compromise. For example, in some cases it could be *good enough* to have a failover cluster with data stored on a highly redundant disk array with asynchronous commit to another server.

The unit of protection is another very important factor to consider. If an AlwaysOn Availability Groups are unavailable, synchronous database mirroring could be a great option that guarantees zero data loss and does not have a single point of failure. However, it works within the scope of a single database, which could be problematic if the system consists of multiple databases that should reside on the same server. A failover cluster is the only option besides an AlwaysOn Availability Group that guarantees that multiple databases will always fail over together.

You can still use database mirroring in such a scenario by implementing a routine that monitors the principal server database location and fails over the databases if needed. One possible implementation is a SQL Agent job that runs every minute and queries the `State` or `State_Desc` columns in the `sys.databases` view for one of the databases in the group. The job could fail over other databases in the group when it detects that the database is in `RESTORING` state, which means that it was failed over to a different server.

It is extremely important to test your High Availability strategy and perform failover after it is implemented in production. The situation where everything works perfectly the first time is extremely rare. You may encounter security issues, incorrect settings in application connection strings, missing objects on the servers, and quite a few other issues that prevent the system from working as expected after failover. Even though testing of the failover process can lead to system downtime, it is better to have a controlled outage with all personnel on deck than a situation where the system does not work after an unplanned disaster.

Finally, you should regularly reevaluate and test your High Availability and Disaster Recovery strategies. Database size and activity growth can invalidate your HA implementation, making it impossible to meet RPO and RTO requirements. It is especially important when secondary (standby) servers are less powerful than the primary ones. It is entirely possible that the system would not be able to keep up with the load after a failover in such cases.

Summary

Even though High Availability and Disaster Recovery strategies are interconnected, they are not the same. A High Availability strategy increases the availability of the system by handling hardware or software malfunctions transparently to users. A Disaster Recovery strategy deals with situations that the High Availability strategy was unable to handle and when the system needs to be recovered after a disaster.

A SQL Server failover cluster protects you from server failures by implementing a clustered model using a SQL Server instance as the shared resource. Only one server/node can handle users' requests at any given time; however, a Windows Server Failover Clustering cluster can host multiple SQL Server clusters. Even though running multiple instances of a SQL Server failover cluster is a common practice that helps to reduce the cost of the solution, you should avoid situations where the cluster does not have spare passive nodes and multiple SQL Server instances running on the same node after failover with unacceptable performance.

A SQL Server failover cluster uses shared storage, which becomes the single point of failure. You should combine the failover cluster with other High Availability technologies that store the data on different storage devices to minimize the possibility of data loss resulting from storage failure.

Database mirroring and AlwaysOn Availability Groups allow you to maintain a byte-to-byte copy of the database on another server(s) by constantly sending transaction log records over the network. With synchronous commit, SQL Server does not commit the transaction on the primary server until the log record is hardened on the secondary server. This approach guarantees no data loss for committed transactions, although it adds extra latency to the transactions. With asynchronous commit, log records are sent asynchronously and data loss is possible. Data loss is possible even with synchronous commit if the secondary server is offline or data is not fully synchronized.

AlwaysOn Availability Groups allow the creation of an infrastructure with one primary server that handles read/write activity and multiple secondary servers that allow read-only access to the databases. AlwaysOn Availability Groups should be installed underneath the Windows Server Failover Clustering cluster, although every node uses separate storage for the databases.

Log shipping allows the maintenance of a copy of the database on multiple secondary servers by applying a continuous stream of log backups. It does not protect against data loss for the period since the last backup was applied.

Replication allows you to replicate a subset of data from the database across multiple databases, allowing read/write access in each location. Transaction replication has low latency for the changes to be distributed across subscribers. However, setting up and monitoring a complex replication topology is a very challenging task.

Designing a High Availability strategy is an iterative and interactive process that requires you to work with other members of the technical team as well as with stakeholders. You must make sure that RTO and RPO requirements are realistic and achievable within the budget allocated to the project.

The choice of High Availability technology depends on the requirements and budget as well as on the version and edition of SQL Server installed. You are not restricted to a single technology—it is often beneficial to combine a few technologies together.

You should consider the performance implications of the technologies that use synchronous commit, especially if the system has a performance SLA that dictates latency for some OLTP transactions.

It is extremely important to test your High Availability technology and perform failover after it is implemented in production. It is better to find and fix any issues in a controlled environment than to fight with them after a disaster occurs.

You should regularly reevaluate the High Availability solution you implement based on database size and activity growth, especially if your secondary standby servers are less powerful than your primary ones.

PART VII

Columnstore Indexes

CHAPTER 33

Column-Based Storage and Batch Mode Execution

Columnstore indexes are an Enterprise Edition feature introduced in SQL Server 2012. They are part of the new family of technologies called *xVelocity* (formerly known as *VertiPaq*), which optimizes the performance of analytical queries that scan and aggregate large amounts of data.

Columnstore indexes use a different storage format for data, storing compressed data on a per-column rather than a per-row basis. This storage format benefits query processing in data warehousing, reporting, and analytics environments where, although they typically read a very large number of rows, queries work with just a subset of the columns from a table.

The design and implementation of data warehouse systems is a very complex process that is not covered in this book. This chapter, however, will reference common database design patterns frequently encountered in such systems. Moreover, it will provide an overview of columnstore indexes and their storage format, discuss batch mode execution, and outline several tips that can improve the performance of data warehouse solutions.

Data Warehouse Systems Overview

Data warehouse systems provide the data that is used for analysis, reporting, and decision support purposes. In contrast to OLTP (online transactional processing) systems, which are designed to support operational activity and which process simple queries in short transactions, data warehouse systems handle complex queries that usually perform aggregations and process large amounts of data.

For example, consider a company that sells articles to customers. A typical OLTP query from the company's *Point-of-Sale* (POS) system might have the following semantics: *Provide a list of orders that were placed by this particular customer this month*. Alternatively, a typical query in a data warehouse system might read as follows: *Provide the total amount of sales year to date, grouping the results by article categories and customer regions*.

There are other differences between data warehouse and OLTP systems. Data in OLTP systems is usually volatile. Such systems serve a large number of requests simultaneously, and they often have a performance SLA associated with the customer-facing queries. Alternatively, the data in data warehouse systems is relatively static and is often updated based on a set schedule, such as at night or during weekends. These systems usually serve a small number of customers, typically business analysts, managers, and executives who can accept the longer execution time of the queries due to the amount of data that needs to be processed.

D. Korotkevitch, *Pro SQL Server Internals*, DOI 10.1007/978-1-4842-1964-5_33

To put things into perspective, the response time of the short OLTP queries usually needs to be in the milliseconds range. However, for complex data warehouse queries, a response time in seconds or even minutes is often acceptable.

The majority of companies start by designing or purchasing an OLTP system that supports the operational activities of the business. Reporting and analysis is initially accomplished based on OLTP data; however, as the business grows, that approach becomes more and more problematic. Database schemas in OLTP systems rarely suit reporting purposes. Reporting activity adds load to the server and degrades the performance and customer experience in the system.

Data partitioning can help address some of these issues; however, there are limits on what can be achieved with such an approach. At some point, the separation of operational and analysis data becomes the only option that can guarantee the acceptable performance of both solutions as well as the ability to meet availability SLA. In many cases, it leads to the physical separation of the data between OLTP and data warehouse databases.

It is important to remember that the data warehouse workload is usually processing a large amount of data, and this adds a heavy load on the I/O subsystem and can flush content of the buffer pool on the server. It is usually better to place OLTP and large data warehouse databases on different servers unless you have enough memory in the buffer pool to cache data from both systems.

OPERATIONAL ANALYTICS

It is also impossible to avoid mentioning another category of tasks called *operational analytics*, which has become very popular nowadays. Consider a *Point-of-Sale* system in which you want to monitor up-to-date sales and dynamically adjust articles' sale price based on their popularity. This requires you to run analytical queries on recent OLTP data.

SQL Server 2016 helps you to improve performance in such a scenario by mixing column-based and row-based indexes on the same table. OLTP queries use regular B-Tree indexes while operational analytics queries utilize columnstore indexes. We will talk about this approach in the next chapter while focusing on the classic data warehouse implementation in this chapter.

OLTP systems usually become the source of the data for data warehouses. The data from OLTP systems is transformed and loaded into a data warehouse with *ETL (Extract Transform and Load) processes*. This transformation is key; that is, database schemas in OLTP and data warehouse systems do not and should not match.

A typical data warehouse database consists of several dimensions tables and one or a few facts tables. *Facts tables* store facts or measures of the business, while *dimensions tables* store the attributes or properties of facts. In our Point-of-Sale system, the information relating to sales becomes facts while the list of articles, customers, and branch offices become dimensions in the model.

Large facts tables can store millions or even billions of rows and use terabytes of disk space. Dimensions, on the other hand, are significantly smaller.

A typical data warehouse database design follows either a *star* or a *snowflake* schema. A star schema consists of a facts table and a single layer of dimensions tables. A snowflake schema, on the other hand, normalizes dimensions tables even further.

Figure 33-1 shows an example of a star schema.

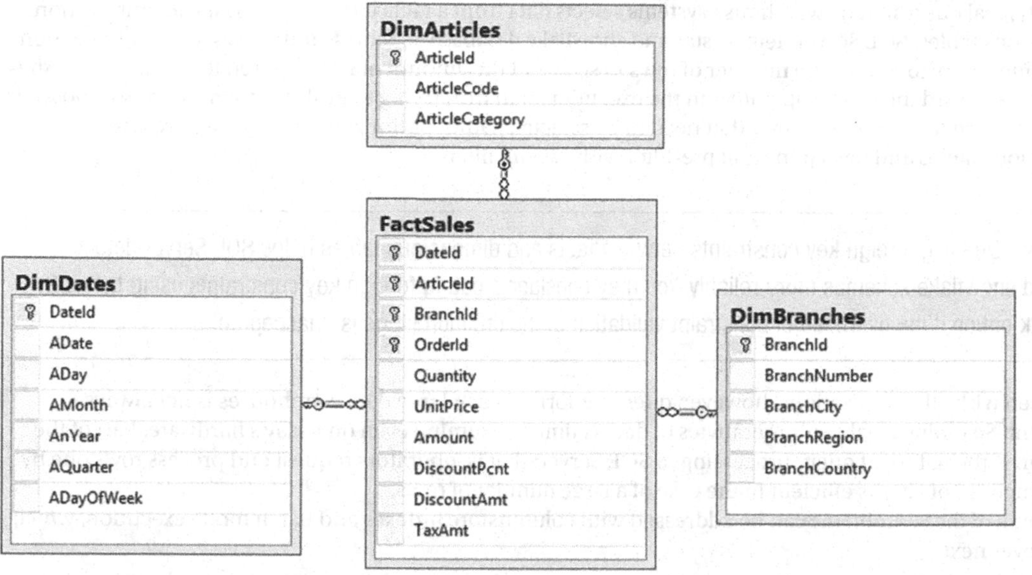

***Figure 33-1.** Star schema*

Figure 33-2 shows an example of a snowflake schema for the same data model.

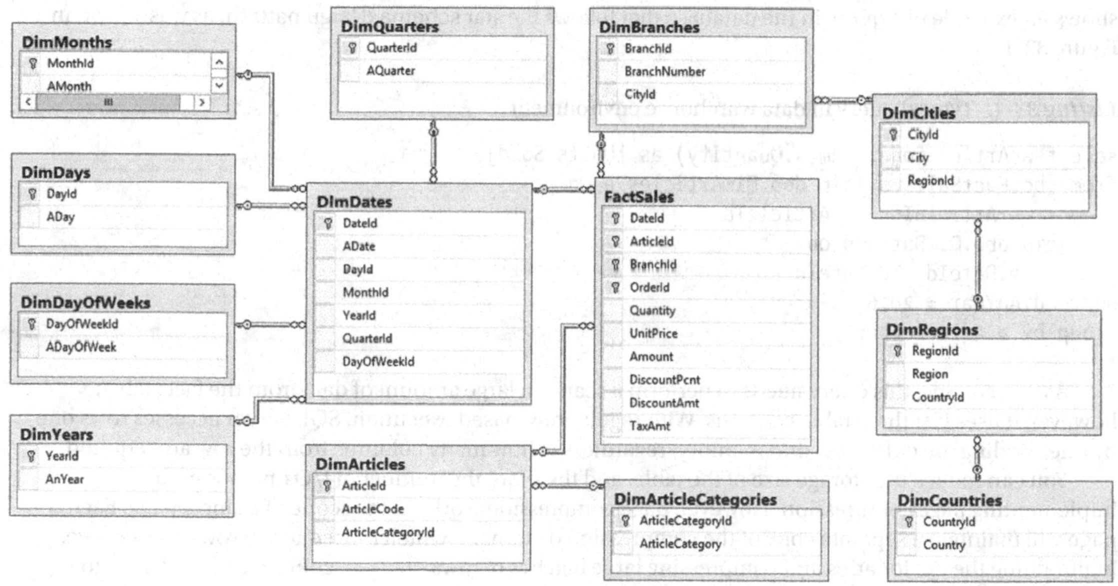

***Figure 33-2.** Snowflake schema*

A typical query in data warehouse systems selects data from a facts table and joins it with one or more dimensions tables. SQL Server detects star and snowflake database schemas, and it uses a few optimization techniques to try to reduce the number of rows to scan and the amount of I/O required for a query. It pushes predicates toward the lowest operators in the execution plan tree, trying to evaluate them as early as possible so as to reduce the number of rows that need to be selected. Other optimizations include a cross join of dimensions tables and hash joins that pre-filter with *bitmap* filters.

■ **Note** Defining foreign key constraints between facts and dimensions tables helps SQL Server detect star and snowflake schemas more reliably. You may consider creating foreign key constraints using the `WITH NOCHECK` option if the overhead of constraint validation at the creation stage is unacceptable.

Even with all optimizations, however, query performance in large data warehouses is not always sufficient. Scanning gigabytes or terabytes of data is time consuming even on today's hardware. Part of the problem is the nature of query processing in SQL Server; that is, operators request and process rows one by one, which is not always efficient in the case of a large number of rows.

Some of these problems can be addressed with columnstore indexes and batch mode execution, which I will cover next.

Columnstore Indexes and Batch Mode Execution Overview

As already mentioned, the typical data warehouse query joins facts and dimensions tables and performs some calculations and aggregations while accessing just a subset of the facts table's columns. Listing 33-1 shows an example of a query in the database that follows the star schema design pattern, as was shown in Figure 33-1.

Listing 33-1. Typical query in data warehouse environment

```
select a.ArticleCode, sum(s.Quantity) as [Units Sold]
from dbo.FactSales s join dbo.DimArticles a on
        s.ArticleId = a.ArticleId
    join dbo.DimDates d on
        s.DateId = d.DateId
where d.AnYear = 2016
group by a.ArticleCode
```

As you can see, this query needs to perform a scan of a large amount of data from the facts table; however, it uses just three table columns. With regular row-based execution, SQL Server accesses rows one by one, loading the entire row into memory, regardless of how many columns from the row are required.

You can reduce the storage size of the table, and therefore the number of I/O operations, by implementing page compression. However, page compression works in the scope of a single page. Each page will maintain a separate copy of the compression dictionary, which is used for all rows on the page. Maintaining the dictionaries and compressing large batches of rows on a per-column basis will lead to significantly better compression results.

Finally, there is another, less obvious problem. Even though access to in-memory data is orders of magnitude faster than access to data on disk, it is still slow as compared to CPU cache access time. With row mode execution, SQL Server constantly reloads CPU cache data with new rows copied from the main memory. This overhead is usually not a problem with an OLTP workload and simple queries; however, it becomes very noticeable with data warehouse queries that process millions or even billions of rows.

Column-Based Storage and Batch Mode Execution

SQL Server addresses these problems with columnstore indexes and batch mode execution. Columnstore indexes store data on a per-column rather than a per-row basis. Figure 33-3 illustrates this approach.

Column-based storage (Columnstore indexes)

DateId	ArticleId	BranchId	OrderId	Quantity	UnitPrice
51	32	10	35412	5.000	$25.99
51	18	3	35413	1.000	$9.99
52	7	4	35414	1.000	$199.99
52	18	10	35415	2.000	$9.49

Row-based storage (B-Tree indexes)

Figure 33-3. *Row-based and column-based storage*

Data in columnstore indexes is heavily compressed using algorithms that provide significant space savings, even when compared to page compression. We will compare the results of different compression methods later in this chapter. Moreover, SQL Server can skip columns that are not requested by a query, and it does not load data from those columns into memory.

The new data storage format of columnstore indexes allows SQL Server to implement a new batch mode execution model that significantly reduces the CPU load and execution time of data warehouse queries. In this mode, SQL Server processes data in groups of rows, or batches, rather than one row at a time. The size of the batches varies to fit into the CPU cache, which reduces the number of times that the CPU needs to request *external* data from memory or other components. Moreover, the batch approach improves the performance of aggregations, which can be calculated on a per-batch rather than a per-row basis.

In contrast to row mode execution, where data values are copied between operators, batch mode processing tries to minimize such copies by creating and maintaining a special bitmap that indicates if a row is still valid in the batch.

To illustrate this approach, let's consider the query in Listing 33-2.

Listing 33-2. Sample query

```
select ArticleId, sum(Quantity)
from dbo.FactSales
where UnitPrice >= 10.00
group by ArticleId
```

With regular row mode execution, SQL Server scans a clustered index and applies a filter on every row. For rows that have `UnitPrice >= 10.00`, it passes another row of two columns (`ArticleId` and `Quantity`) to the *aggregate* operator. Figure 33-4 shows this process.

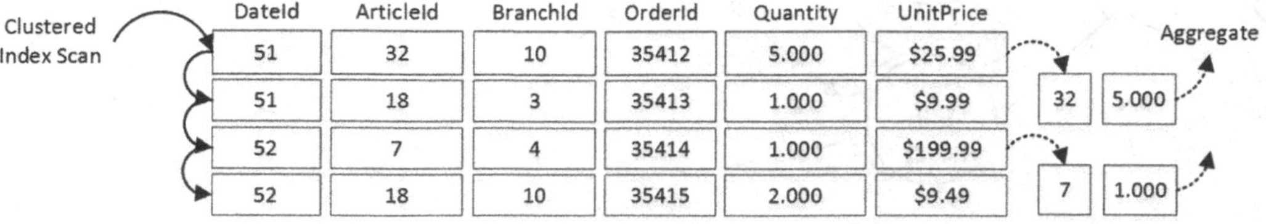

Figure 33-4. *Row mode execution*

Alternatively, with batch mode execution, the *filter* operator would set an internal bitmap that shows the validity of the rows. A subsequent aggregate operator would process the same batch of rows, ignoring non-valid ones. No data copying is involved. Figure 33-5 shows such an approach. It is also worth noting that only the `ArticleId`, `Quantity`, and `UnitPrice` columns would be loaded into the batch.

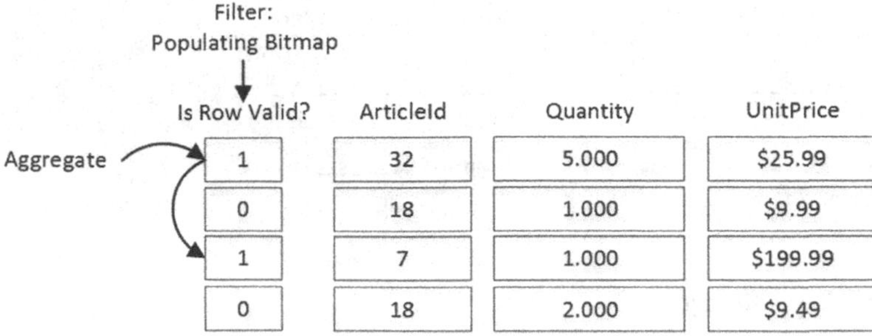

Figure 33-5. *Batch mode execution*

■ **Note** In a real system, SQL Server can push a predicate that evaluates if `UnitPrice >= 10` to the *columnstore index scan* operator, preventing unnecessary rows from being loaded into the batch. However, let's assume that this is not the case in our example.

SQL Server handles parallelism in row mode and batch mode executions very differently. As you know, in row mode execution, an *exchange* operator distributes rows between different parallel threads using one of the distribution algorithms available. However, after the distribution, a row never migrates from one thread to another until another exchange operator gathers or repartitions the data.

Figure 33-6 illustrates this by demonstrating an exchange operator that uses the *Range* redistribution method to distribute data to three parallel threads that perform *hash joins*. The first letter of a join key value would control to which thread row it is distributed and where it is processed.

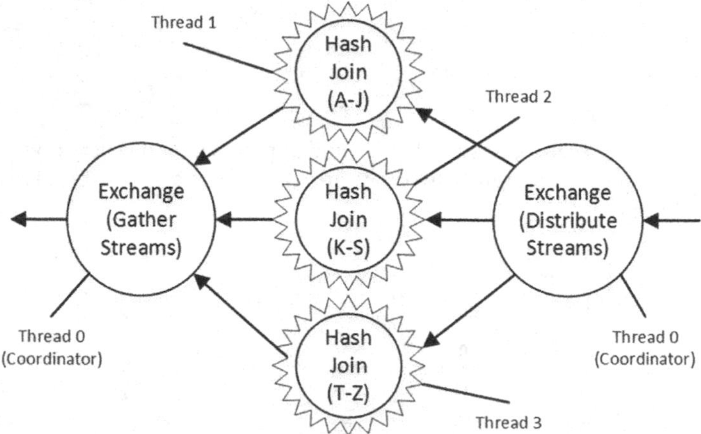

Figure 33-6. *Parallelism in row mode execution*

SQL Server takes a different approach with batch mode execution. In that mode, every operator has a queue of work items (batches) to process. Worker threads from a shared pool pick items from queues and process them while migrating from operator to operator. Figure 33-7 illustrates this method.

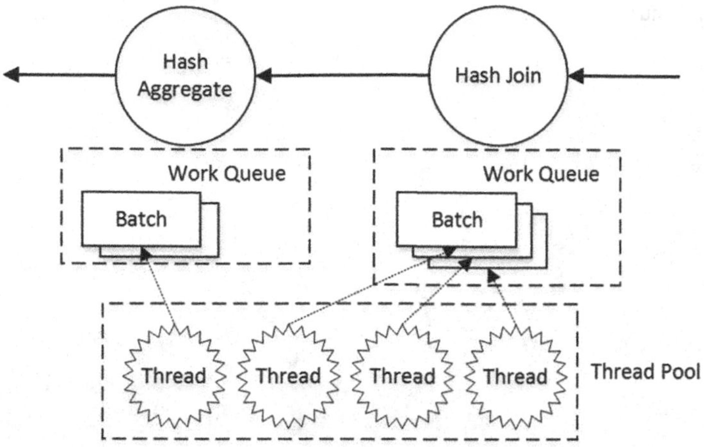

Figure 33-7. *Parallelism in batch mode execution*

One of the common issues that increases the response time of parallel queries in row mode execution is uneven data distribution. Exchange operators wait for all parallel threads to complete; thus, the execution time depends on the slowest thread. Some threads have more work to do than others when data is unevenly distributed. Batch mode execution eliminates such problems. Every thread picks up work items from the shared queue until the queue is empty.

Columnstore Indexes and Batch Mode Execution in Action

Let's look at several examples related to columnstore index behavior and performance. Listing 33-3 creates a set of tables for the database schema shown in Figure 33-1 and populates it with test data. As a final step, it creates a nonclustered columnstore index on the facts table. Based on the performance of your computer, this could take several minutes to complete.

It is also worth noting that nonclustered columnstore indexes are implemented and behave differently in SQL Server 2012/2014 and 2016. These indexes make tables read-only in SQL Server 2012/2014, which is not the case in SQL Server 2016. We will discuss their internal implementation in detail in the next chapter.

Listing 33-3. Test database creation

```
create table dbo.DimBranches
(
    BranchId int not null primary key,
    BranchNumber nvarchar(32) not null,
    BranchCity nvarchar(32) not null,
    BranchRegion nvarchar(32) not null,
    BranchCountry nvarchar(32) not null
);
```

```
create table dbo.DimArticles
(
    ArticleId int not null primary key,
    ArticleCode nvarchar(32) not null,
    ArticleCategory nvarchar(32) not null
);

create table dbo.DimDates
(
    DateId int not null primary key,
    ADate date not null,
    ADay tinyint not null,
    AMonth tinyint not null,
    AnYear smallint not null,
    AQuarter tinyint not null,
    ADayOfWeek tinyint not null
);

create table dbo.FactSales
(
    DateId int not null
        foreign key references dbo.DimDates(DateId),
    ArticleId int not null
        foreign key references dbo.DimArticles(ArticleId),
    BranchId int not null
        foreign key references dbo.DimBranches(BranchId),
    OrderId int not null,
    Quantity decimal(9,3) not null,
    UnitPrice money not null,
    Amount money not null,
    DiscountPcnt decimal (6,3) not null,
    DiscountAmt money not null,
    TaxAmt  money not null,
    constraint PK_FactSales primary key (DateId, ArticleId, BranchId, OrderId)
    with (data_compression = page)
);

;with N1(C) as (select 0 union all select 0) -- 2 rows
,N2(C) as (select 0 from N1 as T1 cross join N1 as T2) -- 4 rows
,N3(C) as (select 0 from N2 as T1 cross join N2 as T2) -- 16 rows
,N4(C) as (select 0 from N3 as T1 cross join N3 as T2) -- 256 rows
,N5(C) as (select 0 from N2 as T1 cross join N4 as T2) -- 1,024 rows
,IDs(ID) as (select row_number() over (order by (select null)) from N5)
,Dates(DateId, ADate)
as
(
    select ID, dateadd(day,ID,'2014-12-31')
    from IDs
    where ID <= 727
)
insert into dbo.DimDates(DateId, ADate, ADay, AMonth, AnYear, AQuarter, ADayOfWeek)
```

```
    select DateID, ADate, Day(ADate), Month(ADate), Year(ADate), datepart(qq,ADate),
    datepart(dw,ADate)
    from Dates;

;with N1(C) as (select 0 union all select 0) -- 2 rows
,N2(C) as (select 0 from N1 as T1 cross join N1 as T2) -- 4 rows
,N3(C) as (select 0 from N2 as T1 cross join N2 as T2) -- 16 rows
,IDs(ID) as (select row_number() over (order by (select null)) from N3)
insert into dbo.DimBranches(BranchId, BranchNumber, BranchCity, BranchRegion, BranchCountry)
    select ID, convert(nvarchar(32),ID), 'City', 'Region', 'Country' from IDs where ID <= 13;

;with N1(C) as (select 0 union all select 0) -- 2 rows
,N2(C) as (select 0 from N1 as T1 cross join N1 as T2) -- 4 rows
,N3(C) as (select 0 from N2 as T1 cross join N2 as T2) -- 16 rows
,N4(C) as (select 0 from N3 as T1 cross join N3 as T2) -- 256 rows
,N5(C) as (select 0 from N4 as T1 cross join N2 as T2) -- 1,024 rows
,IDs(ID) as (select row_number() over (order by (select null)) from N5)
insert into dbo.DimArticles(ArticleId, ArticleCode, ArticleCategory)
    select ID, convert(nvarchar(32),ID), 'Category ' + convert(nvarchar(32),ID % 51)
    from IDs
    where ID <= 1021;

;with N1(C) as (select 0 union all select 0) -- 2 rows
,N2(C) as (select 0 from N1 as T1 cross join N1 as T2) -- 4 rows
,N3(C) as (select 0 from N2 as T1 cross join N2 as T2) -- 16 rows
,N4(C) as (select 0 from N3 as T1 cross join N3 as T2) -- 256 rows
,N5(C) as (select 0 from N4 as T1 cross join N4 as T2) -- 65,536 rows
,N6(C) as (select 0 from N5 as T1 cross join N4 as T2) -- 16,777,216 rows
,IDs(ID) as (select row_number() over (order by (select null)) from N6)
insert into dbo.FactSales(DateId, ArticleId, BranchId, OrderId, Quantity, UnitPrice, Amount
    ,DiscountPcnt, DiscountAmt, TaxAmt)
    select ID % 727 + 1, ID % 1021 + 1, ID % 13 + 1, ID, ID % 51 + 1, ID % 25 + 0.99
        ,(ID % 51 + 1) * (ID % 25 + 0.99), 0, 0, (ID % 25 + 0.99) * (ID % 10) * 0.01
        from IDs;

create nonclustered columnstore index IDX_FactSales_ColumnStore
on dbo.FactSales(DateId, ArticleId, BranchId, Quantity, UnitPrice, Amount);
```

Let's run several tests that select data from a facts table and join it with one of the dimensions tables using different indexes and different degrees of parallelism, which leads to serial and parallel execution plans. I am running the queries in SQL Server 2012, 2014, and 2016 on 4-vCPU virtual machines with 8 GB of RAM allocated.

The first query, shown in Listing 33-4, performs a *clustered index scan* using a serial execution plan with row mode execution.

Listing 33-4. Test query: Clustered index scan with MAXDOP=1

```
select a.ArticleCode, sum(s.Amount) as [TotalAmount]
from dbo.FactSales s with (index = 1) join dbo.DimArticles a on
    s.ArticleId = a.ArticleId
group by a.ArticleCode
option (maxdop 1)
```

All versions of SQL Server produce identical execution plans, as shown in Figure 33-8.

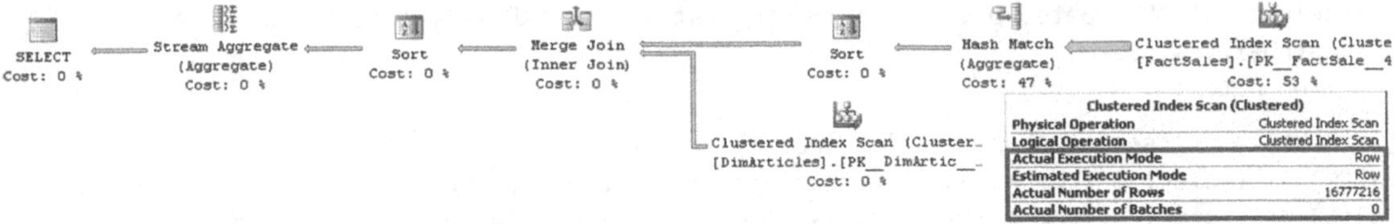

Figure 33-8. *Execution plan with clustered index scan and MAXDOP=1*

Table 33-1 shows the execution statistics for the queries in my environment.

Table 33-1. *Execution Statistics: Clustered Index Scan and MAXDOP=1*

	Logical Reads	CPU Time (ms)	Elapsed Time (ms)
SQL Server 2012	46,254	4,594	4,660
SQL Server 2014	46,245	4,564	4,656
SQL Server 2016	46,781	4,484	4,608

In the next step, let's remove the index hint and allow SQL Server to pick a columnstore index with which to access the data, still using the serial execution plan. The query is shown in Listing 33-5.

Listing 33-5. Test query: Columnstore index scan with MAXDOP=1

```
select a.ArticleCode, sum(s.Amount) as [TotalAmount]
from dbo.FactSales s join dbo.DimArticles a on
    s.ArticleId = a.ArticleId
group by a.ArticleCode
option (maxdop 1)
```

SQL Server 2012 and 2014 generated an identical execution plan, as shown in Figure 33-9. The plan utilizes a columnstore index scan via row mode execution.

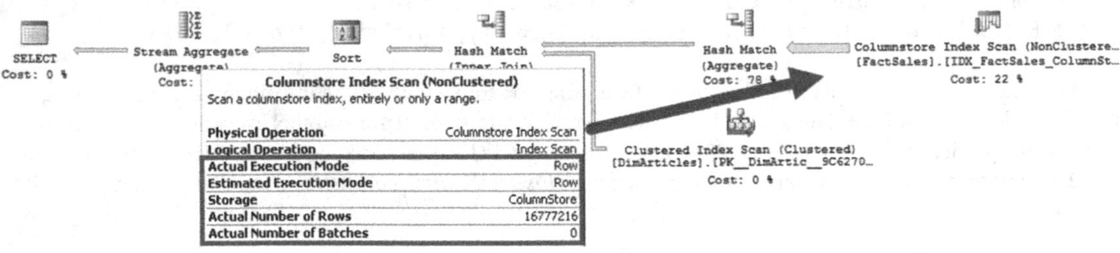

Figure 33-9. *Execution plan with a columnstore index scan and MAXDOP=1 (SQL Server 2012 and 2014)*

One of SQL Server 2016's enhancements is the ability to use batch mode execution in serial plans when the database compatibility level is set to 130. In this mode, SQL Server generates the execution plan shown in Figure 33-10. The plan utilizes a columnstore index scan in batch mode.

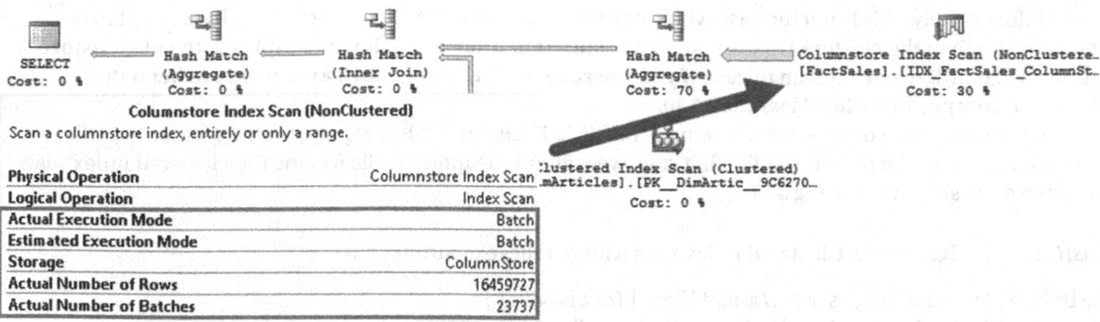

Figure 33-10. *Execution plan with a columnstore index scan and MAXDOP=1 in SQL Server 2016 with compatibility level of 130*

With a database compatibility level of less than 130, SQL Server generates the plan shown in Figure 33-11. This plan uses row mode execution and is less efficient as compared to SQL Server 2012 and 2014. The difference in the plan results from the different (updateable) nature of nonclustered columnstore indexes in SQL Server 2016.

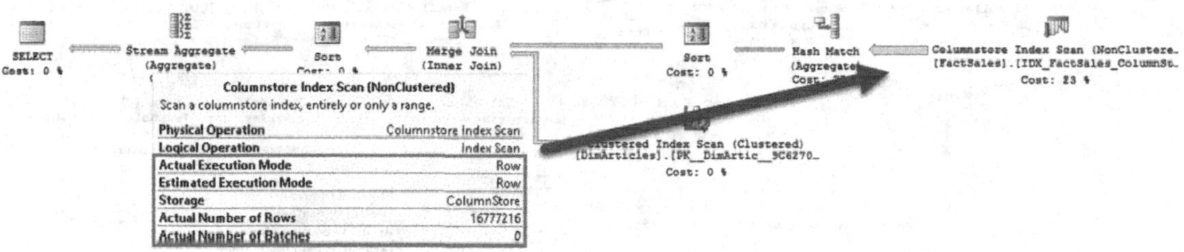

Figure 33-11. *Execution plan with a columnstore index scan and MAXDOP=1 in SQL Server 2016 with compatibility level less than 130*

It is worth noting that the ability to use batch mode execution in serial plans depends on the database compatibility level rather than on the cardinality estimation model. SQL Server 2016 will be able to use it even when the legacy cardinality estimator is enabled in the database scoped configuration, as long as the database compatibility level is set to 130.

Table 33-2 shows the execution statistics for the queries. In SQL Server 2012 and 2014, even with row mode execution, the columnstore index scan introduces more than four times the reduction of the number of reads, and it allowed the query to complete almost two times faster as compared to the clustered index scan. In SQL Server 2016, the query is an order of magnitude faster with batch mode execution.

Table 33-2. *Execution Statistics: Columnstore Index Scan and MAXDOP=1*

	Logical Reads	CPU Time (ms)	Elapsed Time (ms)
SQL Server 2012	10,030	2,703	2,746
SQL Server 2014	12,522	2,563	2,604
SQL Server 2016 compatibility level < 130	29,914	6,985	7,023
SQL Server 2016 compatibility level = 130	29,914	407	475

Unfortunately, this is not the case with row mode execution in SQL Server 2016, where the plan is less efficient than the clustered index scan. **Make sure that queries against the tables with columnstore indexes can utilize parallelism in case if you upgrade to SQL Server 2016 and decide to keep the database compatibility level less than 130.**

In the next group of tests, we will remove the `MAXDOP` hint and allow SQL Server to generate parallel execution plan for the queries. As the first step, we will run the query while forcing the clustered index scan with the code shown in Listing 33-6.

Listing 33-6. Test query: Clustered index scan with parallel execution plan

```
select a.ArticleCode, sum(s.Amount) as [TotalAmount]
from dbo.FactSales s with (index = 1) join dbo.DimArticles a on
        s.ArticleId = a.ArticleId
group by a.ArticleCode
```

Figure 33-12 illustrates the execution plan for the query running in SQL Server 2012. Even though SQL Server generated a parallel execution plan, it used row mode execution for all operators.

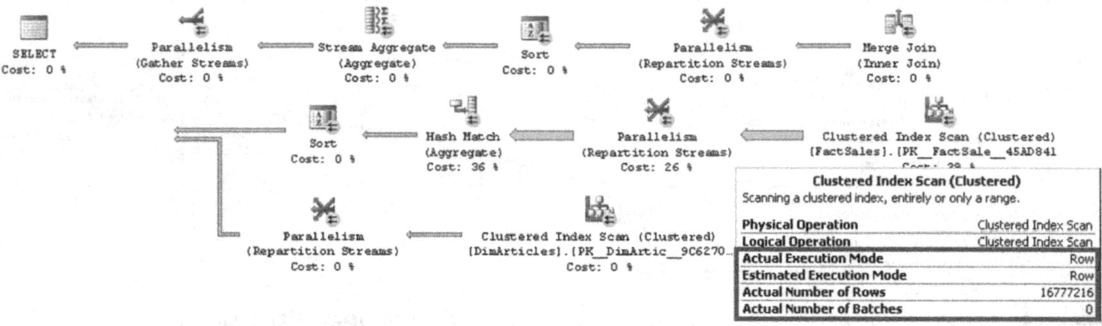

Figure 33-12. *Execution plan with clustered index scan in SQL Server 2012*

If you ran the same query in SQL Server 2014 or in SQL Server 2016 with a database compatibility level of less than 130, you would see different results, as shown in Figure 33-13. SQL Server still used row mode execution during the clustered index scan; however, hash join and hash aggregate operators were used in batch mode execution. It is worth repeating that in SQL Server 2012 and 2014, batch mode execution works only in parallel execution plans.

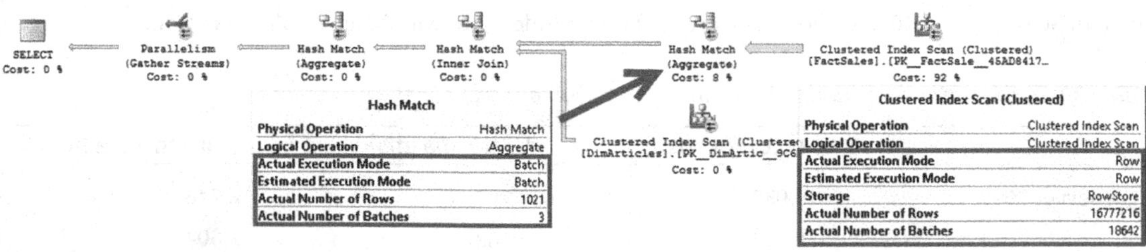

Figure 33-13. *Execution plan with clustered index scan in SQL Server 2014 and SQL Server 2016 with a database compatibility level of less than 130*

Unfortunately, in SQL Server 2016, forcing a non-columnstore index with an index hint on those tables with a columnstore index prevents batch mode execution in databases with a compatibility level of 130. This behavior provides the user with finer control over execution and resource consumption in operational analytics scenarios; however, in our example it led to a less efficient execution plan, as shown in Figure 33-14.

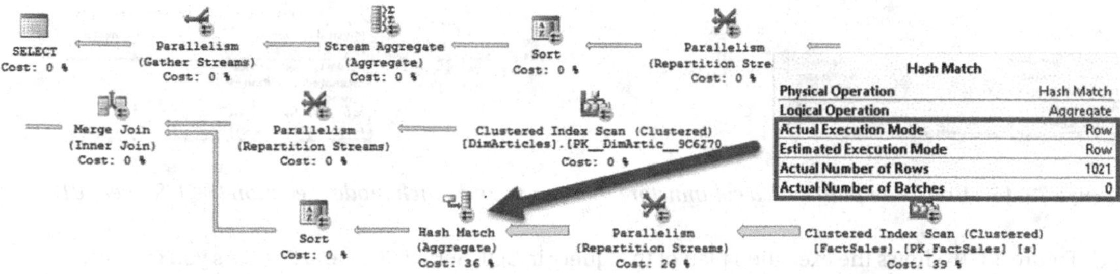

Figure 33-14. *Execution plan with clustered index scan in SQL Server 2016 with a database compatibility level of 130*

Table 33-3 shows the execution statistics for the queries.

Table 33-3. *Execution Statistics: Clustered Index Scan and Parallel Execution Plan*

	Logical Reads	CPU Time (ms)	Elapsed Time (ms)
SQL Server 2012	46,907	5,531	1,825
SQL Server 2014	47,147	4,704	1,716
SQL Server 2016 compatibility level < 130	47,623	4,657	1,673
SQL Server 2016 compatibility level = 130	47,435	5,656	1,819

Finally, let's remove the index hint and allow SQL Server to use a columnstore index and parallel execution plan. This query is shown in Listing 33-7.

Listing 33-7. Test query: Columnstore index scan with parallel execution plan

```
select a.ArticleCode, sum(s.Amount) as [TotalAmount]
from dbo.FactSales s join dbo.DimArticles a on
        s.ArticleId = a.ArticleId
group by a.ArticleCode
```

Figure 33-15 illustrates the execution plan of this query in SQL Server 2012. As you can see, it utilizes batch mode execution. It is worth noting that the *exchange/parallelism* (*repartition streams*) operators in the execution plan do not move data between different threads, which you can see by analyzing the operators' *actual number of rows* properties. SQL Server 2012 keeps them in the plan to support cases where a hash table spills to `tempdb`, which would force SQL Server to switch to row mode execution.

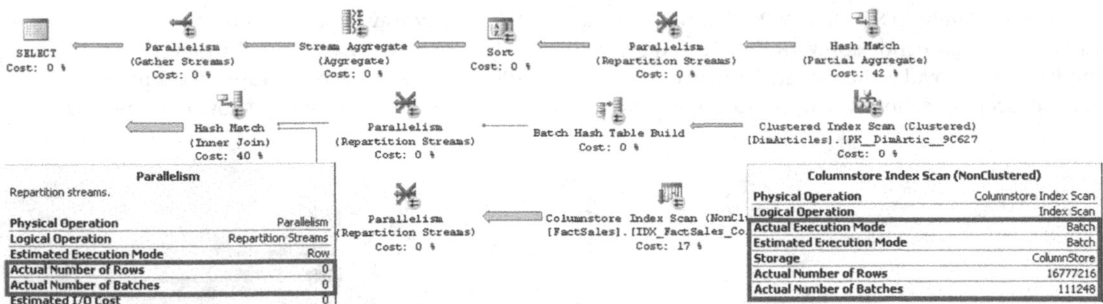

Figure 33-15. *Execution plan with a columnstore index scan and batch mode execution (SQL Server 2012)*

Figure 33-16 shows the execution plan of this query in SQL Server 2014 and 2016. As you can see, the execution plan is significantly simpler and does not include *parallelism/exchange* operators. Both SQL Server 2014 and 2016 support batch mode execution even in cases of `tempdb` spills. SQL Server 2016 generates the same plan regardless of database compatibility level.

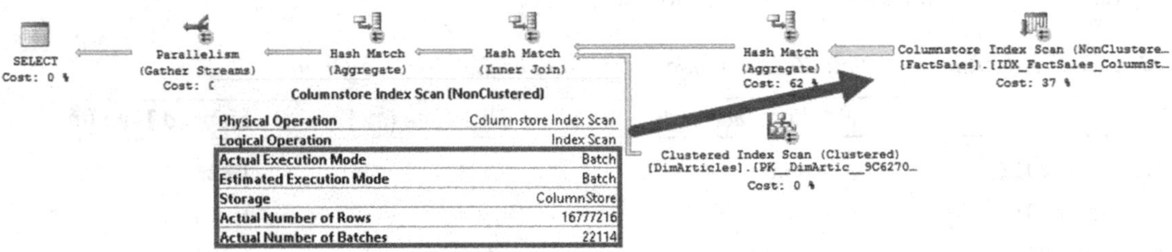

Figure 33-16. *Execution plan with a columnstore index scan and batch mode execution (SQL Server 2014 and 2016)*

Table 33-4 illustrates the execution statistics for the queries. It is worth noting that, even though SQL Server 2014/2016's performance improvements are marginal in batch mode execution, this situation would change if there were a `tempdb` spill, when SQL Server 2012 would switch to row mode execution.

Table 33-4. *Execution Statistics: Columnstore Index Scan and Parallel Execution Plan*

	Logical Reads	CPU Time (ms)	Elapsed Time (ms)
SQL Server 2012	10,048	482	180
SQL Server 2014	25,784	480	181
SQL Server 2016	29,952	469	178

As you can see, columnstore indexes significantly reduce the I/O load in the system as well as the CPU and elapsed times of the queries. The difference is especially noticeable in the case of batch mode execution, where the query ran orders of magnitude faster as compared to a row mode clustered index scan.

Every new version of SQL Server increases the number of operators and use cases that support batch mode execution. As an example, batch mode support in SQL Server 2012 is extremely limited. It does not support any join types with the exception of inner hash joins; it does not support scalar aggregates, nor does it support the `union all` operator, and it has quite a few other limitations.

In SQL Server 2014, batch mode execution supports all join types and outer joins, explores different join orders during the query optimization stage, and supports scalar aggregates and the `union all` operator. Moreover, the execution algorithms for various operators have been improved. For example, the hash join operator in SQL Server 2014 can now spill to `tempdb` without switching to row mode execution, which was impossible in SQL Server 2012.

SQL Server 2016 improves the situation even further. It supports batch mode execution with *sort* operators, allows the pushing of string predicates to the *scan* operator in some cases, and has many other enhancements, including the ability to use batch mode execution in serial execution plans.

All these improvements make upgrading to the latest SQL Server version in data warehouse environments worth the effort, especially in the case of SQL Server 2012, where batch mode execution support is very limited and requires non-trivial query re-factoring.

Column-Based Storage

There are several types of columnstore indexes available in different versions of SQL Server. Even though they have different requirements and behavior, all of them share a column-based storage format under the hood. We will talk about different columnstore index types in subsequent chapters.

It is important to mention that regardless of the type of columnstore indexes, SQL Server does not allow you to define more than one columnstore index per table.

Storage Format

Each data column in column-based storage is stored separately in a set of structures called *row groups*. Each row group stores data for up to approximately one million or, to be precise, `2^20=1,048,576` rows. SQL Server tries to populate row groups completely during index creation, leaving the last row group partially populated. For example, if a table has five million rows, SQL Server creates four row groups of 1,048,576 rows each and one row group with 805,696 rows.

In practice, you can have more than one partially populated row group when multiple threads create columnstore indexes using parallel execution plans. Each thread will work with its own subset of data, creating separate row groups. Moreover, in the case of partitioned tables, each table partition has its own set of row groups.

After row groups are built, SQL Server combines all column data on a per-row group basis and encodes and compresses these groups. The rows within a row group can be rearranged if that helps to achieve a better compression rate.

Column data within a row group is called a *segment*. SQL Server loads an entire segment to memory when it needs to access columnstore data. SQL Server also keeps information about the data stored in each segment in segment metadata—for example, minimum and maximum values—and can skip segments that do not have the required data.

Figure 33-17 illustrates the index creation process. It shows a columnstore index with four columns and three row groups. Two row groups are populated in full, and the last one is partially populated.

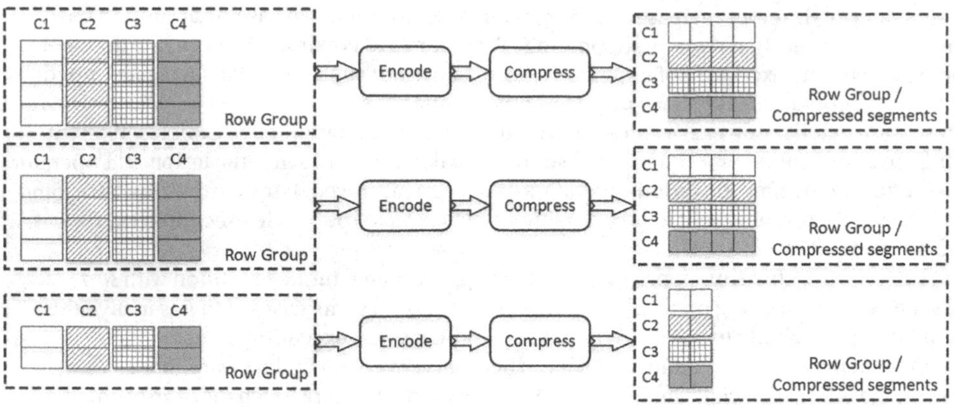

Figure 33-17. *Building a columnstore index*

During encoding, SQL Server replaces all values in the data with 64-bit integers using one of two encoding algorithms. The first algorithm, called *dictionary encoding*, stores distinct values from the data in a separate structure called a *dictionary*. Every value in a dictionary has a unique *ID* assigned. SQL Server replaces the actual value in the data with an *ID* from the dictionary.

SQL Server creates one *global dictionary*, which is shared across all segments that belong to the same index partition. Moreover, SQL Server can create local dictionaries for individual segments using values that are not present in the global dictionary.

Figure 33-18 illustrates dictionary encoding. For simplicity's sake, it shows neither multiple row groups nor local dictionaries in order to focus on the main idea of the algorithm.

Original Data		Dmitri	Dmitri	Niko	Victor	Victor	Niko	Niko	Dmitri	Victor
Dictionary	ID	1	2	3						
	Value	Dmitri	Niko	Victor						
Encoded Data		1	1	2	3	3	2	2	1	3

Figure 33-18. *Dictionary encoding*

The second type of encoding, called *value-based encoding*, is mainly used for numeric and integer data types that do not have enough duplicated values. With this condition, dictionary encoding is inefficient. The purpose of value-based encoding is to convert integer and numeric values to a smaller range of 64-bit integers. This process consists of the following two steps.

In the first step, numeric data types are converted to integers using the minimum positive exponent that allows this conversion. Such an exponent is called *magnitude*. For example, for a set of values such as 0.8, 1.24, and 1.1, the minimum exponent is 2, which represents a multiplier of 100. After this exponent is applied, values would be converted to 80, 124, and 110 respectively. The goal of this process is to convert all numeric values to integers.

Alternatively, for integer data types, SQL Server chooses the smallest negative exponent that can be applied to all values without losing their precision. For example, for the values 1340, 20, and 2,340, that exponent is -1, which represents a divider of 10. After this operation, the values would be converted to 134, 2, and 234 respectively. The goal of such an operation is to reduce the interval between the minimum and maximum values stored in the segment.

During the second step, SQL Server chooses the *base value*, which is the minimum value in the segment, and subtracts it from all other values. This makes the minimum value in the segment number 0.

Figure 33-19 illustrates the process of value-based encoding.

Original Data	Numeric	0.8	1.24	1.1	0.25	9.99	4.99	
	Integer	1340	20	2340	3210	220	3300	
Step 1	Numeric	80	124	110	25	999	499	Exponent: E+2 (value * 100)
	Integer	134	2	234	321	22	330	Exponent: E-1 (value / 10)
Step 2	Numeric	55	99	85	0	974	474	Base: 25 (value - 25)
	Integer	132	0	232	319	20	328	Base: 2 (value - 2)

Figure 33-19. *Value-based encoding*

After encoding, SQL Server compresses the data and stores it as a LOB allocation unit. We have discussed how this type of data is stored in Chapter 1, "Data Storage Internals."

Listing 33-8 shows a query that displays allocation units for the `dbo.FactSales` table we created earlier in the chapter.

Listing 33-8. dbo.FactSales table allocation units

```
select i.name as [Index], p.index_id, p.partition_number as [Partition]
        ,p.data_compression_desc as [Compression], u.type_desc, u.total_pages
from sys.partitions p join sys.allocation_units u on
        p.partition_id = u.container_id
    join sys.indexes i on
        p.object_id = i.object_id and p.index_id = i.index_id
where p.object_id = object_id(N'dbo.FactSales')
```

As you can see in Figure 33-20, the columnstore index is stored as `LOB_DATA`. It is worth noting that this index has `IN_ROW_DATA` allocation units; however, these allocation units do not store any data. It is impossible to have `LOB_DATA` allocation in the index without an `IN_ROW_DATA` allocation present.

	Index	index_id	Partition	Compression	type_desc	total_pages
1	PK_FactSales	1	1	PAGE	IN_ROW_DATA	46265
2	IDX_FactSales_ColumnStore	2	1	COLUMNSTORE	IN_ROW_DATA	0
3	IDX_FactSales_ColumnStore	2	1	COLUMNSTORE	LOB_DATA	16905

Figure 33-20. *dbo.FactSales table allocation units*

Compression and Storage Size

As you already know, the data in columnstore indexes is heavily compressed and can introduce significant space savings compared even to page compression. Moreover, SQL Server 2014 introduces another compression option called *archival compression*. It can be applied on an entire index or on individual partitions by specifying a `DATA_COMPRESSION=COLUMNSTORE_ARCHIVE` columnstore index property, and it reduces storage space even further. It uses the Xpress 8 compression library, which is an internal Microsoft implementation of the LZ77 algorithm. This compression works directly with binary data without any knowledge of the underlying SQL Server data structures.

Archival compression works transparently with other SQL Server features. Columnstore data is compressed at the time it is saved on disk and decompressed before it is loaded into memory.

Let's compare the results of different compression methods. I created four different tables with the same schema, as shown in Listing 33-9. The first two tables were heaps with no nonclustered indexes defined. The first table was uncompressed and the second one was compressed with page compression. The third and fourth tables had clustered columnstore indexes (more about them in the next chapter) compressed with the `COLUMNSTORE` and `COLUMNSTORE_ARCHIVE` compression methods respectively. Each table had almost 62 million rows generated based on the `dbo.FactResellerSales` table from the `AdventureWorksDW2012` database.

Listing 33-9. Schema of test tables

```
create table dbo.FactSalesBig
(
    ProductKey int not null,
    OrderDateKey int not null,
    DueDateKey int not null,
    ShipDateKey int not null,
    CustomerKey int not null,
    PromotionKey int not null,
    CurrencyKey int not null,
    SalesTerritoryKey int not null,
    SalesOrderNumber nvarchar(20) not null,
    SalesOrderLineNumber tinyint not null,
    RevisionNumber tinyint not null,
    OrderQuantity smallint not null,
    UnitPrice money not null,
    ExtendedAmount money not null,
    UnitPriceDiscountPct float not null,
    DiscountAmount float not null,
    ProductStandardCost money not null,
    TotalProductCost money not null,
    SalesAmount money not null,
    TaxAmt money not null,
    Freight money not null,
    CarrierTrackingNumber nvarchar(25) null,
    CustomerPONumber nvarchar(25) null,
    OrderDate datetime null,
    DueDate datetime null,
    ShipDate datetime null
)
```

Table 33-5 compares the on-disk size of all four compression methods.

Table 33-5. *On-disk Data Size for Different Compression Methods*

HEAP Table (no compression)	HEAP Table (page compression)	Columnstore Compression	Archival Compression
10,504 MB	2,440 MB	831 MB	362 MB

Obviously, different table schemas and data lead to different compression results; however, in most cases you will achieve significantly greater space savings when archival compression is implemented.

Archival compression introduces additional CPU overhead at the compression and decompression stages. Let's run a query that performs a `MAX()` aggregation on 20 columns in a table. The result of the query is meaningless; however, it forces SQL Server to read data from 20 different column segments in each row group in the table. Listing 33-10 shows the query.

Listing 33-10. Test query

```
select max(ProductKey),max(OrderDateKey),max(DueDateKey),max(ShipDateKey),max(CustomerKey)
    ,max(PromotionKey),max(CurrencyKey),max(SalesTerritoryKey),max(SalesOrderLineNumber)
    ,max(RevisionNumber),max(OrderQuantity),max(UnitPrice),max(ExtendedAmount)
    ,max(UnitPriceDiscountPct),max(DiscountAmount),max(ProductStandardCost)
    ,max(TotalProductCost)
    ,max(SalesAmount),max(TaxAmt),max(Freight)
from dbo.FactSalesBig;
```

Table 33-6 illustrates the execution times of the query against the tables with different columnstore compression methods. Even though the data compressed with archival compression uses significantly less space on disk, it takes longer for the query to complete because of the decompression overhead involved. Obviously, the results would vary based on the CPU and I/O performance of the system.

Table 33-6. *Execution Time for Different Compression Methods*

COLUMNSTORE Compression (Elapsed/CPU time)	COLUMNSTORE_ARCHIVE Compression (Elapsed/CPU time)
1,458 ms / 4,733 ms	1,774 ms / 6,098 ms

Archival compression is a great choice for static, rarely accessed data, and I would like to reiterate that it can be used on a per-index partition basis. It is common for data warehouses to retain data for a long time, even though historical data is rarely accessed. You may wish to consider applying archival compression on partitions that store old data and benefit from the disk space savings it achieves.

Metadata

SQL Server provides several columnstore index-related catalog and data management views. Two catalog views, described next, work in SQL Server 2012–2016. We will look at other views in the next chapter.

sys.column_store_segments

The `sys.column_store_segments` view returns one row for each column per segment.

Listing 33-11 shows a query that returns information about the `IDX_FactSales_ColumnStore` columnstore index that is defined on the `dbo.FactSales` table. There are a couple of things that you should note here. First, the view does not return the `object_id` or `index_id` of the index. This is not a problem, as a table can have only one columnstore index defined. However, you need to use the `sys.partitions` view to obtain the `object_id` when it is required.

Second, like regular B-Tree indexes, nonclustered columnstore indexes include a *row-id*, which is either the address of a row in a heap table or a clustered index key value. In the latter case, all columns from the clustered index are included in the columnstore index, even when you do not explicitly define them in the `CREATE COLUMNSTORE INDEX` statement. However, these columns would not exist in the `sys.index_columns` view, and you would need to use an `outer join` if you wanted to obtain the column name.

Listing 33-11. Examining the sys.column_store_segments view

```
select p.partition_number as [partition], c.name as [column], s.column_id, s.segment_id
       ,p.data_compression_desc as [compression], s.version, s.encoding_type, s.row_count
       ,s.has_nulls, s.magnitude,s.primary_dictionary_id, s.secondary_dictionary_id,
       ,s.min_data_id, s.max_data_id, s.null_value
       ,convert(decimal(12,3),s.on_disk_size / 1024.0 / 1024.0)  as [Size MB]
from sys.column_store_segments s join sys.partitions p on
           p.partition_id = s.partition_id
       join sys.indexes i on
           p.object_id = i.object_id
       left join sys.index_columns ic on
           i.index_id = ic.index_id and
           i.object_id = ic.object_id and
           s.column_id = ic.index_column_id
       left join sys.columns c on
           ic.column_id = c.column_id and
           ic.object_id = c.object_id
where i.name = 'IDX_FactSales_ColumnStore'
order by p.partition_number, s.segment_id, s.column_id
```

Figure 33-21 shows the partial output of this query. Column 8, which does not have column name displayed, represents the OrderId column, which is a part of the clustered index and has not been explicitly defined in the columnstore index.

	partition	column	column_id	segment_id	compression	version	encoding_type	row_count	has_nulls	magnitude	primary_dictionary_id	secondary_dictionary_id	min_data_id	max_data_id	null_value	Size MB
1	1	DateId	1	0	COLUMNSTORE	1	2	1048576	0	-1	0	-1	9	167	-1	1.001
2	1	ArticleId	2	0	COLUMNSTORE	1	2	1048576	0	-1	0	-1	1	1021	-1	1.334
3	1	BranchId	3	0	COLUMNSTORE	1	2	1048576	0	-1	0	-1	1	13	-1	0.001
4	1	Quantity	4	0	COLUMNSTORE	1	2	1048576	0	-1	0	-1	1000	51000	-1	0.482
5	1	UnitPrice	5	0	COLUMNSTORE	1	2	1048576	0	-1	0	-1	9900	249900	-1	0.003
6	1	Amount	6	0	COLUMNSTORE	1	2	1048576	0	-1	0	-1	9900	12744900	-1	0.905
7	1	ArticleCategory	7	0	COLUMNSTORE	1	3	1048576	0	-1	0	-1	4	54	-1	0.801
8	1	NULL	8	0	COLUMNSTORE	1	1	1048576	0	1	-1	-1	9	16777145	-1	4.001
9	1	DateId	1	1	COLUMNSTORE	1	2	1048576	0	-1	0	-1	6	151	-1	0.889

Figure 33-21. *sys.column_store_segments output*

The columns in the output represent the following:

> column_id is the ID of a column in the index that you can join with the sys.index_columns view. As you have seen, only columns that are explicitly included in an index have corresponding sys.index_columns rows.
>
> partition_id references the partition to which a row group (and, therefore, a segment) belongs. You can use it in a join with the sys.partitions view to obtain the object_id of the index.
>
> segment_id is the ID of the segment, which is basically the ID of a row group. The first segment/row group in a partition has ID of 0.
>
> version represents a columnstore segment format. SQL Server 2012, 2014, and 2016 return 1 as its value.
>
> encoding_type represents the encoding used for this segment. It can have one of the following four values:
>
> > Value-based encoding has encoding_type = 1
> >
> > Dictionary encoding of non-strings has encoding_type = 2
> >
> > Dictionary encoding of string values has encoding_type = 3
> >
> > No encoding has encoding_type = 4
>
> row_count represents number of rows in the segment.
>
> has_null indicates if the data has null values.
>
> magnitude is the magnitude used for value-based encoding. For other encoding types, it returns -1.
>
> min_data_id and max_data_id represent the minimum and maximum values in a column within the segment. SQL Server analyzes these values during query execution and eliminates segments that do not store values that satisfy query predicates. This process works in a way similar to partition elimination in partitioned tables.
>
> null_value represents the value used to indicate nulls.
>
> on_disk_size indicates the size of a segment in bytes.

sys.column_store_dictionaries

The sys.column_store_dictionaries view provides information about the dictionaries used by a columnstore index. Listing 33-12 shows the code that you can use to examine the list of dictionaries. Figure 33-22 illustrates the query output.

	partition	column	column_id	dictionary_id	version	type	last_id	entry_count	Size MB
1	1	DateId	1	0	1	1	729	727	0.018
2	1	ArticleId	2	0	1	1	1023	1021	0.020
3	1	BranchId	3	0	1	1	15	13	0.001
4	1	Quantity	4	0	1	1	53	51	0.001
5	1	UnitPrice	5	0	1	1	27	25	0.001
6	1	Amount	6	0	1	1	1277	1275	0.036
7	1	ArticleCategory	7	0	1	3	54	51	0.001

Figure 33-22. *sys.column_store_dictionaries output*

Listing 33-12. Examining the sys.column_store_dictionaries view

```
select p.partition_number as [partition], c.name as [column], d.column_id, d.dictionary_id
        ,d.version, d.type, d.last_id, d.entry_count
        ,convert(decimal(12,3),d.on_disk_size / 1024.0 / 1024.0)  as [Size MB]
from sys.column_store_dictionaries d join sys.partitions p on
            p.partition_id = d.partition_id
        join sys.indexes i on
            p.object_id = i.object_id
        left join sys.index_columns ic on
            i.index_id = ic.index_id and
            i.object_id = ic.object_id and
            d.column_id = ic.index_column_id
        left join sys.columns c on
            ic.column_id = c.column_id and
            ic.object_id = c.object_id
where i.name = 'IDX_FactSales_ColumnStore'
order by p.partition_number, d.column_id
```

The columns in the output represent the following:

column_id is the ID of a column in the index.

dictionary_id is the ID of a dictionary.

version represents a dictionary format. SQL Server 2012, 2014, and 2016 return 1 as its value.

type represents the type of values stored in a dictionary. It can have one of the following three values:

Dictionary containing integer values is specified by type = 1

Dictionary containing string values is specified by type = 3

Dictionary containing float values is specified by type = 4

last_id is the last data ID in a dictionary.

entry_count contains the number of entries in a dictionary.

on_disk_size indicates the size of a dictionary in bytes.

Design Considerations and Best Practices for Columnstore Indexes

The subject of designing efficient data warehouse solutions is very broad and impossible to cover completely in this book. However, it is equally impossible to avoid such a discussion entirely.

Reducing Data Row Size

Regardless of the indexing technologies in use, most I/O activity in data warehouse systems is related to scanning facts tables' data. The efficient design of facts tables is one of the key factors in data warehouse performance.

It is always advantageous to reduce the size of a data row, and it is even more critical in the case of facts tables in data warehouses. By making data rows smaller, we reduce the size of the table on-disk and the number of I/O operations during a scan. Moreover, it reduces the memory footprint of the data and makes batch mode execution more efficient because of better utilization of the internal CPU cache.

As you will remember, one of the key factors in reducing data size is the use of correct data types for values. You can think about storing Boolean values in `int` data types, or using `datetime` when a value requires up to the minute precision as examples of bad design. Always use the smallest data type that can store column values and that provides the required precision for the data.

Giving SQL Server as Much Information as Possible

Knowledge is power. The more SQL Server knows about the data, the better the chances are that an efficient execution plan is generated.

Unfortunately, the nullability of columns is one of the most obvious but frequently overlooked factors. Defining columns as `NOT NULL` when appropriate helps Query Optimizer and in some cases reduces the storage space required for the data. It also allows SQL Server to avoid unnecessary encoding in columnstore indexes and during batch mode execution.

Consider a `bigint` column as an example. When this column is defined as `NOT NULL`, the value fits into a single CPU register, and therefore operations on the value can be performed more quickly. Alternatively, a nullable `bigint` column requires another, 65th bit to indicate `NULL` values. When this is the case, SQL Server avoids cross-register data storage by storing some of the row values (usually the highest or lowest values) in main memory using special markers to indicate it in the data that resides in the CPU cache. As you can probably guess, this approach adds extra load during execution. As a general rule, it is better to avoid nullable columns in data warehouse environments. It is also beneficial to use `CHECK` constraints and `UNIQUE` constraints or indexes when overhead introduced by constraints or unique indexes is acceptable.

Maintaining Statistics

Creating and maintaining statistics is a good practice that benefits any SQL Server system. As you know, up-to-date statistics help Query Optimizer generate more efficient execution plans.

Columnstore indexes behave differently than B-Tree indexes do regarding statistics. SQL Server creates a statistics object at the time of columnstore index creation; however, it is neither populated nor updated afterward. SQL Server relies on segment information, B-Tree indexes (when available), and column-level statistics when deciding if a columnstore index needs to be used.

It is beneficial to create missing column-level statistics on the columns that participate in a columnstore index and are used in query predicates and as join keys.

Remember to update statistics, keeping them up to date after you load new data to a data warehouse. Statistics rarely update automatically on very large tables.

Avoiding String Columns in Fact Tables

Generally, you should minimize the use of string columns in facts tables. String data uses more space, and SQL Server performs extra encoding when working with such data during batch mode execution. Moreover, queries with predicates on string columns may have less efficient execution plans that also require significantly larger memory grants as compared to their non-string counterparts. SQL Server 2012 and 2014 do not push string predicates down toward the lowest operators in execution plans.

Let's look at an example of such behavior. The code shown in Listing 33-13 adds an `ArticleCategory` column to the `dbo.FactSales` table, populating it with values from the `dbo.DimArticles` table. As a final step, the code recreates the columnstore index, adding a new column there. Obviously, you should not design database schemas this way, as you don't want to keep redundant attributes in facts tables.

Listing 33-13. String columns in facts tables: Table schema changes

```
drop index IDX_FactSales_ColumnStore on dbo.FactSales;
alter table dbo.FactSales add ArticleCategory nvarchar(32) not null default '';
go

update t
set t.ArticleCategory = a.ArticleCategory
from dbo.FactSales t join dbo.DimArticles a on
    t.ArticleId = a.ArticleId;

create nonclustered columnstore index IDX_FactSales_ColumnStore
on dbo.FactSales(DateId, ArticleId, BranchId, Quantity, UnitPrice, Amount, ArticleCategory);
```

As a next step, let's run two similar queries that calculate the total amount of sales for a particular branch and article category. The queries are shown in Listing 33-14. The first query uses a `dbo.DimArticle` dimensions table for category filtering, while the second query uses an attribute from the facts table.

Listing 33-14. String columns in facts tables: Test queries

```
select sum(s.Amount) as [Sales]
from dbo.FactSales s join dbo.DimBranches b on
        s.BranchId = b.BranchId
    join dbo.DimArticles a on
        s.ArticleId = a.ArticleId
where
        b.BranchNumber = N'3' and
        a.ArticleCategory = N'Category 4';

select sum(s.Amount) as [Sales]
from dbo.FactSales s join dbo.DimBranches b on
        s.BranchId = b.BranchId
where
        b.BranchNumber = N'3' and
        s.ArticleCategory = N'Category 4';
```

The partial execution plan for the first query, performed in SQL Server 2012, is shown in Figure 33-23. As you can see, SQL Server pushes both predicates on the `BranchId` and `ArticleId` columns to the columnstore index scan operator, filtering out unnecessary rows during a very early stage of the execution. SQL Server 2014 and 2016 would generate a slightly different plan; however, they would use the same approach, evaluating predicates during a columnstore index scan.

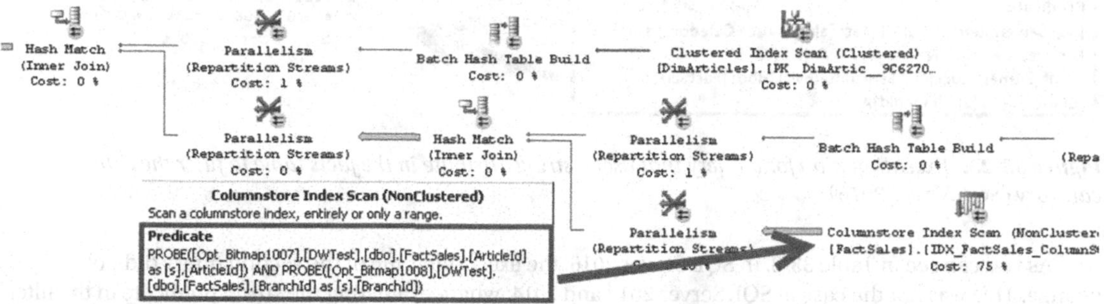

***Figure 33-23.** Execution plan for a query that uses a dimensions table to filter the article category*

Table 33-7 shows execution times of the queries in my environment. As you can see, SQL Server 2014 and 2016 are slightly faster than SQL Server 2012; however, all versions of SQL Server ran efficiently.

***Table 33-7.** Execution Times of the First Query*

	CPU Time (ms)	Elapsed Time (ms)
SQL Server 2012	61	22
SQL Server 2014	32	11
SQL Server 2016	28	10

With the second query, neither SQL Server 2012 nor 2014 pushed a string predicate on the `ArticleCategory` column to the columnstore index scan operator. Both versions of SQL Server used an additional filter operator afterward. This introduced the overhead of loading unnecessary rows during the index scan. You can see a partial execution plan of the second query in Figure 33-24.

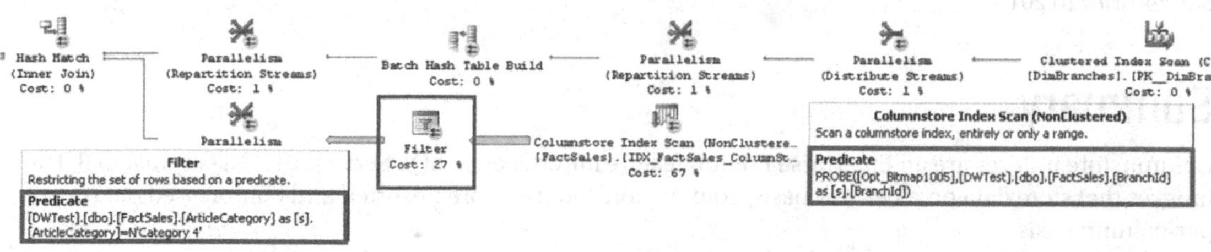

***Figure 33-24.** Execution plan for a query that uses a string attribute in the facts table to filter the article category (prior to SQL Server 2016)*

SQL Server 2016 generates a different execution plan that pushes the string predicate toward the columnstore index scan operator, as shown in Figure 33-25.

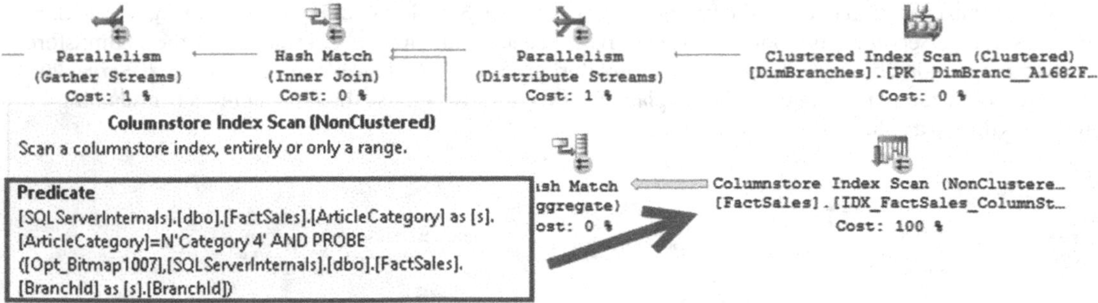

Figure 33-25. *Execution plan for a query that uses a string attribute in the facts table to filter the article category (SQL Server 2016)*

As you can see in Table 33-8, in SQL Server 2016, the execution time of the second query did not change. This was not the case in SQL Server 2012 and 2014, where evaluating the string predicate in the filter operator slowed down queries dramatically.

Table 33-8. *Execution Times of the Second Query*

	CPU Time (ms)	Elapsed Time (ms)
SQL Server 2012	266	90
SQL Server 2014	187	65
SQL Server 2016	30	11

Obviously, in some cases string attributes become part of the facts and should be stored in facts tables. However, in a large number of cases, you can add another dimensions table and replace the string value in the facts table with a synthetic, integer-based ID key that references a new table.

You already saw one such example of this with the `ArticleCategory` data. As another example, you may consider a situation where the facts table needs to specify the currency of a sale. Rather than storing a currency code (USD, EUR, GBP, and so forth) in a facts table, you can create a `dbo.DimCurrency` dimensions table and reference it with a `tinyint` or `smallint CurrencyID` column. This approach can significantly improve the performance of queries against facts tables in data warehouse environments, especially in SQL Server prior to 2016.

Summary

Columnstore indexes are an Enterprise Edition feature introduced in SQL Server 2012. In contrast to B-Tree indexes that store data on a per-row basis, columnstore indexes store unsorted and compressed data on a per-column basis.

Columnstore indexes are beneficial in data warehouse environments where typical queries perform a scan and aggregation of data from facts tables, selecting just a subset of table columns.

Columnstore indexes reduce the I/O load and memory usage during query execution. Only the columns that are referenced in a query are processed. Moreover, SQL Server introduced a batch mode execution model that utilizes columnstore indexes. Rather than accessing data on a row-by-row basis, in batch mode execution SQL Server performs operations against a batch of rows, keeping them in the fast CPU cache whenever possible. Batch mode execution can significantly improve query performance and reduce query execution time.

Several factors improve the efficiency of data warehouse database systems. You should endeavor to reduce row and column sizes by using appropriate data types; avoid nullable columns; use `CHECK` and `UNIQUE` constraints when appropriate, and avoid using string columns in facts tables when possible.

CHAPTER 34

Columnstore Indexes

This chapter provides an overview of the different columnstore index types available in various versions of SQL Server. It discusses their internal structure as well as best practices for data loading and maintenance.

Columnstore Index Types

As mentioned in the previous chapter, there are several different types of columnstore indexes supported in SQL Server. Unfortunately, the terminology is quickly become confusing and version-specific. For example, *nonclustered columnstore indexes* in SQL Server 2012/2014 and in SQL Server 2016 are, in a nutshell, very different objects; however, they are called the same thing in the documentation.

Table 34-1 shows what types of columnstore indexes are supported in different versions of SQL Server.

Table 34-1. *Columnstore Index Types Available in SQL Server*

<table>
<tr><th>SQL Server 2012</th><th>SQL Server 2014</th><th>SQL Server 2016</th></tr>
<tr><td colspan="2">Read-only nonclustered columnstore indexes on heap/B-Tree clustered indexes
(they make a table read-only)</td><td></td></tr>
<tr><td></td><td></td><td>Updateable nonclustered columnstore indexes on heap/B-Tree clustered indexes.</td></tr>
<tr><td></td><td colspan="2">Clustered columnstore index as the single index on the table</td></tr>
<tr><td></td><td></td><td>Clustered columnstore index with nonclustered B-Tree indexes</td></tr>
<tr><td></td><td></td><td>Clustered columnstore index on memory-optimized tables
(will be covered in the Chapter 35)</td></tr>
</table>

Note You can read more about columnstore index features supported in different versions of SQL Server at `https://msdn.microsoft.com/en-us/library/dn934994.aspx`.

Regardless of the type, columnstore indexes have several limitations in common. They cannot have more than 1,024 columns or include sparse columns. You cannot define them as `UNIQUE` or use them with the tables that utilize `FILESTREAM` or replication, nor can they be created on an indexed view.

D. Korotkevitch, *Pro SQL Server Internals*, DOI 10.1007/978-1-4842-1964-5_34

Moreover, the following data types are not supported: binary, varbinary, (n)text, image, (n)varchar(max), timestamp, CLR, sql_variant, and xml. In addition, SQL Server 2012 does not support the following data types: uniqueidentifier, decimal, and numeric with precision greater than 18 digits, or datetimeoffset with precision greater than 2 digits.

Let's look at the different types of columnstore indexes in depth.

Read-Only Nonclustered Columnstore Indexes (SQL Server 2012–2014)

Read-only nonclustered columnstore indexes were introduced in SQL Server 2012, and they were the only columnstore index type supported in this version. In this section, I will refer to them as *nonclustered columnstore indexes* (NCCI); however, I would like to repeat that they are implemented and behave differently from nonclustered columnstore indexes in SQL Server 2016.

A nonclustered columnstore index can include up to 1,024 non-sparse columns. Due to the nature of the index, it does not matter in what order the columns are specified; that is, data is stored on a per-column basis.

Similar to B-Tree nonclustered indexes, nonclustered columnstore indexes include a *row-id,* which is either a clustered index key value or the physical location of a row in a heap table. This behavior allows SQL Server to use the *columnstore index scan* operation to perform a *key lookup* afterward. It is worth repeating that columnstore indexes do not support seek operations, because the data in those indexes is not sorted, as you saw in the previous chapter.

Listing 34-1 shows an example of a query that uses a columnstore index scan with key lookup operators, using the dbo.FactSales table defined in the previous chapter.

Listing 34-1. Query that triggers key lookup operation

```
select OrderId, Amount, TaxAmt
from dbo.FactSales
where ArticleId = 10
```

Figure 34-1 shows the execution plan for this query. You can see that the OrderId column is included in the output list of the columnstore index scan. That column has not been explicitly defined in the columnstore index; however, it is part of the clustered index key in the table.

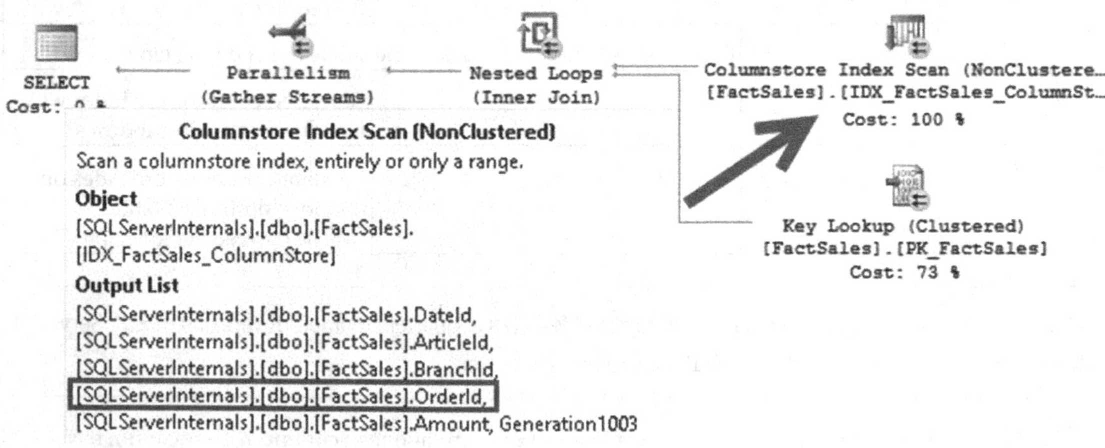

Figure 34-1. *Execution plan for this query*

The creation of a columnstore index is a very memory intensive operation. When you create a columnstore index in SQL Server 2012, it requests a memory grant of a size that you can roughly estimate with the following formula:

```
Memory Grant Request (MB) =
        (4.2 * Number of columns in the index + 68) * (Degree of Parallelism) +
        (Number of text columns in the index * 34)
```

For example, the columnstore index created in Listing 33-3 in the previous chapter requested a memory grant of 394 MB in my environment, which is fairly close to the `(4.2 * 7 (6 index columns + OrderId) + 68) * 4 = 390 MB` calculated with the formula. The size of the memory grant does not depend on the size of the table. As you will see later, SQL Server processes data in batches of about one million rows each.

The index creation process fails in cases of insufficient memory. There are two ways to solve this problem besides adding more memory to the server. The first is to reduce the degree of parallelism with the `MAXDOP` index option. While this option reduces the memory requirements for a query, it increases the index creation time proportionally to the decrease of DOP.

The second option is to change the `REQUEST_MAX_MEMORY_GRANT_PERCENT` property of the workload group in Resource Governor. By default, the size of the query memory grant is limited to 25 percent of the available workspace memory, which you can increase for the duration of the `CREATE INDEX` statement.

The index creation algorithm has been improved in SQL Server 2014. In contrast to SQL Server 2012, which uses a degree of parallelism that matches either the server or index DOP options, SQL Server 2014 automatically adjusts the DOP based on available memory. This behavior decreases the chance that the index creation process will fail due to an out-of-memory condition.

The biggest limitation of nonclustered columnstore indexes is that a table with such an index becomes read-only. You cannot change data in the table after the index is created. This limitation, however, is not as critical in a data warehouse environment where data is usually static and updated on schedule. Unfortunately, this limitation prevents nonclustered columnstore indexes from being used in operational analytics scenarios in SQL Server 2012 and 2014.

Tables with columnstore indexes support a partition switch, which is a great option for importing data into the table. You can create a staging table, use it as the target for data import, then add a columnstore index to the staging table when the import is completed, and then switch the staging table to be the new partition in the main read-only table as the last step of the operation. Listing 34-2 shows an example of this.

Listing 34-2. Importing data into a table with a nonclustered columnstore index using a staging table and partition switch

```
create partition function pfFacts(int) as range left for values (1,2,3,4,5);
create partition scheme psFacts as partition pfFacts all to ([FG2016]);
go

create table dbo.FactTable
(
    DateId int not null,
    ArticleId int not null,
    OrderId int not null,
    Quantity decimal(9,3) not null,
    UnitPrice money not null,
    Amount money not null,
    constraint PK_FactTable
    primary key clustered(DateId, ArticleId, OrderId)
    on psFacts(DateId)
);
```

```
;with N1(C) as (select 0 union all select 0) -- 2 rows
,N2(C) as (select 0 from N1 as T1 cross join N1 as T2) -- 4 rows
,N3(C) as (select 0 from N2 as T1 cross join N2 as T2) -- 16 rows
,N4(C) as (select 0 from N3 as T1 cross join N3 as T2) -- 256 rows
,N5(C) as (select 0 from N4 as T1 cross join N2 as T2) -- 1,024 rows
,IDs(ID) as (select ROW_NUMBER() over (order by (select NULL)) from N5)
insert into dbo.FactTable(DateId, ArticleId, OrderId, Quantity, UnitPrice, Amount)
    select ID % 4 + 1, ID % 100, ID, ID % 10 + 1, ID % 15 + 1 , ID % 25 + 1
    from IDs;

create nonclustered columnstore index IDX_FactTable_Columnstore
on dbo.FactTable(DateId, ArticleId, OrderId, Quantity, UnitPrice, Amount)
on psFacts(DateId);

create table dbo.StagingTable
(
    DateId int not null,
    ArticleId int not null,
    OrderId int not null,
    Quantity decimal(9,3) not null,
    UnitPrice money not null,
    Amount money not null,

    constraint PK_StagingTable
    primary key clustered(DateId, ArticleId, OrderId)
    on [FG2016],

    constraint CHK_StagingTable check(DateId = 5)
);

/*** Step 1: Importing data into a staging table ***/
;with N1(C) as (select 0 union all select 0) -- 2 rows
,N2(C) as (select 0 from N1 as T1 cross join N1 as T2) -- 4 rows
,N3(C) as (select 0 from N2 as T1 cross join N2 as T2) -- 16 rows
,N4(C) as (select 0 from N3 as T1 cross join N3 as T2) -- 256 rows
,N5(C) as (select 0 from N4 as T1 cross join N2 as T2) -- 1,024 rows
,IDs(ID) as (select ROW_NUMBER() over (order by (select null)) from N5)
insert into dbo.StagingTable(DateId, ArticleId, OrderId, Quantity, UnitPrice, Amount)
    select 5, ID % 100, ID, ID % 10 + 1, ID % 15 + 1 , ID % 25 + 1
    from IDs;

/*** Step 2: Creating nonclustered columstore index ***/
create nonclustered columnstore index IDX_StagingTable_Columnstore
on dbo.StagingTable(DateId, ArticleId, OrderId, Quantity, UnitPrice, Amount)
on [FG2016];

/*** Step 3: Switching a staging table to be the new partition of the main table ***/
alter table dbo.StagingTable switch to dbo.FactTable partition 5;
```

■ **Tip** You can use a partitioned view that combines data from updatable tables and read-only tables with columnstore indexes. However, using the `UNION ALL` clause in SQL Server 2012 disables batch mode execution.

Clustered Columnstore Indexes (SQL Server 2014–2016)

The read-only nature of nonclustered columnstore indexes in SQL Server 2012 seriously affected the adoption of the technology. Even though data partitioning and partition switches could help to work around this limitation, they require complex and often cumbersome implementations.

Starting with SQL Server 2014, you can store data in column-based storage using *clustered columnstore indexes* (CCI). In SQL Server 2014, a CCI is a single instance of the data in a table, and tables with clustered columnstore indexes cannot have any other indexes defined—neither B-Tree nor nonclustered columnstore indexes. In SQL Server 2016, however, you can define nonclustered B-Tree indexes on tables with clustered columnstore indexes. Finally, neither SQL Server 2014 nor 2016 allows you to define triggers on the table.

In SQL Server 2014, clustered columnstore indexes have several other limitations in addition to the list provided in the beginning of this chapter. A table cannot reference other tables nor be referenced with foreign key constraints. You cannot query tables with clustered columnstore indexes on readable secondaries in AlwaysOn Availability Groups.

SQL Server 2016 removes those limitations; however, supporting uniqueness, referential integrity, and primary key constraints will require the creation of nonclustered B-Tree indexes.

There are still some features that do not work with clustered columnstore indexes. For example, replication, change tracking, and change data capture are not supported, even in SQL Server 2016.

You can create a clustered columnstore index with the `CREATE CLUSTERED COLUMNSTORE INDEX` command. You do not need to specify any columns in the statement—the index will include all table columns. This adds further restrictions on the column data types, as we discussed in the beginning of this chapter.

Internal Structure

Clustered columnstore indexes use the same storage format as nonclustered columnstore indexes use, storing columnstore data in row groups. However, they have two additional elements that support data modifications. The first is *delete bitmap*, which indicates which rows were deleted from a table. The second structure is *delta store*, which includes newly inserted rows. Both delta store and delete bitmap use the B-Tree format to store data. Moreover, SQL Server 2016 uses several other structures to support nonclustered B-Tree indexes. We will discuss these later.

■ **Note** SQL Server's use of delete bitmaps and delta stores is transparent to users, which makes the relevant terminology confusing. You will often see delta stores referenced as another row group in documentation and technical articles. Moreover, a delete bitmap is often considered a part of a delta store and/or row group.

To avoid confusion, I will use the following terminology in this chapter. The term *row group* references data stored in a column-based storage format. I will explicitly reference *delta stores* and *delete bitmaps* as two separate sets of internal objects as needed.

Figure 34-2 illustrates the structure of a clustered columnstore index in a table that has two partitions. Each partition can have a single delete bitmap and multiple delta stores. This structure makes each partition self-contained and independent from other partitions, which allows you to perform a partition switch on tables that have clustered columnstore indexes defined.

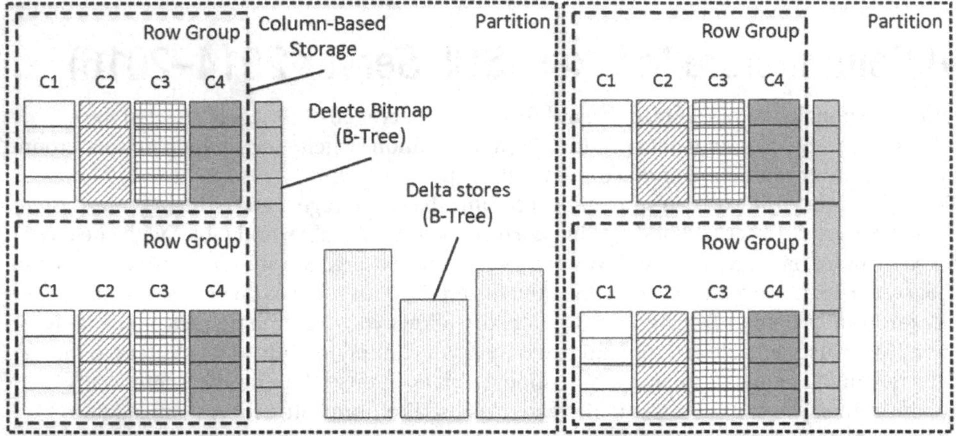

Figure 34-2. *Clustered columnstore index structure*

It is worth noting that delete bitmaps and delta stores are created *on demand*. For example, a delete bitmap would not be created unless some of the rows in the row groups were deleted.

Every time you delete a row that is stored in a row group (not in a delta store), SQL Server adds information about the deleted row to the delete bitmap. Nothing happens to the original row. It is still stored in a row group. However, SQL Server checks the delete bitmap during query execution and excludes deleted rows from the processing.

As already mentioned, when you insert data into a columnstore index, it goes into a delta store, which uses a B-Tree format. Updating a row that is stored in a row group does not change the row data. Such an update triggers the deletion of the row, which is, in fact, insertion to a delete bitmap, and insertion of a new version of a row to a delta store. However, any data modifications of the rows in a delta store are done the same way as in regular B-Tree indexes—by updating and deleting actual rows there. You will see one such example later in this chapter.

Each delta store can be in either an *open* or a *closed* state. Open delta stores accept new rows and allow modifications and deletions of data. SQL Server closes a delta store when it reaches 1,048,576 rows, which is the maximum number of rows that can be stored in a row group. Another SQL Server process, called *tuple mover*, runs every five minutes and converts closed delta stores to row groups that store data in a column-based storage format.

Alternatively, you can force the conversion of closed delta stores to row groups by reorganizing an index with the `ALTER INDEX REORGANIZE` command. While both approaches achieve the same goal of converting closed delta stores to row groups, their implementation is slightly different. Tuple mover is a single-threaded process that works in the background, preserving system resources. Alternatively, index reorganizing runs in parallel using multiple threads. This approach can significantly decrease conversion time at a cost of extra CPU load and memory usage.

■ **Note** You can disable the background tuple mover process with trace flag `T634`.

Neither tuple mover nor index reorganizing prevent other sessions from inserting new data into a table. New data will be inserted into different and open delta stores. However, deletions and data modifications would be blocked for the duration of the operation. In some cases, you may consider forcing index reorganization manually to reduce execution, and therefore locking, time.

You can examine the state of row groups and delta stores with the `sys.column_store_row_groups` view. Figure 34-3 illustrates the output of this view, which returns the combined information of all columnstore index objects. Rows in `OPEN` or `CLOSED` state correspond to delta stores. Rows in `COMPRESSED` state correspond to row groups with data in a column-based storage format. Finally, the `deleted_rows` column provides statistics about deleted rows stored in a delete bitmap.

	object_id	index_id	partition_number	row_group_id	delta_store_hobt_id	state	state_description	total_rows	deleted_rows	size_in_bytes
1	949578421	1	1	4	72057594048217088	1	OPEN	51424	NULL	NULL
2	949578421	1	1	3	72057594048151552	2	CLOSED	1048576	NULL	NULL
3	949578421	1	1	2	NULL	3	COMPRESSED	32	0	176
4	949578421	1	1	1	NULL	3	COMPRESSED	1048576	0	2797376
5	949578421	1	1	0	NULL	3	COMPRESSED	1048576	0	2797376

Figure 34-3. *`Sys.column_store_row_groups` view output*

As you can see, the second row in the view output from Figure 35-2 shows the closed delta store that has yet to be picked up by the tuple mover process. The situation will change after the tuple mover process converts the closed delta store to a row group on its next scheduled run. Figure 34-4 shows the output from a view in SQL Server 2014 after this occurs. As you can see, the `row_group_id` of the converted row group changed. Tuple mover created a new row group, dropping the closed delta store afterward. It is worth noting that in SQL Server 2016 the old row group will be present in the output in `TOMBSTONE` state until it is deallocated.

	object_id	index_id	partition_number	row_group_id	delta_store_hobt_id	state	state_description	total_rows	deleted_rows	size_in_bytes
1	949578421	1	1	5	NULL	3	COMPRESSED	1048576	0	2797376
2	949578421	1	1	4	72057594048217088	1	OPEN	51424	NULL	NULL
3	949578421	1	1	2	NULL	3	COMPRESSED	32	0	176
4	949578421	1	1	1	NULL	3	COMPRESSED	1048576	0	2797376
5	949578421	1	1	0	NULL	3	COMPRESSED	1048576	0	2797376

Figure 34-4. *`Sys.column_store_row_groups` view output after tuple mover process execution*

Data Load

Two different types of data load can insert data into a columnstore index. The first type is *bulk insert,* which is used by the `BULK INSERT` operator, the `bcp` utility, and other applications that utilize the bulk insert API. The second type, called *trickle inserts,* are regular `INSERT` operations that do not use the bulk insert API.

Bulk insert operations provide the number of rows in the batch as part of the API call. SQL Server inserts data into newly created row groups if that size exceeds a threshold of 102,400 rows. Depending on the size of the batch, one or more row groups can be created, and some rows may be stored in a delta store.

Table 34-2 illustrates how data from different batches are distributed between row groups and delta stores.

Table 34-2. *Batch Size and Data Distribution During Bulk Insert*

Batch size	Rows added to row groups (column-based storage)	Rows added to delta store (row-based storage)
99,000	0	99,000
150,000	150,000	0
1,048,577	1,048,576	1
2,100,000	1,048,576; 1,048,576	2,848
2,250,000	1,048,576; 1,048,576; 152,848	0

SQL Server loads columnstore data to memory on a per-segment basis, and, as you remember, segments represent data for a single column in a row group. It is more efficient to load and process a smaller number of fully populated segments as compared to a large number of partially populated segments. An excessive number of partially populated row groups negatively affect SQL Server performance. I will provide an example of this later in the chapter.

If you bulk load data to a table with a clustered columnstore index, you will achieve the best results by choosing a batch size that is divisible by 1,048,576 rows. This will guarantee that every batch produces one or several fully populated row groups, reduce the total number of row groups in a table, and improve query performance. Do not exceed this number, however, because the batch would not fit into a single row group.

Batch size is less important for non-bulk operations. Trickle inserts go directly to a delta store. In some cases, SQL Server can still create row groups on the fly in a manner to similar a bulk insert when the size of the insert batch is close to or exceeds 1,048,576 rows. You should not rely on this behavior, however.

Delta Store and Delete Bitmap

Let's analyze the structure of delta stores and delete bitmaps and look at the format of their rows. As a first step, let's create a table, populate it with data, and define a clustered columnstore index there. Finally, we will look at segments and row groups with the `sys.column_store_segments` and `sys.column_store_row_groups` views.

Listing 34-3 shows the code that does just that. I am using the `MAXDOP=1` option during the index creation stage to minimize the number of partially populated row groups in the index.

Listing 34-3. Delta store and delete bitmap: Test table creation

```
create table dbo.CCI
(
    Col1 int  not null,
    Col2 varchar(4000) not null,
);

;with N1(C) as (select 0 union all select 0) -- 2 rows
,N2(C) as (select 0 from N1 as T1 cross join N1 as T2) -- 4 rows
,N3(C) as (select 0 from N2 as T1 cross join N2 as T2) -- 16 rows
,N4(C) as (select 0 from N3 as T1 cross join N3 as T2) -- 256 rows
,N5(C) as (select 0 from N4 as T1 cross join N4 as T2) -- 65,536 rows
,N6(C) as -- 1,048,592 rows
(
    select 0 from N5 as T1 cross join N3 as T2
```

```
    union all
    select 0 from N3
)
,IDs(ID) as (select row_number() over (order by (select null)) from N6)
insert into dbo.CCI(Col1,Col2)
    select ID, 'aaa' from IDS;

create clustered columnstore index IDX_CS_CLUST on dbo.CCI
with (maxdop=1);

select g.state_description, g.row_group_id, s.column_id
    ,s.row_count, s.min_data_id, s.max_data_id, g.deleted_rows
from
    sys.column_store_segments s join sys.partitions p on
        s.partition_id = p.partition_id
    join sys.column_store_row_groups g on
        p.object_id = g.object_id and s.segment_id = g.row_group_id
where p.object_id = object_id(N'dbo.CCI')
order by g.row_group_id, s.column_id;
```

Figure 34-5 shows the output from the sys.column_store_segments and sys.column_store_row_groups views. The columnstore index has two row groups and does not have a delta store or delete bitmap. You can see Col1 values that are stored in both row groups in the min_data_id and max_data_id columns for the rows that have column_id=1.

	state_description	row_group_id	column_id	row_count	min_data_id	max_data_id	deleted_rows
1	COMPRESSED	0	1	1048576	1	1048592	0
2	COMPRESSED	0	2	1048576	4	4	0
3	COMPRESSED	1	1	16	16145	16160	0
4	COMPRESSED	1	2	16	4	4	0

Figure 34-5. *Delta store and delete bitmap: Sys.column_store_segments and sys.column_store_row_groups output*

In the next step, shown in Listing 34-4, we will perform some data modifications in the table. The first statement inserts two new rows into the table. The second statement deletes three rows, including one of the rows that we just inserted. Finally, we will update another newly inserted row.

Listing 34-4. Delta store and delete bitmap: Data modifications

```
insert into dbo.CCI(Col1,Col2)
values (2000000,replicate('c',4000)), (2000001, replicate('d',4000));

delete from dbo.CCI
where Col1 in
    ( 100              -- Row group 0
      ,16150         -- Row group 1
      ,2000000   -- Newly inserted row (Delta Store)
    );

update dbo.CCI
```

```
set Col2 = replicate('z',4000)
where Col1 = 2000001;    -- Newly inserted row (Delta Store)
```

Now, it is time to find the data pages that are used by the delta store and delete bitmap. We will use the undocumented `sys.dm_db_database_page_allocations` data management function, as shown in Listing 34-5. This function returns us the information about object page allocations.

Listing 34-5. Delta store and delete bitmap: Analyzing page allocations

```
select object_id, index_id, partition_id, allocation_unit_type_desc as [Type]
    ,is_allocated,is_iam_page,page_type,page_type_desc
    ,allocated_page_file_id as [FileId]
    ,allocated_page_page_id as [PageId]
from sys.dm_db_database_page_allocations(db_id(),object_id('dbo.CCI'),null,null,'DETAILED')
```

You can see the output of this query in Figure 34-6. As you know, SQL Server stores columnstore segments in `LOB_DATA` allocation units. Delta store and delete bitmap use `IN_ROW_DATA` allocation.

	object_id	index_id	partition_id	Type	is_allocated	is_iam_page	page_type	page_type_desc	FileId	PageId
1	501576825	1	1	IN_ROW_DATA	1	1	10	IAM_PAGE	1	311
2	501576825	1	1	IN_ROW_DATA	1	0	1	DATA_PAGE	1	308
3	501576825	1	1	IN_ROW_DATA	1	1	10	IAM_PAGE	1	307
4	501576825	1	1	IN_ROW_DATA	1	0	1	DATA_PAGE	1	306
5	501576825	1	1	LOB_DATA	1	1	10	IAM_PAGE	1	310
6	501576825	1	1	LOB_DATA	1	0	3	TEXT_MIX_PAGE	1	309
7	501576825	1	1	LOB_DATA	1	0	3	TEXT_MIX_PAGE	1	2872

Figure 34-6. *Delta store and delete bitmap: Allocation units*

Let's look at the data pages using the `DBCC PAGE` command with the code shown in Listing 34-6. Obviously, the database, file, and page IDs would be different in your environment.

Listing 34-6. Delta store and delete bitmap: Analyzing page data

```
dbcc traceon(3604);  -- Redirecting output to console
dbcc page -- Analyzing content of a page
(   9          -- Database Id
    ,1         -- FileId
    ,306       -- PageId
    ,3         -- Output style
)
```

Figure 34-7 shows the partial content of a data page that is a delta store page. As you can see, SQL Server stores data in regular row-based storage. There is one internal column, `CSILOCATOR`, in addition to two table columns. `CSILOCATOR` is used as an internal unique identifier of the row in the delta store.

```
PAGE HEADER:
Page @0x00000002164EE000
m_pageId = (1:306)                  m_headerVersion = 1                m_type = 1
m_typeFlagBits = 0x0                m_level = 0                        m_flagBits = 0x8200
m_objId (AllocUnitId.idObj) = 188   m_indexId (AllocUnitId.idInd) = 256
Metadata: AllocUnitId = 72057594050248704
Metadata: PartitionId = 72057594044153856                               Metadata: IndexId = 1
Metadata: ObjectId = 501576825      m_prevPage = (0:0)                 m_nextPage = (0:0)
pminlen = 4                         m_slotCnt = 1                      m_freeCnt = 4081
m_freeData = 8122                   m_reservedCnt = 0                  m_lsn = (103:44488:1)
m_xactReserved = 0                  m_xdesId = (0:8857)                m_ghostRecCnt = 0
m_tornBits = -1830688536            DB Frag ID = 1
Allocation Status
GAM (1:2) = ALLOCATED               SGAM (1:3) = ALLOCATED
PFS (1:1) = 0x60 MIXED_EXT ALLOCATED   0_PCT_FULL                       DIFF (1:6) = CHANGED
ML (1:7) = NOT MIN_LOGGED
Slot 0 Offset 0x100d Length 4013
Record Type = (COMPRESSED) PRIMARY_RECORD    Record attributes =  LONG DATA REGION
Record size = 4013
CD Array
CD array entry = Column 1 (cluster 0, CD array offset 0): 0x02 (ONE_BYTE_SHORT)
CD array entry = Column 2 (cluster 0, CD array offset 0): 0x04 (THREE_BYTE_SHORT)
CD array entry = Column 3 (cluster 0, CD array offset 1): 0x0a (LONG)
Record Memory Dump
000000000B21B00D:   2103421a 829e8481 010100a0 0f7a7a7a 7a7a7a7a  !.B..... .zzzzzzz
000000000B21B021:   7a7a7a7a 7a7a7a7a 7a7a7a7a 7a7a7a7a 7a7a7a7a  zzzzzzzzzzzzzzzzzzzz
<SKIPPED>
000000000B21BFAD:   7a7a7a7a 7a7a7a7a 7a7a7a7a 7a                 zzzzzzzzzzzzz
Slot 0 Column 0 Offset 0x4 Length 4 Length (physical) 1
CSILOCATOR = 2
Slot 0 Column 1 Offset 0x5 Length 4 Length (physical) 3
Col1 = 2000001
Slot 0 Column 2 Offset 0xd Length 4000 Length (physical) 4000
Col2 = zzzzzzzzzzzzzzzzzzzzzzzzzzzzzzzzzzzzz <SKIPPED>
Slot 0 Offset 0x0 Length 0 Length (physical) 0
```

Figure 34-7. *Delta store and delete bitmap: Delta store data page*

Finally, it is worth noting that the row with Col1=2000000, which we inserted and deleted after the clustered columnstore index was created, is not present in the delta store. SQL Server deletes (and updates) rows in the B-Tree delta store the same way as in regular B-Tree tables.

You can use the same approach to examine the content of a deleted bitmap data page. In my case, the page ID is 308.

Figure 34-8 shows the partial output of the DBCC PAGE command. As you can see, the delete bitmap includes two columns that uniquely identify a row. The first column is a *row group id* and the second column is the offset of the row in the segment. Do not be confused by the fact that the column names match table columns. DBCC PAGE uses table metadata to prepare the output.

```
PAGE HEADER:
Page @0x00000002164EA000
m_pageId = (1:308)                    m_headerVersion = 1                    m_type = 1
m_typeFlagBits = 0x0                  m_level = 0                            m_flagBits = 0x4200
m_objId (AllocUnitId.idObj) = 187     m_indexId (AllocUnitId.idInd) = 256
Metadata: AllocUnitId = 72057594050183168
Metadata: PartitionId = 72057594044088320                                    Metadata: IndexId = 1
Metadata: ObjectId = 501576825        m_prevPage = (0:0)                     m_nextPage = (0:0)
pminlen = 3                           m_slotCnt = 2                          m_freeCnt = 8074
m_freeData = 114                      m_reservedCnt = 0                      m_lsn = (103:44448:29)
m_xactReserved = 0                    m_xdesId = (0:0)                       m_ghostRecCnt = 0
m_tornBits = -1356155720              DB Frag ID = 1
Allocation Status
GAM (1:2) = ALLOCATED                 SGAM (1:3) = ALLOCATED
PFS (1:1) = 0x60 MIXED_EXT ALLOCATED   0_PCT_FULL                            DIFF (1:6) = CHANGED
ML (1:7) = NOT MIN_LOGGED

Slot 0 Offset 0x69 Length 9
Record Type = (COMPRESSED) PRIMARY_RECORD                                    Record size = 9

CD Array
CD array entry = Column 1 (cluster 0, CD array offset 0): 0x01 (EMPTY)
CD array entry = Column 2 (cluster 0, CD array offset 0): 0x02 (ONE_BYTE_SHORT)
Slot 0 Column 1 Offset 0x0 Length 4 Length (physical) 0
Col1 = 0
Slot 0 Column 2 Offset 0x3 Length 4 Length (physical) 1
Col2 = 99
Slot 0 Offset 0x0 Length 0 Length (physical) 0
KeyHashValue = (875819828e15)

Slot 1 Offset 0x60 Length 9
Record Type = (COMPRESSED) PRIMARY_RECORD                                    Record size = 9

CD Array
CD array entry = Column 1 (cluster 0, CD array offset 0): 0x02 (ONE_BYTE_SHORT)
CD array entry = Column 2 (cluster 0, CD array offset 0): 0x02 (ONE_BYTE_SHORT)
Slot 1 Column 1 Offset 0x3 Length 4 Length (physical) 1
Col1 = 1
Slot 1 Column 2 Offset 0x4 Length 4 Length (physical) 1
Col2 = 5
Slot 1 Offset 0x0 Length 0 Length (physical) 0
KeyHashValue = (b511e0ee3829)
```

Figure 34-8. *Delta store and delete bitmap: Delete bitmap page*

It is worth noting that in SQL Server 2014 delta stores are page compressed. As we already discussed in Chapter 4, compression can increase the row size and, in some edge cases, disallow the creation of columnstore indexes with a very large number of columns. Page compression for delta stores has been removed in SQL Server 2016 to address this problem.

Delete bitmaps, on the other hand, use page compression in both SQL Server 2014 and 2016.

Columnstore Index Maintenance

Updateable columnstore indexes require maintenance that is similar to that of regular B-Tree indexes, even though the reasons for doing the maintenance are different. Columnstore indexes do not become fragmented; however, they can suffer from a large number of partially populated row groups. Another issue is the overhead of delta store and delete bitmap scans during query execution.

Let's run several tests and look at the issues involved in detail.

Excessive Number of Partially Populated Row Groups

For this test, I created two tables with a structure similar to the table we defined in Listing 33-9 in the previous chapter when we tested archival compression. I bulk inserted almost 62 million rows with the bcp utility, using 1,000,000-row batches and 102,500-row batches respectively.

Figure 34-9 illustrates the row groups in both tables after the import.

	row_group_id	state	state_description	total_rows	size_in_bytes
1	61	3	COMPRESSED	847552	11670056
2	60	3	COMPRESSED	1000000	13703040
3	59	3	COMPRESSED	1000000	13720656
4	58	3	COMPRESSED	1000000	13709600
5	57	3	COMPRESSED	1000000	13716384
6	56	3	COMPRESSED	1000000	13708280
7	55	3	COMPRESSED	1000000	13647288
8	54	3	COMPRESSED	1000000	13710112

RTM) | SQL2014\Administrator ... | AdventureWorksDW2012 | 00:00:00 | 62 rows

	row_group_id	state	state_description	total_rows	size_in_bytes
1	603	1	OPEN	40052	NULL
2	602	3	COMPRESSED	102500	1214480
3	601	3	COMPRESSED	102500	1059448
4	600	3	COMPRESSED	102500	1180120
5	599	3	COMPRESSED	102500	1218960
6	598	3	COMPRESSED	102500	1266000
7	597	3	COMPRESSED	102500	1063968
8	596	3	COMPRESSED	102500	1260136

TM) | SQL2014\Administrator ... | AdventureWorksDW2012 | 00:00:00 | 604 rows

***Figure 34-9.** Row groups after bulk import*

During the tests, I ran the query from Listing 33-10. The query required SQL Server to perform MAX() aggregation on 20 columns from the table by scanning all row groups and column segments.

Table 34-3 illustrates the execution time and number of I/O operations for the query against both tables. As you can see, the query against the table with partially populated row groups took a considerably longer time to execute.

***Table 34-3.** Execution Statistics for the Tables with Fully and Partially Populated Row Groups*

		Fully populated row groups	**Partially populated row groups**
SQL Server 2014	Elapsed / CPU Time	1,735 ms / 6,202 ms	2,450 ms / 7,418 ms
	Logical Reads	177,812	192,533
SQL Server 2016	Elapsed / CPU Time	1,405 ms / 5,500 ms	1,603 ms / 6,162 ms
	Logical Reads	118,197	192,533

It is worth noting that the performance of batch inserts was also affected by smaller batch sizes. In the case of 1,000,000-row batches, my system was able to insert about 143,750 rows per second, compared to 129,830 rows per second in the case of the 102,500-row batches.

Loading data in smaller batches puts new data into the delta store and produces fully populated row groups afterward. However, insert performance is seriously affected. For example, when I inserted data in 99,999-row batches, my system was able to insert only 55,500 rows per second.

Large Delta Stores

For the next step, let's look at how large delta stores affect the performance of queries. SQL Server needs to scan these delta stores during query execution.

For this test, I inserted 1,000,000 rows in small batches into the delta store of the first table from the previous test (the table that had row groups fully populated). After that, I rebuilt the columnstore index, comparing the execution time of the test query before and after the index rebuild.

The index rebuild process moved all data from the delta store to row groups. You can see the status of the row groups and the delta store before (on the left side) and after (on the right side) the index rebuild in Figure 34-10.

	row_group_id	state	state_description	total_rows	size_in_bytes
1	62	1	OPEN	1000000	NULL
2	61	3	COMPRESSED	847552	11670056
3	60	3	COMPRESSED	1000000	13703040
4	59	3	COMPRESSED	1000000	13720656
5	58	3	COMPRESSED	1000000	13709600
6	57	3	COMPRESSED	1000000	13716384
7	56	3	COMPRESSED	1000000	13708280
8	55	3	COMPRESSED	1000000	13647288
9	54	3	COMPRESSED	1000000	13710112
10	53	3	COMPRESSED	1000000	13655616

RTM) | SQL2014\Administrator ... | AdventureWorksDW2012 | 00:00:00 | 63 rows

	row_group_id	state	state_description	total_rows	size_in_bytes
1	59	3	COMPRESSED	981568	13475296
2	58	3	COMPRESSED	1048576	14357200
3	57	3	COMPRESSED	1048576	14197680
4	56	3	COMPRESSED	1048576	14333224
5	55	3	COMPRESSED	1048576	14339768
6	54	3	COMPRESSED	1048576	14374088
7	53	3	COMPRESSED	1048576	14348184
8	52	3	COMPRESSED	1048576	14331888
9	51	3	COMPRESSED	1048576	14223872
10	50	3	COMPRESSED	1048576	14362248

TM) | SQL2014\Administrator ... | AdventureWorksDW2012 | 00:00:00 | 60 rows

Figure 34-10. *Row groups and delta store after insertion of 1,000,000 rows*

Table 34-4 illustrates the execution times of the test query in both scenarios, and it shows the overhead introduced by the large delta store scan during query execution. It is worth noting that this overhead is bigger in SQL Server 2016 where the delta store is not using page compression and requires more I/O operations to scan.

Table 34-4. *Execution Time and Delta Store Size*

	Empty delta store (Elapsed / CPU time)	1,000,000 rows in delta store (Elapsed / CPU time)
SQL Server 2014	1,767 ms / 6,235 ms	2,557 ms / 8,781 ms
SQL Server 2016	1,507 ms / 5,723 ms	2,916 ms / 8,512 ms

Large Delete Bitmap

Finally, let's see how delete bitmaps affect query performance. For that test, I deleted almost 30,000,000 rows from a table.

You can see the row groups' information in Figure 34-11.

	row_group_id	state	state_description	total_rows	deleted_rows	size_in_bytes
1	59	3	COMPRESSED	981568	466858	13475296
2	58	3	COMPRESSED	1048576	501344	14357200
3	57	3	COMPRESSED	1048576	494174	14197680
4	56	3	COMPRESSED	1048576	503687	14333224
5	55	3	COMPRESSED	1048576	501017	14339768
6	54	3	COMPRESSED	1048576	498874	14374088
7	53	3	COMPRESSED	1048576	497120	14348184
8	52	3	COMPRESSED	1048576	499543	14331888

QL2014 (12.0 RTM) | SQL2014\Administrator ... | AdventureWorksDW2012 | 00:00:06 | 60 rows

Figure 34-11. *Row groups after deletion of 30,000,000 rows*

The test query needs to validate that rows have not been deleted during query execution. Similar to the previous test, this adds considerable overhead. Table 34-5 shows the execution time of the test query, comparing it to the execution time of the query before the data deletion.

Table 34-5. *Execution Time and Delete Bitmap*

	Empty delete bitmap (Elapsed / CPU time)	Delete bitmap with large number of rows (Elapsed / CPU time)
SQL Server 2014	1,767 ms / 6,235 ms	3,995 ms / 11,421 ms
SQL Server 2016	1,507 ms / 5,723 ms	3,049 ms / 10,611 ms

Index Maintenance Options

You can address all of these performance issues by rebuilding the columnstore index, which you can trigger with the `ALTER INDEX REBUILD` command. The index rebuild forces SQL Server to remove deleted rows physically from the index and to merge the delta stores' and row groups' data. All column segments are recreated with row groups fully populated.

Similar to index creation, the index rebuild process is very resource intensive. Moreover, as with the regular index rebuild process, it holds a schema modification (Sch-M) lock on the table, thus preventing other sessions from accessing it. Unfortunately, a columnstore index rebuild is an offline operation, and so you cannot use the `ONLINE=ON` clause with it.

Similar to B-Tree indexes, you can mitigate the overhead of an index rebuild by utilizing *table/index partitioning*. You can rebuild indexes on a partition basis and only do so for partitions that have volatile data. Old facts table data in most data warehouse solutions is relatively static, and ETL processes usually load new data only. Partitioning by date in this scenario localizes modifications within the scope of one or very few partitions. This can help you dramatically reduce the overhead of an index rebuild.

As we already discussed, columnstore indexes support an online index reorganize process, which you can trigger with the `ALTER INDEX REORGANIZE` command. The term *index reorganize* is a bit vague here; you can think of it as a tuple mover process running on demand. In **SQL Server 2014**, the only action performed by index reorganization, by default, is compressing and moving the data from closed delta stores to row groups. Delete bitmap and open delta stores stay intact.

In **SQL Server 2016**, index reorganize also performs additional defragmentation, as follows:

- It removes deleted rows from row groups that have 10 or more percent of the rows logically deleted.
- It merges closed row groups together, keeping the total number of rows less than or equal to 1,024,576.

Both processes can be done together. For example, if you have two row groups, one that has 500,000 total with 100,000 deleted rows and one that has 750,000 total with 250,000 deleted rows, the defragmentation process will merge them into another row group with 900,000 rows total, physically removing all deleted rows from the merged row group.

You can use the `ALTER INDEX REORGANIZE WITH (COMPRESS_ALL_ROW_GROUPS = ON)` statement to close and compress all open row groups. SQL Server does not merge row groups during this operation.

In contrast to a single-threaded tuple mover process, the `ALTER INDEX REORGANIZE` operation uses all available system resources while it is running. This can significantly speed up the execution process and reduce the time during which other sessions cannot modify or delete data in a table. It is worth noting again that insert processes are not blocked during this time.

A columnstore index's maintenance strategy should depend on the volatility of the data and the ETL processes implemented in the system. You should rebuild indexes when a table has a considerable amount of deleted rows and/or a large number of partially populated row groups.

It is also advantageous to rebuild partition(s) that still have a large number of rows in open delta stores after the ETL process has completed, especially if the ETL process does not use a bulk insert API.

Nonclustered B-Tree Indexes (SQL Server 2016)

As I already mentioned, in SQL Server 2014, the clustered columnstore index is the only copy of the data in the table. You cannot create any other columnstore or B-Tree indexes there. This restriction has been removed in SQL Server 2016, which allows you to define nonclustered B-Tree indexes on tables with clustered columnstore indexes.

Nonclustered B-Tree indexes, in a nutshell, allow you to optimize OLTP queries against those tables. Consider a situation where you store all *current* and *historical* data in a system that handles OLTP activity against current hot data and analysis/reporting activity against historical data. One of the common implementations in this schema is the use of partitioned views that store historical data in tables with column-based storage.

There are still cases, however, when you need to run OLTP queries against historical data. For example, in Point-of-Sale systems customers may want to look up the old order record. Nonclustered B-Tree indexes can help you to optimize those queries and avoid scanning the columnstore index.

Nonclustered B-Tree indexes also allow you to define and enforce primary key and unique constraints on the clustered columnstore index tables. They also allow such tables to reference or be referenced by foreign key constraints. All of this helps to improve data quality in data warehouse systems.

When a table with a clustered columnstore index is partitioned, which is usually the case, SQL Server also partitions nonclustered B-Tree indexes, aligning them with the columnstore index. This may prevent you from defining the uniqueness of the index unless you include a partition column in the index key.

Figure 34-12 shows the partition of the clustered columnstore index with a nonclustered B-Tree index created. Nonclustered B-Tree indexes use the columnstore index locator as the row-id, which references the rows in the clustered columnstore index.

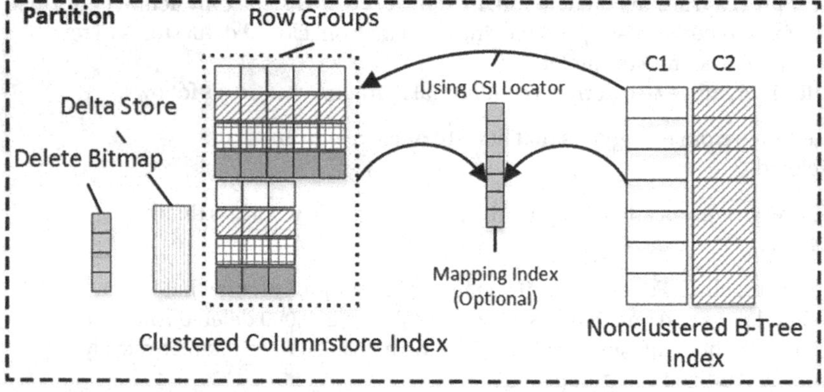

Figure 34-12. *Partition of the table with clustered columnstore and nonclustered B-Tree indexes*

There are cases when rows in the columnstore indexes can be moved to different locations; for example, when delta stores are compressed or row groups are merged. When it happens, SQL Server does not update the row-id in the nonclustered indexes but rather uses another internal component, called the *mapping index*, which contains information about old and new row locations.

Let's look at the following example. Listing 34-7 shows code that creates a table with clustered columnstore and nonclustered B-Tree indexes and populates it with some data.

Listing 34-7. Query that uses nonclustered B-Tree index

```
create table dbo.CCIWithNI
(
    Col1 int not null,
    Col2 int not null,
    Col3 int not null
);

insert into dbo.CCIWithNI(Col1, Col2, Col3)
values(1,1,1), (2,2,2);

create clustered columnstore index CCI_CCIWithNI on dbo.CCIWithNI;

insert into dbo.CCIWithNI(Col1, Col2, Col3)
values(100,100,100),(200,200,200);

create nonclustered index IDX_CCIWithNI_Col3 on dbo.CCIWithNI(Col3);
```

At this stage, the columnstore index will have one compressed row group and one open delta store. You can examine it with the new SQL Server 2016 data management view `sys.dm_db_column_store_row_group_physical_stats`, which provides you with information about row groups in columnstore indexes.

Listing 34-8 shows the query that uses this view. Figure 34-13 illustrates the output of the query.

Listing 34-8. Analyzing the row groups in the index

```
select object_id, index_id, partition_number, row_group_id,generation, state_desc
    ,total_rows, deleted_rows
from sys.dm_db_column_store_row_group_physical_stats
where object_id =  object_id(N'dbo.CCIWithNI');
```

	object_id	index_id	partition_number	row_group_id	generation	state_desc	total_rows	deleted_rows
1	418100530	1	1	1	NULL	OPEN	2	0
2	418100530	1	1	0	1	COMPRESSED	2	0

Figure 34-13. *Columnstore index row groups*

Another new SQL Server 2016 view—`sys.internal_partitions`—provides information about internal columnstore index objects. You can see the query that uses this view in Listing 34-9.

Listing 34-9. Columnstore index internal objects

```
select ip.object_id, ip.index_id, ip.partition_id, ip.row_group_id, ip.internal_object_type
      ,ip.internal_object_type_desc, ip.rows, ip.data_compression_desc, ip.hobt_id
from sys.internal_partitions ip
where ip.object_id = object_id(N'dbo.CCIWithNI');
```

Figure 34-14 illustrates the output of this query. As you can see, at this stage the clustered columnstore index has delta store and delete bitmap without a mapping index present.

	object_id	index_id	partition_id	row_group_id	internal_object_type	internal_object_type_desc	rows	data_compression_desc	hobt_id
1	418100530	1	72057594068205568	NULL	2	COLUMN_STORE_DELETE_BITMAP	0	PAGE	72057594068205568
2	418100530	1	72057594068271104	1	3	COLUMN_STORE_DELTA_STORE	2	NONE	72057594068271104

Figure 34-14. *Columnstore index internal objects*

Let's look at the internal structure of a nonclustered B-Tree index. Listing 34-10 shows a query that returns information about index page allocation. It is using the nonclustered index ID (2) as the parameter of the call. Figure 34-15 shows the output of the query.

Listing 34-10. Getting page allocation information

```
select object_id, index_id, partition_id, allocation_unit_type_desc as [Type], is_allocated
      ,is_iam_page, page_type, page_type_desc, allocated_page_file_id as [FileId]
      ,allocated_page_page_id as [PageId], rowset_id, allocation_unit_id
from sys.dm_db_database_page_allocations(db_id(), object_id('dbo.
CCIWithNI'),2,null,'DETAILED')
where is_allocated = 1;
```

	object_id	index_id	partition_id	Type	is_allocated	is_iam_page	page_type	page_type_desc	FileId	PageId	rowset_id	allocation_unit_id
1	418100530	2	1	IN_ROW_DATA	1	1	10	IAM_PAGE	1	363	72057594068336640	72057594079870976
2	418100530	2	1	IN_ROW_DATA	1	0	2	INDEX_PAGE	1	14568	72057594068336640	72057594079870976

Figure 34-15. *Nonclustered index page allocation*

Now, when we know the file and page IDs of the index, we can examine it with the `DBCC PAGE` command, as shown in Listing 34-11. Obviously, you will get different values when you run the previous query in your environment.

Listing 34-11. Analyzing index page

```
dbcc traceon(3604);  -- Redirecting output to console
dbcc page -- Analyzing content of a page
(   10          -- Database Id
    ,1          -- FileId
    ,14568      -- PageId
    ,3          -- Output style
);
```

Figure 34-16 illustrates the data from the index page. `DBCC PAGE` incorrectly assumes that the second index column is `uniquifier`. In reality, this column is known as the columnstore index *original locator*, which is an eight-byte value that consists of a `row_group_id` in the high four bytes and the offset within the row group in the low four bytes. For example, the decimal value `4,294,967,297` is `0x0000 0001 0000 0001` in hexadecimal format, which corresponds to `row_group_id=1` and `offset=1`.

	FileId	PageId	Row	Level	Col3 (key)	UNIQUIFIER (key)	KeyHashValue	Row Size
1	1	14568	0	0	1	0	(9536464f36de)	20
2	1	14568	1	0	2	1	(98558831a36b)	20
3	1	14568	2	0	100	4294967296	(e6268fbdae9c)	20
4	1	14568	3	0	200	4294967297	(9e41345b5652)	20

Figure 34-16. *Nonclustered index page*

Let's run the ALTER INDEX REORGANIZE statement, closing and compressing the delta store, as shown in Listing 34-12.

Listing 34-12. Reorganizing the index

```
alter index CCI_CCIWithNI on dbo.CCIWithNI reorganize
with (compress_all_row_groups = on);
```

If you looked at the columnstore index's row groups and internal objects again, using the code from Listings 34-9 and 34-10, you would see the output shown in Figure 34-17. As you can see, the delta store is now compressed into the new row group (the old row group is in TOMBSTONE state and will be eventually deallocated). Moreover, SQL Server creates a mapping index to indicate that rows from the old delta store have been moved.

	object_id	index_id	partition_number	row_group_id	generation	state_desc	total_rows	deleted_rows
1	418100530	1	1	2	2	COMPRESSED	2	0
2	418100530	1	1	1	2	TOMBSTONE	2	0
3	418100530	1	1	0	1	COMPRESSED	2	0

	object_id	index_id	partition_id	row_group_id	internal_object_type	internal_object_type_desc	rows	data_compression_desc	hobt_id
1	418100530	1	72057594068205568	NULL	2	COLUMN_STORE_DELETE_BITMAP	0	PAGE	72057594068205568
2	418100530	1	72057594068271104	1	3	COLUMN_STORE_DELTA_STORE	2	NONE	72057594068271104
3	418100530	1	72057594068402176	NULL	5	COLUMN_STORE_MAPPING_INDEX	1	PAGE	72057594068402176

Figure 34-17. *Row groups and internal objects after ALTER INDEX REORGANIZE*

It is worth mentioning that if you look at the nonclustered index page again, the row-id of the rows will not have changed. SQL Server will use the mapping index to locate the new location of the rows.

Internally, the mapping index can track the movement of individual rows along with multiple rows' movements and row group ID changes. As you can see, in our case we have just the single row in the mapping index even though the old delta store had two rows.

When a row in a columnstore index is moved, SQL Server keeps track of the row's *original locator* in an internal nullable column in the columnstore index. This column is created when you add the first nonclustered B-Tree index to the table. This original locator value uniquely identifies corresponding rows in nonclustered B-Tree indexes and is used when you, for example, delete the row from a table. The original locator value is not populated until the row is moved.

■ **Note** You can see the original locator column if you examine the contents of the delta store data page or look at columnstore index segment information with the sys.column_store_segments view. That column has a column_id of 65,535.

The Query Optimizer could use nonclustered B-Tree indexes for OLTP queries that perform point lookups or small range scans. In cases where nonclustered indexes do not cover the queries, SQL Server will get the data from the clustered columnstore index. This operation is shown as a key lookup in the execution plans even though it is different than the key lookup performed on clustered B-Tree indexes.

Listing 34-13 shows a query that could benefit from the IDX_CCIWithNI_Col3 index we defined earlier. Figure 34-18 shows the execution plan of this query, assuming you populated the table with enough data for a *nonclustered index seek* to become more efficient than a columnstore index scan. Alternatively, you can force this execution plan using the WITH (INDEX=IDX_CCIWithNI_Col3) hint.

Listing 34-13. Query that uses nonclustered B-Tree index

```
select Col1, Col2, Col3
from dbo.CCIWithNI
where Col3 = 42
```

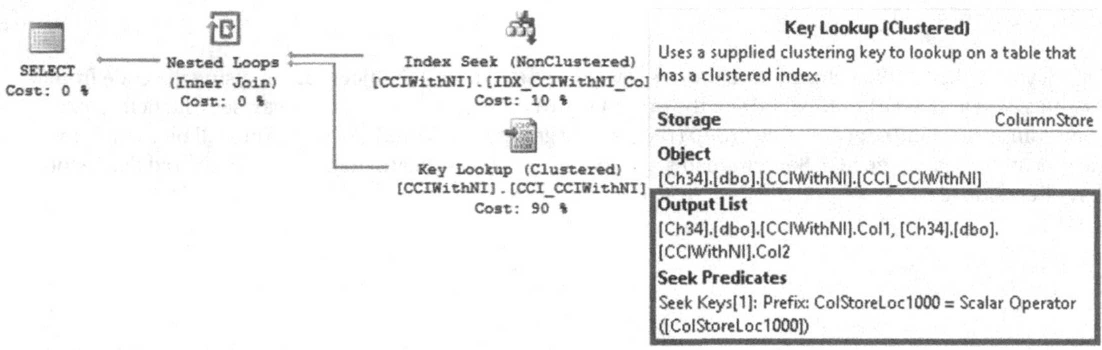

Figure 34-18. *Execution plan with nonclustered B-Tree index seek*

Nonclustered B-Tree indexes need to be maintained in the same way as indexes on B-Tree tables. One thing worth noting is that a rebuild of the clustered columnstore index rearranges rows in the row groups, changing their location. SQL Server will rebuild nonclustered B-Tree indexes and remove mapping indexes as part of this operation.

Updateable Nonclustered Columnstore Indexes (SQL Server 2016)

SQL Server 2016 supports updateable nonclustered columnstore indexes on B-Tree tables. Those indexes can be beneficial in operational analytics scenarios when you need to run reporting/analytics queries against tables with heavy OLTP workload. You can think about a system that should display an operational dashboard with up-to-date information as an example.

Despite the name, nonclustered columnstore indexes in SQL Server 2016 are very different from those in an SQL Server 2012/2014 implementation. Similar to clustered columnstore indexes, they use delta store and delete bitmap to support data modifications. Their delta stores, however, are not limited to 1,048,576 rows and can grow up to about 33.5 million rows (2^25) when you insert a large number of rows in between tuple mover executions.

There is another structure called *delete buffer* that is used as temporary storage for information about deleted rows. It reduces the overhead that delete bitmap managements would introduce to OLTP transactions.

Internally, the delete buffer is implemented as a B-Tree index with a structure that mimics the table row-id, which is either a clustered index key or the location of the row in the heap table. This approach allows SQL Server to avoid a lookup of the columnstore index row locator, which is used in delete bitmap during `DELETE` and `UPDATE` operations.

The tuple mover process updates delete bitmap based on the data from delete buffer during the `ALTER INDEX REORGANIZE` command or when the number of rows there exceeds 1,048,576. At any given point in time, the union of delete buffer and delete bitmap represents all deleted rows in the index.

Figure 34-19 illustrates all components of a B-Tree table partition with a nonclustered columnstore index.

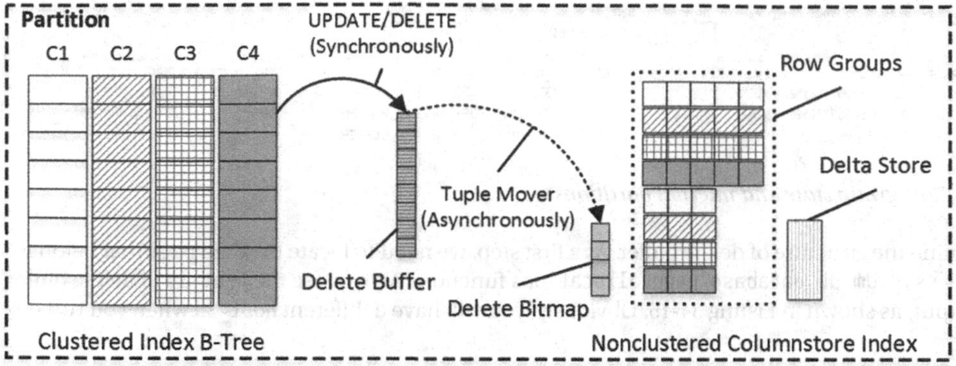

Figure 34-19. *Partition of the table with a nonclustered columnstore index*

Listing 34-14 shows the code that creates a table with a B-Tree clustered index and inserts three rows there. As the next step, the code creates a nonclustered columnstore index and deletes one row from the table. Finally, the code examines the state of the row groups and internal partitions in the columnstore index.

Listing 34-14. Nonclustered columnstore index: Table creation

```
create table dbo.CIWithNCI
(
    Col1 int not null,
    Col2 int not null,
    Col3 int not null,
    constraint PK_CIWithNCI
    primary key clustered(Col1, Col2)
);

insert into dbo.CIWithNCI(Col1, Col2, Col3)
values(1,10,100), (2, 20, 200), (3, 30, 300);

create nonclustered columnstore index NCI_CIWithNCI
on dbo.CIWithNCI(Col2, Col3);

delete from dbo.CIWithNCI where Col1 = 3;

select object_id, index_id, partition_number, row_group_id
        ,generation, state_desc, total_rows, deleted_rows
from sys.dm_db_column_store_row_group_physical_stats
where object_id =  object_id(N'dbo.CIWithNCI');

select ip.object_id, ip.index_id, ip.partition_id, ip.row_group_id, ip.internal_object_type
        ,ip.internal_object_type_desc, ip.rows, ip.data_compression_desc, ip.hobt_id
from sys.internal_partitions ip
where ip.object_id = object_id(N'dbo.CIWithNCI');
```

Figure 34-20 illustrates the output of the two SELECT statements . As you can see, there is one deleted row in the delete buffer; however, delete bitmap is empty. It is also worth noting that SQL Server preallocates extra delete buffer to reduce the overhead of switching buffers during the tuple mover execution.

	object_id	index_id	partition_number	row_group_id	generation	state_desc	total_rows	deleted_rows
1	354100302	2	1	0	1	COMPRESSED	3	0

	object_id	index_id	partition_id	row_group_id	internal_object_type	internal_object_type_desc	rows	data_compression_desc	hobt_id
1	354100302	2	72057594067156992	NULL	2	COLUMN_STORE_DELETE_BITMAP	0	PAGE	72057594067156992
2	354100302	2	72057594067222528	NULL	4	COLUMN_STORE_DELETE_BUFFER	1	NONE	72057594067222528
3	354100302	2	72057594067288064	NULL	4	COLUMN_STORE_DELETE_BUFFER	0	NONE	72057594067288064

Figure 34-20. *Row group state and internal partitions*

Let's examine the structure of delete buffer. As a first step, we need to locate the data page that belongs to it by using the `sys.dm_db_database_page_allocations` function. We can use the `hobt_id` of delete buffer to filter the output, as shown in Listing 34-15. Obviously, you will have a different `hobt_id` when you run this example.

Listing 34-15. Nonclustered columnstore index: Obtaining page_id of delete buffer

```
select object_id, index_id, partition_id, allocation_unit_type_desc as [Type], is_allocated
     ,is_iam_page, page_type, page_type_desc, allocated_page_file_id as [FileId]
     ,allocated_page_page_id as [PageId], rowset_id, allocation_unit_id
from sys.dm_db_database_page_allocations(db_id(),object_id('dbo.CIWithNCI'),null,null
     ,'DETAILED')
where is_allocated = 1 and rowset_id in (72057594067222528)
```

Figure 34-21 illustrates the output of this query.

	object_id	index_id	partition_id	Type	is_allocated	is_iam_page	page_type	page_type_desc	FileId	PageId	rowset_id	allocation_unit_id
1	354100302	2	1	IN_ROW_DATA	1	1	10	IAM_PAGE	1	366	72057594067222528	72057594078560256
2	354100302	2	1	IN_ROW_DATA	1	0	1	DATA_PAGE	1	10880	72057594067222528	72057594078560256

Figure 34-21. *Delete buffer page allocation*

Now that we know file and page IDs, let's look at the internal structure of a delete buffer using the `DBCC PAGE` command, as shown in Listing 34-16.

Listing 34-16. Nonclustered columnstore index: Analyzing delete buffer data page

```
dbcc traceon(3604);  -- Redirecting output to console
dbcc page -- Analyzing content of a page
(   10         -- Database Id
    ,1          -- FileId
    ,10880    -- PageId
    ,3         -- Output style
)
```

Figure 34-22 shows the partial output with the row data. As you can see, it includes three columns. Ignore the column names—`DBCC PAGE` obtains them from the table metadata, which cannot be applied to the delete buffer structure.

```
Slot 0 Column 1 Offset 0x4 Length 4 Length (physical) 4
Col3 = 3

Slot 0 Column 2 Offset 0x8 Length 4 Length (physical) 4
Col1 = 30

Slot 0 Column 3 Offset 0xc Length 8 Length (physical) 8
Col2 = 1
```

Figure 34-22. *Delete-buffer data page*

The first two left-most columns match the structure of the clustered index. The last column indicates the columnstore index `generation` value at the time when the row was deleted. This helps SQL Server to isolate row groups to which the deleted row may belong.

As with any other index, nonclustered columnstore indexes introduce overhead during data modifications. An `INSERT` operation requires SQL Server to insert the row into the delta store. A `DELETE` operation populates the delete buffer. Finally, an `UPDATE` operation performs both of these actions.

In some cases, you can reduce overhead by defining a filter on the index. The filter condition requirements are the same as with regular B-Tree filtered indexes and support simple comparison logic. It is possible to define the filter on a static condition; for example, `OrderStatus='COMPLETED'`. However, you cannot use function calls and non-deterministic expressions, such as `OrderDate < DATEADD(HOUR,-24,GETUTCDATE())`.

Another useful option is `COMPRESSION_DELAY`, which allows you to specify a time interval in minutes for how long a row group should stay in the `CLOSED` state before it is compressed. Consider a system that handles a high rate of inserts and performs some processing when updating the data afterward. Setting `COMPRESSION_DELAY` to a value that exceeds the typical processing time would exclude old (deleted) versions of the rows from compression and improve the performance of the columnstore index.

Metadata

SQL Server 2014 and 2016 provide several catalog and data management views in addition to the `sys.column_store_segments` and `sys.column_store_dictionaries` views, which we already discussed in the previous chapter. Let's look at them in detail.

sys.column_store_row_groups (SQL Server 2014–2016)

The `sys.column_store_row_groups` view returns information about row groups in columnstore indexes. You have already seen this view in action many times in this chapter.

The columns in the output represent the following:

`object_id` and `index_id` provide information about the object and index to which the row group belongs.

`partition_number` is the number of partition in the table.

`row_group_id` is the ID of the row group within the partition.

`delta_store_hobt_id` is the `hobt_id` of the open delta store.

`state` and `state_description` show the state of the row group.

`total_rows` and `deleted_rows` show the number of total and deleted rows in the row group.

`size_in_bytes` indicates the size of the row group on disk.

You should monitor the total number of rows and number of deleted rows in the row groups, rebuilding or reorganizing indexes when needed. As you should remember, small row groups and a large number of deleted rows in the row groups would negatively affect the performance of the queries.

sys.dm_db_column_store_row_group_physical_stats (SQL Server 2016)

The `sys.dm_db_column_store_row_group_physical_stats` view also returns information about row groups in the columnstore index. Some of the columns in the output match the `sys.column_store_row_groups` view; however, there are several additional columns that can be useful during analysis and troubleshooting.

The columns in the output represent the following:

> `object_id`, `index_id`, `partition_number`, `row_group_id`, `delta_store_hobt_id`, `has_vertipaq_optimization`, and `creation_time` provide information about the row group and `hobt_id` of the open delta store.
>
> `state` and `state_description` show the state of the row group.
>
> `total_rows`, `deleted_rows`, and `size_in_bytes` provide information about row count and row group size.
>
> `transition_to_compressed_state` provides the reason why a row group was compressed.
>
> `trim_reason` indicates why a row group has less than 1,048,576 rows.
>
> `generation` shows the sequence number in which the row group has been created.

You can use the `transition_to_compressed_state` and `trim_reason` columns to troubleshoot the situation when a columnstore index has a large number of partially populated row groups in the system.

sys.internal_partitions (SQL Server 2016)

The `sys.internal_partitions` view provides information about internal columnstore objects, such as delete bitmap, delete buffer, delta store, and mapping indexes. We have used this view in this chapter.

The columns in the output represent the following:

> `object_id`, `index_id`, `partition_id`, and `partition_number` provide information about object, index, and partition of the internal columnstore object.
>
> `internal_object_type` and `internal_object_type_desc` show the type of the internal object.
>
> `row_group_id` indicates the row group for the delta store. It is `NULL` for all other object types, which exist on a per-partition basis.
>
> `rows` provides the number of rows in the object.
>
> `data_compression` and `data_compression_desc` provide information about the data compression of the internal object.

This view is useful for the low-level monitoring of columnstore indexes. For example, a large number of rows in mapping indexes or a delete buffer could indicate that the index would benefit from a rebuild. It is worth noting that all internal objects are recreated when you rebuild the index.

sys.dm_db_column_store_row_group_operational_stats (SQL Server 2016)

The `sys.dm_db_column_store_row_group_operational_stats` view provides you with low-level statistics on columnstore index usage, returning information on a per-row group basis. The output includes the following columns:

- `object_id`, `index_id`, `partition_number`, and `row_group_id` indicate the row group in the output.
- `scan_count` and `delete_buffer scan_count` indicate how many times the row group and delete buffer were scanned since the last SQL Server restart.
- `index_scan_count` shows how many times a partition has been scanned. The value in the output is the same for all row groups on the partition.
- `rowgroup_lock_count`, `rowgroup_lock_wait_count`, and `rowgroup_lock_wait_in_ms` provide cumulative locking-related statistics since the last SQL Server restart.

Design Considerations

The choice between columnstore and B-Tree indexes depends on several factors. The most important factor, however, is the type of workload in the system. These indexes are targeted to different use cases, and each has its own set of strengths and weaknesses.

Columnstore indexes shine with data warehouse workloads where queries need to scan a large amount of data in a table. However, they are not a good fit for cases where you need to select one or a handful of rows using point lookup or small range scan operations. An index scan is the only access method supported by columnstore indexes, and SQL Server will scan all the data even if your query needs to select just a single row from a table. The amount of data to scan can be reduced by partition and segment eliminations. In either case, however, a scan would be far less efficient than the use of a B-Tree index seek operation.

Most large data warehouse systems would benefit from columnstore indexes, even though their implementation requires some work in order to get the most from them. You often need to change a database schema to fit into star or snowflake patterns and/or to normalize facts tables and remove string attributes from them. In the case of SQL Server 2012, you need to change ETL processes to address the read-only limitation of nonclustered columnstore indexes, and you must often re-factor queries to utilize batch mode execution.

Clustered columnstore indexes simplify the conversion process. You can continue to use existing ETL processes and insert data directly into facts tables. There is a hidden danger in this approach, however. Even though clustered columnstore indexes are fully updateable, they are optimized for large bulk load operations. As you have seen, excessive data modifications and a large number of partially populated row groups could and will negatively affect the performance of queries. In the end, you should either fine-tune ETL processes or frequently rebuild indexes to avoid such performance overhead. In some cases, especially with frequently modified or deleted data, you need to rebuild indexes on a regular basis, regardless of the quality of the ETL processes.

Table partitioning becomes a *must have* element in this scenario. It allows you to perform index maintenance in the partition scope, which can dramatically reduce the overhead of such operations. It also allows you to save storage space and reduce the solution cost by implementing archival compression on the partitions that store old data.

The question of columnstore index usage in OLTP environments is more complex than it may seem. Even though tables with clustered columnstore indexes are updateable, they are not good candidates for active and volatile OLTP data. Unfortunately, performance issues are easy to overlook at the beginning of development; after all, any solution performs *good enough* with a small amount of data. However, as the amount of data increases, performance issues become noticeable and force the re-factoring of systems.

Nevertheless, there are some legitimate uses for columnstore indexes even in OLTP environments. Almost all OLTP systems provide some reporting and analysis capabilities to customers. The mixed workload can be easily supported with updatable nonclustered columnstore indexes; however, this option will work only in **SQL Server 2016**.

In **SQL Server 2012/2014**, you may consider using columnstore indexes on tables that store old and static historical data while using regular B-Tree tables for volatile operational data. You can combine data from all tables with a partitioned view, hiding the data layout from client applications. However, it will require a complex and thoughtful design process, deep knowledge of the system workload, and considerable effort to implement.

In some cases, especially if data is static and read-only, nonclustered columnstore indexes could be a better choice than clustered columnstore indexes in **SQL Server 2012/2014**. Even though they require extra storage space for B-Tree representation of the data, you can benefit from regular B-Tree indexes to support some use cases and OLTP queries. Obviously, in **SQL Server 2016** you can create nonclustered B-Tree indexes on tables that have clustered columnstore indexes in that scenario.

Finally, it is worth remembering that columnstore indexes are an Enterprise Edition-only feature. Moreover, they are not a *transparent* feature, as are data compression and table partitioning, that can be removed from the database relatively easily if necessary. Implementation of columnstore indexes leads to specific database schema and code patterns, which can be less efficient in the case of B-Tree indexes. Think about the over-normalization of facts tables, changes in ETL processes, and batch mode execution query re-factoring as examples of those patterns.

Columnstore indexes are also available in Microsoft Azure; however, you need to use the premium tier of SQL Databases to utilize them.

Summary

Even though SQL Server supports just two types of columnstore indexes—clustered and nonclustered—they work and behave very differently in the different SQL Server versions.

In SQL Server 2012 and 2014, nonclustered columnstore indexes are essentially read-only. With the exception of a partition switch, you cannot update data in the table once a nonclustered columnstore index is created. It is the only columnstore index type supported in SQL Server 2012.

The clustered columnstore indexes introduced in SQL Server 2014 address the major limitation of nonclustered columnstore indexes in SQL Server 2012/2014, which prevent any modifications of the data in the table. Clustered columnstore indexes are updateable, and in SQL Server 2014 they are the only instance of the data that is stored in the table. No other indexes can be created on a table that has a clustered columnstore index defined.

SQL Server 2016 allows you to create nonclustered B-Tree indexes on tables with a clustered columnstore index. Moreover, it allows you to create updateable nonclustered columnstore indexes in B-Tree tables.

Clustered and nonclustered columnstore indexes share the same storage format for column-based data. Two types of internal objects support data modifications in updateable columnstore indexes. A delete bitmap indicates what rows were deleted. A delta store stores new rows. Both delta stores and delete bitmaps use a B-Tree format to store the data.

The update of rows stored in column-based row groups is implemented as the deletion of old rows, which is insertion to a delete bitmap, and the insertion of a new version of the rows to the delta store. Deletion and modification of the data in a delta store deletes or updates rows in the delta store B-Tree.

Delta stores can store up to 1,048,576 rows. Although, in SQL Server 2016, delta stores of *nonclustered* columnstore indexes can exceed this size if heavy inserts occurred in between tuple mover executions. After this limit is reached, the delta store is closed and converted to a row group in column-based storage format by a background process called tuple mover. Alternatively, you can force this conversion with the `ALTER INDEX REORGANIZE` command.

A large amount of data in delta stores and/or delete bitmaps negatively affects query performance. You should monitor their size and rebuild the indexes to address performance issues. You should partition tables to minimize index maintenance overhead.

Bulk insert operations with a batch size that exceeds 102,400 rows create new, compressed row groups and insert data there. A large number of partially populated row groups is another factor that negatively affects query performance. You should import data in batches with a size divisible by 1,048,576 rows to avoid this situation. Alternatively, you can rebuild indexes after ETL operations are completed.

Columnstore indexes do not support any access methods with the exception of an index scan. They are targeted at data warehouse workloads, and they should be used with extreme care in OLTP environments. In SQL Server 2012 and 2014, you can use them in tables with historical data, storing active OLTP data in B-Tree tables and combining all data with partitioned views. In SQL Server 2016, you can mix B-Tree and columnstore indexes on the same table when you need to support operational analytics or systems with a mixed workload.

PART VIII

In-Memory OLTP Engine

In-Memory OLTP is a complex and fascinating subject that easily merits a book by itself. Unfortunately, it is impossible to cover all aspects of the technology in this book.

The next three chapters will provide you with a good overview of In-Memory OLTP and explain how it works under the hood. Those chapters, however, do not unravel some of the low-level implementation details, nor do they talk about the deployment and management of In-Memory OLTP solutions.

Apress has already published my *Expert SQL Server In-Memory OLTP* book that elucidates In-Memory OLTP implementation in SQL Server 2014. The second edition of the book will be published in 2017, and it will describe SQL Server 2016 implementation. Consider reading those books for a deeper dive into the technology.

CHAPTER 35

In-Memory OLTP Internals

Hekaton was the code name of an In-Memory OLTP Engine introduced in SQL Server 2014. It is an Enterprise Edition feature, and it is available only in the 64-bit version of SQL Server. *Hekaton* is Greek for *one hundred,* which was the target performance improvement goal of the project. Even though this goal has yet to be achieved, it is not uncommon to see a 10X–40X system throughput increase when In-Memory OLTP is used.

This chapter discusses the internal architecture of In-Memory OLTP and explains how In-Memory OLTP stores and works with data in-memory and persists it on-disk.

Why In-Memory OLTP?

Way back when SQL Server and other major databases were originally designed, hardware was very expensive. Servers used to have just one or very few CPUs and a small amount of installed memory. Database servers had to work with data that resided on disk and load it to memory on demand.

The situation has dramatically changed over time. During the last 30 years, memory prices have dropped by a factor of ten every five years. Hardware has become more affordable. It is now entirely possible to buy a server with 32 cores and 1 TB of RAM for less than $50,000. While it is also true that databases have become larger, it is often possible that *active* operational data fits into the memory.

Obviously, it is beneficial to have data cached in the buffer pool. It reduces the load on the I/O subsystem and improves system performance. However, when systems work under heavy concurrent load, it is often not enough. SQL Server manages and protects page structures in memory, which introduces large overhead and does not scale well. Even with row-level locking, multiple sessions cannot modify data on the same data page simultaneously and must wait for each other.

Perhaps the last sentence needs to be clarified. Obviously, multiple sessions can modify data rows on the same data page, holding exclusive (X) locks on different rows simultaneously. However, they cannot update on-page and in-row data simultaneously, because it could corrupt the page structure. As you already know, SQL Server addresses this problem by protecting pages with latches. They protect internal SQL Server data structures by serializing access to them; only one thread can update data on the data page in memory at any given point of time.

In the end, this limits the improvements that can be achieved with the current database systems architecture. Although you can scale hardware by adding more CPUs with a larger number of logical cores per CPU, that serialization quickly becomes a bottleneck and limiting factor in improving system scalability.

Likewise, you cannot improve performance by increasing the CPU clock speed, as the silicon chips would melt down. Therefore, the only feasible way to improve database system performance is by reducing the number of CPU instructions that need to be executed to perform an action.

Unfortunately, code optimization is not enough by itself. Consider a situation where you need to update a row in a table. Even when you know the clustered key value, that operation needs to traverse the clustered index tree, obtaining latches and locks on the data pages and a row. In some cases, it needs to update nonclustered indexes, obtaining the latches and locks there. All of this generates log records and requires writing them and the dirty data pages to disk.

D. Korotkevitch, *Pro SQL Server Internals*, DOI 10.1007/978-1-4842-1964-5_35

All of these actions can lead to a hundred thousand or even millions of CPU instructions to execute. Code optimization can help reduce this number to some degree; however, it is impossible to reduce it dramatically without changing the system architecture and the way the system stores and works with data.

All these trends and architectural limitations led the Microsoft team to the conclusion that a true In-Memory solution should be built using the different design principles and architecture other than the classic SQL Server Database Engine. The In-Memory OLTP Engine is based on three design goals, as follows:

> **Optimize data storage for main memory.** Data in In-Memory OLTP is not stored on on-disk data pages nor does it mimic an on-disk storage structure when loaded into memory. This permits the elimination of the complex buffer pool structure and the code that manages it. Moreover, indexes are not persisted on disk, and they are recreated upon startup when memory-resident tables' data is loaded into memory.
>
> **Eliminate latches and locks.** All In-Memory OLTP internal data structures are latch- and lock-free. In-Memory OLTP uses a new multi-version concurrency control (MVCC) to provide transaction consistency. From a user standpoint, it behaves in a way similar to the regular `SNAPSHOT` transaction isolation level; however, it does not use locking under the hood. This schema allows multiple sessions to work with the same data without locking and blocking each other and improves the scalability of the system allowing fully utilize modern multi-CPU/multi-core hardware.
>
> **Using native compilation.** T-SQL is an interpreted language that provides great flexibility at the cost of CPU overhead. Even a simple statement requires hundreds of thousands of CPU instructions to execute. The In-Memory OLTP Engine addresses this by compiling row access logic and stored procedures into native machine code.

It is also worth mentioning that the In-Memory OLTP design has been targeted toward OLTP workload. As all of us know, specialized solutions designed for particular tasks and workload usually outperform general purpose systems in the targeted areas. The same is true for In-Memory OLTP. It shines with the large and very busy OLTP systems that support hundreds or even thousands of concurrent users. At the same time, In-Memory OLTP is not necessarily the best choice for a data warehouse workload, where other SQL Server components could outperform it. SQL Server 2016, however, allows you to create columnstore indexes on in-memory data, which can help in a system with a mixed workload.

The In-Memory OLTP Engine is fully integrated into the SQL Server Engine, which is the key differentiator of Microsoft implementation as compared to other in-memory database solutions. You do not need to perform complex system re-factoring, splitting data between in-memory and conventional database servers, nor do you need to move all of the data from the database into memory. You can separate in-memory and disk data on a table-by-table basis, which allows you to move active operational data into memory, keeping other tables and historical data on disk. In some cases, that conversion can be even done transparently to client applications.

The first release of In-Memory OLTP in SQL Server 2014 had a large number of limitations and supported just a subset of the SQL Server data types and features. It often required you to perform complex code and schema re-factoring to utilize the technology. Fortunately, SQL Server 2016 removes many of those limitations, as we will discuss in this book.

In-Memory OLTP Engine Architecture and Data Structures

In-Memory OLTP is fully integrated into SQL Server, and other SQL Server features and client applications can access it transparently. Internally, however, it works and behaves very differently than the Storage Engine.

It is important to define the terminology before we discuss In-Memory OLTP internals. I will use the following terms and definitions:

> *Memory-optimized tables* refer to tables with the new data structure that is used by In-Memory OLTP.
>
> *On-disk tables* refer to regular SQL Server tables that are stored in database data files using 8 KB data pages. All tables that we discussed previously in this book were on-disk tables.
>
> *Interop* refers to the ability to reference memory-optimized tables from interpreted T-SQL code.
>
> *Natively-compiled* modules refer to stored procedures, triggers, and scalar user-defined functions compiled into machine code. Those modules will be covered in the Chapter 37.

Figure 35-1 shows the architecture of the SQL Server engine, including the In-Memory OLTP part. As you can see, memory-optimized tables do not share memory with on-disk tables. However, you can access both types of tables from T-SQL and client applications through the Interop Engine. Natively-compiled modules, on the other hand, work only with memory-optimized tables and are unable to access on-disk table data.

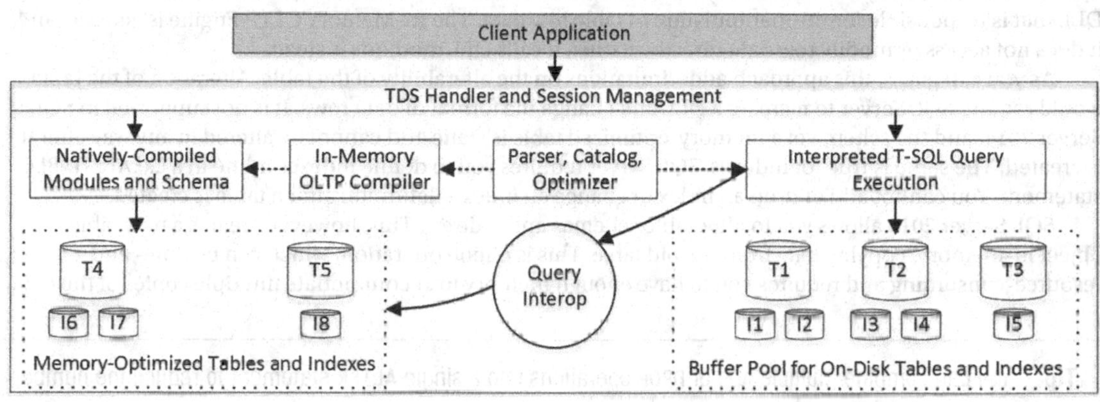

***Figure 35-1.** SQL Server Engine architecture*

In-Memory OLTP stores data in a separate `FILESTREAM`-based filegroup. SQL Server 2014 In-Memory OLTP implementation relies on `FILESTREAM` for all file management. With SQL Server 2016, the `FILESTREAM` filegroup is only used as the container, and all file management and garbage collection is done by the In-Memory OLTP Engine. This makes file management more efficient and allows SQL Server to encrypt in-memory data when you enable *Transparent Data Encryption* (TDE) in the database.

■ **Note** You can read more about `FILESTREAM` at `http://technet.microsoft.com/en-us/library/gg471497.aspx`.

You specify a filegroup that contains memory-optimized tables' data by using the `CONTAINS MEMORY_OPTIMIZED_DATA` keyword, as shown in Listing 35-1. All In-Memory OLTP files used by the database will reside in the `S:\HKData\Hekaton_InMemory` folder after you run the script.

Listing 35-1. Creating a database with the In-Memory OLTP filegroup

```
create database [HekatonDB] on
primary
( name = N'HekatonDB', filename = N'M:\HekatonDB.mdf'),
filegroup [OnDiskData]
( name = N'Hekaton_OnDisk', filename = N'M:\Hekaton_OnDisk.ndf'),
filegroup [InMemoryData] contains memory_optimized_data
( name = N'Hekaton_InMemory', filename = N'S:\HKData\Hekaton_InMemory')
log on
( name = N'HekatonDB_log', filename = N'L:\HekatonDB_log.ldf')
```

It is also worth mentioning that you cannot drop an In-Memory OLTP filegroup from the database once it has been created. It may prevent you from restoring the database on the lower-than-Enterprise editions of SQL Server even after you have removed all In-Memory OLTP objects from there.

Memory-Optimized Tables

Even though the creation of memory-optimized tables is very similar to the creation of on-disk tables and can be done with a regular CREATE TABLE statement, SQL Server works very differently with memory-optimized tables. Every time a memory-optimized table is created, SQL Server generates and compiles a DLL that is responsible for the manipulation of table row data. The In-Memory OLTP Engine is generic, and it does not access or modify row data directly. Rather, it calls DLL methods instead.

As you can guess, this approach adds limitations on the alterability of the table. Alteration of the table would require SQL Server to recreate a DLL and change the format of data rows. It is not supported in SQL Server 2014, and the schema of a memory-optimized table is static and cannot be altered in any way after it is created. The same is true for indexes. SQL Server requires you to define indexes inline in a CREATE TABLE statement. You cannot add or drop an index or change an index's definition after a table is created.

SQL Server 2016 allows you to alter table schemas and indexes. This, however, creates a new table object in-memory, copying data from the old table. This is offline operation, which can be time- and resource-consuming and requires you to have enough memory to accommodate multiple copies of the data.

■ **Tip** You can combine multiple ADD or DROP operations into a single ALTER statement to reduce the number of table rebuilds.

Indexes on memory-optimized tables are not persisted on-disk. SQL Server recreates them at the time when it starts the database and loads memory-optimized data into memory. As with on-disk tables, unnecessary indexes in memory-optimized tables slow down data modifications and use extra memory in the system.

Each memory-optimized table has a DURABILITY option. The default SCHEMA_AND_DATA option indicates that the data in the tables is fully durable and persists on disk for recovery purposes. Operations on such tables are logged in the transaction log, which allows SQL Server to support database transactional consistency and recreate the data in the event of a SQL Server crash or unexpected shutdown.

SCHEMA_ONLY is another option and indicates that data in memory-optimized tables is not durable and would be lost in the event of a SQL Server restart or crash. **Operations against non-durable memory-optimized tables are not logged in the transaction log.** Non-durable tables are extremely fast and can be used if you need to store temporary data in use cases similar to when you would use temporary tables in tempdb. As the opposite to temporary tables, SQL Server persists the schemas of non-durable memory-optimized tables, and you do not need to recreate them in the event of SQL Server restart.

Memory-optimized tables support at most eight indexes. Durable memory-optimized tables should have a unique primary key constraint defined. Non-durable memory-optimized tables do not require the primary key constraint; however, they should still have at least one index to link the rows together.

In **SQL Server 2014**, indexes cannot include nullable columns nor be defined as UNIQUE with the exception of the primary key constraint. Moreover, you cannot index text columns unless they have BIN2 collation. You should remember that these collations are case- and accent-sensitive, which could introduce some side effects, especially if you migrate to In-Memory OLTP, converting on-disk tables to memory-optimized ones.

Other **SQL Server 2014** limitations include missing support of foreign key, check, and unique constraints and DML triggers. All of these limitations have been removed in SQL Server 2016.

Neither SQL Server 2014 nor 2016 support IDENTITY columns with SEED and INCREMENT different than (1,1).

Listing 35-2 shows code that creates a memory-optimized table. You can define a table as memory-optimized by specifying the MEMORY_OPTIMIZED=ON option of the CREATE TABLE statement. Ignore index properties for now; we will discuss them later in this chapter. As I already mentioned, you do not need to store varchar columns in BIN2 collation in SQL Server 2016.

Listing 35-2. Creating a memory-optimized table

```
create table dbo.Customers
(
    CustomerID int not null
        constraint PK_Customers
        primary key nonclustered hash with (bucket_count = 131072),
    Name varchar(128) collate Latin1_General_100_BIN2 not null,
    City varchar(64) collate Latin1_General_100_BIN2 not null,
    SSN char(9) not null,
    DateOfBirth date not null,

    index IDX_Customers_City nonclustered hash(City)
    with (bucket_count = 16384),

    index IDX_Customers_Name nonclustered(Name)
)
with (memory_optimized = on, durability = schema_and_data)
```

High Availability Technology Support

Memory-optimized tables are fully supported in AlwaysOn Failover Clusters and Availability Groups, as well as with log shipping. However, in the case of a failover cluster, data from durable memory-optimized tables must be loaded into memory in case of a failover, which could increase failover time.

In the case of AlwaysOn Availability Groups, only durable memory-optimized tables are replicated to secondary nodes. You can access and query those tables on the readable secondary nodes if needed. Data from non-durable memory-optimized tables, on the other hand, is not replicated and will be lost in the case of a failover.

SQL Server 2016 supports snapshot and transaction replication for memory-optimized tables. In **SQL Server 2014**, you can set up transactional replication on databases with memory-optimized tables; however, those tables cannot be used as articles in publications.

In-Memory OLTP is not supported in database mirroring sessions. This does not appear to be a big limitation, however. In-Memory OLTP is an Enterprise Edition feature that allows you to replace database mirroring with AlwaysOn Availability Groups.

Data Row Structure

Data and index formats in memory-optimized tables are different from those in on-disk tables. Storage is optimized for byte-addressable memory using in-memory pointers rather than for block-addressable disk data using in-file offsets. With the exception of nonclustered (range) indexes, which we will discuss later, in-memory objects do not use in-memory data pages. Data rows have pointers to the next row in the row chain.

The 8,060-byte limit for the maximum in-row data size still applies. Moreover, in **SQL Server 2014**, memory-optimized tables do not support off-row storage, which limits the data types that can be used in tables; only the following data types are supported in SQL Server 2014:

- `bit`
- Integer types: `tinyint`, `smallint`, `int`, `bigint`
- Floating point types: `float`, `real`, `numeric`, and `decimal`
- Money types: `money` and `smallmoney`
- Date/time types: `smalldatetime`, `datetime`, `datetime2`, `date`, and `time`
- `uniqueidentifiers`
- Non-LOB string types: `(n)char(N)`, `(n)varchar(N)`, and `sysname`
- Non-LOB binary types: `binary(N)` and `varbinary(N)`

As was already mentioned, in **SQL Server 2014** you cannot use data types that can use LOB storage in on-disk tables, such as `(n)varchar(max)`, `varbinary(max)`, `xml`, `clr`, `(n)text`, and `image`. Moreover, there is no concept of row-overflow storage in **SQL Server 2014**, so the entire row must fit into 8,060 bytes, including variable-length data. It is impossible to create memory-optimized tables with a row that could exceed that size; for example, a row with two `varchar(5000)` columns.

SQL Server 2016 supports off-row storage and allows data rows to exceed 8,060 bytes. The `(n)varchar(max)` and `varbinary(max)` data types are now supported. There is still no support for `xml`, `clr`, `(n)text`, and `image` data types; however, in some cases you can store them as `varbinary(max)`.

As the opposite to on-disk tables, the decision of what columns need to be stored off-row is made at table-creation stage. The data from row-overflow and LOB columns are always stored off-row regardless of the row size. `(max)` columns are always stored in LOB storage. If the table schema allows the row size to exceed 8,060 bytes, the largest variable-length `(N)` columns are pushed to row-overflow storage. In both cases, the main in-row structure uses an eight-byte identifier to reference them. We will discuss off-row storage in more detail later in this chapter.

Figure 35-2 illustrates the structure of a data row in a memory-optimized table. As you can see, it consists of two sections: *Row Header* and *Payload*.

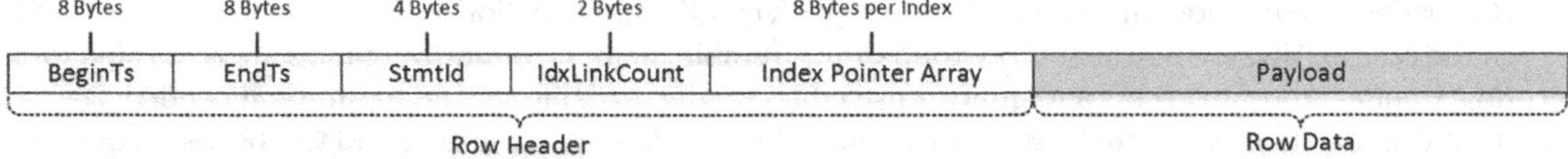

***Figure 35-2.** The structure of a data row in a memory-optimized table*

A SQL Server instance maintains the *Global Transaction Timestamp* value, which is auto-incremented at the time of the transaction pre-commit validation (more on this in the next chapter), and it is unique for every committed transaction. The first two eight-byte elements in the row header, *BeginTs* and *EndTs*, define the data row lifetime. BeginTs stores the Global Transaction Timestamp of the transaction that inserted a row, and EndTs stores the timestamp of the transaction that deleted a row. A special value called *Infinity* is used as EndTs for rows that have not been deleted.

In addition, BeginTs and EndTs control the visibility of a row for a transaction. A transaction can see a row only when the transaction logical start time (Global Transaction Timestamp value at the moment the transaction starts) is between BeginTs and EndTs timestamps of the row.

Every statement in a transaction has a unique four-byte *StmtId* value. The third element in a row header is the StmtId of the statement that is inserted a row. It works as a *Halloween protection* technique, similar to *table spools* in on-disk tables, and it allows the statement to skip rows it inserted. You can think about the `INSERT INTO T SELECT FROM T` statement as the classic example of such a situation, as we discussed in Chapter 25.

In contrast to on-disk tables, where nonclustered indexes are separate data structures, all indexes in memory-optimized tables reference actual data rows. Each new index that is defined on a table adds a pointer to a data row. For example, if a table has two indexes defined, every data row in the table would have two eight-byte pointers that reference the next data rows in the index row chains. This, in a nutshell, makes every index in memory-optimizing tables covering; that is, when SQL Server locates a row through an index, it finds the actual data row rather than the separate index row structure.

The next element in the header, the two-byte *IdxLinkCount*, indicates how many indexes (pointers) reference the row. SQL Server uses it to detect rows that can be deallocated by the garbage collection process. We will talk about garbage collection later in this chapter.

An array of eight-byte index pointers is the last element of the row header. As you can guess, every memory-optimized table should have at least one index to link data rows together. At most, you can define eight indexes per memory-optimized table, including the primary key.

The actual row data is stored in the Payload section of the row. As already mentioned, the Payload format may vary depending on the table schema. SQL Server works with Payload through a DLL that is generated and compiled at the time of table creation.

A key principle of In-Memory OLTP is that Payload data is never updated. When a table row needs to be updated, In-Memory OLTP sets the EndTs attribute of the original row to the Global Transaction Timestamp of the transaction and inserts the new version of the data row with the new BeginTs and EndTs values of Infinity. We will see how this works in more depth in the next chapter.

Hash Indexes

Hash indexes are one of two index types supported by In-Memory OLTP. They consist of an array of hash buckets, each of which contains a pointer to a data row. SQL Server applies a hash function to the index key columns, and the result of the function determines to which bucket a row belongs. All rows that have the same hash value and belong to the same bucket are linked together through a chain of index pointers in the data rows.

Figure 35-3 illustrates an example of a memory-optimized table with two hash indexes defined on the `Name` and `City` columns. Solid arrows represent pointers in the index on the `Name` column. Dotted arrows represent pointers in the index on the `City` column. For simplicity's sake, let's assume that the hash function generates a hash value based on the first letter of the string.

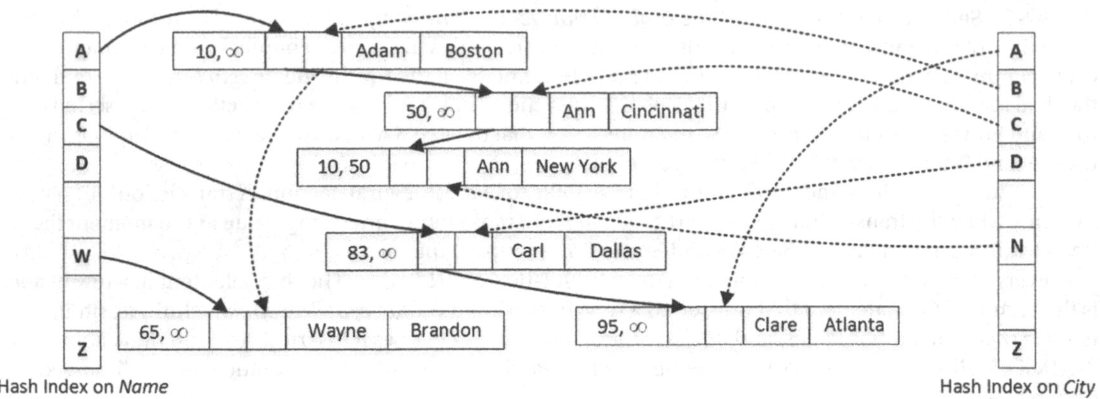

***Figure 35-3.** Hash indexes*

Let's assume that you need to run a query that selects all rows with `Name='Ann'` in the transaction that started when the Global Transaction Timestamp was 65. SQL Server calculates the hash value for *Ann*, which is *'A'*, and finds the corresponding bucket in the hash index, which is displayed on the left side in Figure 35-3. It follows the pointer from that bucket, which references a row with `Name='Adam'`. This row has BeginTs of 10 and EndTs of Infinity; therefore, it is visible to the transaction. However, the `Name` value does not match the predicate, and the row is ignored.

In the next step, SQL Server follows the pointer from the *Adam* index pointer array, which references the first *Ann* row. This row has BeginTs of 50 and EndTs of Infinity; therefore, it is visible to the transaction and needs to be selected.

As a final step, SQL Server follows the next pointer in the index. Even though the last row also has `Name='Ann'`, it has EndTs of 50 and is invisible to the transaction.

Obviously, the performance of queries that scan an index chain greatly depends on the number of rows in the chain. The greater the number of rows that need to be processed, the slower the query is.

There are two factors that affect index chain size in hash indexes. The first factor is index selectivity. Duplicate key values generate the same hash and belong to the same index chain. Therefore, indexes with low selectivity are less efficient.

Another factor is the number of hash buckets in the index, which you should specify during the index creation stage. In an ideal situation, the number of buckets in an array would match the number of unique key values in the index, and every unique key value would have its own bucket. The hash function in SQL Server, however, does not guarantee that. **It is better to define the number of buckets to be about 1.5–2 times larger than the index cardinality, which is the number of unique key values in the index.**

■ **Note** Internally, SQL Server rounds up the number of buckets specified for an index to the next power of two. For example, a hash index defined with `BUCKET_COUNT=100000` would have 131,072 buckets in the hash array.

You should analyze the data and include a projection of future system growth into the analysis when determining the optimal bucket count for the hash index. Underestimation and overestimation are both bad. Underestimation increases the size of the index chain while overestimation wastes system memory. However, in the big picture it is better to overestimate than to underestimate the bucket count.

Unfortunately, it is impossible to change a bucket count after the table has been created. In **SQL Server 2014**, the only option for changing the bucket count is by dropping and recreating the table. **SQL Server 2016** allows you to change the bucket count by rebuilding the index via the `ALTER TABLE` operation, which rebuilds the table in the background.

You can monitor hash index-related statistics with the `sys.dm_db_xtp_hash_index_stats` data management view. This view provides information about the total number of buckets, the number of empty buckets, and the average and maximum row chain lengths. You can read more about that view at `http://msdn.microsoft.com/en-us/library/dn296679.aspx`.

Hash indexes have different SARGability rules than do indexes defined on on-disk tables. They are efficient only in the case of a *point-lookup (equality) search* and *equality joins*, which allow SQL Server to calculate the corresponding hash value and find a bucket in a hash array.

In the case of composite hash indexes, SQL Server calculates the hash value for the combined value of all key columns. A hash value calculated on a subset of the key columns would be different, and, therefore, to be useful a query should have equality predicates on all key columns from the index.

This behavior is different from that of indexes on on-disk tables. Consider a situation where you want to define an index on the `(LastName, FirstName)` columns. In the case of on-disk tables, that index can be used for a *seek* operation, regardless of whether the predicate on the `FirstName` column is specified in the `WHERE` clause of a query. Alternatively, a composite hash index on a memory-optimized table requires queries to have equality predicates on both `LastName` and `FirstName` in order to calculate a hash value that allows for choosing the right hash bucket in the array.

Let's look at the example and create on-disk and memory-optimized tables with composite indexes on the `(LastName, FirstName)` columns, populating them with the same data shown in Listing 35-3. As before, I am using binary collation in the code to make it compatible with both SQL Server 2014 and 2016.

Listing 35-3. Composite hash index: Test tables creation

```
create table dbo.CustomersOnDisk
(
    CustomerId int not null identity(1,1),
    FirstName varchar(64) collate Latin1_General_100_BIN2 not null,
    LastName varchar(64) collate Latin1_General_100_BIN2 not null,
    Placeholder char(100) null,
    constraint PK_CustomersOnDisk primary key clustered(CustomerId)
);

create nonclustered index IDX_CustomersOnDisk_LastName_FirstName
on dbo.CustomersOnDisk(LastName, FirstName);

create table dbo.CustomersMemoryOptimized
(
    CustomerId int not null identity(1,1)
        constraint PK_CustomersMemoryOptimized
        primary key nonclustered hash with (bucket_count = 4096),
    FirstName varchar(64) collate Latin1_General_100_BIN2 not null,
    LastName varchar(64) collate Latin1_General_100_BIN2 not null,
    Placeholder char(100) null,

    index IDX_CustomersMemoryOptimized_LastName_FirstName
    nonclustered hash(LastName, FirstName) with (bucket_count = 1024),
)
with (memory_optimized = on, durability = schema_only);
go
```

```
-- Inserting cross-joined data for all first and last names 50 times
-- using GO 50 command in Management Studio
;with FirstNames(FirstName)
as
(
    select Names.Name
    from ( values('Andrew'),('Andy'),('Anton'),('Ashley'),('Boris'), ('Brian'),('Cristopher')
        ,('Cathy')
        ,('Daniel'),('Donny'),('Edward'),('Eddy'),('Emy'),('Frank'),('George'),('Harry')
        ,('Henry'),('Ida')
        ,('John'),('Jimmy'),('Jenny'),('Jack'),('Kathy'),('Kim'),('Larry'),('Mary'),('Max')
        ,('Nancy')
        ,('Olivia'),('Olga'),('Peter'),('Patrick'),('Robert'),('Ron'),('Steve'),('Shawn')
        ,('Tom'),('Timothy')
        ,('Uri'),('Vincent') ) Names(Name)
)
,LastNames(LastName)
as
(
    select Names.Name
    from ( values('Smith'),('Johnson'),('Williams'),('Jones'),('Brown'), ('Davis'),('Miller')
        ,('Wilson')
        ,('Moore'),('Taylor'),('Anderson'),('Jackson'),('White'),('Harris')  ) Names(Name)
)
insert into dbo.CustomersOnDisk(LastName, FirstName)
    select LastName, FirstName from FirstNames cross join LastNames
go 50

insert into dbo.CustomersMemoryOptimized(LastName, FirstName)
    select LastName, FirstName from dbo.CustomersOnDisk;
```

For the first test, let's run SELECT statements against both tables, specifying both LastName and FirstName as predicates in the queries, as shown in Listing 35-4.

Listing 35-4. Composite hash index: Selecting data using both index columns as predicates

```
select CustomerId, FirstName, LastName
from dbo.CustomersOnDisk
where FirstName = 'Brian' and LastName = 'White';

select CustomerId, FirstName, LastName
from dbo.CustomersMemoryOptimized
where FirstName = 'Brian' and LastName = 'White';
```

As you can see in Figure 35-4, SQL Server is able to use an *index seek* operation in both cases.

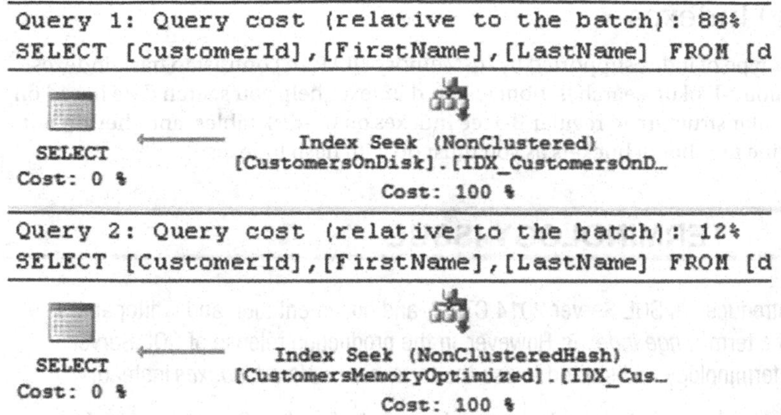

Figure 35-4. *Composite hash index: Execution plans where queries use both index columns as predicates*

In the next step, let's check what happens if you remove the filtering by `FirstName` from the queries. The code is shown in Listing 35-5.

Listing 35-5. Composite hash index: Selecting data using leftmost index column only

```
select CustomerId, FirstName, LastName
from dbo.CustomersOnDisk
where LastName = 'White';

select CustomerId, FirstName, LastName
from dbo.CustomersMemoryOptimized
where LastName = 'White';
```

In the case of the on-disk index, SQL Server is still able to utilize an index seek operation. This is not the case for the composite hash index defined on the memory-optimized table. You can see the execution plans for the queries in SQL Server 2014 in Figure 35-5. SQL Server 2016 will generate a slightly different plan for the second query, scanning the `dbo.CustomersMemoryOptimized` table in a different way. We will discuss it later in this chapter.

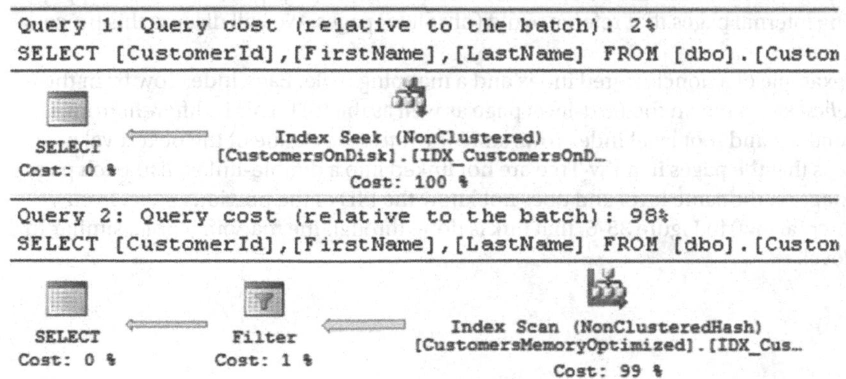

Figure 35-5. *Composite hash index: Execution plans where queries use the leftmost index column only (SQL Server 2014)*

Nonclustered (Range) Indexes

Nonclustered indexes are another type of index supported by In-Memory OLTP. In contrast to hash indexes, which are optimized to support point-lookup searches, nonclustered indexes help you search data based on a range of values. They have a similar structure to regular B-Tree indexes on on-disk tables, and they do not require you to guess and pre-define number of buckets as you must do with hash indexes.

TERMINOLOGY ISSUE

Nonclustered indexes were introduced in SQL Server 2014 CTP 2, and documentation and whitepapers for that version widely used the term *range indexes*. However, in the production release of SQL Server 2014, Microsoft changed the terminology and started to use the term *nonclustered indexes* instead.

That terminology can be confusing because hash indexes are also not clustered. In fact, the concept of clustered indexes cannot be applied to In-Memory OLTP. Data rows are not stored in any particular order nor grouped together on the data pages in memory.

It is also worth mentioning that the minimal `index_id` value of In-Memory OLTP indexes is 2, which corresponds to nonclustered indexes in on-disk tables.

Nonclustered indexes use a lock- and latch-free variation of B-Tree called *Bw-Tree*, which was designed by Microsoft Research in 2011. Similar to B-Trees, index pages in a Bw-Tree contain a set of ordered index key values. However, Bw-Tree pages do not have a fixed size and are unchangeable after they are built. The maximum page size, however, is still 8 KB.

Rows from a leaf level of the nonclustered index contain pointers to the actual chain of the rows with the same index key values. This works in a similar manner to hash indexes, where multiple rows and/or versions of a row are linked together. Each index in the table adds a pointer to the index pointer array in the row, regardless of its type: hash or nonclustered.

Root and intermediate levels in nonclustered indexes are called *internal pages*. Similar to B-Tree indexes, internal pages point to the next level in the index. However, instead of pointing to the actual data page, internal pages use a *logical page ID* (PID), which is a position (offset) in a separate array-like structure called a *mapping table*. In turn, each element in the mapping table contains a pointer to the actual index page.

As already mentioned, pages in nonclustered indexes are unchangeable once they are built. SQL Server builds a new version of the page when it needs to be updated and replaces the page pointer in the mapping table, which avoids changing internal pages that reference old (obsolete) pages. We will discuss this process in detail shortly.

Figure 35-4 shows an example of a nonclustered index and a mapping table. Each index row from the internal page stores the *highest* key value on the next-level page as well as the PID. This is different from a B-Tree index, where intermediate and root level index rows store the *lowest* key value of the next-level page instead. Another difference is that the pages in a Bw-Tree are not linked into a double-linked list. Each page knows the PID of the next page on the same level and does not know the PID of the previous page. Even though it appears as a pointer (arrow) in Figure 35-6, that link is done through the mapping table, similar to links to pages on the next level.

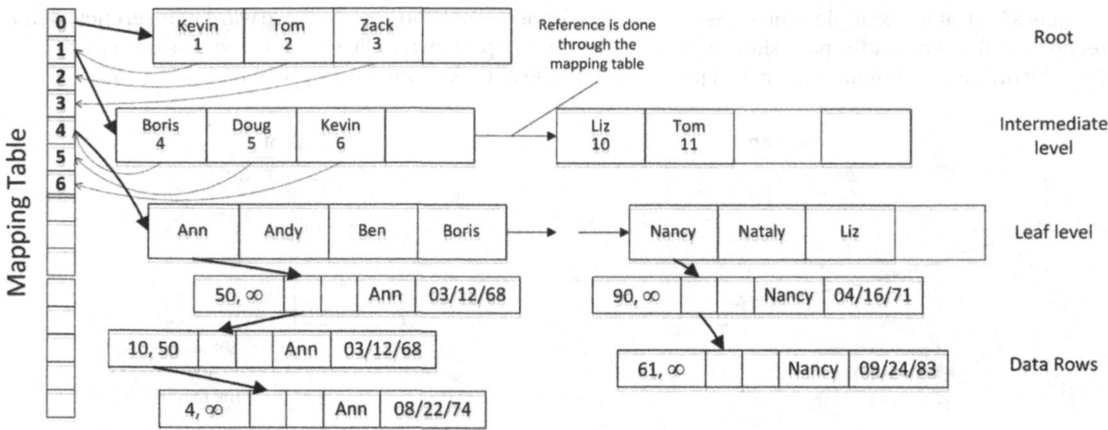

***Figure 35-6.** Nonclustered index*

Even though a Bw-Tree looks very similar to a B-Tree, there is one conceptual difference: The leaf level of an on-disk B-Tree index consists of separate index rows for each data row in the index. If multiple data rows have the same index key value, each row would have an individual index row stored.

Alternatively, in-memory nonclustered indexes store one index row (pointer) to the row chain that includes all of the data rows that have the same key value. Only one index row (pointer) per key value is stored in the index. You can see this in Figure 35-6, where the leaf level of the index has single rows for the key values of *Ann* and *Nancy,* even though the row chain includes more than one data row for each value.

Every time SQL Server needs to change a leaf level index page, it creates one or two *delta* records that represent the changes. `INSERT` and `DELETE` operations generate a single insert or delete delta record, while an `UPDATE` operation generates two delta records, one each for deleting old and inserting new values. Delta records create a chain of memory pointers with the last pointer going to the actual index page. SQL Server also replaces a pointer in the mapping table with the address of the first delta record in the chain.

Figure 35-7 shows an example of a leaf-level page and delta records if the following actions occurred in the sequence: R1 index row was updated, R2 row was deleted, and R3 row was inserted.

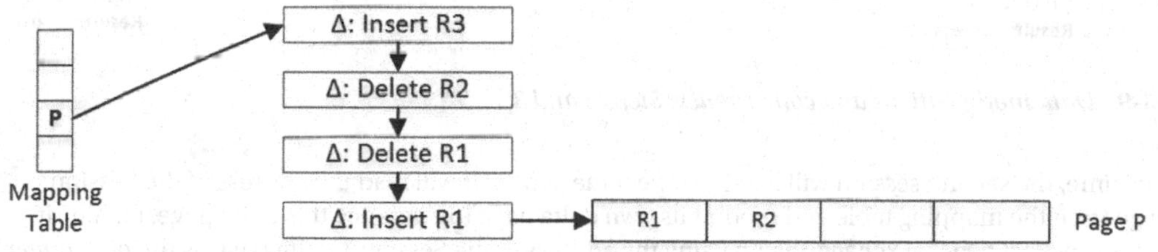

***Figure 35-7.** Delta records and nonclustered index leaf page*

SQL Server uses an `InterlockedCompareExchange` mechanism to guarantee that multiple sessions cannot update the same pointer chain and thus overwrite each other's changes, thereby losing references to each other's objects. `InterlockedCompareExchange` functions change the value of the pointer, checking that the existing (*pre-update*) value matches the expected (*old)* value provided as another parameter. Only when the check succeeds is the pointer value updated. All of those operations are completed as a single CPU instruction.

Let's look at an example, which assumes that we have two sessions in which we want to insert new delta records for the same index page simultaneously. As a first step, shown in Figure 35-8, the sessions create delta records and set their pointers to a page based on the address from the mapping table.

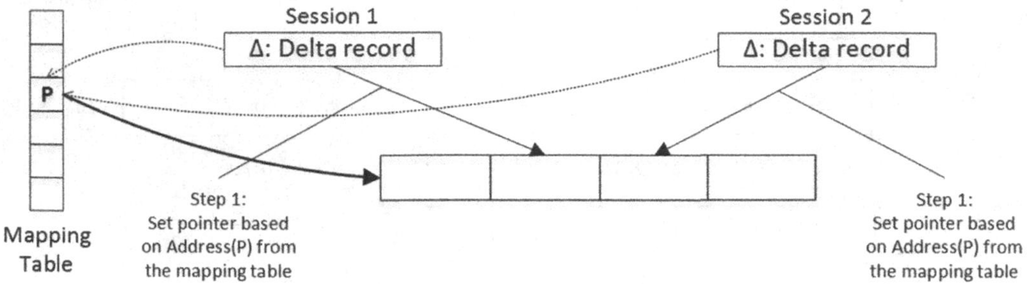

Figure 35-8. *Data modifications and concurrency: Step 1*

In the next step, both sessions call the `InterlockedCompareExchange` function, trying to update the mapping table by changing the reference from a page to the newly created delta records. `InterlockedCompareExchange` serializes the update of the mapping table element and changes it only if its current pre-update value matches the old pointer (address of the page) provided as the parameter. The first `InterlockedCompareExchange` call would succeed. The second call, however, would fail because the mapping table element would reference the delta record from another session rather than the page.

Figure 35-9 illustrates such a scenario.

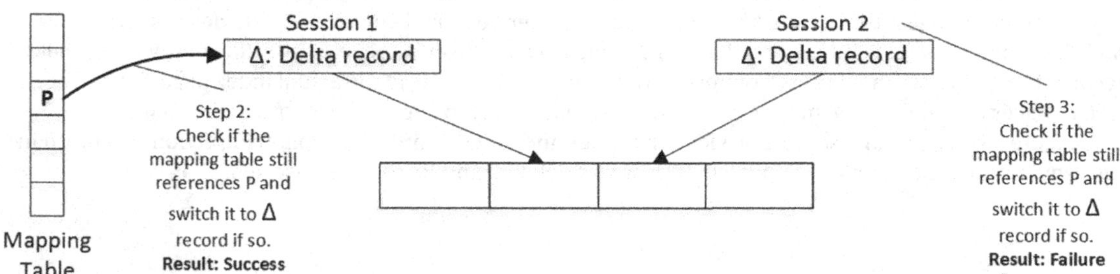

Figure 35-9. *Data modifications and concurrency: Steps 2 and 3*

At this time, the second session will need to repeat the action. It will read the address of the Session 1 delta page from the mapping table and repoint its own delta page to reference this delta page. Finally, it will call `InterlockedCompareExchange` again using the address of the Session 1 delta page as the *old pointer* value during the call. Figure 35-10 illustrates that.

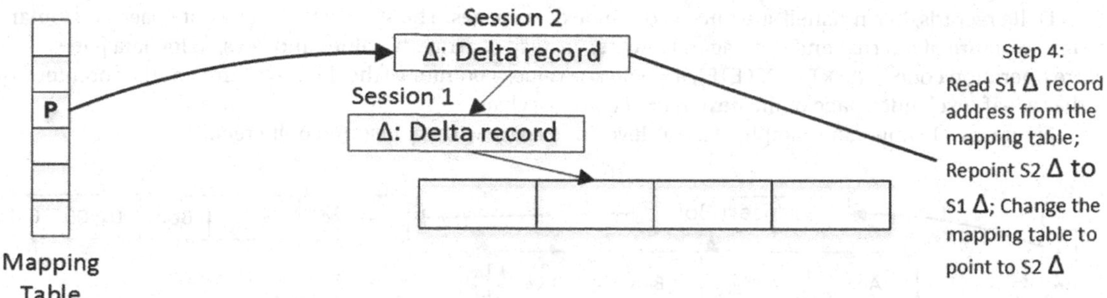

Figure 35-10. *Data modifications and concurrency: Final steps*

As you can see, with the exception of a very short serialization during the `InterlockedCompareExchange` call, there is no locking or latching of the data during the modifications.

■ **Note** SQL Server uses the same approach with `InterlockedCompareExchange` in cases where the pointers chain needs to be preserved; for example, when it creates another version of a row during an update.

The internal and leaf pages of nonclustered indexes consist of two areas: header and data. The header area includes information about the page, such as the following:

PID: The position (offset) in the mapping table

Page Type: The type of the page, such as leaf, internal, delta, or special

Right Page PID: The position (offset) of the next page in the mapping table

Height: The number of levels from the current page to the leaf level of the index

The *Number of key values* (index rows) stored on the page.

Delta records statistics: Includes the number of delta records and space used by the delta key values.

The *Max value of a key* on the page.

The data area of the page includes either two or three arrays depending on the index keys' data types. The arrays are as follows:

Values: An array of eight-byte pointers. Internal pages in the index store the PID of next level pages. Leaf-level pages store pointers to the first row in the row chain with the corresponding key value. It is worth noting that even though PID requires four bytes to store a value, SQL Server uses eight-byte elements to preserve the same page structure between internal and leaf pages.

Keys: An array of key values stored on the page

Offsets: An array of two-byte offsets where individual key values in key arrays start. Offsets are stored only if keys have variable-length data.

Delta records, in a nutshell, are one-record index data pages. The structure of delta data pages is similar to the structure of internal and leaf pages. However, instead of arrays of values and keys, delta data pages store operation code (`INSERT` or `DELETE`), a single key value, a pointer to the data row, and another pointer to either a leaf-level index page or the next delta record in a chain.

Figure 35-11 shows an example of a leaf-level index page with an inserted delta record.

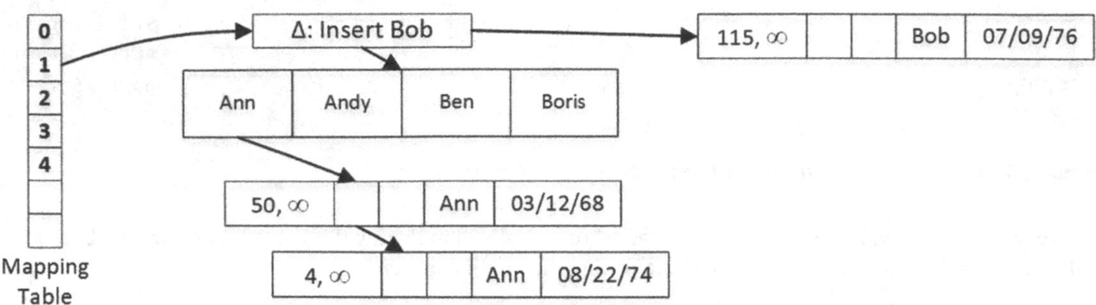

Figure 35-11. *Leaf-level index page with an inserted delta record*

SQL Server needs to traverse and analyze all delta records when accessing an index page. As you can guess, a long chain of delta records affects performance. When this is the case, SQL Server consolidates delta records and rebuilds an index page, creating a new one. The newly created page will have the same PID and replace the old page, which will be marked for garbage collection. Replacement of the page is accomplished by changing a pointer in the mapping table. SQL Server does not need to change internal pages, because they use the mapping table to reference leaf-level pages.

The process of rebuilding is triggered at the moment a new delta record is created for pages that already have 16 delta records in a chain. The action described by the delta record, which triggers the rebuild, will be incorporated into the newly created page.

Two other processes can create new or delete existing index pages in addition to delta record consolidation. The first process, *page splitting*, occurs when a page does not have enough free space to accommodate a new data row. Let's look at this situation in more detail.

Figure 35-12 shows the internal and leaf pages of a nonclustered index. Let's assume that one of the sessions wants to insert a row with a key of value *Bob*.

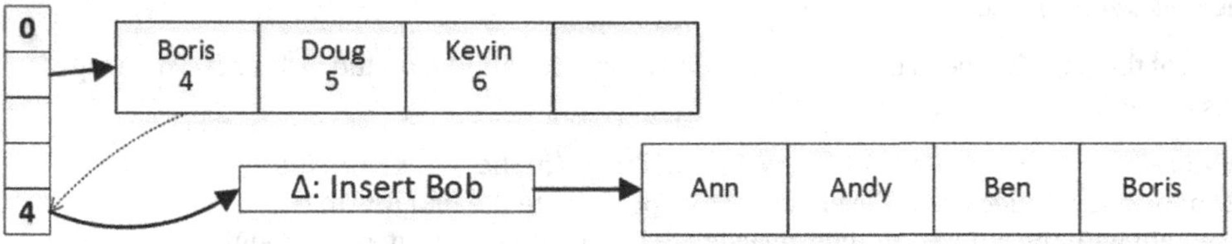

Figure 35-12. *Page splitting: Initial state*

When the delta record is created, SQL Server adjusts the delta records statistics on the index page and detects that there is no space on the page to accommodate the new index value once the delta records are consolidated. It triggers a page split process, which is done in two atomic steps.

In the first step, SQL Server creates two new leaf-level pages and splits the old page's values between them. After that, it repoints the mapping table to the first newly created page and marks the old page and the delta records for garbage collection.

Figure 35-13 illustrates this state. At this point, there are no references to the second newly created leaf-level page from internal pages. The first leaf-level page, however, maintains the link between pages (through the mapping table), and SQL Server is able to access and scan the second page if needed.

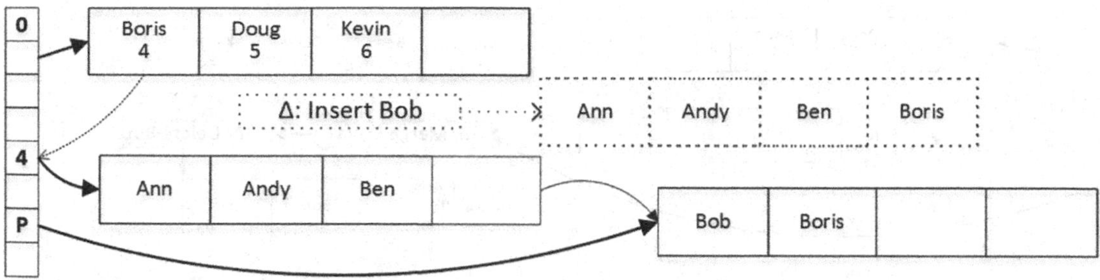

***Figure 35-13.** Page splitting: First step*

During the second step, SQL Server creates another internal page with key values that represent the new leaf-level page's layout. When the new page is created, SQL Server switches the pointer in the mapping table and marks the old internal page for garbage collection. Figure 35-14 illustrates this action.

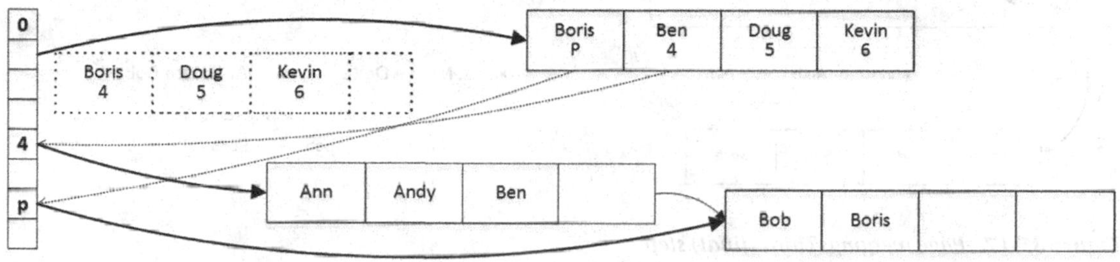

***Figure 35-14.** Page splitting: Second step*

Another process, *page merging*, occurs when a delete operation leaves an index page less than 10 percent from the maximum page size, which is 8 KB now, or when an index page contains just a single row.

Let's assume that we have a page layout as shown in Figure 35-14, and we want to delete the index key value *Bob*, which means that all data rows with the name *Bob* have been deleted. In our example, this leaves an index page with the single value *Boris*, which triggers page merging.

In the first step, SQL Server creates a delete delta record for Bob and another special kind of delta record called *merge delta*. Figure 35-15 illustrates the layout after the first step.

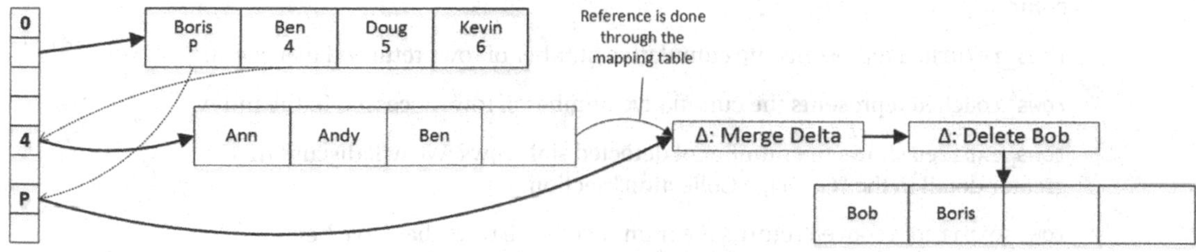

***Figure 35-15.** Page merging: First step*

During the second step of page merging, SQL Server creates a new internal page that does not reference the page with which it is about to merge. After that, SQL Server switches the mapping table to point to the newly created internal page and marks the old page for garbage collection. Figure 35-16 illustrates this action.

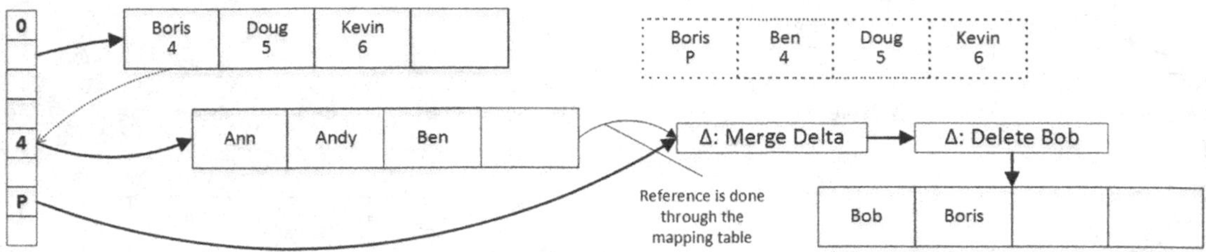

Figure 35-16. *Page merging: Second step*

Finally, SQL Server builds a new leaf-level page, copying the *Boris* value there. After the new page is created, it updates the mapping table and marks the old pages and delta records for garbage collection.

Figure 35-17 shows the final data layout after page merging is completed.

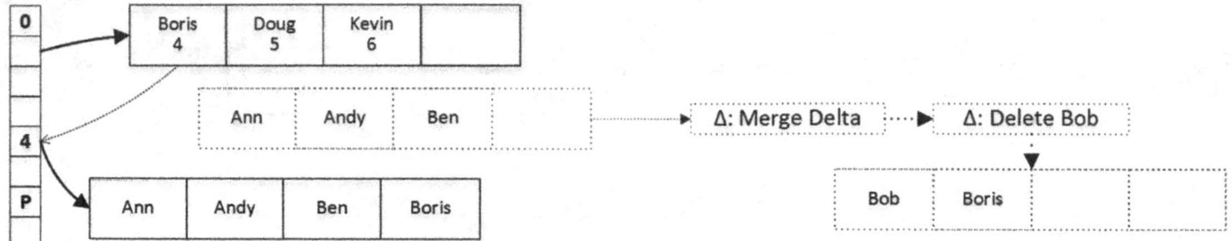

Figure 35-17. *Page merging: Third (final) step*

Indexing considerations for nonclustered indexes are similar to those for on-disk nonclustered indexes. You should remember, however, that In-Memory OLTP in **SQL Server 2014** requires binary sorting for the indexes, which is case- and accent-sensitive.

Finally, the `sys.dm_db_xtp_index_stats` view returns statistics for the indexes defined on memory-optimized tables. Indexes on memory-optimized tables are recreated when SQL Server loads data into memory; therefore, the statistics are collected and kept since that time. Some of the output columns are as follows:

`scans_started` shows the number of times that row chains in the index were scanned. Due to the nature of the index, every operation, such as `SELECT`, `INSERT`, `UPDATE`, and `DELETE`, requires SQL Server to scan a row chain and increment this column.

`rows_returned` represents the cumulative number of rows returned to a client.

`rows_touched` represents the cumulative number of rows accessed in the index.

`rows_expired` shows the number of detected stale rows. We will discuss this in greater detail in the "Garbage Collection" section.

`rows_expired_removed` returns the number of stale rows that have been unlinked from the index row chains. We will also discuss this in more detail in the "Garbage Collection" section.

You can read more about the sys.dm_db_xtp_index_stats view at http://msdn.microsoft.com/en-us/library/dn133081.aspx.

Hash Indexes Versus Nonclustered Indexes

As you already know, hash indexes are useful only for point-lookup searches and equality joins in cases where queries use equality predicates on all index columns. Nonclustered indexes, on the other hand, can be used on a much wider scope, which often makes the choice obvious. You should use nonclustered indexes when your queries benefit from scenarios other than point-lookups.

The situation is less obvious in the case of point-lookups. With hash indexes, SQL Server can locate the hash bucket, which is the entry point to the data row chain, in a single step by calling the hash function and calculating the hash value. With nonclustered indexes, SQL Server has to traverse the Bw-Tree to find a leaf page, and the number of steps depends on the height of the index and number of delta records there.

Even though nonclustered indexes require more steps to find an entry point to the data row chain, the chain can be smaller compared to hash indexes. Row chains in nonclustered indexes are built based on unique index key values. In hash indexes, row chains are built based on a non-unique hash key and can be larger due to hash collisions, especially when the bucket_count is insufficient.

With a sufficient number of buckets, hash indexes outperform nonclustered indexes. However, an insufficient number of buckets and long row chains significantly degrade their performance, making them less efficient than nonclustered indexes. In the end, it all depends on correct bucket_count estimation. Unfortunately, the volatility of the data makes this task complicated and requires you to factor future data growth into your analysis.

In some cases, when data is relatively static, you can create hash indexes, overestimating the number of buckets there. Consider catalog entities; for example, a Customers table and the CustomerId and Phone columns there. Hash indexes on those columns would improve performance of point-lookup searches and joins. Even though the customer base is growing over time, that growth rate is usually not excessive, and reserving one million empty buckets could be sufficient for a long period of time. It will use about 8 MB of memory per index, which should be acceptable in most cases.

Choosing the hash index for the OrderId column in an Orders table, on the other hand, is more dangerous. Load growth and changes in data retention rules can make the original bucket_count insufficient. This still can be acceptable if you are planning to monitor the system and can afford the downtime while rebuilding the index; however, a nonclustered index could be the safer choice in this scenario.

To summarize, for point-lookup and equality join use cases, create hash indexes only when you can correctly estimate the number of buckets and factor future data growth into the analysis. You should also monitor them and be able to afford the downtime involved in rebuilding the indexes when the bucket_count becomes insufficient. Otherwise, use nonclustered indexes, which are the safer choice and do not depend on bucket count.

Statistics on Memory-Optimized Tables

In-Memory OLTP statistics update behavior is very different in SQL Server 2014 and 2016. In both versions, SQL Server creates index- and column-level statistics on memory-optimized tables; however, **in SQL Server 2014 it does not update the statistics automatically.** This behavior leads to a very interesting situation: indexes on memory-optimized tables are created with the tables, and therefore the statistics are created at the time when the table is empty and are never updated automatically afterward.

You need to keep this behavior in mind while designing a statistics maintenance strategy in systems that use SQL Server 2014. You should update statistics after data is loaded into the table when SQL Server or the database restarts. Moreover, if the data in a memory-optimized table is volatile, which is usually the case, you should manually update statistics on a regular basis.

You can update individual statistics with the `UPDATE STATISTICS` command. Alternatively, you can use the `sp_updatestats` stored procedure to update all statistics in the database. The `sp_updatestats` stored procedure always updates all statistics on memory-optimized tables, which is different from how it works for on-disk tables, where such a stored procedure skips statistics that do not need to be updated.

SQL Server 2016, on the other hand, supports automatic statistics updates in the databases that use a compatibility level of 130. It works essentially the same way with on-disk tables, with one exception. With on-disk tables, SQL Server keeps statistics modification counters at the column level and would not count data modification toward the statistics update threshold if the statistics columns were not updated. In memory-optimized tables, statistics modification counters are maintained at the row level.

■ **Important** You should manually update statistics once to enable the automatic statistics update after you upgrade from SQL Server 2014 to SQL Server 2016.

Memory Consumers and Off-Row Storage

In-Memory OLTP database objects allocate memory from separate memory heaps called *varheap*. Varheaps are the data structures that respond to and track memory allocation requests from various database objects and can grow and shrink in size when needed. All database objects that consume memory are called *memory consumers*.

The separation of per-varheap memory consumers allows you to track memory usage on a per-object basis. It also helps SQL Server to optimize some internal operations. For example, it allows the garbage collection process to quickly deallocate the memory when you drop or alter the table. Moreover, **SQL Server 2016** can perform a table scan by going through the allocated memory in the table varheap. This operation is faster than traversing index row chains, and it also supports parallel execution plans when running in Query Interop mode.

It is worth repeating that the varheap scan is the only operation that can lead to parallel execution plans. It happens only in Query Interop mode and requires SQL Server 2016. SQL Server does not support parallel plans in natively-compiled code.

As an example, if you run the second query from Listing 35-5 in SQL Server 2016, you would get the execution plan shown in Figure 35-18. As you can see, SQL Server uses the *table scan* operator rather than the index scan used in SQL Server 2014.

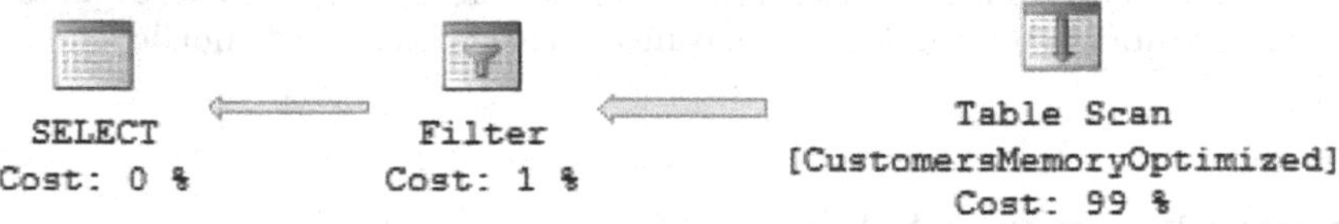

Figure 35-18. *Composite hash index: Execution plans where query use the leftmost index column only (SQL Server 2016)*

You can get detailed information about database-level memory consumers with the `sys.dm_db_xtp_memory_consumers` view. The `memory_consumer_type` column indicates the type of memory consumer and can have one of three possible values, as follows:

- `VARHEAP (2)` indicates the database heap that is used to store data rows, pages of nonclustered indexes, and other objects.

- `HASH (3)` indicates memory used by the hash table in hash indexes.
- `PGPOOL (4)` shows the database page pool used by runtime operations.

Let's create a table with one hash index and one nonclustered index and look at memory consumers, as shown in Listing 35-6.

Listing 35-6. Analyzing memory consumers

```
create table dbo.MemoryConsumers
(
    ID int not null
        constraint PK_MemoryConsumers
        primary key nonclustered hash with (bucket_count=1024),
    Name varchar(256) not null,
    index IDX_Name nonclustered(Name)
)
with (memory_optimized=on, durability=schema_only);

select
    i.name as [Index], i.index_id, a.xtp_object_id, a.type_desc, a.minor_id
    ,c.memory_consumer_id, c.memory_consumer_type_desc as [mc type]
    ,c.memory_consumer_desc as [description], c.allocation_count as [allocs]
    ,c.allocated_bytes, c.used_bytes
from
    sys.dm_db_xtp_memory_consumers c join
        sys.memory_optimized_tables_internal_attributes a on
            a.object_id = c.object_id and a.xtp_object_id = c.xtp_object_id
    left outer join sys.indexes i on
            c.object_id = i.object_id and
            c.index_id = i.index_id and
            a.minor_id = 0
where
    c.object_id = object_id('dbo.MemoryConsumers');
```

Figure 35-19 shows the output of this query. The `xtp_object_id` column represents the internal In-Memory OLTP `object_id`, which is different than the SQL Server `object_id`.

	Index	index_id	xtp_object_id	type_desc	minor_id	memory_consumer_id	mc type	description	allocs	allocated_bytes	used_bytes
1	IDX_Name	2	-2147483641	USER_TABLE	0	281	VARHEAP	Range index heap	2	131072	152
2	PK_MemoryConsumers	3	-2147483641	USER_TABLE	0	280	HASH	Hash index	1	8192	8192
3	NULL	NULL	-2147483641	USER_TABLE	0	279	VARHEAP	Table heap	0	0	0

Figure 35-19. *Memory consumers information*

As you can see in Figure 35-19, the table has three memory consumers. The *range index heap* stores internal and leaf pages of the nonclustered index. The *hash index heap* stores the hash table of the hash index. Finally, the *table heap* stores actual table rows. Figure 35-20 illustrates this.

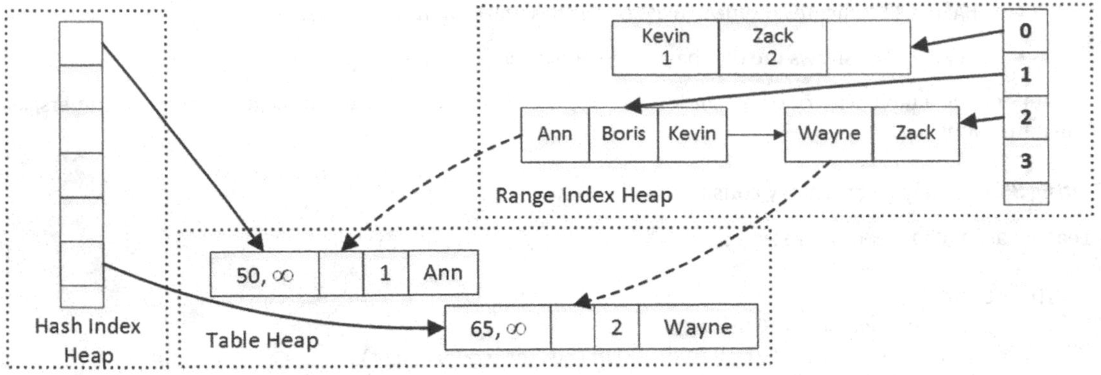

***Figure 35-20.** Table memory consumers*

Let's alter the table and add off-row storage columns, as shown in Listing 35-7. Obviously, this code requires SQL Server 2016 to run.

Listing 35-7. Altering the table

```
alter table dbo.MemoryConsumers add
    RowOverflowCol varchar(8000),
    LOBCol varchar(max);
```

Now, if you get the list of memory consumers using the query from Listing 35-6, you would see the output as shown in Figure 35-21. It is worth noting that the `xtp_object_id` column of the `USER_TABLE` has changed because the `ALTER TABLE` operation rebuilt the table internally.

	Index	index_id	xtp_object_id	type_desc	minor_id	memory_consumer_id	mc type	description	allocs	allocated_bytes	used_bytes
1	IDX_Name	2	-2147483640	USER_TABLE	0	289	VARHEAP	Range index heap	5	196608	608
2	PK_MemoryConsumers	3	-2147483640	USER_TABLE	0	288	HASH	Hash index	1	8192	8192
3	NULL	NULL	-2147483640	USER_TABLE	0	287	VARHEAP	Table Heap	5	65536	400
4	NULL	NULL	-2147483636	INTERNAL OFF-ROW DATA TABLE	4	286	VARHEAP	Range index heap	5	262144	608
5	NULL	NULL	-2147483636	INTERNAL OFF-ROW DATA TABLE	4	285	VARHEAP	LOB Page Allocator	39	458752	304992
6	NULL	NULL	-2147483636	INTERNAL OFF-ROW DATA TABLE	4	284	VARHEAP	Table heap	3	65536	192
7	NULL	NULL	-2147483637	INTERNAL OFF-ROW DATA TABLE	3	283	VARHEAP	Range index heap	5	262144	608
8	NULL	NULL	-2147483637	INTERNAL OFF-ROW DATA TABLE	3	282	VARHEAP	Table heap	3	65536	168

***Figure 35-21.** Memory consumers after table alteration*

As you can see, both off-row columns introduce their own range index heap and table heap memory consumers. In addition, LOB column adds the *LOB page allocator* memory consumer (more about this later). The `minor_id` column indicates the `column_id` in the table to which memory consumers belong.

As you can guess from the output, SQL Server 2016 stores row-overflow and LOB columns in separate internal tables. These tables consist of an eight-byte artificial primary key implemented as a nonclustered index and off-row column value. The main row references the off-row column through that artificial key, which is generated when the main row is created. It is worth repeating that this reference is done though the artificial value rather than the memory pointer.

This approach allows In-Memory OLTP to decouple off-row columns from the main row by using a different lifetime for them. For example, if you update the main row data without touching off-row columns, SQL Server would not generate new versions of the off-row column rows. Vice versa, when only off-row data is modified, the main row stays intact.

In-Memory OLTP stores LOB data in the memory provided by the *LOB page allocator* memory consumer. This consumer is not limited to 8,060-byte row allocations and can allocate a large amount of memory to store the data. The rows in the table heap of LOB columns contain pointers to the row data in the LOB page allocator.

Let's run several DML statements with imaginary Global Transaction Timestamp values, as shown in Listing 35-8.

Listing 35-8. Modifying data in the table

```
-- Global Transaction Timestamp: 100
insert into dbo.MemoryConsumers(ID, Name, RowOverflowCol, LobCol)
values
    (1,'Ann','A1',replicate(convert(varchar(max),'1'),100000))
    (2,'Bob','B1',replicate(convert(varchar(max),'2'),100000));

-- Global Transaction Timestamp: 110
update dbo.MemoryConsumers set RowOverflowCol = 'B2' where ID = 2;

-- Global Transaction Timestamp: 120
update dbo.MemoryConsumers set Name= 'Greg' where ID = 2;

-- Global Transaction Timestamp: 130
update dbo.MemoryConsumers set LobCol = replicate(convert(varchar(max),'3'),100000)
where ID = 1;

-- Global Transaction Timestamp: 140
delete from dbo.MemoryConsumers where ID = 1;
```

Figure 35-22 illustrates the state of the data and the links between the rows. It omits hash table and nonclustered index structures in the main table for simplicity's sake, along with the internal pages of nonclustered indexes for off-row columns.

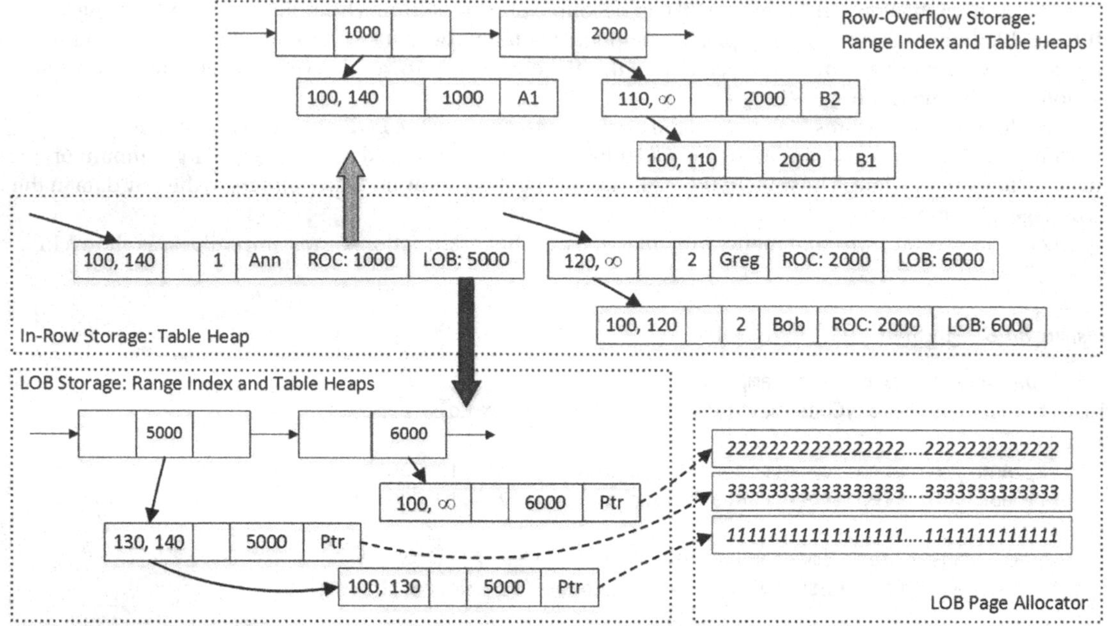

Figure 35-22. *In-row and off-row storage*

The decoupling of in-row and off-row data reduces the overhead of creating extra row versions during data modifications. However, it will add additional overhead when you insert and delete the data. SQL Server should create several row objects during the insert stage and update the EndTs of multiple rows during deletion. It also needs to maintain nonclustered Bw-Tree indexes for off-row columns.

Moreover, indexes defined in the table are not covering the queries that select off-row data. SQL Server needs to traverse nonclustered indexes on off-row columns to obtain their values. Conceptually, it looks very similar to *key lookup* operations in on-disk tables but done in the reverse direction—from the main data row to nonclustered indexes. Even though the overhead is significantly smaller compared to on-disk tables, it is still overhead you'd like to avoid.

You should avoid off-row storage unless you have legitimate reasons to use such columns. It is clearly a bad idea to define text columns as `(n)varchar(max)` *just in case* when you do not store a large amount of data there. Do not forget that In-Memory OLTP would use off-row storage based on table definition rather than size of the data. In our example, `RowOverflowCol` data is stored off-row even though we used just two character values there.

Columnstore Indexes (SQL Server 2016)

In-Memory OLTP is a specialized solution targeted for an OLTP workload. The technology can dramatically improve the performance of OLTP systems that deal with volatile data and process a large number of small transactions in parallel. It does not necessarily perform well in data warehouse and reporting scenarios, where queries scan and process a large amount of static data.

Unfortunately, the line between OLTP and data warehouse workloads is very thin nowadays. Almost every OLTP system has some amount of reporting and analytical workload, and switching to In-Memory OLTP could affect the performance of such queries. It is possible to address some of these challenges by partitioning the data, keeping hot data in memory-optimized tables and cold data in B-Tree or columnstore indexes on disk. However, this approach would not work very well with operational analytics, which scans and aggregates the hot data.

In **SQL Server 2016**, you can solve this problem by creating clustered columnstore indexes on memory-optimized tables. These indexes are updatable and have a structure similar to on-disk clustered columnstore indexes that use compressed segments merged into the row groups. Do not be confused by the definition of columnstore indexes as *clustered*, however. As the opposite of on-disk tables, clustered columnstore indexes on memory-optimized tables are separate data structures that keep a copy of the data. In this context, *clustered* means that those indexes include all columns from the table.

Memory-optimized tables with clustered columnstore indexes have a hidden column—`columnstore RID`—that is used as the row locator in the columnstore index. In-Memory OLTP uses this column as the row locator in the delete bitmap, which is implemented as an internal table with a nonclustered range index. As with on-disk columnstore indexes, it consists of rowgroup ID and position of the row in the rowgroup. It is worth noting that the delete bitmap in In-Memory OLTP is called a *deleted rows table.*

Memory-optimized columnstore indexes do not have a dedicated delta store. The most recent rows in a memory-optimized table *become* the delta store, as shown in Figure 35-23.

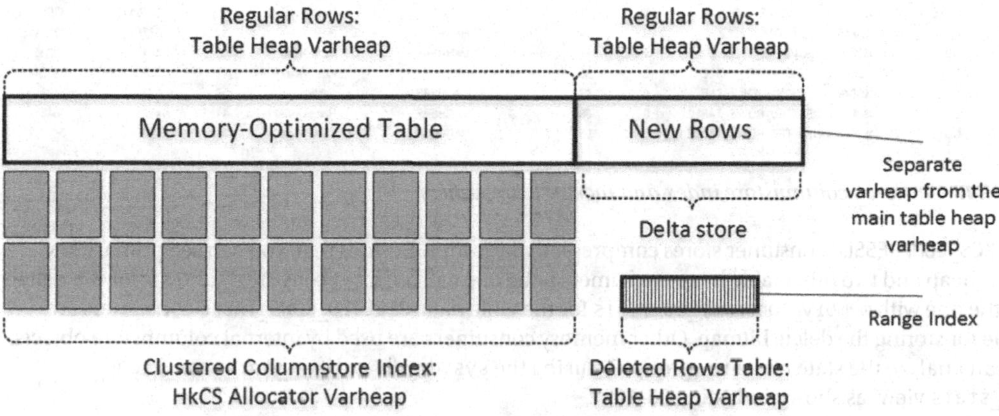

Figure 35-23. *Clustered columnstore index on memory-optimized table*

When you create a clustered columnstore index, In-Memory OLTP uses another memory consumer for the rows in the delta store. All new versions of the rows from `INSERT` or `UPDATE` operations are allocated from this varheap. There is a background process that wakes up about every two minutes and estimates the number of rows in the delta store. In cases where this estimate exceeds one million rows, the process creates a new rowgroup by compressing and encoding the rows in the delta store and then moves them to the varheap of the main table. It is also worth noting that columnstore indexes on memory-optimized tables do not support `COLUMNSTORE_ARCHIVE` compression.

You can add a delay to compression by using the `COMPRESSION_DELAY` index option. This option could be beneficial when the system performs some post-processing that modifies or deletes rows shortly after insert. Deleted versions of the rows in that scenario would not be included in the columnstore index.

Let's look at an example and create a table with a clustered columnstore index, as shown in Listing 35-9. The index has the `COMPRESSION_DELAY=60` option, which defers compression for new rows for an hour.

Listing 35-9. Creating a table with a clustered columnstore index

```
create table dbo.OrdersCCI
(
    OrderId int not null
        constraint PK_OrdersCCI
        primary key nonclustered,
```

```
    OrderDate datetime2(0) not null,
    OrderNum varchar(32) not null,
    Amount money not null,
    index CCI_OrdersCCI clustered columnstore with (compression_delay=60)
)
with (memory_optimized=on, durability=schema_and_data);
```

Figure 35-24 shows memory consumers for the table after I inserted some data there. You can use the query from Listing 35-6 to get memory consumer information.

	Index	index_id	xtp_object_id	type_desc	minor_id	memory_consumer_id	mc type	description	allocs	allocated_bytes	used_bytes
1	NULL	NULL	-2147483648	USER_TABLE	0	77	HKCS_COMPRESSED	HkCS Allocator	2	420814848	420814848
2	PK_OrdersCCI1	2	-2147483648	USER_TABLE	0	76	VARHEAP	Range index heap	31338	194445312	134771824
3	NULL	NULL	-2147483648	USER_TABLE	0	75	VARHEAP	Table heap	10485760	843317248	838860800
4	NULL	NULL	-2147483648	USER_TABLE	0	74	VARHEAP	Table heap	173	99287040	12456
5	PK_OrdersCCI1	2	-2147483644	ROW_GROUPS_INFO_TABLE	0	73	HASH	Hash index	1	1048576	1048576
6	NULL	NULL	-2147483644	ROW_GROUPS_INFO_TABLE	0	72	VARHEAP	Table heap	17	262144	1496
7	NULL	NULL	-2147483645	SEGMENTS_TABLE	0	71	HASH	Hash index	1	33554432	33554432
8	PK_OrdersCCI1	2	-2147483645	SEGMENTS_TABLE	0	70	HASH	Hash index	1	33554432	33554432
9	NULL	NULL	-2147483645	SEGMENTS_TABLE	0	69	VARHEAP	Table heap	64	1048576	15600
10	PK_OrdersCCI1	2	-2147483646	DICTIONARIES_TABLE	0	68	HASH	Hash index	1	33554432	33554432
11	NULL	NULL	-2147483646	DICTIONARIES_TABLE	0	67	VARHEAP	Table heap	16	262144	1408
12	PK_OrdersCCI1	2	-2147483647	DELETED_ROWS_TABLE	0	66	VARHEAP	Range index heap	11	4325376	1648
13	NULL	NULL	-2147483647	DELETED_ROWS_TABLE	0	65	VARHEAP	Table heap	0	262144	0

Figure 35-24. *Clustered columnstore index and memory consumers*

The HKCS_COMPRESSED consumer stores compressed rowgroups. Besides that, you can see primary key range index heap and two other table heap consumers—the one with memory_consumer_id=74 is for the delta store and the one with memory_consumer_id=75 is for the table data. DELETED_ROWS_TABLE consumers are responsible for storing the delete bitmap. Other memory consumers are used by internal columnstore objects.

You can analyze the state of the rowgroups by using the sys.dm_db_column_store_row_group_physical_stats view, as shown in Listing 35-10.

Listing 35-10. Obtaining the rowgroups' status

```
select row_group_id, state_desc, total_rows, deleted_rows, trim_reason_desc, created_time
from sys.dm_db_column_store_row_group_physical_stats
where object_id = object_id('dbo.OrdersCCI')
order by row_group_id
```

Figure 35-25 shows partial output of the query. The trip_reason_desc column indicates the reason why a rowgroup has less than 1,048,576 rows. The value of SPILLOVER indicates that the rowgroup contains rows left over after all full rowgroups were created. The value of STATS_MISTMATCH indicates that the estimate of the number of rows in the delta store was incorrect.

	row_group_id	state_desc	total_rows	deleted_rows	trim_reason_desc	created_time
1	-1	OPEN	1000	0	NULL	NULL
2	1	COMPRESSED	1048576	20815	NO_TRIM	2016-07-29 12:56:48.057
3	2	COMPRESSED	1048576	29059	NO_TRIM	2016-07-29 12:56:48.057
4	3	COMPRESSED	1048576	39245	NO_TRIM	2016-07-29 12:56:48.057
5	4	COMPRESSED	1048576	29674	NO_TRIM	2016-07-29 12:56:48.057
6	5	COMPRESSED	257339	36957	SPILLOVER	2016-07-29 12:56:48.057
7	6	COMPRESSED	348054	45402	SPILLOVER	2016-07-29 12:56:48.057
8	7	COMPRESSED	[illegible]	[illegible]	SPILLOVER	2016-07-29 12:56:48.057

Figure 35-25. *Rowgroups' Status*

You should also monitor the `deleted_rows` value, which indicates how many rows are stored in the delete bitmap. Consider increasing the `COMPRESSION_DELAY` if you see a large number there. It is also worth mentioning that SQL Server drops the rowgroup and moves non-deleted rows back to the delta store varheap after 90 percent of the rows in the rowgroup have been deleted.

There are several limitations related to columnstore indexes in In-Memory OLTP. The most important are the following:

- The columnstore index cannot be created in cases where the table uses off-row storage, and therefore the row size cannot exceed 8,060 bytes.
- Memory-optimized tables with columnstore indexes cannot be altered. You should drop the index, alter the table, and recreate the index afterward.
- Columnstore indexes on memory-optimized tables cannot be rebuilt or reorganized.
- Archive compression is not supported.

Obviously, the system should have enough memory to accommodate columnstore indexes. These indexes, however, are heavily compressed and could use just a fraction of the memory used by non-compressed rows.

Finally, it is important to note that SQL Server can utilize columnstore indexes only in Query Interop mode. These indexes are never used from natively-compiled code.

Garbage Collection

In-Memory OLTP is a row-versioning system. Data modifications generate new versions of rows rather than updating row data. Every row has two timestamps (BeginTs and EndTs) that indicate row lifetime: when the row was created and when it was deleted. Transactions can only see the versions of rows that were valid at the time when the transaction started. In practice, this means that the transaction's *logical start time* (*Global Transaction Timestamp* value at the start of the transaction) is between the BeginTs and EndTs timestamps of the row.

At some point, when the EndTs timestamp of a row is older than the logical start time of the *oldest active transaction* in the system, the row becomes stale. Stale rows are invisible to active transactions in the system, and eventually they need to be deallocated in order to reclaim system memory and speed up index chain navigation. This process is called *garbage collection.*

SQL Server has a system thread dedicated to performing garbage collection; however, the user sessions' threads do most of the work. When a user thread is scanning a row chain in the index and detects a stale row, the thread unlinks that row from the chain and decrements the reference counter (`IdxLinkCount`) in the row header. As already discussed, this counter indicates the number of chains in which the row is present. The row can be deallocated only after it is removed from all chains.

The user thread does not deallocate stale rows immediately, however. When a transaction is completed, the thread puts information about this transaction into the queue used by the garbage collector. Every transaction keeps information about the rows it created or deleted, which is available to the garbage collector thread.

The garbage collector thread, called the *idle worker* thread, periodically goes through that queue, analyzes stale rows, and builds *work items,* which are collections of rows that need to be deallocated. These work items, in turn, are inserted into other queues that are partitioned on a per-logical CPU basis. User (and sometimes idle worker) threads pick up work items and deallocate the rows, reclaiming system memory in the process.

When you use off-row storage in SQL Server 2016, the garbage collection process treats internal tables with off-row data as individual tables. It processes and deallocates the rows from those separately from the main tables.

You can monitor statistics about the garbage collection process with the `sys.dm_xtp_gc_stats` view. This view returns various pieces of information about stale rows, statistics about garbage collection scans, and a few other metrics. You can read more about this view at `https://msdn.microsoft.com/en-us/library/dn268336.aspx`.

The `sys.dm_xtp_gc_queue_stats` view provides information about the garbage collection work item queue, including how many work items have been enqueued and dequeued, how many items are still in the queue, and a couple of other attributes. More information about this view is available at `https://msdn.microsoft.com/en-us/library/dn268336.aspx`.

■ **Note** You can read about the garbage collection process in detail in my *Expert SQL Server In-Memory OLTP* book.

Data Durability and Recovery

The data from durable memory-optimized tables is stored separately from that in on-disk tables. SQL Server uses a streaming mechanism to store In-Memory OLTP data which is based on `FILESTREAM` technology and is optimized for sequential I/O operations. In fact, In-Memory OLTP does not use random I/O operations at all; that is, all In-Memory OLTP I/O operations are sequential.

SQL Server 2014 In-Memory OLTP implementation relies on `FILESTREAM` for all file management. With SQL Server 2016, the `FILESTREAM` filegroup is only used as a container, and all file management and garbage collection is done by the In-Memory OLTP Engine.

In-Memory OLTP stores data in multiple file pairs: *data files* and *delta files,* which often referenced as *checkpoint files*. Each pair of data and delta files covers operations for a range of *Global Transaction Timestamp* values and logs operations on the rows that have BeginTs in this range. Every time you insert a row, it is saved into a data file. Every time you delete a row, the information about the deleted row is saved into a delta file. An update generates two operations—insert and delete—and saves this information to both files.

ON-DISK AND MEMORY-OPTIMIZED TABLES: DIFFERENT STORAGE CONCEPTS

There is a conceptual difference in how on-disk and memory-optimized data are stored. On-disk tables store the single, most recent version of the row. Multiple updates of the data row change the same row object multiple times. Deletion of the row removes it from the database. Finally, it is always possible to locate a data row in a data file when needed.

On the other hand, memory-optimized files store multiple versions of the row. Multiple updates of the data row generate multiple row objects, each of them having a different lifetime. It is impossible to predict where a data row is stored in the files. Nor are there use cases for such an operation. The purpose of data and delta files is to provide data durability.

SQL Server 2016 uses another type of checkpoint file called a *large data* file. These files are very similar to data files and are used to store LOB column data and compressed columnstore rowgroups. The data from row-overflow columns, on the other hand, is stored in regular data files.

Figure 35-26 provides a high-level overview of the information stored in data and delta files. Large data files, in a nutshell, have the same format but can have significantly larger payload size. They also use delta files to indicate row versions that have already been deleted.

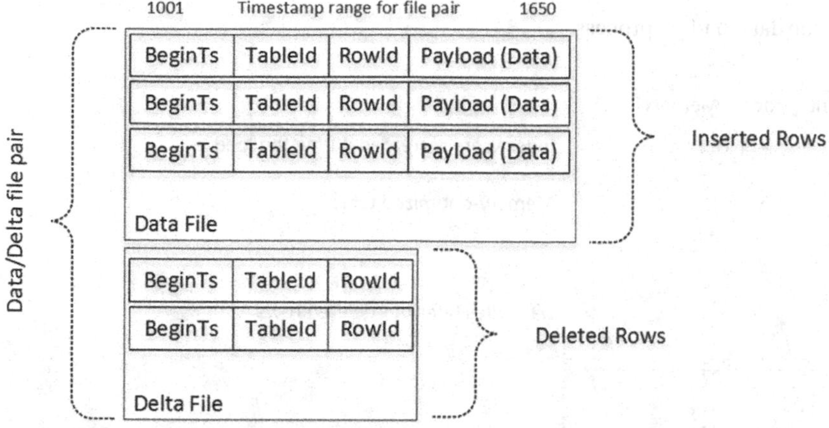

Figure 35-26. Data in checkpoint files

Figure 35-27 shows an example of a database with four pairs of data and delta files. The vertical rectangles with a solid fill represent data files. The rectangles with a dotted fill represent delta files.

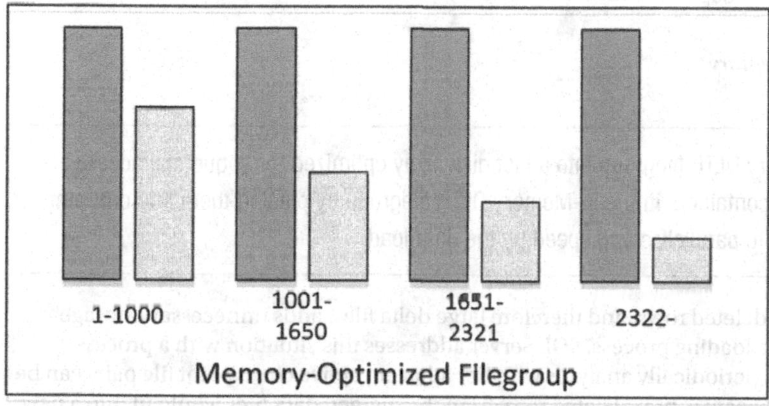

Figure 35-27. Database with multiple data and delta files

Using a separate delta file to log deletions allows SQL Server to avoid modifications in data and large data files and random I/O in cases where rows are deleted. All data, large data, and delta files are append-only. Moreover, when files are closed they become read-only. The size of the data files depends on the amount of memory and number of logical cores installed on the server. It is also worth noting that SQL Server pre-allocates checkpoint files when you create the first memory-optimized table in the database, even when that table is non-durable.

When SQL Server needs to load In-Memory OLTP data to memory—after a restart, for example—it loads only the non-deleted versions of rows, using the delta files as the filter. It checks that a row from a data file is not deleted and is not referenced in the delta files. Based on the results of this check, a row is either loaded into memory or discarded.

The process of loading data is highly scalable. SQL Server creates one thread per logical CPU, and each thread processes an individual pair of data and delta files. In a large number of cases, the performance of the I/O subsystem becomes the limiting factor in data loading performance. Keep in mind that In-Memory OLTP data needs to be loaded to the memory before the database becomes available at startup or after restore.

Figure 35-28 illustrates the data loading process.

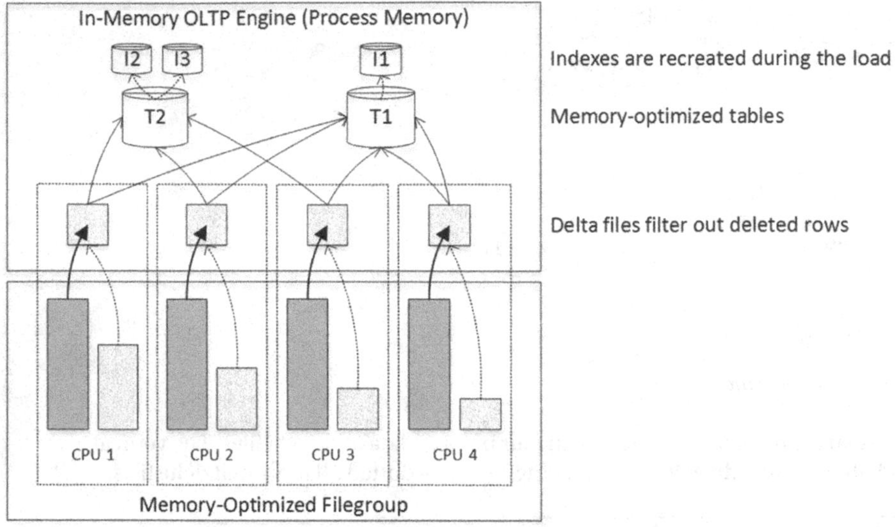

Figure 35-28. *Loading data to memory*

■ **Important** Place the In-Memory OLTP filegroup into a fast disk array optimized for sequential access. Moreover, you can create multiple containers in the In-Memory OLTP filegroup by placing them into different disk drives with different I/O paths to parallelize and speed up the data load.

Having a large percentage of deleted rows, and therefore large delta files, adds unnecessary storage overhead and slows down the data loading process. SQL Server addresses this situation with a process called a *merge*. A background task periodically analyzes whether adjacent active checkpoint file pairs can be merged together in such a way that active, non-deleted rows from the merged data files would fit into a new data file.

In the example shown in Figure 35-27, the first data file, which covers the timestamp range of 1–1000, contains about 40 percent of the active rows. The second data file, which covers the timestamp range of 1001–1650, has about 50 percent of the active rows. Those files can be merged together to cover a timestamp of 1–1650. Figure 35-29 illustrates the data and delta files after a merge.

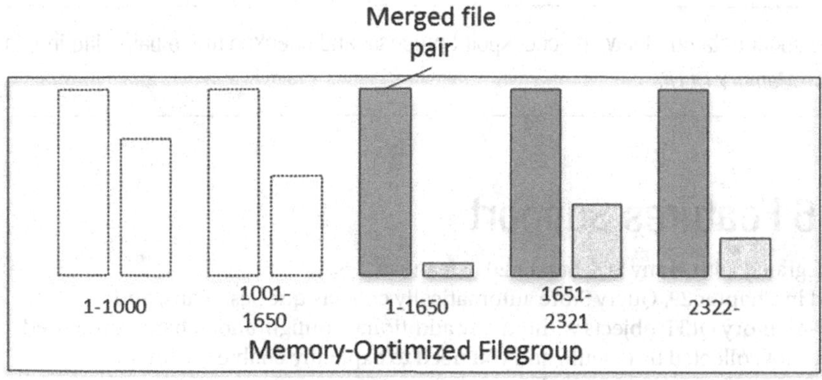

Figure 35-29. *Merge process*

SQL Server uses a similar merge process to combine adjacent large data files. As you should remember, LOB data rows are decoupled from the main rows and have their own lifetime. Therefore, large data files need to be merged separately from the data files.

After the merge process is completed, garbage collection will eventually remove old data and delta files and reclaim the disk space. It does not happen immediately, however. SQL Server needs to make sure that the original files are no longer needed for recovery in case of disaster.

The In-Memory OLTP `CHECKPOINT` is a separate process from the Storage Engine `CHECKPOINT`, and it has its own truncation LSN, which can prevent the transaction log from being truncated. In addition to a manual `CHECKPOINT` operation, which also closes all active data files, it can be triggered under the following conditions:

- Transaction log growth since the last checkpoint exceeds 512 MB in SQL Server 2014 or 1.5 GB in SQL Server 2016. It is also worth mentioning that these thresholds do not differentiate between on-disk and memory-optimized tables' log generation.
- The last automatic or manual `CHECKPOINT` occurred six hours previously.

A `CHECKPOINT` operation persists the current *Global Transaction Timestamp* value and the information about all active checkpoint files. SQL Server 2014 and 2016 use slightly different approaches in how to track checkpoint files. SQL Server 2014 relies mainly on the transaction log while SQL Server 2016 creates another type of checkpoint file called the *root file*.

The In-Memory OLTP checkpoint process is *continuous*. The process constantly analyzes the transaction log records generated by In-Memory OLTP and populates data, large data, and delta files in between checkpoints. This helps avoid bursts in I/O activity for In-Memory OLTP–related checkpoints.

In SQL Server 2014, the checkpoint process is single-threaded. In SQL Server 2016, the operation is multi-threaded. Multiple checkpoint threads are scanning the transaction log in about 1 MB segments and populating checkpoint files in parallel.

Finally, In-Memory OLTP is integrated with the database backup and restore functions. It supports piecemeal restore. However, the In-Memory OLTP filegroup should be backed up and restored together with the `PRIMARY` filegroup. In most cases, it is not a problem because In-Memory OLTP usually contains system critical data that should be online in order for the system to be functional during a piecemeal restore. However, you should analyze how this requirement affects your Backup and Disaster Recovery strategies.

■ **Note** You can read more about data durability, the checkpoint process, and checkpoint file pairs' lifetime in my book *Expert SQL Server In-Memory OLTP*.

SQL Server 2016 Features Support

In-Memory OLTP is fully integrated with many SQL Server 2016 features.

As we already discussed in Chapter 29, Query Store automatically collects queries, plans, and optimization statistics for In-Memory OLTP objects without any additional configuration changes required. However, runtime statistics is not collected by default, and you need to explicitly enable it with the `sys.sp_xtp_control_query_exec_stats` stored procedure.

Keep in mind that the collection of runtime statistics adds overhead, which can degrade the performance of the In-Memory OLTP workload. It is also important to remember that SQL Server does not persist the In-Memory OLTP runtime statistics collection settings, and it will be disabled in case of a SQL Server restart.

You can use system-versioned temporal tables with memory-optimized tables by using on-disk *history* tables to store old row versions. When you enable system versioning in memory-optimized table, SQL Server creates a memory-optimized staging table and synchronously populates it during `UPDATE` and `DELETE` operations. The data from the staging table is asynchronously moved to the on-disk history table by a background process called the *data flush task*. This task wakes up every minute with a light workload and can adjust its schedule to run every 5 seconds under a heavy workload.

By default, the data flush task moves the data from the staging table when it reaches 8 percent of the size of the *current* memory-optimized table. You can also force data movement manually by calling the `sys.sp_xtp_flush_temporal_history` stored procedure.

Memory-optimized tables can be configured for row-level security. The configuration process is essentially the same as with on-disk tables; however, any inline table-valued function that is used as a security predicate must be natively-compiled. We will talk about native compilation in Chapter 37.

Finally, In-Memory OLTP is supported in the premium tiers of SQL Databases in Microsoft Azure. All In-Memory OLTP features will work, considering the limitations on the amount of memory the tiers provide. You should be careful, however, with non-durable tables in SQL Databases. Transient database failovers in Azure will erase the data from those tables.

Memory Usage Considerations

It is obvious that In-Memory OLTP uses server memory. No further data modifications are possible when memory cannot be allocated. Moreover, if SQL Server did not have enough memory for In-Memory OLTP data at database startup, the database would not come online. Be sure to remember this when you need to restore a database backup with In-Memory OLTP data on another server that has less memory available, or when you have secondary nodes in a High Availability solution that are less powerful than the primary ones.

In-Memory OLTP memory usage can affect the performance of other SQL Server components. For example, SQL Server would have less memory available for the buffer pool, and this would degrade the performance of queries against on-disk tables due to the greater amount of physical I/O involved. In-Memory OLTP can consume a maximum of 80 percent of SQL Server memory. However, you can reduce this number by limiting memory usage in the Resource Governor resource pool and binding the database there using the `sys.sp_xtp_bind_db_resource_pool` stored procedure.

■ **Note** You can read more about binding the database to the resource pool at `https://msdn.microsoft.com/en-us/library/dn465873.aspx`.

In a cases of excessive memory usage, you should analyze which objects are consuming the most memory in In-Memory OLTP. You can use the `sys.dm_db_xtp_table_memory_stats` view to detect these tables. Listing 35-11 shows a query that analyzes memory usage on a per-table basis. Figure 35-30 illustrates the output of the query.

Listing 35-11. Detecting memory usage of memory-optimized tables

```
select object_name(object_id) as [Object Name], *
from sys.dm_db_xtp_table_memory_stats
```

	Object Name	object_id	memory_allocated_for_table_kb	memory_used_by_table_kb	memory_allocated_for_indexes_kb	memory_used_by_indexes_kb
1	Customers	645577338	27326	26562	1344	1152
2	HKData	309576141	832	21	0	0

Figure 35-30. *Memory usage information*

■ **Note** SQL Server Management Studio includes a "Memory Usage by Memory-Optimized Objects" standard report that provides similar information.

After you detect the memory consuming tables, you should analyze why they are using memory and look at the data and memory consumers in the table. In cases where a table is storing a large amount of data, you could consider partitioning the data by moving part of it to on-disk tables.

■ **Tip** Adding more memory to the server can be the easiest and cheapest option in the long term. It is often easier and cheaper to upgrade hardware than to invest hundreds of hours redesigning and re-factoring the code and database schema.

Estimating the amount of memory required for memory-optimized tables is not a trivial task. You should estimate the memory requirements of several different components:

Row data size consists of a 24-byte header, an index pointers array, which is eight bytes per index, and the payload (actual row data) size. For example, if your table has 1,000,000 rows and three indexes, and each row is about 200 bytes on average, you will need (24 + 3 * 8 + 200) * 1,000,000 = ~236.5 MB of memory to store row data without any versioning overhead included in this number. Do not forget that every off-row column adds an extra 54+ bytes to store off-row row header and row identifiers.

Hash indexes use eight bytes per bucket. If a table has two hash indexes defined with 1,500,000 buckets each, SQL Server will create indexes with 2,097,152 buckets, rounding the number of buckets specified in the index properties to the next power of two. Those two indexes will use 2,097,152 * 2 * 8 = 32 MB of memory.

Nonclustered indexes' memory usage is based on the number of unique index keys and index key size. If a table has a range index with 250,000 unique key values, and each key value on average uses 30 bytes, it would use (30 + 8(pointer)) * 250,000 = ~9 MB of memory. You can ignore the page header and non-leaf pages in your estimation, as their sizes are insignificant compared to leaf-level row size.

Row-versioning memory estimation depends on the duration of the longest transactions and the average number of data modifications (inserts and updates) per second. For example, if some processes in a system have ten-second transactions and, on average, the system handles 1,000 data modifications per second, you can estimate: 10 * 1,000 * 248(row size) = ~2.4 MB of memory for row-versioning storage.

Obviously, these numbers outline the minimally required amount of memory and do not include memory used by columnstore indexes. You should also factor in future growth and changes in workload and reserve some additional memory just to be safe.

It is almost impossible to estimate the exact disk storage space required for In-Memory OLTP data. It depends on the workload, rate of change of the data, and frequency of the `CHECKPOINT` and merge processes. As a general rule, you should reserve at least two to three times more space on disk than the space used by data rows in-memory. Remember that indexes do not take up any disk space, and they are recreated when the data is loaded into memory.

Summary

Project Hekaton, released as part of SQL Server 2014, is the new latch- and lock-free In-Memory OLTP Engine that provides exceptional throughput for OLTP workload. It is fully integrated into SQL Server, and it lets you store a subset of critical database tables in memory while keeping other tables on disk. You can access in-memory data through the T-SQL Query Interop Engine or through natively-compiled stored procedures, which we will discuss in Chapter 37.

There are plenty of limitations in the first release of the In-Memory OLTP Engine in SQL Server 2014. To name just a few, memory-optimized tables support only a subset of SQL Server data types, rows cannot exceed 8,060 bytes, and no off-row storage is supported. Indexed text columns should have `BIN2` collations. The majority of these limitations have been removed in SQL Server 2016.

SQL Server 2016 supports row-overflow and LOB columns, storing them in separate internal tables. The choice of which columns will be stored off-row depends on the table schema rather than on data size. These columns introduce performance and storage overhead, and you should avoid them unless absolutely necessary.

The In-Memory OLTP Engine supports two types of indexes. Hash indexes are useful for equality searches. Nonclustered (range) indexes are similar to regular B-Tree indexes. At most, a table can have eight indexes, including the unique primary key. With the exception of columnstore indexes, which are supported in SQL Server 2016, In-Memory OLTP does not persist indexes on disk; they are recreated when data is loaded to memory.

SQL Server uses a pairs of checkpoint files to provide data durability. Data files contain inserted versions of rows. Delta files contain information about deleted rows. Each pair of files covers a particular time range and uses a streaming append-only mechanism to maintain the files. SQL Server merges files that cover adjacent time ranges as the percentage of deleted rows grows. SQL Server 2016 also uses large data files to store LOB data and columnstore indexes.

Memory-optimized tables can be either durable or non-durable. Data modifications of the data from durable tables are logged in the transaction log and saved in checkpoint files. That data is included in database backups and is synchronized with secondary nodes in AlwaysOn Availability Groups. Data from non-durable tables is not saved in checkpoint files, nor are data modifications logged in the transaction log.

You should monitor the memory usage of memory-optimized tables. Transactions in the In-Memory OLTP Engine will fail if SQL Server cannot allocate memory. Neither SQL Server nor the database would start if server does not have enough memory to load memory-optimized data.

CHAPTER 36

Transaction Processing in In-Memory OLTP

This chapter discusses transaction processing in In-Memory OLTP. It elucidates which isolation levels are supported by technology, talks about the lifetime of In-Memory OLTP transactions, and explains how In-Memory OLTP addresses concurrency phenomena encountered in the database systems. Finally, this chapter provides an overview of transaction logging in In-Memory OLTP.

Transaction Isolation Levels and Data Consistency

The concurrency model implemented in In-Memory OLTP is quite complex. Before we dive deeper into its internal implementation, it is beneficial to remember the level of data consistency provided by different transaction isolation levels. We discussed this in detail in Part III of this book. However, let's review several points before we start to look at the implementation details in In-Memory OLTP.

Any transaction isolation level resolves write/write conflicts. Multiple transactions cannot update the same row simultaneously. Different outcomes are possible, and in some cases SQL Server uses blocking to prevent transactions from accessing uncommitted changes until the transaction that is making these changes has been committed. In other cases, SQL Server rolls back one of the transactions due to an update conflict. In-Memory OLTP uses the latter method to resolve write/write conflicts and aborts the transaction. We will discuss this situation in detail later, so let's focus now on read data consistency.

There are three major data inconsistency issues that are possible in multi-user environments, as follows:

Dirty Reads: A transaction reads uncommitted (dirty) data from other uncommitted transactions.

Non-Repeatable Reads: Subsequent attempts to read the same data from within the same transaction return different results. This data inconsistency issue arises when the other transactions modified, or even deleted, data between the reads done by the affected transaction.

Phantom Reads: This phenomenon occurs when subsequent reads within the same transaction return new rows (ones that the transaction did not read before). This happens when another transaction inserted the new data in between the reads done by the affected transaction.

Table 36-1 shows the data inconsistency issues that are possible for different transaction isolation levels.

D. Korotkevitch, *Pro SQL Server Internals*, DOI 10.1007/978-1-4842-1964-5_36

Table 36-1. *Transaction Isolation Levels and Data Inconsistency Issues*

Isolation Level	Dirty Reads	Non-Repeatable Reads	Phantom Reads
READ UNCOMMITTED	YES	YES	YES
READ COMMITTED	NO	YES	YES
REPEATABLE READ	NO	NO	YES
SERIALIZABLE	NO	NO	NO
SNAPSHOT	NO	NO	NO

With the exception of the SNAPSHOT isolation level, SQL Server uses locking to address data inconsistency issues when dealing with on-disk tables. It blocks sessions from reading or modifying data to prevent data inconsistency. Such behavior also means that, in the case of a write/write conflict, the last modification wins. For example, when two transactions are trying to modify the same row, SQL Server blocks one of the transactions until another transaction is committed, allowing the blocked transaction to modify the data afterward. No errors or exceptions would be raised; however, changes from the first transaction would be lost.

The SNAPSHOT isolation level uses a row-versioning model where all data modifications done by other transactions are invisible to the transaction. Though it is implemented differently in on-disk than in memory-optimized tables, logically it behaves the same. Aborting and rolling back the transactions resolves write/write conflicts in this model.

SERIALIZABLE VERSUS SNAPSHOT ISOLATION LEVELS

While SERIALIZABLE and SNAPSHOT isolation levels provide the same level of protection against data inconsistency issues, there is a subtle difference in their behavior. A SNAPSHOT isolation level transaction sees data as of the beginning of a transaction. With the SERIALIZABLE isolation level, the transaction sees data as of the time when the data was accessed for the first time.

Consider a situation where a session is reading data from a table in the middle of a transaction. If another session changed the data in that table after the transaction started but before data was read, the transaction in the SERIALIZABLE isolation level would see the changes while the SNAPSHOT transaction would not.

Transaction Isolation Levels in In-Memory OLTP

In-Memory OLTP supports three transaction isolation levels: SNAPSHOT, REPEATABLE READ, and SERIALIZABLE. However, In-Memory OLTP uses a completely different approach to enforcing data consistency rules as compared to on-disk tables. Rather than block or being blocked by other sessions, In-Memory OLTP validates data consistency at the transaction COMMIT time and throws an exception and rolls back the transaction if rules were violated.

- In the SNAPSHOT isolation level, any changes done by other sessions are invisible to the transaction. A SNAPSHOT transaction always works with a snapshot of the data as of the time when transaction started. The only validation at the time of commit is checking for primary key violations, which is called *snapshot validation*.

- In the REPEATABLE READ isolation level, In-Memory OLTP validates that the rows that were read by the transaction have not been modified or deleted by the other transactions. A REPEATABLE READ transaction would not be able to commit if this was the case. This action is called *repeatable read validation.*
- In the SERIALIZABLE isolation level, SQL Server performs repeatable read validation and also checks for phantom rows that were possibly inserted by the other sessions. This process is called *serializable validation.*

Let's look at a few examples that demonstrate this behavior. As a first step, shown in Listing 36-1, let's create a memory-optimized table and insert a few rows there.

Listing 36-1. Data consistency and transaction isolation levels: Table creation

```
create table dbo.HKData
(
    ID int not null
        constraint PK_HKData
        primary key nonclustered hash with (bucket_count=64),
    Col int not null
)
with (memory_optimized=on, durability=schema_only);

insert into dbo.HKData(ID, Col) values(1,1),(2,2),(3,3),(4,4),(5,5);
```

Table 36-2 shows how concurrency works in the REPEATABLE READ transaction isolation level. It is important to note that SQL Server starts a transaction at the moment of first data access rather than at the time of the BEGIN TRAN statement. Therefore, the session 1 transaction starts at the time when the first SELECT operator executes.

Table 36-2. *Concurrency in the REPEATABLE READ Transaction Isolation Level*

Session 1	Session 2	Results

`begin tran`
`select ID, Col`
`from dbo.HKData`
`with (repeatableread)`		

	`update dbo.HKData`
	`set Col = -2`
	`where ID = 2`	

`select ID, Col`
`from dbo.HKData`
`with (repeatableread)`
		Return old version of a row (Col = 2)

`commit`		Msg 41305, Level 16, State 0, Line 0 The current transaction failed to commit due to a repeatable read validation failure.

`begin tran`
`select ID, Col`
`from dbo.HKData`
`with (repeatableread)`		

(*continued*)

Table 36-2. (*continued*)

Session 1	Session 2	Results
	insert into dbo.HKData values(10,10)	
`select ID, Col from dbo.HKData with (repeatableread)`		Does not return new row (10,10)
`commit`		Success

As you can see, with memory-optimized tables, other sessions were able to modify data that was read by the active `REPEATABLE READ` transaction. This led to a transaction abort at the time of `COMMIT` when the repeatable read validation failed. This is a completely different behavior than that of on-disk tables, where other sessions are blocked, unable to modify data until the `REPEATABLE READ` transaction successfully commits.

It is also worth noting that in the case of memory-optimized tables, the `REPEATABLE READ` isolation level protects you from the *phantom read* phenomenon, which is not the case with on-disk tables.

As a next step, let's repeat these tests in the `SERIALIZABLE` isolation level. You can see the code and the results of the execution in Table 36-3.

Table 36-3. *Concurrency in the SERIALIZABLE Transaction Isolation Level*

Session 1	Session 2	Results
`begin tran select ID, Col from dbo.HKData with (serializable)`		
	`update dbo.HKData set Col = -2 where ID = 2`	
`select ID, Col from dbo.HKData with (serializable)`		Return old version of a row (Col = 2)
`commit`		Msg 41305, Level 16, State 0, Line 0 The current transaction failed to commit due to a repeatable read validation failure.
`begin tran select ID, Col from dbo.HKData with (serializable)`		
	`insert into dbo.HKData values(10,10)`	
`select ID, Col from dbo.HKData with (serializable)`		Does not return new row (10,10)
`commit`		Msg 41325, Level 16, State 0, Line 0 The current transaction failed to commit due to a serializable validation failure.

As you can see, the SERIALIZABLE isolation level prevents the session from committing a transaction when another session inserted a new row and violated the serializable validation. Like the REPEATABLE READ isolation level, this behavior is different from that of on-disk tables, where the SERIALIZABLE transaction successfully blocks other sessions until it is done.

Finally, let's repeat the tests in the SNAPSHOT isolation level. The code and results are shown in Table 36-4.

Table 36-4. *Concurrency in the SNAPSHOT Transaction Isolation Level*

Session 1	Session 2	Results

begin tran
    select ID, Col
    from dbo.HKData
        with (snapshot)		

	update dbo.HKData set Col = -2 where ID = 2	

select ID, Col
    from dbo.HKData
        with (snapshot)
		Return old version of a row (Col = 2)

commit		Success

begin tran
    select ID, Col
    from dbo.HKData
        with (snapshot)		

	insert into dbo.HKData values(10,10)	

select ID, Col
    from dbo.HKData
        with (snapshot)
		Does not return new row (10,10)

commit		Success

The SNAPSHOT isolation level behaves in a similar manner to its behavior in on-disk tables, and it protects from the non-repeatable reads and phantom reads phenomena. As you can guess, it does not need to perform repeatable read and serializable validations at the commit stage and therefore reduces the load on SQL Server. However, there is still snapshot validation, which checks for primary key violations and is done in any transaction isolation level.

Table 36-5 shows the code that leads to the primary key violation condition. In contrast to on-disk tables, the exception is raised at the commit stage rather than at the time of the second INSERT operation.

Table 36-5. *Primary Key Violation*

Session 1	Session 2	Results

`begin tran`
`    insert into dbo.HKData`
`        with (snapshot)`
`    (ID, Col)`
`    values(100,100)`		

	`begin tran`
	`    insert into dbo.HKData`
	`        with (snapshot)`
	`    (ID, Col)`
	`    values(100,100)`	

`commit`		Successfully commit the first session
	`commit`	Msg 41325, Level 16, State 1, Line 0 The current transaction failed to commit due to a serializable validation failure.

It is worth mentioning that the error number and message are the same as with the serializable validation failure even though SQL Server validated the different rule.

Write/write conflicts work the same way regardless of the transaction isolation level in In-Memory OLTP. SQL Server does not allow a transaction to modify a row that has been modified by other uncommitted transactions. Table 36-6 illustrates this behavior. It uses the `SNAPSHOT` isolation level; however, the behavior does not change with different isolation levels.

Table 36-6. *Write/Write Conflicts in In-Memory OLTP*

Session 1	Session 2	Results

`begin tran`
`    select ID, Col`
`    from dbo.HKData`
`        with (snapshot)`		

	`begin tran`
	`    update dbo.HKData`
	`        with (snapshot)`
	`    set Col = -3`
	`    where ID = 2`
	`commit`	

`    update dbo.HKData`
`        with (snapshot)`
`    set Col = -2`
`    where ID = 2`
		Msg 41302, Level 16, State 110, Line 1
		The current transaction attempted to update a record that has been updated since this transaction started. The transaction was aborted.
		Msg 3998, Level 16, State 1, Line 1
		Uncommittable transaction is detected at the end of the batch. The transaction is rolled back.
		The statement has been terminated.

(*continued*)

Table 36-6. *(continued)*

Session 1	Session 2	Results

`begin tran`
`select ID, Col`
`from dbo.HKData`
`with (snapshot)`		

	`begin tran`
	`update dbo.HKData`
	`with (snapshot)`
	`set Col = -3`
	`where ID = 2`	

`update dbo.HKData`
`with (snapshot)`
`set Col = -2`
`where ID = 2`
		Msg 41302, Level 16, State 110, Line 1
		The current transaction attempted to update a record that has been updated since this transaction started. The transaction was aborted.
		Msg 3998, Level 16, State 1, Line 1
		Uncommittable transaction is detected at the end of the batch. The transaction is rolled back.
		The statement has been terminated.

	commit	Successful commit of session 2 transaction

Cross-Container Transactions

Any access to memory-optimized tables from interpreted T-SQL is done through the Query Interop Engine and leads to *cross-container transactions*. You can use different transaction isolation levels for on-disk and memory-optimized tables. However, not all combinations are supported. Table 36-7 illustrates possible combinations for transaction isolation levels in cross-container transactions.

Table 36-7. *Isolation Levels for Cross-Container Transactions*

Isolation Levels for On-Disk Tables	Isolation Levels for Memory-Optimized Tables
`READ UNCOMMITTED`, `READ COMMITTED`, `READ COMMITTED SNAPSHOT`	`SNAPSHOT`, `REPEATABLE READ`, `SERIALIZABLE`
`REPEATABLE READ`, `SERIALIZABLE`	`SNAPSHOT` only
`SNAPSHOT`	Not supported

As you already know, internal implementations of `REPEATABLE READ` and `SERIALIZABLE` isolation levels are very different for on-disk and memory-optimized tables. Data consistency rules with on-disk tables rely on locking while In-Memory OLTP uses pre-commit validation. It leads to a situation in cross-container transactions where SQL Server only supports `SNAPSHOT` isolation levels for memory-optimized tables when on-disk tables require `REPEATABLE READ` or `SERIALIZABLE` isolation.

Moreover, SQL Server does not allow access to memory-optimized tables when on-disk tables require `SNAPSHOT` isolation. Cross-container transactions, in a nutshell, consist of two internal transactions: one for on-disk and another one for memory-optimized tables. It is impossible to start both transactions at exactly the same time and guarantee the state of the data at the moment the transaction starts.

As the general guideline, it is recommended to use the READ COMMITTED/SNAPSHOT combination in cross-container transactions during a regular workload. This combination provides minimal blocking and the least pre-commit overhead and should be acceptable in a large number of use cases. Other combinations are more appropriate during data migrations when it is important to avoid non-repeatable and phantom reads phenomena.

As you may have already noticed, SQL Server requires you to specify the transaction isolation level with a table hint when you are accessing memory-optimized tables. This does not apply to individual statements that execute outside of the explicitly started (with BEGIN TRAN) transaction. Those statements are called *autocommitted transactions,* and each of them executes in a separate transaction that is active for the duration of the statement execution. Listing 36-2 illustrates code with three statements. Each of them will run in their own autocommitted transactions.

Listing 36-2. Autocommitted Transactions

```
delete from dbo.HKData;

insert into dbo.HKData(ID, Col) values(1,1),(2,2),(3,3),(4,4),(5,5);

select ID, Col from dbo.HKData;
```

An isolation level hint is not required for statements running in autocommitted transactions. When the hint is omitted, the statement runs in the SNAPSHOT isolation level.

SQL Server allows you to keep a NOLOCK hint while accessing memory-optimized tables from autocommitted transactions. That hint is ignored. A READUNCOMMITTED hint, however, is not supported and triggers an error.

There is a useful database option, MEMORY_OPTIMIZED_ELEVATE_TO_SNAPSHOT, which is disabled by default. When this option is enabled, SQL Server allows you to omit the isolation level hint in non-autocommitted transactions. SQL Server uses the SNAPSHOT isolation level, as with autocommitted transactions, if the isolation level hint is not specified when the MEMORY_OPTIMIZED_ELEVATE_TO_SNAPSHOT option is enabled. Consider enabling this option when you port an existing system to In-Memory OLTP and have T-SQL code that accesses tables that become memory-optimized.

Transaction Lifetime

Although I have already discussed a few key elements used by In-Memory OLTP to manage data access and the concurrency model, let's review them here.

- *Global Transaction Timestamp* is an auto-incremented value that uniquely identifies every transaction in the system. SQL Server increments and obtains this value at the transaction commit stage.
- Every row has BeginTs and EndTs timestamps, which correspond to the *Global Transaction Timestamp* of the transaction that created or deleted this version of a row.

At the time when a new transaction starts, In-Memory OLTP generates a TransactionId value that uniquely identifies the transaction. Moreover, In-Memory OLTP assigns the *logical start time* to the transaction, which represents the *Global Transaction Timestamp* value at the time when transaction starts. This dictates what version of the rows is visible to the transaction. The logical start time should be in between the BeginTs and EndTs in order for the row to be visible.

When the transaction issues a `COMMIT` statement, In-Memory OLTP increments the *Global Transaction Timestamp* value and assigns it to the transaction's *logical end time*. The logical end time will become the BeginTs for the rows inserted and EndTs for the rows deleted by the transaction after it is committed.

Figure 36-1 shows the lifetime of a transaction that works with memory-optimized tables.

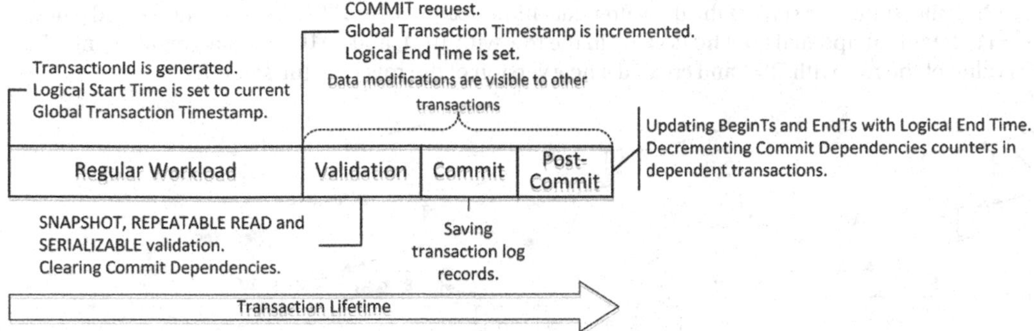

***Figure 36-1.** Transaction lifetime*

When a transaction is active and it needs to delete a row, it updates the EndTs timestamp with the `TransactionId` value. The `INSERT` operation creates a new row with the BeginTs of the `TransactionId` and the EndTs of `Infinity`. Finally, the `UPDATE` operation consists of delete and insert operations internally. It is also worth noting that during data modifications, transactions raise an error if there are any uncommitted versions of the rows they were modifying. This prevents write/write conflicts when multiple sessions modify the same data.

When another transaction—call it `Tx1`—encounters uncommitted rows with a `TransactionId` in BeginTs or EndTs timestamps (`TransactionId` has a flag that indicates such a condition), it checks the status of the transaction with `TransactionId`. If that transaction is committing and the logical end time is already set, those uncommitted rows may become visible for the `Tx1` transaction, which leads to a situation called *commit dependency*. `Tx1` is not blocked; however, it does not return data to the client nor commit until the original transaction on which it has a commit dependency commits itself. I will talk more about commit dependencies shortly.

Let's look at transaction lifetime in detail. Figure 36-2 shows the data rows after we created and populated the `dbo.HKData` table in Listing 36-1, assuming that the rows were created by a transaction with the *Global Transaction Timestamp* of 5. (The hash index structure is omitted for simplicity's sake.)

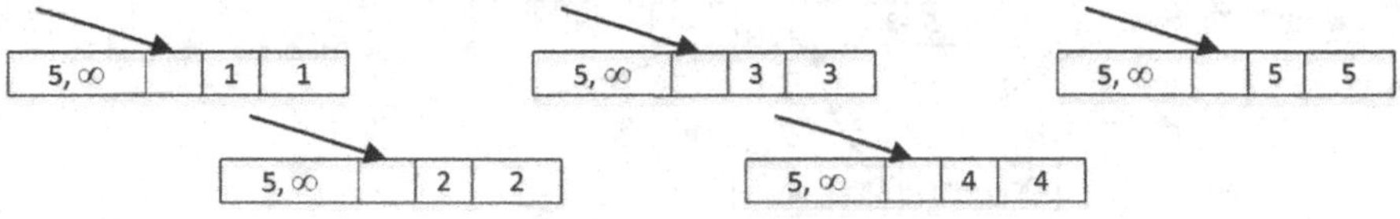

***Figure 36-2.** Data in the dbo.HKData table after insert*

Let's assume that you have a transaction that started at the time when the *Global Transaction Timestamp* value was 9 and the `TransactionId` generated was -8. (I am using a negative value for `TransactionId` to illustrate the difference between two types of timestamps in the figures.)

Let's assume that the transaction performs the operations shown in Listing 36-3. The explicit transaction has already started, and the `BEGIN TRAN` statement is not included in the listing. All three statements are executing in the context of a single active transaction.

Listing 36-3. Data modification operations

```
insert into dbo.HKData with (snapshot) (ID, Col) values(10,10);
update dbo.HKData with (snapshot) set Col = -2 where ID = 2;
delete from dbo.HKData with (snapshot) where ID = 4;
```

Figure 36-3 illustrates the state of the data after data modifications. An INSERT statement created a new row, a DELETE statement updated the EndTs value in the row with ID=4, and an UPDATE statement changed the EndTs value of the row with ID=2 and created a new version of the row with the same ID.

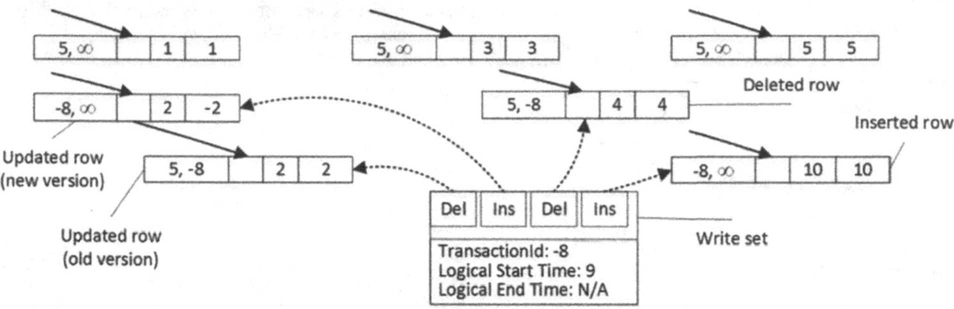

Figure 36-3. *Data in the dbo.HKData table after modifications*

It is important to note that the transaction maintains a *write set*, or pointers to rows that have been inserted and deleted by a transaction, which is used to generate transaction log records.

In addition to the write set, in the REPEATABLE READ and SERIALIZABLE isolation levels, transactions maintain a *read set* of the rows read by a transaction and use it for repeatable read validation. Finally, in the SERIALIZABLE isolation level, transactions maintain a *scan set*, which contains information about the predicates used by the queries in the transaction. The scan set is used for serializable validation.

When a COMMIT request is issued, the transaction starts the validation phase. First, it autoincrements the current *Global Transaction Timestamp* value, which becomes the logical end time of the transaction. Figure 36-4 illustrates this state, assuming that the new *Global Transaction Timestamp* value is 11. Note that the BeginTs and EndTs timestamps in the rows still have a TransactionId at this stage.

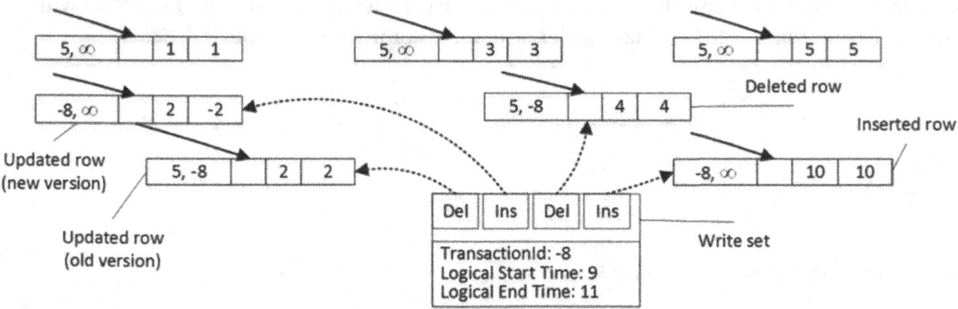

Figure 36-4. *Start of validation phase*

At this moment, the rows modified by transaction become visible to other transactions in the system even though the transaction has yet to be committed, which can lead to commit dependencies. Again, we will talk about them shortly.

As the next step, the transaction starts a validation phase. SQL Server performs several validations based on the isolation level of the transaction, as shown in Table 36-8.

Table 36-8. *Validations Done in the Different Transaction Isolation Levels*

	Snapshot Validation	Repeatable Read Validation	Serializable Validation
	Checking for primary key violations	Checking for non-repeatable reads	Checking for phantom reads
SNAPSHOT	YES	NO	NO
REPEATABLE READ	YES	YES	NO
SERIALIZABLE	YES	YES	YES

■ **Important** Repeatable read and serializable validations add overhead to the system. Do not use REPEATABLE READ and SERIALIZABLE isolation levels unless you have a legitimate use case for such data consistency.

After the required rules have been validated, the transaction waits for the commit dependencies to clear and the transaction on which it depends to commit. If those transactions fail to commit for any reason—for example, validation rules violation—the dependent transaction is also rolled back and error 41301 is generated.

Figure 36-5 illustrates a commit dependency scenario. Transaction Tx2 can access uncommitted rows from transaction Tx1 during Tx1 validation and commit phases, and therefore Tx2 has a commit dependency on Tx1. After the Tx2 validation phase is completed, Tx2 has to wait for Tx1 to commit and the commit dependency to clear before entering the commit phase.

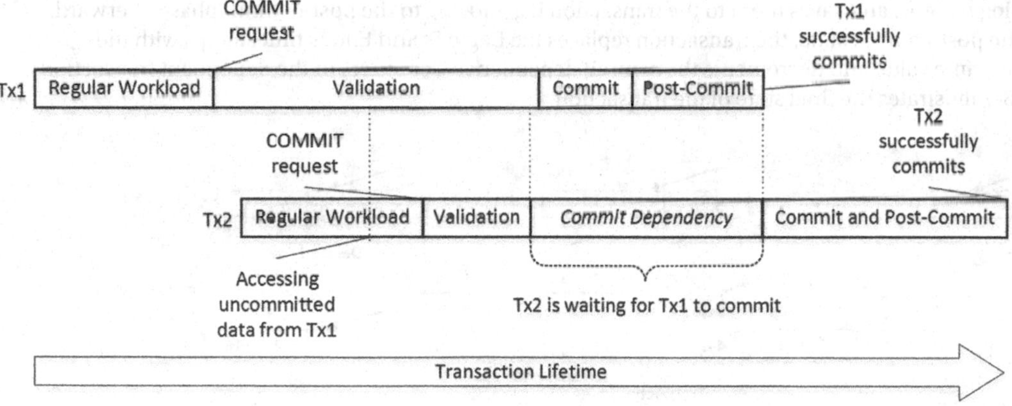

Figure 36-5. *Commit dependency: Successful commit*

If Tx1, for example, failed to commit due to serializable validation violation, Tx2 would be rolled back with Error 41301, as shown in Figure 36-6.

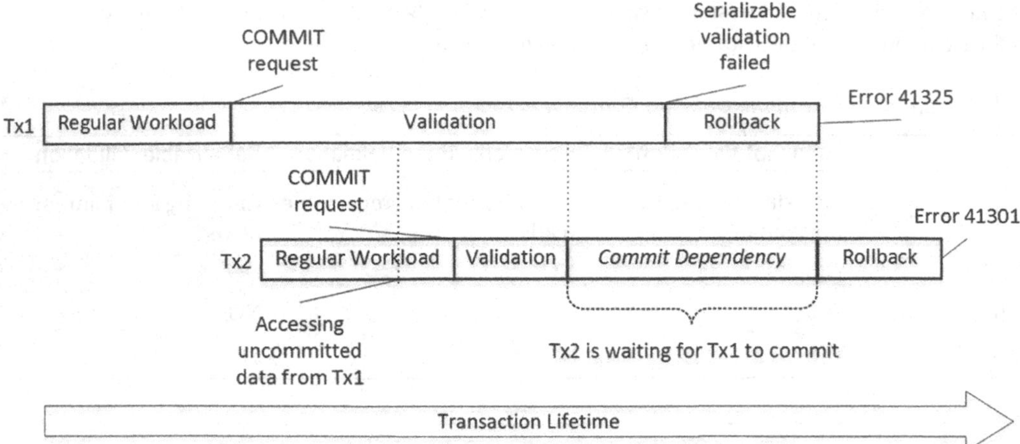

***Figure 36-6.** Commit dependency: Validation error*

Commit dependency is technically a case of blocking in In-Memory OLTP. However, the validation and commit phases of the transactions are relatively short, and that blocking should not be excessive.

SQL Server allows a maximum of eight commit dependencies on a single transaction. When this number is reached, other transactions that try to take a dependency would fail with error 41839.

■ **Note** You can track commit dependencies using the `dependency_acquiredtx_event` and `waiting_for_dependenciestx_event` extended events.

When all commit dependencies are cleared, the transaction moves to the commit phase, generates one or more log records, and saves them to the transaction log, moving to the post-commit phase afterward.

At the post-commit state, the transaction replaces the BeginTs and EndTs timestamps with the logical end time value and decrements the commit dependencies counters in the dependent transactions. Figure 36-7 illustrates the final state of the transaction.

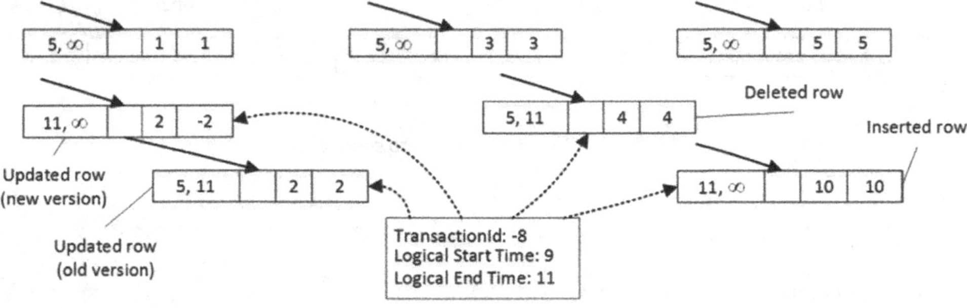

***Figure 36-7.** Completed transaction*

Referential Integrity Enforcement (SQL Server 2016)

It is impossible to enforce referential integrity in *pure* SNAPSHOT isolation level, because transactions are completely isolated from each other. Consider a situation where a transaction deletes a row that is referenced by a newly inserted row in another transaction that started after the original one. In-Memory OLTP addresses this problem by maintaining read and/or scan sets in the SNAPSHOT isolation level for tables and queries that are affected by referential integrity validation.

In contrast to REPEATABLE READ and SERIALIZABLE transactions, these sets are maintained only for affected tables rather than for the entire transaction. They would include all rows that were read and all predicates that were applied during a referential integrity check.

This behavior can lead to issues when a referencing table does not have an index on the foreign key column(s). Similar to on-disk tables, SQL Server will have to scan the entire referencing (detail) table when you delete a row in the referenced (master) table. In addition to the performance impact, the transaction will maintain the read set, which includes all rows it read during the scan, regardless if those rows referenced a deleted row or not. If any other transactions update or delete any rows from the read set, the original transaction would fail with a *repeatable read rule violation* error.

Let's look at an example and create two tables with the code seen in Listing 36-4.

Listing 36-4. Referential integrity validation: Tables' creation

```
create table dbo.Branches
(
    BranchId int not null
        constraint PK_Branches
        primary key nonclustered hash with (bucket_count = 4)
)
with (memory_optimized = on, durability = schema_only);

create table dbo.Transactions
(
    TransactionId int not null
        constraint PK_Transactions
        primary key nonclustered hash with (bucket_count = 4),
    BranchId int not null
        constraint FK_Transactions_Branches
        foreign key references dbo.Branches(BranchId),
    Amount money not null
)
with (memory_optimized = on, durability = schema_only);

insert into dbo.Branches(BranchId) values(1),(10);
insert into dbo.Transactions(TransactionId,BranchId,Amount)
values(1,1,1),(2,1,20);
```

The dbo.Transactions table has a foreign key constraint referencing the dbo.Branches table. There are no rows, however, referencing the row with BranchId = 10. As the next step, let's run the code shown in Listing 36-5, deleting this row and leaving the transaction active.

Listing 36-5. Referential integrity validation: First session code

```
begin tran
    delete from dbo.Branches with (snapshot) where BranchId = 10;
```

The DELETE statement would validate the foreign key constraint and would complete successfully. The dbo.Transactions table, however, does not have an index on the BranchId column, and the validation will require a scan of the entire table, as you can see in Figure 36-8.

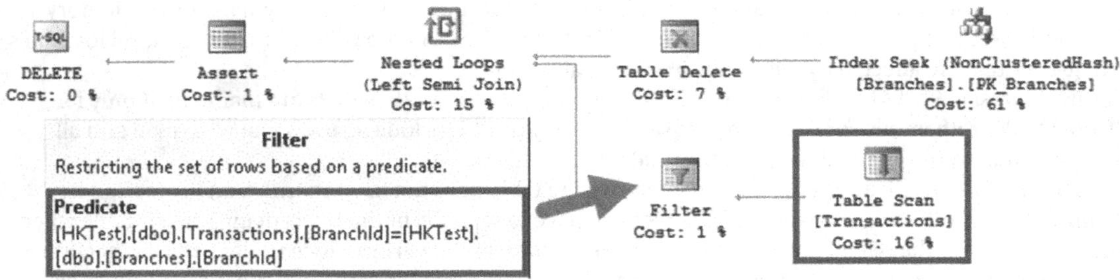

Figure 36-8. *Referential integrity validation: Execution plan of DELETE statement*

At this time all rows from the dbo.Transactions table would be included in the transaction read set. If another session updated one of the rows from the read set with the code shown in Listing 36-6, it would succeed and the first session would fail to commit as a result of a *repeatable read rule violation* error.

Listing 36-6. Referential integrity validation: Second session code

```
update dbo.Transactions with (snapshot)
set Amount = 30
where TransactionId = 2;
```

Similar to on-disk tables, you should always create an index on the foreign key columns in the referencing table to avoid this problem.

Transaction Logging

As mentioned in the previous chapter, transaction logging in In-Memory OLTP is more efficient than the Storage Engine. Both engines share the same transaction log and perform *write-ahead logging* (WAL); however, the log records' formats and algorithms are very different.

With on-disk tables, SQL Server generates transaction log records on a per-index basis. For example, when you insert a single row into a table with clustered and nonclustered indexes, it will log INSERT operations in every individual index separately. Moreover, it will log internal operations, such as extent and page allocations, page splits, and a few others.

All log records are saved in a transaction log and hardened on disk pretty much synchronously at the time when they were created. As you already know, every database caches transaction log records in the log buffers; however, this cache is very small, and it is flushed on disk during COMMIT and CHECKPOINT operations.

Finally, SQL Server has to include *before-update* (undo) and *after-update* (redo) versions of the row to the log records. The checkpoint process is asynchronous and does not check the state of the transaction that modified the page. It is entirely possible for the checkpoint to save the dirty data pages from uncommitted transactions, and the undo part of the log records are required to roll back the changes.

Transaction logging in In-Memory OLTP addresses these inefficiencies. The first major difference is that In-Memory OLTP generates and saves log records at the time of the transaction COMMIT rather than during each data row modification. Therefore, rolled back transactions do not generate any log activity.

The format of a log record is also different and much more efficient. Log records do not include any undo information. Dirty data from uncommitted transactions will never materialize on disk, and therefore In-Memory OLTP log data does not need to support the undo stage of crash recovery or log uncommitted changes.

In-Memory OLTP generates log records based on the transaction's write set. All data modifications are combined in one or very few log records based on the write set and inserted rows' size. Moreover, data modifications in non-durable memory-optimized tables are not logged at all.

Let's examine this behavior and run the code shown in Listing 36-7. It starts a transaction and inserts 500 rows into a memory-optimized table. Then, it examines the content of the transaction log using the undocumented `sys.fn_dblog` system function.

Listing 36-7. Transaction logging in In-Memory OLTP: Memory-optimized table logging

```
create table dbo.HKData
(
    ID int not null,
    Col int not null,

    constraint PK_HKData
    primary key nonclustered hash(ID) with (bucket_count=1024),
)
with (memory_optimized=on, durability=schema_and_data);

declare
    @I int = 1

begin tran
    while @I <= 500
    begin
        insert into dbo.HKData with (snapshot) (ID, Col) values(@I, @I);
        set @I += 1;
    end
commit;

select * from sys.fn_dblog(null, null) order by [Current LSN];
```

Figure 36-9 illustrates the content of the transaction log. You can see the single transaction record for the In-Memory OLTP transaction.

	Current LSN	Operation	Context	Transaction ID	LogBlockGeneration	Tag Bits	Log Record Fixed Length	Log Record Length	Previou
1	0000001f:0000593b:0001	LOP_BEGIN_XACT	LCX_NULL	0000:000003eb	0	0x0000	76	144	00000C
2	0000001f:0000593b:0002	LOP_HK	LCX_NULL	0000:000003eb	0	0x0000	28	9568	00000C
3	0000001f:0000593b:0003	LOP_COMMIT_XACT	LCX_NULL	0000:000003eb	0	0x0000	80	84	00000C

Figure 36-9. *Transaction log content after the In-Memory OLTP transaction*

Let's repeat this test with an on-disk table of a similar structure. Listing 36-8 shows the code that creates a table and populates it with data.

Listing 36-8. Transaction logging in In-Memory OLTP: On-disk table logging

```
create table dbo.DiskData
(
    ID int not null,
    Col int not null,
    constraint PK_DiskData primary key nonclustered(ID)
);
```

```
declare
    @I int = 1

begin tran
    while @I <= 500
    begin
        insert into dbo.DiskData(ID, Col) values(@I, @I);
        set @I += 1;
    end
commit;
```

As you can see in Figure 36-10, the same transaction generated more than 1,000 log records.

	Current LSN	Operation	Context	Transaction ID	LogBlockGeneration	Tag Bits	Log Record Fixed Length	Log Record Length	Previc
1	0000001f:0000598e:0001	LOP_BEGIN_XACT	LCX_NULL	0000:000003fe	0	0x0000	76	144	0000
2	0000001f:0000598e:0016	LOP_INSERT_ROWS	LCX_HEAP	0000:000003fe	0	0x0000	62	108	0000
3	0000001f:0000598e:0018	LOP_LOCK_XACT	LCX_NULL	0000:000003fe	0	0x0000	24	40	0000
4	0000001f:0000598e:002c	LOP_INSERT_ROWS	LCX_INDEX_LEAF	0000:000003fe	0	0x0000	62	116	0000
5	0000001f:0000598e:002d	LOP_INSERT_ROWS	LCX_HEAP	0000:000003fe	0	0x0000	62	108	0000
6	0000001f:0000598e:002e	LOP_INSERT_ROWS	LCX_INDEX_LEAF	0000:000003fe	0	0x0000	62	116	0000
7	0000001f:0000598e:002f	LOP_INSERT_ROWS	LCX_HEAP	0000:000003fe	0	0x0000	62	10[illegible]	0000
8	0000001f:0000598e:0030	LOP_INSERT_ROWS	LCX_INDEX_LEAF	0000:000003fe	0	0x0000	62	116	0000

Query executed successfully. | SQL2014 (12.0 CTP) | SQL2014\Administrator ... | HKDB | 00:00:00 | 1003 rows

Figure 36-10. *Transaction log content after on-disk table modification*

You can use another undocumented function, `sys.fn_dblog_xtp`, to examine the logical content of an In-Memory OLTP log record. Listing 36-9 shows the code that utilizes this function, and Figure 36-11 shows the output of that code. You should use the LSN of the `LSN_HK` log record from the Listing 36-7 output as the parameter of the function.

Listing 36-9. Analyzing an In-Memory OLTP log record

```
select [Current LSN], object_name(table_id) as [Table]
        ,operation_desc, tx_end_timestamp, total_size
from sys.fn_dblog_xtp
(
    '0x0000001f:0000593b:0002'
    ,'0x0000001f:0000593b:0002'
)
```

	Current LSN	Table	operation_desc	tx_end_timestamp	total_size
1	0000001f:0000593b:0002	NULL	HK_LOP_BEGIN_TX	137	17
2	0000001f:0000593b:0002	HKData	HK_LOP_INSERT_ROW	137	19
3	0000001f:0000593b:0002	HKData	HK_LOP_INSERT_ROW	137	19
4	0000001f:0000593b:0002	HKData	HK_LOP_INSERT_ROW	137	[illegible]
5	0000001f:0000593b:0002	HKData	HK_LOP_INSERT_ROW	137	19

Query executed successfully. | SQL2014 (12.0 CTP) | SQL2014\Administrator ... | HKDB | 00:00:00 | 502 rows

Figure 36-11. *In-Memory OLTP transaction log record details*

Finally, it is worth stating again that any data modification made on non-durable tables (DURABILITY=SCHEMA_ONLY) is not logged in the transaction log, nor is its data persisted on disk. This makes these tables great candidates to be the staging tables in ETL processes. You should obviously remember that data in non-durable tables do not survive server crashes or failover; you should handle these conditions in the ETL code.

Summary

In-Memory OLTP supports three transaction isolation levels: SNAPSHOT, REPEATABLE READ, and SERIALIZABLE. In contrast to on-disk tables, where non-repeatable and phantom reads are addressed by acquiring and holding locks, In-Memory OLTP validates data consistency rules at the transaction commit stage. An exception will be raised and the transaction will be rolled back if rules were violated.

Repeatable read and serializable validation add overhead to transaction processing. It is recommended to use the SNAPSHOT isolation level during a regular workload unless REPEATABLE READ or SERIALIZABLE data consistency is required.

SQL Server 2016 performs repeatable read and serializable validations to enforce referential integrity in the system. Always create an index on the foreign key columns in referencing tables to improve performance and avoid validation errors.

You can use different transaction isolation levels for on-disk and memory-optimized tables in cross-container transactions; however, not all combinations are supported. The recommended practice is to use the READ COMMITTED isolation level for on-disk tables and the SNAPSHOT isolation level for memory-optimized tables.

SQL Server does not require you to specify a transaction isolation level when you access memory-optimized tables through the Interop Engine in autocommitted (single-statement) transactions. SQL Server automatically promotes such transactions to the SNAPSHOT isolation level. However, you should specify an isolation level hint when a transaction is explicitly started with a BEGIN TRAN statement. You can avoid this by enabling the MEMORY_OPTIMIZED_ELEVATE_TO_SNAPSHOT database option. This option is useful when you port an existing system to use with In-Memory OLTP.

Transaction logging in In-Memory OLTP is more efficient than on-disk tables. Transactions are logged at the time of COMMIT based on the transaction write set. Log records are compact and contain information about multiple row-related operations.

In-Memory OLTP does not log any data modifications made in non-durable memory-optimized tables. It makes them a great choice to be staging tables in ETL processes.

CHAPTER 37

In-Memory OLTP Programmability

This chapter focuses on the programmability aspects of the In-Memory OLTP Engine in SQL Server. It describes the process of native compilation and provides an overview of the natively-compiled modules and T-SQL features that are supported in In-Memory OLTP. Finally, it discusses several questions related to the design of new systems and migration of existing systems to the In-Memory OLTP architecture.

Native Compilation

As you already know, memory-optimized tables can be accessed from regular T-SQL code using the Query Interop Engine. This approach is very flexible. As long as you work within the supported feature set, the location of data is transparent. The code does not need to know, nor does it need to worry about, if it works with on-disk or with memory-optimized tables.

Unfortunately, this flexibility comes at a cost. T-SQL is an interpreted and CPU-intensive language. Even a simple T-SQL statement requires thousands, and sometimes millions, of CPU instructions to execute. Even though in-memory data location dramatically speeds up data access and eliminates latching and locking contentions, the overhead of T-SQL interpretation and execution limits the level of performance improvements achievable with In-Memory OLTP.

Note The native compilation does not help in operational analytics scenarios in SQL Server 2016. Columnstore indexes can only be utilized in Query Interop mode.

In practice, it is possible to see a 2X–4X system throughput increase when memory-optimized data is accessed through the Interop Engine. To improve performance even further, In-Memory OLTP utilizes native compilation. As a first step, it converts any row data manipulation and access logic into C code, which is compiled into DLLs and loaded into SQL Server process memory. Those DLLs (one per table) consist of native CPU instructions, and they execute without any further code interpretation overhead of T-SQL statements.

D. Korotkevitch, *Pro SQL Server Internals*, DOI 10.1007/978-1-4842-1964-5_37

Consider a simple situation where you need to read the value of a fixed-length column from a data row. In the case of on-disk tables, SQL Server obtains the starting offset and length of the column from the system catalogs and performs the required manipulations to convert the sequence of bytes to the required data type. With memory-optimized tables, the DLL already knows what the column offset and data type are. SQL Server can read data from a pre-defined offset in a row using a pointer of the correct data type without any further overhead involved. As you can guess, this approach dramatically reduces the number of CPU instructions required for the operation.

On the flip side, this approach brings some limitations. You cannot change the format of a row after the DLL is generated. The compiled code would not know anything about the changes. This problem is more complicated than it seems, and simple recompilation of the DLL does not address it.

Consider a situation where you need to add another nullable column to a table. This is a metadata-level operation for on-disk tables and does not change the data in existing table rows. T-SQL would be able to detect that column data is not present by analyzing the various data row properties at runtime.

The situation is far more complicated in the case of memory-optimized tables and natively-compiled code. It is easy to generate a new version of the DLL that knows about new data column; however, that is not enough. The DLL needs to handle different versions of rows and different data formats depending on the presence of column data. While this is technically possible, it adds extra logic to the DLL, which leads to additional processing instructions, which slows data access. Moreover, the logic to support multiple data formats would remain in the code forever, degrading performance even further with each table alteration.

The only way to address this problem is to convert all existing data rows into the new format, rebuilding the table. This is exactly what table alteration performs in SQL Server 2016. In SQL Server 2014 this operation is not supported, so you need to implement it manually by creating another table and copying data there. Keep in mind that you cannot rename memory-optimized tables, and you will need to either change the code referencing the new table name or recreate the original table by persisting data in the staging table during the process. You can also use synonyms to reference the new table under the old name.

To reduce the overhead of T-SQL interpretation even further, the In-Memory OLTP Engine allows you to perform native compilation of stored procedures and, in SQL Server 2016, DML triggers and scalar table-valued functions. These modules are compiled in the same way as table-related DLLs and are also loaded to SQL Server process memory. We will discuss natively-compiled stored procedures and other modules in greater detail later in the chapter.

Native compilation utilizes both the SQL Server and In-Memory OLTP Engines. As a first step, SQL Server parses the T-SQL code and generates an execution plan using Query Optimizer. At the end of this stage, SQL Server generates a structure called *MAT (Mixed Abstract Tree)*, which represents metadata, imperative logic, expressions, and query plans.

As a next step, In-Memory OLTP transforms MAT to another structure called *PIT (Pure Imperative Tree)*, which is used to generate source code that is compiled and linked into the DLL.

Figure 37-1 illustrates the process of native compilation in SQL Server.

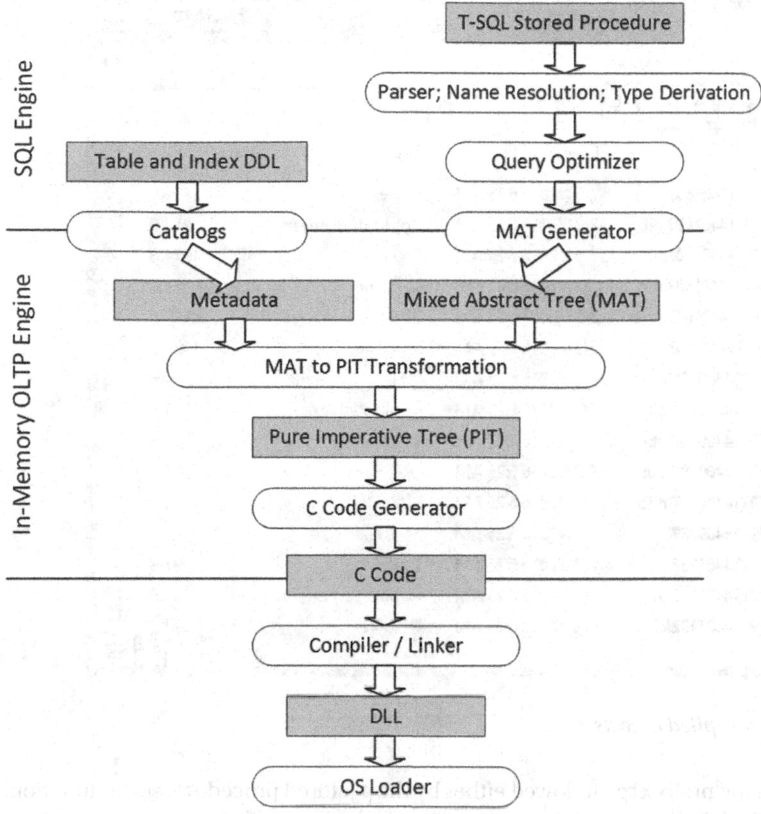

Figure 37-1. *Native compilation in SQL Server*

The code generated for native compilation uses plain C language and is very efficient. It is very hard to read, however. For example, every method is implemented as a single function, which does not call other functions but rather implements its code inline using GOTO as a control-flow statement. You should remember the intention has never been to generate human-readable code. It is used as the source for native compilation only.

Binary DLL files are not persisted in a database backup. SQL Server recreates table-related DLLs on database startup and stored procedure-related DLLs at the time of first call. This approach addresses security risks from hackers, who can substitute DLLs with malicious copies.

SQL Server places binary DLLs and all other native compilation-related files in an XTP subfolder under the main SQL Server data directory. It groups files on a per-database basis by creating another level of subfolders. Figure 37-2 shows the contents of a folder for a database (with ID=9) that contains several In-Memory OLTP objects.

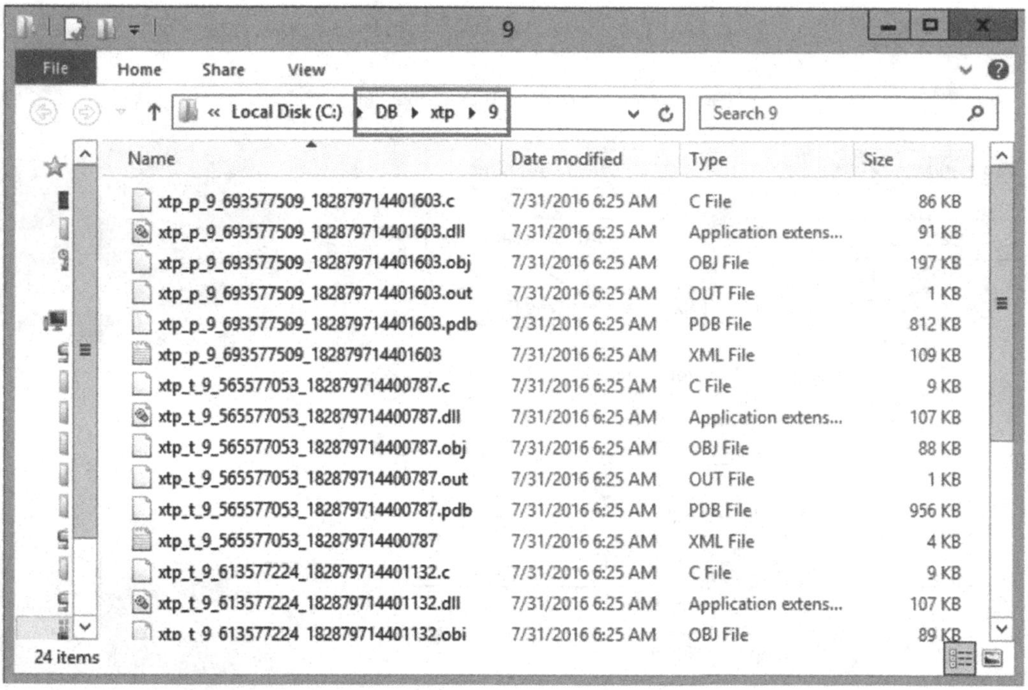

Figure 37-2. *Folder with natively-compiled objects*

All of the file names start with the prefix `xtp_` followed either by the `p` (stored procedure, scalar function, or trigger) or `t` (table) character, which indicates the object type. The two last parts of the name include the database and object IDs for the object.

File extensions determine the type of the file, such as the following:

- `*.mat.xml` files store an XML representation of the MAT structure.
- `*.c` files are the source file generated by the C code generator.
- `*.obj` are the object files generated by the C compiler.
- `*.pub` are symbol files produced by the C compiler.
- `*.out` are log files from the C compiler.
- `*.dll` are natively-compiled DLLs generated by the C linker. These files are loaded into SQL Server memory and used by the In-Memory OLTP Engine.

Listing 37-1 shows how to obtain a list of the natively-compiled objects loaded into SQL Server memory. It also returns the list of tables and stored procedures from the database to show the correlation between a DLL file name and object IDs.

Listing 37-1. Obtaining a list of natively-compiled objects loaded into SQL Server memory

```
select
    s.name + '.' + o.name as [Object Name], o.object_id
from
    (   select schema_id, name, object_id
```

```
        from sys.tables
        where is_memory_optimized = 1
        union all
        select schema_id, name, object_id
        from sys.procedures
    ) o join sys.schemas s on
            o.schema_id = s.schema_id;

select base_address, language, description, name
from sys.dm_os_loaded_modules
where description = 'XTP Native DLL';
```

Figure 37-3 illustrates the output of the code.

	Object Name	object_id
1	dbo.WebRequests_Memory	565577053
2	dbo.WebRequestHeaders_Memory	613577224
3	dbo.WebRequestParams_Memory	645577338
4	dbo.InsertRequestInfo_NativelyCompiled	693577509

	base_address	language	description	name
1	0x00007FFFBC550000	67699940	XTP Native DLL	C:\DB\xtp\9\xtp_t_9_565577053_182879714400787.dll
2	0x00007FFFBC520000	67699940	XTP Native DLL	C:\DB\xtp\9\xtp_t_9_613577224_182879714401132.dll
3	0x00007FFFB92E0000	67699940	XTP Native DLL	C:\DB\xtp\9\xtp_t_9_645577338_182879714401367.dll
4	0x00007FFFBC500000	67699940	XTP Native DLL	C:\DB\xtp\9\xtp_p_9_693577509_182879714401603.dll

***Figure 37-3.** Natively-compiled objects loaded into SQL Server memory*

SQL Server 2016 allows you to ALTER natively-compiled modules. This is online operation; SQL Server uses an old version of the module during the compilation and replaces it with the new DLL when compilation is completed. Alteration is not supported in SQL Server 2014, and the only choice you have is dropping and recreating the stored procedure.

Natively-Compiled Modules

Natively-compiled stored procedures are stored procedures that are compiled into native code. They are extremely efficient, and they can provide major performance improvements when working with memory-optimized tables, as compared to interpreted T-SQL statements, which access those tables through the Query Interop component. In addition, SQL Server 2016 allows you to natively compile triggers and scalar user-defined functions.

■ **Note** In this chapter, I will reference regular interpreted (non-natively compiled) modules as *T-SQL modules*.

Natively-compiled modules can access only memory-optimized tables. Moreover, they support a smaller set of T-SQL features as compared to the Query Interop Engine. We will talk about those limitations in more detail shortly after we discuss when SQL Server compiles and how it optimizes natively-compiled modules

Optimization of Natively-Compiled Modules

Interpreted T-SQL stored procedures and other modules are compiled at the time of first execution. Additionally, they can be recompiled after they are evicted from the plan cache and in a few other cases, such as outdated statistics, changes in database schema, or recompilation, that are explicitly requested in the code.

This behavior is different from natively-compiled modules, which are compiled at creation time. They are never recompiled except for SQL Server or database restart. In these cases, recompilation occurs at the time of the first call.

SQL Server does not sniff parameters at the time of compilation, optimizing statements for `UNKNOWN` values. It uses memory-optimized table statistics during optimization, which may or may not be up to date, especially in SQL Server 2014 where statistics are not updated automatically.

Fortunately, cardinality estimation errors have a smaller impact on performance in the case of natively-compiled modules. Contrary to on-disk tables, where such errors can lead to highly inefficient plans due to the high number of *key* or *RID lookup* operations, all indexes in memory-optimized tables reference the same data row and, in a nutshell, are covering indexes for in-row columns. Moreover, errors will not affect the choice of join strategy—*nested loop* is the only physical join type supported in natively-compiled modules in SQL Server 2014 and 2016.

Outdated statistics at the time of compilation, however, can still lead to inefficient plans. One such example is a query with multiple predicates on indexed columns. SQL Server needs to know the index's selectivity to choose the most efficient index.

It is better to recompile natively-compiled modules if the data in the table has significantly changed. In **SQL Server 2016**, you can do it by calling the `sp_recompile` stored procedure. Unfortunately, it is not supported in **SQL Server 2014**, so you have to recreate natively-compiled stored procedure with the following set of actions:

1. Update statistics to reflect the current data distribution in the table(s).
2. Script permissions assigned to natively-compiled stored procedures.
3. Drop and recreate procedures. Those actions force recompilation.
4. Assign required permissions to the procedures.

Finally, it is worth mentioning that the presence of natively-compiled modules often requires you to adjust the deployment process in the system. It is common to create all database schema objects, including tables and stored procedures, at the beginning of deployment. While the time of deployment does not matter for T-SQL modules, such a strategy compiles natively-compiled modules at a time when database tables are empty. You should recompile (or recreate) natively-compiled modules later; after the tables are populated with data and statistics are updated.

Creating Natively-Compiled Stored Procedures

Natively-compiled stored procedures and other modules execute as atomic blocks, which is an *all or nothing* approach. Either all statements in the module succeed or all of them fail.

When a natively-compiled stored procedure is called outside of the context of an active transaction, it starts a new transaction and either commits or rolls it back at the end of the execution.

In cases where a procedure is called in the context of an active transaction, SQL Server creates a savepoint at the beginning of the procedure's execution. In case of an error in the procedure, SQL Server rolls back the transaction to the created savepoint. Based on the severity and type of the error, the transaction is either going to be able to continue and commit or became doomed and uncommittable. The same is true for natively-compiled DML triggers, which always execute in the context of an active transaction.

Let's look at an example and create a memory-optimized table and natively-compiled stored procedure, as shown in Listing 37-2. Do not focus on unfamiliar constructs in the stored procedure body. I will explain those shortly.

Listing 37-2. Atomic blocks and transactions: Objects' creation

```
create table dbo.MOData
(
    ID int not null
        primary key nonclustered hash with (bucket_count=16),
    Value int null
)
with (memory_optimized=on, durability=schema_only);

insert into dbo.MOData(ID, Value) values(1,1), (2,2)
go

create proc dbo.AtomicBlockDemo
(
    @ID1 int not null
    ,@Value1 bigint not null
    ,@ID2 int
    ,@Value2 bigint
)
with native_compilation, schemabinding, execute as owner
as
begin atomic
with (transaction isolation level = snapshot, language=N'us_english')
    update dbo.MOData set Value = @Value1 where ID = @ID1;
    if @ID2 is not null
        update dbo.MOData set Value = @Value2 where ID = @ID2;
end;
```

At this point, the dbo.MOData table has two rows with values (1,1) and (2,2). Now, let's start the transaction and call a stored procedure twice, as shown in Listing 37-3.

Listing 37-3. Atomic blocks and transactions: Calling stored procedure

```
begin tran
    exec dbo.AtomicBlockDemo 1, -1, 2, -2;
    exec dbo.AtomicBlockDemo 1, 0, 2, 999999999999999;
```

The first call of the stored procedure succeeds, while the second call triggers an arithmetic overflow error, as shown here:

```
Msg 8115, Level 16, State 0, Procedure AtomicBlockDemo, Line 49

Arithmetic overflow error converting bigint to data type int.
```

You can check that the transaction is still active and committable with this select: `SELECT @@TRANCOUNT AS [@@TRANCOUNT], XACT_STATE() AS [XACT_STATE()]`. It would return the following results:

```
@@TRANCOUNT XACT_STATE()
----------- ------------
1           1
```

If you commit the transaction and check the content of the table, you will see that the data reflects the changes caused by the first stored procedure call. Even though the first update statement from the second call succeeded, SQL Server rolled it back because the natively-compiled stored procedure executed as an atomic block. You can see the data in the table below.

```
ID          Value
----------- -----------
1           -1
2           -2
```

As a second example, let's trigger a critical error, which dooms the transaction, making it uncommittable. One such situation is a write/write conflict. You can trigger it by executing the code in Listing 37-4 in two different sessions.

Listing 37-4. Atomic blocks and transactions: Write/write conflict

```
begin tran
    exec dbo.AtomicBlockDemo 1, 0, null, null;
```

When you run the code in the second session, it triggers the following exception:

```
Msg 41302, Level 16, State 110, Procedure AtomicBlockDemo, Line 13
The current transaction attempted to update a record that has been updated since this
transaction started. The transaction was aborted.
Msg 3998, Level 16, State 1, Line 1
Uncommittable transaction is detected at the end of the batch. The transaction is rolled
back.
```

If you check `@@TRANCOUNT` in the second session, you will see that SQL Server terminated the transaction as follows.

```
@@TRANCOUNT
-----------
0
```

As you can see, when an atomic block executes in the context of an active transaction, severe errors in the atomic block roll back the entire transaction while non-critical errors roll back the transaction to the savepoint that corresponds to the beginning of the block.

You should specify that the natively-compiled module is an atomic block by using BEGIN ATOMIC..END at the top level of the module. It has two required and three optional settings, as follows:

TRANSACTION ISOLATION LEVEL is the required setting that controls transaction isolation level in the atomic block. You can use SNAPSHOT, REPEATABLEREAD, or SERIALIZABLE isolation levels.

LANGUAGE setting is required. It dictates the date/time format and system messages language in the block.

DATEFORMAT is optional and it allows you to override the default date format associated with the language.

DATEFIRST is optional and it overrides the default value associated with the language.

DELAYED_DURABILITY is optional and it specifies the durability option for the transaction if it is started by the atomic block.

It is also worth noting that atomic blocks are not supported in interpreted T-SQL modules.

All natively-compiled objects are schema-bound, and they require you to specify the SCHEMABINDING option. Finally, in **SQL Server 2014**, natively-compiled stored procedures do not support the EXECUTE AS CALLER execution context and require you to specify EXECUTE AS OWNER, EXECUTE AS USER, or EXECUTE AS SELF contexts in the definition. This limitation is removed in **SQL Server 2016**, and execution context is optional.

■ **Note** You can read about execution context at http://technet.microsoft.com/en-us/library/ms188354.aspx.

As you have already seen in Listing 37-2, you can specify the required parameters by using the NOT NULL construct in the module's definition. SQL Server raises an error if you do not provide the parameter values at the time of the call.

Finally, it is recommended that you avoid type conversion and do not use named parameters when you call natively-compiled stored procedures. It is more efficient to use exec Proc value [..,value] rather than the exec Proc @Param=value [..,@Param=value] calling format.

■ **Note** You can detect inefficient parameterization with the hekaton_slow_parameter_parsing extended event.

Natively-Compiled Triggers and User-Defined Functions (SQL Server 2016)

SQL Server 2016 allows you to create natively-compiled scalar user-defined functions and DML triggers on memory-optimized tables. As with natively-compiled stored procedures, these modules cannot access on-disk objects.

Listing 37-5 shows the code that creates both types of objects.

Listing 37-5. Natively-compiled trigger and user-defined function

```
create trigger NativelyCompiledTrigger on dbo.MemoryOptimizedTable
with native_compilation, schemabinding
after insert
as
begin atomic with
(
    transaction isolation level = snapshot, language = N'English'
)
    if @@rowcount = 0
        return;
    /* Trigger Body */
end
go

create function dbo.NativelyCompiledScalarFunction(@Param1 int not null)
returns int
with native_compilation, schemabinding
as
begin atomic with
(
    transaction isolation level = snapshot, language = N'us_english'
)
    declare
        @Result int = 0
    /* Function Body */
    return @Result;
end
```

As with T-SQL triggers and scalar user-defined functions, you should consider the overhead these modules introduce. Let's run a couple of tests and compare the performance of interpreted T-SQL and natively-compiled scalar functions. Listing 37-6 creates two very simple functions that just run an empty `WHILE` loop without any data access.

Listing 37-6. Natively-compiled versus interpreted function: Functions' creation

```
create function dbo.ScalarInterpret(@LoopCnt int)
returns int
as
begin
    declare
        @I int = 0
    while @I < @LoopCnt
        select @I += 1;
    return @I;
end
go

create function dbo.ScalarNativelyCompiled(@LoopCnt int)
returns int
with native_compilation, schemabinding
```

```
as
begin atomic with (transaction isolation level = snapshot, language = N'us_english')
    declare
        @I int = 0
    while @I < @LoopCnt
        select @I += 1;
    return @I;
end
```

As the next step, let's call the functions running a 1,000,000-execution loop inside them, as shown in Listing 37-7.

Listing 37-7. Natively-compiled versus interpreted function: Running the loop within the function

```
select dbo.ScalarInterpret(1000000);
select dbo.ScalarNativelyCompiled(1000000);
```

Table 37-1 illustrates the execution time in my environment. As you can see, the natively-compiled function is orders of magnitude faster than its interpreted T-SQL counterpart.

Table 37-1. *Execution Time When Functions Run 1,000,000-Execution Loop*

Interpreted T-SQL Function	Natively-Compiled Function
454 ms	5 ms

Let's run another test and call the functions in the loop, as shown in Listing 37-8. The functions do not execute a `WHILE` loop internally but rather being invoked 1,000,000 times. Table 37-2 shows the execution time in my environment.

Listing 37-8. Natively-compiled versus interpreted function: Multiple calls

```
declare
    @Dummy int
    ,@I int = 0

while @I < 1000000
begin
    select @Dummy = dbo.ScalarInterpret(0);
    select @I += 1;
end;

set @I = 0;
while @I < 1000000
begin
    select @Dummy = dbo.ScalarNativelyCompiled(0);
    select @I += 1;
end;
```

Table 37-2. *Execution Time of 1,000,000 Function Calls*

Interpreted T-SQL Function	Natively-Compiled Function
12,344 ms	11,392 ms

Even though natively-compiled functions are significantly faster than interpreted T-SQL functions, the execution overhead is very similar in both cases. You should avoid scalar user-defined functions in your code even when they are natively-compiled.

SQL Server 2016 also allows you to mark inline table-valued functions as natively-compiled. However, they behave differently than other modules. When you mark these functions as natively-compiled, SQL Server just validates that they are using the language constructs supported by native compilation. The functions are not actually compiled but rather are embedded into the other natively-compiled modules that reference them.

When you call natively-compiled inline table-valued functions from T-SQL via Query Interop, SQL Server treats them as regular T-SQL inline table-valued functions, embedding their statement to the referenced query.

Listing 37-9 illustrates a natively-compiled inline table-valued function.

Listing 37-9. Natively-compiled inline table-valued function

```
create function dbo.NativeCompiledInlineTVF(@Param datetime)
returns table
with native_compilation, schemabinding
as
return
(
    select count(*) as Result
    from dbo.MemoryOptimizedTable
    where DateCol >= @Param
)
```

Supported T-SQL Features

Natively-compiled modules support only a limited set of T-SQL constructs. In SQL Server 2014, the list of limitations is extensive. Fortunately, many of those limitations were removed in SQL Server 2016.

Let's look at the supported features in different areas.

Control Flow

The following control flow options are supported:

- `IF` and `WHILE`
- Assigning a value to a variable with the `SELECT` and `SET` operators.
- `RETURN`
- `TRY/CATCH/THROW` (`RAISERROR` is not supported). It is recommended that you use a single `TRY/CATCH` block for the entire stored procedure for better performance.
- It is possible to declare variables as `NOT NULL` as long as they have an initializer as part of the `DECLARE` statement.
- **SQL Server 2016** supports nested natively-compiled modules execution. For example, natively-compiled stored procedure can call another natively-compiled procedure or function.

Operators

The following operators are supported:

- Comparison operators, such as =, <, <=, >, >=, and <>.
- Unary and binary operators, such as +, -, *, /, and %. The + operators are supported for both numbers and strings.
- Bitwise operators, such as &, |, ~, and ^.
- Logical operators, such as AND, OR, and NOT. However, in **SQL Server 2014**, the OR and NOT operators are not supported in the WHERE and HAVING clauses of the query.
- **SQL Server 2016** supports IN, BETWEEN, and EXISTS operators.

Built-In Functions

The following built-in functions are supported:

- Math functions: **SQL Server 2016** supports all mathematical functions. **In SQL Server 2014**, the following functions are supported: ACOS, ASIN, ATAN, ATN2, COS, COT, DEGREES, EXP, LOG, LOG10, PI, POWER, RAND, SIN, SQRT, SQUARE, and TAN
- Date/time functions: CURRENT_TIMESTAMP, DATEADD, DATEDIFF, DATEFROMPARTS, DATEPART, DATETIME2FROMPARTS, DATETIMEFROMPARTS, DAY, EOMONTH, GETDATE, GETUTCDATE, MONTH, SMALLDATETIMEFROMPARTS, SYSDATETIME, SYSUTCDATETIME, and YEAR
- String functions: LEN, LTRIM, RTRIM, and SUBSTRING
- Error functions: ERROR_LINE, ERROR_MESSAGE, ERROR_NUMBER, ERROR_PROCEDURE, ERROR_SEVERITY, and ERROR_STATE
- NEWID and NEWSEQUENTIALID
- CAST and CONVERT. However, it is impossible to convert between a non-unicode and a unicode string.
- ISNULL
- SCOPE_IDENTITY
- You can use @@ROWCOUNT within a natively-compiled stored procedure; however, its value is reset to 0 at the beginning and end of the procedure.
- **SQL Server 2016** supports the @@SPID function.
- **SQL Server 2016** supports the following security functions: IS_MEMBER, IS_ROLEMEMBER, IS_SRVROLEMEMBER, ORIGINAL_LOGIN, SESSION_USER, CURRENT_USER, SUSER_ID, SUSER_SID, SUSER_SNAME, SYSTEM_USER, SUSER_NAME, USER, USER_ID, USER_NAME, and CONTEXT_INFO.

Query Surface Area

The following query surface area functions are supported:

SELECT, INSERT, UPDATE, and DELETE. **SQL Server 2016** supports the SELECT DISTINCT operator and allows you to use the OUTPUT clause with INSERT, UPDATE, and DELETE operators.

SQL Server 2016 supports UNION and UNION ALL operators.

CROSS JOIN and INNER JOIN are the only join types supported in **SQL Server 2014. SQL Server 2016** also supports LEFT OUTER JOIN and RIGHT OUTER JOIN. You can use joins only with SELECT operators.

Expressions in the SELECT list and WHERE and HAVING clauses are supported as long as they use supported operators.

SQL Server 2016 supports subqueries in FROM and WHERE clauses and scalar subqueries in the SELECT clause.

IS NULL and IS NOT NULL

GROUP BY is supported with the exception of grouping by string or binary data.

TOP and ORDER BY. However, you cannot use these with WITH TIES and PERCENT in the TOP clause. Moreover, the TOP operator is limited to 8,192 rows when the TOP <constant> is used, or an even lesser number of rows in the case of joins. You can address this last limitation by using a TOP <variable> approach. However, it is less efficient in terms of performance.

The native compilation in SQL Server 2016 still has several limitations and unsupported T-SQL constructs. You can think about unsupported CASE and MERGE statements as examples.

Execution Statistics

By default, SQL Server does not collect execution statistics for natively-compiled stored procedures because of the performance impact it introduces. You can enable such a collection at the procedure level with the exec sys.sp_xtp_control_proc_exec_stats 1 command. Moreover, you can use the exec sys.sp_xtp_control_query_exec_stats 1 command to enable a collection at the statement level. SQL Server does not persist these settings, and you will need to re-enable statistics collection after each SQL Server restart.

■ **Note** Do not collect execution statistics unless you are troubleshooting performance.

As you can guess, the collection of execution statistics introduces overhead in the system. Do not enable it unless you are performing troubleshooting, and be sure to disable it as soon as troubleshooting is done.

Listing 37-10 shows the code that returns execution statistics for stored procedures using the sys.dm_exec_procedure_stats view.

Listing 37-10. Analyzing stored procedure execution statistics

```
select top 50
    object_name(object_id) as [Proc Name]
    ,execution_count as [Exec Cnt]
```

```
    ,total_worker_time as [Total CPU]
    ,convert(int,total_worker_time / 1000 / execution_count) as [Avg CPU]
    ,total_elapsed_time as [Total Elps]
    ,convert(int,total_elapsed_time / 1000 / execution_count) as [Avg Elps]
    ,cached_time as [Cached]
    ,last_execution_time as [Last Exec Time]
    ,sql_handle
    ,plan_handle
    ,total_logical_reads as [Reads]
    ,total_logical_writes as [Writes]
from sys.dm_exec_procedure_stats
order by [Avg CPU] desc
```

Figure 37-4 illustrates the output of the code from Listing 37-10. As you can see, neither the sql_handle nor plan_handle columns are populated. Execution plans for natively-compiled stored procedures are embedded into the code and are not cached in the plan cache, nor are I/O-related statistics provided. Natively-compiled stored procedures work with memory-optimized tables only, and therefore there is no I/O involved.

	Proc Name	Exec Cnt	Total CPU	Avg CPU	Total Elps	Avg Elps	Cached	Last Exec	sql_handle	plan_handle	Reads	Writes
1	InsertCustomers	2	6234000	3117	7069937	3534	2014-04-02 21:09...	2014-04-03 07:...	0x0000000000000000...	0x0000000000000000...	0	0
2	DeleteCustomers	2	328000	164	868088	434	2014-04-02 21:19...	2014-04-03 07:...	0x0000000000000000...	0x0000000000000000...	0	0

Figure 37-4. *Data from* `sys.dm_exec_procedure_stats` *view*

Listing 37-11 shows the code that obtains execution statistics for individual statements using the sys.dm_exec_query_stats view.

Listing 37-11. Analyzing stored procedure statement execution statistics

```
select top 50
    substring(qt.text, (qs.statement_start_offset/2)+1,
        (( case qs.statement_end_offset
                when -1 then datalength(qt.text)
                else qs.statement_end_offset
            end - qs.statement_start_offset)/2)+1) as [SQL]
    ,qs.execution_count as [Exec Cnt]
    ,qs.total_worker_time as [Total CPU]
    ,convert(int,qs.total_worker_time / 1000 / qs.execution_count) as [Avg CPU]
    ,total_elapsed_time as [Total Elps]
    ,convert(int,qs.total_elapsed_time / 1000 / qs.execution_count) as [Avg Elps]
    ,qs.creation_time as [Cached]
    ,last_execution_time as [Last Exec Time]
    ,qs.plan_handle
    ,qs.total_logical_reads as [Reads]
    ,qs.total_logical_writes as [Writes]
from
    sys.dm_exec_query_stats qs
        cross apply sys.dm_exec_sql_text(qs.sql_handle) qt
where
    qs.plan_generation_num is null
order by
    [Avg CPU] desc
```

Figure 37-5 illustrates the output of the code from Listing 37-11. Like procedure execution statistics, it is impossible to obtain the execution plans of the statements. However, you can analyze the CPU time consumed by individual statements and the frequency of their execution.

	SQL	Exec Cnt	Total CPU	Avg CPU	Total Elps	Avg Elps	Cached	Last Exec	plan_handle	Reads	Writes
1	delete from dbo.Custo...	2	218000	109	212116	106	2014-04-02 21:19:57...	2014-04-03 07:24:52...	0x000000000...	0	0
2	insert into dbo.Custom...	1999998	3174000	0	2348175	0	2014-04-02 21:09:11...	2014-04-03 07:24:56...	0x000000000...	0	0

Figure 37-5. *Data from the* `sys.dm_exec_query_stats` *view*

Interpreted T-SQL and Memory-Optimized Tables

The Query Interop component provides transparent, memory-optimized table access to interpreted T-SQL code. In interpreted mode, SQL Server treats memory-optimized tables pretty much the same way as it does on-disk tables. It optimizes queries and caches execution plans, regardless of where table is located. The same set of operators is used during query execution. From a high level, when the operator's `GetRow()` method is called, it is routed either to the Storage Engine or to the In-Memory OLTP Engine, depending on the underlying table type.

Most T-SQL features are supported in interpreted mode. There are still a few exceptions that are not supported in either version of SQL Server:

- `TRUNCATE TABLE`
- `MERGE` operator with memory-optimized table as the target
- Context connection from CLR code
- Referencing memory-optimized tables in indexed views. You can reference memory-optimized tables in partitioned views, combining data from memory-optimized and on-disk tables.
- `DYNAMIC` and `KEYSET` cursors, which are automatically downgraded to `STATIC`
- Cross-database queries and transactions
- Linked servers

As you can see, the list of limitations is pretty small. However, the flexibility of Query Interop access comes at a cost. Natively-compiled modules are usually several times more efficient as compared to their interpreted T-SQL counterparts. In some cases—for example, joins between memory-optimized and on-disk tables—Query Interop is the only choice; however, it is usually preferable to use natively-compiled modules when possible.

Memory-Optimized Table Types and Variables

SQL Server allows you to create memory-optimized table types. Table variables of these types are called *memory-optimized table variables*. In contrast to regular disk-based table variables, memory-optimized table variables live in memory only and do not utilize `tempdb`.

Memory-optimized table variables provide great performance. They can be used as a replacement for disk-based table variables and in some cases temporary tables. Obviously, they have the same set of functional limitations as memory-optimized tables.

Contrary to disk-based table types, you can define indexes on memory-optimized table types. The same statistics-related limitations still apply. However, as we already discussed, due to the nature of indexes on memory-optimized tables, cardinality estimation errors yield a much lower negative impact as compared to those of on-disk tables.

SQL Server does not support inline declaration of memory-optimized table variables. For example, the code shown in Listing 37-12 would not compile and would raise an error. The reason behind this limitation is that SQL Server compiles a DLL for every memory-optimized table type, which would not work in the case of inline declarations.

Listing 37-12. (Non-functional) inline declaration of memory-optimized table variables

```
declare
    @IDList table
    (
        ID int not null
            primary key nonclustered hash with (bucket_count=1024)
    )
    with (memory_optimized=on)
```

```
Msg 319, Level 15, State 1, Line 91
Incorrect syntax near the keyword 'with'. If this statement is a common table expression,
an xmlnamespaces clause, or a change tracking context clause, the previous statement must
be terminated with a semicolon.
```

You should define and use a memory-optimized table type instead, as shown in Listing 37-13.

Listing 37-13. Creating a memory-optimized table type and table variable

```
create type dbo.mtvIDList as table
(
    ID int not null
        primary key nonclustered hash with (bucket_count=1024)
)
with (memory_optimized=on)
go

declare
    @IDList dbo.mtvIDList
```

Using memory-optimized table variables and table-valued parameters as the replacement for `tempdb` temporary objects improves performance of the system and reduces `tempdb` load. It requires very few code changes. For example, you can switch from on-disk to memory-optimized TVP by marking the table type as memory-optimized. It is completely transparent to the other code.

As you might remember, in Chapter 13 we tested several methods of importing a batch of rows into the database. On-disk table-valued parameters outperformed all other methods, including the `SqlBulkCopy` class. By changing the table type definition to become memory-optimized, I was able to reduce the import time another 40 percent as compared to on-disk implementation.

You can use memory-optimized table variables to imitate row-by-row processing using cursors, which are not supported in natively-compiled stored procedures. Listing 37-14 illustrates an example of using a memory-optimized table variable to imitate a static cursor. Obviously, it is better to avoid cursors and use set-based logic if at all possible.

Listing 37-14. Using a memory-optimized table variable to imitate a cursor

```
create type dbo.MODataStage as table
(
    ID int not null
        primary key nonclustered hash with (bucket_count=1024),
       Value int null
)
with (memory_optimized=on)
go

create proc dbo.CursorDemo
with native_compilation, schemabinding, execute as owner
as
begin atomic
with (transaction isolation level = snapshot, language=N'us_english')
    declare
        @tblCursor dbo.MODataStage
        ,@ID int = -1
        ,@Value int
        ,@RC int = 1

       /* Staging data in temporary table to imitate STATIC cursor */
    insert into @tblCursor(ID, Value)
        select ID, Value from dbo.MOData;

    while @RC = 1
    begin
        select top 1 @ID = ID, @Value = Value
        from @tblCursor
        where ID > @ID
        order by ID;

        select @RC = @@rowcount
        if @RC = 1
        begin
            /* Row processing */
            update dbo.MOData set Value = Value * 2 where ID = @ID
        end
    end
end
```

In-Memory OLTP: Implementation Considerations

As with any new technology, the adoption of In-Memory OLTP comes at a cost. You will need to acquire and/or upgrade to SQL Server 2014 or 2016, spend time learning the technology, and if you are updating an existing system, re-factor code and test the changes. It is important to perform a cost/benefits analysis and determine if In-Memory OLTP provides you with adequate benefits to outweigh the costs.

In-Memory OLTP is hardly a magical solution that can help you improve server performance by simply flipping a switch and moving data into memory. It is designed to address a specific set of problems, such as latch and lock contentions on very active OLTP systems. It is less beneficial in the case of data warehouse systems with low concurrent activity, large amounts of data, and queries that require complex aggregations. While in some cases it is still possible to achieve performance improvements by moving data into memory, you can often obtain better results by implementing on-disk columnstore indexes, indexing views, data compression, and other database schema changes.

This remains true even in SQL Server 2016, which supports columnstore indexes on memory-optimized tables. Such indexes are targeted toward systems with a mixed workload, and they help with the performance of reporting and analytics queries that work in parallel with OLTP workload. You should not treat In-Memory OLTP columnstore indexes as an in-memory data warehouse solution.

It is also worth remembering that most performance improvements are achieved by using natively-compiled modules, which can rarely be used in data warehouse workloads due to the limited set of T-SQL features that they support. Moreover, SQL Server 2016 does not use columnstore indexes from natively-compiled code.

Another important factor is whether you plan to use In-Memory OLTP during the development of new or the migration of existing systems, and it also greatly depends on the version of SQL Server being used. You need to make changes in existing systems to address the limitations of technology. In **SQL Server 2014** the list of limitations is extensive and includes missing support of triggers, foreign key constraints, check and unique constraints, calculated columns, and quite a few other restrictions.

I would like to discuss a few less obvious items that can greatly increase the migration cost in **SQL Server 2014**. The first is the 8,060-byte maximum row size limitation in memory-optimized tables without any off-row data storage support. Such a limitation can lead to a significant amount of work when the existing active OLTP tables use LOB data types, such as `(n)varchar(max)` or `xml`. While it is possible to change the data types by limiting the size of the strings and/or storing xml as text or in binary format and/or storing large objects in separate tables, such changes are complex, time consuming, and require careful planning. Do not forget that In-Memory OLTP in SQL Server 2014 does not allow you to create a table if there is a possibility that the size of a row exceeds 8,060 bytes. For example, you cannot create a table with three `varchar(3000)` columns.

The indexing of memory-optimized tables is another important factor. **SQL Server 2014** requires the binary collation of indexed text columns. This is a breaking change in system behavior, and it often requires non-trivial changes in the code and some sort of data conversion.

Consider a situation where an application performs a search on the `Name` column, which uses case-insensitive collation. You will need to convert all values to upper- or lowercase in order to be able to utilize a nonclustered index after the table becomes memory-optimized. That will change the user experience in the system.

It is also worth noting that using binary collations for data will lead to changes in the T-SQL code. You will need to specify collations for variables in stored procedures and other T-SQL routines, unless you change the database collation to be a binary one. However, if the database and server collations do not match, you will need to specify a collation for the columns in temporary tables created in `tempdb`.

You should also remember that nonclustered Bw-Tree indexes behave differently than B-Tree indexes on on-disk tables. Nonclustered Bw-Tree indexes are implemented as a single-linked list, and they would not help much if the data needed to be accessed in the opposite sorting order of an index key. To make matter worse, an *index* or *table scan* of large memory-optimized tables can be less efficient as compared to such scans of on-disk tables, especially when data resides in the buffer pool. All of that often requires you to re-evaluate your index strategy when a table is moved from disk into memory in both versions of SQL Server.

SQL Server 2016 addresses many of technology limitations that existed in SQL Server 2014. However, there are still limitations as compared to on-disk tables. Most notable are missing support for `xml` and `clr` data types, calculated columns, and different off-row storage behavior. **Upgrading to SQL Server 2016 could be the easiest and cheapest way to address the technology limitations in SQL Server 2014.**

There are plenty of other factors to consider. However, the key point is that you should perform a thorough analysis before starting a migration to In-Memory OLTP. Such a migration can have a very significant cost impact, and it should not be done unless it benefits the system.

SQL Server Management Studio provides a set of tools that can help you analyze if In-Memory OLTP will improve your application's performance and identify the objects that would benefit the most from the conversion. While these tools can be beneficial during the initial analysis stage, you should not make a decision based solely on the tools' output. Take into account all of the other factors and considerations we have already discussed in this chapter.

■ **Note** You can read about the In-Memory OLTP ARM tool at `http://msdn.microsoft.com/en-us/library/dn205133.aspx`.

New development, on the other hand, is a very different story. You can design a new system and database schema while taking In-Memory OLTP limitations into account. It is also possible to adjust some functional requirements during the design phase. As an example, it is much easier to store data in a case-sensitive way from the beginning as compared to changing the behavior of existing systems after they are deployed to production, in the case if you use SQL Server 2014.

You should remember, however, that In-Memory OLTP is an Enterprise Edition feature, and it requires powerful hardware with a large amount of memory. It is an expensive feature because of its licensing costs. Moreover, it is impossible to *"set it and forget it."* Database professionals should actively participate in monitoring and tuning the system after deployment. They need to monitor system memory usage, analyze data and recreate hash indexes if bucket counts need to be changed, update statistics, redeploy natively-compiled modules, and perform other tasks as well.

All of that makes In-Memory OLTP a bad choice for independent software vendors who develop products that need be deployed to a large number of customers. Moreover, it is not practical to support two versions of a system—with and without In-Memory OLTP—because of the increase in development and support costs.

Finally, if you are using the Enterprise Edition of SQL Server or the premium tier of SQL Database in Microsoft Azure, you can benefit from some of the In-Memory OLTP features, even if you decided that In-Memory OLTP migration is not cost-effective for your organization's needs. You can use memory-optimized table variables and/or non-durable memory-optimized tables as a staging area and for the replacement of on-disk temporary tables. This will improve the performance of calculations and ETL processes that need to store a temporary copy of the data.

Another possibility is using memory-optimized tables as session state storage for ASP.Net applications and/or as distributed cache for client applications, avoiding the purchase of expensive third-party solutions. You can use either durable or non-durable tables in this scenario. Durable tables will provide you with transparent failover, while non-durable tables will have incredibly fast performance. Obviously, you should remember the 8,060-byte maximum row size limitation and address it in code if you are using SQL Server 2014.

■ **Note** My *Expert SQL Server In-Memory OLTP* book covers many other questions related to the deployment, monitoring, and management of the systems utilizing In-Memory OLTP.

Summary

SQL Server uses native compilation to minimize the processing overhead of the interpreted T-SQL language. It generates separate DLLs for every memory-optimized object and loads it into process memory.

SQL Server 2014 supports the native compilation of regular T-SQL stored procedures. SQL Server 2016 also supports the native compilation of DML triggers and scalar user-defined functions. It compiles them into DLLs at creation time or, in the case of a server or database restart, at the time of the first call. SQL Server optimizes natively-compiled modules and embeds an execution plan into the code. That plan never changes unless the module is recompiled after a SQL Server or database restart. You should drop and recreate the module in SQL Server 2014 or recompile it with the `sp_recompile` stored procedure in SQL Server 2016 if data distribution has been significantly changed after compilation.

While natively-compiled modules are incredibly fast, they support a limited set of T-SQL language features. You can avoid such limitations by using interpreted T-SQL code that accesses memory-optimized tables through the Query Interop component of SQL Server. Almost all T-SQL language features are supported in this mode.

Memory-optimized table types and memory-optimized table variables are the in-memory analog of table types and table variables. They live in-memory only, and they do not use `tempdb`. You can use memory-optimized table variables as a staging area for the data and to pass a batch of rows to a T-SQL routine. Memory-optimized table types allow you to create indexes similar to memory-optimized tables.

In-Memory OLTP is an Enterprise Edition feature that requires the monitoring and tuning of systems in the post-deployment stage. It makes In-Memory OLTP a bad choice for independent software vendors who develop systems that need to be deployed to multiple customers.

The migration of existing systems could be a very time consuming and expensive process that requires you to address various limitations and differences in the behavior of memory-optimized and on-disk tables and indexes. You should perform a cost/benefit analysis, making sure that the benefits of migration overweigh its implementation costs.

Index

A

D. Korotkevitch, *Pro SQL Server Internals*, DOI 10.1007/978-1-4842-1964-5

B

C

■ D

■ E

F

G

H

I

N

O

P

Q

R

S

T

U

V

W

X, Y, Z

Printed in the United States
By Bookmasters